Contemporary
Literary Criticism

Guide to Gale Literary Criticism Series

When you need to review criticism of literary works, these are the Gale series to use:

If the author's death date is:	You should turn to:

After Dec. 31, 1959
(or author is still living)

CONTEMPORARY LITERARY CRITICISM

for example: Jorge Luis Borges, Anthony Burgess,
William Faulkner, Mary Gordon,
Ernest Hemingway, Iris Murdoch

1900 through 1959

TWENTIETH-CENTURY LITERARY CRITICISM

for example: Willa Cather, F. Scott Fitzgerald,
Henry James, Mark Twain, Virginia Woolf

1800 through 1899

NINETEENTH-CENTURY LITERATURE CRITICISM

for example: Fedor Dostoevski, Nathaniel Hawthorne,
George Sand, William Wordsworth

1400 through 1799

LITERATURE CRITICISM FROM 1400 TO 1800
(excluding Shakespeare)

for example: Anne Bradstreet, Daniel Defoe,
Alexander Pope, François Rabelais,
Jonathan Swift, Phillis Wheatley

SHAKESPEAREAN CRITICISM

Shakespeare's plays and poetry

Antiquity through 1399

CLASSICAL AND MEDIEVAL LITERATURE CRITICISM

for example: Dante, Homer, Plato, Sophocles, Vergil,
the Beowulf Poet

Gale also publishes related criticism series:

CHILDREN'S LITERATURE REVIEW

This series covers authors of all eras who have written for the preschool through high school audience.

SHORT STORY CRITICISM

This series covers the major short fiction writers of all nationalities and periods of literary history.

POETRY CRITICISM

This series covers poets of all nationalities, movements, and periods of literary history.

ISSN 0091-3421

Volume 66

Contemporary Literary Criticism

Excerpts from Criticism of the
Works of Today's Novelists, Poets,
Playwrights, Short Story Writers, Scriptwriters,
and Other Creative Writers

Roger Matuz
EDITOR

Cathy Falk
Mary K. Gillis
Sean R. Pollock
David Segal
ASSOCIATE EDITORS

Jennifer Brostrom
Susan M. Peters
Janet M. Witalec
ASSISTANT EDITORS

 **Gale Research Inc.** • DETROIT • LONDON

STAFF

Roger Matuz, *Editor*

Cathy Falk, Mary K. Gillis, Marie Lazzari, Sean R. Pollock, David Segal,
Robyn V. Young, *Associate Editors*

Jennifer Brostrom, Jay P. Daniel, Rogene M. Fisher, Christopher Giroux, Ian Goodhall,
Susan M. Peters, Bruce Walker, Janet M. Witalec, *Assistant Editors*

Jeanne A. Gough, *Production & Permissions Manager*
Linda M. Pugliese, *Production Supervisor*
Maureen A. Puhl, Jennifer VanSickle, *Editorial Associates*
Donna Craft, Paul Lewon, Lorna Mabunda, Camille P. Robinson, *Editorial Assistants*

Maureen Richards, *Research Supervisor*
Paula Cutcher–Jackson, Judy L. Gale, Robin Lupa, Mary Beth McElmeel, *Editorial
Associates*
Amy Kaechele, Julie K. Karmazin, Tamara C. Nott, *Editorial Assistants*

Sandra C. Davis, *Permissions Supervisor (Text)*
Josephine M. Keene, Denise M. Singleton, Kimberly F. Smilay, *Permissions Associates*
Maria L. Franklin, Michele Lonoconus, Shalice Shah, Nancy K. Sheridan,
Rebecca A. Stanko, *Permissions Assistants*
Shelly Rakoczy, *Student Co-op Assistant*

Patricia A. Seefelt, *Permissions Supervisor (Pictures)*
Margaret A. Chamberlain, *Permissions Associate*
Pamela A. Hayes, Keith Reed, *Permissions Assistants*

Mary Beth Trimper, *Production Manager*
Shanna Philpott-Heilveil, *External Production Associate*

Art Chartow, *Art Director*
C. J. Jonik, *Keyliner*

Contents

Preface   vii

Acknowledgments   xi

Preface

Named "one of the twenty-five most distinguished reference titles published during the past twenty-five years" by *Reference Quarterly,* the *Contemporary Literary Criticism (CLC)* series provides readers with critical commentary and general information on more than 2,000 authors now living or who died after December 31, 1959. Previous to the publication of the first volume of *CLC* in 1973, there was no ongoing digest monitoring scholarly and popular sources of critical opinion and explication of modern literature. *CLC,* therefore, has fulfilled an essential need, particularly since the complexity and variety of contemporary literature makes the function of criticism especially important to today's reader.

Scope of the Series

CLC presents significant passages from published criticism of works by creative writers. Since many of the authors covered by *CLC* inspire continual critical commentary, writers are often represented in more than one volume. There is, of course, no duplication of reprinted criticism.

Authors are selected for inclusion for a variety of reasons, among them the publication or dramatic production of a critically acclaimed new work, the reception of a major literary award, revival of interest in past writings, or the adaptation of a literary work to film or television.

The present volume of *CLC* includes Dawn Powell, Felipe Alfau, and Rosario Castellanos, all of whom had past works recently reissued in the United States and gained significant acclaim; Janet Frame and Rick Hillis, who won important literary awards in 1990; Sembène Ousmane and David Lynch, prizewinning scriptwriters and filmmakers; and Jim Harrison and Ian McEwan, authors of the recent popular and critically respected novels *Dalva* and *The Innocent,* respectively.

Perhaps most importantly, works that frequently appear on the syllabuses of high school and college literature courses are represented by individual entries in *CLC.* Philip Roth's *Portnoy's Complaint* and Flannery O'Connor's *Wise Blood* are examples of works of this stature appearing in *CLC,* Volume 66.

Attention is also given to several other groups of writers—authors of considerable public interest—about whose work criticism is often difficult to locate. These include mystery and science fiction writers, literary and social critics, foreign writers, and authors who represent particular ethnic groups within the United States.

Format of the Book

Each *CLC* volume contains about 500 individual excerpts—with approximately seventeen excerpts per author—taken from hundreds of book review periodicals, general magazines, scholarly journals, monographs, and books. Entries include critical evaluations spanning from the beginning of an author's career to the most current commentary. Interviews, feature articles, and other published writings that offer insight into the author's works are also presented. Students, teachers, librarians, and researchers will find that the generous excerpts and supplementary material in *CLC* provide them with vital information needed to write a term paper, analyze a poem, or lead a book discussion group. In addition, complete bibliographical citations note the original source and all of the information necessary for a term paper footnote or bibliography.

Features

A *CLC* author entry consists of the following elements:

• The **author heading** cites the form under which the author has most commonly published, followed by birth date, and death date when applicable. Uncertainty as to a birth or death date is indicated by a question mark.

• A **portrait** of the author is included when available.

• A brief **biographical and critical introduction** to the author and his or her work precedes the excerpted criticism. The first line of the introduction provides the author's full name, pseudonyms (if applicable), nationality, and a listing of genres in which the author has written. Since *CLC* is not intended to be a definitive biographical source, cross-references have been included to direct readers to these useful sources published by Gale Research: *Short Story Criticism* and *Children's Literature Review,* which provide excerpts of criticism on the works of short story writers and authors of books for young people, respectively; *Contemporary Authors,* which includes detailed biographical and bibliographical sketches of more than 98,000 authors; *Something about the Author,* which contains heavily illustrated biographical sketches of writers and illustrators who create books for children and young adults; *Dictionary of Literary Biography,* which provides original evaluations and detailed biographies of authors important to literary history; and *Contemporary Authors Autobiography Series* and *Something about the Author Autobiography Series,* which offer autobiographical essays by prominent writers for adults and those of interest to young readers, respectively. Previous volumes of *CLC* in which the author has been featured are also listed in the introduction.

• A list of **principal works,** arranged chronologically and, if applicable, divided into genre categories, notes the most important works by the author.

• The **excerpted criticism** represents various kinds of critical writing, ranging in form from the brief review to the scholarly exegesis. Essays are selected by the editors to reflect the spectrum of opinion about a specific work or about an author's literary career in general. The excerpts are presented chronologically, adding a useful perspective to the entry. All titles by the author featured in the entry are printed in boldface type, which enables the reader to easily identify the works being discussed. Publication information (such as publisher names and book prices) and parenthetical numerical references (such as footnotes or page and line references to specific editions of a work) have been deleted at the editor's discretion to provide smoother reading of the text.

• A complete **bibliographical citation** designed to help the user find the original essay or book follows each excerpt.

• A concise **further reading** section appears at the end of entries on authors for whom a significant amount of criticism exists in addition to the pieces reprinted in *CLC.* In some cases, this annotated bibliography includes references to material for which the editors could not obtain reprint rights.

Other Features

• An **Acknowledgments** section lists the copyright holders who have granted permission to reprint material in this volume of *CLC.* It does not, however, list every book or periodical reprinted or consulted during the preparation of the volume.

• A **Cumulative Author Index** lists all the authors who have appeared in the various literary criticism series published by Gale Research, with cross-references to Gale's biographical and autobiographical series. A full listing of the series referenced in the index appears on page 426 of this volume. Readers will welcome this cumulated author index as a useful tool for locating an author within the various series. The index, which lists birth and death dates when available, will be particularly valuable for those authors who are identified with a certain period but whose death date causes them to be placed in another, or for those authors whose careers span two periods. For example, Ernest Hemingway is found in *CLC,* yet a writer often associated with him, F. Scott Fitzgerald, is found in *Twentieth-Century Literary Criticism.*

• A **Cumulative Nationality Index** alphabetically lists all authors featured in *CLC* by nationality, followed by numbers corresponding to the volumes in which they appear.

• A **Title Index** alphabetically lists all titles reviewed in the current volume of *CLC.* Listings are followed by the author's name and the corresponding page numbers where the titles are discussed. English translations of foreign titles and variations of titles are cross-referenced to the title under which a work was originally published. Titles of novels, novellas, dramas, films, record albums, and poetry, short story, and essay collections are printed in italics, while all individual poems, short stories, essays, and songs are printed in roman type within quotation marks; when published separately (e.g., T.S. Eliot's poem *The Waste Land*), the title will also be printed in italics.

• In response to numerous suggestions from librarians, Gale has also produced a **special paperbound edition** of the *CLC* title index. This annual cumulation, which alphabetically lists all titles reviewed in the series, is available to all customers and will be published with the first volume of *CLC* issued in each calendar year. Additional copies of the index are available upon request. Librarians and patrons will welcome this separate index: it saves shelf space, is easy to use, and is disposable upon receipt of the following year's cumulation.

A Note to the Reader

When writing papers, students who quote directly from any volume in the Literary Criticism Series may use the following general forms to footnote reprinted criticism. The first example pertains to material drawn from periodicals, the second to material reprinted from books:

[1]Anne Tyler, "Manic Monologue," *The New Republic* 200 (April 17, 1989), 44-6; excerpted and

reprinted in *Contemporary Literary Criticism,* Vol. 58, ed. Roger Matuz (Detroit: Gale Research, 1990), p. 325.

²Patrick Reilly, *The Literature of Guilt: From 'Gulliver' to Golding* (University of Iowa Press, 1988); excerpted and reprinted in *Contemporary Literary Criticism,* Vol. 58, ed. Roger Matuz (Detroit: Gale Research, 1990), pp. 206-12.

Suggestions Are Welcome

The editors welcome the comments and suggestions of readers to expand the coverage and enhance the usefulness of the series.

Acknowledgments

The editors wish to thank the copyright holders of the excerpted criticism included in this volume, the permissions managers of many book and magazine publishing companies for assisting us in securing reprint rights, and Anthony Bogucki for assistance with copyright research. We are also grateful to the staffs of the Detroit Public Library, the Library of Congress, the University of Detroit Library, Wayne State University Purdy/Kresge Library Complex, and the University of Michigan Libraries for making their resources available to us. Following is a list of the copyright holders who have granted us permission to reprint material in this volume of *CLC*. Every effort has been made to trace copyright, but if omissions have been made, please let us know.

COPYRIGHTED EXCERPTS IN *CLC*, VOLUME 66, WERE REPRINTED FROM THE FOLLOWING PERIODICALS:

African Arts, v. 5, Spring, 1972 for "Ousmane Sembene and the Cinema of Decolonization" by Robert A. Mortimer. © 1972 by the Regents of the University of California. Reprinted by permission of the author.—*African Literature Today,* n. 12, 1982. Copyright 1982 by Heinemann Educational Books Ltd. All rights reserved. Reprinted by permission of Africana Publishing Corporation, New York, NY.—*America,* v. 162, April 28, 1990 for "Getting Down with Documentaries, Sending Up with Satire" by Thomas H. Stahel. © 1990. All rights reserved. Reprinted by permission of the author.—*The American Book Review,* v. 9, September-October, 1987; v. 11, September-October, 1989. © 1987, 1989 by *The American Book Review*. Both reprinted by permission of the publisher.—*The American Poetry Review,* v. 3, July-August, 1974 for "How Did You Come to Write That Book, Anyway?" by Philip Roth; v. 14, September-October, 1985 for "Georgraphies and Languages and Selves and What They Do" by Frederick Garber. Copyright © 1974, 1985 by World Poetry, Inc. Both reprinted by permission of the respective authors.— *The Atlantic Monthly,* v. 204, November, 1959 for a review of "Act One" by Charles Rolo; v. 223, April, 1969 for "The Journey of Philip Roth" by Theodore Solotaroff; v. 265, May, 1990 for a review of "Chromos" by Phoebe-Lou Adams. Copyright 1959, renewed 1987; copyright 1969, 1990 by The Atlantic Monthly Company, Boston, MA. All reprinted by permission of the respective authors.—*Belles Lettres: A Review of Books by Women,* v. 4, Spring, 1989. Reprinted by permission of the publisher.—*Best Sellers,* v. 33, April 15, 1973. Copyright 1973, by the University of Scranton; v. 37, December, 1977. Copyright © 1977 Helen Dwight Reid Educational Foundation. Both reprinted by permission of the publisher.—*The Bloomsbury Review,* v. 10, May-June, 1990 for a review of "The Theory and Practice of Rivers and New Poems" by James Grinnell. Copyright © by Owaissa Communications Company, Inc. 1990. Reprinted by permission of the author.—*Book World—The Washington Post,* October 29, 1978; August 5, 1979; June 28, 1981; March 6, 1988; April 23, 1989; March 18, 1990; April 22, 1990; September 2, 1990. © 1978, 1979, 1981, 1988, 1989, 1990, *The Washington Post*. All reprinted by permission of the publisher.— *Booklist,* v. 85, October 15, 1988. Copyright © 1988 by the American Library Association. Reprinted by permission of the publisher.—*Books,* London, v. 3, June, 1989. © Gradegate Ltd. 1989. Reprinted by permission of the publisher.—*Boston Review,* v. XV, October, 1990 for a review of "Chromos" by Gregory Rabassa. Copyright © 1990 by the Boston Critic, Inc. Reprinted by permission of the author.—*Canadian Book Review Annual,* 1988. Copyright © 1989 Simon & Pierre Publishing Co. Ltd. All rights reserved. Reprinted by permission of the publisher.—*The Canadian Forum,* v. LXVI, April, 1989 for "In the Aftermath of Empire: Indentities in The Commonwealth of Literature" by Keith Garebian. Reprinted by permission of the author.—*Canadian Review of African Studies,* v. 18, 1984. Reprinted by permission of the publisher.—*Carnegie Magazine,* July-August, 1990. Reprinted by permission of the publisher.—*The Catholic World,* v. 209, June 1969. Copyright 1969 by The Missionary Society of St. Paul the Apostle in the State of New York. Used by permission.—*The Centennial Review,* v. 30, Fall, 1986 for a review of "The Theory and Practice of Rivers" by John Rohrkemper. © 1986 by *The Centennial Review*. Reprinted by permission of the publisher and the author.—*Chicago Tribune,* August 12, 1990. © copyrighted 1990, Chicago Tribune Company. All rights reserved. Used with permission.—*Chicago Tribune—Books,* March 20, 1988. © copyrighted 1988, Chicago Tribune Company. All rights reserved/ April 22, 1990. © Copyrighted 1990, Chicago Tribune Company. All rights reserved. Used with permission.—*The Christian Century,* v. 105, May 18-25, 1988. Copyright 1988 Christian Century Foundation. Reprinted by permission from *The Christian Century*.—*The Christian Science Monitor,* February 5, 1988. © 1988 The Christian Science Publishing Society. All rights reserved/ February 5, 1988, June 13, 1988. © 1988 The Christian Science Publishing Society. All rights reserved. Both reprinted by permission from *The Christian Science Monitor*.—*Christianity Today,* v. XXIII, May 25, 1979. © by Christianity Today, Inc. Reprinted by permission of the publisher.—*CLA Journal,* v. XX, December, 1976. Copyright, 1976 by The College Language Association. Used by permission of The College Language Association.—*Commentary,* v. XI, April, 1951 for "The Path to Total Terror" by David Riesman; v. 36, September, 1963 for "Hannah Arendt on Eichmann: A Study in the Perversity of Brilliance" by Norman Podhoretz. Copyright 1951, renewed 1979, 1963 by the American Jewish Committee. All rights reserved. Both reprinted by permission of the publisher and the respective authors.—*The Critic,* Chicago, v. 31, May-June, 1973; v. XXXIV, Spring, 1976. © The Critic 1973, 1976. Both reprinted with the permission of the Thomas More Association, Chicago, IL.—*Commonweal,* v. CIII, April 9, 1976. Copyright © 1976 Commonweal Publishing Co., Inc. Reprinted by permission of Commonweal Foundation.—*The Drama Review,* v. 21, December, 1977 for "A Growth of Images" by Adrienne Kennedy. Copyright © 1977, *The Drama Review.* Reprinted by permission of The MIT Press, Cambridge, MA and the author.—*English Studies,* Netherlands, v. 65, December, 1984. © 1984 by Swets and Zetlinger B.V. Reprinted by permission of the publisher.—*Esquire,* v. 96, September, 1981. Copyright © 1981, Esquire Associates.—*Études Anglaises,* v. XXVI, January-March, 1973. Reprinted by permission of the publisher.—*Film Comment,* v. 26, November-December, 1990 for "Dead Heat on a Merry-Go-Round" by Kathleen Murphy. Copyright © 1990 by the author. Reprinted by permission of the author.—*The Flannery O'Connor Bulletin,* v. 15, 1986. Reprinted by permission of the publisher.—*Freelance,* September, 1988 for "The Blue Machines of Night" by Gerald Hill. Reprinted by permission of the author.—*The Georgia Review,* v. XIX, Fall, 1965 for "Passionate Pilgrim: Flannery O'Connor's 'Wise Blood' " by Robert M. Rechnitz; v. XLII, Fall, 1988 for a review of "Next" by Greg Kuzma. Copyright, 1965, 1988, by the University of Georgia. Both reprinted by permission of the publisher and the respective authors.—*The Globe and Mail,* Toronto, February 9, 1991. Reprinted by permission of the publisher.—*Great Lakes Review,* v. 8, Fall, 1982. Copyright © 1983 by Central Michigan University. Reprinted by permission of the publisher.—*The Hudson Review,* v. VI, Spring, 1953. Copyright 1953 by The Hudson Review, Inc/ v. XXII, Summer, 1969. Copyright © 1969 by The Hudson Review, Inc. Reprinted by permission of the publisher.—*Humor,* v. 2, 1989 for "Rosario Castellanos: Demythification Through Laughter," by Nina M. Scott. © 1988 Mouton De Gruyter. Reprinted by permission of the publisher and the author.—*Kirkus Reviews,* v. XLIII, August 15, 1975; v. XLV, August 15, 1977. Copyright © 1975, 1977 The Kirkus Service, Inc. All rights reserved. Both by permission of the publisher.—*The Listener,* v. 101, April 12, 1979 for an interview with Ian McEwan by Christopher Ricks. © British Broadcasting Corp. 1979. Reprinted by permission of Ian McEwan & Christopher Ricks.—*London Review of Books,* v. 7, December 5, 1985 for "Janet and Jason" by T. D. Armstrong; v. 12, May 10, 1990 for "Well Done, Ian McEwan" by Michael Wood; v. 12, September 13, 1990 for "What His Father Gets Up to" by Patrick Parrinder. All appears here by permission of the *London Review of Books* and the respective authors.—*Los Angeles Times Book Review,* September 20, 1987; August 19, 1990. Copyright, 1987, 1990, *Los Angeles Times.* All reprinted by permission of the publisher.—*Midstream,* v. 15, June-July, 1969, for "Portnoy Psychoanalyzed" by Bruno Bettelheim. Copyright © 1969 by The Theodor Herzel Foundation, Inc. Reprinted by permission of the publisher and the author.—*The Missouri Review,* v. VIII, 1985. Copyright © 1985 by the Curators of University of Missouri.—*MLN,* v. 103, December, 1988. © copyright 1988 by The Johns Hopkins University Press. All rights reserved. Reprinted by permission of the publisher.—*Monthly Film Bulletin,* v. 46, March, 1979. Copyright © The British Film Institute, 1979. Reprinted by permission of the publisher.—*Ms.,* v. V, October, 1976 for "Lucille Clifton: Making the World 'Poem-Up' " by Harriet Jackson Scarupa. © 1976 Ms. Magazine. Reprinted by permission of the author.—*The Nation,* New York, v. 240, June 1, 1985. Copyright 1985 *The Nation* magazine/ The Nation Company, Inc/ v. 208, March 10, 1969; v. 243, October 18, 1986; v. 244, March 28, 1987; v. 248, July 26, 1989; v. 251, September 17, 1990; v. 251, December 17, 1990. Copyright 1969, 1986, 1987, 1989, 1990 *The Nation* magazine/The Nation Company, Inc. All reprinted by permission of the publisher.—*National Review,* New York, v. 33, January 23, 1981; v. 38, November 7, 1986; v. 42, October 1, 1990. © 1981, 1986, 1990 by National Review, Inc., 150 East 35th Street, New York, NY 10016. All reprinted by permission of the publisher.—*The New Leader,* v. LXIII, September 22, 1980. © 1980 by The American Labor Conference on International Affairs, Inc. Reprinted by permission of the publisher.—*The New Republic,* v. 148, June 15, 1963. © 1963 The New Republic, Inc. Reprinted by permission of *The New Republic.*—*New Statesman & Society,* v. 1, September 30, 1988. © 1988 Statesman & Nation Publishing Company Limited. Reprinted by permission of the publisher.—*New York* Magazine, v. 16, April 25, 1983. Copyright © 1991 by News America Publishing Incorporated. All rights reserved. Reprinted with the permission of *New York* Magazine.—*The New York Review of Books,* v. XXVI, January 24, 1980; v. XXXIV, November 5, 1987; v. XXXVII, November 8, 1990; v. XXXVII, December 6, 1990. Copyright 1980, 1987, 1990 Nyrev, Inc. All reprinted with permission from *The New York Review of Books.*—*The New York Times,* May 18, 1952; October 3, 1980; August 28, 1990. Copyright 1952, 1980, 1990 by The New York Times Company. All reprinted by permission of the publisher.—*The New York Times Book Review,* February 23, 1936; March 29, 1936; September 4, 1938; September 6, 1942; November 19, 1944; September 5, 1954; June 5, 1960; October 14, 1962; April 22, 1973; July 5, 1981; October 11, 1987; January 22, 1989; February 19, 1989; May 13, 1990; September 16, 1990; September 23, 1990. Copyright © 1936, renewed 1964; Copyright 1936, 1938, 1942; Copyright 1944, renewed 1971; Copyright 1954, renewed 1982; Copyright 1960, 1962, 1973, 1981, 1987, 1989, 1990 by The New York Times Company. All reprinted by permission of the publisher.—*The New Yorker,* v.LXVI, July 23, 1990. © 1990 by the author/ v.XX, November 11, 1944 for "My Home is Far Away" by Edmund Wilson; v. XXXVIII, November 17, 1962 for "Dawn Powell: Greenwich Village in the Fifties" by Edmund Wilson. © 1944, renewed 1971; 1962 by The New Yorker Magazine, Inc. Both reprinted by permission of Farrar, Straus and Giroux, Inc./ v. LVI, October 27, 1980 for "The Frog Who Turned into a Prince, The Prince Who Turned into a Frog" by Pauline Kael. © 1980, 1981, 1982, 1983, 1984 by the author. Reprinted by permission of Henry Holt and Company, Inc./ v. LXII, September 22, 1986 for "Out There and in Here" by Pauline Kael. © 1986 by the author. Reprinted by permission of the publisher, Dutton, an imprint of New American Library, a division of Penguin Books USA Inc./ v. LXV, June 5, 1989; v. XXX, October 16, 1954; v. LIV, June 26, 1978; v. LXVI, December 10, 1990. © 1989 by the author; © 1954, 1978, 1990

COPYRIGHTED EXCERPTS IN *CLC,* VOLUME 66, WERE REPRINTED FROM THE FOLLOWING BOOKS:

Joyce Carol. From *New Heaven, New Earth: The Visionary Experience in Literature.* Vanguard Press, 1974. Copyright © 1974 by Joyce Carol Oates. Reprinted by permission of the publisher, Vanguard Press, Inc.—Paquet, Sandra Pouchet. From *The Novels of George Lamming.* Heinemann Educational Book Ltd., 1982. © Sandra Pouchet Paquet 1982. Reprinted by permission of the author.—Rushing, Andrea Benton. From "Lucille Clifton: A Changing Voice for Changing Times," in *Coming to Light: American Women Poets in the Twentieth Century.* Edited by Diane Wood Middlebrook and Marilyn Yalom. The University of Michigan Press, 1985. Copyright © by The University of Michigan 1985. All rights reserved. Reprinted by permission of the publisher.—Updike, John. From "The World Called Third," in *Hugging the Shore: Essays and Criticism.* Knopf, 1983. Copyright © 1977 by John Updike. All rights reserved. Reprinted by permission of Alfred A. Knopf, Inc.—Wallenstein, Barry. From "James T. Farrell: Critic of Naturalism," in *American Literary Naturalism: A Reassessment.* Edited by Yoshinobu Hakutani and Lewis Fried. Carl Winter, 1975. © 1975. Carl Winter Universitatsverlag, gegr. 1822, GmbH Heidelberg. Reprinted by permission of the author.—Wright, Richard. From an introduction to *In the Castle of My Skin.* By George Lamming. McGraw-Hill Book Company, Inc., 1953. Copyright 1953, by George Lamming. All rights reserved. Reprinted by permission of the Literary Estate of Richard Wright.

PHOTOGRAPHS APPEARING IN *CLC,* VOLUME 66, WERE RECEIVED FROM THE FOLLOWING SOURCES:

© Jerry Bauer: pp. 14, 89, 142, 274; Photograph by Layle Silbert: p. 63; UPI/Bettmann Newsphotos: pp. 109, 352; © Rollie McKenna: p. 152; Courtesy of Kitty Carlisle Hart: p. 172; Billy Rose Theatre Collection, The New York Public Library, Astor, Lenox and Tilden Foundations: p. 187; Photograph by Richard Clements, courtesy of University of Pittsburgh Press: p. 193; Photograph by Jim Goodman, courtesy of Beth Turner and Black Masks: p. 201; Michael Joseph Ltd.: p. 216; © Kelly Wise: p. 234; AP/Wide World: p. 255; Reproduced by permission of the Memory Shop: p. 271; Joseph DeCasseres/Photo Researchers: p. 297; © George Hallet; reproduced by permission of Heinemann Educational Books Limited: p. 332; Courtesy of New Yorker Films: p. 345; © Nancy Crampton: p. 384.

Felipe Alfau

1902-

Spanish-born novelist.

Alfau's highly experimental novels, which are frequently compared with the works of Jorge Luis Borges, Italo Calvino, and Vladimir Nabokov, are characterized by ironic wit and layered, self-reflexive narratives. Focusing on traditional Spanish culture, Alfau self-consciously explores the relationship between reality and fiction, often presenting himself as a character in his own works. His first novel, *Locos: A Comedy of Gestures,* drew little attention upon publication in 1936 due to limited distribution. Those who did publish reviews of the work praised its eccentric humor and complex structure, classifying it as a form of baroque romanticism. When *Locos* was reprinted in 1988, critics recognized the novel's innovative, modernist approach, and Alfau is now considered a neglected pioneer of modern fiction.

Alfau emigrated to New York City during World War I, where he found work as a music critic on a Spanish newspaper. Several commentators have maintained that *Locos* employs a musical motif in its variations on the theme of ironic absurdity, and the novel's form has been frequently described as a series of closely linked short stories. Critics have also characterized *Locos* as a modernist detective novel in which the true identity of every character is a mystery. For example, in a chapter titled "Fingerprints," a character named Don Gil argues that fingerprints discovered at the scene of a crime offer indisputable proof of a person's guilt, regardless of contradictory evidence. Shortly thereafter, his own fingerprints are discovered at the site of a murder and, despite his innocence, Don Gil prefers imprisonment to admitting the fallibility of his theory. The real murderer's identity is obscured among the elusive characters who appear in continually shifting circumstances. Alfau himself is a recurring character in *Locos;* in the first chapter, "Identity," he observes an eccentric gathering at the Cafe de los Locos, and selects the cast of his novel. His chosen characters behave as though they have minds independent of the author, and periodically become uncooperative, as when a character named Gaston attempts to escape from the writer's grasp in order to shape his own adventure in "reality." Alfau's tenuous control over his characters has been interpreted as a means of expressing the relationship between reality and the writer's imagination. Michael Dirda asserted: "[Alfau] does everything to call attention to the fact that what we are reading are fictions, artificial constructions. He pursues the novelistic equivalent of Brecht's epic theater, where the actors play at their roles with casual detachment and may even gesture knowingly to an audience required to judge the action rather than simply swallow it."

Alfau's second novel, *Chromos,* published forty-two years after its completion in 1948, was nominated for a National Book Award in 1990. Focusing on a group of Spanish im-

migrants in Manhattan during the 1930s, this work satirizes such Spanish institutions as bullfighting and Catholicism. Reviewers have described *Chromos* as a series of stories within stories, reflecting the layered, musical pattern of *Locos.* Alfau again appears as a character at the novel's opening; he is encouraged by a friend to write about Spaniards living in New York City. Later, in his writing room, Alfau discovers faded chromolithographs of traditional Spanish scenes and dreams of the novel he will write. The imagined book juxtaposes sections from his friend Garcia's novel about a stereotypical Spanish family, with another story about a man who can jump forward in time, and with Alfau's conversations about Spain at various cafés and parties. Critics praised the novel's humor and discussed how its themes of failure and loss are associated with the Americanization of Spanish culture, the constraints of Spanish traditions, and the frustrations of writing. A reviewer in *Publishers Weekly* asserted: "Alfau's prose lurches from conversational banter to baroque sentences that nearly explode under the strain of their internal contradictions and subversive wit. This remarkable, if verbose, novel is a worthy successor to Alfau's *Locos.*"

PRINCIPAL WORKS

NOVELS

Locos: A Comedy of Gestures   1936
Chromos   1990

OTHER

Old Tales from Spain   (children's book)   1929

Edith H. Walton

[*Locos: A Comedy of Gestures*], obviously, is just the book for connoisseurs of the bizarre. Felipe Alfau, who calls himself an author at the mercy of his characters, is a young Spaniard living in America and writing, very wittily, in English. His scene, however, is Spain, and his brand of exotic romanticism is definitely Latin. He has, it seems, been influenced by [Luigi] Pirandello—indeed, he barely troubles to disguise it—but one suspects that he does not take the Pirandellian theories very seriously. Plaintively proclaiming that his characters are anarchic and uncontrollable, he proceeds to guide them into ingenious, diverting mazes.

If one is to believe Mr. Alfau, he first encountered his characters at a certain rendezvous in Toledo called the Café de los Locos, or Café of the Crazy. (It is, he explains, frequented by bad writers in quest of types for their books.) There are gathered all those fantastic people who are destined to dance strange fandangoes through the pages of his novel. They are glimpsed only briefly at first, but the attitudes in which one surprises them prove to be wholly characteristic.

Having set his stage, so to speak, Mr. Alfau insouciantly shifts the scene to Madrid and gets down to business. His characters, transferred from Toledo, begin to strut and talk and to disobey their author's behests with an alarming stubbornness. When they behave inconsistently, infringe the laws of time and space, are detected in a double role, Mr. Alfau disclaims responsibility. These characters are new at the game, he says, and not yet disciplined. They are playing out a meaningless "comedy of gestures," the details of which must not be scrutinized too carefully.

To be more concrete, Mr. Alfau builds up his book as a series of short stories which at first appear to be almost unrelated. Gradually, however, a pattern emerges; the paths of his characters cross, and cross again; the same drama is rehearsed a second time, but from a different and often contradictory angle. The point, if it can be made clear, is this: these characters always behave like themselves, but the circumstances of their life are apt to vary slightly. Sometimes Lunarito, the most elusive of them all, is the mistress of Gaston Bejarano and sometimes she is his wife; again she will turn up as a servant girl of the unhappy poet Garcia—who also shifts rôles a bit as this bewildering comedy progresses.

Since they are so variable, one cannot be too precise about

these extraordinary creatures. Among them, however, are Don Gil Bejarano, who went to prison rather than admit his theory of fingerprints wrong; Donna Micaela Valverde, that weird, alluring woman who fell in love with Death; Don Laureano Baez, the king of Madrid beggars; Chinelato, the mongrel giant with Oriental blood whose cruel, adventurous career approached the fabulous. Among them also is Gaston, or El Cogote, who fell in love—much to Mr. Alfau's embarrassment—with his sister, Carmen, and kidnapped her from the convent where she was a most unconventional nun.

In piecing together this pastiche of strange, interlocking tales, Mr. Alfau's technique is as variable as his characters. Sometimes he will tell his story practically straight; again he will supply a running commentary of footnotes, indicating that his characters are behaving badly; at another time his puppets will comment on their creator; still later he will befuddle the reader by having one of his characters fall in love with a "real" person, or by having a "real" person clamor to become a character. It is all very complex and amusing, and the best thing to do, as Mr. Alfau says, is to remain unsurprised by anything that happens.

Locos, then, is no book for the forthright. It is perverse, a little decadent and extremely self-conscious. Also, however, it is most entertaining—effecting as it does a unique blend of wit and baroque romanticism. Mr. Alfau, when he goes Pirandello, often overreaches himself, but his better episodes—**"The Beggar," "Fingerprints," "The Wallet"**—are very good and very funny indeed. *Locos* is a *tour de force* which would not bear repetition, but of its kind it is clever and unmistakably original.

> Edith H. Walton, "The Pirandello Manner,"
> in The New York Times Book Review, *March 29, 1936, p. 7.*

Groff Conklin

[Alfau's *Locos: A Comedy of Gestures,* is a] goofy book. Written in 1928; probably in search of a publisher for eight years. The second subtitle of the book reads: *An Author at the Mercy of His Characters.* It's like that: self-conscious, cute. It turns out to be a book of short stories, most of them containing the same characters. Scene, Madrid. Psychologies, abnormal. Style, affectedly simple. And yet there is a haunting quality about the setting and the characters—necrophiles, suicides, harlots, professional beggars, and a West Indian Don Juan, name of Chinelato, who is revealed in glimpses. A funny story about the infallibility of fingerprints, another about Madrid's plague of thieves; the last story in the book the best, about a man who had a phobia of dogs and of spring. Delicate, spun-glass, affected, irritating, eccentric stuff; not dull. (pp. 323-24)

> Groff Conklin, in a review of "Locos: A Comedy of Gestures," in The New Republic, *Vol. LXXXVI, No. 1116, April 22, 1936, pp. 323-24.*

Mary McCarthy

[The Discoverers club is] that little circle of the intimate friends of literature which has recently coalesced under the chaperonage of Farrar and Rinehart. To these Discoverers, five to eight times a year at approximately bimonthly intervals, that publisher introduces his debutant authors. In the course of a year the members of the club receive five to eight limited, autographed, numbered first editions of the work of new writers. The snob appeal of this sales promotion stunt is plain. The idea is, of course, that these books will not be just any old first novels, but the first shy efforts of potentially valuable talents—"books," in Farrar and Rinehart's own words, "that cause an unmistakable sense of excitement to sweep our editorial offices."

The tragic flaw in the scheme is, clearly, the fact that in one year there are not five to eight new talents per publisher; indeed, there are not five to eight new talents. Farrar and Rinehart were lucky enough to get for its first Discoverers' selection *Locos,* a bright, eccentric novel by Felipe Alfau, a young Spaniard writing in English. . . .

Locos was a witty, fantastic novel of modern Spain, a novel of forms and surfaces, demanding comparison not with literature but with art. In a general way it was related to the baroque tradition of architecture. More intimately and specifically it was concerned with the surréaliste movement in painting. The characters of the story, habitués of a bohemian resort called the Cafe of the Crazy, were dark, extravagant, grotesque. The laws that governed their behavior were the laws of the dream world: the plot was built out of time shifts, shifts of attributes, out of dislocations and distortions. Yet all that was strange, wild, and irrational in the matter of the novel was gracefully contradicted by the blandness of the manner. The style was an instrument of very great precision. It recalled the smooth miniature technique of Dali, the high polish of Pierre Roy. Those reviewers who were inspired by the instability of the characters of *Locos* to compare it with the plays of Pirandello missed the point. They ignored the glittering finish of the novel, the dégagé air of the author. Doggedly they tried to grapple with it as a novel of ideas, to writing philosophical concepts out of a formal decorative piece which Alfau himself described [in the subtitle] as "a comedy of gestures."

Mary McCarthy, "Two 'Discoveries'," in The Nation, New York, Vol. CXLII, No. 3704, June 27, 1936, p. 848.

Mary McCarthy

[*The essay excerpted below appears as an afterword in the 1988 edition of* Locos.]

Fifty-two years ago, on June 27, 1936, I reviewed [*Locos*] in the *Nation.* Very favorably [see McCarthy's excerpt above]. The author, Felipe Alfau, was said to be a young Spaniard writing in English. Spain was Republican then; the Franco revolt that turned into the Spanish Civil War began on July 19, three weeks and a day later. The charm exercised on me by *Locos,* therefore, cannot have been a matter of politics. And I was ignorant of Spain and Spanish. It was more like love. I was enamored of that book and never forgot it, though my memory of it, I now perceive on rereading, is somewhat distorted, as of an excited young love affair. Alfau, or his book, was evidently my fatal type, which I would meet again in Vladimir Nabokov's *Pale Fire* and more than once in Italo Calvino. But *Locos* was the first. And it appears to have been the author's unique book, fittingly, as it were. I never heard of Alfau again, though for a time I used to ask about him whenever I met a Spaniard; not one knew his name. Maybe that was because he lived in the United States, if indeed he did. But in this country I never found anyone besides me who had read *Locos.* Now the book is being reissued. (p. 145)

To come back to it has been a bit eerie, at least on first sight—a cross between recognition and non-recognition. For example, what has stuck in my memory is a lengthy account of a police convention in Madrid that coincided merrily with a crime wave, the one giving rise to the other: crooks converged on the city, free to practice their trade while the police attended panel discussions and lectures on criminality. Well, it would be too much to say that none of that is in *Locos*; it *is* there but in the space of a few sentences and as a mere suggestion.

The fifth chapter, **"The Wallet,"** begins: "During the 19— police convention at Madrid, a very unfortunate occurrence took place. Something went wrong with the lighting system of the city and the whole metropolis was left in complete darkness." It is the power failure that offers the assembled criminals their opportunity.

> It was a most deplorable thing, for it coincided with the undesirable immigration of a regular herd of international crooks who since the beginning of the World War had migrated into Spain and now cooperated with resident crooks in a most energetic manner. . . . [it] came to pass that during the Police Convention of 19—, Madrid had a criminal convention as well. Of course, the police were bestowing all their efforts and time upon discussing matters of regulation, discipline and now and then how to improve the method of hunting criminals . . . and naturally, after each session . . . had neither time nor energy to put a check to the outrages. . . . Therefore all crooks felt safer and freer to perform their duty in Madrid, where the cream of the police were gathered, than anywhere else.

That is all, a preamble. The body of the chapter has to do with the stolen wallet of the Prefect of Police. The power failure, which provides a realistic explanation, had slipped my memory, and I was left with the delightful illogic—or logic—of parallel conventions of police and criminals. The purest Alfau, a distillate.

"The Wallet," actually, may be the center of the book, whose subject is Spain regarded as an absurdity, a compound of beggars, pimps, policemen, nuns, thieves, priests, murderers, confidence artists. The title, [*Locos*], meaning "The Crazies," refers to a Café de los Locos in Toledo, where in the first chapter virtually all the principal characters are introduced as habitués suited to be "characters" for the bad fiction writers who, like the author, drop in to observe them. There are Dr. de los Rios, the medical attendant of most of the human wreckage washed up at those tables; Gaston Bejarano, a pimp known as El Cogote; Don Laureano Baez, a well-to-do professional beggar; his maid/daughter Lunarito, Sister Carmela, who is the same as Carmen, a runaway nun; Garcia, a poet who becomes a fingerprint expert; Padre Inocencio, a Salesian monk; Don Benito, the Prefect of Police; Felipe Alfau; Don Gil Bejarano, a junk dealer, uncle of El Cogote; Pepe Bejarano, a good-looking young man, brother of El Cogote; Doña Micaela Valverde, a triple widow and necrophile.

Only missing is the highly significant Señor Olózaga, at one time known as the Black Mandarin, a giant, former galley slave, baptized and brought up by Spanish monks in China, former butterfly charmer in a circus, former potentate in the Spanish Philippines, now running a bizarre agency for the collection of delinquent debts and another for buying and selling dead people's clothes. But he is connected with the other "characters" of the Café de los Locos both in his own right and by marriage to Tía Mariquita, his fifth wife, who lives in a house that coughs—their secretary, mistaken for her husband, is murdered by Don Laureano Baez and his daughter/maid Lunarito—one of many cases of mistaken identity. As the Black Mandarin in the Philippines, he has sought the hand of the blue-eyed daughter of Don Esteban Bejarano y Ulloa, a Spanish official, and been rejected because of his color. This, precisely, was the father of Don Gil Bejarano (see above), the brother-in-law of the Prefect of Police and inventor of a theory of fingerprints, which pops up in Chapter 4, where, incidentally, we find Padre Inocencio playing cards with the Bejarano family while the young daughter, Carmen, is having sex with her brother Gaston.

Such underground—or underworld—links are characteristic and combine with the rather giddy mutability displayed by the characters. Lunarito is Carmen, who is going to be Sister Carmela; at one point we find her married to El Cogote, none other than her brother Gaston, who cannot, of course, *be* her brother if she is the daughter of the beggar, Don Laureano Baez. And yet Don Laureano's wife, when we are introduced to him as the bartender of the Café de los Locos, is Felisa, which is the name of Carmen's mother, the sister of Don Benito, the Prefect of Police. . . . In the Prologue, and occasionally thereafter, the author makes a great point of the uncontrollability of his characters, but this familiar notion (as in "Falstaff got away from Shakespeare") is the least interesting feature. The changing and interchanging of the people, resembling "shot" silk, has no need of the whimsy of a loss of auctorial control. If any aspect of the book has aged, it is this whimsicality.

It is not only the characters of *Locos* that have that queer shimmer or iridescence. Place and time are subject to it as well. A fact I think I missed back in 1936 is the discrepancy between the location of the Café de los Locos—Toledo—where the "characters" are gathered for inspection, and their actual residence—Madrid. What are these Madrileños doing in Toledo? I suppose it must be because

of the reputation of Toledo as a mad, fantastic city, a myth, a city, as Alfau says, that "died in the Renaissance"; he speaks of "Toledo on its hill . . . like a petrified forest of centuries." The city that died in the Renaissance and lives on, petrified, can of course figure as an image of Spain. One more quotation may be relevant to the underlying theme of impersonation as a national trait: "the action of this book develops mainly in Spain, a land in which not the thought nor the word, but the action with a meaning—the gesture—has grown into a national specialty. . . ."

Spain and its former possessions—Cuba and the Philippines—constitute the scene; their obverse is China, for a Spaniard the other end of the world, and here the provenance of Señor Olózaga, baptized "Juan Chinelato" by the bearded, tobacco-smoking monks who raised him.

One thing that certainly escaped me as a young reviewer is the hidden presence of this "Juan Chinelato" in the first chapter, the one called **"Identity"** and laid in the Café of the Crazies. He is there in the form of a little Chinese figure made of porcelain being hawked by Don Gil Bejarano in his character of junk dealer. "Don Gil approached us," writes Alfau.

> 'Here is a real bargain,' he said, tossing the porcelain figure on the palm of his hand. 'It is a real old work of art made in China. What do you say?' I looked at the figure which was delicately made. It represented a herculean warrior with drooping mustache and a ferocious expression. He had a butterfly on his shoulder. The color of the face was not yellow but a darker color, more like bronze. . . . 'Perhaps it is not Chinese but Indian.' Don Gil . . . looked slightly annoyed. 'No, it is Chinese,' he said." And he continues to praise it: " 'Yes, this is a real Chinese mandarin or warrior, I don't know which, and it is a real bargain.'

A minute later, thanks to an inadvertent movement, the figure is smashed to pieces on the marble-topped café table.

This is a beautifully constructed book and full of surprises. Another example: one does not notice in this opening chapter the unusually small hand of Don Gil, seen only as a mark on a whitewashed wall. The lightly dropped hint is picked up unobtrusively like a palmed coin several chapters later when Don Gil is being arrested at the reluctant order of his brother-in-law because his fingerprints have been found all over the scene of a crime: "Don Gil had very small hands . . . and the handcuffs did not fit securely enough. . . . 'Officer, those handcuffs are too big for me. You had better get a rope or something.' " In his conversations with the Prefect, he has kept working "the man from China," that is, the man who has the perfect alibi but is tracked down by science through the prints his hands have left. His last article, published in a Madrid newspaper on the day of his apprehension, is entitled "Fingerprints, a sure antidote against all alibis," and his last words, which he keeps reiterating as he is carried off in the police wagon, are "I am the man from China. . . . Fingerprints never fail."

Perhaps police work and criminality, just as much as mad, fantastic Spain, are the subject of *Locos.* And considerable detection is required on the reader's part, to be repaid, as in the hunt for "Wanted" lawbreakers, with a handsome reward. For instance, among the clues planted to the mute presence of Señor Olózaga in the Café of the Crazies there is simply the word "butterfly"; I failed to catch the signal until the third reading. And I still have a lot of sleuthing to do on Carmen-Carmela-Lunarito and the beauty spot on Lunarito's body that she charges a fee to show. A knowledge of Spanish might help. In the Spanish light, each figure is dogged by a shadow, like a spy or tailing detective, though sometimes the long shadow is ahead: "She stood at the end of her own shadow against the far diffused light of the corner lamp post and there was something ominous in that." It may be that this is the link between the theme of Spain and the theme of the criminal with his attendant policeman. In some moods *Locos* could be classed as "luminist" fiction. But I must leave some work (which translates into pleasure) for the reader.

If *Locos* is, or was, my fatal type, what I fell in love with, all unknowing, was the modernist novel as detective story. There is detective work, surely, supplied by Nabokov for the reader of *Pale Fire.* I mentioned Calvino, too, but there is another, quite recent example, which I nearly overlooked. [Umberto Eco's] *The Name of the Rose,* of course. It is not only a detective story in itself but it also contains an allusion to Sherlock Holmes and *The Hound of the Baskervilles.* But in *Locos* Sherlock Holmes is already present: while in England Pepe Bejarano pretends to have studied under him, which explains his uncanny ability to recover his uncle, the Prefect's, wallet. The grateful police officer, who does not know whether Conan Doyle's creation is a real person or not, wants to express his thanks. " 'Yes, Pepe, yes. I should like to write an official letter to that gentleman, to that great man—Cherlomsky, is that the name?' "

Yes, there is a family resemblance to Nabokov, to Calvino, to Eco. And perhaps, though I cannot vouch for it, to Borges, too. (pp. 145-49)

Mary McCarthy, "Felipe Alfau's 'Locos'," in
The Review of Contemporary Fiction, *Vol. 8,
No. 3, Fall, 1988, pp. 145-49.*

Michael Dirda

When the novelist Balzac lay dying, he is reported to have cried out, "Send for Bianchon! Bianchon will save me!" There was, however, no physician by that name in Paris. Then someone remembered that Balzac himself had created Horace Bianchon, the worldly yet brilliant doctor of the *Comédie humaine.*

Writers often remark that characters can take on a life of their own, but in a small subset of novels this is literally true: When the authors step away from their desks for a cup of coffee, their creations go off to play on their own. Modern examples include Flann O'Brien's comic masterpiece *At Swim-Two-Birds* and Gilbert Sorrentino's gargantuan *Mulligan Stew.* To this company must now be added Felipe Alfau's *Locos. . . .* Alfau's inventive "comedy of

gestures" is, like any hall-of-mirrors fun house, disorienting, maddening and greatly entertaining.

It has everything any modern best seller needs: murder, incest, fallen priests, lascivious nuns, a couple of suicides, several mysteries, the living dead, pimps and whores and poets, locales that shift from China to the Philippines to the Caribbean to Europe. The action, most of which occurs in or near Madrid, commingles the seemingly real and the clearly fantastic, with dashes of romance. Alfau's English is neat, often epigrammatic, continually ironic:

> Fulano had come to this world with the undaunted purpose of being famous and he had failed completely, developing into the most obscure person. He had tried all possible plans of acquiring importance, popularity, public acknowledgement, etc., and the world with a grim determination persistently refused to acknowledge even his existence . . . One day he stood in the middle of La Puerta del Sol shouting: 'Fire . . . Fire . . . ' But no one seemed to hear him and at last he had to quit his post because a trolley car nearly ran him down. . . . Not even beggars approached him for alms.

Poor Fulano pops up in the first story of *Locos,* where he meets the author at the Cafe de los Locos, a bar where fictional characters hang out between assignments. (Don Quixote sits forlornly at one table.) Alfau gradually picks out some half dozen or so figures, who will be the protagonists of the interconnected tales in his book. Of course, Alfau himself appears in most of the stories, so the strands of fictional discourse already begin to twist into a Möbius strip, with characters who jump back and forth "real" and "fictive" life.

For instance, in **"A Character"** Alfau sits down to write about Gaston Bejarano, who he admits is "quite a bad influence . . . and on more than one occasion has completely demoralized the cast." Before Alfau really gets started on his story though, he is interrupted by the supposedly fictional Don Laureano Baez—which allows the lightly sketched Gaston to go off on a spree: "Now that I am free from his attention I am able to do as I please." He proceeds to describe a romantic encounter late one night with Lunarito, Don Laureano Baez's "ward," an enigmatic seductress graced with an unforgettable beauty spot somewhere on her body: For one peseta you can see it, for two pesetas it can be touched, and for three pesetas . . .

In most fiction we are encouraged to surrender to the smooth surface of the storytelling, to follow the characters, even to identify with them, allowing the author's narrative skills to hypnotize us. We call this getting lost in a story. Alfau's esthetic is, by contrast, precisely the opposite of such illusionism: He does everything to call attention to the fact that what we are reading are fictions, artificial constructions. He pursues the novelistic equivalent of [Bertolt] Brecht's epic theater, where the actors play at their roles with casual detachment and may even gesture knowingly to an audience required to judge the action rather than simply swallow it.

For instance, at one point a barbaric adventurer known as

Juan Chinelato apparently roasts his infant son and serves him up to his wife, who naturally enough goes mad. At this point there is a footnote.

> Several persons have objected to this passage which they find distasteful to say the least . . . It is not my fault if, although personally preferring to have actual roast pork, Chinelato should prove unyielding in his culinary prerogatives. Besides like all stage dinners this is a make-believe one and the platter really held a cardboard dummy.

Now, I suppose, you either like this sort of thing or you don't. . . . Here fictiveness is a structural principle, and the book exuberantly mocks and undercuts its own stories, emphasizing their literariness, their invention: Here is art, not life.

Yet Alfau knows that every writer must, above all, be interesting, so *Locos* is also witty, hair-raising, touching. During a police convention the electricity fails in Madrid and the city is overrun by crooks—who then hold their own convention and ultimately grow so numerous that they are reduced to robbing each other. In another tale, the handsome, worldly Padre Innocencio wins the favor of the ladies, who "would either confess their sins to no one else, or confess to anyone but him." Like most of the characters, his fate is sad.

But should one feel sorry for such puppets? Underneath the "comedy of gestures" Alfau suggests there lurks the "vulgar aspects of a common tragedy." Just as the fictional characters dream, like Pinocchio, of becoming real, so the people they play yearn to become someone: They want to be recognized, appreciated, loved, but their stories show them repeatedly beaten down by religion, family and Spanish tradition. The cool avant-garde fictioneer, it seems, hides an angry moralist.

Unhappily, appreciation eluded the author of *Locos,* as it does his creations. When the novel was published, it apparently sank like a stone and Felipe Alfau never wrote another. Nearly 90 now, he lives in New York, a retired translator and, on the evidence of this single book, a superb if all too little known artist.

> *Michael Dirda, "Crazy Like a Fox," in* Book World—The Washington Post, *April 23, 1989, p. 9.*

Anna Shapiro

[In an afterword to *Locos,* Mary McCarthy] rightly compares this cool, teasing, wistful work with Nabokov's *Pale Fire* and with the experiments of Calvino [see McCarthy's second excerpt]. *Locos was* before its time: an extraordinarily polished modernist novel, very much preoccupied with the nature of fiction, that takes the form of a series of stories, at least some of which can be read as classic Spanish tales of rogues and con men—picaresques.

In a prologue, Alfau invites one to read the stories in any order, but his tone, like Nabokov's, is sardonic and flagrantly disingenuous, and the invitation should not be taken too much to heart: *Locos* is not a story collection—though its status as a novel is ectoplasmic, floating somewhere off the page in the connections the reader can make between one story and another. It's a pleasure to read *Locos* with pencil in hand, riffling backward to pounce on a clue as suggestive as a detail remembered from a dream, though the book's richness can also tempt one to graduate-student exegesis. *Locos* is a detective story, as McCarthy points out, but one in which the mystery is identity and the detective is the reader.

Take **"Fingerprints,"** a deceptively simple story, like most of the others, with an O. Henry-like "ironic" ending. Don Gil, the brother-in-law of the Prefect of Police, is obsessed with fingerprints, and claims that they are more trustworthy than any alibi. He says, "If a man were in China, and while he was there . . . his fingerprints appeared on a given spot here in Madrid . . . I would say to him, 'You are the author of those fingerprints.'" As it happens, while Don Gil and a priest are drinking chocolate together Don Gil's fingerprints are discovered all over the scene of a grisly murder, and the Prefect, who has been expected the whole time, to play cards, arrives and reluctantly arrests him. Don Gil, a law-abiding family man, allows himself to be carted away, idiotically repeating, "I am the man from China . . . Fingerprints never fail."

And that's the end of that. Except that in the previous story you might have noticed an aside about its main character, Garcia, in which it is mentioned that Garcia has been taught all that Don Gil knows about fingerprints and "perhaps more," and that Don Gil has offered him a job "provided Garcia were willing to let Don Gil have part of his pay." The story also slips in a sly hint that Garcia has agreed but "this was, of course, a secret pact of which Garcia expected to rid himself as soon as he could devise a plan to do so." Since in **"Fingerprints"** Garcia is the man who identifies the prints, one deduces that this may have been his way of getting rid of Don Gil and that he may have committed the murder himself. Yet the only thing you can depend on is that to be absolutely certain of anyone's identity here is to echo the idiocies of Don Gil.

Further stories only add to uncertainty. A story named for its hero, **"Juan Chinelato,"** is about an actual man from China—a term that has come to be synonymous in the reader's mind with the perpetrator of the murder. But then the last of the stories shows Garcia again, this time as a young student, brutally stoning a dog who gets in his way, and, of course, a dog in his way was very much what Don Gil became for him. Still, none of this proves Don Gil innocent; the man was taking kickbacks, after all.

Alfau is dealing here in the identity of indiscernibles, if you remember that philosophy-class mind bender. It's about distinguishing, in the most famous example, between the meanings of "the morning star" and "the evening star." Both morning star and evening star are manifestations of the planet Venus, so aren't they the same thing? But "the morning star" doesn't mean what "the evening star" means: you don't say "I saw the evening star" when you've looked at Venus at dawn. What you are looking for in *Locos* is, in a sense, whatever it may be that the characters are manifestations of, regardless of what they're called or where they happen to appear.

Alfau started out in New York as a music critic, and the shape of *Locos* is musical—a set of themes and variations. One motif is an elusive woman called Lunarito, who at times seems also to occupy the role of a woman named Carmen. They start out as clearly defined, separate people. In an early story, Don Gil's son Gaston meets Lunarito and then goes home to his mistress, Carmen. But later Gaston talks about a nightmare in which he destroys his sister, who in the dream seems to be Lunarito. Chapters later, it is Carmen who is Gaston's sister, and the nightmare recurs—this time, however, as farce, with Carmen seducing her brother. Elsewhere, it is not Carmen who is Gaston's mistress but Lunarito. Carmen is allowed to turn up as a sister with a capital "S"—a nun—in Garcia's nightmarish memories, where Lunarito acts as his maid. Similarly, shadows and the reflected glow of a fire on the front of a house play like refrains through these stories. They work the way music does, and trying to find an explicit meaning in them seems as pointless as seeking meaning in a melody. If they are arrows, they are all pointing at each other.

One suspects that what appears in any given story as a dropped hint began modestly as a bit of background and sprouted ramifications only on second thought, and that the first story, in which we are taken to the Café de los Locos, was, like most introductions, written last. The entire cast appears in this café, where bad writers hang out to pick up secondhand characters (Don Quixote can't find a taker) and also "some fairly good, cheap, new material." (This no doubt is why several reviewers called the book "Pirandellian.") Each of the characters featured in the novel displays here in the café an emblem of his or her story. Don Gil's hand, for instance, leaves a dirty mark on the wall, and Garcia kicks a dog. The introduction thus serves as a kind of witty index (which McCarthy, in her afterword, cross-references) to the myriad and contradictory identities that the characters will take on, and it also establishes their habit of trying to climb out of the world of fiction into "reality." (Living in an alternate reality is one way to describe being crazy—loco.) In the self-animating conceit of being poised between one kind of reality and another, the characters are like Betty Boop pulling herself out of the inkwell in a Max Fleischer cartoon. All in all, *Locos* makes a *Who Framed Roger Rabbit* of literature: its characters are like the Toons, who indestructibly defy the laws of reality but observe with strict, if unwilling, obedience the conventions of fiction, afraid of nothing except, possibly, the eraser.

In this respect, the *Locos* characters are also a little like writers. There is a certain amount of rib-nudging to indicate that they are merely stand-ins for the author, and at one point Alfau chides a character—Gaston, as it happens—for taking over the typewriter to invent his own story. Gaston, having, as he thinks, leaped into reality by means of writing, can't tell whether the woman he meets is fictional or real, but he knows when he falls in love that it is reality he is in love with. This is Alfau's dilemma, too. He is in love with reality, and to enact this love he turns it into—embalms it in—fiction. When Alfau writes about a necrophile, a woman who adores funerals and corpses and periodically falls into epochs of apparent death herself, it is surely authorship he is both mocking and mourning. Pervasively, the stories embody a romance about the fatalism of writing—about living in characters and literary conventions, and therefore living a shadow life vexed by conundrum.

One of Alfau's stand-ins has been educated in England, so he looks at Spain as an outsider and "a spectator witnessing extraordinary things in a strange land." This is Alfau's position precisely. Yet the stories are very, very Spanish. There are phrases in *Locos* that read like translations or like the overcorrect diction of a non-native speaker ("a rogue after whom the police had been for some time"), and the stories hew to the hearty, energetic traditions of picaresque writing. Like Nabokov (again), Alfau is writing in the language of his adopted country, and one wonders what his history, or that of his book, would have been if he had written in Spanish and published in Spain or Latin America, where readers might not have been scared off by an air of "foreignness."

In this country, it wasn't until at least the middle of the century that Alfau's sort of novel began to have currency: structured narratives that can be read more or less straightforwardly as stories but whose stories are about the structures of their own narrative. Recent readers have compared Alfau not only with Nabokov and Calvino but with García Márquez and Borges. McCarthy, who fell in love with *Locos* when she reviewed it for *The Nation* fifty-three years ago [see McCarthy's first excerpt], in her afterword rather sweetly calls it "my fatal type," and her affectionate reassessment begins like a continuation of her intellectual autobiography. There is something in *Locos* that evokes such a response—something more personal, modest, or melancholy than the customary grandeur of modernist fiction. Though Alfau wrote with a confidence astonishing in a twenty-six-year-old, beneath the comedy and the surrealistic effects and the glare and shadows of his book's imagery its formalism is like a whispered secret, a shy way for an ingenious author to gesture to his public from his side of the peculiar one-way mirror that is reflexive art. (pp. 105-08)

Anna Shapiro, "Sixty-One Years of Solitude," in The New Yorker, Vol. LXV, No. 16, June 5, 1989, pp. 105-08.

William Mooney

Locos: A Comedy of Gestures appeared in 1936 in a special subscription edition that allowed Alfau to remain obscure in spite of some favorable reviews. . . . In fact he is a figure more probable in a Borges fiction than in the real world. All the more so since now the book has surfaced and seems entirely postmodern.

The story **"Identity,"** for example, has all the impenetrable lucidity of Borges, whose fictions began to appear after Alfau had left off writing. A character named Fulano (slang Spanish meaning any John Doe) has the problem that no one notices him. He is advised to fake a suicide. Before he can relish the notoriety this should bring, an escaped convict changes the name on the suicide note to his own and adopts Fulano's identity, not only replacing him but afterward attaining a certain celebrity. Left without any identity at all, Fulano has no choice but to jump in the river and become the drowned convict. In another story the defender of the uniqueness of fingerprints must go to prison for a crime he could not have committed, because his fingerprints are found on the murder weapon.

One story calls to mind [Julio] Cortazar's *Continuity of Parks.* Calvino's voice can often be heard, and there is the trainer of butterflies who would be entirely at home in García Marquez's Macondo. Pirandello's *Six Characters* (1921) is Alfau's only point of contact with the world in real time; in **"Character,"** Alfau's protagonist escapes his control, pursuing a "real" person the way the descending angel does in the recent Handke/Wenders film *Der Himmel über Berlin.* A brilliant book, *Locos* seems to have fallen prey to the discontinuities that are its subject. Imagine the discovery of a fifteenth-century *Paradise Lost* that Milton could not have known, or perhaps a twentieth-century *Don Quixote* by someone named Pierre Menard. Influencing and influenced by almost no one in an invisible passage through time, what does Alfau tell us of the workings of history?

William Mooney, "Missing Persons," in The American Book Review, Vol. 11, No. 4, September-October, 1989, p. 15.

Abigail Lee Six

[*Locos*], one other novel, *Chromos,* and a children's book, constitute the complete works of [Felipe Alfau], the retired expatriate Spaniard, who was born in 1902 and has lived in the United States since the First World War. He writes in a rather strange English: at times it reads like translation or sounds too careful to be a native speaker's; occasionally it is surprisingly street-wise American. The mixture of registers has a positive effect, however: the foreign ring harmonizes with the Spanish setting, while the transatlantic English acts as a constant reminder that the author is viewing his country and people from afar.

The text is structured like a collection of short stories; indeed, this is what Alfau claims it is in his prologue, inviting us to read the parts in any order. But while a different sequence would probably work, this is not because the stories are unconnected; on the contrary, they are closely knit, with characters reappearing, now at a different stage of life, now seen from another perspective.

The first part, **"Identity"**, makes an ingenious introduction, although re-reading it at the end will reveal much that is bound to pass unappreciated at the start. Unlike the rest of the stories, this one is set in Toledo, for which Alfau creates a ghostly atmosphere among the ancient buildings and ramparts. The Café de los Locos here—the "Madmen's Café", though Alfau translates very few of the Spanish words he uses—assembles the author himself and all the principal characters before they are transfigured for literary purposes, yet this does not mean that an illusion of reality is created for the first story in order to throw the self-consciously fictional nature of those that follow into relief. Paradoxically, the café has a fantastic quality; there we find, for example, "a poor and shabby lean fellow",

who claims to have been [Alfonso J.] Cervantes's inspiration, but is now quite redundant, except of course that his presence as an extra in Alfau's scene reinforces the phantasmagorical atmosphere of the old capital, haunted by an ageless, literary Spain.

The author follows in the long tradition of all those who, one way or another, have questioned the reality of the flesh-and-blood world compared to its literary counterpart. The relationship between cast and creator seems, at first, reminiscent of Pirandello, but the focus is in fact the reverse of the characters in search of an author, for Alfau in **"Identity"** sets up his premise thus: "Bad writers", he says (and his presence implies his own inclusion in this category), "were in the habit of coming to that café in quest of characters." And in the course of the work, one rebel called Gaston strains at the leash, trying to escape from his author and strike out on his own.

In **"A Character"**, the second story, he succeeds, but Alfau then has to rescue him from the narrative cul-de-sac into which he has stumbled, lacking the technique of a human writer to control a plot. **"Fingerprints"** demonstrates that logic and science are useless in the fictional world, for a man is here trapped into admitting guilt for a murder he did not commit, to vindicate his own faith in fingerprints. Here too, Gaston and his sister strike another blow for the characters' self-determination when they make a noise in the bedroom, interrupting the scene next door. Alfau registers his annoyance in a footnote.

"The Wallet" deals with an international police convention that happens to coincide with a city-wide power-cut of several days' duration. . . . The reaction of the population to this opportunity to take the law into their own hands is observed by an expatriate called Pepe, just back from England, so providing a perspective that one is tempted to imagine might resemble Alfau's own. At first, Pepe "felt like one who is dreaming", and the narrator adds parenthetically that this "is a feeling shared by most Spaniards who return to Spain after a long absence". Within minutes, however, Pepe loses his "foreign veneer", unlike the narrative voice, which retains the distance to observe that he is "witnessing the phenomena of an extraordinary land without present reality".

What is extraordinary, though, is not Spain, but Alfau's imaginary, timeless location of the same name, along with its inhabitants. Gaston thinks he "has stepped past the edge of the paper" by falling in love with a woman he believes to be real. But the author has the last laugh and we with him, for like all the characters in *Locos,* she is a fiction created from a fiction: the *femme fatale* fashioned from a waitress in the oneiric Madmen's Café.

Even if literary personages have tried to escape into reality before and since *Locos,* this text is original enough in the way it rehearses the problems of a writer's relationship with his creatures—and theirs with him—to be more than a historical curiosity, and makes thought-provoking as well as entertaining reading, curiously timeless like the world in which it unfolds. Perhaps the title is a Latin-Spanish pun, for this is a work as much about fiction's creation of places outside time as about the antics of madmen.

Abigail Lee Six, "Stepping past the Edge of the Paper," in The Times Literary Supplement, *No. 4530, January 26, 1990, p. 86.*

Publishers Weekly

[In Alfau's *Chromos,* a] man drops dead moments after a life insurance agent pays a sales call; grieving family members conduct their lives around his immobile corpse, preserved with frown, spectacles and pen in hand. That bit of black comedy conveys the absurdist flavor of Alfau's experimental novel, written in 1948 but never before published. It concerns a motley band of "Americaniards" (émigré Spaniards) in Manhattan in the 1930s who discover that the American "melting pot" is a great maw that threatens to devour their Spanish identity. As one of the group, a struggling novelist, reads aloud portions of his melodramatic work-in-progress (a novel within this novel), Spain's machismo, pride, stormy emotionalism, code of honor, bullfighting, Catholicism and sundry other preoccupations are skewered. Alfau's prose lurches from conversational banter to baroque sentences that nearly explode under the strain of their internal contradictions and subversive wit. This remarkable, if verbose, novel is a worthy successor to Alfau's *Locos.*

A review of "Chromos," in Publishers Weekly, *Vol. 237, No. 6, February 9, 1990, p. 46.*

Tom Whalen

Chromos is not quite as intricate, glittering and self-reflexive a fun house as *Locos* . . . The reader needs to know that about a third of *Chromos* is intentionally bad prose. It has, however, like *Locos,* many false bottoms for the reader to fall through. Alfau was exploring the essential artifice of fiction long before Barth's story "Autobiography" narrated itself, or before Donald Barthelme in "Daumier" folded up his characters and put them in a drawer.

Finished in 1948, but published now for the first time, Alfau's second and only other novel appears to have been written with some reluctance. In the novel's opening, the character Alfau is walking on the streets of New York with his friend Jose de los Rios and the Moor, Don Pedro Guzmán O'Moore Algoracid (a name "at once sonorous, lofty and unconvincing"), when he is encouraged by the latter to begin to write again. De los Rios (whom the Moor calls "Dr. Jesucristo") tells Alfau not to "sell his soul to this devil," but Alfau is tempted to write the novel the Moor suggests about the Americaniards (Spaniards living in New York City) and lets himself be led into his old writing room.

While the Moor waits outside, Alfau lights a match and sees some "old calendar chromos" (chromolithographs), faded color reproductions of two typical Spanish images: a man "serenading a young lady with high comb and very black, mournful eyes" and a dying bullfighter with a woman's "face buried in his bloody chest" while a priest performs the last rites. Before this match has time to burn

down, the next 320 pages of the novel are written, or better, dreamed.

And what a riotous dream it is. If, among the pantheon of 20th-century works of self-reflexive fiction, *Locos* aligns itself with the novels of Raymond Queneau, *Chromos* is closer to those of Flann O'Brien. Of course in Alfau there is no question of influence from or upon these masters or upon the other authors whom reviewers have called forth to help describe him, among them Nabokov, Barth, Barthelme, Borges, Calvino, Pynchon and Eco. (Pynchon fans will appreciate the Moor's answer when Alfau asks what the party they are attending is about: "Well, nobody knows. Nobody knows what it's all about, but they all come simply to increase the total entropy of this vale of tears.") For influences upon Alfau, one would have to go back to, say, Cervantes or Calderon, with the understanding that this [Jose Vasconcelos] Spanish-American, a former music critic and retired translator for a bank in New York, was writing his curiosities all on his own.

In outline the novel that Alfau dreams while his match burns goes something like this: Alfau, a translator, listens to excerpts from his friend García's novel-in-progress about the rise and fall of a stereotypical Spanish family and to García's story about a man who can jump forward in time. These stories' "stock situations and cast-iron sentimentalities" frequently dismay and anger Alfau, as at times they will the reader, though as often I found myself oddly engaged by the plights of García's constructs. When not alone with García (a character revived from *Locos,* as are many others), Alfau is usually at the cafe El Telescopio or at parties presided over by the Moor that always turn bacchanalian. Here discussions occur about what typifies the Spanish soul, about the Americanization of Spaniards in New York, about bullfighting, dancing and music. In one *tour-de-force* section, Don Pedro's discourse on Romantic composers is juxtaposed with excerpts from his mathematical theory that attempts to prove the universe is motionless, "extending in undreamt of directions."

Chromos has moments of startling inventiveness and comedy, and even passages of remarkable lyricism, such as this description of a bus ride down 72nd Street: "All the way down, the shadows of the trees kept growing to immense proportions until they were the shadows of the buildings and the streets themselves were ropes of fire holding down a prostrate giant." But this is rare. In *Chromos* Alfau's prose concentrates on parodying and satirizing Spanish tales and types.

By the end Alfau has

> seen only a kaleidoscope of fancies materialized
> by forgotten chromos, dirty, discolored chro-
> mos. This is what the possible visions of great-
> ness suggested by the conquistadors had finally
> come to: rhapsodic, nomadic incidents with
> hanging tarnished threads of past splendor out
> of time and out of place. Chromos in disrepute.

Rather than accompany our Mephistophelian Moor, Alfau joins de los Rios in Saint Patrick's Cathedral where he feels safe—protected, perhaps, from the sin of writing.

Would Alfau have written more than just these two wondrous novels if his work had been better received? The stories within **Chromos** are stories about loss, about failures told by failures. The further loss for this reader is knowing that there is not a career's worth of books by Felipe Alfau to read and reread.

Tom Whalen, "Felipe Alfau's 'Kaleidoscope of Fancies'," in Book World—The Washington Post, *April 22, 1990, p. 10.*

Phoebe-Lou Adams

Mr. Alfau's provocatively complicated novel [**Chromos**] starts simply enough. The narrator, a Spaniard long entrenched in New York City, quotes his friend Don Pedro, according to whom "a Spaniard speaking English . . . emerges with all other English-speaking persons in complete incapacity to understand the obvious." As all Mr. Alfau's characters are what he calls "Americaniards," the obvious is not to be expected in their activities. García is writing an old-fashioned family saga, which he reads aloud to the helplessly disapproving narrator. Dr. de los Rios is a successful neurologist with much time for conversation. A small-time entrepreneur imports, along with the usual dancers and musicians, a bull-fighter who is surprised and distressed to find his art superfluous. Don Pedro constructs theories of social improvement, all superbly impractical. The thinking of these people constantly harks back to Spain, providing their creator with an excuse to poke wry fun at Spanish preoccupations and character. This is a delightful, if sometimes bewildering, novel.

Phoebe-Lou Adams, in a review of "Chromos," in The Atlantic Monthly, *Vol. 265, No. 5, May, 1990, p. 133.*

John Brenkman

[In Alfau's **Chromos,** the] Spanish-born narrator and his cohort of émigré "Americaniard" friends live in New York, but they meet regularly to preserve their nostalgia for Spain and ward off their feelings of alienation. Mr. Alfau's aim in the novel seems to have been twofold. He reaches in one direction toward a metaphysical reflection, playing with the idea that the experience of time and change is illusory. And he also pursues a cultural commentary on a displaced community's fear of losing its identity. At the various gatherings, the unnamed narrator picks up stories through gossip, works in progress, memories and fantasies. Reams of a manuscript are read aloud to him by his friend García, a writer who cannot bring himself to revise his increasingly sensational and trite novel because all the episodes really did happen to a family back in Spain. Another of García's manuscripts tells of a man tortured by chronic impatience who magically acquires "the power to skip time at will." But he is then left to suffer a kind of amnesia turned inside out, as he is thrown forward into situations whose origins he can never know. Unfortunately, the paradoxes of time-skipping and the parody of family sagas do not ultimately enliven these manuscripts enough to illuminate Mr. Alfau's questioning of time and identity. Nor is **Chromos** much enhanced by

the narrator's practice of mind-reading, his satirical digressions on grieving widows and suicidal landladies or even his parody of a treatise on physics. Mr. Alfau's experiments with pastiche end up obscuring rather than linking his central concerns.

John Brenkman, in a review of "Chromos," in The New York Times Book Review, *May 13, 1990, p. 25.*

Albert Mobilio

When [writers like Borges, Nabokov and Stendhal] speak of the soul's dark nights, they do so breezily, without a trace of sweat. Lacquering pain in effortless grace, these sly foes of the too earnest ache reveal how much show biz shapes every written tragedy.

Felipe Alfau, the Spanish expatriate novelist rescued from obscurity by the Dalkey Archive Press, can now be numbered among the dégagé sophisticates. His two novels, **Locos** and **Chromos,** are glimmeringly honed expressions of the will to artifice. Subtitled *A Comedy of Gestures,* **Locos** details in a soothing, wise, but airy tone the suicides, murders, arrests, and general melancholy of a gallery of Madrid eccentrics. Only if you attend closely to the wry and overly precise narrator will you detect a throaty groan beneath the polished voice. It is the sound of strangled desire: Spanish Catholicism suffocating all evidence of carnality. Alfau doesn't indulge in anger at the loss; instead, he preens over how skillfully passion has been suppressed in his prose. Likewise, in **Chromos,** he cruises close to the bitter side of memory as he examines the bleak isolation of the Spanish exile in New York. But confession's particularities and the stylistic mark of the personal remain packed in salt and ice while the game of author as brinksman predominates.

Alfau exhibits a peculiarly Spanish taste for the extravagant gesture that is tightly reined, willfulness suffused with damning gloom. One thinks of Juan Goytisolo's *Count Julian,* a novel bound by a discomfiting grammatical constraint—the only punctuation is the semicolon—in which the semihero spends hours in the library crushing insects between the pages of Spanish classics. There's also Buñuel's strictly choreographed affection for sacrilege. Alfau partakes of this clerically inspired rigor, and he, too, holds Spain and his heritage in deep but troubled regard. . . .

When novelist Chandler Brossard knew him in the '40s and '50s, Alfau was living alone in a basement apartment, taking pleasure in the intertwined pursuits of music and mathematical puzzles. "He is the most reclusive person I've ever known," Brossard recalls. "He wouldn't talk about writing and had no interest in American literature." Brossard's unsuccessful attempts to get **Chromos** published only bothered Alfau. (His current publisher also reports that Alfau wasn't mightily thrilled by the prospect of being in print again.) Characterizing him as a "sophisticated alien" who disliked his adopted homeland, Brossard remembers Alfau expressing the belief that life is a "labyrinthine joke." Certainly this capsulized philosophy lies behind the dour laughter and intricate brooding of his first novel.

The Madrid of *Locos* is an otherworldly place, a city of closed, heavily draped rooms and persistent shadows lit only for flickering seconds by the narrator's cinematic attention. It has the feel of a movie soundstage so thinly contrived that the narrative camera cannot move much from the characters' faces lest it expose propped walls and doors to nowhere. Alfau confines us to its citizens, specifically the habitués of the Café de los Locos—"Bad writers were in the habit of coming to that café in quest of characters . . . "

If Alfau's shopping for "some very good secondhand bargains" among characters seems coy and dated, it's useful to keep in mind he was writing in the mid-'20s. Pirandello's famous play had been completed only a few years before, so the notion of the self-reflexive author, admittedly as old as Sterne or even Cervantes, was not quite the ragged trope it sometimes seems today. His characters wear their badge of literary creation with style and discretion; they are fanciful concoctions, to be sure, but a healthy dollop of fatalism leavens the dish. Consider Señor Olózaga and his gourmet résumé. Born of mixed parentage, raised by Spanish monks in China, this former galley slave wins and loses fortunes through shady dealings in the Spanish colonies, then becomes a butterfly charmer in a circus. Known as Juan Chinelato, or the Black Mandarin, Olózaga "often must have appeared in the dreams of many, sometimes like a black ogre, sometimes like a Chinese dragon, always spitting fire and devouring children." In his crosshatched ethnicity and Catholic baptism, he bears the brand of Spanish colonialism; to his fellow Madrileños, he's a nightmarish reminder of a spoiled imperial past.

Quixotic and ingeniously brutal, Olózaga exerts a fascination that wins him many wives and mistresses. Yet the virulent specter of miscegenation hovers close by. When he proposes to Don Esteban Bejarano for his daughter's hand, the aristocrat is barely unnerved by the suitor's current marriage—rather, he points out, "It is useless, Señor Chinelato. . . . My daughter is white." Olózaga himself has internalized the stigma. He makes his first wife sick with his cruelty—"The man who knew used to tell me that it was a shame that an aristocratic white lady like her had run herself to death for such a nigger"—then claims that their child is a bastard, even though the baby is "the living image of Chinelato." In a macabre gesture of self-abnegation, he murders, cooks, and serves the child to his wife for dinner. Of course, Alfau maintains his fingernail-paring distance even in the face of atrocity. A footnote to the scene says, "like all stage dinners, this is a make-believe one and the platter really held a cardboard dummy." The cleverness works as a magician's cape thrown over the grotesque—a twisted consequence of race hatred and lust—to make what has burst from the hat disappear. Although he enjoys sparking these eruptions of the uncanny, Alfau cloaks them, investing the horror with a still greater charge.

By chilling the heat of the feral psyche in coolly dispassionate prose, Alfau reenacts Catholicism's purple ritual of repression and guilt. In **"Fingerprints,"** Don Gil Bejarano wants to have every Spaniard's digit on file. Not surprisingly, no one volunteers except Don Gil, who has written an article: "Fingerprints, a sure antidote against all alibis." When the prefect of police, Don Benito, informs him that his prints have been found at a murder scene, Don Gil insists upon his own arrest even though he didn't commit the crime. Don Benito begs him to deny the infallibility of his fingerprint theory, but Don Gil refuses to recant his own canonical law. Alfau glosses this tidy parable of original sin with an episode of incest in the Bejarano household. Related obliquely—"the muffled voices of his son and daughter in an adjoining room, wrapped in an exasperating, mocking laughter . . . and also the broken exclamations of his wife"—this replay of Cain and Abel doesn't unveil sin so much as enhance its mystery. Guilt is a luscious thing in Alfau's Spain, a sought-after delicacy best savored from afar.

Although he employs most of the characters from *Locos,* Alfau offers a very different book in *Chromos,* his only other novel. An extended meditation on exile, especially the linguistic limbo that divides the new language from the old, *Chromos* lacks the detectivelike intricacy and sinister undercurrent of *Locos.* Alfau makes the dilemma clear in the opening sentence: "The moment one learns English, complications set in." Transplanted to New York; the *Locos* cast have become "Americaniards," expatriates strung between the world that made them and the one in which they live. They meet in cramped apartments or in a Spanish café, El Telescopio, and tirelessly mull over the subject of their Spanishness. The revelations, while true, tend toward the obvious: "Spaniards always find in this country a lack of space and a lack of time. One can obtain any number of gadgets which was the privilege of the very rich . . . but no space or time, which is what one has plenty of in Spain." Alfau shines most brightly when bringing his morbid eye to bear on the cityscape: "There is something about most of the East Side. . . . It is the quality of a memory that has lain forsaken like an unattended grave. Nowhere else in New York can one find so everpresent the spirit of the has-been . . . " He shrouds the town in dyspeptic gloom, repelled by "the grimaces and yelpings of industrialism."

These descriptions show this refined outsider's resistance to the New World's rough embrace. Less successful is the evocation of the past's unrelenting grip. During much of the novel, we listen along with the narrator as the poet García reads long sections of two works in progress—a Spanish family romance and a screenplay about the death of a rich Americaniard on the Bowery. The too generous inclusion of these fictions within a fiction and the setups required for each reading grow wearisome. Alfau's mimicry of the traditional Spanish potboiler is witty and ably represents a sensibility given to "abnormal psychology and stormy emotionalism," but the job was accomplished with more exacting finesse in *Locos*; here a little goes a long way. *Locos* is a masterwork written by a 26-year-old prodigy, *Chromos* the first novel he would have written had he not been so gifted. *Chromos* concludes with an admission that seems to acknowledge its flaws, the limits Alfau had reached: "In Spanish I don't have to explain my nation or countrymen. In English, I can't. . . . In Spanish one sees and things remain unquestioned and clear. In English, one studies and uncovers meanings that one does not understand."

By abandoning Spanish to write about Spain and Spanishness in a language whose literature and culture he apparently cared little for, Alfau committed an exalted act of suppression; he buried his heart's own speech so as to recreate its essence in a foreign tongue. An ascetic's sacrifice or perhaps a penance, the decision to abide within English, to command its nuances so persuasively, required demonic faith in the power of artifice. While self-expression finds its strongest voice in the urgent immediacy of the sincere, self-omission models a porous diction, a prose that ritualizes absence. Alfau's richly secretive Spain sifts through the gaps. It is vivid because only partly seen. In **Locos,** a priest is asked if a repressed instinct will degenerate. "Leave the flesh alone for a month," he answers, "and [it] will leave you alone for three." He later commits suicide over a lost love. Alfau left his native home and language alone, but like love, it cannot be hidden long.

Albert Mobilio, "Loco Heroes: Felipe Alfau's Alien Nation," in VLS, *No. 86, June, 1990, p. 18.*

Gregory Rabassa

When the Casa Moneo, a general store on Fourteenth Street in New York, closed down a few years back, one of the last centers of the Peninsular Spanish colony in the city disappeared. Today this relatively small and little known ethnic group, with antecedents that go far back, has been engulfed by the waves of new Hispanic immigrants from Latin America, just as the essentially Peninsular daily *La Prensa* has been absorbed by the mainly Spanish American *El Diario.*

Chromos, a "discovered" novel written in the 1940s, preserves the memory of a way of life that held on for some years against absorption by the Anglo-Saxon culture on the one hand and by that of Hispanics from the New World on the other. It is a society peopled by those the author, Felipe Alfau, calls "Americaniards."

What it means for an individual to speak English or Spanish, to think in Spanish or English, how the constraints of a language change you as a person—these linguistic considerations begin the book, set its tone, and function as theme for much that is to happen:

> The moment one learns English, complications set in. Try as one may, one cannot elude this conclusion, one must inevitably come back to it. This applies to all persons, including those born to the language, and, at times even more so to Latins, including Spaniards. It manifests itself in an awareness of implications and intricacies to which one had never given a thought; it affects one with that officiousness of philosophy which, having no business of its own, gets in everybody's way and, in the case of Latins, they lose that racial characteristic of taking things for granted and leaving them to their own devices

> without inquiring into causes, motives or ends, to meddle indiscreetly into reasons which are none of one's affair and to become not only self-conscious, but conscious of other things which never gave a damn for one's existence.

The action takes place in New York, mostly on the lower East Side and in a bar nicknamed El Telescopio. The larger-than-life characters who forgather there are a varied crew, but all are transplanted Spaniards. Foremost is Don Pedro Guzmán O'Moore Algoracid, a sometime orchestra leader who is known to the American public as Pete Guz, to Spanish friends as the Moor. He is described as "an absurd combination of a slightly daffy Irish-Moorish Don Quixote with sinister overtones of Beelzebub and the only Irishman I ever heard speak English with an Andalusian brogue." Interspersed with the action (or lack of it) are stories of Spain, told by a certain García, who says he may put them into a novel someday.

It is reminiscent of the old writer Morelli in Julio Cortázar's *Hopscotch,* whose ideas on the novel correspond nicely to the form of the one in which he appears. García is the Morelli of this remarkable story, anticipating, as does Alfau's earlier book **Locos: A Comedy of Gestures,** that great outpouring of good fiction that has come to be known as the Latin American "boom" and which, in light of this book, might well have resulted from some condition that is inherently Hispanic and which goes back to *Don Quixote.*

Chromos refers to the gaudy commercial prints of the period, calendar art, as it were. It is a fitting name for the book as it contains what otherwise might be called vignettes. One Guignolesque episode dealing with the mummification and subsequent deterioration of the lawyer Don Hilarión is reminiscent of García Márquez and *The Autumn of the Patriarch.* Moments like this and the anarchic structure of the book (one of the chromos is a lengthy discussion of time, space, and the fourth dimension, all quite solid and erudite) bring us back to the ideas put forth at the beginning of the novel, for at the end Alfau goes back to that theme and explains his difficulties:

> To express this in my own language would be superfluous. To attempt to describe it in another's impossible. In Spanish I don't have to explain my nation or my countrymen. In English, I can't. It is the question of the synthetic method as opposed to the analytical. In Spanish one sees and things remain unquestioned and clear. In English, one studies and uncovers meanings that one does not understand. It is then that, as I said in the beginning, complications set in.

Alfau is strikingly aware of linguistic differences, the very language of his narration is perfectly good English, and yet it is not English. Nor is it Spanish either in a free or in a literal translation. The closest one can come to describing it is as meta-English, with recourse to a regnant cliché. We might be witnessing linguistic transformation here, what happened when the Franks and Goths began to speak Latin or the Normans Anglo-Saxon. This is therefore a remarkable book, not only for what it says, but also for what it is struggling to say, often with strangely successful insights. (pp. 29-30)

Gregory Rabassa, in a review of "Chromos," in Boston Review, *Vol. XV, No.5, October, 1990, pp.29-30.*

The New Yorker

Stories within stories within stories: that is the form of this oblique tease of a novel, [Alfau's **Chromos**], composed in 1948. The narrator's story is straightforward enough: he hangs out with various colorful types who are members of New York's Spanish community, and they regale or oppress him with their tales. First and foremost is García, endlessly writing novels and screen treatments, some of which he insists are true, even while he fiddles with sequence and plot. Another is Don Pedro, who has written a thesis solving all problems of physics, on which he can discourse while brilliantly playing Chopin. To him all music is narrative; the author, for his part, makes literature musical, not in sound but in synchronicity and patterning. If this novel were music, it might be by Shostakovich, for its tone is so ironic as to approach sarcasm—as if anything anyone might do is necessarily faintly ridiculous. But it gives some of the more ridiculous things people do, like falling in love with a store-window mannequin, a strangely regal air, because they are held at such a distance. In a café called El Telescopio, Don Pedro, setting up bottles to look like the skyline, comments, "Now Manhattan is in El Telescopio—the situation reversed, the world inside out. The absurdity typical but the results good. Nothing to it. You know?"

A review of "Chromos," in The New Yorker, *Vol. LXVI, No. 43, December 10, 1990, p. 158.*

Hannah Arendt

1906-1975

German-born American philosopher, journalist, editor, and translator.

Arendt is respected as an important political theorist for her insights into modern governmental, social, and economic conditions that contribute to strife and the rise of totalitarian regimes. She viewed political activity as expressive of what is most valuable in human endeavor, arguing that individuals achieve a sense of purpose and meaning by participating in decision-making processes involving social change or preservation of ideas and artifacts. Accordingly, when people are denied or dispossessed of these political powers they become superfluous and easily dominated by governments, bureaucracies, and other authoritative bodies, which Arendt noted as a disturbing trend in modern life. Indeed, in her work *On Revolution* Arendt linked the major issue confronting twentieth-century civilization with that "most ancient of all [political causes], the one, in fact, that from the beginning of our history has determined the very existence of politics, the cause of freedom versus tyranny." Her elaborations on this theme encompassed such topics as racism, war and revolution, culture and the mind, the nature of evil, and the effects of technology. Stephen Klaidman observed: "[Arendt's] penetrating analyses of totalitarianism and democracy, the problems of mass society, the reasons for revolution and political image-making are widely regarded as required reading for a thorough understanding of modern political history."

Arendt was born in Germany to well-educated Jewish parents involved in socialist causes. Her childhood was spent in Germany and in Königsberg, a Baltic seaport where her parents were raised that was part of East Prussia before World War I. Her happy childhood was disrupted when her father suffered a debilitating illness and died in 1913, by ethnic tensions in multicultural Königsberg, and by World War I. In 1924, Arendt entered Marburg University. There she met Martin Heidegger, who was developing his reputation for studies in phenomenology and with whom she shared a brief romance. Arendt later studied philosophy at the University of Heidelberg under the tutelage of Karl Jaspers, an independent, non-methodological theorist who fervently insisted upon the necessity of freedom. Through such esteemed philosophers as Heidegger and Jaspers, Arendt was introduced to innovative approaches to issues concerning language and consciousness, complemented by her thorough education in Greek, Roman, and German intellectual traditions, all of which are reflected in her writings. After receiving her doctorate at age twenty-two, Arendt wrote essays and articles on political issues and other topics for various periodicals. As anti-Semitism began sweeping through Germany, she became involved with organizations providing safe passage for Jews. Because she was an obvious target for persecution for her anti-fascist ideals and her Jewish heritage, Ar-

endt left Germany for Paris in 1933 when the Nazi party gained power. In Paris, Arendt worked on behalf of Jewish refugees. She moved to the United States in 1940, settling in New York and continuing to work with Jewish support organizations while gaining a reputation through essays and book reviews as an incisive political commentator.

In her writings, Arendt stressed the importance of free public spheres within societies where individuals can debate and participate in political action, a concept that derives in part from Greek and Roman intellectual ideals. This public realm, or "space," as she termed it, is separate from a private realm where personal concerns predominate. Arendt believed that diminishment of space corresponds with loss of freedom and thought. This view informs *The Origins of Totalitarianism,* Arendt's first major study, which examines utter domination of society as practiced in Nazi Germany and Stalinist Russia. Arendt traces the roots of totalitarianism to such trends as imperialism and racism as they have been manifested since the Enlightenment. Through racism, for example, groups of people are denied political power and are particularly vulnerable to persecution by other social groups and by the state. Arendt discusses the structures and methods used by totalitarian regimes to gain and maintain power, the simplistic and distorted logic employed in these systems, and reasons for their popularity. She claims that totalitarian systems' uniqueness in the history of despotism lies in their rigidly institutionalized control of all facets of society and their use of terror to maintain power. *The Origins of Totalitarianism* generated widespread debate among commentators from various fields. The book's non-methodological structure and tone were faulted by some specialists in the social sciences uncomfortable with what they considered unsubstantiated generalizations, particularly Arendt's linking of Nazi and Soviet forms of oppression that differed in various ways. Others argued that this approach made her discussion of vital issues concerning contemporary life more accessible, particularly those relating to human rights. *The Origins of Totalitarianism* has been cited in several court decisions protecting the rights of displaced persons and expatriates.

In *The Human Condition* Arendt outlines her views on public and private spheres. She distinguishes three types of human activities: labor, the production of things immediately consumed by society; work, the production of durable objects; and action, defined as human endeavors that provide a sense of value and meaning to existence. The first two activities, through which human beings satisfy basic necessities, occur in the private sphere, while "action"—which Arendt considers the highest human good—occurs in the public realm and generally encompasses intellectual activities. Humankind suffers, Arendt argues, when action is deemed less valuable than work or labor, as when governments impose controls upon society and dominate the decision-making process. This theme is explored further in *On Revolution,* where Arendt assesses revolts of the modern age. She favors rebellions such as the American Revolution, which created space for society to purge itself of wrongs, rather than those like the French Revolution or ones based on Marxist tenets, where authorities impose cures to social and economic ills. Mixed reaction to these two works mirrors general commentary on Arendt's theories. Detractors considered her insensitive to the plight of the masses and contended that her theories are divorced from historical realities and necessities, while supporters note that she promotes freedom and dignity by placing responsibilities on individuals to better the human condition.

Arendt's most notorious work and the one which garnered the most widespread attention upon publication is *Eichmann in Jerusalem: A Report on the Banality of Evil,* originally presented as a series of articles in the *New Yorker.* The magazine commissioned Arendt to report on the trial of Adolf Eichmann, a Nazi official held responsible for genocide of Jews in concentration camps. At the trial Arendt was surprised to observe that Eichmann, who was placed in a glass booth as part of elaborate security precautions, appeared subdued and simple rather than monstrous and hateful. She viewed him as representative of the effects of totalitarianism, where individuals become automatons, performing duties without reflection or debate. She argued that Eichmann should not be held personally responsible for murder and that Nazism itself was reflec-

tive of a general moral collapse throughout Europe. This conclusion and other observations concerning Eichmann, Nazism, anti-Semitism, and the roles of Jews in Nazi Germany provoked intensive public debate, including charges that Arendt herself harbored anti-Semitic sentiments. As the furor waned, critics viewed *Eichmann on Trial* as being consistent with Arendt's theories expressed in previous works. Several topics discussed in *Eichmann on Trial,* including evil and violence, Jewish identity, and the processes of thought are explored further in Arendt's later works—*On Violence, The Jew as Pariah: Jewish Identity and Politics in the Modern Age,* and *The Life of the Mind.*

(See also *Contemporary Issues Criticism,* Vol. 1; *Contemporary Authors,* Vols. 17-20, rev. ed., Vols. 61-64 [obituary]; and *Contemporary Authors New Revision Series,* Vol. 26.)

PRINCIPAL WORKS

ESSAYS

Der Liebsgriff bei Augustin: Versuch einer philosophischen Interpretation   1929
The Origins of Totalitarianism   1951
The Human Condition   1958
Rahel Varnhagen: The Life of a Jewess   1958
*Between Past and Future: Six Exercises in Political Thought   1961
Eichmann in Jerusalem: A Report on the Banality of Evil   1963
On Revolution   1963
Men in Dark Times   1968
On Violence   1970
Crises of the Republic   1972
The Jew as Pariah: Jewish Identity and Politics in the Modern Age   1978
The Life of the Mind   1978
Lectures on Kant's Political Philosophy   1982

*Expanded version: *Between Past and Future: Eight Exercises in Political Thought*   1968

David Riesman

Hannah Arendt's extraordinarily penetrating book [*The Origins of Totalitarianism*] makes plain that totalitarianism, whether Nazi or Stalinist, cannot be understood so long as we continue to use the traditional categories of common sense: it cannot be explained by the mere desire for power, for national expansion, for class revenge—for any motives that are simply human, though evil. Totalitarians are "inhuman" in that they are motivated toward total domination of the globe, toward total destructiveness of human individuality everywhere. Their goals are based neither on specific, narrow interests nor even on the utopianism of earlier ideologies, religious or socialist, which sought to extend in the future the sway of certain already given values. (p. 392)

Dr. Arendt, building on the work of such writers as Kravchenko, Rousset, and Bettelheim (she criticizes Dallin for his "utilitarian" theory that the Soviet camps are simply an inefficient forced labor supply), shows how the Soviet Union, in eliminating mere whimsical bestiality and sadism from its treatment of people, in forcing friends and families to denounce anyone among them on whom arbitrary suspicion falls, has gone further than the Nazis in the direction of total domination. On this point, I entirely agree with her: most of the Nazis were too corruptible, in their still human desires for money or revenge, to succumb (save in the one sphere of racial policy) to complete and fanatical ideals of total domination. But then, Himmler had less time at his disposal than Stalin has had to create in his own image men who are not even attached to their own lives, let alone to their ease, their advancement, or even their cruel satisfactions.

Without a certain amount of fanaticism on her own part (she reminds one of Simone Weil in her passion and eloquence, though she is not mystical and is much more closely tied to the data of historical experience), Dr. Arendt would perhaps have been less well equipped for the enormous task of understanding she has set herself: namely, to make sense of just those excesses which strike the non-totalitarian world as madness; to feel her way into the mentality of both the leaders and the followers of totalitarian movements, which requires showing just what it was they despised in the bourgeois 19th-century world they wanted to destroy. At times this leads her perilously close to assuming that this world, because it fell and because it bred its destroyers, did in fact "deserve" to be destroyed. Such an attitude assumes a historical rationality and inevitability which, in other aspects, Dr. Arendt rejects; yet this attitude is significant precisely because it is arguable that very little major work of the last hundred years in philosophy and social science—whether we think of Marx, of Comte, of Freud, of Nietzsche—has been produced without some degree of fanaticism. And *The Origins of Totalitarianism* must be placed on that small shelf of truly seminal works whose very errors, exaggerations, and oversystematizations so often turn out, in the unpredictable history of ideas, to be liberating and fructifying for thought.

Dr. Arendt begins by tracing the fateful way in which the Jews became the first near-total victims of near-total domination. (Had the Nazis remained longer in power, the Poles, Ukrainians, and "unhealthy" Germans would have followed suit; the Gypsies actually were wiped out.) It is her aim to show that the Jews were not accidental and wholly innocent victims, as the "scapegoat" theory would have it, and that modern exterminatory anti-Semitism has virtually no connection with medieval or czarist attitudes and outrages—let alone with mere social anti-Semitism in the Western countries. She observes that the Jews lost, with the decline of absolute monarchy, and the later maturing of the national state into the imperialist state, their economic and political function as state bankers and financial-diplomatic intermediaries (of course, this function was monopolized by a very small number, who thereby "led" their fellow Jews). At the same time, the Jews did not find a functional place in the basic industries of the developing mass societies, but remained "between parvenu

and pariah"—either parasitic diamond jobbers or stock manipulators or seekers of fame and the aura of fame in the cosmopolitan glow by which their Jewishness would be erased. Drawing on Proust's work, she shows how in aristocratic and highly anti-Semitic French circles Jewishness, like homosexuality, became a "vice" the more titillating the less it was disguised. Many mobile Jews were put in the position of employing or appearing to employ precisely their social marginality as Jews for their ticket of entry to society. Under such conditions, these Jews lost not only their economic and, in the widest sense, their social function, but also their bearings; and the author shows the consequences of this in her brilliant account of the Dreyfus Affair. The French Jews, with hardly any exceptions, were unable to see that the clearing of Dreyfus involved more desperately political issues than those embodied in a business deal; unlike Bernard Lazare, Zola, and Clemenceau, they kept insisting that it must all have been a mistake, that nobody—least of all Dreyfus's military and reactionary enemies—really meant ill, either to France or to the Jews. Dr. Arendt suggests that the failure to fight the issue through, and the acceptance instead of the compromise of Dreyfus's pardon, made it plain that political anti-Semitism could be used to undermine democracy and the nation-state.

In her attitude, Dr. Arendt may be a bit too uncharitable to the weakness, the lack of heroism, of Dreyfus's family and of the other comfortably fixed French Jews; she admires courage and despises middle-class pretense, blindness, and vacillation. At the same time, she tends to assume not only that the selection of the Jews as political game was no accident but that the success of the game was no accident either but a tribute to the political discernment of the anti-Semites (who "really understood" the masses' longings) and to the cowardice and illusions of the Jews and their liberal friends. The danger of assuming that what happened had to happen (which is different from assuming that one can explain it retroactively) always confronts the historian who attempts to be more than a narrator of antiquities.

However that may be, Dr. Arendt brilliantly uses the French "rehearsal" to show how anti-Semitism becomes a platform uniting the "elite" and the "mob" in contempt for bourgeois society and its laws; and in seeing that this alliance lies at the heart of the totalitarian movements of the 20th century, she makes one of her most important contributions. For instance, her analysis helps account for the success of such a play as *The Madwoman of Chaillot* (written, by the way, by an anti-Semite), which allows people to laugh at the spectacle of the witty bohemians (i.e. the intellectual elite), the wisely mad, and the charming mob leading wicked, rapacious oil financiers (the bourgeois) into a deathtrap; even businessmen enjoy the spectacle of their arty and fashionable demise. The real "merchants of death" under conditions of modern malaise and discontent with middle-class society become writers who, like Céline, passionately argue for the massacre of all Jews, not insomuch as they are Jews but insomuch as they are symbols of what these writers cannot stand in their society. (pp. 392-94)

As things turned out, it was not the Jews at home but the blacks of Africa abroad who suffered in the 19th century from racist doctrine and practice. Dr. Arendt's account of what happened when the Boers in South Africa confronted tribes of "savages" who could neither be quickly killed nor quickly domesticated—but who served as a frightening image of what "going native" meant under the nomadic life of the veld—is one of the many dramatic chapters in her series of moving historical tableaux. Modern anthropology has so accustomed us to assume the fundamental ethnocentrism of such a ferocious value judgment as is implied in the term "savages" that it is startling to the reader to find that Dr. Arendt herself regards the Zulus and other African people as savages and not merely as "preliterates" with a valuable and interesting culture. Yet it is perhaps this bias, which she shares with the wonderful short novel of Conrad, *Heart of Darkness,* which provides her with the empathy required to comprehend the mind of the Boer. In his deracination from all civilized values, the Boer lost not only anything that might be called a Christian attitude toward the indigenous population; he also lost whatever he had possessed of a "capitalist" mentality. Without developing a new ideology, he regressed to a bitter agrarianism, fundamentalism, and anti-urbanism; and became himself metaphorically a member of a lost tribe. Thus, he lost the skills and motives that might have led him to exploit the diamond mines of the Rand, rather than leave this to the hated Jews and to Cecil Rhodes.

The South of Africa thus contributed (by what route Dr. Arendt never makes quite clear) a theme of virulent racialism to the developing pattern of totalitarian theory and practice inside Europe. Meanwhile, in Egypt, at the other end of Africa, the British were facing a very different problem from that of the Boers: they had taken Egypt, not for its loot or to colonize it nor for purposes of future incorporation, but simply because of the need to protect the seaway to India. If the Boers got too close to the natives to be distinguished from them save by skin color, the British proconsuls in Egypt remained wholly detached from the natives whom they supervised. Lord Cromer stands, in Dr. Arendt's account, as the epitome of the cold, correct bureaucratic mentality that could equally well massacre or protect an alien people. Proceeding in the face of what he considered the sentimentality of the British public, he developed techniques for systematic and disingenuous rule. He did this selflessly, capably, anonymously, much as T. E. Lawrence and other foreign agents later served British imperial policy. Dr. Arendt seems to be asserting that such techniques of organization were precursors of totalitarian bureaucracy, as necessary as were the French mobs who stoned Dreyfusards, or the Boers who wantonly murdered Zulus, for the dynamism of the totalitarian movement.

Yet the line which runs from Cromer's imperialistic tendencies, chastened as these were by his exalted ethic and his devotion to reason, to the brutality of a Nazi governor-general in occupied territory, seems to me slim indeed, though no more tenuous than many similar chains of guilt which historians of ideas and of institutions have been drawing in our day. Dr. Arendt is torn between her partial

recognition of this fact in addition to her well-justified sympathy for the heroes and poets of the British foreign service, on the one hand, and her belief that imperialism, along with anti-Semitism, laid the groundwork for totalitarianism, on the other. The second third of her book is in fact devoted to imperialism. She sees this movement as tending, for example, in the case of Cecil Rhodes, to expansion for expansion's sake; Rhodes' famous remark, "I would annex the planets if I could," has the ring of totalitarian inhumanity and fanaticism. Beyond that, she sees imperialism more or less as Hobson does—as an expression of the political power of the bourgeoisie and as the last desperate move of capitalism after people and produce and capital become surplus. In my opinion, she gives insufficient weight to Schumpeter's criticisms of Hobson. Schumpeter suggests that imperialism has its roots largely in pre-capitalist habits rather than late-capitalist crisis; imperialism is out of keeping with the 'soft' moral climate and free-trade economic ethic of mature capitalism. (pp. 394-95)

Dr. Arendt observes that those countries which missed out in the race for empire abroad tended to develop their prologues to totalitarian impulses in the midst of the European homeland. Thus, she describes the "Pan-movements" of Central and Eastern Europe (Pan-Germanism and Pan-Slavism) as a kind of internal imperialism divorced from the restraints imposed by economic interest, collecting followers (and foes) on the basis of mere tribal identities:

> In psychological terms, the chief difference between even the most violent chauvinism and this tribal nationalism is that the one is extroverted, concerned with visible spiritual and material achievements of the nation, whereas the other, even in its mildest forms (for example, the German youth movement) is introverted, concentrates on the individual's own soul which is considered as the embodiment of general national qualities. . . . It claims its people to be unique, individual, incompatible with all others, and denies theoretically the very possibility of a common mankind long before it is used to destroy the humanity of man.
>
> (pp. 395-96)

The Origins of Totalitarianism shows the decisive importance of a belief, on the part of mob and elite alike, that there is a conspiratorial, numerically small power which rules History—the Jews in the case of the Nazis, "Wall Street" today in the case of the Bolsheviks; the existence of this alleged power serves both as a model to be imitated, and as a justification for counter-secrecy, and, more important perhaps than either, as an "explanation" for the bewildering life experiences of the movement's followers.

The most significant of these experiences for attitude formation is that of feeling oneself as an actual or potential "surplus" in an industrial society, as one who is vulnerable to dislocation in the class system by shifts of economic fortunes and to dislocation in the nation-state system by loss of communal roots. (In the reviewer's opinion, Dr. Arendt does not pay enough attention to the closing down of emigration routes after the First World War as a notification to the surplus ones that they no longer had a place of hope and refuge. With the hardening of national, and especially American, boundaries, the growth of "tariffs on people" becomes as explosive an international force as the growth of tariffs on commodities.) Dr. Arendt observes that, whereas the slave had a place in earlier societies because he had a function in them, the new de-classed and de-nationed of the 20th century are just what the exported ones have since come to be called: DP's, people without place. They perforce depend on their mere humanity as the source of their only claim on mankind. (p. 396)

The DP's within and without a country are forced by circumstance to regard all respectable society as a racket, impure and simple, at the same time that their helpless presence symbolizes the puzzling breakdown of national communities and of international comity. In their contempt and cynicism, not only they themselves but also those who observe them and fear the same fate, fall all the more readily for the "keys" which reduce history to the manifestation of class or tribal identities.

Does this not show the importance, in the development of totalitarianism, of sheer confusion as to what is going on in the world? Dr. Arendt makes it very plain that confusion serves to rally people to the movements which claim to be "above parties" and which argue that parties are simply part of the facade, the swindle, of the "dying" democratic state—whose engineered death later "proves" the rightness of the earlier label. The confused ones who rally to these movements are people whose disorientation is far different from the sheer political ignorance in which premodern peasant societies lived; they are people who are troubled by a literate disorientation which seeks ideological answers no longer given by religion or by the sheer presence of an obvious and obviously oppressive ruling group. And confusion also serves to bewilder, on the other hand, the enemies of the totalitarian movements, who suppose that the latter have limited objectives and that, once they have conquered a place in the sun, appeasement will keep them from wanting the sun itself.

In this connection, Dr. Arendt demonstrates that, if the concentration camp is the sign of the existence of totalitarianism in power, the front organization is the means by which it gains power. The front organizations fool not only the outside world about the aims of the movement, by presenting that world with "normal" unfanatical sympathizers, gullible or cynical apologists, and interpreters who put down a barrage of rational explanations ("provocation" or "excesses in the lower ranks") to explain away what the movement does; but the fronts also serve just as much to fool the inner core of members about the nature of the outside world. For this world presents itself to the inner core not as it is, but through the "reasonable" sympathizer of the front organizations. Until iron curtains and mass terror can shut out the non-totalitarian reality, all but the most tenacious of the inner core need the reassuring existence of the sympathizer in order to remain convinced that their ideological key to history is actually correct and that their beliefs that the Jews or the "60 Families" rule, and that they deserve death for this, are not simply crazy and monstrous creeds. (pp. 396-97)

In view of the contributions of Dr. Arendt's book, it is important that its imaginative historical reconstructions be subjected to professional criticism; there are a number of points where I think Dr. Arendt, on shaky evidence, skates daringly over documentary gaps. In general, as I have already implied, she tends to make totalitarianism appear as consistently fanatical; she therefore overinterprets specific actions in terms of long-range goals, and does not allow for any more or less accidental concatenations of bureaucratic forces, slip-ups, careerisms, as explanatory factors. Thus, she sees the duplication of agencies by Nazis and Bolsheviks as a device for mystification, and as serving other totalitarian ends. She does not suggest that such duplication might appear (as it did under Franklin Roosevelt) only partly as a means to keep various people and policies in suspense but also partly because it is hard, even for a dictator, to end the life of an agency. This general slant makes her assume that totalitarianism, while thoroughly un-utilitarian in pursuit of such older human goals as wealth and power, is ferociously efficient in seeking total domination as such. (p. 397)

But such questions of detail and emphasis are relatively minor in comparison with the achievement of [*The Origins of Totalitarianism*]. It is not only an achievement in historiography, but also in political science and, as in its extraordinarily illuminating discussion of the rights of man, in philosophy and ethics. It is throughout a densely imaginative work, truly serious, which makes great demands on the reader, for intellectual readjustments as much as for historical background. I happen to think such an experience in understanding our times as this book provides is itself a social force not to be underestimated. (p. 398)

> David Riesman, "The Path to Total Terror," in Commentary, *Vol. XI, April, 1951, pp. 392-98.*

Eric Voegelin

[*The Origins of Totalitarianism*] is an attempt to make contemporary phenomena intelligible by tracing their origin back to the eighteenth century, thus establishing a time unit in which the essence of totalitarianism unfolded to its fullness. And as far as the nature of totalitarianism is concerned, it penetrates to the theoretically relevant issues. . . . It abounds with brilliant formulations and profound insights—as one would expect only from an author who has mastered her problems as a philosopher—but surprisingly, when the author pursues these insights into their consequences, the elaboration veers toward regrettable flatness. Such derailments, while embarrassing, are nevertheless instructive—sometimes more instructive than the insights themselves—because they reveal the intellectual confusion of the age, and show more convincingly than any argument why totalitarian ideas find mass acceptance and will find it for a long time to come.

The book is organized in three parts: Antisemitism, Imperialism, and Totalitarianism. The sequence of the three topics is roughly chronological, though the phenomena under the three titles do overlap in time. Antisemitism begins to rear its head in the Age of Enlightenment; the imperialist expansion and the pan-movements reach from the middle of the nineteenth century to the present; and the totalitarian movements belong to the twentieth century. The sequence is, furthermore, an order of increasing intensity and ferocity in the growth of totalitarian features toward the climax in the atrocities of the concentration camps. And it is, finally, a gradual revelation of the essence of totalitarianism from its inchoate forms in the eighteenth century to the fully developed, nihilistic crushing of human beings.

This organization of the materials, however, cannot be completely understood without its emotional motivation. There is more than one way to deal with the problems of totalitarianism; and it is not certain, as we shall see, that Dr. Arendt's is the best. Anyway, there can be no doubt that the fate of the Jews, the mass slaughter and the homelessness of displaced persons, is for the author a center of emotional shock, the center from which radiates her desire to inquire into the causes of the horror, to understand political phenomena in Western civilization that belong to the same class, and to consider means that will stem the evil. This emotionally determined method of proceeding from a concrete center of shock toward generalizations leads to a delimitation of subject matter. The shock is caused by the fate of human beings, of the leaders, followers, and victims of totalitarian movements; hence, the crumbling of old and the formation of new institutions, the life-courses of individuals in an age of institutional change, the dissolution and formation of types of conduct, as well as of the ideas of right conduct, will become topical; totalitarianism will have to be understood by its manifestations in the medium of conduct and institutions just adumbrated. And indeed there runs through the book—as the governing theme—the obsolescence of the national state as the sheltering organization of Western political societies, owing to technological, economic, and the consequent changes of political power. With every change sections of society become "superfluous," in the sense that they lose their function and therefore are threatened in their social status and economic existence. The centralization of the national state and the rise of bureaucracies in France makes the nobility superfluous; the growth of industrial societies and new sources of revenue in the late nineteenth century make the Jews as state bankers superfluous. . . . As far as the institutional aspect of the process is concerned totalitarianism, thus, is the disintegration of national societies and their transformation into aggregates of superfluous human beings.

The delimitation of subject matter through the emotions aroused by the fate of human beings is the strength of Dr. Arendt's book. The concern about man and the causes of his fate in social upheavals is the source of historiography. The manner in which the author spans her arc from the presently moving events to their origins in the concentration of the national state evolves distant memories of the grand manner in which Thucydides spanned his arc from the catastrophic movement of his time, from the great *kinesis,* to its origins in the emergence of the Athenian polis after the Persian Wars. The emotion in its purity makes the intellect a sensitive instrument for recognizing

and selecting the relevant facts; and if the purity of the human interest remains untainted by partisanship, the result will be a historical study of respectable rank—as in the case of the present work, which in its substantive parts is remarkably free of ideological nonsense. With admirable detachment from the partisan strife of the day, the author has succeeded in writing the history of the circumstances that occasioned the movements, of the totalitarian movements themselves, and above all of the dissolution of human personality, from the early anti-bourgeois and antisemitic resentment to the contemporary horrors of the "man who does his duty" and of his victims.

This is not the occasion to go into details. Nevertheless, a few of the topics must be mentioned in order to convey an idea of the richness of the work. The first part is perhaps the best short history of the antisemitic problem in existence; for special attention should be singled out the sections on the court-jews and their decline, on the Jewish problem in enlightened and romantic Berlin, the sketch of Disraeli, and the concise account of the Dreyfus Affair. The second part—on Imperialism—is theoretically the most penetrating, for it creates the type-concepts for the relations between phenomena which are rarely placed in their proper, wider context. It contains the studies on the fateful emancipation of the bourgeoisie that wants to be an upper class without assuming the responsibilities of rulership, on the disintegration of Western national societies and the formation of elites and mobs, on the genesis of race-thinking in the eighteenth century, on the imperialist expansion of the Western national states and the race problem in the empires, on the corresponding continental pan-movements and the genesis of racial nationalism. . . . The third part—on Totalitarianism—contains studies on the classless society that results from general superfluity of the members of a society, on the difference between mob and mass, on totalitarian propaganda, on totalitarian police, and the concentration camps.

The digest of this enormous material, well documented with footnotes and bibliographies, is sometimes broad, betraying the joy of skillful narration by the true historian, but still held together by the conceptual discipline of the general thesis. Nevertheless, at this point a note of criticism will have to be allowed. The organization of the book is somewhat less strict than it could be, if the author had availed herself more readily of the theoretical instruments which the present state of science puts at her disposition. Her principle of relevance that orders the variegated materials into a story of totalitarianism is the disintegration of a civilization into masses of human beings without secure economic and social status; and her materials are relevant in so far as they demonstrate the process of disintegration. Obviously this process is the same that has been categorized by Toynbee as the growth of the internal and external proletariat. It is surprising that the author has not used Toynbee's highly differentiated concepts; and that even his name appears neither in the footnotes, nor in the bibliography, nor in the index. The use of Toynbee's work would have substantially added to the weight of Dr. Arendt's analysis. (pp. 69-72)

This excellent book, as we have indicated, is unfortunately

marred, however, by certain theoretical defects. The treatment of movements of the totalitarian type on the level of social situations and change, as well as of types of conduct determined by them, is apt to endow historical causality with an aura of fatality. Situations and changes, to be sure, require, but they do not determine a response. The character of a man, the range and intensity of his passions, the controls exerted by his virtues, and his spiritual freedom, enter as further determinants. If conduct is not understood as the response of a man to a situation, and the varieties of response as rooted in the potentialities of human nature rather than in the situation itself, the process of history will become a closed stream, of which every cross-cut at a given point of time is the exhaustive determinant of the future course. Dr. Arendt is aware of this problem. She knows that changes in the economic and social situations do not simply make people superfluous, and that superfluous people do not respond by necessity with resentment, cruelty, and violence; she knows that a ruthlessly competitive society owes its character to an absence of restraint and of a sense of responsibility for consequences; and she is even uneasily aware that not all the misery of National Socialist concentration camps was caused by the oppressors, but that a part of it stemmed from the spiritual lostness that so many of the victims brought with them. Her understanding of such questions is revealed beyond doubt in the following passage:

> Nothing perhaps distinguishes modern masses as radically from those of previous centuries as the loss of faith in a Last Judgment: the worst have lost their fear and the best have lost their hope. Unable as yet to live without fear and hope, these masses are attracted by every effort which seems to promise a man-made fabrication of the paradise they longed for and of the hell they had feared. Just as the popularized feature of Marx's classless society have a queer resemblance to the Messianic Age, so the reality of the concentration camps resembles nothing so much as mediaeval pictures of hell.

The spiritual disease of agnosticism is the peculiar problem of the modern masses, and the man-made paradises and man-made hells are its symptoms; and the masses have the disease whether they are in their paradise or in their hell. The author, thus, is aware of the problem; but, oddly enough, the knowledge does not affect her treatment of the materials. If the spiritual disease is the decisive feature that distinguishes modern masses from those of earlier centuries, then one would expect the study of totalitarianism not to be delimited by the institutional breakdown of national societies and the growth of socially superfluous masses, but rather by the genesis of the spiritual disease, especially since the response to the institutional breakdown clearly bears the marks of the disease. Then the origins of totalitarianism would not have to be sought primarily in the fate of the national state and attendant social and economic changes since the eighteenth century, but rather in the rise of immanentist sectarianism since the high Middle Ages; and the totalitarian movements would not be simply revolutionary movements of functionally dislocated people, but immanentist creed movements in which mediaeval heresies have come to their fruition. Dr.

Arendt, as we have said, does not draw the theoretical conclusions from her own insights.

Such inconclusiveness has a cause. It comes to light in another one of the profound formulations which the author deflects in a surprising direction: "What totalitarian ideologies therefore aim at is not the transformation of the outside world or the revolutionizing transmutation of society, but the transformation of human nature itself." This is, indeed, the essence of totalitarianism as an immanentist creed movement. Totalitarian movements do not intend to remedy social evils by industrial changes, but want to create a millennium in the eschatological sense through transformation of human nature. The Christian faith in transcendental perfection through the grace of God has been converted—and perverted—into the idea of immanent perfection through an act of man. And this understanding of the spiritual and intellectual breakdown is followed in Dr. Arendt's text by the sentence: "Human nature as such is at stake, and even though it seems that these experiments succeed not in changing man but only in destroying him . . . one should bear in mind the necessary limitations to an experiment which requires global control in order to show conclusive results." When I read this sentence, I could hardly believe my eyes. "Nature" is a philosophical concept; it denotes that which identifies a thing as a thing of this kind and not of another one. A "nature" cannot be changed or transformed; a "change of nature" is a contradiction of terms; tampering with the "nature" of a thing means destroying the thing. To conceive the idea of "changing the nature" of man (or of anything) is a symptom of the intellectual breakdown of Western civilization. The author, in fact, adopts the immanentist ideology; she keeps an "open mind" with regard to the totalitarian atrocities; she considers the question of a "change of nature" a matter that will have to be settled by "trial and error"; and since the "trial" could not yet avail itself of the opportunities afforded by a global laboratory, the question must remain in suspense for the time being.

These sentences of Dr. Arendt, of course, must not be construed as a concession to totalitarianism in the more restricted sense, that is, as a concession to National Socialist and Communist atrocities. On the contrary, they reflect a typically liberal, progressive, pragmatist attitude toward philosophical problems. We suggested previously that the author's theoretical derailments are sometimes more interesting than her insights. And this attitude is, indeed, of general importance because it reveals how much ground liberals and totalitarians have in common; the essential immanentism which unites them overrides the differences of ethos which separate them. The true dividing line in the contemporary crisis does not run between liberals and totalitarians, but between the religious and philosophical transcendentalists on the one side, and the liberal and totalitarian immanentist sectarians on the other side. It is sad, but it must be reported, that the author herself draws this line. The argument starts from her confusion about the "nature of man": "Only the criminal attempt to change the nature of man is adequate to our trembling insight that no nature, not even the nature of man, can any longer be considered to be the measure of all things"—a sentence which, if it has any sense at all, can only mean that the nature of man ceases to be the measure, when some imbecile conceives the notion of changing it. The author seems to be impressed by the imbecile and is ready to forget about the nature of man, as well as about all human civilization that has been built on its understanding. The "mob," she concedes, has correctly seen "that the whole of nearly three thousand years of Western civilization . . . has broken down." Out go the philosophers of Greece, the prophets of Israel, Christ, not to mention the Patres and Scholastics; for man has "come of age," and that means "that from now on man is the only possible creator of his own laws and the only possible maker of his own history." This coming-of-age has to be accepted; man is the new lawmaker; and on the tablets wiped clean of the past he will inscribe the "new discoveries in morality" which Burke had still considered impossible.

It sounds like a nihilistic nightmare. And a nightmare it is rather than a well considered theory. It would be unfair to hold the author responsible on the level of critical thought for what obviously is a traumatic shuddering under the impact of experiences that were stronger than the forces of spiritual and intellectual resistance. The book as a whole must not be judged by the theoretical derailments which occur mostly in its concluding part. The treatment of the subject matter itself is animated, if not always penetrated, by the age-old knowledge about human nature and the life of the spirit which, in the conclusions, the author wishes to discard and to replace by "new discoveries." Let us rather take comfort in the unconscious irony of the closing sentence of the work where the author appeals, for the "new" spirit of human solidarity, to Acts 16: 28: "Do thyself no harm; for we are all here." Perhaps, when the author progresses from quoting to hearing these words, her nightmarish fright will end like that of the jailer to whom they were addressed. (pp. 69-76)

> *Eric Voegelin, "The Origins of Totalitarianism," in* The Review of Politics, *Vol. 15, No. 1, January, 1953, pp. 68-76.*

Anthony Hartley

One of the more depressing features of British culture today is a shortage of sages. On the death of George Orwell that peculiar *genus,* the English moralist, seems to have become extinct. And this is no small loss. One can laugh as much as one likes at the majestically whiskered procession of liberal or not so liberal thinkers who move throughout the nineteenth and early twentieth centuries uttering gravely acute remarks on a variety of topics, but what has replaced them today is an almost total lack of self-criticism about the deeper trends of our society. There has been a good deal of talk about 'angry young men' sounding off in a symposium called *Declaration,* but most of the opinions expressed there were about as perceptive as the yelp of a dog into whom someone has just stuck a pin. A generalised state of irritation in intellectuals can only be a symptom, never a diagnosis, of the discontents of our age. If we want the genuine article with the wearisome effort towards actual thinking that it implies, we must go either to France, where a traditional concern for

general ideas still exists, or to America, where the trends of modern technocratic society are easier to discern for the simple reason that they have developed farther. . . .

With this in mind it is not surprising to find that a book called *The Human Condition* is published in America—such a title would appear intolerably ambitious in Oxford or Cambridge. Hannah Arendt has made a most interesting attempt to study man in action, or, as she puts it, his *vita activa.* Her analysis divides this into three categories: *labour* (the biological operation through which man produces enough to keep himself alive and to ensure his own reproduction), *work* (the production by *homo faber* of objects which are for 'use' not for 'consumption' and which, therefore, offer the possibility of the creation of a semi-permanent world of objects) and *action* (which comprises man's relations in the public world of other men and is therefore essentially political in character). In the Greek and Roman worlds the first two categories were regarded as essentially 'private'; only *action* on the stage of the Greek *polis* (the community of the city state) was public, serving the human need for noble self-expression and regarded as being superior to other human activities. The first thing that happened to upset this scheme was the value attributed to the contemplative life following the development of post-Socratic thought and the rise of Christianity. Discredit was thus cast upon *action,* and, after the Cartesian undermining of contemplation as a way of access to truth, *work* and the values of *homo faber* took up a predominant position in the hierarchy.

Now, however, *labour* powerfully aided by the techniques of mass production (the earlier supremacy of the *homo faber* ethos was extinguished when 'tools' became 'machines' and objects were made for consumption rather than for use) has asserted itself over the other two categories of *vita activa,* and, corresponding to this movement, there has been a fusion of 'private' and 'public' into 'social'—a world in which human beings display those characteristics which they share as members of the same species of the animal kingdom. The only people left who can *work* are artists and writers. As for *action,* it is the prerogative of scientists acting on nature. The sheep have eaten up the men, and, for Dr. Arendt, the *polis* as *polis* in our day and age is null and void.

This summary of Dr. Arendt's work is inadequate, but, I hope, not too oversimplified. The book is difficult, proceeding by brilliant flashes and abounding in intuitions and subtleties, which I cannot discuss here. What emerges from its main line of argument is that any highly developed industrial society is now faced with a grave crisis centred around the nature of work (taken in its usual sense). Labouring to live has produced a mass society, which lives to labour, just at the very moment when technical discoveries have reached the point where life may be sustained with infinitely less trouble. 'A society of jobholders' is likely to find itself out of a job, not because of mass unemployment, but because the level of production required to keep the human race going can be attained and exceeded with the utmost ease by automatically controlled machines rather than by human sweat. Mankind, therefore, will soon be in the position of some prehistoric animal which, having evolved webbed feet over thousands of years in order to cope with a marshy environment, suddenly finds itself faced with climatic change and the transformation of swamps into deserts. There will soon be a surplus of human activity and no purpose to which it can be put, all other purposes than survival having been eliminated by the modern emphasis on simply continuing to live. We shall be stranded with a dinosaur of a society and no mutations in sight.

The eternity of passive boredom, with which Dr. Arendt threatens mankind, may be a good way off yet, and, in any case, her analysis is schematic rather than strictly historical. But there are a number of signs which suggest that she is not far wrong when she points to the submersion of all other activities by that of labouring to keep alive as a potentially dangerous characteristic of the twentieth century. If we take Science Fiction as in part an expression of the innate desires of our time—it is certainly more like the eighteenth-century philosophic fable than it is like any other literary form—then the continued protests uttered by its authors against modern mass society must be considered to be significant. The values put forward in SF are nearly always aristocratic: courage, individualism, decision, solitude, beauty, austerity. Many of the stories even show an unconscious longing for some return to the Greek city state, to a society where individual qualities could make some visible impression on events. Then there is the phenomenon of adolescent gangsterism, which, occurring in countries apparently so ideologically different as America and Russia, also points to some deep flaw in the structure of modern industrial society. And it is worth noting that all this has little to do with whether that society is democratic in its political forms or not. Every individual in a modern society is in the position of suffering too much from it and of being able to affect it too little. It is harder now than at any time in history to be either a hermit or an anarchist. Society is determined that nobody shall contract out, and, this being so, the only safeguard for individual freedom lies in the inefficiency of the instruments by which it imposes its will. It might be held that a rackety and decaying dictatorship allows more freedom to its citizens than an up-to-date parliamentary democracy disposing of an efficient bureaucracy.

Without going as far as this, however, it is easy to see that the present well-ordered mass society, where all States are Welfare States (it is hard to think of a modern State that is not a Welfare State in some degree), suppresses some human instincts and presses too hard upon others. And it is equally easy to predict that this will not continue for ever. Sooner or later we shall be in for a reversal of values, when those elements in man, which liberal humanitarianism has refused to admit to decent company, will take their revenge. If violence is to be to the mid-twentieth century as shocking as sex was to the nineteenth, then we may expect that it will be to the twenty-first century what sex has been to the twentieth: a means of liberation. This is not an entirely comfortable thought, but it is the inevitable result of sitting on bits of human nature in the name of a system.

Anthony Hartley, "The Age of Boredom," in

The Spectator, *Vol. 201, No. 6796, September 26, 1958, p. 411.*

A. Alvarez

In 1953 Miss Hannah Arendt delivered the preliminary draft of *The Human Condition* to that burning fiery furnace of intellectual discussion, the Christian Gauss Seminars in Criticism at Princeton. At the end of her first lecture she was asked for a brief reading list. Instead of producing the expected handful of articles in learned journals, she replied 'Plato, Aristotle and Marx. And of course, I'll also be using Aquinas, Hobbes, Locke, Montesquieu, and Adam Smith'. This, as it turned out, was by no means bravado. And it was certainly fair warning of the breadth and intensity of what was to follow.

Two years before, she had published her massive analysis of *The Origins of Totalitarianism,* called in [England] *The Burden of Our Time.* It was an extraordinary work, for not only was it closely argued, immensely learned, original and difficult, it was also strangely moving. Miss Arendt indulged in no rhetoric, she paraded no horrors and waved no flags, but there was a kind of passionate energy in her thinking that was more effective than any conventional special pleading. She is an intellectual in the rarest sense of the term: not someone who suffers received ideas glibly, but someone whose intuitions about what she calls 'the pains and troubles of living' are most powerfully expressed through abstractions and logic. Quite simply, she responds to experience by thinking for herself, and that, our popular academics notwithstanding, is a rare gift. Her most abstruse arguments have a suppleness and relevance that is more usually the mark of a creative artist than of a political philosopher.

The Human Condition follows directly from *The Origins.* Only the form of the totalitarianism is different; instead of the political tyrannies of Hitler and Stalin, she has now turned to their subtler but no less deadly Western equivalent—the consumer totalitarianism of mass society:

> In both instances, men have become entirely private, that is, they have been deprived of seeing and hearing others, of being seen and being heard by them. They are all imprisoned in the subjectivity of their own singular experience, which does not cease to be singular if the same experience is multiplied innumerable times.

Modern democracy may be privileged, rich and easy, but it is also queerly sterile. It no longer provides a proper common world in which free independent people can act, talk and create significantly. The modern citizen, that eternal jobholder, may have all the trappings of the independent property-owner—semi-detached house, car, TV, refrigerator—but they weigh on him like chains on a slave. Miss Arendt's concern is with this inner, socialised slavishness of the human condition: 'What I propose, therefore, is very simple: it is nothing more than to think what we are doing'. It is, in fact, far from 'very simple'; it involves her in the philosophy of science, sociology, economics, semantics, history, aesthetics, theology, the theory of labour movements, psychology and, most surprisingly of all in this kind of abstract work, in private human experience. It is not cheerful reading, nor is it easy. Miss Arendt's lucid but compressed and muscular style is hard to keep up with. But it is profound and vitally important.

According to Miss Arendt, there are three ways in which man can express his humanity: action, work and labour. Action, the deeds and words of an individual moving in the public realm, is the unpredictable stuff of politics and history, the prerogative only of free men who want 'to make a name for themselves'—to immortalise their individuality through their deeds. In Ancient Greece the *vita activa* was the ideal to which all free citizens aspired. Perhaps it survives in a debased way, in the log-cabin-to-White-House, private-to-public realm, myth of American politics.

So far so clear. But what of *work* and *labour?* They seem on the surface almost the same thing. But Miss Arendt starts from the simple fact that in most European languages—French, German and Italian, as well as Greek, Latin and English—there are two words for what seems to be one process. And the words correspond to different functions, different classes, different mentalities; essentially, to the freeman and the slave. A man who makes a pot, or a pair of shoes, or a boat, who writes a play, builds a table, or carves a statue is producing *work,* or rather *a work,* created out of his skill and imagination and care, complete in itself and made, more or less, to last. 'By his works shall ye know him,' for they are, in their limits, memorials to their maker. They are also unnatural, made by forcing natural materials to human ends. By our works we create a habitable world within the world of nature.

Once created, however, this world must be maintained. And this is the function of *labour.* A Greek slave or a Victorian slavey washed a floor, drew water, chopped firewood; within hours the floor would be dirty again, the water drunk, the wood burned. The Greeks justified slavery because, without it, free citizens would have been enslaved by the necessities of life. Perhaps the Victorians had the same excuse for child-labour. Nowadays, instead of servants, we have *labour-saving* kitchens. . . .

The ideal of the *vita activa* perished with the Greeks. It was already finished when Plato, in the allegory of the cave, suggested that the political world of action was shadowy, delusive; reality lay beyond, in a world of eternal ideas to be discovered only through contemplation. With the rise first of the philosophers, then of Christianity, the life of contemplation replaced that of action as the highest good; which meant that the human condition at its finest was unworldly, unpolitical. Even doing good, 'the one activity taught by Jesus', lost its value immediately it became public—rewarded, praised, or even acknowledged.

The ideal of contemplation held until the Renaissance. It was destroyed not by any great philosophical revolution but by an instrument, Galileo's telescope. It was this that gave the lie to the basic evidence of the senses. And when the senses failed, the old philosophy and the old order failed with them. There arose what Nietzsche called 'the school of suspicion'; at its head was Descartes, with his abiding principle of doubt: *de omnibus dubitandum est.*

But what was most important about the new philosophy was not that it called all in doubt but that it followed and depended upon a manmade instrument: when Descartes heard that Galileo had recanted he thought of burning his papers, since 'if the movement of the earth is false, all the foundations of my philosophy are also false'. Man the maker had taken precedence over both the thinker and the active, eloquent political being. For only *homo faber* could defend himself adequately against his continual destructive doubt by building up a world of his own works, certain and controllable.

The final transformation came when Marx replaced the ideal of *work* with that of *labour* as the fullest expression of man's humanity. The division of labour broke down the individual work of the craftsmen into a series of automatic, largely meaningless labour processes. The result was that 'use objects' (Miss Arendt's unfortunate name for the more or less permanent products of work) were replaced by 'consumer goods', produced in vast abundance and designed to be worn out and replaced as quickly as possible, so that the cycle of labour could proceed as remorselessly as the cycle of life. It takes, for example, three years to buy a car on the hire purchase, by which time the car is both worn out and out of date. And the whole business begins again. No wonder they call it the Never-Never system. (p. 336)

Miss Arendt is not much concerned with the products of the labour process: the paper plates and handkerchiefs, the flimsy veneered cardboard that is sold as furniture, the tinny cars (Packard, the rumour goes, collapsed financially because their pre-war cars were too solid and lasting). Nor is she concerned with the appearance of wealth that goes with the system. Her business, instead, is with the disastrous impoverishment of the human condition itself. The question is not that the labourers have, at last, been given equal rights,

> but that we have almost succeeded in levelling all human activities to the common denominator of securing the necessities of life and providing for their abundance. Whatever we do, we are supposed to do for the sake of 'making a living' . . . The artist . . . is the only 'worker' left in a labouring society.

In mass society the individual is submerged in the vast, anonymous process of life itself. He no longer acts, he behaves. Instead of history, there are the laws of statistics. Only when the unique and the unpredictable can be ruled out as being too rare to count does history become meaningless, and economics and the social studies properly scientific.

> The last stage of the labouring society, the society of jobholders, demands of its members a sheer automatic functioning, as though the individual life had actually been submerged in the over-all life processes of the species and the only active decision still required of the individual were to let go, so to speak, to abandon his individuality, the still individually sensed pain and trouble of living, and acquiesce in a dazed, 'tranquillised', functional type of behaviour. The trouble with modern theories of behaviourism is

not that they are wrong but that they could become true, that they actually are the best possible conceptualisation of certain obvious trends in modern society. It is quite conceivable that the modern age—which began with such an unprecedented and promising outburst of human activity—may end in the deadliest, most sterile passivity history has ever known.

It is a Kafka situation. The horror of Kafka's novels depends not on any dreamlike, symbolic shiftiness but on the simple fact that the protagonist is always an intelligent, human, three-dimensional person who suddenly finds himself thrust into a two-dimensional world. He is bewildered not because he does not understand, but because he understands too much. He is the unique individual plunged into an anonymous, motiveless, mass society. This is the situation Miss Arendt analyses in all its twists and coils. She offers no pat solutions which can be extracted from their context and used as slogans. Her politics are those of human dignity, not dogma. There is in fact, only one 'solution' to the predicament she has so profoundly analysed: that is the example of her book itself, and the free, serenely mature and disinterested intelligence it exhibits at every turn. Her plan to do 'nothing more than to think what we are doing' has involved her in an intense, systematic critique of the whole tradition of political philosophy and the full sterility of our contemporary situation. The result is the first important revaluation of the human condition since Marx. (p. 337)

> *A. Alvarez, "The State of Man," in* New Statesman, *Vol. LVII, No. 1460, March 7, 1959, pp. 336-37.*

John W. Bennett

This important work [*The Human Condition*] could easily be preempted by our field and considered a contribution to "philosophical anthropology": that view of man as a creature who works out his destiny in the framework of Earth, but who also aspires to the benefits and glory of Heaven. Philosophical anthropology attempts to unify the "scientific" and "philosophical" modes of inquiry about man—a difficult task because, as Arendt shows, these have become detached from one another in Western thought. The scientist avoids value judgments as contaminating, while the philosopher is not allowed to cite scientific evidence for his judgments. Hence, inquiry into the nature of man, which must be both empirical and valuational, drops into an excluded middle ground. Arendt's attempt to work in this no-man's-land resembles Greek intellectualism, and there is no doubt that she is practicing a kind of classical revival. She styles herself a "thinker" and her work "thoughts"; that is, she is a phenomenologist, confronting reality and making sense out of it by rational cognition. (p. 684)

[The basic concepts of work, labor, and actions] are discussed at length, and many subsidiary ideas are brought into play. One of the most interesting of these is "society." I use quotation marks because for Arendt society is not an enduring feature of man's condition, but rather a special historical emergent. Society developed only recently, as

housekeeping—that is, all of "labor" and a good deal of "work"—became the chief mission of the body politic (now more accurately the "body social"). It means also that the "private" domestic concerns of love and hate, violence and obedience, and other responses derived from familial relations have become the "public" norms of the whole social cosmos—whereas in classical civilization these remained hidden behind private doors. Society symbolizes for Arendt the over-turning of the hierarchy of the *vita activa*. The intellectual history of the West can read as a progressive inversion of this hierarchy: labor and work, once denigrated, rise to the very top, while action, once the highest type of human activity, sinks to the bottom. Hence politics is a dirty occupation, and the making and selling of toothpaste a shining accomplishment. The artist and the intellectual hover somewhere between, in limbo. (Actually this doesn't represent much of a change—they were there even for the Greeks.) The decay of language in the modern world is for Arendt a symptom of society: you don't communicate articulately with spouses, children, and lovers; you simply emote or use vulgar, truncated speech. The externalization of the social means that one can find identity not in what one does or contributes to the world, but only in one's status: the judgment of others as to one's worth (Riesman's other-direction?). This results in a limitation of perspective, and men are imprisoned in the subjectivity of their own personal experience. The fabric of humanity becomes drab, reality is ambiguous and fleeting, and the psychiatrist prospers.

While Arendt's presentation of her categories and concepts lends them the appearance of precision, upon careful examination they dissolve into blurs. How does one really tell whether an actual, particular human activity belongs to labor or to work? Or do her concepts merely refer to ideological conceptions held by men, and not to real activities? We are not told, but one suspects the latter, since she makes much out of the modern elevation of life itself to the status of the highest human good; hence the assimilation of all activities into labor, since they serve merely to prolong life.

More uncertainty as to the status of these concepts appears in Arendt's exclusive use of the history of ideas, and the etymology of labor, work, and action in European languages, to demonstrate their validity and importance in human affairs. Phenomenology aside, one has the right to wonder precisely who has determined that these three concepts are basic and essential: Arendt, philosophers, Greeks, social analysts, or the speakers of European languages? Surely anthropology's knowledge of biological and cultural history has something to contribute. Could not Arendt have filled the gap between her declarations of ontological status for these concepts, and her inadequate derivation of them from the realm of idea and semantics, by analyzing the findings of historical social science on the life and culture of societies and civilizations? Possibly Arendt would reply that this is our job, not hers. But we have the right to take her to task for neglecting a valuable source of information, even though she claims no more than the status of thinker.

I find it equally curious that while Arendt's position is aggressively humanistic, her presentation is devoid of data on the rich texture of human existence as it is endured, or on the human meaning and experience associated with labor, work, and action. The anthropologist, despite his confused rationalism, is closer to all this, and therefore less sure of his categories and far more receptive to alternative models of man. Considering her humanism, Arendt seems overly committed to rationalistic categories— something which may result from her phenomenalist preoccupation with thought and ideas and her consequent ignoring of data on society, culture, and human affairs in general.

I hesitate to make another criticism, because Arendt could justifiably say she is not concerned with non-Western cultures. At any rate, she fails to recognize cultural variability. Arendt speaks of "the condition of man," and the entire book is cast in this mood of Olympian generality, but it is entirely a work about Western civilization. Not a shred of evidence from the rest of the world is introduced, and the whole complex pattern of Oriental civilization is ignored. Even if we grant her the right to focus on the West, we must observe that this is no time in world history to write books on the condition of man and ignore most of the men. One suspects that without being aware of it, Arendt shares in the ethnocentric ambivalence of modern Western man: on the one hand, Western (American?) civilization is the only really important human accomplishment, since it has had the most momentous consequences; but on the other, it has taken the wrong direction and thus endangers mankind as a whole. To what extent is this view an artifact of Western history? Are not other, longer perspectives possible? The emerging modern societies of Asia and Africa resemble the West, but are clearly taking their own distinctive and indigenous paths, and it seems to the anthropologist that there may be a variety of "conditions of man." And precisely how important are the Western contributions? What of Oriental art, philosophy, and statecraft?

Still another anthropological objection. Arendt (as a phenomenologist) appears to recognize no evolutionary change in man. The inversion of the hierarchy of the *vita activa* since the Mediterranean civilizations is her way of conceptualizing all the technological revolutions, changes in social structure, and alterations in man's intellectual powers of the past 2000 years. Thus she nowhere recognizes that the development of technology represents a continuous expansion of human capabilities, and even, if we follow Washburn and Hallowell, a favorable selection of a large-brained type. The use of human cultural apparatus, material or otherwise, to construct a more elaborate human world and a mastery over nature, seems to her a dangerous thing: it has led to the dehumanization of man. At least she never compliments man on his accomplishment. But could we not argue with equal plausibility that it is man's nature to do these things, and since this is so, human bio-psycho-technical evolution has been inevitable, and we must learn to use it? The pessimism that underlies Arendt's discussion gives us no way out, no way to manage the world. I do not criticize criticism, and Arendt's work has the great merit of calling our attention to

many spiritual shortcomings and social problems. But we need something more: a constructive viewpoint, based on recognition of man's evolution, which accepts that evolution and defines the ends it must serve. Arendt is most correct when she shows how difficult it is for modern man to formulate ends, but perhaps her own book is an example of the difficulty. Clearly we cannot go back to the Greeks, not with all this technological evolution. (Arendt regards the digital computer as dehumanizing, since you cannot talk to it. Of course the computer will do only what men program it to do, out of their talk. Therefore the problem is to make sure they talk about important things, so the computer can help them. The computer by itself does not constitute the problem, and removing it will not make men talk sense.)

This type of argument also has its roots in Arendt's classical separation of man and nature. This is inherent in her distinction between labor and work, and it appears in her doctrine that man has made his mastery over nature a dehumanizing experience. Arendt holds that man, through his work, learns about growth and decay, whereas in reality nature is everlasting. But how does she or can she know what nature really is, if she knows it only through the mind? Why shouldn't growth and decay be just as natural, as real, as everlastingness? Following Whitehead, I would prefer to believe that men can conceive of nature in various ways, apprehending different aspects and yet being part of what they apprehend—the apprehending itself being part of nature. But more important is the fact that the relationship between man and nature simply cannot be categorized with elementary dualities and logical distinctions. This is the trait of an earlier age that had little natural science and therefore had to speculate. We have found that man is to a degree independent of nature, to a degree shares identity with other natural phenomena, and self-consciously conceives of relationships between himself and nature—itself limited by times, places, and circumstances. The issue is too complex to be clarified with rational thought alone, and the rich store of data provided by ecology, physiology, geography, and anthropology cannot be ignored. A phenomenological approach, like Arendt's, leads to simplified and one-sided conceptualizations.

There is, I think, a fundamental contradiction in Arendt's mode of analysis. In the first chapter she asserts that everything with which men come into contact is thereby transformed into a condition of human existence—an aggressively humanistic approach, anthropocentric in the classic Western sense (that is, a cosmic plan or pattern which man imperfectly strives to live up to, as in Oriental philosophy, occupies no place in her thoughts). However, she does not follow this anthropocentric philosophy consistently, as I have already implied, since to do so would lead straight to solipsism. She even struggles against it when she criticizes the tendency to throw all values into the realm of free choice as a result of making man the sole judge of reality. But as already noted, in her ontology she defines reality in a profoundly rational fashion, as if she were God, not a mere human. In other words, she is laboring within the ancient Western dilemma: how to attain certainty within the limits of human fallibility—the very dilemma that she sees lying at the root of so much evil (and which has never, at least until recently, bothered the Orient).

Arendt holds that the contemporary human condition brings about a failure to articulate the nature of this condition, due to the decline of speech, the referral of everything to a common social reality, and so on. But she is a vociferous critic of all this, along with C. Wright Mills, Joseph Wood Krutch, and many others. Her very intellectual existence is at least partial proof of the fact that the condition of man cannot be entirely as she sees it. Taken literally, her diagnosis would rule out her own critical labors. Perhaps she needs a philosophy of culture, an "anthropological" philosophy, which recognizes that human cultures always contain opposites, reactions to conditions or responses to ideology. Like many historians of ideas, she often makes ideology the active force, a primary condition, whereas there seems to be a complex interplay between ideas and activities, the terms of which always vary by situation. The fact is that Arendt is just not humanist enough, or at least not sufficiently aware of the great humanistic significance of the findings of social science. It is probably true that social scientists themselves have not exploited the humanistic implications of their findings, but this is no reason to ignore these findings and to imply that social science has been part and parcel of the dehumanization process. (pp. 685-87)

The reality that Arendt perceives is frightening enough, but I believe that it is only one side of the coin. Men have been in the habit of ritualizing or rationalizing their outdated ideologies and their inadequate social arrangements, perhaps to a degree not always recognized by Western intellectuals steeped in concepts and ideals. (Here is where knowledge of the Orient, and its patience with human foibles and its willingness to compromise, is a help.) I admit the danger of the present situation—the infinite capacity for destruction—perhaps man will destroy the earth, his basic condition of existence, in his overweening, normless confidence in technology. But while things are very bad, man does not, as Arendt's analysis sometimes suggests, lack a capacity for change. This, too, is part of the human condition as taught us by the historical record of human culture.

In conclusion, I want to say that this is a brilliant, important, and very difficult book. It contains much with which any serious observer of modern society and culture must agree, but it also contains attitudes and twists of reasoning based on particular assessments which require serious criticism. And Arendt, as a phenomenologist, would be the first to admit this. The book is full of important ideas for the anthropologist, and any number of theoretical disquisitions could be written on the similarities and differences between Arendt's views and those of anthropology. I hope my review will stimulate a few anthropologists to do just that, because if Arendt is right about anything, it is about the desirability of bringing science and philosophy together in a cooperative attempt to chart new courses for humanity. (p. 688)

> *John W. Bennett, in a review of "The Human Condition," in* American Anthropologist, *Vol. 61, No. 4, 1959, pp. 684-88.*

Bruno Bettelheim

Hannah Arendt's *Eichmann in Jerusalem: A Report on the Banality of Evil* is largely a reprint of articles that appeared in *The New Yorker*. Still, I recommend it even to those who read the articles, not because the book's content is very different, but because the impact is even more powerful in its unbroken sequence. The task she sets for herself far transcends the crimes of one man since it deals with the greatest problem of our time and not merely with genocide, one of its ugliest outcroppings. Totalitarianism in one form or another is the most important issue of our day, and if the trial had dealt only with that it would truly have been the trial of the century, for it is also totalitarianism when a nation plans for atomic destruction on a grand scale, even if that nation is democratic and plans only for defense. This is because such plans fail to set limits within the human scope. To entertain the possibility of risking atomic destruction for millions is to toy with totalitarianism because it implies the right of a state to pursue its goals no matter what.

This then is the virtue of Arendt's book—that it views Eichmann and his trial as posing the problem of the human being within a modern totalitarian system. But in a way it is also its shortcoming: the issues are so vast that we do not seem able yet to cope with them intellectually, though her book is certainly a most serious and in part successful effort to do so.

In order to deal with totalitarianism on a human scale she had somehow to reduce it to its human basis. This she does by pursuing three basic threads of the problem: the man Eichmann; the impossibility of judging totalitarianism from our traditional system of thought, including our legal system; and the hapless victims. But so interwoven are these three issues because of the nature of the subject and the way the trial was conducted, that neither I nor Dr. Arendt can deal with them separately.

Hannah Arendt's previous contributions to our understanding of *The Human Condition* and of *The Origins of Totalitarianism* find her singularly well equipped to understand how Eichmann's deed, his trial, and his victims, are all part of the same problem. So while her book is nominally about Eichmann in Jerusalem and though the trial is discussed in a very personal, erudite, and critical way, in a deeper sense it is not even an essay on the banality of evil, as the subtitle suggests; though it is an essay on that too. Essentially it is a book about the incongruity of it all, greatest of which is the fact that by all "scientific" standards Eichmann was a "normal" person. "Half a dozen psychiatrists had certified him as 'normal'—'More normal, at any rate, than I am after having examined him', one of them was said to have exclaimed, while another found that his whole psychological outlook, his attitude toward his wife and children, mother and father, brothers, sisters, and friends, was 'not only normal but most desirable'—and finally the minister who paid regular visits to him in prison . . . reassured everybody by declaring Eichmann to be 'a man with very positive ideas'." Obviously our standards of normality do not apply to behavior in totalitarian societies.

It is the incongruity of the murder of millions, and of one man being accused of it all. It is so obvious that no one man can exterminate millions. The incongruity is between all the horrors recounted, and this man in the dock, when essentially all he did was to talk to people, write memoranda, receive and give orders from behind a desk. It is essentially the incongruity between our conception of life and the bureaucracy of the total state. Our imagination, our frame of reference, even our feelings, are simply not up to it. (p. 23)

[*Eichmann in Jerusalem*] is a book about our inability to comprehend fully how modern technology and social organization, when made use of by totalitarianism, can empower a normal, rather mediocre person to play so crucial a role in the extermination of millions. By the same incongruity, it becomes theoretically possible for a minor civil servant—say a lieutenant colonel, to keep the parallel to Eichmann—to start the extermination of most of us by pressing a button. It is an incongruity between the image of man we still carry—rooted though it is in the humanism of the Renaissance and in the liberal doctrines of the 18th Century—and the realities of human existence in the middle of our current technological revolution. Had this revolution not permitted us to view the individual as a mere cog in the complex machinery, dispensable, a mere instrument, Eichmann would never have been possible. But neither would have been the slaughter at Stalingrad, Russia's slave labor camps, the bombing of Hiroshima, or the current planning for nuclear war. It is the contradiction between the incredible power technology has put at our disposal, and how unimportant the individual has become just because of it.

It is the incongruity between the banality of an Eichmann, and that only such a banal person could effect the destruction of millions. Had he been more of a man, his humanity would have kept him from his evil work; had he been less of a man, he would not have been effective at his job. His is exactly the banality of a man who would push the button when told, concerned only with pushing it well, and without any regard for who was pushed by it, or where.

Even our language has become incongruous; it fails us because our words are symbols for events occurring in an entirely different context; they refer only to matters of a different magnitude. To kill applies to the murder of an enemy in war, or for personal gain, or out of personal hate. It implies something akin to a face to face encounter. Dillinger was a killer. Eichmann was an instrument in the destruction of millions; anything that he did not consider strictly legal revolted him. As he truthfully stated, he never killed a man. Legalized mass murder, by order of the state—this he did not mind; on the contrary, he could enjoy the efficiency, the "scientific" attitude with which he executed his duty. His "expert" knowledge of the Jewish problem was in all respects woefully inadequate, as Arendt describes in detail; it mainly consisted of his having read two books. But to him this seemed a scientific approach to the problem of emigration and extermination. This again is of crucial importance, because without such legalistic or scientific detachment, the inhumanity of totalitarianism cannot be understood. It was not simply one

person's pseudo-scientism leading him astray. These facts are amply documented by the legalized, murderous "scientific" experiments carried out by persons to whom, according to their training and position, the qualification of scientist could not be denied. I am referring here to the physicians who engaged in human experimentation, as described in the Nuremberg Trials and many other reports. These were—in many cases—prominent physicians, distinguished university professors and what not, all trained in pre-Nazi times, all sworn to the Hippocratic oath. And some of the greatest physicians of Germany knew and officially approved of what their colleagues were doing. They too did what they did only because it all seemed perfectly legal; all was in order within the frame of reference of the totalitarian state. Certainly it is misleading to apply to these doctors the old-fashioned term of physician or healer. But neither does the old-fashioned term murderer apply to them, or to Eichmann, because it is a term remaining within the human orientation.

Despite the judges' efforts to fit Eichmann into the old categories, his location in history, like the magnitude of his deeds, defied their efforts. That is why they tried to establish in vain that he had once killed a Jewish boy, as if that would have made any difference when he had helped to exterminate millions. But if they had been able to prove he had murdered one person, he would somehow have done a deed we could comprehend and punish within existing law and our familiar concept of retribution.

Our language is just as inadequate for discussing the victims. By now an entire literature has sprung up glorifying the martyrdom of the Jewish victims. Yet the term martyrdom applies to them as little as the ordinary term murderer applies to an Eichmann, or to the plane crews who dropped atomic bombs. Had Japan been victorious, they would probably have been tried as murderers.

According to Webster, a martyr is a person "who voluntarily suffers death as the penalty of witnessing to and refusing to renounce his religion or a principle." In this sense the early Christians were martyrs, not because they were murdered—that only makes them victims of the state—but because they could have saved their lives by embracing the state religion, and chose not to. Arendt is right not to grant the murdered Jews the sainthood of martyrs, and to view them simply as men. To those who claim they were martyrs, this is a sacrilegious position, and whoever holds that their actions may have contributed to their fate is accused of wishing to assert that the Jews were guilty—or that the Nazis were not. (pp. 23-5)

When in 1939, fresh out of the concentration camp, I tried to tell Americans about my experiences, I was told by most, including psychiatrists, that my views were incorrect, or that I was suffering from a prisoner psychosis, because I warned that the SS were not demented sadists or (in the words of the Eichmann trial) monsters, but in the vast majority mediocre men—banal, to use Arendt's term—but nonetheless deadly effective. I was told to let the after-effects of my camp experience subside before I said any more, because my theories were apt to mislead Americans. To believe that the SS acted according to purposeful plan ran so counter to what most people then wished to believe, that it was also unacceptable to them when I said that the camps had a crucial role in the master plan of the Reich. When I spoke about a concentration camp society and how it was intended to break the individual's ability to resist, once he was caught, this too met with little acceptance. It was just too contrary to our humanistic frame of reference.

I mention it here because Arendt's book may well meet with similar reactions. Those who will view it as an account of the trial—critical, highly personal, perhaps even biased in part—will be dismayed by it because they will miss what her book has to teach. Yet to write the history of just another prominent Nazi was hardly worth her effort, nor to describe a trial that served propaganda as much as justice. If only one more miserable political criminal was being tried, then it would have seemed petty to take the court to task for the way it conducted the trial, because the accused's guilt was clear to begin with, and he admitted to it. Or why drag into her account of the trial that Jews, and even Jewish leaders, lent an unwilling heavy hand in the extermination of Jews? This had nothing whatever to do with trying the accused. His guilt was not an iota less because they did so.

Many will harp on all this because they fail to grasp the real issue. Judge Musmanno, who reviewed her book in *The New York Times Book Review,* could see it only as a most unfair account of a trial, as if the trial itself had been her topic. He failed to see that the issue was not Eichmann, but totalitarianism. He writes, for example, that "Miss Arendt devotes considerable space to Eichmann's conscience and informs us that one of Eichmann's points in his own defense was 'that there were no voices from the outside to arouse his conscience'." Musmanno adds, "How abysmally asleep is a conscience when it must be aroused to be told there is something morally wrong about pressing candy upon a little boy to induce him to enter a gas chamber of death?" To ask such a rhetorical question is playing up to the gallery, or the emotions of the audience, as did Attorney General Hausner (according to Arendt) because it was never proved that Eichmann did such a thing, or knew about it. Of course, he knew about the killings; he never denied it. But what Arendt was talking about was the dreadful situation that in a totalitarian state there were no voices from the outside to arouse one's conscience. This is the important issue she deals with, as Musmanno's emotionally loaded question tries to make us forget. For us who were not Nazis, the issue is the absence of these voices, our voices. This is what makes living in a totalitarian society so desperate, because there is nobody to turn to for guidance, and there are no voices from the outside. (pp. 25-6)

Since Arendt views the importance of the trial as revealing the nature and the still very present dangers of totalitarianism, she is critical of the legal basis of this trial. She does not accuse the judges or Attorney General Hausner because they failed in meting out justice, or for failing to conduct a trial that was as fair as one could expect it to be under the circumstances. She is critical because the court vacillated between trying a man and trying history, and to this she objects.

To try Eichmann for the deeds of the state which he carried out—this the legal system by which he was tried did not permit. Had that been attempted, then hundreds of thousands of others would have had to be tried too. All the Germans, and many Jews too, who in some fashion helped in the killing of Jews. As those who arranged for the Nuremburg Trials recognized, it was nearly impossible to bring to justice all who participated in the crimes against humanity. (pp. 26-7)

To avoid all these and many other difficulties, Eichmann had to be tried as a person. But to do so required that he be viewed as a man of extraordinary qualities; that is, as a monster. This Eichmann certainly was, but as part of a monstrous system; as a man, he was blatantly not. That is why neither Arendt nor the court were able to restrict themselves to the trial of one man, but resorted to "painting the broader picture." To the court this larger picture was that of anti-Semitism, and Arendt is critical of the court on this score (or so it seemed to me), because it obfuscates the fact that only one individual was on trial for his life, and to mix up his trial with that of a system is questionable if one wishes to uphold individual responsibility.

That is, both the prosecuting attorney and the judges wanted to see Eichmann's deed as horrendous—which it was—but not as something radically different from other persecutions of the Jews. That is why, as far as the prosecution was concerned, "it is not an individual that is in the dock at this historic trial, and not the Nazi regime alone, but anti-Semitism throughout history." And this is why Israel's Attorney General Hausner began his opening address with Pharoah in Egypt, and with Haman's edict, "To destroy, to slay, and to cause them to perish." Not by the farthest stretch of imagination could Eichmann be justly put to death for Pharoah's deeds. Nor can any court within our legal system try an idea, such as anti-Semitism, nor can events in the history of man, such as the history of anti-Semitism, be tried. If we begin to try ideas, we end up with witch-hunts; or condemnations without due process, such as characterized the McCarthy era in America.

Why, then, were all these images evoked? The court did so because it viewed Hitlerism as a chapter, though the most lurid chapter, of anti-Semitism. But in Arendt's opinion, which I share, this was not the last chapter in anti-Semitism but rather one of the first chapters in modern totalitarianism. For this reason it is unfortunate, as Arendt stresses, that Eichmann was not tried by an international tribunal. To ensure against further chapters, as much as a writer can, Arendt tries to show the full horrors of totalitarianism, which go very far beyond those of anti-Semitism. A full understanding of totalitarianism requires that we see Eichmann as basically a mediocrity whose dreadful importance is derived only from his more or less chance position within the system.

To believe otherwise, to believe that there exists true freedom of action for the average individual within such system, is so contrary to fact that neither prosecuting attorney nor judges attempted to show that Eichmann enjoyed such a freedom. Only the extraordinary person, at great risk to himself, retains limited freedom in such a state.

It is in this sense that totalitarianism exists wherever the state abrogates the rights of the individual and makes state reason the supreme principle. That principle in the Hitler state was to make the German people supreme, and to eliminate all racial impurity from the soil of the greater German Reich. Toward this end he exterminated not only Jews but also millions of Poles and Russians, and virtually the entire gypsy population of Europe. Individuals counted for nothing, and if they hampered the unfolding of this supreme goal they were exterminated—not to serve individual hatred or personal advantage, but to obey the supreme law. Hence Eichmann's revulsion at those who enriched themselves, and his outrage at what he considered the barbarity of the Rumanian pogroms. Hence also, as Rousset has pointed out, the requirement of the state that wherever possible, the victims should acquiesce to their destruction so that they, too, like victims in some barbarous rite, should be part of the universal effort to do what is best for the state.

Thus if one translates the extermination of the Jews as part of the history of anti-Semitism, then Eichmann and his kind are indeed the greatest anti-Semitic monsters of all. And this the court tried to establish. If, on the other hand, the extermination of the Jews was merely one part of the master plan to create the thousand year totalitarian Reich, then Eichmann becomes a cog, sometimes an important one, sometimes less so, depending on his position in the over-all machinery. In this case the cog was of such personal mediocrity that he really could not quite comprehend his role. Arendt shows again and again how he was beholden to clichés, was in many ways unable to form opinions or think on his own, was carried away by his own phrases. (pp. 27-8)

To decide whether or not Eichmann was guilty of the crime he was accused of, this was supposedly the purpose of the trial. He admitted his guilt, which was also well established through corroborating evidence. Then why call all these witnesses for the prosecution? For the trial it was immaterial to discuss why Jews did not fight back. Yet the court asked witness after witness: "Why did you not protest?" "Why did you board the train?" "Fifteen thousand people were standing there and hundreds of guards facing you. Why didn't you revolt and charge and attack?"

Arendt is probably correct about the motives of the court. She believes that these questions were asked to convince all Jews that there can be no strength in Jewry unless it is vested in the state of Israel. She feels that by dragging out the lack of Jewish resistance, the Israeli authorities were trying to show that no such resistance was possible because no Jewish state existed to support it. If this was the reason of the court, perhaps it was also why the same court neglected to shed light on the unfortunate and desperate cooperation of Jewish leadership with the SS.

Because, like the court in Israel, it was the misfortune of the Jews of Europe that they too saw Hitlerism as only the worst wave of anti-Semitism. They therefore responded to it with methods that in the past had permitted them to survive. That is why they got involved with executing the orders of the state; that is why the Jewish leaders and elders, with heavy hearts, cooperated in arranging things for the Nazi masters. Arendt claims, and her thesis will long be fought over, that without this collaboration Hitler could never have succeeded in killing so many Jews.

This is the part of her book that will be most widely objected to. I do not claim to know whether she is right or wrong in her argument: that if the Jewish organizations had not existed, the extermination of the Jews could never have attained such tremendous proportions. But she certainly makes her point effectively. No doubt the stories of the ghettos would have been different if most Jews and their leadership had not been more or less willing, out of anxiety, to cooperate with the Germans, if they had not opposed the small minority that called for resistance at all costs, including violent fighting back. No doubt many Jews would have been quicker to support the pitifully small fighting minority had they been told what lay in store for them by Jewish leaders who knew, or should and could have known, what fate awaited them. Many others might have tried to escape. It is another question whether more Jews could have been saved if no Jewish organizations had existed, as Arendt claims.

Here too, objections will be raised against the book. Because of her concentration on the injustice bred by totalitarianism, Arendt at times creates an ambiguity in her evaluation of guilt. Thus on cursory reading she seems to plead that Eichmann was a victim and that Jewish leaders were heavy with guilt. In fact, Arendt saw rightly that Eichmann was not the greatest villain of all. But to say so leaves her open to the misunderstanding that she did not think him much of a villain, which she certainly thought he was.

Conversely, there seems little doubt that Jewish leaders who made up lists of those to be shipped to the gas chambers became accessories to Eichmann's crimes. Others who made up similar lists, not knowing about the extermination policy and thinking their choices were merely being shipped East, acted less reprehensibly. Again others concerned with saving their own lives and those of relatives were ready to sacrifice the lives of others. Finally there were those who gave the SS a helping hand only because they believed that in doing so they reduced hardship; they may merely have been lacking in foresight, in understanding of the situation, in courage. The terrible tragedy was that they, no less than those who collaborated fully with the SS, were helping Eichmann to perpetrate his crimes.

But again, these issues are immaterial in trying one individual for the crimes he committed. Why then did Hannah Arendt spend such a large part of her book on a discussion of Jewish willingness to cooperate and on the Jews' contribution to their own extermination?

I believe that her purpose was to paint the broader context of the trial as she saw it, which went far beyond that of anti-Semitism. This was of greatest interest to me, because it has to do with the much more important issue: how and where can an individual resist, or fight back in a totalitarian society? Jewish witnesses who testified seemed to think that nobody could, certainly not the persecuted Jews. Arendt's point—and it is well taken—is that any organization within a totalitarian society that compromised with the system became immediately ineffectual in opposing it and ended up helping it. "The gravest omission from the 'general picture' [that the court tried to paint of the extermination of the Jews] was that of a witness to testify to the cooperation between Nazi rulers and the Jewish authority." Eichmann himself asserted that without such cooperation the extermination would have run into serious difficulties. (pp. 28-30)

This cooperation the court deliberately refrained from bringing to light, though it freely brought out the absence of resistance. To quote Arendt, the court did not raise the question, "Why did you cooperate in the destruction of your own people?" but this question was shouted by spectators who were only too familiar with the contribution of prominent Jews to the Jewish fate. When the former Baron Philip von Freudiger, formerly of Budapest, gave testimony, this question was screamed at him, so that the court had to interrupt the session. Arendt reports: "Freudiger, an orthodox Jew of considerable dignity, was shaken: 'There are people here who say they were not told to escape. But fifty percent of the people who escaped were captured and killed—as compared with ninety-nine percent, for those who did not escape.'" A fateful comment on the consequences of Jews being kept in the dark by Jewish leaders. . . .

In retrospect it is quite clear that only utter non-cooperation on the part of the Jews could have offered a small chance of forcing a different solution on Hitler. This conclusion is not an indictment of Jews living or dead—but an empirical finding of history. To deny or ignore it may open the door to the genocide of other races or minority groups. Active resistance arouses strong admiration, permits most of us to put it out of our minds fairly soon.

Perhaps an example from the American scene may illustrate. Many of us are impressed by the way Negroes in Birmingham marched, singing and upright, to jail. But much deeper feelings are aroused in us when we see pictures of a solitary Negro being dragged down by policemen because he refuses to march to jail on his own. This experience did not often confront the German people. Certainly from my experience in the concentration camps, and with German civilians there, it made a difference. The reaction of the German people to the crimes committed against the Jews might have been very different if each Jew who was taken had to be dragged down the street, or shot down on the spot. Again and again when German citizens witnessed utter brutality against Jews, there was at least some reaction among the civilian population; and the Nazis were extremely sensitive to it. (p. 30)

Eichmann's trial was not the trial of the century, because as a trial it had altogether too many shortcomings. It was a trial where the witnesses had their day in court, but hardly the accused. It was a trial where there was no balance between the machinery available to the prosecuting attorney when compared to that of the defense. It was a trial where important witnesses for the defense were prevented from appearing in court because they were given no assurance of immunity. (Obviously only those who had intimate knowledge of Eichmann's work could have borne witness on his behalf as to whether or not he wanted the

Jews exterminated, or was only following orders. But the only ones who could solve these questions were those who had seen him at his gruesome work, because they had been his collaborators. Hence they risked prosecution under the same Nazi Collaborator Law that Eichmann was tried under. They could have come to Israel and appeared as witnesses only if immunity had been granted them. This Israel refused to do, depriving Eichmann of his chance to produce witnesses on his own behalf.) It was a trial where most of the time was spent on issues that had no direct bearing on the guilt of the accused.

It was a trial where the state spoke with rightful moral indignation about crimes against humanity, to an accused it had kidnaped in violation of international law. The legal background of this trial also illustrates the incongruity of our legal concepts for dealing with 20th Century totalitarianism. And here again I speak not as an expert or as a lawyer, but rather as a citizen concerned with what our laws can, and cannot do for us all.

The basic principle underlying the law under which Eichmann was tried is derived from the charter of the Nuremberg Trials. They served as precedent, for example, for convicting a man without his having been found guilty by a jury of his peers. According to this charter of the Nuremberg Trials the greatest crime of all was the crime against peace which was called "the supreme international crime . . . in that it contains within itself the accumulated evil of the whole: war crimes, and crimes against humanity." Of those who sat in judgment at Nuremberg, at least one nation had engaged in unprovoked aggressive war against Finland, while two had committed crimes against humanity according to this charter; one by using slave labor. (In addition, that nation has been accused of the killing of 15,000 Polish officers at Katyn Forest. This was never proved, or disproved, because it was never brought to trial.) Another nation had clearly acted against the Hague convention by dropping atomic bombs, indiscriminately killing civilians. Still, these things happened before the Nuremberg Trials.

Since then, Israel, together with France and England, have waged war against Egypt and hence, according to the charter, committed the supreme international crime. But no court has tried them. While England and France could at least claim that Egypt had abrogated certain of their rights, Israel could not even make this claim. Crimes against humanity are unfortunately still tried only by the victors, with only the vanquished as the accused.

Such are the realities of political life in our 20th Century. I regret them but I do not object to them, because I know that these same realities induced me (in my more optimistic moments I like to think, forced me) to do things in the concentration camp (and probably outside as well) that would not stand up too well under closest scrutiny.

Unlike Arendt—and despite her cogent argument for an international court—I do not object to Israel's trying Eichmann, or to their trying him the way that they did, because I believe we must deal in some fashion with the Eichmanns of this world. That our legal procedures are not adequate for doing so does not mean they should go untried. I mean only to show that our existing laws are as incongruous for dealing with totalitarianism as we are unprepared as individuals to meet its challenge. Despite my many objections to details, if I were asked whether I preferred the trial to Eichmann's remaining free, I have no doubt that I am glad there was a trial.

Arendt seems to object to the trial as propaganda. This to me is its main justification, given the irregularities of the trial and Eichmann's having been kidnaped. Personally I would have preferred the solution Arendt suggests, that Eichmann should have been killed by a Jew, as Tindelian killed Talaat Bey (the great killer in the Armenian pogroms of 1915) and Schwartzbard killed Simon Petlyura (who was responsible for the pogroms during the Russian civil war). If such executioner of Eichmann had then been tried, through that trial all the crimes of Eichmann could have been forced on the conscience of the world without extraneous questions such as kidnaping and legality of the trial interfering with the clear message of the murderous nature of totalitarianism. If Eichmann's trial did not serve justice well, it did something much more important, and this for the living rather than for the dead: It brought the world face to face with those dangers of totalitarianism that it seems all too willing to avoid examining.

So while I would recommend this book for many reasons, the most important one is that our best protection against oppressive control and dehumanizing totalitarianism is still a personal understanding of events as they happen. To this end Hannah Arendt has furnished us with a richness of material. (pp. 32-3)

> *Bruno Bettelheim, "Eichmann; the System; the Victims," in* The New Republic, *Vol. 148, No. 24, June 15, 1963, pp. 23-33.*

Norman Podhoretz

One of the many ironies surrounding [*Eichmann in Jerusalem: A Report on the Banality of Evil*] is involved in the fact that it should have been serialized in the *New Yorker* so short a time after the appearance in the same magazine of James Baldwin's essay on the Black Muslims. A Negro on the Negroes, a Jew on the Jews, each telling a tale of the horrors that have been visited upon his people and of how these horrors were borne; and each exhorting the prosperous, the secure, the ignorant to understand that these horrors are relevant to them. The two stories have much in common and they are both, in their essentials, as old as humankind itself—so old and so familiar that it takes a teller of extraordinary eloquence, or else of extraordinary cleverness, to make them come alive again. (p. 201)

If Baldwin is all eloquence and no cleverness, Miss Arendt is all cleverness and no eloquence; and if Baldwin brings his story unexpectedly to life through the bold tactic of heightening and playing exquisitely on every bit of melodrama it contains, Miss Arendt with an equally surprising boldness rids her story of melodrama altogether and heavily underlines every trace of moral ambiguity she can wring out of it. What she has done, in other words, is translate this story for the first time into the kind of terms

that can appeal to the sophisticated modern sensibility. Thus, in place of the monstrous Nazi, she gives us the "banal" Nazi; in place of the Jew as virtuous martyr, she gives us the Jew as accomplice in evil; and in place of the confrontation between guilt and innocence, she gives us the "collaboration" of criminal and victim. The story as she tells it is complex, unsentimental, riddled with paradox and ambiguity. It has all the appearance of "ruthless honesty," and all the marks of profundity—have we not been instructed that complexity, paradox, and ambiguity are the sign manifest of profundity?—and, in addition, it carries with it all the authority of Miss Arendt's classic work on *The Origins of Totalitarianism.* Anyone schooled in the modern in literature and philosophy would be bound to consider it a much better story than the usual melodramatic version—which, as it happens, was more or less the one relied upon by the prosecution at the Eichmann trial, and which Miss Arendt uses to great effect in highlighting the superior interest of her own version. But if this version of hers can from one point of view be considered more interesting, can it by the same token be considered truer, or more illuminating, or more revealing of the general situation of man in the 20th century? Is the gain she achieves in literary interest a matter of titillation, or is it a gain to the understanding?

Let us be clear about these questions: they cannot be answered by scholarship. To the extent that *Eichmann in Jerusalem* parades as history, its factual accuracy is of course open to critical examination. But it would be unwise to take the scholarly pretensions of the book at face value. This is in no sense a work of objective historical research aimed at determining "the way things really were." Except in her critique of the trial itself, which she attended, Miss Arendt's sources are for the most part secondary ones (she relies especially on Raul Hilberg's *The Destruction of the European Jews*), and her manipulation of evidence is at all times visibly tendentious. Nevertheless, a distorted or exaggerated picture drawn in the service of a suggestive thesis can occasionally bring us closer to the essential truth than a carefully qualified and meticulously documented study—provided that the thesis accords reasonably well with the evidence. The point to begin with, then, is Miss Arendt's thesis, and the problem to settle is whether it justifies the distortions of perspective it creates and the cavalier treatment of evidence it impels.

According to Miss Arendt, the Nazis, in order to carry out their genocidal plan against the Jews, needed Jewish cooperation and in fact received it "to a truly extraordinary degree." This cooperation took the form of "administrative and police work," and it was extended by "the highly assimilated Jewish communities of Central and Western Europe" no less abundantly than by "the Yiddish-speaking masses of the East." In Amsterdam as in Warsaw, in Berlin as in Budapest, Miss Arendt writes,

> Jewish officials could be trusted to compile the lists of persons and of their property, to secure money from the deportees to defray the expenses of their deportation and extermination, to keep track of vacated apartments, to supply police forces to help seize Jews and get them on trains, until, as a last gesture, they handed over the as-

sets of the Jewish community in good order for
final confiscation.

All this has long been known. What is new is Miss Arendt's assertion that if the Jews (or rather, their leaders)
had not cooperated in this fashion, "there would have
been chaos and plenty of misery but the total number of
victims would hardly have been between four and a half
and six million people."

So much for the Jews. As for the Nazis, carrying out the
policy of genocide required neither that they be monsters
nor pathological Jew-haters. On the contrary: since the
murder of Jews was dictated by the law of the state, and
since selfless loyalty to the law was regarded by the Germans under Hitler as the highest of virtues, it even called
for a certain idealism to do what Eichmann and his cohorts did. Miss Arendt in this connection quotes the famous remark attributed to Himmler: "To have stuck it out
and, apart from exceptions caused by human weakness, to
have remained decent, that is what has made us hard."
Eichmann, then, was telling the truth when he denied having been an anti-Semite: he did his duty to the best of his
ability, and he would have performed with equal zeal even
if he had loved the Jews. Thus also, the Israeli prosecutor
Gideon Hausner was absurdly off the point in portraying
Eichmann as a brute and a sadist and a fiend: Eichmann
was in actual fact a banal personality, a nonentity whose
evil deeds flowed not from anything in his own character,
but rather from his position in the Nazi system. (pp. 201-
02)

Obviously, though, this ordinary man could not have been
turned into so great and devoted a perpetrator of evil if the
system had not been so tightly closed—if, that is to say,
there had been voices to protest or gestures of resistance.
Such voices as existed, however, were in Miss Arendt's
judgment pathetically small and thin, and such gestures
of resistance as were displayed she finds relatively insignificant. Not only did "good society everywhere" accept the
Final Solution with "zeal and eagerness," but the Jews
themselves acquiesced and even cooperated—as we have
seen—"to a truly extraordinary degree." Here, then, is the
finishing touch to Miss Arendt's reading of the Final Solution, and the explanation she gives for dwelling on Jewish
complicity: this chapter of the story, she says, "offers the
most striking insight into the totality of the moral collapse
the Nazis caused in respectable European society—not
only in Germany but in almost all countries, not only
among the persecutors but also among the victims."

An interesting version of the story, no doubt about that.
But let us look at it a little more closely. Assuming for the
moment that Jewish leadership did in fact cooperate with
the Nazis "to a truly extraordinary degree" (the degree is
the point under contention), why did the Nazis *want* their
cooperation? A reader of *The Origins of Totalitarianism*
might have expected Miss Arendt to reply that they wanted it for its own sake. And indeed, she does quote David
Rousset to this effect in dealing with the "cruel and silly
question," as she calls it, that Hausner kept putting to his
witnesses at the trial ("Fifteen thousand people were
standing there and hundreds of guards facing you—why
didn't you revolt and charge and attack?"). . . .Yet when

Miss Arendt arrives a hundred pages later at the matter
of "Jewish help in administrative and police work," considerations of a strictly mundane and thoroughly utilitarian nature suddenly enter as the decisive ones. The Nazis
wanted Jewish help, for without it, "there would have
been either complete chaos or an impossibly severe drain
on German manpower."

Coming from Miss Arendt, this is surprising—"to a truly
extraordinary degree," we might say. It is surprising because one of the major points she makes in *The Origins
of Totalitarianism* is that the Nazi will to murder every
Jew in Europe was so powerful that resources badly needed at the front in 1944 and early 1945 were tied up so that
the ovens of Auschwitz could be kept working at full capacity. Certainly it was more *convenient* for Eichmann
that the Jews took some of the burdens upon themselves
that would otherwise have fallen to him. But to contend
that such burdens would have put enough strain on German resources to force the Nazis to ease off on the Jews
is ridiculous by Miss Arendt's own account.

For by her own account, the Nazis were determined at almost any cost to "cleanse" Europe of the Jews; nothing
in their program had higher priority. But was there no
possibility of stopping them? Miss Arendt now argues that
there was. Whenever they encountered determined opposition, she says, they backed down, and she cites France,
Italy, Belgium, Bulgaria, and (most glorious of them all)
Denmark, where the Nazis succeeded in deporting only a
comparatively small proportion of the resident Jews. In
Holland, Rumania, Hungary, Poland, and the Ukraine,
on the other hand, the slaughter was near complete. Looking at all these countries, one can readily agree that the
determining factor in the number of Jews murdered was
the amount of resistance (either active or passive) offered
to the Final Solution. The important question to be decided, however, is: resistance by *whom?* Miss Arendt knows
of course, that it was the attitude of the local populace that
made the main difference—where they were willing to cooperate in the rounding up and deportation of Jews, most
Jews were deported, and where they were unwilling to cooperate, fewer Jews were deported. But since Miss Arendt
wishes us to believe that the Nazis could never have killed
as many as six million Jews without Jewish help, she tries
very hard to convey the impression that what the Jews
themselves did in any given country mattered significantly
too. And it is here that she becomes most visibly tendentious in her manipulation of the facts. In explaining, for
example, why not a single Belgian Jew was ever deported
(though thousands of stateless Jews living in Belgium
were), she tells us how the Belgian police and the Belgian
railwaymen quietly sabotaged deportation operations, and
then adds: "Moreover, among those who had fled were the
more important Jewish leaders . . . so that there was no
Jewish Council to register the Jews—one of the vital pre-
requisites for their seizure." But there *was* a Jewish Council in Belgium. There was also one in France, and Miss Arendt simply neglects to mention it. Quite right, too, for the
U. G. I. F. made no more difference to the situation in
France than the *Association des Juifs en Belgique* made to
the situation in Belgium, or than any other *Judenrat* made
to the situation in any other country.

So far as the *Judenräte* were concerned, the chief difference between Western countries like Belgium and France on the one hand, and the Eastern territories on the other, was that the Germans did not set up ghettos in the West. The reason is suggested in Léon Poliakov's account of the role of the French *Judenrat:* "In France you never had a situation where Jews were systematically presiding over the deportation of other Jews. [For] *the attitude of the French population, which strenuously opposed the policy of segregation and isolation of the Jews, made such degradation impossible*" (my italics). . . . As for Jewish opposition, all *it* ever did was bring out more German troops. Certainly the Nazis showed little concern over the drain on their manpower when the Warsaw Ghetto revolted.

But not only is Miss Arendt wholly unwarranted in emphasizing Jewish cooperation as a significant factor in the number of victims claimed by the Final Solution; the irony is that her insistence on doing so also involves her in making the same assumption about the Nazis that lay behind Jewish cooperation itself. This assumption was that the Nazis were rational beings and that their aims must therefore be limited and subject to negotiation. . . . As many historians have pointed out, the policy of appeasement was not in itself foolish or evil; it was a perfectly traditional diplomatic tactic, and its foolishness in this case lay in the fact that it was being applied to an aggressor who was *not* politically prudent and whose aims were *not* of the traditionally limited kind. The mistake of the appeasers, in other words, stemmed from their failure to recognize the unprecedented and revolutionary character of the Nazi regime. Almost every Jewish leader in Europe made the same mistake regarding the intentions of the Nazis toward them and their people—a mistake that the Nazis incidentally did everything they could to encourage.

If, then, we ask why Jewish leadership cooperated with the Nazis, the answer would seem to be that they were following a policy of appeasement, and that there was nothing in the least "extraordinary" about this. That, however, is not the answer we get from Miss Arendt; her answer is more interesting and complicated and paradoxical. A distinction must be made, she argues, between the Jewish masses and the Jewish leaders. It was "cruel and silly" of Hausner to ask why the masses went passively to their deaths, "for no non-Jewish group or people had behaved differently." But it is apparently compassionate and intelligent to ask much the same question of the Jewish leaders, even though no non-Jewish leaders had behaved differently. (pp. 202-04)

[What] is Miss Arendt really saying when she tells us that "if the Jewish people had . . . been unorganized and leaderless, there would have been chaos and plenty of misery but the total number of victims would hardly have been between four and a half and six million people." Why, she is saying that if the Jews had not been Jews, the Nazis would not have been able to kill so many of them—which is a difficult proposition to dispute. I do not think I am being unfair to Miss Arendt here. Consider: the Jews of Europe, even where they were "highly assimilated," were an organized people, and in most cases a centrally organized people. This was a fact of their condition no less

surely than sovereign nationhood was a fact of the French condition. Yet I doubt that Miss Arendt would ever take it into her head to declare that if the French people had not been organized into a nation-state, they could never have been sold out to the Nazis by Pétain and Laval. Throughout this book, Miss Arendt is very nasty about Zionists and Zionism, but the only sense one can glean from her argument is a grain of retroactive Zionist sense. The Jews, she is implying, should have known that anti-Semitism rendered their position in the Diaspora untenable, and they should therefore either have set up a state of their own or renounced their communal existence altogether. She does not explain how such renunciation could have saved them from the Nuremberg laws. Nor does she tell us why the slaughter of Jews in occupied Russia should have been so complete even though there was no central Jewish leadership or communal organization in the Soviet Union.

But it is unnecessary to pursue the absurdities of Miss Arendt's argument on this issue, just as it is unnecessary to enter once again into the endless moral debate over the behavior of the Jewish leaders—the endless round of apology and recrimination. They did what they did, they were what they were, and each was a different man. None of it mattered in the slightest to the final result. Murderers with the power to murder descended upon a defenseless people and murdered a large part of it. What else is there to say?

In stark contrast to the Jews, whose behavior in Miss Arendt's version of the story self-evidently explains and condemns itself, the Nazis—or anyway Adolf Eichmann—need the most careful and the most imaginative attention before they can be intelligently judged. The irony here is of course obvious, and even the Eichmann trial to some extent fell victim to it. As Harold Rosenberg put it in these pages two years ago:

> Why should this self-styled nobody who had hurled into silence so many of the subtlest and most humane intellects of Europe have been permitted to elaborate on each trait of his character, his opinions on all sorts of matters, including Kant's categorical imperative, and his conception of himself as Pontius Pilate and as a "romantic," his reaction to his wife's reading the Bible, his drinking of mare's milk and *schnapps?* One question would have sufficed to complete the formulation of his culpability: "Weren't you the head of Sec. IV B4 of RSHA charged with the extermination of the Jews of Europe, and did you not carry out the function assigned to you to the best of your ability?"

This, in Rosenberg's view, was the main defect of the trial, and it flowed from Gideon Hausner's persistent efforts to prove that Eichmann was subjectively vicious, as well as a perpetrator of objectively criminal deeds. Miss Arendt also disapproves of these efforts by Hausner, but her complaint is against Hausner's particular conception of Eichmann's character and not against the opportunity he gave him to speak. Far from being offended at the idea that *this self-styled nobody who had hurled into silence so many of the subtlest and most humane intellects of Europe* should have been permitted to discourse himself at such great length, Miss Arendt helps the discourse along, develops it, refines it, and in the end virtually justifies it. By this I do not mean that she defends Eichmann, as some of her critics have stupidly charged: she does nothing of the kind anywhere in her book, and she says plainly in the closing chapter that he was guilty of participation in mass murder and deserved to hang. What she does do, however, is accept Eichmann's account of himself and of his role in the Final Solution as largely true. In some sense, he *was* an "idealist"; in some sense, he was *not* an anti-Semite; and the degree of his responsibility for the murder of the six million, while sufficient to hang him, *was* relatively insignificant, and certainly nowhere near what the prosecution claimed. By building Eichmann up into a fiendish Jew-hater and a major Nazi figure, Miss Arendt believes, the prosecution missed the whole point of his crimes, of the system which made them possible, and of the lessons to be drawn for the future.

Taking Eichmann pretty much at his own word, then (except when his own word conflicts with her reading of his character), Miss Arendt treats us to a genuinely brilliant portrait of the mind of a middle-echelon Nazi and, by extension, of the world that produced him and gave him the power to do the things he did. And around this theme of Eichmann's "banality" other themes gather: the almost universal complicity of Christian Europe, and especially of the German people, in Nazism (for in diminishing Eichmann's personal responsibility for the Final Solution, she enlarges the area of European responsibility in general); and the almost total consequent unwillingness of the Federal Republic to prosecute and mete out adequate punishment to Nazi war criminals still at large and in many cases flourishing (Miss Arendt, it should be noted, presents perhaps the most severe indictment of Adenauer's Germany that has yet been seen this side of the Iron Curtain, and whatever comfort the book may bring to the Germans in some respects, it is bound in the main to infuriate them).

The brilliance of Miss Arendt's treatment of Eichmann could hardly be disputed by any disinterested reader. But at the same time, there could hardly be a more telling example than this section of her book of the intellectual perversity that can result from the pursuit of brilliance by a mind infatuated with its own agility and bent on generating dazzle. The man around the corner who makes ugly cracks about the Jews is an anti-Semite, but not Adolf Eichmann who sent several million Jews to their death: *that* would be uninteresting and would tell us nothing about the Nature of Totalitarianism. Similarly, the behavior of the Jewish leaders under the Nazis was "extraordinary," but Adolf Eichmann was ordinary, even unto banality; otherwise, he tells us nothing about the Nature of Totalitarianism. Did he have no conscience? Of course he had a conscience, the conscience of an inverted Kantian idealist; otherwise he tells us nothing about the Nature of Totalitarianism. But what about his famous statement that he would die happy because he had sent five million "enemies of the Reich" to their graves? "Sheer rodomontade," sheer braggery—to believe it is to learn nothing about the Nature of Totalitarianism. And his decision to carry on with the deportations from Hungary in direct defiance of Himmler's order that they be stopped? A perfect

example of the very idealism that teaches us so much about the Nature of Totalitarianism.

No. It finally refuses to wash; it finally violates everything we know about the Nature of Man, and therefore the Nature of Totalitarianism must go hang. For uninteresting though it may be to say so, no person could have joined the Nazi party, let alone the S. S., who was not at the very least a *vicious* anti-Semite; to believe otherwise is to learn nothing about the nature of anti-Semitism. Uninteresting though it may be to say so, no person of conscience could have participated knowingly in mass murder: to believe otherwise is to learn nothing about the nature of conscience. And uninteresting though it may be to say so, no banality of a man could have done so hugely evil a job so well; to believe otherwise is to learn nothing about the nature of evil. Was Hausner right, then, in repeatedly calling Eichmann a liar? Yes, he was right, however successfully Eichmann may have deceived himself by then, and however "sincere" he may have thought his testimony was.

And the Nature of Totalitarianism? What Miss Arendt's book on the Eichmann trial teaches us about the Nature of Totalitarianism is that the time has come to re-examine the whole concept. Apart from the many other weaknesses it has revealed since the days when it was first developed to distinguish between the "simple" dictatorships of the pre-modern era and the ideologically inspired revolutionary regimes of Stalin and Hitler, the theory of totalitarianism has always been limited in its usefulness by the quasi-metaphysical and rather Germanic terms in which it was originally conceived. For what the theory aimed at describing was a fixed essence, not a phenomenon in flux, and the only changes it saw as possible within the totalitarian structure were those leading toward a more perfect realization of the totalitarian idea itself. (pp. 205-06)

But since the perfect totalitarian state did not yet exist, how did the theorists of totalitarianism know what it would look like in a fully realized condition? The answer is that they knew from the Nazi concentration camps, which, as they rightly understood, had in part been set up to serve as models and as "laboratories" for experimenting with techniques of absolute domination. Here was where totalitarianism stood nakedly revealed; here was its essential meaning; here was what the system was really all about.

So far, so good. The trouble began with a tendency to speak of Nazi Germany and Soviet Russia as though they had already attained to the perfection of vast concentration camps, and as though the Nazis in their style and the Communists in theirs had already been transformed into the new men of the transvalued totalitarian future. Yet on the basis of a somewhat more optimistic view of human nature than is implicit in the theory of totalitarianism (which substitutes for the naïve liberal idea of the infinite perfectibility of man the equally naïve idea of the infinite malleability of man), one may be permitted to doubt that the whole world could under any circumstances ever be made over into a concentration camp. As it is, Soviet Russia seems to be moving in the other direction. And so far as the Third Reich is concerned, it lasted for less than thirteen years and conquered only a small section of the globe, with the result that: (1) Nazi Germany never had a chance to seal itself off completely from outside influences; and (2) the people who participated actively in Nazism *knew* they were being criminal by the standards under which they themselves had been raised and that also still reigned supreme in the "decadent" culture of the West.

This is why it is finally impossible to accept Miss Arendt's conception of Eichmann's role and character. Eichmann was not living in the ideal Nazi future, but in the imperfect Nazi present, and while we can agree with Miss Arendt that, as a mere lieutenant-colonel, he probably did not enjoy the importance that the Israeli indictment attributed to him, neither can he have been quite so banal as she makes him out to be. After all, there *was* enough opposition to the Final Solution to have persuaded him that not everyone looked upon the murdering of Jews as a fine and noble occupation, and after all, he *was* a first-generation Nazi and an important enough one to have been trusted with a large measure of administrative responsibility for a top-priority item in the Nazi program. Now, if we are not to lose our own minds in the act of trying to penetrate into the psychology of the Nazi mind, we must be very careful to keep it clear that this item of the Nazi program—the "cleansing" of Europe, and ultimately the whole world, of Jews—was literally insane. It is one thing to hate Jews, but it is quite another to contemplate the wholesale slaughter of Jews; it is one thing to believe that no nation-state can be healthy when it contains "alien" elements, but it is quite another to decide upon the murder of eleven million people (the estimated target of the Final Solution) as a means of achieving ethnic homogeneity. Ponder the difference between the Germans and the Rumanians in this connection. The Rumanians were the worst anti-Semites in Europe and were delighted to join in the butchering of Jews, until they discovered that there was money to be made from the saving of Jews, whereupon they began saving Jews: this is pathological anti-Semitism bounded by rational limits. The Germans, on the other hand, regarded the Jews, whom they had rendered utterly helpless with a stroke of the pen, as dangerous enemies, and they were so convinced of the necessity to do away with these enemies that they were willing to let the war effort suffer rather than let up: this is pathological anti-Semitism bounded by no rational limits. Insanity, in short.

It is in this insanity, I believe, and not in the pedestrian character of Adolf Eichmann, that whatever banality attaches to the evil of the Final Solution must be sought. And because Hitler and his cohorts were madmen on the Jewish question, there is probably little of general relevance we can learn from the Final Solution beyond what the Nuremberg trials established concerning the individual's criminal accountability when acting upon superior orders, even within a system guided by insane aims. There is, however, much to be learned from the Final Solution about other matters, and principally about anti-Semitism. When Miss Arendt speaks of the amazing extent of the moral collapse that the Nazis caused "everywhere," she must be referring specifically to the Jewish question. The will to fight the German armies did not collapse everywhere, and the will to defend democracy against the Nazi

onslaught stood up well enough to triumph in the end; the only collapse that took place "everywhere" was a collapse of the will to prevent the Nazis from wiping the Jews off the face of the earth. Here again, Miss Arendt can be refuted out of her own mouth, for acquiescence in the Final Solution (as she demonstrates) was far from universal in Europe (though it may well have been nearly universal in Germany). The fact remains, however, that there was acquiescence enough to allow this insane Nazi ambition to come very close to succeeding. Nobody cared about the Gypsies because nobody ever thinks about the Gypsies—except the police. But how did it happen that nobody cared about the Jews when everyone seems always to be thinking about the Jews? The question surely answers itself, and the answer incidentally provides the justification for Ben Gurion's statement that one of the purposes of the Eichmann trial was to make the nations of the world ashamed.

Miss Arendt dislikes that statement, but no more than she dislikes every other statement Ben Gurion made about the trial. She is also unhappy with the trial itself—the fact that Eichmann was tried before an Israeli court instead of an international tribunal, the substance of the indictment, the way Hausner handled the prosecution, the way Servatius conducted the defense. The only aspect of the trial that pleases her is that the judges behaved with scrupulous regard for the interests of Justice: she is as unstinting in her praise of them as she is relentless in her contempt for Hausner and Ben Gurion ("the invisible stage manager of the proceedings"). A few of Miss Arendt's criticisms of the trial seem reasonable, but given the animus she exhibits from the very first sentence of the book, it becomes extremely difficult to look upon these criticisms as anything other than further instances of the inordinate demands she is always making on the Jews to be better than other people, to be braver, wiser, nobler, more dignified—or be damned. (pp. 206-08)

The Nazis destroyed a third of the Jewish people. In the name of all that is humane, will the remnant never let up on itself? (p. 208)

> *Norman Podhoretz, "Hannah Arendt on Eichmann: A Study in the Perversity of Brilliance,"* in Commentary, *Vol. 36, No. 3, September, 1963, pp. 201-08.*

George McKenna

[The essay excerpted below originally appeared in the Winter 1970 issue of Salmagundi.]

It is against [a] background of apology for mass apathy and oligarchic control that the political thought of Hannah Arendt stands in sharp relief. In a land where politics is a sideshow and flying saucers are serious business, something more is needed than bland description of how the system works: what is needed is a political discipline which asks, broadly, about the ends toward which the system works, which undertakes a critical analysis of those ends, and, if they are wanting, which provides alternatives that are viable and attainable, or at least worth striving for. Arendt's political thought, taken as a whole, is an important step toward such a reconstruction. Her unique contribution is an attempt to recapture the meaning of political action as it was understood by the actual participants in great political enterprises, and, using them as a guide, to measure the areas where politics has declined or altogether collapsed in today's world. What emerges is a radical critique of all those aspects of the modern world which either result from or contribute to the political environment in which most of us live. It is radical in the sense that it attempts to go to the roots of the problem by tracing it to its historical origins; it is a critique because it makes no attempt to treat phenomena such as totalitarianism in a "value free" manner: Arendt is convinced that to describe, say, concentration camps *sine ira,* "is not to be 'objective,' but to condone them." (p. 107)

[It is necessary] to see what Arendt means by political action if we are to understand what she has to say about its decline. (p. 108)

The best way to begin studying her definition of politics is to note this observation which she makes of it in *The Human Condition:*

> Action [i. e., political action], the only activity that goes on directly between men without the intermediary of things or matter, corresponds to the human condition of plurality, to the fact that men, not Man, live on the earth and inhabit the world.

In other words, politics has three characteristics: First, it does not require the intermediary of things or matter but goes on directly between man and man. Second, because of this fact, it cannot be performed in solitude and always requires the presence of others. Third, and following from the first and second, it corresponds to the plurality of men. Her meaning here ought to be explained.

What sets men apart from animals, in Arendt's thoroughly secular philosophy, is not the presence of an immortal soul or even a rational faculty, but the fact that men are mortals whereas animals have, in a sense, an eternal life. This seems to be the exact opposite of the Christian understanding. What she means is that animals have eternal life because they are properly viewed, not as individuals, but as parts of their encompassing species; and the species "dog," for example, will go on living indefinitely, whatever may befall individual dogs. Of course, the same is also true in the case of the species "mankind." But the difference, for Arendt, is that man admits of more than *en masse* classification. Man, properly understood, is really individual *men:* each member possesses his own life, a *"bios,* with a recognizable life-story from birth to death," rising out of the eternal cycle of biological life or zoe. In short, "men are 'the mortals,' the only mortal things there are, for animals exist only as members of their species and not as individuals." Anyone who has owned pets might object to this line of reasoning. Her elaboration of it makes it more defensible while bringing it closer to the Christian understanding. Very simply, what she has in mind is the uniqueness of the human person. All things, including even inanimate objects, possess the quality of *alteritas,* "otherness." But only individual men are able, actively, to express their distinctive qualities and not merely, passive-

ly, to be considered distinct. Each man, in other words, is able to "communicate himself," to reveal himself as a "who" rather than a "what."

Political action corresponds to this human plurality—the fact that men, not Man, live in this world—because it is the means by which men are able to communicate their distinctness without recourse to anything other than themselves. Painters and poets also communicate themselves, but they must perform their works in solitude and require the intermediary of things—if only pen and ink—to express themselves. Political action is the most completely human of activities.

Politics, as Arendt understands it, is indissolubly bound up with speech. A whine or growl might communicate anger or hunger, the use of mathematical symbols might communicate certain concepts, a computer can analyze and communicate data with superhuman accuracy, but only human speech can communicate man's distinctness as a person, can reveal him as a "who" and not simply a "what."

"Action and speech are so closely related because the primordial and specifically human act must at the same time contain the answer to the question asked of every newcomer: 'Who are you?' " . . . At any rate, she is convinced that without the accompaniment of speech action would be meaningless and subjectless.

> Without the accompaniment of speech . . . action would not only lose its revelatory character but, and by the same token, it would lose its subject, as it were; not acting men but performing robots would achieve what, humanly speaking, would remain incomprehensible. Speechless action would no longer be action because there would no longer be an actor, and the actor, the doer of deeds is possible only if he is at the same time the speaker of words. The action he begins is humanly disclosed by the word, and though his deed can be perceived in its brute physical appearance without verbal accompaniment, it becomes relevant only through the spoken word in which he identifies himself as the actor announcing what he does, has done, and intends to do.

For Arendt, "speechless action" is a contradiction in terms, for action without speech is no longer politics but violence. Because of the contemporary confusion between political power and violence, this point is particularly relevant today, and I will return to it presently.

"The *raison d'être* of politics is freedom. . . ." Although Arendt claims to be stating but a truism, it would be disputed by a number of premodern and modern political thinkers from Hobbes to Reinhold Niebuhr. The latter has made these observations:

> It is our common assumption that political freedom is a simple *summom bonum.* It is not. Freedom must always be related to community and justice. Every community seeks consciously and unconsciously to make social peace and order the first goal of its life. It may pay a very high price in the restriction of freedom so as to establish order; but order is the first desideratum for

the simple reason that chaos means non-existence.

Yes, Arendt might reply, it is quite true that communities—except during times of revolution—seldom make freedom the first order of business. But this anthropological fact does not negate the principle of the primacy of freedom. (All communities also have some form of ritualized cruelty, but this is hardly a justification for it.) Political life might well be impossible without order, but it would be, she believes, meaningless without freedom. Niebuhr's observation, moreover, assumes an antithesis between freedom and order which Arendt would not accept. Freedom, Arendt believes, produces its own order, an order not imposed from without but growing out of mutual agreement. In Niebuhr's frame of reference, Arendt would almost certainly be classified among the "foolish children of light," for she goes the length of identifying politics with freedom. "Men are free, as distinguished from possessing the gift for freedom, as long as they act, neither before nor after, for to be free and act are the same." Arendt acknowledges a debt to Martin Heidegger and other *existenz* philosophers, and her own writings emphasize the concrete and the existential. She would not be put in the position of saying that man is "essentially" free for the same reason that she will not discuss an absolute, unchanging "human nature"; fixed essences have no place in her thinking about man and his activities. Man, she believes, is as he acts and "the appearance of freedom, like the manifestations of principles coincides with the performing act." She is interested in freedom as a phenomenon, a "demonstrable fact" rather than a metaphysical category. She compares the appearance of freedom to the actions of the performing artist: it exists *only* in the moment of performance It is, therefore, unrealizable—in an environment from which politics is excluded—in tribal societies, in the privacy of the household, or in "despotically ruled communities which banish their subjects into the narrowness of the home and thus prevent the rise of a public realm." When she says that freedom needs a "worldly space" to make its appearance, we might put it again in terms of the performing arts and say that freedom needs a stage or platform to be seen in public.

Politics, as she understands it, does not depend upon any particular physical location. When she says that it requires a "public space" or "space of appearances," she uses these expressions in a figurative or social, rather than a literal, physical sense. The ancient *polis,* for example, was not the city-state as a geographical entity, but an organization of people that was, ultimately, independent of material factors; hence, the watchword, "Wherever you go, you will be a *polis.*" The space of appearances is therefore to be interpreted in the widest sense of the word as "the space where I appear to others as others appear to me, where men exist not merely like other living or inanimate things but make their appearance explicitly." It is a space that "comes into being wherever men are together in the manner of speech and action," hence speech and action provide their own public realm and are not dependent upon buildings or even constitutions. Arendt is simply taking note of the fact that one need not go to Washington or City Hall to take part in politics and that the real centers of po-

litical action may be far removed from the formal centers, from the "paraphernalia of officialdom." A letter to an individual or newspaper can be a supremely political act. *The Federalist* papers and the letters of Thomas Jefferson (who spent the better part of his life at his writing desk in Monticello) are examples of how independent of location the "space of appearances" may be.

Political action, in Arendt's analysis, can appear in unlikely places because it goes on directly between man and man, without the intermediary of things. Wherever men gather it is found potentially; but, she emphasizes, only potentially. The rise and fall of civilizations is to be explained, not by material things or their absence, but the actualization and loss of *power*. Power, elusive and intangible as it is, plays a key role in Arendt's notion of politics.

> What first undermines and then kills political communities is loss of power and final impotence; and power cannot be stored up and kept in reserve for emergencies, like the instruments of violence, but exists only in its actualization. Where power is not actualized, it passes away, and history is full of examples that the greatest material riches cannot compensate for this loss.

Power, as its etymological roots reveal, always has a potential character. In order for it to be actualized, it is not sufficient for men to be gathered together. They could be collected together like slaves, or inmates in a concentration camp or passengers on a bus. It is only actualized when men undertake joint action. And since action, as she understands it, always involves speech, her concept of power must be distinguished from another term frequently used as a synonym: violence. (One hears "black power" invoked by those who mean "black violence" and "power politics" used when "politics through violence" is really meant.) The hallmark of power is speech combined with creative action.

> Power is actualized only where word and deed have not parted company, where words are not empty and deeds not brutal, where words are not used to veil intentions but to disclose realities, and deeds are not used to violate and destroy but to establish relations and create new realities.

Violence by itself is capable only of producing "an array of impotent forces that spend themselves, often spectacularly and vehemently but in utter futility, leaving behind neither monuments nor stories, hardly enough memory to enter into history at all." Impotent while armed to the teeth: as examples Arendt could point to the last years of Rome, the Court of Louis XVI, the Romanoffs, the succession of petty tyrants in South Vietnam since 1954, our own Southern sheriffs of whom the freedom song prophesies: "All their dogs will lie there rottin'/All their lives will be forgotten." What she does use to illustrate a confrontation between impotent violence and non-violent power is the example of the Danish refusal to cooperate with the Nazis during World War II in the matter of deporting the Jews. So determined were the Danes to protect the Jews and so concerted were their efforts that they succeeded, even converting some high-ranking Nazis to their side. "One is tempted to recommend the story as required reading in political science for all students who wish to learn something about the enormous power potential inherent in non-violent action and in resistance to an opponent possessing vastly superior means of violence." This does not mean that Arendt is a pacifist. Indeed, her model of political action is derived in large part from the revolutions of the past two centuries, and the Resistance movement during World War II, none of which could have succeeded without violence of some sort. But that is the point. Organized violence—warfare—may be necessary to *protect* the operation of the political process but it must not be *confused* with it. Arendt's approach to politics is thus sharply at variance with that school of realpolitik which proceeds on the maxim that "war is the continuation of politics by other means." The adoption of this principle might have the effect of limiting war (although this has hardly been demonstrated by the events of the last few years), but it also destroys the distinction between politics and violence by making politics the continuation of war by other means. And, far from being simply the attitude of a Prussian military officer, the maxim of Clausewitz is really a concise summary of the whole modern world's confusion between politics and violence, persuasion and force, debate and mute savagery. The United States policy, pursued with utter futility for three years, of bombing another country to "persuade" its leaders to negotiate only serves to underscore the danger in these confusions. Politics, for Hannah Arendt, comprises both word and deed. When men fall silent and turn to their weapons, politics comes to an end: "for man, to the extent that he is a political being, is endowed with the power of speech."

By sharply distinguishing between power and violence, Arendt is also freeing power from all the negative connotations attributed to it by the classical liberals—that power corrupts, that the state is an instrument of oppression or at best a necessary evil, a badge of lost innocence and so on.

On the contrary, power, in Arendt's view is essential to the freedom of man and the survival of the body politic. "Power is what keeps the public realm, the potential space of appearance between acting and speaking, men in existence."

Let us pause to consider the implications of Arendt's notion of politics and its connection with freedom. What she is saying is that no man can be free unless he participates in the political life of his community. It is important to keep in mind that Arendt considers politics in terms of active participation, not simply passive acceptance. Hence, the expression "government by consent of the governed" is, for Arendt, misleading if it is meant to imply that the governed are thereby taking part in politics. Consent alone does not constitute political activity. Government by consent, whether that consent be expressed in terms of periodic elections, referenda, plebiscites or whatever, is not government by the people but government by an elite which occasionally gets the approval of the people. Perhaps she would consider the act of voting itself as political (Arendt is not clear on this question), but when the voter returns to his private life for another year or two or (most usually) four, he is no more free than the subject of an oriental despot, though he may be treated more decently. This should

hardly fail to provoke a number of questions. Is it not possible for activities other than political participation to be considered free? And what is freedom after all—does it not ultimately depend upon whether one *thinks* he is free, regardless of his political status? Is not free will and freedom from neurosis a much more fundamental measure of freedom than political freedom, which is, after all, only a matter of externals?

To the first question her answer here would seem to be a somewhat equivocal "no."

She admits that there is such a thing as freedom *from* politics, understood at various periods of history as the freedom to spend one's time in philosophic or religious contemplation, the freedom to make money without state interference, the freedom to go to work or play without worrying about the burden of political participation. But it is clear from the context in which she discusses freedom from politics that she does not regard this negative freedom very highly. Such an understanding of freedom, which she considers either Platonic or Christian in origin, seems to her more an obstacle to the enjoyment of political freedom than anything that could be called a positive contribution.

But what of the activities themselves? Cannot man find freedom in the pursuit of monetary gain, visions of Truth, the joy of labor, or simply diversion? She would deny that any of these activities are, properly speaking, free acts. Contemplation is not even, as she understands it, an activity but a motionless state of wonder. Contemplation is "an experience of the eternal," a confrontation with Being, or perhaps The Being, which rules all of the universe with iron laws. Far from being an experience of freedom, it is a surrender to necessity: the philosopher can only gaze in helpless awe at a universe "where no beginning and no end exist and where all natural things swing in changeless, deathless repetition." As for labor, business and play, since they serve nature's life processes (they are meant to feed the demands of the body which requires both food and rest), they are as much ruled by necessity as the "changeless, deathless" universe which surrounds and encloses all life. Hence, Arendt would probably agree that the prototype American, whose major preoccupations are his job, his golf and his home workshop, and who takes no part in political life, is not a free man. This is not to say that he is not, in his own way, happy. The Negroes in the antebellum South may also have been happier than those trying to liberate themselves today.

All of this underscores the difficulty of defining freedom as a state of mind. If freedom ultimately depends upon whether a man *thinks* he is free, then the term ceases to have meaning, for even a slave can be led to think he is free. (Arendt considers it more than a coincidence that "free will" originated with Epictetus, the slave-philosopher.) We are plunged into a sea of subjectivity with one man's feelings as valid as another's with no commonly identifiable landmarks. Thus, she is suspicious of "free will" for the same reason that she distrusts psychiatry: "the human heart, as we all know, is a very dark place and whatever goes on in its obscurity can hardly be called a demonstrable fact." Arendt's concept of freedom is political freedom, which is not a phenomenon of the will—or heart, or psyche—but a "worldly, tangible reality." (pp. 109-17)

Politics, as she understands it, is concerned with the extraordinary; a political act is to that extent an extraordinary act. To Americans who are used to thinking of politics as anything but extraordinary—"politics as usual"—Arendt's assertion needs to be explained.

Since she considers politics as the most human activity, it is necessary, even at the expense of some repetition, to reflect on the meaning of man's mortality. "This is mortality: to move along a rectilinear line in a universe where everything, if it moves at all, moves in a cyclical order." What she means is that, while every creature exclusively natural is bound to nature's cycle of eternal recurrence and is incapable of beginning anything new, man alone is able to move forward in a straight line, i. e., to have a history.

Arendt's cosmology is postmedieval but pre-Darwinian. The medievalists lived in a universe in which natural bodies and forces had appetites for certain things while abhorring others—a human universe not always friendly but at least on speaking terms with man. The effect of Galilean science was to divest nature of these traits. Yet Darwin's discoveries opened up the possibility that the medieval view, purged of its naiveté, could be restored on an even better footing. The opportunity was not lost on Pierre Teilhard de Chardin, the Jesuit paleontologist whose posthumous writings have already been enormously influential not only upon scientific thought but on secular and religious attempts to find a place for man in what otherwise seems a hostile and alien universe. The starting point for Teilhard's cosmic humanism is Darwin's key discovery: that nature does not go round and round, it goes forward. Toward what? Toward Parousia, the consummation and end of the world, but not before man somehow raises himself, evolves, to a spiritual level. (pp. 117-18)

Arendt's view is directly opposite. From the standpoint of man, or more accurately *men,* living in the here and now, nature is not progress but circularity: the change of seasons, the cycle of birth, growth, reproduction, death, and so on and on again. Teilhard measures a time not our time: million-year units are for scientists and mystics to contemplate, but they are too vast for acting men. The progress of nature is a scientific hypothesis without political relevance; it has no meaning for this generation, or the next, or even a hundred succeeding ones. In the long run nature may move forward, but in the long run we are dead. (pp. 118-19)

The present essay, however, does not deal with Arendt's view of man's plight but with her model of his capacities. If Teilhard's man is thoroughly at home in the universe, Arendt's man uneasily coexists with it. When Arendt describes political action as a straight line in a universe of circularity, the line must not be taken as a path (either upward or downward) marked out by nature but as a sword thrust into nature. Human activity is not in and through nature but against it and in spite of it; it is not the smooth process of natural evolution but the sudden intrusion into

nature of something unexplainable by any natural laws, Newtonian or post-Newtonian. Since man is the only surprise in a universe of calculables, it follows that human action consists in reasserting and augmenting man's unpredictability, his unnaturalness, his insistence upon *not* being a phenomenon.

If man did nothing but his housework, he would, from the standpoint of what he left behind for future generations, be no different from the birds who work industriously, even "intelligently," but begin nothing new. The extraordinary act, then, is that which runs counter to nature's circular pattern of birth, procreation, death. What sets men apart from beasts is their capacity to defy nature by starting something new in a universe otherwise bound to a cycle of eternal recurrence. What makes politics extraordinary is that men leave the privacy of the household, meet together in public, and decide to undertake something new, something which then enters into history. (pp. 119-20)

It is here that Arendt's philosophy becomes concerned with the problem of the perishability or "futility" of politics. The danger, as Arendt sees it, is that unless someone is around to see and record the extraordinary deeds of man, they will sink into oblivion without a trace. Speeches and deeds, considered by themselves, "lack not only the tangibility of other things, but are even less durable and more futile than the things which we produce for consumption." Politics is "as futile as life itself." Human greatness, seen in terms of man's extraordinary words and deeds, requires some means of preservation. Arendt suggests two: "The whole factual world of human affairs depends for its reality and its continued existence, first, upon the presence of others who have seen and heard and will remember, and, second, on the transformation of the intangible into the tangibility of things." The first condition assumes a body politic which will not only be witness but have sufficient durability to pass from generation to generation the record of human greatness. This was the role assumed by the ancient *polis* which was supposed to "offer a remedy for the futility of action and speech."

> The *polis*—if we trust the famous words of Pericles in the Funeral Oration—gives a guaranty that those who forced every sea and land to become the scene of their daring will not remain without witness . . .; without assistance from others, those who acted will be able to establish together the everlasting remembrance of their good and bad deeds, to inspire admiration in the present and future ages.

But the *polis* itself did not endure, nor did Rome, and the whole record of human greatness would have been lost were it not for a group of men whose activities have not yet been discussed: the artists, writers, and other makers of things whom she classifies together as *homo faber*.

The task of the fabricator is to transfer the intangible "into the tangibility of things." In this connection she considers the role of historians, poets, sculptors, architects and the like, who "reify" or make into things the memory of human greatness. *Zoon politikon,* by himself, produces nothing; if his words and deeds are to be remembered, they must be recorded. "Acting and speaking men need the help of *homo faber* in his highest capacity, that is, the help of the artists, of poets and historiographers, of monument-builders or writers, because without them the only product of their activity, the story they enact and tell, would not survive at all." The task of poets and historiographers thus "consists in making something lasting out of remembrance. They do this by translating *praxis* and *lexis*, action and speech, into that kind of *poeisis* or fabrication which eventually becomes the written word." Fabrication in its "purest" form is a handmaiden or auxiliary to politics. When things are made not for use but to endure and commemorate the great words and deeds of man, they put the stamp of immortality upon the activities of mortal men.

This brings us to the role which Hannah Arendt has assumed. Arendt is convinced that for a number of reasons, the meaning of politics as the ancients understood it—the meaning of politics explored in this essay—has become lost or obscured over the past nineteen centuries since the decline of Rome. It is this "lost treasure" which Arendt attempts to unearth, not simply for the sake of scholarly curiosity, but with the hope that modern man may derive lessons from it. In other words, Arendt herself has undertaken the role of *"homo faber* in his highest capacity": in being a philosopher of politics, she must also be an historian commemorating what otherwise might be forgotten. Whether or not "all historiography is necessarily salvation," it is clear that hers is.

But it is not only the "lost treasures" of the past that she would have us remember as a means of understanding and perhaps even beginning to resolve our predicament. We need also to remember how we got into the predicament in the first place. Some of the forgotten fragments of the past such as those which set the stage for the appearance of modern alienation, mass society and totalitarianism also have to be recalled so as to "free" ourselves from their "burden," for the past presses upon the present and shapes it. "Not even oblivion and confusion, which can cover up so efficiently the origin and responsibility for every single deed, are able to undo a deed or prevent its consequences." In her study of totalitarianism, for example, she attempts to isolate those events of the past two centuries which became the chief elements of present-day crisis. These events, or at least their connection with totalitarianism, have become obscure. Nevertheless, this "subterranean stream," as she calls it in her preface to *The Origins of Totalitarianism,* "has finally come to the surface and usurped the dignity of our tradition." To find the source of this stream and to survey its course before it broke the surface—in less metaphorical language, to find the hidden connections between events in our past and the crises of our own times—is not an easy task, and in many ways it is painful both to writer and reader because it raises the question of what might have been. Nevertheless, Arendt believes that the "tears of remembrance" are cathartic and essential to understanding our present predicament.

> The scene where Ulysses listens to the story of his own life is paradigmatic for both history and poetry; the "reconciliation with reality," the catharsis, which, according to Aristotle, was the

essence of tragedy, and, according to Hegel, was the ultimate purpose of history, came about through remembrance.

The task which Hannah Arendt has set for herself as political philosopher and historian is to bring the forgotten past to our attention—not only its "lost treasures" but also its "subterranean streams." (pp. 120-22)

> *George McKenna, "On Hannah Arendt, Politics: As It Is, Was, Might Be," in* The Legacy of the German Refugee Intellectuals, *edited by Robert Boyers, Schocken Books, 1972, pp. 104-22.*

FURTHER READING

Bernstein, Richard J. "Hannah Arendt: The Ambiguities of Theory and Practice." In *Political Theory and Praxis: New Perspectives,* edited by Terence Ball, pp. 141-58. Minneapolis: University of Minnesota Press, 1977.
> Lecture addressing Arendt's view of political decline as resulting from a divorce between theory and practice.

Bradshaw, Leah. *Acting and Thinking: The Political Thought of Hannah Arendt.* Toronto: University of Toronto Press, 1989, 162 p.
> Emphasizes Arendt's commentary on the relation between political thought and action.

Canovan, Margaret. *The Political Thought of Hannah Arendt.* New York: Harcourt Brace Jovanovich, 1974, 136 p.
> First full-length critical overview of Arendt's work.

Hill, Melvyn A., ed. *Hannah Arendt: The Recovery of the Public World.* New York: St. Martin's Press, 1979, 362 p.
> Collection of essays written between 1972 and 1978 examining Arendt's controversial philosophy.

Jacobson, Norman. "Parable and Paradox: In Response to Arendt's *On Revolution."* *Salmagundi,* No. 60 (Spring-Summer 1983): 123-39.
> Attempts to illuminate the historical foundation of *On Revolution* "to permit Arendt's political theory to be tested and contested on its grounds, rather than dismissed . . . as parable only."

Jay, Martin. "The Political Existentialism of Hannah Arendt." In his *Permanent Exiles: Essays on the Intellectual Migration from Germany to America,* pp. 237-56. New York: Columbia University Press, 1985.
> Reprinted essay from 1978 tracing the influence of existential thought on Arendt's philosophy.

Kateb, George. *Hannah Arendt: Politics, Conscience, Evil.* Totowa, New Jersey: Rowman and Allanheld, 1984, 204 p.
> Overview of Arendt's work emphasizing her critique of modern democracy.

Laqueur, Walter. "Re-Reading Hannah Arendt." *Encounter* LII, No. 3 (March 1979): 73-9.
> Examines Arendt's early journalistic articles for their in-

sights into the conception of her later works, *The Jew as Pariah* and *Eichmann in Jerusalem.*

McCarthy, Mary. "The Hue and Cry." *Partisan Review* XXXI, No. 1 (Winter 1964): 82-94.
Characterizes negative reviews by Jewish reviewers of *Eichmann in Jerusalem* as politically motivated and slanderous.

May, Derwent. *Hannah Arendt.* Middlesex, England: Penguin Books Ltd., 1986, 136 p.
Brief biographical portrait. Includes illustrations, a chronology of Arendt's life, and a short primary and secondary bibliography.

Nordquist, Joan. *Social Theory: A Bibliographic Series—Hannah Arendt.* Santa Cruz, California: Reference and Research Services, 1989, 64 p.
Bibiography of works by and about Arendt.

O'Sullivan, N. K. "Politics, Totalitarianism and Freedom: The Political Thought of Hannah Arendt." *Political Studies* XXI, No. 2 (June 1973): 183-98.
Explicates Arendt's political philosophy as expressed in her works as a whole.

O'Sullivan, Noel. "Hannah Arendt: Hellenic Nostalgia and Industrial Society." In *Contemporary Political Philosophers,* edited by Anthony de Crespigny and Kenneth Minogue, pp. 228-51. New York: Dodd, Mead and Company, 1975.
Examines the classical roots of Arendt's political philosophy.

"More on Eichmann." *Partisan Review* XXXI, No. 2 (Spring 1964): 252-83.
Series of responses by various authors to Mary McCarthy's critique of the controversy surrounding Arendt's *Eichmann in Jerusalem* (see McCarthy's citation above).

Ricoeur, Paul. "Action, Story, and History: On Rereading *The Human Condition.*" *Salmagundi,* No. 60 (Spring-Summer 1983): 60-72.
Assesses *The Human Condition* from a perspective "closer to philosophical anthropology than to political science."

Riley, Patrick. "Hannah Arendt on Kant, Truth and Politics." *Political Studies* XXXV, No. 3 (September 1987): 379-92.
Voices disagreement with Arendt's reading of Kant in her *Lectures on Kant's Political Philosophy* and her essay "Truth and Politics."

Rotenstreich, Nathan. "Introspection without Insight." *Midstream* XXVI, No. 3 (March 1980): 47-53.
Faults Arendt's posthumous publication, *The Jew as Pariah,* as lacking in "sensitivity to nuances."

Shklar, Judith N. "Hannah Arendt as Pariah." *Partisan Review* L, No. 1 (1983): 64-77.
Examines Arendt's refusal to assimilate into Christian society and her belief in "the bizarre notion that being Jewish was an act of personal defiance."

Suchting, W. A. "Marx and Hannah Arendt's *The Human Condition.*" *Ethics* LXXIII, No. 1 (October 1962): 47-55.
Surveys Arendt's use and understanding of Karl Marx's theories in *The Human Condition.*

Tlaba, Gabriel Masooane. *Politics and Freedom: Human Will and Action in the Thought of Hannah Arendt.* Lanham, Maryland: University Press of America, 1987, 205 p.
Examines the concept of freedom in Arendt's works.

Whitfield, Stephen J. *Into the Dark: Hannah Arendt and Totalitarianism.* Philadelphia: Temple University Press, 1980, 338 p.
Close reading of *The Origins of Totalitarianism* and *Eichmann in Jerusalem* incorporating factual historical support unavailable at the time of Arendt's writing.

Young-Bruehl, Elisabeth. *Hannah Arendt: For Love of the World.* New Haven: Yale University Press, 1982, 563 p.
Detailed biography including illustrations and a primary bibliography.

Rosario Castellanos

1925-1974

Mexican poet, novelist, short story writer, essayist, and critic.

Castellanos is best known for poetry and fiction that reveal structures of social domination in her native Mexico. Gradually developing a tone of ironic humor with which she mocked social conventions, Castellanos employed historical and religious metaphors to illuminate a cultural tradition of oppression in which women and Indians are deprived of individual freedom. Personal concerns with solitude, sadness, and mortality also recur throughout Castellanos' works. She is recognized as a forerunner of Mexican feminism and a predecessor to many contemporary feminist literary critics.

Castellanos grew up on her parents' coffee plantation near Comitán, a village with a large Chamula Indian population close to the Guatemalan border. The farm was expropriated after President Lázaro Cárdenas introduced land reforms that deprived the provincial elite of their property holdings, forcing the family to move to Mexico City. Castellanos became attuned to the concerns of Mexican Indians during her childhood in Comitán, which became the setting of her first novel, *Balún-Canán* (*The Nine Guardians*). She wrote her first two published poems, *Trayectoria del polvo* and *Apuntes para una declaración de fe,* while a philosophy student in Mexico City. These long, rhetorical verses, which Castellanos herself later scorned for their pretentious tone, develop a hopeful vision of humanity despite the world's overriding decadence and injustice. Soon abandoning the style of her first poems, Castellanos attempted to create a disengaged voice that could still express intimate thought. She adopted this voice most successfully in "Lamentación de Dido." Often considered Castellanos's best poem, "Lamentación de Dido" is a retelling of Dido and Aeneas' love affair from Vergil's *Aeneid.* In Castellanos's version, the betrayed Dido, rather than Aeneas, is the focus of the poem.

Strongly influenced by such authors as Simone de Beauvoir, Virginia Woolf, and Simone Weil, much of Castellanos's verse utilizes allusions to three traditional Mexican figures—La Malinche, La Virgen de Guadalupe, and Sor Juana Inés de la Cruz. In her essay "Once Again Sor Juana," she argues that these female archetypes encompass the Mexican ideal for women, who are expected to be mothers, faithful lovers, or virtuous old maids. Women in Castellanos's work reflect these patterns, often waiting patiently for marriage and happiness and unwilling to challenge or resist traditional expectations. Castellanos identified language as a significant instrument of domination and often used dialogue to express her characters' subjugation: women's effusion or loss of articulation indicate their inability to liberate themselves from subordinate roles. Castellanos's concern for feminist issues reflects not only women's oppression, but that of all repressed groups; Helene M. Anderson noted: "[It] is precisely because [Castellanos] deals with the question of women within the larger context of questions of freedom and liberation, that there is, in her work, an important synthesis of social issues that goes beyond the female and has to do with the fundamental structures of power and the theme of domination and submission within society."

Castellanos participated in archeological studies in the Chiapas region of Mexico and spent two years writing scripts for an indigenous language puppet show that traveled to Indian villages. These experiences heightened her understanding of the marginalized Mexican Indian population that was the focus of her two novels and many of her poems. While *The Nine Guardians,* which won the Mexican Critics' award for the best novel of 1957, was faulted by some for obscure historical references, most critics praised this work for providing an unprecedented humanistic portrait of Indians. Following Castellanos's death, José Emilio Pacheco wrote: "When the commotion passes and people reread [Castellanos's] works, it will become evident that nobody in her time had as clear a consciousness of the twofold condition of being a woman and a Mexican. And no one else has made of that consciousness the subject matter and the central line of a body of literary work. Of course we didn't know how to read her."

Much of Castellanos's later poetry, including *Materia memorable* and *Lívida Luz,* for which she won the Xavier Villaurrutia Prize, is more personal than her earlier work. Following a divorce, two miscarriages, and the birth of a son, she created works that reveal an increasing preoccupation with suicide and solitude.

(See also *Contemporary Authors,* Vols. 53-56.)

PRINCIPAL WORKS

POETRY

Trayectoria del polvo   1948
Apuntes para una declaración de fe   1948
De la vigilia estéril   1950
Dos poemas   1950
Presentación en el templo   1951
El rescate del mundo   1952
Poemas (1953-1955)   1957
Salomé y Judith: Poemas dramáticos   1957
Al pie de la letra: Poemas   1959
Lívida luz: Poemas   1960
Materia memorable   1969
Poesía no eres tú: Obra poética, 1948-1971   1972

Meditación en el umbral: Antología poética 1985 *(Meditation on the Threshold: A Bilingual Anthology of Poetry,* 1988)
The Selected Poems of Rosario Castellanos 1988

SHORT FICTION COLLECTIONS

Ciudad Real: Cuentos 1960
Los convidados de agosto 1964
Album de familia 1971

NOVELS

Balún–Canán 1957 (*The Nine Guardians,* 1958)
Oficio de tinieblas 1962

ESSAYS

Sobre cultura femenina 1950
Juicios sumarios: Ensayos 1966
Mujer que sabe latin . . . 1973
El uso de la palabra 1974
El mar y sus pescaditos 1975

DRAMA

El eterno femenino: Farsa 1975

OTHER

A Rosario Castellanos Reader: An Anthology of Her Poetry, Short Fiction, Essays, and Journals 1988

Selden Rodman

Still in her twenties and generously endowed as poet and novelist, Rosario Castellanos is almost unique among Mexican writers for the respect her work inspires among the embattled cliques of both Left and Right. **The Nine Guardians,** her first novel to reach us in translation, shows why.

Written during a period when she was employed as an anthropologist by the Indian Bureau in Chiapas, it deals with the social upheaval of the Cárdenas period in such a way as to give little comfort to either the die-hard *hacendados* or the sentimental *indianistas.* Though never explicit, the author's sympathy for the sufferings of both parties is always felt. Bedeviled by the hatreds, fears and superstitions of a five-hundred-years-old unnatural relationship, the inevitable clash of peasant and landlord was bound to end in horror; yet the reader never feels that horror is being exploited for mere literary advantage. Only in the first few pages, as a matter of fact, is one conscious of anything highly wrought: poetical descriptive passages and characters vibrating with exquisite sensibility. And this is the more remarkable in a literary tradition that is apt to strike us as excessively style-conscious.

The novel is divided into three parts. Part I, the scene of which is laid in the outpost village of Comitán, reveals a landowner's family in process of disintegration as seen through the eyes of the little daughter. The father retains vestiges of dignity, but is neither strong enough to resist the revolution nor intelligent enough to meet it halfway

by gaining the confidence of his laborers. The mother hates the Indians for their sullen or cunning responses to the unexpected prospect of power, and her hatred becomes pathological.

Part II takes place on the doomed sugar plantation. The focus shifts to Ernesto, an illegitimate child of the landlord's brother, and Matilde, a neurotic poor-relation whom he casually seduces—and despises. Ernesto, who can't speak a word of the Indian's language, is forced to play teacher to conform to the letter of the new law. When the Indians demand a genuine teacher—not because they want to learn, but to embarrass the masters—the landlord orders them back to work and they retaliate by burning the sugar mill. Ernesto is shot on his way to deliver a futile message of protest to the Governor. As his body is brought into town strapped to the saddle of his horse, Matilde confesses that she bears his unwanted child, and is driven heartlessly into the forest for "betraying" the family's hospitality.

Part III completes the family's ruin with the death (by psychological terror) of the little boy who is its only heir.

What saves this Faulknerian tale from being merely a case history in degeneracy, is the degree to which the author (like Faulkner) manages to invest the degradation of the present with a brooding sense of the meaningfulness of the past. But this, unfortunately, she does too subtly, or ambivalently. The reader unversed in the Maya background or the Cárdenas foreground would never guess that any spirit of illuminating aspiration had ever crossed this dark terrain. (pp. 5, 26)

> Selden Rodman, "Children Caught in a Storm," in The New York Times Book Review, *June 5, 1960, pp. 5, 26.*

Rosario Castellanos

[*The following excerpt was originally published in Spanish in* Mujer que sabe latín *in 1973.*]

Justify a book? It's easier to write another one and leave to the critics the task of transforming confusion into something explicit, vagueness into precision, erratic matter into a system, arbitrariness into substance. But, in my case, when all my books of poetry are collected in a single volume that opens to a first line that affirms

the world cries out sterile, like a mushroom,

there's nothing left to do but quickly proceed to explain. Well, as commentators made me see in their good time, the mushroom is the antithesis of sterility since it proliferates with shameless abundance and nearly a total lack of stimulation. Actually, what I wanted to say then was that the world had a genesis as spontaneous as that of the mushroom, that it had not sprung from any divine plan, that it was not the result of the internal laws of matter, nor was it the *conditio sine qua non* for the development of the human drama. That the world was, in short, the perfect example of fortuitousness.

If this was what I wanted to say then why didn't I say it? Simply because I don't want to do so. And I must add that inertia more than conviction dragged me into taking up the banner of faith that declaimed an America more rhetorical than real. I was not an optimist in those days but pessimism seemed to me to be a private and mistaken attitude, the product of childhood traumas and a difficult adolescence. Neither did I have the slightest notion of what that "continent that lies dying" was, but I had thought about it so little that it had not been lost together with all my other beliefs, after a serious crisis of values that had left me in the most absolute of Cartesian winters.

But (now I realize it) I've moved from cover to cover of the book without stopping to look at it. There's a title there—(*Poesía no eres tú*) *You Are Not Poetry*—that merits a separate paragraph. Is it a reaction at this stage of the game, against the Spanish romanticism that Bécquer so well embodied? We're anachronistic but not that much. Is it a contradiction, in more recent terms, of Rubén Darío when he decides that one cannot exist without being romantic? It's not that either. What happened is that I developed very slowly from the most closed subjectivity to the disturbing discovery that the other existed and, finally, to the rupture of the pattern of the couple to integrate myself into the social sphere that is the one in which the poet defines, understands, and expresses herself. The *zoon politikon* does not achieve such a category unless it be composed of a minimum number of three. Even in the Gospels, Christ assures us that wherever two persons meet in His name, the Holy Spirit will come to rescue them from their solitude.

Well, then, is it triangles in the French style? Naughty vaudeville? Nothing could be further from my intentions. At least the link between the related parties does not have to be an amorous one. But if it is, I have always conceived of love as one of the instruments of catastrophe. Not because it doesn't achieve fullness or permanence. That's a minor matter. The major matter is that, like St. Paul, it takes the blinders off our eyes and we see each other as we are: needful, mean, cowards. Careful not to risk ourselves in our giving and not to commit ourselves in our reception of gifts. Love is not a consolation, declared Simone Weil. And she added something terrible: It is light—that light from which the soul draws back so that its crevasses cannot be illuminated, that clamor for us to dive into them, that will annihilate us and then . . . the promise is not clear. Afterward it might be the void that is not conceivable for our intelligence even though it may be desirable, due to the sensitivity that strives for the definitive cessation of suffering. Or perhaps rebirth on another plane of existence, marvelously serene, that paradise that Jorge Guillén condenses to a single line: "*where love is not anguish.*"

So it seems that, after so much hopping about and comings and goings, I am only a poetess ("poetriste" or "poetresse," Mejía Sánchez proposed as alternatives) who *also* writes about love! Shades of Delmira Agustini, Juana de Ibarbourou, and Alfonsina Storni, [Latin American women poets best known for their erotic, romantic, and vanguard poetry based on passionate love affairs] be still!

It is not precisely the same thing. I would not want to resign myself to its being the same. It is true that I read them with the application of an apprentice. It is true that I admired Agustini's sumptuous imagery and Storni's ironic similes and in both of them the oblique and direct suicidal impetus. It is true that from Ibarbourou I learned that everything of hers was alien to me. But my problem sprang from other sources and consequently demanded other solutions.

At the time when one discovers one's vocation, I found out that mine was one of understanding. Until then, unconsciously, I had identified this need with that of writing. Whatever came out. And rhymed, eleven-syllable lines are what came out. Four by four and three by three. Sonnets. Their composition offered me some relief from the anguish, as though, for a moment, I had been emancipated from the dominion of chaos. Order reigned, laughable perhaps, certainly provisional, but order at last.

Someone revealed to me that what I was doing was called literature. Later I found out that there was a college at the university where one studied its history and techniques. I went to register for it, simply to convince myself that the list of dates and names, the catalogs of styles, and the analysis of the techniques did not help me in the least in understanding anything. The programs of studies in humanities not only were lacking answers to the major questions but they also didn't even ask the main questions, which are, for example, Why? What for? How? And, naturally, I am referring to everything.

My Guardian Angel made me see that next to the classes of literature they were giving philosophy classes, where, yes, they asked all those questions. And I refer again to everything.

I changed classrooms. "Happy, unwarned, and confident," I began to receive instruction about the pre-Socratics—who wrote, if I remember correctly, poems. Parmenides and Heraclitus gave the body of an image to their conception of the world. Plato, too, although he already struggles to draw a dividing line between the two ways of knowledge and expels poets from his Republic because by nature they contain the undesirable germ of dissolution. Aristotle came later and the separation between philosophy and letters was consummated.

When I realized that philosophic language was inaccessible to me and that the only notions within my reach were those disguised as metaphors, it was too late. Not only was I just about to finish my degree but I also no longer wrote hendecasyllables or rhymed verse or sonnets. Now it was something else. Amphibea. Ambiguity. And like the mating of different species, it was sterile.

Evidence? A lot of destroyed manuscripts and the first two poems of the book that we've been talking about, **"Apuntes para una declaración de fe"** and **"Trayectoria del polvo."** (Which, in parenthesis, maintain a chronological order distinct from that of their location in the book. It is not obvious, there is so little development from one text to the other.) The unforgivable sin of both poems is the abstract vocabulary that I used in them. It was indispensable for me to substitute for it another vocabulary that would refer to objects at hand, with which themes could acquire a consistency that could be felt and touched.

I could find no better way out of this blind alley than to place a model or example in front of me and then laboriously copy it as faithfully as possible. I chose Gabriela Mistral, the Gabriela of "Matter," "Creatures," and "Messages," the reader of the Bible, a reading which I then of course also applied. The image of such exemplary models casts its shadows and some of its substance over the pages of *De la vigilia estéril.*

An unfortunate title that enabled my friends to make plays on words. Sterile or hysterical? I was still single against my will and the drama of rejection of the most obvious aspects of femininity was genuine. But who could guess that, if I covered it up with so much clutter and rubbish? I had arrived at the same conclusion as the sculptor: the statue is what remains after you have removed the excess stone.

So my goal was, then, simplicity. I advance much more quickly to *Rescate del mundo.* And, nearly weightless, I get carried away with **"Misterios gozosos"** and **"El resplandor del ser."**

But as St. Augustine said, it is the heart that is heavy. It is similar weight that upsets the balance of a poem. *Eclipse total,* yes, briefly. Suffering is so enormous that it spills over the vessel of our bodies and goes in search of more capable vessels. It finds the paradigmatic figures of a tradition. Dido, who raises the triviality of an anecdote (is there anything more trivial than a scorned woman and an unfaithful man?) to majestic heights where the wisdom of centuries resounds. **"Dido's Lament"** (**"Lamentación de Dido"**), in addition to being the story of individual misfortune, is the convergence of two readings: Virgil and St. John Perse. One gave me matter and the other form. And from that privileged moment of felicitous intercourse the birth of a poem took place!

It immediately rose up before me like a barrier. I was afraid to write again and I was afraid not to write again, until I decided to ignore it and to start from zero in *Al pie de la letra.*

Among so many echoes I begin to recognize my own voice. Yes, I'm the one who writes **"La velada del sapo"** as well as **"Monologue of a Foreign Woman."** Three cardinal points to follow: humor, solemn meditation, and contact with my carnal and historical roots. And everything is bathed in that *livid light* of death that makes all matter memorable.

I say that I was detained at this stage because I don't like to recognize that I'm stagnating. There has to be a very strong jolt from outside in order for perspective to change, style to be renewed, in order to open up to new themes, new words. Some of them are vulgar, crude. What can I do about it? They are the ones that are useful to say what I have to say. Nothing important or transcendent. A few

insights into the structure of the world, some guidelines to some of the coordinates that help me locate myself in it, the mechanics of my relationships with other beings, which are neither sublime nor tragic. Perhaps, a bit ridiculous.

We have to laugh. Because laughter, we already know, is the first evidence of freedom. And I feel so free that I can begin with "dialogue of the most honorable men," I mean, with other writers. On an equal basis. On a first-name basis. A lack of respect? A lack of culture, if culture is what Ortega defined as a sense of hierarchies? It could be. But let us give ourselves the benefit of the doubt. Let the *reader-accomplice* go to the bother of elaborating other hypotheses or other interpretations. (pp. 254-58)

Rosario Castellanos, "If Not Poetry, Then What?" translated by Maureen Ahern, in her A Rosario Castellanos Reader: An Anthology of Her Poetry, Short Fiction, Essays, and Drama, *edited by Maureen Ahern, translated by Maureen Ahern and others, University of Texas Press, 1988, pp. 254-58.*

Beth Miller

[*The following essay was originally presented as a lecture at the Conference on Latin American Women Writers at Carnegie-Mellon University in March, 1975.*]

[Rosario] Castellanos developed a habit of mind which permitted her to see her personal problems as social ones, to identify her subjective experiences with those of women historically, to understand sex roles as cultural and women's struggles as political. A young Mexican critic, José Emilio Pacheco wrote at Castellanos' death in August of 1974: "When the commotion passes and people re-read her works, what will become evident is that nobody in her time has as clear a consciousness as she did of the meaning of the double condition of woman and Mexican. And no one else has made that consciousness the subject matter of a literary production, the central line of a body of work. Of course we didn't know how to read her." (p. 198)

In **"Malinche,"** [Malinche was the native interpreter and mistress of Cortez] the embracing of literary tradition (pre-Columbian poetry, Greco-Roman drama) adds dimension to Castellanos' sketch of a woman and universalizes its cultural particulars—a matrilinear inheritance of rejection and covert competition, a paternal legacy of abandonment and alienation. Malinche's search for identity is not that of a divided self, but that of an outsider, a displaced person, attempting to understand her lost birthright, to recover a sense of roots in language and the past, and to find in these a source of courage and a path to the blurred world. (p. 199)

Castellanos is expert at conveying feminist statement through literary allusion and dramatic monologue. Malinche/Electra is not Woman, but a woman, one with whose suffering the poet identifies her own. Similarly, Dido's memories of her girlhood in **"Lamentación de Dido"** (**"Dido's Lament"**) are abstract and impersonal enough to evoke the generalized experience of time lost, capacities wasted, and boredom. . . . Castellanos has said that this poem is "a kind of interior biography transfigured by a great metaphor, Dido." Here again her re-creation of literary, historical, and legendary figures provides vehicles for connecting personal and social experience.

There are few aspects of life—childhood to childbirth, puberty to divorce—not covered in Castellanos' poetry. In her choice of such themes she recalls Alfonsina Storni, an Argentine poet who committed suicide in 1938, from whose works Castellanos first learned how to use irony for social protest and self-defense. Her social concerns sometimes lead necessarily to moral imagery and to political statement, as in **"Emblema de la virtuosa"** (**"Emblem of a Virtuous Woman"**) and **"Memorial de Tlatelolco"** (about the student uprising and slaughter in Mexico City in 1968).

The image of woman in **"Metamorfosis de la hechicera"** (**"Metamorphosis of a Witch"**) is "obedient and sad" and full of wiles:

> A woman, she had her masks
> and played at deceiving herself
> and everyone else

In a militantly feminist essay, **"La mujer y su imagen"** (**"Woman and her Image"**), Castellanos analyzes this stereotype in political terms: "Women have been accused of being hypocrites, and the accusation is not without ground. But hypocrisy is the response of the oppressed to their oppressors, of weak persons to strong, of subordinates to a master. Hypocrisy is . . . a self-defensive conditioned reflex—like a chameleon's protective change in color—when there are many dangers and not many options."

Another recurrent "feminine trait" in Castellanos' work, one which she explored obsessively, is patience. While deception may be considered a weapon, patience implies inaction, mere passivity. . . . Both themes are significant because of the threat these traditional characteristics pose to personal authenticity (or psychological integration) and, therefore, to dynamic social and political participation. Castellanos credits women themselves with being the effective transmitters and most patient teachers of passivity. . . . Castellanos puts it eloquently in an essay:

> The audacity to investigate oneself, the need to make oneself conscious of the meaning of one's own bodily existence or the unheard of pretension of conferring meaning on one's own spiritual existence is severely repressed and punished by the social apparatus. Society has decreed . . . that the only legitimately feminine attitude is waiting. . . . Sacrificed, like Iphigenia on the patriarchal altars, a woman doesn't die: she just waits.
>
> (pp. 200-02)

Castellanos sees these feminine traits as a series of con-

stants in the feminine ideal of Western culture through the centuries and traces them back to Christianity:

> The strong woman who appears in the Holy Scriptures is strong because of her prenuptial purity, her fidelity to her husband, her devotion to her children, her laboriousness in the house, her care and prudence in administering a patrimony which she wasn't able to possess or inherit. Her virtues are constancy, loyalty, patience, chastity, submission, humility, caution, abnegation, the spirit of sacrifice, the governing of all her acts by the evangelical precept that the meek will inherit the earth [*Mujer que sabe latín*]. Those particular virtues have been used of course to restrict a woman's possibilities and keep her at home. . . .
>
> (pp. 202-03)

Castellanos, with practiced understatement, is able to create tragedy out of soap-opera materials. In the following excerpt from **"Monólogo de la extranjera"** (**"Monologue of a Foreign Woman"**), the traditional verses (lines mainly of seven and eleven syllables) and religious vocabulary help make her case. Her intentionally hackneyed phrasing ("supreme pride," "supreme renunciation") make the painful turn of phrase at the end neatly effective:

> Supreme pride is found
> in supreme renunciation. I refused
> to be an extinguished star
> that comes alive by borrowed light.
> Without a name, without a memory,
> in spectral nudity I revolve
> in a brief domestic orbit.

The "domestic orbit" of an Indian woman's experience is poignant in this monologue, one of Castellanos' earliest and best known. The poem dramatically combines Mexican social reality and myth. . . . (p. 203)

Much of Castellanos' later poetry is what has come to be called "open," that is, not dependent on metaphor. This trend, most evident in her last works, is historically significant in that it represents the accomplishment of a sought-after break with the dominant symbolist tradition—a much discussed goal of her contemporaries in the Generation of 1950 from the time they were schoolmates at the National University. Secondly, to the degree that it is true that a poem may present "its case and its meaning by the very form it assumes" (William Carlos Williams), the "social-realist" mode is appropriate for Castellanos for much the same reasons as the dramatic monologue form and the literary allusions to legendary women. (p. 204)

A "Third World specimen," Castellanos explores the root of *machismo,* which she believes has a double source. Mexico, she writes in her essay, **"The Participation of Mexican Women in Formal Education,"** is heir not only to the European culture of the fifteenth and sixteenth centuries, but to a series of severely patriarchal civilizations. The Conquest brought about a deeply divided culture in which "the violence of the clash between conquerors and conquered came to preside even over sexual unions" (*Mujer*).

Castellanos was a woman who read women. She has acknowledged the early influence not only of Storni, but of Juana de Ibarbourou and, especially, of Gabriela Mistral, the 1945 Nobel prizewinner. The anti-symbolist direction is already apparent as early as 1959 in poems such as **"La velada del sapo"** (**"The Toad's Watch"**) whose featured animal recalls Marianne Moore's "poetry garden" with "real frogs." In *Al pie de la letra* (**Starting from Scratch,** 1959) and *Lívida luz* (*Livid Light,* 1960), her poetry is less abstract and intellectual, increasingly socially committed. As she sees her own evolution: "Among slow echoes I began to recognize my own voice. . . . Three threads to follow: humor, grave meditation, and contact with my rootedness in history and my body" (*Mujer*). (pp. 204-05)

By 1960, her esthetic values have changed, and the world, as she sees it, is no longer "an object of contemplation, but . . . a battle ground for the struggle we're engaged in." (p. 205)

In her works [Castellanos] explores, describes, and works against cultural patterns of dominance-submission—between men and women, whites and Indians, Mexicans and Europeans or North Americans, lower class and elite, parents and children. What she sees as the goal for women is liberation from deceptive, long-suffering femininity. But she believes that the "feat of becoming what you are" is always problematical, a matter of mind as well as of political, social, and economic circumstances. . . . (p. 208)

> *Beth Miller, "Women and Feminism in the Works of Rosario Castellanos," in* Feminist Criticism: Essays on Theory, Poetry and Prose, *edited by Cheryl L. Brown and Karen Olson, The Scarecrow Press, Inc., 1978, pp. 198-210.*

Helene M. Anderson

In 1950 Rosario Castellanos (1925-1974) presented a thesis on feminine culture which has come to be considered the intellectual point of departure for the women's liberation movement in Mexico. According to Mexican essayist, Carlos Monsiváis, no one up to that time had expressed so clearly what it meant to be both a woman and a Mexican. This became, in effect, the central line of Castellanos' work, but always from a very particular perspective: the relationship of women to their culture within the broader relationship in Mexican society of those with power to those deprived of it.

Although her 1973 book of essays, *Mujer que sabe latín . . .(Woman Who Knows Latin . . .)* is considered the first provocative Mexican analysis of the image of women within the framework of Western culture in general and Mexican culture in particular, it is well within a national tradition of polemical literature which has existed since the seventeenth century. In this tradition Castellanos examines the issues of image and reality, and submission and domination from a consistently unique, female perspective. (p. 22)

For Castellanos . . . the three elements which are a symbolic synthesis of woman's image and reality in Mexican culture are sexuality, or betrayal leading to the fall of (Mexican) man; motherhood, which is chaste and excludes any recognition of sexuality; and intellectuality, which is a negation of both motherhood and sexuality. These elements, whose equivalent counterparts are considered integrative in the male, are thus displaced and fragmented in the image of woman in Mexico.

Rosario Castellanos has stated that, when she wrote *Mujer que sabe latín . . .,* her purpose was to raise consciousness, to awaken the critical spirit, to disseminate it and make it infectious, and not to accept any dogma until one is sure it is capable of "resisting a good joke." The "good joke" is perpetrated by the author in her play *El eterno femenino* (*The Eternal Feminine*), a farce set in modern Mexico which satirizes the typical female roles in Mexican society and visualizes projects of defiance and rebellion against them. Ironically, all of the action takes place in a beauty parlor under a hair dryer.

In *El eterno femenino* there are those female characters who do not wish to challenge the status quo, who have managed to adapt to the "cult of the venerated slave"—that comfortable role of mother, wife, or lover. They play the roles of innocent virgins, analytical, pragmatic wives, and self-sacrificing mothers. The fantasy counterparts of these women are the characters who have rejected all stereotypic and conventional behavior, women who establish either tacitly or overtly the necessity of finding another way of being human and free. These are key words in Castellanos' work; it is precisely because she deals with the question of women within the larger context of questions of freedom and liberation, that there is, in her work, an important synthesis of social issues that goes beyond the female and has to do with the fundamental structures of power and the theme of domination and submission within society.

In the beauty salon that serves as the setting for *El eterno femenino,* a device is being sold by an agent for use by women while under the dryer. This device is guaranteed to avoid what the salesman considers to be the greatest danger to which women are susceptible while doing nothing—that is, thinking. Thought in itself is dangerous and must be avoided at all costs. The little device plugged into the dryer triggers a series of scenes which are, in fact, projections of distorted and surrealistic situations in which women either contemplate wild extrapolations of their own image of their roles as proper wives and mothers, or else they are fantasies which absolutely destroy all traditional roles.

Castellanos uses techniques of the theater of the absurd to project fantasies through the little device in the hair dryer. She also inserts herself into the world of her play by having the characters express a variety of speculations on what the author's purpose is in setting up these absurd situations. One character says:

> Do you realize that our most venerated traditions, our dearest symbols, are right now objects of mockery in a theater in the Capital? Against whom are they speaking out? Against one who is the pillar of our society, the one who transmits the values that sustain all of us to future generations, against the one who is the source of

our strength and wholeness—the Mexican woman. . . . The attack is specific: and is against the self-sacrifice of mothers, the chastity of sweethearts, the virtue of wives, that is, against all our proverbial attributes. These are attributes in which our most solid institutions are rooted—family, religion, country!

By having a character comment on the dire consequences of allowing a playwright to mock the very pillars of society, Rosario Castellanos takes the question of women out of a limited focus and sets it in a more general perspective: the way in which women are conditioned to uphold the structures of power and how, therefore, within the family unit one finds a symbolic synthesis of the social, economic, and cultural structures of society at large. As in her other essays, novels, and short stories, Castellanos goes beyond the limits of conventional discourse on feminist questions and examines the whole question of social justice and economic exploitation, not unlike the concerns of Simone Weil, a writer she greatly admired. This is precisely the preoccupation that binds together the themes of the woman and the Indian in Castellanos' work.

Neither women nor Indians are given the privilege of choice. As an instrument of repression, the mythification of the traditional role models for Mexican women has glorified the negation of choice as one of the most desirable qualities in a "proper" woman. . . . (pp. 23-5)

Because Rosario Castellanos sees both women and Indians as occupying a confined space within Mexican society, the small town of Comitán in Chiapas becomes the perfect emblem of this confinement. Castellanos spent a good part of her early life in the southern Mexican region of Chiapas, an area deeply permeated by Indian (Tzotzil) culture. It is alive in the stories, traditions, and legends passed on from generation to generation in the language which is still spoken by a majority of the population there. It has also been rocked by repeated political and economic upheavals due to the confrontation between the landless Indian peasants and the white landed gentry. This area is also extremely provincial in its attitude toward the roles of male and female in society. Thus Comitán becomes the natural setting for Rosario Castellanos' narrative. It is here that the dominant problems of Mexican society intersect in the theme of submission vs. liberation. (p. 26)

Delving into the "lives of the obscure" in this remote town, she writes about people of no great social, political, or economic import. They are those who consider themselves *gente decente* (proper citizens). Basically, they are small voices heard in a minor key. Yet it is precisely this dramatic counterpoint between the obscurity of the voice and the emblematic magnitude of the situation that gives such force to Castellanos' narrative.

In *Los convidados de agosto* (*The Guests of August*), a collection of short stories, various female characters in the town of Comitán confront their *situación límite*. These characters, reflecting the archetypes Castellanos discusses in her essays, are, among others, restless adolescents on the threshold of womanhood, impatient to claim its experience and rewards; or spinsters who, in a desperate attempt to break the structures that enclose them, surrender

themselves on summer nights to strange men, "without resistance, without enthusiasm, without sensuality, without remorse," but in some last effort to give meaning to their lives which, "like water, seem to filter through the fingers of the hand." They are women left at life's periphery, abandoned by fathers and lovers, whose role it is to wait, for there is nothing more dishonorable than initiating a thrust into life. Time and again, the female characters in Castellanos' stories wait. (p. 27)

The *soltera,* or spinster, is a prominent figure in Castellanos' stories because if the duty of woman is to wait passively to be chosen, the ultimate embodiment of waiting is the maiden lady. In ["**Los convidados de agosto**"], Emelina, a spinster of thirty-five, is caught between the possibility of life and the abandonment of hope. In a last, desperate attempt to break out of the structures that have confined her to a sterile waiting, she impulsively decides to attend the fair that is being held in honor of the patron saint of the town. Her solitary flight to freedom and an encounter with a stranger dissolves into public humiliation as her brother takes a very inebriated Emelina home by force. Protesting that the stranger did not do anything to her, that he was just going to teach her how to live, she is berated by her brother who sees her behavior as an ineradicable stain on the honor of his name. One final, composite image in the story—very much in keeping with Castellanos' critical vision—is Emelina howling in the streets with the desperation of an animal, while her brother, after satisfying the affront to his honor, is seen knocking at the door of the town brothel.

For Castellanos, spinsterhood within the confines of a small Mexican town is the constant recollection of time, the constant aspect of time slipping away and death slipping in. (In this aspect her stories are not unlike those of Sherwood Anderson's *Winesburg, Ohio.*) *Soltería* is the absolute opposite of everything that constitutes energy, activity, and affirmation of life. The anguished point in the lives of these characters is the approaching moment when hope and resignation lie in the balance. It is within this moment, with its desperate awareness of being the last chance for a thrust into life, that many of her *solteras* are fixed. These women—the unmarried, the abandoned, the aged—will never be free of the conflict between a potential for life that they still feel, and the social impositions that forever determine the channels of their existence.

Castellanos' novel, *Balún-Canán,* fuses the theme of the Indian and the woman. It is set in Chiapas during the time of the presidency of Lázaro Cárdenas when Mexico undertook a program of land redistribution. It was a time of anticlerical legislation as well as of the division of large expanses of land into smaller parcels to be distributed to the Indians, and was thus a time that threatened all the traditional power structures. This novel deals with the repercussions of these events on both the relationships in Chiapas between Indians and ladinos (persons of Indian-Spanish racial origin, or mestizos, who identify with the dominant culture), and the relationships between men and women. (pp. 28-9)

[One] aspect of the structures of power, as they relate to Indians and to women, is brought out in *Balún-Canán* when an Indian nursemaid says to the little girl who is the narrator and the daughter of a well-to-do ladino family: "It is very bad to love those who rule, those who possess." When the child, who worships this woman who raised her, looks at her father dismissing his Indian workers, she thinks of him for the first time as "one who rules, one who possesses." The newly raised consciousness in the child's perception of her father's role is Castellanos' way of pointing to the family structure as a microcosm of society as a whole. The same young narrator, for example, finds a notebook in her father's desk which contains a text, obviously taken from an Indian source, which recounts the conquest and suffering of the Indians under the *caixlanes,* or ladino overlords. The child reads it furtively. When her mother discovers her, she admonishes her for playing with things that are part of her brother's inheritance. In other words, the knowledge of the world around her, as represented by the text, is denied to her. It can only be filtered to her through her male counterpart.

In yet another revealing incident in **Balún-Canán,** a ladino visits his family ranch at Chactajal. The owner of the ranch has "inherited" his Indian laborers as well as his property. He boasts to his visitor of the Indian women at his disposal, the number of children he has had with them and the advantages this entails, since the children stay close to the big house and serve with loyalty. Thus, the Indian woman—akin to La Malinche—becomes a mechanism for perpetuating the servitude of her people and the structures of colonialism. Hers is a double submission—as Indian and as woman.

Castellanos signals the fusion of the Indian and the woman's theme in other ways as well, such as in the selection of quotes from Indian texts to serve as epigraphs to her stories. In **Balún-Canán,** she chooses the following lines from a Mayan text:

> We are only returning. We have fulfilled our
> task. Our days are finished. Think of us. Do not
> erase us from memory. Do not forget us.

The Indian vision of life is as part of a continuity of the past in the present; one's life is part of an inherited, collective experience. For non-Indians, life is unique and individual, ending in nothingness, thus heightening the panic felt by the lonely spinster. The Indian woman, on the other hand, is transformed by the consciousness of being part of a process that has preceded her and will survive her. (pp. 30-1)

Rosario Castellanos' awareness of herself as an articulator of the dilemmas of Mexican culture, as a responsible and committed writer, is summed up by some comments she made about the profession of writing and the nature of language in a collection of articles entitled **El uso de la palabra (The Use of Words).** Language, for Castellanos, is an instrument of command over one's self and one's reality. She interprets the literary vocation as being rooted in profound levels of human experience. By virtue of having written the words, tensions are released and a sense of liberation achieved.

Language is also a structure of power. When one of her Indian characters speaks in Spanish to the ticket-taker at the ferris wheel, the ladino comments mockingly: "Just listen to him, this Indian who thinks he's equal! He's speaking Spanish! Who ever gave him the right?" Spanish, says the narrator, is a privilege that belongs to us (the ladinos), and we use it by addressing our superiors as *usted,* our equals as *tú,* and Indians as *vos.* One of Castellanos' Indian characters, as he is learning to read and write, thinks: "What a feeling, to discover the names of things, to pronounce them, to write them, and to take possession of the world!"

It is this consciousness of the significance of language as a key to taking possession of the world that infuses all of Rosario Castellanos' work. It is through her language as an author that Mexican women and Mexican Indians finally break the invisible space to which they have been confined and, by clamoring to be heard, claim their portion of the world. (p. 31)

> *Helene M. Anderson, "Rosario Castellanos and the Structures of Power," in* Contemporary Women Authors of Latin America, *edited by Doris Meyer and Margarite Fernández Olmos, Brooklyn College Press, 1983, pp. 22-32.*

Frank Dauster

Much of Rosario Castellanos's work as a poet . . . lies in the effort to create a poetic persona, a mask that would serve a double purpose. First, it would give some degree of objectivity or distance to her work, because of the wish to hide or at least disguise the extent to which the work reflected autobiographical features. At the same time, through this distancing it would help her to control her language. Nothing could be further from the confessional poet than this earlier period of her work. . . . That she later almost abandoned this kind of poetic disguise and adopted another voice is, at least in part, a recognition that she had created so well that unless she developed another kind of persona, she would become frozen behind a mask that had served its purpose. (pp. 135-36)

Castellanos's poetry does not divide easily into periods, although she said that she passed from closed subjectivity to the discovery of the other and from that to social reality. Nor does her work usually reflect drastic long-lasting shifts from one book to the next. Although there are frequently rather considerable changes, she tends to return to earlier modes, at least partially, in succeeding volumes. What is clear is that over the total course of her production there is a visible evolution, although not quite the one pointed out by the author herself. . . .

[One of Castellanos's first published works, **Apuntes para una declaración de fe**], is a relatively long attempt at a syncretic poetic vision of the history of humanity and of the world, a vision of the possibility of hope for the hemisphere in spite of apparent present decadence. Later, the author spoke mockingly of the poem's presumptuous conception and pretentious wordiness, but even so there is a tone that would characterize the very last poems. . . . (p. 137)

One of the most surprising notes of this early volume is the importance of ironic humor, which would then nearly disappear and not again play an important role until almost the very last poems. There is much in *Apuntes* that recalls the Salvador Novo of *"Elegia,"* a poet for whom Castellanos repeatedly expressed her admiration. . . . [Another early work], *Trayectoria del polvo* lacks the irony that is the principal poetic virtue of *Apuntes,* and often the author resorts to an incantatory, almost biblical, tone of limited success. This may represent the influence of *Muerte sin fin* of José Gorostiza. . . . Yet the poem achieves far greater success than *Apuntes,* particularly in the earlier sections, because the focus is more personal and the expression denser. . . . The expression is more concentrated, less diffused by the conscious effort to write philosophically or grandly, and in a brilliant image the author fuses humanity's search for self with the personal voyage in search of definition that would be the theme of so much of her own work. . . . The ironic vision of humanity facing life and its inevitable corollary recalls key sections of *Muerte sin fin* and the tone of Novo, but it also indicates a vision that would surface again years later, and seems to hint at Castellanos's own ambivalence toward the experience of life. (pp. 137-38)

De la vigilia estéril (1950) represents a considerable step forward, avoiding in large measure the youthful rhetoric of the two books published only two years before. It establishes the themes for the more mature work: solitude, sadness, death. There is also a marked religious tone that soon disappears, as well as a significant love element and a few poems in which motherhood, actual or anticipated, plays an important role. This last is from sources recognized by Castellanos, who had deliberately read Mistral and the Bible in order to overcome the abstractness of her earlier books. Unfortunately, these influences also became stylized to the point of becoming another rhetoric. The best poems are those that deal with immediate matters in concrete specific imagery: **"La casa vacía"** or **"Destino."** Castellanos said that she had wanted to create poems whose images referred to concrete objects, but she was less than pleased with the result. . . . That she was at least partially successful is evidenced by poems such as **"Distancia del amigo"** in which she abandons the mannerisms of much of the book in favor of a rhythmic colloquial tone that presents a religious content in deceptively simple terms.

Much of *De la vigilia estéril* seems to bear an autobiographical stamp. Despite Castellanos's remarks about "pudor," [modesty or shame] her attempt to create a mask that would let her express her inner vision without revealing it to the reader had not yet been fully developed. For example, in **"Tinieblas y consolación,"** although the situation is referred directly to God, it recalls what we know of Castellanos's childhood, when she was relatively forgotten in her parents' absorption with her younger brother. . . . Not surprisingly, there are anticipations of such major poems as **"Lamentación de Dido,"** especially in the three **"Elegías del amado fantasma,"** but in the **"Dos poemas"** there is an important new note: the poet's

realization that there exists a world outside her, composed of other suffering human beings. . . . She has become aware of the existence of her fellows, a fact that was to be of crucial importance in her novels, but that would also impact in a major fashion on the poetry.

This discovery led to *El rescate del mundo,* a short volume of fourteen poems published in 1952. They are concerned exclusively with indigenous and popular themes: people and occupations . . . or with the simple things that are a fundamental part of rural life. . . . (pp. 138-40)

El rescate del mundo is a slender volume, but it indicates the course of a drastic change that would take place in Rosario Castellanos's development as poet. This change was not yet complete; *Poemas* (1957) is one of her most important collections and represents in some ways the culmination of earlier tendencies. There are several poems written in short meters and with a vaguely popular tone, especially several of the sections of the **"Misterios gozosos,"** which are composed primarily of poems with no fixed referent in the objective world, but the most important characteristic of the volume is the shattering sense of nostalgia that imposes itself on the reader. In addition to the emotion of loss, the poems of the collection reflect a movement that takes on mythic migratory dimensions, as in **"Exodo,"** **"Destierro,"** or **"Relación del peregrino."** Common to virtually all is the sense of timelessness, of being unrelated to daily reality. Frequently they may be read from a Christian point of view (**"El ungido," "El hermano mayor"**) but this is not true of all. They seem rather the expression of the vision of all of humanity as temporal voyager, alone with the purified emotionalism of the voyage and a few others who share the need to pursue the journey. More than anything else, these poems are reminiscent of St.–John Perse for the sense of timelessness of these mythic migrations, and of Jaime Torres Bodet for the direct presentation of the emotional implications of such a situation. One of the most interesting of the poems here is a lovely **"Elegía"** that recalls the opening of *Rescate. . . .* Unlike the poems of *Rescate,* this is not an affirmation of the consciousness of a living way of life, but a lament for something gone; it is the silence of her dead, broken only by the desolate music of the bone flute. The poem is anchored in the broken remnants of the small concrete details of life of nontechnological civilizations: sleeping mats, bone flutes. . . . It begins at the cosmological level: a fallen star, cold now. Firmly rooted in the immediate level, the poem can contrast it with the larger cultural manifestations: temples, now destroyed; trodden earth for the communal dance, abandoned now; paths, buried beneath the dust. **"Elegía"** is saved from archeologism or abstraction by its base in the homely detail that gives it immediacy. This specific subject matter does not again appear in *Poemas,* but the nostalgic tone pervades the volume. More to the point, unlike the remainder of the volume, **"Elegía"** gives the situation a specific Mexican referent. The sadness is no longer a remote and placeless generalized sense of longing, but rooted in the Mexican *meseta.* Anyone who has traveled the central highlands of Mexico will recognize the description. As we have seen, Castellanos was preoccupied with the need to deal with concrete images and specific objects. Here she applies this technique to a poetic theme that normally uses such techniques to prevent the sense of timelessness from deteriorating into sheer vagueness, but in **"Elegía"** rather than simply use objective correlations more or less at random, she has anchored them in a specific contextual reality. She has said of these poems that they represent a return to religiosity, but not to an orthodox Catholicism. (pp. 140-42)

The high point of the volume is two of her best poems, and quite possibly two of the best produced by her entire generation in Mexico: **"Resplandor del ser"** and the splendid **"Lamentación de Dido."** They present a remarkable contrast; **"Resplandor del ser"** is as close as Castellanos ever comes to achieving the moment of total immersion in the felicity of the universe. The motive, if there is a specific one, is not made clear. It appears to be the sheer joy of the word and of the creative act, but this creativity is also hinted at in more personal or physiological terms, and it may very well be the double fecundity of the word and of biological birth about which she speaks. In any event, the poem captures a moment that is rare in Castellanos's poetry. It avoids the abstraction that is a major peril for this kind of statement by beginning with very concrete images of the natural world that reflect the emotional state of the speaker. . . . The joy opens out from this initial image, but the poem returns periodically to such natural imagery as a sort of underpinning to its more metaphysical developments. At the poem's end, we have come full circle and are once again before the renewed joy, expressed . . . in the image of the returning life of the cyclical natural world. (pp. 142-43)

"Lamentación de Dido" is another matter entirely, a poem all fire and passion. It presents Castellanos's view of the failed love of Dido and Aeneas as presented by Vergil in Book IV of the *Aeneid*. The **"Lamentación"** is much briefer than its Latin model, only slightly more than five pages, and highly condensed, which is one of the principal reasons for its power . . . The theme is an obsessive one in her work: the betrayal by an absent lover, for whatever reasons, seems to have haunted her. . . . [In an] interview Castellanos openly admitted that the poem reflected an autobiographical episode, another example of her willingness to discuss openly what she seemingly made every effort to veil in her poetry. It seems quite clear that this discretion in her poetry is really more an effort to avoid the excesses of emotionalism. . . . The myth of Dido, as Vergil had presented it, provided Castellanos with the kind of objective correlative to her own feelings that would allow her to control them, to objectify them in a poetic mask. Jaime Labastida has pointed out how Castellanos changes the focus of the poem so that Dido is the center, not Aeneas. It is, in the best of senses, a poem distilled from autobiographical experience and controlled by the use of poetic tradition.

"Lamentación de Dido" also uses a distinctive verse form, an irregular line that looks more like rhythmic prose than verse. It consists of an irregular series of units predominantly of seven and eleven syllables, organized in long lines, at times as though a whole verse had been run on in prose fashion. . . . Castellanos was consciously at-

tempting to achieve . . . a solemn but musical line she called a "versículo" that would serve to hide her personal and emotional investment behind the mask of a traditional theme and a classical-seeming meter, and would permit her to avoid the excesses of confessional poetry. (pp. 143-45)

[Her] consciousness of the formal aspect of poetic creativity is the other side of her own vision of her mission as a writer. Rosario Castellanos quite clearly wished to be a "major" poet, as is visible in the overreaching of *Apuntes* and *Trayectoria,* both works conceived as encompassing visions of life and human existence, far too great a task for such a young poet. Even so early she had been reaching for a kind of stately but flexible language, something like a combination of [St.–John] Perse and the Bible. When she achieved it, she was so fearful that it might become a recipe for concocting poems that she reacted against it strongly in later books, although echoes remain until the end. But her work through the best-known poems reveals this search, and it is illuminating to examine her translations of three of her favorite poets, [Paul] Claudel, Perse, and Emily Dickinson. The two French authors often used a long, stately line which Castellanos reproduced rather closely, but her translations of Dickinson are quite another matter. She has a problem with the short, sharply rhythmic character of Dickinson's verse, and the Spanish versions use a more measured, less staccato line. Where the originals are frequently made up of four iambs, the translations tend toward a steady seven-syllable line, but she alters and expands Dickinson's crabbed and intricate syntax, with the result that the translations lose a good deal of movement and agility. Where Castellanos is closest to Dickinson is in those of her own later poems where she abandoned the search for stateliness and returned to a more popular traditional verse.

Obviously, the success of **"Lamentación de Dido"** has little to do with these specifics of the possible sources of the line; this is important only in that it provided her with a measured control against which she plays the uncontrolled passion of the anguished Dido. After the slow regal measures of her lament, Dido's confession comes as a chilling cry. . . . The nearly normal spoken rhythms permit Castellanos to handle this passion with effective moderation and occasional telling understatement, while at the same time she controls the outbursts of the agonized queen. The overwrought emotions with which the poem deals contrast with the almost colloquial speech, a contrast that is implicit in that of the legendary tragic queen with her modern counterpart. A vocabulary rich in terms like booty, daggers, "el de la corva garra de gavilán," "nave de airosas velas," rapidly establishes the barbaric atmosphere of a remote semimythical kingdom, only to be contrasted again with the restraint of Dido's statements. The result is a poem in which the betrayed queen speaks in remarkably modern rhythms and words, and we realize doubly that Dido is much more than a convenient figure about whom to compose a paean to the past.

There is another dimension to this technique. Certain obsessive themes recur in Castellanos's work, among them the situation of Dido, the abandoned lover. It is not unlikely that the repeated effort to create the nearly classical line she uses here, the progressive abandonment of a specific external referent in so much of her poetry, and the adaptation of the figure of Dido are a masking of the real circumstances, whatever they may have been, that led to this obsessive usage. Castellanos's Dido, unlike Vergil's, shuns suicide . . . but this will not always be the case.

This tendency toward impersonal poetry as a masking device is carried to an extreme in *Al pie de la letra* (1959). Few of the volume's eighteen poems have any visible individual reference or are placed in the mouth of a speaker who could by any stretch of the imagination be a double for Rosario Castellanos. . . . She has again attempted to mask the specific circumstances that gave rise to the poems in order to attain a less individual expression, one that would also obscure her own participation as a *character* within the poems, as well as their author. The majority of the poems deal with subjects that are impersonal, broadly human, or apparently external to the author, and in several she deals once more with themes reminiscent of Perse's fables of migration. (pp. 145-47)

Nearly all the books mentioned thus far are characterized by a tension between short personal poems and the longer attempts at a poetic persona, but *Lívida luz* (1960), winner of the Villaurrutia Prize, marks a substantial break. The volume consists primarily of brief and highly personal lyrics that are simultaneously a statement of the author's social commitment, as though this emerging commitment had provided her with a means to react poetically against her own efforts at masking her emotions. (p. 149)

But this newly apparent commitment does not produce euphoria. . . . Much less is it the communal march to the radiant future that some would have preferred; the poems are more anxiously individual than before. Castellanos may have varied the masks she used to protect herself from the exposure her poetry would otherwise have meant, but she could not use the mass mask of the proletarian poet hymning doctrinaire slogans. She was too thoughtful and self-aware, too conscious of her individuality and her role as writer to be able to mesh into a collective communal voice. In two fundamental texts, she clarified her conception of the conflictive nature of poetry and the artist's commitment. . . . [In *Lívida luz*] there are no prefabricated formulae leading to the "only" road to the future. We find, on the contrary, pessimism and frustration in the face of ingratitude and violence. . . . It is as though the masks were all beginning to crack and leave the poet naked before the accumulated suffering of all time. At moments the frustration is expressed in almost everyday language, as in **"El excluido."** (pp. 150-51)

This frustration is apparent everywhere, as in the second of the **"Tres poemas,"** which presents a pure vision of an enormous fish whose eyes never close, fixed always on someone, something, incapable of doing any more than observing, a comment on humankind's incapacity that leads us inevitably to the apocalyptic vision of **"Los distraídos."** . . . This is a poetry that becomes more and more pessimistic, more and more the expression of a per-

ception of the tragic nature of existence. . . . The growing negativism of her poetry is due only in part to a socially-based pessimism; whatever other personal factors were influencing the process, the inexorability of advancing time and the loss of any hope of the instant of plenitude were also at work.

But there is an important new element in *Lívida luz.* Several poems include direct comments, in first person singular, as if the author were suddenly to be transformed into a confessional poet in the manner of Robert Lowell, for example. . . . **"Jornada de la soltera"** [is] the clearest, most intimate poetic expression to date of Castellanos's often-expressed personal feelings. Indeed, [**"Jornada de la soltera"**] is so intensely personal, and Castellanos spoke so often and so freely of her private life, that one is tempted to suspect the creation of another and different persona. One of the Mexican poets most admired by Castellanos was Salvador Novo, who perfected the art of appearing to be a confessional poet revealing his most personal feelings while in fact adopting an ironic self-mocking mask. There is a thread that recurs in a number of these poems: a speaker who is more observer than participant, remote from those about her (or him), whose suffering is somehow disconnected. . . . Even in as intensely personal a work as **"Jornada de la soltera,"** the poem is written in third person, paradoxically distancing it from the author herself. In the swing from the mask of Dido, Castellanos has here created the mask of a third person, never really identified as Rosario Castellanos, never quite willing (or able) to take the definitive step into autobiographical or confessional poetry, yet drawn obsessively to certain themes that clearly concerned her deeply. One of these was the looming shadow of death, of possible suicide, which was to become a constant, almost obsessive presence. . . . Of the overtly socially-oriented human solidarity that had been so important only a few years earlier, there remain barely traces.

Perhaps as a reaction against the extreme personalism of *Lívida luz, Materia memorable* (1969) is in a much calmer and apparently more objective mode, as though the poet were engaging in a sort of dialectic to-and-fro in her struggle to discover the most effective and at the same time the least revealing poetic idiom and stance. The title comes from the final stanza of **"Toma de conciencia,"** a poem that expresses much of the familiar recognition of the solitude and frustrations of a woman who regularly faces the "mínimas tragedias cotidianas," but there is also, as the poem's title indicates, a new perception. She is no longer entirely alone; she forms part of all creation, known and unknown to her. She participates in all living kind, in a new—or recalled?—solidarity which defies the ever-present Tempter. (pp. 151-54)

Emerging in *Materia memorable* is a new kind of poem which fuses the longer line and use of a poetic persona of the earlier works with a calmer, more colloquial idiom approximating the rhythms of normal speech. The rhetoric of the earlier years is definitely gone, and the tensions of subjectivism and wordiness are effectively harmonized. **"Nocturno,"** for example, consists of irregular combinations of seven and four syllables, with the majority of lines ranging around eleven; it echoes quite clearly the form of **"Lamentación de Dido,"** but the subject matter is much more openly modern and personal. It is one of Castellanos's most controlled performances, with short phrases balanced against longer combinations. The poem is a straightforward portrait of two people who have quietly betrayed their pact, until now there is no further opportunity. In a perfectly calm tone, the speaker asks for a truce. But the chief characteristic of the poem is its vocabulary, which, like the form, still echoes the migration-epic based earlier works. . . . **"Nocturno"** is again a potentially highly personal and revealing poem; Castellanos has chosen to express the strictly *personal* aspect . . . against a background that both highlights the major theme and at the same time removes it from confessionalism. The poet is still struggling with the dual temptation to confess openly her personal life and to screen it against a distancing background.

The extent to which *Materia memorable* is anchored in the ongoing struggle is visible in the persistence of the creation of masks. **"Testamento de Hécuba"** uses as a framework the legend of the Trojan queen, mother of Paris, enslaved by Ulysses after the fall of Troy. Castellanos's version follows closely the classical outline and does not seem to have been adapted directly to her personal circumstance, although clearly the fallen queen's hinted equivalence between her slavery and her previous life struck an echo in Castellanos. Considerably different is **"Metamorfosis de la hechicera"** in that it has no fixed referent and does not rely on a historical setting. (pp. 154-55)

It is important to stress the presence of death in this volume, even in the relatively peaceful poems. Castellanos's insistence on finding her own name is prefigured ironically and, given the circumstances of her premature death. . . . Suicide is never really absent from her poems, after the earliest ones, and *Materia memorable* includes the overt **"Privilegio del suicida,"** in which the sufferer is the survivor, condemned to life.

Materia memorable was the last separate volume of poetry published during the life of Rosario Castellanos; the collected poems, *Poesía no eres tú,* appeared in 1972, two years before her death. It includes four sections of previously unpublished poems: *En la tierra de en medio, Diálogos con los hombres más honrados, Otros poemas,* and *Viaje redondo.* It would seem that the multiple obligations of which she wrote so often—wife, mother, columnist, teacher, and finally diplomat—had interfered with her creative work. There is nothing here of the sustained power of the mature longer poems, which does not mean at all that there are not poems, here which do her honor. Perhaps the most striking aspect is the almost complete disappearance of the masks we have noted so often. *En la tierra de en medio,* a title that reflects her increasing vision of this world as a no-man's-land, bears as epigraph Eliot's "Human kind/cannot bear very much reality." For the first time, Castellanos is writing overtly autobiographical poetry or, at the very least, poetry whose speaker bears a life that conforms to the outward details of Castellanos's own life. The tone is of resigned, ironic sadness, acceptance of the fact that her existence has become hopelessly

mediocre. . . . Rarely does the poet use her old trick of the poetic mask of mythic structures; it is visible only in the unseen absence of **"Bella dama sin piedad,"** or the familiar story of the Aztec princess in **"Malinche."** There is no longer any need for such forms; Castellanos has learned to control her rhetorical exuberance, and the result is an **"Autorretrato"** where the tutelary voice is no longer Claudel or Perse but the master ironist, Salvador Novo. No longer does Castellanos take refuge behind lengthy rhetorical verses dealing with remote people and remoter places. In **"Autorretrato"** she can use clearly autobiographical materials . . . as she creates her ironic self-portrait as a housewife advancing in years whose stable life is in danger of collapse. (pp. 157-59)

Two poems deserve further comment in that they return to a deeply humane commitment. **"Poesía no eres tú"** is an extension of what we have already seen in *En la tierra de en medio,* but there is also the formulation of a commitment and of the belief that poetry can no longer be the expression of the intimate lyric, even though during this stage of her career Castellanos herself was writing predominantly intimate lyrics. It is impossible to say how much the attitude was influenced by the trauma of 1968, but one of the strongest poems of the volume is the denunciation of the massacre, **"Memorial de Tlatelolco."** She avoids high-pitched political rhetoric; instead, she portrays in a controlled voice the complete absence of any record of the crime, of any official or public recognition that it had ever transpired. Nor does she cast exclusive blame on the government that perpetrated and then covered up the slaughter; like Octavio Paz, she finds something ancestral in it all. . . .

Castellanos's remaining works do not give the impression of being finished collections. *Diálogos con los hombres más honrados* is a group of semiaphorisms, responses to lines by other writers, ironic comments rather than poems. Others are longer but they share the same wry pessimism. They are all pretexts for commenting on the life and character of the Mexican, but even here death is ever present. (p. 160)

We have seen how the struggle to control her own verbal facility led to a characteristic style, how this style gradually evolved into a much more personal vision of the individual, and how this vision, with its view of human solidarity and responsibility, slowly gave ground before an increasingly despairing vision. More and more her poetry is the expression of the search for a real self as a reaction against the slogans and recipes with which we are surrounded, with no exit except the universal one. (p. 162)

> *Frank Dauster, "Rosario Castellanos: The Search for a Voice," in* The Double Strand: Five Contemporary Mexican Poets, *The University Press of Kentucky, 1987, pp. 134-62.*

Maureen Ahern

Rosario Castellanos was the first Mexican writer to draw the essential connections among sex, class, and race as factors that define women in Mexico. The keys to that ideology are her essays. First written as weekly pieces for *Excélsior* and other newspapers in Mexico City, they constitute a fascinating mosaic of cultural life and thought in Mexico between 1960 and 1974. In touch with her roots, ahead of her time, and laughing at herself, she establishes in these texts an immediate rapport with a wide variety of readers. As part of the lively tradition of the *crónica,* or short creative prose popular in Latin American writing, they are akin to the pieces that her countryman Carlos Monsiváis was publishing during the same decade or the provocative texts that Ellen Goodman presently writes for the *Boston Globe* and the *New York Times.*

Juicios sumarios, the first collection that Castellanos edited, in 1966, passed largely unnoticed. However, her second collection of essays, *Mujer que sabe latín,* which analyzes women's issues and women writers, was avidly read by women all over Latin America, particularly the younger generation of feminists and writers, when it was published in 1971. There had been nothing like it since *Letter in Reply to Sor Philotea,* the intellectual autobiography of the seventeenth-century nun, Sor Juana Inés de la Cruz, in whose extraordinary life and work many patterns coincide with those of her twentieth-century countrywoman. The status of women in Mexico in the fifties and sixties had in essence changed little over the centuries, and the saying on which Castellanos based her title was still popular: *Mujer que sabe latín, ni tiene marido ni buen fin* (A woman who knows Latin will find neither husband nor happy end). Just before her death, Castellanos edited a third collection, *El mar y sus pescaditos* (1975), a compilation of her reviews of other contemporary authors. José Emilio Pacheco compiled sixty-five more chronicles that had first appeared in the editorial pages of *Excélsior,* in *El uso de la palabra* (1974). My own research, conducted in Mexico in 1978, located approximately ninety more uncollected essays that are recorded in my annotated bibliography in *Homenaje a Rosario Castellanos* (p. 39)

Although Rosario Castellanos began to examine the question of feminine culture when she wrote her master's thesis in philosophy, *Sobre cultura femenina,* in 1950, Beth Miller [in *Rosario Castellanos: Una conciencia feminista en México*] has shown that she actually used the arguments of Schopenhauer, Weininger, Simmel, Nietzsche, and Freud to establish female inferiority based on biological determinism. Even in this early academic project, Castellanos was concerned with women as part of culture as a whole and the tradition and potential of feminine achievement within it. Looking ahead to the directions in which this thesis actually led her, I agree with Miller that "it is actually Castellanos' point of departure." It was clearly an academic exercise that worked through traditional male authorities, whom she soon outgrew. That same year, 1950, study and travel in Europe brought Castellanos into contact with the ideas of Simone de Beauvoir, Simone Weil, and Virginia Woolf, three intellectual and aesthetic mentors who stimulated the development of her own thinking in the decades that followed. (p. 40)

In *Mujer que sabe latín,* Castellanos presents the magisterial texts of a wide range of women writers from both European and American traditions and a number of essays that attend to silences in women's lives in Mexico and silences in their texts.

"Woman and Her Image" takes issue with the forces that have kept woman outside history. "In the course of history (history is an archive of deeds undertaken by men and all that remains outside it belongs to the realm of conjecture, fable, legend, or lie) more than a natural phenomenon, a component of society, or a human creature, woman has been myth," Castellanos wrote. She used arguments by Simone de Beauvoir and Virginia Woolf to refute the biological inferiority postulated by male authorities. Scientific arguments for the inferior capacity of the female cranium are reenforced by listing "the inventions that our civilization owes to female talent"—among them rose petal cigarette wrappers, a marker for rubber clogs, and aromatic toothpicks. This parody of scientific report through the enumeration of ludicrous evidence demolishes the scientific hypothesis. It is an example of Castellanos' talent for producing ironic humor by reversal, in this case by using the discourse of scientific reporting as a caricature of itself.

Another principal strategy in this essay is the skillful use of intertextual fragments and references to other feminine figures from texts by or about other women. Virginia Woolf's description of her famous "Angel in the House," the embodiment of woman as the Victorian ideal of "materialism, order, and cleanliness," is introduced into the essay as "the model of virtue to which every female creature must aspire." The older text is inserted into the new one by use of quotation marks that enable it to serve as "an image and metonymic device through which a former text in its totality is alluded to." The results are powerful: first, Woolf's figure reinforces Castellanos' argument through illustration and, second, it produces a new and dual awareness of Woolf's text. The chilling idea that this ludicrous creature from late Victorian England is still alive, sitting in drafts to shield others, that she is still in some way relevant in the twentieth-century world of Hispanic women, revalidates Woolf's metaphor, its relevance to our times, and the tragedies of women who still embody it.

Similar, although more subtle, effects are achieved with the enumerations of female characters from Hispanic and European literatures, among them Melibea, Ana de Ozores, Hedda Gabler, and la Pintada; "each one in her way and in her own circumstances denies the conventional, making the foundations of the establishment tremble, turning hierarchies upside down, and achieving authenticity," Castellanos wrote. These figures are examples of "the road that leads from the strictest solitude to total annihilation," embodying the destructiveness of stereotypes imposed upon the lives of women who dared to struggle for access to their authentic selves. These intertextual mirrors serve to match textual representation with intellectual arguments. In this aspect her work reflects the same features as the writing of her textual mentor, Virginia Woolf. . . . The integration of feminine intellectuality with feminine textuality distinguishes Castellanos' essays. By using the sign systems of other women authors to enrich and feminize her own, Castellanos actually familiarizes their writing, resulting in a new awareness of the network of women writers and thinkers through their relativization in a new context. In this case, the use of female examples for Sartre's "limit situation" prepares the reader for Castellanos' conclusions: "The feat of *becoming what one is* (a feat belonging to the privileged whatever their sex or condition) not only demands the discovery of the essential features beneath the spur of passion, dissatisfaction, or surfeit, but above all the rejection of those false images that false mirrors offer woman in the enclosed gallery where her life takes place."

From the examination of women as national signs in Mexico to the ways that myth keeps women outside history, Castellanos turned her inquiry to women's lives within history in Mexico: "the actual *experiences* of women in the past." Her essay **"The Nineteenth-Century Mexican Woman"** shares the concerns of historians of women about "the quality of [women's] daily lives, the conditions in which they lived and worked, the ages at which they married and bore children; . . . their relations to other women; their perceptions of their place in the world." When Castellanos inquired about women at the beginning of the republican period in Mexico, she found so few sources written in her own country that she turned to the testimony of another woman of that time, the diary of Fanny Calderón de la Barca, the Scottish wife of the first Spanish ambassador to independent Mexico. Calderón's *Life in Mexico,* first published in Boston in 1843, is now recognized by historians as one of the prime sources for the social history of the independence period, from 1839 to 1841.

Castellanos braids excerpts from this journal into her own essay. The technique consists of inserting extended fragments of direct quotations from Calderón's daily entries, then juxtaposing Castellanos' own commentary. The result is the creation of a dialogue across 170 years of Mexican life, a kind of double window on the images of those nineteenth-century matriarchs, wives, daughters, sisters, and nuns. For example, on the topic of their appearance, Calderón's comparative description prompts Castellanos to reply: "Aristocracy and indolence? Have they not been synonymous among us? To such a point that even the order of courtesy is altered."

In other spheres of feminine life, Castellanos inserts Calderón de la Barca's chilling account of the glittering ceremony a young Mexican girl underwent when she took the veil. This quotation imbeds the direct discourse of the diarist as well as that of another female speaker who together express their horror "at the sacrifice of a girl so young, that she could not possibly have known her own mind . . . but many young girls, who were conversing together, seemed rather to envy their friend—who had looked so pretty and graceful, and 'so happy,' and whose dress 'suited her so well'—and to have no objection to 'go and do likewise.'" Castellanos is quick to deduce: "It is obvious that there is a relationship of cause and effect between these options and the ignorance of the world that is so strongly supported by general ignorance."

The interplay between Calderón's vision of nineteenth-

century Mexico transmitted by the actual words of her diaries and Castellanos' twentieth-century comments creates a powerful new one when they are fused in a single frame. By enabling her text to both speak and be spoken about, it takes on renewed life across the centuries. When both perspectives converge, many women's voices generate clusters of meanings centered in their experiences, intensifying the feminization of the discourse. When Calderón's eyes also bear on the same discursive object, the Mexican woman, the clarity and strength of the discursive lens are doubled. It recharges our vision of Calderón, renewing our awareness of the roots of present-day Mexico.

This dialogue among Mexican women and their texts is a cogent example of Castellanos' talent for what Adrienne Rich calls *"re-vision*—the act of looking back, of seeing with fresh eyes, of entering an old text from a new critical direction": Castellanos' skill at creating new verbal meaning from old, her ability to look at a specific case and draw the wider cultural application. Castellanos' grim tongue-in-cheek conclusion produces just such a re-vision: "Devout nuns, impeccable housewives, docile daughters, wives and mothers. The other side of the coin Madam Calderón de la Barca saw in the insane asylums and jails. There most of the cases were madness due to love and murder of the spouse. What a shame that she did not pay a visit to the brothels to make her picture complete!" Rosario Castellanos searched for the silences that must make our understanding of texts complete. As this remarkable closure converts us into *listeners* of women's voices, not only do Calderón's words speak, but so also do her silences. (pp. 44-7)

Self-oppression has as its correlation the oppression of other women. **"Herlinda Leaves"** applies this axiom to Castellanos' own life when she discusses how "servanthood" affects the relationships between women of different social classes in modern Mexico. Using the biography of four women's lives, among them a wrenching confession about her own, Castellanos includes herself as an example of the maternal colonialism which servanthood thrives on and must, therefore, defeat. "There I was off playing Quetzalcoatl, the great white civilizing god, while right next to me someone was walking around ignorant. I was ashamed. I made a promise that the next time (if there was to be a next time) it would be different. My policy in regard to Herlinda Bolaños was totally different. But I would not venture to say that it was more appropriate."

Castellanos is aware, as few women were in her time, that freedom based on the dependence and exploitation of other women and classes is false. Although her stay in the United States coincided with the march commemorating the fiftieth anniversary of women's suffrage in this country, and the demonstrations that dramatized the Women's Liberation Movement throughout it, she thought about them in terms of Mexico. What meaning did these events hold for Mexican women and how were they being interpreted in their own country? How liberated is a woman whose freedom is dependent upon another's servitude? (pp. 49-50)

"We have to create another language, we have to find another starting point," Castellanos wrote in **"Language as an Instrument of Domination"** in 1972. Understanding that our knowledge of the world is through language, Castellanos viewed language both as an instrument of oppression and as a way to combat it—it was the point of access to our authentic selves. While we do not know what the specific qualities of this new language would be, we can speculate that it would look for a way out of the negativity, the false images, and the codified male systems that have excluded women from history and social freedom that Castellanos examines in her poems and her essays. [In "Rosario Castellanos: On Language"] Regina Harrison MacDonald has demonstrated that, for Castellanos, "language serves as a codifying system for examining false institutions, antiquated prejudices and iron-clad hierarchies which have been erected in the name of Mexican culture."

"An Attempt at Self-Criticism" and **"If Not Poetry, Then What?,"** written a decade apart, trace the formation of Castellanos' literary vocation, affirming the liberation from traditional literary canons and language that she achieved in her mature writing. These two texts are our critical guides to Castellanos' work, in which writing, identity, and language are linked, not separate, constants. They were her survival, she declared, the way she transformed her reality into memorable material.

Considering the privileged position that language holds in Castellanos' work, we are struck by the many points of convergence with that of the French feminists Hélène Cixous, Julia Kristeva, Luce Irigaray, and Monique Wittig, whose recognition of language as an instrument of oppression, repression, and exclusion and whose call for another language Castellanos clearly anticipates. "Briefly, French feminists in general believe that Western thought has been based on a systematic repression of women's experience. Thus their assertion of a bedrock female nature makes sense as a point from which to deconstruct language, philosophy, psychoanalysis, the social practices, and direction of patriarchal culture as we live in it and resist it." Clearly, there is a great deal more to say about the points of affinity between this Mexican writer and the wide spectrum of attitudes formulated by these younger French writers five to ten years later, the many coincidences of her writing with their practice of what is now recognized as *l'écriture féminine,* or women's writing. This chapter remains to be written. Yet, even briefly, it is clear that Castellanos' penchant for punning titles, the orality of her discourse, her multiple feminine speakers and addresses, her sarcastic challenges to "you self-sacrificing little Mexican housewives," and the open-ended stories and essays are closely akin to Luce Irigaray's practice of *parler femme,* female writing.

Castellanos' predilection for female body metaphors and the habit of inscribing herself into her discourse in ways I have pointed out in this study relate her writing to Hélène Cixous' call: "Write your self. Your body must be heard." Like Castellanos, Cixous saw writing "as one of the sites of resistance or liberation in this phallocentric universe": "Everything turns on the Word: everything is the Word and only the Word . . . we must take culture at its word, as it takes us into its words, into its tongue . . . no political reflection dispenses with reflection on language, with work on language." Castellanos took culture at its word in the many essays that she wrote about language—imbuing it with transforming as well as oppressing powers—revealing its negativity in order to search for "another beginning."

"My style, as you already know, consists of taking a completely insignificant fact and trying to relate it to a transcendent truth," Castellanos tells her readers in **"The Moment of Truth"** (*El uso de la palabra*). Reflecting on the tropes that organize her essays, it becomes evident that many that generate some of her best writing are essentially domestic, yet they convey some of her most controversial discussions about women's experiences.

Several strategies fuse domesticity into the discursive organization of Castellanos' essays. Frequently, a text begins with an utterance by an autobiographical I, who tosses out a provocative personal detail or an aside on a domestic event that sets up the discussion of an issue of cultural, political, or artistic importance. "As I was putting on my makeup to attend the dinner that the Israeli government is offering President Nixon and his Secretary of State, Professor Kissinger (I'm not presuming anything, right?), I was thinking about the way things happen" (**"A pesar de proponérselo"**). **"A Man of Destiny"** begins by mentioning the author's forty-fifth birthday and the fact that she's not interested in ignoring dates as one does gray hairs and wrinkles. Many essays in that same collection, like **"Herlinda Leaves,"** meditate on topics that are intrinsically domestic, such as the relationships between mistress and servants in modern Mexico. By using communication elements from areas of human activity that are intrinsically domestic or feminine, that is, supposedly innocuous, Castellanos enables the reader to initially perceive them to be harmless and non-threatening. But in Castellanos' prose they function either as springboards for a dive into the deep water of controversy that immediately follows or to hold a mirror up to our faces—and follies. In other words, the author uses referents, images, or structures from areas that because they are domestic have been stereotyped as safe, discountable, or insignificant, articulating dialogues or monologues that are just the opposite.

If a woman's body is an object, her image distorted, and language makes her an alien in her own country, little is left for her but the domestic sphere. Domesticity as trope becomes a way of access to the self in Castellanos' writing. As a discursive strategy, it creates a textual sleight-of-hand that is inherently ironic by startling or amusing the reader with a referent from an area not usually permitted or found in the discourse of male writers. When feminine or domestic referents trigger the production of a text, they defuse their topics by bringing them on to familiar ground, engaging the reader's attention and setting the stage for acceptance of the message. Once the analogy is made, it *recharges* or *resemanticizes* the familiar sign with new meaning. Wrinkles and gray hair, putting on makeup, or a charm school metonymically become original, ironic, and appropriate message bearers of significant ideas. Feminine experience converts the ordinary into the relevant and the significant through feminine tropes that articulate spheres of experiences that are usually "devalued or not admitted by the dominant discourse."

Domesticity is a sign of dual value in Castellanos' writing. The domestic sphere is a space where women dwell, excel, and create, but it is also a space that may have demeaned or diminished its inhabitants. Perhaps part of that other language that Castellanos was searching for is to be found in those codes that are nearest to us—our bodies, our spaces—the ways and places to invent ourselves as her writing urges us to do. (pp. 50-3)

> *Maureen Ahern, "Reading Rosario Castellanos: Contexts, Voices and Signs," in* A Rosario Castellanos Reader: An Anthology of Her Poetry, Short Fiction, Essays, and Drama, *by Rosario Castellanos, edited by Maureen Ahern, translated by Maureen Ahern and others, University of Texas Press, 1988, pp. 39-53.*

Nina M. Scott

Rosario Castellanos (1925-1974), one of modern Mexico's best writers and most outspoken feminists, is famous for the wit and humor that characterize her multifaceted literary production. Ever since the publication in 1950 of her master's thesis *Sobre cultura femenina* [*On Feminine Culture*], Castellanos used her writing not only to discover her own particular identity as a woman but to foreground the absurd and conflictive customs of Mexican society which prevented women in general from developing their selfhood. (p. 20)

[Beneath a lighthearted exterior] lay intense seriousness of purpose and constant tension, a tension which stemmed from an inability to reconcile herself to her cultural context and manifested itself in a dialectical opposition between understanding and rebellion. In quasi-melodramatic terms Castellanos delineates both her feminist goals and the function which humor assumes in the realization thereof:

> I would suggest a campaign: not to rush to attack our customs with the flaming sword of indignation nor with the mournful tremolo of tears but by showing up that which makes them ridiculous. I assure you that we have inexhaustible material for laughter. And we need to laugh so badly because laughter is the most immediate form of freeing ourselves from that which oppresses us the most, of distancing ourselves from that which imprisons us!

Castellanos uses wit and humor as classic weapons of attack against authority, taking pride in becoming one of the "iconoclasts who apply the 'corrosive acid of laughter' to institutions in order to destroy them because they are absurd, because they are unjust, because they lack foundation and meaning . . . ". Like her model Democritus, she is a revolutionary "who has a good time deconstructing mechanisms, showing their inconsistencies, reducing to ashes with one breath a construction which defied the centuries."

Much of Castellanos's efforts to speak out on behalf of women's issues took place on the editorial pages of *Excelsior*. As I said in a previous study on the interrelationship between Castellanos's journalism and her creative writing ["Rosario Castellanos: Communication Strategies as Columnist and Creative Writer"], "The editorial page has traditionally provided men with a forum from which to express their opinion; a woman's voice was unusual in this context and Castellanos' overt feminism was controversial enough to both attract and alienate readers." Aware of this, Castellanos often adopted an attitude of humorous self-deprecation in order to defuse potential reader hostility: "My column is the mirror, mirror on the wall whom I ask every Saturday who is the most marvelous woman on this planet, and just as in the fairy tale, it always tells me that Snow White is"; however, [Norma] Alarcón is also right in her assessment that "Rosario Castellanos controls and masks her intellectual rage through the self-conscious assumption of inferiority." The lightness of touch was a useful tactic in that it masked her real intention, that of using humor as a means of liberation, for in her opinion "to laugh at something is the most immediate form of putting yourself out of reach of that something." What Castellanos as iconoclast wished most to destroy were the myths which reduced the existence of the Mexican woman to a living cliché. The use of the verbal cliché is one of the hallmarks of Castellanos' humor, a point to which I shall return later.

The introductory essays of *Mujer que sabe latín* provide the reader with a resumé of Castellanos's feminist credo and are a useful point of departure for the examination of her ideas. Castellanos begins by pointing out the male tendency to reduce woman to myth and thereby to nullify her authentic existence. . . . She cites three categories of myth—esthetic, ethic, and intellectual—all of which contribute to the psychological and physical deformation of women. Castellanos provides numerous examples to illustrate her thesis, and an examination of several of these will provide a sense of the characteristic forms in which her brand of humor is expressed.

Esthetic myths transform woman into muse, Castellanos noted, "and in order to achieve this one must maintain distance and be silent. And be beautiful." In the process of undermining this myth Castellanos points out that, whereas it is a woman's obligation to be beautiful, standards of beauty and fashion are often dictated by men who ignore factors such as physical comfort or well-being. (pp. 20-2)

But it is not only men who impose absurd esthetic expectations: women, too, participate actively in keeping them alive and well. . . . Another major culprit is the media, for example the popular women's magazines which project false or conflictive images to their readers and thereby foster guilt feelings in women unable to measure up to these expectations. . . . (p. 23)

The second type of myth is of an ethic nature and relates to the fact that in Mexican society women are taught that their ultimate fulfillment can only come through being, as Alarcón calls it, "Beloved or Mother." "Among the institutions which cynical wit is wont to attack," Freud observed, "there is none more important and more completely protected by moral precepts, and yet more inviting of attack, than the institution of marriage." Castellanos would agree. On the one hand she faults an educational system which fails to educate girls so that they can become independently functioning human beings and on the other a culture which encourages women to remain in a permanent state of passive immobility: "The social apparatus . . . has decreed, once and for all, that the only legitimate attitude for womanhood is that of waiting around." Poets, too, have told a woman that domesticity is her principal function: "As the bard Díaz Mirón's verses said, she was born like the dove for the nest. And as don Melchor Ocampo instructed her . . . her mission is that of being the balsam that soothes the wounds which a man incurs in his daily confrontation with life." As in her discussion of the esthetic myth, here, too, Castellanos avoids Manichean oversimplification by underscoring women's complicity in its perpetuation. She once observed that Mexican women tend to be parasites more than victims and noted that, in Mexican society, "complicity between the executioner and his victim [is] so long-standing that it is impossible to distinguish who is who." The newlywed protagonist of **"Lección de cocina"** [in *Album de familia*] ruefully acknowledges this type of complicity. In an imaginary conversation with her friends about her sex life, she knows that instead of articulating her growing disenchantment therewith she would most likely extol and thereby falsify her husband's prowess in bed. . . . (pp. 23-4)

Within the parameters of this discussion of ethic concerns, Castellanos points out that the myth of the glories of motherhood is one of the most powerful in Hispanic culture and, in her opinion, one of the most insidious. To a great extent she blamed the creation and perpetuation of this myth on the teachings of the Church:

> Motherhood redeems woman from the original sin of being one, [and] confers meaning and justification onto her life (which would otherwise be superfluous). It anoints with holy unguents the sexual drive which, by itself, is considered an unpardonable sin when it is a female being who feels it. It exalts the institution of matrimony to the point of absolute stability, makes the domestic yoke easy and the scourge of responsibilities a delight. It serves as an infallible panacea for the deepest and most wrenching personal frustrations.

The unctuous clichés in the above lines are paralleled by the hyperbolic sentimentality of those directed at the venerable mother whose life has consisted of abnegation and sacrifice: "Praise the little gray heads! Eternal glory to 'the one who loved us even before she knew us'! Statues in the parks, days set aside to honor her, etc. etc." On the other hand, Castellanos also reminds her readers that the basest insults the Spanish language has to offer refer to mothers and motherhood, "which is nothing more than the other side of the shining coin of her importance." She points out that the universal exaltation of motherhood as "the fast lane to sanctification" excludes any element of choice on

the part of the woman, for Mexican society rejects women who might prefer to be single, choose not to have children, or aspire to an education and a career. This point leads Castellanos to examine the third kind of myth, that which concerns a woman's intellectual development.

With mock seriousness she cites a number of scientific sources, most of them Germanic, to prove that women are endowed with minuscule brains which render them biologically unfit to think. She again faults both society and the Church for limiting the instruction of many women to purely religious subjects, taught by rote memorization or drill in devotional rituals of whose deeper meanings the students are never apprised. An intellectual woman such as Sor Juana, the brilliant, seventeenth-century Mexican nun, was considered "a devouring monster," and even in modern times an intelligent young woman who aspires to a university education is classified by both men and women as "abnormal, pedantic, impertinent, Miss-know-it-all, a ridiculous stuck-up, etc." Supposing that a woman persists and succeeds in entering the career world? Well, Castellanos asks, would *you* entrust a woman architect with the building of *your* house?

> A house is too much money, too many years of dreams and doing without to let some hysterical woman or some lady who's worrying about where her husband is nights throw it all overboard. Besides which, neither one of them would know how to be boss to the kind of people construction workers are. No, as a last resort better hire a contractor.

The above barrage of clichés may be humorous, but unfortunately it also echoes the opinion of many a potential client. The effect of such attitudes on a trained professional cannot help but be destructive: "Efficiency depends to a large degree on interior equilibrium. An equilibrium which everything conspires to destroy."

The examples cited above show several types of humor characteristic of Castellanos's writing: direct, colloquial dialogue, irony, of course, apparent self-denigration, witty asides, and, most of all, the accumulation *ad absurdum* of the hackneyed cliché. The use of the cliché is so constant in her writing that it becomes necessary to ask why Castellanos had such a predilection for this particular form of expression.

In her perceptive article on Castellanos's language ["Rosario Castellanos: On Language"], Regina Harrison Macdonald notes that "Language serves as a codifying system for examining false institutions, antiquated prejudices and iron-clad hierarchies which have been erected in the name of Mexican culture." Because men tend to reify women it is not surprising that they speak of them in clichés. The fact that many women are not trained to think or speak responsibly contributes not only to their continued cultural passivity but also, on a linguistic plane, to their own affinity for the cliché. For those accustomed to mental passivity the cliché is a useful form of expression, for it can be appropriated without thinking. Because of the anonymity of its origin, the cliché avoids responsibility for the opinion stated, yet by dint of repetition it has acquired universal authority and acceptance. For Castellanos the articulation of concepts into language was far too serious a matter to be relegated to a passive act:

> Just the way that the precision of the stamp on a coin, which is what defines its value, is worn off by constant use, so do words become equivocal, multivalent. After too much handling and being spit upon they must undergo a purifying bath in order to recover their original condition.
>
> (pp. 24-6)

Aside from the cliché. Castellanos also calls attention to the way in which women are victimized by the use of the euphemism, which by its nature masks and displaces real meaning. Because of their lack of experience in life and in critical thought, she saw women as especially vulnerable to this kind of linguistic deception, so that what is hailed by society as a young woman's "purity" and "virginity," for example, turn out on closer inspection to mean "ignorance" and "confinement." The protagonist of **"Lección de cocina"** has learned something of this lesson of shifting meanings; musing on her lack of physical coordination she observes, "Now it's called clumsiness; before [we got married] it was called innocence and you loved it."

Language as a tool of domination is a frequent topic in her writing. Castellanos was raised in rural Chiapas, near the Guatemalan border, and knew firsthand that the Spanish language had long been used as a tool to keep the Indian and the mestizo in a state of subjection; in her opinion, it had been utilized equally effectively with respect to the female sector of Mexican society. In her campaign to make women linguistically aware, Castellanos does not limit herself to questions of vocabulary and meaning but also points out the power of structural aspects of language to influence thought patterns and attitudes. The suggestive power of passive grammatical constructions is a good example hereof. . . . The character of Eve, as presented in **El eterno femenino,** . . . rebels against the use of the passive construction. When a worried Adam asks her, "Who put those ideas in your head?," she replies tartly, "Ideas are not put in heads; they come out of heads." In Castellanos's case the rejection of the passive—in both grammatical and behavioral terms—is much more than a personal linguistic peeve: it is a cornerstone of her feminist ethic. (pp. 26-7)

The affirmation of an active, conscious role in life, especially for women, is thus inseparably linked to Rosario Castellanos's concept of humor. From her close association with both women and the Indian population of her native Chiapas she understood the pernicious psychological damage to people who are permanently marginalized and silenced. As Freud had observed, wit unleashes immediate psychic energy, and Castellanos, too, conceived of humor as "the demand for an immediate physical response." Humor as immediate stimulus is therefore a first stage in combatting physical as well as mental passivity. Longer-term strategies involved making patent to Mexican women the absurdity and injustice of widely accepted cultural beliefs and institutions which continued to imprison them. Castellanos, who often made use of mirror imagery in her writing, also applied it to the function of humor as a means to make these absurdities more evident:

"Sometimes it's good to go into the fun house and to see our image reflected in mirrors which distort it." By establishing distance between herself and the institutions of which she is critical, laughter was for her especially useful for keeping a balanced perspective: "Only that person is able to laugh who has been able to safeguard a lightness of spirit because he [sic] has not been tied to any dogma, who has been able to preserve freedom of judgment. . . . " An indispensable ingredient of Castellanos's humor is irony, precisely because "the grain of salt of irony . . . [is] distrust" and therefore "irony adds a grain more of freedom." For women to learn to distrust both appearances and verbal messages was essential in the battle to achieve authentic selfhood. (pp. 27-8)

But in the final analysis self-discovery alone is not sufficient: "It is not enough . . . to discover what we are. We have to invent ourselves." In this process of self-creation, humor is again indispensable: "We are agreed on one point: to form our conscience, to awaken the critical spirit, to defend it, to spread it. Not to accept any dogma until we see if it is able to withstand a good joke."

This brief analysis of the function of humor in some of Rosario Castellanos's works offers convincing evidence that laughter was an indispensable part of her feminist stance precisely because it was an extremely serious matter. And whereas she repeatedly stressed the ability of laughter to provide distance, in her role as narrator Castellanos never adopted a peripheral position with respect to her reader. She consistently shared in the painful process of battling for self-affirmation—at considerable personal cost. (p. 28)

[Castellanos'] gift turned out to be her humor, by means of which she probed, questioned, and exposed to view the absurd myths and social inequalities endemic to women's roles in Mexico. In this process she was unafraid to make public testimony of her own fears and foibles, which not only attracted the sympathy and loyalty of her readers but gave other women the encouragement to strive for a sense of self. (p. 29)

> *Nina M. Scott, "Rosario Castellanos: Demythification through Laughter," in* Humor, *Vol. 2, No. 1, 1989, pp. 19-30.*

Suzanne Ruta

Castellanos was spared a destiny of "marriage and death" by the land-reform program of President Lázaro Cárdenas. When her parents' *finca* was expropriated in 1941, the family moved to Mexico City, where they lived in shabby gentility and slow decline. But for Rosario, Mexico City was liberation. She studied philosophy at the National University, moved in a circle of promising writers later known as the Generation of 1950, went off to Spain for a year, and then, influenced by her reading of Simone Weil, returned to Chiapas to work among the Indians. For two years she traveled the back country with an indigenous language puppet theater, writing educational scripts in collaboration with a group of young Indian men. Education for Indian women would have to wait a generation at least, as Castellanos recounts in a heart-breaking essay, **"Incident at Yalentay,"** in which a Mayan village elder refuses to let his daughter go off to the town school, but offers to sell her to the teachers for a few thousand pesos.

The return to Chiapas gave Castellanos a chance to review her childhood through the appalled eyes of an adult. The result of this newborn vision was a southern Gothic first novel, *Balún-Canán (The Nine Guardians,* 1957), which evokes, in a manner sometimes reminiscent of the young Truman Capote, Castellanos's early years in the kitchen with her family's Indian servants. Her second novel, *Oficio de Tinieblas (Rite of Darkness,* 1962), which is a somber account of a fictional Indian rebellion set in the early '40s, foreshadows recent cycles of revolt and repression in Central America. The novel begins with the rape of an Indian girl by a wealthy rancher with half an hour to kill. Through a series of interwoven subplots, Castellanos shows the machinations of a hateful rural oligarchy. The subject is as up to date, alas, as the latest Amnesty International report from Chiapas.

[A] good sampling of Castellanos's output—eight volumes of poetry, three books of stories, two novels, plays, and numerous essays—is now available in [*A Rosario Castellanos Reader: An Anthology of Her Poetry, Short Fiction, Essays, and Journals,* edited by Maureen Ahern] and in Magda Bogin's bilingual edition of selected poems [*The Selected Poems of Rosario Castellanos*]. *The Reader* gives a better account of Castellanos's public career, the Bogin translations of her private moments of doubt.

Castellanos can sometimes sound earthbound, especially when she writes as a guilty observer. Her sociological agenda vis à vis her Indian brethren weighs down her first collection of stories, *Ciudad Real,* set in the gloomy Chiapas highlands. *The Reader* offers one example, **"The Eagle,"** the tale of a ne'er-do-well mestizo who invents a lucrative scheme to exploit the superstitions of an Indian village.

When, however, Castellanos writes about her own great leap from the provinces to Mexico City, she's quite wonderful. The heroine of the story **"Fleeting Friendships"** is a tropical version of Chekhov's Darling, ready to embrace and adore any man life sends her way. This is one of Castellanos's most original feminist creations: instead of the familiar long-suffering Mexican woman, *la Llorona,* she gives us a heroine who slips blithely through life barely touched by all the fuss her macho menfolk are kicking up. But she pays a price: she is so elusive that in the end she vanishes without a trace and the narrator must grab a pen in order to reinvent her in a story full of deadpan lines— "Gertrudis began to get bored the moment they took the corpse away"—and Southern gothic atmosphere. . . .

In **"Three Knots in the Net"** Castellanos flays her parents alive. She shows us a loveless couple, each hoarding bitter secrets, eking out a déclassé life in post-Cárdenas Mexico City. She puts herself into the picture as a daughter who

strangles birds and skins live lizards with the same cruel pleasure of the writer dissecting her own flesh and blood: "She also took pleasure in stripping lizards of their green skin covering. Beneath the fat and roughness appeared a whitish membrane almost transparent enough to observe the violent palpitations of its viscera."

By the mid-'60s, Castellanos had had her fling with the two traditional subjects in Mexican novels—provincial life and the revolution—and by then the hallowed topics were beginning to lose their appeal. (p. 33)

By the '70s Castellanos had begun to write, often outrageously, on feminist themes. *The Eternal Feminine* not only makes light of sacred moments in Mexican history, it mocks such macho shibboleths as the cult of virginity and the division of womankind into saints and whores. A newly deflowered bride, still in her blood-stained wedding gown, is interrogated by her husband. "Did you like it?" She knows just how to reply. "Like it? Me? A decent girl? Who do you take me for?" In **"The Cooking Lesson"** one of Castellanos's last stories, the sight of a raw steak reminds of bride of her Acapulco honeymoon and the terrible sunburn she had. Her husband's back was sunburned too, but at night he got to lie on top of her in comfort, while she lay beneath him in pain, thinking, like the Aztec emperor Cuauhtémoc under Spanish torture in 1521, "My bed is not made of roses." If, as Octavio Paz has written, Mexican history began with a rape, so, as Castellanos sees it, does every Mexican marriage. The sardonic wit Castellanos musters on behalf of her sex in her later work reveals a woman in confident middle age, at peace with her status as renegade daughter, divorcée, and—uncomfortable anomaly in Mexican history—"a woman who knows Latin."

But the peace was hard won. The pain of a late marriage, an early divorce, and two miscarriages is felt in the poems. . . . Death and solitude prevail. The solitude of the mystic, precondition for religious ecstasy. The solitude of the woman whose lover has gone, or worse yet, wishes he would go away. The solitude of the woman intellectual.

The long poems of religious ecstasy (**"Joyful Mystery,"** **"The Splendor of Being"**) are hard to embrace. They lack the confessional detail, the revelation of ideas in things. Instead, things—birds, bees, branches, streams—are emblems for ideas and mental states. This is early Castellanos, still swayed by multiple influences: St. John of the Cross, St.-John Perse, Gabriela Mistral, Claudel.

Her later poetry is more original and direct both in Spanish and English. She had learned to loose the satiric verve of her native south against a broad range of targets. Her last poems are irreverent, chatty, personal, and not a bit plaintive. **"Meditation on the Threshold"** recalls Villon's catalogue, but Castellanos turns her back respectfully, on the *Dames du Temps Jodis.* The specific weight of their names and histories, presented in iconographic detail, contrasts with the emptiness of the last lines. The past is rich in detail and in suffering. The future is hopeful but a blank. (pp. 33-4)

Suzanne Ruta, "Adios, Machismo," in VLS, No. 75, June, 1989, pp. 33-4.

Dan Bellm

Mujer que sabe latín, goes an old Mexican saying, *ni tiene marido ni tiene buen fin*: A woman who knows Latin will find no husband and come to no good. Few Mexican women have so thoroughly spurned the warning as Rosario Castellanos, a poet, novelist and feminist pioneer who dissected her culture and disclosed her own heart with unsparing candor. Her influence has been immense. She insisted on making words her work—a refuge from life, a magnet for its pain, an act of liberation—and in the end she had shown the way, for the first time since Sor Juana in the seventeenth century, for other Mexican women to do the same. Predictably, male critics judged her work sentimental, bitter, domestic, *feminine.* . . .

Castellanos's poetry remains her most illustrious gift—vivid and startling, rooted in solitude and death but abundant with life. . . .

Among five books of fiction, Castellanos's great achievement was her poignant first novel, *Balún-Canán,* translated into English and published in 1960 . . . as *The Nine Guardians.* . . . *The Nine Guardians* chronicles an Indian uprising in the time of Cárdenas and the death of a favored son in a family much like Castellanos's own. The novel begins and ends with her Indian *nana,* her black dove, who bequeathed her not only love but words, stories, the memory-box of a vanishing culture. . . . (p. 891)

The four short stories and one novella in the *Rosario Castellanos Reader* [edited by Maureen Ahern] are lesser works, but still of great interest. In **"Three Knots in the Net,"** a small-town girl grows up in the shadow of bitter, quarreling parents, convinced she does not exist, entertaining herself by "twisting the necks of birds" and "stripping lizards of their green skin." In **"Fleeting Friendships,"** the bored adolescent Gertrudis runs away with the first drifter who walks into her parents' store—but takes her baby sister along. Castellanos eventually felt she had exhausted "that vein of archaic provincial life," and the late story **"The Cooking Lesson"** ventured into a new style of wicked satire: A young newlywed delivers a monologue on marriage while broiling to death her first home-cooked meal for her husband, a piece of frozen meat akin to her own body, "red, as if it were just about to start bleeding."

In poetry, too, Castellanos's sense of solitude, her own and other women's, led to the dramatic monologue form, a public voice brutally frank about private pain, a voice stripped bare. Her disastrous marriage at 32, her two miscarriages, the birth of her son Gabriel, her divorce, an exhilarating sense late in life of "becoming what one is," all became the stuff of poetry:

> They have pierced my nocturnal water, my original
> silences, the first forms
> of life, the struggle,

> the broken membrane, the horror and
> the blood.
> And I, who have been a net spread in
> the deep,
> return to the surface without a fish.

Like **"The Cooking Lesson,"** a few of her poetic monologues tapped a new vein of domestic humor. . . . But others, such as **"Home Economics,"** are rather predictable tracts, and the late **"Self Portrait"** is annoyingly self-mocking: "I am more or less ugly. . . . I am mediocre. . . . I would be happy, if I knew how."

In a critique of her own work, included in her essay collection *Mujer que sabe latín,* Castellanos wrote, "The mechanics of my relationships with other beings . . . are neither sublime nor tragic. Perhaps, a bit ridiculous. We have to laugh. Because laughter, we already know, is the first evidence of freedom." The nearly unstageable but sporadically brilliant farce she wrote in the last year of her life—*The Eternal Feminine,* included in Ahern's *Reader*—is as close as Castellanos came to mastering this freedom to laugh. Her last three years, spent in Israel with her son, were among her happiest; if not for an absurd, untimely death by electrocution at 49, she might have charted a bold and joyful new direction. The voice she *did* master was more stoic and contemplative—a woman alone in a numinous natural world, alone with death. Castellanos herself seems to have devalued her earlier accomplishments; new freedom did not necessarily make for better poetry. (pp. 891-92)

Dan Bellm, "A Woman Who Knew Latin," in The Nation, New York, Vol. 248, No. 25, July 26, 1989, pp. 891-93.

FURTHER READING

Ahern, Maureen and Vásquez, Mary Seale, eds. *Homenaje a Rosario Castellanos.* Valencia: Albatros Hispanófila Ediciones, 1980, 174 p.
  Bilingual collection of criticism on Castellanos's essays, poetry, drama, and fiction.

Fox-Lockert, Lucía. *Women Novelists in Spain and Spanish America.* Metuchen, N.J.: The Scarecrow Press, Inc., 1979, 347 p.
  Detailed exposition of social issues presented in *Balún-Canán.*

Lindstrom, Naomi. "Women's Expression and Narative Technique in Rosario Castellanos's *In Darkness.*" *Modern Language Studies* 13 (Summer 1983): 71-9.
  Examines the ways Castellanos "explores the problems of women's expression through the writing in her novel *Oficio de tinieblas.*"

Schlau, Stacey. "Conformity and Resistance to Enclosure: Female Voices in Rosario Castellanos' *Oficio de tinieblas.*"

Latin American Literary Review XII, No. 24 (Spring-Summer 1984): 45-57.

    Examines female characters in *Oficio de tinieblas* and the "cultural norms which distort their voices or silence them all together."

Stoll, A. K. " 'Arthur Smith salva su alma': Rosario Castellanos and Social Protest." *Crítica Hispánica* VII, No. 2 (1985): 141-47.

    Examines "Arthur Smith salva su alma" as a story of social protest expressed through mythic structures.

Lucille Clifton

1936-

(Born Lucille Sayles) American poet and author of children's books.

A prolific author whose works frequently concern the well-being of black families and youth, Clifton is highly praised for her strong affirmation of African-American culture. She writes in a style that echoes black speech and music. Although Clifton has been named Poet Laureate of Maryland, has been nominated for the Pulitzer Prize, and has won two grants from the National Endowment for the Arts, critics consistently assert that her work has not received the level of popular and critical attention it deserves. Describing Clifton's poetry, Marilyn Hacker stated: "Clifton mythologizes herself: that is, she illuminates her surroundings and history from within in a way that casts light on much beyond. She does this with a penetrating brevity in a verse that mirrors speech as a Japanese ink drawing mirrors a mountain."

Clifton was born in Depew, New York, where her father worked in the steel mills and her mother in a laundry. In a 1976 interview she described her family as "[poor, but] not downtrodden. We didn't have much money, but we had a lot of love." Although neither of Clifton's parents finished elementary school, they both valued literature, and her mother wrote poems that she read to her four children. "A lot of feelings went into her poetry," Clifton stated. "From Mama I knew one could write as a way to express oneself." Clifton's father often told stories about his ancestors, particularly his grandmother Caroline, who was abducted at a young age from her home in the Dahomey Republic of West Africa and brought to New Orleans as a slave. In Clifton's autobiography, *Generations*, "Ca'line" appears as a woman of almost mythical endurance and courage, reflecting the author's characteristic portrayal of women as strong and deeply nurturing. The memoir was lauded for its celebration of a black family's survival through great hardships. Within the work Clifton asserts: "Things don't fall apart. Things hold. Lines connect in thin ways that last and last, and lines become generations made out of pictures and words just kept."

In 1953 Clifton attended Howard University in Washington, D. C., where she associated with such writers as LeRoi Jones (Amiri Baraka), A. B. Spellman, Owen Dodson, and Sterling A. Brown. A drama major, she acted in the first performance of James Baldwin's *The Amen Corner*. Clifton left Howard after two years to attend Fredonia State Teachers College, where she read and performed plays with a small group of black intellectuals and further developed her poetic voice, experimenting with sparse punctuation and a lyricism that reflects speech patterns. Clifton described her writing style: "I use a simple language. I have never believed that for anything to be valid or true or intellectual or 'deep' it had to first be complex. . . . I am not interested if anyone knows wheth-

er or not I am familiar with big words, I am interested in trying to render big ideas in a simple way. I am interested in being understood not admired." In 1969, she made her first submission of poems to Robert Hayden, a respected black poet, resulting in her receipt of the YW-YMHA Poetry Center Discovery Award—an event that was followed by the publication of her first poetry collection, *Good Times*. The work was cited by the *New York Times* as one of the best books of the year. Since then, Clifton has been a prolific poet and children's author, and she credits her six children with inspiring much of her work: "They keep you aware of life. And you have to stay aware of life, keep growing to write."

In *Good Times* Clifton focuses on difficulties and poverty in urban life while also evoking a sense of strength and celebration in the face of adversity: "My daddy has paid the rent / and the insurance man is gone / and the lights is back on . . . / and they is good times. . . ." Critics emphasized the collection's portraits of dignity and strength in the face of suffering and praised its rejection of negative sociological stereotypes. The poem "in the inner city," for example, juxtaposes affection for one's home with the reality of an urban wasteland made up of "houses straight as

/ dead men." The collection stresses the importance of family and characterizes black males as integral family members, countering a tendency of some contemporary writers to depict them as conspicuously absent from domestic responsibilities. Haki Madhubuti asserted: "At the base of [Clifton's] work is concern for the Black family, especially the destruction of its youth. Her eye is for the uniqueness of our people, always concentrating on the small strengths that have allowed us to survive the horrors of Western life."

Some critics have associated Clifton with the Black Arts Movement of the 1960s and 1970s, which promoted African-American arts as means to overcome racial oppression. Many of Clifton's poems castigate racist attitudes: "pity this poor animal / who has never gone beyond / the ape herds gathered around the fires / of Europe . . . / his mind shivers against the rocks / afraid of the dark. . . ." Clifton's poetry, as well as her juvenile literature, is recognized for its cultivation of identity and pride through awareness of black history. Her second volume of verse, *Good News About the Earth,* contains several poems dedicated to social activists, including Malcolm X, Eldridge Cleaver, Bobby Seale, and Angela Davis. Clifton's political conscience is also revealed in the collection, *Next: New Poems,* which laments broken promises in the political poems "at gettysburg," "at nagasaki," and "at jonestown."

Clifton frequently explores African-American experience from a female perspective, presenting women who are simultaneously fierce, heroic, and loving. For example, the "Kali Poems" trilogy of *An Ordinary Woman* evokes a metaphysical and forceful image of feminity through an aboriginal Indian goddess associated with blood, violence, and murder. Andrea Benton Rushing observed that in the "Kali Poems," Clifton "frees herself from the feminist tendency to see women as hapless victims and explores the psychic tensions of an introspective modern woman negotiating the dramatic changes in contemporary attitudes about culture, race and gender at the same time that she juggles the roles of daughter, sister, artist, writer, and mother." Clifton's following collection, *Two-Headed Woman,* reveals a more personal exploration of womanhood. Many of the poems are written in a confidential tone, focusing on Clifton's changing relationship with her children as they grow up, and the emotional experience of her husband's death.

A number of reviewers have noted Christian tenets in Clifton's poetry, particularly a faith in the deliverance of an oppressed people. Biblical imagery appears in much of her work; for example, the Virgin Mary is frequently depicted as an ordinary woman chosen for a miraculous experience. Written in a Caribbean dialect, the poem "holy night" portrays Mary as an uneducated young girl: "joseph, i afraid of stars, / their brilliant seeing. / so many eyes, such light. . . . " Critics have consistently linked Clifton's Christian optimism with her strong belief in the power of human will. According to Greg Kuzma, "[Clifton's poems reveal] an implicit conviction that there is evil in the world because people allow it, and that life would be infinitely

better, even perfect, could we but forgive each other and truly love."

(See also *CLC,* Vol. 19; *Contemporary Authors,* Vols. 49-52, rev. ed.; *Contemporary Authors New Revision Series,* Vol. 24; *Children's Literature Review,* Vol. 5; *Dictionary of Literary Biography,* Vols. 5, 41; *Black Writers;* and *Something about the Author,* Vol. 20.)

PRINCIPAL WORKS

POETRY

Good Times: Poems   1969
Good News About the Earth: New Poems   1972
An Ordinary Woman   1974
Two-Headed Woman   1980
Good Woman: Poems and a Memoir, 1969-1980   1987
Next: New Poems   1987

JUVENILE FICTION

The Black BCs   1970
Some of the Days of Everett Anderson   1970
Everett Anderson's Christmas Coming   1971
All Us Come Cross the Water   1973
The Boy Who Didn't Believe in Spring   1973
Don't You Remember?   1973
Good, Says Jerome   1973
Everett Anderson's Year   1974
The Times They Used to Be   1974
My Brother Fine with Me   1975
Everett Anderson's Friend   1976
Three Wishes   1976
Amifika   1977
Everett Anderson's 1 2 3   1977
Everett Anderson's Nine Month Long   1978
The Lucky Stone   1979
My Friend Jacob   1980
Sonora Beautiful   1981
Everett Anderson's Goodbye   1983

OTHER

Generations: a Memoir   (autobiography)   1976

Erica Jong

I began dog-earing pages of poems that struck me in Lucille Clifton's *Good News About The Earth,* and after a while, there were so many that the book seemed twice as fat as it was to start with. Listen:

"the lost baby poem"

the time i dropped your almost body down
down to meet the waters under the city
and run one with the sewage to the sea
what did i know about waters rushing back
what did i know about drowning
or being drowned
you would have been born into winter
in the year of the disconnected gas

and no car we would have made the thin
walk over Genesee hill into the Canada wind
to watch you slip like ice into strangers' hands
you would have fallen naked as snow into winter
if you were here i could tell you these
and some other things
if i am ever less than a mountain
for your definite brothers and sisters
let the rivers pour over my head
let the sea take me for a spiller
of seas let black men call me stranger
always for your never named sake

That last line has Lucille Clifton's unique cadence: the pause after the first word, and the economy of the rest of the line. Everybody talks about aural values in poetry but nobody does anything about them—except Lucille Clifton (and a few others). Everyone talks about breath units and breath pauses—but the truth is that few poets know how to achieve them. This poet knows. The spaces in her poems are not just typographical blanks.

Listen again:

Wise: having the ability to perceive and
            adopt the best means for accomplish-
      ing an end.

all the best minds
come into wisdom early.
nothing anybody can say
is profound as
no money no wine.
all the wise men
on the corner.

Lucille Clifton writes about what it means to be a black woman who grew up in the 1940s hating her own blackness, wearing "bleaching cream to bed," "Trying to be white"—and who finally came of age in the sixties to discover an affirmation of selfhood in being black. For the sensitivity and artfulness with which she portrays this coming of age, she reminds me a little of Toni Morrison, the remarkable author of *The Bluest Eye*. The story Clifton and Morrison tell is the story of what it means for a soul to discover its oppression and finally its own identity, and, in a way, it is not so different from the story Eleanor Ross Taylor tells [in *Welcome Eumenides*] when she evokes the southern woman oppressed by her wifehood and her whiteness.

There is a particular sort of movement rhetoric—it could belong either to the black movement or to the woman's movement—which subverts the ambiguity of literature. Lucille Clifton avoids it much of the time. It must be a difficult thing to be a black writer in an age which demands political polarization of everyone—especially those who belong to oppressed groups. At times that demand for ideological clarification must interfere with a writer's freedom to be herself in all her complex selfhood. Lucille Clifton's definition of blackness is an organic part of her consciousness and therefore rightly pervades her work, but when she takes to self-conscious black myth-making, she loses the subtlety which is her greatest strength. For example, in **"after Kent State"**:

only to keep

his little fear
he kills his cities
and his trees
even his children oh
people
white ways are
the ways of death
come into the
Black
and live

I find the simple equation White = Death, Black = Life, unworthy of the more difficult truths poetry has to offer. The tendency of all movement poetry to divide the world into Manichean opposites: black versus white, female versus male, freak versus pig—is objectionable whether it comes from the left or the right, the oppressed or the oppressor. Poetry has more to tell us than that.

Whatever disappointments I have with **Good News about the Earth** spring mostly from that. Too many poems are Agit-prop, not art. Too much Socialist Realism. On second reading, when the shock of Lucille Clifton's perfect lines has been absorbed, some of the poems seem to collapse. The poems about the Panthers, Malcolm X, Eldridge Cleaver, Bobby Seale, Angela Davis, Richard Penniman are artfully written, but they are not much more durable than the headlines which inspired them. They have practically no substance in and of themselves and rely principally upon the gut response of the reader. There is a place for writing like this—both as entertainment and as inspiration. Certainly it moves people, but then so do the most banal popular songs and so do angry slogans.

The question of politics and literature is ancient, and I do not pretend to be able to solve it here. I value Clifton and other black writers for reinterpreting black history, and thus reinterpreting American history, for daring to deal with their own internal racism and self-hatred, but I often feel they do not press their self-knowledge far enough. Surely there is *more* to say about the fantastic history of black/white relations in America (and the world over) than "White ways are the ways of death." A writer is supposed to be first of all a *knower* and a *self-knower*. If a poem contains no more *knowing* than an editorial, something is missing.

I won't speak for other writers, but Clifton doesn't lack subtlety. Or sensitivity. Her first book and many of the poems in this book show an extraordinary subtlety. A poet whose favorite theme is reverence for life, reverence for birth and rebirth, she is capable, if anyone is, of bearing witness to the maelstrom of African-American experience in all its horror. Why then does she content herself with lines like,

I grieve my whiteful ways?

Not that it isn't a skillful line, but the logic is so pat, so *closed,* so unprobing. I would like to see a black poetry which truly mirrors the insanity, blood thirstiness, and inconsistencies of black/white experience. Whites don't dare to write it, both for fear of being called patronizing, and because they only know part of the story. But why don't blacks write it? Why do they content themselves with easy slogans which are simply the reverse of easy white slogans? Why do they imitate the very things they hate the oppressor for? I am waiting for the black poet who will answer that question once and for all. Lucille Clifton could well be that poet. I only wish she would probe deeper and push harder. (pp. 84-8)

Erica Jong, "Three Sisters," in Parnassus: Poetry in Review, *Vol. 1, No. 1, 1972, pp. 77-88.*

Harriet Jackson Scarupa

Browsing through a volume of Lucille Clifton's poems or reading one of her children's books to my son always makes me feel good; good to be black, good to be a woman, good to be alive. **Generations,** her newest book and first prose work for adults, makes me feel like joining with her in a song of celebration to family and heritage and survival.

Still, something about Lucille Clifton irritated me. It was the title of her respected poetry collection, **An Ordinary Woman,** and what that title seemed to imply. It bothered me that this woman whose latest book has been called a "lyrical rapture" in the *New York Times Book Review,* who has written three other well-received books of poetry and a dozen children's books, and who has acquired a good handful of literary awards—all within the last seven years—persisted in calling herself "ordinary." What, I wondered, did that make all of us—me, for instance—with so many lesser accomplishments? So when I went to see Lucille Clifton, I think I expected to meet some kind of superwoman, despite all her claims to the contrary.

It was a weekday evening when I dropped by the big, rambling old house she shares with her husband Fred, an administrator for community development, and their six children in a predominantly black, middle-income Baltimore neighborhood. Lucille Clifton settled back on a worn, comfortable loveseat in her large living room. She is a tall, soft-spoken woman with a smooth round face set off by a gray-speckled Afro.

"One of the things I was saying in the title is that the extraordinary woman *is* the ordinary one," she explains. "Take the woman with eight kids and a small income, who manages to feed them, keep sane, even have fun. It's very ordinary to do what a woman can do." As for herself, she adds, "It isn't that hard to have six kids. The things you care about you can do."

Lucille Sayles Clifton was born 40 years ago in Depew, New York, a little town outside Buffalo. (*I entered the earth in a woman jar—* from **Generations.**) Her father worked in the steel mills; her mother, in a laundry. There were four children in the family. "We were poor. But not downtrodden. We didn't have much money, but we had a lot of love."

Her father would tell her of the history of his family in this country, starting with Caroline, "born among the Dahomey people in 1822," who walked from New Orleans to Virginia when she was eight years old. And he would repeat Caroline's legacy, passed down through the years—through slavery and struggle and survival: *Get what you want, you from Dahomey women* (from **Generations**).

Although neither parent was graduated from elementary school, both valued books. "And they both loved to read about all kinds of things," she remembers. "For instance, China, for some strange reason. I saw reading as a natural part of life and grew up loving books and words. How I do love words!"

Her mother loved words too and set them down in poems—in straight iambic pentameter—which she read to her children. "My mother was a rather sad person," she recalls now. "She had epilepsy and died, too young, at forty-four. A lot of feelings went into her poetry. From Mama I knew one could write as a way to express oneself." (*Oh she made magic, she was a magic woman, my Mama. She was not wise in the world but she had magic wisdom*—from **Generations.**)

In 1953, Lucille Sayles went to Howard University on a full scholarship. It was her first time away from home, and she felt homesick and a little out of place in the cosmopolitan Howard world. "I went to college with my clothes in my grandmother's wedding trunk held together with rope, and here were all these kids with matching luggage." But it was a good time for a budding writer to be at Howard—people like LeRoi Jones (now Amiri Baraka), A. B. Spellman, Owen Dodson, and Sterling Brown were there, writing and reading their works. She gravitated toward them and majored in drama, playing in the first performance of James Baldwin's *The Amen Corner.*

She left Howard after two years ("I forgot to study," she says wryly). Besides, as she told her disappointed father: *I don't need that stuff [college]. I'm going to write poems. I can do what I want to do. I'm from Dahomey women!* (from **Generations**). While attending Fredonia State Teachers College near Buffalo, she joined a small group of black intellectuals who got together to read plays and perform them wherever they could. One member of the group was the novelist Ishmael Reed. Another was Fred Clifton, then teaching philosophy at the University of Buffalo. In 1958, Fred and Lucille were married.

"It was in Buffalo that I began finding my own voice as a writer," Lucille Clifton recalls. "But I still never thought about publishing. What I was writing was not like the poems I'd been reading." But Ishmael Reed showed some of her poems to Langston Hughes, who selected a few for the anthology, *Poetry of the Negro, 1746-1970.* In 1969, she sent poems to Robert Hayden, a respected black poet then teaching at Fisk University, who took them to Carolyn Kizer, another well-known poet. She, in turn, sent them along to the YW-YMHA Poetry Center in New York City. That year Lucille Clifton received the prestigious Discovery Award from the Poetry Center, given annually to promising but undiscovered poets, and Random House published her first book, **Good Times.** The New York Times cited it as one of the 10 best books of the year. Since then, her books have flowed with regularity.

These days Clifton writes either on the dining room table or on a cluttered desk in a sunlit room at the back of the house. "I write in spurts," she says. "I'm completely undisciplined. I never do all the things you're supposed to, like write at a set time every day. And I can't write if it's quiet." So she sits in front of her electric typewriter, having worked out a lot of things in her head beforehand, with Aretha on the stereo if she's in the mood, and the children wandering in and out. Every time she makes a mistake, even an innocent typing error, she dramatically rips paper from the typewriter. "One of the kids says something like, 'Look at all the paper mama's wasting.' I yell, 'How can I do anything with you kids? . . . ' " The whole scene brings to mind her words from *Good Times:*

> children
> when they ask you
> why is your mama so funny
> say
> she is a poet
> she don't have no sense

"They get on your nerves sometimes," Clifton says of her children, her smile, almost, but not quite, betraying her words. "It's important for my children to know there are some things I need to do for myself, for them to know I'm a woman who's thinking things, that I have days when I get tired of them. But they actually help with my writing, especially the children's books." As an example, she cites the time one of her sons threatened to run away from home—and got as far as the bottom step. She used the experience in *My Brother Fine with Me.* And when her children referred to Africa as "the dark continent," she included many positive images about Africa in the book *The Black BC's* to counteract that stereotype.

But Clifton's children have helped her as a writer in a larger way than by suggesting specific ideas for stories. As she puts it, "They keep you aware of life. And you have to stay aware of life, keep growing to write." And, she adds ironically, "They also keep me sane." She continues: "I did this reading at the Library of Congress once. It was a great honor. Next day, I was ironing and I said, 'What is this great *poet* doing ironing?' The kids laughed, said, 'Are you crazy?' and I came back to earth."

Clifton gets ideas "by staying awake to things. Sometimes something hits me, 'That's it.' It's not like I really think about it. It's more intuitive. You just know when something will poem up."

When Clifton began to meet many a child with an African name, she decided to focus on one in *All Us Come Cross the Water.* In the story, a boy named Ujamaa (Unity) worries that he can't pinpoint where his ancestors come from in Africa. A friend at the Panther bookstore helps him see that black Americans have roots in all African countries; *All us crossed the water. We one people, Ujamaa. Boy got that name oughta know that.*

All Lucille Clifton's works have a lot to say about blackness and black pride, as in the poem **"after Kent State"** from *Good News About the Earth:*

> . . . oh
> people
> white ways are
> the way of death
> come into the
> Black
> and live.

Some critics reading such lines have concluded that Clifton hates whites. She considers this a misreading. When she equates whiteness with death, blackness with life, she says: "What I'm talking about is a certain kind of white arrogance—and not all white people have it—that is not good. I think airs of superiority are very dangerous. I believe in justice. I try not to be about hatred."

Generations is a virtual celebration of the survival of the black family. Clifton looks back at her parents and her father's ancestors, at their struggles and their joys, and she draws strength:

> And I could tell you about things we been through, some awful ones, some wonderful, but I know that the things that make us are more than that, our lives are more than the days in them, our lives are our line and we go on. I type that and I swear I can see Ca'line standing in the green of Virginia, in the green of Afrika, and I swear she makes no sound but she nods her head and smiles.

Clifton also writes about being a woman, but in many ways she's on a different wavelength from the Women's Movement. "I believe the smartest one in the family should be deferred to, and in most cases my husband is the smartest one. Yet he's never tried to keep me from being myself.

"The Movement is helpful to some women," Clifton acknowledges. "It's good for them to realize they can be something or do something and not have to follow some prescribed role." But as a black woman, with a long history behind her, she feels she has some good reasons to be wary. In *An Ordinary Woman,* she writes about them in the poem **"To Ms. Ann"**:

> i will have to forget
> your face
> when you watched me breaking
> in the fields,
> missing my children . . .
> and you never called me sister
> then, you never called me sister
> and it has only been forever and
> i will have to forget your face.

Clifton also faults the Movement—and too many people today—with not paying enough attention to love. "When people love each other, they'll accept a lot of things they wouldn't otherwise. They can deal with things they couldn't deal with otherwise. It has to do with the nature of love."

One of her early poems in *Good Times* is about what concerns her most—as a woman, as a writer—and is also her favorite:

> Here we are
> running with the weeds
> colors exaggerated
> pistils wild.
> embarrassing the calm family flowers
> Oh
> here we are
> flourishing for the field
> and the name of the place

is Love.

(pp. 118, 120, 123)

*Harriet Jackson Scarupa, "Lucille Clifton:
Making the World 'Poem-Up'," in* Ms., *Vol.
V, No. 4, October, 1976, pp. 118, 120, 123.*

Joyce Johnson

[Clifton's] first book of poetry, *Good Times,* published in
1969, was selected as one of the ten best books of the year
by the *New York Times,* and her latest, ***Two-Headed
Woman,*** published in 1980, was a Pulitzer Prize nominee
and won the Juniper Prize, an award presented annually
by the University of Massachusetts Press. In 1969, she received both the YM—YWHA Poetry Center Discovery
Award and a grant from the National Endowment for the
Arts. Clifton has contributed to American Poetry Review
and several other poetry magazines; her work has been anthologized in many books, including Louis Simpson's *Introduction to Poetry* and Dudley Randall's *The Black
Poets.* Clifton enjoys the distinction of being Poet Laureate
of Maryland.

Recently, responding to the question, "Why do you
write?" Clifton answered, "I write to celebrate life." This
personal sense of celebration, this affirmation of black life,
is apparent in much of her work. Her vision is not marred
by sentimentality, for she sees all too clearly the bitterness
and pain which are the offspring of racism; however, she
consciously elects to accentuate Black life positively,
thereby shaping—poetically—the reality of Black people
through emphasis on their strength and beauty.

Clifton's poems are generally brief, delicate and incisive.
Often they reach pointed conclusions which come to the
reader as re-reactions. Her short lines are sinewy and lithe;
her diction, plain; her poetry, lean, hard, and graceful.
The leanness of her poetry depends, in part, on her use of
what Stephen Henderson calls "mascon" images, a phrase
he uses to mean Afro-American archetypes that represent
a "massive concentration of black experiential energy."
Mascons are not always images per se; often they are simply "verbal expressions which evoke a powerful response
in the [reader] because of their direct relationship to concepts and events in the collective experience."

The poem **"in the inner city"** employs the euphemism for
what was once referred to as the "ghetto" or "slum"—
words which conjure up negative images of negative people living on the edge, separated from the rest of society
by some unclear, unnamed criteria:

> in the inner city
> or
> like we call it
> home
> we think about uptown
> and the silent nights
> and the houses straight as
> dead men
> and the pastel lights
> and we hang on to our no place
> happy to be alive
> and in the inner city

> or
> like we call it
> home

Clifton makes the clear distinction between the view from
within and the view from without. The words "inner city"
describe a place which is "home" to those who live there.
"Home," a universal term, is also a mascon image—note
the expressions "down-home," "back-home," "home-
boy," "homey," "homebase," words used by blacks which
suggest an additional dimension to the concept of warmth,
security, love and family we all associate with the word.
It lacks the negative sociological overtones which hang relentlessly to the other expression. By using "inner city"
and "home," Clifton creates contrast and tension by juxtaposing the two concepts. One invites a kind of sympathetic
head shaking resulting from the bad mouthing done by sociologists who peer in from the outside and are blinded by
their outsideness and their theories. The other is a view
shared by those inside who participate in the vitality of
their home and who recognize their good fortune to be
there. The contrast is implied rather than stated. Uptown,
the nights are silent, the houses, straight as dead men, the
lights, pastel. "Silence," denoting the absence of sound
and the lack of communication, also suggests a kind of
death, an idea which is supported by the metaphor "houses straight as dead men." The houses, like the uptown area
itself, are lifeless, cold, silent, and pale. Like the lights, the
area lacks intensity and color; it is pallid. The language is
as abstract as the community it is used to describe. Then,
with a note of irony, the speaker says "we hang on to our
no place / happy to be alive / and in the inner city."
"Alive" is the key word in this passage, for through the
artful use of understatement, the message is made clear
that the inner city is vibrant not only with colors, but also
with life.

As if to provide support for this view, the poem **"Good
times"** offers strong mascon images which the poet uses
to effectively awaken in the reader the appropriate emotional response. The emotion in this instance is jubilation
and the sense of celebration associated with the good times
that come by way of the small triumphs in the community
dwellers' battle to survive.

> My daddy has paid the rent
> and the insurance man is gone
> and the lights is back on
> and Uncle Brud has hit
> for one dollar straight
> and they is good times
> good times
> good times
> My momma has made bread
> and Grandpaw has come
> and everybody is drunk
> and dancing in the kitchen
> and singing in the kitchen
> oh these is good times
> good times
> good times
> oh children think about the
> good times

The fact that *Daddy* has paid the rent challenges by implication the notion advanced by many white sociologists

that all black fathers are conspicuously absent from their familial responsibilities. It attests to the courage of many of these fathers who, despite the power structure's efforts to destroy their image of themselves as men, continue to struggle to support and protect their families. The reference to the insurance man supports this contention. Years ago, and perhaps even today, insurance men came each week to houses in the black community to collect the fifty cents or one dollar insurance premium for the family head. Many families paid faithfully, year after year, only to collect a mere $150-200 when the policy matured, a sum which rarely covered the expenses of the funerals for which it had been planned. But in the black community, keeping the insurance paid was a number one priority, and making that weekly payment was often an accomplishment that evoked a sigh of both relief and celebration.

That Uncle Brud has "hit for one dollar straight" is a sure signal that "they is good times." The reference is to the numbers game, "policy" as it is called in some cities. Hitting the numbers is the dream many in the community hold, for it spells the end of struggle, the answer to prayers, the beginning of a new life, or so they think. Millions of the community's dollars are poured into this elusive dream, but the hope of hitting is held fast. Uncle Brud's one dollar hit assured a $500-600 return, and calls for a party. There is dancing and singing and food and family—and together, they spell good times.

The last line, "oh children think about the / good times" speaks directly to black youth whose assessment of their community is often shaped by those on the outside, those who fail to recognize the measure of good times in a culture and community they don't understand.

In **"listen children,"** the poet again offers direction to black youth:

> listen children
> keep this in the place
> you have for keeping
> always
> keep it all ways
> we have never hated black
> listen
> we have been ashamed
> hopeless tired mad
> but always
> all ways
> we loved us
> we have always loved each other
> children all ways
> pass it on

Again, Clifton alludes to the outsider's view of the black community, a view which fosters the notion of self as well as group hate. The pun or play on the words "always" and "all ways" adds to the subtle meaning of the poem, a meaning sustained throughout by repetition, and the words effectively reinforce each other. "We have always loved each other / all ways." The first, meaning for all times, and suggesting without end, forever; the second, meaning in every way, totally, entirely. The line "pass it on" alludes to and celebrates the continuity of generations, the title of one of her books and a theme which prevails in much of Clifton's work.

In **"lucy and her girls,"** this theme, though unstated, is communicated by the poet's employment of one line to serve as the end of one statement and the beginning of another. The effect creates a resonance which contributes to the musical quality of the poem and re-enforces the theme of continuity through generations.

> lucy is the ocean
> extended by
> her girls
> are the river
> fed by lucy
> is the sun
> reflected through
> her girls
> are the moon
> lighted by
> lucy
> is the history of
> her girls
> are the place where
> lucy was going

The use of ocean and sun, river and moon as metaphors for lucy and her girls, respectively, demonstrate, through traditional archetypes, the continuation of generations. Each line looks at once backward to the preceding line (and by implication to the preceding generation) and forward to the following line or the present and future generations. The former is extended and reflected through the latter. The girls, in turn, are fed and lighted by lucy, that is, just as the rivers are nourished by the ocean, they are nourished by her, and as the moon reflects the sun's light, her wisdom is reflected through them. And while lucy represents their history—their past—they represent her future and the continuation of her unfulfilled dreams and aspirations. The density of the work contributes to its overall effect and to the sense of generations building and growing stronger as the natural order of things. The rhythm, achieved through the interconnectedness of the lines, creates a celebratory tone.

In **"homage to my hair,"** Clifton harks back to an earlier poem entitled **"the Way it Was"** in which she writes of straightening her hair and "trying to be white." In this poem, she pays homage to a part of her of which she was once ashamed:

> when i feel her jump and dance
> i hear the music
> i'm talking 'bout my nappy hair!
> she is a challenge to your hand
> Black man
> she is as tasty on your tongue as good greens
> Black man
> she can touch your mind
> with her electric fingers and
> the grayer she do get, good God!
> the blacker she do be!

"Nappy hair" provides a powerful mascon image, for it has been the mainstay of an endless cycle of shame and humiliation which was psychologically debilitating, particularly for many black women. The word "hair," innocent enough in its own right, took on modifiers which for generations seemed inseparable from the word they modified. "Good" and "bad," adjectives which hung tenaciously to the word hair, not only described the texture and quality of a person's hair, but somehow were extended to measure the beauty and worth of that person as well. The change in this attitude is captured in Clifton's poem. The verbs "jump" and "dance" are appropriate, for they authentically capture the character and vitality of nappy hair; together with the word "music," they present images we readily associate with celebration, and thus, operate on two levels, as description and exultation. The diction in the last lines of the poem shifts from mainstream English to black dialect, reinforcing her recognition of and pride in her blackness.

The genesis of this celebration in Clifton's poetry seems to spring from her expressed world view. In a recent taped interview, she said that we must come to understand that "we are more than today, and our lives are more than today." She is concerned with the danger of our becoming disconnected from our distant and recent past. As a poet, Clifton sees the whole of things, for she takes the responsibility for seeing beyond the obvious. She says that it is her artistic responsibility to bring more order into the universe. She sees it as worthy of remark that we still *do* live and love and dance and party and hope, despite the long history of slavery and deprivation we have suffered. She constantly juxtaposes static images of this deprivation against animated images of great joy.

Often, our collective life, as reflected in the literature, is one of "coping" and "making do," and certainly these are elements of black life that are real; however, it is all too often the case that these are depicted as the major elements in our lives. In such a context, "celebration" is usually presented as just another way we have of "coping" with the overwhelming negativity with which Black American life is portrayed. Clifton takes us beyond this narrow and dependent notion to a concept of celebration under which the others may be subsumed. That is to say, celebration is the mainstay of our survival, and "coping" and "making do" are merely ways of getting over the obstacles to celebrating. We cope with rats and roaches, which seem to be so natural a part of our environment that they cannot be escaped; we "cope" with the absence of light when the power company cuts us off for being unable to pay the bill. We "make do" when we stuff newspaper in the spaces beneath the doors or tape it over the cracks of the windows. Celebration makes these things bearable. We do not celebrate the coming of the light or the going of the roaches, we celebrate the life that we are more fully aware of as such small annoyances are removed.

Lucille Clifton celebrates life. Not just her life, or even our life, but all of life. She celebrates its realities, its mysteries, and perhaps, most of all, she celebrates its continuity.

The last poem ["**Roots**"] expresses as well as any Lucille Clifton's view about life and that quality of it that allows us to celebrate so fully. It also says how she feels about naming that quality:

> call it our craziness even
> call it anything
> it is the life thaing in us
> that will not let us die.
> even in death's hand

> we fold the fingers up
> and call them greens and
> grow on them,
> we hum them and make music.
> call it our wildness then,
> we are lost from the field
> of flowers, we become
> a field of flowers.
> call it our craziness
> our wildness
> call it our roots,
> it is the light in us
> it is the light of us
> it is the light, call it
> whatever you have to,
> call it anything.

(pp. 70-6)

Joyce Johnson, "The Theme of Celebration in Lucille Clifton's Poetry," in Pacific Coast Philology, *Vol. XVIII, November, 1983, pp. 70-6.*

Lucille Clifton

[*The following essay, which appears in* Black Women Writers (1950-1980): A Critical Evaluation, *is Clifton's response to a questionnaire focusing on her views about her role in society and the ideology and methods behind her poetry.*]

I write the way I write because I am the kind of person that I am. My styles and my content stem from my experience. I grew up a well-loved child in a loving family and so I have always known that being very poor, which we were, had nothing to do with lovingness or familyness or character or any of that. This doesn't mean that I or we were content with whatever we had and never hoped tried worked at having more. It means that we were quite clear that what we had didn't have anything to do with what we were. We were/are quite sure that we were/are among the best of people and not having any money had nothing to do with that. Other people's opinions didn't influence us about that. We were quite sure. When I write, especially for children, I try to get that across, that being poor or whatever your circumstance, you are capable of being the best of people and that best, as a human, does not come from the outside in, it comes from the inside out.

I use a simple language. I have never believed that for anything to be valid or true or intellectual or "deep" it had to first be complex. I deliberately use the language that I use. Sometimes people have asked me when I was going to try something hard or difficult, as if my work sprang from my ignorance. I like to think that I write from my knowledge not my lack, from my strength not my weakness. I am not interested if anyone knows whether or not I am familiar with big words, I am interested in trying to render big ideas in a simple way. I am interested in being understood not admired. I wish to celebrate and not be celebrated (though a little celebration is a lot of fun).

I am a woman and I write from that experience. I am a Black woman and I write from that experience. I do not feel inhibited or bound by what I am. That does not mean that I have never had bad scenes relating to being Black and/or a woman, it means that other people's craziness has not managed to make me crazy. At least not in their way because I try very hard not to close my eye to my own craziness nor to my family's, my sex's, nor my race's. I don't believe that I should only talk about the beauty and strength and good-ness of my people but I do believe that if we talk about our room for improvement we should do it privately. I don't believe in public family fights. But I do think sometimes a good fight is cleansing. We are not perfect people. There are no perfect people.

I have been a wife for over twenty years. We have parented six children. Both these things have brought me great joy. I try to transmit the possible joy in my work. This does not mean that there have been no dark days; it means that they have not mattered. In the long run, I try to write about looking at the long run.

I have been writing things down all my life. I was first published in 1969 due to the efforts of Robert Hayden and Carolyn Kizer among others. I did not try to be published; it wasn't something that I thought that much about. I had had a short short story published in an issue of *Negro Digest* magazine earlier in the sixties. That had been my try.

When my first book was published I was thirty-three years old and had six children under ten years old. I was too busy to take it terribly seriously. I was very happy and proud of course, but had plenty of other things to think about. It was published by Random House and that seemed to bother some of my friends. At first my feelings were a little hurt that anyone would even be concerned about it but I got over that. I decided that if something doesn't matter, it really doesn't matter. Sometimes I think that the most anger comes from ones who were late in discovering that when the world said nigger it meant them too. I grew up knowing that the world meant me too but that was the world's insanity and not mine. I have been treated in publishing very much like other poets are treated, that is, not really very well. I continue to write since my life as a human only includes my life as a poet, it doesn't depend on it.

I live in Baltimore and so I do not have sustained relationships with many of my peers. I am friends with a lot of the people who do what I do but my public and private lives tend to be separate. At home I am wife and mama mostly. My family has always come first with me. This is my choice due to my personal inclination. As the children have grown up I have been able to travel more and I enjoy it. I very much enjoy the public life and I also very much enjoy the private.

My family tends to be a spiritual and even perhaps mystical one. That certainly influences my life and my work. I write in the kitchen or wherever I happen to be though I do have a study. I write on a typewriter rather than in longhand. My children think of me as a moody person; I am shy and much less sunny than I am pictured. I draw my own conclusions and do not believe everything I am told. I am not easily fooled. I do the best I can. I try. (pp. 137-38)

> *Lucille Clifton, "A Simple Language," in*
> Black Women Writers (1950-1980): A Criti-

cal Evaluation, *edited by Mari Evans, Anchor Press/Doubleday, 1984, pp. 137-38.*

> "You have to have ego to write—to attempt a poem—but when it comes down to the actual writing, I leave my ego at the door."
>
> —Lucille Clifton, 1988

Audrey T. McCluskey

"Lucille Clifton was born in Depew, New York, in 1969. She attended Howard University and Fredonia State Teachers' College. She now lives in Baltimore with her husband and their six children. Mrs. Clifton also writes children's books."

Four sparse sentences constitute most of what has been written as a biographical and critical statement about Lucille Clifton and her work. The lack of critical attention afforded this writer who has been steadily producing poetry and books for children for well over a decade is a major oversight in literary criticism.

We can only guess at the reasons. Lucille Clifton is a soft-spoken poet. She writes verse that does not leap out at you, nor shout expletives and gimmicks to gain attention. A public poet whose use of concrete symbols and language is easily discernible, Lucille Clifton is guided by the dictates of her own consciousness rather than the dictates of form, structure, and audience. She is not an "intellectual" poet, although she does not disdain intellect. She simply prefers to write from her heart. Her poetry is concrete, often witty, sometimes didactic, yet it can be subtle and understated. Her short-lined economical verse is often a grand mixture of simplicity and wisdom. Repeated readings of her work show her to be a poet in control of her material and one who is capable of sustaining a controlling idea with seemingly little effort. Clifton is a poet of a literary tradition which includes such varied poets as Walt Whitman, Emily Dickinson, and Gwendolyn Brooks, who have inspired and informed her work.

Lucille Clifton writes with conviction; she always takes a moral and hopeful stance. She rejects the view that human beings are pawns in the hands of whimsical fate. She believes that we can shape our own destiny and right the wrongs by taking a moral stand.

> I [always] wanted to make things better.
> I wanted to make things right. I always
> thought I was supposed to.

Lucille Clifton's belief in her ability (and ours) to make things better and her belief in the concept of personal responsibility pervade her work. These views are especially pronounced in her books for children.

Her children's books are her most prolific literary product, and no analysis of her work could ignore their overall importance. Her books for children introduce themes, ideas and points of view that may sometimes find their way into her poetry. It is important to note that she does not greatly alter her style as she moves from one genre to another. Her language remains direct, economical, and simply stated. She does not patronize the children for whom she writes. She gives them credit for being intelligent human beings who do not deserve to be treated differently because of their age. Being the mother of six children must certainly give her material for her books, but it is her respect for children as people and her finely tuned instincts about what is important to them—their fears, their joys—that make her a successful writer of children's literature.

One of her favorite characters in her books for children is Everett Anderson. He is a boy of six or seven, living with his working mother, who teaches him responsibility, pride, and love. He is reminded to "walk tall" in the world and to be proud of who he is. He is always referred to by his complete name, which helps to underscore his sense of identity and belonging. Yet Everett Anderson does not exist in a world of bliss and fantasy. He experiences periods of loneliness—when he remembers the good times that he had with his Daddy when he lived with them—and frustration—when he wants to bake a cake but finds that "the sugar is almost gone and payday's not 'til later on." He will survive these momentary frustrations because he feels secure and loved. . . . The understated message in the Everett Anderson books is that a loving, caring environment more than makes up for any real or perceived deprivations when it comes to the development of a positive self-concept. Everett Anderson seems to understand that. (pp. 139-40)

In her poetry, Clifton continues to advocate that Black children be taught self-worth and encouraged to develop the mental and spiritual toughness that they will require to survive in a society that is hostile to their development. In the following poem, the children are called upon to make decisions for themselves and to begin to take control of their lives. They must become socially responsible—for they shall someday lead.

> Come home from the movies
> Black girls and boys.
> The picture be over and the screen
> be cold as our neighborhood.
> Come home from the show,
> don't be the show . . .
> Show our fathers how to walk like men,
> they already know how to dance.

The movies serve as a metaphor for the fantasies and falseness in society that stunt our children's growth. She believes that what is important in life is found, not in the movies but in the values that are passed through generations. (pp. 141-42)

Clifton's view of herself as a writer is based, in part, upon her belief that "things don't fall apart. Things hold. Lines connect in ways that last and last and lives become generations made out of pictures and words just kept." She is interested in the continuity of experience and the writer's unique ability to connect generations of people and to remind them who they are and from whence they came.

As a poet, her connections include the works of other poets such as Emily Dickinson, Walt Whitman, and Gwendolyn Brooks, who serve as literary predecessors for many of her concerns. Like that of Emily Dickinson and Gwendolyn Brooks, Clifton's work is heavily influenced by Christian optimism. To these poets, the world is defined by possibility. Also, like Emily Dickinson and Gwendolyn Brooks, Clifton prefers to experience life through her senses, producing a poetry that is not devoid of wonder and ebullience. Like her predecessors, Clifton can marvel at nature and find worthy themes in everyday and commonplace occurrences. Clifton's short elliptical verse, her simultaneous acknowledgment of pain and possibility, and her use of domestic images are especially Dickinsonian. **"I Am Not Done Yet"** is a poem which highlights these comparisons.

Also like Emily Dickinson, Clifton finds joy in "not having" and in being out of step with public opinion.

The preference for "our no place" over "houses straight as / dead men" is a rejection of established opinion and an assertion of an independent view of reality. She seems to relish being different and is not concerned that others may consider her odd. (p. 142)

Among her identifiable predecessors, it is Gwendolyn Brooks with whom Mrs. Clifton shares her racial and spiritual legacy. Although her poetry does not contain the variety of form and experimentation or breadth of subject matter found in the poetry of Gwendolyn Brooks, they share a sensibility rooted in the Black experience and in Christian idealism. The religious values translate into poems that value simplicity, despise injustice, and identify with the common, uncelebrated man and woman. Lucille Clifton, like Gwendolyn Brooks, gives identity and substance to the everyday people in her poems by giving them names, and therefore a history, such as "Willie B.," "Tyrone," and "Everett Anderson." (pp. 142-43)

Clifton's feminine sensibility, like her Blackness, runs deep. The femaleness in her poems—children, family, domesticity, and the concerns of the ordinary woman—derive not from a newly spawned feminine consciousness but from historical role models of Black, keeping-on women who are her inspiration.

> Harriet
> if i be you
> let me not forget
> to be the pistol
> pointed
> to be the madwoman
> at the river's edge
> warning
> to be free or die

This poem merges a collective and personal past and serves to renew the speaker's acceptance of the challenges faced by her ancestors.

The female voice in Clifton's poetry is her most sustained and her most introspective. Her female poems reflect her personal journey toward self-discovery and reconciliation. She traces her origins to the Dahomey woman who was the founder of Clifton's family in America. Mammy Ca'line is the link with Africa and a lost-found past. In

"Ca'line's prayer," Mammy Ca'line speaks through the poet, whose function is to keep alive the aching memory and to pass on her cry for redemption.

> Remember me from Wydah
> Remember the child
> running across Dahomey
> black as ripe papaya
> juicy as sweet berries
> and set me in the rivers of your glory.
> Ye Ma Jah.

At birth, the weight of this history is passed on to the poet, who inherits not only Mammy Ca'line's discontent, but the legacy of her namesake—her grandmother Lucille—the first Black woman legally lynched in the state of Virginia.

> . . . who waited by the crossroads
> in Virginia
> and shot the whiteman off his horse,
> killing the killer of sons.
> light breaks from her life
> to her lives . . .
> mine already is
> an Afrikan name.

The "light" that she inherits is an avenging light that is activated by the special circumstances of her birth.

> i was born in a hotel,
> a maskmaker
> my bones were knit by
> a perilous knife.
> my skin turned round
> at midnight and
> i entered the earth in
> a woman jar.

By saying yes to her legacy, Clifton acknowledges a responsibility to the Dahomey women who have preceded her and to all unsung Black warriors who await vindication.

The unsung, the unvindicated for whom the poet speaks include those like **"Miss Rosie,"** whom society has cast aside.

> . . . wrapped up like garbage
> sitting, surrounded by the smell
> of too old potato peels
> . . . sitting, waiting for your mind
> like next week's grocery
> . . . you wet brown bag of a woman
> who used to be the best looking gal in Georgia

The poem emanates from a fusion of language and meaning. The language denotes highly charged sensory images of an old woman discarded by society and left to rot like garbage. The theme of human waste and uselessness is suggested throughout the poem by the placement of key words and phrases like "sitting," "waiting for your mind" and metaphors like "too old potato peels" and "wet brown bag of a woman." The tragedy of Miss Rosie's present state is heightened by the knowledge that she "used to be called the Georgia Rose—the best looking gal in Georgia." Although she is the commanding presence in the poem, this poem is not only about the destruction of Miss Rosie; it also conveys the speaker's resolve to fight the

forces that caused that human waste and suffering. "I stand up," the speaker says, "through your destruction. I stand up."

The tenacious spirit and resolve of the speaker in **"Miss Rosie"** is also the theme of the poem **"For deLawd."** It is a poem which seeks to merge the speaker's individual optimism and faith with a larger, well-articulated historical tradition of women who, under adverse circumstances fought the good fight and just kept on pushing. The speaker has inherited her mantle and thus proclaims:

> . . . I got a long memory
> and I came from a line
> of black and going on women.

This poem is another illustration of Clifton's belief in the continuity of human experience and in our indebtedness to the generations that preceded us.

The "going on" women that Clifton writes about are like their counterparts in blues songs. They know that the world is not a sane and rational place, but it is the only world that we have. So they have learned to manipulate the chaos—not to control it—to ensure their individual and collective survival. This cold reality of that statement can force undesirable alternatives, as in **"the lost baby poem,"** a poem in which a mother speaks to the unmade child that poverty has forced her to abort. As in a blues song, she only wants to explain to her lost baby the *necessity* of her actions.

> You would have been born into winter
> in the year of the disconnected gas
> and no car we would have made the thin
> walk over Genesee hill into Canada wind
> to watch you slip like ice into strangers' hands
> you would have fallen naked as snow into winter.

"the lost baby poem" is also structured like a blues song in three parts, with a statement, an embellishment, and a resolution or rebuttal. It is one of Clifton's most lyrical poems. The longer length allows for the development of sustained images and for the use of extended metaphor which in both instances suggests coldness, bleakness, and death. In the resolution of the poem, the speaker vows to join the lost baby in his watery death if she is ever less than a "mountain" to her "definite" children.

> if i am ever less than a mountain
> for your definite brothers and sisters
> let the rivers pour over my head
> let the sea take me for a spiller.

The long untitled "the thirty-eight year" poem, is another example of a female blues lament. It depicts an ordinary woman—"plain as bread, round as cake"—attempting to reconcile the reality of her ordinary existence with her unfulfilled expectations.

> i had expected to be
> smaller than this,
> more beautiful,
> wiser in Afrikan ways
> more confident,
> i had expected
> more than this.

In doubting her own accomplishments, the speaker begins to feel that she is destined to relive her mother's fate.

> my mother died at forty four
> a woman of sad countenance.

Although she has become a mother herself and is

> surrounded by life,
> a perfect picture of
> blackness blessed,

she is unable to free herself from the ghost of her mother's unfulfilled life.

This poem, like the traditional blues song, is a frank confrontation with self that bears no traces of self-pity or bitterness. It is a statement of the speaker's condition in an attempt to cope with its unflattering implications.

> i had expected more than this
> i had not expected to be
> an ordinary woman.

A more diffuse view of Clifton's family is presented in *Generations,* a stylized family memoir, which uses Walt Whitman as a literary model to suggest celebration and self-discovery. It represents an ultimate attempt at reconciliation and synthesis of family, history, and the artist. Through the use of Whitmanesque cinematic cuts and cadences, *Generations* tells the story of the Sayles family in America.

The story is told to Clifton, in part, by her father, whose voice and presence dominate the book. Just as the Dahomey women are ideals of feminine strength and virtue, her father, Sam Sayles, is Clifton's ideal of masculine strength and fortitude. "He was a strong man, a rock," who is described in near-mythic proportions.

> He used to go to dances and sometimes in the
> middle of a dance he would get tired and throw
> his hat down and shout The Dance Is Over, and
> all the people would stop playing music and
> dancing and go home.

In her poem **"Daddy"** written after his death, Clifton remembers him as

> . . . a confident man
> "I'll go to heaven," he said,
> "Jesus knows me."
> When his leg died, he cut it off.
> "It's gone," he said, "it's gone
> but I'm still here."

Clifton's family in general and her father in particular are the stabilizing force upon which her work is drawn. Acknowledging suffering and simultaneously asserting the will to overcome it, as exemplified by her father, is a central tenet of her philosophy and a recurring theme in all of her work. This philosophy allows the poet to reconcile the dichotomy of personal/racial history—its mix of hopelessness and hope, of tragedy and triumph—with the realities of the present condition and to still feel fortunate. As Clifton's father once told her, "We fooled them, Lue, slavery was terrible but we fooled them old people. We came out of it better than they did."

The optimism that permeates all of Clifton's work is fu-

eled by her Christian faith. The tenets of Christianity are a natural vehicle for the espousal of her belief in the ultimate triumph and deliverance of an oppressed people. The biblical heroes and heroines that are cited in her poetry are examples of personal triumph over adversity, such as Daniel:

> I have learned
> some few things,
> like when a man
> walk manly
> he don't stumble
> even in the lion's den.

(pp. 143-48)

In the final analysis, the vindication that is promised the oppressed will come not only because it is just, and right and overdue—it will come because it is mandated by Divine Will.

> While I was in the middle of the night
> I saw red stars and black stars
> pushed out of the sky by white ones
> and I knew as sure as jungle
> is the father of the world
> I must slide down like a great dipper of stars
> and lift men up.

This, then, is the good news that Lucille Clifton tells. She dwells not on what Black people have been through but on the qualities that have enabled us to survive it all—and to keep right on. (p. 148)

> *Audrey T. McCluskey, "Tell the Good News:
> A View of the Works of Lucille Clifton," in*
> Black Women Writers (1950-1980): A Critical Evaluation, *edited by Mari Evans, Anchor
> Press/Doubleday, 1984, pp. 139-49.*

Haki Madhubuti

In everything she creates, this Lucille Clifton, a writer of no ordinary substance, a singer of faultless ease and able storytelling, there is a message. No slogans or billboards, but words that are used refreshingly to build us, make us better, stronger, and whole. Words that defy the odds and in the end make us wiser. (p. 50)

Lucille Clifton is a woman of majestic presence, a full-time wife, over-time mother, part-time street activist and writer of small treasures (most of her books are small but weighty). That she is not known speaks to, I feel, her preoccupation with truly becoming a full Black woman and writer. Celebrity,—that is, people pointing you out in drugstores and shopping malls—does not seem to interest her. When she was almost assured of becoming the poet laureate of Maryland, she wrote Gwendolyn Brooks (poet laureate of Illinois) asking if she should consider such a position. I suggest that she really wanted to know: (1) Are there any advantages in the position for her people? and (2) Would she significantly have to change her life by accepting the honor? Brooks' response was, "It is what you make of it." Clifton accepted.

The city of Baltimore, where she and her family reside, does not figure heavily in her work. The "place" of her poetry and prose is essentially urban landscapes that are examples of most Black communities in this country. Clifton's urge is to live, is to conquer oppressive and nonnatural spaces. Her poetry is often a conscious, quiet introduction to the real world of Black sensitivities. Her focus and her faces are both the men and the women connected and connecting; the children, the family, the slave-like circumstances, the beauty, and the raw and most important the hideouts of Black people to Black people.

Her poetry is emotion-packed and musically fluent to the point of questioning whether a label on it would limit one's understanding. Her first book of poetry, *Good Times,* cannot be looked upon as simply a "first" effort. The work is unusually compacted and memory-evoking.

There is no apology for the Black condition. There is an awareness and a seriousness that speak to "houses straight as / dead men." Clifton's poems are not vacant lots; the mamas and daddies are not forgotten human baggages to be made loose of and discarded. Much of today's writing, especially much of that being published by Black women writers, seems to invalidate Black men or make small of them, often relegating them to the position of white sexual renegades in Black faces.

No such cop-out for Clifton. There is no misrepresentation of the men or women. And one would find it extremely difficult to misread Clifton. She is not a "complicated" writer in the traditional Western sense. She is a writer of complexity, and she makes her readers work and think. Her poetry has a quiet force without being pushy or alien. Whether she is cutting through family relationships, surviving American racial attitudes, or just simply renewing love ties, she puts something heavy on your mind. The great majority of her published poetry is significant. At the base of her work is concern for the Black family, especially the destruction of its youth. Her eye is for the uniqueness of our people, always concentrating on the small strengths that have allowed us to survive the horrors of Western life.

Her treatment of Black men is unusually significant and sensitive. I feel that part of the reason she treats men fairly and with balance in her work is her relationship with her father, brothers, husband, and sons. Generally, positive relationships produce positive results.

> my daddy's fingers move among the couplers
> chipping steel and skin
> and if the steel would break
> my daddy's fingers might be men again.

Lucille Clifton is often calling for the men to be Black men. Asking and demanding that they seek and be more than expected. Despite her unlimited concern for her people, she does not box herself into the corner of preaching at them or of describing them with metaphors of belittlement. Clifton has a fine, sharp voice pitched to high C and tuned carefully to the frequency of the Black world. She is a homeland technician who has not allowed her "education" to interfere with her solos.

The women of *Good Times* are strong and Dahomey-made, are imposing and tragic, yet givers of love. Unlike most of us, Clifton seemed to have taken her experiences and observations and squeezed the knowledge from them, translating them into small and memorable lessons:

> . . . surrounded by the smell
> of too old potato peels
> you wet brown bag of a woman
> who used to be the best looking gal in Georgia
> used to be called the Georgia Rose
> I stand up
> through your destruction
> I stand up

Standing up is what *Good Times* is about. However, Clifton can beat you up with a poem; she can write history into four stanzas and bring forth reaction from the most hardened nonreader. Listen to the story of Robert:

> Was born obedient
> without questions
> did a dance called
> Picking grapes
> Sticking his butt out
> for pennies
> Married a master
> who whipped his head
> until he died
> until he died
> the color of his life
> was nigger.

There is no time frame in such a poem. Such poems do not date easily. Robert is 1619 and 1981, is alive and dying on urban streets, in rural churches and corporate offices. "Niggers" have not disappeared; some of them (us) are now being called by last names and are receiving different types of mind whippings, mind whippings that achieve the same and sometimes greater results.

Clifton is a Black cultural poet. We see in her work a clear transmission of values. It is these values that form the base of a developing consciousness of struggle. She realizes that we do have choices that can still be exercised. Hers is most definitely to fight. From page to page, from generation to generation, the poems cry out direction, hope, and future. One of the best examples of this connecting force is from her book *An Ordinary Woman;* the poem is **"Turning."**

> Turning into my own
> turning on in
> to my own self
> at last
> turning out of the
> white cage, turning out of the
> lady cage
> turning at last
> on a stem like a black fruit
> in my own season
> at last.

It is the final voyage into oneself that is the most difficult. Then there comes the collective fight, the dismantling of the real monsters outside. But first we must become whole again. The true undiluted culture of a people is the base of wholeness. One way toward such wholeness is what Stephen Henderson calls "saturation," the giving and defining of Blackness through proclaiming such experiences as legitimate and necessary, whereas the Black poetic experience used often enough becomes natural and expected.

Clifton "saturates" us in a way that forces us to look at ourselves in a different and more profound way. For every weakness, she points to a strength; where there are negatives she pulls and searches for the positives. She has not let the low ebbs of life diminish her talents or toughness. She is always looking for the good, the best, but not naïvely so. Her work is realistic and burning with the energy of renewal.

Clifton is an economist with words; her style is to use as few words as possible. Yet she is effective because, despite consciously limiting her vocabulary, she has defined her audience. She is not out to impress, or to showcase the scope of her lexicon. She is communicating ideas and concepts. She understands that precise communication is not an easy undertaking; language, at its root, seeks to express emotion, thought, action. Most poetry writing (other than the blues) is foreign to the Black community. It is nearly impossible to translate to the page the changing linguistic nuances or the subtleties of body language Blacks use in everyday conversation; the Black writer's task is an extremely complicated and delicate one. But understand me, Clifton does not write down to us, nor is she condescending or patronizing with her language. Most of her poems are short and tight, as is her language. Her poems are well-planned creations, and as small as some of them are, they are not cloudy nor rainy with words for words' sake. The task is not to fill the page with letters but to challenge the mind:

> What I remember about that day
> is boxes stacked across the walk
> and couch springs curling through the air
> and drawers and tables balanced on the curb
> and us, hollering,
> leaping up and around
> happy to have a playground
> nothing about the emptied rooms
> nothing about the emptied family

Her originality is accomplished with everyday language and executed with musical percussion, pushed to the limits of poetic possibilities. Lucille Clifton is a lover of life, a person who feels her people. Her poems are messages void of didacticism and needless repetition. Nor does she shout or scream the language at you; her voice is birdlike but loud and high enough to pierce the ears of dogs. She is the quiet warrior, and, like the weapons of all good warriors, her weapons can hurt, kill, and protect.

Language is the building block of consciousness. To accurately understand the soul of a people, you not only search for their outward manifestations (e.g., institutions, art, science and technology, social and political systems), but you examine their language. And since the Black community, by and large, speaks a foreign language, the question is to what extent have we made the language work for us, i.e., build for us? All languages to some degree are bastards, created by both rulers and the ruled, kings and proletariat, masters and slaves, citizens and visitors. The greatness and endurance of a people to a large degree lies in their fundamental ability to create under the most adverse conditions using the tools at hand. Language is ever growing and a tool (weapon) that must be mastered if it is to work for us.

Language used correctly (communicating and relating at the highest) expands the brain, increases one's knowledge bank, enlarges the world, and challenges the vision of those who may not have a vision. *One of the most effective ways to keep a people enslaved, in a scientific and technological state which is dependent upon a relatively high rate of literacy, is to create in that people a disrespect and fear of the written and spoken word.* For any people to compete in the new world order that is emerging, it is absolutely necessary that study, research, and serious appraisal of documentation that impact on people's lives become second nature. Fine poetry is like a tuning fork: it regulates, clears, and challenges the brain, focusing it and bringing it in line with the rest of the world. Therefore, it is a political act to keep people ignorant. We can see that it is not by accident that Black people in the United States watch more television than any other ethnic group and that more of our own children can be seen carrying radios and cassettes to school than books. The point is that it is just about impossible to make a positive contribution to the world if one cannot read, write, compute, think, and articulate one's thoughts. The major instrument for bringing out the genius of any people is the productive, creative, and stimulating use and creation of language.

Lucille Clifton has expanded the use of small language. Very seldom does she use words larger than four syllables. She has shaped and jerked, patched and stitched everyday language in a way that few poets have been able to do. In her book *An Ordinary Woman* she fulfills her promise of greatness. The book is a statement of commitment and love. The songs are those that stretch us, and in this final hour mandate the people immortal. Her nationalism is understated, yet compelling, with short stanzas and fistlike lines.

The imposing images in *An Ordinary Woman* are bones. Bones are used as the connecting force of Black people. The word is used fourteen times in a multitude of ways throughout the volume. The image is profoundly effective because bones represent strength. . . . The bones are connectors and death, lineage and life.

> More than once
> I have taken the bones you hardened
> and built daughters
> and they blossom and promised fruit
> like Afrikan trees.

She is what John Gardner describes as the moral writer and what Addison Gayle, Jr., refers to [in *The Way of the New World*] as a writer's writer in the Black nationalist tradition: "The Black writer at the present time must forgo the assimilationist tradition and redirect his (her) art to the strivings within . . . to do so, he (she) must write for and speak to the majority of Black people; not to a sophisticated elite fashioned out to the programmed computers of America's largest universities."

Clifton's nationalism is sometimes subtle and bright, sometimes coarse and lonely; it is fire and beaten bodies, but what most emerges from the body of her work is a reverence for life, a hope for tomorrow, and an undying will to live and to conquer oppressive forces.

By customary standards she *is* no ordinary woman. In another time and place, that might have been the case, but here in never-never land, the make-believe capital of the world, she exemplifies the specialness we all need to be. However, the ordinariness she speaks of is an in-group definition between sister and sister:

> me and you be sisters
> we be the same.
> me and you
> coming from the same place.

She too is the mother who has had sons and brothers, uncles and male friends, and seems to have learned a great deal from these relationships. I am excited about her work because she reflects me; she tells my story in a way and with an eloquence that is beyond my ability. She is sister and mother, lovingly fair; her anger controlled, her tears not quite hidden. She knows that mothers must eventually let sons and daughters stand on their own; she also knows that the tradition and politics of the West conspire to cut those sons and daughters down before they are able to magnify their lives:

> those boys that ran together
> at Tillman's
> and the poolroom
> everybody see them now
> think it's a shame
> everybody see them now
> remember they was fine boys
> we have some fine Black boys
> don't it make you want to cry?

Her tears are not maudlin, however: she strides, face wet with a fierce and angry water. And she keeps getting up from being down, keeps stealing future space. She is the woman of "long memory" coming from a long line "of Black and going women / who got used to making it through murdered sons." Clifton is an encourager, a pusher of the sons and daughters; a loving reminder of what was, is, must be.

She brings a Black woman's sensitivity to her poetry—brings the history of what it means to be a Black woman in America, and what she brings is not antagonistic, not stacked against Black men. When she speaks of the true enemy, it is done in a way that reinforces her humanity yet displays a unique ability to capture the underlying reasons Europe wars on the world. Speaking of the "poor animal" and the "ape herds" of Europe, she says of them:

> he heads, always, for a cave
> his mind shivers against the rocks
> afraid of the dark
> afraid of the cold
> afraid to be alone
> afraid of the legendary man creature
> who is black
> and walks on grass
> and has no need for fire . . .

For the Buffalo soldiers and for the Dahomey women, the two images that flow throughout the body of much of her work, she sees a bright and difficult future. And she knows how to hurt, and she knows how to heal:

> me and you be sisters

> we be the same.
> me and you
> coming from the same place.
> me and you
> be greasing our legs . . .
> got babies
> got thirty-five
> got black . . .
> be loving ourselves
> be sisters
> only where you sing
> i poet.

Indeed, she poets. An understatement, she is like quality music; her works make you feel and care. She is also a folk historian, dealing not in dates and names but concepts. She is the original root woman, a connector to trees, earth, and the undestroyables, as in **"On the Birth of Bomani"**:

> We have taken the best leaves
> and the best roots
> and your mama whose skin
> is the color of the sun
> has opened into a fire and
> your daddy whose skin
> is the color of the night
> has tended it carefully with
> his hunter's hands and
> here you have come, Bomani,
> an Afrikan Treasure-Man.
> may the art in the love that made you
> fill your fingers,
> may the love in the art that made you
> fill your heart.

Clifton's style is simple and solid, like rock and granite. She is a linear poet who uses very little of the page, an effective device for the free and open verse that she constructs. She is not an experimental poet. She has fashioned an uncomplicated and direct format that allows great latitude for incorporating her message.

She writes controlled and deliberate lines moving from idea to idea, image to image, building toward specific political and social concepts. She is at her best when she is succinct and direct:

> Love rejected
> hurts so much more
> than Love rejecting;
> they act like they don't love their country
> No
> what it is
> is they found
> their country don't love them.

To conclude, Europeans put up statues for their dead poets or buy their homes and make them into museums. Often, they force their poets into suicide or nonproduction. Neglect for any writer is bitter, bitter salt, and Lucille Clifton's work has not seemed to take root in the adult segments of the Black reading community. Is it because she does not live in New York, may not have "connections" with reviewers nor possess Madison Avenue visibility? Is it that she needs more than a "mere" three books of poetry and a memoir? Is it that the major body of her work is directed toward children? Is it that her expressed moral and social values are archaic? All these possibilities are significant because they speak to the exchange nature of the game played daily in the publishing world; the only business more ruthless and corrupted is the Congress.

Clifton without doubt or pause is a Black woman (in color, culture, and consciousness); a family woman whose husband, children, and extended family have represented and played roles of great importance in her life and work, and a superb writer who will not compromise. She is considered among some to be *a literary find;* she is widely published and talked about, but, like most Black women writers, not promoted, and again, like most, her work can often be found in remainder bins less than a year after publication. (I bought fifty copies of **Generations** from a used-book store.) Finally, she is serious about revolutionary change. Most writers that "make it" in this country have to become literary and physical prostitutes in one form or another. Clifton's work suggests that if she is to sell herself, it will be for benefits far greater than those which accrue from publishing a book. In recent Black literature, she is in the tradition of Gwendolyn Brooks, Mari Evans, and Sonia Sanchez. She will not compromise our people, is not to be played with, is loved and lover (". . . you are the one I am lit for / come with your rod that twists and is a serpent / I am the bush / I am burning / I am not consumed"), is revolutionary, is, all beauty and finality, a Black woman. . . . (pp. 150-59)

When we begin to rightfully honor the poets, Clifton will undoubtedly be gathering roses in her own community and miss the call. She is like that, a quiet unassuming person, yet bone-strong with vision of intense magnitude. She is *new bone* molded in Afrikan earth, tested in Western waters, ready for action:

> Other people think they know
> how long life is
> how strong life is / we know.

To be original, relevant, and revolutionary in the mouth of fire is the mark of a dangerous person. Lucille Clifton is a poet of *mean* talent who has not let her gifts separate her from the work at hand. She is a teacher and an example. To read her is to give birth to bright seasons. (p. 160)

> *Haki Madhubuti, "Lucille Clifton: Warm Water, Greased Legs, and Dangerous Poetry,"* in Black Women Writers (1950-1980): A Critical Evaluation, *edited by Mari Evans, Anchor Press/Doubleday, 1984, pp. 150-60.*

Thema Bryant

Hello! My name is Thema Bryant. I'm in the 6th grade at Mt. Royal Elementary Middle School. When I get older I would like to be a teacher and to write poetry. After hearing some of my poetry I was asked to do an interview with the great Lucille Clifton. In case you don't know, Lucille Clifton is a poet and also writes children's books. If you would like to know more about her, read the following interview and get her books.

This year I had the pleasure of interviewing a great Black woman writer by the name of Lucille Clifton. When she first answered the phone I told her my name and how hon-ored I was to give the interview. She said how honored she was to be interviewed. The first question I asked her was, "How old were you when you first became aware of your talent as a writer? She needed no time at all. "Well, when I first became interested I was ten but I never thought my books would be published."

After this question I asked, "Did you have an opportunity to read many Black women poets and writers during your childhood?" Again she needed no time. She just plain out said, "No." Then after a moment of silence she said, "I'd never ever heard of them."

After this answer I needed to know, "Who gave you the most encouragement during your childhood?" She said, "My mother. She told me that nothing was impossible and she encouraged me to try." I said, "Do you have a favorite time to do your writing?" This time she waited a second and then she said, "Not much. When I first started writing, I had a lot of little children and whenever I got a chance I would write, but now I mostly write at night."

Then I asked, her, "We know what your writing does for others; what does it do for you?" She replied, "Oh! it's very satisfying. It makes me satisfied with myself and what I'm doing." Then I said, "What authors' books do you enjoy reading?" She replied, "Lots of them . . . lots . . . of . . . them." She said, "I like reading children's books, even though I'm not a child, and Black women's books."

Later I asked her, "Does listening to music help?" She replied gaily, "Yes . . . Yes." I then asked her which did she prefer. She said, "All kinds, especially classical. I like the composer Bach, Aretha Franklin, and Gladys Knight and the Pips." After that answer we both laughed. Then I asked her, "Are you writing something special now?" She replied with a sigh, "Well, I'm working on a book **New and Old Selected Writings,** where new and old poems will be together, and I may be also writing a children's book because I have an idea."

Afterwards I asked her, "What recommendations do you have for someone who would like to follow in your footsteps?" She replied, "I think I would recommend that they write a lot, don't get discouraged, have patience." Then I said, "When you are not writing how do you enjoy spending your time?" She replied, "Well right now I teach at the University of California, I read, and I like to sit by the ocean."

I asked her, "Do you ever get writer's block, and if so how do you get rid of it?" She said unashamedly, "Yes! Sometimes I do, but when I do I just remain patient and relax, and it goes away." Then I said, "Which book that you have written do you enjoy the best." She again replied without a pause, "Um, well, let's see, I most enjoy what I am working on now." Then I asked her, "What is the most challenging thing you think someone who is a writer will come up against?" She said, "One challenging thing is when you think that being a writer is more important than writing."

For my final question I asked, "What is your advice to children." She said, "I would like for all children to remember, especially Black children, that all that you want to be you can be and just because you are not doing well on the outside doesn't mean you can't do good on the inside." After that we said our good-byes.

> Thema Bryant, "A Conversation with Lucille Clifton," in SAGE, Vol. II, No. 1, Spring, 1985, p. 52.

Andrea Benton Rushing

Like all the other contemporary African-American women poets, Clifton was deeply affected by the Black Arts movement of the sixties and seventies. Although subsequent experiences like the women's movement and her own heightened religious consciousness have also left their imprint on her, we must consider that soul-changing crusade the crucible which most searingly shaped her art.

A concomitant of the separatist Black Power campaign, the Black Arts movement enlisted such cultural workers as musicians, visual artists, and writers to address the masses of African-Americans about the liberation struggles which confronted them. Propelled by slogans like "I'm Black and I'm proud" and "Black is beautiful," artists pronounced European and Euro-American critical norms inadequate yardsticks for African-American creations and viewed African-American arts as cultural tools with which to destroy three centuries of racial oppression and degradation.

While many bourgeois Euro-American and African-American readers and critics deplored the rage, obscenity, and violence of "New Breed" poetry, respected African-American critics like Bernard Bell, Hoyt Fuller, Addison Gayle, and George Kent recognized its merits. More importantly, young African-Americans in pool rooms and bars (as well as on street corners and college campuses) read it attentively and imitated it widely. . . . According to [Stephen Henderson in his essay "Understanding the New Black Poetry"] both oral and written African-American poetry clusters around the motif of political, sexual, and spiritual liberation. In analyzing structure, Henderson terms it the poetry's reflection of spoken language and performed music. "Whenever Black poetry is most distinctively and effectively Black, it derives its form from . . . Black speech and Black music." Saturation is Henderson's rubric for "the communication of Blackness in a given situation and the sense of fidelity to the observed and intuited truth of the Black Experience."

Clifton's early verse clearly indicates the influence of the Black Arts movement. In accord with its dictates about how poetry should raise the cultural and political consciousness of "the Black community," Clifton dedicates **Good News About the Earth** to those killed in student uprisings at Orangeburg, South Carolina, and Jackson, Mississippi. It contains an apology to the militant Black Panther Party.

> i became a woman
> during the old prayers
> among the ones who wore
> bleaching cream to bed
> and all my lessons stayed
> i was obedient

> but brothers i thank you
> for these mannish days
> i remember agin the wise one
> old and telling of suicides
> refusing to be slaves
> i had forgotten and
> brothers i thank you
> i praise you
> i grieve my whiteful ways

The volume also features verse to Angela Davis, Eldridge Cleaver, and Bobby Seale. In addition to treating these political subjects, Clifton mirrors the tenets of the Black Arts movement by directing herself to a general African-American audience using the grammar, vocabulary, and rhythm of idiomatic African-American speech. Interestingly, none of Clifton's verse on these vivid figures parallels so many of the tributes to them in relying on typographical quirks, like capitalized words and slashes, or haranguing either African-American or Euro-American readers.

In light of Clifton's later poetry, it is crucial to indicate the ways in which her early work diverges from the creations of her contemporaries. Many of the women poets who came to prominence during the sixties and seventies shocked readers. Despite their slight stature and (in a few cases) bourgeois upbringing, they mirrored the strident stance, profane language, and violent imagery of urban, male poetry. Part of my interest in Clifton's lyrical verse arises from my admiration for the acumen with which she found her own voice during a turbulent period when so many poets sounded the same chords of outrage and militancy. Rather than merely imitating the sarcasm and fury of male poets, Clifton anticipated the concern with women's issues which is—like opposition to the war in Vietnam, support of homosexuals' rights, and the crusade for environmental protection—in deep, though often unacknowledged, debt to the strategies and moral vision of the Civil Rights and Black Power campaigns. Furthermore, while other poets have tended to focus on historical figures such as Harriet Tubman, Sojourner Truth, Frederick Douglass, and Malcolm X, Clifton anticipated Alex Haley's *Roots* in personalizing history and using her own natal family as a symbol of the anguish and triumph of the African-American experience. Moreover, in an era when many African-American nationalists were harshly critical of their accommodating "Uncle Tom" and "Aunt Jemima" elders, the "opiate" of African-American Christianity, and the Anglo-Saxon proper names which are a living legacy of chattel slavery and cultural assimilation, Clifton wrote in a different key. While others complained of their elders' failures, she celebrated her ancestors, while others converted to Islam, she wrote about the life-giving power of African-American religion; and, though others assumed African and Arabic names, Clifton justified her own.

> light
> on my mother's tongue
> breaks through her soft
> extravagant hip
> into life.
> Lucille
> she calls the light,

which was the name
of the grandmother
who waited by the crossroads
in Virginia
and shot the whiteman off his horse,
. . . .
mine already is
an Afrikan name.

Beginning with an allusion to the origins of the name "Lucille" in the Latin for "bright light," Clifton goes on to affirm a throbbing connection between Africa, the slave experience, and her own twentieth-century life.

Despite the considerable achievements of *Good Times, Good News About the Earth,* and *Generations,* it is with the publication of *An Ordinary Woman* and *Two-Headed Woman* that Clifton strides to center stage among contemporary African-American poets. These two fine collections parse the female sector of African-American life and give vivid testimony to the terse brilliance which alerted readers of her early work to Clifton's enormous potential. Not only do they explore a broad swath of rarely examined experience; they do so in an appealing personal voice with an attractive infusion of self-revelation and wit. By now, all the major contemporary African-American women poets have written verse about women's lives: the mother-daughter dyad, heterosexual relations, oppressive standards of female beauty, and loneliness are common themes. The verse is often autobiographical, its saturation in African and African-American culture is explicit, and its tone varies from aggrieved to nostalgic to exultant. Several things set Clifton's work apart from the strophes of others. First, she has written more poems about women's lives than any other African-American poet except Gwendolyn Brooks. Second, she has consistently done so in the African-American demotic with sinewy diction, a confiding voice, and stark imagery.

With the Kali poems in *An Ordinary Woman,* Clifton makes a bold innovation in poetic presentation of African-American women. Rather than limning heroic embodiments of female power and triumph, or depicting lifelike women victimized by parents, racism, poverty, and sexism, Clifton invokes an aboriginal ebony-faced Indian goddess associated with blood, violence, and murder. Since the paternal slave ancestor Clifton celebrates in her memoir, *Generations,* came from Dahomey, with its well-known tradition of heroic women, Clifton could have crafted poems around an African-based tradition. In turning to Kali, however, she frees herself from the feminist tendency to see women as hapless victims and explores the psychic tensions of an introspective modern woman negotiating the dramatic changes in contemporary attitudes about culture, race, and gender at the same time that she juggles the roles of daughter, sister, artist, wife, and mother. Written in standard English, these lyrics differ from Clifton's earlier work in syntax and diction; they are also tighter and more forceful. Like her earlier work, however, they also employ short lines, few rhymes, brief stanzas, and recurring images of women's blood and bones. The three Kali poems are striking enough to be quoted at length.

"Kali"

queen of fatality, she
determines the destiny
of things. nemesis.
the permanent guest
within ourselves.
woman of warfare,
of the chase, bitch
of blood sacrifice and death.
dread mother. the mystery
ever present in us and
outside us. the
terrible Hindu Woman God
Kali.
who is Black.

"The Coming of Kali"

it is the Black God, Kali,
a woman God and terrible
with her skulls and breasts.
i am one side of your skin,
she sings, softness is the other,
you know you know me well, she sings,
you know you know me well.

"Calming Kali"

be quiet awful woman,
lonely as hell,
and i will comfort you
when i can
and give you my bones
and my blood to feed on.
gently gently now
awful woman,
i know i am your sister.

In these poems, Clifton juxtaposes archetypal imagery about female generative and destructive power and insists on the tense mystery implicit in that union of opposites. Furthermore, she combines awe about Kali's violence and power with a fierce, almost protective, tenderness toward the fearful figure she refers to as "sister."

The thematic connections between *Two-Headed Woman* and Clifton's previous verse are immediately apparent. The opening **"homage to mine"** section demonstrates her continuing attention to family and friends and religious themes. In other ways, however, Clifton's latest volume of verse marks some sort of threshold experience for her. Unlike most other African-American women poets of the sixties and seventies, Clifton's marriage has been stable, and she has had six children. None of her verse articulates either the strains between men and women or the loneliness which often characterizes the work of other female poets, and her sons and daughters have been sources of pleasure and affirmation for her. A pivotal poem in *Two-Headed Woman* indicates new timbres in her life.

the light that came to lucille clifton
came in a shift of knowing
when even her fondest sureties
faded away. it was the summer
she understood that she had not understood
and was not mistress even
of her own off eye. then
the man escaped throwing away his tie and
she could see the peril of an
unexamined life.

Here the poet's children grow up, her husband "escapes," and (despite all the introspective verse she has written) she terms her life "unexamined." One indication of the difference between the texture of *An Ordinary Woman* and *Two-Headed Woman* is that while the former invokes Kali to personify the furious tensions between women's creative and destructive powers, the latter concentrates on the smaller (though equally intense) landscape of one woman's searching psyche.

> see the sensational
> two-headed woman
> one face turned outward
> one face
> swiveling slowly in.

Another indication of the difference appears in the religious verse in the volume. On the one hand, Clifton uses a lower-class Caribbean accent rather than the African-American idiom in which she usually writes. On the other, she concentrates on the near ineffability of the interface between divine call and human response. Many of her religious poems are about Mary. Rather than depicting her as the wise poised figure of Renaissance painting, Clifton portrays her as an uneducated young girl inexplicably chosen for miraculous experience. . . .

"holy night"

> joseph, i afraid of stars,
> their brilliant seeing.
> so many eyes, such light.
> joseph, i cannot still these limbs,
> i hands keep moving toward i breasts,
> so many stars. so bright.

Clifton's focus on Mary not only reflects her heightened concern with extraordinary religious experience but also resonates with the emphasis on motherhood which has characterized poetry about her family.

One comes away from Clifton's powerful recent verse knowing that while it shares its lyric qualities, lucidity, and compression with her earlier work, it also marks significant steps beyond her past achievements. Using many of the same tools which molded the stanzas of *Good Times* and *Good News About the Earth* and maintaining her interest in female experience, Clifton has broadened her range and deepened her perspective. (pp. 214-21)

> *Andrea Benton Rushing, "Lucille Clifton: A Changing Voice for Changing Times," in* Coming to Light: American Women Poets in the Twentieth Century, *edited by Diane Wood Middlebrook and Marilyn Yalom, The University of Michigan Press, 1985, pp. 214-22.*

E. K. Laing

Though not yet as well known as Maya Angelou, Gwendolyn Brooks, or Nikki Giovanni, Lucille Clifton is admired by many other authors for her integrity and skill. She deserves a wider audience.

Her two most recent books, *Good Woman: Poems and a Memoir* and *Next,* take their place among her best. They leave no doubt why Clifton has been nominated for the Pulitzer Prize.

She was born in Depew, N.Y., raised on the East Coast, and tenured on the West (University of California at Santa Cruz). The 51-year-old mother of six has never attended a poetry workshop.

Good Woman, with its 177 poems and 53-page memoir, is a kind of "selected poems." Clifton challenges her readers, romantics and rebels alike, to do more than grieve over life's inconsistencies. . . .

Clifton's power lies in her ability to celebrate both the extra and the ordinary in the human spirit and experience. Often fusing declarative structure and narrative tone, she relies on line endings and spacing for punctuation and achieves self-effacing transparency.

We see her art in **"The Lesson of the Falling Leaves,"** where repetition speeds the rhythm of each phrase.

> the leaves believe
> such letting go is love
> such love is faith
> such faith is grace
> such grace is god
> i agree with the leaves

Like the leaves' own logic, her poems neither defy nor defer. They are observations of innocence, and in that way penetratingly pure and uncompromisingly sincere.

Black and white on the page, black and white in society, Clifton's poems do not equivocate. If ever they are gray, it is because they are as exacting as a steel blade cutting to central issues. They say a lot about black being white in America.

Clifton's poems have an internal brilliance—here the repetition underscores the theme of pushing on. Chanting, droning, humming, her poems almost always work something out.

With Clifton, nothing is reckless—neither her multifaceted use of "i," nor the absence of titles on most poems, nor the lack of punctuation. Each poem appears as a meditation on power; what it means to control, withhold, or relinquish power as an ultimate demonstration of mastery.

Unadorned, Clifton's gemlike forms are resplendent, refracting the author's themes of family, the grace that can mean survival, the environment, and perhaps most of all, individual responsibility for the future.

"I grieve my whiteful ways," she says. But this is not the limit of her scope. She uses her experience as black, woman, mother, and child to describe relationships more far-reaching than those labels would admit. . . .

The slimmer volume of her two recent publications, *Next,* is a streamlined collection of 65 new poems.

Next can be best appreciated as further condensation where none was thought possible. The book is punctuated with words describing, documenting, denouncing finality, endings in themselves.

The poem **"the woman in the camp,"** about Lebanon in

1983, is an indictment of our times: "a woman in this camp has one breast and two babies. . . . "

Clifton, however, is not a guilt-tripping political poet. Her frustration with cruelty, whether intentional or random, is as steady and calm as it is enduring. *Next* includes a trilogy of what may be seen as political dirges. Her poems **"at gettysburg," "at nagasaki," "at jonestown,"** mourn promises unkept. In these, she speaks of freedom, peace, faith, eternal values that can neither be granted nor ultimately diminished.

These poems on public themes shed light on the universality of her more personal poems. Clifton titles one extremely succinct poem with a phrase half as long as the poem itself. An eight-word title on the 19-word poem reads: **"why some people be mad at me sometimes."**

Often, as in this case, black English takes the subjunctive form, expressing a possibility, or what is wished or imagined. Imagined, not because the condition, topic, or idea does not exist, but most often because blacks have had to wish things were otherwise. With such a cultural heritage it is no wonder "be" is commonly used.

> they asked me to remember
> but they want me to remember
> their memories
> and i keep on remembering
> mine.

One recalls the wonder of the black child who in elementary school asks her teacher, "Why is the color of this crayon called 'flesh?' It doesn't look like anyone I know."

The final pages contain one poem in particular—**"the death of fred clifton"**—that shows Clifton's metaphysical view of life. It recalls Bergman's film *Through a Glass Darkly,* or perhaps the Bible passage in I Corinthians for which it was named. The poem, the film, the biblical reference, are all about transition transcended and the impetus that makes it possible.

> i seemed to be drawn
> to the center of myself
> leaving the edges of me
> in the hands of my wife
> and i saw with most amazing
> clarity so that i had not eyes
> but sight,
> and rising turning
> through my skin
> there was all around not the
> shape of things
> but old, at last, the things
> themselves.

This poem perhaps best of all suggests Clifton's method, her form of understanding. In its simplest and most potent version, that "method" is love. For Clifton, love is the means by which each transforms and transcends his or her own vision to become witness to things themselves.

> E. K. Laing, *"The Voice of a Visionary, Not a Victim,"* in The Christian Science Monitor, *February 5, 1988, p. B3.*

Marilyn Hacker

Clifton is a poet of astonishing economy: five or ten pared lines can tell volumes.

> i am the sieve she strains from
> little by little
> every day
> i am the rind
> she is discarding.
> i am the riddle
> she is trying to answer.
> something is moving
> in the water.
> she is the hook.
> i am the line.

Lorine Neidecker and Hilda Morley limn in such strokes; Clifton contains, though, in her craft, the force, anger and hope of the Afro-American experience.

She also renders character with precision. Readers of her earlier books will recognize some of the ancestors and companions whose images Clifton had previously etched: her mother Thelma, her husband Fred, the twelve-fingered Dahomey foremothers. Their lives and deaths counterpoint farther-flung presences: Crazy Horse and Black Buffalo Woman, Winnie Mandela, the women of Lebanon and Johannesburg.

[The first section of her new collection *Next*] takes a global perspective, from Johannesburg to Jonestown to Nagasaki to the Middle Passage; its concentration is on women of color suffering violence they did not incite, a celebration of their wisdom and connection:

> this is the tale
> i keep on telling
> trying to get it right:
> the feast of women,
> the feeding
> and being fed.
>
>   **"this is the tale"**

The book's second section is a brave and devastating roll-call of elegies: deaths, the messages of the departed, the resurrecting power of words and names:

> White Buffalo Woman who brought the pipe
> Black Buffalo Woman and Black Shawl
> sing the names of the women sing
> the power of name in the women sing
> the name i have saved for my daughter sing
> her name to the ties and baskets and
> the red tailed hawk will take her name and
> sing her power to Wakan Tanka sing
> the name of my daughter sing she is
> They Are Afraid Of Her.
>
>   **"crazy horse names his daughter"**

"The death of crazy horse" and **"the message of crazy horse,"** whose "medicine is strong in the Black basket / of these fingers," are followed by the early death and testament of Thelma Sayles, the poet's mother, and the death, from leukemia, of a 21-year-old woman:

> i can hear her repeating my dates:
> 1962 to 1982 or 3. mother
> forgive me, mother believe
> i am trying to make old bones.
>
>   **"she won't ever forgive me"** . . .

The cumulative effect Clifton achieves through these testimonies, these elegies, is not despair, though grief fueled their making, but a mustering of strength and belief in the unkillable connecting spirit. Clifton mythologizes herself: that is, she illuminates her surroundings and history from within in a way that casts light on much beyond. She does this with penetrating brevity in a verse that mirrors speech as a Japanese ink drawing mirrors a mountain. (p. 24)

Marilyn Hacker, "A Pocketful of Poets," in The Women's Review of Books, *Vol. V, Nos. 10 & 11, July, 1988, pp. 23-4.*

> **"Poetry doesn't just come from the mind. Art is not just a thing of the intellect, but of the spirit. It's a balancing act. It is a thing of wonder to me."**
>
> **—Lucille Clifton, 1988**

Greg Kuzma

Lucille Clifton solves the problem of seeing continuity in life by never asking for it. Her poems do not pretend to be all-inclusive or to reconcile inhospitable realities. They are instead brief encounters, small disturbances of idea or language which over a few lines find a resolution and conclude. They seem oral, very much the product of doing poetry out loud, and they seem particularly dependent upon what one can safely absorb and bear in mind over a few moments, hearing them, without a text. No loose ends are allowed. Everything is neatly tucked into place, properly subordinated, arranged, and pointed toward the punch line.

Clifton too is a poet in middle age, but she seems protected from disillusionment and despair by having had children and by the patterns of changes and growth that envelop people in families, and by her blackness and her sisterhood. The very source of her grief and pain, in the collective history of her race and in her identification with the weak and the oppressed, is the source of her strength. She is rooted in many ways, and even in her poems of loss and grief, personal or cultural, she speaks always as a rooted person. We always know that someone of a large and multiple identity is speaking, and as we read through the poems we are not so much learning more of her depth and variousness as we are witnessing this same woman alive in the world. The poems are strong; they emanate from a collected and whole personality, one that is at home with itself, but they do not quest or question against absurdities. There is instead an implicit conviction that there is evil in the world because people allow it, and that life would be infinitely better, even perfect, could we but forgive each other and ourselves and truly love.

The danger with this vision is that things will be resolved too quickly, or that the treatment will seem simplistic. In **"winnie song,"** [of the collection *Next*] we hear "a dark wind is blowing / the homelands into home"—which sounds good, and might even serve as a slogan, but this poem does little to address the complex and almost impossible realities of South Africa. In another South Africa poem, **"there,"** she seems to penetrate to an essential level of reality and irony, where a white woman smiles at her own child on the lawn and at her husband "home from / arresting children." Regarding her own children, Clifton is amazingly sensitive to how they have become different from herself and different from each other. . . . Clifton works well in images that become metaphors of conditions and that are also open-ended and mysterious. The above poem is small, but it seems to embrace an essential truth about human experience: for all our complexity, our dilemmas are often explicable in simple terms. Elsewhere these same daughters defy her expectations:

> how they bewitch you into believing
> you have thrown off a pot that is yourself
> then one night you creep into their rooms and
> their faces have hardened into odd flowers
> their voices are choosing in foreign elections and
> their legs are open to strange unwieldy men.
> **"here is another bone to pick with you"**

Memorable phrases abound in the poems. Writing what is closely cropped, Clifton is conscious of the need for economy but also of how much can be achieved with the carefully drawn or apt phrase. In **"at creation"** she rises with "the dusky beasts" and a few lines later concludes with "all life is life / all clay is kin and kin." In **"at gettysburg"** she experiences the "bloody voices" of the ghosts, and remembers the battle as "this clash of kin across good farmland." In **"my dream about the cows"** she discovers "how all despair is / thin and weak and personal . . ." In **"morning mirror"** she remembers her mother, "whose only sin was dying, whose only / enemy was time. . . . whose only strength was love. . . ." Clifton's language carries a high degree of authority. Where the poems sometimes seem fragmented or enigmatic we work to understand them, so well do they usually understand themselves.

In part two of the book there are a number of death poems, or rather a number of poems devoted to each of a number of deaths. A different poet might have grouped all the poems about Joanne's death from leukemia together in one or two longer poems, but Clifton leaves them to make what seems a casual assortment. Where each of the poems as we read might well be the last, we become unusually alert and attentive, only to find on the next page another Joanne poem taken from a slightly different perspective. Here is one of the poems:

> the death of joanne c.
> 11/30/82
> aged 21
> i am the battleground that
> shrieks like a girl.
> to myself i call myself
> gettysburg. laughing,
> twisting the i.v.,
> laughing or crying, i can't tell
> which anymore,
> i host the furious battling of
> a suicidal body and
> a murderous cure.

Other poems are **"leukemia as white rabbit," "incanta-tion,"** and **"chemotherapy"** with its haunting and power-ful line, "my mouth is a cave of cries." There are nine in all, or perhaps ten, running from page 54 through 63, all of them brief, and though each is compact and tidy, to-gether they make a ragged sequence. The method is a strange one, unsettling and unnerving. We go from page to page not knowing if Joanne is still alive, or what the last word might be, or whether it will all add up or make sense once it is over. Clifton in effect re-creates some of the anxi-ety and tension that accompany any long terminal illness. Life progresses day by day from terror to remission, from moments of anguish to moments of calm and insight and a suspension of hostilities. Any day offers a fresh perspec-tive, or may, or holds out hope for the kind of seeing that may bring an ultimate and healing knowledge. Clifton's technique with these poems makes us aware of these reali-ties, however painful they are, however frustrating it is to read her. Some readers may come away longing for a poem of monumental design and address, one that might through eloquence and sweep of gesture put to rest these many uneasy and desperate cries, one that will make death seem orderly and neat in its lessons and meanings. Clifton offers us, wisely, only fragments. (pp. 628-30)

> *Greg Kuzma, in a review of "Next," in* The Georgia Review, *Vol. XLII, No. 3, Fall, 1988, pp. 628-30.*

Liz Rosenberg

The writer Clarence Major once noted that black Ameri-can poetry is almost always, in some sense, a reaction to slavery—and therefore often concerns itself with the right to Being. Lucille Clifton is a poet who grapples mightily with such questions. Her poetry is direct and clear: full of humor and forthrightness, tenderness and anger. She has no sentimental hankering after the past: " 'Oh slavery, slavery,' my Daddy would say. 'It ain't something in a book, Lue. Even the good parts was awful.' "

Her work is grounded in her own personal history, re-vealed most beautifully in the long memoir at the end of *Good Woman: Poems and a Memoir.* A sure sense of self reverberates throughout her poetry. . . .

Ms. Clifton resists, undermines myths of hierarchy, place-ment, entitlement (many of her poems are untitled), privi-lege—hers is a poetry of democracy, full of jumpy and lovely music:

> say skinny manysided tall on the ball
> brown downtown woman
> last time i saw you was on the corner of
> pyramid and sphinx.

She is a storyteller, as is clear throughout *Good Woman.*

> . . . I was in the kitchen washing dishes and all of a sudden I heard my Mama start screaming and fall down on the floor and I ran into the room and she was rolling on the floor and Daddy hadn't touched her, she had just started scream-ing and rolling on the floor. 'What have you done to her,' I hollered. Then 'What should I do, what should I do?' And Daddy said 'I don't

know, I don't know, I don't know, she's crazy,' and went out. When he left, Mama lay still, and then sat up and leaned on me and whispered, 'Lue, I'm just tired, I'm just tired.'

All of Ms. Clifton's best work falls into this space between comedy and tragedy—even melodrama. Her concerns are both earthbound and mystical, and what may appear sty-listically simple is, upon close examination, an effort to free the true voice clear and plain. BOA Editions has si-multaneously issued a book of her most recent poetry, *Next.* The poems here are about death and loss, in which: "the one in the next bed is dying. / mother we are all next. or next." The loss is not only personal, but spreads out-ward:

> it is late
> in white america.
> i stand
> in the light of the
> 7-11
> looking out toward
> the church
> and for a moment only
> i feel the reverberation
> of myself
> in white america
> a black cat
> in the belfry
> hanging
> and
> ringing.

Ms. Clifton's poetry is big enough to accommodate sorrow and madness and yet her vision emerges as overwhelming-ly joyous and calm:

> Things don't fall apart. Things hold. Lines con-nect in thin ways that last and last and lives be-come generations made out of pictures and words just kept. 'We come out of it better than they did, Lue,' my Daddy said, and I watch my six children and know we did. They walk with confidence through the world, free sons and daughters of free folk, for my Mama told me that slavery was a temporary thing, mostly we was free and she was right.

> *Liz Rosenberg, "Simply American and Mostly Free," in* The New York Times Book Review, *February 19, 1989, p. 24.*

Deborah Plant

Out of a history that can be traced to great-great-grandmother Caroline Donald come the realities and the wishes, the gaieties and grief, the worlds and words of Lu-cille Clifton, in her book *Good Woman: Poems and a Memoir 1969-1980. Good Woman* is a collection of Clif-ton's previously published poetry and prose: *Good Times, Good News about the Earth, An Ordinary Woman, Two-Headed Woman,* and *Generations: A Memoir.*

The title poem, **"Good times,"** informs the first book. It speaks of hard times at home, in the community, and in a present often assailed by a past haunted with slavery and struggle. The awful beauty Clifton brings to her poetry is that in spite of all, "still it was nice": "the sharp birdcall of the iceman," the sparks shooting from the rolling wheel of the scissors man, the street music of black voices looking for space to be, and home, Buffalo, New York, Purdy Street, where we all "hang on to our no place / happy to be alive." And when the rent is paid, the bread is baked, and grampaw is here, "everybody is drunk / and dancing in the kitchen / and singing in the kitchen." It's about making it, making something from what might be mistaken as nothing. It's about being able to go on because "i come from a line / of black and going on women."

The "Good News about the Earth" is that it remembers. The bad news is that its dust and waters have soaked up and swallowed much tormented red and black blood: "the bodies broken on / the trail of tears / and the bodies melted / in the middle passage / are married to rock and / ocean by now / and the mountains crumbling on / white men / the waters pulling white men down / sing for red dust and black clay . . ." The earth remembers and Clifton reflects on the state of slavery and the chaotic '60s when "white ways" killed white children at Kent State and black women and men taught her not to be ashamed of her kinky hair and dark skin. *Good News* ends with good news. The poem **"Spring Song"** promises a future, but a spiritual cleansing of the earth is required before the promise can be fulfilled. **"Spring Song"** says it is possible.

The journey to self-discovery and authenticity begun in *Good News* becomes more complex and intent in *An Ordinary Woman* and *Two-Headed Woman*. Clifton reassesses her life in **"the light that came to lucille clifton."** That light shone on "an unexamined life" and showed she had not understood the phenomenon that she was. In poems like **"what the mirror said,"** the poet begins to understand who she is and can be. The mirror said, "listen, / woman, / you not a noplace / anonymous girl." In **"I Am Not Done Yet"** she finds that she is "as possible as yeast / as imminent as bread / . . . a changed changer / i continue to continue." As the past and future exist simultaneously in the present, so Clifton comes to see herself as a totality of all that was, is, and will be. Her sense of herself as a totality of all that was, is, and will be. Her sense of herself underscores and reinforces all her connections—to her environment, herself, her children, her mothers: "i have dreamed dreams / for you mama / more than once, / i have wrapped me in your skin / and made you live again."

In *Generations: A Memoir,* Clifton brings to life those lives that live in her. Among others, she writes of her mother, Thelma Moore Sayles, with whom she shares close bonds—she was her mother's daughter, though her father's child; her father, Samuel Louis Sayles, Sr., who believed a man's goals in life were to buy a house, have a son, and plant a tree; her great-grandmother, Lucille Sale, who was the first woman hanged in Virginia; and her great-great-grandmother, Caroline Donald, who walked from New Orleans to Virginia when she was eight and told her children: "Get what you want, you from Dahomey women."

The memoir is a story of the lives of generations interwoven with the story of the death of Clifton's father. It tells a tale of quiet grief, assuaged anger, and lasting love. The prose memoir, like the poetry, is about relationships, connections, interconnections, and bonding, especially bonding between women. It's about life. And Clifton's artistry brings the poetry and prose to life. Like the edict of her great-great-grandmother, Clifton's style is straightforward, stark, and potent. Though subtle, her writing is intense; though spare, it is far-reaching. And it is infused with the power of the spoken word: one listens.

Good Woman: Poems and a Memoir 1969-1980 is all of a piece. It is life laid bare, a celebration of life celebrated. (pp. 115-17)

Deborah Plant, in a review of "Good Woman: Poems and a Memoir, 1969-1980," in Prairie Schooner, *Vol. 63, No. 1, Spring, 1989, pp. 115-17.*

Hank Lazer

Lucille Clifton's name is fairly well known, but perhaps her writing is not. With each new book she receives consideration for a Pulitzer Prize, and, up to a point, her poems are widely anthologized. But due to the deceptive simplicity of Clifton's work—a function of its conciseness, compression, and reliance on an oral tradition—her poetry is undervalued. When written about, her poems are described and praised but rarely given a reading that grants their depth and complexity. As readers, we fail to appreciate Lucille Clifton's full accomplishment if we exclude from the scope of our attention her twenty-one children's books. For they too, as fully as the poetry, establish the ethical and artistic dimensions of her work as a writer. With the publication of *Good Woman: Poems and a Memoir, 1969-1980* and *Next: New Poems,* all of Clifton's previously published poetry is back in print, and we can begin to see the magnitude of her accomplishment.

Beginning with her first book of poems [*Good Times*], Clifton attends to the enigma of pain fused with grace: . . .

> i forget
> while the streetlights were blooming
> and the sharp birdcall
> of the iceman and his son
> and the ointment of the ragman's horse
> sang spring
> our fathers were dead and
> our brothers were dying

Usually the ethic of the poetry, unlike the children's stories, is subdued or indirect. Wonder and suggestion often replace didacticism, as in the example of the scissors man and his sharpening wheel:

> still
> it was nice
> in the light of maizie's store
> to watch the wheel
> and catch the wheel—
> fire spinning in the air
> and our edges
> and our points
> sharpening good as anybody's

When the ethical imperative of the poetry gets stated, it

takes the form of solidarity, celebration, and witness, as in the act of commemoration and community which concludes **"Miss Rosie,"** one of Clifton's most often anthologized poems:

> when i watch you
> you wet brown bag of a woman
> who used to be the best looking gal in georgia
> used to be called the Georgia Rose
> i stand up
> through your destruction
> i stand up

As in the first poem in her first book of poems, the physical setting is usually urban, with a mixture of death and joy. That place or setting—"the inner city"—gets defined by someone else (who holds the power of definition), but it is also given another name by its actual inhabitants:

> in the inner city
> or
> like we call it
> home
> we think a lot about uptown
> and the silent nights
> and the houses straight as
> dead men
> and the pastel lights
> and we hang on to our no place
> happy to be alive
> and in the inner city
> or
> like we call it
> home

That "or" by itself on a line typifies the care of Clifton's writing: it is the pivot upon which the names "inner city" and "home," the opposed definitions of place, turn to face each other.

But the primary task of Clifton's writing is for "us" "to learn ourselves," which in the context of "album" (the first poem in Clifton's volume of new poems) means resisting the desire (in 1939) to turn young black children into images of Shirley Temple. Instead, to gain self-possession, or at least the dignity of fashioning and naming themselves in and by a history of their own devising, "we had to learn ourselves / back across 2 oceans / into bound feet and nappy hair." As Houston Baker has made abundantly clear, African-American literature constitutes "an expressive tradition grounded in the economics of slavery." For Baker and for Clifton that fact leads to a refiguring of American history, where, as Baker describes it, "the transportable stock on American vessels is no longer figured as a body of courageous Pilgrims but as 'black gold.' " For Clifton, who early in her poetry asks what "if the sea should break / and crash against the decks / and below decks break the cargo" and what "if the seas of cities / should crash against each other / and break the chains / and break the walls holding down the cargo," this refiguring of history takes several forms: her own familial history as recounted in *Generations: A Memoir* (included in *Good Woman*), her twenty-one children's books (especially *The Black BC's* and *All Us Come Cross the Water*), and her employment of and insistence upon the richness and beauty of vernacular expression. The latter strategy matters precisely for the reasons developed by Baker, who concludes "that writing the culturally specific is coextensive with discovering vernacular inscriptions in American culture. What must be summoned to view are not Grecian urns, but ancestral faces." And thus for Clifton, the last poem in *Two Headed Woman* asserts

> in populated air
> our ancestors continue.
> i have seen them.
> i have heard
> their shimmering voices
> singing.

The story of Clifton's ancestral lineage goes back to Caroline Donald, born in Dahomey in 1822, seized and taken to America, but who as a child of seven walked all the way from New Orleans to Virginia. A portion of that history appears in *Good News,* juxtaposed to Clifton's own shorter walk:

> walked twelve miles into buffalo and
> bought a dining room suit
> mammy ca'line
> walked from new orleans
> to virginia
> in 1830
> seven years old
> always said
> get what you want
> you from dahomey women.

Caroline's child Lucille shoots and kills the white father of her only son. Out of respect for the much admired Caroline, the mob that seizes Lucille does not lynch her; instead, they try her and accord her the "dignity" of being the first black woman legally hanged in Virginia. Lucille's son Genie was the father of Samuel, who married Thelma Moore, and they are Thelma Lucille Sayles Clifton's parents. Beginning with this accounting—"Who remembers the names of the slaves? Only the children of the slaves. The names are Caroline, and Lucy and Samuel, I say. Slave names"—Clifton tells and re-tells her history in *Generations.* After her first recording of that history, Clifton writes, "I look at my husband and our six children and I feel the Dahomey women gathering in my bones."

The history that Clifton records and affirms, as relayed to her by her father, is one of a community of strong women: "and she [Caroline Donald] used to always say, 'Get what you want, you from Dahomey women.' And she used to tell us about how they had a whole army of nothing but women back there and how they was the best soldiers in the world." *Generations* tells and re-tells Clifton's lineage, clarifying and verifying as it goes. Clifton's father's version of it begins, "The generations of Caroline Donald, born free among Dahomey people in 1822 and died free in Bedford Virginia in 1910 . . . and Sam Louis Sale, born a slave in America in 1777 and died a slave in the same place in around 1860." His account ends with his daughter Lucille, the poet, to whom he says, "We fooled em, Lue, slavery was terrible but we fooled them old people. We come out of it better than they did." (pp. 760-64)

In **"a simple language,"** [see Clifton's excerpt], the poet explains:

I use simple language. I have never believed that for anything to be valid or true or intellectual or "deep" it had to first be complex. I deliberately use the language that I use. Sometimes people have asked me when I was going to try something hard or difficult, as if my work sprang from my ignorance. I like to think I write from my knowledge not my lack, from my strength not my weakness. I am not interested if anyone knows whether or not I am familiar with big words, I am interested in trying to render big ideas in a simple way.

Such a poem as **"light,"** depending as it does on the Latin root *lux,* meaning light, at the heart of Lucille, begins to demonstrate how much Clifton accomplishes with a few simple words. Besides explaining why Clifton did not change her name to an Afrikan name—her name was already figured into an Afrikan-based history—the poem offers a motivation for her grandmother's deed, as well as establishing her own lineage as one based on light. So that in subsequent poems, when Clifton declares "the light that came to lucille clifton / came in a shift of knowing," or in the impressive sequence of poems entitled "the light that came to lucille clifton" when she asks "who are these strangers peopleing this light?," we know that that light is a history, a narrative refiguring of an otherwise often ahistorical image of inward illumination. The strength of Clifton's mysticism is that it is grounded in history and in a familial mother tongue:

> someone calling itself Light
> has opened my inside.
> i am flooded with brilliance
> mother,
> someone of it is answering to
> your name.

Clifton answers back with her poetry and prose. In the poetry, one other definition of that light occurs in **"roots":**

> call it our wildness then,
> we are lost from the field
> of flowers, we become
> a field of flowers.
> call it our craziness
> our wildness
> call it our roots,
> it is the light in us
> it is the light of us.

Clifton's literary accomplishment is simultaneously political and aesthetic. In "Race, Gender, and the Politics of Reading," Michael Awkward points out that "whenever the question has arisen as to whether black literary expression should be analyzed in terms of its internal formal structures and attempts at aesthetic sophistication or, in Richard Wright's famous autobiographical words, as an extratextual 'weapon' in the war against American racism, more often than not the Afro-American reader came down on the side of weaponry." According to Awkward, what that has meant in practice is a sociopolitical reading of black texts which assesses the text's potential to increase racial pride. Clearly, that production of dignity and pride has been a crucial aspect of Clifton's work, especially in her children's books such as *The Black BC's* and *All Us Come Cross the Water.* (pp. 764-66)

As both her poetry and *All Us Come Cross the Water* illustrate, ownership is linked to language and to naming. Telling the story, choosing the dialect, and picking the name are acts of power with direct consequences in terms of dignity and autonomy. Clifton's acts of naming are *not* the transcendental "perfect fits" imagined by Ralph Waldo Emerson, whose Adam-poet gives the "true" and "original" names to the creatures of the earth. It seems to me that Emerson's ideal is imaginable *only* from a position of power and privilege, not from within a family and a race where names are imposed as a brand and an exercise of power by someone else. Clifton's position as namer gets written in "the making of poems":

> the reason why i do it
> though i fail and fail
> in the giving of true names
> is i am adam and his mother
> and these failures are my job.

But Lucille Clifton's failure is her success. That is, Clifton affirms most effectively when she fuses limitation and grace, as in her finest poem . . . which begins "the thirty eighth year / of my life / plain as bread / round as cake / an ordinary woman" and which ends

> if in the middle of my life
> i am turning the final turn
> into the shining dark
> let me come to it whole
> and holy
> not afraid
> not lonely
> out of my mother's life
> into my own.
> into my own.
> i had expected more than this.
> i had not expected to be
> an ordinary woman.

In her newest poems, Clifton's revisionary history focuses more insistently on women. In one poem, she rewrites woman's power relationship to God, concluding "i am the good daughter who stays at home / singing and sewing. / when I whisper He strains to hear me and / He does whatever i say." Earlier in her writing, Clifton found herself "turning out of the / white cage, turning out of the / lady cage"; now, the poem she writes goes by the title **"female"** and affirms

> there is an amazon in us.
> she is the secret we do not
> have to learn.
> the strength that opens us
> beyond ourselves.
> birth is our birthright.
> we smile our mysterious smile.

Thus, her newest poems continue her work in defining and affirming "us."

The other equally effective affirmation in Clifton's poetry is akin to a power of the blues, what Houston Baker hears as the blues' "powers at the junctures of American experience—its power to wed quotidian rituals of everyday American experience to the lusters of a distinctively American expressive firmament." For Clifton, that wedding is accomplished in poems such as **"homage to my hips," "homage to my hair,"** and **"what the mirror said,"** but nowhere as effectively as in **"cutting greens":**

> curling them around
> i hold their bodies in obscene embrace
> thinking of everything but kinship.
> collards and kale
> strain against each strange other
> away from my kissmaking hand and
> the iron bedpot.
> the pot is black,
> the cutting board is black,
> my hand,
> and just for a minute
> the greens roll black under the knife,
> and the kitchen twists dark on its spine
> and i taste in my natural appetite
> the bond of live things everywhere.

If, as many readers and writers of poetry are aware, a dominant feature of poetry in our time is its diversity, the absolute fragmentation of audience and the decentralization of its production and distribution, then many important consequences ensue from Ron Siliman's conclusion that "the result has been a decentralization in which any pretense, whether from the 'center' or elsewhere, of a coherent sense as to the nature of the whole of American poetry is now patently obvious as just so much aggressive fakery." It especially matters that white male readers, writers, and professors reach out and resist the drawing of xenophobic boundaries so that they can begin to live in the fullness of the present moment, so that we might have, as Gertrude Stein had wished, "all of our contemporaries for our contemporaries." In so doing, we can begin to undo one of the most damaging, lingering, and conservative goals of high modernist poetry. Instead of seeking to "purify the language of the tribe," we can begin to ac-

knowledge with and through Lucille Clifton's writing, and the poetry of many other African-American poets, that "there are / too many languages for / one mortal tongue." What we need is not a purification of the language of the tribe, but an attentiveness to the languages of the many tribes constituting American expression. (pp. 768-70)

Hank Lazer, "Blackness Blessed: The Writings of Lucille Clifton," in The Southern Review, *Vol. 25, No. 3, July, 1989, pp. 760-70.*

FURTHER READING

Johnson, Dianne. "The Chronicling of an African-American Life and Consciousness: Lucille Clifton's Everett Anderson Series." *Children's Literature Association Quarterly* 14, No. 3 (Winter 1989): 174-78.

Examines themes of black identity and pride in Clifton's juvenile fiction.

Laing, E. K. "Making Each Word Count." *The Christian Science Monitor* (5 February 1988): B3.

Interview in which Clifton describes the personal philosophies and values that have influenced her writing.

Waniek, Marilyn Nelson. "Black Silence, Black Songs." *Callaloo* 6, No. 1 (1983): 156-65.

Discusses the visionary quality of poems in Clifton's *Two-Headed Woman*.

J. M. Coetzee

1940-

(Full name: John M. Coetzee) South African novelist, essayist, critic, editor, and translator.

Widely regarded as one of South Africa's most accomplished contemporary novelists, Coetzee examines the effects of racism, oppression, and fear. While addressing the brutalities and contradictions associated with the South African policy of apartheid, Coetzee writes from an apolitical viewpoint that extends beyond geographic and social boundaries to achieve universal significance. This effect is enhanced through his use of such literary devices as allegory, unreliable narrators, and enigmatic symbolic settings.

Coetzee lived in numerous small towns in rural Cape Province as well as the suburbs of Cape Town, where he was born. He attended the University of Cape Town, where he received undergraduate degrees in mathematics and English by 1961. Moving to London, Coetzee worked for International Business Machines (IBM) as a computer programmer while writing poetry and studying literature in his spare time. "[I spent] the evenings in the British Museum reading Ford Madox Ford," Coetzee wrote, "and the rest of the time tramping the cold streets of London seeking the meaning of life." He eventually gave up computer programming and traveled to the United States to complete his graduate studies in English at the University of Texas. While there he became troubled by such events as the Vietnam War and the assassination of South African Prime Minister H. F. Verwoerd. Coetzee's moral questioning of violence and war informs his first work, *Dusklands,* written in 1971 after he returned to South Africa. Comprised of two long stories, "The Vietnam Project" and "The Narrative of Jacobus Coetzee," *Dusklands* explores Western imperialism by juxtaposing the Vietnam War in the first story with a fictional account in the second of the exploitation of native Africans by one of the country's Boer settlers.

In the Heart of the Country was the first of Coetzee's novels to be published in both South Africa and the United States. Presented in stream-of-consciousness form, *In the Heart of the Country* is the story of Magda, a troubled white woman who murders her father, ostensibly due to his affair with a young black woman. Unable to adjust to change and doomed by her isolation, Magda is said to represent the stagnant policies of apartheid. Blake Morrison commented: "Coetzee manages through [Magda] to present a powerful image of outdated conventions and of the struggle to erode them." Coetzee's strong international reputation was established with *In the Heart of the Country* and solidified with his next novel, *Waiting for the Barbarians.* This work addresses oppression through its depiction of a magistrate in an unspecified setting who must choose between helping to dominate a group of people known as "the Barbarians" and his desire to ally himself

with them. Declaring that when "some men suffer unjustly . . . it is the fate of those who witness their suffering to suffer the shame of it," the magistrate offers powerful commentary about the perpetuation of injustices by the ruling class in an authoritarian society. *Life and Times of Michael K* corresponds thematically to Coetzee's earlier works but includes a new dimension in its focus on the oppression of a single character. Michael K is a slow-witted outcast who searches with his mother for a home during a turbulent period of an unnamed country's civil war. Although Coetzee has denied the similarities, critics frequently compare Michael K and the character K in Franz Kafka's novel *The Trial.* Like Kafka's K, Michael K is victimized by social forces he can neither control nor understand.

Although his novels usually address political injustice, Coetzee deviated from this trend with *Foe.* A retelling of Daniel Defoe's *Robinson Crusoe, Foe* examines the complexities of communication and the relationship between authorship and authority. In this story, a woman attempts to relate her impressions of Crusoe and Friday to an author called "Foe." Later changing his name to Defoe, Foe alters the woman's story by presenting its characters as idealistic and enterprising rather than indigent and depressed, as the woman had originally described them. Through this scenario, many critics assert that Coetzee creates a viable philosophical parable of how language can contribute to oppression.

In his collection of essays, *White Writing: On the Culture of Letters in South Africa,* Coetzee continues to investigate the power of language by analyzing the works of white South African writers. Attempting to expose the relationship between language and cultural identity, Coetzee focuses on how European values and conventions are reflected in South African policies and attitudes concerning property and government. The novel *Age of Iron* traces the experiences of Elizabeth Curren, a white South African woman suffering from cancer who writes long letters to her daughter in the United States. Some critics considered this Coetzee's most brutal and pessimistic novel due to its detailed explication of the viciousness of apartheid and of the physical deterioration of disease; however, several noted that Elizabeth's sentimental musings on childhood and maternal love signify rebirth and human continuity. While representing Coetzee's abiding concerns with human suffering and the dissolution of oppressive and racist regimes, *Age of Iron* also reflects recent positive changes in South Africa, among them the release of Nelson Mandela from prison and the easing of some social restrictions that are based on race. At the end of *Age of Iron,* the protagonist declares, "[It is] time for fire, time for an end, time for what grows out of ash to grow."

(See also *CLC,* Vols. 23, 33 and *Contemporary Authors,* Vols. 77-80.)

PRINCIPAL WORKS

Novels

Dusklands   1974
In the Heart of the Country   1977; also published as *From the Heart of the Country,*   1977
Waiting for the Barbarians   1980
Life and Times of Michael K   1983
Foe   1986
Age of Iron   1990

Other

Land Apart: A South African Reader   [coeditor, with André Brink]   1987
White Writing: On the Culture of Letters in South Africa (essays)   1988

J. M. Coetzee   [Interview with Tony Morphet]

[The following interview was conducted in February, 1987.]

[Morphet:] *Foe might be seen as something of a retreat from the South African situation. Certainly one, if not the major, interest of the book is the nature and the processes of fiction—of words and stories. Would you comment on the prominence of this theme in the book?*

[Coetzee:] *Foe* is a retreat from the South African situation, but only from that situation in a narrow temporal perspective. It is not a retreat from the subject of colonialism or from questions of power. What you call "the nature and processes of fiction" may also be called the question of *who writes?* Who takes up the position of power, pen in hand?

Your attitude to stories has always been ambivalent—they create and bestow meanings but they also construct false worlds (Crusoe's island with its cannibals!). In Foe you sharpen the critical side of this ambivalence by constant references to the market in books ("Their trade is in books not truth"). How do these reflections bear on your own position as a successful author?

"Successful author" is a barbed phrase here, a highly barbed phrase. Foe in the book, or Daniel Defoe in "real" life, is the type of the successful author. Am I being classed with Foe, though my interest clearly lies with Foe's foe, the *un*successful author—worse, author*ess*—Susan Barton? How can one question power ("success") from a position of power? One ought to question it from its antagonist position, namely, the position of weakness. Yet once again, in this interview, I am being installed in a position of power—power, in this case, over my own text.

Part of the pleasure of the book is tracking the detailed divergences between Susan's narrative and Defoe's book. There are two features, though, which stand out with especial prominence: Susan herself and Friday. Would you like to say something about your choice of narrator—the begetter of the story? Is there a feminist point here?

I would hate to say either that there is a feminist point or that I *chose* the narrator. The narrator chose me. There is a flippant way of saying that, and a serious way. The book deals with choosing in the serious sense.

Friday has no tongue. Why?

Nobody seems to have sufficient authority to say for sure how it is that Friday has no tongue.

He is an uncomfortable presence but he is more potent as an absence. Is the absence directly related to his blackness—his Africanness?

In Robinson Crusoe's story, Friday is a handsome Carib youth with near-European features. In *Foe* he is an African. Whether Friday is potent or not I don't know. What is more important, Susan doesn't know. (pp. 461-63)

Friday appears to be a close relative of Michael K's, as well as of a number of other figures in your work—the barbarian girl, for example, in **Waiting for the Barbarians.** *Would you comment on the recurring presence of this "family" in your writing?*

You have pointed out this "family" to me before. I am intrigued by its existence, but I don't think it is in my best interests to look too deeply into it.

In **Dusklands** *you describe Jacobus attempting to reach into the interior life of a stone by cracking it into pieces.*

There is no interior because at each splitting he is faced with yet another surface. I read this as an image of resistance and it seems to me that Friday (and his relatives) embody a similar form of resistance to efforts to comprehend their interior "meanings." Is that a fair and reasonable reading? Would you like to comment further on the importance which you attach to the notion of resistance?

Yes, it is a fair and reasonable reading. I hope that a certain spirit of resistance is ingrained in my books; ultimately I hope they have the strength to resist whatever readings I impose on them on occasions like the present one.

To return to South African issues. Your writing seems to me radical in the sense that it goes beneath the specific phenomena of history and culture but also deeply conservative in that it throws into doubt the whole significance of created meanings. Would you accept the implication that your work contradicts the idea of a "master narrative"—whether religious or socio-historical—and that therefore human-meaning making can only appear as a series of arbitrary games played out against the innocence and unconcern of nature or being? Susan and Foe against Friday and Crusoe? And where then is Art?

Your questions again and again drive me into a position I do not want to occupy. (But what legitimacy has that "want"?) By accepting your implication, I would produce a master narrative for a set of texts that claim to deny all master narratives. Let me therefore simply say that certain things get put in question in my novels, the notion of arbitrariness being, I hope, one of them. (pp. 463-64)

> *J. M. Coetzee and Tony Morphet, in an interview in* TriQuarterly, *No. 69, Spring-Summer, 1987, pp. 454-64.*

George Packer

J. M. Coetzee's first four novels—all slim, all intense, but increasingly spare and lucid—are so distinctive in their style and atmosphere that almost any sentence plucked at random from them is bound to seem unmistakably his. Coetzee has been pursuing one theme for some time now: the fate of conscience in the face of its own oppressive power. His new novel seems to me to be a wrong, if interesting, step, but one needs to get at the qualities that make the earlier books "Coetzean" before considering whether *Foe* is a departure or simply a development along lines already implicit in the other work.

Coetzee is an allegorist, or fabulist, even though his work contains the precise details of naturalistic fiction. Something in the remoteness of his settings liberates his imagination: the second novella in *Dusklands* is the narrative of an eighteenth-century Boer frontiersman; *In the Heart of the Country* is set in the wasteland of the Western Cape in the early nineteenth century; *Waiting for the Barbarians* has no specific time or place; and *Life and Times of Michael K* takes place in a dimly recognizable South Africa of the future, with even the crucial fact of K's race left unclear. In these indeterminate settings Coetzee's strangely archaic physical world of pumpkins and packhorses and linseed oil can strike the reader with the force of a leather lash.

But it is the human body that he puts most disturbingly before us. Think of *Barbarians,* and the broken ankles and scarred eyes of the barbarian girl stick uneasily in your mind; think of *Michael K,* and it is the hero's harelip; from *In the Heart of the Country,* Magda's grotesque face, and the father she has shot, steeping in his own blood and feces. These images of mutilation and decay evoke the atmosphere of horror from which Coetzee rarely allows relief: he lingers on them until they become emblems of his central theme.

The aging magistrate in *Barbarians,* a hedonistic but humane official in an outpost town at a time of impending war, beds the barbarian girl whom the agents of his own empire have tortured. "Until the marks on this girl's body are deciphered and understood," he thinks, "I cannot let go of her." She yields, but he experiences neither pleasure nor escape, and his intentions turn out to be barely different from those of the interrogators he thinks he is opposing. . . . After an act of rebellion, after his own imprisonment and torture at the hands of the empire, the Magistrate reaches this insight into his equivocal position: "I was not, as I liked to think, the indulgent pleasure-loving opposite of the cold rigid Colonel. I was the lie that Empire tells itself when times are easy, he the truth that Empire tells when harsh winds blow. Two sides of imperial rule, no more, no less." And also: "The crime that is latent in us we must inflict on ourselves."

That last remark might stand as an epigraph for Coetzee's central vision. In the world of his novels the oppressed are almost always the other, the oppressor the ambivalent self; the works locate the place in the human soul where oppression and injustice begin. Coetzee is too penetrating to say that cruelty exists only in this or that regime or because of such and such events. He pursues the nature of cruelty relentlessly, and in *Michael K* it leads him to a position very near a kind of nostalgic quietism.

That strain is latent in all his novels.. . . . But in *Michael K,* quietism—lying low—is the only possible escape from war and internment camps. Half-starved and "simple," K finds a harsh freedom in the mountains, surviving on the fruit of the earth: "Perhaps the truth is that it is enough to be out of the camps, out of all the camps at the same time. . . . How many people are there left who are neither locked up nor standing guard at the gate?" The pastoral is no sentimental idyll; K's bare existence hardly represents a triumph over the state. But in Coetzee's vision there is no real alternative to hiding in the mountains or being crushed by history, except in madness.

Foe seems a playful respite from that nightmare. The tone is lighter; the allegory takes place at the level of philosophical speculation rather than engaging disturbing images and events. Among other things, the book is one long jest based on *Robinson Crusoe.* (pp. 402-03)

Foe reads as if Coetzee started out to reinvent Defoe's famous tale through a woman's eyes, became intrigued with the linguistic and philosophical implications, and ended up writing a commentary on the elusiveness of his own project. This kind of metafiction is not new to Coetzee: *Dusklands* blurs the distinctions between author and character, and between history and fiction; in *In the Heart of the Country* much of Magda's agony is directed toward language itself. But in his masterpieces, *Barbarians* and *Michael K,* Coetzee drops these concerns and lays out a straightforward story that seems too urgent to be diverted.

In general, *Foe* avoids the excessive cleverness of the self-regarding novel. Instead of a puzzle's complacent smile the book engages its mystery. And yet you close the novel feeling that almost nothing in it approached the intensity of Coetzee's best work. Its diction and syntax are often burdened by its stiff, vaguely eighteenth-century style. Neither the island nor London comes alive with the specificity of Coetzee's other imagined landscapes. Friday is an utterly passive figure, hardly a character at all; compare him with the barbarian girl, whose quiet physical presence dominates the first half of her book. The image of his severed tongue is far less forceful than the physical mutilations in the earlier books; it remains an abstraction, a symbol. These problems seem to me signs of a hollowness in *Foe* that goes back to the vision Coetzee left us with in *Michael K.* One place to start asking what happens to that vision in *Foe* is at the central image of the tongue. What does it signify? (p. 404)

The oppressive system in *Foe* is language, and the mark of the oppressed is Friday's missing tongue. The story's allegory expresses a profound skepticism about the ability of speech and writing to tell the truth about the mute and thereby free them. In that sense Friday is a Michael K who has no J. M. Coetzee. And by her obsession with his story Susan, his would-be interpreter, is betrayed—like the Magistrate—into making him her "helpless captive." For all its enigmas and inventions, *Foe* follows directly from Coetzee's recent work.

Readers may criticize or embrace *Foe* as escapist, but neither response is an accurate measure of its worth, and neither recognizes how it or something like it was almost inevitable, given the direction of Coetzee's other novels. The vision that led to *Barbarians* and *Michael K* has led Coetzee temporarily into a blind alley. *Foe* is a brilliant and in some ways jocose philosophical novel, but at its center lies the pessimism implicit in his earlier work. *Foe* leaves us with the impossible choice of either withdrawing into an ideal world of nature, of the uncorrupted precolonial past, or enduring the violence of just about everything else: civilization, history, sexuality, referential language, novel-writing.

This is Coetzee's strain of quietism, here occupying vast tracts of the territory. In the end it may be an untenable position for a novelist. It means leaving out too much— among other things, the possibility of change. It amounts to a negation, and perhaps a writer can't keep producing good novels on that basis. Coetzee has seen more deeply into the solitary nightmare at the origin of oppression than any contemporary writer I can think of. The only way out is to soften the nightmare; to accept it but search for a meliorating principle in spite of what one knows; or to adopt some type of quietism. Coetzee is too honest for the first, and too pessimistic for the second. He is left with the ste-

rility of the third, and it is this that robs *Foe* of the power of his best work. (pp. 404-05)

George Packer, "Blind Alleys," in The Nation, New York, Vol. 244, No. 12, March 28, 1987, pp. 402-05.

Maureen Nicholson

In his earlier, remarkable novels, *Waiting for the Barbarians* (1980) and *Life and Times of Michael K* (1983), J.M. Coetzee subtly examined brutal actions in what appeared to be an allegorized South Africa. His writing in these novels was moving, convincing and frank. Coetzee seemed to understand and could represent for his readers a grasp of the workings of social injustice and its outcomes for marginalized individuals. I found his writing especially impressive as literature that didn't oversimplify a social reality that might easily have provoked a defensive response of incomprehension and helplessness—as well as profound despair. Mutilation, obsession, jealousy, oppression and madness—issues at the distraught heart of Coetzee's writing—could, presented in his spare prose, make the reader sicken with recognition and realization. Coetzee struck me as brave.

With his most recent novel, *Foe* (1986), Coetzee initially appeared to me to have all but abandoned his usual concerns and literary techniques. I was mistaken. More importantly, though, I was worried about why he has chosen *now* to write this kind of book; I found his shift of focus and technique ominous. Could he no longer sustain the courage he had demonstrated, turning instead to a radically interiorized narrative? For, in *Foe,* Coetzee has written what is for him a self-reflexive, experimental work, partly derived from Defoe's *Robinson Crusoe,* with a brooding quality most reminiscent of his own *In the Heart of the Country* (1977). 'Textuality' is here the central issue: how the story is told and what gets hidden or suppressed; whose voices are heard in the story and in history; the relationships between author and characters; and the demands of readers and booksellers whose 'trade is in books, not in truth'.

Given this explicit emphasis on textuality, *Foe* is a departure from what readers have come to expect of Coetzee. But his strength was and remains the literary representation of race and personal relations, *not* intertextual relations. For example, we found in *Waiting for the Barbarians* Coetzee's willingness to explore the attraction one can feel for the mutilated, especially when this mutilation is the result of injustice, and corresponds to a deep emotional wound. We were given the central character of the Magistrate whose principal obsession is washing the feet, calves, and thighs of a 'barbarian' girl. A victim of torture, she has had her ankles broken and eyes seared. In *Life and Times of Michael K,* the central character's name was obviously intended to associate him with Kafka's K. At the novel's austere conclusion, Michael, whose obliging spirit is undercut by a body that simply wants to die, proposes to live a straitened life: 'he would lower [a teaspoon] down the shaft deep into the earth, and when he brought it up there would be water in the bowl of the spoon; and in that way, he would say, one can live'. These powerful examples of Coetzee's concern with injustice and human need, shaped by his strong literary sensibility, do find further expression in *Foe,* but in a laboriously articulated narrative marred by incessant contrivance and good intentions. While his novels have never been conventionally realistic, they have never before been so consistently 'literary' in emphasis, nor so emotionally distant. His demands on his readers with *Foe* sadden me, requiring a patience with literary contrivance that many will give grudgingly.

Coetzee starts with the Crusoe story, especially the 'mythologizing' of Crusoe's individuality and economic industriousness, thoroughly subverting the tale. He tells what he proposes as the *hidden* stories of *Robinson Crusoe:* he tells of *his* Cruso's slothfulness (Cruso says: 'We have no need of tools', and his first and only bit of furniture is a bed); of the barrenness of the island (the trees are stunted and unusable for building; there is no clay to bake into pots; the diet is solely wild bitter lettuce, fish and birds' eggs); of the mundanity of the dangers ('The danger of island life . . . was the danger of abiding sleep'). To disabuse 'readers raised on travellers' tales', expecting high adventure, Coetzee creates a truthteller: Susan Barton, a woman who, after spending several years in Brazil searching for her stolen daughter, is a passenger on a ship whose crew mutinies. She is assaulted, then set adrift in a small boat with the ship's dead captain (he has a handspike in his eye-socket). She rows, then swims to safety on an island where she finds Coetzee's Cruso and Friday. (Defoe's Friday is tawny with rather delicate features whereas Coetzee's Friday is 'black: a Negro with a head of fuzzy wool'.) Their major activity is futile work, which involves building elaborate, well-ordered terraces that remain unplanted since there is no seed. Once Susan Barton and Friday are back in England (Cruso dies on the voyage home), she represents herself as Mrs Cruso, and finds that, for her, 'all that Cruso leaves behind . . . is the story of his island'. This she offers to a Mr Foe, 'who had heard many confessions and . . . [was] reputed a very secret man'.

Susan's introductory monologue or confession to Mr Foe (Daniel Defoe's 'true' name) is the first of four sections; the second section begins with accounts of her life in London, then shifts into a series of letters to Mr Foe, and ends with some notes on her walk to Bristol with Friday, a 'castle in the air' adventure, as she calls it, to send Friday by boat back to Africa (or, as she initially sees it, to return him to his freedom). What emerges in these two sections are Susan's desire to tell her story well and her fascination with Friday and what he represents for both her and Foe. When she reflects on her year and a half on the island, she wonders, 'Are these enough strange circumstances to make a story of ? . . . Alas, will the day ever arrive when we can make a story without strange circumstances?' (When I was little, 'telling stories' was the same as telling lies; Susan struggles with this kind of moralized conflation of art and ethics.) From doubting the likelihood of making an interesting *and* truthful story from her experience, as well as doubting her ability to write, she moves toward a liberating, though possibly irresponsible, realization: '[T]he words themselves do the journeying. I had not guessed it was so easy to be an author'. She writes her ac-

count while suspecting that Foe has already decided that the story would work better *without the woman.* The irony here is that the reader knows her story forms no part of Defoe's *Crusoe;* and it is to Coetzee's credit that, at least for this reader, Susan's absence or silence in that novel provides some grounds for bewildered indignation. In *Foe,* she points to what is lacking in Defoe's book, for that narrative shows no sign of the historical birth Coetzee proposes—none of the racial and sexual tensions, the loneliness of the characters, and the frustration of their needs, as well as Defoe's financial and legal difficulties.

Is it fair to blame Defoe? Of course not; and that's scarcely Coetzee's point: he uses Susan Barton to address the issue of what happens to historical experience as it is transformed into story, to address the question of what or who gets left out, 'for art's sake'. Susan asserts: 'I am not a story, Mr Foe . . . I am a free woman who asserts her freedom by telling her story according to her own desire'. There is great pride here; Susan is saying that her voice *will* be heard; and it is in part her belief in the power of language that attracts her to Friday, for unlike Defoe's Friday, who mastered some English, Coetzee's Friday can't speak: he has no tongue. As Susan fears ('the lost tongue might stand not only for itself but for a more atrocious mutilation') and later discovers, Friday is also castrated. (Coetzee's thematic obsessions, as well as their links to literary and language theory, break through into *Foe* at this point.) Friday's powerlessness and his unknown past—whether he was indeed a slave or, as Cruso once claimed, a former cannibal—fascinate Susan as mysteries: 'Friday has no command of words and therefore no defence against being reshaped day by day in conformity with the desires of others'.

The relationship between Susan and Friday provides Coetzee with ample opportunities to consider at length, explicitly or analogously, the ethical position of the writer vis-à-vis people who may later be represented in writing; specifically, in his case, South African blacks and coloureds, but, more generally, all people who have been silenced, suppressed or misrepresented. Cruso had said earlier that the slavers who may have cut out Friday's tongue perhaps 'wanted to prevent him from ever telling his story'; and Foe states (it is difficult not to attribute this to Coetzee himself) that 'the true story will not be heard till by art we have found a means of giving voice to Friday'.

Coetzee is obviously making important points. Yet that's part of the problem with *Foe*—its obviousness. Coetzee has said before much of what he seems to say here, but in a dramatic way that was far more likely to engage a reader than this thoughtful, didactic, arid prose. There's a bitter, earnest, well-intentioned rationality at work in this novel. There is irony, too, but not enough to counter the contrivance of incidents and set monologues. Only Susan is allowed any development as a character; the others fulfill their roles in an ungenerous scheme which inexorably leads the reader to the work's final pages.

In the third section the novel opens, a crack, for the reader. We are given much less of Susan speaking aloud, with no response except Cruso's occasional few words; we have instead some semblance of dialogue and an attempt at fuller characterization. Susan attempts to communicate with Friday (and it *is* 'communication', with all this word's connotations, not just talk) in other than a rudimentary way; she tries pictures, music, but with little success; her speeches become transparently reminiscent of Miranda's to Caliban [in Shakespeare's *The Tempest*]. (Symbolically and thematically important in African literature, Caliban's brutishness has been seen as analogous to what some whites saw in blacks, a brutishness which may be tempered by language; as Miranda rebukes Caliban: 'When thou didst not, savage, / Know thine own meaning but wouldst gabble like / A thing most brutish, I endow'd thy purposes / With words that made them known'. So, Susan's adoption of Miranda's attitude before Friday's inarticulateness may be seen as at once presumptuous and inevitable, given her intention of being a teacher of language. This predicament may well represent Coetzee's own; that is, how dare he—and he must—speak for others.) Friday in London, grown fat and unhappy on sleep and oatmeal, is ultimately attracted to writing by Foe's writing accoutrements—his robes, a filthy wig, his writing table, pens—*not* by Susan's efforts. When Susan tells Foe she is afraid Friday 'will foul your papers', he replies: 'My papers are foul enough, he can make them no worse.' Friday begins to learn to write.

Foe's 'foulness' is seen in the fact that he tries to foist onto Susan a daughter, a family history, and a five part adventure novel, in which the island 'adventure' provides novelty. (For Foe, 'foul papers' would mean unrevised manuscript.) Coetzee represents this tension between the imperatives of Susan's 'true' experiences and Foe's artistic wilfulness as a struggle; yet the struggle itself remains subdued and distant, elaborated usually in the form of long paragraphs of questions. Faced with Foe's wilfulness, Susan begins to mistrust her own authorship: '[A]ll my life grows to be a story and there is nothing of my own left to me. . . . Now I am full of doubt. Nothing is left to me but doubt. I am doubt itself. Who is speaking me? Am I a phantom too? To what order do I belong? And you: who are you?' At this outburst, Foe, the writer who 'never before had . . . failed for words', is speechless; he kisses Susan.

To the key phrase 'Who is speaking me?' the response is an embrace. Susan, attempting to fathom her relationships with the characters who surround her, is clearly changed: her illusions of simple autonomy, of self-sufficiency, of being her own author, crumble. I suspect that Coetzee, too, prods himself with this question; and it seems to me that, in *Foe,* what we can read is the writing of a man who is now explicitly questioning his right to speak through his characters, who is engaging in a protracted examination of his own influences, ethics and power. In *Foe,* at least, his characters do have an autonomy of sorts: they are aware that they speak within a story, and they are intimately concerned with questions of authorship and ethics. (In one of Coetzee's few traces of humour, Susan reflects before sleeping with Foe: 'I hesitated awhile, wondering what it augured for the writing of my story that I should grow so intimate with its author'.)

Coetzee's examination of the ethics of interpretation find

an ideal starting point in *Robinson Crusoe,* that paragon of 'realistic' narrative and early capitalist endeavour. For how truthful was Defoe's presentation of Crusoe's psychological integrity and resilient industriousness after twenty-eight years on the island, practically all spent in isolation? Coetzee's Cruso says: 'I ask you to remember, not every man who bears the mark of the castaway is a castaway at heart'. This is only one of Coetzee's many examples showing that, despite appearances, social connectedness exists or is desired. In fact, it is Cruso's *degeneracy* in isolation that serves as an affirmation of this need for social experience. And, as Coetzee makes clear, such experience is riddled with the politics of competing, conflicting interpretations—and interpreters. This realization provides the link with his previous concerns: interiorized though this narrative may be, it is still a narrative that struggles to become *social,* to be articulated and situated in society. What is at issue then is power.

In the brief final section of *Foe,* we are introduced to a new interpreter—'I'—who is not identified except by what he or she does; it is tempting to conclude that the 'I' is Coetzee himself (especially once one has realized this dreamlike sequence's significance). Early in the novel, Susan had watched Friday paddle out to sea, where, over a particular spot, he sprinkles white petals; she identifies this act as the first sign that Friday has some 'spirit or soul [that] stirred beneath that dull and unpleasant exterior'. With Foe, Susan further speculates that, at this place, Cruso's ship—a slaver—went down; Foe and Susan together imagine that 'Friday is beckoned from the deep' by his submerged community, the bones of his fellow slaves. They elaborate a descent into the wreck, for 'till we have spoken the unspoken we have not come to the heart of the story'. Now, the 'I' of the last section of *Foe* undertakes this descent, after briefly ascending to Foe's London rooms.

There he finds Susan and Foe in bed, 'quietly composed', their skin taut across their faces. Friday is also in the room, barely alive, his pulse faint, 'as if his heart beat in a far-off place'. For the first time, we are allowed to note a scar around Friday's neck, 'left by a rope or chain'; the 'I' unsuccessfully attempts to pry open Friday's mouth. Then the dreamlike, darkly passionate and sorrowful movement of the last section intensifies, with the 'I' descending into the wreck, 'slipping overboard' into the waters where Friday had strewn the petals. In the wreck are 'Susan Barton and her dead captain, fat as pigs in their white nightclothes, their limbs extending stiffly from their trunks, their hands, puckered from long immersion, held out in blessing, float like stars against the low roof'. Again Friday is sought, and found, dominant in death: '[T]his is not a place of words. . . . This is a place where bodies are their own signs. It is the home of Friday'. The narrator is successful, this time, in opening Friday's mouth, from which a slow stream 'runs northward and southward to the ends of the earth. Soft and cold, dark and unending, it beats against my eyelids, against the skin of my face'. Coetzee has had his characters talk their way through to this silenced character's opened mouth.

But this is where Coetzee's novels usually appear to *begin.*

The remarkable conclusion, with its ambiguous communion, cannot make up for the contrivance of much that has come before. The lighthearted *zeal* that makes similar writing work—say, in Italo Calvino's 'novels'—simply isn't *in* Coetzee; his sombre imagination is too grounded in a politicized reality that leaves him grieving. Throughout the novel, he seems to be considering for himself another of the questions Foe asks Susan: imagining a life without sleep, Foe wonders: 'Would we be better or worse . . . if we were no longer to descend nightly into ourselves and meet what we meet there?' Coetzee's answer is clearly that we would be worse; and his own 'descents' have previously made for excellent novels. Perhaps *Foe* is best viewed as a pause for recapitulation and evaluation, transitional in Coetzee's development as a writer, though I frankly can't imagine what will come next—whether he will return to the artistic potency of *Waiting for the Barbarians* and *Life and Times of Michael K,* remain with the ethical uncertainty expressed in *Foe,* or move toward some form of resolution of what he sees as the exigencies of art and 'truth'. I do know that Coetzee no longer trusts his readers and that *his* voice, brave and revelatory, ought not to be silenced, as it has been in so much of *Foe.* (pp. 52-8)

> Maureen Nicholson, " 'If I Make the Air around Him Thick with Words': J. M. Coetzee's 'Foe'," in West Coast Review, Vol. 21, No. 4, Spring, 1987, pp. 52-8.

Ashton Nichols

J. M. Coetzee is an archeologist of the imagination, an excavator of language who testifies to the powers and weaknesses of the words he discovers. His first four works of fiction, *Dusklands, In the Heart of the Country, Waiting for the Barbarians,* and *Life and Times of Michael K,* have provided sparse, rich allegories of the South African system and, more widely, of all forms of injustice. In his most recent novel, *Foe,* Coetzee examines the relationship between authorship and authority. The result is an enigmatic, powerful work that reveals the complex interplay between words and silence, and the ultimate limitation of all our attempts to linguistically transform our experience.

Susan Barton is a castaway; she washes up on an island with Robinson Cruso and Friday, where she lives until the time of her rescue. As a result, she has the opportunity to tell the story once told in *Robinson Crusoe* from the vantage point of a woman. But Susan Barton lacks the sense of authority needed to organize her experience into words. Once she and Friday return to England, she seeks out the author Daniel Foe (later Defoe) in hopes that he will chronicle her tale of shipwreck, life on the island, and subsequent rescue. While waiting for Foe to write her story, however, Barton ends up writing a narrative of her own, first begging the famous man to do the job ("Return to me the substance I have lost, Mr. Foe: that is my entreaty"), later realizing her own power to interrogate her experience ("I ask these questions because they are questions any reader of our story will ask"), finally realizing the power that is given her by language: "I am a free woman who asserts her freedom by telling her story according to

her own desire." In the process of discovering the means of telling her story, Barton is also learning something about the limits of language. "I do not know how these matters can be written of in a book unless they are covered up again in figures," Barton admits of the deep mysteries contained in her narrative. Later she wonders how even the most straightforward story could be simplified to the extent that would allow it to be enclosed between the covers of a book.

If Susan Barton is a new character in the Crusoe story, Coetzee's Cruso is not the confident island dweller we recall from Daniel Defoe's earlier novel on the same subject. Defoe's ingenious, colonial master of his own destiny has given way in Coetzee's version to a smug, complacent, castaway, unconcerned about improving his lot on the island or about the prospect of rescue. Cruso may be master of all he surveys, but his mastery is worth very little to him or to anyone else. Susan Barton realizes what Cruso clearly suspects: "in truth the island no more belonged to Cruso than to the King of Portugal or indeed to Friday or the cannibals of Africa." His sole occupation in his isolation is the building of vast stone walls and terraces, fertile sites for future cultivation by the settlers he claims will come after him. But Cruso refuses to cultivate the terraces himself, or to make the tools that would simplify his life. Nor does he seem interested in the idea of rescue. He is a stubborn anchorite, committed only to day-to-day survival: "We sleep, we eat, we live. We have no need of tools." Cruso dies shortly after his rescue; there seems to have been little to live for on the island, and even less to live for once the island sojourn ends.

The man known as Friday plays a crucial, if silent, role in Coetzee's retelling of the tale. Friday's arrival on the island is wrapped in mystery, as are his origins, his knowledge, and his desires. He has had his tongue cut out by the slavers who imprisoned him—or perhaps by Cruso—yet his silence takes on the intensity of any of the language that is used in the book. "Oh, Friday," Susan Barton pleads at one point, "how can I make you understand the cravings felt by those of us who live in a world of speech to have our questions answered! It is like our desire, when we kiss someone, to feel the lips we kiss respond to us." Both Susan Barton and Foe use Friday's silence as a stimulus to their own imaginative recreations of experience. In the absence of Friday's ability to tell his own story, they are able to imagine and articulate stories for him. Friday's speechlessness is an index of his powerlessness, yet even the sound of his breathing seems to possess a legitimacy denied to the words of the two literary artists who wonder about him. Foe sees Friday's silence as a function of hierarchical authority: "as long as he is dumb we can tell ourselves his desires are dark to us, and continue to use him as we wish." Before the story ends, however, Friday does open his mouth, and though he does not speak, the energy that emerges from between his lips has the power to overwhelm the "ends of the earth."

Foe is also a fiction about authorship. Coetzee's training as a linguist is evident in his demand that every reader interrogate the text. Foe, the famous author, wants to tell Susan Barton's story in his own way. He wants to decide the relative merits of the pieces of the narrative as he understands them. In the process, he is tempted to add facts that never occurred, to heighten "reality" for the sake of literary interest, to alter the story to fit his own purposes. Is this moulding of words to purposes any less the case when we tell our own stories? For Coetzee, all language is in one sense a lie, an almost grotesque simplification of circumstances that human beings use to gain a measure of control over their lives. Words are a drug we use to lull ourselves into a false sense of security about our ability to alter events. The author is thereby implicated as the consummate dispenser of lies. Authors are parasites, vampires, and shamans who manipulate, control, and seize power over experience for their own purposes. Like Coetzee's earlier fictions, *Foe* struggles to get behind the façade of fiction implied in all verbal exchange, to seek a deeper level of experience out of which all words flow.

Foe is finally a sustained meditation on a series of unanswered—need we say unanswerable—questions about language and writing. Who has the right to tell a story? Who has the right to speak for someone else? Who is denied the right to speak? Who needs someone else to speak for them? Beyond the question of rights, who has the confidence and authority necessary to organize experience into a coherent verbal structure? The real foe is language itself, or rather the complex interplay between language and silence that produces the texture of our lives as speakers and writers. We don't need words in order to live, so why do we invest so much power in our use of words? At this level, *Foe* leaves the reader with an additional series of nagging queries. Who has been allowed to learn to write? What is the purpose of any narrative? Where does the truth lie in any story? Is truth perhaps to be found only outside of stories and words?

Like all of Coetzee's earlier works, *Foe* retains a strong sense of its specifically South African origins, a sociopolitical subtext that runs along just below the surface of the narrative. Coetzee's Cruso is a descendant of the Boer foot-trekkers, a rooted, complacent Afrikaner settler who sees himself as a survivor and refuses to acknowledge the injustice and the limitations of his situation. Susan Barton reminds us of an English housewife in Johannesburg, who sees the black man living so close to her as her "shadow," and yet feels for him the way a mother feels for an unwanted child: "A woman may bear a child she does not want, and rear it without loving it, yet be ready to defend it with her life. Thus it has become, in a manner of speaking, between Friday and myself. I do not love him, but he is mine. . . . That is why he is here." Daniel Foe is Coetzee himself, the author who will grow rich and famous telling the stories of others, yet who senses the extent to which he revises and controls all the details of the telling. The author, whether Foe or Coetzee, also wonders if he has any right to speak for the one person whose story most needs to be told.

Friday is—perhaps most vividly of all these parallels—the tongueless voice of millions. Susan Barton wonders how a just God could have created a world in which Friday's tongue has been cut from his mouth—"Was Providence sleeping?" Cruso's answer snaps us back from Coetzee's allegory to the present: "If Providence were to watch over all of us . . . Who would be left to pick the cotton and cut the sugar cane?" Friday has a story to tell, a story that involves a sunken slave ship with the remains of its captives still in chains. But Friday's right to speak has been denied him by a culture that determines who will have the right to give utterance to a new truth. Toward the end of the novel, Foe convinces Susan Barton that Friday can learn to write, even if he is unable to speak. Once Friday learns to write, a new story will be told for the first time. The new story will not be a story we have heard before, nor will it be a story designed to satisfy our preconceptions about the world. But it will be a story that has long been silenced, and a story, however unsettling, that will be well worth the telling. (pp. 384-86)

Ashton Nichols, in a review of "Foe," in The Southern Humanities Review, *Vol. XXI, No. 4, Fall, 1987, pp. 384-86.*

Michael Scrogin

[J. M. Coetzee] has fashioned a method of storytelling that is closer to classical myth than to modern realism. Some critics have compared him to Franz Kafka, and the comparison is apt. Like Kafka, Coetzee often sets his work in unspecified or unnamed locations, or else in the distant past or not-too-distant future. *Waiting for the Barbarians* (1980), for example, is about a mythical regime, called "the Empire," and its main character is known only as "the Magistrate." The Magistrate is a petty official of the Empire who has run the government outpost for years and who finally concludes that the Empire well deserves to fall to the Barbarians. *Foe,* Coetzee's most recent work, a retelling of the Robinson Crusoe tale (hence the title's allusion to Daniel DeFoe), is set on a desert island. And *Life and Times of Michael K* (1984), Coetzee's most fully realized work and one of his few stories set in South Africa, involves not the present but the future, at a time during and following a great race war. Despite this oblique approach, however, it is clear that the central question which fascinates Coetzee is how to end, and finally to transcend, the master-slave relationship which defines the races in South Africa.

Coetzee's main resource in fashioning his myths, aside from his South African upbringing, is the great wellspring of biblical motifs. Though he does not explicitly allude to Scripture, again and again the central themes of Scripture inform and shape his works. Coetzee simply assumes, for example, an apocalypse. All his tales start from the premise that the old order—of government, law, religion—is falling apart or has completely disappeared. We are on a desert island, in a town at the edge of a crumbling empire, at an obscure farm in the remote heart of the country, or in the middle of a war. Coetzee apparently believes that this is what the future holds, at least for South Africa, and perhaps for the rest of the world.

Those characters who resist this apocalypse, this ending of the old order, do so cynically, half-heartedly, hopelessly. The Magistrate in *Waiting for the Barbarians* realizes that the only way the Empire can survive is to start over—

which means first of all eliminating the Barbarians. Otherwise there is no hope. Yet he cannot bring himself to approve this course. "That will not be my way. The new Men of Empire are the ones who believe in fresh starts, new chapters, clean pages; I struggle on with the old story, hoping that before it is finished it will reveal to me why I thought it was worth the trouble." But the story is soon finished, and the Magistrate concludes that the Empire was never worth the trouble.

It is a mistake to see Coetzee's works as messages of despair, however. Indeed, his vision further mirrors the biblical motif in regarding apocalypse not as mere punishment but as transformation, a sign of hope that points toward reconciliation. But Coetzee's hope is not a revolutionary one—that is, it does not rest on the destruction and reorganization of the state under a new, more just order. He distrusts such political or military resolutions. The hope he offers is based on what he sees as a natural, inherent possibility for the healing of individuals and relationships. And the focus of that healing is in the land— just as, in the Bible, the wilderness is the site of healing, renewal, recommitment and restoration.

For Coetzee, it is almost as though the land has a power and sense of its own, even a power to do justice. In *Waiting for the Barbarians,* the Magistrate, who has begun to sympathize with the Barbarians, tells us that they will win because they will outlast the Empire. And even the land and the water of the nearby lake, which gets saltier each year because of the Empire's pollution, will assist this victory. "Every year the lake-water grows a little more salty. There is a simple explanation—never mind what it is. The Barbarians know this fact. At this very moment they are saying to themselves, 'Be patient, one of these days their crops will start to wither from the salt, they will not be able to feed themselves, they will have to go.' That is what they are thinking. That they will outlast us."

But the land not only punishes; it can also heal and restore. *Life and Times of Michael K* is the story of a young black man who has been labeled retarded by the white authorities. As a race war engulfs Cape Town, where Michael lives with his aging and critically ill mother, he makes plans, as best he can, to return her to her ancestral home so that she can die among her people. But she does not survive the trip, and against Michael's wishes her body is cremated by the authorities. Determined to keep his promise to her even in her death, Michael returns his mother's ashes to the ancestral home and in the process begins a healing relationship with the land itself.

Unable to dig a deep hole for burial because of an underlying ledge, Michael turns over the topsoil and scatters his mother's remains. Then, because he does not want to return to Cape Town, and because he wishes to live apart from the world of history and war, he plants a few pumpkin and melon seeds, found in an abandoned farmhouse, and so begins his life as a cultivator.

The earth gives back to Michael generously. He is pleased by the great silence of the land and by its bounty. When struck with dysentery, he nurses himself through the fever and relies for healing on his crop of melons and pumpkins.

"When food comes out of this earth . . . I will recover my appetite, for it will have savor." And it is finally the land and his cultivation of it that give him a new and healing vision of who he is, and place him, at least temporarily, beyond the apocalypse—the war going on all around him.

One night a group of black guerrillas camp near Michael's garden and help themselves to his pumpkins and melons. Michael hides out of sight, listening to the proud laughter and tales of battle. He is at first entranced, and even thinks that in the morning he will come out of hiding and ask to join the warriors. But a moment's reflection reminds him of his new and sacred vocation, one which he cannot abandon "because enough men had gone off to war saying the time for gardening was when the war was over; whereas there must be men to stay behind and keep gardening alive, or at least the idea of gardening: because once the cord was broken, the earth would grow hard and forget her children." The land has exercised its power: Michael is not a soldier, or a retarded boy, an orphan or a refugee, but a gardener.

The land has the power to heal but not, finally, to bring peace. Peace in Coetzee's vision—as in the Bible's—lies outside, not inside, history. And, indeed, it is the desire to find some location outside history that characterizes all of Coetzee's protagonists. Michael K, in his flight from Cape Town to the countryside, takes comfort in the fact that "now that in all the world only I know where I am, I can think of myself as lost." The very act of becoming lost puts Michael beyond the apocalypse. The Magistrate in *Waiting for the Barbarians* thinks to himself as the Empire crumbles: "I wanted to live outside history. I wanted to live outside the history that Empire imposes on its subjects, even its lost subjects. I never wished it for the Barbarians that they should have the history of Empire laid upon them."

Though peace comes outside history, the vision of peace which Coetzee's protagonists reach is not without consequences within history. Coetzee's heroes are signs and symbols for those who have eyes to see and ears to hear. They represent the possibility of another way of living in relationship to history and to people, a way beyond the master-slave relationship. Michael K's simplicity and courage become such a sign to one of the white authorities he encounters. At the end of his story, when he has again grown ill and has been found by the military, he is turned over to the care of a certain medical officer. In treating Michael the man comes to see his remarkable and peaceful strength, and he seeks Michael's guidance.

> I am not asking you to take care of me, for example by feeding me. My need is a very simple one. Though this is a large country, so large that you would think there would be space for everyone, what I have learned of life tells me that it is hard to keep out of the camps. Yet I am convinced that there are areas that lie between the camps and belong to no camps . . . certain mountain-tops, for example, certain islands in the middle of swamps, certain arid strips where human beings may not find it worth their while to live. I am looking for such a place in order to settle there, perhaps only till things improve, perhaps

forever. I am not so foolish, however, as to imagine that I can rely on maps and roads to guide me. Therefore I have chosen you to show me the way.

Coetzee's several improbable heroes serve to show the way, to point to the reconciliation, hope and freedom that lies on the other side of apocalypse. In that new place freedom is not brought about by guns nor is it assured by institutions of government. It is an inherent freedom, the natural right of human beings, a right that emerges almost spontaneously when people live in right relationship with one another. It is this minimal but profound and irreducible freedom to which Michael K aspires and which he finally achieves, the freedom to be who one pleases and to stand on one's own. "Perhaps the truth is that it is enough to be out of the camps, out of all the camps at the same time. Perhaps that is enough of an achievement, for the time being. How many people are there left who are neither locked up nor standing guard at the gate?" Coetzee holds out the small, fragile, but very potent hope that beyond the apocalypse we will no longer have to divide ourselves into those who are locked up and those who stand guard. (pp. 503-05)

> *Michael Scrogin, "Apocalypse and Beyond: The Novels of J. M. Coetzee," in* The Christian Century, *Vol. 105, No. 17, May 18-25, 1988, pp. 503-05.*

"Why should one automatically try to interpret my thinking in political terms? It is not necessary to know my ideas to understand my novels."

—J. M. Coetzee, 1985

Barbara Eckstein

[In *White Writing: On the Culture of Letters in South Africa*], South African novelist J. M. Coetzee provides analyses of dominant ideas in South African white writing from 1652, when Europeans settled at the Cape of Good Hope, to 1948, when apartheid was institutionalized in South Africa. Focusing on writers of English and of Afrikaans, Coetzee traces the writers' relationship to the African land as landscape and as landownership (the farm). He articulates many of the paradoxes inherent in the practice of African pastoral art by people of European heritage. One such paradox involves the European descendants' search for a language which "can speak to Africa and be spoken to by Africa": "In order to convince the European that he appreciates Africa [the colonial] must give evidence of a degree of alienation from it; once he is thus alienated he can no longer claim to be by nature at one with it."

United States and European readers—and perhaps South African readers as well—can benefit from Coetzee's cross-cultural analyses of white writing and the ideas which

shaped it. Unlike the settling of the Americas, for example, the settling of Africa was not described as a myth of the new Eden or a city on the hill. From the beginning, Coetzee argues, there was far more uncertainty about the African enterprise.

White Writing may encounter criticism for its choice of subjects, particularly Gertrude Millin's novels of mixed "blood" and degeneracy. Still, Coetzee deserves appreciation for his necessary analyses of mostly conservative white writing, as does, say, Robert Lifton for his analysis in *The Nazi Doctors*. Coetzee's book elucidates how (self-justifying) ideas develop in a land and culture and find expression in its art. In apparent defense of his subject and method, Coetzee somewhat mysteriously expresses criticism of "reading *the other*: gaps . . . undersides. . . . It is a mode of reading which, subverting the dominant, is in peril, like all triumphant subversion, of becoming the dominant in turn." Nevertheless, in his reading and his writing, Coetzee is a master of the gaps. (pp. 718-19)

> *Barbara Eckstein, in a review of "White Writing: On the Culture of Letters in South Africa," in* World Literature Today, *Vol. 62, No. 4, Autumn, 1988, pp. 718-19.*

Shaun Irlam

J. M. Coetzee is widely known for his steady production of some of South Africa's finest "white writing." To date he is author of five novels, most recently *Foe,* and several articles on linguistics, stylistics, and literary topics. Now, in the seven essays composing *White Writing,* he collects his critical reflections on the mixed fortunes of "white writing" in South Africa, "a body of writing [not] different in nature from black writing," but "generated by the concerns of people no longer European, not yet African." The essays, arranged chronologically, range from the seventeenth century to the mid-twentieth century.

The collection quite explicitly avoids any claim to be comprehensive; the author reminds us that these essays "do not constitute a history of white writing, nor even the outline of such a history." The modesty of these claims should not let one underestimate the scope, wisdom and care of these thoughtful and thought-provoking discussions of "the great intellectual schemas through which South Africa has been thought by Europe." Rather than attempt to summarize these rich and diverse essays individually, I shall mention a couple of abiding concerns that resonate throughout the collection.

Coetzee suggests that there are two "rival dream topographies" dominating white South African literature. The first is a kind of pastoral that withdraws into utopian fantasies where every farm would be "a separate kingdom ruled over by a benign patriarch." Examples of this topography occur in the work of Pauline Smith, the Afrikaans *plaasroman* and, in a more complex fashion, in the farm novels of C. M. van den Heever.

The "rival dream topography" is one that would construe Africa either as dystopia (Olive Schreiner's *Story of an African Farm*) or "a vast, empty, silent space" in which "the poet scans the landscape with his hermeneutic gaze, but it remains trackless, refuses to emerge into meaningfulness as a landscape of signs."

Since the utopian "dream topography" manifests itself as primarily wish-fulfillment with few aspirations to historical veracity, Coetzee does not devote much attention to it. On the other hand, he asserts that "the lone poet in empty space is by no means a peripheral figure in South African writing," and here one might include the artists of chapter two and even the travel-writers of chapter one (with their illustrious progenitor from *Dusklands,* Jacobus Coetzee). Consequently this figure becomes an abiding concern of the book, most obviously in **"The Picturesque, the Sublime, and the South African Landscape"** and in **"Reading the South African Landscape."** In this latter essay, Coetzee remarks that "the project of landscape-writing in English comes to be dominated by a concern to make the landscape speak, to give a voice to the landscape, to interpret it." This same concern prevails in different and more attenuated ways in **"Idleness in South Africa," "Simple Language, Simple People: Smith, Paton, Mikro,"** and even **"The Farm Novels of C. M. van den Heever"** in as much as these essays are concerned too, with a language to address, represent or comprehend an inscrutable "other," or alternatively, assert a sense of communion with it.

In addition to dwelling on these rival dream topographies, another persistent concern, of chapters one, four, and six especially, is with what one might call "exigencies of narrative." Coetzee proposes, for example, that such narrative exigencies inform Sarah Gertrude Millin's novels (**"Blood, Taint, Flaw, Degeneration"**). Her racist rhetoric, reflecting her influence by certain epigones of Social Darwinism, is not informed exclusively by racist prejudices, he concludes, but responds, in the absence of alternative social structures in the colony sufficiently adaptable to tragic forms, to a double imperative:

> Any view of Millin as a woman imbued with the racial prejudices of white South African society and using her novels as a means of propagating and justifying these prejudices must . . . be tempered by a view of her as a practising novelist adapting whatever models and theories lie to hand to make writing possible.

Similar narrative exigencies, he argues, lie at the heart of van den Heever's farm novels: the need to motivate moments of epiphany, or *vergestaltiging,* . . . [is] also a factor motivating the moral indignation expressed by early travel writers over the spectacle of Hottentot idleness: the dozing Hottentot yielded no story and proved a mere frustration to their taxonomic and narrative aspirations. Coetzee writes:

> [T]he laziness of the Hottentot aborts one of the more promising discourses about elemental man. . . . The moment when the travel writer condemns the Hottentot for doing nothing is the moment when the Hottentot brings him face to face (if he will only recognize it) with his own preconceptions.

Chapters one, two, and seven are chiefly concerned with obstacles to reading and interpretation and the inadequacy of European anthropological and aesthetic schemata. As a corollary, the search for an adequate vocabulary becomes a prevalent concern. The anxiety behind the poet's/painter's "hermeneutic gaze" is epitomized by the question in chapter two "is it possible for a European to acquire an African eye?"

The last piece in the collection, **"Reading the South African Landscape,"** is an essential companion to chapter two. In the work of Butler, Clouts, and others, Coetzee analyzes previous answers to the questions posed there: "How are we to read the African landscape? Is it readable at all? . . ."

Readers of Coetzee's novels may already be sensitized to the problems these questions raise. Anxieties about interpretation and "demeanour" before the *want* of a story commonly constitute a surrogate story. One recalls the magistrate's musings about the captive barbarian woman in *Waiting for the Barbarians,* the doctor's speculations about the eponymous hero of *The Life and Times of Michael K,* and Susan Barton's fascination with the untold story of the tongueless Friday in *Foe.*

The enigma of the idle Hottentot or the blank South African landscape are structural cognates of these enigmatic characters. Into this repertoire Coetzee admits one more character at the close of *White Writing;* it is perhaps the mother of them all. He construes the abiding predicament of the "white writer" in these emblematic terms:

> The desert of the South African plateau becomes the home of a Sphinx, a Sphinx all the more baffling for having no material form, for being everywhere present yet nowhere apprehensible. The Sphinx does not speak; yet, indifferent, more than indifferent because not even personally present to be indifferent, it forces upon the poet the role of a man answering a riddle, a riddle which he must, faute de mieux, lacking any interlocutor, pose to and for himself. The Sphinx he confronts is in fact no different from nothing. . . .
>
> (pp. 1147-1149)

Coetzee's critique of white writing's persistent navigation within dream topographies emerges most sharply in response to this perennial phantasy of the Sphinx. The imaginative projection of "the lone poet in empty space," he concludes, is the product of wilful negative quixotism. Its fancied epistemological crisis ("a man answering a riddle") is a deliberate self-mystification and, serving "the imperial calling," perhaps an unacknowledged desire to see the *blank* landscape in Afrikaans as " 'n *blanke* land" [a white country]:

> In all the poetry commemorating meetings with the silence and emptiness of Africa—it must finally be said—it is hard not to read a certain historical will to see as silent and empty a land that has been, if not full of human figures, not empty of them either.

Earlier Coetzee remarked that, "The literature of empty landscape . . . is a literature of failure, of the failure of the historical imagination." Initially it may appear that a "literature of failure," connoting involuntariness, consorts ill with the intentionality of "a certain historical will." The terms of the discussion are complex and Coetzee passes over this subtle moment in his analysis somewhat too quickly.

There are in fact two dimensions of failure that Coetzee diagnoses in this "literature of failure" and it is important to distinguish them. It is not the testimonies of involuntary failure to read the landscape or comprehend the Sphinx, i.e., the *thematization* of failure, that define the literature of empty landscape as a literature of failure. Indeed, one might argue conversely that this literature of failure, in thematic terms, succeeds all too well: first, the absence or failure of an historical imagination is evidently the triumph of an imperial lyric imagination capable of fashioning by fiat, a compelling "dream topography"; moreover, by imagining this topography as the site of its own involuntary failure, such a literature succeeds in diverting attention from its triumph, and deriving a compensatory pathos from the drama of its failure. The resources of such a rhetoric of failure are not to be underestimated.

Coetzee recognizes however, that the rhetoric of failure is merely a decoy, a surrogate failure to mask the other sense in which it is a "literature of failure," i.e., as a wilful *omission* or evasion of history. It is a credit to Coetzee's critical acuity that he does not succumb to the considerable persuasive force of this decoy rhetoric, but remains alert to this other failure, this other silence in South African landscape poetry. He writes:

> [T]he failure of the listening imagination to intuit the true language of Africa, the continued apprehension of silence (by the poet) or blankness (by the painter), stands for, or stands in the place of, another failure, by no means inevitable: a failure to imagine a peopled landscape, an inability to conceive a society in South Africa in which there is a place for the self.

The strength of Coetzee's collection is to interrogate succinctly and lucidly the presuppositions inhabiting the language with which "white writers" have addressed and presumed to ventriloquize Africa. With an alert and responsive eye, he discloses the mystifications and blind-spots inherent in European schemata for thinking Africa. His penetrating analyses continually isolate the acute difficulties a writing that conceives its destiny as "finding a language to fit Africa . . . that will be authentically African" creates for itself. This collection must considerably raise the standards by which criticism of South African literature is judged. (pp. 1149-50)

Shaun Irlam, in a review of "White Writing: On the Culture of Letters in South Africa," in MLN, *Vol. 103, No. 5, December, 1988, pp. 1147-1150.*

Barbara Temple-Thurston

[In *White Writing*], J. M. Coetzee looks back as far as the writings of European travelers of the late seventeenth and eighteenth centuries to seek the foundations and attitudes that influenced the consciousnesses of the nineteenth- and early twentieth-century white South African writers. He claims to have two concerns: one with the influence of certain European ideas that shaped attitudes about South Africa—the idea of Man, of cultural progress, of "natural" racial divisions, and of people in harmony with their landscape; the other with the South African landscape and landed property itself. These concerns attempt to unite thematically what often seem rather disparate essays, many of which have been published previously in some form or other.

Coetzee begins by considering the major European idea of the garden myth, or the new Eden, so popular with travelers in the New World. He notes that this myth failed to take hold in South Africa, and blames this failure on the fact that Africa was regarded as the *old* world, rather than the new, which wrought, in Conradian fashion, a degeneration from man to brute. Travelers' disgust with the Hottentots' habits, particularly their seeming idleness, confirmed the idea of degeneration.

While the "new Eden" myth failed, what did take hold among South Africa's early white writers was the Western genre of pastoral writing, though it took a conservative and nostalgic form. South African writers of the early twentieth century hearkened back to a rural patriarchal social order found on early Afrikaner farms. Afrikaans novelists adapted the *Blut-und-Boden* romantic earth mysticism of Germany to create the South African farm novel, while English novelist Pauline Smith drew on the great country house of the Tory tradition to endorse the same rural patriarchal order in her works. Coetzee's extensive discussion of Afrikaans farm novelist C. M. van den Heever, whose use of the pastoral promotes Afrikaner ideology, will be of sociological interest. The essay demonstrates that the Afrikaners viewed themselves as a nation whose rule as family farm owners and patriarchs was God-given. Coetzee points out that the notion of ennobling labor so significant to the pastoral genre, and the notion of degenerative idleness perceived in Hottentot and black lifestyles, became obsessive issues in white writing. He traces the seeds of this preoccupation to the European post-Reformation attitudes that idleness is sinful, and to the Enlightenment views that idleness betrays one's humanity. These culture-bound attitudes led to a denunciation of the native Hottentots, who refused to be drawn into the colonial economy as laborers, because colonists could not conceive of "idleness" as a sign of fulfilled desire.

Linked to the issues of idleness and labor is man's relationship to the land. No longer of Europe yet burdened with its notions, and not yet African, the colonial writers struggled to express the experience of their new land. They sought a voice to make Africa speak authentically through their art as the English landscape spoke through Wordsworth's. Besides the adopted pastoral genre which seeks to humanize the land through hand and plough, Coetzee identifies a portrayal of the landscape as "alien, impenetrable, a land of rock and sun." We see this portrayal in English writer Olive Schreiner's bitterly antipastoral novel, *Story of an African Farm,* and in the English poets of landscape who listen for an African voice but hear only silence. Coetzee traces the poets' struggle out of silence, as well as their efforts to break free of the inappropriate picturesque language of the French and English landscape schools, through South African writers and poets like Burchell, Thomas Pringle, Francis Carey Slater, Roy Campbell, Guy Butler, and Sydney Clouts.

The question of appropriateness of language, voice, and form is further explored in a chapter examining the works of Pauline Smith, Alan Paton, and Mikro (pen-name for Afrikaans novelist C. H. Kuhn). Coetzee analyzes the writers' manipulation of language and expression, thereby revealing their endorsement (unconscious perhaps) of certain Western cultural and racial views of the times. Pauline Smith, using a syntax common to Afrikaans and a style evocative of the Authorized Version of the Bible, creates "in the echo chamber of the English prose tradition felicitous effects that cohere neatly with the Afrikaner's myth of himself as Israelite." Paton's use of language in *Cry, the Beloved Country* evokes the sense of a Zulu speaking Zulu. Coetzee holds that Paton, in a patronizing nostalgia, comes close to joining those writers of the 1930s and 40s who were anxious to stop change and wished for a return to patriarchal times gone by. However, Paton's recognition at the end of the novel that "economic, and hence the political, basis of feudalism has been eroded by demographic forces" separates him from those other writers.

Coetzee shows that Mikro, unlike Paton, fails to face the reality of change. He contends that Mikro, using stylistic and sociolinguistic features to differentiate between "coloured" and "white" Afrikaans, introduces into the subtext a racial hierarchy and a concept of separateness. Notions of racial inferiority stem, in Mikro's feudal world, largely from the fear that the Afrikaners' economic independence and cultural identity would be lost through change. In the case of Sarah Gertrude Millin, however, racial difference and inferiority is explained through pseudo-scientific notions popular in the mid-nineteenth and early twentieth centuries. In his chapter titled **"Blood, Taint, Flaw, Degeneration,"** Coetzee points out that Millin was well read in this so-called science. Millin, says Coetzee, "decides to see conflict in South Africa in terms of race, class, and caste rather than in terms of class alone." In a fascinating discussion of some of the scientific theories regarded as respectable in Millin's time and her application of those theories to her work, Coetzee makes us realize that "any view of Millin as a woman imbued with the racial prejudice of white South African society and using her novels as a means of propagating and justifying these prejudices must . . . be tempered by a view of her as a practising novelist adapting whatever models and theories lie to hand to make writing possible."

Coetzee's book reiterates impressively how cultural ideas and language bind and limit the way in which we interpret our world. It demonstrates that when our world changes, ingrained cultural views and patterns often cannot, and that attempts to adapt can be awkward and sometimes offensive. It enhances our understanding of the development of white South African culture as well as its writing. *White Writing*'s most frustrating aspect is its studious avoidance of discussion of or connection to the growing body of out-standing white contemporary South African fiction and poetry today, but is nonetheless a book of considerable insight. Through an examination of colonial heritage (one wonders why only a comparison with America and not with Australia), it explains much about today's South Africa as the culture writhes in pain, not daring to let go of its petrified perceptions of cultural identity. (pp. 85-7)

> *Barbara Temple-Thurston, in a review of "White Writing: On the Culture of Letters in South Africa," in* Rocky Mountain Review of Language and Literature, *Vol. 43, Nos. 1-2, 1989, pp. 85-7.*

Patrick Parrinder

In J. M. Coetzee's *Age of Iron* Elizabeth Curren, a retired Classics lecturer, is dying of cancer in Cape Town. . . . Though it is less a realist novel than an allegorical fable about contemporary South Africa, *Age of Iron* suggests the extent to which [South African writer Nadine] Gordimer's writings have set an agenda for her younger compatriots. The imminent death of white society and the problem of inheritance overshadow a novel which, once again, centres on what may be called illicit relationships.

Elizabeth's story is a monologue, supposedly designed to be read after her death by her only child, a daughter who has emigrated to the United States. The daughter has a new life in which it is no longer possible for her to care for a dying parent, though her mother never reproaches her for her absence. Instead, Elizabeth finds herself sharing her house with a trio of uninvited guests: Mr. Vercueil, a white down-and-out, and Bheki and John, two teenagers on the run from the Police. Bheki is the son of Florence, Elizabeth's black housemaid (Florence also has two baby daughters significantly named Hope and Beauty). But Florence has come to realise that, in a country where children have learnt to burn down their schools and to take on the Security Forces, 'there are no more mothers and fathers.' Through Florence and Bheki, Elizabeth is led into the world of terrified shanty-dwellers and riot-torn townships. . . . At the same time, the white lady who becomes involved in black politics through her concern for her domestic, and who finds herself giving sanctuary to an armed fugitive, is almost a stock character in South African fiction. The truly unconventional relationship in this novel is that between Elizabeth and Mr. Verceuil.

To her stuffy neighbours, it is almost unimaginable that she should tolerate a vagrant living on her property in a house of plastic sheeting and cardboard boxes. Vercueil, however, becomes a reliable companion as well as the only audience for the moral homilies to which, as a former teacher, Elizabeth remains addicted. Their partnership gives the novel an air of inspired eccentricity, yet (like Elizabeth's fondness for mythological allusions and Classical parallels) it also has a transparently allegorical intent. When the drunken old man eventually lies down with the cancer-ridden heroine there can, of course, be no chance of issue, no hope of inheritance. Vercueil's semen would be 'dry and brown, like pollen or like the dust of this country', Elizabeth reflects. His dog, and for that matter his smelly feet, are also found to embody the state of contemporary South Africa. Vercueil is an angel of death who becomes progressively more attentive to Elizabeth as her decline continues; and it is the dying narrator herself who, inevitably, stands as the novel's principal emblem for the once beloved country.

She takes a long time dying, and since she is the author of her narrative, she is, of course, not dead when it ends. Coetzee's piling-up of images of South Africa's national destiny can seem over-insistent, so that *Age of Iron* is more a cry of agony and disgust than . . . a machine to think with. Nevertheless, the novel has its share of lyrical moments and acute insights. Elizabeth, who is nothing if not a liberal, is shamed but not completely silenced by the atrocities committed by a collapsing social system which claims to represent her colour and her class. Once she finds her voice, she has stern admonitions for the black revolutionaries, the people of the future. It is hard not to agree with her own assessment that she is a good person, even if she is also a back number. 'What the times call for is quite different from goodness,' she concedes. 'The times call for heroism.' In an iron age there is no longer any time for the private virtues. (pp. 17-18)

> *Patrick Parrinder, "What His Father Gets Up to," in* London Review of Books, *Vol. 12, No. 17, September 13, 1990, pp. 17-18.*

Lawrence Thornton

"When some men suffer unjustly . . . it is the fate of those who witness their suffering to suffer the shame of it." This observation by the Magistrate in J. M. Coetzee's *Waiting for the Barbarians* (1982) could easily stand as an epigraph to *Age of Iron,* his superb new novel, which lays bare the effects of apartheid on the psyches of both the oppressor and the oppressed.

Like the Magistrate, Mrs. Curren, the narrator of *Age of Iron,* awakens to her own complicity with South Africa's regime after years of silence. But there is a profound difference between these characters. *Waiting for the Barbarians* concludes with the Magistrate pressing on "along a road that may lead nowhere." By the time we reach the end of *Age of Iron,* Mrs. Curren's crisis, compounded by terminal illness, becomes part of a larger vision of a time when justice and decency will return to her country. The novel's prophecy comes to us in her splendidly articulated voice, sometimes sharp, sometimes laconic, but always calibrated to her growing awareness of how things are.

For the last 20 years Mr. Coetzee, a professor of literature at the University of Cape Town, has gone his own way, ignoring the trends of contemporary fiction in favor of allegorical narratives that focus on life under regimes capable of endless brutality. Each novel has its own idiosyncratic shape, but within that broad scope of difference, there is a constant focus on questions of power and position and the claims of conscience. Now, in *Age of Iron,* the wall of apartheid is finally cracking. The killings and oppression continue, but we are witnessing the death throes of the system. The action unfolds in Cape Town, "where a century ago the patricians . . . gave orders that

there be erected spacious homes for themselves and their descendants in perpetuity, foreseeing nothing of the day when, in their shadows, the chickens would come home to roost."

Age of Iron takes the form of a long letter from Mrs. Curren, a former classics professor now dying of cancer, to her daughter, who has moved to America to avoid the complicity of living under a regime she despises. Mrs. Curren entrusts its mailing to an alcoholic homeless man called Vercueil, who has taken shelter in a pile of boxes and plastic sheeting in the alley behind her house. The transient Mr. Vercueil is reluctant to speak. Soon after, on the day her doctor gives her the bad news, Mrs. Curren meets him and muses about his silence and inattention, aware that he barely listens to her. "Perhaps, despite those keen birdeyes, he is more befuddled with drink than I know. Or perhaps, finally, he does not care. Care: the true root of charity. I look for him to care, and he does not. Because he is beyond caring. Beyond caring and beyond care." Although they are linked through hopelessness and disease, whose double tragedy seems to marginalize them, Mrs. Curren is wrong. Care will bring her and Mr. Vercueil a measure of unexpected salvation, even though the full flowering of *caritas* in their homeland lies off in the future.

Mrs. Curren's letter to America chronicles her awakening to apartheid's last vicious gasps as well as her own impending death. She is thus a witness to the *dies irae*—the days of wrath—of her inner and outer being and to the coming of the age of iron—the future of the country's black youth. Appalled that her housekeeper Florence cannot control her son Bheki and his friends, she asks how Florence and other mothers can turn their backs on their children, for surely the violence they engage in will deform their adult lives. Florence answers that she is only acknowledging necessity. All the children are good: "They are like iron, we are proud of them."

"Children of iron," she thinks.

> Florence herself, too, not unlike iron. The age of iron. After which comes the age of bronze. How long, how long before the softer ages return in their cycle, the age of clay, the age of earth? A Spartan mother, iron-hearted, bearing warrior sons for the nation. "We are proud of them." We. Come home either with your shield or on your shield.

Understanding the true meaning of this metaphor allows Mrs. Curren to open her eyes to the struggle and see it whole for the first time. When she ponders its ramifications she tells her daughter that she writes "not so that you will feel for me but so that you will learn how things are." But the time for words has already passed. The historical process of revolution sweeps them aside in its indefatigable rush toward the future. She understands this after speaking to a friend of Bheki's and discovering that her "words fell off him like dead leaves the moment they were uttered. The words of a woman, therefore negligible; of an old woman, therefore doubly negligible; but above all of a white." White words, then, are futile, and their lack of authority extends to her stock in trade, the words of Greek and Roman artists, lovingly read and interpreted in lectures.

The first overt crisis of the novel occurs when Mrs. Curren's concern for Bheki's disappearance takes her to a place the authorities call Site C in the township of Guguletu. As she and Mr. Vercueil enter the township the full horror becomes apparent. Bheki has been murdered by the police. His body is laid out with four others, eyes open to the terror of death but also to what she intuits as a kind of triumph. In going to Site C she has abandoned the sanctuary of her middle-class life, and afterward she can never forget those "desolate flats" where she had no choice but to "smell the smoke in the air, see the bodies of the dead, hear the weeping."

Mrs. Curren's journey to Guguletu allows her to see that no one is free, neither white or black. "When madness climbs the throne," she thinks, "who in the land escapes contagion?" The madness follows her home when a friend of Bheki's goes to the boy's room for a gun. Later he is trapped in her house by the police. Despite her protests, the police commandeer her house, and in one of the novel's most chilling scenes, they force her outside, where she hears the explosion of a concussion grenade, then shots, then sees the boy's body being taken away.

Devastating as these two murders are in their illustration of the regime's limitless brutality, the power of *Age of Iron* is nowhere more apparent than in Mrs. Curren's relationship with Mr. Vercueil, whose slovenliness and drinking she resents until she realizes that he is as doomed as she is, because he is not a man of iron. What she has taken for laziness is a profound malaise deeded him by the madness on the throne. It is quite simply too late for either of them.

Yet a deeply moving attachment develops between this dying woman and castoff man that is all the more compelling because the reasons for it remain unspoken. After the boy is murdered in her house, she wanders off, falls ill and finds shelter beneath an overpass. A gang threatens her until Mr. Vercueil appears and runs them off. They spend the night together in a heap of cardboard boxes and the next day he carries her home. From this moment forward, she is increasingly forced to depend on him for the most intimate things because of her growing weakness. Just as the Magistrate washes the broken feet of a barbarian girl, so Mr. Vercueil washes Mrs. Curren's underwear when the pain prevents her from doing it. He prepares her meals, shops, becomes her guardian. He is, she constantly reiterates, her messenger. In her loneliness, she asks to sleep with his dog. "He won't stay. He sleeps where I sleep." "Then sleep here too," she says, binding herself even more completely to this "rudimentary man."

"When it comes to last things," she tells her daughter,

> I no longer doubt him in any way. There has always been in him a certain hovering if undependable solicitude for me, a solicitude he knows no way of expressing. I have fallen and he has caught me. It is not he who fell under my care when he arrived, I now understand, nor I who fell under his: we fell under each other, and have tumbled and risen since then in the flights and swoops of that mutual election.

Mrs. Curren and Mr. Vercueil are thus harbingers of the *caritas* that is slowly, even glacially, returning to South Africa. It is not yet time when "mutual election" will heal the old wounds, but the process has begun with these two unlikely avant-gardes. . . .

Despite the brutal killings and Mrs. Curren's excruciatingly detailed recording of the progress of the disease eating away at her, *Age of Iron* emerges from its smoky, apocalyptic images as a finely wrought prophecy that should send chills down the spines of the Voortrekkers. In this chronicle of an aged white woman coming to understand, and of the unavoidable claims of her country's black youth, Mr. Coetzee has created a superbly realized novel whose truths cut to the bone. His readers will "suffer the shame" of injustice that came to occupy the old Magistrate's heart, but they will also witness the inevitable flowering of the age of iron.

Lawrence Thornton, "Apartheid's Last Vicious Gasps," in The New York Times Book Review, *September 23, 1990, p. 7.*

An excerpt from *Age of Iron*:

Days ago I caught a cold, which has now settled on my chest and turned into a dry, hammering cough that goes on for minutes at a stretch and leaves me panting, exhausted.

As long as the burden is a burden of pain alone I bear it by holding it at a distance. It is not I who am in pain, I say to myself: the one in pain is someone else, some body else who shares this bed with me. So, by a trick, I hold it off, keep it elsewhere. And when the trick will not work, when the pain insists on owning me, I bear it anyhow.

(As the waves rise I have no doubt my tricks will be swept away like the dikes of Zeeland.)

But now, during these spasms of coughing, I cannot keep any distance from myself. There is no mind, there is no body, there is just I, a creature thrashing about, struggling for air, drowning. Terror, and the ignominy of terror! Another vale to be passed through on the way to death. *How can this be happening to me?* I think at the height of the coughing: *Is it fair?* The ignominy of naïveté. Even a dog with a broken back breathing its last at the roadside would not think, *But is this fair?*

Living, said Marcus Aurelius, calls for the art of the wrestler, not the dancer. Staying on your feet is all; there is no need for pretty steps.

Yesterday, with the pantry bare, I had to go shopping. Trudging home with my bags, I had a bad spell. Three passing schoolboys stopped to stare at the old woman leaning against a lamppost with her groceries spilled around her feet. In between the coughing I tried to wave them away. What I looked like I cannot imagine. A woman in a car slowed down. "Are you all right?" she called. "I have been shopping," I panted. "What?" she said, frowning, straining to hear. "Nothing!" I gasped. She drove off.

How ugly we are growing, from being unable to think well of ourselves! Even the beauty queens look irritable. Ugliness: what is it but the soul showing through the flesh?

Peter Reading

J. M. Coetzee's new novel [*Age of Iron*] is short and simple. There is no clutter and the writing even seems to have been purged of "style". The allegorical element, while present, is not laboured. But even though Coetzee reduces the action, setting and number of characters to a bare minimum (a few days in Cape Town recording the progress of a dying old lady, her black domestic and a drunk tramp), Coetzee none the less manages to address the large issues of life, love, death, South Africa and internecine political intractability.

Elizabeth Curren is a retired classics teacher. Her doctor has diagnosed that she has terminal cancer. She returns home from the surgery to discover a smelly wino dossing in a cardboard-and-plastic lair in her garden. This no-hoper, the strange, taciturn Mr. Vercueil, is an ambiguous presence from the outset—"A visitor, visiting himself on me on this of all days." Vercueil is allowed to stay, occupying a position of gradually increasing importance in Mrs Curren's life as he moves from the woodshed to the house (and finally to the bed) of his benefactress. Indeed, the roles of protector and protected become slyly reversed as the derelict begins to assume the burdens of comforting and counselling the carcinomatous woman. An "unclean" visitor, however, Vercueil retains, to the end, an ominous whiff of the Angel of Death: "He took me in his arms and held me with mighty force, so that the breath went out of me in a rush. From that embrace there was no warmth to be had." This first-person account of moribundity is addressed by Mrs Curren to her daughter, who has quit the untenable mess of South Africa to life in self-imposed exile in America, and, of course, the *dégringolade* of the two protagonists implicitly mirrors the rapid degeneration of a whole society.

It is the frequently more specific indictments of the ship of state, however, that produce a contrasting tension in this affectingly sad chronicle of personal decline. Elizabeth's rueful reflection that "life in this country is so much like life aboard a sinking ship, one of those old-time liners with a lugubrious, drunken captain and a surly crew and leaky lifeboats" is given substance by graphic accounts of hardship, injustice, gratuitous police brutality and ignorant, incorrigible viciousness. Florence, the bigoted black housekeeper, has two little daughters ironically named Hope and Beauty ("Hope and Beauty. It was like living in an allegory") as well as a young son, Bheki, who is summarily butchered while taking part in a local riot. To an accompaniment of appropriately harsh-sounding Afrikaans prattle, Bheki's pistol-wielding playmate is gunned down by the police in Elizabeth's house while she tries to safeguard the boy.

In one memorably described, Dantesque sortie to a squalid shanty community of poor blacks on the outskirts of Cape Town, Elizabeth is guided by a ten-year-old towards the rim of a crater where rioting gangs of men are engaged in burning down their rivals' shacks:

> Save for an old woman with a sagging mouth standing in a doorway, there was no one in sight. But as we walked further the noise we had heard, which at first might have been taken for wind and rain, began to break up into shouts, cries, calls, over a ground-bass which I can only call a sigh: a deep sigh, repeated over and over, as if the wide world itself were sighing.

And throughout this book Coetzee releases similar utterances of powerful compassion, repeatedly causing Elizabeth to raise her voice in condemnation of inhumanity and hatred in favour of reason and tolerance. Hers is an unassuming wisdom, though, which the author renders in a manner which seems effortlessly natural and without sententiousness: "There are no rubbish people. We are all people together" is Elizabeth's quiet defence of the drunkard; while her portentous caution to Florence about the fearlessness of the Children of the Revolution ("Be careful: they may start by being careless of their own lives and end by being careless of everyone else's") is canny yet convincingly conversational.

As the heroine's time runs out, her brief but concentrated commentary becomes more urgent and all-embracing. She is eloquently moving on the subject of maternal love, almost mystical in her musing on human continuity through childbirth and the act of writing, and by turns sagaciously trenchant and lyrical about her cancer, her country and the human condition in microcosm: "Monstrous growths, misbirths: a sign that one is beyond one's term. This country too: time for fire, time for an end, time for what grows out of ash to grow."

Peter Reading, "Monstrous Growths," in The Times Literary Supplement, *No. 4565, September 28-October 4, 1990, p. 1037.*

Gabriele Annan

J. M. Coetzee's new novel [*Age of Iron*] is more overtly about apartheid than any others he has written, and about the same of living with it. The word "shame" throbs through the text like a recurrent pain. The principal character thinks she is dying of it: "I have cancer from the accumulation of shame I have endured in my life," she says. "That is how cancer comes about: from self-loathing the body turns malignant and begins to eat away at itself." Mrs. Curren is a liberal, a retired teacher of classics at Cape Town University. She lives alone. Her divorced husband is dead. Her only child emigrated to America years ago, vowing never to set foot in South Africa so long as the existing regime remained in power. Mrs. Curren yearns for her daughter and writes to her all the time, an endless letter not to be sent until after her own death. The letter is the book.

Age of Iron begins with her return from the doctor, who has told her that her cancer has spread to the bone and is terminal. As she parks her car she sees a vagrant sleeping in a cardboard box behind the garage—"an unsavoury smell about him: urine, sweet wine, moldy clothing, and something else too. Unclean." She tries to get rid of him, but he returns with his dog. Reluctantly, Mrs. Curren feeds him. He is an alcoholic with a crippled hand. Uncommunicative and uncooperative, he won't help around the place or earn a little money, and this irritates Mrs. Curren. Still, he is useful: he can push her old car which doesn't start by itself. So with no enthusiasm on either side, he becomes her constant companion: she has to take him along wherever she goes. In the course of the novel a grouchy symbiosis develops between the derelict and the old woman, and when she finally dies he is the one entrusted to mail the manuscript to her daughter.

The man's name is Vercueil, which could be Afrikaner or Huguenot. He has long, greasy black hair and green eyes: I thought he was meant to be a Coloured (who often have European names); but Professor Parrinder, reviewing the novel recently in the *London Review of Books* [see excerpt above] thinks he is white. It seems just possible that Coetzee has deliberately left his color in doubt. Vercueil's chief characteristic is idleness, and in Coetzee's volume on *White Writing* (in and about South Africa), he has an arresting Foucault-inspired essay called **"Idleness in South Africa"**: he shows that from the year of the country's settlement in 1652 until the present day, foreign observers were scandalized by the idleness of the inhabitants—first black, then white as well. The Dutch Calvinists were shocked by the Hottentots' sloth and by their—to Europeans—disgusting personal habits. But soon they themselves succumbed to sloth. By the nineteenth century, "the true scandal . . . was not the idleness of the Boers," Coetzee claims:

> The history of idleness in South Africa is not a side issue or a curiosity. One need only look at the face of South African labour in the twentieth century to confirm this. The idleness of the Boer is still there in taboos on certain grades of manual work (*hotnotswerk, kafferwerk*), as well as in rituals of leisure indistinguishable from idleness (sitting on the porch, lying on the beach). The idleness of the native is still present in a tradition of overemployment and underpayment, maintained from both sides of the fence. . . . The luxurious idleness of the settler is still denounced from Europe, the idleness of the native still deplored by his master.

And Coetzee concludes:

> I hope that I have opened a way to the reading of idleness since 1652 as an authentically native response to a foreign way of life, a response that has rarely been defended in writing. . . .

Vercueil could be read as its defense in fiction, but only if you have read the essay on idleness: the man comes across not as a specimen or a symbol, but as an individual with eschatological implications: the angel of death. Physically he is only too real—filthy, clumsy, smelly, hawking, snoring, spitting. His inner life is inscrutable, but never in doubt. Coetzee likes to write about primitive characters who hang loose on the society where fate has placed them: the barbarian girl in *Waiting for the Barbarians,* the simpleton Michael K in *The Life and Times of Michael K,* and now Vercueil. But whereas the reader is let into Michael K's consciousness and experiences his life and times

from his point of view, Vercueil is as opaque as the barbarian girl.

All three have physical defects: the girl has been lamed and partly blinded by her captors, Michael K has a harelip, and Vercueil his crippled hand. Their defects may be intended as symbols (like Mrs. Curren's cancer: she has already had a breast removed), but you sense a compulsion to write about them. Both Michael K and Vercueil have inappropriately remained virgins through a tragic combination of incompetence and detachment. The old, dying, and disfigured Mrs. Curren initiates Vercueil out of pity for his condition: an act performed and described in such a low-key, matter-of-fact manner that the shock and the scandal of it have a delayed effect. This is typical of Coetzee's method: his prose is rich with marvelous descriptive detail and illuminating poetic metaphor; but its pace is even and resigned, like an army on the march: it's not until it has disappeared over the horizon that the devastation begins to tell.

Mrs. Curren is not exactly a female Saint Julian, her relationship with Vercueil is reciprocal; but the thought of the saint and the leper must be meant to cross one's mind and probably crossed hers, filled as it is with learned references and snatches of Thucydides and Virgil. She is not so much concerned with saintliness as with heroism: "I have been a good person," she says.

> I freely confess to it. I am a good person still. What times these are when to be a good person is not enough! . . . What the times call for is quite different from goodness. The times call for heroism.

She does not aspire to heroism, although there is something heroic about her refusal to bother her daughter with her dying. She has never been an activist and does not like to be thought of as a do-gooder. She believes in life and happiness and hates both the Calvinist puritanism of the Afrikaners and the revolutionary puritanism of the young blacks committed to liberation by violence. She is always lecturing her servant on the subject; her didactic streak is an endearing *déformation professionelle:*

> The more you give in, Florence, the more outrageously the children will behave. You told me you admire your son's generation because they are afraid of nothing. Be careful: they may start by being careless of their own lives and end by being careless of everyone else's. What you admire in them is not necessarily what is best.

But she realizes that "Florence had no desire to be preached to"; neither does Vercueil. Mrs. Curren accepts their contempt for her high-minded, sometimes semimystical ramblings about love and humanity, motherhood and death. She is a sharp old thing, and her deflationary self-irony never sleeps for long. That is what makes her an attractive heroine, along with her casual goodness and her scholar's compulsion to go after truth and examine and face it.

Florence is the perfect servant, supremely conscientious and hard-working, but dour. Mrs. Curren is not in her confidence. Florence doesn't tell her the true names of her children, or that Mr. Thabane, whom she calls her cousin, is really her brother and a leading activist. Mr. Thabane sells shoes: he was once a school teacher, but was dismissed.

Terrible things happen. Florence's son Bheki takes part in a school-children's strike organized by Mr. Thabane against a system of education that prepares them only to be slaves. Shortly afterward two policemen contrive a road accident outside Mrs. Curren's house: fifteen-year-old Bheki and his friend John are severely injured. A little later Mrs. Curren witnesses the police burn and sack the township where Florence lives, and sees Bheki's body neatly laid out in a row with other murdered schoolchildren. She thinks of driving her car to Government House and setting herself alight in it as the noonday gun goes off. She is dying anyway: "I want to sell myself, redeem myself." Vercueil eggs her on.

"I was outraged. But was I fair to him? It seems to me now," she writes much later, when death is very close and the failed immolation long past,

> that he has no more conception of death than a virgin has of sex. But the same curiosity. The curiosity of a dog that sniffs at one's crotch, wagging its tail, its tongue hanging out red and stupid as a penis.

But it is Vercueil who aborts the suicide by getting drunk and angry and throwing away the car key as they wait for noon to come.

After Bheki's death Mrs. Curren allows his friend John to hide in her house. The police arrive, surround his bolthole, and shoot him down. The beastliness of his killing is emphasized by the presence of a friendly policewoman whose job it is to try and remove the sick old woman from the scene with a display of caring solicitude. By this time Mrs. Curren is very ill and in great pain, but wrapped in her pink quilt she escapes from the policewoman and runs into the town. She collapses under an overpass. Vercueil finds her and carries her home. She needs stronger pills: they make her hallucinate, but the pain is still there. Vercueil offers to kill her. She won't let him, but she asks if his dog can share her bed to keep her warm.

> "He won't stay. He sleeps where I sleep."
>
> "Then sleep here too."

And so he does, and she doesn't mind his smell anymore and dies in his arms.

One can, of course, read her death as a metaphor for the doom of liberalism in South Africa: the age of iron has set in, there is no possibility left for reconciliatory solutions. But *Age of Iron* is about dying as much as it is about apartheid, and that raises it above the level of a political novel or a *roman a thèse,* and gives resonance to the political message: except that there is no message, nothing to be learned—only disgust and grief and, of course, shame. Coetzee is an extraordinarily powerful writer, and sadness is his strongest suit. The sadness grips like frost; by the last page one is numb with it. (pp. 8-10)

Gabriele Annan, "Love and Death in South Africa," in The New York Review of Books, *Vol. XXXVII, No. 17, November 8, 1990, pp. 8-10.*

George Packer

[When South African writer Nadine] Gordimer criticized J. M. Coetzee for excluding "social destiny" from a work of art, she was pointing to a theme of all his novels: that there is no salvation inside history and politics, but only in inwardness, silence, cultivating one's garden—which is literally the way the simple hero of *Life and Times of Michael K* survives during civil war. One can claim that this is a skewed, defeatist, even false vision, but a more affirmative one would require Coetzee to shut off the very source of his power. One couldn't ask him to turn his gifts to the cause of liberation and expect him to keep writing good books. Coetzee's quietism imposes limits on his novelistic range—in the case of *Foe* (1987) it led to a lukewarm novel of ideas—but it is central to the intense feeling in his work.

Age of Iron deepens quietism into pessimism; it spreads a sadness over the reader that is all the heavier for the lack of *Michael K*'s or *Waiting for the Barbarians'* imaginative brilliance. For the first time Coetzee does without allegory and fantasy: *Age of Iron* is set in Cape Town around the year 1986, and events like police raids on squatter camps are more than just social background. So the novel goes partway toward righting the balance between "private and social destiny." Coetzee's narrator is an old white woman, a classics professor, alone and dying of cancer. The novel is her letter to a daughter, long since fled to America, about her final days in a doomed country. (pp. 778-79)

Mrs. Curren hates the apartheid regime and its props: "What absorbs them is power and the stupor of power. Eating and talking, munching lives, belching." But only as she's dying does the hard violence of South Africa break in on her life. Her maid's son Bheki and the son's friend, student activists fleeing the police, take refuge in Mrs. Curren's house; at the same time, a homeless wino named Vercueil has begun sleeping on her property in a cardboard box. Vercueil is one of Coetzee's nearly speechless primitives, like Michael K (and like K's, his race is left indeterminate), who hover on the margin of social life as haunting counterpoints to the world of power and intellect. Vercueil hardly exists as a character beyond drinking, cadging money and quietly taunting Mrs. Curren for her garrulous despair. More than anything, he is a figure of death.

So history and death visit at the same time, and it's hard to say which intrusion causes her more pain. Mrs. Curren accuses her maid of abdicating responsibility for the behavior of the rebellious youths. "These are good children, they are like iron, we are proud of them," the maid declares, but for the white woman their hardness, arrogance and contempt for Vercueil bode ill: "If this is how the new guardians of the people conduct themselves, Lord spare us from them." Yet something like maternal instinct, the need to love, draws her to Bheki and his friend in danger. When Bheki disappears in the burning township, Mrs.

Curren and her maid go to look for him. The night sequence in a squatter camp is as powerful as anything Coetzee has written. . . . (pp. 779-80)

"I want to go home. I am in pain. I am exhausted," the sick old woman moans amid the overwhelming sights of violence and destruction. Her maid's brother, a schoolteacher, turns on her.

"But what of the people who live here? When they want to go home, this is where they must go. What do you think of that?" A crowd suddenly gathers; the atmosphere becomes coercive, accusing. "What sort of crime is it that you see? What is its name?"

"These are terrible sights," Mrs. Curren stammers, still trying to keep a soul alive. "They are to be condemned. But I cannot denounce them in other people's words. I must find my own words." At last they discover Bheki's bullet-torn body along with the bodies of other township youths. Mrs. Curren thinks: "Now my eyes are open and I can never close them again." . . .

This woman will continue to die, in deepening shame now as well as isolation, Vercueil her only companion. And she will end in his cold embrace. *Age of Iron* offers absolutely no hope, no sanctum for the soul against either social or private destiny. Yet neither death nor revolution can bring freedom. . . . [*Age of Iron* shows] that the "unity of art and life" has less to do with social truth than with intense private feeling. (pp. 780)

> *George Packer, "Manifest Destiny," in* The Nation, *New York, Vol. 251, No. 21, December 17, 1990, pp. 777-80.*

FURTHER READING

Bishop, G. Scott. "J. M. Coetzee's *Foe:* A Culmination and a Solution to a Problem of White Identity." *World Literature Today* 64, No. 1 (Winter 1990): 54-7.
  Examines Coetzee's use of a dissipating authorial voice, through which he questions language as a tool of oppression.

Castillo, Debra A. "The Composition of the Self in Coetzee's *Waiting for the Barbarians.*" *Critique: Studies in Modern Fiction* 27, No. 2 (Winter 1986): 78-90.
  Academic analysis of social and personal history as presented in *Waiting for the Barbarians.*

Clayton, Cherry. "Uprooting the Malignant Fictions." *The Times Literary Supplement,* No. 4460 (23 September 1988): 1043.
  Review of Coetzee's *White Writing* and Nigerian author Chinua Achebe's *Hopes and Impediments: Selected Essays, 1965-1987* in which Clayton compares and contrasts the depiction of white culture in both books.

Dodd, Josephine. "Naming and Framing: Naturalization and Colonization in J. M. Coetzee's *In the Heart of the Country.*" *World Literature Written in English* 27, No. 2 (Autumn 1987): 153-61.
  Asserts that early criticism of *In the Heart of the Country* was limited in scope and based on inaccurate assumptions regarding the narrator.

Gallagher, Susan Van Zanten. "Torture and the Novel: J. M. Coetzee's *Waiting for the Barbarians.*" *Contemporary Literature* 29, No. 2 (Summer 1988): 277-85.
  Examination of Coetzee's attempts to explore state-approved torture in *Waiting for the Barbarians* without the use of realistic detail. According to Gallagher, Coetzee believes that "the novelist participates vicariously in the atrocities, validates the acts of torture, assists the state in terrorizing and paralyzing people by showing its oppressive methods in detail."

Gardiner, Allan. "J. M. Coetzee's *Dusklands:* Colonial Encounters of the Robinsonian Kind." *World Literature Written in English* 27, No. 2 (Autumn 1987): 174-84.
  Examines similarities and differences between the treatment of colonialism in Coetzee's *Dusklands* and Daniel DeFoe's *Robinson Crusoe.*

Hewson, Kelly. "Making the 'Revolutionary Gesture': Nadine Gordimer, J. M. Coetzee and Some Variations on the Writer's Responsibility." *Ariel: A Review of International English Literature* 19, No. 4 (October 1988): 55-72.
  States that Nadine Gordimer relies on explicit critical realism to expose the brutalities of South African politics while Coetzee presents a less regionalistic view of oppression by distancing himself from the specifics of apartheid.

Martin, Richard G. "Narrative, History, Ideology: A Study of *Waiting for the Barbarians* and *Burger's Daughter.*" *Ariel: A Review of International English Literature* 17, No. 3 (July 1986): 3-21.
  Scholarly comparative analysis.

Moore, John Rees. "J. M. Coetzee and Foe." *The Sewanee Review* XCVIII, No. 1 (Winter 1990): 152-59.
  Briefly discusses Coetzee's earlier novels while providing a detailed analysis of *Foe.*

Olsen, Lance. "The Presence of Absence: Coetzee's *Waiting for the Barbarians.*" *Ariel: A Review of International English Literature* 16, No. 2 (April 1985): 47-56.
  Asserts that Coetzee deconstructs South Africa's "dominant cultural myths" in *Waiting for the Barbarians* by presenting an arbitrary text replete with expressions of absence and desolation that refer to such institutions as "civilization, authority, humanism, and truth."

Penner, Dick. "Sight, Blindness and Double-thought in J. M. Coetzee's *Waiting for the Barbarians.*" *World Literature Written in English* 26, No. 1 (Spring 1986): 34-45.
  Attempts "to demonstrate Coetzee's skillful handling of the leitmotif of blindness and insight" in *Waiting for the Barbarians.*

——. "J. M. Coetzee's *Foe:* The Muse, the Absurd, and the Colonial Dilemma." *World Literature Written in English* 27, No. 2 (Autumn 1987): 207-15.
  Analysis of *Foe* in which Penner describes the novel as "a retelling of *Robinson Crusoe* with Absurdist overtones, a commentary on the art of fiction, and an analogue of South Africa's political and racial dilemmas."

Post, Robert M. "Oppression in the Fiction of J. M. Coetzee." *Critique: Studies in Modern Fiction* 27, No. 2 (Winter 1986): 67-77.
> Discusses Coetzee's ambiguous portrayal of both the oppressed and the oppressor. Since apartheid "oppresses and restricts freedom" for both, "neither the oppressed nor the oppressor is really free."

————. "The Noise of Freedom: J. M. Coetzee's *Foe.*" *Critique: Studies in Contemporary Fiction* 30, No. 3 (Spring 1989): 143-54.
> Detailed analysis of the themes of colonialism, powerlessness, women's liberation, and silence in Coetzee's novel.

Renders, Luc. "J. M. Coetzee's *Michael K:* Starving in a Land of Plenty." In *Literary Gastronomy,* edited by David Bevan, pp. 95-102. Amsterdam: Rodopi, 1988.
> Examines the allegorical structure and the "opposition between creative and destructive forces" in *Life and Times of Michael K.*

Watson, Stephan. "Colonialism and the Novels of J. M. Coetzee." *Research in African Literatures* 17, No. 3 (Fall 1986): 370-92.
> Discusses different facets of colonialism in Coetzee's major works.

James T. Farrell

1904-1979

(Born James Thomas Farrell; also wrote under pseudonym Jonathan Titulescu Fogarty) American novelist, short story writer, essayist, and editor.

One of the most notable American novelists to emerge during the 1930s, Farrell initially garnered critical attention as an innovative contributor to naturalism. Naturalism as a literary movement closely parallels philosophic naturalism, a doctrine which holds that all observable phenomena exist in nature and are therefore explainable in scientific terms. Farrell's novels and short stories, which are often set in the south side of Chicago and are organized as multi-volume cycles, frequently feature protagonists who either succumb to elements of immoral urban life or escape through the pursuit of self-knowledge. Although praised for convincing characterizations, detailed settings, and unsentimental treatment of Chicago street life, Farrell's works are sometimes considered outdated or lacking in grace and style. However, AlfredKazin, while generally concurring with the latter assessment, declared that "[Farrell's] gracelessness seemed so methodical that it became a significant style in itself—not awkward . . . , but an automatic style, a style rather like a sausage machine, and one whose success lay in the almost quantitative disgust with which Farrell recorded each detail."

Farrell was part of a large, working-class family; the parents were first-generation Irish Catholic immigrants with a very limited income. Farrell was raised by his more wealthy maternal grandparents on the south side of Chicago. In 1925, Farrell enrolled at the University of Chicago, where his interest in realism and naturalism was shaped by reading the fiction of Theodore Dreiser and Sherwood Anderson and philosophical treatises by such American pragmatists as George H. Mead and John Dewey.

Farrell began publishing short stories and criticism as early as 1925 but first achieved serious critical recognition with his first novel, *Young Lonigan: A Boyhood in Chicago Streets*. Set in the south side Chicago neighborhood where Farrell grew up, *Young Lonigan* portrays the adolescence of Studs Lonigan, an intelligent and inquisitive middle-class boy who blindly adopts "tough-guy" values. In *The Young Manhood of Studs Lonigan* and *Judgment Day*, Farrell extends his examination into Studs's young adult life, demonstrating how such institutions as marriage, family, education, and the Church are incapable of eradicating what Farrell called his protagonist's "spiritual poverty." Farrell's Studs Lonigan novels, which are sometimes referred to as a single work, were collectively published as *Studs Lonigan: A Trilogy*. Written in a sharp, accusatory tone, these works chronicle Studs's descent into despair as he participates in such activities as gambling, excessive drinking, and gang rape. The trilogy culminates in Studs's death at the age of thirty after he develops pneu-

monia from sleeping drunk in a gutter. While some reviewers initially accused Farrell of glorifying an immoral character, most contemporary critics agree that Studs achieves the status of a sympathetic tragic figure not because he is a criminal or social rebel but because his life is devoid of purpose or meaning. Walter Allen referred to *Studs Lonigan* as "among the most depressing novels ever written, and one of the most honest and disturbing," and Walter B. Rideout called the trilogy one of the "most durable achievements of the radical novel of the thirties."

Farrell wrote many short stories and several independent novels featuring characters who recur throughout his various series, but most of his novels belong to cycles organized around individual protagonists. For example, Farrell's "O'Neill-O'Flaherty" series, also referred to as the "Danny O'Neill" cycle, features a character similar to Studs who becomes a social and artistic rebel. Like Farrell himself, O'Neill is raised by his maternal grandparents (the O'Flahertys), and observes harsh family conflicts from a young age. In the novels *A World I Never Made, No Star Is Lost, Father and Son, My Days of Anger,* and *The Face of Time,* Farrell portrays Danny's relationships with such characters as his father, a laborer who works his way up to shipping clerk only to be paralyzed by a series of strokes; his hysterical, fanatically religious mother, who finds relief from her family's poverty in alcohol and extra-marital affairs; his grandfather, an aging teamster and Irish immigrant; and his Irish-American grandmother, an illiterate, sanctimonious matriarch whose disapproval of the Danny's penury creates constant tension within the family. Although Farrell's "O'Neill-O'Flaherty" series is sometimes regarded as diffuse or episodic and never attained the popular status of *Studs Lonigan,* most scholars consider the cycle more comprehensive than the previous series, contending it projects a society with more realistic opportunity for social ascension.

Throughout his career, Farrell believed that literature could function as both an instrument of social change and an art form divorced from political considerations. He was a supporter of the American Communist Party from 1932 until 1935, when he became disenchanted with Stalinism. Some politically-minded reviewers chastised him during the 1930s for not dealing directly with class-related issues in his fiction. Farrell responded in periodicals and in *A Note on Literary Criticism,* a volume of essays in which he opposed the political manipulation of literature by the American Communist Party and both defended and attacked the techniques and theories of Marxist literary critics such as Granville Hicks and Michael Gold. Farrell's encounters with the Marxist critics informed his next cycle, the "Bernard Clare" trilogy. This series, which includes the novels *Bernard Clare, The Road Between,* and *Yet Other Waters,* describes the emergence of a young, working-class Chicagoan of Irish heritage who attains success as a writer in New York City. Bernard, whom reviewers often compare to Stephen Dedalus, the protagonist of two novels by James Joyce, encounters a vivid assortment of artists and communists while opposing Catholicism, communism, and other forces that he feels threatening to his artistic integrity. Farrell's "Bernard Carr" trilogy is esteemed primarily for its realistic portrayal of left-wing intellectuals of the 1930s.

During the 1940s, such critics as Alfred Kazin, Irving Howe, and Leslie Fiedler declared the possibilities of naturalism to be exhausted, citing Farrell as a case in point. The emphasis on determinism in works of naturalism led critics to fault Farrell's worldview as rigid, asserting that his emphasis on environmental factors disallows for the possibility of free will in his characters. This view has been challenged by others and remains an outstanding issue of critical debate concerning Farrell's fiction. Farrell commented: "I've never been the economic determinist that critics made me. I first read Zola in 1937. I have a functional conception of environment and character; I don't believe in environment over character or anything like that." Undeterred by critical hostility, Farrell continued to naturalistically explore the primary theme of all his works—that of the individual's provident use of his brief lifetime.

Farrell stated that in his "A Universe of Time" series he was attempting "a relativistic panorama of our times" that would address "man's creativity and his courageous acceptance of impermanence." This cycle, which was originally projected to run to thirty volumes, was intended to present Farrell's autobiographical experience more comprehensively than before and to reflect his more mature acceptance of conditions that had earlier engendered only resentment. In the eleven volumes he completed before his death in 1979, Farrell focused principally on the life of Eddie Ryan, a working-class Irish-American from Chicago who becomes a successful writer in New York City but is unable to forge lasting personal relationships. Although many critics contended that "A Universe of Time" represented no significant advance in Farrell's writing and was outdated in both subject and style, Joseph W. Slade commented that the cycle is intended to demonstrate that the romantic self "is bankrupt. In demonstrating its exhaustion, Farrell shows that he understands human isolation, and that he understands what it means to be without significant resources to alleviate isolation. That understanding makes him very modern indeed."

(See also *CLC,* Vols. 1, 4, 8, 11; *Contemporary Authors,* Vols. 5-8, rev. ed., Vols. 89-92 [obituary]; *Contemporary Authors New Revision Series,* Vol. 9; *Dictionary of Literary Biography,* Vols. 4, 9; and *Dictionary of Literary Biography Documentary Series,* Vol. 2.)

PRINCIPAL WORKS

Novels

*Young Lonigan: A Boyhood in Chicago Streets   1932
Gas-House McGinty   1933
*The Young Manhood of Studs Lonigan   1934
*Judgment Day   1935
Ellen Rogers   1941
This Man and This Woman   1951
What Time Collects   1964

The "O'neill-O'flaherty" Series

A World I Never Made   1936
No Star Is Lost   1938
Father and Son   1940; published in Great Britain as *A Father and His Son,*   1943
My Days of Anger   1943
The Face of Time   1953

The "Bernard Carr" Trilogy

Bernard Clare   1946; also published as *Bernard Clayre,* 1948, and as *Bernard Carr,*   1952
The Road Between   1949
Yet Other Waters   1952

"A Universe of Time"

Boarding House Blues   1961
The Silence of History   1963
Lonely for the Future   1966
New Year's Eve, 1929   1967
A Brand New Life   1968
Judith (novella)   1969
Invisible Swords   1971
Judith and Other Stories (short stories)   1973
The Dunne Family   1976
The Death of Nora Ryan   1978

Olive and Mary Anne (short stories) 1978

SHORT FICTION COLLECTIONS

***Calico Shoes and Other Stories* 1934; published in
    Great Britain as *Seventeen and Other Stories,* 1959
***Guillotine Party and Other Stories* 1935
***Can All This Grandeur Perish? and Other Stories* 1937
Tommy Gallagher's Crusade (novella) 1939
†*$1000 a Week and Other Stories* 1942
Fifteen Selected Stories 1943
†*To Whom It May Concern and Other Stories* 1944; also
    published as *More Stories,* 1946
Twelve Great Stories 1945
More Fellow Countrymen 1946
When Boyhood Dreams Come True 1946; also published
    as *Further Short Stories,* 1948
A Hell of a Good Time and Other Stories 1947
†*The Life Adventurous and Other Stories* 1947
Yesterday's Love and Eleven Other Stories 1948
A Misunderstanding (story) 1949
An American Dream Girl 1950
French Girls Are Vicious and Other Stories 1955
A Dangerous Woman and Other Stories 1957
Saturday Night and Other Stories 1958
The Girls at the Sphinx (stories) 1959
Looking 'em Over (stories) 1960
Side Street and Other Stories 1961
The Short Stories of J. T. Farrell 1962
Sound of a City 1962
Childhood Is Not Forever and Other Stories 1969
Eight Short Stories and Sketches 1981

ESSAY COLLECTIONS

A Note On Literary Criticism 1936
The League of Frightened Philistines and Other Papers
    1945
The Fate of Writing in America 1946
Literature and Morality 1947
Reflections at Fifty and Other Essays 1954
Selected Essays [ed. by Luna Wolf] 1964
Literary Essays, 1954-1974 [ed. by Jack Alan Robbins]
    1976

OTHER

The Name Is Fogarty: Private Papers on Public Matters
    1950
*Poet of the People: An Evaluation of James Whitcomb
    Riley* [with others] ·1951
*My Baseball Diary: A Famed Author Recalls the Wonder-
    ful World of Baseball, Yesterday and Today* 1957
It Has Come to Pass (nonfiction) 1958
Dialogue with John Dewey [editor; with others] 1959
The Collected Poems of James T. Farrell 1965
The Letters to Theodore Dreiser 1966
When Time Was Born (prose poem) 1966

---

*These novels were published together in 1935 as *Studs Lonigan: A
Trilogy.*

**These three volumes were published collectively as *The Short Sto-
ries of James T. Farrell,* 1937; also published as *Fellow Countrymen: Collected Stories,* 1937

†These three volumes were published together as *An Omnibus of
Short Stories,* 1956.

Robert Morss Lovett

Five years ago the name of James Farrell was unknown.
Today it is read on the title-pages of five novels, two volumes of short stories, and a challenging book of
criticism. . . . [Farrell] is among the foremost in the
group of younger writers who are taking the stage in succession to those whom we already think of as the old
guard: Theodore Dreiser, Upton Sinclair, Sinclair Lewis,
Sherwood Anderson, and Ernest Hemingway. In his external career he recalls Dickens in the rapidity of his production and his sudden rise to notability as a writer and
as a public figure—a defender of human rights.

My first acquaintance with Farrell at the University of
Chicago was in connection with a letter which he wrote
to the college newspaper protesting against the exclusion
by the dramatic club of colored students from plays which
introduced characters belonging to their race. At our second meeting he brought me the manuscript of a story
about Studs Lonigan, a boy who grew up in the changing
neighborhood a mile or so west of the University. If my
recollection is correct—that I told him his material was
fitted for longer treatment than the short story—I take it
as an "appropriation to my own good parts." At all events
I soon heard my colleague Professor Linn roaring about
a student who had turned in a theme of sixty thousand
words on Studs Lonigan. Later I was in consultation with
Mr. Henle of the Vanguard Press about its publication,
when we decided to ask Professor Trotter, authority on
boys' gangs, to write an introduction calling attention to
the extraordinary sociological value of the story, the result
of Farrell's keen observation and intimate knowledge of
adolescent life. I do not apologize for these early recollections, however gratifying they are to me, because they
bring out the things that have made Farrell an important
writer today—the richness of his material within sharply
defined limits, the robust naturalism of his treatment, the
social significance of his view of the American scene, and,
it must be added, the strain of pity which humanizes while
it never distorts the picture.

It is quite proper to take as a starting-point for a consideration of Farrell's work in fiction the lucid account which
he has given of the artist's function and process in *A Note
on Literary Criticism.* He rejects the view that the purpose
of art is to give an enhanced and exalted impression of reality; to leave us with a sense of life as more intense and
important than the life we usually lead; a means of rising,
in Matthew Arnold's words, from our ordinary selves to
our highest and best selves. "When we experience through
a work of art," he argues, "we call on fewer of our senses
than when we experience directly. Hence, when we ask of
art that it be more than life we are asking not only for the
impossible; we are asking for a downright absurdity." The
enhancement-of-life theory of art implies that "a part can
be greater than the whole." One might quarrel with Far-

rell's thesis in the name of Leonardo, Michelangelo, Beethoven, Dante, and Goethe—but not on the basis of his own work. One of his earliest short stories, written in 1929—a sketch of the funeral of Studs Lonigan, which became the germ of the trilogy dealing with that hero—illustrates the principle announced in 1936 that "art is a reproduction and reaction of a sense of elements from life that interest man," and that "within the pattern and structure of events of a literary work necessity flows out of the essential factors of environment, situation, milieu, characters." In his consistent loyalty to this creed he has remained close to the objective material of his observation and experience—the boy gangs centering about the corner of Indiana Avenue and Fifty-eighth Street in Chicago, the express office where he and McGinty worked, the family circles of the Lonigans and the O'Flahertys, St. Patrick's Church where the young men received spiritual nourishment, and the baseball games, parks, bathing beaches, saloons, and worse places whither they resorted for recreation. In his effort to make his senses yield all possible evidence, he has drawn upon the baser as well as the nobler of them. I know of no episode more poignant or more revealing than that in which Studs Lonigan at mass in St. Patrick's Church is swept by recurrent waves of emotion at the sight of Father Gilhooley eating the body of Christ to the rich accompaniment of music and incense, and the disturbing beauty and odor of the girl beside him.

One feature of Farrell's realism has received undue emphasis—his use of a few short words pertaining to physical properties and processes, colloquially current but until recently never seen on the printed page. Such words invariably attract the attention of the censor and, indeed, serve to illustrate the futility of censorship. From the time when Jeremy Collier published his *Short View of the Immorality and Profaneness of the English Stage* in 1697 the language described as bawdy disappeared from the drama and, under the further disapproval of *The Spectator,* from polite literature. Naturally in two centuries such words stored up a tremendous explosive force, so that when they were heard in Messrs. Stallings' and Anderson's *What Price Glory?* and in Sidney Howard's *They Knew What They Wanted,* audiences received a terrific shock. Censorship had given these words an extra-realistic value from which realists were bound to benefit. One or two examples show their heads timidly in most novels of today which affect the hard-boiled attitude. Farrell uses them boldly as necessary parts of speech in his dictaphonic record of conversation among his people. Unlike Lawrence in *Lady Chatterley's Lover,* he has no ulterior purpose of cultivating a phallic consciousness in his readers. He uses them because his characters use them; under expurgation their speech would become unreal, and in this unreality would falsify, in his own view, the writer's presentation. (pp. 347-50)

A work of art the Studs Lonigan trilogy assuredly is. Farrell tells us somewhere that in his opinion Dreiser's *An American Tragedy* is the greatest American novel of this century. In the manner of that masterpiece he follows the career of his hero through successive phases of mental and physical growth and deterioration to the Judgment Day, which is determined with Calvinistic inevitability out of the factors given of heredity, environment, and circumstance. *A World I Never Made,* which opens a tetralogy based upon similar data of Irish-American family life, shows gain in firmness of texture and precision of drawing. The appearance of Margaret in her lovely nakedness is unforgettable. Here again convention has stored up dynamic power for the bold defier of it. Painters of the nude have discovered the difference between academic purity and realistic truth. Farrell merely follows them. The quarrel between Margaret and her mother in which each combatant fires volleys of verbal filth in the face of the other is a scene with the fine abundance of Fielding, though it will be long before this displaces the famous quarrels of Brutus and Cassius and of Marmion and Douglas as an appropriate exercise for graduation from high school.

Besides Dreiser the writers whom Farrell mentions with most approval are Proust and Joyce. These three were the literary gods in the years when he was beginning to find himself, and it is natural to see something of each in his work. The stern logic of the career of Studs Lonigan [in *Young Lonigan*] is comparable to that of *An American Tragedy,* but it may be inferred that in the more extensive and deeply implied human pattern which emerges in *Judgment Day,* with its ampler sense of "the individual human being in interaction with other human beings in society," we have the influence of Proust. Certainly the first volume of *A World I Never Made* suggests a definitely Proustian approach to a segment of society which the author knows from the inside. The external realism by which we follow the characters through the section of Chicago which lies between Washington Park and Wabash Avenue is reminiscent of Joyce's Dublin; and the stream of consciousness which carries us down the years of Patrick J. Lonigan's life, once in triumph in the first pages of *Studs Lonigan,* again in defeat in the last pages of *Judgment Day,* is suggestive of Mrs. Bloom. It may be added that Farrell's short stories are of the family of Joyce's Dubliners.

Farrell's short stories are chips off the blocks of his novels. They are sketches of characters and episodes, casual and often trivial, thrown off with the prodigality of a Chekhov. Two qualities which are implicit in all Farrell's work stand out more distinctly than elsewhere in these fragments of life: irony and pathos. Sometimes the mere factual statement carries the bitter meaning: the dull vulgarity of city life in Don Bryan's Sunday stroll in **"Looking 'Em Over"**; and the atrocious sacrifice, meditated by priestly teachers, of the young lives intrusted to their charge in the resolutions set for Alvin Norton to read in **"Accents of Death."** The pathos of wasted youth in **"A Front Page Story," "Soap,"** and **"Honey, We'll Be Brave"** is released the more effectively by the author's determined understatement. The reader knows, however, that behind the literal manner of the case reporter there is pity for the broken shards of humanity—a pity that has its most sustained expression in the drunken odyssey of the elder Lonigan, back through the years and the city of his success to the starting-point which now denotes failure—on the evening of his son's dying.

His admiration of Dreiser, Farrell limits by recognizing

the inadequacy of his general ideas. In this respect the younger writer has already surpassed the older master, and, judging by his growth in intellectual power evinced by *A Note on Literary Criticism,* he bids fair to go farther yet. When the first volume of the *Studs Lonigan* series appeared [*Young Lonigan*] was recognized as a valuable contribution to the social problem of adolescence in metropolitan life. Professor Trotter wrote in his Introduction:

> Life on the street is the most potent educative influence for the majority of boys in such areas and one which contradicts traditional definitions and values as represented by the home, the church, the social agency, and the school. The street gives no diplomas and grants no degrees, but it educates with fatal precision. In *Young Lonigan* there is clearly portrayed a process of assimilation of boys to the attitudes and behavior patterns of the street and its characteristic play groups, gangs, poolrooms, et cet., which represent the juvenile community in this type of area. The process of demoralization as it takes place in a natural and inevitable way among boys in such an environment is vividly illustrated in the life of Studs Lonigan and his *confrères.* The influence of the streetcorner tramp, the role played by social status in the gang, the neighborhood processes of rivalry and conflict, and the immense importance attributed to sex are revealed as important elements in the boy's social life. This is the process of informal education, the significance of which as yet has hardly penetrated the ken of psychologists and educationists, to say nothing of parents and teachers.

An aspect of urban life which appears with sinister clearness is the decline of institutions in their ability to hold or influence youth. The impotence of the church is always a theme of Farrell's social criticism. It is traced to one source in two short scenes from clerical life: **"Reverend Father Gilhooley"** and **"The Little Blond Fellow."** A mild indorsement of its influence appears in the belief of Studs Lonigan's companions that Catholic girls do not fall as easily as others, but its services have become a bore and the confessional has no terrors. The school is an unexplainable trespass on personal liberty. The family is a field of wrangling in which parental authority is constantly flouted. A theme of great significance in late nineteenth-century literature is that of the revolt of youth seeking freedom from institutions of the past—the war between the generations—which received its classic treatment in Turgeniev's *Fathers and Sons.* The tragedy of Studs Lonigan is that he is not a rebel; not even a criminal. He does not war against his family and against society, though he preys upon both. His life is tragic because it is empty of any purpose whatever. His experience is terrible and pitiful to his audience because it is meaningless to himself. It is Farrell's ferocious indictment of American life.

As I remarked at the outset, Farrell's addiction to general ideas and social criticism is by way of making him a public figure concerned in various movements for the reform and renovation of society. He has, however, succeeded in keeping his fiction free from the entanglements of partisanship. It is perhaps as a prophylactic treatment against the infection of his art by the virus of propaganda that he wrote

his *Note on Literary Criticism.* At all events a reader sees in this unpretentious little book the evidence of the writer's assimilation of ideas from Marx, Engels, Lenin, Dewey, and others, according to their usefulness to himself in making clear the purpose and necessary processes of his art.

Farrell begins by distinguishing between the aspects of literature as a fine and a useful art, according to whether it depends upon the aesthetic or the functional elements in human experience. Exclusive emphasis upon the aesthetic as represented by Pater or upon the functional as represented by St. Thomas Aquinas and Professor Babbitt he rejects. His chief battle is with the critics of the Marxist school: Granville Hicks, Michael Gold, Edwin Seaver, and others, who conceive literature largely in terms of economic environment and evaluate it according to its consciousness of the class struggle and the aid which it brings to one side or the other, bourgeois or proletarian. Against these interpreters of Marx, Farrell cites the authority of Marx himself:

> Marx, then, conceived societies in motion, and he perceived that the factor of change is ever present in social relationships. Because of this factor, the effects of one set of relationships become causal factors for the next set, and thus there is ever evolving a whole network of influences; so that cultural manifestations, such as formal art, thought, and literature, which *may be* directly related to the basic material and economic relationships upon which a society is founded in one era, evolve away from that set of relationships as the process unfolds with the passage of time, and they in turn become part of the network of causal factors and conditioning influences in the general stream of social tendencies and forces.

This description, as Farrell points out, provides an explanation of the process "in which thought, art, and literature possess a carry-over value" from the past and bring aesthetic enrichment to the present as part of the inheritance of tradition.

The fact that Farrell is himself a Marxist in politics makes him the more anxious to defend his position that individual and collective, bourgeois and proletarian, as categories have no place as standards of judgment. He does not deny that a collective novel can be written but he rejects the notion that "the extent of the geographical territory covered in a novel and a prolixity of characters treated with relatively little detail will convey a stronger sense of the pressure of social circumstances and a stronger feeling of group or class or continent." His citation of John Dos Passos' *The 42nd Parallel* as an example of a so-called collective novel which "has to rely for unity on mechanical interlardings—his news-reel, his camera's eye, his use of free verse biographies of contemporary and historical figures," seems to me ill chosen. For Dos Passos, unity depends on atmosphere diffused through a technique which Professor Joseph Warren Beach has happily called "breadthwise cutting," and further made palpable by the explicit interludes which remind us of what the country at large was reading, seeing, and thinking. Again one must agree with

Farrell's protest that men have other interests besides the class struggle, and that to use "proletarian" and "bourgeois" as terms of eulogy or reprobation is to substitute labels for analysis. It is true, nevertheless, that experiments in fiction and drama which emphasize the concept of group or mass, and criticism which takes account of literary values to be found in the exploited class, whose immediate interest is bound up with a world-process leading to a classless society, are in accord with the great and characteristic theme of modern literature: the theme of human solidarity—of "social union in a rationally ordered state." That Farrell in his stories of the degradation of human beings under the decay of human institutions is contributing to the emergence of this theme is my own conviction. Within the categories of growth and decay in literature, to which he devotes his last chapter, I place his own work in that of growth. (pp. 350-54)

> *Robert Morss Lovett, "James T. Farrell," in* English Journal, *Vol. XXVI, No. 5, May, 1937, pp. 347-54.*

Joseph Warren Beach

The three books of the *Studs Lonigan* series amount to less than half of Farrell's output so far in the novel. Before the completion of the trilogy, he had already published *Gas-House McGinty* (1933), and since its completion he has brought out the first three volumes of a series of four—*A World I Never Made* (1936), *No Star Is Lost* (1939), and *Father and Son* (1940). These books deal with much the same class of people as *Studs Lonigan,* but in somewhat different aspects and more comprehensively, so that we have a greatly enlarged view of the social conditions of which Studs was a product. In *Studs Lonigan* it is the life of the young man on the streets that is featured; in *Gas-House McGinty* it is the working life of the adult; in the beginning novels of the new tetralogy it is, more broadly, family life. Many of the same basic motives of action are present in all the novels; but in *Studs Lonigan* they are shown leading a young man into gross and dreary dissipation; in *Gas-House McGinty* we see how they are affected by conditions of employment and display themselves under those conditions; in the later series we see them working in the larger theater of family life, with the effect on parents at home and on their families of growing children.

Gas-House McGinty has for its special subject the men who drive the express wagons and the men who take the calls and route the wagons for the "Continental Express Co." in Chicago. Most of the action takes place in the office, where the men fill in the time between taking calls wisecracking and playing practical jokes. The central character is Ambrose J. McGinty, who is boss in the call office until he is transferred and put on the street as the result of a shindy in the office. The narrative is almost entirely made up of what the men say to one another, together with some sprinkling of their thoughts, their daydreams, and their dreams at night. But out of this unplotted pandemonium we gather a very adequate notion of the ways of life, and above all of the dominant preoccupations, ideals and motives in this little industrial microcosm.

These men are of course concerned with keeping their jobs, supporting their families, and bringing up their children. And they are also bent on finding entertainment and relaxation in their leisure time. But all this would seem to be secondary to the more essential compulsion to maintain their self-esteem, to keep up, each one, a sense of his personal importance or build up defenses against the realization that he is a "mutt." The work is hard and leads nowhere; employment is precarious, subject to the whim of a boss or to the accident of ill-health or crippling injury. They work not in their own vineyards but are constantly subject to command and abuse from patrons and superiors. They live meanly, and enjoy only the social prestige which attaches to having fairly steady jobs. In spite of this they are men, and they have the ineradicable need to demonstrate to themselves and to all the world their force and worth as men. (pp. 287-88)

For some of them—and notably for Ambrose McGinty (Mac)—the chief of such means is the satisfaction he takes in his work, his personal efficiency, and the importance he derives from his connection with the Continental—great and powerful organization indispensable to the carrying on of the world's work. Mac has in the business a position of responsibility and command. He can be proud of the order which he puts into things; he has even worked out the percentage of reduction in overhead which he has brought about.

But he has his troubles too. His wife is a despotic, suspicious woman, a mountain of flesh, and he has not the satisfaction of being master in his own house. He has no children to make him proud of his manhood. And for some reason which he cannot comprehend, he is the object of constant razzing on the part of the other men, who regard him, in spite of his efficiency, as a "fat slob." It is impossible for the reader to make out whether or not to like Mac, he is such an assorted bundle of natural impulses, the mean and generous all mixed up together. Which means, I suppose, that he is all too human, or, as the French say, *l'homme moyen sensuel.*

He certainly has his provocations. His friends humiliate him by getting a "fairy" to make up to him and then joking him in the office on his Oscar Wildean propensities. When in a fit of showy generosity he gives his last dime to a beggar, expecting his friends to pay his street car fare, they decline to acknowledge his acquaintance until he is on the point of being put off by the conductor. When he brings pillows to the office to lighten his suffering from the piles, they hide the pillows and provoke the hullabaloo that results in his being demoted. And, dirtiest trick of all, they telephone his wife that back pay has been distributed, so that she thinks he is keeping his pay envelope from her. This results in a period of sourness and alienation under which he suffers acutely. . . . He has urgent need of psychological compensations, and the mechanism works automatically. He falls asleep and dreams.

The account of his dream, which fills one of the longest chapters, is a perfect primer in the ways of the unconscious—at least in the more direct and obvious ways. The dream takes its start from his bodily condition, and the "manifest content" is much of it derived from the experiences of the day. But the dreaming mind ranges widely among images and symbols that free him from the restrictions of commonplace reality and morality. Long passages of anxiety, shame, fear, and baffled seeking resolve themselves in a burst of triumph and liberation. The dream begins with naked girls inviting him to join them. But shame and confusion come upon him when a girl he is chasing turns out to be Josephine, his little stepdaughter. He finds himself in hell, but even Satan cannot abide him and he is thrown out and told to go dig his own hole in the bottom of the sea. All through there is much made of this theme, derived from Mac's dream-identification with the hero of the popular song. McGinty jumps from towers, defies lions, and lands in a dreary Nowhere. Then begins his process of recovery. He is soothed by a sweet girl-voice (the voice of Josephine) bidding him arise and fight. The man in him asserts himself. "McGinty arose, brandishing a sword with monkey-glands tied to the handle, faced the blankly forward-marching Legions of Death, and declaimed: McGinty never, never dies!" There are many relapses into fear and humiliation; there is long searching for a woman whom he cannot identify or visualize. But at length the notes of victory prevail. McGinty is crowned King of all Ireland, and St. Patrick himself says a nuptial mass. . . . But McGinty has not reached the zenith in his dream-flight until he has slain God and freed himself from the last constraint and mastership under which mortal man must labor.

Thus by the fantasy of dreams McGinty has raised himself above the humiliations to which he has been subject and set his manhood above all question. A similar process is shown in the daydreaming of Danny O'Neill, the office boy, who is supposed to be more or less modeled after the author; in the boastful lies of Dusty Anderson, who pretends that he keeps his driver's job merely for exercise and to relieve his mind, that his main earnings are from his tony gambling house, or that he has turned down lucrative offers from big league baseball teams; and in the vicarious adventures indulged in by men at the moving pictures. In all of this, as well as in McGinty's dreams, we are often reminded of the fantasies of Leopold Bloom and other characters in Joyce's *Ulysses.*

In many cases the men support their sense of manhood in more socially constructive ways. They are concerned for the coming child; they take satisfaction in the thought of educating their little girls, sending a sick boy to a farm out West to restore his health, or putting their mother in steam heat. The most touching case is Jim O'Neill, Danny's father, a poor teamster with a large family, who has served the company for many years, and now has an office job, with some prospect of a raise if he can stand the gaff. But he has much to suffer from the insolence of his bosses, and he has had a stroke and is in fear that his health will not hold out. As he looks at himself in the washroom mirror his heart rises up in desperate prayers. "If God would only give him ten more years. God, please! God, please give the kids a chance." He was nothing but a workman; but he had been honest. He had done his share of drinking, but a man had a right to some diversion, and he had provided for his wife and kids with his hand and his back. (pp. 288-92)

More prominent, at least as a subject of conversation, are the pleasures of the bed, which are rightly understood by Farrell as having far more than a sensual character—as constituting, quite as much, a means of gratifying the vanity and restoring a man's sense of his own dignity and importance. Indeed, I cannot think of an author who has shown a better understanding of the psychological importance—we might almost say the spiritual importance—of the sexual act. These teamsters and route inspectors are often embarrassingly frank on this theme, and sometimes foul enough; but there is occasionally a simple eloquence in reference to the subject on the part of married men that should not be mistaken for obscenity. And the author is clearly aware of the unique value of this common experience for relieving nervous tensions and delivering poor devils from the indignities of life and from the burden of themselves.

With unmarried men the whole business has a more unsavory cast, because of its casual, promiscuous and hugger-mugger nature, the social irresponsibility, and the mainly commercial and mechanical character of the transaction. There is nothing very appetizing about the atmosphere of the Elite Hotel where the expressmen assuage their carnal hungers. But it is clear how large a part is played in the whole affair by the ideal or psychical element in these men's make-up—the need they have to satisfy the demands of the "persona" or ideal image a man has of himself, including the view of himself as a virile being. Even the diseases incident to purchased love are invested with some of the glamour attaching to the whole subject. The risk of disease adds to the adventurous nature of the enterprise; a man shows himself more manly by recklessness in the face of danger, and "you ain't a man till you get a dose."

But an even more constant and unattractive way for men to raise themselves is by lowering others. It is not that these men are by nature unfriendly or disinclined to do a good turn to one who needs it. But they are constantly eaten up with a gnawing sense of their being nobodies. There is so little chance to establish their worth by skill and knowledge; of doing so by goodness of heart or urbanity of manner the idea has not occurred to them. Where someone rises above the common level the impulse of the rest is to bring him down with ridicule. The language of these men is racy and vivid within a narrow range; but the use of any words from beyond that range, however exact or expressive, is universally frowned upon as affectation and show-off. These men would profit materially by a little education, but they make no end of fun of those among them who take pains to acquire it. This is no conspiracy, but the automatic working of an instinct to depreciate whatever you do not have. These men have a natural gift for conversation, but it takes the form of wisecracking and scurrility. You salve your own wounds by getting under the skin of another; and when he retaliates, it is a question of who can be most insulting. Your wife and in-laws are subject to abuse, and nothing is too intimate to be dragged in the mud.

If you have authority, however humble, you use it to humiliate those beneath you. You bawl them out on the slightest occasion. You make them toe the line. The blackest mark against McGinty was his procuring the discharge of Jimmy Horan, who was a good workman and had nothing against him except that he was sick of his job and had expressed the usual grudge against the boss. The report of this came to McGinty at a time when he was peculiarly down in the mouth. There is no indication that he understood the reasons for his action. His superior had told him that the call department needed jacking up. His vanity demanded a victim, and he persuaded himself that the firing of Horan was necessary for the good of the service. When the other men protested that Horan was a good workman, it was too late to reverse his decision without losing face. He had to go through with his injustice in order not to fall into lower depths of self-depreciation. McGinty was not a bad sort as human nature goes, but the strongest urge of his nature was to establish his own superiority.

The same mechanism is shown at work in his meeting with Jim O'Neill. Jim is a sad and dreary figure since he has had his stroke and goes limping about. And Mac is really sorry for him. But his dominant sentiment is self-congratulation over his own good health.

> Mac strode away, feeling sorry for Jim. Jim was through. Well, it hadn't gotten him yet, he thought with a pride that he immediately regretted. It was lousy for a healthy man to feel proud when he sees a sick friend. But he couldn't help feeling that it hadn't gotten McGinty yet.

Self-maximation is the word applied by some psychologists to the motive here at work. It is the clue to nearly every aspect of human nature displayed in this novel. It is a motive that may work for good or ill; and here, through lack of enlightenment, it comes out almost altogether in cheap and ugly ways. These lives are like pictures painted in a mean tradition through want of knowledge or through bad instruction. The fine energies of the ego are turned into foul channels. It is a pitiful want of economy of spiritual forces from which there was so much to be hoped. Instead of fair and goodly lives we are left to mourn "the expense of spirit in a waste of shame."

A broadly similar motivation is much in evidence in the later novels, *A World I Never Made, No Star Is Lost,* and *Father and Son.* Only, here the scene is transferred from the office to the home, and we have the more tragic spectacle of young children subjected to the same blighting and deforming influences. The central character here is Danny O'Neill as a young boy. The series is not completed. We know that in the end this boy was destined to break the evil spell and make his way out of the foul labyrinth, though it is not yet clear by just what turn of fortune he was granted light and strength to perform this feat.

The scenes are laid in two households, those of the O'Flahertys and the O'Neills. Mrs. O'Flaherty is Danny's grandmother, who is kept in steam heat and electricity by her son Al, a traveling salesman in shoes. She lives with her daughter Margaret, a cashier in a hotel. Lizz O'Neill is Danny's mother. She is supported by his father Jim, the teamster, whose acquaintance we have made in *Gas-House McGinty.* In the period covered by the first two books, he has not had his stroke; he is strong and hard-

working. But he has too many children, and they must live in squalid quarters, without even gas or water-closet. . . . (pp. 292-96)

The O'Flahertys have come to the rescue, taking Danny and later his little sister Margaret to live with them. The old woman is "shanty Irish"—completely illiterate, vain, boastful, foul-mouthed, violent, superstitious, stingy, and as hard as nails. But she is fond of her children and grandchildren. She claims Danny for her son, does her best to spoil him, and centers on him her hopes for the future honor of the family. She is proud of her son Al and grateful to him for making her comfortable. She is ashamed of the poverty of Lizz and Jim, and on public occasions dissociates herself from them as persons beneath her notice. She never admits being Irish, since in the old country only landlords and the English had social caste. And yet in her cups she often speaks of the time when she was "a wisp of a girl running the bush in the old country, barefooted and with her backside showing through her dress." Jim O'Neill is deeply resentful of her vulgar toploftiness and of having his son brought up to scorn his father; and this is the occasion of many quarrels between him and Lizz. At bottom they are tenderly devoted to each other and to their children; but poverty puts a heavy strain upon them. It has turned Lizz into a slattern and brought out in her the gutter strain she had from her mother.

The other O'Flahertys are all in reaction against this gutter strain. Ned has married someone who passes for a lady. Al has remained a bachelor, his heart set on lifting the family out of the bog of vulgar indigence. He reads the letters of Lord Chesterfield; he shuns the drinking and obscene storytelling of his comrades of the road, their boasting and fighting; he strives to improve the speech of his relatives, and recommends to his drummer friends "the touch delicate and the retort adroit." He takes seriously his obligations to Danny O'Neill, teaches him to walk properly, plays baseball with him, disciplines him considerately. In the family circle he strives for harmony, good feeling, urbane manners, and "constructive" ideals. He dreams of a happy fireside, with the "Rosary" sung by self-respecting wives or "Kathleen Mavourneen" played on the victrola while children sport about the Christmas tree. It is only the dread of vice in the home that rouses his temper and leads him to violence and brutality. Altogether, Al O'Flaherty is one of the great creations of modern fiction—a slightly ridiculous old bachelor, priggish and limited, but a man of genuine character and goodwill, struggling valiantly with circumstances that make of him a profoundly pathetic figure.

His sister Margaret is a tragic figure. She is by endowment the richest and finest of all the family. She is warmly affectionate and generous by nature, an Irish heart of gold, full of romantic sentiment. She should have been a devoted wife and the life-giving mother of a family of children. Her fine nature has been warped by unhappy experiences— dreary meanness and quarrelsomeness in the home, cruel beatings as a child, the cynical construction placed by Irish puritanism on her association with boys. Her romantic nature has found satisfaction not in marriage and home but in a secret liaison with a married man—a Protestant lumber tycoon—who after a few years of furtive meetings ceases to answer her letters and leaves her to blank misery and despair. She tries to console herself with other men and with gin; she falls into terrible fits of drunkenness culminating in attempts at suicide and fearful visions of snakes and devils. There are dreadful scenes where her mother calls her a whore, puts upon her the curse of a parent, or exorcises the devils with prayer and holy water. And the worst of it all is the presence of terrified young children, who must stay up all night to keep their aunt from turning on the gas, or sit by helpless while aunt and grandmother engage in foul exchanges of insult and recrimination.

The real subject of the whole study is the plight of children reading in such a book their first lessons in the art of living. One hardly knows which of the children are the more unfortunate—Danny and little Margaret, who pay for cleanly surroundings and steam heat with subjection to spectacles like these, or the children who remain in the slums with their mother, or the one who passes back and forth between the two infernos and picks up on the way the criminal inspirations of the street. This one is Bill, Danny's older brother (an incipient Studs Lonigan), who comes to play with Danny and teach him the facts of life as observed in his home.

As for the younger children, we see them in their sordid home playing the games of children, sedulously copying their parents in every detail of speech and behavior, especially in the scolding exercise of authority and in the use of foul and abusive language. As babies they are adorable little animals; their parents sincerely love them and fiercely defend them against all comers. But it is alarming to see how fast they take on the less attractive features of adulthood; and one looks forward dolefully to a new generation repeating the errors and imbecilities of the last.

It is the moral blight that is most distressing to contemplate. But more immediate is the physical peril. They live in filth and ignorance, with no defense against disease but prayers and holy water. *No Star Is Lost* concludes with a series of scenes in which the baby of the family is struck down with diphtheria and dies before a doctor or priest can be had, and all the other children are bundled off in the police wagon to a hospital for contagious diseases. Meantime, at the O'Flahertys', little Margaret has been taken down with the same malady. But the O'Flahertys have better standing with the doctor, and he comes promptly to their call. What is most bitter for Jim O'Neill is the thought that his poverty is so great he cannot even command a doctor for his dying child. No doubt, with a little more enterprise or imagination, he could have had free medical care; but enterprise and imagination do not thrive in the midst of so much ignorance.

Perhaps I have laid too much stress on the unfavorable influences brought to bear on these children. After all, their father and mother were honest, religious, well-intentioned people; the father wrought manfully to support his family; and they and all the other relatives duly preached the gospel of industry, sobriety and Christian goodness. In *Father and Son,* Farrell shows the O'Neills in a period of greater prosperity, with Jim now in the supervision end of the ex-

press business and Bill, too, settled down and bringing home his pay envelop from the express company. It is not quite clear what turn of heart has brought Bill to a sense of responsibility. But there is every prospect of his marrying and setting out on a way of life that is an exact duplication of his father's.

Danny is destined to emerge upon another cultural level, but the process of his emancipation is distressingly protracted. The psychologist would doubtless find in this record plentiful indications of how the character of Danny O'Neill was beaten into shape and given its bent by his childhood experience. And the discerning psychologist could even make clear how the most apparently unfavorable influences were working, by some logic of reaction, to free him from the dark web which circumstance was weaving about him. We see him playing the games and thinking the long, long thoughts of youth. Every defeat begets daydreams of success and triumph. (pp. 296-99)

The most poignant scenes in *No Star Is Lost* are those of his birthday party. Danny has managed to secure the attendance of several of the most attractive girls from school, and the refreshments are of the best. His great dread is that Aunt Peg will get drunk and cause a scandal; but she is persuaded to stay in her room and babble tearfully of her innocence as a child. Danny hopes by this party to make himself popular with the kids and get pretty Virginia Doyle for his girl. But the kids resent his choosing the prettiest girl for his partner, and the girls do not take to the game of postoffice. The net result is that the girls avoid him and the boys kid him more than ever. He is greatly relieved when the family moves to a new neighborhood. He hopes that Aunt Margaret will give up drinking and he may make a fresh start in his social life. One of the first acquaintances he makes in the new street is young Studs Lonigan. Ominous portent! But Danny O'Neill has not the making of a tough guy. His very deficiencies will drive him into the larger life of the mind, the liberator.

But that is a long process, which will take more than the four years at St. Stanislaus high school, recorded in *Father and Son.* This is one of the most frank and convincing studies of adolescence ever made in fiction. It is a most uncomfortable affair for all concerned. Young O'Neill is determined to make himself respected by the boys and admired by the girls, and this he achieves in some degree by dint of thoughtful application to the arts of pugilism, baseball, football and basketball. But he never succeeds in getting himself accepted by the other boys as quite one of them, in spite of being an athletic star, dressing like a dude, and spending all his money on fraternity dances. As a ladies' man he is a flop, and the harder he tries the less he enjoys himself. He cannot seem to strike the right tone with boys or girls, and is censured by his fraternity brothers for wisecracking and want of dignity. Everybody insists on treating him as a goof, and he is more and more impressed with his ineptness and his difference from other boys. For a time, under the suggestions of Sister Magdalen, he thinks he has a call to the priesthood; perhaps his awkwardness with the girls is an indication that way. But he is glad enough to have the support of father and uncles in giving up that idea. In the final year at high school he does a good deal of heavy drinking, but that satisfies nothing but his social vanity. Altogether it is a painful and obstinate case of growing pains—a disease common enough at Danny's age, but likely to be most severe and protracted under conditions that do nothing to feed the mind or employ the faculties of the growing organism. . . . (pp. 300-01)

Dramatically, the most interesting and moving theme in the last book is Danny's relation to his father—Jim crippled, dying and anxious over the fate of his family, Danny all absorbed in the crude desires and ambitions of adolescence. It is the familiar tale of a father angered and dismayed at the sight of a son precariously entrenched on the top of "Tom Fool's Hill" (to use the term most often on my own father's lips) and a son too much preoccupied by his own urgencies to appreciate his father's merits or understand his point of view. There are many beautiful and poignant touches in the account of Jim's decline. As for the blind egotism and crudity of the boy, they were a measure of his inexperience and the desperation of his spirit, starved and bewildered in a world that had so little to offer for its satisfaction. In his conscientious portrayal of Danny's relation to his father, Farrell has done bitter penance for us all.

On his father's death, Danny came down to earth. He went to work dutifully for the support of the family and gave up his dreams of life as a college man. Work in the wagon call department was anything but congenial, and leaden skies closed down upon him.

But there is a lightening on the horizon in one direction. Danny has sometimes thought that he might be a writer. He has read much in a battered volume of poetry cherished by his father, and in the little blue books of his Uncle Al. The men at the express office make fun of him for reading Shakespeare between calls. But the reader knows better. The reader knows that the written word is the key for which he is seeking, the key to all the doors of the mind and imagination. . . . (pp. 301-02)

Farrell's writing is perhaps the plainest, soberest, most straightforward of any living novelist. There is nothing commonplace about it, for there is none of the prosing self-consciousness of an author displaying his skill or his wisdom. The acts and thoughts of the characters are stated in the simplest terms, and the rest is their very speech, with the edge and tang of what is said in deadly earnest. It is, in Wordsworth's phrase, a "selection from the real language of men." Selection because the author eliminates everything trivial and superfluous, leaving only what will illuminate the primary concerns of his people. Real language of men; for it has an unmistakable ring of authenticity. There is no attempt to point up the dialect, exaggerate the slanginess, or give phonetic representation to the local accent. Nor, on the other hand, is there any prudish toning down of the grossness of language. There is nothing facetious, nothing smartly satirical in the author's tone. These are linguistic documents, as they are social documents, of high seriousness and value, but not slavishly photographic. Farrell is obviously more concerned with the spirit than the letter of truth.

The fictional method is purest naturalism, unrelieved by the traditional interest of plot and drama, mystery and suspense, unalloyed with "idealism," with theory, moralizing, sentimentality, or humorous comment. The pathos is the pathos of human suffering; the tragedy is the tragedy of act and fact. The naturalism is not that of elaborate documentation; there is no suggestion of the notebook and the subject worked up for literary use. Nor is there any suggestion of data collected and forced into the frame of theory. The documentation is really prodigious, but it did not require the author's going beyond the limits of experience and memory. Scene crowds on scene with suffocating profusion, till the reader cries out for mercy. But no scene has the air of being made up; none is forced, not many can be spared. They spring like geysers from the seething burdened depths of the author's being. They are not the cold and labeled cases of the sociologist. Each one is presented in the concrete terms of story; the appeal is first to the imagination, and only in retrospect to the mind and conscience.

In so far as anything is lacking it is some principle of relief. And this is felt most in the third volume of the Danny O'Neill series. Too many of the episodes are on the same level of interest. This is the price paid for fullness and sobriety in the recording. One is conscious of something like monotony of effect. When the series is completed this may seem a frivolous objection. The level stretches of *Father and Son* may fit in perfectly in the planned perspective of the whole. Let it be stated then not as criticism but as simple matter of fact that one grows a little tired of the delays and repetitions of Danny O'Neill. One is impatient to see him get his toes and fingers in the clefts and make a start at scaling the cliff that towers above him.

The best single test for a writer of fiction is the creation of characters that live in the imagination. Farrell has brought to life an unusual number of such living characters. Studs Lonigan, Ambrose McGinty, Jim O'Neill, Al O'Flaherty, Aunt Margaret, and grandmother O'Flaherty are among the memorable people in English fiction. I have not been able to do justice to any of them, and above all to Mary O'Flaherty.

There is one scene that must not be passed without mention—that in which the old woman visits the grave of her dead husband. It will remind us that Farrell is not unprovided with that type of imagination which we associate with poetry and with the most famous of the Irish dramatists. The old woman sits on a bench in a well-tended plot, nibbling her sandwiches, and looks toward the weed-grown sandy lot where her husband and daughter Louise are buried. She thinks of the hard days they led together in the past and of the evil life of her daughter Margaret, of the grievous sorrow which her Tom has been spared by death. Her indignation is roused at the thought of how her daughter has neglected the father's grave. And as she sits there in the gentle breeze from the lake, with the sounds of the city distant and dreamlike, the limits between real and imaginary fade away. She sees her husband rise from the grave in his habit as he was; and she finds herself talking with him, complaining of her daughter, recalling their days together as children in the old country—their first communion—and exchanging views at last on his character and hers, and the obligations laid upon her as the spiritual head of the house. He asks her if she "do be missing" him. "Indeed, I do," she answers. "You were a good man, but I had to make you toe the mark." "You're a good woman yourself, Mary, but, ah, you're a hard woman, you are," he seemed to say. And to this she agrees, taking it as a compliment. "Hard I am, and hard I'll be till they'll be carrying me sorry old bones out here to be laid at rest beside you, Tom," she said. And almost the last thing he has to say to her is to bid her make the children all toe the mark—"Be hard on them, Mary," he seemed to say.

It is a ticklish undertaking for anyone to record the visions of an old woman communing with the spirits of the departed, and doubly ticklish in the context of hard facts provided by Farrell. But this whole scene is managed with a simple naturalness (born of a grudging tenderness) which is a signal triumph of literary tact. To any reader who thinks that in Farrell he has to do with a commonplace or insensitive spirit, I heartily recommend this eighth chapter of *No Star Is Lost*.

Farrell's type of naturalism is not of a kind to appeal to the common run of readers. It has little to offer those who go to fiction for light entertainment, the glamour of the stage, or the gratification of their bent for wishful thinking. There is no reason why the squeamish or tender-minded should put themselves through the ordeal of trying to like his work. But there will always be a sufficient number of those whom life and thought have ripened and disciplined, who have a taste for truth however unvarnished provided it be honestly viewed, deeply pondered, and imaginatively rendered. For many such it may well turn out that James T. Farrell is the most significant of American novelists writing in 1940. (pp. 302-05)

> *Joseph Warren Beach, "James T. Farrell: The Plight of the Children," in his* American Fiction (1920-1940), *The Macmillan Company, 1941, pp. 287-308.*

Alfred Kazin

The two most formidable left-wing naturalists, Erskine Caldwell and James T. Farrell, brought a zest to their documentation of "capitalist decay" that was strangely irrelevant to Socialism, but actually the very secret of their power. Caldwell's twisted comic sense was defended on the strength of a suspicion that he really belonged to the tradition of Southern frontier humor, and it was significant that when he was not energetically grotesque, he was merely cute. His delight in cruelty and outrage, in sharecroppers being devoured by hogs and little girls sold into prostitution for a quarter, was as gamin in its quality as his delight in the sexual antics of his poor whites, and equally reflective of a primitive, sly, and stuttering romanticism. But Farrell was hardly a naïf, and certainly never a purveyor of Gothic tidbits for the delectation of urban sophisticates who thought Jeeter Lester a representative Southern citizen, but amusing. Passionately honest and passionately narrow, he brought to his novels the intensity of an autobiographical mission as tortured and complex

in its way as Proust's. Like Proust, Farrell seems to have endured certain personal experiences for the sole purpose of recording them; but he also desired to avenge them, and he charged his work with so unflagging a hatred of the characters in them, and wrote at so shrill a pitch, that their ferocity seemed almost an incidental representation of his own. Like Caldwell, he wrote with his hands and feet and any bludgeon within reach; but where Caldwell's grossness seemed merely ingenuous, or slick, Farrell wrote under the pressure of certain moral compulsives that were part of the very design of his work and gave it a kind of dreary grandeur. He had the naturalist's familiar contempt for style, but his gracelessness seemed so methodical that it became a significant style in itself—not awkward, as in Dreiser at his worst, or grandiose as in Frank Norris, but an automatic style, a style rather like a sausage machine, and one whose success lay in the almost quantitative disgust with which Farrell recorded each detail.

Farrell was perhaps the most powerful naturalist who ever worked in the American tradition, but the raw intensity of that power suggested that naturalism was really exhausted and could now thrive only on a mechanical energy bent on forcing itself to the uttermost. There is a total and moving design unfolded in his conflicting histories of Studs Lonigan and Danny O'Neill—the history of the South Chicago world out of which both sprang; the history of these two careers, one descending and the other ascending, with the ascendant Danny O'Neill giving back the life that had almost crushed him as a youth—*giving it all back*. But scene by scene, character by character, Farrell's books are built by force rather than imagination, and it is the laboriously contrived solidity, the perfect literalness of each representation, that give his work its density and harsh power. As an example for novelists Farrell was as much a blind alley as Dreiser, but where Dreiser remained a kind of tribal poet, a barbaric Homer who exercised a peculiar influence because of his early isolation and his place in the formation of naturalism, Farrell, so much less sentient a mind, grew out of the materialism of the early thirties. For while Dreiser was the epic recorder of the American tragedy in the first great period of naturalism, his awkwardness seemed merely a personal trait, and one that did not conceal the great depths in his work. Farrell was the archetypal novelist of the crisis and its inflictions, and the atmosphere of crisis supported his work as appropriately as his own conception of life satisfied the contemporary need to shock and to humiliate. It is not only that all the rawness and distemper of the thirties seem to live in Farrell's novels; though written as the story of his own education, they are at the same time the most striking example of that literalness of mind which showed all through the depression literature in the surrender of imagination and in the attraction to pure force and power.

It is this literalness, this instinctive trust in the necessity of violence, which make Farrell's practice in fiction so livid a symbol of the mind of depression America. In his hands the cult of violence was something different from Faulkner's overstylized Gothic, which had to be seen through a maze of confused lyricism and technical legerdemain, or Caldwell's pellagra Frankenstein, which was wryly comic. It was naturalism proving its bravado to itself, and expanding by the sheer accumulation of sensations. The technique was a kind of arithmetical progression, notably in such furious scenes as the famous New Year's Eve bacchanal in *The Young Manhood of Studs Lonigan,* the nightmare initiation scene in *Judgment Day,* and that apocalyptic passage in *No Star Is Lost* which portrayed Aunt Margaret O'Flaherty, drunk to the hilt, thrown out by her latest lover, sitting on the steps and counting her fingers in a devouring rush of the D.T.'s. Farrell's style was like a pneumatic drill pounding at the mind, stripping off the last covers of the nervous system. Primitive in their design, his scenes aroused a maximum intensity of repulsion by the sheer pressure of their accumulative weight. If one submitted to that pressure, every other consideration seemed irrelevant or falsely "literary," like Farrell's tone-deafness, or the fact that he improvised his scenes within so narrow a range that the final impression was black unrelieved dullness. This was Life, or at the very least the nerve-jangled and catastrophic life the thirties knew.

What gave Farrell his edge over other left-wing naturalists, many of whom perished singly even before their movement did, was his complete confidence in his material and gifts, in the very significance of his literary existence. . . . Farrell's will to endure gave him the energetic faith to write a trilogy and to launch one of the most expansive autobiographical epics in literary history. If his grimness often became the very tone of his work, it also served as a rationale, a formal conception as grandiose as Jules Romains's. Farrell's very need to write along a line of single concentration was, like his complete dependence upon his own resources, a kind of spiritual autarchy—there was only one subject in his work, and the spirit with which he pursued it soon became one with it. For Farrell was not "making" subjects out of proletarian life, like those occupational novelists whose books reflected their special knowledge of automobile workers, textile hands, relief supervisors; or those nationality novelists who were as crude as the Communist party's program for a "black belt" in the South to be composed exclusively of Negroes. He never wrote about his fellow Irish in that fake sociological spirit; Studs Lonigan's gang, the Flaherty and O'Neill families, the priests and nuns, were all dramatis personae in the story of Danny James Farrell O'Neill, whose story *was* his will to endure, to be free of the influences that had threatened to stifle his spirit.

Farrell's distinction was thus a very real one: in a period of moral collapse, he believed in himself with an almost monumental seriousness. Far more than Dreiser, whose career was spotted with failure, who wrote his books by intermittent and devastating exertions, Farrell represented the supremacy of the naturalist's imagination in, rather than over, a period of tormented materialism. He did not rise above the hazards of writing, he was fiercely unconscious of them; his personal victory over the first enemies of his freedom—the Church and Studs Lonigan and the slums of Chicago—became a literary victory by the sheer force of his remorseless attack upon them. If all writers remember longest what they learned in their youth, Farrell's work suggests that he remembered nothing and learned from nothing but his youth. Unlike all the little people in

left-wing letters who loved the working class to death but could never touch them, Farrell was joined by every instinct to men and women who have never known the barest security, who have clawed the earth to live from one day to the next. What more was needed in *Studs Lonigan* than the literal transcription of the Irish Babbittry's inhuman yammering, with abysmal cruelty banging against animal insolence, where only Celtic blood could get back at Celts with so much grisly humor? What more was needed in *A World I Never Made* and after than the toneless saga of drink, of a new child every year, of meat once a week, of endless, life-shattering recrimination, of a little boy named Danny O'Neill who wanted baseball and a quiet table, but who could never forget, though his grandmother took him away, that at home his parents and brothers and sisters were slowly dying together?

Unlike some sentimentalists, Farrell certainly never defended his work by calling it "sociology." Although he quickly became a convenient symbol to cultural historians who saw in him a student of the American city, to sociologists and social-settlement liberals and literary anthropologists of the lives and morals of the poor, Farrell insisted, with the traditional justice and something more than the traditional vehemence of the naturalist, that his work had the self-sufficient form and self-justifying power of a solidly written and precise literary record. And it was not the Marxist critics alone—who, indeed, were often cold to Farrell's work because it was not formally "revolutionary"—who supported this view; it was a kind of collective esthetic simplicity, or paralysis, of men of goodwill in the thirties who, having rejected genteel objections that *Studs Lonigan* was sociology, decided that it must be art—and obviously very powerful art. These genteel objections, which occurred only to those who feared the widest possible democracy of subject in the novel, were, as John Chamberlain wrote in his introduction to [*Studs Lonigan: A Trilogy*],

> an incantation designed to exorcise the uncomfortable memory of Studs and his frightening palsy-walsies, with their broads, their movies, their pool, their alky, their poker and their craps. . . . Like all incantations, it masks a real respect. People don't usually bother to spin fine distinctions between documentary and artistic excellence when they are not disturbed by a book.

Whereupon one asked, as Mr. Chamberlain did, impatiently, "What in hell is art, anyway?"

What was it indeed? To a democracy slowly arming against Fascism and conscious of its latent forms in the United States, *Studs Lonigan* did, at the very least, rank as a brilliant exposure of brutality and ignorance and corruption. If a healthy literature, as the Marxists insisted, meant an aroused concern with social analysis and the pressure of class forces in capitalist society, *Studs Lonigan* was a dynamic naturalism whose depth of insight and furious vitality gave it the stamp of creative power. To an America obsessed by the atmosphere of dissolution, proud of its "realism" and urgently in need of stimulation, Farrell's violence was salutary—a vigorous demonstration that art had to respond, at some stage of human development, with as much vigor as the strident life that gave it birth. "When a book has depth and pace," John Chamberlain wrote of **Studs Lonigan,**

> when it continually flashes with meanings, when it coördinates one's own scattered and spasmodic experiences and reflections, when it mounts to climaxes that suddenly reveal by artistic mutation what has been imperceptible and latent in a character, then aren't we justified in calling it art, no matter how "photographic" the realism?

Yes; but in these terms art became only another abstraction, a hypothetical end-product as unreal as the famous "withering away of the state" in Leninist theory. For what if the realism was as brutal in its way as the brutality it exposed? It was not that Farrell's work was "amoral"; on the contrary, the moral judgment Danny O'Neill was forever making on his world—though familiarly mechanical as in most books of the kind, forever declaiming *J'accuse!*—was the most pervasive element in his work. It was art, powerful and vital art; but it was also a perfect example of that unconscious and benevolent philistinism which believes that one escapes from materialism by surrendering to it; that the principle of action, for writers as well as for revolutionaries, is to gain freedom for oneself by denying it to others. In the Marxist-Leninist theory of the state, one began as a terrorist and ended theoretically as a free man living in a more "human" world that had never practiced a conscious humanity. In the left-wing theory of literature, which was so riddled with determinism that it employed only half one's mind and soul, spiritual insight was to be won only by proving how little there was of it in life. (pp. 380-85)

> *Alfred Kazin, "The Revival of Naturalism," in his* On Native Grounds: An Interpretation of Modern American Prose Literature, *1942. Reprint by Harcourt Brace Jovanovich, Inc., 1963, pp. 363-99.*

Charles Child Walcutt

The work of James T. Farrell offers a remarkable study in the process by which form or technique controls content. He began writing in a convention of selection (to be described presently) which undertook to present the whole truth more fully and precisely than previous novelists had done but which had the unexpected effect, in a few years, of leading Farrell to take a different view of his subject matter from what he had had at starting. In writing about certain aspects of modern life he not only purged himself of his bitterness but also achieved a different conception of his material. What he began by assailing he ended by defending. He thus in a sense wrote himself inside out, and the process reveals something about the implications and consequences of attempting to fulfill the naturalistic goal of telling the whole truth.

In his great **Studs Lonigan** trilogy Farrell wrote of the Chicago South Side with a conscious and conscientious naturalism. He presented a character and revealed his destiny in the closest possible (so it seemed at the time) relation to the social, economic, and spiritual conditions in

which he lived. The presentation is ostensibly objective; certainly it satisfies the literary canons of objectivity. The point of view is controlled and consistent. But the attitude that appears in almost every page is the author's cold, furious loathing of the spiritual barrenness of Studs' life. The values of school, playground, church, and home are revealed in their naked poverty. Studs does not reach beyond them, and he exhibits the terrible spectacle of humanity wasted. If one read only the **Studs Lonigan** trilogy, he would lay it down, I believe, with the conviction that its dominant emotion was concentrated despair and disgust for the conditions that dwarfed and then blighted Studs' spirit. **Studs** is magnificent writing. It is naturalistic in the tradition of Dreiser, with its careful accumulation of detail, its pretense of naïveté, its obvious inclusion of the reader in the tragic agon—for here as in *An American Tragedy* the reader is made aware that the forces which blight the growth of Studs' spirit are not fatal but social: the reader cannot stay outside of the conflict. Whereas the emotions aroused by classical tragedy are pity and terror, the emotions aroused by such naturalistic tragedies as this are pity and guilt. The Greek and Shakespearean tragedy exhilarates, the modern depresses.

Yet depressing as it is, the **Studs Lonigan** trilogy owes much of its power and unity to its tragic form. Studs' consciousness, his personality, and his economic status are three strands of a life that moves as it ends, in waste. The tragic form is not marked by a great ethical issue and a critical choice, but by the relentless dissipation of energy, idealism, and intelligence in the futile and purposeless activities of a young man who does not know what to do with his life.

In **Young Lonigan** (1932) it is shown that Studs yearns with the fervent idealism of youth for a good life. He has undefined aspirations, which come nearest to definition in his love for Lucy Scanlan and in certain tentative responses he has to church ritual and to the beauty of nature. The concrete ambitions upon which he can focus, however, are the idea of being a tough guy, a gang leader, and of growing up to be a lawyer, a politician, or a workman getting his pay on Saturday night and going out, independent, to drink beer with the guys. The code of his friends is never give a sucker an even break, never allow oneself a noble thought, never express pity or sympathy or charity or respect—for these are signs of weakness and will inevitably subject one to ridicule and even physical persecution. (pp. 240-42)

Ashamed of his rare impulses toward beauty and goodness, ignorant of any single creative outlet, Studs turns to drink, brutality, and sex. The tough guy can express himself by ganging up on a Jew or a Protestant, breaking a window, or robbing a store. Every night the gang roams the streets, dawdles in the poolroom, or stands on the corner looking at the girls. And always the tough "goofing" goes on—hard talk to show that one has neither softness nor tolerance. The dominant notes of this life are boredom and frustration. Violence as a form of self-expression palls; it can satisfy only while it increases in intensity; and so the limit is very soon reached where violence and filth provide no relief from boredom. Studs passes before us time after time in a dull twilight reverie of sexual desire. He is increasingly aware as the years pass that he has missed his chance to amount to something or to do any of the things that important people do, and his waking consciousness is dominated by a weary, bitter sense of defeat.

The foil that sets off this bitterness is his memory of Lucy Scanlan. Lucy was pure beauty and goodness, and Lucy liked Studs; but the tough guy was violently shy before a nice girl, and if he mastered his shyness for a moment he was still unable to talk to her in respectable language. One of the profound insights in Farrell's books is the knowledge that communion between individuals demands a medium. Whether it be politics, art, creative work, literary background, or social conventions or traditions—or all these together—both friendship and love communicate through shared experience. One may go even further and say that they grow and live through shared experience. Even love cannot sustain itself and must be nourished by common interests and activities. All of Studs' loves and friendships are exactly as poor, as thin, as unsatisfying as the meager and tawdry content of his mind. His relation with Lucy goes no further than a couple of walks and one beautiful scene in which she and Studs sit in a tree in the park, singing and swinging their legs and enjoying the sunshine. This glimpse of bliss stays with Studs for the rest of his life. It alone embodies the vague search for goodness that haunts his defeat.

The story of Studs' dreary life, which ends when, at about thirty, he contracts pneumonia from lying drunk in a gutter, need not be rehearsed in greater detail. Farrell has conveyed a sense of Studs as a real and sympathetic personality, an individual perfectly capable of a good life who achieves only the status of a minor tough guy and feels that he is always on the outside looking in. He has shown the sources of Studs' mind and accounted for the terrible poverty of his intellectual and emotional life. The work is dominated by a tone of furious irony which rises occasionally to shrill denunciation (when we accompany Studs to a movie) or sinks to repulsion when we assist at a drunken brawl that ends with a brutal rape. Paradoxically, the bitterness of tone is justified by the profusion of evidence, for whereas bitterness usually evokes suspicion that the writer is giving a distorted picture, here the detail is so rich, so almost tediously exhaustive, that it justifies this tone, which brings to it a certain aesthetic relief.

It is noteworthy that the naturalistic form of this work does not involve the assumption that a strict pattern of cause and effect is being worked out step by step, in the rigidly "experimental" manner of Zola, before our eyes. Farrell's naturalism is descriptive rather than explicitly deterministic insofar as it appears in the form of the novel. We are not, in short, persuaded that Studs must on that particular night of his life have contracted pneumonia or that the forces behind any single incident in the work are scientifically or systematically demonstrated. Farrell is not interested in this sort of pattern. What he does make entirely convincing is that we are in possession of all the elements that go into Studs' life, so that we have a complete understanding of his mind and character and so that the events of his career are made probable. Different things could have happened to Studs just as probably, but barring extraordinary accidents we feel that what did happen was perfectly typical. Typical and probable but not inevitable. This is why I say the naturalism is descriptive rather than formally deterministic.

I have already attempted to account for the tone of this work. The violent sense of outrage derives from the other half of the divided stream of transcendentalism—from the idealism which assumes the dignity of man and the inherent right of every individual to self-development and social justice. Because of this tone and the assumptions which accompany it, *Studs Lonigan* is a reproach to every American who reads it.

Part of the tragic effect of *Studs* comes from the fact that Studs is always on the edge of the action. Just as he feels that the big opportunities are always passing him by, so he is never the toughest guy in his gang, never does the dirtiest deeds, never achieves the extremes of depravity and cynicism that are evinced by the characters who carry the action. The wildest drinking, raping, and destroying are not performed by Studs himself. The really depraved ones are part of the environment in which Studs moves. This quality of watching, of drifting, and of being led into evil because there are no influences to lead him into good attracts the tragic sense of waste, the emotions of pity and fear, to Studs in a way that might not occur if he were the leader in evil. We can deplore the forces which fail to lead and inspire Studs and the forces which debauch him. But what of the really vile fellows? Are we to understand that at heart they are no tougher than Studs? Are we to believe that they too are tragic figures? Perhaps, but in the process of "accounting" for Studs' fall the writer has to make his cronies appear absolutely vile; he has to give them a drive toward evil which operates like a force in nature. What I believe all this shows is how the introduction of ethical values—values derived from the transcendental tradition—controls the form and consequently the effect of the *Studs Lonigan* trilogy. The result is another version of the tragic form of Norris's *Vandover and the Brute*. Whereas Vandover struggled against the weakness in his own character, and failed, Studs struggles very feebly against evil companions and likewise fails. Farrell's tragedy therefore approaches the qualities of melodrama.

After the *Studs Lonigan* trilogy and *Gas-House McGinty* (1934) Farrell turned to a different slice of the same kind of life. He turned to a four-volume study of the childhood, the family life, and the young manhood of Danny O'Neill, who finally gets to the University of Chicago and promises to escape—as the author, who has never hesitated to acknowledge the autobiographical elements in this work, himself escaped to a literary career and a different life. Danny O'Neill comes from about the same milieu as Studs—he plays in the same neighborhood and would like to be one of Studs' gang instead of being bullied because he is a few years younger than they. Danny's family is not spiritually or culturally superior to Studs', nor are Danny's boyhood thoughts and ideals very much nobler; but they are a little more successfully directed. Danny has a spark of ambition, he is subject to constant friction at home and in school, and somehow he continues to study and grow until he is firmly able to criticize the world from which he has come.

Similarities of style, setting, detail, and general tone, however, do not conceal differences between these books and the *Studs* books which make their total effect entirely different. The reader is constantly among the thoughts of Studs, although he does not identify himself with Studs. But he does become identified with Danny, and he therefore does not see in the environment a controlling force. Danny's family, likewise, presented with much fuller and much harsher detail than Studs', become people who are interesting in and for themselves. In a sense they are wasted humanity, but in a more immediate sense they have personal qualities which are not accountable to the environment. They are all alive and kicking. They are loved and hated by the author, and to Danny they appear to possess an independent, nay a willful perversity: as characters and as people they take the bit in their teeth and run. The blighting environment is still acknowledged. Close attention is given to the effect of the Church on Danny's mother, who year after year slips so much money surreptitiously into its swollen coffers that the O'Neill family never have enough of anything and live like pigs.

But the author has again and again taken sides with these people against America. Values of integrity and fortitude and courage begin to emerge. The cold fury of the *Studs* trilogy is now tempered with what appears to be admiration. One gets the impression that the emancipated author looks with no little wonder upon the dogged persistence of those who never are able to rise above their milieu. He has maintained that they have more guts and integrity than carloads of liberals and intellectuals who jump from left to right, from isolationism to interventionism, at the slightest prickings of social change. Thus the spiritual barrenness which is the main concern of the *Studs* trilogy is now still hated, yes, but also defended, admired, and even set up as having virtues of integrity rare in the flabby and corrupt capitalistic world above these people.

It is impossible within my limits to do justice to the variety and abundance of human insights in this two-thousand-page work. It takes Danny from the time when he is a little boy to his college days. It gives an almost incredibly detailed picture of the family soul, of childhood and adolescent activities, and of the society in which these lives have their setting. Danny's father, Jim O'Neill, does not earn enough to support all of his children, and so Danny is taken to live with his grandmother O'Flaherty and his aunt Margaret in a household that is largely supported by his uncle Al O'Flaherty, a traveling shoe salesman. Danny thus from the beginning is torn between love, pride, and shame. At the O'Flahertys' he must listen to constant abuse of his parents. When he goes to his parents' (a few blocks away) for a visit he is ashamed of them and also tortured by guilt because he enjoys a better life at the O'Flahertys'. (pp. 242-47)

The old grandmother is the most amusing figure in the books. Illiterate, mean, shrill, truculent, vindictive, profane, and sanctimonious beyond belief, she has the power again and again to embarrass her whole family by her ridiculous pride and her violent efforts to defend them where they do not want to be defended. She picks a quarrel with the most innocent bystander and screams like a witch. Her ignorance is equaled only by her evil and superstitious piety. In her home there is rarely a quiet hour; Danny lives between extremes of murderous hate and slobbering sentiment. This is the surface; but the longer Danny lives the more he becomes attached to the old harpy. From time to time she is presented in reverie of her youth in Ireland, when she was beautiful and desired; and this evocation of the pathos of nostalgia invests her with dignity. She becomes a strong and simple person who has been uprooted and transported to a brassy new world of commerce and gadgets. If her piety is repulsive, one gathers the impression that in a simpler life it would be admirable. Her cruel vituperation of Jim O'Neill, who cannot support his family, rises to poetic heights and thus gains a kind of wild grandeur. At her death, in the fourth volume, our hearts are wrung, for something has passed for which the cheap modern world can have no substitute.

Uncle Al, the shoe salesman, is the pitiful epitome of 100 per cent Americanism. He recites all the maxims of bigotry and conservatism, the confident old saws about supply and demand, Protestants, communism, and the value of education. Al loves Danny with all the intensity his starved heart can summon. He gives him advice which Danny ignores; he sees in Danny the promise of his own frustrated ambitions. Most of all—and most pathetic—he imagines developing between him and Danny a relation of love, trust, and communion such as he has always dreamed of and never known. But as Danny grows up he finds Al's advice platitudinous, his mind empty, his enthusiasms boring, and he shrinks from his company. And then toward the end of the series attitudes of guilt, pity, and admiration are associated with Al. His limitations become strengths. What at first appeared as narrowness of outlook now seems the stubborn determination of a limited man to do good as he knows it. What at first appeared as the timidity of a man caught in a rut which he did not have enterprise enough to get out of now seems to be self-sacrifice and love of family. The violent rages do not appear so often. Al's single-minded devotion to his family stands out against the general background of an America full of vacillating intellectuals. We are led to consider the vast difference between lip-service and action: Al acts by what light he has; the sophisticated world talks and talks and commits itself to nothing.

Another unforgettable character, drawn with pity and repulsion, is Danny's aunt Margaret. In Farrell's books women deteriorate less gracefully than men. Drink, scolding, and piety, sloppy dependence alternating with screaming independence, fatuous chastity with revolting promiscuity, rudeness with cowardice—these qualities make of home a hell. Margaret loves a prosperous businessman who loves her, leaves her, and after sending her money for a time withdraws completely. Margaret meanwhile takes to drink and self-pity. With a different set of circumstances, Margaret might have made a respectable wife; but she is so undisciplined, so vapid, so nasty that the reader cannot feel any considerable sense of waste. Occasionally he does, to be sure, but the image of Margaret as a "respectable" housewife dispels it quickly.

The most effective and moving passages in these volumes, nevertheless, are those which render in one way or another the waste of human potential and the poverty of human relationships among people whose ignorance, insecurity, and emotional maladjustment prevent them from attaining the dignity of which they are presumably capable.

If this statement appears to be a direct contradiction of what I have written about Farrell's defending these people against America and endowing them with "virtues of privation" (i.e., integrity, loyalty, fortitude, and faith) beside which the idle rich look cheap and silly, I can only say that this paradox is in the books and that it defines my sense of their somewhat confused total effect. I would also urge that such an effect cannot be functionally related to naturalism, for it does not proceed necessarily from any of its premises or theories. The effect derives rather from the author's relation to his materials. I see him performing at once acts of penance, of denunciation, and of purgation. He is purging himself through these books of the pent-up exasperations and frustrations of his childhood. He is denouncing the nation and the social system which he deems guilty of the waste of these and millions of other lives. He is doing penance for his own early impatience, his failure of sympathy, his inability to know his father.

Through the Danny O'Neill tetralogy the purgation has been effected; having effected it Farrell has discovered that his own traumata do not differ in essence from those of hundreds of other people who have achieved workable adjustments; and so now he can return a third time to the same materials and treat them another way. The boy whose childhood was blighted by his family's stupidity and crudeness is now seen as not greatly different from thousands of other boys who struggled through unhappy years to security and confidence in themselves. In a new preface to **Studs Lonigan** Farrell explains that Studs was not a "hard guy" but a typical youth from a lower-middle-class family. He does not wish the reader to look down upon Studs but to see that he is presented more realistically than most writers present their characters. Penance has been done, too, and so there is no longer the dammed-up tide of indignation and exasperation with the family and the shame that went with them.

Now if the expression of penance, purgation, and denunciation have rendered the effect of the Danny O'Neill books ambiguous, it should be possible to begin again—to give a complete, objective, and unconfused account of how a young writer fights his way through doubts, discouragements, and indifference to the full realization and recognition of his powers. **Bernard Clare** is the beginning of a third enterprise in autobiography. It is a third look at the material that went into the two earlier works. Bernard has come to New York, at the age of twenty-one, to defy his parents and be a writer. His thoughts move in a narrow orbit of girls, diffidence, scorn, the desire to be a writer, and hatred of all organized business. The novel shows Bernard trying to impress a girl in the New York Public Library; deeply but fruitlessly moved at the execution of Sacco and Vanzetti; at work for United Cigar, where he despises his co-workers and puts out the absolute minimum of effort; engaged in an affair with a married woman

whom he tortures with his own scruples; selling advertising in Queens and, again, working only a fraction of the required hours; and finally living in the Y.M.C.A. and attempting to confuse the uplift of that organization by asking cynical questions. Bernard is callow, desperate, earnest, contemptible, unscrupulous. He lives with shyness and desire every waking hour, and when he escapes from these pangs he suffers fearful doubts of the means by which he does so. No emotion or idea possesses him to the point of freeing him from tormented self-consciousness. I know of no character in fiction farther removed from the ideal of personal integration, no one who "thinks with the blood" less than Bernard.

Bernard's thoughts are forever tied to the immediate situation in which he finds himself, and the method of Farrell's writing is to present Bernard's thoughts as he reacts to what he sees. If he is to meditate on the danger of failing and subsequently becoming a worthless bum, it will be because (and when) he is approached in the park by a pitiful old drunk who boasts of his talent. If he despises business, it is when he is listening to businessmen talking business. When Sacco and Vanzetti are executed, Bernard goes to Union Square and is caught up in a surge of proletarian defiance. This constant dependence of thought upon concrete situation keeps the novel rigorously concerned with the personality of the protagonist. It is a source of strength because it is so concrete and immediate; it is impossible for the reader to doubt that what he is reading about is real. The only question is whether experience is properly represented when measured out thus piece by piece. One insight may mean more in a man's life than a thousand hours of reverie or depression.

Viewed in the same scale, Bernard is less admirable than Danny and even than Studs. He is more narrowly self-centered, more contentious, more supercilious, more arrogant, less imaginative. Yet this volume indicates that Bernard is destined to amount to something in the literary world, and the subsequent volumes take him further toward success. The narrowness of outlook, the tendency to ride a single interminable groove of reverie, which were given as evidences of spiritual sterility in Studs, now appear as normal qualities of the questing spirit—the growing pains of all men. In this shifting of perspective the very qualities that were by implication deplored in Studs are now defended in Bernard. "Here," Farrell seems to say, "is what people are really like. Bernard is the way a young man actually is today. He is narrow, self-centered, confined by his fears and doubts. And if you consider him dull, barren, and contemptible you are merely admitting that you prefer a fanciful and idealized image of man to the Real Thing."

Here a very significant shift in the intention of a major naturalist appears. It is a shift in the novelist's conception of truth and in his notion of the purpose of naturalistic writing. The world which he began by denouncing he now proposes to accept and explore, watching the actual so closely that he brings to bear upon it no discernible force of the ideal. Let us see how this new intention affects the conventions of fiction. Bernard wants to write, if we are to judge by the facts given, in order to be able to sneer at Babbitry.

Does this make Bernard contemptible, or does it reveal to the reader that most writers' (and therefore most people's) motives are "lower" than we like to suppose? I suspect that neither is true, that Farrell, impelled by the same sense of guilt that leads him in all his books to emphasize the appalling waste of time, energy, and talent which is characteristic of all men, is actually dealing with the ignoble motives of his own experience. We all acknowledge Thoreau's sentence, "I never knew, and never shall know, a worse man than myself," as a just verdict. Whitman makes the same confession ("The wolf, the snake, the hog, not wanting in me") in order to establish contact with Everyman. Do we not all despise ourselves? Do we not all waste our talents and debase the purity of our better selves? But do we get at truth by exposing the hog and the snake in ourselves? Is man fairly represented by a literal account of everything he thinks and does? If Bernard Clare is to become a successful writer, he will have had qualities which are not revealed in this novel. If he is to be just a cheap fourflusher and heel, for all his inner torments, then we are misled by the constant suggestion that he is an important person.

The ironic fact is that every reader of **Bernard Clare** will be able to identify beneath his own respectable exterior impulses and thoughts considerably more vicious than Bernard is credited with—and yet I believe he will consider himself essentially superior to Bernard. This paradoxical situation derives, as I have suggested, from the fact that characterization in the novel has always been highly artificial, representational, conventionalized, selective, and symbolic. According to the convention, characters in novels are not photographed, nor are their lives transcribed factually, with full accounts of every meal eaten and bodily function performed. But these facts are not denied just because they are not dwelt upon. Writers have sought to represent the reality of their characters by dealing with traits, motives, and qualities that are several degrees more interesting, worthy, and able than those of the actual people they represent. We all know this, or we should not dare, for example, to condemn Hamlet's mother as morally insensate—since most of us have on occasion acted more ignobly than she. Farrell has wrenched this convention several degrees in the direction of complete literal reportage, but he has not gone all the way by any means, and the result is an ambiguity: with reference to the convention Bernard is a despicable worm, but with reference to actuality he is "better" than the average pious citizen. . . . The effect of Farrell's method, in short, is to make his hero appear worse than he "really" (!) is.

Art has always idealized its materials. It has done so, I suppose, because man lives so constantly with his lower nature that he wants, in art, to study his rare best self in patterns of beauty and virtue. This is the source of the convention to which I have referred. It is also true that this convention has always spread a virus of delusion and hypocrisy for which it has been treated by the perennial ministrations of literary radicals, whether in characterization or metrics. The convention was pretty inane when the early naturalists swung into action, but they were working with the convention as well as on it. Let it not be supposed that they were attempting to transfer the bare and stinking actuality of life into the novel.

Farrell writes on after the early assault of his cohorts has succeeded in greatly modifying the convention in the direction of actuality. He is no longer in the context of c. 1930 whence his magnificent **Studs Lonigan** emerged; and to dwell upon Bernard's "lower" nature is to slip into the ambiguity of anachronism, of pushing against something that is no longer there in the same form to push against. Writers today are abundantly aware of the hoggish and snakelike elements that Anthony Trollope barely brushed. With Trollope the convention was perhaps drawing, graciously and exquisitely, somewhat far from actuality. But the James Cains and the John O'Haras have changed all that, and in doing so they have made this aspect of Farrell's naturalistic method supererogatory. The assumption I see in **Bernard Clare** is that this material is important because it is *true;* I believe that Farrell is one of our important writers, but the truths for which I value him are still his insights into the ideal of Man and its struggle for realization and fulfillment—truths which emerge from his books almost in spite of the dogged banality of his style and his masochistic kneading of the gray dough of life.

To recapitulate: between **Studs Lonigan** and **Bernard Clare,** Farrell has inverted himself in two ways. In the first place, with each book he has developed a more literal and exhaustive presentation of the facts of life and the quality of thought. Where he began by representing the boredom and limitedness of Studs' outlook, he has come to the point where he gives a much fuller account of the tedious and self-centered reveries of Bernard Clare. He has extended the convention of representation, by which all novelists select and indicate without ever pretending to give the true (and boring) proportion of creative thinking to dull reverie, until his latest manner comes closer to being transcription than representation. Thus the personality of Bernard Clare is less attractive than that of Studs. At the same time, in the second place, Farrell has been constantly modifying his conception of what is admirable. What he first set down as a picture of Studs' appalling spiritual barrenness he has come to defend as a reasonable account of the mind of a typical young American—and he has gone on in the direction of literalness in describing Bernard Clare until a promising writer appears tedious, selfish, and almost contemptible.

The tone of Mr. Farrell's three major works has evolved in a continuing organic relation to their structures. In **Studs Lonigan** the tone of indignation and contempt accompanies the formal tragic structure of the protagonist's disintegration under the impact of his environment; the writer is definitely outside of this work. In the Danny O'Neill books the tone wavers ambiguously, as we have seen, between indignation and defensiveness; the writer is alternately inside and outside of his action; and the structure involves little more than a chronological succession of situations and impressions which could end at any point where the author chose to stop writing. In **Bernard Clare** the tone is far more nearly objective; the writer is pretty consistently inside of his action watching the world through Bernard's eyes, presenting Bernard's mind and personality without judgment other than what I have described as the assumption that Bernard is typical of questing youth; the structure again is merely a chronology of situations and impressions. There is no action beyond the suggestion of self-discovery, and this we must consider somewhat further.

The characterization of Bernard Clare reveals certain very modern ideas about personality which have always been present in Mr. Farrell's work. The tragedy of Studs Lonigan is that he has no moral center, no ethical focus. He never achieves that sense of "moral certainty of self" which marks a fulfilled and effective personality. And this semi-vacuum which is Studs does not ever notably affect anyone. Modern society is responsible for this depersonalizing of personality. Our schools, far from deploring it, stress doing rather than being. An active child cannot pine; if he acts in and with a group he need not even think, for he participates in a mass life and a mass mind. . . . The world must appear different to this sort of consciousness from the way it appears to a focused personality. Judging from the way one hears them talk, events happen to these children. The world is a spectacle in which they are not ethically involved. Life is like a day at Coney Island. You visit the fun-houses, take the rides, and perhaps you hit a jackpot or meet the girl of your dreams. It can be interesting, dangerous, or dull; you never know till it happens, for you are doing nothing to control your destiny. This is of course an extreme statement of the case against modern man. It would be nearer the truth to say that this is the pattern against which modern men have to rebel if they are to become *persons*—and many do. Bernard Clare is completely unintegrated, but he does have in extraordinary measure the impulse to rebel, and he is forever trying to find himself, to define his own character against the pattern of gray stupidities in the lives around him. There is an ethical impulse in his rebelliousness, but Bernard is too utterly self-centered to care about anything so abstract as a value. He cares only about himself.

A symposium entitled *Naturalism and the Human Spirit,* published in 1947 and containing essays by such distinguished contemporary philosophers and critics as John Dewey, Sidney Hook, and Eliseo Vivas, contains many passages in which the writers attempt to formulate a statement that will retain naturalism's attack on supernaturalism without denying the practical freedom of the will. I say practical because I do not see in these passages statements of ontological or epistemological positions that define the naturalistic cosmos. What I do see is a constantly reiterated identification of naturalism with scientific method. The naturalist sees the world not in timeless abstractions but as a succession of concrete problems. Such problems constitute reality. The naturalist proposes to approach them with an open-minded and dispassionate use of available concrete data. Thus he will discover himself and the world as he responds to the problems which successively present themselves to him. The inference I draw is that the good life will emerge in proportion to the scientific method employed. There is also the implication here that action is more productive than contemplation, that problems which are in theory insoluble dissolve when submitted to the pressure of concrete action. The opposition involved in any theoretical formulation of the problem of will versus determinism disappears under the impact of action. Do not look back to explain how and why something occurred; look forward to discover what lies in the future and can be known only through action.

These formulations reflect a stage in the development of naturalistic theory which can be identified in the evolving forms of Farrell's novels. The first stage assumed perfect determinism, reduced will to a fiction and thought to a chemical reaction; it found its most nearly perfect formal expressions in clinical studies of disease and degeneration and in tragedies of environment where the hapless protagonist was destroyed by the social and economic pressures of his milieu. The second stage followed when these very limited forms were exhausted and when it became increasingly apparent that it was in actual fact quite impossible to demonstrate in a novel a scientific, experimental sequence of causes and effects. The second stage is descriptively naturalistic; it describes the stream of consciousness, or it describes the mind and the experience of a Studs Lonigan in a way that makes what happens to him appear typical and probable. So far as I can see, however, this stage of naturalism, if it does not use the simple tragic form of *Studs,* is either structurally formless or else derives its structure from other sources than naturalistic theory. Most modern psychological novels, if they do not take shape around an act of violence and its violent consequences, lack the structural definition which has been traditional in the novel. We are no longer sure where the novel stops and personal history or reportage begins. The third stage, which eschews abstractions in favor of problem solving, must perforce exist in the flux of its own explorations.

I believe Farrell's *Bernard Clare* can be interpreted as an application of this latest formulation of naturalistic theory. Bernard's past is not presented as an inevitable, lawbound continuum. Rather his present is seen as a threshold to the problems of the future. Bernard finds his way into this future. He *makes* himself by his response to the series of problems with which he is confronted. This statement may be an accurate account of Bernard's relation to his world, but I do not see in it a description of a very effective form for the novel. The writer may indeed present Bernard groping through problem after problem, but in Farrell's style the application of this thesis does not constitute an illuminating organization of reality—except insofar as it is illuminating to see how personalities emerge when they grow without values, without moral certainty of self, and without the conception of personal responsibility. (pp. 247-57)

> *Charles Child Walcutt, "James T. Farrell: Aspects of Telling the Whole Truth," in his* American Literary Naturalism, A Divided Stream, *University of Minnesota Press, 1956, pp. 240-257.*

Edgar M. Branch

In addition to the major works—*Studs Lonigan,* the O'Neill-O'Flaherty pentalogy, the Bernard Carr trilogy, and *A Universe of Time*—Farrell has published five other novels and well over two hundred short stories. These tales and individual novels round out and complicate his fictional world; for . . . they interlace with his multivolume works in settings, characters, and themes. The story **"Shorty Leach"** from *Sound of a City* (1962) illustrates the relationship. This tale brings us back to the Washington Park-Chicago Loop axis; and the narrator is Danny O'Neill, a man in his late forties, whose memories of his boyhood friend Shorty reveal his own maturity and his intense attachment to his personal past, as well as details of his early life.

Danny tells of two conversations twenty-five years apart that he had with Shorty, a character from the tale **"A Practical Joke"** and *The Young Manhood of Studs Lonigan*, where he sings the blues at the famous New Year's Eve party. Initially, the tale returns us to August, 1925, when Danny is in his first quarter at the university and when Shorty anticipates a happy future. It skips briefly back to a time before Danny moved to the Fifty-eighth Street neighborhood in 1917 and when he knew Shorty's reputation as a fine athlete. Then it moves ahead to Danny's last meeting in 1950 with the beaten Shorty. By giving the essentials of Shorty's unsuccessful life over a period of thirty-five years, the tale traces one more American destiny in the populous society of Farrell's world. It also displays Shorty's relationships to familiar characters from earlier books: Phil Rolfe, Jack Morgan, Marty Mulligan, Milt Rosenplatz, and Sonny Green. Shorty, like so many of his contemporaries, is firmly fixed in his time and place. Similarly, most of the other tales and the individual novels add depth and detail to Farrell's picture.

During the fall of 1931, while in Paris, Farrell wrote *Gas-House McGinty* (1933), his second novel. This work directly influenced *The Young Manhood of Studs Lonigan* and *Judgment Day*—for example, Farrell wrote its dream chapter in preparation for the death fantasies of Studs. As recently as the preceding July, Farrell had sent the prospectus of his new book to James Henle, who promised him an advance when his manuscript was under way. By September 13, Farrell had completed 329 pages; and Henle's immediate response of September 28, 1931, was favorable: "I like them, I like your method of work and I like everything about you." Henle sent an advance of two hundred dollars and issued the contract. With this encouragement, Farrell worked at top speed, and, by October 7, he had completed most of the first draft. He made final revisions in February, 1933, while in New York City.

Gas-House McGinty had simmered in Farrell's mind since 1927 when he submitted a story **"Harry and Barney"** (the original versions of McGinty and Willie Collins) to Professor Linn. In 1931, he designed his novel as the first part of a trilogy on the Amalgamated Express Company in Chicago, for which Farrell, his father, and two of his brothers had worked. The action of the three books was to revolve around the Wagon Call Department under the successive direction of four chief dispatchers. Much of the manuscript for the unpublished second and third volumes was destroyed by the 1946 fire in Farrell's New York apartment; but revisions of unburnt portions

may be seen in about a dozen of Farrell's Chicago tales, including the four about Willie Collins, who was to have been the central character of the final book.

Farrell linked the expressmen of his trilogy to the more prosperous middle-class circles in which the Lonigans moved, and he made the sixteen-year-old Danny O'Neill and his father, the stricken Jim, important characters in *Gas-House McGinty.* There we read Jim's prayer for his children: "God, I know the game; and it's beat me. Please don't let it beat them! Please God! God, make them sluggers, make them slug, and take it, and slug again." We see Danny's growing feeling of being a nobody as he flounders in a nether commercial world that is poles apart from the enlightenment he later found at the University of Chicago.

Farrell originally called his new work "The Madhouse" and described it as "a Romance of Commerce and Service." In the undated prospectus sent to Henle, he stated: "it cannot be written as a straight novel, but must have its own structure worked out; and I do not favor having that a simple series of stories, as, say, Seaver did in his 'The Company.' Rather it should be something in which the characters are massed, and in which the sense of the composite picture is more developed, so that one gets a sense of them squirming inside this large institution." He wrote in a letter to Henle, dated September 13, 1931, that plot and movement could be "developed by allowing the incidental jokes, quarrels, jealousies, promotions, deaths, and felt-pressures of the external environment (economic depression) to lead from scene to scene." Somewhat later, before he reworked the first draft, he decided—as he told Henle on January 8, 1932—to make McGinty the dominant character in order to "give an added coherence to the book" beyond that gained by "a style, a common scenery, and . . . a loose connection of the characters' work."

The completed novel focuses on the hectic Wagon Call Department during the summer of 1920, and the slight narrative follows the fortunes of frustrated Chief Dispatcher Ambrose J. McGinty, a proud man whose eventual demotion to route inspector parallels the "fall" of the hero in the song "Down Went McGinty." But, in a real sense, the office itself remains the protagonist. The anonymous, blaring telephone conversations of the call clerks and the incessant sadistic banter create a nightmarish collective personality; and all the office workers from the lowliest to the supervisor merge into one commercial function. Paradoxically, the irritations of the job intensify a crude individualism within the hierarchy of authority. In the give and take of the Call Department, the men release their hostilities through aggressive speech and practical jokes. They unguardedly reveal some deep concerns of their personal lives, and they reflect current events in their talk and inner consciousness. As Farrell accurately wrote to Henle on September 13, 1931, his characters "bring everything down to the Call Department, and, so to speak, dump it." The crowded, claustrophobic office thus remains the central stage, one rich in social implication. Otherwise, Farrell tellingly indicates the social context through scenes of McGinty and other office workers at home or on the street and through interchapters about the wagon men. Only rarely do company executives of the upper managerial level, men remote and feared like gods, step into the action.

McGinty is a small triumph of characterization. This vain, restless fat man can be petty and cruel; but his vulnerability and his clumsy, naïve search for satisfaction in love and work arouse our sympathy. His existence affords him no dignity and little opportunity for affection, yet he is his own worst enemy. He longs for power, but he can neither master his wife nor command the respect of others. Only in his troubled, erotic dreams can he triumph, and even in them his guilts and apprehensions drag him down. (pp. 117-20)

Despite the dreary human material with which the novel deals, it remains a fresh, meaningful treatment of an area rarely explored. It vividly dramatizes the shaping—and scarring—of character through occupation and thus complements the stories of Studs and Danny, which constantly return to the effect of leisure activity and family relationships upon personal growth. It vigorously re-creates the human significance of the commercial purgatory Danny fled.

This Man and This Woman (1951), a successful minor novel, returns to the milieu of the Express Company a quarter of a century later in relating the domestic catastrophe of the aging couple Walt and Peg Callahan. Walt is sixty-three, ten years older than Peg. He is a respected and capable terminal dispatcher who has worked his way up from the wagons. A veteran of almost fifty years with the company, he is one of the few survivors of the old free-wheeling days of Gas-House McGinty, Jim O'Neill, and Porky Mulroy. A kind, likable man, his great desire is to live out his years happily and actively with his wife and grandchildren, enjoying the comforts of life he feels he has earned. Instead, he is stabbed to death by Peg, herself a victim of advanced paranoiac delusions, of voices saying "He'll kill you."

This short novel thus becomes a concentrated study in paranoia. Its theme, as Farrell noted in a letter to Henle on May 11, 1954, is a variation on the idea of "biological tragedy," earlier developed in the stories of Jim O'Neill, Tom O'Flaherty, and Bernard's parents, as well as in Farrell's unpublished novel *Invisible Swords.* The erosion of human life through physical and psychological causes is seen here particularly in Peg's aberration. The action is limited to the last six days in Walt's life, and it builds upon Peg's growing paranoia that suffocates her former buoyant spirit. The novel roots Peg's illness in her childhood and conveys her sense of the loss of all that made her life as a young woman desirable. It convincingly depicts the critical transition from an extreme form of irrational nagging to murderous action. Farrell achieves his effect by switching back and forth between the viewpoints of Peg and Walt, the two major characters.

Farrell sees his aging couple, once so much in love, with an unsentimental detachment and an implicit sympathy. He does not skim over the dreary and often ugly details of their daily relationship; he invokes no easy, soothing explanation of the monstrous torment in Peg; and he shows Walt in all his stolid, well-meaning obtuseness. He thor-oughly understands the Callahans. Perhaps the novel's greatest strength lies in the convincing and sympathetic portrayal of Peg's change into the very thing she thinks she sees in the likable Walt. Appropriately minimizing the social background, Farrell in this bare and unadorned story explores seemingly unbridgeable differences between man and wife—between the masculine and the feminine—with an intensity suitable to Peg's obsessional character.

Ellen Rogers (1941), also a story of blighted love in Chicago, concerns an affair in 1925 between twenty-one-year-old Edmond Lanson and Ellen, two years his junior and just out of high school. The novel is Farrell's first sustained study of a woman, and he adds in Ed Lanson an original character to his gallery of men. Farrell, who began serious work on his story in December, 1940, felt the need of a vacation from writing about the O'Neills and the O'Flahertys. At first he intended no more than a novelette centering on Ellen, conceived as a shallow flapper not unlike the character Eloise in his story **"Seventeen."** But before long his imagination fastened upon Ed Lanson, who is modeled after a close friend of Farrell's from the 1920's. Early in March, as Farrell revealed to John Dewey, he was rereading Nietzsche as background study for Ed's character. The work developed rapidly into a chronicle whose events are tied together by Ellen's growing passion for Ed, and whose mounting climax, as Mencken wrote to Farrell in September, 1941, is managed with impressive effect. By the middle of 1941, Farrell had completed the writing except for a few revisions.

Compared to his earlier novels, ***Ellen Rogers*** depends only slightly upon minor characters and upon dense social background, partly because Farrell had begun his work as a novelette. But, when his book became the history of an affair, Farrell continued to play down the social context and the supporting cast of characters; he felt he should concentrate on his lovers' personal relationships. He also believed that his earlier books adequately gave the essential middle-class background for Ellen and Ed. Here, then, was an opportunity to carry out his plan of gradually expanding his "social universe" from its carefully laid base. He would still keep to Chicago; but he could proceed, as he explained in a letter to C. A. Pearce of May 8, 1941, to unfold new characters "from the background that I have tried firmly to establish in the books I've already written." The story thus lacks the massive social impact of ***Studs Lonigan,*** where we see Studs in a full context and where we observe his habits, shared by many friends, as they are being formed. The origins of Ed's destructive egotism are left in obscurity, and he is presented as a loner, unique in his revolt against established values.

The narrow focus of the novel is suggested by Thomas Mann's judgment, expressed in a letter to Farrell of September 26, 1941, that ***Ellen Rogers*** "is one of the best love-stories I know, of unusual truthfulness and simplicity." Mann believed that Ellen's agony and humiliation following her abandonment by Ed were brilliantly portrayed. She is, indeed, Farrell's far lesser Anna Karenina, the female in the grip of passion. Once she is in love, her calculating worldliness and her self-sufficiency disappear. Her superficial life assumes increased meaning as depths of devotion and suffering develop. In a sequence of effective episodes, we see her growing helplessness before Ed, but her floundering efforts to win him back lead only to fury and desperation. Then Farrell presents her final abasement and her sense of numb emptiness before she takes her life. One thinks, almost inevitably, of Theodore Dreiser's portrayal in *Sister Carrie* of Hurstwood's dissociation from life and his suicide. The two actions appropriately differ in the characters' psychology and in the pace of the decline; moreover, Dreiser employs no "villain" comparable to Ed. Of the two stories Dreiser's is the more fateful and reveals greater depths of suffering humanity, but Farrell's accomplishment is nevertheless memorable and affecting.

Although Ellen is the source of emotional strength in this novel, her destroyer, Ed Lanson, interests us more as an individual and as a symbolic figure of the 1920's. Farrell imagined him as a mixture of a middle-class Sanine, a shallow Raskolnikov, and an eighteenth-century rogue transplanted to the 1920's. In short, as Farrell indicated in his letter to C. A. Pearce of April 25, 1941, Lanson is a vulgarized product of "the Ben Hecht, Bodenheim, Cabell, Nietzsche influence." Ed, a character of calculated ambiguity, is not merely morally starved or conventional; he directs his charm, his courage, and his intelligence toward wicked ends. He is a rebel in the cause of Romantic individualism, a kind of debased version of Max Stirner's egotist, a would-be superman. Lanson "uses" others, for whom he shows utter contempt; and he rationalizes his actions through his misconception of Nietzsche's philosophy. He is more dangerous than Studs because he is aware—an accomplished technician in evil.

Like Studs, Ed Lanson is a foil to Danny (significantly *Ellen Rogers* came just before *My Days of Anger*), for essentially he is uncreative and he grows toward irresponsibility and ill will. He takes a road more deathlike than Studs's; he is incapable of true love even in dream. *Ellen Rogers* is remarkable as a love story and as a study of the deceitful heart that awakens love for the pleasure of strangling it. As Hortense Farrell noted when she read the manuscript, it catches much of the spirit of the 1920's in its portrayal of youth's careless squandering of human emotions, even the throwing away of human lives. The theme of waste is evident in *Ellen Rogers* as in *Studs Lonigan.* (pp. 121-24)

Years before Farrell conceived *Studs Lonigan,* he had been writing short stories, beginning with the juvenilia published in his high school magazine, *Oriflamme.* At the University of Chicago he continued to write stories. **"The Open Road"** and **"Mary O'Reilley"** were composed in 1928; and James Weber Linn's praise in 1929 of **"Calico Shoes"** in manuscript triggered renewed efforts at story writing that soon led to publication (conversation with Farrell, September 8, 1963). Every year since then Farrell has written many stories. Typically, he keeps them by him for a few years, and sometimes much longer, a practice usually permitting several revisions and explaining the presence of early writings in even his most recent collections, *Side Street and Other Stories* (1961), *Sound of a City* (1962), and *Childhood Is Not Forever* (1969). To date, he has published approximately two hundred and

twenty-five tales, most of them collected in thirteen volumes beginning with *Calico Shoes and Other Stories* (1934), an impressive group of sixteen Chicago pieces that he first wanted to bring together as *These Chicagoans.* In addition, he has published two omnibus collections, several paperback editions of selected stories, and a limited edition of *A Misunderstanding* (1949). A good many other tales are still uncollected or in manuscript.

Farrell's tales are additional evidence of his intention to shake reality like a sack until it is empty. A few of them, as Robert Morss Lovett said, literally are chips off the blocks of his novels: early versions or preliminary experiments (**"Studs," "Jim O'Neill"**), deletions (**"Boys and Girls"**), or parts of abandoned works (**"The Hyland Family," "Pat McGee"**). The great majority were written as independent pieces, yet many of these mesh with the novels and among themselves, thereby helping to complete the design of Farrell's fiction. All the stories remain faithful to his version of reality while reflecting his continuing experience. Thus, they reinforce our impression of his writing as a loosely organized, expanding work-in-progress.

In this connection, Farrell's use of Danny or his near equivalent in the tales is especially revealing. This autobiographical character may appear as a small boy mourning his dog Lib or as a grown man touring Italy in the mid-1950's. Altogether, he appears in over fifty stories. In a liberal handful of these, tales like **"Boyhood"** or **"Kilroy Was Here,"** Danny is himself the central character. In about ten others the major character who in all essentials is Danny is unnamed or differently named: for example, **"Autumn Afternoon," "Soap,"** and **"$1,000 a Week."** When the focus is on others, Danny or his stand-in often enters as a minor character. Sometimes he is fairly prominent as in **"The Professor"** or **"A Lesson in History,"** but more often he is the observant narrator or a sounding-board for other characters, as in **"After the Sun Has Risen"** and **"On a Train to Rome."** In a dozen stories Danny appears only in the conversation, thoughts, or dreams of others—notable instances are in **"Wedding Bells Will Ring So Merrily," "Spring Evening," "When Boyhood Dreams Come True,"** and **"Shanley"**—a device permitting us to see Danny in different lights. As a result, our familiarity with him and with his many relationships enriches the meaning of single episodes in which he appears. We who know Danny well, for instance, must be aware of his true but carefully hidden feelings in **"Blisters."**

Farrell uses similar tactics with other characters. Red Kelly and Willie Collins, for example, carry on through several tales and appear peripherally in others. As their circumstances change with the years, they establish the lines of their "destinies." Ed Lanson turns up at new times under other names: as Lewis Gordon in **"The Life Adventurous,"** as Mark in **"Yesterday's Love,"** and recently as George Raymond in *The Silence of History* and *Lonely for the Future.* The tales tighten and involve the personal relationships among Farrell's vast body of characters, yet they leave his "social universe" open and permit quick probings of unexplored regions. They add significantly to Farrell's picture of youth and age, boyish aspiration and adult acceptance, ardent love and tired middle-aged infidelity, the social life of the high-school set and young married couples, family life and the tension between the generations.

Similarly, Farrell's tales inspect the Catholic Church and the clergy, education up through the university, unions and laboring men (especially express-company workers and gas-station attendants), the politics of the ward heeler and the radical, Bohemian and literary circles, organized urban violence (sexual aggression, racial strife, criminal racketeering) and organized sports (boxing, baseball, basketball, football, tennis), and the everyday life and death of city people of numerous nationalities (Irish, Greek, Polish, Lithuanian) and of many sorts (the bum, the struggling immigrant, the white-collar serf, the chain-store magnate, to name some). Working outward from many Chicago neighborhoods—not confined to what is loosely called Farrell's "South Side"—the stories eventually reach to New York, Paris, and Europe at large. Increasingly in the last fifteen years Farrell has written of Americans in Europe, as in *French Girls Are Vicious and Other Stories* (1955), and, to some extent, about cultivated Europeans transplanted to America. Beginning with *$1,000 a Week and Other Stories* (1942), his tales often reflect his experience with publishers, writers, actors, Hollywood producers, intellectuals, and persons of some standing met in this country and abroad.

In Farrell's tales relentless pursuit of a fallible humanity is usually tempered by rare understanding, whether the quarry is a sheik "lookin 'em over" on a Chicago beach of the 1920's or a contemporary writer sardonically aware of his self-betrayal. Ben Ray Redman remarked that Farrell's stories show man as a self-deceiving creature, but as one whose self-deception is both suicidal and life-giving. Perhaps the greater emphasis lies upon that side of experience Studs represents: the frustration and blight. In a testimonial for *Calico Shoes and Other Stories* given to Vanguard Press, Evelyn Scott caught the spirit of many of Farrell's tales, particularly a large body of early ones:

> In his stories, he takes what would seem the least promising material and, with a hardy honesty which rejects adornment, projects the lives of those whose minds are trite, those whose habits are unsavory, those who are banal and those who have been made perverse. . . .

Alfred Kazin has remarked that the "rude vigor" of Farrell's manner is appropriate to "the strident life that gave it birth"; and, if some readers object to a monotony of subject and treatment, others feel with S. L. Solon "that it is the monotone of a sea, not a dripping faucet."

In the Preface to the 1937 volume bringing together his first three collections of tales, Farrell has written that an experience may call for translation into an anecdote, sketch, tale, novelette, or novel. His stories, accordingly, range from mere scraps of experience (**"In City Hall Square"**) and simple sketches to *Tommy Gallagher's Crusade* (1939), a novelette about a Studs-like character of the 1930's who gives his floundering life direction through the native fascism advocated by Father Moylan, the radio priest.

Tommy, a bitter, frustrated product of the Depression, finds importance and excitement in breaking up "Red" meetings and in hawking *Christian Justice,* Father Moylan's anti-Semitic paper. As Thomas Mann wrote to Farrell on October 4, 1939, Tommy is an alarming social type; and his story is Farrell's concentrated effort to present in terms of a single character the meaning of American fascism in the 1930's (the original title was *Tommy Gallagher—American Storm Trooper*). But Tommy is perhaps too much of a type—too clear-cut an example of a major social problem—to be entirely convincing. In "The Short Story," the address that Farrell gave to the First American Writers Congress, he argued for the primacy in fiction of the sense of life and human character. Meanings must arise naturally from incidents, and incidents must be unfolded with no sacrifice of human character to ideology or to frozen form. Tommy is a consistent character who conveys terrifying meanings, but we feel that his realization as a complete human being is limited by Farrell's use of him as social illustration.

In attempting to achieve that sense of life that he values so highly in fiction, Farrell has most often, but not invariably, used the "plotless short story," the artifice of an intentionally primitive method. Not surprisingly, his tales have been profoundly affected by Chekhov's short fiction, which also emphasizes character over plot and portrays the ordinary experience of common people. In Chekhov's prodigal output Farrell found strong support for his view of short stories as "doors of understanding and awareness opening outward into an entire world." About the time he read the Russian Realist in 1927, Farrell evinced what he had learned about writing fiction from Sherwood Anderson (in **"Mary O'Reilley"**), from Theodore Dreiser (in **"The Open Road"**), and from Ernest Hemingway (in **"A Casual Incident"**). The first two tales illustrate characteristics of his early style: both are overelaborated and tend toward "fine" descriptive writing. Learning to control his preference for metaphorical language, he rapidly developed his more objective manner of describing his characters' feelings and actions, as in the story **"Jim O'Neill."** (pp. 127-31)

Farrell, like Hemingway and Ring Lardner, came to rely heavily upon his characters' dialogue as a means of narration in his tales and novels. [The title character of **"Jim O'Neill"**] voices a mild complaint to [his wife] Lizz:

> "Jesus, we sure get paper on the floor here, don't we?" Jim said, seeing the paper stacked and piled under the dining-room table as he came into the room, wearing his work clothes.
>
> "Well, Jim, I always think this. When the children are playing, I think to myself that if they got their health, it's good, and the paper they throw on the floor don't hurt the floor, not this floor full of slivers. You couldn't hurt a floor in this dump," Lizz said, standing in the door.
>
> "The floor's sometimes so covered with papers that we can't even see it," Jim said.
>
> "Our Lord was born in a stable. It isn't what the outside looks like. It's what the inside looks like. If your soul is clean, that counts more than if

your house is. Many there are in the world with clean houses and dirty souls. And this morning, the souls in this house are clean. This morning, everyone who's old enough to in my house received the Body and Blood of our Blessed Lord," Lizz said, her voice rising in pride as she drew to the end of her declamation.

"Well, it isn't necessary to have a dirty house in order to have a clean soul," Jim said.

This style has its limitations, as critics have freely asserted. Yet it permits effective, colorful contrasts of idiom, and it achieves dramatic immediacy; for character is directly exposed through the interplay of dialogue or, in other passages, through the free association of interior monologues. At its best, the style *is* the character-in-action.

Experimenting in his new style during the prolific years between 1928 and 1932, Farrell quickly came to his lyrical vein of boyhood loves and sorrows in early stories like **"Autumn Afternoon"** and **"Helen, I Love You,"** and to his fiercely ironic manner in stories like **"The Scarecrow"** and **"Two Sisters."** In a manuscript **"The Origin of 'The Scarecrow,'"** Farrell explains that this story and others like it grew out of his collapsing romanticism and youthful indignation at cruelty practiced on others. At that time he was earnestly striving for objectivity ("letting life speak") as a technical device of style, and he was trying to use dialogue accurately for narration and atmosphere, as well as for characterization. "Strongly determined not to produce received sentiments" in his writing, he was struggling to avoid general words and to dramatize states of mind. In writing **"The Scarecrow,"** he felt he had made "a leap into originality."

He progressively opened up the broader world of his Chicago youth in such tales as **"A Jazz Age Clerk,"** **"Spring Evening,"** and, somewhat later, in **"Comedy Cop"** and in **"The Fastest Runner on Sixty-First Street."** **"Side Street," "They Ain't the Men They Used to Be," "The Girls at the Sphinx,"** and **"An American Student in Paris"** are examples of superior stories completed at later dates that take us outside Chicago. During the past two decades as Farrell has gone farther afield in his settings, he also has increasingly experimented with different styles. He has tried the monologue, the stream-of-consciousness, and other variants of the first-person point of view. In many of the late tales he has moved away from the vocally dramatic method of dialogue and from other methods that yield a direct impression of particularized experience; instead, he relies in them on a generalized narrative manner somewhat like the summary of a rather detached chronicler of human events. Although this manner has enabled him to condense a given character's "destiny" within a few pages while simultaneously permitting him greater freedom for authorial comment and analysis, it has meant a loss in the reader's sense of immediate participation in the experience recorded.

Farrell's stories can be heavy-handed and verbose (**"Honey, We'll Be Brave"**), tendentious (**"Reverend Father Gilhooley"**), synthetic (**"Just Boys"**), more skilled in portraying belching and banalities (**"Thanksgiving Spirit"**) than nuances of feeling or thought (**"The Philoso-**

pher"). Yet time and again they display his sure grasp of complex human relationships and his homing instinct for situations and values central—often elemental—in human experience. Perhaps they are most moving when he gives the illusion of dramatic objectivity to simple, compact action known from the inside. Then, most likely, truth to individual character becomes social revelation, and we feel the story as a self-sufficient unit. At the same time we seem to be confronted not by a discrete and packaged experience but by an ongoing actuality momentarily spotlighted in the stream of time. We might say with Danny O'Neill in *Boarding House Blues:*

> It is not a story at all. It is an account of . . . that which has happened, has come to pass and has passed to become part of the welter of all that has happened.

Although Farrell has succeeded best in his novels, which impressively embody his concern with time and human emergence, his tales are an integral part of his work—and a surprising number of them are individually memorable. (pp. 132-34)

> *Edgar M. Branch, in his* James T. Farrell, *Twayne Publishers, 1971, 192 p.*

Barry Wallenstein

Despite the leveling in sales of his novels and stories—a fact that reveals more about our mercurial fancies than literary merit—James T. Farrell remains an American classic. With close to fifty volumes written and widely read in more countries than one could sensibly list, Farrell has suffered the dubious pleasure of thorough categorization. Once a writer is categorized, placed in a school with narrow lines of definition, whether symbolist, surrealist, or naturalist, readers come to his works with preconceptions defined by formal limitations, ways of receiving the word before the word has reached them.

The literary reputation of James T. Farrell has, to a large extent, been shaped by the word naturalism, first, and apparently irrevocably, affixed to him in the 1930's. In the early years of the depression, those writers who realistically recorded both the struggles of desperate people and of "the workers" with "social consciousness" won accolades from the critics; the expression "proletarian novelist" would assure certain prestige to the most tawdry of novelists. Naturalism in the thirties was likewise an affirmative appellation, but the expressions "Marxist," "proletarian," or "protest" writer, with attendant political beliefs taken for granted, gained precedence over all other critical terminology. After 1936, when Farrell publically broke with the dogmas of Marxian criticism by disparaging the catch phrases of proletarian and protest literature in his brilliant *Note on Literary Criticism,* only the term naturalist remained to be applied to him, and in the mouths of many it was used as a political as well as artistic bludgeon. Before that time the possible artistic evils of naturalism could be subsumed under the probable social benefits of a naturalistic work. . . . The *New York Times* greeted *Young Lonigan* by making special allowance for the more typical, that is, more socially edifying, scenes:

There is no question that this book is no novel. The artistic powers of the author, save where he exercises a selective facility to make his scenes more typical, are in suspension.

(pp. 154-55)

By 1936 the **Studs Lonigan** trilogy had established Farrell as one of the major young talents of the day. He was emerging, as well, as a central figure, in that ongoing drama of literature and politics. However, the stigma associated with the naturalistic tradition was prevailing. Granville Hicks felt there was "significance to his reporting," yet, in *The Great Tradition,* listed him among the sociologists of fiction.

By 1941 the ranks of proletarian novelists had thinned and the old labels, politically inspired, were reserved only for those protestors who went along with Stalin and the Stalinist world view. Farrell, by that time an independent socialist, found few friends in the literary establishment and the convenient apolitical pigeonhole (out of which he apparently did not care to crawl) of "naturalist" stuck. By 1941 this meant, in the words of an anonymous *Time* reporter, "Like Dreiser, James T. Farrell writes with his thumbs. His words are blunt tools that must wield with force and repetition."

Farrell has never been especially concerned with what he was called, but the accumulated meaning of the naturalistic label has been persistent enough to hurt him materially for it influences the reception of even his current fiction. In the more recent reviews distortion sets in and Farrell is not so much criticized as he is misrepresented. A columnist writing in the *Louisville Times* noted that Farrell "popularized naturalism" in 1932 with **Young Lonigan** and that "his newest work **Lonely for the Future** (1966), is a threadbare echo of his earlier successes." Another reviewer of the same novel remembers that Farrell "started if not a school of naturalism, at least a style which inspired many imitators." And Charles Poore, writing in the *Sunday Gazette Mail*, Charlotte, W. Va., noted "there is a rough poetry in his pawky, Dreiserian view." The *Atlantic Journal* reported that Farrell has "united literary naturalism with the documentary novel." The label has held.

The following passage anticipates one of Farrell's own arguments against the narrow definition of naturalism. The *Boston Globe,* in response to **Lonely for the Future,** placed Farrell on a list of those who

> were the dedicated reporters, the social historians, the case-history workers, with a strong indoctrination in pessimism and naturalism. They told us that America was not . . . a land of prosperity and good cheer, but a spreading jungle of poverty and ugliness . . . And the method of all this is the old naturalistic "case history" method. The novels [of Farrell] pile up without much structure.

(pp. 155-56)

When a collection of stories appeared in 1970, the response was the same. Gayle Cox, writing in the *Courier Tribune,* reviewed **Childhood Is Not Forever** by categorizing Farrell as "an American Zola." So the case stands. Similar documents of nominal critical response could be collected from four decades of narrowing focus. I bother to cite these examples not merely as evidence of folly on the part of critics, but as an introduction to a context for Farrell's own views on literary naturalism.

Though Farrell has not written an extended text on naturalism, the pressures set against him as a writer working within an observable tradition have led him to comment frequently and with precision on the subject. His comments, written over a forty year span, reveal a consistency of thought that could be considered his artistic credo. Always aware that writers suffocate in pigeonholes, he has been led to take defensive positions regarding his craft. It is from the vantage point of the artist holding out against a storm that some of his best criticism was written. One could argue that his defense is overly subjective, in the sense of an ego not wanting, in André Gide's words, to be "too easily understood." But after all, Gide's point is well taken, and Farrell's criticism of naturalism, particularly the term's application to his own work, stands as more than the record of one artist defending his individual talent against the Philistines—though he does aim at them constantly and with Arnoldian vigor.

It is not my intention here to show how and where Farrell's fiction is at variance with the naturalism of Zola or that practiced by Norris or Dreiser. I will refrain from commenting about his fiction. Rather, through assembling the various statements by Farrell on naturalism, I will locate his position in a tradition which also includes those practitioners among whom he is often loosely classed. Farrell's own criticism creates a coherent image, both of the man and of the tradition he sets out to define. I will draw from his volumes of essays, **Note on Literary Criticism, Literature and Morality, League of Frightened Philistines, Reflections at Fifty,** and **Selected Essays,** as well as from uncollected essays. Mr. Farrell has assisted me in this labor by granting interviews and allowing me to quote from unpublished manuscripts.

On the back inside cover of *Mind, Self and Society* by George Herbert Mead, the social behaviorist who inspired much of his early ideas on the subject of personal freedom and social action, Farrell, late in the thirties, penciled this note:

> In **Studs Lonigan** and *A World I Never Made—* the writing always concerns itself to a *now*—it is this fact which, I think, often leads critics to call it photographic—to say that the characters are mindless—this restriction to a *now* at all times determines content and the repetitions which are often attributed to other reasons are really often caused by the demands of keeping the action in a *now*. Develop this point sometime—

The critics' response to his fiction did lead him to develop "this point." The development, sporadic though it may be, is toward the citing of a tradition he identifies with. In defining this tradition Farrell goes well beyond a personal defense against the clichés that are usually employed by the detractors of naturalism. He investigates the causes behind the clichés, their origins which lie in a basic misconception of the novelist's craft, and develops what may be termed an aesthetics of realism. This aesthetics allies him with Henry James more than with Zola; for it was James who sought definitions for a method he was already practicing while Zola was, it seems to me, more interested in proclaiming a particular function for the novel, a program for the novelist, than he was in describing a literary activity. In the light of Farrell's aesthetics, the label naturalist takes on new and possibly ironic meanings.

The rise of the naturalistic novel in France and elsewhere was not met with a simultaneous acceptance in the consciousness of the reading public. There was the outcry against amoral (often called immoral) fiction which was answered in turn by the novelists themselves. From Zola and James, from Garland and Norris, the message went forth that the modern novel was as worthy a medium for telling the truth as books of history. Prior to these pioneering efforts in behalf of realism in fiction, the reading public went to novels for entertainment and to biography and history for their enlightenment. Zola made use of the physical sciences to deepen the texture and make incontrovertible the material of his fiction while James used psychology as a device for opening up points of view not only toward character but the character of Truth. Each defended his own separate method of perceiving and transmitting reality. . . . Out of defense came exploration and definition. If Farrell belongs to the naturalistic tradition it is in his ceaseless effort to define a procedure by which the literary artist can tell the truth.

The difficulty of locating any figure in the naturalistic school stems from the fact that it is really not a school at all. Such schools as the Imagists, the Dadaists, even the Surrealists, are implanted with their own individual manifestoes signed, as it were, by many hands. The manifestoes of naturalism are all separate statements—hardly adding up to a school—which could be considered at best as comprising touchstones of a tradition. (pp. 156-58)

Émile Zola, writing in *The Experimental Novel* (1880) noted that

> naturalism was not a school . . . like romanticism, that it consisted simply in the application of the experimental method to the study of nature and of a man. . . . Therefore in naturalism it would be impossible for there to be either innovators or leaders of a school. There are simply workmen, some of whom more powerful than others.

Yet, his own definitions were thoroughly fixed and thus would provide the most likely basis for any discussion of naturalism.

Zola's points were first set down in 1871 when, as apologist for naturalism, he wrote a preface for his Rougon-Macquart series. He argued at the outset that his interest was in "temperament" not character, and temperament here is shorn of free will. Working out of "pure scientific curiosity," Zola wrote, "I have simply done on living bodies the work of analysis the surgeons perform on corpses."

Zola's ideas and finally the passion of his beliefs were drawn from Dr. Claude Bernard's *Experimental Medi-*

cine. Using Bernard to affirm his own application of Taine's thesis of heredity and environment, Zola reveals less of an interest in science proper than in theory, crude enough, of naturalistic determinism. Nevertheless, his apparent preoccupation with experimental science led Zola to formulate a methodology for a certain kind of fiction, and these formulations, for better or for worse, stand as the cornerstones of naturalism. He began his Preface by arguing that he wanted

> to explain how a family, a small group of human beings, comports itself in a society, flowering to give birth to ten, twenty individuals, who, at first glance, seem very dissimilar, but who upon analysis are seen to be intimately bound one to the other. Heredity has its laws, like weight.

Zola's interest is in the "total will" of individuals in society which creates "the general drive of the whole body." Soon he composed what could stand as a definition of naturalism, including the aesthetic of determinism with which later figures, principally James Farrell, differed:

> Physiologically the members of this family are the slow working-out of accidents to the blood and nervous system which occur in a race after a first organic lesion, according to the environment determining in each of the individuals of this race sentiments, desires, passions, all the natural and instinctive human manifestations whose products take on the conventional names of virtues and vices.

Zola extended his meanings in *The Experimental Novel,* again relying on the "authority" of Claude Bernard. He used the words "doctor" and "novelist" interchangeably, thereby establishing an active role for the novelist. Experimentation was pitted against observation. The experimentor controlled his materials; the observer passively recorded:

> The observer in him presents data as he has observed them, determines the point of departure, establishes the solid ground on which his characters will stand and his phenomena take place. Then the experimentor appears and institutes the experiment, that is, sets the characters of a particular story in motion, in order to show that the series of events therein will be those demanded by the determinism of the phenomena under study.

Zola concluded that "the novelist starts out in search of a truth." Zola's battle cry reminds us of his spiritual affinity with Farrell.

We must remember one important consideration: *The Experimental Novel* was written in an age when traditional faith had been shaken by the new science. Modern man stood at the cross-roads of a dilemma; either fall victim to doubt and despair, a path recorded in so much of the English Victorian poetry, or develop a new faith in the very science which had toppled the old one founded on religion. A third possibility was available, a return to the dogma of the church, but this possibility was not feasible for Zola. Instead he waged an open war on doubt and mystery. It was the "task" of the naturalistic novelist "to make an experiment, in order to analyze the facts and become master of them." Like the scientist who searches for "fixed laws," the novelist, through his controlled experimentation, searches for the explanations behind obscure truths and inexplicable phenomena. . . . (pp. 158-60)

The laboratory method was difficult to resist in the age that followed Darwin; no less a mind than Thomas Huxley shared Zola's naturalistic faith. The "fallacy," as Joseph Wood Krutch called it, of "basing an estimate of our welfare upon the extent to which our material surroundings have been elaborated," came into existence "at the same moment with scientific method itself . . . [and] is still the foundation stone in the faith of the more naive of contemporary materialists who assume that we have . . . bettered ourselves" through material advances. Farrell's own practice as a novelist and his stance regarding materialism in general, as we shall soon see through his criticism of Zola, show him to be nearer to the mind of Mr. Krutch than to that of the French novelist.

So, fearing the "metaphysical chaos" of the idealists and others who leaned "on the irrational and the supernatural," Zola affirmed his faith in science only to be later disproven by science itself, which has, in its own way, indicated how large a role mystery plays in our physical condition. Not long after Zola's death, there arose a new kind of novelist, dedicated to truth but with one foot in the "chaos." Such writers as Conrad, Ford and, in his extraordinary way, Kafka, provide a bridge from Zola to the twentieth century. Farrell, who is more influenced and moved by Kafka's works than Zola's, is at the twentieth-century end of that bridge. From that position he stands as a critic of naturalism.

The facts that Farrell did not read Zola until 1937, after *Studs Lonigan* was published, and only picked up *The Experimental Novel* late in the fifties, lend some amusement to the appellation "the American Zola." His remarks on Zola are scattered and demonstrate more than the awkward irony of literary reputation. Zola's ideas of basing a fictional method on current scientific theories; his attempt to imitate the very methods of science in his fiction; the deliberateness with which he chose his subject as if he were a biologist working with specimens; and his confidence that the facts in fiction equalled or were synonomous with the laboratory reports of scientists—all these are irrelevant and in some instances repellant to Farrell. He believes, along with Krutch, that the essence of the laboratory method is indifferent to man's aims, his values and his destiny, and that "the physical world we are aware of through the senses is almost equally remote from that which the laboratory reveals." Farrell's remarks in **"Some Observations on Naturalism, So-Called, in Fiction"** have a similar ring:

> He [Zola] equated art and science without making any clear distinction. For instance, Zola did not look upon the questions he raised in terms of the difference between problems in the laboratory and those in the writer's study.

But, unlike the humanistic Krutch, Farrell does not disregard materialistic approaches to reality; he is often on Zola's side once certain points are made clear:

> To apply Zola's theory in a literal-minded way to his own works and by it also to damn the work of many later writers, as they have been damned [he is speaking from direct experience] would be to blind ourselves to understanding and to blind those we might influence.

Farrell has frequently acknowledged the relationship between literature and science and while in more recent writing he reveals a distrust of modern technology, that early acknowledgment places him in the naturalistic tradition, which is not the same thing as branding him a naturalist in any constrictive sense. In **"Moral Censorship"** (1958) Farrell notes how literary methods have changed as a result of the progress of science. Describing naturalism in literature as "an attempt to embody the method and objectivity of science in the writing of literature," he soon quoted Zola on the objective method and spoke of the naturalistic current without much qualification:

> During Zola's life, materialism was a dominant trend in the thought of the time. Materialism posited the premise that character is the product of environment, and this was the basis for Zola's naturalism. Thanks to science, the minds of many men were turned more and more to the data of experience. This tendency had its effects on writing. Writers looked all around them to facts. They attempted to embody in their work the direct patterns of the life they saw and lived: "the two-fold life of character and its environment."

He went on to a further affirmation: "The naturalistic movement has not died out in literature. It is through tendencies we call naturalism and realism that untold possibilities of writing have been perceived and utilized."

There are, however, essential qualifications regarding Farrell's appreciation of Zola, and through his criticism of naturalism is discovered. In 1965 his voice rang in an angry disclaimer. When asked in "An In-Depth Interview" for *Writers' Forum* why his characters seem "defeated by their surroundings," Farrell answered that he did not accept the casual relationship between surroundings and defeat:

> I've never been the economic determinist that critics made me. I first read Zola in 1937. I have a functional conception of environment and character; I don't believe in environment over character or anything like that.

He added significantly, "Characters are effected by environment and effect it in turn," making an explicit allowance for free-will. (pp. 160-61)

Farrell's belief in the various options open to man, upon which all his fiction rests, was registered in his early writing on *Studs Lonigan* with his attempt to set the record straight on the central issue of determinism in his works. In **"The Story of Studs Lonigan"** Farrell explained succinctly: "Environment affected character, and character itself is a social product which is a result of society. In turn, character affects and changes environment." And in the essay **"How *Studs Lonigan* Was Written"** (which appears as the introduction to the 1938 edition of the Modern Library's **Studs Lonigan**), Farrell made this key observation, which should stand beside all later reconsiderations of the subject:

> Had I written **Studs Lonigan** as a story of the slums, it would then have been easy for the reader falsely to place the motivation and causation of the story directly in immediate economic roots. Such a placing of motivation would have obscured one of the most important meanings I wanted to inculcate into my story: my desire to reveal the concrete effects of spiritual poverty.

Farrell's testament led to the further consideration that his hero

> is not . . . caught in a net of circumstances beyond his control. If he has drawn delusive sustenance from outmoded cultural values, he has done so by his own choice. His tragedy is that he has never been willing to understand the conditions of his action and freedom. He has neither heeded the problematic nor altered his attitudes and values when they have been obstructed by reality.

The protagonist is far from being a puppet pulled here and there by the indifferent fingers of destiny or circumstance or even environment. Rather it is his self-informing being that molds character, and free will is as important as environment itself. In the interview for *Writers' Forum* Farrell pointed out that in part Studs was destroyed by his acceptance of false value standards of his environment. He was destroyed, in the spiritual sense, for he "took everything for granted, and his environment betrayed him."

In the 1938 introduction to **Studs Lonigan** he reminded the reader of the importance of Dewey's epigrams: "The poignancy of situations which evoke reflection lies in the fact that we do not know the meaning of the tendencies that are pressing for action." By remarking that "this observation crystallized for me what I was seeking to do," Farrell admitted his vital curiosity about causation, denying a belief in determinism. As he said in **"Some Observations on Naturalism . . . ":**

> Recently, a reader asked me why my character Danny O'Neill . . . escaped from his environment, and did not end as did Studs . . . Danny O'Neill was a character who determined and who chose to change. Frequently, at least, defeat and disintegration, when described, appear as though inevitable, and thus determined: to the contrary, growth and change do not at all seem inevitable, and, in fact, even seem to be so inexplicable as to appear fortuitous or accidental.

When he defended himself against the listing of his name among a group of writers loosely called naturalists, Farrell noted that the "lumping together" of certain authors "failed . . . to give a final and conclusive answer to the question of free will versus determinism." At the same time, he declared that the question is not especially vital for literary criticism and can be damaging when the terms are allowed categorical value "as a means of judgment." Final judgment must emerge from the reader's emotional response to the literature at hand and not to any idea or thesis intruding into the investigation. In a footnote to that same essay, Farrell spoke directly and with finality on determinism:

> It is my personal opinion that a number of the literary critics of "Naturalism" who base their criticism on Free Will do so on grounds of temperament. . . . Personally, let me add that I am not a monistic determinist. I do not, moreover, look on free will as an inherent attribute of man; rather, I believe that free will is an achievement of men, gained individually and collectively, through knowledge and the acquisition of control; both over nature and over self.

There is a kind of outrageous futility in attempting to prove Farrell either a determinist or a "free-will-ist" for when he says the question has been "outlived" he is admitting the palpable truth that the precise definition of each defies practicable application.

Farrell departs from the naturalism of Zola in two separate yet interrelated developments. The first is his view of reality, which includes the roles character and personality play in narrative fiction, and the second involves his notion of the social value of literature. In **"Some Observations on Naturalism . . . "** Farrell stated flatly that Zola was "mistaken" when he denied that the naturalistic novel "was an expression of personal views." He added that Zola's insistence that scientific authority overrides the personal authority of the artist was equally erroneous. The error lies, according to Farrell, in Zola's optimism regarding the amount and extent of knowledge science can provide for the human condition.

> We know that we can know less, and that the unknown is much more vast than many imagined it to be in the 19th century . . . Proof is a much more complicated process than he thought it would be. With this, it might be added that some scientific warrant can be given, at least tentatively, to substantiate the possible validity of types of art which Zola might have described as unrealistic, idealistic, metaphysical or romantic—as lies.

Thus when he describes his novel **Gas House McGinty** (1933), in the prefatory note, as "an imaginative representation of American life . . . it contains descriptions of dreams and processes of thought so intimate and personal that they cannot be considered as descriptions of the dreams and thought processes of any living person," he was not disqualifying himself from the realistic-naturalistic tradition: rather, he was adroitly extending Zola's search for the nature of reality. (pp. 162-64)

Farrell's first writing exercises were in the form of a diary. He noted in **"My Beginnings as a Writer"** that the early entries were "factual and brief," but that at the same time he wanted to write of his dreams, of love, of fame. Soon the personal data of Farrell's dream world would prove real enough to undergo the filter of his artistic imagination. Together fact and fancy add up to the fact of fiction, a personal yet objectified observation of the real world.

Clearly, and from the start, Farrell's "unreality" was rooted in personal experience rather than in any sociological or data-oriented mode of perceiving and communicating the world. In that same radio interview Farrell said "serious fiction" is one of the most considerable and powerful means of assimilating emotions and experiences. As his comments on **Studs Lonigan** bear out, the trilogy sprang from an emotional source, his own personal needs and desires to tell a story that was close to him, and in the telling he realized "character." "Situation" is, of course, essential to his theory of naturalism, but not in the sense of being motivated by a problem, a thesis or an intellectual idea. Human character motivates not only action but the presentation and shape of situation as well. In the interview published in 1965 he criticized Dos Passos as being a "better historian" than novelist for "he was inclined to make his characters local and historical and the function of a situation. His characters are not individualized so it is not art."

Characters—and Farrell mentioned those in his Danny O'Neill tetralogy as examples—carry in their consciousness the values of their past and their society. Thus, as he stated in the introduction to the 1947 edition of **A World I Never Made,** the problem the novelist is concerned with is not the context but the "precise content of life of people in environments such as the environment described in this work." He explained that the novel does not "seek to answer" questions concerning the problems of poverty, etc., "in any formal and sociological manner"; rather "it seeks to describe, to recreate, to present in terms of immediate characterization." The introduction closes on these words: "This novel is one of the efforts I have made to go as deeply as possible into the nature of experience during the period of my own lifetime."

Farrell's most dramatic statements of his position *vis à vis* Zola's socio-scientific approach to character were presented in the radio interview of 1956. When questioned about the "raw material" of his fiction Farrell replied that so much transformation takes place that to treat it as if it were "merely a photograph, or as though it were sociology" would be to violate the process of re-imagining events or "how you guess." Regarding the theory about direct or literal recreation of the data of experience, Farrell remarked how even "the actual circumstances of the material that started the idea going" are often changed in order to conform to character development. His is an organic theory of fiction at odds with any mechanistic or, as already established, deterministic thesis that would dictate the form or substance of art.

For Farrell, the novel has an important social function; what underlies this function is its freedom from dogma stemming from ideological or positional characterization, even when it seems to come from society itself. (pp. 164-65)

[In] the "In-Depth Interview" printed in *Writers' Forum,* Farrell extended his "personal bias," to borrow a phrase coined by Edgar M. Branch, far enough to place himself on the opposite side of naturalism's emphasis on objectivity. In noting that the literary artist "must be selective" in the choice of events, Farrell made the point that such selectivity "means that they [the chosen events] are subjective." This is a corrective statement, part of his developing antipathy to being classed as a follower of the Zola-

Dreiser "school" of objective reportage, a school he characterized here as the "I-am-dumb-school" in which "natural" is a word used to describe one who does not use his intellect in the shaping of his art. And when he sounded almost Jamesian—"There's as much fiction in what people think of as fact as there is fact in fiction"—he seemed to be denying an aspect of objective aesthetic reality. This is not quite true, however, and Farrell soon tempered his statement on subjectivity by taking up the use of psychology in fiction. Referring to **Studs Lonigan** he noted that "the language, the objective impressions were filtered through his mind through a controlled use of free-association." When asked if he "wrote from the unconscious," he replied that much came, of course, from the unconscious, but he also veered toward the naturalistic credo: "I evolved the idea of being as completely objective as I could and as concrete as I could and also of using [Studs'] own language so that it was his world, his culture."

Earlier I argued that Farrell diverged from Zola's naturalism mainly on the grounds of his more personal, or we could say emotional, conception of character, and that this was related to his ideas on the social function of literature. With some historical perspective these two currents in his thought can be seen as the two sides of his theory of fiction. During the 1930's Farrell registered an entire generation of American writers' faith in literature as a positive social force, as part of the vanguard in the march toward truth. Despite his disillusionment with the Marxian criticism of the more dogmatic spokesmen of that decade, Farrell held firm to fundamental Marxian concepts. His naturalism is based on the belief, as he wrote in **Literature and Morality** (1947) that there is

> no necessary polarity between a moral code based on what I here term social morality [in a Marxian sense] and one based on a personal morality.
>
> Man lives out his personal drama on the plane of society; man's very self and his personality are socially directed, socially delineated, socially organized. The self is a social product, not a separate individual entity, superior to, anterior to, separable from, society.

This is not to suggest a deterministic world view. For example, it is the individual will to exploit, not society in the abstract, that creates exploitive situations. (pp. 165-66)

[Farrell's characters], as his portrayals and comments on them indicate, are not passive victims of crushing environment; rather they, in embodying Farrell's moral and political vision, are active participants in the struggle for personal and social reconstruction. Development of character and personality is never without social dimension, and in this sense Farrell's aesthetics *advocates* a stance regarding society and the destiny of man.

When praising a contemporary of the thirties, Richard Wright, Farrell noted that his socially conscious literature differs from the naturalism of preceding generations. His literature, first of all, in Farrell's words, "is sharply realistic and . . . depicts conditions of dirt, physical misery and inner frustrations," and second, differs in its use of the problems of self-awareness combined with an "account of conditions of life in America." This literature, which he earlier called "bottom-dog literature,"

> states social problems, not in terms of general-
> izations but rather in terms of direct character-
> ization, of the immediacy of life described on the
> printed page. . . . social causation is translated
> into individual motivation and into immediacy
> of action, thought, dream, and word. This litera-
> ture deals concretely and directly with the major
> phases of American life which now seriously in-
> terest scores of sociologists, social workers, psy-
> chiatrists, criminologists, jurists, and others. It
> seeks to present in the more humanizing terms
> of literature, much of what the newspapers sen-
> sationalize and view with alarm.

Literature is more "humanizing" than sociology or fiction predicated on beliefs and methods borrowed directly from the social sciences, for "the purpose of a novel, no matter how realistic it may be, is not that of being a literally true record of life. It is a recreation, a concentrated image of what life is or may be like." Furthermore, novels function as autonomous worlds in which the reader becomes personally involved. He can not become equally involved in a mere pile of statistics, which are meaningful only in terms of other statistics.

Thus, Farrell's writing on the novel continually emphasizes the importance of character, but character is rarely conceived apart from society. On the contrary, novels enrich, or humanize, when the development of character is complete enough for the reader to sense the communality of spirit between the persons in the fiction and the experience of his own life. The "personal bias" operates on a social level. In **"On the Function of the Novel"** he observed that novels help us increase the "ability to attain what the American philosopher G. H. Mead called 'the sense of the other.' By gaining a better sense of the other we can expand our image, our sense of ourselves."

Approaches to the novel before World War II had been somehow dominated by Zola's materialistic stance on the one hand and James' sensibility on the other. Farrell's naturalism, or more accurately his criticism of the term, acts as a necessary corrective for a sensible view toward post World War II fiction. He has no sympathy for the "materialist's gratuitous mechanism," for his determinism or for the attendant attitude toward human values and ideals. His naturalism is both more political and moral, more personal and extensive than that set down by Zola in the 19th century and continued by Dreiser in Farrell's own lifetime.

Yet it is to the tradition of naturalism that Farrell adheres, despite the validity and richness of his corrective adjustments. It is necessary, therefore, to define that tradition in the terms Farrell himself set down. In 1939 the *Partisan Review* conducted a symposium on "The Situation in American Writing." To the first question, "Are you conscious, in your writing, of the existence of a 'usable past'?" Farrell answered in the affirmative. His tradition was "the modern tradition of realism and naturalism," but his list of exemplary authors revealed a wider range than any previously defined school of naturalism would allow. The

principal figures he included were Dreiser, Lewis, Anderson, Hemingway, Lardner, Masters, Sandburg, Proust, and Joyce. This tradition, comprised of many diverse styles and attitudes is unified in that, for Farrell, the serious books were all written "in the spirit of truth" and oppose what is known as the "genteel tradition" in American fiction. (pp. 166-68)

[Farrell was asked in 1965] if naturalism was still a vital force in literature. This time he answered in the negative:

> Not the kind of naturalistic writing that they're
> talking about, but I'm not that kind of writer.
> Zola was a great writer, but you can't repeat
> Zola or Dreiser. I'm a philosophical naturalist
> in the John Deweyian sense . . . They say that
> I pile up facts; I don't. I take facts from all kinds
> of sources, but they're not just piled up to build
> up a case for environment. The environment and
> the people more or less come together.

Farrell's "philosophical naturalism," best defined in **"Some Observations on Naturalism, So-Called, in Fiction"** and in isolated notes in *Note on Literary Criticism,* attempts to extend the range of fiction beyond the boundaries set by Zola and the older generation of naturalists. Farrell seeks to do this by freeing the term from the narrowness and spiritual vacuity of being so closely identified with materialism. Farrell wrote in **"Some Observations on Naturalism . . . "** that he had made a mistake early in his career (though I have not been able to locate such a statement) of using the word naturalism as if it were synonomous with materialism.

> I would really prefer the word naturalism, and
> I would define it in a Deweyian sense. By natu-
> ralism, I mean that whatever happens in this
> world must ultimately be explainable in terms of
> events of this world. I assume or believe that all
> events are explainable in terms of natural origins
> rather than extranatural or supernatural origins.

And he repeated, significantly, that "although this assumption underlies what I have written, I do not write novels to prove or disprove this assumption. I write novels in order to reveal what life seems to me to be like. I write novels as part of an attempt to explore the nature of experience." So finally, the importance of exact or scientific knowledge, given Farrell's personal emphasis coupled with his strong sense of social consciousness, is to be measured in terms of man's needs. The resultant naturalism becomes both a philosophical and moral enterprise, one which takes into account the philosophical and psychological needs of man as corollary to any progress in the total integration of faith and fact, data and felt experience. The social orientation given to sense of self allows Farrell's naturalism, unlike Zola's, to explore value judgments which might operate for society, or at least, in his words, "one third of society." Zola's biological reduction is thus impossible for a writer like Farrell. By opening his fiction to greater social considerations than those thrust upon him by time past and time present, Farrell would necessarily complicate the issue of how one perceives and assesses reality.

Farrell's tradition nevertheless includes Zola and, as we

shall see, Dreiser, too, in its acceptance of the categories of science, if not fact itself, as clues or signs of reality. There remains the persistent search for a knowable truth, even though Farrell's new naturalism encompasses ephemeral truths of transient episodes or experiences. (pp. 168-69)

The connection between Dreiser and Farrell has, by most commentators, been improperly drawn. Certain lines by Dreiser, e.g., "The sum and substance of literary as well as social morality may be expressed in three words—tell the truth" and "The extent of all reality is the realm of the author's pen, and a true picture of life, honestly and reverentially set down, is both moral and artistic whether it offends the conventions or not," written in 1903, contain the spirit of Farrell's naturalism, but this should not lead to the conclusion that Farrell was either a disciple of Dreiser or that he held to the older novelist's plan and practice of narrative fiction.

Farrell, just out of college in 1927 (though he did not complete the B.A.) perceived a power in Dreiser that had nothing to do with the applied category. When in a review of *Sister Carrie* he called Dreiser "an American classic," he made a judgment that literary history has sustained. From the start he considered Dreiser both as a hero and a writer not to be classed or easily placed in an arbitrary or even logically considered list of writers.

Farrell's **"A Note on Sherwood Anderson"** revealed, however, that it was the author of *Winesburg, Ohio,* not Theodore Dreiser, who most influenced Farrell's development as a writer.

> I felt closer to Anderson's intimate world than I did to that depicted in Dreiser's massive novels. The neighborhoods of Chicago in which I grew up possessed something of the character of a small town. They were little worlds of their own.

Unlike Dreiser, who did feel the wonder, size, and ambition of Chicago, having come from the village to the city, Farrell admits that he had not felt the wonder of Chicago until he returned to it many times. Thus Anderson's

> work was closer to my own experience. . . . I had sometimes felt that I was a goof. Anderson's sympathy for the grotesque, the queer, the socially abnormal . . . struck immediate chords of response within me. I was more like Anderson's characters than I was like Dreiser's.

Farrell read *Tar* in 1927. The book's development of character, its emotional range, directly influenced Farrell at this critical time in his own career:

> I lived in this book . . . If the inner life of a boy in an Ohio country town of the 19th century was meaningful enough to be the material for a book like *Tar,* then perhaps my own feelings and emotions and the feelings and emotions of those with whom I had grown up were important . . . My ambition to write was solidified and strengthened. I thought of writing a novel about my own boyhood, about the neighborhood in which I had grown up. Here was one of the seeds that led to **Studs Lonigan.**

There does remain, and not without reason, the persistent connection to Dreiser which needs to be fully examined for the light it sheds on Farrell's criticism of naturalism and his use of the term. In a recent conversation, he stated that Dreiser was a thoroughgoing determinist. This point, more than any other, dissociates Farrell and Dreiser. Farrell's objections are specific: Dreiser "rejected the idea that there was any discreteness to individuality." A truth narrowly perceived from one perspective may not be true in terms of social behavior or our understanding of the behavior of people in society. Farrell emphasized that we see people as individuals, as different:

> We do differentiate. He denied that. Dreiser was not a good thinker. I once said of Theodore Dreiser that he had no talent, he had little education, he thought badly and sloppily, he had not a damn thing in the world to recommend him but genius.

The relationship is defined in Farrell's **"Some Correspondence with Theodore Dreiser"** where he has written:

> Despite the statement of many critics, I had never regarded myself as his disciple. His example, his strength and persistence in the fact of opposition, the sympathy and depth of feeling in his writings—all this had encouraged me . . . At the same time I had never, except in moody moments and perhaps for a short period, agreed with his general ideas.

By 1927 he had read all of Dreiser in print, yet he insists that he did not "borrow Dreiser's attitudes, acquire some so-called method of writing or accept a deterministic view of man that regards them as rats in traps or cages." (pp. 169-71)

In a 1942 essay, **"Dreiser's *Sister Carrie*,"** Farrell, with more deliberation than is often the case in his occasional criticism, developed in a footnote his ideas on Dreiser's naturalism, ideas that serve as reference points to much of his later writing on the subject:

> His determinism, more emphasized in *The Financier* and *The Titan,* can be analyzed as embodying two important elements: (1) He accepted as science generalizations based on the ideas of nineteenth century materialism. From these he adduced a deterministic idea, and this, in turn, was represented as biological determinism. In *The Financier* and *The Titan* this biologic determinism is usually explained by the word "chemisms." Paradoxically enough, Dreiser's appeal to "chemisms" is made quite frequently in specific contexts concerning motivations of character, where we can now see that the real rationale of these motivations can be most satisfactorily explained by Freudianism. Often his "chemisms" are overall generalizations of impulses of which the character is not aware. In this respect Dreiser asserted a biologic determinism, which, in terms of our present state of knowledge of man, is crude. (2) The other and decidedly more important element in Dreiser's determinism is social. He sought to grasp the working and operation of social laws as they effect human fates.

His sympathy for Dreiser rests on the last point. His appreciation resides in their common struggle against Philistinism and censorship, and in Dreiser's "probing effort to identify social forces, to grasp them, and then to correlate them with human destiny." In these respects Farrell saw Dreiser as a "great moral force," an ideal spirit worthy of emulation. (p. 171)

In 1947 the valuable footnote in his essay on *Sister Carrie* was expanded into a larger essay published in the *Chicago Review* (Summer, 1947) entitled **"Theodore Dreiser."** Here Farrell differentiated Dreiser's determinism from Zola's and latter-day popularizations of the term. He noted that though Dreiser was indeed a determinist, an heir to social-Darwinian thought, he had as well a mystical side. Farrell, reflecting his own practices as a novelist which are within the naturalist tradition, directed our attention to the autobiographical or subjective in Dreiser, who was "not merely an objective realist who gathered facts impersonally, and who then used them in order to write realistic novels; he lived in his dreams, his hopes, his broodings, his observations." Later Farrell wrote: "The connection between [Dreiser's] own life and his fiction is an intimate one. In one way or another, he felt and saw everything he described. His novels may be called autobiographies of the American dream." The connection between the two writers is not to be found in any definition of naturalism, but rather in a kind of distilled subjectivity and in Zola's line, "the truth is on the march." Farrell chose this line as an epigraph for his tribute **"Theodore Dreiser: In Memoriam."** He most clearly sympathized with Dreiser "as the living example of a writer who had stubbornly struggled to express himself sincerely; he did not surrender to the censors or to the prudes."

To Farrell, Dreiser was a liberating force. Both participate in the naturalist's faith that truth, in the largest sense which includes the moral ordering of society, is available to the literary artist. The artist's responsibility to "tell the truth" is one which includes both treatment and theme; it entails the use of as much material as is needed, and then some, to present a full picture of reality; it opposes the exclusive selection of detail employed in the genteel tradition. (pp. 171-72)

Many of the books that influenced Farrell's thinking were not literary books at all. Recently he told me that Dewey, Mead, Tawney, Veblen, Charles E. Marion, Freud, Marx, and even Irving Babbitt were the major influences. He learned to handle facts from his own personal experience and from reading the likes of Dewey and Mead, not from Zola or Dreiser despite the judgments of a Granville Hicks or Philip Rahv.

In Rahv's "Notes on the Decline of Naturalism" (*Ideas and Image,* 1949), Farrell was listed as one who ascribes to naturalism's two part code: (1) pessimistic determinism, and (2) the exposure of socio-economic conditions. Rahv declared that Farrell's work is "mostly a genre-record," where human behavior is a function of its social environment. Such inaccurate criticism develops when these precede direct examination of the record. Farrell's observations on naturalism, the application of those ideas in his own fiction, all point in the direction Rahv himself

was looking when he remarked, "Imaginative writing cannot include fixed and systematic definitions of reality without violating its own existential character." And, too, Farrell would agree with Rahv that "naturalism, which exhausted itself in taking an inventory of this world while it was still relatively stable, cannot possibly do justice to the phenomena of its disruption." The kind of naturalism Rahv was speaking of is that materialistic 19th century brand espoused in the 1870's and 1880's by Zola and in this country by Garland, Howells, and Norris, all of whom, in attempting to "keep the record straight," failed to predict the day when no record could possibly account for "the dissolution of this familiar world," to use Rahv's words. Farrell's naturalism is much more flexible and does take into account the unpredictable mass of events, the crisis of our own unknowing, which makes up modern life.

As a practical critic, Farrell has written memorable essays on works as diverse as *Huckleberry Finn* and *A Portrait of the Artist as a Young Man*; his inclination is not toward a literature of solutions or even that which best delineates the raw materials of physical reality. It is the energetic spirit of naturalism that connects him to its tradition more than any other element. He is constantly, in his criticism and in his novels, outdistancing the formal definitions, even those he has proposed at one point or another, for the imaginative process of making literature involves breaking codes while it preserves the passion which might even be found in political ideology or in a viable scientific method.

Malcolm Cowley, too, in his often incisive essay, "A Natural History of American Naturalism," makes an error of judgment when he applies Farrell's name in his definition of naturalism:

> Naturalism is not what we have learned to call literature "in depth." It is concerned with human behavior and with explanations for that behavior in terms of heredity or environment. It presents the exterior world, often in striking visual images; but unlike the work of Henry James, or Sherwood Anderson or William Faulkner—to mention only three writers in other traditions—it does not try to explore the world within.

Clearly Farrell attempts inner exploration, and if his novels are records of the times, they are conceived as individual records, or as he has said, "one man's record." He does not nor did he ever believe in complete objectivity; his interest in time and continuity (he likes to speak of Proust's conception of the continuous novel, which he himself has been working on for over thirty years) prevails over the narrower considerations of direct reportage. He has said to me that some of these ideas were put into *The Silence of History* (1963), the first novel in his latest tetralogy. The notion that "once something happens, you can't predict its consequences, you can't erase its influences" is so simple and evocative that no school or codified discipline would properly carry its meaning. (pp. 172-73)

Barry Wallenstein, "James T. Farrell: Critic of Naturalism," in American Literary Naturalism: A Reassessment, *edited by Yoshinobu*

Hakutani and Lewis Fried, Carl Winter, 1975, pp. 154-75.

FURTHER READING

Adams, J. Donald. "The Heavy Hand of Dreiser." In his *The Shape of Books to Come,* pp. 54-83. New York: The Viking Press, 1945.

> Briefly traces Farrell's naturalism to that of Theodore Dreiser.

Branch, Edgar M. "American Writer in the Twenties: James T. Farrell and the University of Chicago" and "James T. Farrell's *Studs Lonigan." The American Book Collector* XI, No. 10 (Summer 1961): 9-19, 25-32.

> Delineates Farrell's technique in *Studs Lonigan: A Trilogy,* focusing on such details as the work's autobiographical origins and Farrell's relationship to the actual Studs Lonigan.

————. "Freedom and Determinism in James T. Farrell's Fiction." In *Essays on Determinism in American Literature,* edited by Sydney J. Krause, pp. 79-96. Kent, Ohio: Kent State University Press, 1964.

> Relating Farrell's ideas to those of American pragmatists such as John Dewey, Branch rejects as inadequate the prevalent critical view that Farrell's fiction "reveals a thoroughgoing naturalistic determinism" in its emphasis on degrading social environments.

————. "The 1930's in James T. Farrell's Fiction." *The American Book Collector* 21, No. 6 (March-April 1971): 9-12.

> Comments upon the critical tendency to classify Farrell as a writer of the 1930s due to his occasional emphasis on the American Depression and his prominence during that era.

————. "James T. Farrell: Four Decades after *Studs Lonigan."* In *A Question of Quality: Popularity and Value in Modern Creative Writing,* edited by Louis Filler, pp. 80-91. Bowling Green, Ohio: Bowling Green University Popular Press, 1976.

> Defends Farrell against prevailing critical hostility and neglect, asserting that Farrell's fiction "has a prominent place within a distinctively American tradition of art and thought."

Cowley, Malcolm. "James T. Farrell: Time Obliterated." In his *The Flower and the Leaf: A Contemporary Record of American Writing Since 1941,* edited by Donald W. Faulkner, pp. 279-84. New York: Viking, 1985.

> Reprints an unfavorable review of *Yet Other Waters,* the third novel in the "Bernard Carr" trilogy. Cowley assesses the strengths and weaknesses of Farrell's writing method as of 1952.

Curley, Thomas F. "Catholic Novels and American Culture." *Commentary* 36, No. 1 (July 1963): 34-42.

> Addresses the critical inclination to exclude Farrell and other American writers of Catholic upbringing from the category of Catholic novelists because they had renounced their religion prior to writing.

Douglas, Ann. "*Studs Lonigan* and the Failure of History in Mass Society: A Study in Claustrophobia." *American Quarterly* XXIX, No. 5 (Winter 1977): 487-505.

> Contends that Farrell's trilogy comments upon the American sense of historical purpose, which, according to Douglas, "predicates a vision of Anglo-Saxon progress and expansion which our intellect no longer supports."

Gelfant, Blanche Housman. "James T. Farrell: The Ecological Novel." In her *The American City Novel,* pp. 175-227. Norman, Okla.: University of Oklahoma Press, 1954.

> Identifying Farrell as a writer of the city who "could present with extraordinary precision its language and manners," Gelfant examines form and technique in Farrell's fiction.

Glicksberg, Charles I. "The Criticism of James T. Farrell." *Southwest Review* XXXV, No. 3 (Summer 1950): 189-96.

> Analyzes Farrell's critical involvement in Marxist controversies of the 1930s. Glicksberg asserts that Farrell inflicted "more heavy damage in exposing the contradictions and rank absurdities of the Marxist aesthetic . . . than any of the so-called 'bourgeois' critics."

Grattan, C. Hartley. "James T. Farrell: Moralist." *Harper's Magazine* 209, No. 1253 (October 1954): 93-4, 96, 98.

> Dismissing Farrell's neglect in critical circles as arbitrary, Grattan groups his works with those of such literary moralists as Henry James and Leo Tolstoy.

Gregory, Horace. "James T. Farrell: Beyond the Provinces of Art." *New World Writing* (April 1954): 52-65.

> In response to those who fault Farrell's works as artless, Gregory asserts that the author's realistic evocation of his boyhood places his autobiographical fiction "beyond the provinces of art."

Hatfield, Ruth. "The Intellectual Honesty of James T. Farrell." *College English* 3, No. 4 (January 1942): 337-46.

> Reacting to critics who fault Farrell's dialogue as profane and his subject matter as monotonous, Hatfield asserts that these elements sincerely reflect the author's naturalistic intentions.

Howe, Irving. "James T. Farrell: The Critic Calcified." *Partisan Review* XIV, No. 5 (September-October 1947): 545-6, 548, 550, 552.

> Negative assessment of Farrell's essays collected in *A Note on Literary Criticism, The League of Frightened Philistines,* and *Literature and Morality.* According to Howe, these "may be read as an attempt to formulate, solve, or escape his problems as a novelist."

Mitchell, Richard. "*Studs Lonigan:* Research in Morality." *The Centennial Review* VI (Spring 1962): 202-14.

> Declares that Farrell's trilogy is informed by "a scientific morality" based on the observable facts of human experience, "a morality of men, not gods."

O'Malley, Frank. "James T. Farrell: Two Twilight Images." In *Fifty Years of the American Novel: A Christian Appraisal,* edited by Harold C. Gardiner, S. J., pp. 237-56. New York: Charles Scribner's Sons, 1952.

> Sees Farrell's "gruesome image of civilization" and "his image of the Catholic Church" as stemming from "the particular circumstances and pressures of modern, urban, secular existence."

Pizer, Donald. "James T. Farrell: *Studs Lonigan.*" In his *Twentieth-Century American Literary Naturalism: An Interpretation,* pp. 17-38. Carbondale, Ill.: Southern Illinois University Press, 1982.

> Determines some prevailing views of Farrell's trilogy to be superficial or reductive and identifies Studs as a tragic figure.

Janet Frame

1924-

New Zealand novelist, autobiographer, short story writer, and poet.

Frame is considered one of New Zealand's most innovative contemporary writers because of her use of unconventional narrative techniques that feature elaborate symbolism and imaginative explorations into the nature of truth. Drawing upon her personal experiences in numerous mental hospitals, where she was placed after suffering a nervous breakdown and being incorrectly diagnosed as schizophrenic, Frame explores misconceptions about insanity by juxtaposing madness and fantasy with reality. She also uses language that is intellectually and figuratively complex to delve into the oppressive nature of society and empathetically address the negative consequences of abnormality and nonconformity.

Frame began to write as a young child to liberate herself from what she termed "a background of poverty, drunkenness, attempted murder, and near-madness." Reflecting her abiding concerns for destructive familial relationships and the consequences of miscommunication between individuals and societies, Frame's novels address the plight of people who are perceived as being psychologically, physically, or intellectually inferior by those possessing political power. Frame's early novels are generally regarded as disturbing and powerful. These include *Owls Do Cry,* which concerns a woman struggling to survive in a psychiatric hospital; *Intensive Care,* a story about the creation of a legislation that would rid the world of its misfits; and *Scented Gardens for the Blind,* an allegorical tale about the possible atomic destruction of Britain. Robert Osterman commented on Frame's early work: "No one can call Janet Frame an easy novelist to come to terms with. Her imagination is most comfortable with subjects like madness, personal dislocations in time and place, and the use of dreams and illusions to keep life at bay. And deep in all her fiction lies a passionate concern for language and the betrayals of human purpose it can be made to serve."

Frame began publishing in the late 1950s, and her fiction often contains autobiographical elements, but it was not until the publication of her three-volume autobiography in the 1980s that Frame revealed the details of her family life and the eight years she spent in and out of mental hospitals as a young woman. *To the Is-Land* traces Frame's poverty-stricken childhood in New Zealand and investigates some of the incidents that would later lead to a series of nervous breakdowns. In the second installment, *An Angel at My Table,* Frame recounts her experiences as a student at a teacher's training college and the events that caused her to flee from an assignment when an inspector entered her class to observe her lesson. After this incident Frame attempted suicide for the first time, was diagnosed as schizophrenic, and sent to a mental hospital where "the squalor and inhumanity were almost indescribable." The

narrative of *The Envoy from the Mirror City* begins after Frame was released from psychiatric care. Deciding to move to England "to broaden [her] experience" and to develop her talents as a writer, Frame learns that she was never schizophrenic after visiting a respected mental facility in London. Although unnerved by the implications of this discovery, Frame continues to rely upon the rejuvenative powers of writing to which she had always been drawn: "It is a little wonder that I value writing as a way of life when it actually saved my life."

The Carpathians, Frame's most recent novel and winner of the Commonwealth Literary Prize, takes place in the fictional town of Puamahara, New Zealand, where legend has it that a young Maori woman gained unequivocal knowledge of human history after tasting the fruit of an unknown tree. The story of Mattina Breton, a wealthy New Yorker who journeys to New Zealand to attempt to learn the source of the folktale from Puamahara's eccentric residents, *The Carpathians* explores such issues as death, illness, and old age. While investigating the legend, Mattina also becomes fascinated by reports about the Gravity Star, an astral phenonenon that if real would challenge common perceptions of time and space and destroy the world. Although some critics faulted *The Carpathians* for complex and interrelated elements of reality and fantasy, they nonetheless lauded Frame's continuing exploration of the relationships between language, conformity, and the mysteries of time and space. Jayne Pilling commented: "As so often in Frame's novels, there's a curious, combustible mix of modes at work here. An apparently straightforward narrative is exploded from within by a mother-load of metaphor. . . . Yet its possibilities are so rich that Frame needs several different narratives, Chinese-box style, to contain them."

(See also *CLC*, Vols. 2, 3, 6, 22.)

PRINCIPAL WORKS

NOVELS

Owls Do Cry   1957
Faces in the Winter   1961
The Edge of the Alphabet   1962
Scented Gardens for the Blind   1963
The Adaptable Man   1965
A State of Siege   1966
*The Rainbirds   1968
Intensive Care   1970
Daughter Buffalos   1972
Living in the Maniototo   1979
The Carpathians   1988

SHORT STORY COLLECTIONS

The Lagoon   1951
The Reservoir: Stories and Sketches   1963
Snowman, Snowman: Fables and Fantasies   1963
You Are Now Entering the Human Heart   1984

AUTOBIOGRAPHIES

To the Is-Land   1982
An Angel at My Table   1984
The Envoy from the Mirror City   1985

POETRY

The Pocket Mirror   1967

---

*Published in the United States as *Yellow Flowers in the Antipodean Room.*

Fleur Adcock

The first volume of Janet Frame's absorbing autobiography, *To the Is-Land,* told of her childhood in the South Island of New Zealand with her railwayman father, her harassed "poetic" mother who talked of books but never had time to read them, her brother, and her three sisters. The oldest sister drowned, the brother was seriously epileptic, there was never enough money; but Janet, in her skimpy home-made uniform and embarrassing homemade sanitary towels, got through High School and was accepted for training as a teacher. *An Angel at My Table* begins

with her journey south from Oamaru, from a family that seemed "enveloped in doom", to the Training College in Dunedin. She was a quiet, shy student, "no trouble at all" to lecturers or landladies. Just after her twenty-first birthday, when she was in her probationary teaching year, the inspector arrived in her classroom; she excused herself politely and walked out of the school. A few weeks later she was taken to the first of several mental hospitals and diagnosed as schizophrenic.

The numbingly terrible history of the following nine years (1945 to 1954) is condensed here into some forty pages. For a fuller account of what Frame endured in Seacliff, Sunnyside, and the brutal, squalid "refractory ward" of Avondale Hospital it is necessary to read her second novel, *Faces in the Water* (in which the events described are all factual although the central character is invented), a fuller account, but not the whole story—that book, for all its horrors, omitted a good deal in order not to seem "over-dramatic". The present volume makes no attempt to fill these gaps; instead it adds details of the external events which lay between the periods in hospitals—and which, as they include the drowning of her second sister and her mother's heart attack, cannot fail to have been causally related to them.

It also adds explanations. What seems to have happened is that after her first brief stay in Seacliff and the hasty, inaccurate diagnosis of schizophrenia she simply taught herself, out of books, to be what she was thought to be. As a schoolgirl and a young student she had learnt to cope with her anxieties by turning on performances—the child-poet, the clever examinee—for approval. Later, she writes, it did not occur to her "that people might be willing to help me if I maintained my ordinary timid smiling self ". And anyway, great artists had always suffered from disabilities; here was hers. So for the first few months of 1946, in between working on her stories, worrying about her decaying teeth, and having "little talks" with a young psychology lecturer assigned to her as a therapist, she swotted up the symptoms of her supposed illness until she could "turn on schizophrenia" at will. When things got out of hand there was no way back: to use her grammatical metaphor, she had moved from the first person into the third—no longer "I" nor a part of "we" but "she", one of "them".

Her first book of stories, *The Lagoon,* was published while she was a committed patient, and its choice for a literary award saved her from an imminent leucotomy and led to her eventual release. But what next? "After having received over two hundred applications of unmodified E. C. T., each the equivalent, in degree of fear, to an execution" she arrived home, smiling, meek, and fearful, sure by now (from knowing genuine cases) that she was not schizophrenic, but unable to detach that largely self-affixed label. "How is Janet?" people asked in her presence. "Would she like some shortbread?"

The second part of the book records her gradual return to something like confidence. Under her superficial timidity ran the wiry thread of her determination to find her own place in the world and, above all, to write. She left her parents' dilapidated cottage and began work as a waitress in a Dunedin hotel ("I had no impatience, irritation, anger to subdue: I seemed to be a 'born' servant", she had written of an earlier, even more menial job—suspecting that she had inherited this submissiveness from her mother.) When after her six months' "probation" she was declared officially sane she celebrated by going to Auckland to visit her married sister June. There she was sought out and befriended by a benefactor who was to direct the progress-chart of her life into a firm upward curve at last. The writer Frank Sargeson, "a bearded old man in a shabby grey shirt and grey pants tied with string", was already a literary hero to her. He lived frugally in a small house with, in its vegetable garden, an army hut which he was in the habit of offering to needy protégés. He installed Janet Frame there, arranged with a friendly doctor for her to receive a sickness benefit, cooked for her, taught her to play chess, and imposed his own strict daily time-table on her. By the time she left, to travel overseas on a grant he had insisted she apply for, her first novel was finished and accepted for publication.

Throughout her schooldays she had longed to acquire imagination, which she thought of as some kind of all-purpose magical possession, absent from her competent, contrived little poems. Instead she was praised in class for being "original": different, perhaps a little peculiar. "I did not think of myself as original; I merely said what I thought" she noted afterwards. Saying what she thinks, and saying it with a fidelity to what she has seen and heard and a cool sharpness of language, is one of her great strengths as a writer. Another, of course, is imagination. Those of her short stories which rework episodes from her childhood may not have required fertile powers of invention, but they have been beautifully organized into their shapes, and her people speak and think in ways which sound like real speech; they are grim, pathetic, funny and authentic. Frame has spoken of her difficulties in creating characters, but those she has drawn from life (particularly the children) cannot be faulted.

In *You Are Now Entering the Human Heart,* her new selection of stories (chosen by herself from three earlier collections, with the addition of some hitherto unpublished work) realism alternates with bizarre fantasy and semi-didactic allegory. All three modes are equally natural to their author, but the mixture of flavours is startling, and it is possible to quarrel with the selection itself—a few of the briefer sketches seem too slight to have been worth including, while other, more substantial pieces may be missed. There is a great deal here to admire and enjoy, however. The childhood stories are classics of their kind, in the tradition of Katherine Mansfield but speaking with their own recognizable accent. At a time when New Zealanders were still only tentatively finding out how they spoke and behaved (as distinct from how people in English literature did), these economical, seemingly casual little pictures of small-town life were something new. Then there is another typical Janet Frame genre, the study of a lonely person in later life, perhaps a widow or widower, keeping up appearances. She is, not surprisingly, very good on isolation. If her fables and fantasies for the most part stand up less well than their neighbours in this book it is perhaps because of the contrast, or because they do not have time to establish themselves properly: Frame

seems to need the spaciousness of a novel in order to engage the reader fully in her invented worlds. One exception is **"Snowman, Snowman"**, the longest piece in this collection, which just manages to overcome the cuteness of having a snowman as its narrator through the use of a deadpan, faux-naïf voice which is very much the author's own: she allows no convenient assumption and no human motive to pass unchallenged; she questions everything.

Her fictional and autobiographical writings are so closely interrelated that to read one work creates an appetite for the others; her various treatments of any subject enhance, rather than diminish, each other. Everything she presents is illuminated and thrown into sharp focus by the limpid clarity of a highly individual vision; she can be detached and passionate at the same time. The autobiography lacks the occasional flamboyance of some of her fiction—it is a deliberately subdued exercise in establishing the facts—but it is irresistibly readable, commendably honest, and, as a lesson in how courage and the will to survive defeated the effects of a ghastly mistake, inspiring.

*Fleur Adcock, "The Road to Independence,"
in* The Times Literary Supplement, *No. 4258,
November 9, 1984, p. 1281.*

T. D. Armstrong

Few writers can claim to have quite literally saved their own lives through writing. In [*An Angel at My Table*], the second volume of her autobiography, Janet Frame describes how she was rescued from the leucotomy then fashionable in New Zealand mental hospitals by attracting the attention of the superintendent. Her first volume of short stories, **The Lagoon,** had won the Hubert Church Award, the first of many literary prizes which she was to receive in her climb to an international reputation (one, it should be said, which has always flourished in the USA rather than England). Some ten novels and four other volumes of poems and stories later, she is at 60 close to being the grand old woman of New Zealand literature.

The legacy of Frame's seven years in and out of psychiatric institutions is described in **An Angel at My Table:** 'I inhabited a territory of loneliness which I think resembles that place where the dying spend their time before death and from where those who do return living to the world, bring inevitably a unique point of view that is a nightmare, a treasure, and a lifelong possession.' The novels which she wrote after her final release in 1954 put this 'treasure' to good use in describing characters who live on the edge of society, and of the alphabet of human discourse. Often they were drawn almost directly from her experience. The leucotomised Daphne Withers of **Owls Do Cry** is based both on her own experience and on the friend Nora whom she describes in the autobiography as lingering on for years in the twilight world of those who did undergo the operation. Frame has described the life of the 'mad', and the terrors of the institutions set up to 'care' for them, with considerable sympathy, finding in those rooms with no doorhandles and the constantly threatened ECT a powerful measure of society's need to control and impose limits on its members. Her writing can be attuned to the domestic realities of everyday life, but an awareness of the connection between 'sanity' and an acceptable language (suggested by the euphemistic names of the institutions— Seacliff, Avondale, Sunnyside) constantly shifts her prose towards the condition of poetry. Many of her novels include poetic interludes. In a parallel fashion, her career has included volumes of poetry, and has shifted from its autobiographical base towards a greater attention to the task of writing as a subject in itself and an attempt to control experience and understand life and (increasingly) death. The later Frame is an internationalist. Her life has become that of the modern writer, with periods spent in Europe, New York, residences at Yaddo and elsewhere. Her most recent novel, *Living in the Maniototo,* has as many affinities with the work of the Latin American fabulists or with that of Doris Lessing as it does with her own early works.

In the first volume of her autobiography, *To the Is-Land,* Frame combines an evocative and clear-sighted account of growing up in small-town New Zealand with a self-conscious sub-plot which offers an explanation of how she was to become a psychiatric patient and a writer. She grew up in a poor but close-knit railway family, her overworked Christadelphian mother planting the first seeds of her imaginative life. Childhood was, she suggests, the time of the 'we' rather than the troubled 'I'. But even as a child she began to cultivate a difference from her richer, prettier peers: a difference expressed in the poetry she wrote for the columns of the local newspaper, and in the rhapsodic 'imaginative' essays which she produced for her English mistresses. Literary talent became the adolescent's vocation, though there was still the need for some external confirmation: 'the question of a disability—Coleridge and Francis Thompson and Edgar Allan Poe had their addiction to opium, Pope his lameness, Cowper his depression, John Clare his insanity.' Family disasters fed the desire for dark afflictions: her brother's epilepsy, the death by drowning of a sister, like Browning's Evelyn Hope 'sixteen years old when she died'. Life and literature became inextricably tangled for the young girl in a quiet province. Frame is skilled at describing the almost tactile presence of words for the child and adolescent: the physical shock when she encounters her dead sister Myrtle's name hidden in the opening line of 'Lycidas', the violent effect of an obscenity on the family dinner-table. She emphasises (and perhaps protests too much) that literature was not an escape but something to be 'brought home'; and she pleads for the organicity of literature's 'special vision'. The 'special vision' was also that, eventually, of madness. Desperately lonely at Teachers' College (her family could not afford University, but she attended some lectures), she found an eager listener in a young lecturer in psychology, and entered into a Freudian comedy in which she learned to become the ideal subject of analysis, spinning out her fantasies on demand. After a pill-swallowing episode the comedy turned tragic. She was committed for the first time, assigned the label 'schizophrenic', and embarked upon her psychiatric career. She had found her 'disability', and her 'treasure'. Frame's story reverses what is often expected of the relationship between madness and art. The appearance of madness was almost a prerequisite, a product of the dangerous desire to write rather than of any ma-

ture creative conflict. Form precedes meaning in a way reminiscent of some of Freud's later thoughts on psychic mechanisms (a parallel suggested by Frame's description of analysis as a form of creative writing class), or even his thoughts on cultures in *Moses and Monotheism:* a society needs victims before it can have a literature.

The process of becoming a writer is thus a more fundamental subject of the autobiography than the experiences Frame had in hospital. Indeed, she refers the reader here to her second novel, *Faces in the Water,* rather than attempt to repeat her evocation of that world. Her emergence from seven years of suffering (an almost Biblical span) is described in more detail in the second half of *An Angel at My Table,* subtitled 'Finding the silk'. The subtitle draws on a complex family of metaphors which Frame has used throughout her career: threads, cocoons, warmth, cloth. In her first novel it is the strand by which, Theseus-like, we seek our way out of the labyrinth. In later elaborations it is the thread from which art is spun, as in the golden blanket which is described in *Living in the Maniototo,* as well as a cocoon and shelter which can take on dangerous overtones: a metamorphosis of the image suggested by her comment in the autobiography that 'I had woven myself into a trap, remembering that a trap is also a refuge.' After her final release, Frame stayed for a period with the Auckland writer Frank Sargeson, who had been one of the first to recognise her skills. In a review of *The Lagoon* he commented on the 'piercing flavour of anguish and suffering' in the stories: the review appears in the present collection of his pieces, which do much to evoke the sense of a developing literature, and literary professionalism, in New Zealand. In the hut in his backyard Frame found, at last, a refuge. Sargeson provided an objective version of thread-gathering, bringing home a box of silk-worms and offering them to her over the following months as a silent poem in the mode of Blake's 'Mental Traveller'. The spinning of the cocoons, the cutting free of the silk-worms, their metamorphosis, breeding and death, and the burying of the eggs in the earth, are all suggestive of the writer's career. An experienced literary sericulturalist, Sargeson fed his pupating novelist with the disability pension which he arranged for her, and with a potent mixture of toleration, discipline, Dostoevsky and Proust.

The autobiographical volumes show just how much of her experience is woven into her writings, often risking a redundancy in which the autobiography repeats the novels. The deaths of her two sisters, for example, are described in her 1972 novel *Daughter Buffalo,* and the silkworm story also occurs in that work. A number of the episodes mentioned briefly in the autobiography, even some of the seemingly irrelevant detail, can be fleshed out by turning to works of 'fiction'. *Living in the Maniototo* can be taken as a commentary on the autobiographical project. Alice Thumb, with all her aliases, is recognisably a version of Janet Frame, and willingly describes herself as a gossip and a ventriloquist, 'a secret sharer of limited imaginings'. The novel describes the 'real' and imaginary adventures of Frame & Co, beginning with Alice Thumb's inheriting a house from two admiring Californian readers, but becoming increasingly complicated by the entanglement of life and fiction as characters vanish into mid-air, die, return to life, or threaten to take over the story. The narrator's visible battle with the materials of her life is suggested by a fight over a golden blanket which Alice Thumb describes herself as winning from the other characters. She comments that 'the price of warmth is often too high for too close a scrutiny of the means of getting it'—a remark which brings out the dangers of exposing too much of an author's limited resources of memory and imagination in the kind of autobiography which Frame now offers.

In fact, the effect of writing her own story seems to be liberating rather than restraining for Frame, as if the burden of fiction were removed and she were free to write a linear narrative. This is especially true, as she remarks, of her description of childhood, the time before the thread of narrative becomes tangled. This illusion of simplicity can be allied to her occasional statements to the effect that she lives 'outside fiction' in the coldness of reality. Such claims are ingenuous. Frame's life has always been at the centre of her fiction, the ventriloquist on stage with her puppets. As the title-piece of her most recent collection of short stories suggests, the journey into 'the human heart' (or the heart of Frame) is a cliché. The heart in the story is a huge walk-in model, and the author in search of her material is diverted by accidents along the way. For all her courage, Frame has never lived 'outside' fiction, but always inside fictions which are both refuge and snare, therapy and pathology. She is skilled at capturing that moment when the silk is cut, our illusions and fantasies violently stripped from us, and a reconstruction of experience demanded. In the autobiography she describes the cold winds which sweep through family life as her parents age and grow ill, and her own subsequent estrangement. She tells of the web of paralysing social fears and dangerous objects or situations (meals, sanitary towels, dances) in which the adolescent is caught, and tells of her attempted escape when she walks out of her teaching job. Meanwhile, beyond the family, the Depression arrives, and the war. But the silk is always respun, the recourse to art irresistible.

The largest danger for Frame's writing, as apparently for Frame herself, is the tendency to strain towards the literary. It too readily becomes rhapsodic—relentless and even humourless in its pursuit of the imaginative. In the third volume of the autobiography, [*The Envoy from Mirror City*], Frame describes her personal encounter with the reality principle. Travelling to England on a literary scholarship, she went to Ibiza, beguiled by the fantastic world of the Mediterranean. She tells of her first sexual experiences there, of becoming pregnant, and miscarrying. In escaping from Ibiza, she fell into another trap: an interlude in Andorra during which she became absorbed into her boardinghouse family and engaged to a fellow lodger, an Italian, before escaping again to London, where she set out to 'discover by objective means whether I had ever suffered from schizophrenia' and attended the Maudsley Clinic. She seems to have been treated remarkably humanely and was told that she had never been mentally ill: the garment, as she puts it, finally removed.

The remainder of the book describes her years in London: living in a small way in Clapham, Camberwell, Kentish Town, and, more affluently, in Kensington; a season in Suffolk; working in a hospital, a cinema, attending concerts; writing and suffering setbacks and triumphs, meeting literary agents and authors. Like many writers, she found in London's vastness a sense of freedom and human variety. London became the 'Mirror City' of the imagination, a world to which the 'real' self is an envoy. Her eventual voyage home was prompted by the death of her father, but the reasons for it were also literary. She wished, she says, to regain the advantages of a country still open to the imagination: 'Living in New Zealand would be, for me, like living in an age of mythmakers.'

Frame's story is an important one for New Zealand literature, for reasons which have to do with a good deal more than the fascination of some of her brief portraits—the aesthetic and distant Charles Brasch, Frank Sargeson's pioneering bluntness and determination. In the struggle to write the cost is high. She has served time for her ambitions, and gained from her struggles a literary treasure which has brought the golden fleece home to the land of the woolmark. At the same time, Frame the word-spinner can seem like that other woman faithful to her vocation, ravelling and unravelling her supply of threads each night in a display of skill designed to disguise her vulnerability. . . .

T. D. Armstrong, "Janet and Jason," in London Review of Books, *Vol. 7, No. 21, December 5, 1985, p. 26.*

Publishers Weekly

A fearful sense of unnamed and unnamable disaster haunts the pages of [*The Carpathians*], the 11th novel by . . . acclaimed New Zealand writer [Janet Frame] (*Faces in the Water, Living in the Maniototo*), whose topsy-turvy vision of a world beyond bearing reminds us uneasily of our own. News of the Gravity Star, so-called because the nearer it hovers, the farther it recedes, and of the Memory Flower, Puamahara, which unleashes the land's memories and unites them with the future, so stirs rich New Yorker Mattina Brecon that she flies to New Zealand to visit the town of Puamahara, where the Memory Flower took palpable form. Driven to possess places that capture her fancy and the people therein, she rents a house on Kowhai Street, and sets out to know, possess, her neighbors. But they, like Mattina herself, are strangers, imposters, activated by the memory of another time and place. Increasingly, Puamahara resembles a graveyard, silent, unmoving, except for the great lolling exotic flower heads. As Mattina begins to discover the secrets of Kowhai Street, she senses in her bedroom a shape, quiescent but clearly there, akin to the formless pain inside her body. The grace and power of Frame's prose illumines this inventive, delicately structured narrative.

A review of "The Carpathians," in Publishers Weekly, *Vol. 234, No. 9, August 26, 1988, p. 76.*

Fleur Adcock

In Janet Frame's new novel the Carpathians are a symbol of remoteness: if distance could be abolished "you'd have the Carpathians in your garden". Instead the mountains visible from the windows of Kowhai Street, Puamahara, are the Tararuas in New Zealand. Puamahara is an imaginary small town in the south-west of the North Island; the local industry is horticulture, and the local legend, recently rediscovered and promoted by the tourist board, is that of the Memory Flower. In the legend the young Maori woman who "tasted the yesterday within the tomorrow" of the Memory Tree became a storyteller, and the dominating motifs of the novel relate to the art of fiction and the powers, and dangers, of language.

As well as the Memory Flower there is an even more slippery concept to be grasped, or grappled with, by the reader: the Gravity Star. This is an astral phenomenon which "appears to be both relatively close and seven billion light years away"; it has contradictory effects on distance, and is potentially capable of catastrophic damage to language and logical thought, as the bizarre fate visited on the inhabitants of Kowhai Street demonstrates.

Distance is an obsession with New Zealanders, who have suffered from a sense of being marooned out on the edge of the world, ignored by its other inhabitants. The central character in [*The Carpathians*] is a rich American, Mattina Brecon, who has a compulsion to understand the lives of people in other countries by living among them and listening to their stories. In Puamahara she visits her neighbours in Kowhai Street, politely admiring their gardens and their whirlpool baths, louvre cupboards and shagpile carpets, being mildly deferred to as a visitor from "out there" (New Zealand is plagued by anxiety about the impression it makes overseas), hearing their reminiscences, and being told by one solidly local resident after another, "I'm a stranger here myself." This is a country where everyone was, not many generations ago, a settler. Even the descendents of the original settlers, the Maori people Mattina meets, feel strange now that it has suddenly become fashionable to speak their own language: they are having to learn it.

These sociological observations occur naturally, given Mattina's mission, and they are studded into a richly textured fabric of events, covering her American life as well as her stay in New Zealand. The large cast of characters is expertly manipulated, and apart from a few bumpy patches caused by the Gravity Star (an awkward presence) the narrative flows easily and has Frame's usual eccentric charm. One of its joys is her characteristic tone, a mixture of innocence and acuteness, equally at home with fantasy and domestic detail, often slightly detached, sometimes amused: it is like the voice of a very grown-up child.

Janet Frame never lets us forget that we're reading fiction. There are recurring, sometimes joky references to "point of view" (linked with both memory and distance, but also a novelist's device). Narratives are enclosed within narratives, ingeniously interlocked: a third of the volume consists of an account by Dinny Wheatstone, Kowhai Street's self-proclaimed "imposter novelist", incorporating Mat-

tina's own experiences and perceptions and read by her during the course of the events it describes. Mattina's husband is a novelist; the ostensible "author" of the novel is another. At the end of it he, or rather Janet Frame, cuts the ground from under our feet by revealing why none of

---

An excerpt from *The Carpathians*

At the time of the discovery of the Gravity Star, Kowhai Street, Puamahara, had its usual variety of residents. The street itself, the architecture of the houses, the arrangement of the lawns, the fences and garden sheds and garages were 'suburban comfortable', with the houses at each end of the street bordering the two busy highways, Gillespie Street and Royal Street, descending to 'suburban struggling' or 'poor'. An ordinary street in an ordinary cluttered town made extraordinary, perhaps, only by the Memory Flower and the Gravity Star.

The Memory Flower grows always from the dead. Where are they, the long dead, the recently dead, the poets, the painters, the toilers, the housekeepers, the murderers, the imposters: all who have held the memory blossom? If you walk in mid-afternoon through the streets of Puamahara you might suppose you walk through a neatly kept cemetery where the graves are more spacious than usual, with flowers and vegetable gardens, fences, concrete paths leading to the door of the family mausoleum. The silence, cavelike, may be entered. No sound of cars, trains, planes, radios, people, dogs; and just as you become certain that you walk in a cemetery, the sounds of the living intrude, the dream vanishes, and those whom you thought to be dead appear in the doorways with brooms and brushes and motormowers and hedge-clippers to perform the daily sweep and cut and snip, while others wheeling shopping trundlers, riding bicycles, driving cars, set out in search of substance to feed on, to sleep on, make love on, die on; to clean with, to look at, to spit on, to sigh over, to read, to admire, to wear: all to make certain of one more day of life, that is, to protect the habits of being human: housekeeping their lives.

Kowhai Street is little different from other streets in Puamahara. You may shiver with a sudden inkling of eternity as you sense or imagine that perhaps your street is unique in the world, with the last two houses at each end facing not a noisy frontier of State Highways but a verge of darkness on the furthermost boundaries of the earth, that you and your street may be suspended as a capsule in space and if you dig the thin skins of your garden you may stare down at the spinning earth and the stars or upward at the stars. Such feelings are common, too, in the largest cities of the world where, walking to the end of your block, you gaze and gaze at the seemingly endless street of similar houses, on and on to the ends of the earth, and the further you gaze the easier it is to lose your sense of being somewhere, of having your familiar place, with the warmth of being in your street changed to the desolation of realising that distance may transform your feeling and knowing into nothingness, that you yourself may destroy and declare not to exist what you do not now know and have ceased to become a part of. Then, desperately, you must forge links or deny whatever lives in time and space, your denial meaning the constant possibility that you may fall into the the darkness at the edge of the earth and may never be known again.

---

it could have happened. But it doesn't matter: we knew it was fiction. It just happens to be good fiction. (pp. 42-3)

Fleur Adcock, "An American in New Zealand," in New Statesman & Society, *Vol. 1, No. 17, September 30, 1988, pp. 42-3.*

Mary Ellen Quinn

This forceful and original novel [*The Carpathians*] tells the story of Mattina Brecon, a wealthy New Yorker who spends a few months in the small New Zealand city of Puamahara. Mattina rents a house on Kowhai Street and spends her time trying to get to know her neighbors. All of them, she discovers, consider themselves strangers despite their close proximity. In fact, one of the novel's several themes has to do with the relativity of distance: what is close is also far away, while what seems distant is at the same time next door. The novel mixes the mundane, expressed in the details of the lives of the residents of Kowhai Street, with the surreal. At the time that Mattina is scheduled to return to New York, all of her neighbors suddenly disappear. This incident is never explained. Also unanswered is the question of who actually controls the narrative point of view. It may be Mattina; it may be Dinny Wheatstone, known as the "impostor novelist" of Kowhai Street; it may be Mattina's son. Despite its thematic and symbolic complexity, the novel is made accessible by the author's beautiful prose.

Mary Ellen Quinn, in a review of "The Carpathians," in Booklist, *Vol. 85, No. 4, October 15, 1988, p. 364.*

David Nokes

Post-modernist fiction has breathed new life into the corpse of the literary whodunit, arming its readers with clues to track down not the murderer, but that culprit-in-chief, the novelist himself. Janet Frame's latest novel, *The Carpathians,* is one of those books in which everyone turns out to be a character in some other character's fiction. Ostensibly solid citizens inhabiting suburban semis collapse into alphabetical heaps at the sudden revelation of their fictiveness. People are reduced to punctuation; an only child shrinks to 'a comma, a full-stop or a question-mark'.

For most of the novel we are in the mind of Mattina, a rich Manhattan matron drawn to small-town New Zealand in quest of the legendary Memory Flower. Unfortunately, Mattina, unlike her husband, her son and even her neighbour, is not herself a novelist. So while these three are busily creating her imaginative world, she merely offers us an inventory of impressions, collecting 'a purseful of people' and rendering a detailed account of their world of shagpile carpets, herbaceous borders and up-and-over garage doors.

Readers may feel justifiably cheated when, her purse bulging with the small change of suburban life, Mattina suddenly confesses that all these people are merely 'cut-outs between the pages of a book'. There is one marvellously surreal moment when these cut-outs re-materialise as a kind of lexical fall-out settling over the town. But the contrivances by which estate-agent realism is transformed into fairy-tale fantasy seem more than a little forced.

David Nokes, "Lexical Fall-out," in The Observer, *October 23, 1988, p. 42.*

Jayne Pilling

"Interesting. Episodic. But it shows novelistic greed—you've taken all points of view, all time—it's an act of dreamlight robbery!" This comment, made by Mattina Brecon, protagonist of Janet Frame's new novel, might also be a mischievous aside by the author herself on the book's ambitions. Language, in everyday use and in fiction, and its relation to experience—of self and others, nature and the denaturing effects of modern life—is the theme of *The Carpathians.*

Mattina is a rich American, married to a novelist whose thirty-year writing block drives her to exotic trips abroad in search of contact with other people's experience. She settles for a couple of months in a small New Zealand town, attracted by its newly discovered legend of a Memory Flower, repository of the "land-memory." Her project to know and record the lives of her neighbours is apparently, and disconcertingly, appropriated by one of them, an elderly female eccentric called Dinny Wheatstone, whose novel charting Mattina's own investigations and reflections elicits the response quoted above. Dinny is self-appointed "Official Imposter", in whom

> all points of view are burgled because the imposter has no point of view. Locked within the language of my own imposture I further bind myself with every word I use, and yet I acknowledge the treasure of my deceit because it is within the human country of birth, meeting, parting and death—the sanctuary of the imposter. And although the inevitable deceit also of language has built for us a world of imposture, we do survive within it, fed by the spark, at times by the fire of the recognition of the hinterland of truth.

The relativity of truth, symbolized by the Gravity Star, a recent scientific discovery which annihilates conventional notions of time and space, challenging language's ambitions to capture truth, is another preoccupation of the novel.

When Dinny Wheatstone disappears, along with all the other inhabitants of Kowhai Street, after a howling night when language rains down like atomic fallout, leaving dusty jumbled heaps of letters and punctuation marks in its wake, the strands of literary-philosophical enquiry are magnificently embodied. Yet ultimately the sheer weight of ideas packed in to the novel works against its coherence.

The individual narratives of Kowhai Street's inhabitants, for example, are idiosyncratic, sometimes cruelly witty—and each says something about the relation of language to life, individual and collective. They also speak for the variety of the New Zealand experience: a quest for cultural identity is confused by simultaneous impulses to revalue ancient Maori traditions, discard colonial influences and ape the American way of life. Mattina's retrospectively recounted marital history seems at first unnecessary and un-convincing despite, or perhaps because of, its obvious re-working in another key of ideas about fiction-making, its sources, frustrations and achievements.

As so often in Frame's novels, there's a curious, combusti-ble mix of modes at work here. An apparently straightfor-ward narrative is exploded from within by a mother-load of metaphor. Perhaps the problem is that the author has been trapped in her own "discovery" of the Gravity Star as a pseudo(?)-scientific concept, infinitely (and somewhat repetitiously) useful for explicating parallels to the cre-ative process of writing. Yet its possibilities are so rich that Frame needs several different narratives, Chinese box-style, to contain them.

Janet Frame has already given us the opportunity to see how a creative imagination works with felt and observed experience, since her autobiographical works can be read alongside her fiction, and it is richly rewarding to do so. *The Carpathians* feels like a new approach, or at least a transitional phase. And if there's a touch of "novelistic greed", and a certain indigestability as a consequence, it is never less than interesting. The novel makes more sense on a second reading—or at least the thinking in it does—and there are moments when the language sings.

> *Jayne Pilling, "Relativities," in* The Times Literary Supplement, *No. 4470, December 2-8, 1988, p. 1350.*

Frame on Writing

My main interest is writing. I write from obsession, habit, and because I have a thorn in my foot, head and heart and it hurts and I can't walk or think or feel until I remove it. When I was a child and I used to ask my father why he worked, I could not understand the answer he gave—'To keep the wolf from the door.' I understand now, though it's a different kind of wolf that writing keeps at bay and the writer has no hope of keeping it from the door: the impor-tant task is to stop it from getting in!

Though I am regarded as a novelist I do not look on myself as such. I look on my writing as exploration in no favourite form. It is hard work: it is easier to write about it than to write. One must be an apprentice to solitude and silence with the terrible realisation that the term of apprenticeship may never end and if it does one may meet a locked door, one may be denied the final silence and solitude, or find it only in death when one cannot speak or make sentences in writing.

Nancy Wartik

[*The Carpathians*], is an unconventional fantasy. Told for the most part from the viewpoint of a wealthy, compulsive globe-trotter, a middle-aged New Yorker named Mattina Brecon, it describes her two-month stay in the fictional New Zealand town of Puamahara. The book takes as its starting point the discovery of a strange celestial phenom-enon: a galaxy that, paradoxically, appears at the same time "both relatively close and seven billion light years away" as a result of light's passage through intervening gravitational forces. *The Carpathians* examines what might happen if this so-called Gravity Star phenomenon suddenly affected our own world—starting in the street in Puamahara where Mattina takes up residence—and "de-stroyed the concept of nearness and distance as oppo-sites." Fascinating, frustrating, obscure, complex, with a deceptively haphazard plot and confoundingly shifting points of view, *The Carpathians* is not a fast, entertaining read. But it *is* a small masterpiece of literary craftsman-ship, the work of an original thinker with a poet's ear for the sound and cadence of language. The catastrophic ef-fects of the Gravity Star paradox on one New Zealand neighborhood prefigure Ms. Frame's vision of the world-wide destruction "of the old ways when distance is near and the eastern mountains of Puamahara could be the Carpathians; and weight becomes lightness; and the trees . . . have their roots in the sky." In just under 200 pages, Ms. Frame conveys volumes: her book yields new facets of meaning with each rereading.

> *Nancy Wartik, in a review of "The Carpathi-ans," in* The New York Times Book Review, *January 22, 1989, p. 22.*

Cecilia Konchar Farr

If all of our conceptions of time and place suddenly disap-peared, would memory become the only real field of expe-rience? Would language be necessary to guarantee our ex-istence? New Zealand writer Janet Frame gives this fasci-nating idea free rein in her latest novel, *The Carpathians,* inspired by her musings about the Gravity Star, "a galaxy that appears to be both relatively close and seven billion light years away." The Gravity Star "by itself could ban-ish distance, nearness, weight, lightness, up, down, today, yesterday, tomorrow," she says.

And in the tiny town of Puamahara, New Zealand, it does just that. People living on Kowhai Street, whether they have lived there for twenty years or two, identify them-selves as strangers and newcomers. They set up temporary camp in their "suburban comfortable" homes, adding rumpus rooms, new wiring, overhead garage doors, and flower gardens, then camouflaging themselves in "clothes patterned with flowers and leaves, of all colours," and talking constantly of moving somewhere else. When Mat-tina Brecon, a wealthy stranger from New York, journeys to Puamahara in search of the Memory Flower, she dis-covers instead the threat of sudden annihilation among the uprooted, alienated residents of Kowhai Street.

"You see," Mattina explains to her writer-husband when she returns to New York, "I had to fight for my life, my very days, and my point of view." She talks to him of memory, "not as a comfortable parcel of episodes to carry in one's mind, and taste now and then, but as a naked link, a point, diamond-size, seed-size, coded in the world, of the human race; a passionately retained deliberate focus on all creatures and their worlds to ensure their survival."

The power of memory and its link with language is the ambitious focus of Frame's story. The story itself is claimed by three different authors in the course of the novel. Its disjointed style lurches us from everyday experience into the world of Frame's imaginings. And Frame intends us to be uncomfortable there, where our very selves are as threatened as Mattina's—by the loss of our Memory Flower, our collective land-memory, by the loss of our point of view, and of our language.

"The Carpathians are a great mountain system, extending from Bratislava to Orsovo," chants one of the characters of this strange and vivid world. "You'd have the *Carpathians,*" he repeats, revelling in the sound of the cherished word, "the *Carpathians* in your garden." The dissonance created by the character's joy in language and his odd disjuncture of places and dimensions is the secret to the success of this extremely creative, sophisticated novel. Frame's skilled prose and her powerful evocation of a reality that is slightly out of kilter make her novel both a pleasure and a challenge to read. Like Mattina, we do not come out of the land of the Memory Flower and the Gravity Star quite the same as we went in. Frame successfully dislodges our comfortable realities.

> *Cecilia Konchar Farr, in a review of "The Carpathians," in* Belles Lettres: A Review of Books by Women, *Vol. 4, No. 3, Spring, 1989, p. 21.*

Keith Garebian

Janet Frame's **The Envoy From Mirror City** (1985), the third and final volume of autobiography by this remarkable writer from New Zealand, traces Frame's travels to Paris, Barcelona and Ibiza, her often touching and bewildering introductions to love, work, and self-sufficiency, and finally her growing self-assurance and sense of vocation. The fundamental questions for readers' concern is the publicly shared conception of self: Just how much can a writers ego be trusted? How much is literary mythology, how much a caricature of reality?

Frame's autobiographical trilogy is a sequence of revelations of her need to be protected. This impulse for refuge and self-concealment goes back to childhood, a time of life endearingly described in her first installment **To The Island** (1982). Written with vivid detail about her railway family's sequence of uprootings and journeys, and streaked with tragedy—the death of a sister by drowning, an epileptic brother—the book reveals Janet Frame's developing literary sensibility, at first colonial and conventional (imagination is reduced to a dreary poeticism), but gradually moving away from stereotypes of fantasy.

An Angel At My Table (1984), her second installment, is, perhaps, the most psychologically revealing of her personal history, for it traces her bizarre student life, her startling exit from schoolteaching, her mental breakdown and its subsequent stigma, and her continual attempt to hide her vocation *within* herself. Frame's self is like a festering wound in this book. Her schizophrenia (an incorrect diagnosis, as it turns out) marks her as a victim without hope, and she adopts a formidable schizophrenic repertoire.

> I'd lie on the couch, while the handsome John Forrest, glistening with newly-applied Freud, took note of what I said and did, and suddenly I'd put a glazed look in my eye, as if I were in a dream, and begin to relate a fantasy as if I experienced it as a reality. I'd describe it in detail while John Forrest listened, impressed, serious. Usually I incorporated in the fantasy details of my reading on schizophrenia.

Her first meeting with compatriot and noted writer Frank Sargeson leads to a deep friendship, which helps her break out of a sealed-in world of literature. Through him she meets other writers and wins a travel grant to broaden her experience, and escape from the awful stigma of schizophrenia. But when she sails for New Zealand on the *Ruahine,* anxiety still consumes her. Consequently, her final autobiographical installment is shot through with apprehension in search of a cure. She arrives on the grimy steps of the London YWCA after finding that a letter she had sent from New Zealand had gone astray, leaving her stranded for lodging. For a moment, however, the loss of the letter seems unimportant beside "the fictional gift of the loss as if within every event lay a reflection reached only through the imagination and its variant servant languages, as if, like the shadows in Plato's cave, our lives and the world contain mirror cities revealed to us by our imagination, the Envoy." Quickly, then, within two chapters, Frame gives us the symbolic framework for her literary autobiography, choosing to read her life as a contemplation of the parallel between fact and fiction.

This second book is very definitely a writer's vision of reality. The words of London newspapers, magazines, sheets of advertisements in the shop widows, the names and buses, the street signs, the restaurant menus, the posters in the underground stations, and the graffiti in public lavatories and road tunnels provide her with a generous opportunity for public reading and private fascination. Haunting names (High Wycombe, Shepards Bush, Swiss Cottage, Mortlake) and expressions (Giant Toad and Two Veg., Shepherd's) become a source of linguistic pleasure. Hampstead Heath and the neighbourhood where Keats lived, bring to mind a quotation from "La Belle Dame Sans Merci". But the psychological attitude is very much a colonial's sense of awe, and she adopts a defensive strategy when faced with revealing her own literary identity. Thrilled by the literary ferment of London, she writes a group of poems in the persona of West Indian arrivant, and sends them to the *London Magazine:* her literary pretence is a "safeguard" against the discovery by others that her "real" poetry is worthless: it is also a reflection of a New Zealander's "search for identity beyond her own country where being thought 'more English than the English' was felt to be more insulting than praise-worthy." Perhaps, most of all—though this she does not ever say directly—her literary preference is her way of living securely within "the city of the imagination" whenever the real city becomes threatening.

The Envoy From Mirror City, however, is unsatisfactory even on its own limited terms. Its diffidence is not simply psychological, but literary as well. On her return to New Zealand, (where she hopes that living in her homeland will be "like living in an age of mythmakers; with a freedom of imagination among all the artists because it is possible to begin at the beginning and to know the unformed places and to help to form them, to be a mapmaker for those who will follow"), she is asked by a shy, pale, young man about the titles of her books, but her primitive shyness about naming prevents her from disclosing her titles. This reluctance "to reduce or drain into speech the power supply of the mind" is what is fatal to the book.

The autobiography tells us only that she has made laborious journeys to and from Mirror City. It is controlled by the "politics of use." Frame confesses that although she has "used, invented, mixed, remodelled, changed, added, subtracted from all experiences," she has never written directly of her own life and feelings. She has created "selves" by mixing herself with other characters who "themselves are a product of known and unknown, real and imagined,"

but she has never written of herself. Why? "Because if I make that hazardous journey to the Mirror City where everything I have known or seen or dreamed of is bathed in the light of another world, what use is there in returning only with a mirrorful of me?"

Her return to New Zealand is sad and desolate—her beloved father having just died—yet she relishes its importance to the Envoy from Mirror City, "that watching self." For her readers, however, that "watching self" is too censorial and does not allow Mirror City its complete reflection in its twin reality. (pp. 31-2)

Keith Garebian, "In the Aftermath of Empire: Identities in the Commonwealth of Literature," in The Canadian Forum, *Vol. LXVIII, No. 780, April, 1989, pp. 25-33.*

Jim Harrison

1937-

(Full name James Thomas Harrison; has also written under the name James Harrison) American novelist, poet, essayist, scriptwriter, and critic.

Often considered an experimental novelist, Harrison has reworked such literary forms as the memoir, adventure tale, and romance. He frequently employs allusion and figurative language in narratives that offer energetic and humorous explorations of displacement, violence, and the destruction of the environment. Reflecting his skills as a poet, Harrison's novels are frequently interlaced with metaphorical descriptions and fragmentary impressions. Harrison has stated: "I never start with an idea. . . . I usually start, even on a novel, with a collection of sensations and images. A form is a convenience that emerges out of what I have to say rather than something I impose on the material."

Born in Grayling, a rural town in northern Michigan, Harrison grew up amidst forests, rivers, and wildlife, images of which figure largely in both his poetry and prose. He began writing poetry in college, and published his first collection, *Plain Song,* while studying for his Master's degree at Michigan State University. Harrison has experimented with various poetic forms throughout his nine collections. For example, *Locations,* his second volume of poetry, contains his own variations on the suite, a lyric form related to musical composition, and the ghazal, a grouping of flexible couplets first used by the ancient Persians. In his verse, Harrison effects a unique blend of rural colloquialisms, metaphysical speculations, and natural and surrealistic images to create multiple layers of meaning. His most recent collection, *The Theory and Practice of Rivers and New Poems,* draws heavily on landscapes of northern Michigan while exploring the complexities of self-deception and the relationship between past and present.

Initial reaction to Harrison's poetry was generally favorable—M. L. Rosenthal called him "one of our finest young poets"—but he remained virtually unknown until the publication of his first work of fiction, *Wolf: A False Memoir,* which he wrote on a whim while recovering from a hunting accident. The story of a disillusioned young man who abandons urban life to seek renewal in the Michigan woods, *Wolf* addresses feelings of displacement and the struggle for self-identity in contemporary American society. Harrison further explores these themes in *A Good Day to Die,* in which an unnamed protagonist journeys in search of romance in an anti-romantic age. The novel also comments on the repercussions of environmental disasters and the destruction of Native American cultures. *A Good Day to Die* received disparate reviews, with some critics praising Harrison's imagery and others faulting his simplistic portrayal of America in the 1960s. William Crawford Woods commented: "[*A Good Day to Die* is] a work of art. A bad novel but a work of art. What a strange ac-

complishment!" The theme of individuals struggling with feelings of inadequacy is developed in Harrison's next novel, *Farmer,* which concerns a man suffering a mid-life crisis.

Harrison received both critical and popular acclaim for *Legends of the Fall,* a collection of three novellas. Although differing in plot and subject matter, these pieces are bound by a common focus on obsession, revenge, and violence. Critics generally concur that the volume's success derives from Harrison's poetic talents, including his economic language, apt phrasing, and structural experimentation. Robert Houston opined that *Legends of the Fall* "may well be the best set of novellas to appear in this country during the last quarter-century."

In his next major novel, *Dalva,* Harrison departs from the exploration of male concerns and experiences that dominate his earlier works. The story of a woman of Sioux heritage in search of the son she gave up for adoption years before, *Dalva* is divided into three sections, two of which are narrated by Dalva, and one by her lover, Michael. The novel was praised for its tender and respectful portrayal of a strong, intelligent woman. Jonathan Yardley commented: "[Dalva] is that rare fictional character whom the reader would dearly love to meet. That she is the creation of a man makes her all the more interesting." Harrison again utilized a female protagonist in *The Woman Lit By Fireflies*. A collection of three novellas—"Brown Dog," "Sunset Unlimited," and the title work—*The Woman Lit By Fireflies* explores such diverse topics as the exploitation of Native American culture, the radical politics of the 1960s, and a middle-aged wife's dissatisfaction with her boorish husband. Reflecting the author's belief that "an incredible playfulness about language" is necessary to creativity, *The Woman Lit By Fireflies* evidences Harrison's continuing use of innovative narrative techniques and poetic imagery.

(See also *CLC*, Vols. 6, 14, 33; *Contemporary Authors*, Vols. 13-16, rev. ed.; *Contemporary Authors New Revision Series*, Vol. 8; and *Dictionary of Literary Biography Yearbook: 1982.*)

PRINCIPAL WORKS

NOVELS

Wolf: A False Memoir   1971
A Good Day to Die   1973
Farmer   1975
Legends of the Fall   (novellas)   1979
Warlock   1981
Sundog   1984
Dalva   1988
The Woman Lit By Fireflies   (novellas)   1990

POETRY

Plain Song   1965
Locations   1968
Walking   1969
Outlyer and Ghazals   1971
Letters to Yesenin   1973
Returning to Earth   1979
Selected and New Poems, 1961-1981   1982
The Theory and Practice of Rivers and Other Poems   1986
The Theory and Practice of Rivers and New Poems   1989

General

William H. Roberson

The basic theme in Harrison's prose is the individual's attempt to come to terms with, and to survive in, contemporary society. Modern life is depicted as shapeless. Society inevitably provides no stability or security for the individual. He must create his own sense of meaning and belonging by finding something to personally place his faith in, an event or belief that will give his life form. Harrison's characters are wanters and dreamers, existing on the edge of failure, their dreams perverted by the reality of contemporary society, but possessing an ability to survive. The support that is lacking in society, but is necessary for their

survival, is often found in nature or natural or primitive activities—rituals. In the general sickness and confusion of modern life, stability and a joy of living are derived from physical pleasures and an immersion into the natural world. Central to the characters' attempt to live with purpose is their understanding that death offers nothing: "one first realizes one is alive and that like all other living creatures one has a beginning, a middle and a terribly certain end." Death in Harrison's work emphasizes life. Life is all there is, all that is offered; it should therefore be made meaningful and purposeful.

Harrison's first novel *Wolf: A False Memoir* (1971) clearly demonstrates this sense of disengagement from the social world and entry into the natural. *Wolf* is the narrative and reminiscences of Carol Severin Swanson, age 33, during a week's camping trip in the Huron Mountains of the Upper Peninsula of Michigan. His intent is to see a wolf, a creature he strongly identifies with. Swanson is a loner, an anachronism, a person outside of society, "a one-man pioneer movement looking for a new country." Just as he is unable to read a compass and repeatedly becomes lost in the woods, Swanson is lost in life. He possesses a strong urge to live and to live fully and meaningfully but is thwarted by the circumstances that exist in life—"I don't want to live on earth but I want to live." His pursuit of the wolf is a symbolic quest for the freedom and wildness which he enjoyed during his twenties in an extended *Wanderjahr* across America. The chronicle of these adventures is told through flashbacks interspersed with the events of the camping trip.

The book is a stream of consciousness of ribald and boisterous philosophizing and observations on contemporary society: business, ecology, politics, love, and drugs. Yet despite all of Swanson's hip rantings and ravings, he is a failure. Leaving the woods after seven days he craves cigarettes, whiskey, the comfort of a hotel room and a shower, and drinking "myself into the comatose state I knew I deserved." He is unable to make any lasting connections with life, not with people, the family homestead he revisits, or even the wolf he seeks. He connects only with himself. His criticisms regarding contemporary life camouflage his own failures and inabilities, his lack of determination and personal strength.

Wolf has strong autobiographical elements in it. Harrison has termed it "an extremely direct, nontherapeutic attempt to come to terms with my life in the present." Swanson's experiences in New York, Boston, and San Francisco have been, in some measure, derived from Harrison's own in the same cities as he worked as farm laborer, carpenter, hod carrier, and salesman. One reviewer has observed that *Wolf*, as well as *A Good Day To Die*, Harrison's second novel, "fail as novels precisely because they triumph as poetry, diatribe and personal memoir."

A Good Day To Die (1973), a darker, more unsettling, and less successful work, continues Harrison's theme of being out of sync with the twentieth century. A trio of characters sets out from Florida to blow up dams in the West in a vague and ill-formed ecological protest. All three are alienated from society. The narrator is a young, intelligent ne'er-do-well and fisherman who has abandoned his wife and child. His companions are two Georgians who "didn't seem to belong to the twentieth century though they bore so many of its characteristic scars," Tim, a burly wildly naive and suicidal Vietnam veteran and his girlfriend Sylvia.

The book is the story of the slow suicide of Tim from a combination of drugs and alcohol and the growing love of the narrator for Sylvia and the resulting relationship among the three. Although they travel together, they remain individuals, each struggling to resolve their own spiritual dilemma through an act of violence against society and government, trying to achieve some sense of control through acts of aggression. They are unable, however, to maintain a constancy in either their actions or relationships. They remain in a perpetual state of flux: "there was no sense of balance left in anything we were doing." Yet, for the narrator, although he views his interest in life as tentative, he recognizes that the desire for it remains, "the juice still seemed to be there," and this desire is supported by natural and basic pleasures: "the delight in the air and water and trees and in such rare creatures as Sylvia, and the food that even now Rosie was slinging on the table. And in whiskey and fishing." In their one attempt to destroy a dam, Tim is killed. The narrator and Sylvia are left in disarray, not knowing what to do or where to go. Because of their inability to help one another achieve a sense of stability and purpose in their lives, the story ends in the ultimate futility and tragedy of their actions.

Farmer (1976), arguably his finest novel, strengthens Harrison's theme of the individual's realization of the certainty of death and his subsequent search for identity. Joseph Lundgren is a forty-three year old schoolteacher/farmer undergoing a mid-life identity crisis. The school where he teaches is being closed, his mother is dying of cancer, and he is faced with a classic dilemma concerning a question of love. He is caught between a relationship with his long-time mistress and friend Rosealee and a sexual relationship with Catherine, a young student in his class. Harrison unfolds this all too familiar story slowly, actually presenting its resolution in the first two pages, yet revealing its development only gradually through flashbacks and flash-forwards. In so doing he presents a beautifully real meditation of a complex sensitive person against the background of a gracefully drawn description of rural northern small town and farm life in 1956.

In the dichotomy that he creates between Lundren's two relationships, Harrison presents the individual's struggle for constancy in a world of imbalance. Lundgren teaches, hunts, fishes, reads Keats, and dreams. He dreams of the ocean and the world that lies beyond the farm. In his relationship with Catherine he is experiencing the freedom and wildness he has dreamed about. She and her parents have moved to northern Michigan from the city. She is contemporary and new, she is unknown: "she was from the outside world and this clearly interested him no matter how dangerous the situation was." Their relationship, however, offers him no stability, only confusion and uncertainty, fear and guilt. . . . In comparison, Lundgren's relationship with Rosealee is regular, at times dull, but real. "With Rosealee it was sweet and pleasant, precisely

what he imagined it would be like to be married to someone you deeply cared for." She represents his roots to his past forty-three years, his family, his life, the land. Lundgren recognizes that at this time of crisis in his life, "all of the strictures, habits, the rules of order for both work and pleasure seemed to be rending at even the strong points."

In his ultimate choice between the two Harrison establishes his point. Life is a "death dance." It goes on and on, proceeding to its only certainty, death, and death, as Harrison has stated, is "ineluctably death and nothing else." The meaning of one's life is therefore established in its pattern, and continuity and satisfaction come from pursuing the pattern that has been developed. Constancy is achieved through habit. This is not to say that one has to be perfunctory and unchanging, but that the orbits of personal experience need to have a solid axis to maintain stability. A way of life must be established.

"The Man Who Gave Up His Name," one of three novellas comprising Harrison's next work, *Legends of the Fall* (1979), is clearly a continuation of this theme and of the Swanson-Lundgren protagonist. Nordstrom is "a man of forty-three years, a father, formerly a husband, magna cum laude University of Wisconsin 1958, and so on," who is experiencing a crisis of identity. At mid-life, recently divorced, his daughter graduating from college, Nordstrom questions his up-to-now successful pursuit of the American dream: "what if what I've been doing all my life has been totally wrong?"

Nordstrom realizes that although he has been successful by the standards of contemporary society, he has not followed his "heart's affections." He attempts to find the proper niche in life to satisfy himself. In his "pilgrimage away from an unsatisfactory life" he refines and elevates Swanson's earlier lament of wanting to live but not on earth, for Nordstrom has "either lost or given up everything on earth" and in so doing has found the peace within himself that is needed to survive.

Nordstrom does not want to escape from the world but into it. He resigns his position as a vice-president for a book wholesaler in Boston, begins to dance by himself and learns gourmet cooking (culinary activity is central to all of Harrison's characters, himself a gourmet cook, the ingestive appetite being the most primitive human need). He recognizes that "life is only what one does every day," and confronted by his father's death and the killing he is forced to commit as a result of a scam operation by a small-time hood, he perceives "how biologically flimsy we are. We go along for forty-three years then someone pokes a knife in us or a .38 slug and it's goodnight." Over. Finished. Again Harrison forces his character into life by confronting him with the absence of it: "most days I'm excited about living for no particular reason." (pp. 29-32)

The other two novellas in *Legends of the Fall* are, like **"The Man Who Gave Up His Name,"** stories of obsession. Like Nordstrom, the protagonists are well-educated, well-off men in their forties, who are compelled to acts of violence in attempting to achieve some type of self-realization.

"Revenge," Harrison's only work that is not set, at least in part, in the Key West area of Florida or the northern Midwest, tells the story of Cochran, a retired air force pilot who is having an affair with Miryea, the wife of a Mexican friend and associate, Tibey, Spanish slang for "the shark." Ignoring hints and opportunities from Tibey to end the affair, the couple is surprised in a cabin by him and his men. Cochran is severely beaten and left for dead in the desert. Miryea is disfigured with a razor, addicted to heroin, terrorized by snakes, and placed in a whorehouse. Cochran survives his ordeal and seeks revenge on Tibey and tries to find Miryea. The story ends in embarassing sentimentalism and triteness as Miryea dies in Cochran's arms after he and Tibey have reconciled.

"Revenge" is surely Harrison's most violent and stark piece of work. It lacks the touches of humor and self-deprecation that marked his previous stories. The character of Miryea, who supposedly motivates the dual cycle of revenge, is one of Harrison's weakest and least developed portraits of a woman. Indeed, all the characters are sketched out rather than fully developed. They are merely props for the strongly cinematic sets Harrison creates.

"Legends of the Fall," the title piece and concluding story, is a similarly stark and violent tale with baroque pretensions. It is a dense and busy work, a novella of epic proportions. The story concerns Tristan Ludlow, one of three brothers from a Montana ranch, who in 1914 go to Calgary, Alberta to fight in the First World War. The work is essentially composed of three parts, each comprised of adventure, violence, romantic obsession, and death, all connected by the angry and brooding figure of Tristan Ludlow.

Tristan is a marked man. His youngest brother, Samuel, is killed in the war and Tristan nearly goes insane. He escapes from a mental ward and becomes an adventurer and smuggler. He returns home and marries Samuel's intended wife, Susannah, leaves her to return to the sea and more adventures involving spying and smuggling. He returns home again and marries a sixteen-year old Indian girl, ranches and continues to smuggle. After six years of relative quiet his wife is killed in a freak accident. Meanwhile Susannah has married Albert, Tristan's older brother, who becomes a United States Senator. Susannah, however, is insane and becomes suicidal over what she believes to be Tristan's lack of love for her. Their subsequent tryst is discovered by Albert who eventually spends time in an asylum himself, and at the death of Susannah, sends her body to Tristan. The story fades to a close amidst more violence as Tristan, plagued by guilt over his betrayal of his brother, finally achieves some sense of peace in a solitary existence in Cuba and then Alberta.

"Revenge" and "Legends of the Fall" are among the best known of Harrison's work, both having been published in *Esquire* accompanied by much hyperbole and fanfare. Although both are impressive stylistic achievements and exemplary pieces of storytelling, in the final analysis they lack heart or substance. The characterizations are shallow and undeveloped. Harrison has allowed the violent and elemental nature of the works to dominate. He has moved away from the minds of his characters, the mental and

emotional lives that his other works are centered around, and focused more upon action and physical activity. Although they are the most atypical of his work, "Revenge" and "Legends of the Fall" are also the basis for the critical charges that Harrison is simply a writer of "macho fiction."

Since *Wolf* reviewers have termed Harrison's work Hemingwayesque because of his understated plots and prose and use of simple declarative sentences as well as what is perceived to be his overstressed masculinity. To accuse him, as some critics do, of advocating "male power" and labelling his writing "macho fiction" is, however, a serious error.

One reviewer has defined macho fiction as

> fiction women won't readily enjoy—not because it is pornographic (on the contrary, it is resolutely antierotic), but because it celebrates a fantasy of masculine self-sufficiency. It is above all solemn stuff.

To further explain the type of characters that populate this genre, a description from James Salter's novel *Solo Faces* is given:

> There are men who seem destined to always go first, to lead the way. They are confident in life, they are first to go beyond it. Whatever there is to know, they learn before others. Their very existence gives strength and drives one onward.

This clearly does not relate to the majority of Harrison's characters. Although his stories may be crowded with what some may narrowly perceive to be male-oriented elements: drinking, fishing, hunting, and sex, Harrison deflates the extravagantly male animal by making him in a term he uses more than once, "goofy."

With the exception of Cochran and Tristan, Harrison's male protagonists do not exhibit characteristic macho tendencies. Both Swanson and the narrator of *A Good Day To Die* are self-serving, self-pitying, weak individuals. Harrison himself has described Swanson as a "not very heroic hero" and an "essentially . . . comic figure." In *A Good Day To Die* the narrator is helpless to prevent another man's slow suicide before his own eyes and questions his own worthiness of a woman's love. These two characters do not represent the epitome of manliness and virtue. They are not leaders, they are lost. They are weak and self-indulgent, ineffective and helpless. They cannot achieve a break with societal reality. They remain defined and sustained by society, unable for all their protestations and scoldings to preserve and attain a life of purpose. They are unable to commit themselves successfully to women or families, and this is portrayed not as a strength but as a failure of the characters, a point Harrison makes clear in the relationships that evolve in his other works.

None of Harrison's work celebrates a masculine self-sufficiency. The male characters are not confident in life. On the contrary, they are all deficient in one aspect or another. The protagonists of *Farmer,* "The Man Who Gave Up His Name," and *Warlock* particularly, are sensitive, fallible characters with questions of self-doubt and concern, who experienc fear and anxiety. A central theme in

Harrison's work is man's quest to acquire that intangible element that will bring stability and completeness to his life. In at least two of his works, *Farmer* and *Warlock,* a woman eventually satisfies a major portion of that need, no small irony if masculine self-sufficiency is Harrison's intent.

Although both Cochran and Tristan may certainly be viewed as possessing machismo, there is no sense of fulfillment or strength at the conclusion of **"Revenge"** or **"Legends of the Fall."** There is instead an emptiness and exhaustion, a sense of pity and loss. Indeed, even though all of his prose work, at one time or another, suffers from the threat of sentimentality and romanticization it is in these two works, with the strongest elements of "male power," that Harrison comes closest to succumbing to that threat.

Warlock is Harrison's most recent novel and continues his line of Swedish-American mock-heroes undergoing identity crises in the twentieth-century United States. Emphasizing the continuity of Harrison's themes and characters, the protagonist of *Warlock* has the same last name as the "hero" in *Farmer,* Lundgren. Similarly, he is not a macho figure. He fears, among other things, fire, the dark, sexually aggressive women, fist fights, and death, and he too gets lost in the woods. Harrison wastes little time in re-establishing the death-life impetus. Within the first two pages of narrative Lundgren has had a dream of his death and awoken with a renewed vigor for life: "he really wasn't so much a fool as he was giddy about still being alive." He figured out that he was going to die some day.

In *Warlock* Harrison fully develops his concept of the individual in conflict with the real world. John Milton Lundgren has been fired from his job as a foundation executive. He is "a goofy fop and terribly intelligent, no longer to any particular effect." He and his wife, Diana, an emergency room nurse, move to rural northern Michigan where he experiments with gourmet cooking and philosophizes concerning life and reality. Diana, confronted with death every day as a surgical nurse, is a pragmatist. Lundgren, however, is a Keatsian romanticist. He is cognizant of the attraction of an imaginative dream world without the disagreeable aspects and remorseless pressures of reality. He "tingled with a gentle warmth" watching *Man of La Mancha,* and decided "there was something to the old saw about grasping for straws."

Lundgren, or Warlock, his secret Cub Scout name that he resurrects along with his new view of life, accepts a job, arranged through his wife, from Dr. Rabun, a rich eccentric researcher. He is hired to investigate possible infringements of Rabun's timber and real estate investments by Rabun's wife and son whom he describes as being free-spending and gay respectively. After a series of bumbling adventures, Lundgren uncovers the truth and is almost destroyed by the reality of the situation. Rabun is robbing his relatives of their rightful trust funds, and is testing his experimental sexual devices with the help of Diana. Unlike the stories of *Legends of the Fall,* Lundgren's revenge stops short of physical violence and Harrison neatly and peacefully resolves the story.

Harrison's affectionate spoof of the detective genre is marred only by the flawed pacing of the work. He takes too long to establish his story and then too quickly concludes it, but the tale of Johnny Lundgren clearly demonstrates the major elements of Harrison's prose work: the testing of the individual in his search for identity outside of the restrictions of society, the beauty and support of the natural environment, and the perceptions of death and reality in one's life.

Harrison's works have something more to offer than the simplistic motto that one reviewer of *Legends of the Fall* credited it with: "live with gusto, die with dignity." He is relentlessly examining the place and purpose of man in the twentieth century. His characters are in a struggle to control the effects of the twentieth century upon their lives, a struggle between the reality of self and the reality of society. They are in search for a truth about themselves, striving for personal affirmation or achievement within the human limitations of the present age.

Harrison's novels are sparsely populated because the focus is upon the individual in a crisis situation, the individual who endures under difficulties. This effort to survive and establish an identity and purpose causes them to be self-occupied, they must depend upon themselves because society offers them no support: "you were either obsessive and totally in control or you were nothing." They are not heroic or brave, but they are survivors. There is almost a total absence of God or religion in these novels. The individual must assume religion's role in society, the responsibility for the salvation of the emotional and spiritual self. The physical self is maintained by nature in the process of primitive activities and the following of rules and rituals.

In a brief autobiographical essay commenting upon his family's move from northern Michigan to a more urban southern Michigan when he was thirteen, Harrison states that it took him "two decades to comprehend the unhappiness of this move from a basically agrarian culture into the twentieth century." In his prose work Harrison attempts to articulate the problems inherent in America's progress from a rural to an urban society into the twentieth century and its impact upon individual lives. Formerly the basis for a person's life and well-being was found in the land. Nature was a touchstone with the past. It offered continuity and consistency and, therefore, stability. Modern urbanized and industrialized America has moved away from this agrarian tradition and Harrison's work explores the effect of uncertainty caused by a fast-moving, fast-evolving society on the individual. As Lundgren observes, "civilization certainly hasn't panned out."

Harrison's characters are reaching out for something to hold on to, searching for answers to their questions. He suggests that that something, that answer, is within themselves. That the questions, however, are ultimately unanswerable, and that Harrison's solutions are not totally successful, do not diminish his achievement in so honestly, sensitively, and stylishly documenting the problem of contemporary American ways and needs. (pp. 32-7)

> *William H. Roberson, " 'A Good Day to Live':*
> *The Prose Works of Jim Harrison," in* Great

Lakes Review, *Vol. 8, No. 2, Fall, 1982, pp. 29-37.*

Jim Harrison   [Interview with Jim Fergus]

[*The following interview was conducted over a period of five days at Harrison's farm in Leelanau County, Michigan, in October 1986.*]

[Harrison]: I wrote this in my notebook: "My favorite moment in life is when I give my dog a fresh bone." That comes from being the blinded seven-year-old hiding out in the shrubbery with his dog, whom he recognized as his true friend.

[Fergus]: *Do you think your childhood accident when you lost sight in one eye gave you a different way of looking at things?*

Probably. I understand they believe that in other cultures, especially when it's the left eye.

You seem to have a remarkable memory for the events of your childhood, which you use a lot in your work.

It's nondiscriminate and that's why you have to work hard at it. In terms of classic Freudianism, if you have a knot in your past that stops the flow of your life, it's a psychic impediment. Your memories enlarge in ways proportionally to how willing you are to allow them to enlarge.

Do you believe that a good memory is an essential attribute for a writer because it gives one a deeper well to draw from?

Sometimes I wish I could forget more things. I have to make a conscious effort to free my mind, open it again because memory can be tremendously rapacious. Was it to you that I said jokingly that I had to go out and collect some new memories, I'm going dry? That's why I like movement.

This idea of movement and the metaphor of the river, seem to be central to your work.

It's the origin of the thinking behind **The Theory and Practice of Rivers.** In a life properly lived, you're a river. You touch things lightly or deeply; you move along because life herself moves, and you can't stop it; you can't figure out a banal game plan applicable to all situations; you just have to go with the "beingness" of life, as Rilke would have it. In **Sundog,** Strang says a dam doesn't stop a river, it just controls the flow. Technically speaking, you can't stop one at all.

But you have to work at it, make a conscious effort so that your life flows like a river?

Antaeus magazine wanted me to write a piece for their issue about nature. I told them I couldn't write about nature but that I'd write them a little piece about getting lost and all the profoundly good aspects of being lost—the immense fresh feeling of really being lost. I said there that my definition of magic in the human personality, in fiction and in poetry, is the ultimate level of attentiveness. Nearly everyone goes through life with the same potential perceptions and baggage, whether it's marriage, children, education, or unhappy childhoods, whatever; and when I say at-

tentiveness I don't mean just to reality, but to what's exponentially possible in reality. . . . This attentiveness is your main tool in life, and in fiction, or else you're going to be boring. As Rimbaud said, which I believed very much when I was nineteen and which now I've come back to, for our purposes as artists, everything we are taught is false—everything.

How did you think at age fourteen that you might want to be a poet?

Those years, fourteen, fifteen, sixteen, are a vital time in anybody's life, also a tormenting time. I wanted to be a preacher for a while, but then it seemed to me that whatever intelligence I had wouldn't allow it. That again would be a question of leaving out the evidence. So I think all my religious passions adapted themselves to art as a religion.

Did you always read a lot?

Yes. My father was a prodigious reader and passed on the habit. He was an agriculturist but he also read all of Hemingway and Faulkner and Erskine Caldwell. He read indiscriminately. Both my parents did.

That had to have been valuable training for you.

A large part of writing is a recognition factor, to have read enough to know what good writing is. Finally, what Wallace Stevens said, which I love and which is hard to explain to younger writers, is that technique is the proof of your seriousness. (pp. 55-8)

Having begun your career as a poet, how did you make the transition to fiction?

I fell off a cliff while bird hunting and hurt myself, and I had to be in traction for a month. I had a long convalescence. Fortunately, I had the Guggenheim that year, or we would have been bankrupt. Tom McGuane suggested I write a novel while I was convalescing, and that's how I wrote **Wolf.** I sent it off and for a month it was lost in the mail strike. It was the only copy. When they accepted it for publication I was somewhat surprised. I thought, oh good, here's something else I can do, because the dominant forces in my life had always been novelists, along with a few poets.

In its form, **Wolf** *is quite unconventional. It has a very personal, almost confessional quality. Does that reflect your background as a poet?*

At the time I hadn't written any fiction other than juvenilia, so naturally **Wolf** was a poet's book. I even have grave doubts whether it's a novel at all. That's why I called it a false memoir. I certainly came to the novel backwards, because poets practice an overall scrutiny habitually, and what's good later for their novels is that they practice it pointillistically. You read some reasonably good novelists who tell a story well enough in terms of a flat narrative, but they never notice anything interesting, whereas a poet has folded and unfolded his soul somewhat like an old-fashioned laundry girl with the linen. His self is his vocation. As W. C. Williams said, "no ideas but in things."

Wolf *is a very angry book.*

Wolf reminds me somewhat of a heartbroken boy up on

the barn roof, just sort of yelling. I've certainly become a nicer person over the years. (pp. 60-1)

After **Wolf***, your next novel,* **A Good Day To Die***, took a more traditional form as a narrative. Was that a natural progression from poetry into fiction?*

No, I think it was the influence of Raymond Chandler and John D. MacDonald. I wanted to tell one of those simple tales that has a great deal of narrative urgency, propelled by characters who, once you've met them, you know it's going to be a godawful mess. These are people that nobody wants in their living room . . . except maybe Sylvia, in her white cotton underpants.

I can see where some people might find these characters objectionable. That's a disturbing book.

The book came out of the feeling of the late sixties. In a sense it was the first Vietnam book. A critic in New York told me that such people don't exist, and I said, well, I'm afraid they do, in enormous quantity, as we were to see later.

Do you think the fact that you often write about people who are not exactly "mainstream" type characters has hurt you in terms of critical acceptance?

It's occurred to me that some of the awkwardness I have in reception—not that I can't write badly—is because the kind of people I write about are utterly alien to almost everyone in the reviewing media. (pp. 63-4)

Did you ever get to the point where you thought you were just never going to make it?

Yes, I did. **Wolf** actually did quite well for a first novel, and **A Good Day To Die** did all right, but the heartbreaker for me was the absolute failure of **Farmer**. That was something I couldn't handle because it just slipped beneath the waters. I think Viking took out one one-inch ad for it. That was a difficult period and I couldn't maintain my sanity. I had a series of crack-ups. I was at the point where I couldn't pay my taxes, which were a feeble amount. My oldest daughter won a full scholarship but I couldn't fill out the forms because I had no IRS returns to show what I made. That was the period out of which I wrote **Letters to Yesenin,** which is the book I've gotten the most mail on.

Letters to Yesenin *deals with the consideration of suicide. At the end you come out against it as a valid option in your own life. Did you know right then that it was totally out of the question?*

I knew I'd been thinking about it during that bad period in the back of my mind, but I finally couldn't entertain the thought because I'd seen it in my circumstances as an utterly selfish and stupid thing to do, and then I evolved this theory that even the next meal is worth waiting for. Also I wrote, "My three-year-old daughter's red robe hangs from the doorknob shouting stop." (pp. 67-8)

After you'd made that decision, "decided to stay," as you put it at the end of **Letters to Yesenin,** *what happened then?*

Curiously, things kept going downhill. I would get cheat-ed on the most minor little screenplay. I'd write one for money and then they wouldn't pay me. These things kept happening. My older daughter is still angry about what we went through, and I must admit I am occasionally. But there's nothing unique about it, and all it does is make you enormously cynical. At the end of that ghastly time I met Jack Nicholson on the set of McGuane's movie, *The Missouri Breaks.* We got talking and he asked me if I had one of my novels with me, and I had one, I think it was **Wolf.** He read it and enjoyed it. He told me that if I ever got an idea for him, to call him up. Well, I never have any of those ideas. I wasn't even sure what he meant. I think he said later that I was the only one he ever told that to who never called. A year afterwards, I was out in L.A. and he called up and asked me to go to a movie. It was really pleasant, and I was impressed with his interest in every art form. It was right after *Cuckoo's Nest* and all these people tried to swarm all over him after the movie. Anyway, later he heard I was broke and he thought it was unseemly. So he rigged up a deal so that I could finish the book I had started, which was **Legends of the Fall.** (pp. 68-9)

In the last few years you've done a good deal of screenplay writing. Does it worry you that you're spending too much time at it, to the detriment of your fiction?

Naturally, I worry about that. But it's the only way I can make a living. I don't have any other way of getting any money. I have no other gifts except what I can pull out of my hat, my imagination. I made a very conscious choice between teaching and the film business. If I hadn't made a mess of my life, I could make a reasonably good living off my novels. I'm close to it. (pp. 69-70)

This is perhaps [an] old horse that doesn't need to be beaten any more, but you've been accused of being a "macho" writer. Anything more to say about that one?

All I have to say about that macho thing goes back to the idea that my characters aren't from the urban dream-coasts. A man is not a foreman on a dam project because he wants to be macho. That's his job, a job he's evolved into. A man isn't a pilot for that reason either—he's fascinated by airplanes. A farmer wants to farm. But you know what it's like here and up in the Upper Peninsula. This is where I grew up. How is it macho that I like to hunt and fish? I've been doing it since I was four. I have always thought of the word "macho" in terms of what it means in Mexico—a particularly ugly peacockery, a conspicuous cruelty to women and animals and children, a gratuitous viciousness. You don't write—an artist doesn't create, or very rarely creates—good art in support of different causes. And critics have an enormous difficulty separating the attitudes of your characters from your attitudes as a writer. You have to explain to them: I am not all the men in my novels. How could I be? I'm little Jimmy back here on the farm with my wife and two daughters and, at one time, three female horses, three female cats, and three female dogs, and I'm quite a nice person. So how can I be all these lunatics?

Nevertheless, there is clearly a lot of you in many of your protagonists, and though they are very different people in many ways, with different backgrounds and professions, you can almost see them growing from one to the next. More recently, you seem to be coming off that a bit.

I think so. That's what I've become exhausted with. The reason I revere Faulkner is that he was such a pure story-teller, in the Conradian sense. He created a whole world, a whole reality, and any time you don't aim to do that, you're somehow involved in contemporary gossip. I don't want to piss myself away on that kind of nonsense. And it's always this hyper gossip that turns out to be the most popular in any given age. Frankly, I can't imagine a nasti-er or more exhausting profession because in the long run you spend your life pulling everything out of your ass. Re-member Coleridge's great quote: "What webs of deceit the spider spins out of his big hanging ass." That's in Cole-ridge's notebooks. I love that.

Has there been a conscious progression from the intensely personal material of your first novel to what you're trying to do now?

Hopefully. This time, in **Dalva**, the first third and last third of the book are written from the voice of a woman. Why that's been brutally hard is that you don't get to use any of your easy accumulation of male resonances.

How do you give yourself the voice of a woman?

It's taken about three years of hard work and, as such, is a trade secret.

As long as we're on the subject, who are some of the women novelists you admire?

I don't think of women novelists but writers. Who do I read when they have something coming out? Denise Levertov, Joan Didion, Joyce Carol Oates, Diane Wakoski, Renata Adler, Alison Lurie, Toni Morrison, Leslie Marmon Silko, Ellen Gilchrist, Anne Tyler, Ad-rienne Rich, Rebecca Newth, Rosellen Brown, Gretel Ehrlich, Annie Dillard, Susan Sontag. Those come imme-diately to mind. Also Margaret Atwood.

You have said that you can't be a good artist unless you have a very well-developed feminine side.

That's largely unaccepted but absolutely true. It comes from an idea in the area of psychology. The work of a man named James Hillman, an unbelievably brilliant man, has helped me to understand certain things. He asks, what have we done with our twin sister who we abandoned at birth? A man usually gives up the feminine because of our culture.

When you're writing about something that you can't know personally, is there ever any question of cheating?

No, because you live through it in your imagination, and you have to trust the truth of your heart's affections and the imagination.

You've always written your novels very quickly. Are you changing your work habits on this one?

Writing out of this woman's voice has been so enormously difficult. I've never had more than a three-page day with her. It makes you feel like an ineffective bulldog, you keep worrying it and worrying it and nothing has come fast at

all. And you have to wait until the bread comes fresh from the oven. I don't know if she's going to talk to me today or not. It's been sort of spooky.

Does the speed with which you usually write your novels have something to do with the poetry process?

Yes, because you've already thought and brooded about it a lot. I think I wrote **"Legends of the Fall,"** the title story, in about ten days. **"Revenge"** in about ten days. **"The Man Who Gave Up His Name"** was a little slower, that was probably two weeks. It just came that fast, it all came at once, and I couldn't "not" write it down that fast. Of course, those were some real long days—some eigh-teen-hour days. And I've never done that before or since.

Do you keep to a specific schedule when you're working?

With this woman, [the title character of **Dalva,**] I've had good luck starting very early in the morning which I've never been able to do before. My optimum hours are be-tween two and four in the afternoon. I don't know why and it aggravates me. It's a circadian rhythm I can't avoid. And then between eleven and one at night. I always work a split shift.

Does it require a discipline to maintain that schedule?

After you've been in it this long there's no such thing as discipline. You write it when it's ready to be written. And I've tried several times to start novels when they weren't there and that's tremendously discouraging and anguish-ing. It's dog-paddling, and fraught with the stupidest kinds of anxieties.

What do you do when you can't write?

I wonder, when a writer's blocked and doesn't have any resources to pull himself out of it, why doesn't he jump in his car and drive around the U.S.A.? I went last winter for seven thousand miles and it was lovely. Inexpensive too. A lot of places—even good motels—are only twenty-five dollars in the winter, and food isn't much because there aren't any good restaurants. You pack along a bunch of stomach remedies and a bottle of whiskey.

Is the gestation period a conscious process?

Much of it, although the best things seem to arrive uncon-sciously, somewhat in the manner that your dreams invent people you don't know.

You said earlier that one's dream life is the foundation of art.

It is for everyone whether they like it or not. Or that sleep-ing/waking period early in the morning. Your brain has spent the night evolving a sequence of metaphors that al-lows you to survive the day, and sometimes it comes out in such poignant, distinctive terms.

Hemingway spoke about stopping work when it was going well and then not thinking about it until the next day. Can you actually shut down the process at the end of the work-day?

Not altogether successfully. You want to give it as much chance to occur as possible, but not too much. It's similar to that Faulknerian notion that if you grovel before the muse, she'll only kick you in the teeth. You have to court her, do little dances, all these things you do to keep right with her.

Don't you also do very little rewriting?

That's just an artificiality. The people who do a lot of rewriting haven't thought about it for three years. Some writers work it out on paper and I work it out mentally beforehand. It's only a habit.

I know that you allow very little, if any, editing of your work once it goes to the publisher. Why is that?

Because I know what I want to say. If they want to publish the novel, fine, if not, not. I've been over it four or five times, so why should I let them fool with it? They're not writers.

I don't know many writers who don't feel that they couldn't benefit at some point from sound editorial assistance.

A woman at Viking, Pat Irving, did an extraordinary thing. On *Farmer* she suggested that chapter five should be chapter three and chapter three should be chapter five. So I switched it around and she was totally right. That's wonderful. (pp. 71-7)

You've always seemed interested in form, and in experimenting with form.

I diagrammed the form of *Wolf* before I wrote it—just a picture of the form, no words. In *Farmer,* for example, I tell the reader how the book is going to end in the first two pages, then attempt to make the reader forget. It's similar to a Greek tale that people listen to two hundred times and still enjoy. The idea is that you make little suggestions, little parts to suggest a whole. (p. 77)

One reviewer called **Sundog** *"a novel teeming with ideas." How has your interest in philosophy influenced your work?*

I think ideas are as real as trees. *Sundog* is actually a philosophical novel. I live around that structure although those ideas tend to emerge in my work as sort of irrational and metaphoric. What Bergson called *elan vital* interested me very early. You can see me as a fifteen year-old reading Kant's *Critique of Pure Reason,* wondering why I didn't understand every bit of it. Then I went from Kant to Kierkegaard, to Bergson, to Nietzsche. Those questions started very early in my life, once I gave up temporarily on the Bible, though I still seem to write totally within a Christian framework in an odd way.

In what way?

Well, I realized a couple of years ago that never has it occurred to me not to believe in God and Jesus, and all that. I never questioned it particularly. I was quite a Bible student, pored over and over it, both the Old and New Testament in the King James Version.

Do you feel that your style has evolved or changed in any particular direction?

Well, I'm no longer interested in anyone getting fancy for the wrong reasons. I'm not interested in showing off anymore. I think what's important in style, which of course

is someone's voice finally, is that you have a firm sense of the appropriate. There's a temptation to enter into rhetorical sections because they're fun to write. That's probably a problem William Styron has, particularly as he's so good at it. It was very difficult for me in **"Legends of the Fall,"** the title story, to subdue that impulse, because I think I'm pretty good at it too when I cut loose, and I had to consciously subdue my more grandiose impulses.

So sometimes you have to consciously hold a style in?

Absolutely, because you want the style, in that book especially, to burst at the seams. One editor told me that if **"Legends"** was four hundred and fifty pages rather than one hundred pages, I could make a fortune. But the whole reason it works is that it's only a hundred pages. Tristan isn't Tristan if he's babbling. And the grandeur is in people's minds.

*Will this new book [***Dalva***] be longer than your others?*

This will be the first time I've written a novel that's five hundred pages.

Was it your intention from the beginning to try a longer work?

No, but this was a larger idea and I couldn't do it in less. And what I did again is I over-researched it. That seems to be a nervous habit I've been involved in recently.

Do you dislike didacticism in literature?

I hate it. I can't use most of what I know but I think it should be there as a resonating board. You should read enough to know what's going on throughout the world. Poets should know the history of the United States and South America. . . . It's amazing to me, for instance, how few people know anything about nineteenth-century American history. They don't know what happened to the hundred civilizations represented by the American Indian. That's shocking. I'm dealing with that in [***Dalva***]. To me, the Indians are our curse on the house of Atreus. They're our doom. The way we killed them is also what's killing us now. Greed. Greed. It's totally an Old Testament notion but absolutely true. Greed is killing the soullife of the nation. You can see it all around you. It's destroying what's left of our physical beauty, it's polluting the country, it's making us more Germanic and warlike and stupid.

Does it ever discourage you that the artist can do so little to prevent this?

No, he's doing all he can by writing well. (pp. 78-81)

You've never been afraid of poking fun at yourself in fiction, have you?

Who wants to read about another nifty guy at loose ends? There's not a lot of self-knowledge in those novels which are published by the hundreds.

Are there any of your own novels that you like better than others?

I actually never think about it. I'm always interested when reviewers compare my current work unfavorably to work that they never reviewed at all, like *Farmer.*

Do literary prizes mean anything to you—say, winning a Pulitzer Prize?

No, not really. Any kind of prize is pleasant—especially to your mom, your wife, and kids—but I never got one. After you've written novels or books of poetry for a long time, your concerns become very different. That's just what you do, you've given your entire life over to it, and luckily it's panned out to the point that they're printing your books. So as far as reputation goes, I'm not interested in any reputation that has to be sought. If there's anything more gruesome than Republican politics, it's literary politics.

So you don't feel any pressure at this stage in your career to write the "Big Book"?

I feel absolutely no pressure of any kind. People don't realize how irrational and decadent an act of literature is in the first place, and to feel pressure in a literary sense is hopeless. I always think of an artist in terms of his best work, which I think is what he deserves. If he can do this, if he's taken the trouble, then this is what I think of him. The before and after is always there, but so what? He wrote well and nobody should wish to take it away from him. That's what people forget about James Jones, who wrote far and away the best war novel I can imagine. Why did they flog him senseless for the rest of his life? I always felt, strangely, a real kinship with Jones, whom I never met, being from the Midwest. (pp. 83-4)

Do you feel any sense of competition with other writers?

I don't know what that would be for. I can't see the art processes as being a sack race. I've thought that over as part of the idea that when people whom you love very much die, why would you get in a sack race over the novel? And I think sometimes that bitterness of competition leads people to write the wrong kind of novel, the kind of novel they wouldn't otherwise write. I think Keats is still right in that the most valuable thing for a writer to have is a negative capability.

In what sense?

Just to be able to hold at bay hundreds of conflicting emotions and ideas. That's what makes good literature, whereas opinions don't, and the urge to be right is hopeless. Think of the kind of material Rilke dealt with all his life. It's stupefying. Did you read Stephen Mitchell's new translation of *The Sonnets to Orpheus*? You see that the depth of his art is so dissociated from what we think of as literary existence. Your best weapon is your vertigo. (pp. 84-5)

Do you have any advice for younger writers?

Just start at page one and write like a son of a bitch. Be totally familiar with the entirety of the western literary tradition, and if you have any extra time, throw in the eastern. Because how can you write well unless you know what passes for the best in the last three or four hundred years? And don't neglect music. I suspect that music can contribute to it as much as anything else. Tend to keep distant from religious, political, and social obligations. And I would think that you shouldn't give up until it's plainly

and totally impossible. Like the Dostoyevskian image—when you see the wall you're suppose to put your hands at your sides and run your head into it over and over again. And finally I would warn them that democracy doesn't apply to the arts. Such a small percentage of people get everything and all the rest get virtually nothing. (p. 87)

*Many of your protagonists seem to be seeking escape from their lives. Joseph in **Farmer** laying his farm to rest. Nordstrom in **"The Man Who Gave Up His Name"** very deliberately disassembling his life. Lundgren in **Warlock** trying in his fatuous way to fill the vacuum. Is there some metaphor at work here through which the artist can then move on to something else himself?*

I think part of that is a literary device. You don't want to catch the man on the job, you want to catch him quitting the job, because when he's on the job all he gets to do is work. You have to think of him as escaping into life rather than from it. Somebody gives you the most banal and demeaning life in the way of making a livelihood, and if you abandon that, you're escaping—well, you'd have to be a nut case not to abandon it. It's that whole notion that Strang has of meaningful work. If you're an intelligent human being and you don't have meaningful work, then you'd better find it because your death, in those spooky terms, is stalking you every day. What those characters have in common, I suspect, is that they all want more abundance—mental heat, experience, jubilance. As a young man, Henry Miller saved my neck by offering these qualities.

And does that quest for abundance satisfy a similar need in the artist?

The closest I've come to a perception of it keys off that prime metaphor of Neruda's—the interminable artichoke, the unfolding, a process which never stops. What people forget is that this is not a goal-oriented operation. The Buddhists say the path itself is the way. It's a matter of not stopping your perceptions and of the courage involved in following them. It's why you have to think of Rilke as the most courageous poet, and certainly Rimbaud, potentially, in terms of the sheer daring of his consciousness. But that's an interesting question, because to tell you the truth, I've never thought about it. What you've done is created these people who fascinate you, created them perhaps because they'll try to answer some questions that you deeply need to be answered. Frankly, a writer should be a hero of consciousness. (pp. 88-9)

Jim Harrison and Jim Fergus, in an interview in The Paris Review, *No. 107, 1988, pp. 53-97.*

Reviews of Poetry

John Rohrkemper

Jim Harrison's newest volume [***The Theory and Practice of Rivers***] contains eleven poems, but its success or failure must rest on the long title poem which is almost thirty pages long and runs to nearly seven hundred lines. In the first stanza, Harrison declares: "to speak it clearly, / how the water goes / is how the earth is shaped," and, it might be added, how the poem is shaped. For Harrison is a nature poet in theory and practice. In this poem he explores, as he often has before, the perils, the transcendental beauty, and the rejuvenative powers of nature, but with a technique more fluid than ever before. We are inclined to accept the rather banal basic assumption that Harrison's rivers are symbolic of life because his method wonderfully conveys the flux and flow of real rivers. Ostensibly written for his niece who we see his brother burying alongside a river in the fifth stanza, the poem in fact is an exploration of the poet's life and career at midstream. It again posits a belief which informs most of Harrison's poetry and fiction: the world of nature offers life at the risk of death; the other world—the urban social world—offers only the seduction of death. The question remains: "What kind of magic, or rite of fertility / to transcend this shit-soaked stew?"

Early in the poem, Harrison declares that he is less interested in destinations than in "the shape of the voyage," a shape always moving and changing, as in this stanza in which the states of sleep and wakefulness flow together:

> Sitting on the bank, the water
> stares back so deeply you can hear
> it afterwards when you wish. It is the water
> of dreams, and for the nightwalker
> who can almost walk on the water,
> it is most of all the water of awakening,
> passing with the speed of life
> herself, drifting in circles in an eddy
> joining the current again
> as if the eddy were a few moments' sleep.

In contrast to the river, Harrison offers, throughout the poem, the sterile wasteland of urban life. In Los Angeles, for instance, the poet cannot find a river, "except the cement one behind the Sportsman's Lodge / on Ventura" where he feels his "high blood pressure like an electric tiara" around his head. To save himself from drowning in the "shit of skewed dreams and swallowed years," he must turn always again to the river. . . . (pp. 535-36)

Since his first volume of poems, twenty years ago, Harrison has been compared to another nature poet from Michigan, Theodore Roethke, and it is not surprising that in **"The Theory and Practice of Rivers"** we hear echoes of Roethke's poetry, particularly his late masterpiece, the "North American Sequence," in which Roethke acknowledged his "foolishness with God" in his recurring desire for "the unsinging fields where . . . light is stone." Roethke turned to redemptive nature and to the "pure serene of memory" which he found inspired there. Harrison's journey, in **"The Theory and Practice of Rivers,"** also takes him there, to the extraordinary and distinctively human place of memory: "The involuntary image that sweeps / into the mind, irresistable and without evident / cause as a dream or thunderstorm, / . . . / the longest journey taken in a split-second: / from there to now, without pause."

Still, Harrison is no mere imitator, of Roethke or anyone

else, and if we hear a kinship with Roethke in Harrison's voice we should celebrate it. In a time when so much of our poetry attempts to replicate the hum of commercial air conditioning and record the banalities of contemporary life, it is a pleasure to hear again in this volume the strong river voice of Jim Harrison. (p. 536)

John Rohrkemper, in a review of "The Theory and Practice of Rivers," in The Centennial Review, *Vol. 30, No. 4, Fall, 1986, pp. 535-36.*

James Grinnell

There is danger in trying to write about someone else's poetry when that poetry is about deep personal loss, about trying to make sense out of the accumulating years and all that implies. Writing about Jim Harrison's **The Theory & Practice of Rivers** is something like trying to prune away an overripe blossom; you may get the job done but you're likely to make a mess in the process. Already complete distillations, the poems need to be read, not talked about. And yet, one wants others to read them; that is why, after all, poetry is written.

As the complete title suggests, there are two groupings. The "Theory" section was written in the years following the 1979 death of Harrison's fifteen-year-old niece to whom the volume is dedicated, and presumably, the "New Poems" were written in the second half of the eighties decade. Yet, there is great continuity and unity throughout. The recurring images of northern Michigan supply part of this oneness: birds, bears, horses, hearth fires, wolves, and—most centrally—streams and rivers.

Often the poet's voice speaks to us from a figure waist-deep in a stream, in an eddy where a tributary from behind him pauses in a small maelstrom before joining, if you'll pardon the expression, the mainstream. While standing at this pivotal spot, half in and half out, he ponders the unfathomable. For example:

> This man in his over-remembered life
> needs to know the source of the ache
> which is an answer without question.

In this case, the speaker was halfway between sleep and wakefulness, but the effect is the same. . . .

The title poem accounts for well over one-third of the book's length, and at least that much of its substance. Within **"Theory and Practice"** is a recurring couplet, a kind of refrain that says, "the days are stacked against / what we think we are." Although there are multiple meanings in this key passage, I don't think Harrison intends the phrase, "stacked against us" to mean stacked as a deck of cards are stacked (except insofar as our deaths are inevitable) so much as that the days past are stacked as a cord of wood is stacked against an oncoming winter and/or that those days are stacked against any false images we might have or be tempted to have about ourselves.

And so one thinks, reading these poems, about many things, some profound, some shallow, about the past and its alluvial deposits which mix in the swirling present with the even greater flow of the future and its separate past.

One thinks of wet times and dry, about Raymond Carver's poem, "Where Water Comes Together with Other Water," about old man river who just keeps rolling along.

One thinks, finally, about one's own life. Therein lies the strength of [*The Theory and Practice of Rivers and New Poems.*]

> *James Grinnell, in a review of "The Theory and Practice of Rivers and New Poems," in* The Bloomsbury Review, *Vol. 10, No. 3, May-June, 1990, p. 27.*

Reviews of *Dalva*

Jonathan Yardley

Jim Harrison's literary career has lasted for two decades and produced 14 books, half of them fiction and half poetry, but his impressive productivity has brought him relatively little renown. This is unfortunate, for he is one of our better writers, but it is perhaps explicable by his persistent refusal to play the literary game. He has lived in places, primarily the West and Midwest, not greatly frequented by literary folk, and he has written about subjects—farmers, hunters, ordinary people—that are scarcely fashionable among the literati. Stubbornly, and to my view admirably, he has gone his own way, writing not to suit the bookish or commercial markets but to explore and expand his own themes and visions.

Like that of many other serious writers, his fiction is erratic. It has been most successful when he has resisted the temptation to flex his literary muscles—I think in particular of a quiet, lovely novel called *Farmer*—and least so when he has come forth as northern representative of the southern good-ol'-boy school. In *Dalva,* fortunately, his contemplative side is to the fore, and the result is a novel that, though uneven in certain respects, is moving, interesting and satisfying. It is his most ambitious book to date; he fulfills this ambition to a degree that, if there is any such thing as literary justice, should bring him a substantial and appreciative readership.

The title character was given her unusual name because before she was born her mother and father loved to dance to a recording of a samba called "Estrella Dalva": Portuguese for "Morning Star." Now she is 45, a woman whose great physical allure has not significantly dimmed and whose appetite for life is as insatiable as ever. She comes from a well-to-do Nebraska farming family, but "I had always worked because nothing whatsoever in my background had prepared me to act like a rich person, a notorious non-profession, the dregs of which everyone has witnessed in life, or in magazines and on television."

She is vigorous, independent, tough-minded—even ornery, if circumstances call for that—and in this sense she is of a piece with a number of male characters in Harrison's previous books. But she is a woman, and one haunted by the losses of her life: the deaths of her father and grandfather, the memory of her ardent love affair with her Sioux half-brother, Duane, and the disappearance of the son she had by him when she was a girl, a son she gave up for adoption immediately upon his birth. . . .

She is back in Nebraska for the first time in years, following an extended period of roaming in New York, Los Angeles and points in between, as well as "short, unsuccessful attempts to live in foreign countries—France, England, Mexico, Brazil." She has been lured back by her friend and occasional lover Michael, an alcoholic historian at Stanford who is desperate to attain tenure. He has learned of her family's papers, dating "from the end of the Civil War to the massacre at Wounded Knee in 1890," and he offers to help Dalva find her son in exchange for access to the papers. After some hesitation, she decides to accept the deal.

Michael's presence in the novel is at once amusing and distracting. He narrates the middle section—Dalva herself narrates the first and last—and the book runs a bit off course while he is at center stage. In part this is because his voice is so different from Dalva's that for a hundred pages we forget what she sounds like, and in part because his research into the Northridge family's past yields more for him (a discovery that "life was indeed larger and much more awesome than I presumed it to be") than it does for the reader. Obviously Harrison means to contrast the charming but self-destructive Michael with the doughtily self-reliant Northridges; the point is made, but it does little to enhance our understanding of Dalva, who is far and away the book's most arresting figure.

The other figure of particular interest is in the past. Michael's inquiry into the history of the Northridges focuses on Dalva's great-grandfather, J. W. Northridge, a strange and messianic man who, coming to the West as a settler, soon became a passionate supporter of the Indians. He was a "horticulturist and botanist, an agricultural missionary," who gave much of his adult life to an effort "to help the defeated native population adapt to an agrarian existence, but the native population [was] driven hither and yon by the government and . . . never had a good piece of land that [wasn't] removed from them instantly." He is posed in contrast to the soldiers who brutalized the Sioux: he is the white man's conscience. Yet he is also, such being the contradictory nature of white settlement, an unwitting exploiter as well, for the family that he establishes in the West gains its wealth by farming land that once belonged to the Indians.

This is interesting, and the Northridge journals that Harrison invents have a solid ring of authenticity, but in the end it is merely peripheral to the story of Dalva herself. Little of surpassing moment happens to her in the course of these pages, for *Dalva* is indeed a contemplative novel. Rather, what arouses our curiosity and sympathy is her quiet self-exploration—her meditations upon her family, her loves, her losses and gains, her sense of the world she inhabits. She is that rare fictional creation, a character whom the reader dearly would love to meet. That she is the creation of a man makes her all the more interesting, for Harrison took a great risk in attempting to put himself into the mind of a woman. As a man I am perhaps not the one to pass final judgment on this, but it seems to me that he has succeeded admirably.

Jonathan Yardley, "A Lonely Heart in the Heartland," in Book World—The Washington Post, March 6, 1988, p. 3.

Louise Erdrich

[*Dalva*, Jim Harrison's seventh novel], is a fascinating mixture of voices that cut through time and cross the barriers of culture and gender to achieve a work in chorus. The book feels monumental, though it is occasionally flawed. Perhaps the mark of a work that can rise above its problems is a certain generosity of spirit. *Dalva* is big-hearted, an unabashedly romantic love story, a grim chronicle of changing time, an elegantly crafted set of imaginary diaries, a work of humor and a unified lament.

It is also a novel driven by a satisfying plot, a device rather out of fashion, which clunks from time to time but is in the main intriguing. There is no putting aside the book until the time-bombs go off, the identities are revealed, and the skeletons almost literally tumble from closets. *Dalva* is also rich in language and characterization, exploiting the possibilities of its form.

Diaristic novels are nothing new, but few manage to appear authentic, or to incorporate so many various accounts realistically and naturally into the plot. The book begins in the voice of Dalva, a woman who is wildly emotional but courageous and decisive, romantic but level-headed, beautiful but careless, rich but socially conscious. She sounds too good to be true, but isn't. Her strengths are her flaws. Dalva has remained self-destructively attached to the ghost of her first lover, Duane, whose son she bore and gave up for adoption when she was 16. Her diary is meant to be read by her lost son. . . .

Almost immediately, Dalva seems to forget to whom she is speaking. If we read this diary strictly as a letter to an unknown child we might wonder why Dalva includes in the next few pages an account of her sister Ruth's sexual liaison with a priest. Fortunately we don't care, since Dalva's anecdotes are in and of themselves so compelling that the spell remains unbroken.

Of course, curiosity about Dalva's son or his mixed-blood father, Duane, an altogether melodramatic figure, is reason enough to keep reading. And beyond that, there is business to be resolved regarding another diary in the family. This document is a historical treasure written by Dalva's great-grandfather, an eccentric agriculturalist who attempted to aid the Oglala Sioux during the desperate years that preceded and followed their confinement to South Dakota reservations. This account, tantalizingly concealed by the family, is the focus of an ambitious professor, whose research diaries form the middle section of the book.

Harrison's account of the skullduggery and murder that changed Sioux (Lakota) culture, robbing Indians of treaty-protected sacred land, is unflinching and timely. In 1988, the Senate will consider an act to restore federally held Black Hills land to the Sioux, who have already stated that they will not forsake their claims to land, even for millions of dollars in recompense.

Although the narrative in *Dalva* is occasionally diverted by bookchat or description that runs on too long, the trove of information—advice on wine, horses, and observations on desert flora and fauna, birds, and the work of Edward Curtis—is interesting. This is less true for the virtual saturation of the text in descriptions of drinking. The characters in *Dalva* imbibe on any and every occasion.

Yet, finally, this is an emotional story, a complicated and lovely cat's cradle of a novel. Pull one string—the sentimentalism, a tendency to lecture—and one can dangle a straight piece of rope. But *Dalva* is a configuration that should not be over-analyzed, rather celebrated, suspended in its own beauty, a book to be met halfway and read with trust and exuberance.

Louise Erdrich, in a review of "Dalva," in Chicago Tribune—Books, March 20, 1988, p. 1.

"My only defense against the world [is] to build a sentence out of it."

—Jim Harrison, 1985

Michael C. M. Huey

On the surface, Jim Harrison's new novel, *Dalva,* is a collection of narratives written by a contemporary Western woman, her boyfriend (Michael), and her pioneering great-grandfather. Their stories sometimes enhance, sometimes interrupt each other, but each is told in a voice the reader quickly grows fond of. As different as the writers/speakers are, they have one thing in common: Writing offers them a quiet medium for confronting the boundaries of their lives.

The characters lead beautiful but chaotic lives, and despite their glib and bantering conversations they have a hard time expressing themselves orally. As writers they come into sharper focus, and one sees other ways in which they and their accounts are closely related.

Dalva's book records her feelings as she searches for a child she gave up when she was 16. At age 45, she listens to the ticking of her biological clock and longs for both the boy and his father, Duane, who disappeared during her pregnancy. When she fell in love with him, Duane was just a farmhand—now she knows he was also her half brother. While looking for the "others," Dalva is also looking for herself.

Her strength is gleaned from the Western plains—its certainty and mystery made manifest in her poise. In dealing with the misfortunes of her past she appeals to her sense of "the now," and instead of losing herself to what she cannot change, she seeks to heal what she can. Her memoir often returns to the present.

She invites Michael to her mother's Nebraska farm, which sits in the shadow of the cultured patriarchs who earlier retreated there. During his stay at the farm, Michael confronts a host of real and remembered persons—"ghosts" of spirit and flesh. A professor on sabbatical, he is researching the journals of Dalva's great-grandfather, J. W. Northridge. Michael narrates the second book. His writing is curiously casual.

The issues that preoccupied Northridge in the journals, on the other hand, are not superficial; and they concern Dalva still: coming to terms with the strife between the white man and the American Indian; finding, and then quickly losing, love; identifying with the "sacred landscape"; and leaving behind a written record.

Harrison has written novels, stories, and poems. His style is flexible and capable of great intimacy. Reading his new novel, *Dalva,* one feels that, like his characters, he is half writing and half telling it. (pp. 19-20)

Harrison deals with the eccentricities of Dalva and her family with tact and humor. Dalva drives around on the plains, dodging thunderstorms in a convertible that's missing its top. She keeps a folding cot stashed away in the Arizona mountains in case she should be near enough to hike in and spend the night. Her mother, a widow for several decades, finds solace each night by sitting on the porch swing and conversing with her late husband. Michael describes with pride how by age 16 he "knew the birthdates of all the kings and queens of England."

Ultimately, the quirkiness of these characters expresses their sanity. *Dalva* turns out to be a festival of life's poetry. (p. 20)

> *Michael C. M. Huey, "Writing and Telling in Harrison's Latest," in* The Christian Science Monitor, *June 13, 1988, pp. 19-20.*

Roz Kaveney

Harrison is known as the novelist of American regional male tough-mindedness; in [*Dalva,*] in both its strengths and in its truly awful weaknesses, he refuses any such straightforward labelling. The book centres on the life of Dalva, a part-Sioux beauty with a ranching background, a social conscience and a not especially secret sorrow; contrasted with her are Michael, an academic and her occasional lover, a sorry drunk with a slavering taste for firm young flesh, and her great-grandfather, Northridge, a missionary and botanist notorious on the frontier for his sympathy with the Sioux's resistance. This is a book about the bad conscience that any thinking Mid-Westerner has to have about the past, and about the reservations that any thinking male has about the models of masculinity associated with the West.

The interpolated fragments of Northridge's journal are the best thing in this scrappy book; the imitation of a Nineteenth Century style, echoing the Bible even at those moments when Northridge is furthest from faith, is exemplary, and the righteous anger at the pretexts under which modern America built itself on genocide both passionate and coherent. Much of the time indeed we are sufficiently

interested in the years over which Northridge wins the trust of the Sioux, and comes to respect and love their values, to resent being dragged away from them back to Dalva's search for her lost son, and Michael's struggle and tenure and alcoholism. Harrison is trying to rub our noses in the shallowness of what has replaced the Sioux's vibrant consciousness, but most of the time he tries too hard.

Michael spends too much of the novel being set up for mockery; he blunders around the countryside of Nebraska, getting drunk with elderly Scandinavians and getting beaten up for ogling local teenagers. Too much of the time, he is there as a foil for the impossibly perfect Dalva, whose mixed ancestry qualifies her to be heir and synthesis of American and Native American worlds. Perhaps because of his awareness of the difficulty of writing in a female voice, of his vulnerability to feminist critique, Harrison tries too hard with Dalva. . . .

Harrison is a fine writer of novellas; his problem as a novelist is that here at least he is not writing a novel—he is writing three novellas of varying quality and shuffling the pages together. The general effect is patchy—he has to rely on effects like the gaudy image of Dalva's dying lover riding his horse into the sea. Worse, in order to give the book the appearance of coherence, he builds an armature from whatever lengths of contemporary cliche he has lying around his stockroom; the lover Duane has, just has, to have been poisoned by Agent Orange, just as one of the major plot facilitations has to be Dalva's gay brother-in-law, who is being sensible about AIDS.

Nonetheless, Harrison is a fine writer; he has a good eye for both social occasion and the natural world, so that even as we are irritated by the manipulative presentation of Dalva as a demi-goddess, we are thrilling to the landscape we see so brightly through her eyes, or delighting in the complexities and embarrassments of her sexual and family life. The freedom with which the novel moves around in time is one of the areas in which we never feel Harrison to be clumsy or careless; the occasional shock of recognition with which we learn what we had never earlier understood about the purging of the plains is the product not only of the material but of Harrison's hard and honourable effort to make us see. In the end, [*Dalva*] is a powerful and inspiring book, even though on many pages we want to take the author and shake him for his sentimentalities and lazinesses.

> *Roz Kaveney, "An Eye for the Regional and Social," in* Books, London, *Vol. 3, No. 3, June, 1989, p. 16.*

John Clute

For some time now, Jim Harrison has been known as a singer of the psyche for the caring, outdoor American male. At once euphoric and testy, his novels have tended to feature men of the furthest Mid-West who affirm the world, who are wounded by it yet do not surrender. *Dalva,* whose central character is a life-celebrating woman therapist and rancher, might not seem a markedly convincing attempt to broaden this palette, but there are moments of insight and pleasure throughout its considerable length which make the effort worthwhile.

Harrison on writing fiction:

I like grit, I like love and death, I'm tired of irony. As we know from the Russians, a lot of good fiction is sentimental. I had this argument in Hollywood; I said, 'You guys out here in Glitzville don't realize that life is Dickensian.' Everywhere you look people are deeply totemistic without knowing it: they have their lucky objects and secret feelings from childhood. The trouble in New York is, urban novelists don't want to give people the dimensions they deserve. The novelist who refuses sentiment refuses the full spectrum of human behavior, and then he just dries up. Irony is always scratching your tired ass, whatever way you look at it. I would rather give full vent to all human loves and disappointments, and take a chance on being corny, than die a smartass.

Jim Harrison in a 1990 interview in Publisher's Weekly.

Just the same, Dalva Northridge, fourth of the Northridge line of Indian-loving ranchers and conservationists who dominate much of northern Nebraska, is at times rather difficult to swallow. In southern California she works as a therapist with damaged children, generally of Mexican ancestry; in Nebraska she shares, with her exuberant mother Naomi and her sister Ruth, doyenne-status over the upper reaches of the Niobrara River. As a lover she is flamboyant and generous; on horseback she is superb; she cooks well and knows wine; she drives her car like a man. She is rich.

It is her current lover, a grotesquely inadequate college professor, who moves *Dalva*'s slender plot into action by finagling an invitation to examine the family papers. This, and her longing to trace the child born of her teenage romance with a tortured young Indian, bring Dalva back to Nebraska, where the novel soon takes on a graver cast. The journals of the first Northridge cover the last decades of the nineteenth century, the period of the American government's campaign of genocide against the Sioux Indian Nation, and Harrison crafts these journals with great care. A botanist and minister without faith, the first Northridge is deeply believable in his frustration and anguish as the Indian world around him begins to die. It is only when Harrison allows Dalva and the other Northridge descendants an unquestioned moral hegemony over these papers, and the truths they embody, that the novel begins to demonstrate a paucity of invention. Harrison has always seemed to be a striking teller of tales who rarely chances on a story complex enough to justify his efforts; and *Dalva* is an example of this. In the absence of narrative structure that might legitimize Dalva's enthronement as Northridge's spiritual heir, Harrison falls back on a congested assertiveness, wheezily poetical, clearly uneasy.

But Dalva is a remarkably charismatic protagonist for a failed novel, and no failures of structure should blind one to Harrison's success in making one wish to believe in her.

Nor does Harrison ever insist on parallels between the death of the Indians last century and the death of the land now, though innumerable details attest to such parallels, and the extent to which *Dalva* is an elegy for the continent is clear, though unspoken.

> *John Clute, "Elegiac Heirs," in* The Times Literary Supplement, *No. 4486, March 24, 1990, p. 299.*

Reviews of *The Woman Lit By Fireflies*

Joseph Coates

For almost the last 20 years, Jim Harrison has been developing into one of our finest novelists, even though he declines to live what late 20th Century America considers to be a writer's life, which these days usually revolves around the universities with their MFA programs and teaching jobs.

Harrison remains essentially the same man who spent years "at manual labor as a block layer, a carpenter, a digger of well pits," as he indicated in a *Paris Review* interview a few years ago, [see excerpt above] and he believes "that rural, almost white-trash element . . . stood me in good stead as an artist, in the great variety of life it forced me into. . . ." He legitimately has the kind of resumé that writers used to display on the jackets of their first novels: Mr. So-and-So has worked as a bartender, bricklayer, census-taker and member of a magazine subscription crew.

As a result, Harrison writes the kind of bedrock Americana that Hemingway might have turned out if he had come home from the Great War, moved up in Michigan and stayed there, with occasional side trips to Key West, Idaho and other points west. He is a poet who wrote his first eccentric novel (*Wolf*) during the enforced ennui of being in traction after a hunting accident. And his combination of poetic attentiveness to detail with the exemplary commonplaceness of the life he has continued to lead gives his work a genuine mythopoeic quality that is rare, if not unique, among contemporary American writers.

Part of that power has to do with Harrison's feeling for the spirit of a land or place and his identification with the kind of people, Native Americans among others, who routinely believe that the natural world is contiguous with an unseen one. "Why are people," he has asked, "incapable of ascribing to the natural world the kind of mystery which they think they are somehow deserving of but have never reached? . . . For our purposes as artists, everything we are taught is false—everything."

Harrison and his characters believe in that continuity between the natural and the unseen solidly enough to mock the phony veneration of it among professional mystifiers and modern-day shamans—like the team of anthropologists who get involved with an Upper Peninsula layabout and fake Indian named Brown Dog, title character of the hilarious first novella among the three in Harrison's new book, *The Woman Lit By Fireflies,* which is in many ways a companion volume to the three epic tales in his *Legends of the Fall* (1979).

Brown Dog's amused, wary and edgy affair with the beautiful academic Shelley could be a paradigm for the quintessential Harrison man's relationship with the whole modern world. He meets her when she and "two fellows who wore beards and hundred-dollar tennis shoes" come into a bar looking for the old Chippewa herbalist with whom Brown Dog is drinking. Brown Dog appreciates her beauty while noting that she "is a fair-size girl by modern standards, but not in the Upper Peninsula. . . . In a cold climate a larger woman is favored by all except transplants from down below. . . . " If Brown Dog and his friends want beauty, they watch the "exercise programs on television as you don't get to see all that many girls in bathing suits in the U. P., what with summer being known locally as three months of bad sledding."

From Shelley and her friends, including an equally beautiful cousin named Tarah, Brown Dog gets sex, free psychoanalysis and "a book of poetry by a fruitcake Arab by the name of Gibran that I couldn't understand, so I gave it to a tourist girl and it made her horny as a toad."

From Brown Dog, Shelley gets sex plus limited and grudging access to a Chippewa burial mound that would make her name in anthropology of the Hillman period if only she could get him to pin down its location.

Brown Dog, who works as a salvage diver, meanwhile pursues his own disastrous project of raising an Indian corpse perfectly embalmed by the cold at the bottom of Lake Superior so he can sell it for $20,000 to a shady Chicago dealer in nautical artifacts.

Amid the farcical crescendo of these intertwining plots, something real and quite moving takes place. All three novellas are about midlife crises that are really unresolved adolescent problems, actions defining selfhood that are delayed for 20 or 30 years.

In **"Brown Dog,"** the 42-year-old title character finally catches up with Rose, the Chippewa girl who wanted nothing to do with him in high school. **"Sunset Limited,"** the second story, is "The Big Chill" played for keeps, as the former members of "a pacifist Wild Bunch" who did time in the late sixties for vandalizing a local draft board regroup in middle age to save the one of their number who has continued his radical activism and is now under sentence of death in a Mexican prison.

Gwen, the divorced rancher with an adopted Cambodian teenage daughter; Billy, who has been "destructively manipulated by his father" into becoming a brilliant and wealthy corporate lawyer; Patty, a vice-president at a Hollywood movie studio; and Sam, the mystical former Green Beret who has become a naturalist "studying coyotes in the mountain fastness of northern New Mexico," have all enacted the rite of passage from Yippiehood to some compromise with Yuppiehood." But each will have to sacrifice something to save Zip, the half-mad but essentially harmless revolutionary.

In the title story, the woman ultimately lit by fireflies is Clare, who would be 50 in another week but up till now has been "so fair-minded as to be frequently rendered immobile." She ends her immobility and makes her first real bid for independence during a drive across Iowa in an Audi 5000 as "her husband on the seat beside her punched in a tape called Tracking the Blues which contained no black music, but rather the witless drone of a weekly financial lecture sent from New York City."

At a rest stop she leaves a note to the police in a toilet stall saying "My husband has been abusing me. Do not believe anything he says," and escapes among endless rows of corn into freedom and an oncoming migraine. Improvising shelter according to half-learned survival lessons and reviewing her life, she recognizes some important truths and revives some old dreams during a long rainy night lit only by fireflies. The hardest truth of all is simple recognition of how much time it took her to begin living:

> The beauty and dread of time was that nothing was forgiven. Not a single minute. The years she had spent in consideration of this act were not only lost, irretrievable, but the recognition of the loss was so naive as to leave her breathless.

Brown Dog's retrieval of his sunken Indian, whom he dazedly comes to identify as his father, proves to be an effective metaphor for the psychic action of all three of these marvelous stories: something painful, unfaceable is brought to the surface of a half-lived life, and recognition of it allows life to resume being lived as it should be.

And the advice Brown Dog gets from "the chief . . . who spoke to me there in the ice-cold dark" of a stolen refrigerator truck, is after all pretty good:

> "Beware of women with forked tongues. Buy yourself a hat, because your hair is thinning on top. Don't rely on alcohol so much for good times . . . [D]on't come tromping into the Halls of Death, but live your life with light feet. Before I forget, bury me in the Forest where I belong, not with the fish."

(pp. 1, 4)

Joseph Coates, "Bedrock Americana," in Chicago Tribune, *August 12, 1990, pp. 1, 4.*

Judith Freeman

Having now published six novels, seven books of poetry and two collections of novellas, Jim Harrison has reached a wonderful place in his writing. There was always great strength to his novels and stories, a compelling sense of movement and character, prose marked by clarity and beautifully eclectic erudition, ribaldry and humor. Set in the West and Midwest, his stories feature rebel characters, outsiders living close to nature, dissolute in their appetite for alcohol and women but guided by a strong conscience and a penchant for honesty.

With his last two books, something else has graced the work, a tender, almost androgynous understanding of the human condition, which allows him to write convincingly in either a male or female voice, widening even further the range of his work.

This was most evident in *Dalva,* published two years ago—a novel written largely from the perspective of a woman who is searching for the son she gave up for adoption 20 years earlier. In *Dalva,* Harrison wrote: "Most women have intimations of a higher fidelity to the spirit and to a love beyond human weakness and imperfection." In a sense, it is to that higher fidelity that Harrison's books aspire—an enlarged and generous vision of a troubled but remarkably beautiful world, where a sensuous passion for life may be not just the best but the only revenge.

In each new work of Harrison's—and this includes his often hilarious and erudite magazine articles on food and travel—the same distinctively personal voice is present. He is unfailingly entertaining but he is much more—a haunting, gifted writer who can't be shoved into any category. Furthermore, his work seems to be getting stronger, and one wonders if he won't finally move beyond the small but passionate following he has built up over the years to receive the wider recognition he deserves.

The Woman Lit by Fireflies should help. It is—like an earlier work, *Legends of the Fall*—a collection of three novellas, each of which is written in a distinctly different voice. His basic power comes from his directness. (It's rebel voices we hear, not the timid squeaking of a dandified stylist.) One story is written from the perspective of a man (**"Brown Dog"**), one from that of a woman (**"The Woman Lit by Fireflies"**) and one, **"Sunset Limited,"** mixes the voices. . . .

[In **"The Woman Lit by Fireflies"**], Clare, a 50-year-old woman with two grown children, is driving down the freeway with her husband, who is listening to his weekly financial lecture on tape. A migraine is closing in on her. She is deeply unhappy. Quite recently, her closest friend Zilpha died, as did her beloved dog. Her husband is a dried-up, condescending boor.

When they pull over at a rest stop, Clare goes into the ladies room and leaves a note attached to the toilet stall: "I am in the small red car driving east. My husband has been abusing me. Do not believe anything he says. Call my daughter." She then heads out the door, scales a fence behind the Welcome Center and disappears into a cornfield, having chosen this moment to finally leave her husband.

Most of the novella takes place during the night Clare spends hiding in the cornfield, reviewing her life as she rests in the little cave of dried husks she's constructed: "It was the nest of a not very skilled animal, a temporary measure like a deer bed in high grass." She boils ditch water, nurses a fire, tests her small knowledge of survival and paces under the moon, remembering the accidents and events that have brought her to this point. (p. 1)

Harrison understands how women react to things, how they examine things up close. Women have an intimate relationship with nature: Clare sees not only a rabbit but the little engorged ticks in its ears. In this lovely novella, nature itself becomes the cocoon in which a woman enshrouds herself.

In **"Brown Dog,"** we hear another kind of voice, the voice of the Man of Nature and Appetite, the hard-drinking,

womanizing B. D., or Brown Dog—not quite Indian, not quite white, a failed Bible student who has found a corpse while scavenging shipwrecks:

> Just before dark at the bottom of the sea I found the Indian. It was an island sea called Lake Superior. The Indian, and he was a big one, was sitting there on a ledge of rock in about seventy feet of water. There was a frayed rope attached to his leg and I had to think the current had carried him from far deeper water.

Who could not go on? There's a feeling in this opening paragraph that a fascinating story is about to unfold, and it does, a hilarious, wild tale of how Brown Dog is hunted down for the murder of the drowned Indian whose body he retrieved from the lake in order to give him a proper burial, and how his girlfriend cons him into showing her some ancient Indian burial grounds. It's a wonderful, raucous tale that pokes a good deal of fun at otiose academics and law-enforcers.

"Sunset Limited" is arguably the least successful novella in the collection, and it's still a story you don't want to put down. According to *Smart* magazine, where it first appeared, the piece started out as a treatment for a screenplay. Maybe that's why it feels slightly staged, why the characters seem to act out roles. But the interesting part, in terms of this collection, is how it balances the other two stories. It has a larger plot and a bigger cast, presenting four old friends—Billy, Patricia, Sam and Gwen—all of whom were jailed briefly in the '60s for defacing a draft center. Now they are reunited, 20 years later, in an attempt to save Zip, a fifth friend from college, who has been thrown into a Mexican jail as a revolutionary. Ultimately the story is about making friends in one's youth in a way that's never duplicated in maturity, and what it means to see those friends after a long period of absence when everyone's life has changed and become more settled.

Harrison is a consummate story teller—truly one of those writers whose books are hard to put down. He creates appealingly vulnerable characters who inhabit palpably real worlds. His passion for food and wine, his affection for animals, connect us to the sensual. These three accomplished novellas are remarkably different. What they have in common is Harrison's deepest strength, a rich and nourishing sense of pleasure. (pp. 1, 5)

Judith Freeman, "Women's Intimations," in Los Angeles Times Book Review, *August 19, 1990, pp. 1, 5.*

Michiko Kakutani

Although they have almost nothing else in common, the three protagonists in Jim Harrison's new collection of novellas [*The Woman Lit by Fireflies,*] are all at turning points in their lives. Having somehow managed to reach middle age without too many bouts of introspection, they suddenly find themselves forced—by circumstance or self-doubt—to reassess their lives, and the reader is invited to listen in on their efforts to come to terms with the past. Each of the stories is told, with varying degrees of effectiveness, in a series of dreamlike flashbacks and flash-forwards that cut back and forth in time. Each is meant to convey the shape and texture of a life caught in medias res.

The title character of the first tale, **"Brown Dog,"** will be instantly familiar to readers of the author's earlier books. Brown Dog, or B. D., as he is called by some of his pals, is another one of those macho men of the wilderness who are fond of solitude, alcohol and women (in more or less that order). . . .

As he has done so many times before, Mr. Harrison conjures up life in the Michigan wilderness in strong, authoritative prose, and he proves equally adept at satirizing the ecological-minded yuppies who arrive there intent on writing dissertations about Indian burial mounds and local storytelling customs. It is B. D.'s luck to become involved with just such a yuppie—a sexy young woman named Shelley, who becomes his lover and later his legal guardian.

Shelley seduces B. D. to get him to show her some secret Indian burial grounds—or so he later suspects. Their affair, along with a series of other developments, will cause B. D. to start re-evaluating his attitudes toward family and tradition. Some of those developments (including the vindictive torching of a campsite, and the discovery of a frozen corpse in a lake) sound ridiculously melodramatic when described in isolation, but as depicted by Mr. Harrison they are smoothly knit into the narrative, lending it both suspense and a heightened sense of legend.

Similar elements conclude the second story, **"Sunset Limited,"** but unfortunately they turn a well-observed account of a "Big Chill"-like reunion into a moralistic fable about guilt and redemption, revolutionary zeal and liberal piety. This time, the dynamic between rich city slickers and nature-loving country folks is illustrated by two pairs of former 60's radicals.

On one hand, there are Patty, an uptight movie executive known for mixing risky pictures, and Billy, an enormously wealthy lawyer, who takes corporate planes back and forth to his favorite baseball games. Opposing them are Gwen, a plucky woman who ekes out a living on a small ranch in the Arizona desert after her divorce, and Sam, an eccentric naturalist who prefers the company of coyotes to that of human beings. Although the four have had little contact with one another since their draft-board-protest days, they are unexpectedly reunited when a fifth friend—an ardent revolutionary named Zip, who has stubbornly clung to his radical politics—is jailed in Mexico for outside agitation.

What happens when Patty, Billy, Gwen and Sam try to rescue Zip is not only tricked up in the worst movie-of-the-week-fashion, it is also delineated in such baldly manipulative terms that the reader is never able to forget that Mr. Harrison is there behind the scenes, pushing and pulling his characters hither and thither to illustrate his own theses.

The last novella in this volume, **"The Woman Lit by Fireflies,"** also suffers from an air of contrivance. Like the author's last novel, *Dalva,* it attempts to give a portrait of a middle-aged woman as she searches her past for clues to her identity. This time, the woman in question is a wealthy and genteel Midwesterner married to a horribly supercilious businessman.

As they're driving home after a visit with their daughter, Clare suddenly bolts: at a rest stop on the highway, she leaves a note in the ladies' room saying she is running away from an abusive husband, and she sets off alone through the cornfields. She spends the night in a farmer's field; she catches rainwater in an empty can, builds a fire with some twigs and roasts an ear of corn for dinner. In the process, she reviews her life and marriage.

Though there are some genuinely moving moments in Clare's reminiscences, much of her story feels hokey and sentimental. Her husband is described in such thoroughly obnoxious terms that the reader finds it difficult to understand why Clare has stayed with him all these years. Worse, Clare's own maudlin memories—which mainly have to do with her beloved dog, Sammy, who dies of cancer within weeks of her best friend, who also dies of cancer—sound more like someone's impersonation of a woman on the verge of a nervous breakdown than the thing itself.

In the end, Clare, like Mr. Harrison's other two protagonists, finds fulfillment and a measure of redemption in moving on to the next chapter of her life. The reader is ultimately less satisfied, finishing [*The Woman Lit by Fireflies*] with decidedly mixed feelings.

> *Michiko Kakutani, "The Shapes and Textures of 3 Lives," in* The New York Times, *August 28, 1990, p. C16.*

Arthur Krystal

Ever since the appearance of *Legends of the Fall,* the three novellas Jim Harrison published in 1979, his admirers have been awaiting another superlative work of fiction from this author. Three novels have followed that collection—*Warlock, Sundog, Dalva*—all in certain respects successful and in certain respects flawed. None has had the clarity, sureness of phrase and cumulative power of the novellas. Is it fair to hold an author accountable for the expectations raised by past work? Probably not. No writer should defer to the critics, expecially when they attach greatness to specific efforts. Instead, writers should, and most do, go their own way, letting the books fall where they may.

Harrison's latest offering lands, so we must assume, exactly where he intended it. Ten years after *Legends,* Harrison has put together another collection of novellas, [*The Woman Lit By Fireflies,*] which naturally is nothing like the earlier book, though it has the same enviable quality of gaining in depth as the novellas proceed. The first, **"Brown Dog,"** is an amiable romp in the Upper Peninsula of Michigan with B. D., an orphan of uncertain lineage, more than likely part Indian, who is usually involved in something a tad illegal. While salvaging artifacts from Lake Michigan, B. D. discovers the body of an Indian sitting bolt upright on the lake's floor. More remarkably, he

---

An excerpt from "The Woman Lit By Fireflies":

Something brushed against her leg and she bolted upright from the waist in alarm, with hundreds of yellow dots whirling about her and above the rabbit that paused beside the dim coals of the fire. The moon made shadows of the rabbit's twitching ears. She scrambled out of the green cave and stood, gulping air in fright, the rabbit shooting back into the thicket. She prayed that her heart would stop thumping, and looked up at the moon, and there were fireflies above her. As her heartbeat slowed she still did not want to look down at her body or touch herself because she thought she might be seven again. The fireflies were denser in some places above the thicket, blinking off and on, whirling toward each other so that if you blurred your eyes there were tracers, yellow lines of light everywhere. She thought, *Laurel should see this, Laurel would love this,* and then she was no longer seven.

Clare rebuilt the small fire to break the unearthly mood but the fireflies weren't disturbed. She walked up the path fifty feet, turned and looked back, hoping that she wouldn't see herself standing there. The countless thousands of fireflies stayed just outside and within and above the thicket. Quite suddenly she felt blessed, without thinking of whether or not she deserved it. She went back to her nest, lay down and wept for a few minutes, then watched a firefly hovering barely a foot above her head. She tried out *Now I lay me down to sleep* despite its failure to reassure. *All souls will be taken, including the souls of fireflies.*

---

finds a buyer for the corpse in Chicago; and the matter of transporting the Indian, though not for mercenary purposes, constitutes whatever straight plot the story has.

As the none-too-bright 42-year-old B. D. recounts his tribulations to his girlfriend, a 24-year-old anthropologist studying Indian gravesites, Harrison indulges in a lot of fanciful cussin' and raucous sexism. Sometimes it's funny; at other times it only distracts from the tale's serious themes: B. D.'s search for an identity and the exploitation of the North American Indians' heritage. Sex and shenanigans, however, are not the problem. Rather, it's the triteness of B. D.'s persona and the predictability of his relations with women. The picaresque is nothing if not obvious, and yet Harrison, by allowing B. D. to tell his story in his own bald, profane way, wears us out long before the story is done.

"Sunset Limited" is a slightly more believable, though slicker, tale of four middle-aged ex-radicals who join forces to spring a friend locked in a Mexican jail on a trumped-up murder charge. The prisoner, "Zip," is the only one of the group who has remained faithful to the politics they shared at the University of Colorado in the '60s. The others—two men and two women—have become a hot-shot West Coast lawyer, a movie executive, a marginal rancher and a wildlife biologist. Lingering resentments and passions surface as the four travel to Mexico, and Harrison valiantly attempts, in too short a space, a convincing portrait of their characters. Although there are some nice touches, especially in the depiction of the

rancher, Gwen, the overall plot is so facile that the people never really matter. Call it a "Big Chill" with high stakes.

The title novella, which first ran in the *New Yorker,* represents a departure for Harrison, although it's hardly a typical *New Yorker* story—unless, that is, one recalls Cheever's early short stories. Consider the bare outline: A middle-aged woman walks out on her husband and her life at a rest area somewhere along I-80 in Iowa. She walks into a cornfield, makes a rough nest for herself, and lies down to reflect. By now, midlife crisis applies equally well to women as to men, and in **"The Woman Lit by Fireflies"** Harrison adroitly manages to get inside a woman's mind—no small feat for the burly, rough-looking guy on the dust jacket. To quibble with his portrayal of Clare is only to note that sometimes she seems too good to be true: smart, sensitive, well-read, well-meaning, she's also unlucky enough in life to be interesting. Her memories and her imaginary conversations with her daughter reveal a life unequal to the spirit that endured it. As she lies amid the alien corn, Clare's character takes on deeper and deeper resonance, and Harrison's voice seems finally at home with its material.

However one feels about Harrison's evolution as a writer, he is always worth a look. He continues to write beautifully about a landscape where the horizon is not foreshortened by smog or construction, and where the population density is unimaginable to city dwellers. Like Thomas McGuane, Barry Hannah and Richard Ford, whose work is alike only in its dissimilarity to the slick fictions by and about urban professionals, Harrison has a narrative voice that fairly defies the reader to ignore it.

> *Arthur Krystal, "Jim Harrison: Three for the Road," in* Book World—The Washington Post, *September 2, 1990, p. 7.*

Robert Houston

A dozen years ago, Jim Harrison published a collection called **Legends of the Fall,** which may well be the best set of novellas to appear in this country during the last quarter-century. But if [**The Woman Lit By Fireflies**], which also consists of three novellas, doesn't move at the breakneck speed of its predecessor, there's no cause for Harrison fans to become alarmed. No writer who tries to extend his range, as good writers must, can allow himself to repeat effects only because they worked well the first time around. **The Woman Lit by Fireflies** demonstrates, in fact, a powerful talent in search of its limits.

All three novellas explore, to varying extents, a familiar Harrison theme, which is summed up in a line one of his characters remembers from a Robert Duncan poem: "Foremost we admire the outlaw / who has the strength of his own / lawfulness."

In the first story, a rogue tale called **"Brown Dog,"** the narrator is literally an outlaw, if only a petty one—a fellow called B. D., shortened from the nickname Brown Dog, which was given to him by his Chippewa neighbors in Michigan's Upper Peninsula when he was a boy. B. D. is the most vivid of the book's characters, a scoundrel and folk philosopher whose impeccably done voice swings from humor to pathos as easily as a blues song. B. D. may or may not be part Indian himself; he was raised as an orphan and has pretty much had to make himself up as he goes along. Now he's got involved with a graduate student in anthropology who's using their love affair to wangle out of him the location of an ancient Chippewa burial ground; B. D., however, refuses to comply, since he's sworn to the Chippewas that he won't. On the other hand, he's discovered an intact Indian corpse in the cold waters of Lake Superior and is trying to peddle it to a shady artifacts dealer, an endeavor for which the cops have branded him an outlaw.

What's truly lawful, then? For B. D. (and, one suspects, for Jim Harrison, too), lawfulness lies in respecting what's worth respect—in B. D.'s own terms.

The second novella, **"Sunset Limited,"** moves with a hard narrative drive that makes it the closest cousin to the stories in *Legends of the Fall.* It's a kind of political melodrama that brings four 60's radicals, now middle-aged and "reformed," back together to rescue their onetime leader from a Mexican jail. For a while, they become outlaws again to fight the greater outlaws in the still-intact System. In the process, they must come to terms with old betrayals, loves and ironies.

But while the issues the novella deals with are valid, the story itself is marred by a not terribly credible action-movie ending. One of the characters, for example, redeems a long-ago betrayal by staying behind to cover the others' escape from the C.I.A. In the process, he gets himself blown apart by an AK-47, but manages to die with "a trace of a smile" on his face. Actors, one imagines, are much more likely to die smiling than real people who are torn to shreds by assault rifles. Because it fails to live up to its promise, **"Sunset Limited"** is the weakest of the three stories.

The title novella, which originally appeared in a slightly different form in *The New Yorker,* represents the greatest departure from Mr. Harrison's earlier work. Its protagonist, a more subtle outlaw, is a wealthy, fiftyish suburban Detroit housewife who simply walks away from her husband at a freeway rest stop, leaving a note in the bathroom and making her escape over a fence out back. She spends the night in a cornfield, and in the course of that night— complete with flashbacks that allow the reader to understand how things have come to such a startling pass—she is reborn into a new, more authentic self.

At one level, **"The Woman Lit by Fireflies"** is very much a classic *New Yorker* story, with all the blessings and limitations that almost-genre has come to imply: an emphasis on subtext and character over immediacy and plot, a narrative that digresses as much as it progresses, an "interior" approach to storytelling. In the hands of lesser writers, the form can produce pretty bloodless fiction. But it is Mr. Harrison's characteristic energy—in the prose, in the individual moments—that ultimately saves the piece. Instead of being overwhelmed by the form, he has transcended it, created a tension with it.

As he did in his most recent novel, *Dalva,* Mr. Harrison proves again in **"The Woman Lit by Fireflies"** that he can convincingly handle a woman's point of view, once more giving the lie to the inane argument that a writer must stick only with his or her own sex, race, region and so on. A talented writer who understands the human heart, as Mr. Harrison does, understands essence; the rest of a character is accident, and can be learned.

Overall, then, while it is quite different from the earlier collection, *The Woman Lit by Fireflies* provides a sampler of just what Jim Harrison is up to *these* days. And though it's not without its flaws, what he's up to is still exciting and impressive.

> *Robert Houston, "Love for the Proper Outlaw," in* The New York Times Book Review, *September 16, 1990, p. 13.*

Moss Hart

1904-1961

(Also wrote under the pseudonym Robert Arnold Conrad) American playwright, scriptwriter, and autobiographer.

For related criticism, see the entry on George S. Kaufman in *CLC,* Vol. 38.

An important dramatist of the 1930s and 1940s, Hart is best known for his comedies written in collaboration with George S. Kaufman. Their most famous works, which are primarily valued as escapist entertainment, include *You Can't Take It with You,* a farce about a family of eccentric individualists, and *The Man Who Came to Dinner,* a comedy about an obnoxious guest who overstays his welcome. Some commentators have criticized Hart for failing to address the social issues of his times. Nevertheless, Hart is recognized for his contributions to the development of Broadway theater, and his works remain popular in revival.

Born in the Bronx, a borough of New York City, Hart was the son of English-born Jewish immigrants. As a child, he frequently attended performances at the Alhambra Theatre and the Bronx Opera House with his maternal aunt. After his father became unemployed, Hart dropped out of school at the age of twelve to help support his family. While working as an office boy for Augustus Pitou, a theatrical manager nicknamed "the King of the One Night Stands," Hart wrote *The Beloved Bandit,* a three-act comedy, under the pseudonym Robert Arnold Conrad. Produced by Pitou in 1923, *The Beloved Bandit* was a commercial and critical failure; one leading drama critic wrote a review of the opening night in Chicago in the form of an obituary for the play, and Pitou fired Hart after losing $45,000 on the production.

After losing his job, Hart returned to New York City and obtained a role in a revival of Eugene O'Neill's *The Emperor Jones.* For the next six years Hart spent his summers working as a social director of various resort camps in the Catskill Mountains and his winters directing amateur theater groups. During this period Hart wrote six plays, all of which were rejected by theater companies. Encouraged by favorable commentary about the humor in several scenes in his rejected plays, however, Hart began writing *Once in a Lifetime,* a comedy about a trio of vaudeville actors who go to Hollywood to give elocution lessons at the advent of the "talking" motion picture era. In 1929, producer Sam H. Harris agreed to stage *Once in a Lifetime* if Hart would revise the play with the well-established playwright George S. Kaufman. Hart and Kaufman worked together for several months, and in 1930 *Once in a Lifetime* opened on Broadway to widespread critical and popular acclaim. In *Once in a Lifetime,* Hart and Kaufman introduced the large casts, outrageous incidents, and humorous dialogue that became hallmarks of their come-

dies. Over the next decade, Hart and Kaufman collaborated on seven more plays.

You Can't Take It with You, for which Hart and Kaufman won a Pulitzer Prize, ran for over two years on Broadway and remains one of their most popular works. This play concerns the eccentric Sycamore family and their friends, whose assorted activities include ballet, candy making, the manufacture of fireworks, playwriting, and snake collecting. The contrast between the mad confusion of the Sycamore household and the staid behavior of Mr. and Mrs. Kirby, who are visiting to meet the family of their son's new fiancée, provides much raucous humor. In a review of a revival of *You Can't Take It with You,* Richard Watts, Jr. commented: "A time comes toward the end of the play when the authors apparently thought they should offer some kind of philosophical moral about the advantages of not toiling or spinning over the struggle for practical success, but their hearts were obviously not in it, and it's just as well. They weren't writing a preachment but a carefree comedy on some likeable people whose oddities are amusing and charming without being fantastically excessive, and they managed it delightfully."

Hart and Kaufman also wrote *The Man Who Came to*

Dinner, which many critics consider their most accomplished and enduring work. The authors loosely based the personality of the play's main character, Sheridan Whiteside, on that of their friend Alexander Woollcott, a famous writer and radio commentator who was noted for his mercurial temperament and caustic wit. During a visit to the Stanleys, a middle-class Ohio family, Whiteside slips on a patch of ice on the doorstep and is carried into their home. Because his injuries preclude moving him, Whiteside's doctor orders him to remain with the Stanleys for the next six weeks while recovering. Whiteside quickly takes over their home, receiving a constant stream of visitors and deliveries while harassing his hosts with petty demands and the threat of a lawsuit. Whiteside also meddles in the romantic relationship of his secretary and encourages the Stanley children to run away from home. In the final act, Whiteside is evicted by the Stanleys only to be dropped on the doorstep and returned, threatening an even larger lawsuit than before.

Other collaborations by Hart and Kaufman include *Merrily We Roll Along,* a serious play about a playwright who betrays his artistic integrity in his pursuit of material success. Hart's contributions to this work include the innovative arrangement of its episodes in reverse chronological order, beginning at the peak of the main character's career and moving backwards in time to his high school graduation. *The Fabulous Invalid,* which concerns the decline and restoration of the Alexandria, a fictional theater house, is considered the least successful of their collaborations. Their last work, *George Washington Slept Here,* a farce about a city dweller attempting to refurbish a country home, never achieved the popular or critical acclaim of their earlier comedies.

Fearing that he would only be remembered as half of a writing team, Hart ended his partnership with Kaufman after their collaboration on *George Washington Slept Here.* Hart's next play, *Lady in the Dark,* featured music by Ira Gershwin. This piece, which Hart directed, portrays a woman undergoing psychoanalysis. Praised particularly for its skillful transition between scenes of fantasy and reality, *Lady in the Dark* became Hart's most popular individual effort. During the next decade, Hart wrote and directed four more plays. His 1943 production of *Winged Victory,* a patriotic play which follows the training of bomber crew, included several hundred members of the armed forces. His other works include *Christopher Blake,* which concerns the effects of divorce on a young boy, and *Light Up the Sky,* a light-hearted comedy about the theater. His last play, *The Climate of Eden,* is an adaption of Edgar Mittelhölzer's novel *Shadows Move among Them.* Although Hart considered this his "most interesting" work, the play was poorly received by critics and audiences.

In addition to stage plays, Hart wrote several screenplays, including the script for *Gentleman's Agreement,* a film on anti-Semitism that was nominated for an Academy Award in 1947. Hart received a Tony Award in 1957 for his direction of Alan Jay Lerner's *My Fair Lady,* a musical adaption of George Bernard Shaw's *Pygmalion.* Shortly before his death, Hart completed *Act One: An Autobiography,* a memoir of his early years that has been praised for its honesty and insight into the theater. A critic for the *Saturday Review* called the book "a distinguished personal history," while Hollis Alpert praised *Act One* as "the most engrossing autobiography I have yet to read by an important figure of the theatre."

(See also *Contemporary Authors,* Vols. 89-92, Vol. 109; and *Dictionary of Literary Biography,* Vol. 7.)

PRINCIPAL WORKS

PLAYS

The Beloved Bandit [as Robert Arnold Conrad] 1923; also produced as *The Hold-Up Man,* 1923
Jonica [with Dorothy Heyward] 1930
Once in a Lifetime [with George S. Kaufman] 1930
Face the Music [with Irving Berlin] 1932
As Thousands Cheer [with Irving Berlin] 1933
Merrily We Roll Along [with George S. Kaufman] 1934
Jubilee [with Cole Porter] 1935
You Can't Take It with You [with George S. Kaufman] 1936
I'd Rather Be Right [with George S. Kaufman] 1937
The Fabulous Invalid [with George S. Kaufman] 1938
Sing Out the News 1938
The American Way [with George S. Kaufman] 1939
The Man Who Came to Dinner [with George S. Kaufman] 1939
George Washington Slept Here [with George S. Kaufman] 1940
Lady in the Dark 1941
Winged Victory 1943
Christopher Blake 1946
Inside U.S.A. 1948
Light Up the Sky 1948
The Climate of Eden [adaptor; from the novel *Shadows Move among Them* by Edgar Mittelhölzer] 1952

OTHER

Gentleman's Agreement (screenplay) 1947
The Eddy Duchin Story (screenplay) 1954
A Star Is Born (screenplay) 1954
Prince of Players (screenplay) 1955
Act One: An Autobiography 1959

Frank Hurburt O'Hara

[If] we are looking for a moral in a farce, for a real spiritual boost wrapped up in the cellophane of a jolly philosophy, we might as well turn at once to that Pulitzer prize-winner . . . , *You Can't Take It With You.* This is indeed sentimental comedy gone farce, and it is easy to understand the concern for the state of the nation's drama which was aroused in the minds of some persons when the sages of Columbia awarded the prize to Moss Hart and George S. Kaufman for their dramatization of a national Urge To Be Cheerful. For this is hokum, timed to the theatrical minute, boldly and boisterously executed, and—what seems worst of all to the objectors—spotted with moments of apparent sincerity and even "feeling." No evident shafts of satire in this, as in *Susan and God,* Rachel Crothers' comedy on the same general theme, or in the journalistic *tours de force* which the Kaufman-Hart team manages in ***The Man Who Came to Dinner.***

For indeed ***You Can't Take It With You*** is patently absurd and hilariously preposterous. It is the story of a household which couldn't possibly be like that. And yet to many in any audience it is more persuasive than most farces. Persuasive because, without staying its fierce tempo, it makes them feel that they are getting glimpses into the inner nature of the characters. Characterization? Of course not, really; yet the members of this wild household do seem to reveal themselves, so deft is the playwrights' sketching of them, until there comes a kind of recitative spell in the midst of hilarities when the onlooker is made to feel that after all these people are a little wistful as well as absurd. In this peculiar effect the work of Hart and Kaufman illustrates a marked tendency to be seen in a number of farces of today—the tendency to sink a shaft, as it were (geographically toward the end of the second act) into a deeper level of character interest. The mirth stands aside for a moment and something almost poignant, too swift for tears and too sentimental for intellectualizing, comes to the fore. This nuance of seriousness is the reverse of tragedy's old use of the comic. The older writers of tragedy protected the sensibilities of the audience by giving strained nerves a chance to relax in laughter; the new writers of farce give hilarity a chance to relax in an instant's quiet perception. Then the audience can laugh again with renewed gusto, having been given a sort of second breath for merriment. An extra quality of persuasiveness in performances of this play undoubtedly came from actors seasoned in the timing of these nuances as well as in the pacing of straight farce. (pp. 224-26)

The philosophy of ***You Can't Take It With You*** is stated plainly in the title; a "thesis," really, if so dignified a term may be applied to an idea which is as much mood as thought. It was Grandpa's idea.

> . . . . Thirty-five years ago he just quit business one day. He started up to his office in the elevator and came right down. He just stopped. He could have been a rich man, but he said it took too much time. So for thirty-five years he's just collected snakes and gone to circuses and commencements.

The whole family are that way. They do the things they hanker to do, instead of just hankering. Their side lines are their main lines. When we have met the family we practically know the story, for the story is just the family going on being themselves in all sorts of strange juxtapositions. The family (and therefore the play) consists of: Penelope Vanderhof Sycamore, known as "Penny," a comfortable, round little woman in her fifties who writes plays "because eight years ago a typewriter was delivered here by mistake"; Paul Sycamore, Penny's husband, who maintains a youthful air well into middle life and manufactures fireworks in the basement; Essie, daughter of the Sycamores, now in her late twenties, who dances for the love of it but

makes candy for sale as a side line; Ed Carmichael, Essie's husband, who composes for the xylophone and sells Essie's candy—each box with a neatly printed quotation from Trotsky or someone else who has caught Ed's fancy; Alice, young, fresh, and lovely, who works down town and has a slightly practical air which does not make her any less charmingly a member of the family; Rheba, the colored servant, and her friend, Donald, who is always at hand to assist with the work, although not for pay because he is on relief; Mr. De Pinna, serious, bald-headed assistant in the manufacture of the fireworks. And Grandpa. Grandpa is about seventy-five if one insists upon being statistical, but he is youthful and wiry and exuberantly at peace with the world. The household revolves about Grandpa as naturally as spokes about a hub. On the other hand, the plot, such as it is, revolves around Alice because Alice is interested in a young man who is interested in her—Anthony Kirby, vice-president of Kirby and Company—the boss's son. "Just like the movies." Tony comes to see her and meets the family; and he's shocked in spite of all her warnings, but he's pleasantly shocked. However, Alice refuses to let him marry into such a "cock-eyed" family.

> . . . I'd want *you,* and everything about you, everything about *me,* to be—one. I couldn't start out with a part of me that you didn't share, and a part of you that I didn't share. Unless we were all one—you, and *your* mother and father—I'd be miserable. And they can never be, Tony—I know it. They couldn't be.

Just by way of proof, she invites Tony's mother and father to dinner. They come, but come a night early, when the house is at its maddest: a slightly disheveled actress, cordial but rather drunk, is asleep on the living-room couch; a Russian ballet dancer who wrestles as a side line—with the guests—assists in doing the honors; each member of the family is doing his own particular stunt—typing, dancing, making fireworks, or caring for snakes, as the case may be. Not a successful evening, and climaxed by sudden arrival of the police. They have come to search the house, and they don't like what they find. So the entire party lands in jail. Why? Well, Ed has taken to printing subversive sentiments on the candy cards; it isn't that he cares about the sentiments, but he likes to print things. After their release from jail next day, the senior Kirby comes back to call. The Grand Duchess Olga Katrina is already there; the Grand Duchess has "not had a good meal since the revolution" and she has come with the wrestler-dancer Kolenkhov for dinner, forgetting her job in Child's for the ecstatic pleasure of making blintzes for the family. Grandpa and Mr. Kirby exchange philosophies in the interest of Tony's and Alice's future happiness. Mr. Kirby wants to know what he is expected to do; live the way Grandpa and the rest of them do—doing nothing?

> GRANDPA. Well, I have a lot of fun. Time enough for everything—read, talk, visit the zoo now and then, practice my darts, even have time to notice when spring comes around. Don't see anybody I don't want to, don't have six hours of things I *have* to do every day before I get *one* hour to do what I like in—and I haven't taken

bicarbonate of soda in thirty-five years. What's the matter with that?

Mr. Kirby thinks it is a ridiculous life; he is not aware of missing anything in his own life; moreover, Grandpa's philosophy is dangerous, "it's un-American." And that's why Mr. Kirby is opposed to this marriage. But his opposition does not restrain Tony's appearing in order to restrain Alice's disappearing. And the end of the matter is that they all have dinner together with stacks of blintzes for all.

If the main plot is skimpy, the stunts and byways of stage business and dialogue do a generous job of feathering out. There is the case of Grandpa and the federal agent who comes to collect his back income tax which Grandpa has not paid since 1914. Grandpa does not intend to pay it; anyone who wants to can pay for Congress and the President, but not Grandpa; except maybe seventy-five dollars. Grandpa's attitude is all right with us, and we do not object when the tax-collector has to shout over xylophone music, dodge snakes, and jump at the blast of a new bomb firecracker banging off in the cellar beneath him. Indeed, when there is a chance of any lag in interest in *You Can't Take It With You*, there are always the firecrackers to go off, solo or ensemble. All in all, a mad family; and a mad idea to try to make a play of such complete nonsense. To accomplish it, the playwrights have managed to stir up all the ingredients of farce in this household, and flavor the mixture with an essence of sentiment; so that, strange as it seems afterward, in every audience some heads beside Grandpa's and the family's are bowing mentally when this family and their assorted guests sit down just before the blintzes are brought in and the old gent taps on his plate for silence before he begins his friendly and respectful remarks to make the tag of the play.

> Well, Sir, here we are again. We want to say thanks once more for everything You've done for us. Things seem to be going along fine. Alice is going to marry Tony, and it looks as if they're going to be very happy. Of course the fireworks blew up, but that was Mr. De Pinna's fault, not Yours. We've all got our health and as far as anything else is concerned, we'll leave it to You. Thank You.

Almost all the way through this farce, as through other farces, we laugh. That's what we came for. Not to solve any of our problems, but merely to expose ourselves to the release of laughter. Indeed, if we think of the theater at all in terms of our own problems, it is usually only to pick one of these rollicking plays and decide to "laugh it off"; although what sometimes happens is that we are able to laugh ourselves into a sense of proportions. The absurdities upon the stage serve as a sort of social safety valve, an antitoxin which we can receive painlessly and more or less unconsciously.

Most plays in these days—comedies and melodramas as well as tragedies—depict the social order as mowing us down or propping us up, and emphasize the kind and variety of this new Fate with which we have to deal. Farces, on the other hand, have a way of depicting the funny pigmy man as taking his Fate too seriously. They restore a sense of human importance, not by dwelling upon the roots of character motivation but by showing us how many circumstances are not important. We spend an evening with these plainly preposterous Vanderhofs, watching them on the stage daring hard-masked Fate and getting away with it, and we come out of the theater feeling of course that the Vanderhofs are burlesquing life, but feeling also that maybe we are bungling life a bit ourselves. (pp. 227-33)

> *Frank Hurburt O'Hara, "Farce with a Purpose," in his* Today in American Drama, *The University of Chicago Press, 1939, pp. 190-234.*

Brooks Atkinson

[Moss Hart and George S. Kaufman] have contributed something distinctive to American drama. For fantastic wit and humor, compact in form, swift in tempo, it would be hard to improve upon *Once in a Lifetime* of 1930, *You Can't Take It with You* of 1936 and *The Man Who Came to Dinner* of 1939. All those comedies added to the gaiety of the nation during a period, incidentally, when gaiety was not unconfined and the theatre was declining in scope and originality. *You Can't Take It with You* won the Pulitzer Prize.

None of the other plays is in their best style. Although I enjoyed *Merrily We Roll Along* in 1934 and *The American Way* in 1939, the one study of character with moral overtones and the other study of American democracy with moral overtones lack the gusto of the three memorable works. As pieces of theatrical showmanship they were as vivid as any of the others, but as writing they are guarded and their values are acquired. *The Fabulous Invalid* . . . can hardly be separated from Donald Oenslager's brilliantly naturalistic scenery and a long sequence of nostalgic theatrical posters; nor . . . [can] the script of *I'd Rather Be Right* . . . be separated from the Rogers and Hart score and lyrics. As for *George Washington Slept Here*, which was a box-office success, it seems to me no more than a dutiful chore in playwriting and it does not convey the real enjoyment the authors take in their country estates. But [*Once in a Lifetime, You Can't Take It with You,* and *The Man Who Came to Dinner*] bustle and flare with a kind of comedy that is peculiarly American. No one can write a complete history of the nineteen thirties without reckoning with them.

Probably Mr. Kaufman and Mr. Hart have written brilliantly together because they like each other. Ever since they first met in 1930 in the office of the late Sam H. Harris to work on Mr. Hart's script of *Once in a Lifetime* they have gotten on famously. They have much in common in their point of view toward Broadway and the dim world that lies beyond, and they complement each other in other respects. Mr. Kaufman, who was born in 1889, is the older by fifteen years. He was operating in the theatre with immense success and acclaim while Mr. Hart was enviously staring at Broadway from the outside. Before 1930 Mr. Kaufman had written, among other works, *Merton of the Movies* and *Beggar on Horseback* with Marc Connelly and *The Royal Family* with Edna Ferber. Working without a collaborator, he had also written *The Butter and Egg Man,* which was as hilarious as anything that bears his name, and the book of *The Cocoanuts* for the Marx Brothers, who were just then beginning to destroy the logic and sobriety of the Western world.

Meanwhile, Mr. Hart was going through a bedraggled apprenticeship. While employed as secretary to the late Augustus Pitou, the Erlanger booking agent, he wrote *The Hold-Up Man,* which succeeded in failing obscurely in Chicago in 1923. He acted with a group of amateurs. He directed amateur groups and staged shows in summer hotels and camps. In the Spring of 1930 *Jonica,* a musical comedy he had written with Dorothy Heyward, appeared on Broadway to reviews that were not unappreciative. A serious drama, entitled *No Retreat,* was staged that Summer by the Hampton Players on Long Island before a society audience that stole all the press notices, although some Broadway managers saw it and expressed interest in the author's abilities. Shortly afterward Mr. Hart submitted the script of *Once in a Lifetime* to six managers, all of whom accepted it. He sold it to Mr. Harris on the promise that Mr. Kaufman would work on it as collaborator. That was the beginning of their association. (pp. ix-xi)

Apart from [Hart's] collaborations with Mr. Kaufman he has written the scripts of several illustrious musical shows—*Face the Music* and *As Thousands Cheer* with Irving Berlin, *Jubilee* with a score by Cole Porter and *Lady in the Dark* which is a co-ordinated musical play as contrasted with the routine form of musical show. A part of Mr. Hart's spontaneity derives from the fact that he is artistically ambitious.

No one knows exactly what each man contributes to their collaborations. People who know both of them might hastily conclude that Mr. Kaufman supplies the discipline and Mr. Hart the spirit. Indeed, I fancy there is more of Mr. Hart than of Mr. Kaufman in the tone of *You Can't Take It with You,* which is the most sympathetic of their comedies. Although Mr. Hart wrote the original script of *Once in a Lifetime* under that title, I confess I can perceive no individual traits in their whirling satire of Hollywood, unless it is the acid character of Lawrence Vail that Mr. Kaufman played in the original production; and I cannot distinguish individual notes in *The Man Who Came to Dinner,* which Mr. Kaufman and Mr. Hart wrote about the cyclonic personality of their crony, Alexander Woollcott. The truth seems to be that these plays are genuine collaborations. They are not jobs of assembly, but a blending of ideas and phrases, brought to a furious boil.

Mr. Kaufman and Mr. Hart collaborate somewhat as follows: They first discuss various ideas casually, sometimes letting an idea develop at random for several months before they begin to take it seriously. When they feel that an idea has become sufficiently tangible, they go to work on a daily schedule in some place where they can be free from interruption. Even New York has served that purpose on one occasion. At first they continue talking for two or three weeks, hoping to enlarge and clarify the idea and to run up stray notions into fantastification. The whole thing begins to change proportion and direction once they get both heads working at it systematically. When the details

of character and narrative have begun to take shape, Mr. Kaufman and Mr. Hart start putting them on paper, Mr. Kaufman usually sitting at the typewriter, Mr. Hart roaming the house and hoping for interruptions. An orderly person who likes to attack everything on plan, Mr. Kaufman feels happy if they produce four pages a day. They are likely to overwrite the first draft, confident that it is easier to improve a play by cutting than by expanding. Working after this general fashion, *You Can't Take It with You* was finished in five weeks, but *The Man Who Came to Dinner* took six months.

By the time the play is finished Mr. Kaufman and Mr. Hart know what actors they need and usually they have an opening date set for the next October. . . . Both gentlemen suffer acutely on opening nights, but happily in individual fashion, and both hate opening-night audiences. Since the opening-night audiences usually scream with neurotic pleasure Mr. Kaufman's and Mr. Hart's antipathy toward them may be dismissed as a temperamental phobia. There are no other authors held in higher esteem by the bizarre assembly of New York people who regard opening-night performances as essential to their prestige in the community.

Even the best plays [of Kaufman and Hart] are not notable for plot or theme, and you will search them in vain for passionate adventures of the heart. Mr. Kaufman and Mr. Hart are not poetic writers. The plots serve as frames for the fireworks; the romantic scenes are dutiful gestures toward conventions of the stage. But the fury of the gags, the bitterness and speed of the attacks upon stupidity, the loudness of the humor, the precision of the phrasing are remarkable in the field of popular comedy. Mr. Kaufman and Mr. Hart have made their best plays out of dynamite. (pp. xiv-xvi)

> *Brooks Atkinson, in an introduction to* Six Plays by Kaufman and Hart, *by George S. Kaufman and Moss Hart, The Modern Library, 1942, pp. ix-xvi.*

Joseph Wood Krutch

Moss Hart's *Light Up the Sky* is a great deal more entertaining than I, for one, expected it to be. The preliminary hoopla—of which there was considerable—centered around its allegedly daring topicality and the promise that it would give so much inside dope on show business that only the initiated would be able to know what it was all about. There were hot tips in the gossip columns to the effect that Billy Rose would—and then that he would not—sue for libel. The public was, by implication, invited to guess whose dirty linen was being washed in this scene or that and promised a generally rip-roaring time. Now topicality is one of the curses which lie heavily upon nearly every branch of contemporary letters, from the magazines full of "profiles" to the novels full of low-downs on the true inwardness of this racket or the other, and the prospect of a super Gridiron Club skit in place of a play was a bit depressing.

One of the reasons why *Light Up the Sky* turns out to be genuinely entertaining is, paradoxically, that it does not try to be too funny. It is a farce and at times a rather extravagant one, but it knows, as a good many recent farces have not known, where to stop. Ever since Hart, Kaufman, and others discovered, almost a generation ago, that it was possible to make farce faster and more extravagant than it had ever been before, the tendency has been to try to make a good thing better, although the point at which speed, noise, and improbability began to pay diminishing returns was reached a good while ago. I do not know who discovered the word "fabulous" as a convenient term to be used whenever it became desirable to suggest that wildly improbable triviality was really poetic imagination in its most truly sophisticated form, but the word has done a lot of harm. Nevertheless, in the present play Mr. Hart's "fabulous" actress, his "fabulous" director, and his "fabulous" backer are kept within the generous limits of acceptable farce. I was a little nervous when it developed that the Shriners were having a jamboree in the hotel where the action takes place. That is precisely the sort of noisy irrelevance which has helped ruin a good many recent extravaganzas, but even in this dangerous case Mr. Hart exhibits a refreshing temperance.

The plot turns around an earnest new playwright possibly suggested by Tennessee Williams but not, it would appear, actually modeled on him. His somewhat obscure script is taken up with unrestrained enthusiasm by an all too utter director, by an easily recognizable wonder-boy of the amusement world, and by a "glamorous" actress whose mannerisms strongly resemble those of a very successful star. When the play flops at the Boston try-out, they all run for cover, snarling as they go, while the playwright, understandably enough, renounces the profession he had once had some illusions about. Then, instead of falling back on the *Butter-and-Egg Man* or ***Once in a Lifetime*** conclusion—which, by the way, merely implies that success is as meaningless as failure—Mr. Hart arranges, more probably as well as more significantly, that the critics shall find some promise in the play and that everybody shall get together again to see if rewriting can salvage the possibilities inherent in the author's script. Obviously ***Light Up the Sky*** is intended to say something, and that something seems to be that while show business necessarily involves the antics of maniacal egocentrics who, their temperaments being what they are, can hardly be expected to know when they mean what they say, the fact nevertheless remains that even they function most successfully when they manage occasionally to deviate into sense. (p. 674)

> *Joseph Wood Krutch, in a review of "Light Up the Sky," in* The Nation, *New York, Vol. 167, No. 24, December 11, 1948, pp. 674-75.*

George Jean Nathan

If a reviewer were to write of Mr. Hart as in [***Light Up the Sky,*** a] road-revised and toned-down play he has written of a number of painly recognizable New York theatre people, that worthy, judging by his past performances, would so seethe with indignation that you could boil a fifty-pound salmon on him. I speak from intimate personal acquaintance with his ire, which has erupted with such gusto on the one or two occasions when I have timidly ventured

to reflect on the magnitude of his genius that one would have thought I had defied Jehovah Himself. Yet what I wrote of him was the purest Rouennaise sauce compared with what he sees fit to remark about his well-known and, despite his cagey disclaimers, scarcely disguised characters, some of whom, report has it, even figure among his buddies.

As a playwright, Mr. Hart of course has a perfect right to do what he has done. Playwrights have been doing much the same thing ever since Aristophanes more than twenty-three centuries ago in *The Frogs* did to Euripides and others what shouldn't happen to a dog. Nor is the questionable taste which he displays properly a consideration of criticism, since questionable taste has also been displayed in similar directions by such creditable dramatists as Wycherley and Sheridan, among various others. Yet further, the thinness of disguise practised by him is no more criticizable, since it is not any thinner than that of Shaw in his ridicule of his fellow-critics in *Fanny's First Play*. The difference, however, is the difference between the banana peel and the broken leg. Where the eminent others made us laugh at their characters' slips and prattfalls, Hart—as did Leo Trevor in *Dr. Johnson*—bids us laugh at his characters' fractured limbs. And the worst of it—human nature being as despicable as it is—is that we do.

Our apology in such a situation is that, since he does not really call his characters by name, we can get away with our amusement and still preserve the punctilio. But we are charlatans. . . . When Hart sticks his finger into one of his victims' eyes the eye is injured and drips blood, yet, like jitney Neros, we nevertheless every now and then bounderishly chuckle. It is something of a commentary on both Hart and us, and also very probably on changed times and changed morals. But down at bottom, pain or no pain, it is the nasty quirk in all our natures that impels us willy-nilly to find amusement in others' discomfiture, even indeed when those others are our friends. Lamentable as it may be, let a friend sit on and wreck his hat, or rip his breeches, or tumble on his rear, or have a waiter spill hot soup on him, or step on a pasture muffin, or be besmirched by a dog, and our mirth knows small bounds. Similarly, so odious are we, that let a crony get the barber's itch, or swell from poison ivy, or deposit his corpus on a tack, or be sprayed by a polecat, and one would think the show was provided by Bobby Clark. And it is much the same if our friend at his age contracts mumps or the measles, loses his money on bogus gold-mine stocks, is vouchsafed a Mickey Finn, or is caught *in flagrante delicto* with a lady of color. There is apparently nothing that can be done about it. We are lice.

To give him his due, Hart doubtless appreciates all this just as well as we ourselves do and I, for one, though I do not commend him for doing what he has done, on the other hand can not without hypocrisy condemn him for doing it. So I stick to business and fairly report that his play has some very funny stuff in it along with its forced and spurious, and that I guffawed at much of it like any other cad.

What the exhibit in essence amounts to is a comic valentine of the show business and, like a comic valentine, it is crude and pretty vulgar. Its thread of story is simply a variant of the many plays in which a fraternal group of people turn acrimonious under catastrophe of one kind or another and, when the sun again shines, return to cheer and goodwill. Hart's former collaborator, George Kaufman, wrote a basically not altogether dissimilar and better play all of twenty-three years ago in *The Butter and Egg Man,* to which at several points this later specimen bears a resemblance. But, as I have said, the current paraphrase has some high and saucy sport in it, and most of the performances, notably those of Phyllis Povah as the stage mother, Audrey Christie as the brassy wife of the producer, Glenn Anders as the epicene director, Virginia Field as the temperamental star, and Barry Nelson as the idealistic novice playwright, are all they should be.

The underlying weakness of the play is its author's inability to reinforce his often malicious comment on his characters with the wit that might shade malice into sharp critical appraisal. His humor, furthermore, is uneven and teeters between some genuinely hilarious barbs and such lines as "She'll develop a cough that'll make Camille's sound like hay fever." And his characters range from the freshly observed and freshly drawn to, however factually portrayed, the long familiar and stencilled star actress with her tantrums and miscellaneous use of "darling," her dumb, stuffy businessman husband, and the elderly playwright who has gone through the mill and lounges about the stage with an inner smile at the other characters' perturbations. (pp. 181-84)

> *George Jean Nathan, in a review of "Light Up the Sky," in* The Theatre Book of the Year, *1948-1949, pp. 181-84.*

George Jean Nathan

Moss Hart's dramatization of Edgar Mittelhölzer's novel, *Shadows Move Among Them,* retitled **The Climate of Eden,** brings the central character of Ugo Betti's *The Gambler* out of Italy and into the jungle of British Guiana, along with his full cargo of psychopathic aches and alarms. As in the earlier play, he is tormented by the recollection of a savagely hated wife, in this case not murdered through his apparent connivance but the victim of an accidental death that interrupts his own plans for slaughter. And also as in the Italian play he is brought finally to a realization that he himself was really the guilty one in his marriage relations and that the wife he detested was undeserving of his contumely. The character in the Betti incarnation was introduced to God and through Him learned the value of mercy and grace; now he is introduced to a missionary instrument of God and through him comes to learn the same thing. Though a less tortuous play than the Italian's, Mr. Hart's is still too complicated for comfort and is at its comparative best when he leaves off his involved excursions into Freud, Adler, Stekel and other such sleuths of the psyche and allows the story of the missionary and his family to enjoy its more placid course.

In this latter regard the play offers some ingratiating facets and there is pleasure in a contemplation of the missionary's philosophy of evasion and illusion in contrast to hypothetical civilization's determination in pursuing everything to a pragmatic conclusion. The uninhibited life of the jungle colony as opposed to the morality and conduct of the cities, winningly argued and defended, provides the materials for considerable whimsical charm. But the melodramatic introduction into this gentle atmosphere of the tormented psycho, which the playwright doubtless prized as a remarkably fetching idea, particularly in respect to dramatic catalysis, jars the exhibit out of itself and gives it the effect of being not a single play but two different ones operating at one and the same time. The consequence is puzzlement and mad disorder. (pp. 65-6)

> *George Jean Nathan, "American Playwrights, Old and New," in his* The Theatre in the Fifties, *Alfred A. Knopf, 1953, pp. 40-112.*

Moss Hart

I think **The Climate of Eden** is by far the most interesting piece of work I have ever done for the theatre. I wrote it because it represented a challenge to me as a writer; a departure from anything I had ever done before; in style, in content, in my whole creative personality. (Note how astonishingly easy it is to be pompous in two short sentences. And how very pleasant, I might add.) I am aware, however, that those two sentences are rash ones, and the answer I must give as to why I feel this way is a good deal less short and a trifle complicated.

It is no secret, to begin with, that I have been very successful in my own bailiwick of satire and light comedy. Beginning in 1930 with **Once in a Lifetime,** I have been represented through the years by a series of plays that pleased both me and a large public. (Arrogance is even easier, you will note.) In the plays I wrote with George Kaufman I consider **The Man Who Came to Dinner** and **You Can't Take It with You** comedies of a high order, and on my own I consider **As Thousands Cheer** a first-rate satirical revue and **Lady in the Dark** a musical comedy of substance and humanity—particularly in the frame of the time it was written and produced.

With **Lady in the Dark,** however, I felt a growing disaffection with the kind of work I had been doing. I stopped all work momentarily and directed *Junior Miss* and *Dear Ruth* to keep me trotting through a stage door, and then wrote **Winged Victory** to order for the Air Force. **Winged Victory** turned into a three-year stint, what with the additional job of writing the motion picture, and I took the first big jump with a play after that. **Christopher Blake** was faulty in many respects, but it represented, whatever it lacks, an abrupt departure from anything I had ever written before. I had hoped, in **Light Up the Sky,** my next play, to say a number of things I wanted to say under the masquerade of hard-hitting comedy, but the result, whatever its comedic value to an audience, was a disappointment to me personally, for I did not succeed at all in my own terms.

I am conscious, as I write, of the faintly obituary flavor of the foregoing, to say nothing of the fact that it would seem that I am taking myself pretty seriously, to put the matter mildly. The only truthful answer to be given is an uninhibited "yes." Of course I am taking myself seriously and I always have, as does any playwright worth his salt. Playwriting is not a gentle or sentimental profession, nor, may I add, is any part or portion of the theatre. It is ironic indeed that the public at large thinks of us all, playwrights, actors, composers, et al., as "show-folks," a wonderfully childish and sentimental lot. They could not be less right. Irving Berlin has even further perpetrated the "show-folks" legend in his song, "There's No Business Like Show Business," by the lines:

> Yesterday they told you you would not go far,
> That night you opened and there you are,
> Next day on your dressing room they hung a
> star.

The improvement made by Professor Abe Burrows is more to my liking and much nearer the truth, to wit:

> Yesterday they told you you would not go far,
> Tonight you opened and they were right!

Actually, we are the least sentimental people in the world, and woe betide the amateur of any kind who wanders into the coldly surgical precincts of the professional theatre. It is the audiences, thank God and bless them in their ignorance, who are sentimental about the theatre and its people, and long may they continue to remain so.

But the practicing playwright must take himself seriously, whether he writes comedies, satires, farces or tragedies. For make no mistake about it—I do not look down my nose at comedies; they are an ancient and honorable form of making certain truths palatable with laughter, and an age can be understood as well by its comedies as by its tragic drama. Nevertheless, it is most necessary for a writer to grow and expand in his craft; the too constant use of the same writing tools must dull the edge of them. Moreover, though it seems to be irritatingly backward and laggard, the theatre is constantly changing. As a youngster longing to break into even the fringes of it, I watched the revolutionary change in the theatre of the twenties, the turmoil of the thirties via the WPA and the Group Theatre, and the excitement of the late forties, represented by Tennessee Williams, Arthur Miller, Giraudoux and Christopher Fry. The proud chalice of the theatre is not to be judged on the record of one or two dreary seasons and the excrescences of a few fly-by-night managers backed by fly-bitten angels. If the theatre is your profession it avails you nothing to bewail its present economic disorder or its suicidal live-or-die, roulette-wheel, opening-night neuroticism; it behooves you all the more to be part of the changing scene, whatever its penalties. And for a playwright to grow in such unhealthy soil means, perforce, that he must have the courage to make mistakes.

Now, mistakes these days are not easy to bear by managements and investors alike (to say nothing of the burden on the playwright himself; plays, good or bad, are not exactly tossed off—*The Climate of Eden* was almost two years in the making), but the playwright must nevertheless take the chance of making mistakes. I found nothing that excited or pleased me enough to write for almost two years after *Light Up the Sky,* and I was determined not to put that blank piece of paper in the typewriter until I did. I

> **"[The] practicing playwright must take himself seriously, whether he writes comedies, satires, farces or tragedies. For make no mistake about it—I do not look down my nose at comedies; they are an ancient and honorable form of making certain truths palatable with laughter, and an age can be understood as well by its comedies as by its tragic drama."**
>
> **—Moss Hart, 1954**

---

read Edgar Mittelholzer's novel *Shadows Move Among Them.* I liked it immensely as a novel, but I paused long and hard, a little appalled at the job of making a play out of it. Most often the exact things that make a novel a good one, its very strength and virtues as a novel, defeat it as a play. Also, I had never adapted anything in my life before, and as I remarked earlier, I am not without my share of that virus that runs strong through every author's bloodstream—vanity. Yet, the very difficulties of Mr. Mittelholzer's novel attracted me; and I was drawn back again and again by the prospect of departing almost completely from the style and content of all my other work. More than that, its setting seemed to present the very chance I had been looking for—an ability to explore and set down my own feelings on what I can most easily and quickly term "a utopia of the heart." I had been searching for some such structure in my own mind for a long while, and Mr. Mittelholzer's book seemed ideal for the purpose.

Unfortunately, one does not get "A" for effort in the theatre. Perhaps the least fortunate part of our theatre setup today is that it allows so little margin for error. And by error I mean also growth. A writer, to my mind, is to be judged not by an isolated play, but by a body of work over the years, and in that body of work there must be of necessity growth and recession, good mistakes and bad mistakes. It is by the quality of the very mistakes he makes that the playwright is to be judged, rather than in the grotesque Broadwayese of success or failure. Still I foolishly continue to hope for a theatre in which an audience will be achieved that is as interested in a writer's or actor's progress and growth as in the "hot ticket" at McBride's. A foolish hope, but then I am part of a foolish profession.

At any rate, I have stated in a roundabout and fairly presumptuous way my feeling about *The Climate of Eden* and the reasons I felt compelled to undertake it; stated it a shade unblushingly, I have no doubt. It would be footling, by the same token, to deny that I had deep hopes for its success. Even before production however, I already had received in some measure, sufficient reward. I have said that the theatre is a foolish profession. It is. To depend upon it for an honest livelihood is lunacy, and its working conditions are idiotic. But there is no other profession, I think, that can possibly give one that feeling of exhilaration and joy—that indescribable excitement of walking toward a first rehearsal with a play under your arm that you believe in, to meet the cast that is going to bring that play alive. There is no other feeling like it in the world. (pp. 32-3)

Moss Hart, "No Time for Comedy . . . or Satire: My Most Interesting Work," in Theatre Arts, *Vol. 38, No. 5, May, 1954, pp. 32-3.*

Hollis Alpert

There are so many wonderful things Moss Hart does not do in his autobiography, **Act One,** that there may not be enough space to list all the wonderful things he *does* do. He is not, for instance, pretentious, sententious, overly modest, smug, egotistic. He doesn't name-drop, or place-drop; he doesn't give the weekly grosses of **Lady in the Dark** or **You Can't Take It with You.** He doesn't tell how he almost did not direct *My Fair Lady.* He has instead written a delightful, candid, totally absorbing book about a chap, incidentally named Moss Hart, who fell in love with the theatre when he was seven years old, who maintained that love through failure, chagrin, and near-starvation, and who is willing to admit with utter frankness that the money he eventually made was one of the most pleasant things ever to happen to him.

The book may be slightly Alger-like as pluck, luck, and a series of fortunate and unfortunate circumstances led the boy to one of the most illustrious careers in the modern American theatre, but that pattern doesn't detract in the least from the charm of the most engrossing autobiography I have yet to read by an important figure of the theatre. Mr. Hart is the first to acknowledge that this life somehow fell into a familiar pattern; but beyond that he has such a wealth of anecdote and incident to relate that you soon forget it and become as involved as the author in how he happened to make his quite fabulous way. Don't expect him, however, to finish the story in this volume. The book is exactly as the title implies, and after an intermission, which I hope won't be long, there is more to come. . . . It is possible that some will carp that Mr. Hart typifies the hit psychology of Broadway theatre, but they will be carping at success and at a man who has done much to brighten it. As I suspected, I lack the space to describe the many qualities of the book. Let me say, at least, that this chronicle of an admittedly stage-struck man is witty, funny, poignant, and delightful, and that it is told with rare polish and skill. In other words, I loved it.

Hollis Alpert, "Thespis Made His Mind Up," in Saturday Review, *Vol. XLII, No. 41, October 10, 1959, p. 41.*

Charles Rolo

Moss Hart's venture into autobiography, **Act One,** is altogether more substantial than the conventional theatrical memoir.

Mr. Hart has confined himself to the story of his youthful struggles, which were motivated by two compelling forces—hatred of poverty and a vision of Broadway as the Promised Land. His father was a cigar maker of English origin, and the son grew up in the Upper Bronx with "the dark, brown taste of being poor" always in his mouth. A wildly eccentric aunt, with the pretensions of a *grande dame,* aroused in him a sense of the theater's infinite glamour; and at fourteen he got a job as messenger boy to a producer known as "the King of the One Night Stands." Presently young Hart found himself starring in a real-life version of soap opera. His boss suddenly lost the services of the author who dished out all the plays he sent on tour— she hit the jackpot with *Abie's Irish Rose.* Hart promptly offered to bring the desperate impresario a fine drama by one Robert Arnold Conrad, and he proceeded to compose it in three nights. Miraculously, **The Beloved Bandit** not only delighted his employer (who forgave him his trickery) but found an enthusiastic backer who deemed it worthy of Broadway. The play flopped catastrophically in the tryout stage, and at eighteen Hart was "a fully-fledged failure."

During the following six years, he wrote unproduced plays and worked as a social director in summer camps, rising to be "King of the Borscht Circuit." Though etched with loathing, his picture of the frenzied, uninhibited life of these camps in the late 1920s is wonderfully fresh and funny.

The rest of the book (some 200 pages) is devoted to the long-drawn-out and harrowing journey of his play **Once in a Lifetime,** through a collaboration with George Kaufman to success on Broadway. It is a good, frequently amusing tale of the dolors and doldrums of playwriting, rehearsals, and tryouts, but there is certainly much too much of it.

Mr. Hart has written with candor, vitality, and a lack of vanity rare in books about the theater. He speaks of himself as one of "the less honorably inspired" who finds highly satisfying "the mess of pottage that success offers." This honesty gives his lively memoir a much greater solidity and human interest than one might expect in a success story of the commercial theater. **Act One** is a distinguished personal history. (pp. 175-76)

Charles Rolo, in a review of "Act One," in The Atlantic Monthly, *Vol. 204, No. 5, November, 1959, pp. 175-76.*

Richard Mason

The comedies of Moss Hart, written alone or in his famous collaboration with George S. Kaufman, are among the most popular of recent American theater. To the American theater, which begins on Broadway, Hart also contributed musical books, dramas, and revues. At least once he was called America's most famous playwright, and often he was complimented for the satirical tone of his comedies.

Yet, despite the popularity of many of Hart's works, many critical histories of his period tend to relegate him to the annotated margin rather than the body of their texts. Hart appears, for example, as but one of many collaborators of George S. Kaufman in John Gassner's *Masters of the Drama;* therein Hart is considered as but one practitioner in a movement of comedy which Gassner calls "The Kaufman Cycle."

One reason affecting the seeming eclipse of Hart's reputation is that critical history tends to diminish the dramatic respectability of the comic genre. Perhaps this tendency is due to comedy's general commitment to the topical, which often causes it to date quickly. Most comedy does, it is true, contain within itself the seeds of its own ephemerality. Another reason may be that historical analysis tends to concentrate on serious drama which the written page accommodates with considerable ease. This differs from the nature of comedy, especially the low forms whose essence is, in a very real sense, identical to its stage life. According to this view, then, comedy demands a theatrical emphasis, and one often gained at the expense of the idea or the language, which are drama's more enduring elements and which are responsive to analysis beyond their performance qualities.

Another circumstance which directly affects the Hart reputation is his identification with Broadway rather than a body of drama. This is a subject to explore. For if it is true that Hart reflected Broadway taste, then judgments of his work would naturally extend into his theatre and its audience.

A French translation of Hart's autobiography, *Act One,* is revealingly re-titled *Un Homme de Broadway, A Man of Broadway.* The title goes directly to the heart of its subject: the making of a Broadway playwright. Consideration of either the man or the playwright reveals that neither can be meaningfully removed from the Broadway background. Such must inevitably inform any substantial evaluation of Moss Hart and his work.

In his *A History of the American Theater,* Glenn Hughes surveys theatrical activity in ten and twenty-year periods. As he approaches the contemporary theatre, Hughes explains that he is dealing with only ten per cent of Broadway's productions. In that ten per cent, however, he has included almost every production of artistic importance, as well as a considerable number of popular hits which were artistically inconsequential. "The remaining ninety per cent may with good conscience be ignored."

A substantial part of that ninety per cent were comedies, which Bernard Hewitt [in *Theatre U.S.A.*] has defined as being "almost exclusively satire and farce, frequently softened with sentiment." This is the genre in which Hart did the notable bulk of his writing. It is a genre which always satisfied, like television today, the voracious appetite of the theatre-goers, [whom Kenneth MacGowan referred to in *Famous American Plays of the 1920s* as] "the mass audience that wanted melodrama and farce."

As playwright and collaborator, and later as director and film writer, Moss Hart achieved remarkable success in a competitive and commercial milieu long noted for its obstacles to such success. It was his first comedy that attracted the already successful playwright, Kaufman. Consequently, this study attempts to maintain a focus on Hart independent of attention he must share merely as a collaborator of Kaufman, a name with which his is inextricably linked. Although never substantiated, Kaufman's role in

the famous team is generally considered to concern language and pace, the theatrical polish, as it were, of the dramatic plot and characters offered him by his many partners. An evaluation of Hart's contributions to their joint efforts will be based on this assumption. It is an assumption that can be reasonably supported by an analysis of Hart's solo efforts and Kaufman's many other collaborations.

One goal of this study is to determine and evaluate the structural and satirical nature of Hart's comedies. A secondary goal is to determine what links there might be among his various plays or to identify sources common to them all. The foregoing emphasis on the Broadway milieu is necessary, for the fact that Hart wrote explicitly for the Broadway theatre might exert a common influence on the Hart repertory. Observable throughout the Hart works are certain repeated characteristics which might be interpreted as compromises of his material with the expectations of the Broadway theatre in mind. This pattern of repetition includes such effective theatrical and comic devices that Hart's concept of "theatricalism" could be said to provide a common source for the theatrical elements in his plays regardless of their genre. This pattern of repetition is consistent enough to prompt the subtitle of this study, "the persistence of a formula."

Undoubtedly, Hart was fortunate in that his "formula" had a parallel in the work of George S. Kaufman, with whom he entered into a most fruitful collaboration after the success of *Once in a Lifetime.* In between, however, he had tested this formula as it buttresses many a musical book or revue sketch. Later, he was less fortunate in seeing fit to extend this formula into some serious works which reflect an ambition for his craft as do his comedies for his career.

Throughout this study distinctions between drama (content) and theatre (drama on stage) are continually made and must be continually understood. Such a distinction is inevitable in considering comedy—which gains so much from performance.

Further, comedy is accepted as [what Robert Lewis Shayon identified as] "a form of rational discourse, questioning and exposing absurdities and vices." Although the comic form may range from slapstick to verbal gymnastics, Louis Kronenberger, a connoisseur of comedy, identified a consistent characteristic when he writes [in *The Thread of Laughter*] that it is "a trenchant way of regarding life."

The nature and the effect of the comic have intrigued the poet and the philosopher from Aristotle to Sigmund Freud. Indeed, the theatre's comic mask has as many expressions and evokes as many varying responses as there are mirrors of distortion in an amusement park, but in pinning labels on them all, one runs the risk of echoing Polonius' category of plays.

Moss Hart took to the stage as a writer of comedy at the end of one of its most productive periods, and was highly active during its bleaker period when laughter was a precious commodity and cultural introspection unavoidable.

We propose to gauge how Moss Hart met the challenge of his time, his theatre, and the venerable tradition of comedy. Hart's autobiography ended with the successful premiere of *Once in a Lifetime.* This study begins with it.

There is little doubt or mystery that Hart's involvement with Kaufman made a deep effect on his work. An investigation of Hart's plays can neither neglect *Once in a Lifetime* nor observe it cursorily. Fortunately, two versions exist: Hart's original, submitted to Kaufman, and the final, collaborative result. A comparison not only reveals the development of a play from its rough beginnings to a craftily polished stage piece, but it also indicates the authors' disposition toward the nature of comedy, their audiences, and the demands of their theatre as well. Importantly, a comparative study reveals characteristics repeated in the body of Hart's subsequent work, whether it be the product of collaboration or of solitary labor. These plays, *Once in a Lifetime* included, must be viewed partially in light of Hart's own recorded sentiment concerning an important aspect of his dramatic material:

> An audience is not interested in how hard an author has worked at his research, or how much material he has unearthed, and they do not take kindly to his parading in front of the footlights his hard-earned knowledge. They are quite right. They have not come to a school room; they have come to a theatre.

This was the theatre for which he desired to write, an inspiration notably described and detailed in his famous autobiography. Even its title, *Act One,* becomes particularly interesting in the context of Hart's lifelong preoccupation with the theatre world. It offers a somewhat tantalizing self-view of the author as a man of the theatre whose life runs like a play, and entices one to investigate the playwright on a psychological level. His plays, coupled with the available library of his personal papers, offer ample evidence that the work was an exceedingly personal extension of the man.

Here, it must suffice to record that Moss Hart's personal preoccupation with the theatre influenced his work to the extent that a substantial portion of it deals with the theatre itself (*Face the Music,* 1932; *Light Up the Sky,* 1948); with themes realized in purely theatrical terms (*Lady in the Dark,* 1941; *Christopher Blake,* 1946); and with the theatrical-in-life, represented by characters who behave in a *bravura* or "grand" manner (Eva Standing in *Jubilee,* 1935; the Russians in *You Can't Take It with You,* 1936; Alison du Bois in *Lady in the Dark,* 1941, to name but a few out of an entire repertory).

It is crucial to note that Hart wrote but one serious, realistic play, the Broadway failure, *Climate of Eden* (1952). It is equally pertinent to note that the plot was not original with him, being based on a British novel, *Shadows Move among Them* by Edgar Mittelholzer.

Although Kaufman wrote in a fairly late letter to Hart "of those twin targets at which I have aimed so many times, business and politics. . . . " he too, had an affinity for the theatrical theme which must have contributed to the bond that was established between them with *Once in a Lifetime.*

Show-business satire is contained in many of Kaufman's early works. In collaboration with Moss Hart, other plays involving theatrical personalities are *Once in a Lifetime* (1930), *Merrily We Roll Along* (1934), and *The Man Who Came to Dinner* (1939); and actors make appearances in *You Can't Take It with You* (1936) and *George Washington Slept Here* (1940). Their *Fabulous Invalid* (1938) is, indeed, the history of a theatre.

On his own, Moss Hart dealt with the actual theatre or with some of its inhabitants in an early play, *No Retreat* (1930), and the musicals *Face the Music* (1932), *Jubilee* (1935), and *Lady in the Dark* (1941). After the termination of his collaboration with Kaufman, his drama *Christopher Blake* (1946) and the comedy *Light Up the Sky* (1948) still reflect various aspects of theatrical life in whole or in part. His unproduced television script, *These Pretty People,* and his adapted film plays, *The Eddy Duchin Story* (1954), *A Star Is Born* (1954), and *Prince of Players* (1955), all deal with theatrical life.

Admittedly, it is Kaufman rather than Hart upon whom the spotlight is mainly turned whenever their collaboration is under focus. In his eulogy to Kaufman, Hart admitted his "debt to George is incalculable." The beginnings of indebtedness would seem to have been established some time before Kaufman ever saw the young Hart's script, for there is much evidence of the strong influence of Kaufman's comedies in *Once in a Lifetime.* This initial influence stimulated Hart into (1) treating a theatrical milieu in (2) a farce frame.

Once in a Lifetime, a Comedy with Sound and Fury by Moss Hart, reads the title page of the script. It bears no copyright date but was written in either September or October of 1929. The garish film industry and its newly found "sound" are the subjects of Hart's play. This original version of *Once in a Lifetime* is obviously an apprentice work, but a highly promising one when it is considered that Hart was just past twenty years old, had never visited Hollywood, nor even written a comedy. [The critic adds in a footnote: "Hart tells us he had already written six serious plays."] What it lacks in structure and character development, it compensates for in energy and extravagance, and a sense of parody and satire. It is certainly "native" in its lack of cerebral subtleties, in the popularity of its aggressive farce form, and in its theme of the innocent (a Kaufman analogue) who stumbles his way to success, winning a beautiful bride along the way.

The script is so topical in its theme that the passage of time and the passing of a particular Hollywood era have robbed it of much of its original pertinence. Yet, Hart's script can claim an abundance of amusing moments and comic invention of situation and character. Although unsatisfactorily episodic in its dramaturgy, it is in its Hollywood caricatures that Hart's original is the most theatrically telling: Dahlberg, the man who rejected sound, who will not make a film without a "name" no matter how miscast the "name" may be, and to whom everything, regardless of subject, is "just too colossal," is in performance actually more humorously drawn than a description might indicate. It is the same with the narcissism of the mass-manufactured starlets; the ire of the foreign film director; and the ubiquity of the Hollywood hopeful, auditioning by way of vigorous, kaleidoscopic facial expression whenever important studio personnel appear.

It is of particular interest to note the grandly intense and "tragic" demeanor of the studio receptionist, a pose which anticipates the "bravura" manner of the theatrical and royal folk of the later comedies.

But for all the theatrical heightening and comic absurdity, one repeatedly concludes that the reach exceeds the grasp as one fertile idea after another fails realization in a dramatically sustained way, or is so overdrawn as to blunt the edge of laughter. Repeated promise of genuine satire is lost or weakened amid the general and increasing extravagance.

The impression emerges, at least from a reading of *Once in a Lifetime,* that the play is a series of comic vignettes held together by a loose narrative rather than a dramatic plot. A lack of development in character treatment accounts for much of this. There is little conflict or story development, since Hart sacrifices narrative for burlesque sequences.

This native facility for "extravagance" can be traced throughout Hart's work. It contributes not only to the unique character of the comedies, but also to the later theatrical ingenuity of *Lady in the Dark* and the dramatic weaknesses of *Christopher Blake.*

Although the intent and spirit of the collaborative version sustains intact those of the original, it may be called an entirely new play in light of its more deliberate comic air and direction. The quality of burlesque remains the same as often does the incident of the original, but the accumulative effect is overwhelmingly superior to Hart's. This is mainly achieved through the infusion of an obvious theatrical skill and sureness of effect, a more sophisticated narrative, more dimensionalized characters, and smoother dialogue. A filling out of the drama's connective tissues has been added to Hart's skeletal schemes. An impression is gained that where Hart worked through intuition and an imitative sense, producing but the healthy embryo of an idea, Kaufman's theatrical disciplines helped "humanize" it.

Should one, however, find it failing to achieve on a satirical level what it has the potential to achieve, one could predicate of it the following view [expressed by James Agee in *Films in Review*]:

> Farce, like melodrama, offers very special chances for accurate observation, but here accuracy is avoided ten times to one in favor of the easy burlesque or the easier idealization which drops the bottom out of farce. Every good moment frazzles or drowns.

Even this collaborative version of *Once in a Lifetime* is, essentially, a parody less of Hollywood life and filmmaking than it is a parody of a typical genre film story, film decor, and the people involved in their production.

Although possessed of moments of satire and satirical allusion, it is essentially a sympathetic lampoon.

On the other hand, as a carefully constructed farce containing timely and irreverent allusion, the collaborative version of *Once in a Lifetime* certainly possesses the merit to be included in the comedies which reflect the American scene as described by Alan Downer [in *Revolution in the American Drama*]:

> Here, in the mockery of the serious, the classic, the formal, and the eventual victory of the much-beaten underdog, is the theatrical equivalent of the tall talk and the comic folk story which reflect so accurately the American temper. Here, waiting for a playwright to put them to use, or give them form or purpose, were the elements of American comedy.

Twenty-four years later, Hart looked over his original script. He recorded his reaction in his journal:

> It was quite well constructed, the lines extremely funny, and I think perhaps, if a manuscript like this were submitted to me today, I would have to admit that the author had real talent for the theatre.

In 1954, Moss Hart entered the following observation in his journal:

> Again, I was struck by the fact that the three biggest hits of the season—*Teahouse Of The August Moon, Tea and Sympathy,* and *The Caine Mutiny Court Martial*—violate almost every theatre rule. It is a lesson that there are no rules whatever about the theatre, but one which is very hard to remember.

Yet, guided by principles of the theatre which had made their *Once in a Lifetime* a notable success, Hart and Kaufman apparently established a set of rules for themselves which they applied to their joint comedies and to which Hart returned with his *Light Up the Sky.*

A certain pattern emerges from the merest reading or viewing of these plays, and certain broad judgments are unavoidable. *You Can't Take It with You* is the most imaginative and exudes the most warmth and sentiment. Tonally, *The Man Who Came to Dinner* is reminiscent of the earlier Kaufman satires. It is of superior construction and, by way of Sheridan Whiteside, its caustic and principal role, proves a particularly effective sounding board for Kaufmanesque dialogue. Neither a reading nor viewing can disguise the fact that *George Washington Slept Here* is the weakest of the group, and strong in evidence that the collaboration was wearing thin or losing fire. Their joint authorship terminated with this play, but the influence of Kaufman thoroughly permeates the writing of *Light Up the Sky.* Although varying in degrees of accomplishment, the comedies suggest, by their very similarities, that the authors were writing for a theatre they knew and that they knew what that theatre wanted.

Once in a Lifetime proved to be the prime example of a formula constructed earlier by Kaufman and his various collaborators: the successful rise in a jungle world of the helpless innocent almost despite himself. Although such a theme has been replaced in the comedies written with Hart which are under scrutiny here, the formula persists in the theatrical frame and theatrical devices which are common to both.

The change of theme from *Once in a Lifetime* to the theme of these collaborative comedies and Hart's *Light Up the Sky* is the replacement of the strong narrative of the bumbling innocent's success story with a situation the "normal" state of which has had its equilibrium jarred (*You Can't Take It with You* and *The Man Who Came to Dinner*) or, of which, the "normal" state is one of a lack of equilibrium (*George Washington Slept Here* and *Light Up the Sky.*)

More specifically, *You Can't Take It with You* concerns itself with the problems which occur when the daughter of a highly non-conformist family falls in love with the Boss's son who is from a very conservative background. Breaking up and then patching up the romance of a secretary he loathes losing, while an injury confines him to a middle-class Ohio home, comprises the catalyst of plot by which *The Man Who Came to Dinner,* a renowned celebrity, is enabled to verbally attack all who come within hearing distance. *George Washington Slept Here* deals with the efforts of an urban, middle-aged couple to adjust to country life, while *Light Up the Sky* exposes the manic-depressive cycle striking theatre folk while awaiting a new play's critical reviews.

Thus, the term "situational comedy" (now common to television) is quite an appropriate label for these plays. Rather than following a change in the status of a character's fortunes against a series of changing backgrounds, the play's concern is to set aright an ordinary, normal routine which has been violated.

The situational rather than narrative themes of the comedies are reflected by the sets called for. Whether influenced somewhat by the Depression or not, the multiplicity of sets typical of *Once in a Lifetime* and the earlier Kaufman plays has been replaced in each of these instances with a single setting. This serves to diminish a broad scope of action and forces treatment to remain close to the situation which the single set frames. Each of them is, however, multifunctional (i.e., combination living room-dining room as in *You Can't Take It with You*) and capable of containing great diversity of action.

Whether we call the "situations" of the comedies "plotless" or use some other label, it would seem that a construction whereby a single situation is exploited from a number of different angles would enable the authors to delve deeply within that situation for all its satirical and dramatically comic possibilities; *but in each case a plethora of farce incident and farce character* precludes such exhaustive treatment of theme. Large casts and an especial use of character vignette are one of the "constants" or repeated theatrical devices contributing to the "Persistance of a formula."

In 1929, before the saga of writing *Once in a Lifetime,* Hart directed a production of George Kelly's *The Show-Off* for an amateur drama group. In a program editorial, he promised audiences the best and most serious of theatre, but added, "What we must not forget, however, is that the theatre demands an audience."

Neither Moss Hart nor George Kaufman were ever unmindful of their audiences. Consideration of the comedies reveals a common intention energizing them all: *the construction of a steady stream of constant stimuli to the ear and eye of the beholder.* Like the relationship of one frame of film to the next, these stimuli are so placed and so generated as to appear to flow smoothly one into the other. They are geared to startle and shock us repeatedly into risible attention. Taken alone, the ever-present wisecrack is an example of such stimulus.

It must be borne in mind that the playing style of each of the foregoing comedies remains in the sheerest farce tradition. For the most part, the abundance of farce incident, the extravagant number of characters, the comic turn of dialogue, all serve to preclude satirical treatment-in-depth while appealing to immediate response. The more serious an issue becomes, the deeper must its probings go and the more complex does its thought become. It is not with such concerns that these authors are preoccupied.

Because the comic spectrum may range from sheer physical action on the one hand to a preoccupation with language and idea on the other, pace, plot, and character are unavoidably affected if only because these extremes take utterly diverse attitudes toward aesthetic use of time: in short, situation comedies need less of it and cram more into it, than do comedies of language and idea which are more dependent on the time-consuming intellectual faculties of the audience.

For example, as soon as the Kirby-Grandpa meeting in the final act of *You Can't Take It with You* succeeds in establishing a basic opposition of views necessary to the plot, the Russian Grand Duchess is immediately reintroduced to quicken the proceedings, recharge them with a comic energy, and to remind us we are still within a comic world. She serves as a perfect example of the comic stimulus so abundant in these comedies, as well as a vignette use of comic character. Neither satire nor any weighty preoccupation with issues is allowed to get in the way of the comedy sequence in any of these comedies. In this particular play, there is such a preoccupation with mayhem that any metaphorical values possessed by the play are quite overshadowed by its farce exuberance.

Indeed, the main characters of *You Can't Take It with You* must all be performed with the lightest touch, else "the mild insanity that prevades . . . them," (as a direction reads), might easily impress as a genuine, psychological eccentricity. Such an impression could make it seem that Grandpa was both protecting and shielding the others from the world, which is hardly the author's intent.

In terms of playing "style," what has been written of *You Can't Take It with You* remains predicative of *The Man Who Came to Dinner,* but with one added dimension. The speeches of Sheridan Whiteside, expert in syntax, imaginative of vocabulary, and commanding in total expression, add a "literary" quality to the play. Although many of these speeches are "wisecracks" by way of construction— and thus extensions in dialogue of the farce or low comedy form—their freedom from slang elevates them qualitatively just as the character of Whiteside elevates the comic level of his scenes. This is not in essence successful for the play as a whole because Whiteside is offered nothing of import or depth to utter. His utterances are sharply pointed and acerbic comments (if not downright insults) on the surrounding farce action and characters. They are not intended to provoke thought beyond that.

The glimpses of high comedy achieved by *The Man Who Came to Dinner* may possibly have influenced the authors to attempt a less broad canvas in *George Washington Slept Here,* and to produce a "realistic" domestic comedy. The effects are curious. The steady stream of alternating comic stimuli, ranging from the wisecrack to visual gag, is absent, and yet is not replaced with any higher comic forms. Thus, without that steady stream of comic adornments, the formulating construction and placing of elements stands exposed to analysis. We notice the melodramatic plot, the lack of necessary explanations, the unfinished business, and the spirited exaggerations of character or episode which also occur in the other comedies. If *The Man Who Came to Dinner* contains elements forcing it to the highest level of comedy attained by the authors, the very lack of those elements relegates *George Washington Slept Here* to the lowest. *George Washington Slept Here* would absolutely require an artificially rapid pace, imposed upon it by the director, to compress its lengthy, arid areas and to conceal its flaws from an audience.

In terms of dramatic "style," *Light Up the Sky* rendered more of a piece than any of the other three comedies. A study of several versions reveals that this is the result more of the omission of a variety of comic modes than success in concentration on character. For when Hart indulges himself in the type of comic element typical of the collaborative comedies, it is in the broad, exaggerated style we have come to expect as a staple of the Kaufman-Hart canon.

The theatrical characters, being mock-heroic, are cut from that mold of parody introduced with *Once in a Lifetime.* Each is immediately established, and once again, it is the time-tested pace of farce that must help in sustaining them with theatrical interest for three acts. There are no depths to fathom so surface speed is mandatory. It is observable, though, that a change of rhythm is provided in the Owen-Peter playwriting debates and Peter's disillusionment with his theatrical colleagues. A typical danger is that these "serious" if shallow sequences can dissipate the comedy without offering a compensatory dramatic value. Playing "speed" avoids this.

You Can't Take It with You is the richest of the Kaufman-Hart plays in terms of a broad, seemingly satirical canvas. And yet, an analysis of it suggests that while many comic films and plays of the period reflect a time of inescapable social consciousness and introspection, this famous comedy by Hart and Kaufman reflects a time for escape.

Despite the success of *You Can't Take It with You* and the sharp contemporary aura enveloping *The Man Who Came to Dinner* this latter play is the first to drop substantially the use of the comic form as satirical metaphor; and what

we are offered in the three subsequent comedies are reflections in varying hue of the private world of the playwrights.

Indeed it may be said that in them we have comedies *à clef:* that is, with characters and situations based on original personalities and events. The caricature of types was unavoidable in *Once in a Lifetime.* Shortly thereafter, it was actual celebrities who were used as barely disguised models. In *As Thousands Cheer,* the famous were actually names, as well as depicted on stage, as were national figures in *I'd Rather Be Right,* the musical which followed *You Can't Take It with You.* In *The Man Who Came to Dinner,* Beverly Carlton is Noel Coward to all but the uninitiated, and Alexander Woolcott and Harpo Marx are disguised in name only. Originally, Salvador Dali was parodied as a Miguel Santos, but this vignette was deleted before the New York opening. It is a matter of newspaper fact prior to each opening of the comedies, guessing games were popular as to which celebrity or intimate of Kaufman or Hart would be characterized.

So, from an analysis of the various versions of Hart's plays, two impressions emerge: that he was substantially more successful with comic than "serious" elements in his plays; and that, although we may call his comedies *à clef* (offering an illusion of "comment"), he seems unable to move away from the essentially autobiographical or the personal experience. These are observations to which we must return when considering his "serious" plays.

In *You Can't Take It with You,* a theatrically oriented character pattern emerges. As might be predicted from the preceding remarks about pace requirements and superficial concern for issues, the notion of "individuality" or "non-conformity" in *You Can't Take It with You* is expressed in external behaviour patterns. The characters are comic in view of their observable eccentricities rather than anything ideological. The leading roles are never "straight" heroes or heroines (i.e., "romantic" leads) but those known as "character" roles. Both a "character" role and a caricature can rely heavily on externals for quick impression. Indeed, they must in a farce. Such characters do not require that precision of delineation or probing of personality which more realistically drawn or "straighter" characters demand. There is much in the comedies to substantiate this formulistic and habitual working equation of the authors.

A vignette use of character is an especial characteristic of Kaufman, later absorbed by Hart because of the collaboration. It is a use of character distinct from that of supporting characters, such as De Pinna and Kolenkhov of *You Can't Take It with You* who are woven into the action and whose comic natures are realized to reflect and further it. The vignette is used principally to earn immediate laughs rather than to complicate the plot. It is the comic "moment" that is served. With a minor exception, vignettes are not at all in evidence in Hart's 1948 *Light Up the Sky,* when both rising costs and expensive labor behooved the playwright to cut corners. In that play a number of original vignettes were ultimately deleted.

Analysis indicates that much of the comedy of all the

Kaufman and Hart farces and *Light Up the Sky* flows from a bi-streamed fountainhead. One is the effect produced by the juxtaposition of unlike parts whose union is aptly labeled the "incongruous;" the second stream is calculated exaggeration of those parts. What is consequently produced is an effect quick to impress the eye or ear, which in its "unexpectedness" arouses the risibility of the audience. Thus, it is a formula of placing two cross and unlike "things" closely together to produce a single effect that results in the "startling" comic stimulus that so often earns for the playwrights the appreciative response of the guffaw or the loud belly-laugh. The "things" that are so manipulated refer to the varying equations of character with dialogue, a particular action or "business" with props, with the immediate background, or with other distinct characters.

In considering some basic aspects of comic dialogue, as utilized in the comedies, several typical constructions emerge: one involves the use of opposing concepts; another a terminal "punch" word or phrase; and another concentrates on the style or language of the speech, be it mock-heroic or argot.

For example, a brief dialogue sequence from *You Can't Take It with You* is as follows:

> PENNY. (talking of her current play) I've just got Cynthia entering the monastery.
>
> RHEBA. Monastery? How'd she get there? She was at the El Morocco, wasn't she?
>
> PENNY. Yes, I sort of got myself into a monastery and I can't get out.
>
> ESSIE. Oh, well, it'll come to you, Mother. Remember how you got out of that brothel?

The contrasts between "monastery" and "El Morocco," and "monastery" and "Brothel" are sharp and extreme enough to shock us into an automatic response. Such extremes bound together in close utterance are repeated throughout the script, reaching down even to Rheba's dinner announcement:

> Cornflakes, watermelon, some of those candies Miss Essie made and some kind of meat, I forget.

The food Donald rushes out to get for the unexpected Kirby's is almost anticipated: pickled pigs' feet.

Whatever *The Man Who Came to Dinner* may lack in satirical point is compensated for in the quality and consistency of its dialogue. The dialogue pattern of *You Can't Take It with You* not only extends into *The Man Who Came to Dinner* but finds there its apotheosis. Quantitatively, *The Man Who Came to Dinner* derives more comedy from its dialogue than its farce sequences. The obvious cause is that Whiteside's many speeches abound in the wisecrack, and the destructive wisecrack it is as it falls from his acid-dipped tongue. "What do you want, Miss Bed Pan?" he asks of Nurse Preen. Even his occasional compliments are stripped of their sentimentality, as when he says to Maggie, "Don't look up at me with those great cow-eyes, you sex-ridden hag," or "Don't be bitter, Puss, just because Lorraine is more beautiful than you are." The

very frequency, audacity, and outrageousness of Whiteside's epithets prove continuously stunning, drawing an attention to this play's dialogue not shared by any of the other comedies.

Where *The Man Who Came to Dinner* abounds in the gymnastics of dialogue, *George Washington Slept Here* is surprisingly spare. The afore-mentioned dialogue construction appears with less frequency, but is consistent in structure when it does. Rena, for example, refers to Raymond as "Huckleberry Capone," and to Newton, carrying garden utensils, as "Sears and Roebuck." After waxing lengthily poetic on the simple, earthy joys of country life, Newton is reminded by Mr. Kimber of the need "for a cesspool." Their very infrequency here illustrates their importance in sustaining a steady stream of laughter. The isolated "crack" does not seem to earn quite the risible response it may deserve, because its energy is dissipated in the arid areas separating one area of comic dialogue from another.

The dominantly visual nature of low comedy is further indicated by *the essentially incongruous meeting of certain characters,* as, for example, Gay Wellington's attraction to both Donald and Mr. Kirby in *You Can't Take It with You,* or Rheba's girlish giggle at Kolenkhov's teasing attentions. This is a special character relationship, containing the element of extremism or blatant exaggeration. An amused response is gained merely by viewing such disparate characters together in a common situation. (A classic illustration of such a combination was that of high society dowager Margaret Dumont who for years on stage and films was foil to the Marx Brothers.)

The initial entry of Banjo in *The Man Who Came to Dinner* further illustrates this generation of easy laughter. He enters carrying a screaming Nurse Preen in his arms, fondling and kissing her. If he had been carrying Maggie instead, a distinctly different impression would have been produced. And although Banjo has a unique relationship with Whiteside, their mutual appreciation of talent makes their unlikely friendship both plausible and understandable, and, consequently, less "shocking" in effect.

Additional "free" laughs, by way of basically visual gags which earn an appreciate response without intolerably taxing the writer's imagination, may be provided by *judicious use of a prop.*

In describing weakening audience reaction to a production of an early version of *Once in a Lifetime,* Hart wrote that the audience was "perfectly prepared to laugh at costumes and props until the play came to life again." And in *You Can't Take It with You,* De Pinna poses for Penny atop a table. He is costumed in a Roman toga, and studies the same Racing Form held by "The Bishop" in the marriage sequence of *Once in a Lifetime.* The Racing Form itself earns part of the laughter. Penny, absent-mindedly nibbling on candy taken from a human skull, or Eddie suddenly "scaring" Essie with his mask of "Mrs. Roosevelt" are similar examples. In *George Washington Slept Here,* the sight of Annabelle carrying in a few "puny radishes," culled from her garden, is certain to elicit appreciative laughter without a word being uttered.

George S. Kaufman and Moss Hart

Perhaps the most famous prop in all the comedies is the Egyptian sarcophagus of **The Man Who Came to Dinner,** a gift to Sheridan from the Khedive of Egypt, in which Lorraine Sheldon is spirited away. Should we imagine that Lorraine might suffocate, the authors assure us that air can seep in. We should, then, be able to hear her yells. Yet, the inventive hilarity of the sequence overrules any sensible objection, and the scene pleased even George Jean Nathan who is not as enthusiastic in his review of the play as was Brooks Atkinson [see excerpts above].

In general then, part of the Kaufman and Hart comedy formula is the use of these various comic "tricks," in differing proportions, to construct a "steady stream of stimuli to the eye and ear."

Both the construction of the wisecrack (whose point is usually made clear with the last word) and many of the visual comic forms (possessed of exaggerated or gross outlines) are related by having a demonstrably common source in the incongruous and the unexpected. Indeed, the incongruous moment, a totally parenthetic moment in life (when the ordinary sequence of events is suddenly jarred out of its routine) is comically effective in so much as it is unexpected and unanticipated. Its effect is thus, a "startling" one, and we are "shocked" into risibility.

Also, since theatrical rather than dramatic forms are here being scrutinized, it must be noted that a heightening or broadening of the comic form to assure quick audience assimilation is usually affected. An obvious exaggeration of theatrical personality, or costume, or meeting of characters, is constructed. If there is one thread that runs through the entire Kaufman-Hart repertory of comedies and chronicle plays, it is this of the obvious exaggeration. That such a device or characteristic lends itself admirably to farce is apparent. Its projection, as we shall see, into a more serious format, results substantially in melodrama.

In addition to those dramatic and theatrical elements which run in alternate fashion consistently through the Kaufman-Hart works, there are certain additional devices of dialogue or construction. In light of their consistency, these elements may be said to assist the persistence of a formula. They are:

a. the use of famous names
b. the use of animals, seen and unseen
c. the use of "loud" curtain and "quiet" scene,

The first two are obvious. Each functions consistently according to the "low comedy" formula: each is capable of immediately startling or shocking the audience into attention or risibility. In the use of the third category, the "quiet" scene allows for relaxation of the pitch, often a noisy one, terminating the second act.

When Hart deleted the third-act night club sequence from *Once in a Lifetime* and replaced it with the conversational scene between May and Lawrence Vail, he stumbled upon a rhythmic device from which the collaborative comedies and *Light Up the Sky* do not vary.

It is a dramaturgical principle that the second act be the strongest of the three (the climax ordinarily occurring therein) because it can be the Achilles' heel of either a drama or comedy. It is difficult to revive, with a third act, an audience whose attention has been lost in the second act, whereas a first act generally has a momentum of its own. Hart himself stated [in *Act One*] that "it is the second acts that seperate the men from the boys." In the comedies, an energetic first act curtain is "topped" by a second act curtain descending on a veritable *coda* of action or high pitch of tension. This is followed in the opening of the third act with a quiet, conversational scene which quickly gains momentum, however, and firmly builds to the end of the play.

There is a difference between immediate pleasure and the cerebral retention of its cause, and it is precisely in that difference that the diametrically opposed reputations of Kaufman and Hart, as comedy writers, lie rooted. It explains in part why their plays, written singly and in collaboration, can total an amazing number of performances on Broadway and yet, in anthologies and histories of the period, be relegated to an annotational position in the text. In effect, the comedies of Kaufman and Hart are there to be thoroughly enjoyed on the stage, but it is fatal to think about them. In this regard, the comedies decidedly belong to the tradition of low comedy which finds its life, like the wisecrack, in a moment and of a time, and in theatrical action rather than between the covers of a book.

Although we cannot consider the books of the musicals with which Hart was associated, a view of them appears to demonstrate that the musical form was most adaptable to the often extreme exaggeration of character and the good-natured mockery of events that seem keynotes to his instinctive and energetic talents. The ease with which the musical form radiates visual and audible stimuli and creates a heightened, delightfully unreal and imaginative world, allied to worlds of fantasy, dream and escape, is the essence of the form. In effect, the musical is above all, totally theatrical. And it is precisely these elements in Hart's writing manner that were confirmed by his participation in the musical field, that contribute much to the unique character of the later collaborations, and account so much for the failure of his serious plays.

When designer Robert Edmond Jones states that "elaborate 'scenic productions' are an infallible sign of low vitality in the theatre," he is actually referring to low vitality in a drama which has theatre do much of its work for it. By having his senses titilated, one is distracted from the awareness that his brains and sensibilities are not being titilated.

The very "ingenuity" or theatrical novelty of *Lady in the Dark,* Hart's "musical drama," serves as a bridge into consideration of the chronicle plays, issue of Hart's collaboration with Kaufman, and his singly written three serious plays.

Lady in the Dark was a pivotal point in Hart's career. Earlier, lay a decade of comedy, musicals, collaborations and forays into the drama with the three "chronicle" plays discussed below. This was his first and only serious musical book, launching a decade of solo writing, directing, motion picture adaptations, and several original scripts for television.

But a theatrical strain, that is, an emphatic reliance on form, permeates so much of his writing that formulistic elements extend into the serious plays.

These plays fall into two groups, those written in collaboration with Kaufman and those written alone. It is a fact rich in implication that *Lady in the Dark* comes between them.

Let us consider first the collaborative dramas. These are *Merrily We Roll Along* (1934), *The Fabulous Invalid* (1938), and *The American Way* (1939). *Merrily We Roll Along* was the first play to reunite Hart with Kaufman since *Once in a Lifetime.*

So distinct in form are the serious plays that they are here labeled "chronicle plays," a record of events in historical order. The very fact that these serious plays are "chronicle" (or episodic) in construction is a factor of extreme importance in assessing Hart's talent and in underscoring the theatrical bent of that talent.

The loss of a playwright's ideals in a money-conscious culture which equates the "fashionable" with success is the theme basic to *Merrily We Roll Along.* More pertinently, each of its nine scenes takes place at an earlier time than the preceding one.

The *novelty* of such a construction is a strong feature of the play, as were Jo Mielziner's nine elaborate sets: fashionable homes and apartments, the restaurant Le Coq d'Or, a court house corridor, an artist's studio, tenements, a park, and a college chapel.

It would be unfair to the authors to suggest that the novelty of form saves a rather sentimental story melodramatically told. Despite the novelty, there is considerable dramatic excitement in seeing the promise of a talent grow after we have witnessed its failure. The inverse chronology is, in itself, part of the action conceived as drama. Still, it *is* novel, even if that novelty is not sleight-of-hand.

Merrily We Roll Along is another example, then, of Hart's desire to write serious themes, but it is executed with a dependence on a novel form to assure its theatricality.

The very broadness of the comic elements in the later comedies seems applicable here as well. Such broadness of character and action seems, when comic elements or design are lacking, to result in melodrama. Low comedy and melodrama seem to exist on the same level, having much in common in terms of their treatment of character and action. Like a straight line changing color, they exist in different colors on the same continuum. Low comedy, then becomes melodrama as it loses its comic hue.

The broad treatment and the novel form which may be said to form a pattern, are evident in the other plays as well.

History itself is the theme of Hart and Kaufman's blatantly patriotic *The American Way.*

The panoramic sweep necessary to cover the fortunes of three generations of a family, and friends intimate with it, is by itself not necessarily unique; it is a device, however, more common to literature than to the stage. Considered with the other serious plays, the three-generation device does sustain the image of the authors' dependence upon a rather special form and a theme that will demand the full resources of their stage. The vivid effects possible in the theatre will appeal immediately to the senses, and make possible a colorful frame for the dramatic action.

The form of *The American Way* was as special as the form of *Merrily We Roll Along* was unique. With a total focus on the mores and people of the theatre, which so often emerge in his work, Hart is able in *The Fabulous Invalid* to completely indulge himself.

The Fabulous Invalid combines scenic elaboration and novelty of form with greater focus than in any other of Hart's plays. This greater focus results from the absence of dramatic action and complication. The "story" is composed of episodic but historical highlights in the life of a theatre, the Alexandria. These highlights are uniquely punctuated by lengthy montage sequences. Such sequences are composed of fragments of famous scenes and musical production numbers that have played at the Alexandria in addition to giant reproductions of the original billboards flashed on a screen.

Christopher Blake opened on 30 November 1946 for a run of 114 performances. With the exception of the Air Force spectacle, *Winged Victory* (1943), it was Hart's first play after *Lady in the Dark.* Except for the musical element, the theme and construction of *Christopher Blake* are identical to those of *Lady in the Dark.* The insecure Liza Elliot is here replaced by twelve-year-old Christopher Blake, whose parents are divorcing and who must choose between them. As he sits in the judge's chambers waiting to be called, his dream wishes and fantasies are dramatically realized.

As in *Lady in the Dark,* the dream sequence format of *Christopher Blake* theatrically assists the presentation of a dramatically prosaic story. Both are particularly interesting in two respects: one, as examples of Hart's persistent theatricalism, and two, the increasing psychological theme of his dramas, paralleling his own psychoanalysis.

His last play, *The Climate of Eden,* explores the psychological terrain in a traditional mode, but, for the first time, abandons any particularly eye-catching theatrical form. *The Climate of Eden,* however, was not original. It was based on an English novel, *Shadows Move Among Them,* by Edgar Mittelholzer.

Other than in the novel's psychological preoccupation, a cursory glance at the original story does not reveal a story that one might predict would have attracted Hart. It is precisely this fact which suggests that Hart's undertaking an adaptation was a very ambitious move. However, the story does deal with the unorthodox and the exotic, a family that lives by theatrical make-believe on a tropical island. Here the novelty exists completely within the theme and in no way within its form.

Both the strong psychological focus of the narrative and the theatre-in-life philosophy must have appealed to Hart and in his adaptation he was remarkably faithful to the novel. He focused completely on the theme, and, in only two acts, dealt with all the major incidents of Mittelholzer's story of 334 pages.

The very absence of those typical theatrical elements that divert the senses throws Hart's dramatic talent under the sharpest light of his career. And with all respect to his endeavor, it must be stated that this dramatic talent was found wanting. It is not believed that the novel was any kind of unusual success, but Mittelholzer had the novelist's facility to probe and define the minds of his characters. By being rigidly faithful to the story, Hart actually robs it of a necessary expansion and vitality. And most ironically, by not theatricalizing it in some way, he did not replace the deleted material with any of compensatory value.

The Climate of Eden, Hart's most ambitious project and thus his most personal failure, was the last play he ever wrote. It is the only work he ever undertook determined to make a break with a pattern and a formula that was so obvious a characteristic of his work.

The reverse chronology of *Merrily We Roll Along,* the three-generation span of *The American Way,* the montages of *The Fabulous Invalid,* and the stylized presentation of the fantasies in *Lady in the Dark* and *Christopher Blake* constitute heightened theatrical forms for the treatment of serious themes. Collectively considered, these theatrical forms may be called novel expressions of themes in themselves not novel. They are theatrical forms precisely because they aspire to the unique, and thus freshly stimulate the eye and the imagination.

Therefore, it may be said that Hart's "chronicle" and "dream sequence" constructions have a common source with his comic technique. This statement is possible when it is recalled that the basis of much of what is comic in the collaborative comedies is "the incongruous, the unexpected, and the exaggerated." A source common to all three of these comic principles or qualities is found in the notion of "novelty." When these qualities are predicated on a character, action, or dialogue, such are endowed with rather special characteristics removing them from the ordinary, common routines of life. They have been made to stand out from the ordinary background in a special and, often, novel way. If, then, we consider the "novelty" of theatrical form as an extension of the "novelty" which is the source of "the incongruous and the unexpected," we have glimpsed a source common to both Hart's theatricality and comic technique.

In sum, a consideration of Hart's serious plays suggests two principles: the broad lines of character and action delineation, which contribute strongly to making his comedy low, contribute to making his serious themes melodramatic; and the conspicuously theatrical forms of Hart's serious plays are related to his comic technique by the extension of the notion of "novelty."

It appears to be the historical view that farce is more indigenous to American culture than high comedy, which to many analysts has seemed an important form.

Perhaps, because the American personality has been practical and active rather than contemplative, and informal and irreverent more than formal and polite, the farce, because possessed of these same characteristics, is more popular with American audiences than are the higher comic forms which deal so dominantly with manners and ideas.

The dominance of the farce form in the American comic scene is obvious not only by the number, but, indirectly, by the rarity of high comedies on the American stage and the attention these endeavors receive in critical histories and anthologies.

With many theatrical energies increasingly absorbed by the musical format, it seems as if the clever farce is becoming even more scarce than heretofore. The comic form has, however, proved amazingly versatile. Farce itself has been able to combine the ever-funny low comic construction, which frames a zestful pace and abundant physical activity, with an increasing sophistication of content and character. Testimony to this felicitous state of affairs is suggested, in the Hart canon, by *The Man Who Came to Dinner.*

Therefore, with farce the dominant comic form upon the American stage, the occasion for a literature of comedy was minimal. Some critics have felt that if farce, no less than high comedy, "is to survive its hour upon the stage, it must have some literary merit." But as a general rule, American farce has not contained it.

By definition, the repeated characteristics of Hart's writings are farcical or melodramatic: the exaggerated character, the stress on action, the emphasis on plot complication and complex situation, and the dialogue best expressed in the wisecrack. The "broad stroke" is a term in which such characteristics may all be summed up, and through which it may be said that Hart entered the mainstream of American comedy.

Of all his work, Hart's farces are the most successful in attaining their objectives, and upon his farces will the more enduring elements of his theatrical reputation rest. His farce-burlesque, *Once in a Lifetime,* can stand alone as a low comedy when the purpose of its parody is forgotten. Only the utter topicality of *As Thousands Cheer* and the passing of the revue prevents its revival. The second act of *You Can't Take It with You* is a classic of farce construction and *The Man Who Came to Dinner* is one of the most elevated farces of its decade. Indeed, Hart's very dexterity with the farce form inhibits his more ambitious

works, such as *The Climate of Eden,* from being his most successful.

Hart himself may not have been happy with this state of affairs, for after the failure of *The Climate of Eden* he wrote in his journal, "It is extremely foolish, as Mr. Mencken so sagely pointed out, ever to underestimate the low taste of the American public."

Yet, the foregoing analysis concludes that as much as Hart may have aspired to create plays of dramatic stature, he often readily settled for the "American public's low taste" since, obviously, a Broadway hit was so often dependent upon it. Perhaps it is more generous to state that the American public has a collective preference for farcical action and Hart was able to satisfy it with skill.

The device of "overstatement," or "the broad stroke," is the principal characteristic of the comic element in the musical books as well as the later comedies. Characters are either types (to sustain the romantic interest) or broadly drawn (the comic character leads), the action tends toward the situational and the absurd, and the dialogue toward the wisecrack or the speech containing exaggerated or opposing concepts. Even when the musical book became serious with *Lady in the Dark,* the dramatic elements tended toward the simple and the naive while the theatrical elements, seemingly to compensate for the lack of the "startling" effect, grew ingenious and complicated, as if to assure audience attention.

In the collaborative comedies and *Light Up the Sky,* the comic formula continues to be drawn from manipulation of the exaggerated, the incongruous, and the unexpected. This is the stuff of low comedy and low comedy is the basic stuff of farce. A source common to all three principles is contained, then, in the notion of "novelty."

On but a slightly different level, "novelty" is the basis of the special forms given Hart's chronicle plays, and his solo *Lady in the Dark* and *Christopher Blake.* A reverse chronology, a three-generation span, lengthy montage sequences, dream sequences and the use of revolving stages all stamp the serious plays with a particularly novel and theatrical cast. The theatrical form is strengthened in each case precisely because a certain novelty is an essential characteristic of it. It must be noted that none of the above-mentioned devices are original to Hart, but taken collectively they reflect his tendency to identify theatricality with novelty.

Thus, a source common to both Hart's comic technique and his theatrical forms is to be found in the basic quality of novelty which characterized both throughout his writing career.

Hart's dependence on novelty is unquestionably indicative of a limited dramatic ability. It may be recalled that it was even the unorthodox and novel philosophy of the jungle family in *The Climate of Eden* which attracted Hart to adapt it. Hart's lack of dramatic depth—ironically, a depth attained only in his autobiography—makes none of his plays, especially his dramas, acceptable as art; his theatrical flair makes all of them, especially the comedies, at least artful. Hart's theatricalism and his comedies found

Broadway the most hospitable, precisely because they are the easiest appreciated by the larger number of audiences and the most acceptable, therefore, to theatre managers.

The very fact that all of Hart's writing was for the theatre of Broadway serves to explain partly the pattern of repetition, the persistence of a formula, running throughout the body of his work. The deliberate, polarizing use of popular names, the dialogue playing with opposing concepts, a devotion to strong situation and pace, and variations on the bases of low comedy, once proven efficient in drawing attention or exciting laughter, are among the devices that find a second life in new plays. If a mock-heroic actress proved theatrically popular in one play, Hart had no dramatic scruples about reintroducing the character in another play if it would assist in its popularity. Thus, the Broadway theatre itself is an important, ever-present influence to consider in an evaluation of the works of Moss Hart.

The constructional principal that appears to inform the Hart plays, regardless of their genre, is a continual stream of stimuli to both the eye and ear. Although as in *Once in a Lifetime, You Can't Take It with You,* and *The Man Who Came to Dinner,* his comedies often possess an illusion of satire, none of them possesses a genuine probing of ideas. The immediate effect draws Hart's attention and skill more than the challenge of dramatic possibilities.

It does appear that in the Hart comedies a cerebral preoccupation with ideas is never allowed to get in the way of comic pace, a comic turn of dialogue, or a comic action. This preference may not serve satire, but it may assist good farce, especially when that farce often offered an illusion of satire. This preference may not serve enduring drama, but it may serve a part of the theatre's immediate needs. Hart's preference for fortifying his comedy, even at the expense of dramatic depth, may not necessarily prove a fatal criticism. For as a genre intrinsic to the theatrical taste of a people, farce is worth all the attention, talent, and skill native playwrights can bring to it. To farce, Hart contributed these things. There is, perhaps, a touch of irony in crediting Hart for his enrichment of the farce form: it is possible that where Hart imagined he was being commercial and safe in attending to farce, he was actually being his most contributive to the comedy of a native drama. (pp. 60-87)

> *Richard Mason, "The Comic Theatre of Moss Hart: Persistence of a Formula," in* The Theatre Annual, *Vol. 23, 1967, pp. 60-87.*

Brendan Gill

[*Once in a Lifetime*] is a literary curiosity—a comedy that stumbles and rights itself again and again in the course of stringing together by hook or by crook the greatest possible number of funny lines and sight gags. . . . The first of several successful collaborations by Moss Hart and George S. Kaufman, it is now almost fifty years old, and it unquestionably shows its age. By contemporary standards, it is far too long; moreover, it is in three acts, and one sees with what difficulty the authors wove the three acts into a coherent whole. Moss Hart devotes almost half of his delightful autobiography, *Act One,* to the genesis of *Once in a Lifetime;* it is one of the most instructive accounts ever written of how plays can be hammered into actable shape by dogged hard work and showbiz knowhow. In 1930, *Once in a Lifetime* was a big hit (Kaufman himself making a hit in the role of a Broadway playwright hired by a Hollywood studio and then entirely forgotten); the play was slangy, headlong, and irreverent, in a fashion that we tend to associate today largely with the Marx Brothers. It poked fun at the vulgarity and egomania then rampant in Hollywood, making it clear at the same time that these qualities were to be found everywhere throughout the country.

The plot of *Once in a Lifetime* deals with the coming of the "talkies" to Hollywood. George Lewis, an unemployed vaudeville straight man of little intelligence and no talent, arrives in Hollywood and through a series of preposterous accidents is hailed as a genius; he becomes the right-hand man of the noisiest, most manic, and most important of Hollywood producers. Every error Lewis makes pays off; everything he clumsily blunders into turns to gold. . . . First read Moss Hart's autobiography, then go see the play; you will have a good time.

> *Brendan Gill, "In Praise of Lemmon," in* The New Yorker, *Vol. LIV, No. 19, June 26, 1978, p. 51.*

John Simon

It is a sorry theater in which *You Can't Take It with You* becomes a classic, as this ramshackle, simplistic wish-fulfillment farce is most often uncritically hailed. That it is almost plotless would not matter if the characters were less mechanistically contrived, the situations at least remotely related to reality, and the wit not so consistently primitive. Of course, in 1936, when the Depression was not yet over, there must have been something vastly comforting about a happy-go-lucky family and friends, one zanier than the other, surviving in style with two black servants without having to work, and free to pursue their lunatic hobbies to their full hearts' and empty heads' content.

The principals come schematically equipped with two unrelated hobbies each. For Grandpa Vanderhof, it's collecting snakes and frequenting commencements at nearby Columbia University; for his daughter, Penny Sycamore, it's painting and playwriting, because a typewriter was mistakenly delivered to the house (didn't the rightful owner ever claim it, or was it destined for George S. Kaufman or Moss Hart of the famous duo-typewriting team Kaufman and Hart, responsible for *You Can't Take It with You,* either of whom could make do with the other's machine?); for granddaughter Essie, it's ballet dancing and making candy; for her husband, Ed, it's a printing press and a xylophone. Penny's husband, Paul, has only one hobby, making fireworks, but he has a sidekick, Mr. DePinna, who came to deliver ice but stayed on to help make heavenly fire in the basement; so here it's one hobby but two practitioners.

Essie has a lovely elder sister, Alice, who is normal and a secretary, but somehow exempt from the opprobrium heaped on other workers. She and the boss's son, Tony Kirby (the ineffectual drone of his father's Wall Street firm, and thus, obviously, lovable), are in love; by play's end, the senior Kirby, a workaholic millionaire, is likewise converted to the saxophone—and, in due time, perhaps even to his other secret passion, the trapeze—so he can be saved. For his wife, a typical society matron, no immediate redemption is in view, though she may yet take up, say, clinometry and scrimshaw. That Essie, DePinna, and Ed (who prints Trotskyist slogans and distributes them in his wife's candy boxes, but is astounded when the F.B.I. takes an interest) are authentic imbeciles, that Mr. Vanderhof is made into a hero for cheating the government out of a lifetime of income tax, that the émigré Boris Kolenkhov should be thought charming because he lives off fraudulent ballet lessons to unteachables, surprisingly bothers no one. That Penny, who writes god-awful plays, should seem delightful to the authors of **You Can't Take It with You** is, however, perfectly understandable.

That farce can and should make a modicum of sense has been amply demonstrated by such playwrights as Feydeau and Courteline, Nestroy and Goldoni. In a letter to his wife, Kaufman said that the play "has a point . . . that the way to live and be happy is just to go ahead and live, and not pay attention to the world." It may be all right for the dramatis personae not to pay such attention and suffer the consequences; but dramatists guilty of the same inattention are sure to end up on the junk heap of theatrical history. (pp. 89-90)

John Simon, "Dubious Blessings," in New York Magazine, Vol. 16, No. 17, April 25, 1983, pp. 89-91.

FURTHER READING

Ferber, Edna. "A Rolling Moss Gathers Considerable Heart." *Stage* 14 (December 1936): 41-3.
Discusses Hart's early career and childhood.

Gould, Jean. "Some Clever Collaborators: George S. Kaufman and Moss Hart." In her *Modern American Playwrights,* pp. 154-67. New York: Dodd, Mead & Company, 1966.
Focuses on the early careers of Kaufman and Hart and their professional relationship during the 1930s.

Harriman, Margaret Case. "Hi-Yo, Platinum!" *The New Yorker* XIX, No. 30 (11 September 1943): 29-34, 37-8, 40, 42-3.
Discusses Hart's "enthusiasm for riches," his early career, and his collaborations with George S. Kaufman and Cole Porter.

Hart, Moss. "Men at Work." *Stage* 14 (November 1936): 58-62.
Comments on Hart's collaborations with George S. Kaufman, Cole Porter, and Irving Berlin.

———. "Graduate Academy." *Theatre Arts* 34, No. 4 (April 1950): 54-5.
Briefly outlines Hart's ideas for training actors and other theater professionals.

———. "How a Lady Kept a Playwright in the Dark." *Theatre Arts* 36, No. 11 (November 1952): 80-2.
Reminisces about Gertrude Lawrence, the lead actress in the original production of *Lady in the Dark.*

Rick Hillis

1956-

(Born Richard Lyle Hillis) Canadian poet and short story writer.

Often drawn from personal experience, Hillis's poems and stories recount the daily trials of pipeline workers, construction crews, and boys coming of age in the author's native Saskatchewan. Hillis's insightful depictions of the lives and intimate concerns of blue collar workers have prompted many critics to liken his works to Raymond Carver's short stories about working class communities in the Pacific Northwest. Many commentators praised Hillis's use of simple, often terse language to develop characters with convincing depths of emotion. Ellen S. Wilson stated: "Hillis has a talent for selecting the telling details, not so much summing up a life in a sentence as hinting at the complexity that transcends the ability of fiction to recount it."

The Blue Machines of Night, Hillis's first collection of poetry, contains loosely autobiographical verse about boyhood in a small Saskatchewan community and work on a pipeline crew. Reviewers agreed that Hillis's poems successfully evoked common experience and emotion without sacrificing the poet's personal voice. Gerald Hill noted: "[Hillis's] poems are close to action, are sharp reflections of concrete event. 'Trust me,' says the 'Photographer of Snow' 'to curve myself around your edges.' The poems in [*The Blue Machines of Night*], then, not only mark clear edges of image and idea but also point the way to contexts beyond."

The nine stories in *Limbo River,* for which Hillis won the 1990 Drue Heinz Literature Prize, are also set in rural Canada, and range from realistic accounts of working class families to an absurd tale of a man obsessed with sight after staring into a pig's eye as it was butchered. Two stories, "Blue" and "Big Machine," that address concerns of workers on a gas line, are peopled by characters struggling to adjust to changes in their families and jobs. One character, for example, is a welder who is insulted when he is assigned to work with a woman and shocked that his son doesn't plan to follow his working class lifestyle. Most critics commended Hillis's use of humor in these realistic, often harsh stories, and agreed that the author succeeded in creating complex, absorbing characters. Robert Olen Butler declared: "The characters in Mr. Hillis's world get blown in with commonplace clutter like tumbleweeds against a chain link fence, and in response they yearn. Mr. Hillis gives us something that is all too rare in the modern short story—characters with discernible desires that move them to action."

PRINCIPAL WORKS

The Blue Machines of Night   (poetry)   1988
Limbo River   (short fiction collection)   1990

Gerald Hill

What follows is an appreciation more than a review. I already admire much of the work in [*The Blue Machines of Night*], having seen much of it published in magazines in recent years.

The "Aneroid" section covers a prairie boyhood. Naturally, things like hawks, heat, gophers (the "stupid heroes of springtime"), pennies on train tracks, and the "Pressure/of growing older with no future" appear in this sequence. But within such a familiar context Hillis's poems nip sharply and unpredictably in little bursts of image and story. See **"Accidental Bird Murder,"** one of a half-dozen or so prose poems in this book, in which an arrow, after killing a bird, is "painting a brand new emptiness on the wind."

And one need not have grown older under the south Saskatchewan sky to appreciate the range of meaning implied in lines like these from **"A Boy, Dreaming"**:

> Listen to the dead whine in the wind.
> They are the ones who wouldn't believe
> if you live to be eleven
> you will live.

Fine line-making, sure but not constrictive, occurs throughout this book:

> So, he slept his youth on
> the shore of her. Awoke
> denuded, shattered
> remains, her alluvial fan.
>
> **("Photographer of Snow")**

The "Hands" section, ten poems related to life with a gas line crew in rural Saskatchewan, has this to say:

> You know what you are doing.
> It is called work—known as doing
> time in some circles, and you suspect
> time is doing you
> no favours on this road.
>
> **("The Road")**

The sound in Hillis's lines carry much of the content in these work poems: "Young bronk saddles the hog/ and hooks the chain on a brain-size rock./Choking diesel . . . "

> **("Bottleneck Blues")**.

There are many other highlights. **"Photographer of Snow,"** with its shifting tone and point of view, is a series of fragments which are nonetheless true to the whole of love. In this poem, as in others, images pass, then recur in slightly altered form. The lines "You will sleep smooth as stone/in a child's palm, a quite pebble/beneath my tongue" become, three pages later, "you will sleep smooth as a pebble/on my tongue a stone/in a child's palm."

The humourous **"Bob and Bing Visit Saskatchewan,"** wherein Hope and Crosby "came to Saskatchewan to kill/birds," works, for me, as a dandy anti-free trade piece:

> Hope killed everything in sight.
> He'd kill a Hungarian Partridge for
> example and Bing would go,
> "Nice shot, Robert." And Bob would
> tilt his famous ski-slope nose and blow
> smoke off his weapon.

Generally, Hillis is a poet of great vigour. His poems are close to action, are sharp reflections of concrete event. "Trust me," says the **"Photographer of Snow"** "to curve myself around your edges." The poems in this book, then, not only mark clear edges of image and idea but also point the way to contexts beyond. Hillis is indeed a poet to trust.

> *Gerald Hill, in a review of "The Blue Machines of Night," in* Freelance, *September, 1988.*

Brian Burch

Joe Fafard's *DC-neuf,* the cover of Rick Hillis's **The Blue Machines of Night,** provides a powerful introduction to Hillis's first collection of poetry. The image of fertile life buried beneath an urban nightscape seems to underlie much of the book.

In **The Blue Machines of Night** we are confronted with images of Hillis's youth on the farms and in the small communities of Saskatchewan. He is not showing a retrospective of an idealized rural past or attacking his early experiences, but rather giving us something of our own experiences of growing up transported to another setting.

The Blue Machines is not entirely devoted to life in the Saskatchewan countryside. A favorite poem in the collection is **"Crossing the Border,"** a story of an encounter between Hillis and a large American red-neck who both breaks the front window of Hillis's car and, after convincing Hillis that he can replace the glass, gets Hillis lost in the back roads of Montana. It is a fine narrative poem.

Hillis's short section of poems, "What Time Can Do," is an intense delving into the coming to terms of the aging of one's father and the death of one who has given you life. There is no cheap sentimentality in these poems. **"Old Man"** and **"My Father"** are vivid descriptions of the experience of continuing in time while a history you are a part of has ceased.

Hillis is not an academic writer, despite good academic qualifications. He writes in a popular, accessible style somewhat reminiscent of Milton Acorn or Gwen Hauser. He is, like too few of those writing in Canada, a product primarily of the Canadian experience, and his writing reflects our shared realities.

> *Brian Burch, in a review of "The Blue Machines of Night," in* Canadian Book Review Annual, *1988, pp. 200-01.*

Publishers Weekly

This fine debut collection of stories [**Limbo River**], winner of the 1990 Drue Heinz Prize, is set largely in central and western Canada, but is not regionalist in flavor. Having gazed into the strangely impassive eye of a pig being butchered, the schoolteacher in **"The Eye"** is plagued by intrusive dreams and loses the ability to make eye contact. Not all the characters in these nine stories can identify the sources of the massive psychological blocks they live with, but the struggle of blunted sensibilities against fierce or whimsical destructive forces is a common theme. Hillis maneuvers well in his chosen fictional milieu of redneck pipefitters, deer hunters and neglected children, yet readers may find it easy to separate themselves from the pain of characters—partly due to a pervading element of farce, and partly because an indulgent sense of poetic justice directs the worst of the devastation against the more obnoxious characters. Nonetheless, in rich and figurative language so controlled that it at times seems terse, the author considers human behavior with empathy and impressive depth.

> *A review of "Limbo River," in* Publishers Weekly, *Vol. 237, No. 26, June 29, 1990, p. 87.*

Ellen S. Wilson

The construction workers, taxi drivers, and street musicians that people Rick Hillis' **Limbo River** are rather familiar. Hillis focuses, however, on the bizarre aspects found in these generally ordinary personalities, the obsessions, the illogical desires, the lengths to which, at times, we all must go to be reconciled with our lives. The result is a series of wholly absorbing yet surprising worlds, the mark of successful short fiction. More important, these stories are fun.

Of the nine stories in this new collection, winner of the 1990 Drue Heinz Literature Prize, four stand out as remarkable. **"Blue"** and **"Big Machine"** are both about a three-person team of gas-line construction workers. The world of Ed Lubnickie, veteran welder, has been stable until now, distilled to a system of essential truths. When a woman named Norma is put on his team, he tells his foreman, "I don't work with a woman," as though stating irrevocable fact. But Lubnickie does work with this woman, and her presence is the first in a series of circumstances that contradict what Lubnickie has always believed.

Hillis has a talent for selecting the telling details, not so much summing up a life in a sentence as hinting at the complexity that transcends the ability of fiction to recount it. The complicated character of Ed Lubnickie, for example, is illustrated in part by the way he sees other people. "Ed understands Murdoch. What Murdoch wants is to be a welder, but needs practice. . . . He is twenty years old, two years older than Chris, Ed and Myrtle's son, whom Ed believes to be a queer." A man, according to Ed, is what he does, and he does what he does because he has a family to support . . . which he has because he is a man.

In **"Big Machine,"** every life seems to have gone just over the line into catastrophe. Lubnickie's wife Myrtle, in **"Blue,"** is thoroughly complacent about what she can and cannot control, never troubled by self-doubt, and spends her time "making bread and buns because a home needs these." In short, "her life is what she wants." In **"Big Machine,"** even Myrtle's well-organized life is falling apart: "She can't put her finger on what's going on with Ed and Chris. How come things can't get back to the way they were? Myrtle bakes, irons, cleans—her home is in order. So how come she feels lost inside it?" These characters don't want to see the world as fluid. They can't quite keep up. As one character says, "Somebody changed the rules on me and I don't know what to do." **"Big Machine"** ends with too much unsettled for a reader to be willing to leave it there, and in fact these two stories are part of a novel in progress.

These prize-winning stories create a series of wholly absorbing and surprising worlds

---

The shifting perceptions of reality in **"Summer Tragedy Report,"** and the shifting sympathies on the part of the reader, are due to the fact that the narrator is a small, intellectual 13-year-old boy. Alex is spending the summer on his aunt and uncle's farm being terrorized, initially, by his brawny 15-year-old cousin, who is also visiting for the summer. Roy beats up Alex on their first day at the farm, but very quickly Alex learns to manipulate his less-intelligent cousin by pretending he wants to do whatever it is he wants Roy to do. Roy then can't resist taking away whatever he thinks Alex wants.

In the final episode in the story, Roy shoves Alex aside and goes after a rat in the pump room, only to have the rat run up inside his pants leg. Their aunt blames Alex for this, which seems unfair. How could he have directed the course of the rat? But Alex has found ways to stay out of trouble all summer and, in doing so, reveals a certain amount of cruelty in himself. He takes too much pleasure in exploiting Roy, and there is also a disturbing scene in which Alex shoots a young frog merely for the pleasure of demonstrating control. Here is something that he, small as he is, can bully. His perceptive aunt may have sensed this in him. But as Alex explains, "To them, I was the bad guy because they couldn't understand the only weapons I had to fight with."

"Limbo River," the last story in the collection, is also a first-person account by a young boy. Sean, only eight or nine years old, moves to a shabby apartment complex with his mother and becomes friendly with Marcel, a middle-aged man on welfare who spends his time sitting on the lawn drinking and boasting. Marcel's view of his life, which includes time in prison, the loss of a son, and at least one failed marriage, is that he is an incredibly lucky guy. Always, at the last minute, things work out for him. And as he frequently tells Sean, "You remind me of myself at your age."

The story is filled with images of imprisonment and the only time Sean feels free, feels that anything is possible, is when he briefly owns a bike that Marcel finds for him and then later takes away and sells. The story is named both for the way Sean thinks of the river that flows by the complex, "a different river every day," and the dance that Marcel, a man with many unusual talents, can do better than anyone. "Roll with the punches," Marcel tells Sean. "We're here for a good time, not for a long time." That is the best advice that Sean, imprisoned in childhood, can get at the moment.

It may be no coincidence that the best stories in this collection are the longest ones. Hillis' fully-developed characters have lives that must continue long after their tales are told. Award-winning fiction does not always go down as easily as this does, and sometimes requires an intellectual effort merely to figure out what it means. In Hillis' stories there is a real sense of adventure, in the chances he takes with his characters, his plots, his details.

> *Ellen S. Wilson, in a review of "Limbo River,"*
> *in* Carnegie Magazine, *July-August, 1990.*

Robert Olen Butler

A gas pipeline worker named Murdoch lies awake in the dark listening to the highway traffic outside his window. Murdoch's fear and yearning—and all the fear and yearning resident in the working-class world he's part of—are matters of great concern to the Canadian writer Rick Hillis. "The thin walls of his apartment shake," Mr. Hillis writes in the story **"Big Machine,"** "and Murdoch feels like his future is leaking away, oil from a bad gasket."

The metaphor is direct and pitch-perfect, and it is typical of Mr. Hillis's work in *Limbo River,* his first collection of short fiction, which won the 1990 Drue Heinz Literature Prize. There's a scruffy thingness in Mr. Hillis's stories. He lingers with the contents of a welder's rumpus room, a farmer's kitchen, a teen-age girl's truck stop hangout, even the contents of a blue-collar working woman's shopping cart. What makes this elaboration of detail effective is its intimate integration into Mr. Hillis's larger vision. Consider, for example, this glimpse of a character as he listens to his heart:

> How did he get here?—frozen in the middle of an oil-stained parking lot in the dark. The sodium lights put a bluish tint on the cars. The chain link fence, blown in with tumbleweeds, rings softly in the wind making a lonely sound. A few tumbleweeds have drifted over the fence, pinned against car bottoms.

The characters in Mr. Hillis's world get blown in with commonplace clutter like tumbleweeds against a chain link fence, and in response they yearn. Mr. Hillis gives us something that is all too rare in the modern short story—

An excerpt from "Blue"

Norma hates these guys. The one called Finch and the red-neck Eddy. They make fifteen bucks an hour and welfare pays her three hundred and fifty a month. She's supposed to feed and clothe two kids on this, yet. This is her chance, nobody's taking it away. She thinks of last night, nervous about the job, cranking tobacco filter tubes at the kitchen table. Her two kids, Terry and Tracy, watching TV, eating a whole box of Ritz. Tracy, her fourteen year old, copping the odd cigarette before Norma can put them in the Tupperware case. Colin coming home stoned and sad. He can't find a job because of the times and because nobody wants a thirty-eight-year-old laborer on the payroll, and now he can't afford to license his Harley.

"I don't want my woman working on the pipeline," he said. "Don't do this to me, honey."

It was strange to see him sad like that, with his face in his hands at the kitchen table.

"Somebody changed the rules on me and I don't know what to do," he said. He was referring, Norma knew, to the poster she found at the welfare office: Blue Women Wanted. A work project created to expose women to the trades; to share a bit of the grant money the government paid to construction. She told Colin about it, but welfare dads weren't wanted. The only work for them was sporadic labor from Temporary Manpower if you could get down there early enough in the morning. Unloading semis and whatnot. Colin was too old to be doing that.

---

characters with discernible desires that move them to action.

An old-time, hidebound pipeline welder in the story called **"Blue,"** coping not only with his disaffected son but also with a new woman partner at work, longs for the world to be as ordered as it once was. A 13-year-old boy in **"Summer Tragedy Report"** seeks a way to defend himself from a bullying older cousin when he is sent for a long visit to his uncle's farm. A weekend hunter in **"The Storyteller"** tries to understand death—of animals and of men—as he hunts with a near stranger who has an odd story to tell.

And in **"Big Machine,"** the story in which Mr. Hillis's vision is most fully and complexly realized, six characters' hopes are woven intricately together. To try to write from six emotionally intense points of view in one short story is a risky matter, but Mr. Hillis pulls it off brilliantly by making the characters themselves, the particularities of their yearning, part of his over-arching vision of the welter of things. A man's striving for a better job, for example, skiffs as loosely as the tumbleweed around this world of oil-stained parking lots.

As in almost any collection, there are a few weak stories. At times Mr. Hillis seems to force a story, usually by building it too tightly around one symbol, as in **"The Eye,"** in which a man becomes obsessed with eyes after seeing the expression of a pig that is about to be killed. But the best of *Limbo River* is splendid work indeed.

> *Robert Olen Butler, "A Scruffy Thingness," in* The New York Times Book Review, *September 23, 1990, p. 40.*

John Godfrey

Rick Hillis read my mind. I had just finished reading **"Blue,"** the first of nine short stories in Hillis' *Limbo River,* and I was rabid for more.

I wanted to read more about Lubnickie, the hardened welder who attains all he ever wanted yet remains curiously discontent; more about Norma, the streetwise housewife driven to tough labor by her husband's laziness; and more about Murdoch, the bachelor who wants to belong to something but isn't sure what that something is.

The story ends beautifully just as the three blue-collar workers are on the verge of discovering something crucial about themselves. I wasn't ready to leave their world, but the story was over. I shrugged it off, turned the page and read on.

The stories in *Limbo River* astonish in part because of Hillis' ability to look into his own back yard and see the world

---

An afternoon and five stories later, **"Big Machine"** kicked into gear with Lubnickie, Norma and Murdoch behind the wheel again. I felt as if I were visiting old friends. We went for a spin, saw the sights, and this time, when we parted company, I knew it was for good.

More important, *I knew it was good. Better than good . . . outstanding, transcendent, inspirational*—I'm gushing, I know, but this is a fantastic collection of stories.

Hillis spent his formative years on the northern edge of civilization in small towns like Moose Jaw, Saskatchewan. The stories in *Limbo River* astonish in part because of Hillis' ability to look into his own back yard and see the world.

"The Eye" bears witness to Hillis' sense of the bizarre. The opening line seems innocent enough: "Harvey McKinnon was hopelessly eye-shy, whatever the situation." But what follows is a macabre journey through the depths of severe psychosis.

McKinnon's inability to look anyone in the eye costs him his job, his family and eventually leads the pained man into a world of dream analysis and thoughts of eye exorcism.

Hillis deftly walks the line between psychological realism and surreal absurdity. **"The Eye"** begins with a serious, almost pitiful tone and spirals wildly to a close in a hilarious scene in which McKinnon battles and conquers his demons between bites of a ham-and-egg break fast at the local diner.

> Using the fork as a decoy, he splattered a dollop of ketchup onto the hash browns, effectively blinding the eye.
>
> A shrill cry of pain rang out.
>
> "Yes!" Harvey speared the eye with his fork and rammed it between his teeth where it wriggled and squirmed like an oyster. He sucked it down without chewing, hoping to scald it with coffee.

The flow of *Limbo River* rises and falls easily between stories. **"Summer Tragedy Report"** brings a change of climate as it follows **"The Eye"** and demonstrates Hillis' mastery over a more conventional writing style.

At first, **"Summer Tragedy Report"** appears to be ridden with clichés: Pre-pubescent Alex is farmed off to the sticks to spend some time with his childless aunt and uncle on a sprawling Alberta ranch. Joining him is his older, tougher, cousin Roy—a rowdy 14-year-old jock who brutalizes Alex and promises to make his younger kinsman suffer as much as possible.

This scenario has been realized in literature before, but Hillis makes it new.

Alex relies on his wits to survive the three-month haul. Through subtle turns of phrase and action, Alex's delicate manner and finesse eventually overpower the bully. Applause seems in order as the story matures to a close and Alex stands triumphant.

"Eagle Flies on Friday; Greyhound Runs at Dawn" explores still different territory—the inextricable link between suffering and art.

"My name is Art Sweet and yours is the last heart I'll break," it reads. "If you follow music, you probably heard of me. I was the young cat who stepped onto the stage at the Newport Folk Festival and became instantly famous. I was eighteen years old and played jazz guitar . . . "

On the verge of stardom, Sweet suffers the loss of his right hand in a freak farming accident. Devastated, he loses touch with his instrument for years, but eventually comes to grips with his handicap and heads to the mountains of Calgary to draw inspiration and play under the stone spires.

Playing on the street for food money one day, he meets Ava: "You rarely find someone absorbed by music the way she was then. Her walk was a dance and my heart fell for her."

Soon after they fall in love, they fall out. And Sweet's final, painful expression, a song called "Tunnel Mountain Breakdown," wraps the story together touchingly, with just enough ambiguity to draw the reader into post-story speculation.

Limbo River is the perfect title for this collection. Hillis' flexible writing style lends depth to the pools and eddies of human behavior. Test the waters.

> *John Godfrey, "Stories from 'Limbo' Kick into High Gear," in* San Diego Tribune, *October 12, 1990.*

Perry Glasser

[*Limbo River*] is a young man's collection. There's a hunting story, and there are two stories about boys learning hard truths about the unrelenting world. These situations are not a surprise, though they are written here with grace, wit, and sad irony. However, because Rick Hillis has an acute eye, and because Rick Hillis selects telling details, he is at his best when he abandons the profluent plot and allows a story to accrue rather than progress. Two connected stories in the collection, **"Blue"** and **"Big Machine"** are more than a string of anecdotes selected to lead a reader to The Big Insight.

"Blue" focuses on the lives of people involved in constructing pipelines, specifically a welding gang that as part of an affirmative action program has been assigned a woman, Norma, as a member of the crew. Norma's presence is met with deep resentment by Lubnickie, a master welder. Hillis observes them sharply.

> Lubnickie's rumpus room sports a stuffed fish, two deer heads, a framed hunter safety diploma. This is where he goes to feel at home. There is a stand-up gun rack that looks like a china cabinet, a Remington pump action 30-06, a rare Winchester lever-action single shot .22 by Ithaca . . . Everything Lubnickie ever wanted in a home is in this room. . . . He comes down here to remember that these are the things he dreamed of having someday, and why he worked so hard.

Of course, Lubnickie feels truly at home nowhere, least of all in something called a rumpus room.

As they say in Intro to Fiction Writing, once you establish conflict, a story ought to write itself. Lubnickie's antagonist, Norma, is married to a philandering parasite, an unemployed creep who borrows money from his wife and vanishes on his motorcycle for days at a time. Norma's daughter, Tracy, is a foul-mouthed tramp and petty thief. Murdoch, a third member of the welding crew, drinks beer and is open to a good time, though he's a bit too stupid and confused to know how to go out and pursue it. Lubnickie fears his only son is a homosexual. The kid does things like read, a sure sign of twisted desires. Eventually, through her desperation, Norma learns to operate heavy equipment and earns grudging acceptance by Lubnickie. It's not a victory; just a change in state, like liquid to gas.

But this story doesn't write itself. **"Blue"** evades being a contrived examination of a "hot" social topic because Rick Hillis delivers to us a cross section of attitudes, histories, worries and fears for all of his characters. Our eye is directed rapidly from one to the other and then back again by highly polished passages never much longer than a few hundred words. The story has no center, no character toward whom the writer and reader are supposed to direct all their empathy, and the result, contrary to expectation, is very pleasing. It shouldn't work; it does because each character is depicted with great compassion. The end result is a story less about character than about a determined time and a gritty place. Narrative by mosaic is Rick Hillis's greatest talent.

"Big Machine," another mosaic, puts us among the lives of the children of the focal characters in **"Blue."** Same place, same time, different universe. Keg parties at "Beer Flats," high spirits with no outlet, frustrated teachers, high school graduates enraged by parents with the temerity to believe that their kids should begin to earn a living. In the reader's mind the two stories resonate off each other so that their sum is more than the addition of two parts. There isn't a sentence in these stories that doesn't ring hard and true.

Other stories in *Limbo River* are less startling, but no less engaging. **"Summer Tragedy Report"** is a narrative about what happens when two young cousins, who have not previously met, summer at a third relative's farm. The older cousin is a rude, loud, unruly bully. The younger cousin reads magazines, prefers to be alone, and plays chess. The story is in first person. Quick now, guess which is the point of view character. The boys become adversaries, and the younger uses the only weapons he has, cleverness and wit. As the summer progresses, the warfare between the two mounts in severity until one bests the other. The final resolution of this story turns on a weak ironic epiphany, one that many readers will have guessed before the story's end, though it is nevertheless pleasing to see the story fulfilled. **"Summer Tragedy Report"** works pretty well. And the title story of the book also resolves with an epiphanic moment. A boy who has drifted with his alcoholic mother finally comes to terms with his life at the Alamo Apartments—his last stand. Hillis's debut is indeed fine. Go. Introduce yourself. His stories dance before your eyes. (p. 61)

Perry Glasser, "Making Introductions," in

The North American Review, *Vol. 275, No. 4, December, 1990, pp. 60-4.*

Rick Groen

Pardon my breathlessness, but talent is a rare commodity, and you don't often see so much of it in so small a space. The venue is *Limbo River,* the talent is Rick Hillis—one being a first collection of short stories set in Western Canada, the other being a thirtysomething writer born into the same setting. A regional voice, then? Hardly. What interests Hillis, and what he impeccably captures, is a geography of mind, not of place—a mental state perfectly mirrored in the book's parodoxical title.

Yes, Limbo River—emprisoned souls floating on an interminable current, a kind of "motion in stasis." Yet don't think these are bleakly existential tales. The characters—mainly blue collar, usually rural—may be trapped in a world spinning beyond their control or understanding, but Hillis never condescends to them. There's joy amidst their sorrow and humour amidst their pain; in fact, there's all the bittersweet residue of what Faulkner called the "human heart in conflict with itself."

The two longest pieces—**"Blue"** and **"Big Machine"**—feature recurring characters along with interlocked incident and imagery. Apparently, the pair are part of a novel-in-progress, but their ability to double as short stories is a tribute to the elliptical tautness of Hillis's style. Indeed, in a spot of technical bravado, he keeps spinning the telescope on us, narrating the account from no fewer than five separate perspectives: Ed, the aging pipe-layer, with attitudes as inflexible as his rapidly fusing spine; his assistant Murdoch, a beer-guzzling "motorhead" caught in that hyphenated greyness between young and adult; his son Chris, a highschool jock quickly losing his athletic arrogance; Norma, the on-and-off welfare mom, saddled with a deadbeat for a husband and a thief for a daughter; and Guttenberg, the sometime schoolteacher, only a few years removed from the kids who now mock him.

Each of these lives swirls around the others, but there's no real point of intersection, except in the shared solitude of troubled dreams and unvoiced yearnings. Yet Hillis does connect them to us, by sketching these remote souls in accessible colours. His language is picture-precise, so precise that Ed, ensconced in the relative peace of his basement den, can be elevated by a single phrase into the essence of middle-class compromise: "He is populated by fulfilled dreams, emptied by them." Likewise, Murdoch, alone behind the thin walls of his high-rise cubby, echoes the universal cry of impatient youth: "He feels like his future is leaking away, oil from a bad gasket." And Norma, after a kitchen spat with her wayward daughter, sighs the lament of every discouraged parent: "Just tired. Weary of feeling so young when she's expected to be wise."

In two other pieces, equally good, Hillis switches to the first-person and the limited consciousness of a young boy. A 13-year-old in the case of **"Summer Tragedy Report,"** where our callow narrator spends a few months on the farm with his rustic uncles and bullying cousin. The result is a marvellously ironic and multi-textured story, with

Hillis bringing off a difficult feat: He turns the tables on his protagonist and on us, first eliciting our sympathy and then withdrawing it, forcing us to see this polite boy as the grown-up he will surely become—a cold-eyed schemer and an inveterate snob, more bully than bullied.

Some of the shorter pieces, notably **"The Eye"** and **"Rumours of Foot,"** are less effective, the poetic volume turned up too high, too fast. But with the title story, he's back on track—it's both funny and wry, an elegant summing-up. This time, the teller is a nine-year-old, a true innocent, flanked by an alcoholic mother and a parade of instant uncles, including the drunken Marcel. Once again, perception is a shifting function of your point-of-view. The pathetic Marcel, for example, fancies himself a truly lucky man, content in his only skill: seems he's an expert "limbo dancer" (the pun is delicious), blessed with a knack for getting "snakebelly low".

Here, the imagery is quietly organic, arising naturally from the text—like the boy's bicycle, literally fished from the river, a found object that "was more than transportation, it *transported me,* changed the way I saw myself." And then disappeared, stolen. *Limbo River* is similarly transporting, found art pulled from the welter of words. But it stays with you; it flows on.

> *Rick Groen, in a review of "Limbo River," in* The Globe and Mail, *Toronto, February 9, 1991.*

Rick Hillis [In correspondence with *CLC*]

Comment on the process of writing **Limbo River,** *including the amount of time it took to complete, your writing habits, the process of revision, and significant editorial input.*

The earliest of these stories **"The Eye"** was written in 1980, the latest **"Big Machine"** in 1989. A number of the stories were written at various "artists colonies" between stints in the work force. In an intense six week period at St. Peter's Abbey in Saskatchewan (a writer's haven) I wrote **"Blue," "The Storyteller,"** what became part of **"Big Machine"** and a few other published stories not included in *Limbo River.*

Generally, when I have time ahead of me, I like to do the Hemingway thing: revise what I did in the days before and then add a few pages on, as I did with **"Big Machine"** and **"Summer Tragedy Report"** specifically, the longer pieces. What happens more often is that I write the opening page or two a few dozen times before I find a voice, then I continue to the climactic scene. For one reason or another I will then put the piece aside for a couple of months and then revise, tacking on the climactic scene (which it seems is almost pre-written) when I get to it, usually in a draft or two. This process is common to most of my stories. . . .

How is your own experience incorporated into your fiction?

I suppose in complex ways; I'm not really sure. Many of my settings are actual places I've spent a lot of time in, which helps in terms of detail, but I doubt anybody living in these places would recognize them from my stories.

Most of my characters have jobs that I've had myself (teacher, construction worker, prison guard). My characters are, I think, largely imagined. A few might have attributes of people I've known, but you wouldn't recognize them, or at least I don't. I think my own interests find their way into my stories: music, sports, how to make a buck, dreams for a better life. I suppose some of my fears find their way in too, at least I hope they do.

Was there a particular event or person that inspired you to compose this work?

No, but the Canadian writer Guy Vanderhaeghe influenced what I'm working on now, a novel based on my story **"Blue."** He'd read the story and said it read in a way like a novel. He put the bug in my ear.

What do you hope to accomplish through your writing?

My chief aim is to entertain, to somehow find a way to pull the reader through the story. I also try very hard to make my fiction aesthetically pleasing—the idea of poem as artifact, imagistically fresh and energetic. But I fear this aspect is likely overlooked because of the class of people I've so far focused on in my work, generally blue collar and below. Raymond Carver and others have rightly pointed out that poorer, less educated folks have the same dreams and anxieties as everybody else, but I think many readers are still blind to the rough hewn beauty and humor of the rundown and marginal. I want my fiction to capture this.

As you write, do you have a particular audience in mind or an ideal reader?

I just write for myself. Often I'll have books I admire scattered around me and I try to live up to them, do justice to their risk taking, diction, all of it. But no, I don't think I have an audience, imaginary or real. It's just me.

Whom do you consider your primary literary influences, and why?

I am influenced by the comic realism, or comic inventiveness of Mordecai Richler, Kingsley Amis, Tom McGuane, John Irving, and John Nichols, to name a few. I think to an extent these kind of writers have shaped my vision; they certainly have made me want to write and be entertaining about it. Canadian poet Patrick Lane was an early, remaining influence. There is something about the lyrical violence, the gritty detail, the *westerness* of his poetry that strikes me, literally, where I live. Hemingway's *In Our Time* was an early influence in the short story, in terms of style and clarity. Lately writers such as Tobias Wolff and Alice Munro, to name a few, have influenced me. I think I am also influenced by more playful, risk-taking writers such as Michael Ondaatje whose poetry collections *The Collected Works of Billy the Kid* and *There's a Trick With a Knife I'm Learning to Do* are probably the two books I reread most, next to Patrick Lane's *New And Selected Poems.* I was influenced early by an old collection of stories by W. P. Kinsella called *Shoeless Joe Jackson Comes To Iowa,* and lately, T. C. Boyle has my vote. I am influenced by fiction that attempts what Gogol did: to push realism, comically, beyond naturalism into a kind of poetic realm.

Describe any works-in-progress.

I've always worked piecemeal, which may account for my slow output. At the moment I'm 2/3 done [with] a novel based on my story **"Big Machine."** In a drawer I have part of a manuscript from a much larger novel, which I abandoned a couple of years ago to work on short stories. I plan to get back to it in the next year or so. Also I'm working on a book of poems, or a cycle of poems, rather, on prairie scout Jerry Potts.

Adrienne Kennedy

1931-

(Full name Adrienne Lita Kennedy) American play-wright and memoirist.

Kennedy's controversial, often violent plays use symbolism to portray African-American characters whose multiple or uncertain identities reflect their struggle for self-knowledge in a white-dominated society. Although some audiences have expressed discomfort with the dark, brutal nature of Kennedy's plays, critics have consistently praised their lyricism and expressionistic structure, frequently comparing them to poetry. Wolfgang Binder observed: "[These] dramas are to some degree exorcizing personal and collective racial traumas and have anger, the urge to communicate and (attempted) liberation as the motivating forces."

Kennedy grew up in a multi-ethnic, middle-class neighborhood in Cleveland, Ohio. A gifted child, she learned to read at the age of three. Kennedy credits her mother as an early literary influence: "I really owe writing to her in a sense, because my mother is a terrific storyteller and I feel that all my writing basically has the same tone as the stories she told about her childhood. She used to tell funny stories, but they always had this terror in them, a blackness." Kennedy's memoir, *People Who Led to My Plays,* presents the diverse people and images that have influenced her writing, and conveys her early fascination with glamorous film stars, and discusses her reverence for the work of Tennessee Williams, whose play *The Glass Menagerie* first attracted her to the theater. She did not begin writing, however, until she enrolled in a course on twentieth-century literature at Ohio State University: "That course fired something in me. I suddenly found myself writing short stories instead of studying." Shortly after graduating, Kennedy was married, had her first child, and began writing plays while staying up late with her baby. Although her work was praised by writing instructors, she became discouraged by consistent rejections from publishers. At the age of twenty-nine, however, Kennedy traveled to West Africa, which induced a turning point in her writing: "I couldn't cling to what I had been writing—it changed me so. . . . I think the main thing was that I discovered a strength in being a black person and a connection to West Africa." During this time, she also traveled to Rome, and the contrast between her African and European experiences provided the background for her first play, *Funnyhouse of a Negro.* When Kennedy returned to the United States, she submitted the drama to a workshop taught by playwright Edward Albee. Soon afterward, the play enjoyed a successful off-Broadway run and won an Obie Award in 1964.

Funnyhouse of a Negro won praise for its innovative depiction of characters with multiple personalities. The play focuses on a young girl named Sarah whose confused identity is linked with her ambiguous feelings toward her white

mother and black father. Simultaneously obsessed with and alienated from Western culture, she is tormented by visions of her light-skinned mother, Queen Victoria, the Duchess of Habsburg, and Jesus Christ. Reviewers were intrigued by the use of historical figures to represent various aspects of Sarah's identity, noting Kennedy's own fascination with many personalities of European royalty. When discussing this work, Kennedy commented: "I struggled for a long time to write plays—as typified by *Funnyhouse*—in which the person is in conflict with their inner forces, with the conflicting sides to their personality, which I found to be my own particular, greatest conflict. . . . I finally came up with this one character, Sarah, who, rather than talk to her father or mother, talked with these people she created about her problems."

Kennedy's following work, *Cities in Bezique,* consists of two one-act plays, *The Owl Answers* and *A Beast Story.* Like *Funnyhouse of a Negro, The Owl Answers* portrays a black woman's quest for self-knowledge in a world dominated by white people. The main character, named She, is the illegitimate daughter of a wealthy white man and his black cook, who is also "the town whore." Rejected by both parents, She is consumed by feelings of estrangement, and her psyche is fragmented into several identities that manifest themselves as Clara, the Virgin Mary, the Bastard, and the Owl. Throughout the play, her black, white, and mythical personalities transform and merge in a dreamlike manner until She finally appears as a lonely teacher who threatens her lover with a butcher knife, and then changes into an owl. Critics emphasized the recurring symbol of this nocturnal bird, citing its ambiguous legendary associations with death, ill fortune, the occult, quests for love, and feminine mythology. Contrasting with the multiple identities in *The Owl Answers, A Beast Story* presents stark characters who enact a pattern of destructive family relationships. At the opening of the play, Beast Girl's father performs her ominous wedding ceremony to Dead Human: "My father preached our wedding service and a black sun floated over the altar. A crow flew through an open window while my mother played the organ and the black sun floated. . . ." Throughout the play, Beast Girl is victimized by her family; she is stalked by her lustful father and then raped by Dead Human when she refuses his advances. Later, her parents force her to kill her child; in an apocalyptic fit of rage and despair, she murders her husband as well. Kimberly W. Benston observed: "[A Beast Story] deals with the impossibility of maintaining a dream untarnished—specifically, the dream of identity achieved through love—amid the corruption which is life. The play is unrelentingly melancholy—we have sublimations and deaths, tiredness and disillusion, frustration and disenchantment."

Other critically acclaimed works by Kennedy include the lesser-known *A Rat's Mass* and *Lesson in a Dead Language,* which portray worlds of surrealistically distorted religion, focusing on the loss of childhood innocence through sexual initiation rites. *Sun: A Poem for Malcolm X Inspired by His Murder,* a short play about creation, is one of Kennedy's few dramas dominated by a male voice.

(See also *Contemporary Authors,* Vol. 103; *Contemporary Authors New Revision Series,* Vol. 26; *Contemporary Authors Bibliographical Series,* Vol. 3; *Black Writers;* and *Dictionary of Literary Biography,* Vol. 38.)

PRINCIPAL WORKS

PLAYS

Funnyhouse of a Negro   1962
The Owl Answers   1963
A Rat's Mass   1966
The Lennon Play: In His Own Write [with John Lennon and Victor Spinetti] 1967
A Lesson in a Dead Language   1968
A Beast Story   1969
Boats   1969
Sun: A Poem for Malcolm X Inspired by His Murder   1970
An Evening with Dead Essex   1973
A Movie Star Has to Star in Black and White   1976
Black Children's Day   1980
A Lancashire Lad   1980
Orestes and Electra   1980

OTHER

People Who Led to My Plays   (memoir)   1987
In One Act   (collection of plays)   1989

Robert L. Tener

One of the most provocative and least studied black American dramatists to emerge in the sixties is Adrienne Kennedy. Set in the surrealistic theatre of the mind, her dramas are rich collages of ambiguities, metaphors, poetic insights, literary references, and mythic associations, all of which provide a dramatic form unique to Miss Kennedy. Having the power of myths, her dramas suggest an awareness of reality contingent upon the images that man is conditioned to expect in his culture. Moreover, they draw upon that peculiar quality of myths which enables man to externalize his deepest feelings about his own nature, identity, and relationship with the sacred. In ***The Owl Answers,*** one of Miss Kennedy's most compact plays, this effect of myths is achieved through extending the metaphoric values of the owl. While on one level of literary meaning the owl stands for evil omens and darkness, in association with the fig tree it is the controlling metaphor in the play anchoring the heroine's problem of identity with the worlds of her white and black parents and her many self-images.

The Owl Answers, a one act play, takes place in a New York Harlem subway which changes at times into the Tower of London, St. Peter's Chapel, or a Harlem hotel room. As the action moves from the present time on the subway to the past time of memories and dreams, the setting becomes variously one of the other three areas. There are three major actions blurring and blending with each other so that setting as well as identity become fragmented and swirl through time and memory as in a dream. Characters pass from one role to another with the removal of an item of clothing or a change in hair. The heroine is named She, the bastard daughter of a black cook and a white man.

The first major action, created partly from memory and fantasy, takes place largely in London. According to She's fantasy, she and her white father, William Mattheson, visit London on a literary pilgrimage. There he dies of a heart attack, and she is locked in the Tower to prevent her attending his funeral. Her guards are Chaucer and Shakespeare, their names suggesting the white literary heritage she had studied. Another historical character appears, Anne Boleyn, who apparently reflects attitudes toward love as expressed in Western literature and political history. She turns to Anne and asks for her help.

Blending with the events in London and in the Tower, the second major action takes place in the past and, representing expository reality, communicates religious and social attitudes. In his home town in Georgia, the white father who had conceived She on his black cook calls his daughter a bastard and apparently rejects her. She is adopted and brought up by the Reverend Passmore and his wife, both of whom are black, who call her Clara. Occasionally, however, they refer to her as an owl and lock her in a fig tree. When her white father died, she wanted to attend his funeral and was told not to. She also wants to make a literary pilgrimage to Europe. Sometime in the past she had been married once and has become a school teacher in Savannah, Georgia. Her adopted parents, the Passmores, like She, are associated with specific attitudes. Seeing herself as God's bride, the Virgin Mary, the wife refuses to allow her husband to touch her. Her bed she turns into an altar by means of owl feathers and there she commits suicide with a butcher knife. As for her husband, Reverend Passmore believes in the white man's Christian religion and has as his symbol the white bird of the church which flies into a canary cage.

The blurring together of both actions develops when the Reverend Passmore's wife becomes successively She's real black mother and then Anne Boleyn. She's white father is presented just as ambiguously. In the events located in London and in the Tower, he is apparently emotionally close to his daughter; in those placed in the real past, he has obviously ignored her. As for his daughter, she appears at times as Clara; in other instances she is the Bastard, or the Virgin Mary, or the Owl. The consequent merging of the two actions emphasizes She's feelings of love and estrangement.

The third major action develops in the present time on a subway in New York. Here Clara sits, a thirty-four-year-old lonely school teacher who searches for love and spends her summers hunting men in New York to take to her hotel room. As Clara brings to life in her memory the events and actions of the first two plots, her latest pick-up, a black man watches her. Eventually she calls him God and asks him to take her so that she can go to St. Paul's chapel. When he tries to undress her, the setting shifts to the hotel room and the bed transforms into an altar. Now she wants him to call her Mary and shows him her letters written daily to her dead father on her trip to Europe (it is not clear if she has really taken the trip or if it was made only in her fantasy). Then she takes a bloody butcher knife from the letters and attacks him. Frightened, he runs away. Now alone, she kneels at the bed-altar which catches on fire, and in its light gradually she begins to look more and more like an owl.

The play suggests no simple answers to its complexities. It would appear that She is confused by her multiple identities or their sources, none of which seems to be really her, yet all of which help determine her inner relationships. Some of them, like Bastard and daughter, come from the black world; others like Virgin Mary come from the white man's religious world; but one, the Owl, comes from the world of myth and legend. She is on a quest for her identity, and her identity cannot be separated from love for which she also searches. Nor can her need for identity and love be divorced from her desire for a father. Her multiple father images are her blood father (a white man), her adopted father (a black man), and her religious father (God); the love which she searches for is love for a father image: love for a real father whom she can be close to, love for a man whom she hunts for in the subways, and reli-

gious love which she identifies with God. Her sense of personal identity is equally fragmented as it is confused by her fractured living as a black person in a white world filled with white images and concepts, none of which is directly related to herself as a black woman.

The play focuses on the problems of identity as conceived in She's mind on two different levels of complexity. In a sense her least complicated roles are that she is a woman, she is a black, and she is a bastard. Her other roles are, however, culturally more complex. She has been educated in college in the white man's literary and political heritage; she has been brought up in the white man's Christian religion none of whose symbols have the mythic power of uniting man with the sacred for the black person; and she has been forced to live in two worlds, one black and one white, because she is a mulatto.

The major thematic content of the play then is the problem of how She's fragmented identities relate to her quest for a stable and unified self-image. The problem is an internal one for She, and Adrienne Kennedy has externalized it by joining the metaphor of the owl with the mythic qualities of the fig tree. (pp. 1-2)

It is clearly more than merely a bird of ill omen. In the more common mythologies of the world, the owl is, among many things, a symbol for non-believers in God who dwell in darkness; a messenger of witches or the bird transformation of a witch; another name for a harlot who works the night; one of the epiphanies of Athene, the Greek goddess of wisdom and the female domestic arts; or the metamorphosis of the baker's daughter who begrudged Christ her father's bread. Its hooting cry is the call of death; at night its voice is the spirit of a woman who has died in childbirth and is crying for her dead child; its presence in a tree near a home presages ill fortune to the inhabitants. Its legendary associations with death, trees, ill fortune, anti-Christian nuances, quest for love, and a female principle thus make it a richly ambiguous metaphor suitable for Kennedy's intentions.

In the play the owl is She, the mulatto daughter of a rich white man. Her identity has historical roots both in the English literary, political, religious world of her white blood father and in the white-black world of her mother, the town's black whore. In addition her identity has an anchorage in the mythical world of folklore and legend from which Kennedy draws her controlling metaphors. If in the white world the owl has one set of governing associations, in the world of myths it has another.

The structure for Adrienne Kennedy's use of the owl and fig tree is one of association with different events, situations, attitudes, and persons. First, as a bird, the owl balances the white bird identified in the play with Christianity and the Reverend Passmore. Like a canary, the white bird prefers to fly into a cage. On the other hand, while the white bird is not related to She, the owl is. The obvious inference is that Christianity as a religion of white men is not psychologically and historically suited to She.

Second, in the play the owl is associated with a fig tree. As the bastard daughter of William Mattheson and the black whore (or as the adopted daughter of the Passmore's, the point of view not being clear on this matter), she is "locked" in a fig tree. The metaphoric term "locked" relates this action with her being locked in the Tower of London. Both situations suggest that what is important is not what happened but how she responds to or feels about the events. Thus as an owl, She sits in the fig tree.

Third, the bird is associated with the dead. In She's memory it occurs in relation to her white father, now dead, who had called her an owl, and somewhat like her white father, she is similar to a dead thing. She feels sterile, barren, loveless.

Fourth, the owl is presented in the context of the beginning of things and in relation to sacred notions. When her mother tells her that "the Owl was your beginning," she says that she belongs to "God and the owls." Her bastard birth is thus anchored by the owl. In addition the owl extends some of its meaning to her black mother who uses owl feathers to construct an altar. Exploring her responses to the owl, She says that she calls "God and the Owl answers." Later she exclaims that

> it haunts my Tower calling, its feathers are blowing against the cell wall, speckled in the garden on the fig tree, it comes feathered great hollowed-eyed with yellow skin and yellow eyes, the flying bastard. From my Tower I keep calling and the only answer is the Owl God. . . . I am only yearning for our kingdom God.

Fifth, the owl is presented against a background of personal and religious ritual which suggests the frustrations of the three black women who dominate the play in their tripartite roles as the biological mother, the religious mother, and the maiden. The black whore mother sits like an owl and pecks at red rice on the floor. She becomes more owl-like as owl feathers appear on her and as she drags in a "great dark bed." At this point the real mother's identity fuses with those of Mrs. Passmore and of the owl. She acquires more owl feathers and her hair becomes black and long and straight like that of the Reverend's wife. In this transformation she turns her bed into a high altar with owl feathers and candles. There she sits. And now as all three concepts (mother, adopted mother, and owl), with a white dress and "wild kinky hair," and partly covered with owl feathers, the figure calls to She, the "Owl in the fig tree," and says that "there is a way from owldom." That way, however, is to St. Paul's Chapel. As both figures kneel in prayer, a green light suffuses the tableau, and the mother image kills herself with a butcher knife.

Sixth, the owl is always associated with She, as can be seen in the many references already suggested. But especially is the association stressed in the final scene of the play. When the black man tries to undress She on the altar-bed, she "screams like an owl," struggles, and begs to be allowed to go to St. Paul's Chapel to see her white father. Suddenly from her notebooks, she draws the butcher knife, bloody and covered with feathers and attacks him. As he runs away frightened, she falls onto the bed which begins to burn. In the background up in the dome, as though suggestive of the Chapel, the white bird laughs.

She is transformed almost magically into an owl-like figure and can only say "Ow . . . oww."

Quite clearly the owl is intended by Adrienne Kennedy to be a black woman lost intellectually and emotionally in a white world. Confused about her black identity and its related basic values of love, father, and religion. She becomes at times a harlot. As the owl who answers, she is the nonbeliever, the harlot, the woman anguished by the lack of love, the spirit of the dead. But being black she feels related to the night; she cries of the woe to come. (pp. 2-3)

In the play She is the composite overlay of her father's cultural heritage and her mother's racial background. Her identity is fragmented because half of her physical roots are black but almost all of her intellectual heritage is white. The consequence is that she feels alienated from her many selves and cannot integrate them. She asks herself on her literary pilgrimage to London if this is her past. And she says that she is never going back there. When her white father died, he returned to the home of his ancestors, but she cannot.

Within the context of the play then, She is the owl for whom instead of solace Christianity offers only the vision of the white virgin Mary equated with a black Christian step-mother who had called her a child of darkness. She is a harlot who hunts for love at night time, a prophetess of death. Especially is she a barren woman crying for the love and children which she does not have. But the owl is also her alter ego, her bird sister, her epiphany. She sits in the fig tree and her presence reflects the death of her father and of Mrs. Passmore and of all those like them. The two metaphors suggest that her anguish is profound and timeless, growing from her basic sense of self. Sitting like an owl in the tree of knowledge about good and evil, she has learned about the white man's literature, but she has also acquired a sense of her personal loss.

Specifically Adrienne Kennedy in *The Owl Answers* appears to focus on the concept that the black in America has no historical or literary heroes to identify with and to achieve personal unity through, a unity necessary to prevent the self from being alienated from the continuity of life. This is a theme that Amiri Baraka has developed many times also. But Kennedy has restricted the idea by treating it from a woman's point of view. In this way the owl and the fig tree become uniquely appropriate images because they are historically associated with the female principle and reflect the rootless aspects of She's nature. They strongly emphasize her mythic qualities as well as her need for a spiritual or sacred relationship with her dead. In addition they provide metaphorical comments on her problems as a woman in finding a love and a religion which can be meaningful for her within the framework of her two disparate worlds.

If she accepts herself as a Christian (Christianity being a religion which reflects white culture), then she can identify with the virgin Mary and become symbolically the wife of God. In this way her bed becomes an altar on which she surrenders to God, and every man whom she picks up is transformed by her into God. On the other hand if she accepts herself as an owl, her bed is the place of a sacred and non-Christian marriage that she has with both a real man and her ancestral spirit; it remains barren despite her yearning for life. This polarized ambivalence overlaps with her submergence at times in the identity of Mrs. Passmore who commits suicide to become God's bride, finding Christianity and release from the pains of the flesh in death. Here the owl metaphor suggests the confusion of the woman's role in sex, in love, and in religion when it is conceived in the frame of Christianity set against the awareness of its non-Christian associations. Uniquely She becomes a collage of many roles and in one of them must be the bride of God (an alien spirit in her owl transformation), literally and repetitively sacrificing herself (that is, her physical self). That belief forces her to repulse the real man before he can become her lover. In the end her search for love becomes hopelessly involved with religion, sex, and self. Perhaps then, her essence, her soul or her spirit, is the only positive thing that she has. But her essence also has to be owl-like because when she kneels at the altar confused by what she is, she looks more and more like an owl.

Adrienne Kennedy uses in the play the images of historical and religious figures and those of birds and the fig tree to make a bitter and satirical comment on the American black female trapped by the conflict of cultures and sexual roles in twentieth-century America. As a mulatto, an educated school teacher, the daughter of a white man, and an intellectual inheritor of his English historical and literary past, She can find no meaning or solace in that past, nothing to reassure the continuity of her own life. She finds kinship only with man's mythic assertions about his nature and its identification with the non-human forms of life.

In this view the setting of *The Owl Answers* is the mind of She and reveals through metaphors her internal responses to external events. Thus past and present and different places become one in a dramatic montage.

It is no wonder then that with her confused dream of love, She becomes lost in the insistence on the dream of the virgin Mary and can not find satisfaction with men. She calls God, but only the owl, the ambivalent fusion of non-Christian forces and of her alter ego, answers. Living in owldom, the land of ambivalence, the vague featureless past of darkness, she feels as though she is locked in a prison from which there is no escape. Because her mother in the role of Mrs. Passmore had denied life by approaching God through suicide, every embrace with a man becomes for She a perpetual religious sacrifice. Trapped in the mystery of the sacred, she sits alone in the fig tree and remains barren. For the Christian the dove as a symbol bridges the gap between the transitory nature of physical identity and the more permanent transcendental spiritual identity which extends like some power from the past into the future as a unifying element. But for the half-white, half-black, part-Christian, part-pagan, the owl and the fig tree emphasize the gulf between the physical self and the spiritual center. (pp. 3-4)

> *Robert L. Tener, "Theater of Identity: Adrienne Kennedy's Portrait of the Black Woman," in* Studies in Black Literature, *Vol. 6, No. 2, Summer, 1975, p. 1-5.*

Kimberly W. Benston

Afro-American drama has, until recently, been rooted in the mimetic tradition of modern Euro-American realism. Yet contemporary black playwrights have come to reject increasingly the formal limitations of the theatrical mainstream to which they are heirs. For the naturalism of which Hansberry's, Baldwin's, Bullins's, and Imamu Baraka's early works are exemplary seems to be satisfied, more or less, with the forms it finds in life: prose; nonfigurative language; an illusion of non-selected events; a "natural" sense of emphasis; and a nonmusical (not necessarily cacophonous) sound. The most distinctive attribute of this form is its guiding sociological and materialistic conception of man. Naturalism takes man to be a part and function of his environment and depicts him as a being who, instead of controlling concrete reality, is himself controlled and absorbed by it. The milieu takes a preponderant part in shaping human destiny; all actions, decisions, and feelings contain an element of the extraneous, something that does not originate in the subject and that makes man seem the unalterable product of a mindless and soulless reality. So long as Afro-American drama maintained naturalism as its dominant mode, then, it could do little more than express the "plight" of black people. Its heroes might declare the madness of reality but reality inevitably triumphed over them. (p. 235)

For the Black Arts Movement, Baraka's *Four Black Revolutionary Plays* showed the way to putting new life into sterile forms, and even though the salient feature of these works is their platitudinous satire, stirrings of a more profound insight were evident. Yet more quietly, less influentially, the strange, surrealistic plays of Adrienne Kennedy had already taken the first steps toward a complete departure from naturalism. The overall effect of her *oeuvre,* from *Funnyhouse of a Negro* (1962) to *Sun* (1970), is one of mystery, mythic fantasy, and poetic ambiguity. The growing interest in and appreciation of her work among Afro-American artists and critics attest to their increased acceptance of expressionistic, or "subjective" explorations of the black psyche.

Cities in Bezique—a dramatic distich composed of *The Owl Answers* and *A Beast Story*—is one of Kennedy's most complex and lyrically beautiful pieces. Though written at different times, these plays are quite clearly complementary investigations of black identity organized around a specific cluster of themes (sexuality, family/tribal structure, death) and symbols (animals, light/dark motifs, musical accompaniments, and innumerable objects of all kinds). Together they provide an excellent model of Kennedy's dramaturgy and vision.

Cities in Bezique is enacted in scenes of strange power, achieved by Kennedy's departures in method: the breakdown of autonomous "characters"; the elaboration of a pattern of verbal themes; and rejection of the representational stage for a kaleidoscope of imaged expressionistic scenes. Kennedy's settings, for example, are a mixture of real and surreal which reinforces the plays' thematic ambiguities: *The Owl Answers* takes place in a subway that is simultaneously St. Peter's, the Tower of London, and a Southern black preacher's den; the set of *A Beast Story* is the "gloomy house of a minister in a drab section of a midwestern city" that is transformed into a bleak landscape of monsters, apparitions, and nightmares. Kennedy includes with her text a "costume plot" and set design, thereby emphasizing the importance of visual elements in the total meaning of her work. Most crucial is the way in which an economy of symbols and motifs, usually concretized by objects such as the ax in *A Beast Story* or by symbolic figures such as *The Owl Answers*'s Negro Man, join with spectacular and supernatural effects to create an aura of lyric other-worldliness and a conciseness of dramatic statement.

The result of such an assembling and ordering of symbols is to add a function to action itself. Instead of treating a plot that explores human relations in their moral aspect, Kennedy makes action into another signature of emotion. It is not an end in itself, flowing from and dependent on what we naturalistically call "character," but invokes instead the intimacies, ecstasies, and anguish of the Afro-American's soul-life. In her plays, relations between men matter less than the struggle of a soul with an all-enveloping spiritual mystery. The coherent action-sequence that illustrates the moral nature of black life (*vide* Hansberry's *A Raisin in the Sun* or Bullins's *The Corner*) gives place to a complex pattern communicating a spiritual insight. In this pattern action is sometimes, it is true, an element of the life of human relations; more often it is an element of the unseen life of the soul and of spiritual powers, presented in poetry through anthropomorphic images.

In the mingling of these elements of seen and unseen, of natural and fantastic, of human and divine, "action" comes to have the force of symbol, and conversely symbol assumes sometimes the character of action. Kennedy opened the way for black writers to become poetic dramatists rather than simply dramatic poets. Her plays allow the spectator to close the gap between himself and the spectacle only by an act of interpretation. Thus, a typical Kennedy drama invades the spectator's mind, putting him in intimate contact with the inner visions he and the playwright share. Ultimately, the characters' struggles become the audience's empathic concern.

The Owl Answers is what Paul Carter Harrison would call a *Hantu* form; that is, its structure turns upon a fluid time/space relationship which eschews linear presentation of images in favor of a more interpretive and poetic design. Thus the multiple personalities of the characters and their various environments change rapidly, often obscurely, and together form an intricate matrix of associations which alone defines the totality of their world. The main figure is "She Who Is Clara Passmore who is The Virgin Mary who is The Bastard who is the Owl"; she has come from Georgia to London to mourn her Dead White Father who was once "Goddam Father who is the richest White Man in the Town" and who is also her stepfather, the black Reverend Passmore. She Who Is is held prisoner in the Tower of London by a chorus composed of Shakespeare, Chaucer, William the Conqueror, and Anne Boleyn (who is also both the Bastard's Black Mother—once a cook for Goddam Father—and the Reverend's wife).

SHE's attempt to assume the white, English patrimony of the Dead Father by visiting his bier, which lies in St. Paul's, is the play's central action. SHE's claim is to the lineage of her blood ancestors, a claim made poignant by the juxtaposition of her love for English culture and her brutal rejection by the chorus of exemplary Anglo-Saxon heroes:

SHE. My father loved you William . . .

THEY. (*Interrupting.*) If you are his ancestor why are you a Negro? . . .

SHE. Let me into the chapel. He is my blood father. I am almost white, am I not? . . . I am his daughter.

For SHE . . . the search for the father and the quest for identity become one. While the individual roles of the father and mother are unique beings, each representative of a distinct and partially valid aspect of SHE's ancestry, SHE's roles are fragments of a single personality, either designated imperialistically by others or personally embraced in her desperate pursuit of selfhood. THEY are cold, abstract, aloof; she moves among their apparitions desiring love in a lifeless world:

DEAD FATHER. (*Rises, goes to her, then dies again. Great clang.*)

BASTARD'S BLACK MOTHER. (*Shakes a rattle at SHE.*)

SHE. (*Screams at the DEAD FATHER and the MOTHER.*)

SHE. You must know how it is to be filled with yearning.

THEY. (*Laugh.*)

Finally, a dark Negro Man, whom SHE calls "God," tries to supplant her vision of love with the sordid sexuality of a Harlem hotel:

NEGRO MAN. What is it? What is it? What is wrong? (*He tries to undress her. Underneath her body is black. He throws off the crown SHE has placed on him.*) . . . Are you sick?

SHE. (*Smiles*) No, God. (SHE *is in a trance.*) No, I am not sick. I only have a dream of love. A dream.

Her dream-world bursts into flame as she and the Negro Man grapple in a space that is suddenly transformed from hotel room to High Altar. SHE's once-calm demands upon the past give way to a final hysteria in which she strips through each available identity—Clara, the Negro child of Reverend Passmore; Mary, the martyred Virgin; Bastard, the Mulatto daughter of Dead White Father—until, enflamed and dripping in her suicidal mother's blood, she at last becomes the mysterious Owl. The owl, solitary, wise, dispassionate, cries out the question embedded within the name "SHE WHO IS"—*Whooo?* Denied the complex legacy of her blood ancestors, surrounded by deception and death, SHE nearly answers by asserting an identity with the nocturnal creature. Yet this concluding statement is only a muted, seemingly painful, and ultimately enigmatic moan: "Ow . . .ow."

One of the most notable features of this play is the addition to naturalistic psychological torment of symbolic overtones that actually alter the character's psyche as they resonate at climactic moments, so that, as the play progresses, character becomes symbol and the work moves into another dimension entirely. Kennedy's plays require of their audiences a sensitivity to these shifts in aesthetic key—some slight, some abrupt, some daring—and especially to those moments of symbolic expansion when the characters lunge forward, thrusting their significance at the beholder. The feeling of dislocation that the audience experiences as the plays move back and forth between the realistic psychological mode and the symbolic one involves it in a constant, conscious process of readjustment to the fictional world. It also accounts, in considerable part, for the sense of menace that pervades Kennedy's work. But it is the threat of meaning, of horrible or blinding revelation, rather than the threat of violence that lies at the root of this menace. It is the fear that what lurks in the inner self and the collective past will emerge stillborn, grotesque, or useless. The result is that when the audience begins to hear the play's symbolic resonances it also begins to feel the special frightening unease characteristic of them. For that sense of menace is intimately related to a paradoxical phenomenon: the further the plays move into the symbolic realm, the nearer they come to the world of the audience itself.

In a work like *The Owl Answers,* Kennedy is pioneering for black theatre a subjective-critical mode which is a deeply innovative dramatic response to the visionary aspect of the Black Arts Movement. The conventional nature of her drama should be clear; borrowing from both the folk-tale and the Strindbergean dream-play, it crashes the barriers of realism by establishing a lyric metaphysical emphasis. *A Beast Story* is essentially an extension of *The Owl Answers* in theme and technique. Yet in the later play pretensions to realism are shed even more while the symbolic investigations of identity, sexuality, and death are rendered with greater clarity. In addition, *A Beast Story* adds to *The Owl Answers* an interest in the confused relation between Nature and the self—the animal and the social being inscribed into and enacted out of a single consciousness.

The multi-dimensional personalities of *The Owl Answers* are reduced in *A Beast Story* to stark, monolithic figures whose only role-fragmentation is evinced in their dual nature of "beast" and Negro. The four characters—Beast Woman, Beast Man, their daughter Beast Girl, and Beast Girl's husband Dead Human—form a "black family" locked in a timeless struggle of wills, desires, and antipathies. *The Owl Answers*'s study of ancestral connection is here supplanted by a concern with the poisonous inheritances possible within a given family structure. Beast Man, a minister, has performed the marriage rite for his daughter and her now dead lover. This event was shrouded in uncertainty and accompanied by evil portents. Yet for Beast Girl it seemed a moment of perfection in which the truth of selfhood was found:

> BEAST GIRL. My father preached our wedding service and a black sun floated over the altar. A crow flew through an open window while my mother played the organ and the black sun floated. . . . He had to stop singing, he had to stop singing, the room was silent. . . . It was morning when I awakened, a red sunrise morning, the first day of my marriage. At last I knew who I was . . . no shadow of myself, I was revealed . . . to myself.

The darkened sky, ominous bird, and interrupted ceremony are merely outward signs of the horror that awaits the young couple. Beast Girl, stalked by her enigmatically lustful father and frightened of her sexuality by her mother's passionate denial ("I cut the throat of a pigeon poult to keep myself untouched"), shuns her husband's advances. They struggle and he wins. Their child seems to her a reward of sin; her parents force her to kill it and, with a countenance of ravaged innocence, she slays her husband also.

Beast Girl's acts of murder are to be seen in two terms: the religious outrage of life's denial and the chaotic sensuality of passion in which death, too, plays its part. Beast Girl is forced into a criminal position which is repulsive to her. She accepts her acts as final and yet her obligation remains to herself, a conscience which will not allow her an artificial martyrdom. It is plain that in the background of elemental, sexual struggle between father and mother—initiated by Black Man and Black Woman and tragically repeated by Beast Girl and Dead Human—is the issue of the emergence of woman as an individual. She comes to recognize the destructive cycle of suppressed desire, bestiality, and death which her forebears—"southern Negroes who came to the city"—have traversed:

> BEAST GIRL. My father built a crib. (*Staring at her father.*) How he loved me, saw me in the crib, circled by the golden aureole. My mother. Black shadows were etched under those pale eyes, for she hardly slept at night and suffered endless wakeful fits. . . . Above the bed hung a doleful picture of the Virgin and Child. . . . Now the moon is out. A bird perches on my bedpost, a great toad runs through the house. I killed his baby with quinine and whiskey.

Beast Girl seems to divine, as the play progresses through moments of accusation and insight, that the antidote to her parents' sublimation of inherited burdens is violent repudiation. Killing her husband and child, however, is useless and cowardly—their ever-present forms and the wild beasts (jackal, toad, crow) who are "glad" at their passing attest to her continued weakness. Haunted by the "nightmares and visions" of her mysterious father (Beast Girl: "My father comes toward me, saying something I do not comprehend and the sky turns black"), Beast Girl is finally driven to an apocalyptic destructiveness. As her parents look on with satisfaction, she hacks away at the monsters and loved ones of her life, ending in utter despair:

> (*A blue crow behind her, she turns and instantly kills it with the ax. A giant toad hops to the room, Croaking. She sees it and wildly axes it to pieces. Beast noises. She swings the ax, wildly screaming.*

Noises louder. She drops the ax, falls down weeping.)

(Silence.)

BEAST MAN and BEAST WOMAN. Now the sky above our house is blue, three robins with red chests appear on the horizon. All is warm and sunlit.

(Silence. Strange bright sunlight, then darkness.)

I have traced the narrative of *A Beast Story* in a summary way, omitting a mass of detail, because it is necessary to assert that the play is a controlled formulation of a specific theme. The play's inquiry, when its pattern is accepted, can be seen, not as obscure, but as a powerfully original projection of deeply considered experience. It deals with the impossibility of maintaining a dream untarnished— specifically, the dream of identity achieved through love— amid the corruption which is life. The play is unrelentingly melancholy—we have sublimations and deaths, tiredness and disillusion, frustration and disenchantment. The cultural institutions it probes, from the family to the "Old Spirituality" represented by Beast Woman's insidious prayers and vanity-table altars, are depicted as vapid and ruinous. As the sun turns black at Beast Girl's wedding, so her world grows dark until only the "strange" light of her failure illumines it again.

Nevertheless, the final impression left by *Cities In Bezique* is painfully complex. Though Kennedy's heroines are caught in webs of congenital horrors, products of both the history of race and the human condition, they still pass through crisis to epiphany, shattering though this process may be. Moreover, a more concrete, positive apologue is discernible in both plays: neither SHE nor Beast Girl fully embrace the realities of her past, her sexuality, or her blackness. The menacing quality of their unfulfilled quests is perhaps less a reflection of the author's nihilism than a warning to those who look on. Kennedy furnishes her plays with a reality of motives and inclinations but her world is like a beachhead on the edge of a darkness teeming with a host of spirits, generally inimical to man. Her plays leave an impression of restlessness and an unresolved longing to believe. They have helped infuse an overriding and overt spiritual impulse into black theatre. Thus far, it has been left to others to evolve in this spiritual mode from search to celebration. (pp. 236-44)

Kimberly W. Benston, " 'Cities in Bezique': Adrienne Kennedy's Expressionistic Vision," in CLA Journal, *Vol. XX, No. 2, December, 1976, pp. 235-44.*

Adrienne Kennedy

[*In the following essay, transcribed from an interview with Lisa Lehman, Kennedy discusses the personal experiences and perceptions that have influenced her writing.*]

Autobiographical work is the only thing that interests me, apparently because that is what I do best. I write about my family. In many ways I would like to break out of that, but I don't know how to break out of it. In fact I would really like to write more about the people who were before my own immediate family, like my grandparents and their family. I have two children, but I've never been able to write about them.

I feel overwhelmed by family problems and family realities. I see my writing as being an outlet for inner, psychological confusion and questions stemming from childhood. I don't know any other way. It's really figuring out the "why" of things—that is, if that is even possible. I'm not sure you can figure out the "why" of anything anymore.

You try to struggle with the material that is lodged in your unconscious, and try to bring it to the conscious level. You try to remain as honest about that as possible, without fear. I don't believe you intentionally set out to write the things you write. For instance, I would like to write mystery stories like Agatha Christie, or much lighter things which are far less torturous, but I feel you must be honest by letting the material come to the surface. And just accept it.

It's not necessarily that easy, because I think your intellect is always working against you to censor. You must just let the material come out and not be frightened about it and not censor it. Just trust yourself and do not have an opinion of your previous work. One must always fight against that imitation of oneself.

My writing, therefore, really requires a certain amount of time-lapse between the event and the written product. I do keep a journal and have always kept some type of written diary, but I have never been happy with that. Diaries and journals always seem so time-consuming.

You can only spend so many hours a day writing about yourself or your world. I trust those periods when I'm not writing constantly. I believe in long periods of resting, not working against yourself by forcing yourself to write when you don't want to. I believe in being relaxed but not in letting things lie dormant for a long time or in between times.

Work does, however, play a very big part in my life. I do write and then go back and work on it some more. Most important, it's really a lot of hard work.

I think about things for many years and keep loads of notebooks, with images, dreams, ideas I've jotted down. I see my writing as a growth of images. I think all my plays come out of dreams I had two or three years before; I played around with the images for a long period of time to try to get to the most powerful dreams.

As an example, *A Rat's Mass* was based on a dream I had once when I was on a train. I was very frightened, doing something I had never done before. I was on a train going from Paris to Rome, and I was going to try to live in Rome for a few months. I was with my seven-year-old son. It was very difficult thing for me to do because I'm not really that adventurous. I had never tried to do something like this. In a way, I just wanted to turn around and go back. I had this dream in which I was being pursued by red, bloodied rats. It was very powerful dream, and when I woke up the train had stopped in the Alps. It was at night. I had never felt that way. It was a crucial night in my life. So, I was just haunted by that image for years, about being pursued by these big, red rats.

Then I try to take these images and try to find what the source for them are. All this is unconscious, all this takes a long time. I'm not in that much control of it. In the case of *A Rat's Mass,* there was a connection to my brother. At that time my brother was in an automobile accident, from which he subsequently died. This evoked an almost unreal memory of when we were children we used to play in the attic and there used to be a closet in the floor of the attic. I didn't like to go up there by myself because I would imagine that there would be something in that closet.

In *Cities in Bezique,* the character of Clara Passmore was a composite of my aunt and my mother and, of course, myself. Clara was very much my aunt's life. She was this girl who grew up in a small Georgia town. She was quite brilliant. Her father was white. She came to live with us when I was in high school. They wanted her to go to school in Cleveland because they figured she was so smart. This was many, many years ago—more than twenty-five years ago she got her Masters at Teacher's College at Columbia. She teaches English somewhere in the South now. I used to listen to her talk a lot. She was very hysterical. I haven't seen her for many years now, but what struck me as a child—as a young person, not necessarily as a child—was how she used to talk, how she didn't belong anywhere. She's very much a basis to that girl in *The Owl Answers,* and my mother also, in a different way, talks about things like that.

Yes, those two people did have a very big influence on me; they both are very articulate and, in different ways, both are very pretty. Somehow, it always struck me, unconsciously, what a tragedy that these very pretty women seemed so tormented. So of course I used them as a model.

I was always interested in English literature and I've traveled in England. There's always been a fascination with Queen Victoria. It always seemed to amaze me that one person could have a whole era named after them. I find the obsession with royalty fascinating. Not only Queen Victoria, but other great historical literary figures such as Patrice Lamumba and, it's obvious, Jesus Christ. Well, I took these people, which became a pattern in *The Owl Answers,* and then used them to represent different points of view—metaphors really.

Obviously there was always great confusion in my own mind of where I belonged, if anywhere. It's not such a preoccupation now, since I see myself as a writer I don't worry about the rest of it anymore.

I first had my plays done in the early sixties and, as a result, I'm really a product of that time of when [Edward Albee's] *Zoo Story* and *American Dream* were the models of success. I studied with Edward Albee at one point, just after I had written *Funnyhouse of a Negro.* I would never have even gone for the one-act, except for the fact that everyone was going to see *Zoo Story* and because I was not happy with any of the three-acts I had written up to that point. I couldn't seem to sustain the power and still can't seem to write really long, huge works.

I admire Tennessee Williams and Garcia Lorca, and I struggled for a long time to write plays—as typified by *Funnyhouse*—in which the person is in conflict with their inner forces, with the conflicting sides to their personality, which I found to be my own particular, greatest conflict. I am a relatively quiet person who just mulls over all these things and, in a sense, it was an attempt to articulate that—your inner conflicts. I had worked for a long time before I did *Funnyhouse* on having people in a room with conflicts. I was very much in awe of Tennessee Williams at the time and so I imitated him. Somehow it just didn't work. It didn't have any power. I just didn't believe it when I read it. Starting with *Funnyhouse,* I finally came up with this one character, Sarah, who, rather than talk to her father or mother, talked with these people she created about her problems. It's very easy for me to fall into fantasy.

Most people seem to feel that *Funnyhouse of a Negro* is still my most powerful play. Of course I find that depressing, seeing that I wrote that over sixteen years ago. But *Funnyhouse* was a build-up of an idea I had been working on for over five years. Finally that idea just suddenly exploded. The subsequent plays were ideas that I had been trying to work on in my twenties, but then they just suddenly came at the same time, because all those plays were written quite close together. They all came out eleven months to a year from the time *Funnyhouse* came out. All those plays are a product of ideas I've been working on from the time I was twenty-five to thirty. I was struggling with those ideas for a long time. Once I found a way to express them in *Funnyhouse,* I think that was when I found a technique. I employed that technique for the rest. (pp. 42-8)

> *Adrienne Kennedy, "A Growth of Images," in an interview with Lisa Lehman, in* The Drama Review, *Vol. 21, No. 4, December, 1977, pp. 41-8.*

Rachel Koenig

With *People Who Led to My Plays,* Adrienne Kennedy has invented a new form of autobiography. Presented to the reader as a "scrapbook" of words, pictures and memories, this slim volume is more accurately an odyssey which poetically documents the coming to artistic maturity of one of the most daring voices in American theatre. Like her lyrical, surrealistic plays, in which the psyche is alternately masked and laid bare, this memoir reveals a disturbing confusion/convergence/juxtaposition of cultures, histories, mythologies, symbols, landscapes, dreams and personal experience.

Covering a period of 25 years, the book is divided into five sections, from "Elementary School" and "High School" through "College," "Marriage and Motherhood" and "A Voyage." Within each time-frame, Kennedy identifies recurring themes, images and experiences that both obsessed and shaped her. In the first section, the seemingly enchanted and safe world of childhood is revealed in all its terror and uncertainty. At sea in a racist and violent wartime society in which watchtowers are erected in schoolyards to ward off Hitler and his armies (who may at any moment invade Cleveland), Kennedy was anchored and nurtured by her social-worker father who urged her to become a "great woman" like "Marian Anderson, Eleanor Roosevelt, Mary Bethune and Helen Keller," by her beautiful, imaginative and mystical mother, and by an extended family which included aunts, uncles, "distant" cousins, grandparents, neighbors and even a specter, Kennedy's Great Aunt Ella.

An endless source of fascination, Kennedy's mother is perhaps the most frequent entry in the book. Kennedy recalls how her mother's dreams were as exciting to her as movies of Frankenstein and Dracula:

> When my mother was making oatmeal on winter mornings as I sat waiting with my bowl at the kitchen table, I secretly yearned that my mother would talk *more* about the people she had dreamed about. There is no doubt that a person talking about the people in his or her dreams became an archetype for people in my monologues, plays and stories.

Swiss psychologist Alice Miller has explored the early childhood experience of literary artists. Thinking about Kafka's childhood, she wrote:

> I would say that Kafka was not imitating the structure of dreams in his work but that he was dreaming as he wrote. Without his realizing it, experiences from early childhood found their way into his writing, just as they do into other people's dreams. Looking at it this way, we get into difficulty: for either Kafka is a great visionary who sees through the nature of human society and his wisdom somehow "comes from on high" (in which case this can have nothing to do with childhood) or his fiction is rooted in his earliest unconscious experiences and would then, according to popular opinion, lack universal significance. Could it be, however, that we cannot deny the truth of his works for the very reason that they *do* draw upon the child's intense and painful way of experiencing the world, something that has meaning for all of us?

Kennedy's dreamlike plays bear out Miller's suggestion; their universality lies precisely in their power to portray what Miller calls "knowledge of the world as it is actually absorbed." The same could be said of *People Who Led to My Plays,* which is a kind of map of the psyche, an exploration of the ways in which a culture imprints itself on a child.

The book also captures the process of modeling, the psychic work which the artist from a very early age engages in as her quest for an authentic voice unfolds. The modeling process often begins with a much beloved parent: Kennedy writes,

> As much as it was possible, I used to imagine that I had been my mother when she was a little girl. . . . when she told me stories, I almost believed they had happened to me: her life at boarding school, her pictures in the red scrapbook . . . the people in her dreams and maybe most of all her incredibly pretty hair . . .

I think now that I often thought they were mine. They all belonged to me.

In the "College" section (1949-1953), we bear witness to how the virulent racism of American Society affected the developing artist. Kennedy coped with this brutal reality by conjuring the image of Jesse Owens, which "helped and sustained" her through the "dark rainy winters" and the dehumanizing, "often open racial hatred of the girls in the dorm." Again and again, we watch the artist imagining her way out of isolation by creating a psychic community.

In the final time-frame, "A Voyage," Kennedy comes to artistic maturity. In the fall of 1960, she traveled to Africa with her husband. During this voyage—via London, Paris and Madrid to Casablanca—image, memory, feeling and impression began to collect and intensify. Directly upon her arrival in Ghana, Patrice Lumumba, the Congo's young and heroic Prime Minister, was murdered.

> Just when I had discovered the place of my ancestors, just when I had discovered this African hero, he had been murdered. Ghana was in mourning. . . . Even though I had known of him so briefly, I felt I had been struck a blow. He became a character in my play [*Funnyhouse of a Negro*] . . . a man with a shattered head. . . . I remembered my father's fine stirring speeches on the Negro cause . . . and Du Bois' articles in *Crisis* which my father had quoted . . . There was no doubt that Lumumba, this murdered hero, was merged in my mind with my father.

(In *Funnyhouse of a Negro* Patrice Lumumba becomes both a raping father and a husband in the confused mind of the central character, Sarah.)

In Ghana, Kennedy writes,

> The sun and the moon seemed to have a powerful effect on my senses. I felt on fire. We bought masks, cloth, musical instruments made of gourds, drove to the north of Ghana where men ran naked, drove to a village where vultures sat atop every tree, sat in a circle and sang with an African family, had tea with Ghanaian ambassadors in the lavish dining room of the Ambassador Hotel, and drove to the white beaches where wild white horses were running free.

As Kennedy told me, "I couldn't cling to what I had been writing—it changed me so. I didn't realize it was going to have such a big impact on me . . . the main thing was that I discovered a strength in being a black person and a connection to West Africa." During this period, she began to work in a surrealistic mode. In Rome, she made an artistic breakthrough—her characters began to have other personas. All of the historical people who fascinated her became an extension of her heroine, Sarah, in *Funnyhouse.*

"My plays are meant to be states of mind," wrote Kennedy. *People Who Led to My Plays* is as dramatic, as personal, as disturbing and as radical as the rest of her oeuvre. Now through her generous work, more young writers may come to understand how the artist selects material from a myriad sources and transforms it into a vision. (p. 15)

Rachel Koenig, "Revolutions on Stage," in
The Women's Review of Books, *Vol. V, No.
1, October, 1987, pp. 14-15.*

Adrienne Kennedy [Interview with Kathleen Betsko and Rachel Koenig]

[Betsko and Koenig]: *When did you begin writing?*

[Kennedy]: I really started to write when I was a senior at Ohio State University. The year I was a junior, I took a course which was very inspirational; we studied Faulkner, Fitzgerald, D. H. Lawrence, T. S. Eliot. That course fired something in me. I suddenly found myself writing short stories instead of studying.

You once said that you were disappointed with college.

It was an ordeal. There were twenty-seven thousand students attending Ohio State, and southern Ohio was almost like the deep South in those days, much more bigoted than northern Ohio where I'd grown up. I majored in education. I expected to be a teacher like my mother. Then I majored in social work for a while. All the women—black women, especially—I knew majored in education and a few wanted to be social workers. I was a poor college student, I found college extremely boring, something to just get through. But there were these few English courses; when I was a senior, I had a couple of credits left over and took a survey course in twentieth-century drama. I did better in that than I did in any course the whole time I was at Ohio State. Looking back, it was important.

Did you pursue a profession in social work?

I managed to graduate and got married a month later. From then on, I wrote. My husband went to Korea, and while he was away I gave birth. I lived with my parents and when I wasn't taking care of the baby, I wrote. After my husband returned, we came to New York. I remember the exact date, January 4, 1955. We drove in the snow from Cleveland. Joe worked while he was in graduate school, and I had a certain kind of energy; I would stay up all night and write. You have to do that when you have a baby! I wrote parts of plays . . . then I started taking courses, which I did for ten years, at various places such as Columbia University and the American Theatre Wing. I was always in a writing course. I wrote my first play about a year after I came to New York.

Did you write as a child?

I always kept diaries on people in my family. My mother used to sneak into my room and read them. I really owe writing to her in a sense, because my mother is a terrific storyteller and I feel that all my writing basically has the same tone as the stories she told about her childhood. She used to tell funny stories, but they always had this terror in them, a blackness. I was the only daughter, and we were very close. I feel that my writing is an extension of my relationship with my mother, of talking with her.

How does she feel about your writing?

It makes her edgy. My writing has a lot of violence in it.

As a mother myself, I would find it disturbing if my sons were writing that kind of violence and darkness.

What attracted you to dramatic writing?

Like most people at that age, I was always writing poetry and short stories. But I really admired Tennessee Williams because he was the leading playwright then, and I'd seen *The Glass Menagerie* when I was sixteen, and I'd read his plays at Ohio State. I saw a lot of theater in New York. I worked two years on my first play in my spare time and it was very imitative of Williams, of *The Glass Menagerie.* I still have it. I was twenty-three then, and I sent the play to Audrey Wood (Williams's agent), who wrote me a long letter which said she couldn't take me as a client, but that she thought I was very talented. That was a great encouragement to me. I had written the play in a course at the New School taught by Mildred Kuner. She said I wrote the best play in the class, and entered it in a play contest in Chapel Hill, North Carolina, which also meant a lot to me. Well, I didn't win. And that was a pattern I had for a long, long time. People would respond very enthusiastically to my writing, then it would fall through.

How did you maintain the stamina to continue writing plays?

I became discouraged from playwriting and went back to writing stories and a novel. I went to the General Studies Program at Columbia University where I met John Shelby, the former editor of Rinehart, who played a very big part in my life. I had written some short stories and part of a novel which Shelby read. I remember one cold winter afternoon, I went to his office and he said: "I don't know if you will ever have a big success, but I think you are touched with genius." He took the novel and sent it around. He felt the novel would definitely get published. It never did, though he sent it everywhere. Then he moved to San Francisco, but before he left he put me in touch with another editor who'd done some work for *The New Yorker.* I worked with him on my stories off and on for two years. We sent the stories around and an agent . . . Richard Gilston, decided to represent me. By this time, I was twenty-seven and had been writing for six years. Gilston sent the stories around, but he could never get them published. One well-known editor tried to get me to write a novel based on a character in one of the short stories. I was unable to do that, although I worked on it for nine months. It is hard for me to take another person's idea and write about it. I was very frustrated by this time. I used to get despondent, and I must confess my former husband was extremely encouraging. He had his doctorate by this time and was teaching at Hunter College. I became discouraged; it bothered me that I'd begun at twenty-one and by twenty-eight, nothing had happened. I stopped writing for a year or so, and then Joe got a grant from the Africa Research Foundation to do a study in Africa. We went to Europe first, then Ghana, Nigeria . . . we traveled for over a year and it totally changed my writing.

In what way?

In the fourteen months I spent out of this country, my writing became sharper, more focused and powerful, and less imitative. It was a tremendous turning point. I was exactly twenty-nine when I wrote *Funnyhouse of a Negro* (1964), which many people still consider to be my best play. The masks in the play were very specific. I would say almost every image in *Funnyhouse* took form while I was in West Africa where I became aware of masks. I lived in Ghana at a most fortunate time. Ghana had just won its freedom. It was wonderful to see that liberation. And I thought the landscape of Africa was so beautiful, and the people were beautiful—it gave me a sense of power and strength. We lived in a huge house. I went into the bush and visited many villages. My husband went into the bush every day, and my son, who was five, went to school; I had a lot of time to write. More time probably than I'd ever had in my entire life. I tend to be restless in hot weather, so I'd wake up very early and could not sleep until very late. That combination produced some of the most powerful images I'd ever had. And we'd been to London, Paris, Madrid, Casablanca—it was a total regeneration. I couldn't cling to what I'd been writing—it changed me so. I didn't realize it was going to have this big impact on me. I think the main thing was that I discovered a strength in being a black person and a connection to West Africa.

Did it bother you to be constantly referred to as a "new writer" in the Funnyhouse of a Negro *reviews, even though you had already been writing for ten years?*

No. Finally being recognized as a writer was tremendously gratifying. But *Funnyhouse of a Negro* presented some other problems; it is such an intense play, and so very revealing of my psyche—if not me, personally . . . It was very dramatic. People who know me think of me as quiet, and to suddenly have this play staged which, again, is quite violent, put a lot of tension in my relationships. Also, to read about yourself in the newspaper is very anxiety producing. I found *Funnyhouse* created tremendous anxiety for me for at least two years.

Was this anxiety solely connected to being in the public eye, or were there other factors which contributed to it?

Well, it was also going through the production which, as you know, is always full of tension and hatreds and personality problems. To this day, I have fear when a production is started. I wonder how I will get along with the director, and how I will relate to the actors. Even though I had a great director, Michael Kahn, and was thrilled to be working with the people in Edward Albee's workshop, *Funnyhouse of a Negro* wasn't what I would call a good experience simply because I am a writer who is happier at the typewriter than in the arena. (pp. 246-49)

It seems your work is either highly praised or harshly criticized.

That's right. My reviews are always split. It was clear early on that many people hated my writing. The initial shock came at the Edward Albee workshop production of *Funnyhouse of a Negro* at Circle in the Square. Nothing has ever been as shocking to me as that particular night . . . many people hated my writing. Then, when it went on to a production at Actor's Studio (1964) and people said things like, "It's really nothing—you've just written the same lines over and over again . . . " Rumors went around that people were saying, "She's psychopath-

ic." So you see, I got it all at once, and from the very beginning. Other people felt the play was very lyrical, et cetera. But I realized then that many people disliked my writing. When I said it took two years to recover from *Funnyhouse,* that was part of it. Even now, there is that fear—that's why I want to leave town on opening night. You never know when the critics will attack you.

Was the darkness and violence evident in your early writing, the stories, the novel?

Yes, but it was tempered. I censored my writing more.

Because you felt your work might shock people?

Oh, I don't think it had anything to do with what other people might think. I wasn't that sophisticated. When I would read my work over and write a second draft, I would censor things which I, personally—sitting there at the typewriter—found uncomfortable. I had a certain image—even my friends thought of me as quiet and shy, and because I am small, I was labeled "sweet" from the time I was a kid. My writing, quite naturally, turned out to be just the opposite. It was a surprise for me when I would write stories which were so dark. I was censoring my work all the time. In that sense, I owe a lot to Edward Albee. I joined his workshop at Circle in the Square several months after I returned to the United States with my husband. I had written *Funnyhouse of a Negro* in Rome and handed it in to Albee's workshop. There was a lot of suspense about which sixteen people Albee would select for his workshop. After they accepted me, I went through *Funnyhouse* and edited it, very carefully. When they were ready to do my workshop production, I gave Michael Kahn, who was then Albee's assistant, my edited-out version. I'll never forget sitting in Michael's office; he said, "Isn't there something different about this play?" I said, "This is the version I want done in the workshop." He said okay, but mentioned it to Albee. After class, Albee said, "I hear you've given Michael another version of your play." I said, "I don't want that original version done in the workshop, that would be too upsetting. I used the word *nigger* throughout and I'm worried about what I said about my parents, even though it's fictionalized. I don't want it performed." That was a very big moment. We were standing at the back of the stage, and he said, "I really think you should try—I know it's hard—but maybe we should try to put the first version on." Then he said, "If a playwright has a play on, it should be his guts on that stage. . . . If you really think you can't, it's okay. But you should try." I was in tears. But I made the effort. I was the only black person in the workshop. I became very worried.

Did you ever get strong, negative response when your writing was more censored?

People always liked my writing in those early workshops. It was softened, and highly imitative of Tennessee Williams and Garcia Lorca.

In an earlier interview, you said that during this imitative phase, you realized that Williams's style would not work for you. Why?

The structure wouldn't work. I couldn't sustain a three-act play. It was a huge breakthrough for me when my main characters began to have other personas—it was in fact my biggest breakthrough as a writer, something I really sweated over, pondered. It was very clear to me that my plays and novels lacked something. I read my work over and over, and found there was a stilted quality. I kept intensive diaries. I can remember the room I was sitting in when I said to myself, "You are very drawn to all these historical people, they are very powerful in your imagination, yet you are not interested in writing about them historically." That's when I decided to use historical people as an extension of the main character, and also to give up the idea that I had to write a full-length play. I would say those were my two big realizations, and to me, they were *really* worth the ten years.

Returning to the **Funnyhouse of a Negro** *productions, we read that the play almost closed after twenty-two performances and then was extended by private funds.*

Isabel and Fredrick Eberstadt came to the last performance and decided they would like to contribute money to extend the run. It's hard to explain, but those in the theater really loved that play, and other people were alienated from it and felt that it was bad or offensive—which I still find amazing. It was catastrophic when it was a failure. . . .

A box-office failure?

Yes. When it closed, I thought it was the end of the world. But other things came out of it, like Rockefeller grants and a Guggenheim. And it gave me a feeling of affinity for people in the theater which has lasted to this day. I still consider writers my best friends. I trust writers.

Were you surprised, then, at winning an Obie?

Yes. Yes. It was a very strange period. I was barely able to handle the extremes. The play closed, I was very upset—almost suicidal—then it won an Obie. It was utterly confusing. (pp. 250-52)

How did the black arts community react to **Funnyhouse of a Negro?**

A lot of blacks hated this particular play and said it was pretentious and imitative. It was upsetting. People wanted me to be part of the movement but, frankly, I was always at home with my children. So apart from my temperament, the hours didn't exist.

You were not outspoken in your politics?

That's right. I remember there was an article written in the sixties that attacked my writing specifically and said that I was an irrelevant black writer. That sort of criticism was pretty pervasive at the time, so I built up a little resistance to it. I was criticized because there were heroines in my plays who were mixed up, confused. But I knew what my alliances were. My father was a social worker and went to Morehouse College, where Martin Luther King studied. He even had the same cadence in his voice, and was always giving speeches. I grew up in a house where people wrote and we were members of the NAACP and the United Negro College Fund. I knew my alliances.

Would you discuss your symbolism, the repeated motifs such as blood, birds . . . (p. 252)

I've always been drawn to the written word and have found solace in symbolism, even as far back as when I was eleven years old and read *Jane Eyre.* I have an affinity for symbolism as a way of surviving. What always impressed me, whether it was Brontë or Fitzgerald, T. S. Eliot or Lorca, was the way that writers took anguish and turned it into symbolism.

Do you have a strong religious background?

I was expected to go to Sunday School and church. I think all those stories at Sunday School played a big part in my imagination. And I am overlooking the influence of my grandparents, whom my brother and I went to visit every summer. They lived in Georgia, in a town of about five hundred people. I remember the red clay of Georgia, the white churches, going to prayer meetings with my grandmother on Thursday night and to church on Sunday morning. All of that was so powerful. Everybody in my family is very dramatic. I look exactly like my grandmother and express myself like her. The whole family is emotional; people tend to cry a lot. . . .

Are you conscious of the religious imagery in your work?

Oh, sure. I'm drawn to religious symbols. They are very powerful. Yet I did not have parents who were constantly preaching to me and I did not go to church more than the average person. I did grow up in a neighborhood which was at least sixty percent Italian. I did see people going to catechism in their white dresses (an image from **A Rat's Mass,** 1967). So that and those summers in Georgia played a huge role.

What is the source of the imagery in your work? How do you get in touch with it?

When I was in my twenties, I studied the symbolism of other writers such as Ibsen, Lorca, Chekhov. And my dreams were very strong. I used to write them down in a few sentences: "Last night I dreamed I was running through white walls . . . " It appeared to me that those sentences had a certain power. I began to feel that my diaries had much more life than my work. I began to examine them. I started using the symbolism in my journals that came from dreams. Realizing that my dreams had a vitality that my other writing did not was another breakthrough.

How did you begin to incorporate the dream imagery into your work?

I had many recurrent dreams, so I started to write tiny stories based on them, never thinking that they could be a "work," and not really seeing how I could turn them into a short story. I started to let the images accumulate by themselves. When I made the breakthrough where I discovered that the character could have other personas, the images then seemed more indigenous. Another source of imagery which I am overlooking is the fact that my father used to read to me every night when I was growing up. Sometimes just two or three lines of poetry from Langston Hughes, Paul Laurence Dunbar, James Weldon Johnson.

That, too, must have played a role in my development. There is obviously a lot of pleasure in having someone read poetry to you.

Do you agree with critic Rosemary K. Curb's analysis of the menstrual blood in **Lesson in a Dead Language** *(1964): "A sign, almost the antisacrament of the inherited guilt of womanhood"?*

(Laughter) Let me tell you something, I get very upset when I read people's analysis of my work. I try not to read it. It makes me uncomfortable.

More uncomfortable than reviews?

Yes. Yes . . . to have people sort of dissect my psyche . . . I think I fear that it will inhibit me in my future work. I find it disturbing. Reading a review compels me because it concerns whether or not the play is going to run.

Would you tell us about **Lesson in a Dead Language** *in your own words? How did the play begin in your mind?*

Apparently—because it is hindsight—I just have this thing about blood. I had always wanted to write something about menstruation. To me, menstrual periods, no matter how long you've been having them, are traumatic—simply the fact that you bleed once a month. I wanted to write about the fear . . . the fear that you will get blood on your clothes. . . . I tend to forget that play, but I like it very much. That play has almost been lost because it was published so long ago. Gaby Rogers did an exquisite production of it at Theatre Genesis (1970). She captured it.

You have dealt with many "taboo" subjects in your work— rape, incest, domestic violence. How did you find the courage to reveal such volatile truths?

I wouldn't use the word *courage.* I got the *impetus* from **Funnyhouse of a Negro.** In the decade after, I wrote many one-act plays in rapid succession. It was a confident period . . . I felt confident because I knew I had revealed my obsessions in **Funnyhouse.** Many people like Ellen Stewart at La Mama and Joe Papp (New York Shakespeare Festival) were very responsive and receptive to my work. I'm not sure I could write those plays now. I was riding an emotional crest. After all those years of rejection slips, people suddenly wanted to do my plays. I got letters from Paris, London, Germany . . . it made me very productive. Then, maybe twenty years later (I was about forty), I realized that although I had many first-class productions, apart from grants my plays did not seem to generate an income. That produced another set of conflicts. I had been living on grants, and hadn't quite realized that. (pp. 252-55)

Were you affected by the women's movement?

No. First of all, I hate groups. Secondly, I'd been through all of those struggles . . . alone. I'd been through that decade from age twenty to thirty, 1955 to 1965, trying to write with babies, trying to be a wife, and then experiencing divorce.

You once described your divorce as "a choice for writing. . . ." Would you elaborate?

I don't know whether I ever said that. There were so many tensions and writing was a comfort. It was much more complicated. I think my husband and I had a typical marriage of that time. He was very busy and on his way "up" and tensions built between us.

Because you were a two-career family?

I didn't have a career. I was a housewife. I wrote on the side at night and my husband was constantly busy. Each year was a step and the tensions built. Looking back, I think that people put those words in my mouth, because the divorce was not that clear-cut. One paradox I've never quite recovered from is that I feel my former husband encouraged me to write more than anybody has since then. And he supported me financially, and wanted to, and enjoyed doing it.

How did he feel about your success?

I don't know. By that time there was a lot of sadness that we weren't together. I had known him since I was nineteen. We were married thirteen years. So it wasn't that clear-cut. I am not a heroine who chose writing over marriage. It's not like that at all. I think divorce is futile. I would never divorce again, not with children.

What inspired **Evening with Dead Essex** *(1973), which dealt with the Mark Essex snipings? (Mark Essex, a troubled black ex-Navy man left six persons dead and fifteen wounded after sniping from the tower of a seventeen-story New Orleans Howard Johnson's Motor Lodge in January, 1972).*

When I go through periods when I can't write, I'm glued to the television news. I was following the Munich Olympics, and the Mark Essex snipings happened around the same time.

How did you come up with the multimedia dramatic form—headlines are read, slides are shown . . .

I was trying to capture how you feel when you hear all that on television. Isn't that funny? I've almost forgotten that play.

Evening with Dead Essex *was the first play by a woman to be produced at the Yale Repertory Theater. Were there subsequent productions of the play?*

It was done at The American Place Theatre first, in a small space, directed by Gaby Rogers, who is brilliant. It did not work well on the main stage at Yale; the actors got lost. Then it was done by a theater company in Louisiana; but nothing ever happened to that play. Apparently, my plays are sometimes expensive and hard to put on. They seem to be taught more than they are produced.

How did your unusual and imaginative use of stage space evolve?

Martha Graham was very popular in the fifties. I was in my own way attempting to imitate her. I also had a fixation for Picasso. I read everything Picasso had written about his work. Then, in Cleveland, there was one foreign movie house where in my teens I saw all of the French surrealist films, by people like Cocteau, Buñuel . . . my writing is definitely influenced by French film, Martha Graham and Picasso.

What, specifically, were you drawn to in Martha Graham's staging?

There were always many things happening simultaneously. And everything seemed to come out of darkness. People played many parts, she used a lot of black and white—there was a fluidity and a deemphasis on the narrative. The narrative was being presented to you in another way. I want to say that I wasn't yet capturing this in my short stories or in my plays, though there is no doubt that from 1955, it was on my mind. I'm sure I was also influenced by O'Neill's long monologues about people's torments—by the use of interior monologue.

Do you believe there is a female aesthetic in drama?

Yes, I think we can make a special contribution to theater.

Virginia Woolf said that however much we may go to the work of male artists for pleasure, it is difficult to go to them for help in finding a voice. . . .

That is a fascinating statement. I remember reading the stories of Colette when I was young. We carry that around with us. Women writers do affect me differently than male writers. That is probably the female aesthetic at its height. You see, *Jane Eyre* is my favorite novel. I'm glad that Charlotte Brontë was a woman. I think if you can bring your woman's experience to something, it is really great. It's important not to censor or inhibit that experience. Alice Childress has also been a great inspiration to me.

Do you teach the work of women writers in your courses?

That is a problem. I taught an American drama course at UC (University of California at) Davis and used O'Neill, Sam Shepard, Lorraine Hansberry . . . many writers. The girls complained that there weren't enough women in the course and they complained about the female characters in the plays. I'm not sure what the answer is for that particular period. Not many women playwrights have had recognition. And they are not in the textbooks.

How do you feel about being called a "Woman Playwright," or a "Black Woman Playwright?"

Ten years ago, it might have bothered me because I would have felt that people were saying I was lesser than say, Norman Mailer. [Laughs] I am a woman writer and a black writer and that doesn't disturb me anymore.

Playwright Wendy Wasserstein says that our cultural idea of a playwright is a white male—anything else is some kind of subset.

In some ways I have made peace with that. But when I

say I have made peace, it is crystal clear to me what is really the issue: as a black woman, or as a woman writer, or as a black writer, I don't stand in line for the income and the rewards, and that bothers me a lot. The white male writer can take steps. He's Off Broadway and the next thing you know, he's writing screenplays for Sidney Lumet. He does stand eighty percent more chance of getting his writing career to pay off. It's that simple. (pp. 255-58)

> *Adrienne Kennedy, with Kathleen Betsko and Rachel Koenig in an interview in* Interviews with Contemporary Women Playwrights, *by Kathleen Betsko and Rachel Koenig, Beech Tree Books, 1987, pp. 246-58.*

FURTHER READING

Barnes, Clive. "*Cities in Bezique* Arrives at the Public." *The New York Times* (13 January 1969): 26.
> Favorable review emphasizing poetic aspects of *Cities in Bezique.*

Binder, Wolfgang. "A *MELUS* Interview: Adrienne Kennedy." *MELUS* 12, No. 3 (Fall 1985): 99-108.
> Kennedy discusses the events leading to the production of *Funnyhouse of a Negro.*

Diamond, Elin. "An Interview with Adrienne Kennedy." *Studies in American Drama* 4, (1989): 143-57.
> Focuses on personal experiences that have influenced Kennedy's writing.

Forte, Jeanie. "Realism, Narrative, and the Feminist Playwright—A Problem of Reception." *Modern Drama* XXXII, No. 1 (March 1989): 115-27.
> Feminist critical analysis of *The Owl Answers.*

Kolin, Philip C. Review of *In One Act,* by Adrienne Kennedy. *World Literature Today* 63, No. 1 (Winter 1989): 101-02.
> Positive review that briefly summarizes works included in the collection.

Solomon, Alisa. "Stardust Memories: Adrienne Kennedy Shows and Tells." *The Village Voice* XXXII, No. 44 (3 November 1987): 61, 65.
> Positive review of *People Who Led to My Plays.* Highlights excerpts from the memoir.

George Lamming

1927-

(Full name George William Lamming) Barbadian novelist, poet, and essayist.

Lamming's works explore the colonial experience of the West Indies. His novels are commended for their nationalistic spirit and poetic prose style. Lamming depicts the enduring effects of European colonization on the West Indies, focusing on the inhabitants' search for a distinct political, economic, and cultural identity free from the pervasive influence of early colonial rule. Ian Munro has called Lamming "the most outspoken nationalist of the generation of West Indian novelists who grew to maturity in the turbulent 1930s and 1940s."

Lamming has witnessed and participated in much of the social and political upheaval that has taken place in the West Indies during his lifetime. Throughout the 1930s such factors as rapid population growth, widespread economic depression, and the shift from a primarily agrarian to an industrial economy inexorably and profoundly altered traditional Barbadian village life. Trade unions became an increasingly effective political force during the 1930s and 1940s, and organized labor led the agitation for political reform that ultimately resulted in the Barbadian independence movement. All of these historical factors had an impact on Lamming's life and are reflected in his fiction. In 1946 Lamming went to Trinidad, where he worked as a teacher and met a number of Trinidadian writers, including Clifford Sealy and Cecil Herbert. During this time he published poems in literary magazines. In 1950 he moved to England, working for the British Broadcasting Corporation and as a journalist while pursuing his literary career. His first novel, *In the Castle of My Skin,* was published in 1953; three other novels and a book of essays, *The Pleasures of Exile,* appeared over the next seven years. In 1955 Lamming visited the United States on a Guggenheim Fellowship, serving as writer-in-residence at the University of Texas. Returning to the Caribbean a year later, he became involved with various political causes, including the movement for Barbadian independence, which was realized in 1966. He published two further novels, *Natives of My Person* and *Water with Berries,* in 1972. Lamming remains associated with the educational and cultural projects of the Barbados Workers' Union and the Barbados Labour College, and divides his time between England, the West Indies, and the United States.

Regarded as a national classic of West Indian literature, *In the Castle of My Skin* is a semiautobiographical story. Set on the fictional island of San Cristobal in the 1930s and 1940s, the novel follows a male protagonist identified only as G. from age nine to eighteen, and concludes with his preparations to leave the island to pursue his education. This work has been commended for its poetic narrative, close observation and faithful depiction of village life, ac-

curate portrayal of the social changes of the period, meticulous recreation of Barbadian speech, and local color. Michael Gilkes called *In the Castle of My Skin* "one of the earliest novels of any substance to convey, with real assurance, the life of ordinary village folk within a genuinely realized, native landscape: a 'peasant novel' . . . written with deep insight and considerable technical skill."

In the Castle of My Skin is the first of four novels that outline the cycle of expatriation and return undergone by many West Indians of Lamming's generation. His next novel, *The Emigrants,* follows a diverse group of people from the West Indies and the Caribbean who move to England, which they have been educated to believe is culturally superior to their native islands. There they find what is to them an unsatisfactory way of life that leaves them longing for home. The next two novels, *Of Age and Innocence* and *Season of Adventure,* feature protagonists who return to San Cristobal after living abroad. A prominent theme of these works is the futility of attempting social and political progress without a full understanding of the past.

Natives of My Person and *Water with Berries,* published almost simultaneously, continue Lamming's exploration of

West Indian history, chronicling the profound impact of the colonial past on the present circumstances of the region. These novels have been assessed as only partially successful, with many commentators contending that Lamming's combination of fantasy, allegory, and symbolism with social realism results in dense, complex prose that often proves obscure.

The nationalistic sympathies evident in Lamming's fiction also inform *The Pleasures of Exile.* This essay collection addresses the role of the artist, maintaining that it is incumbent upon the West Indian writer to challenge the values and beliefs that colonizers have imposed on native populations. For his repudiation of the assumption that the culture of the European colonizers is superior to indigenous culture, and for his affirmation of a distinctly West Indian national identity, Lamming remains an important figure in West Indian literature.

(See also *CLC,* Vols. 2, 4; *Contemporary Authors,* Vols. 85-88; and *Contemporary Authors New Revision Series,* Vol. 26.)

PRINCIPAL WORKS

NOVELS

In the Castle of My Skin   1953
The Emigrants   1954
Of Age and Innocence   1958
Season of Adventure   1960
Natives of My Person   1972
Water with Berries   1972

OTHER

The Pleasures of Exile   (essays)   1960

Richard Wright

[*One of the most influential American authors of the twentieth century, Wright was among the first black American literary figures to attain international prominence. In the following essay, Wright commends Lamming's portrayal of Barbadian life in transition from agrarianism to industrialism in* In the Castle of My Skin.]

Accounting for one of the aspects of the complex social and political drama in which most of the subject people of our time are caught, I once wrote: " . . . to a greater or less degree, almost all of human life on earth today *can* be described as moving away from traditional, agrarian, simple handicraft ways of living toward modern industrialization."

These words deal with vast, cold, impersonal social forces which are somewhat difficult to grasp unless one has had the dubious fortune of having had one's own life shaped by the reality of those forces. The act of ripping the sensitive human personality from one culture and the planting of that personality in another culture is a tortured, convo-

luted process that must, before it can appeal to peoples' hearts, be projected either in terms of vivid drama or highly sensual poetry.

It has been through the medium of the latter—a charged and poetic prose—that George Lamming, a young West Indian Negro of Barbados, has presented his autobiographical summation of a tropical island childhood that, though steeped in the luminous images of sea, earth, sky, and wind, drifts slowly toward the edge of the realms of political and industrial strife. Notwithstanding the fact that Lamming's story, as such, is his own, it is, at the same time, a symbolic repetition of the story of millions of simple folk who, sprawled over half of the world's surface and involving more than half of the human race, are today being catapulted out of their peaceful, indigenously earthy lives and into the turbulence and anxiety of the twentieth century.

I, too, have been long crying these stern tidings; and, when I catch the echo of yet another voice declaiming in alien accents a description of this same reality, I react with pride and excitement, and I want to urge others to listen to that voice. One feels not so much alone when, from a distant witness, supporting evidence comes to buttress one's own testimony. And the voice that I now bid you hear is sounding in Lamming's *In the Castle of My Skin.* What, then, is this story that Lamming tells?

Without adequate preparation, the Negro of the Western world lives, in *one* life, *many* lifetimes. Most whites' lives are couched in norms more or less traditional: born of stable family groups, a white boy emerges from adolescence, enters high school, finishes college, studies a profession, marries, builds a home, raises children, etc. The Negro, though born in the Western world, is not quite of it; due to policies of racial exclusion, his is the story of *two* cultures: the dying culture in which he happens to be born, and the culture into which he is trying to enter—a culture which has, for him, not quite yet come into being; and it is up the shaky ladder of all the intervening stages between these two cultures that Negro life must climb. Such a story is, above all, a record of shifting, troubled feelings groping their way toward a future that frightens as much as it beckons.

Lamming's quietly melodious prose is faithful not only to social detail, but renders with fidelity the myth-content of folk minds; paints lovingly the personalities of boyhood friends; sketches authentically the characters of schoolmasters and village merchants; and depicts the moods of an adolescent boy in an adolescent society. . . . Lamming rehearses the rituals of matriarchal families so common to people upon whom the strident blessings of an industrial world are falling—families whose men have been either killed, carted off to war, or hired to work in distant lands, leaving behind nervous mothers to rule with anxious hysteria over a brood of children who grow up restless, rebellious, and disdainful of authority.

Lamming recounts, in terms of anecdote, the sex mores of his people, their religious attitudes, their drinking habits, their brawls in the sunlit marketplaces, the fear of the little people for the overseers, and the fear of the overseers for the big white boss in the faraway house on the hill. (Unlike the population ratio in the United States, the English in these tiny islands comprise a minority surrounded by a majority of blacks; hence, that chronic, grinding, racial hatred and fear, which have so long been the hallmark of both white and black attitudes in our own Southland, are largely absent from these pages.)

Lamming objectifies the conscience of his village in those superbly drawn character portraits of Pa and Ma, those folk Negroes of yesteryear whose personalities, bearing the contours of Old Testament, Biblical heroes, have left their stamp upon so many young Lammings of the Western world. I feel that Lamming, in accounting for himself and his generation, was particularly fortunate in creating this device of a symbolic Pa and Ma whose lineaments evoke in our minds images of simple, peasant parents musing uncomprehendingly upon the social changes that disrupt their lives and threaten the destinies of their children. . . .

The clash of this dying culture with the emerging new world is not without its humor, both ribald and pathetic: the impact of the concept of marriage upon the naïve, paganlike minds is amusingly related by Lamming in his story of Bots, Bambi, and Bambina. The superstitions of his boyhood friends are laid engagingly before us. And there's a kind of poetry suggested even in the outlandish names of his boyhood playmates: Trumper, Boy Blue, Big Bam, Cutsie, Botsie, Knucker Hand, Po King, Puss-in-Boots, and Suck Me Toe. . . .

Just as young Lamming is ready to leave Barbados Island for Trinidad, Trumper, who has gone to America and has been influenced by mass racial and political agitation, returns and, in a garbled manner, tells of the frenzied gospel of racial self-assertion—that strange soul-food of the rootless outsiders of the twentieth century. The magnetic symbol of Paul Robeson (shown here purely in racial and *not* political terms!) attracts as much as disturbs young Lamming as he hears Robeson sing over a tiny recording device: *Let My People Go!*

Even before Lamming leaves his island home, that home is already dying in his heart; and what happens to Lamming after that is something that we all know, for we have but to lift our eyes and look into the streets and we see countless young, dark-skinned Lammings of the soil marching in picket lines, attending political rallies, impulsively, frantically seeking a new identity. . . .

Filtered through a poetic temperament like Lamming's, this story of change from folk life to the borders of the industrial world adds a new and poignant dimension to a reality that is already global in its meaning.

Lamming's is a true gift; as an artist, he possesses a quiet and stubborn courage; and in him a new writer takes his place in the literary world. (pp. ix-xii)

> *Richard Wright, in an introduction to* In the Castle of My Skin *by George Lamming, McGraw-Hill Book Company, Inc., 1953, pp. ix-xii.*

V. S. Naipaul

[*A Trinidadian novelist and critic, Naipaul is considered one of the most gifted novelists in world literature. In the following excerpt, he assesses* Of Age and Innocence *as unnecessarily complicated by symbol and allegory and maintains that Lamming is most successful with autobiographical themes.*]

It is easy to understand the incomprehension which has greeted Mr George Lamming's third book. Mr Lamming is a Barbadian Negro, and unless one understands the West Indian's search for identity, *Of Age and Innocence* is almost meaningless. It is not fully realised how completely the West Indian Negro identifies himself with England. Africa has been forgotten; films about Africa tribesmen excite derisive West Indian laughter. For the West Indian intellectual, speaking no language but English, educated in the English way, the experience of England is usually traumatic. The foundations of his life are removed. He has to look for new loyalties.

> I discovered that until then, until that experience, I had always lived in the shadow of a meaning which others had placed on my presence in the world, and I had played no part at all in making that meaning. . . . My rebellion begins with an acceptance of the very thing I reject, because my conduct cannot have the meaning I want to give it, if it does not accept and live through that conception by which the others now regard it. What I may succeed in doing is changing that conception of me, I cannot ignore it.

So speaks the newly-made politician of 'this feeling which had disfigured his innocence and separated him from himself'. The other attitude is one of detachment or 'disinclination'. Both attitudes, Mr Lamming states, are destructive; and coldly, step by step, he works out his tragedy of love and politics on a Caribbean island.

I thought this a better novel than *The Emigrants.* But Mr. Lamming creates difficulties for the reader. He has devised a story which is fundamentally as well-knit and exciting as one by Graham Greene. But you have to look hard for it. Mr Lamming suppresses and mystifies; he shies away from the concrete, and grows garrulous over the insignificant. He is not a realistic writer. He deals in symbols and allegory. Experience has not been the basis of this novel. Every character, every incident is no more than a constituent idea in Mr Lamming's thesis; the reader's sympathies are never touched. San Cristobal, the imaginary island which is the setting of Mr Lamming's novel, could never exist. I can understand Mr Lamming's need for fantasy. His conception of the search for identity is highly personal; it has arisen from a deep emotion which he has chosen to suppress, turning it instead into an intellectual thing which is fine in its way, but would be made absurd by the comic realities of West Indian political life. Here is one West Indian writer who feels hindered rather than inspired by the West Indian scene. Mr Lamming is only thirty. He is one of the finest prose-writers of his generation. Purely as a work of fantasy *Of Age and Innocence* is really quite remarkable. It fails through its sheer unreadability. Mr Lamming should be warned by this that his best subject, as in *In the Castle of My Skin* and the first 50 pages of this novel, is himself.

V. S. Naipaul, in a review of "Of Age and Innocence," in New Statesman, *Vol. LVI, No. 1447, December 6, 1958, p. 827.*

Wilson Harris

[Harris is a Guyanese novelist and critic. In the following excerpt, originally a lecture given on May 15, 1964 to the London West Indian Students Union, he examines reasons for the perceived failure of Lamming's novel Of Age and Innocence.*]*

One of the most interesting novelists out of the West Indies is George Lamming. Lamming was—and still is—regarded as a writer of considerable promise. What is the nature of his promise? Let us look at his novel *Of Age and Innocence.* This is a novel which somehow fails, I feel, but its failure tells us a great deal. The novel would have been remarkable if a certain tendency—a genuine tendency—for a tragic feeling of dispossession in reality had been achieved. This tendency is frustrated by a diffusion of energies within the entire work. The book seems to speak with a public voice, the voice of a peculiar orator, and the compulsions which inform the work appear to spring from a verbal sophistication rather than a visual, plastic and conceptual imagery. Lamming's verbal sophistication is conversational, highly wrought and spirited sometimes: at other times it lapses into merely clever utterance, rhetorical, as when he says of one of his characters: 'He had been made Governor of an important colony which was then at peace with England.' It takes some effort—not the effort of imaginative concentration which is always worthwhile but an effort to combat the author's self-indulgence. And this would not arise if the work could be kept true to its inherent design. There is no necessary difficulty or complexity in Lamming's novels—the necessary difficulty or complexity belonging to strange symbolisms—and I feel if the author concentrated on the sheer essentials of his experience a tragic disposition of feeling would gain a true ascendancy. This concentration is essential if the work is not to succumb to a uniform tone which gives each individual character the same public-speaking resonance of voice. I would like to stress a certain distinction I made earlier once again. In the epic and revolutionary novel of associations the characters are related within a personal capacity which works in a poetic and serial way so that a strange jigsaw is set in motion like a mysterious unity of animal and other substitutes within the person. Something which is quite different to the over-elaboration of individual character within the conventional novel. And this over-elaboration is one danger which confronts Lamming. For in terms of the ruling framework he accepts, the individuality of character, the distinctions of status and privilege which mark one individual from another, must be maintained. This is the kind of realism, the realism of classes and classifications—however limited it may be in terms of a profound, poetic and scientific scale of values—the novel, in its orthodox mould, demands. Lamming may be restless within this framework (there are signs and shadows of this in his work) but mere extravagance of pat-

tern and an inclination to frequent intellectual raids beyond his territory are not a genuine breakthrough and will only weaken the position of the central character in his work. He must school himself at this stage, I believe, to work for the continuous development of a main individual character in order to free himself somewhat from the restrictive consolidation he brings about which unfortunately, I find, blocks one's view of essential conflict. This becomes a necessity in terms of the very style and tone of his work. He cannot afford to crowd his canvas when the instinctive threat of one-sidedness is likely to overwhelm all his people and in fact when this one-sidedness may be transformed into a source of tremendous strength in a singleness of drive and purpose which cannot then fail to discipline every tangential field and exercise. The glaring case is Shephard whom you may recall in *Of Age and Innocence.* Here was an opportunity which was not so much lost—as lost sight of—to declare and develop the tragic premises of individual personality by concentrating on the one man (Shephard) in order to bring home a dilemma which lay in his coming to terms with the people around him by acting—even when he was playing the role of the great rebel—in the way everyone else appeared to see him rather than in the way he innocently may have seen himself.

It is illuminating . . . to compare V. S. Naipaul's *A House for Mr Biswas* with George Lamming's *Of Age and Innocence.* Naipaul never loses sight of his Mr Biswas throughout a very long chronicle in the way Lamming disposes of Shephard again and again. Naipaul's style is like Lamming's in one respect: it is basically conversational though without the rhetoric and considerable power Lamming displays and it follows a flat and almost banal everyday tone. On this flat conversational level the novel has been carefully and scrupulously written. The possibility for tragedy which lay in *Of Age and Innocence,* the vein of longing for a lost innocence associated with Shephard's world is nowhere apparent in *A House for Mr Biswas.* Mr Biswas is essentially comic—a mixture of comedy and pathos—where Shephard may have been stark and tragic. Naipaul's triumph with Mr Biswas is one which—in the very nature of the novel—is more easily achieved, I feel, than a triumph with Shephard for Lamming would have been. To achieve the nuclear proportions of tragedy in Shephard, Lamming needed a remarkable and intense personal centre of depth; this he never held, overlooking the concrete challenge which stems from such a presence in his novel whose status is obscure. (pp. 37-9)

Wilson Harris, "Tradition and The West Indian Novel," in his Tradition, the Writer and Society: Critical Essays, *New Beacon Publications, 1967, pp. 28-47.*

Ian Munro

Barbados-born George Lamming is the most outspoken nationalist of the generation of West Indian novelists who grew to maturity in the turbulent 1930s and 1940s. His six novels chronicle the sweep of West Indian history, from the colonial setting of *In the Castle of My Skin* (1953) through the achievement of independence in *Season of*

Adventure (1960) to a post-independence uprising in *Water with Berries* (1971). His most recent novel, *Natives of My Person* (1972), is the culmination of his work, reaching back to the beginnings of colonialism and, through allegory, suggesting the underlying, recurrent patterns of Caribbean history. Each of his novels is both complete in itself and part of a continually developing vision linked to the changing political scene in the Caribbean, with its urgent problems of political and psychological decolonisation, and to Lamming's evolving understanding of the human condition.

His earliest writing, the poetry and short prose he wrote before emigrating to England in 1950, expresses primarily a rejection of West Indian society and politics. From 1946 to 1950, while living in Trinidad, he devoted himself to the creation of an 'artistic personality' through poetry. Romantic and ethereal in the earliest poems, the persona soon came into conflict with West Indian colonial society. [In **"West Indian Dutch Party"**, a 1948 broadcast for the BBC program *Caribbean Voices*], Lamming describes a Trinidadian 'Dutch party', with the poet on one side, brooding on the 'permanent disease of society', and the 'glittering chatter' of the party on the other. The West Indies in Lamming's poetry is a spiritually sterile prison for the creative spirit: 'islands cramped with disease no economy can cure'. In the short story **"Birds of a Feather"**, his young protagonist dreams of a 'way of escape'. The colonial politics of the time are seen as an exercise in futility:

> Contestant and onlooker,
> The leading and the led fusing danger and de-
>   light
> In an original pattern, an automatic violence.

In a later poem, Lamming speaks of retreating from 'the multitude's monotonous cry / For freedom and politics at the price of blood', to an aesthetic world where the spirit can 'Live every moment in the soul's devouring flame, [**"Birthday Poem (For Clifford Sealy)"**].

Emigration to England marked a turning point in his attitude towards the West Indies. A black West Indian in an unfriendly city, he discovered not creative freedom, but alienation. His feelings are best expressed in his poem **"Song for Marian"**, about a concert given in London by the black American Marian Anderson. Her songs awaken him to their common experience as blacks confronting white civilisation:

> Now I venturing from scattered islands
> To rediscover my roots
> Have found an impersonal city
> Where your tales are incredibly true.

His experience in England showed Lamming the need to define himself not only as an artist but as a West Indian. The poems he wrote before beginning work on *In the Castle of My Skin* return to the society he had earlier rejected. **"The Boy and the Sea"** celebrates the freedom of boyhood, and **"The Illumined Graves"** introduces a central motif of his later work: the living seeking communion and reconciliation with the dead on All Souls' Day:

> To renew the contagion of living,
> So these by similar assertion of love

> Promote their faith in flame,
> Remembering the ceremony of undying souls
> With a meek congregation of candles.

In the Castle of My Skin is the best-known of his works and is perhaps the most widely read West Indian novel. It is Lamming's most autobiographical work, covering nine years in the life of G., the novel's artist-hero, from his ninth birthday to his departure for Trinidad. Interwoven with G.'s story is that of his village, which also undergoes dramatic changes during the course of the novel. From the outset, G.'s sensibility is distinct from that of the other villagers. His birthday coincides with a flood which threatens to wash Creighton's village into the sea. The villagers' resistance to the flood is signified by a song taken up from house to house until 'the whole village shook with song on its foundation of water'. But the song has a second purpose: it is started by G.'s mother to suppress the boy's inquiry into his past—this 'always happened when I tried to remember'. His attempt to find out who he is by probing into his family's history poses another threat to the village, since the past, with its story of slavery and oppression, has been buried. Even teachers at the village school know nothing of it and Barbados, the villagers believe, has always been a junior partner of England, 'Little England'—not a subservient colony.

It is not only curiosity which separates G. from the village, but his mother's ambition. Education gradually separates him from his friends like Bob and 'the gang at the corner'. The long poetic chapter describing G.'s day at the beach with his friends opens with a quarrel between G. and Bob, and the chapter is concerned mainly with change, as the boys perceive it through games, stories and symbols. 'You never know as you yourself say,' says Boy Blue, 'when something go off pop in yuh head an' you ain't the same man you think you wus.'

G.'s transition to manhood coincides with fundamental changes in village life. In the opening chapters of *In the Castle of My Skin* the village is united by common values, a deep attachment to the land and faith in the landlord, the 'Great'. Lamming shows, in his ironic handling of the school inspection scene, that their faith is based on illusions about England and ignorance of the slave past; yet he also shows, through the periodic appearances of Ma and Pa, the quiet stability and continuity of peasant consciousness.

Chapter 5 is pivotal. It contrasts the timeless patterns of their lives, as the villagers gather around the pastry cart to gossip and quarrel, with a group of working men watching the clock, waiting to hear from Mr Slime whether they are to go on strike against a shipping firm owned by the landlord. The strike meshes with others going on throughout the West Indies, and begins a chain reaction of events culminating in the village's invasion by a band of city workers intent on killing the landlord. A new political power, represented by the trade union leader Mr Slime, threatens to assume the landlord's position.

When G. reappears in the novel he is on the verge of leaving for Trinidad. In an act of cleansing for a new life ahead, he wades into the sea. His imagination focuses on a pebble he had hidden earlier; its disappearance embodies for him the qualities of village life from which he has become irrevocably separated by his high school education. Though a part of his sensibility remains in the village, 'It was as though my roots had been snapped from the centre of what I knew best.' The uprooting of the village itself begins, as the land is sold to outsiders, middle-class men with legal deeds laying claim to the estate that Mr Creighton had sold them through Slime's company. Like Slime himself, they are rootless men, 'intransit passengers', who want to own property. For the villagers, whose life is ruled by almost feudal customs, the law is irrelevant, but in the new capitalist economic and social system which Slime and his colleagues are introducing into the island, land has become a commodity. Change has accumulated throughout the novel, but the dispossession of the villagers happens in the novel's penultimate chapter when the three central village characters are uprooted: first, the shoemaker, who had earlier defended change but believed himself uninvolved in the outcome; next, Mr Foster, who at the opening of the novel had refused to leave his home during the flood; and finally Pa. G. and the village undergo a similar experience of displacement and breaking with the past, though for different reasons. Both events, G.'s departure and the destruction of the semi-feudal system of Creighton's village, are inevitable, but G., as a writer forced to leave the source of his creativity, is divided in his attitude toward them.

In the Castle of My Skin ends the evening before G.'s departure. His new maturity is suggested by his use of a diary to record his thoughts and by an ironic, affectionate distance from his formerly dominating mother. Yet he is still far from discovering the identity he had sought nine years earlier, and the ideas of his boyhood friend Trumper about black pride and political struggle are almost incomprehensible to him. He departs for Trinidad as bewildered and rootless as the society he leaves behind. Although the artist-hero plays a less important role in Lamming's subsequent novels, his quest for his roots remains a recurrent and significant part of the struggle of West Indian society for freedom.

Lamming's second novel, *The Emigrants* (1954), begins where the earlier book leaves off. 'Those four years in Trinidad', recalls the novel's first-person narrator, 'seemed nothing more than an extension of what had gone before, but for this important difference. I had known a greater personal freedom.' As Lamming's poetry suggests, personal freedom soon became less important than the spiritual limitations of a colonial society, and on his birthday the narrator becomes aware of the need for something more: 'to get out . . . go elsewhere . . . start all over again'. Educated to believe in England's cultural superiority, he chooses the Mother Country as his natural destination.

But the artist-narrator plays a minor role in the novel; he soon merges into Collis, a young poet whose experience cannot easily be separated from that of the other emigrants. 'We're all in flight,' he thinks, 'and yet as Tornado says we haven't killed. We haven't stolen.' Lamming's concern in the novel is less with personal experience than with the powerful myth of colonialism that draws West

Indians to emigrate to England. 'This *myth*,' Lamming writes in his book of essays *The Pleasures of Exile* (1960), 'begins in the West Indian from the earliest stages of his education. . . . It begins with the fact of England's supremacy in taste and judgement: a fact which can only have meaning and weight by a calculated cutting down to size of all non-England. The first to be cut down is the colonial himself.

During the long first section of the novel, the emigrants discuss their reasons for emigrating; each shares Collis's desire to begin again. As England—which Tornado calls 'the land of the enemy'—nears, the emigrants draw closer together and seek a basis for West Indian unity. But their tenuous shipboard nationalism is never stronger than the myth of England, for colonials 'whose only certain knowledge said that to be in England was all that mattered'. Once they land, the emigrants disperse and the leisurely movement of the voyage gives way to a series of episodes.

Despite their fragmentary effect, the episodes are carefully plotted to show the inevitable disintegration of the emigrants' unity and their faith in England. At first they maintain a degree of contact in barber and hairdressing shops and their hostel, although the subterranean, shabby nature of these gathering places emphasises exclusion from English life. Their windows look out from basement level rooms through bars onto walls which proclaim the compulsive privacy of English life. Of the twenty-one scenes which follow their arrival in England, only two occur outside, in contrast to *In the Castle of My Skin,* where most of the action takes place in backyards, on street corners or beaches, where the villagers are free to move about. Later, the emigrants are found in even smaller rooms and flats, 'alone, circumscribed by the night and the neutral staring walls'. Even the middle-class emigrants, though enjoying a more comfortable existence, live amidst fear and intrigue. Their dilemma is typified by Dickson, a respectable schoolteacher from Barbados, who forms a liaison with an Englishwoman, and then discovers that she is curious about him only as a stereotyped sexual object, the black male. The episode shatters his concept of himself as a 'black Englishman'. In various ways, each of the emigrants undergoes a similar experience of disillusionment and loss of identity, including Collis, whose ambitions for a writing career are reduced to doing liner notes for record albums. He makes his living as a factory worker, at which he is unlucky and incompetent. His alienation from people is expressed in a tendency to see them as objects.

A similar division from community affects the Governor, who plays the role of the political leader, a recurrent figure in Lamming's fiction. His main quality is a determination to control events, but after arrival in England his control of situations slips away and he loses all sense of responsibility to his people. By the end of *The Emigrants,* both the Governor and Collis have lost all relation to the society in which they should have functioned. 'I have no people,' Collis says; and indeed his fellow emigrants no longer exist as a community after emigration has exposed the colonial illusions about the Mother Country upon which their identity had been based. For Lamming, emigration is a phase of discovery that leads back to the West Indies and the rejuvenation of the spiritually moribund society the emigrants fled. In his next two novels, his characters struggle to create what Tornado—in exile in London—could only dream of: 'some new land where we can find peace . . . a place where they can be without making up false pictures 'bout other places'.

In the four years before the publication of his third novel, *Of Age and Innocence* (1958), Lamming travelled widely in Europe, the United States and the Caribbean. His travels broadened his artistic concerns. In his address to the First Congress of Negro Writers and Artists in Paris in 1956, he argued that the black colonial experience of being partly defined in terms of racial and cultural stereotypes, confronting the white 'Other' in conditions that make understanding impossible, is an example of a contemporary human condition. 'It is . . . the universal sense of separation and abandonment, frustration and loss, and, above [all] else, of some direct inner experience of something missing.' Nationalism is one form of the human effort to overcome the separation between men; another is the desire to participate in a close fraternity with other individuals. In Lamming's earlier novels, his English characters had been mostly unsympathetic; in *Of Age and Innocence* his four English visitors to San Cristobal play an important role in extending the novel's themes.

The novel is set on Lamming's fictional island of San Cristobal. With its multiracial population, and place names and geographic features drawn from throughout the Caribbean, San Cristobal is a Caribbean microcosm. *Of Age and Innocence* was published in the year the short-lived West Indies Federation came into existence, and is prophetic in its treatment of the failure of Isaac Shephard's multiracial People's Communal Movement. While it affirms the yearning of West Indians for unity and freedom, it is also a critique of independence movements and their leaders.

Despite their ideals of harmony, Shephard and his allies Singh and Lee turn toward violence against colonialism, without realising the extent to which their actions are dictated by the historical circumstances against which they are struggling. The drift towards violence begins after a conference in which the three leaders discuss meeting with the English Governor about a threatened strike. The response of each man is shaped by his racial experience and upbringing. Shephard, the descendant of slaves and most 'colonised' psychologically of the three, is indecisive. As Lamming has pointed out in a separate discussion of Shephard, he never overcomes the division within himself between his commitment to nationalism and his need to 'achieve the approval and ultimate embrace of a spiritual authority which is dedicated to his perpetual self-imprisonment'. Through Shephard, Lamming offers a brilliant comment on the nature of West Indian political leadership, with its roots in religious demagogy. His analysis of Shephard's character reaches back to reveal a lifetime of struggle for recognition against petty humiliations, and an obsession with absolute power beginning from his competition with his aggressive father, a preacher. Neither Singh's nor Lee's ancestors had been victims of slavery,

and Singh's uncompromising stance reflects the attitude of one who has no doubts about his identity: 'The point is,' he says, 'that we must never trust them. That is like a golden rule in this movement.'

The issue of the meeting is still in balance when it is interrupted by the arrival of Bill Butterfield. The leaders' fatal weakness is revealed by their hostility towards Bill, 'a perfect example of teamwork in ill-will'. Unable to trust any Englishman—though in fact Bill has come to warn of a plot against Shephard's life—they find themselves distrustful of one another. Challenged to prove their unity, they give way to Singh's extreme position. But their distrust remains: 'From now on I must be careful with Singh', thinks Shephard, while Singh wonders if Shephard has been collaborating with 'the enemy'.

Shephard, Singh and Lee have in common a failure to escape from the conditions history has imposed upon them. The future ideal of community is represented instead by the four boys of the Secret Society, who are inspired by a legend of the island's primordial harmony and spirit of resistance, the Tribe Boys. Like the Guyanese novelist Wilson Harris, Lamming reaches back to the aboriginal past for a model of community in which West Indian consciousness has its roots. *Of Age and Innocence* is a clear statement of Lamming's conviction that political change must be accompanied by a profound change in outlook: 'In order to change [his] way of seeing,' he writes in *The Pleasure of Exile,* 'the West Indian must change the very structure, the very basis of his values.' Failure to do so leads to the sort of violence and murder in which the novel ends, initiated by the madhouse fire. The fire's 'red wall . . . transparent and impenetrable' parallels the vengeful wall of hostility the leaders create.

Interwoven with the public political drama is a private one, the story of four English visitors to San Cristobal who have only a tangential involvement in the political struggle. They too have an ideal of community, a 'little world, made by four people' in the tranquillity of the Balearic Islands. But in the turbulent milieu of San Cristobal, each undergoes a crisis of identity which divides him from the others. England, for the quartet, is the Old World of established self-concepts and relationships; San Cristobal is a New World, an abrupt break with the settled past and a confrontation with the realities of existence. Penelope Butterfield's concept of herself is jeopardised when she discovers her lesbian desire for Marcia and is afraid of revealing it to the others. She becomes isolated from them by her awareness of the stigma she bears. 'The Negro, the homosexual, the Jew, the worker', she realises, suffer a similar stigma, and the realisation enables her to understand the motives behind Shephard's rebellion.

Mark Kennedy's cold distance from his girlfriend Marcia—leading to her insanity and death in the madhouse fire—is part of a similar existential detachment from the world. Mark is an exile and drifter, like G. and Collis; he has lived away from San Cristobal for twenty years. He returns there with a vague sense of searching for his origins. After drifting apart from his friends he briefly joins Shephard's movement and gives a speech at a party rally expressing his deep yearning for identification with the land. But he remains unable to escape his alienation or, as a biographer, to make a pattern out of the fragments of West Indian history.

While Mark's failure is in part a comment on the continued inability of the colonised West Indian intellectual to return to his roots, the story of the four English visitors illustrates the contemporary problem of human isolation and lack of communication that Lamming had explored in his 1956 address. *Of Age and Innocence* continues Lamming's concern with the private search for identity—focused on the problem of understanding between men and women—but expands it into a universal quest.

The novel ends with San Cristobal's occupation by British troops. When *Season of Adventure* (1960) opens, the island has become independent, but power is in the hands of a new indigenous ruling elite, shaped by colonialism and divorced from the working and peasant masses. As *Of Age and Innocence* proved prophetic of the failure of the West Indies Federation, *Season of Adventure* anticipates the fall of the 'First Republic', a society controlled by an elite with alien values.

The focus of contention between the elite and the masses in the novel is the Ceremony of the Souls, an African retention. In the vodun ceremonies he witnessed in Haiti in 1956, Lamming found a suitable metaphor for communication between the present and a buried past. The ceremonies were also a reminder of an African and slave past that middle-class West Indians would prefer to forget. In San Cristobal, the Ceremony is practised only by those living in wretched areas like Forest Reserve, who are also the guardians of the steel bands, symbols of the survival and continuity of West Indian peasant consciousness. The Ceremony of the Souls at the *tonelle,* the canopied space where vodun ceremonies take place, is the route which Fola, the novel's middle-class mulatto heroine, follows back to her roots. Her quest leads not back to Africa but to the common folk of the West Indies in whom the society's essential values survive. During the Ceremony of the Souls that she witnesses at the beginning of the novel, Fola is shocked into an awareness of a part of herself, 'her forgotten self', that her upbringing has concealed. Her subsequent quest for her father forms the narrative thread of *Season of Adventure.* It overlaps with conflict between the inhabitants of Forest Reserve and the elite, who attempt to suppress the steel bands and the *tonelle.*

A mediator between the two levels of society appears in the painter, Chiki, who had been separated from his origins in Forest Reserve by his education, but who has returned to live there. Like the other artist figures in Lamming's novels he is plagued by a loss of creativity, but nevertheless plays an important role as teacher in relation to several characters. Chiki persuades his friend Powell to see the 'gift' of independence as another form of enslavement, he inspires the drummer Gort, and leads Fola through her 'backward glance' into an understanding of her past, painting a portrait of her father—who could be either African or European in origin—as they imagine him.

The portrait becomes in turn the link between Fola's pri-

vate quest for her father and the political conflicts in San Cristobal. Fola's personality undergoes a split between the Fola who had been formed and imprisoned by alien middle-class values and another self, Fola 'and other than, outside and other than', whose reality must be discovered through a re-examination of her personal past and the secret of her parentage. When Vice-President Raymond is assassinated, Fola chooses to side with Forest Reserve against her own class. Wading through water, like a dead soul in the Ceremony seeking release from its imprisonment, Fola steps into the Reserve and declares it was her father—represented by the portrait—who had murdered him. Her announcement throws the Republic into disarray, as people are forced to see in the appearance of this mythical ancestor the mirror of their own abandoned past. As Fola's stepfather and the rest of the San Cristobal elite prepare to use the assassination as an excuse for wiping out the steel bands and *tonelle,* steelbandsmen from throughout the island gather under Gort's leadership to play the forbidden drums. The First Republic falls, to be replaced by the Second, led by Kofi James-Williams Baako.

Baako's name suggests a synthesis of European and African, but he speaks only vaguely of possibilities for the future. If the novel concludes on a more hopeful note than Lamming's earlier fiction, it is clear that the process of renewal initiated by Fola's quest has only begun. *Season of Adventure* takes the historical and political development of the West Indies up to the present stage—the stage of the 'First Republic' dominated by a Europeanised elite without a clear vision of a truly West Indian future—and suggests the potential source of renewal in the experience of the common man, 'the very soil from which our consciousness springs'. The danger of failure is suggested by the fact that Powell, the Vice-President's murderer whose lessons from Chiki had been corrupted into fanaticism, remains at large.

Thus Lamming's first four novels trace the evolution of West Indian society from the disintegration of a tradition-bound colonial society through the dispersal of the displaced West Indians by emigration to the struggle for a still-unrealised form of community. At that time, Lamming later commented, there was 'no further point for me to go without in a sense going beyond what had actually happened in the society' [see Further Reading]. Over a decade separated the publication of *Season of Adventure* from that of *Natives of My Person* (1972), in many ways the culmination of Lamming's work. Lamming has described the novel as 'a way of going forward by making a complete return to the beginnings; it's actually the whole etiology of *In the Castle of My Skin, The Emigrants* and *Season of Adventure.* I think it might be possible to find in *Natives of My Person* elements, parallels and so forth in each of the preceding volumes.'

The novel returns to the roots of Caribbean colonialism, gathering four centuries of history into a span of six months, the time it takes the *Reconnaissance* to complete two legs of the triangular route from Europe to the Guinea Coast and thence to the West Indies. Moving freely forward and backward in time, Lamming establishes the es-

sential pattern of West Indian history, from the subjugation and looting of its Indian civilisations to the terrifying
monstrosities of slavery, to the exploitation of the islands
under various forms of European colonialism.

Europeans believe that non-Europeans lack humanity and
use this belief to justify their exploitation. To the ship's
carpenter, Pierre, and his fellows, Africans are less than
human: they go 'naked everywhere like beasts' and are
possessed of unusual sexual powers. Pierre's view, and indeed much of the section of the novel describing the Guinea Coast, is adapted from Hakluyt's *Voyages*. As early as
1960, when he was writing *The Pleasures of Exile,* Lamming's imagination had been fired by Hakluyt's narratives, as a record of the period when England's experiment
in colonisation was beginning. In the attitude of Hakluyt's
adventurers toward Carib Indian and African slave he discovered the roots of an outlook which continues to affect
coloniser and colonised alike. 'The slave whose skin suggests the savaged deformity of his nature becomes identical with the Carib Indian who feeds on human flesh . . .
both seen as the wild fruits of Nature, share equally that
spirit of revolt which Prospero by sword or Language is
determined to conquer.' Like Hakluyt's Englishmen, both
the Commandant in his persecution of the Tribes and the
crew in their treatment of African slaves are morally blind
and cannot comprehend the stubborn 'spirit of revolt' of
the oppressed.

Lamming's Lime Stone represents England and Europe,
as its House of Trade and Justice combines in a single entity the whole spirit and thrust of colonialism over several
centuries. The slave trade has brought both wealth and
moral corruption to the Kingdom, symbolised by the Sev-
ern asylum, the hell-like repository of the nation's ills. The
Commandant, a philosopher-adventurer like Shakespeare's Prospero, envisages a new society in San Cristobal, cleansed of the Kingdom's corruption. But he is himself a veteran of the extermination of the Tribes, and his
vision of a New World society is based on the tainted
model of the Old.

The origin of the Commandant's obsession lies in his relation to his lover, the Lady of the House, who had abandoned him after he had repeatedly broken his promise not
to go to sea again in pursuit of imperial goals. The expedition is intended to establish a new society where he and
the Lady can be reunited. The officers of the *Reconnaissance* have different reasons for joining the illegal expedition, but share in a sense of the insecurity of their power
and fear of the 'men below'. Each—with the exception of
Priest and Pinteados—has in his background a woman he
has wronged in pursuing his private obsessions. The officers' failure to show humanity and compassion towards
their women—who have seen beyond their 'purity of intention' into their innermost anxieties and weaknesses—is
the ultimate cause of the expedition's failure. When Surgeon and Steward learn of the Commandant's intention to
reunite them with their wives in San Cristobal, they murder the Commandant and are themselves murdered by the
cabin boy Sasha.

The officers' inhumanity towards the women is, Lamming
has said elsewhere, symptomatic of the 'pervasive corrup-

tion of the society in which they lived', a society built on
the exploitation and dehumanisation of others. But their
failure is given a wider significance by Pinteados, the pilot
and architect of the expedition. 'To feel authority over the
women! That was enough for them. But to commit themselves fully to what they felt authority over. That they
could never do. Such power they were afraid of.' Pinteados's remark intersects with the underlying allegorical
themes of the novel, in which the Commandant is a type
of the early independence leaders in the West Indies, men
like Cipriani, Manley and Bustamante, whose goal of independence was tempered by their admiration for England and commitment to her economic system. The
Commandant and his group of officers representing the
middle-class inheritors of power in ex-colonial territories
fail to escape from the colonial legacy of conquest, command and exploitation, as their relation to the women testifies.

The determination of the men, under Baptiste, in alliance
with the painter Ivan, to continue the expedition without
the officers may be seen as a statement of the role of the
common man in shaping a future West Indian society.
Like Lamming's other novels, *Natives of My Person* ends,
however, without a conclusive resolution. The women
wait alone and isolated in a cave on San Cristobal, the 'future they must learn', as the Lady of the House observes.
Natives of My Person draws together the complex themes
of Lamming's previous work: his concern with the quest
for identity and the enduring myth of colonialism, and
with the problem of human misunderstanding as a reflection of the distortions in relationships created by colonialism.

The novel also marks Lamming's most significant stylistic
achievement. For Lamming, style is more than a manner
of writing: it is an expression of artistic identity. 'Nothing
matters more than a man's discovery of his *style,*' he writes
in a tribute to the late Edgar Mittelholzer, 'a discovery
which is also part of his own creation, and style—not a
style—but *style* as the aura and essence, the recognised example of being in which and out of which a man's life assumes its shape' [**"But Alas Edgar"**, *New World: Guyana
Independence Issue,* 1966]. In his first two novels, his style
is often imitative of other writers, notably James Joyce,
though strongly influenced by the rhythms and idioms of
West Indian speech. Lamming's style, his creation of characters, events and even landscapes, is characteristically
concerned with underlying meanings, expressed through
highly symbolic descriptions. An allegorical level is present in all his fiction, in characters like Ma and Pa in *In the
Castle of My Skin,* for example, who embody the historical will of their community, or in the symbolic descriptions of the boys' day at the beach.

Lamming's use of language as a means of symbolic exploration and interpretation is perhaps the most distinctive
stylistic feature of his work, but in *Of Age and Innocence*
and *Season of Adventure* it too often overwhelms the narrative. Descriptions of the weather or the landscape are invariably used to reinforce the mood of an episode or as a
comment on events, and while the results are often successful and striking, the technique is so insistent that it be-

comes difficult to read such dense passages with real attention.

Lamming's concept of the artist as teacher has led him toward the adoption of an entirely allegorical mode in his most recent novels, *Natives of My Person* and *Water with Berries.* In *Natives of My Person,* the metaphor of the journey imparts a new structural control to Lamming's work. The novel's structure enables him to put to work the whole range of his stylistic abilities as a novelist, combining concrete and abstract, realistic and fabulous, since allegory allows a separation of the two levels and suggests at the same time a synthesis between them. An advantage of allegory, for a writer with Lamming's political ideals and concept of the artist as teacher, is that once the allegorical meaning has been established it does not have to be repeatedly returned to and insisted upon in every scene and event.

Water with Berries (1971) was written after *Natives of My Person,* though published almost simultaneously. In the broad line of development of Lamming's work from realism towards an allegorical form based on West Indian history, the novel appears a digression, returning to the life of West Indian exiles in London dealt with in *The Emigrants.* The novel's main concern, however, is with creative sterility and the artist's relation to English society, a problem which may have been especially urgent for Lamming during the long process of writing *Natives of My Person.*

On a 'realistic' level, *Water with Berries* is the story of three impoverished artists from San Cristobal living in London. During the two weeks the narrative covers, the West Indian past they had rejected encroaches on their private, routine worlds. Roger, a musician of East Indian descent, repudiates his pregnant wife Nicole, out of an unconscious fear of racial mixing, arising from his childhood horror at the creolised 'impurity' of West Indian society. The actor Derek is driven by his Christian upbringing to reveal Roger's accusations of infidelity to Nicole; his idealism ends in her suicide. And Teeton, a painter, learns that his wife has committed suicide in San Cristobal. He had abandoned her after she became the wife of the American ambassador in order to secure Teeton's release from prison after an uprising.

The suicides of Randa and Nicole mark the end of the isolated, aesthetic lives the three had created for themselves. In their quest for artistic freedom they had betrayed the love of women for whom self-sacrifice was the only virtue. The suicides assume a wider significance, however, on an allegorical level, with the introduction of motifs from Shakespeare's *The Tempest,* which Lamming treats in his non-fiction work, *The Pleasure of Exile,* as an allegory of colonialism.

In *Water with Berries,* Shakespeare's Prospero is dead, but his widow is represented by the Old Dowager, who as a survivor of the spirit of colonialism exerts a subtle, mothering control over her colonial tenant, Teeton. Shakespeare's Miranda is resurrected both as Randa, Teeton's wife, and as Myra, a prostitute he meets on the heath. Myra had been brutally ravaged by her father's servants in San Cristobal, but makes no connection between her fate and her father's demonic treatment of his servants. Like the Old Dowager, who was deserted by him, Myra still admires her philosopher-father: 'Never showed any interest in personal fortunes,' she recalls. 'No taste at all for possession. Must have been a saint.' Ironically, the three artists share a similar indifference to the materialism of the 'social herd' and a commitment to the purity of art as a style of life. Myra's fate is thus linked to Randa's and Nicole's, as Caliban's is to Prospero's, by a common relation to what Fernando calls the 'curse' of colonialism. Fernando, the Old Dowager's lover and Myra's true father, alone realises that Myra's rape had been the result of Prospero's 'experiment in ruling over your kind', as he tells Teeton. But the knowledge has driven him mad; he is convinced that the curse will last until 'one of us dies'. The novel indeed ends with murder, arson and rape as the artificial harmony between the English and the West Indian immigrants disintegrates.

Lamming's use of *The Tempest* provides a framework for his argument that the experiences of slavery and colonialism have left a lasting mark on coloniser and colonised alike which can only be exorcised through some collective Ceremony of the Souls of the sort Teeton envisages on the heath before events overtake him. 'Sometimes they argue all through the night,' he tells Myra. 'For hours. The living and the dead. It will go on until they reach a point of reconciliation. Then you know it's the end. The end of all complaint from the dead, the end of all retribution for the living.'

If Teeton's, Roger's and Derek's final acts of violence proceed from a will to freedom and a desire to escape from the false 'safety' of their refuge in London, they also renew the pattern of violence begun by Prospero's conquest and enslavement of Caliban. Derek's assault on the actress on stage duplicates Caliban's attack on Miranda, as Roger's arson parallels Caliban's firing of Prospero's home. It is a blind and tragic striking out in reaction to brutalisation, without the re-examination of the past and the collective Ceremony of the Souls that Lamming believes is necessary if the spirit of Prospero's imperial enterprise is to be finally exorcised. Not surprisingly, for Lamming the Ceremony of the Souls is an imaginative rather than political quest.

Lamming's concern with the function of the imaginative contact with, and purgation of, the past goes back to his poem **"The Illumined Graves"**, published twenty years earlier, and forward through his methodical treatment of the struggle for independence and decolonisation in his first four novels to his realisation, in *Natives of My Person,* of the process Teeton envisages. *Natives of My Person* is a journey into the souls of both coloniser and colonised by a writer who feels himself part of both worlds, in search of a new, imaginative vision of human community. For Lamming, political change in the Caribbean must be accompanied by a profound psychic transformation which it is the artist's responsibility to articulate 'at the deepest levels of our reflective self-consciousness'. The imaginative journey into the psyche, 'the symbolic drama, the drama of redemption, the drama of cleansing for a commitment towards the future', is as vital to Lamming's creative purpose as the drama of political struggle and change. Lamming's fiction has been a means of exploration into the self, and an important argument for the necessity of art and the imagination in shaping a new vision of human freedom and Caribbean unity. (pp. 126-43)

Ian Munro, "George Lamming," in West Indian Literature, *edited by Bruce King, Archon Books, 1979, pp. 126-43.*

Sandra Pouchet Paquet

The colonial experience is a matter of historical record. What I'm saying is that the colonial experience is a *live* experience in the *consciousness* of these people. And just because the so-called colonial situation is over and its institutions may have been transferred into something else, it is a fallacy to think that the human-lived content of those situations are automatically transferred into something else, too. The experience is a continuing psychic experience that has to be dealt with long after the actual colonial situation formally 'ends' [George Lamming (see Kent's entry in Further Reading)].

The colonial experience is the subject matter of all George Lamming's novels to date. In each work he explores aspects of this experience with a comprehensiveness and skill that distinguish him as a major political novelist. His novels characteristically describe the structure and organization of society and the extent to which these shape individual response and action. Private experience is examined in relation to the larger public events at the centre of every novel. There is no separation of the business of politics and private life. Lamming insists always on the 'direct informing influence from the subsoil of life outside', and this emphasis organizes and informs the shape of his fiction. He writes out of an acute social consciousness that is vitally concerned with politics and society, that is, with the function of power in a given society, and its effects on the moral, social, cultural, and even aesthetic values of the people in that society.

Lamming's pursuit of the colonial theme gains authority from the broad range of his concern with this experience. His novels deal specifically with colonization as the political and economic history which informs the quality of life in his home island of Barbados, the Caribbean and Western Europe. Lamming explores the influence of this history on three levels which he distinguishes as the province and responsibility of the writer: the world of the private and hidden self; the world of social relations; and the community of men, to whom the writer is directly responsible in his 'essential need to find meaning for his destiny' [Lamming, **"The Negro Writer and His World,"** *Caribbean Quarterly* 5, No. 2, 1958]. He explains further that the writer's 'responsibility to that other world, his third world, will be judged not only by the authenticity and power with which his own private world is presented, but also by the honesty with which he interprets the world of his social relations.' For Lamming, these three worlds influence each other intimately and complexly, so that his concern with the politics of colonialism is a concern with the precise quality of individual experience, as it reflects the weight of history on the total society. As Lamming conceives it, this is the proper function of the novelist and the responsibility of the Caribbean writer in particular.

In his fiction Lamming characteristically examines the present in relation to the past and the future. He returns to this theme continually in references to the Haitian Ceremony of Souls. It is his symbol of a meaningful reconciliation of contemporary post-colonial experience with its historical past, with the artist as pilot in this hopeful venture. The Ceremony of Souls is crucial to an understanding of the politics of Lamming's novels. In **"The West Indian People"** [in *New World Quarterly* 2, No. 2, 1966], Lamming describes the ritual and spells out its significance for him as a writer.

. . . in the republic of Haiti there is a Ceremony of Souls at which all the celebrants are relatives of the dead who return for this occasion to give some report on their previous relations with the living. The dead are supposed to be in a purgatorial state of Water, and it is necessary for them to have this dialogue with the living before they can be released into their final eternity. The living, on the other hand, need to meet the dead again in order to discover if there is any need for forgiveness. This dialogue takes place through the medium of the Priest or *Houngan*. . . . It is not important to believe in the actual details of the ceremony. What is important is its symbolic drama, the drama of redemption, the drama of returning, the drama of cleansing for a commitment towards the future.

These are major concerns in Lamming's fiction. The drama of redemption, of returning, of cleansing for a commitment towards the future; these define the perspective which organizes his fiction and shapes his treatment of the colonial theme.

Lamming locates the determining factor for contemporary Caribbean and European experience in the European colonial experiment which gained momentum in the seventeenth century, and in the subsequent exploitation and enslavement of peoples native to Africa and the Americas. His fiction engages in a comprehensive examination of this past and the present in relation to each other: 'It's very central to me in the sense that the world in which one lives is not just inhabited by the living. It is a world which is also the creation of the dead. And any architecture of the future cannot really take place without that continuing dialogue between the living and the past.' The Ceremony of Souls is Lamming's symbol of this exercise of the creative imagination. But more than this, it articulates his conception of the public role of the artist in the figure of the Priest or *Houngan*.

This conception of the artist's public role is elaborately treated in an early collection of essays, *The Pleasures of Exile.* This book, Lamming writes, was 'intended as an introduction to a dialogue', between descendants of the colonizers and the colonized, or as he names them, the descendants of Prospero and Caliban. As an artist whose language is that of the colonizer, and who is nonetheless a descendent of Caliban, he claims singular authority in articulating a perspective that is to create new possibilities for the future:

> For I am a direct descendant of slaves, too near to the actual enterprise to believe that its echoes are over with the reign of emancipation. Moreover, I am a direct descendant of Prospero, worshipping in the same temple of endeavour, using his legacy of language—not to curse our meeting—but to push it further, reminding the descendants of both sides that what's done is done, and can only be seen as a soil from which other gifts, or the same gift endowed with different meanings, may grow towards a future which is colonized by our acts in this moment, but which must always remain open [**"In the Beginning,"** *The Pleasure of Exile*].

Lamming offers an alternative to Caliban's curse. He intends 'a calculated challenge to the habitual way of seeing that has become a normal part of colonization.' He wants to change the inherited values and rationalizations of colonization that stymie both sides, and to offer the descendants of Prospero and Caliban an alternative 'way of seeing'. His artistic purpose is no less than to shape the consciousness and to influence the perspective of both the Caribbean community and the world community at large. He states categorically that the Caribbean writer has a 'public task' beyond the 'creating of so-called works of Art'. He sees the artist as engaged in 'the shaping of national consciousness, giving alternative directions to society'.

While the organization of political movements is not the artist's function, he has social responsibilities similar to the politician's, says Lamming [in an interview with Ian Munro and Reinhard Sander in *Kas-Kas,* 1972]:

> So although I would make a distinction about *functions,* I do not make a distinction about *responsibilities.* I do not think that the responsibility of the professional politician is greater than the responsibility of an artist to his society.

More recently, in a graduation address at the University of the West Indies, Cave Hill, Lamming assigns to the Caribbean writer a variety of specific functions. He is educator, social historian and priest:

> Throughout the literature of the Caribbean, this theme of spiritual dispossession and self-mutilation remains central to the thought and perception of your writers; and it's no wonder that the gradual infiltration of their books into the education of our youth is made a cause of grave concern. But it is the function of the writer to return a society to itself; and in this respect, your writers have been the major historians of the feeling of your people. To separate them by open or hidden forms of censorship from a generation which needs to be provided with a firm sense of historical continuity would be to inflict upon us a second stage of isolation.

According to Lamming, the writer records and interprets the world of social relations; he provides historical continuity; and he liberates a new generation from a cycle of 'spiritual dispossession and self-mutilation'. He emphasizes the revolutionary character of the region's literature.

The writer is an arbiter of social change. His art is at once subversive, liberating and restorative.

In the light of such clearly delineated views on the nature of fiction and the social obligations of the artists, Lamming's novels can be termed political not only because the matter they investigate is of a political nature, but because they reflect his commitment to reorganize the imbalance in personal and social relationships engendered by a colonial history. The novels are intended as political acts. In his fiction, Lamming offers no easy solutions and no programme for government. What he offers is a careful evaluation of the social laws and values that perpetuate a colonial mentality, and also an evaluation of those elements in the society that contribute to the making of a new social order.

Lamming's emphasis on colonial history as the appropriate context for exploring the peculiarities of contemporary West Indian experience, and his preoccupation with fiction as an instrument of social transformation, shape the distinctive features of his art. In his novels, individual human experience is always circumscribed by historical and political circumstance. Political events are linked to the development of plot and character. In fact, character and action frequently embody the social and political confrontations around which the plot develops. This allows him to portray the complexities of the total society within the parameters of personal and social relationships among a representative community.

Lamming's fiction typically presents a crowded canvas. His novels are dense and panoramic in scale, at times covering territory that ranges from one end of the Caribbean to the other in the fictive island of San Cristobal, or all of Europe in the Kingdoms of Lime Stone and Antarctica. It is often difficult to focus on a single most important character in the conventional sense of hero or heroine. This is certainly the case in *The Emigrants, Of Age and Innocence, Water with Berries,* and to varying degrees in the other novels, where competing elements in the society, or the society itself, are as important as the unfolding history of any single character. Even in *In the Castle of My Skin,* where autobiography identifies a central character, G. shares the focus of the novel in a complementary way with the village community. In *Season of Adventure,* Fola's predicament individualizes the external drama of a class war and the fall of the second republic; she is interesting because she embodies an important aspect of the upheaval around her. She shares the focus of interest with a variety of other characters. The same is true of the Commandant in *Natives of My Person* even though his enterprise provides the narrative framework of the novel.

Lamming characteristically isolates what is most significant about the structure and development of the society at a particular moment in history, and embodies these trends in characters and confrontations that are representative of social and political forces at work in the society. It is his way of individualizing the general social condition. The motivation for character and action derives from the individual's attachment to the values and images which tie him to a particular class and social function. The complexity of warring elements in the society is reflected in the individual psychology of characters, their relationships with each other, and their choices as private and public crises arise.

As early as *In the Castle of My Skin,* characters and actions have a symbolic resonance that invests the plot with poetic denseness. Lamming relies heavily on what he calls 'collective character'. Such characters are representative of a group or class or value system within the society. Collective characters are often composites fashioned in the way Richard Wright describes in 'How Bigger Was Born'; 'there was not just one Bigger, but many of them, more than I could count and more than you suspect.' Lamming himself describes Powell in *Season of Adventure* as 'a composite member of West Indian society'. Characters such as Ma and Pa in *In the Castle of My Skin* are collective characters in the sense that they express the cumulative experience of the village community. The different responses to social and political change which they articulate reflect a division in the village to which they belong. The dilemma of the village in turn articulates the dilemma of the island, and the frame of reference broadens indefinitely. Lamming says he wanted to make Creighton's village 'applicable to Barbados, to Jamaica, and to all of the other islands. I wanted to give the village that symbolic quality.' With this emphasis in mind it is not surprising to find Lamming moving away from the limitations of a known setting in *In the Castle of My Skin* and *The Emigrants,* to the imaginary island of San Cristobal in subsequent novels, and even the fictional European kingdoms of Lime Stone and Antarctica in *Natives of My Person.*

In keeping with Lamming's early reliance on the symbolic representation of experience in *In the Castle of My Skin,* there is a definite movement in his fiction towards what he describes as 'an allegorical interpretation of experience' as opposed to 'a naturalistic rendering of society'. This is especially apparent in his last two novels: *Water with Berries* and *Natives of My Person.* In *Water with Berries,* characters act out their inherited roles as colonizer and colonized in a post-colonial setting with devasting results for all. Plot and characters are loosely derived from Shakespeare's *The Tempest.* This provides a Ceremony of Souls framework for the struggle to be freed from the burden of an inherited colonial relationship to the mother country. When Teeton, the West Indian artist in exile, murders his landlady, Mrs Gore-Brittain, in order to escape the menace of her hospitality and affection turned vindictive, their interests are mutually exclusive and his life and freedom depend on this extreme action. The political comment is abundantly clear as Lamming uses the cloying quality of their relationship and its latent hostilities to describe the destructiveness of a post-colonial attachment to old colonial ties. In *Natives of My Person,* Lamming describes a late-sixteenth century voyage to settle in the New World, with a view to elucidating the dilemma of post-colonial societies, so that the House of Trade and Justice in the Kingdom of Lime Stone functions as a symbol of its modern equivalent:

> I was thinking of the House as a symbol of our contemporary situation, of the post-colonial world like that of San Cristobal. Today, it's the *international corporation.* That is the stupendous body that now rises above what ordinary people and their leaders imagine to be the domestic authority of the land. A country becomes what is called 'independent', attempts, like the *Reconnaissance* to set out on a journey of very serious *breaking away,* but discovers instead the international corporation—that gigantic arrangement of modern life has the capacity to control or redirect decisions democratically decided by people and their leaders.

The novel is both an analysis of politics and society in the late sixteenth and seventeenth centuries, as well as a political commentary on the lingering influence of that social and political system in post-colonial societies.

Lamming approaches language with the same political awareness that determines the quality of his fiction at large, and his efforts are not always understood. While Stuart Hall remarks [in "Lamming, Selvon, and Some Trends in the West Indian Novel," *Bim* 6 No. 23, 1968] that in Lamming's 'hand, the rhythms and idioms of West Indian speech are brought to a condition of sensitivity where language is capable of expressing the deepest reaches of West Indian personality,' Wilson Harris complains about its 'self-indulgence', about 'a verbal sophistication rather than a visual, plastic and conceptual imagery' [see excerpt above]. What Hall credits with the richness of poetic expression, Harris dismisses as superfluous. More recently, Elizabeth Nunez-Harrell charges that conversational dialect in Lamming's fiction lacks organic spontaneity [see Further Reading list]. She is particularly unhappy about the language of the village boys in *In the Castle of My Skin,* as they struggle to verbalize their impressions of the adult world about them. The search for criteria that transcend individual preference is an elusive one.

Lamming argues that the language of Caribbean literature is weighted with 'the cultural and historical associations and discontinuities which the area has experienced'. He identifies three areas of influence at work in Caribbean literature, all of which feature in his novels in a variety of combinations: the British literary tradition, the influence of the King James Bible on the language of the masses in Jamaica and Barbados, and the influence of popular speech. What is important about language in Lamming's Caribbean novels is that, however stylized, it is historically and linguistically based in the experience he describes. Consider the dream vision of Pa, the old man in *In the Castle of My Skin.* In Chapter Ten, the old man struggles to describe a vision of the future that draws on the whole range of memory and accrued experience. His language is a wonderfully creative approximation of Biblical language—the most sophisticated expression of the colonizer's tongue to which Pa has been exposed. The transformation of language which occurs in his attempt to articulate a vision that transcends the mental and physical limitations of slavery and colonization, reflects Lamming's own efforts to free the language from its historical role as a major colonizing agent. The mixture of Biblical rhythms and popular speech are appropriate both to the old man's language experience and to the epic journey of return and discovery he describes.

Lamming contends that once Prospero's language had

been accepted by Caliban, 'the future of his development, however independent it was, would always be in some way inextricably tied up with that pioneering aspect of Prospero. Caliban at some stage would have to find a way of breaking that contract, which got sealed by language, in order to reconstruct some alternative reality for himself.' The adoption of a foreign language initiated a spiritual exile from Caliban's native inheritance. The writer's function and responsibility is to alter the pattern of values that came with the colonizer's language. In Lamming's words: 'the language of modern politics is no longer Prospero's exclusive vocabulary. It is Caliban's as well; and since there is no absolute from which a moral prescription may come, Caliban is at liberty to choose the meaning of this moment.' Lamming's fiction is an attempt to realize this liberty in a continuing dialogue concerning various aspects of the colonial experience. He makes no distinction between aesthetics and politics, that is, between his pursuits as an artist and his commitment to change the bias of a colonial inheritance.

Politics becomes a necessary consideration in any critical assessment of Lamming's fiction because it is so much a part of the content and form of the novels. Much in his aesthetic as a political novelist invites comparison with Marxist critical concepts, especially those of totality, typicality and historical overview. But there is a sharp divergence between Lukács' anti-modernism and Lamming's movement towards political allegory. Lukács argues that modern allegory is ahistorical and static, and sacrifices typicality to abstraction. Lamming clearly finds the allegorical rendering of experience perfectly compatible with social criticism and analysis in an historical context. *Water with Berries* is inspired in form and content by his interpretation of Shakespeare's *The Tempest* as political allegory. In this novel, he combines social realism with allegory as a way of linking past history with typical conflicts in the present. Another obvious point of connection with Marxism and literature lies in the Marxist concepts of art as an instrument of social development, and the artist as social enlightener. There is ample evidence of Lamming's commitment to both these principles in both his life and his art.

While he stays clear of propaganda or dogmatism in his fiction, the political bias that shapes Lamming's perspective as a novelist is obviously anti-colonialist and anti-imperialist. But even more basic to the political bias implicit in his fiction, are the peasant and working class sympathies that distinguish the novels in varying degrees. Not only is his fiction nationalistic in its devotion to the concept of a distinct West Indian identity, but it consistently embodies the islands' progression towards independence and nationhood in the motions, aspirations, language and lifestyles of the peasant and working class majority. It becomes increasingly clear in his novels, that Lamming measures the evolution of West Indian society in terms of the peasant struggle against a middle class pursuit of privilege and power. In fact he identifies the peasant orientation of the West Indian novelists, with a few exceptions, as their distinguishing characteristic. He argues that it was in the West Indian novel that 'the West Indian peasant became other than a cheap source of labour. He became, through

the novelist's eye, a living existence, living in silence and joy and fear, involved in riot and carnival. It is the West Indian novel that has restored the West Indian peasant to his true and original status of personality.' Whether Lamming's statement is fair or not, it is certainly true of his own art. For as he says of the West Indian novelist, he was 'the first to relate the West Indian experience from the inside. He was the first to chart the West Indian memory as far back as he could go.' (pp. 1-8)

In the six novels he has published since 1953, George Lamming identifies colonialism as the political institution that has shaped the structure and direction of West Indian society. He has striven consistently as a writer to portray the development of this society in its totality. He describes the complex motivations and interrelationships of the West Indian community within the framework of its political history. Each novel explores a stage in, or an aspect of, the colonial experience, so that the novels are finally the 'unfolding of a single work'. Each individual novel is organically related to Lamming's political concern with how the structure of power reflects colonial history and how this in turn affects the intimate details of private and public life in a representative community.

There are two distinct movements in this body of work that mark a clear progression in thematic and artistic method. There is a well-co-ordinated continuity in the first four novels, from *In the Castle of My Skin* to *Season of Adventure,* that gives these volumes epic stature. Together they describe the struggle of the West Indian people to be free of the political, economic, and cultural domination that characterized their history. Lamming describes the breakdown of colonial rule and the emergence of an independent republic in the Caribbean, followed by the fall of this republic and the emergence of the second republic in a continuing struggle to break free of the psychological and political thrall of colonialism. He begins with the initial promise and failure of the emerging labour movement of the 1930s in *In the Castle of My Skin.* This is the prelude to *The Emigrants* in which Lamming describes, with deep sympathy and understanding, the attitudes and the motivations of thousands of West Indians who emigrated to the 'Mother Country' after the Second World War. In *Of Age and Innocence* he describes the return of the emigrant to the Caribbean and the sudden growth of independence movements in the 1950s. *Season of Adventure* is Lamming's last direct fictional statement on the now largely independent, self-governing Caribbean. It marks a high point in Lamming's fiction with the unqualified promise of Gort and Fola, the folk artist and the middle-class revolutionary who ties her educational advantages to the African and peasant values of Gort's drum. In Gort and Fola, the masculine and feminine principles in the society are identified in productive harmony with each other, as an oppressed working class struggles for freedom from the inherited bias and injustices of the post-colonial regime. This is Lamming's concluding and most optimistic statement about the future of an independent Caribbean. Revolution is seen as a continuing process with certain guarantees of success in the Gort/Fola alliance.

Of Age and Innocence and *Season of Adventure* differ from the first two novels in that their setting is a fictional West Indian island called San Cristobal. This suggests a deepening concern in Lamming to address himself to the West Indian people as one, despite the political and geographic divisions that isolate the different territories. What is especially significant, in terms of the texture of these novels, is an intensification of the regional character that distinguished *In the Castle of My Skin* and the first section of *The Emigrants.* Lamming elaborates on details of setting, speech, customs, and legends from different West Indian countries, in his effort to chronicle the history and meaning of emerging West Indian nationhood as a shared experience.

Season of Adventure marks the end of one movement in Lamming's work. He explains that 'there was at that moment no further point for me to go without in a sense going beyond what has actually happened in the society.' For twelve years Lamming published no further novels. Then in 1972, his last two novels were published simultaneously: *Water with Berries* was released in London in October and *Natives of My Person* was released in New York in the same month. The shift in focus and artistic method immediately set these novels apart from his earlier efforts.

In *Water with Berries* Lamming turns his attention to those West Indians, artists in particular, who never re-entered the mainstream of life in the Caribbean. He examines the continuing drama of conflict and rejection that attends West Indians domiciled in Great Britain. Interestingly enough, this is the shortest of Lamming's novels. It offers a much reduced canvas of characters and makes them carry the burden of the book's comment on the immigrant experience. The relative compactness of the novel is clearly tied to its allegorical design and marks a new development in the writer's artistic method. The allegorical structure of *Of Age and Innocence* had been heavily underscored with a wealth of descriptive detail about his characters and their fictional setting. It would seem that working with Great Britain as a known setting in *Water with Berries,* as opposed to San Cristobal, Lamming no longer felt he had to chart the history and structure of the society in the convolutions of an elaborate plot. In *Water with Berries,* as few as eight characters, and the interrelationships among them, sustain the multiple levels of allegory that comprise the novel's statement about the conflict between immigrant and native Briton.

Natives of My Person, with its very different setting and European cast, confirms Lamming's continuing concern to define the scope of the colonial experience. In this instance, he explores the crises of late sixteenth-century and early seventeenth-century Europe which inspired Europe's annexation of the New World. Lamming's political intention is clear in his comment to Raymond Gardner of the *Guardian* [quoted in Gardner's review of *Natives of My Person* and *Cannon Shot and Glass Beads,* in the Manchester *Guardian,* 10 July 1974]:

> There is a tendency to speak of colonialism as though it were exclusively a black experience. That is a very limited understanding. It was a two-way thing. Colonialism has been as much a

white experience as a black one. It is simply that it has taken the white world a very long time to understand the nature of that enterprise and it seems to me that the agents of power in that society have been always very slow to allow that understanding to percolate down to the ordinary person in the street.

In *Natives of My Person* Lamming goes back in history to describe the genesis of colonialism. He describes a sixteenth-century voyage that was the beginning of plantation society in the West Indies. But while the historical fiction is complete within itself, the novel is also a sustained allegory of the structure of power in post-colonial countries. In this novel, Lamming returns to the elaborate architecture of the first four novels as he once again attempts to chart a whole society in the full complexity of the historical moment. But he considerably limits the multiple demands of setting and custom that weight his earlier fiction by structuring this novel around a real and symbolic ship's journey. This is by far the most finely executed of his novels, and especially impressive in that it penetrates the consciousness of another race, another culture, and a distant moment in history.

Lamming's preoccupation with the colonial experience as an organizing point in his fiction has led to the charge that he is Europe-orientated rather than West Indian. In his Introduction to *Wilson Harris and the West Indian Novel,* Michael Gilkes writes:

> The cultural presence of the Old World is always, then, an important and necessary ingredient in Lamming's writing, since his identity as a West Indian Negro can make sense, it would seem, only in the context (albeit a renewed, purged context) of the European presence. His work is therefore Europe-oriented in the sense that it almost always involves a re-statement, a re-examination of the Caliban/Prospero relationship.

It is of course Lamming's stated position that the West Indian cannot wish away or fruitfully ignore three hundred years of European influence in the predominantly African and East Indian communities of the former British Caribbean. He is not alone in this respect. In "The Muse Of History" [*Is Massa Day Dead?,* edited by Orde Coombs, 1974] Derek Walcott describes the fine balance between the Caribbean and Europe, by comparing the Guadeloupian poet, St John Perse, and the Martiniquan poet, Aimé Césaire, as follows:

> men of diametrically challenging backgrounds, racial opposites to use the language of politics, one patrician and conservative, the other proletarian and revolutionary, classic and romantic, Prospero and Caliban, all such opposites balance easily, but they balance on the axis of a shared sensibility, and this sensibility, with or deprived of the presence of a visible tradition, is the sensibility of walking to a New World.

Even Wilson Harris who rejects the victor/victim stasis he finds implicit in the Prospero/Caliban theme, finds it necessary to explore all aspects of the past, whether the recorded bias of history or the obscured perspectives of vanquished peoples [the critic cites "History, Fable, and Myth in the Caribbean and Guianas," *Caribbean Quarterly* 16, No. 2, 1970]. The proximity of Europe in the lives of West Indians is not only a major fictional theme, but a real dilemma in the lives of West Indian writers who, whether resident in the Caribbean or not, are heavily dependent on a reading public outside the West Indies.

In *The Pleasures of Exile,* Lamming wrote that 'the West Indian Novel, by which I mean the novel written by the West Indian about the West Indian reality is hardly twenty years old.' In *The West Indian Novel and Its Background* Kenneth Ramchand agrees and goes on to point out that by this definition, the first known work of West Indian prose fiction appeared in 1903 [see Further Reading]. His statistics are interesting: 'Between 1903 and June 1967, at least 162 works of prose fiction have been produced by fifty-six writers from six West Indian territories.' The statistics are even more to the point when we consider that 141 of the 162 he estimates were published between 1941 and June 1967. Along with the work of Naipaul, Selvon and Harris, Lamming's fiction is the most significant that the West Indies has produced over the last twenty years. Lamming's contribution is distinct and pervasive. It was Lamming who first defined the terms of the West Indian writer's relationship to his society and art that have dominated West Indian literary criticism. In *The Pleasures of Exile,* he in fact defined what he had already achieved in his fiction, and this gave added authority to his pronouncements. The only serious challenge to what Lamming had to say comes from Wilson Harris's *Tradition, the Writer and Society,* in which Harris charged that the West Indian novelists (and Lamming among them) were negatively attached to the traditional nineteenth-century novel, and this was seriously inhibiting their efforts in fiction.

But much that Harris has to say confirms Lamming's stature as a major West Indian writer who is directly attuned to an emerging Caribbean aesthetic. For instance, Harris argues:

> The West Indian artist therefore has a central theme or symbol, and that symbol is man, the human person, as opposed to the European artist whose symbol is masses and materials. In order to develop his theme the West Indian must concern himself with the several levels of his world; he has in short most significantly to influence the architectural problem of his time, since though he may work principally in terms of values in his bare world, the effects will be felt soon or late in terms of masses and structural organization.

For Harris as for Lamming the artist has a vital role to play in shaping the direction of society. Harris explains himself further in terms that echo similar concerns in Lamming's fiction:

> So many walls fall between us and our fellows. Money, myth and numerous obsessions. Yet when we look at the human we must be prepared not to overlook these obsessions but to work them into the structure of art so that all these levels of man are present. It is the only way we can

come close to the real power of man, by showing the interaction of all the levels of his life, thereby not only baring his conflict, but the rhythms within the welter of his existence. These rhythms being after all the source of man's generation of energy yesterday and today, are also the source of man's energy—tomorrow.

In his fiction Lamming examines both 'conflict' and 'rhythms' in terms of man's political and economic history. His special distinction as a West Indian novelist is the wide range of his concern with the colonial experience. He addresses himself consistently to an examination of its multiform parts, and is always sensitive to the private dilemma of the individual in relation to the wider social pressures of a particular moment in history.

Lamming is the most overtly political of West Indian writers in English, in his choice of theme, and in his insistence on the moral and social obligations of the artist in the Caribbean. But he is not isolated in his concern to move beyond the confines of a particular ethnic group or a particular territory, and to address himself to the meaning of the Caribbean experience as a whole. A significant feature of contemporary West Indian literature is precisely Lamming's concern to define the structure of power in the society and to examine the individual dilemma in relation to the function of that power. The central concern is to examine individual experience in relation to the 'subsoil of life outside'. There is a definite movement in this direction in V. S. Naipaul and Derek Walcott, and this is certainly the preoccupation of Edward Brathwaite and Wilson Harris. (pp. 116-20)

Whatever the difference in perspective and the texture of their art, these writers are increasingly in dialogue with each other over the weight and effect of colonial history on the quality of life in the Caribbean. Their sense of the artist's task varies. For Walcott, it is Adam's task of giving things their name. For Harris and Brathwaite, that task is to sound out new directions by entering into authentic dialogue with obscured roots whether Amerindian or African. As Brathwaite explains in ["Timehri," in *Is Massa Day Dead?*]:

> In the Caribbean, whether it be African or Amerindian, the recognition of an ancestral relationship with the folk or aboriginal culture involves the artist and participant in a journey into the past and hinterland which is at the same time a movement of possession into present and future. Through this movement of possession we become ourselves, truly our own creators, discovering word for object, image for word.

Like Lamming, both Harris and Brathwaite have a well-defined sense of the artist's role in shaping the destiny of his people.

In *Season of Adventure,* Lamming goes so far as to suggest an alternative base of values for the society in its peasant and African roots. But Lamming's fiction offers no programme for social change. He has consistently refused to commit himself to a political ideology in his fiction, despite the fact that he still works with the Barbados Workers' Union in that island, and has spoken out publicly in support of Castro's socialist revolution in the Caribbean. Lamming is a political novelist because his fiction is primarily concerned with the relationship between politics and the social and cultural values that shape the quality of human life in a given historical moment. Baako's complaint in **Season of Adventure** remains uncontradicted in Lamming's fiction: 'if Government is rotten, then every activity under its authority will be polluted too. And I don't mean parties. It makes no difference whether they are to the right or left, if the actual way of governing is rotten.' (pp. 121-22)

> *Sandra Pouchet Paquet, in her* The Novels of George Lamming, *Heinemann Educational Books Ltd., 1982, 130 p.*

FURTHER READING

Barthold, Bonnie J. "From Fragmentation to Redemption: Seven Representative Novels—George Lamming, *In the Castle of My Skin.*" In her *Black Time: Fiction of Africa, the Caribbean, and the United States,* pp. 150-57. New Haven: Yale University Press, 1981.
  Examines Lamming's portrayal of his protagonist's growth and maturation in conjunction with a state of change within Barbadian society.

Birney, Earle. "Meeting George Lamming in Jamaica." *Canadian Literature,* No. 95 (Winter 1982): 16-28.
  The Canadian poet reminisces about meeting Lamming while researching Caribbean literature in 1962.

Boxill, Anthony. "San Cristobal Unreached: George Lamming's Two Latest Novels." *World Literature Written in English* 12, No. 1 (April 1973): 111-16.
  Assessment of *Water with Berries* and *Natives of My Person.* Boxill considers *Native of My Person* successful for its insights into the history of colonialism in the West Indies, and maintains that *Water with Berries* fails due to the "pretentious complexity" of its symbolic pattern.

Brown, Carolyn T. "The Myth of the Fall and the Dawning of Consciousness in George Lamming's *In the Castle of My Skin.*" *World Literature Today* 57, No. 1 (Winter 1983): 38-43.
  Analysis of Lamming's first novel, in which Brown identifies the archetypal theme of a fall from a state of grace as necessary to maturity and self-knowledge.

Cartey, Wilfred. "Lamming and the Search for Freedom." *New World Quarterly* 3, Nos. 1 and 2 (Dead Season 1966-Croptime 1967): 121-28.
  Identifies acceptance of the past, anticipation of the future, and establishment of a national identity as prominent themes in works by Lamming and other expatriate West Indian novelists.

Clarke, Austin C. "Some Speculations as to the Absence of Racialistic Vindictiveness in West Indian Literature." In *The Black Writer in Africa and the Americas,* edited by Lloyd W. Brown, pp. 165-94. Los Angeles: Hennessey & Ingalls, 1973.
  Includes discussion of *In the Castle of My Skin* and *The*

Pleasures of Exile in an examination of racial issues in West Indian writing.

Cudjoe, Selwyn R. "Towards Independence: *Of Age and Innocence, Season of Adventure, Water with Berries.*" In his *Resistance and Caribbean Literature,* pp. 179-211. Athens: Ohio University Press, 1980.
  Considers Lamming's exploration of the colonial experience and independence movements in the novels listed.

Gilkes, Michael. "Background to Exile." In his *The West Indian Novel,* pp. 86-115. Boston: Twayne Publishers, 1981.
  Includes discussion of *In the Castle of My Skin* in an examination of the theme of alienation in West Indian expatriate literature. Scattered references to Lamming elsewhere in the book include an assessment of *In the Castle of My Skin* as a national classic.

Griffiths, Gareth. "Childhood and Leavetaking" and "A Sense of Place." In his *A Double Exile: African and West Indian Writing between Two Cultures,* pp. 79-109, 110-39. London: Marion Boyars, 1978.
  Includes discussion of Lamming's novels in chapters devoted to West Indian fiction about childhood, expatriation, and the return of the expatriate.

Jonas, Joyce E. "Carnival Strategies in Lamming's *In the Castle of My Skin.*" *Callaloo* 11, No. 2 (Spring 1988): 346-60.
  Traces the influence on Lamming's first novel of the trickster figure from African folklore.

Kent, George E. "A Conversation with George Lamming." *Black World* XXII, No. 5 (March 1973): 4-14, 88-97.
  Interview in which Kent and Lamming discuss characterization, plot, and influences on Lamming's fiction.

Larson, Charles R. "Toward a Sense of the Community: George Lamming's *In the Castle of My Skin.*" In his *The Novel in the Third World,* pp. 89-107. Washington, D.C.: Inscape, 1976.
  Considers *In the Castle of My Skin* an important developmental novel in West Indian literature for its combination of autobiographical and fictional elements.

McDonald, Avis G. " 'Within the Orbit of Power': Reading Allegory in George Lamming's *Natives of My Person.*" *The Journal of Commonwealth Literature* XXII, No. 1 (1987): 73-86.
  Allegorical interpretation of Lamming's novel.

Moore, Gerald. *The Chosen Tongue: English Writing in the Tropical World.* New York: J. & J. Harper Editions, Harper & Row, 1970.
  Includes mention of Lamming in an account of English-language authors from colonized tropical regions.

Morris, Mervyn. "The Poet as Novelist: The Novels of George Lamming." In *The Islands in Between: Essays on West Indian Literature,* edited by Louis James, pp. 73-85. London: Oxford University Press, 1968.
  Survey of Lamming's novels.

Nunez-Harrell, Elizabeth. "Lamming and Naipaul: Some Criteria for Evaluating the Third-World Novel." *Contemporary Literature* 19, No. 1 (Winter 1978): 26-47.
  Examines protest elements in the fiction of Lamming and V. S. Naipaul. The critic characterizes Third-World writers as "descendants of those people of color whose

history included colonization and, in some cases, en-slavement by peoples of Europe."

Petersen, Kirsten Holst. "Time, Timelessness, and the Jour-ney Metaphor in George Lamming's *In the Castle of My Skin* and *Natives of My Person*." In *The Commonwealth Writer Overseas: Themes of Exile and Expatriation*, edited by Alastair Niven, pp. 283-88. Brussels, Belgium: Marcel Didier, 1976.

> Examines "the theme of the journey" in the novels men-tioned, finding that "his purpose is not to probe the indi-vidual mind for its own sake, but rather to give an imagi-native insight into the growth of West Indian sensibility and through that to offer an interpretation of West Indi-an history."

Ramchand, Kenneth. *The West Indian Novel and Its Back-ground.* London: Heinemann, 1983, 310 p.

> Includes numerous scattered references to Lamming.

Sunitha, K. T. "The Theme of Childhood in *In the Castle of My Skin* and *Swami and Friends.*" *World Literature Written in English* 27, No. 2 (Autumn 1987): 291-96.

> Compares the theme of childhood in novels by Lamming and R. K. Narayan.

Thiong'o, Ngugi Wa. "George Lamming's *In the Castle of*

My Skin" and "George Lamming and the Colonial Situa-tion." In his *Homecoming: Essays on African and Caribbean Literature, Culture and Politics,* pp. 110-26, 127-44. London: Heinemann, 1972.

> Interprets *In the Castle of My Skin* as a study of the forces behind and development toward colonial revolt. The second chapter cited discusses exile as a dominant theme in Lamming's novels.

West, Anthony. Review of *The Emigrants,* by George Lam-ming. *The New Yorker* XXXI, No. 15 (28 May 1955): 122, 124.

> Charges that Lamming's second novel suffers from dis-jointed narrative, but commends the vivid portrayal of characters and events in individual episodes.

Willis, Susan. "Caliban as Poet: Reversing the Maps of Dom-ination." In *Reinventing the Americas: Comparative Studies of Literature of the United States and Spanish America,* edited by Bell Gale Chevigny and Gari Laguardia, pp. 92-105. Cam-bridge: Cambridge University Press, 1986.

> Includes discussion of Lamming's novel *Water with Ber-ries* in an essay contrasting First- and Third-World views of Caribbean culture as portrayed in historiogra-phy and fiction.

Denise Levertov

1923-

English-born American poet, essayist, short story writer, editor, and translator.

A leading post-World War II American poet, Levertov blends the tenets of objectivist and projectivist verse with metaphysical elements from Judeo-Christian religions and the poetry of the nineteenth-century romantics. While her early verse is often described as neo-Romantic, Levertov's later writing reflects the influence of the objectivist poetry of William Carlos Williams and Ezra Pound as well as the projectivist work of "Black Mountain" poets Robert Creeley, Charles Olson, and Robert Duncan. In this poetry, Levertov infuses descriptions of everyday objects with her personal, political, and religious sensibility. She employs such projectivist and objectivist techniques as natural speech rhythms, enjambment, irregular line breaks to allow pauses for breathing, and direct and spontaneous transmission of the poet's emotional and intellectual energy. Levertov frequently examines various aspects of love, encompassing marital, erotic, maternal, and religious themes. In her work of the 1960s and 1970s, Levertov presents these topics in increasingly politicized poems that discuss American military involvement in the Vietnam conflict, the women's movement, and nuclear disarmament. Levertov's craftsmanship, command of style, and imagery place her in the forefront of contemporary poetry. Kenneth Rexroth observed: "Levertov's style is characterized by its low visibility. Her poems are so carefully wrought that the workmanship goes by unnoticed. They seem like speech, heightened and purified. Although her poems are modernistic enough to satisfy any avant-garde editor of the Twenties, they are certainly never obscure, never seem to be doing anything but communicating with presentational immediacy."

Levertov's father, a Russian-Jew who emigrated to Great Britain and became an Anglican minister devoted to combining Christian and Jewish faiths, and her mother, who was well-versed in Welsh and English folklore and literature, both exerted strong influences on her poetry. Her father was descended from Schneour Zalmon, an eighteenth-century rabbi reputed to know the language of birds and a founding member of Habid Hasidism, a Jewish mystical movement that opposes rationalism and celebrates the mystery of everyday events. Likewise, Levertov's mother claimed the Welsh tailor and mystic Angell Jones of Mold among her forebears. In her poem "Illustrious Ancestors" Levertov declares an affinity with her heritage: "I would like to make, / thinking some line taut between me and them, / poems direct as what the birds said, / hard as a floor, sound as a bench / mysterious as the silence when the tailor / would pause with his needle in the air."

Levertov's parents assumed all the responsibility for their two daughters' education, relying on the family library

and programs aired on the British Broadcasting System. Levertov's only formal instruction occurred at ballet school. She began writing poetry at an early age and mailed several verses to T. S. Eliot—who responded with a lengthy and encouraging letter—when she was twelve years old. When she was fifteen, Levertov was corresponding on a regular basis with poet and critic Herbert Read, who wrote: "What history demands in the long run is the object itself—the work of art which is itself a created reality, an addition to the sum of real objects in the world." Her first volume of poems, *The Double Image,* was written during World War II. These lyrical pieces are set in traditional metrical and stanzaic forms, evidencing Levertov's interest in English Romantic poetry.

Following the war, Levertov married American novelist Mitchell Goodman. For two years the couple lived in southern France near Goodman's friend Robert Creeley, whose poetic theories greatly influenced the Black Mountain school of poetry. When Goodman and Levertov moved to the United States in the early 1950s, Levertov studied the American modernist poets—Wallace Stevens, Ezra Pound, and, particularly, William Carlos Williams, whose objectivist edict "no ideas but in things" profoundly influenced her verse. During this period, Levertov befriended American poet Robert Duncan who is also associated with the Black Mountain school and also wrote extensively about mythology, mysticism, and the occult. Levertov published verse in *Black Mountain Review* and *Origin,* prominent magazines that presented Black Mountain theories and literature. Levertov's collections from this period—*Here and Now, Overland to the Islands, With Eyes at the Back of Our Heads, The Jacob's Ladder* and *O Taste and See: New Poems*—firmly established her as an important contemporary poet and contain many frequently anthologized pieces. Her thematic concerns are reflected in the lines "I like to find / what's not found / at once, but lies // within something of a different nature, / in repose, distinct."

While holding teaching positions at several United States colleges during the 1960s and 1970s, Levertov participated in demonstrations against American military involvement in the Vietnam conflict as well as other causes. Her volumes of this period, including *The Sorrow Dance, Relearning the Alphabet,* and *To Stay Alive,* document Levertov's attempt to expand the realm of poetry to encompass social and political themes. In many of these poems, Levertov adopts a more immediate style to convey the urgency of her message. "From a Notebook: October '68-May '69," for example, combines letters, prose passages, and quotations to depict her experiences within the antiwar movement. Many critics faulted this new approach as too harsh and haphazard. Charles Altieri remarked: "The notebook style at best can serve as a historical document dramatizing the problems of a sensitive consciousness at given moments. But it has little reconstructive value because it provides no checks—either formal or in demands for lyric intensity—against the temptations—so strong when one is driven by moral outrage—to easy rhetoric and slack generalizations. Moreover, the form exerts very little authority: it seems only the cries of a passive victim." Many critics agree, however, that Levertov's political themes are more germanely presented in "The Olga Poems." This sequence concerns Levertov's relationship with her older sister, a political activist whose death in 1964 had a tremendous impact on Levertov's public and personal life. Levertov's later collections, including *Footprints, The Freeing of the Dust, Life in the Forest,* and *Breathing the Water,* contain many pieces of a political nature and are also noted for poems that explore such personal topics as her divorce, her son, and feminine themes.

Although Levertov's political beliefs have alienated some critics, she has garnered respect for her ability to craft poems that spring organically from everyday objects and actual events. "The quotidian reality we ignore or try to escape," said Ralph J. Mills, Jr., "Denise Levertov revels in, carves and hammers into lyric poems of precise beauty. As celebrations and rituals lifted from the midst of contemporary life in its actual concreteness, her poems are unsurpassed; they open to us aspects of object and situation that but for them we should never have known."

(See also *CLC,* Vols. 1, 2, 3, 5, 8, 15, 28; *Contemporary Authors,* Vols. 1-4, rev. ed.; *Contemporary Authors New Revision Series,* Vols. 3, 29; and *Dictionary of Literary Biography,* Vol. 5.)

PRINCIPAL WORKS

POETRY

The Double Image   (1946)
Here and Now   (1957)
Overland to the Islands   (1958)
With Eyes at the Back of Our Heads   (1959)
The Jacob's Ladder   (1961)
O Taste and See: New Poems   (1964)
The Sorrow Dance   (1967)
Relearning the Alphabet   (1970)
To Stay Alive   (1971)
Footprints   (1972)
The Freeing of the Dust   (1975)
Life in the Forest   (1978)
Collected Earlier Poems, 1940-1960   (1979)
Candles in Babylon   (1982)
Poems, 1960-1967   (1983)
Oblique Prayers: New Poems with Fourteen Translations from Jean Joubert   (1984)
Selected Poems   (1986)
Breathing the Water   (1987)
Poems, 1968-1972   (1987)

OTHER

The Poet in the World   (essays)   1973
Light Up the Cave   (essays)   1981

Sandra M. Gilbert

In an age of psychic anxiety and metaphysical *angst,* Denise Levertov's most revolutionary gesture is probably her persistent articulation of joy—joy in self, delight in life, sheer pleasure in pure *being.* In different poems, her frequently mystical self-definitions achieve varying degrees of intensity: in **"Stepping Westward,"** for instance, she is "realistic," scrupulously celebrating "what, woman, / / and who, myself, / I am," while in **"Song to Ishtar"** [from *O Taste and See*] she is more "fantastic," exulting that "the moon is a sow . . . and I a pig and a poet." Yet at her best Levertov has always expressed an exuberant self-knowledge, the mysterious self-contact of what in **"The Son"** she called "the rapt, imperious, sea-going river," along with an appreciation of otherness that continually leads her to seek new ways of affirming "Joy, the, 'well . . . *joyfulness* of / joy.'"

Especially in her early collections, from **Overland to the Islands** through **Relearning the Alphabet,** Levertov produces a succinct yet detailed record of experience in which the perceiving mind, confronting the apparent ordinariness of the world, is continually surprised by joy. A section of **"Matins,"** from **The Jacob's Ladder** (1961), reveals the paradoxically insouciant reverence with which this poet of the particular can celebrate the visionary pleasures of daily reality:

> The authentic! I said
> rising from the toilet seat.
> The radiator in rhythmic knockings
> spoke of the rising steam.
> The authentic, I said
> breaking the handle of my hairbrush as I
> brushed my hair in
> rhythmic strokes: That's it,
> that's joy, it's always
> a recognition, the known
> appearing fully itself, and
> more itself than one knew.

Later in this suite of ceremonial praise "the real, the new-laid / egg" and "the holy grains" of a child's breakfast are added to the poet's hairbrush, her "steaming bathroo[m]" and kitchen "full of / things to be done" as *loci* of **"Marvelous Truth,"** of the "terrible joy"—the awesome, eternal delight—which is always, in some sense, waiting to illuminate and transfigure the facade of the ordinary.

That the *lares* and *penates* of the household seem to Levertov to contain such symbolic potential is surely significant. Though she is not an aggressively feminist poet, she is very much a woman poet, or perhaps, more accurately, a poet conscious that the materiality of her life as a woman is not matter to be transcended; it is material in which poetry is immanent. Like "the worm artist" in **The Sorrow Dance** who "is homage to / earth [and] aerates / the ground of his living," this writer consciously inhabits a domestic world whose grounds her words record, revere, transform. Indeed, throughout Levertov's career, the house itself becomes an emblem of not only physical but spiritual shelter, its mysteries the secrets not just of habit but of inhabitation.

The comparatively early **"Overheard,"** from *O Taste and See* (1964) suggests the literal resonance Levertov attributes to her dwelling place:

> A deep wooden note
> when the wind blows,
> the west wind.
> The rock maple is it,
> close to the house?
> Or a beam, voice
> of the house itself?
> A groan, but not
> gloomy, rather
> an escaped note of
> almost unbearable
> satisfaction, a great
> bough or beam
> unaware
> it had
> spoken.

Suavely cadenced, with pauses whose careful timing emphasizes this artist's consistent attention to "where the silence is" as well as to the flow of her verse's "inner song," this piece clearly represents Levertov's commitment to the skillful deployment of "organic form," an aesthetic strategy for which she has often been praised. But the very technique of "organic form," as Levertov defines it, cannot be

separated from attention to, and celebration of, indwelling mysteries. "For me," she has written, "back of the idea of organic form is the concept that there is a form in all things (and in our experience) which the poet can discover and reveal." Thus, with comparable fluency, a number of her other poems also explore both the personal and the poetic meanings of inhabitation.

"From the Roof," for instance begins with the poet in a wild wind, "gathering the washing as if it were flowers," meditating on a move "to our new living-place" and asking "who can say / the crippled broom-vendor yesterday, who passed / just as we needed a new broom, was not / one of the Hidden Ones?" The piece's final answer—"by design / we are to live now in a new place"—suggests the significance of place, of house, of "indwelling" to this artist. Similarly, **"Invocation,"** which concludes *Relearning the Alphabet* (1972), dramatizes a family's preparation for moving with a prayer:

>   O Lares,
> don't leave.
> The house yawns like a bear.
> Guards its profound dreams for us,
> that it return to us when we return.

More playfully, **"What My House Would Be Like if It Were a Person,"** in *Life in the Forest* (1978), incarnates the house itself as a mysterious, even mystical, creature:

> Its intelligence
> would be of a high order,
> neither human nor animal, elvish.
> And it would purr, though of course,
> it being a house, you would sit in *its* lap,
> not it in yours.

At the same time, though, such a Levertovian vision of the house-as-personality is luminously complemented by a vision of the person-as-house. The beautiful **"Psalm Concerning the Castle"** almost seems to follow Gaston Bachelard's *Poetics of Space* in its scrupulously elaborated analysis of "the place of the castle . . . within me":

> Let the young queen sit above, in the cool air,
> her child in / her arms; let her look with joy at
> the great circle, the / pilgrim shadows, the work
> of the sun and the play of / the wind. Let her
> walk to and fro. Let the columns / uphold the
> roof, let the storeys uphold the columns, / let
> there be dark space below the lowest floor, let
> the / castle rise foursquare out of the moat, let
> the moat be a / ring and water deep, let the
> guardians guard it, let / there be wide lands
> around it, let that country where it / stands be
> within me, let me be where it is.

But if the figure of the house itself is cherished by this woman poet, the activities associated with it are equally important to her. For Levertov, the ancient female tasks of keeping and cleaning, sewing and baking, loving and rearing, often become jobs as sacred as the apparently humdrum task of spinning the prayer wheel in the archaic temple—which is not to say that she is the "Dear Heloise" of poetry but rather that she is a sort of Rilke of domesticity, turning her talent for what the German poet called *einsehen* ("inseeing") toward those supposedly mundane but really central occupations which bring order out of the chaos of dailiness. Whether gathering rebellious laundry or stirring holy grains, she means to invest her housework (and her spouse's) with meaning, and she is often awestruck by its implications. As early as *Here and Now* (1957) she celebrates the dull job of **"Laying the Dust"**— "What a sweet smell rises / when you lay the dust"—and a year later, in *Overland to the Islands* (1958), she develops a metaphor of sewing to which she returns in her most recent collection, *Oblique Prayers* (1984). "I would like," she says in the earlier verse, "to make . . . poems . . . mysterious as the silence when the tailor / would pause with his needle in the air," and in the later she notes that "a day of spring" is "a needle's eye / space and time are passing through like a swathe of silk." With the same intensity, moreover, **"The Acolyte,"** in *Candles in Babylon* (1982), enters a large, dark, enigmatic kitchen to explore a woman's sense of the magical ambitions inspired by bread-baking:

> She wants to put
> a silver rose or a bell of diamonds
> into each loaf;
> she wants
>
> to bake a curse into one loaf,
> into another, the words that break
> evil spells and release
> transformed heroes into their selves;
> she wants to make
> bread that is more than bread.

But of course, as the proverb would have it, the loaf that rises in the oven is often really (that is to say, symbolically) the child, and it is the child—her son Nikolai—for whom Levertov most often finds herself stirring the holy grains. From **"The Son,"** in *The Sorrow Dance* (1967), to **"He-Who-Came-Forth,"** in *Relearning the Alphabet,* a poem whose title works off the first line of **"The Son,"** she exults in the miraculous separateness of the life to which she has given birth: "He-who-came-forth was / it turned out / a man," exclaims the first text, while the second marvels that his "subtle mind and quick heart . . . now stand beyond me, out in the world / beyond my skin / beautiful and strange as if / I had given birth to a tree."

Perhaps even more than in her poems about and to her son, however, Levertov elaborates her sense of the strangeness, as well as the joy, of *relationship* in a number of erotic poems about married love. Though her work has often been discussed in terms of stylistic innovations associated with the Black Mountain School, though she is generally classified as a "neo-Romantic," and though she is frequently seen as a determinedly political poet, Levertov is not often defined as what used to be called a "love poet." Yet, especially in *The Jacob's Ladder* (1961), *O Taste and See* (1964) and *The Sorrow Dance* (1967), she has produced a set of remarkable verses, poems which, like Christina Rossetti's sonnet-sequence *Monna Innominata,* dramatize the female side of the story of desire. . . . Thus, mythologizing male beauty the way male poets have traditionally celebrated and sanctified female beauty, they suggest the Song of Songs in which an Eve, untaught silence and submissiveness, might have given voice to her erotic love for Adam. More, melodiously articulated and

passionately phrased, they imply the essential connection between "the authentic" miracles of the physical house and the inescapable authenticity of the body, whose "terrible joy" the house holds and reveals. (pp. 335-40)

In other love poems, however, Levertov explores the tension between the desire for merging with the beloved that is manifested in her erotic verses and the inexorable separateness of lovers. **"Bedtime"** begins with near-fusion— "We are a meadow where the bees hum, / mind and body are almost one"—but moves to an acknowledgement of what Whitman called the "solitary self": "by day we are singular and often lonely." Similarly, **"The Ache of Marriage,"** which deserves to be quoted in its entirety, dramatizes the paradoxes of separateness-in-togetherness, unity and duality:

> The ache of marriage:
>
> thigh and tongue, beloved,
> are heavy with it,
> it throbs in the teeth
>
> We look for communion
> and are turned away, beloved,
> each and each
>
> It is leviathan and we
> in its belly
> looking for joy, some joy
> not to be known outside it
>
> two by two in the ark of
> the ache of it.

"It is leviathan": though, as I have already noted, Levertov is not an aggressively feminist writer, her rigorous attentiveness to the realities of her own life as a woman has inevitably forced her to confront the contradictions implicit in that condition. Desire entraps lovers in an ark—a covenant as well as a Noah's ark steering toward survival—that is also an ache, an institution in which the married pair are buried as in the belly of the whale. "Don't lock me in wedlock, I want / marriage, an / encounter—" the poet exclaims in **"About Marriage,"** yet, despite her reverence for those details of desire and domesticity which manifest "the authentic," she often implies that the wife-mother who is an artist, a woman who *sees* and says what she sees, can never be wholly one with her life, for to see is to be set apart by the imperatives of perception and expression. Where the clean and comely homemaker wears "a utopian smock or shift" and, "smelling of / apples or grass," merges with the nature of her life and the life of nature, the artist-wife, "dressed in opals and rags," separates herself from the kindly routines of the household.

In a number of poems, therefore, Levertov characterizes herself as *two* women—the one who lives, loves, nurtures, and the one who observes, sings, casts spells. Such a strategy of doubling is of course a traditional one for women artists: as Susan Gubar and I have argued elsewhere, nineteenth-century writers from Charlotte Brontë to Emily Dickinson frequently imagined themselves as split between a decorous lady and a fiercely rebellious madwoman. Interestingly, however, where her precursors experienced such splits as painful if liberating, Levertov usually describes them as purely liberating, further sources of "the, 'well . . . *joyfulness* of / joy.'" The early **"The Earthwoman and the Waterwoman,"** from *Here and Now* (1957), dramatizes polarities of female experience that appear throughout most of the poet's subsequent volumes. The wholesome, nurturing "earthwoman" has children "full of blood and milk," while her opposite, the prophetic "waterwoman / sings gay songs in a sad voice / with her moonshine children"; at night, while the earthwoman drowses in "a dark fruitcake sleep," her waterwoman self "goes dancing in the misty lit-up town / in dragonfly dresses and blue shoes." Yet despite the opposition between these two, both are exuberant, both celebrate "the authentic" in its different manifestations.

The speaker of the later **"In Mind,"** from *O Taste and See* (1964), is more frankly confessional about her own relationship to these antithetical selves, and franker, too, about the pain that at least one of them, the mystically self-absorbed waterwoman, may cause to others. "There's in my mind a woman / of innocence," the poet explains, a woman who "is kind and very clean . . . but she has no imagination." But the double of this woman, she adds, is a "turbulent moon-ridden girl // or old woman . . . who knows strange songs"—and *she* "is not kind." Unkind though she may be, however, the visionary singer inexorably exists, and significantly Levertov does not apologize for her existence. On the contrary, even while in **"The Woman"** (*The Freeing of the Dust,* 1975) she concedes the problems that the female split self poses for a "bridegroom"—

It is the one in homespun
you hunger for
when you are lonesome;

the one in crazy feathers
dragging opal chains in dust
wearies you . . .

—she is adamant about this complex psychic reality: "Alas, / they are not two but one," she declares, and her groom must "endure / life with two brides. . . ."

In fact, it is particularly when she undertakes to analyze and justify female complexity that Levertov makes her most overtly "feminist" political statements. **"Hypocrite Women,"** from *O Taste and See,* simultaneously expresses contempt for "a white sweating bull of a poet" who declared that "cunts are ugly" and rebukes women for refusing to admit their own strangeness, their own capacity for prophetic dreaming. Cunts "are dark and wrinkled and hairy, / caves of the Moon," yet

                              when a
dark humming fills us, a

coldness towards life,
we are too much women to
own to such unwomanliness.

Whorishly with the psychopomp
we play and plead . . .

Similarly, **"Abel's Bride,"** in *The Sorrow Dance* (1967), urges acquiescence in the female mystery that is associated with the confrontation of earthwoman and waterwoman,

a confrontation enacted in the interior household where vision and domesticity coexist. Though "Woman fears for man [because] he goes / out alone to his labors" (and by implication, his death), she must recognize her own complex fate: "her being / is a cave, there are bones at the hearth." In fact, those—both male and female—who do not acknowledge the "dark humming" of the spirit that imbues the flesh with meaning are like **"The Mutes"** (also in *The Sorrow Dance*), inarticulate men whose "groans . . . passing a woman on the street" are meant to tell her "she is a female / and their flesh knows it" but say, instead,

'Life after life after life goes by
without poetry,
without seemliness,
without love.'

Finally, indeed, Levertov declares that it is precisely in her womanhood—in its tangible flesh of earthwoman as well as in its fluent spirit of waterwoman—that her artistic power lies:

When I am a woman—O, when I am
a woman,
my wells of salt brim and brim,
poems force the lock of my throat.

Given such a visionary and mystically (if not polemically) feminist commitment to female power, it is not surprising that some of Levertov's strongest and best-known poems offer homage to the muse-goddess whom she sees as patroness of her poetry. Among her earlier verses, the piece called **"Girlhood of Jane Harrison,"** in *With Eyes at the Back of Our Heads* (1960), suggests one of the forces that shaped her thought on this matter, for in her monumental *Prolegomena to the Study of Greek Religion* (1903) the British feminist-classicist had sought to document the dominance of the Great Mother in ancient Greek culture. Levertov's famous poem **"The Goddess,"** also in *With Eyes at the Back of Our Heads,* plainly develops Harrison's theories as it praises the deity "without whom nothing / flowers, fruits, sleeps in season, / without whom nothing / speaks in its own tongue, but returns / lie for lie!"—the goddess who empowers not only the flowering grounds on which the earthwoman lives but also the strange songs of the waterwoman. Similarly, **"The Well,"** in *The Jacob's Ladder,* as well as **"Song for Ishtar"** and **"To the Muse,"** in *O Taste and See,* celebrate "The Muse / in her dark habit" and with her multiple manifestations. Finally, that this divinity inspires and presides over the essential solitude in which the woman poet inscribes her tales of earth and water is made clear in **"She and the Muse,"** from the recent *Candles in Babylon,* a poem which shows how, after "the hour's delightful hero" has said *"arrivederci,"* the "heroine . . . eagerly" returns to the secret room of art, where "She picks a quill, / dips it, begins to write. But not of him." In the last analysis, the joyfulness of this woman's life and love is *made* authentic through the joy of language, the pleasure of musing words in which "the known" appears "more itself than one knew."

Although Levertov's joy is sometimes playful ("The authentic! I said / rising from the toilet seat"), it is rarely ironic or skeptical. Neither the relieved exstasis of the sufferer momentarily released from pain (the kind of exhilaration sometimes enacted by, say, Sylvia Plath) nor the brief tentative reconciliation to things-as-they-are of what we might call the *eiron maudit* (the kind of affirmation sometimes dramatized by Robert Lowell), Levertov's delight in existence depends, rather, on the steady celebratory patience of the believer who trusts that if you wait long enough, if you abide despite forebodings, the confirming moment of epiphany will arrive. Thus she assimilates those metaphysical anxieties which Wordsworth in a very different context defined as "fallings from us, vanishings" into a larger pattern based on faith in the inevitability of joy renewed.

Even some of her verses about absence—the actual or imminent absence of self, body, spirit—suggest confidence in the restoration of presence. **"Gone Away,"** in *O Taste and See,* confesses that "When my body leaves me / I'm lonesome for it," but depends on a knowledge that the physical self will return, while two mirror poems, **"Looking-Glass"** (also in *O Taste and See*) and **"Keeping Track"** (in *Relearning the Alphabet*), trace the "shadow-me" in the glass "to see if I'm there" and, by implication, to verify an expected sense of authenticity. Even more dramatically—and more characteristically—**"To the Muse,"** in *O Taste and See,* maintains that though the poet, the "host" of the house of art, fears that his aesthetic patroness is hiding,

> all the while
>
> you are indwelling,
> a gold ring lost in the house.
> *A gold ring lost in the house.*
> You are in the house!

And the mystery of creativity is precisely that the muse's "presence / will be restored."

Inevitably, perhaps, for a poet of Levertov's bent, a poet who trusts that a thread of potential joy is woven into every inch of the fabric that constitutes daily reality, any ripping or clipping of that secret, sacred thread threatens cataclysm. Thus, like such other poets of affirmation as Blake, Shelley, Whitman, or in our own age Bly, she is a deeply political writer—and I am using the word "politics" in its most ordinary sense, to mean public matters having to do with "the policies, goals, or affairs of a government" (*American Heritage Dictionary*). For in the "real" world, it is political action—the burning of villages, the decapitation of villagers, the building of bombs—that most threatens the authority of daily joy. Yet, paradoxically enough, despite their often revolutionary intensity, Levertov's most artistically problematic poems are precisely those no doubt overdetermined verses in which she explicitly articulates her political principles.

Comparatively early in her career, Levertov began to try to find a way of confronting and analyzing the horrors of a history—especially a twentieth-century history—which denies the luminous integrity of flesh-and-spirit. But even one of her better poems in this mode, **"Crystal Night"** (in *The Jacob's Ladder*), now seems rhetorically hollow, with its generalized description of "The scream! The awaited scream" which "rises," and "the shattering / of glass and the cracking / of bone." The better-known **"Life at War,"** in *The Sorrow Dance,* is more hectic still, in its insistence that

> We have breathed the grits of it [war] in, all our
>   lives,
> our lungs are pocked with it,
> the mucous membrane of our dreams
> coated with it, the imagination
> filmed over with the gray filth of it

and in its editorial revulsion from the complicity of "delicate Man, whose flesh / responds to a caress, whose eyes / are flowers that perceive the stars."

In a splendid essay on verse in this mode (**"On the Edge of Darkness: What is Political Poetry?"** in *Light up the Cave,* 1981), Levertov herself observes, about the "assumption by partisan poets and their constituencies that the subject matter carries so strong an emotive charge in itself that it is unnecessary to remember poetry's roots in song, magic, and . . . high craft," that such a belief is "dangerous to poetry." Yet in most of her political verse she seems herself to have disregarded her own astute warning. . . . [Despite] the impressive sincerity of her political commitment, her exhortations fail to attain (as perhaps post-modernist exhortations inevitably must) the exaltation of, for instance, Shelley's "Men of England, wherefore plough / For the lords who lay ye low?"

Still, as Levertov's personal commitment to the antinuclear movement and to support for revolutionary regimes in Central America has intensified, the proportion of politicized work included in her published collections has risen drastically. *Oblique Prayers* (1984) contains a section of ten manifestoes, most of which, sadly, dissolve into mere cries of rage and defiance. The tellingly titled **"Perhaps No Poem But All I Can Say And I Cannot Be Silent,"** for instance, protests against "those foul / dollops of History / each day thrusts at us, pushing them / into our gullets" while **"Rocky Flats"** depicts "rank buds of death" in "nuclear mushroom sheds," and **"Watching *Dark Circle"*** describes the experimental "roasting of live pigs" in "a simulation of certain conditions" as leading to "a foul miasma irremovable from the nostrils." Though I (along with, I suspect, the majority of her readers and admirers) share most of Levertov's political convictions, I must confess that besides being less moved by these poems than I have been by the more artful verses of Bly, Lowell, and Shelley, I am rather less moved than I would be by eloquent journalism, and considerably less affected than I would be by a circumstantially detailed documentary account of the events that are the subjects of Levertov's verses, for certainly there is little song, magic, or high craft in some of their phrases. The muse is still, I trust, "indwelling" in this poet's house, but she has not presided over some of the writer's recent work.

To be sure, the muse *has* inspired several of Levertov's political verses: **"Thinking about El Salvador,"** in *Oblique Prayers* opens with the poet's confession that "Because every day they chop heads off / I'm silent . . . for each tongue they silence / a word in my mouth / unsays itself," and concludes with a poignant vision

of all whose heads every day
float down the river
and rot
and sink,
not Orpheus heads
still singing, bound for the sea,
but mute.

And the much earlier **"A Note to Olga** (1966)" dramatizes the poet's sudden vision of her dead sister at a political rally:

It seems
you that is lifted

limp and ardent
off the dark snow
and shoved in, and driven away.

But what moves these poems, as opposed to Levertov's less successful polemics, seems to be not ferocious revulsion but revolutionary love—not the hate that is blind to all detail except its own rhetoric ("foul dollops") but the love that sees and says with scrupulous exactitude the terror of the severed heads that are "not Orpheus heads" and the passion of the ghostly Olga, "limp and ardent." And as these works show, such rebellious *caritas,* perhaps as surely as Bly's ironic inventiveness, Lowell's meticulous weariness, or (even) Shelley's hortatory energy, can impel the poetics of politics. (pp. 341-49)

When Levertov is at her best, such love underlies both her celebrations and her cerebrations; indeed, precisely because she is not an artist of irony or disillusionment but a poet of revolutionary love, she succeeds at recountings of the authentic in daily experience and fails at what Swift called *saeva indignatio.* Clearly, moreover, she knows this in some part of herself. One of the best poems in **Candles in Babylon** is **"The Dragonfly-Mother,"** a piece in which Levertov re-examines the split between earthwoman and waterwoman specifically in terms of her own split commitment to, on the one hand, political activism, and, on the other hand, poetry.

I was setting out from my house
to keep my promise

but the Dragonfly-Mother stopped me.

I was to speak to a multitude
for a good cause, but at home

the Dragonfly-Mother was listening
not to a speech but to the creak of
stretching tissue,
tense hum of leaves unfurling.

"Who is the Dragonfly-Mother?" the poem asks, then goes on to answer that she is the muse, "the one who hovers / on stairways of air," the one—by implication—who sees and says the authentic in the ordinary, the revolutionary love continually surprised, and inspired, by joy. Her imperatives are inescapable: "When she tells / her stories she listens; when she listens / she tells you the story you utter."

It is to such imperatives that, one hopes, this poet will continue to be loyal, for what the Dragonfly-Mother declares, over and over again, is that the political is—or must be

made—the poetical: the fabric of joy should not be ripped or clipped, yet the activist artist must struggle to praise and preserve every unique thread of that fabric, against the onslaughts of those who would reduce all reality to "foul dollops." Toward the end of this poem, Levertov seems to me to express the central truth of her own aesthetic, the truth of the joy *and* the pain born from revolutionary love:

Dragonfly-Mother's

a messenger,
if I don't trust her
I can't keep faith.

(pp. 350-51)

Sandra M. Gilbert, "Revolutionary Love: Denise Levertov and the Poetics of Politics," in Parnassus: Poetry in Review, *Vols. 12 & 13, Nos. 2 & 1, 1985, pp. 335-51.*

Frederick Garber

[Denise Levertov understands] the likeness of being and doing and of the poem as radical act. Indeed, the push toward exposing the radical in word and phrase, thing and event, creates and defines Levertov's work. . . . **"Decipherings,"** the first poem of **Oblique Prayers,** offers a set of instructions for reading what is to follow. We see and then make images ("half a wheel's / a rising sun: without spokes, / an arch"); what we see opens out to stand for greater, the greatest, acts ("half a loaf / reveals / the inner wheat: / leavened / transubstantiation"); the life outside, "felt life / grows in one's mind" as children do in the womb, becoming the energy of images which tie themselves and us into moving wholeness: "each semblance / forms and / reforms cloudy / links with / the next / and the next." What follows in the book moves out from this poem, though **"Decipherings"** does it better than some of the poems which follow. The language is characteristic Levertov, brief, tight and spare both in word and phrase, these leading into statements of equal spareness. The ideal is to be lean and rich, dense but never crammed. Levertov has always looked for a kind of essentialism in which seeing and saying are alike, pure and direct and to the bone, no gap in quality between vision and language and therefore no gap between their activities. Such activities ask of the poet a concomitant purity of consciousness, self not only the agent of vision and language but their partner in quality as well. Of course such language comes from Williams but she puts it to the service of an ecstasy especially her own. The best of Levertov shows how she has so mastered economy that she can do minimalist work, shows how the essence of things is inseparable from movement, shows also the alertness of consciousness (itself lean and rich) for moments of surprise. **"Blue Africa"** puts her on a freeway in winter, yet seeing and hearing, in sudden interspace, the stride and quiet of the African elephants as "each in turn / enters . . . a blue river of shadows."

Yet Levertov's poems ride on a razor's edge. She practices a difficult lyricism which always aims for the delicate but often finds only the soft. It is breathtaking and unnerving to see her so frequently waver between Williams and Edna Millay. **"Of Necessity"** hovers between the two, never quite certain of where it is, while **"Mappemonde"** slips effortlessly into the sticky: "O Geography! / On your thick syrops / I float and float, / I glide through your brew / of bitter herbs." But to counter these there are others like the very fine **"Presence,"** on the spirit of Jim Wright in the Ohio landscape, where the touch never falters, the razor's edge becoming the broadest of places on which to work. Essentialism leaves no room, has no mercy, for the slightest hesitation in touch or tonality.

Oblique Prayers builds toward its final section with hints in poems like **"Presence"** of dimensions beyond the tactile, of the making of spaces for the self beyond the textures of Ohio yet somehow contained within them, emergent from them. As the final section shows, this is more than a matter of spooks. That section seeks to put it all together, with some of her most delicate seeing and some subtly intoned moments of (essentially religious) ecstasy. **"Of Rivers," "Of Gods," "The God of Flowers," "This Day"**: these and several others harbor the book's finest moments, where she is fully in touch with things, querying their capacities and showing the range of her own. Self can dwell in dimensions available only in certain conditions, dimensions that she seeks to open within the words that make the poems. The book ends in stillness and peace and (for the most part) a deftness of touch, the blood of El Salvador elsewhere than here, "great suffering, great fear— / withdrawing only / into peripheral vision." The politics which take up the second part of the book are put by for "this need to dance, / this need to kneel. / this mystery." All those moments of Millay have to be countered by moments like these where it all comes together, with seeing, making and being at their surest and most essential. (pp. 18-19)

> Frederick Garber, *"Geographies and Languages and Selves and What They Do,"* in The American Poetry Review, *Vol. 14, No. 5, September-October, 1985, pp. 14-21.*

Joyce Lorraine Beck

In Denise Levertov's poem **"The Instant,"** from *Overland to the Islands,* a moment of illumination occurs when mist and clouds roll away to show forth the distant peak of Mt. Snowdon shining in the gleam of early morning. Suddenly, "Light graces the mountainhead / for a lifetime's look, before the mist / draws in again." Levertov has spoken of this poem and of the title poem of her collection *With Eyes at the Back of our Heads* as one of those stages in her life's journey that are "moments of vision presaging the secret that will bring the seeker to his goal, but which are quickly forgotten again, or hidden again from the imagination, just as the head of Snowdon, Eryri, is hidden again as the mists return." As a representative combination of the sublime and the mundane, Ralph J. Mills finds **"The Instant"** characteristic of Levertov's poetics. It is both "an abbreviated narrative, dramatic in character," and "a spiritual adventure of a nearly ineffable sort." There is indeed a religious meditative element in Denise Levertov. It has at least three sources—the Christian in-

heritance of her immediate background, her upbringing as a child of a Church of England clergyman; her ancestral roots in Judaism and her affinity for Hasidism; and finally the "natural supernaturalism" of her romantic poetics.

If **"The Instant"** is a good example what Mills terms her "visionary disposition," it still retains its status as a "poem of fact," one "emerging from ordinary circumstances and immediate life, and returning there." Levertov often associates the imagination with exquisitely realistic detail. The work of the imagination is "its far-reaching and faithful permeation of those details that in a work of art, illuminate the whole." In **"A Note on the Work of the Imagination,"** she attributes the graphic intensity of a recent dream to the power of imagination to introduce "exquisite realistic detail" into dream as into art. In the dream a radiant glimmer had led her to approach nearer her own image in a mirror where she saw "a network of little dew or mist diamonds" sprinkled in her dark hair. She finds this realistic detail, provided by the creative unconscious—the imagination—surprisingly appropriate to a dream in which she had "been walking in the misty fields in the dew-fall hour," and concludes.

> I awoke in delight, reminded forcibly of just what it is we love in the greatest writers—what quality, above all others surely makes us open ourselves freely to Homer, Shakespeare, Tolstoy, Hardy—that following through, that *permeation* of detail—relevant, illuminating detail—which marks the total imagination at work. . . . It was Imagination put seed pearls of summer fog in Tess Durbeyfield's hair . . . and it was the same holy, independent faculty that sprinkled my hair with winter-evening diamonds.
>
> (pp. 45-6)

Levertov stresses again and again in her prose writings her definition of poetry as a revelation of the meanings or patterns of experience. As the poet contemplates or "muses" in the temple of life, meaning is revealed to her:

> To contemplate comes from 'templum, temple, a space for observation, marked out by augur.' It means, not simply to observe, to regard, but to do these things in the presence of a god. And to meditate is 'to keep the mind in a state of contemplation'; its synonym is 'to muse,' and to muse comes from a word meaning 'to stand with open mouth'—not so comical if we think of 'inspiration'—'to breathe in.'

The organic form of existential experience is revealed to the disinterested, musing, attentive poet as poetry: "So— as the poet stands open-mouthed in the temple of life, contemplating his experience, there come to him the first words of the poem, if there is to be a poem. The pressure of the demand and the meditation on its elements culminate in a moment of vision, of crystallization, in which some inkling of the correspondence between those elements occurs; and it occurs as words." Levertov's poetics, like the art of the poet she refers to in **"Origins of a Poem,"** combines musing or meditation—what Emerson in "Poetry," calls "the intellect being where and what it sees," with articulation—"sharing the path or circuit of things through forms and so making them translucid to others."

According to Albert Gelpi, Levertov deliberately maintains the tension of the meeting of mind and nature. It is in this sense that "hers is a sacramental notion of life; experience is a communion with objects which are in themselves signs of their own secret mystery." Levertov has said herself, in **"Some Notes on Organic Form,"** that organic poetry is based on "an intuition of an order, a form beyond forms in which forms partake, and of which man's creative works are analogies, resemblances, natural allegories." Mills believes that Levertov's art teaches us what the French theologian Jacques Maritain affirms in *Art and Scholasticism,* that "Our art does not derive from itself alone what it imparts to things; it spreads over them a secret which it first discovered in them, in their invisible substance or in their endless exchanges and correspondences." Gelpi notices that while Levertov's All-Day Bird is "gripped by joy," it is "the pressure of his skill as singer," his ability to discriminate, which enables him to shape his song "closer to what he knows." Levertov, in her prose writings, acknowledges two Muses or sources of poetic truth: rational discrimination, the Apollonian guide who directs her in craftsmanship or in deliberate imaginative creation; and meditation, the Beatific "breath" or Spirit who reveals to her the invisible substances of organic forms, or the Archetypes that arise from very deep associations.

Two such archetypes in Levertov's poetry, Knight and Muse, point toward the simultaneously descriptive and meditative poetic described by Mills and Gelpi and by her own prose. In her essay **"A Sense of Pilgrimage,"** she has reflected on both of these symbols, drawing out some of their associations. The questing knight or pilgrim wandering through "imagination's holy forest" may be a successor of Chrétien de Troyes's Percival, Malory's Galahad, or Spenser's Red Crosse Knight. But there are more immediately personal linkings. Levertov remembers also the longing she had as a child to "step backward into time and become a page or knight errant." As a member of "The Church of England's Children's League: Knights of St. Richard," she saw herself as a knight on a journey through states or phases of being in life's pilgrimage, her feelings drawn both from Arthurian legends and from the "Prayer of St. Richard. . . ." Years later, in **"Relearning the Alphabet,"** the letters P and Q recall "petitioner" and the recurrent "quester":

> In childhood dream-play I was always
> the knight or squire, not
> the lady:
> quester, petitioner, win or lose, not
> she who was sought.
> The initial of quest or question
> branded itself long since on the flank
> of my Pegasus
> Yet he flies always
> home to the present

Much more mysterious than the questing knight-errant is the second recurring figure in Levertov's poetry, the Muse. The Muse, who sometimes accompanies and inspires the poet-pilgrim-knight on the quest, and some-

times appears as "she who is sought," as the spiritual home to which the Pegasus flies, seems to be a double figure, corresponding to Levertov's sense of the poet's twofold power for articulation and for contemplation. Her Muse is both seer and maker, prophet and craftsman. She said, in **"A Sense of Pilgrimage,"** that her Muse is one who both sees deeply (often appearing mysteriously or unexpectedly) and sings skillfully. The act of verbalization, when skillful or masterful, leads the poet to the full perception of organic forms or transcendent prototypes. Poets are "instruments on which the power of poetry plays," she says, "but they are also *makers,* craftsmen: It is given to the seer to see, but it is then his responsibility to communicate what he sees, that they who cannot see may see, since we are 'members of one another.' "

The Muse may be a successor of Homer's Athena, Dante's Beatrice, or Spenser's Gloriana. Then again, she may be the type of Hagia Sophia, of Jerusalem the Golden, or of Lady Eloah. But—like the figure of the Knight—this Muse also has deeply personal associations for Levertov. In **"The Well"** and in **"To the Muse"** she notes the resemblance of her vision of the Muse to "the face of a certain actress," but the face resembles in turn the face of a figure who occurs and reoccurs in the tales of George MacDonald, such as "The Princess and the Goblin," "The Princess and Curdie," and such shorter stories as "The Golden Key" or "The Wise Woman." This personage is "the young/old grandmother," whose spinning room in a tower, where the gold ring waits to be found, "is hard to find at will, even though it is part of the house one inhabits." In **"To the Muse,"** she is one who chooses and abides:

> I have heard it said,
> and by a wise man,
> that you are not one who comes and goes
>
> but having chosen
> you remain in your human house,
> and walk
>
> in its garden, for air and the delights
> of weather and seasons.
>
> Who builds
> a good fire in his hearth shall find you at it
> with shining eyes and a ready tongue.

Still, the Muse must be cultivated by any poet who wants her around: when the "host" fails her, she goes into hiding. She cannot be forced or coerced, but only discovered through a kind of "active reticence," or "wise passiveness"—as well as a "leap of faith," a generous and courageous commitment, made in a spirit of fear and trembling, to a loved and mysterious, "known/Unknown" source. (pp. 47-9)

In other places Levertov links the figure of the Muse with an "inexhaustible source," a "vast, irreducible spirit" summoned by the exercise of writing poetry. In her essay **"Origins of a Poem"** she relates the Muse to the divine in both poet and reader: "The poet—when he is writing—is a priest; the poem is a temple; epiphanies and communion take place within it. The communion is triple: between the maker and the needer within the poet; between the maker and the needers outside him—those who need but can't make their own poems (or who do make their own but need this one too); and between the human and the divine in both poet and reader. . . . When the poet converses with this god he has summoned into manifestation, he reveals to others the possibility of their own dialogue with the god in themselves." Writing the poem, in this view, becomes the poet's means of "summoning the divine," or the Muse.

The relationship of the Muse to the poet-pilgrim-knight errant is central in Levertov's poetry. In **"The Well"** the poet stands on a bridge crossing a stream while the Muse, in her dark habit, wades into deep water to a spring where she fills her pitcher to the brim and then opens the doors of the world by spelling the word "water" in the poet's left palm. In this poem the Muse remains a mysterious figure whose connection with the poet is only obscurely suggested. . . . (pp. 50-1)

When the Muse and the questing knight come together, the spirit of here-and-now or of "the present" is united with the romantic spirit of quest, of what she calls "longing to wander toward other worlds." Levertov finds in the **"Olga Poems"** a poem that brings the pilgrim to the end of his pilgrimage, as it were. All her other poems based on the underlying conception of life as **"A Vale of Soulmaking"** are "written, one might say, on the road; this one looks back at a life that has ended, or come full circle." But, she concludes, "The purpose of pilgrimage that I hope emerges is not merely what is known as "a good death"; the candle doesn't just get relit at the end of all the darkness, but is somehow to be miraculously kept alight all the way through." The knight errant who wanders through imagination's holy forest in Levertov's poetry is accompanied and inspired by the Candlelight of Truth. In these paired figures, time and eternity, imaginative detail and a sense of divine presence are reconciled. The figures of the questing knight and the Muse together best constitute a symbol for Levertov's poetic of pragmatic, practical, or peripatetic Neo-Platonism.

If art is, as Levertov has said, "the act of realizing inner experience in material substance," the poet may realize or substantiate in her art, her being, and her actions the inspirations or inner dialogues of her Muse. She may, like Apollo, or the artist Levertov refers to in her **"Origins of a Poem,"** "give body and future to 'the mysterious being hidden behind the eyes' " or the Muse. Levertov's own poetry, when inspired by her Muse, becomes what she calls, following Martin Heidegger, "a realization, quite literally 'realization,' making real, substantiation"; her acts, when inspired by her Muse, become symbolic acts or sacraments; and her visions become revelations. Such, we should expect, is also true of the poet-pilgrim-knight in the poems. The Muse is made apparent, or visible, through and in the figure of the knight errant or traveller and the continuing quest. In her poem **"A Letter to William Kinter of Muhlenberg,"** Levertov finds "the profound Christian symbolism of the stations of the Cross dimly apprehended as the model for spiritual pilgrimage." This pilgrimage is in turn "imaged forth in a reference to the peripatetic discourse of personages in *The Zohar*":

Zaddik, you showed me

the Stations of the Cross

and I saw
not what the most abstract

tiles held—world upon world—
but at least

a shadow of what
might be seen there if mind and heart

gave themselves to meditation,
deeper

and deeper into Imagination's
holy forest, as travelers

followed the Zohar's dusty
shimmering roads, talking

with prophets and
hidden angels. . . .

Levertov's Muse is both the end or goal of the quest and she who is present and inspires all along the way. The Muse is found or realized "when the travelling soul and its Muse are brought together at the Place of Origin by way of a winding road." Yet the Muse is also like a candle or star that is somehow "miraculously kept alight all the way through." Levertov's grail is found in the act of finding, when the seeker and the sought are one. The knight errant and the Muse together constitute the poet's whole Self, her becoming in her Being. In the poem **"The Wings,"** the poet-pilgrim contemplates herself as a traveller sprouting "embryo wings" and going or continuing onward, "on one wing":

But what if,
like a camel, it's

pure energy I store
and carry humped and heavy?. . .

What if released in air
it became a white

source of light, a fountain
of light? Could all that weight

Be the power of flight?
Look inward: see me

with embryo wings, one
feathered in soot, the other

blazing ciliations of ember, pale
flare-pinions. Well—

could I go
on one wing

the white one?

Levertov's Muse is realized when one cannot tell the questing knight from the Muse, the poet-pilgrim from the Light of Truth. In poems such as **"Voyage,"** from *The Freeing of the Dust,* the reticent artist, the Muse or Goddess of Truth, the questing pilgrim, the true inner self are drawn together in revelations of absolute presence and freedom. In her early poem **"Matins,"** she shows that fear of the Divine can be the beginning of wisdom even in the midst of the mundane. In the recent **"Benedictus,"** from

"Mass for the Day of St. Thomas Didymus," she moves into the "known/unknown," de-centered center, drawing together writing with spirit, word with windripple, song with silence, to articulate beatitude in a medieval/contemporary polyphonic sequence:

> Blessed is that which comes in the name of the
>   spirit,
> that which bears
> the spirit within it.
>
> The name of the spirit is written
> in woodgrain, windripple, crystal,
>
> in crystals of snow, in petal, leaf,
> moss and moon, fossil and feather,
>
> blood, bone, song, silence,
> very word of
> very word,
> flesh and
> vision.

Levertov's Apollonian or rational "guide," then, does not dominate the Sacred Muse of beatitude so as to deny her activity and nullify her wisdom; rather, he creates, interacts, and corresponds with her. Levertov's poetic is not defined through, or as, craft alone. Her Apollonian "guide" has not cast out Polyhymnia and set himself up as tyrant or idol. Her knight or squire, the "quester, petitioner" of **"Relearning the Alphabet,"** has come to understand what so many benighted pilgrims, left like Orestes to wander in Hades, have yet to learn, that "transmutation is not / under the will's rule":

> The door I flung my weight against
> was constructed to open   out
>   towards me.
>
> In-seeing
> to candleflame's
> blue ice-cavern, measureless,
>
> may not be forced by sharp
> desire.

Both her poet-persona and her Muse are (simultaneously or intermittently) active and passive, perceptive and receptive. As she reminds us in her conversation with Walter Sutton, her notion of organic form is really "based on the idea that there is form in all things—that the artist doesn't impose form upon chaos, but discovers hidden intrinsic form—and on the idea that poems can arrive at their form by means of the poet's attentive listening, not only his listening but also his experience and by means of his accurate transcriptions of that experience into words." While she recognizes the need for a well-developed ego, a strong conscious intellect, and a mastery of craft on the part of the Apollonian poet-persona, she also stresses the value of that reticence, or restraint, which leaves the door open to Spirit and allows the promptings of the Muse of grace.

Levertov's Muse of beatitude, the holy "breath" and "dim star" of her poetry, is an active faculty, a "source of mind's fire," whose presence she regards with reverence and joyfully celebrates:

> Joy—a beginning. Anguish, ardor.

To relearn the ah! of knowing in unthinking
joy: the belovéd stranger lives.
Sweep up anguish as with a wing-tip,
brushing the ashes back to the fire's core.

Like Julia Kristeva's *"jouissance,"* Levertov's "joy" is born of "cosmic connection," of a realized link between the poet-persona and the Muse of meditation, the personal and the cosmic, a link leading the way to the eternal. As she turns in the forest, relearning the alphabet, all utterance takes the poet step by hesitant step into "that life beyond the dead-end," to a place not evoked, but discovered upriver:

> *Sweep up*
> *anguish as with a wing-tip:*
>
> the blaze addresses
> a different darkness:
> absence has not become
> the transformed presence the will
> looked for,
> but other: the present,
>
> that which was poised already in the ah! of
>   praise.

The Goddess/poet-pilgrim-knight is one of the old yet new metaphors that Denise Levertov has contributed to English and American letters while on her "life's pilgrimage." By travelling through imagination's holy forest, she may, indeed, have approached, now and again, the shrine of the "well or pool of living water" and found there not only continuance, but Spirit's candleflame, holiness:

> The forest is holy.
> The sacred paths are of stone.
> A clearing.
> The altars are shifting deposits of pineneedles,
>   hidden waters,
>   streets of choirwood,
> not what the will
> thinks to construct for its testimonies.

If the end, or purpose, of pilgrimage in Levertov's poetics is holiness—as it has been in most journeys to Jerusalem or traditional grail quests—then holiness, here, is synonymous with wholeness. Such integrity includes wholeness of vision, for Levertov is a poet who "subtly points the way to see with whole sight." But it is also a matter of full humanity. If the poet shares the spirit of theologian Martin Buber in always saying "thou" to the persons, occasions, and objects she encounters, that is simply an expression of "her imagination's essential humanizing gesture toward every aspect of existence." In her essay **"Poems by Women,"** she has written that both women and men have to resist polarization and become more fully human, which is a question of "the humane comprehensions of the perceptive and receptive being in balance." Those poems which enrich the lives of readers and which demonstrate "that transcendence of gender which is characteristic of the creative mind" may, in this very act, have an effect beneficial to the body politic.

Holiness, as wholeness, of both person and place is hinted at in several of her poems. In **"Kingdoms of Heaven,"** for example, the poet-pilgrim asks if "to believe it's there within you / though the key's missing / makes it enough?"

As if / golden pollen were falling / onto your hair from dark trees." In **"The Goddess"** she tells a similar story of a new heaven and new earth about to be more fully manifest: "I bit on a seed / and it spoke on my tongue / of day that shone already among stars / in the water-mirror of low ground." The letter "R" in **"Relearning the Alphabet"** finds the poet suddenly released into "a soft day, western March;" where "a thrust of birdsong / parts the gold flowers thickbranching / that roof the path over." A later poem, **"The Many Mansions,"** presents an expanded view of a whole, or holy, universe—a place of universal harmony and abundance where each is unique yet all are holy, or whole. Here she speaks of "the world of the white herons," perfect yet undefiled, and of the knowledge her vision of that world gave:

> . . . it was not a fragile only other world,
> there were, there are (I learned) a host,
> each unique, yet each having
> the grace of recapitulating
>
> a single radiance, multiform.

We can surmise that the **"Oblique Prayers"** of Levertov's most recent volume have been answered when "no man's land," a gray place without clear outlines, a "mere not-darkness," gives way, in **"The Antiphon,"** to a new land where "all is eloquent," a land very like a regained or re-discovered English garden Paradise, where all is blessed:

> —rain,
> raindrops on branches, pavement brick
> humbly uneven, twigs of a storm-stripped hedge
> revealed
> shining deep scarlet,
> speckled whistler shabby and
> unconcerned, anything—all
> utters itself, blessedness
> soaks the ground and its wintering seeds.

As an awe so quiet she doesn't know when it began fills the poet-pilgrim and a gratitude begins to sing in her, daybreak arrives and the wind begins to shimmer in blue leaves. Then we know, as we did and did not know before, that Denise Levertov's Muse is and has been the Spirit of Holiness, Lady Sophia-Gloriae, the living Light, Wordsworth's "Wisdom and Spirit of the universe." The pilgrim-poet has returned to the Vale, to Grasmere or Stanford Rivers, rediscovered the splendor in the grass, and regained "the glory and the dream," the visionary gleam of the celestial light. (pp. 51-7)

In the last poem of **"Of God and of the Gods,"** the poet celebrates the grace and liberating power of that Muse who has inspired her journey all along the way. She acknowledges the creative strength of Spirit—of "breath," of *"ruach"*—and of those "forms the spirit enters." We are led to understand from **"Passage"** that the "light that is witness and by which we witness" is present still, moving over the meadow of long grass, for, even now "green shines to silver where the spirit passes." Here the speaker addresses a different darkness, a darkness from out of which light has broken anew. We are invited, then, to see and to say, to hear and to sing, to dance and to kneel with the poet:

Wind from the compass points, sun at meridian,
these are forms the spirit enters,
breath, *ruach,* light that is witness and by which
    we witness.

The grasses numberless, bowing and rising, silently
cry hosanna as the spirit
moves them and moves burnishing
over and again upon mountain pastures
a day of spring, a needle's eye
space and time are passing through like a swathe
    of silk.

(pp. 59-60)

Joyce Lorraine Beck, "Denise Levertov's Poetics and 'Oblique Prayers'," in RELIGION & LITERATURE, *Vol. 18, No. 1, Spring, 1986, pp. 45-61.*

Nancy J. Sisko

Many of the poems that appear in *To Stay Alive* were previously published in two collections titled *The Sorrow Dance* and *Relearning the Alphabet,* and Denise Levertov, aware that this is unusual, writes a two and a half page preface providing "justification" for their appearance in this new volume. "Themes recur," she writes, and the artist often discovers that she is "building a whole in which each discrete work is a part that functions in some way in relation to all the others." In *To Stay Alive,* then, Levertov is trying to "assemble separated parts of a whole," to create "a record of one person's inner/outer experience" and present that record in what she sees as its proper order. This paper will explore the poet's struggle to find that "proper order" not only for her poems, but for her life. Levertov sees herself as a poet in a world that requires revolutionaries. The problem is that as a poet, she is unable to be the kind of revolutionary she wants to be. *To Stay Alive* is a record of her struggle to reconcile these two roles, and this paper will examine the dialectic of that struggle.

Very basically *To Stay Alive* is divided into two parts, the first ("Prelude") providing the background for the second ("Staying Alive") in which the struggle between poetry and revolution takes place. Similarly, this paper will have two parts: in the first few pages I will briefly describe and explicate the "Prelude" section; in the rest of the paper, I will trace Levertov's attempt to combine poetry and revolution in **"Staying Alive."**

In "Prelude," Levertov returns to her youth when her feelings about war and peace were formed in response to her sister Olga's example. Levertov does not mention herself very often in this first section, and then only as a young girl watching her older sister as she tries to "save the world." Olga, then, becomes a standard against which Levertov will judge herself throughout the rest of the book. Levertov remembers her sister as a person who "wanted / to shout the world to its senses / . . . to browbeat / the poor into joy's / socialist republic." Olga seeks to make possible the impossible, to "change the course of the river."

Though Levertov doesn't feel as if she can compare with Olga in most categories, she does rival her in some ways. Towards the end of the **"Olga Poems,"** Levertov describes her sister as living in "the year [she was] most alone". All her life she was alone, alone in her dreams, and alone in her failures; Levertov feels much the same way, and the same sense of loneliness and despair pervades the entirety of *To Stay Alive.* After the **"Olga Poems,"** Levertov has included the poem **"A Note to Olga (1966),"** which also appeared first in *A Sorrow Dance,* though it was not originally grouped with the **"Olga Poems"** in that book. In this poem Levertov appears grown up now, marching in a "Stop the War" demonstration. She is reminded of her sister's voice and in the final stanza uses her poetic sensibilities to re-envision the event, transplanting her sister into it, and then seeing Olga arrested: "It seems / you that is lifted / limp and ardent / off the dark snow / and shoved in, and driven away." Wanting to be like her sister, Levertov marches in protest, but symbolically her sister's presence eludes her, is "driven away," leaving Levertov alone, still trying to capture the essence of Olga's vision.

Levertov is the "beady-eyed . . . sister" with her "head / a camera." These are the young eyes of a poet, recording, seeking to understand what has been seen. In the final poem of the Olga group, Levertov memorializes Olga's eyes that "were the brown gold of pebbles under water" and writes that there are "so many questions my eyes / smart to ask your eyes." Her sister's eyes are able to see in a way her "camera" eyes cannot: Olga has "eyes with some vision / of festive goodness." And it is that utopian vision that Levertov will spend the rest of *To Stay Alive* trying to capture.

In the five poems Levertov has chosen to end the "Preludes" section of *To Stay Alive,* the personal tone of the **"Olga Poems"** is, for the most part, dropped, and Levertov begins speaking to and with a more impersonal "we": "The disasters numb within us . . . we have breathed the grits of it in, all our lives." This is the first appearance of the "outer experience" as she described it in her "Preface," the milieu, the landscape, the setting, for the rest of the poem. This is the United States as she sees it during the Viet Nam War: "The same war / continues." And "We are the humans . . . / who do these acts, who convince ourselves it is necessary." (pp. 47-9)

In the "Prelude" section, Levertov feels separated from the outer world; her inner life is the result of her ability to observe and absorb that outer world. These previously published poems are the work of the "young" Levertov. In **"Staying Alive,"** the new poetic sequence that forms the second part of the book, Levertov tries to join the outer world, still observing, but now also acting. To accomplish this the poet adopts a dramatic structure. **"Staying Alive"** consists of eight major sections: a "Prologue," four "Parts," which can be seen as corresponding to the acts of the play, and three "Entr'actes." The "Prologue," the four "Parts" and the three "Entr'actes" are divided into numbered sections. Levertov, in short, is writing an historical play—or, perhaps more accurately, the scenario for a play. The main character of the play is obviously Lever-

tov herself, the "dramatic speaker," the conscientious poet who wanders across the war-torn stage of history.

For Levertov history is a drama, and her sense of the dramatic possibilities of history has already emerged in the **"Olga Poems."** In the third poem of this group, Olga is presented as a director who paces "the trampled grass where human puppets / rehearsed fates," puppets that were "Stun[ned] into alien semblences by the lash of her will." But in the end, Olga's dreams are frustrated and "the stage lights had gone out, even the empty theatre / was locked to [her], cavern of transformation where / all had been possible." If Olga represents a failed director, Levertov represents the sympathetic audience; years ago, while her sister directed and acted, Levertov observed. But in **"Staying Alive"** Levertov tries to pick up where her sister left off.

Despite the numerous sections of the poem, the drama does not really progress from act to act in the same way a play does. The action in all the sections is fairly uniform, which results in a repetition of the main action rather than a progression of action. The primary action is basically a dialectical one and is baldly stated in the title of "Part I": "Revolution or Death." **"Staying Alive"** is a chronicle of the struggle between these two concepts, and certainly there are moments in which this struggle is explicitly highlighted. For example, in "Part II," Levertov retells the story of People's Park and how she and other idealistic revolutionaries attempted to transform it into a workers' paradise:

> May 14th, 1969—Berkeley
> Went with some of my students to work in the
>   People's
> Park. There seemed to be plenty of digging and
>   gardening
> help so we decided, as Jeff had his truck avail-
>   able, to
> shovel up the garbage that had been thrown into
>   the west
> part of the lot.
>   O happiness
>   in the sun! Is it
>   that simple, then
>   to live?
>   —crazy rhythm of scooping up barehanded
>   (all the shovels already in use)
>   careless of filth and broken glass
>   —scooping up garbage together
>   poets and dreamers studying
>   joy together, clearing
> refuse off the neglected, newly recognized
> humbly waiting ground, place, locus of what
>   could be our
> New World even now, our revolution, one and
>   one and
> one and one together . . .

But the happiness is short-lived and in response to "revolution" the state sends "death" in the form of helicopters, "the ominous zooming, war-sound," and the police, who have brought bulldozers and the materials to build a fence, closing off the just recently born "New World." And "Everyone knows . . . / what all shall know / this day, and the days that follow: / now, the clubs, the gas, bayonets, bullets. The War / comes home to us . . . ".

Moments where the opposing forces of revolution and death appear in such stark contrast are few. And as one reads the sequence one realizes that it is not the simple question of "Revolution or Death" that the poem is trying to resolve. Such a formulation leaves out a crucial element: the poet. Levertov frames the question to imply that it is one that everyone is or should be answering: *"Which side are you on?"* asks a disembodied voice which is answered by yet another disembodied voice, "Revolution, of course." But it soon becomes clear that as far as Levertov is concerned she is the only one who is really asking the question seriously, because everyone else she knows has already answered the question to her/his satisfaction. At the end of the first section of "Part I" she writes, "Of course I choose / revolution," but it is a false certainty. Immediately following, in section ii, she writes, "And yet, yes, there's the death . . . ". And though the death spoken of here is not the same kind referred to in section i represented by Mayor Daley ("Death is Mayor Daley"), its very presence in the poem belies the matter-of-fact tone of the "Of course" that preceded it.

"Staying Alive," quite simply, records Denise Levertov's effort to find her place in the dialectical world she has postulated. In fact whether she is aware of it or not, structurally, **"Staying Alive"** is a perfect example of her struggle. Levertov makes it clear that she would like the tension in this poem to reflect her own struggle to choose between "Revolution or Death," though interestingly she does not actually begin to engage that struggle until one third of the way through the sequence. She wants to be a revolutionary, like Olga, and like her husband Mitch, and her friends, but she vacillates repeatedly and despite her attempts to choose never seems to be able to. She is after all a poet, with a camera's eye, and such an eye is remarkably indiscriminate: it records everything, revolution *and* death. And its very inclusiveness, its "objective" reporting nature, prevents integration, prevents the poet from defining a stance. Levertov finds herself seeking revolution and rejecting death, but finally is unable to do either—she is caught in the middle. . . . (pp. 50-2)

The death represented by Mayor Daley, the police, and the military is easy to see, but revolution also demands a high price. Levertov's **"Prologue: An Interim"** makes this very clear. First, she introduces "de Courcy Squire, war-resister," who began a lengthy fast in her jail cell as a way of protesting the war. During her ordeal she was "Denied visitors, even her parents; / confined to a locked cell without running water / or a toilet." And most terrible of all, she was informed that her "fast may cause her permanent brain injury." Levertov presents Mitch as another example, for he too is threatened with a possible jail term. Finally, Levertov describes the most extreme example, "The great savage saints of outrage— / . . . for whom there is no world left— / their bodies rush upon the air in flames, / sparks fly, fragments of charred rag / spin in the whirlwind, a vacuum / where there used to be this monk or that, / Norman Morrison, Alice Hertz." These are the "self-immolators—Vietnamese and American— . . .

flares to keep us moving in the dark" as Levertov describes them in her preface. They are not supposed to be "models," necessarily, but the reader realizes that Levertov does not condemn them in the slightest for what they have done. In fact she reveres them, and she thinks we need more such people:

> But we need
> the few who could bear no more,
> who would try anything
> who would take the chance
> that their deaths among the uncountable
> masses of dead might be real to those who
> don't dare imagine death

Much of the poem is like this: a hagiography cataloging Levertov's personal saints of the War Resistance. It would be ultimately pointless to list every instance in which Levertov invokes another saint's name and her particular saintly act, because the real reason they are included is to establish a contrast to the poet herself. Levertov judges her life and her brand of War Resistance against all of these others she names and admires. Inevitably, she comes up short.

Why? One reason seems to be her hesitation to accept physical discomfort. Certainly she could never "bring [herself] to injure [her] own flesh, deliberately"—her response to the self-immolators. But it is not just the extreme of injuring her own flesh that she avoids; Levertov is unwilling to put herself in any situation that might get her put in jail, or in contact with the police. This is not to condemn Levertov, for certainly most of us would be (for ourselves) in agreement with her on this issue. The point is that Levertov continually condemns herself for what she sees as her own cowardice, her own inadequacy. There are other models of resistance "to aspire to," besides the self-immolators: A. J. Muste, Dennis Riordon, Bob Gilliam, etc. But there is no indication that even these models prompt Levertov to do what she feels she ought to do. A revolutionary must be dedicated to a single-sighted, focused vision; Levertov's poetic, objective camera's eye won't allow her the focus of vision that she thinks she should have. And so she pronounces herself guilty.

But guilty of what? Of being a poet in a time when poetry seems useless. In a letter she includes in the "Prologue," Levertov reacts to Mitch's situation, his possible conviction: "And all I can bring forth out of my anger is a few flippant rhymes." Her poetry is insignificant against the ultimate horror of the war and the detrimental effect that war has on the language, the only tool she thinks she can use well. Again in the "Prologue," Levertov juxtaposes the conversation of two children in which a little boy declares " 'yes means no . . . ' " with that now infamous justification for a bombing raid: "It became necessary to destroy the town to save it." And Levertov then bemoans the fact that the language has become like a "touchstone / worn down by what / gross fiction." As words become more uncertain, poetry becomes harder to write. At one point, there is even the intimation that Levertov's inability to write powerful poetry contributed to the death of a friend. In the fourth part of the poem she writes about two friends who committed suicide. Judy had written Levertov "('If you would write me a poem / I could live for ever')."

But Levertov admits, "still I've not begun the poem, / the one she asked for." And she writes that Robert Duncan "sees me as Kali!" She denies that label because, as she says, "I can't sustain for a day / that anger." She cannot do so because as a poet she is unable to single-mindedly pursue anything. She must remain open to all experience.

Remaining open to all experiences poses a problem early in the poem; Levertov's simple dualism "Revolution or Death" proves to be just that: simple. As **"Staying Alive"** develops we see that there is more than one kind of death; one that is not included in the death of Mayor Daley or the death of the self-immolators, an extremely attractive kind of death that Levertov finds herself drawn to throughout the poem. It first surfaces in the second section of "Part I" (some of which has already been quoted): "And yet, yes, there's the death / that's not the obscene sellout . . . Death lovely, whispering, / a drowsy numbness . . . ". This is the death of Hopkins' "Goldengrove," a passive dying resembling the falling of leaves from a tree: "goldengrove / is unleaving all around me." This is the true temptation, to remain passive, simply to observe "the will to live" with "some photo-eye" and with her poet's words attempt to make them into "a sacrament." But the uncertainty remains: the inability to trust the language. She tells us that her roots which are "in the / 19th century" put her "out of touch." (She explains this in her introduction: "in writing about my childhood in England, my diction became English . . . for the sense my individual history gives me of being straddled between *places* extends to the more universal sense any writer my age—rooted in a cultural past barely shared by younger readers, yet committed to a solidarity of hope and struggle with the revolutionary young—must have of being almost unbearably, painfully, straddled across *time*.") She is homeless except for the home she creates for herself within the language: "language itself is my one home." But it is a home that offers little solace because, as she implied in the passage quoted, her language alienates her, and once again she is alone.

She chooses revolution, "but my words / often already don't reach forward / into it— / (perhaps)." The parenthetical "perhaps" speaks volumes. Such uncertainty prevails: "Whom I would touch / I may not, / whom I may / I would / but often do not" (like Judy above). Out of touch with her language, she also feels out of touch with the whole era: "My diction marks me / untrue to my time; / change it, I'd be / untrue to myself." This is the crux of the matter. Levertov wants to use her poetry to serve the revolution, but discovers that she is unable to bend the poetry to her will. It is as though the poetry contains some unalterable truth that will not allow it to be shaped for political reason into something other than what it is. The truth of Levertov's dictum that "form is never more than a revelation of content" accurately sums up what has happened. Seeking to speak of revolution, Levertov finds herself meditating on death—the death of friends, the death of language, and by extension perhaps the death of herself (as poet, revolutionary).

Trapped in a tunnel and unable to make her words do what she wants them to do, Levertov resorts to what be-comes the major action of the sequence: she runs away. She does not feel good about this course of action but it becomes a necessity despite the words of Gandhi she includes in the second "Entr'acte": " 'Never / run away from the stormcenter. / Cultivate / cool courage, die without killing' " As we have already seen, the idea of getting killed is not one Levertov entertains very readily. And certainly the second half of Gandhi's injunction is even more troublesome:—" 'cultivate / the art of killing and being killed / rather than in a cowardly manner / to flee from danger' ." Neither of these alternatives sits well with Levertov, and though she believes in them, believes them necessary for a successful revolution, a rigid adherence to "Keiner / oder Alle, Alles / oder Nichts" ("No one or everyone, all or nothing") eludes her. And so she flees.

More time is spent away from the "stormcenter" than near it. In the "Prologue" she and Mitch are in Puerto Rico vacationing before he has to return to stand trial. It is a positive experience, one that allows them "To repossess [their] souls" by flying "to the sea." It is during these times of escape that some of Levertov's best poetry is written. She has always had a facility for the meditative lyric that considers the "outer" world in all its wonder and the ways in which the "inner" and "outer" worlds shape one another. There are several such sections within this sequence. She needs to renew herself "To expand again, to plunge / [her] dryness into the unwearying source— / but not to forget. / Not to forget but to remember better." She returns to this theme again in the first "Entr'acte" where instead of being isolated in an eternal summer-like paradise, she and Mitch are isolated by a snowstorm that has "(marooned)" them, taking away their phone, lights, heat, etc. As in Puerto Rico, there is great joy. Instead of jumping into the sea, they jump "into snowbank— / no sound— / pleasure—". But soon, terror mingles with the pleasure, as when the world appears to be a horrible "black-and-white photo" in which everything is "deprived / of color"—even in retreat, the horror of the camera-eye remains. To leave the war behind does not mean forgetting it, and Levertov describes the "pain!" of the "sharp stabs of recall" and "revelations." This retreat becomes a way of "capturing . . . moments and their procession in palm / of mind's hand," to once again "make / of song a chalice / of Time, / a communion wine." The song, her poetry, is elevated to sacrament.

However, the escapes do not help for long. At the beginning of "Part II," immediately after the first "Entr'acte," Levertov exclaims that she is unable to continue with her poems: "Can't go further. / If there's to be a / second part, it's not / a going beyond, I'm / still here"—meaning, of course, that she is still where she was at the end of "Part I": confused, out of sync, despairing. In "Part II" she seeks to get to the root of her malaise by examining her language again, "To dig down, / to re-examine." She asks herself: "What is the revolution I'm driven / to name, to live in?" Robert Duncan has reminded her that "revolution / implies the circular" and Levertov despairs that it is "The wrong word" because "a new life / isn't the old life in reverse, negative of the same photo." But resignedly she admits, "it's the only / word we have." (pp. 52-56)

"Part III" is devoted entirely to another one of Levertov's escapes from the stormcenter. She returns to England and Europe unsure whether she is a "Cop-out . . . / or merely / on holiday?" . . . For many sections the War and the resistance movement are not mentioned at all as she seeks "oblivion." She remembers Olga when she passes streets where her sister used to work for the Revolution, but that is all. Finally the question is asked: "After the American lava / has cooled and set in new forms, / will you Americans have / more peace and less hope?" And Levertov wonders to herself: "when I go back into the writing lava, / will I rejoice in / fierce hope, in / wan hope?" (p. 57)

Levertov [eventually] imagines that her poetry can be of some use to the revolution if it is not indeed synonymous with it. In the last "Entr'acte" she tells of Richard who has a "pulse . . . / that day and night says / revolution revolution revolution / and another / not always heard: / poetry poetry." If the "flame-pulse" of revolution stops beating "life itself / shall cease," but if the pulse of poetry ever grows "faint / fever shall parch the soul, breath / choke upon ashes." The new hope Levertov has is that she can help bring about the conditions "when their rhythms / mesh" so that "though the pain of living / never lets up / the singing begins."

And so in "Part IV," with new resolve she goes back to the United States to try again. For a time there is "Happiness," as section ii of "Part IV" is called, but then death intervenes again. "Judy had killed herself a full two weeks / before my hours of dancing began" and Grandin who "raged bursting with life into death . . . his death a year ago, hits me now." Her poetry disappears and as predicted her breath chokes on ashes: "Dry mouth, / dry nostrils." Again, she denigrates herself: "I'm frivolous." And she is reminded of her primary condition: "I'm alone." She reaffirms her desire for revolution but recognizes that as a poet she will always appear impractical to herself and others. . . . She names those who are doing worthwhile things, living on collectives (Richard and Neil), writing books on "the long revolution" (Mitch); and again, in comparison, her own worthlessness is reiterated when she admits that she cannot "sustain for a day / that anger. / 'There comes / a time / when only anger / is love'— / I wrote it, but know such love / only in flashes." Still she hopes: "I'm trying to learn / the other kind of waiting: charge, or recharge, my / batteries. / Get my head together. Mesh. Knit / idiom with idiom in the / 'push and shove of events' . " She desires to mesh revolution and poetry but, ever impatient, proclaims, "But that *when* must be now!" Unable to act, she holds fast to her "love / of those who dare, who do dare / to struggle, dare to reject / unlived life, disdain / to die of *that*." For them she has these final desperate words: "O holy innocents! I have / no virtue but to praise / you who believe / life is possible . . . "—and the poem ends. It is as though Levertov has torn away the rest of the manuscript. To return to the play analogy, Act V is missing; the poet found it impossible to write. As with Olga, "the stage lights had gone out, even the empty theatre / was locked to [her], cavern of transformation where all / had been possible."

One question that we're left with is: Why did Levertov choose this dramatic form? I suspect that she hoped to maneuver around the possibility of writing "merely confessional" poetry by choosing to use a more impersonal literary form. Compared to poetry or the novel, drama has the potential to allow the author some distance. She hoped that the objectification allowed by this less personal form would help her accomplish her public purpose. The irony, of course, is that the inner life overcomes the outer political life and the dramatic structure highlights her personal struggle rather than hiding it. Note for instance, that the "Entr'actes" always present Levertov in a passive, observing state, a time for her to store energy for her action on stage. But in the four parts of the poem which correspond to the acts of a play, she is once again passive, unable to decide, lamenting her inability to act.

To some degree then, *To Stay Alive* is a poem of self-annihilation. Seeking to celebrate revolution and life and to resolve her questions surrounding these issues in the '60s, Levertov succeeds only in reaffirming for herself her own inadequacy to do either. The poet's fear that she will be unable to do what she hopes to do becomes a self-fulfilling prophecy that dooms her and her poem to continual despair as she meditates upon the uselessness of her endeavour. Seeking to obtain the sainthood she imagines others have gained, she ends up proclaiming herself (and her poem) as one with "no virtue."

But what Levertov doesn't seem to recognize at the close of *To Stay Alive* is that her poetry, that "cavern of transformation," *has* opened to her the possibilities that she longed for in the "Preface" of the book. "It assembles separate parts of the whole. . . . not as mere 'confessional' autobiography, but as a document of some historical value, a record of one person's inner/outer experience in America during the '60's . . . ". She hoped that *To Stay Alive* would reflect "an experience which [was] shared by so many." Her confusions about revolution, war, and the action she felt she *had* to take but was unable to take were shared by many. Therefore when Levertov accurately records her own struggle she in turn mirrors the struggle of others like her during that era. Levertov does not resolve her own problem, but I believe she allows her audience "to achieve the keenest, most open realization" of her/their struggle. (pp. 58-60)

Nancy J. Sisko, " 'To Stay Alive': Levertov's Search for a Revolutionary Poetry," in Sagetrieb, *Vol. 5, No. 2, Fall, 1986, pp. 47-60.*

Marion Lomax

Denise Levertov's first book of poems appeared in 1946, two years before she left Britain. The *Selected Poems* of the woman who has since been hailed "one of the best living poets in America" come from volumes published in New York between 1957 and 1982.

Levertov was associated with the 1950s Black Mountain poets; the influence of Whitman, Williams and Pound is apparent but, although she has clearly adopted the rhythms and diction of America, an awareness of her British inheritance remains, particularly in her skilful sound patterns—"smallest inviolate, stone violet" (**"The Stone-**

carver's Poem"). Levertov reaches back to the Renaissance lyric, the Metaphysicals, and the Romantics; she takes a title from Donne's "The Extasie" (**"Else a great Prince in prison lies"**) or twists a Wordsworth sonnet in **"O Taste and See"** ("The world is / not with us enough"). Her similes are often domestic—"gathering the washing as if it were flowers"—but she has Wordsworth's ability to invest the everyday with mystery, as in the "crippled . . . Ones" (**"From the Roof "**).

What is admirable in this volume outweighs the weaknesses. Levertov's energy, commitment and boldness of expression deserve applause. She writes strongly on women, not sparing herself in the rebuke, "And our dreams / with what frivolity we have pared them / like toenails, clipped them like ends of / split hair?" (**"Hypocrite Women"**).

She ranges from accomplished lyrics like **"The Ache of Marriage"** ("two by two in the ark of / the ache of it") to hard-line protests. She writes clear-sightedly about relationships with the living and the dead who "have no time / to bear grudges or to bless us; / their own present / holds them intent. Yet perhaps / sometimes they dream us." The creative process is explored in several poems: in **"She and the Muse"**, a visit from "the hour's delightful hero" gives us the poem which ends wittily when the heroine "picks a quill, / dips it, begins to write. But not of him."

Above all, Levertov's sense of political responsibility stands out. Although the anti-nuclear poems in **Candles in Babylon** are weakened by the force of her commitment—which tempts her to preach—she handles the issue effectively in **"The Sun Going Down upon Our Wrath"**, her address to the young with its play on "dust to dust". This works because of her own confessed reluctance to contemplate the worst, and the helplessness expressed in her uncertainty for the future. . . .

The **"Olga Poems"**, for her dead sister, are densely autobiographical. Other poems reveal a healthy sense of perspective in relation to ageing, solitude and man's place in the natural world. Stylistically innovative, Levertov also explores the surreal or adapts myths to her own purposes, as in **"A Tree Telling of Orpheus,"** where the tree describes being hacked to pieces by the Thracian women in its own terms: "It is said they felled him and cut up his limbs for firewood".

Her latest volume, **Oblique Prayers,** combines incantatory meditative and protest poetry with translations of Jean Joubert's poems alongside their French originals. The Orpheus myth appears in **"Thinking about El Salvador"**, which begins, "Because every day they chop heads off / I'm silent"—in sympathy with the silence "of raped women, / of priests and peasants, / . . . of all whose heads every day / float down the river / . . . not Orpheus heads / still singing, bound for the sea, / but mute". Levertov has consolidated her position as an effective political and personal poet through a realistic awareness of what restricts us all as fellow human beings. As the swimmer in **"Action"** (**Selected Poems**) lays "everything down / on the hot sand" to float in "Deep water," the poet, too, acknowledges that "Little by little one comes to know /

the limits and depths of power". Denise Levertov has accomplished this through action as well as poetry.

Marion Lomax, "Ebb and Flow," in The Times Literary Supplement, *No. 4371, January 9, 1987, p. 41.*

Matthew Flamm

In the late '60s, a new book of poems by Denise Levertov was almost as important as a new album by The Byrds. Levertov had a following. She was impressionistic in the William Carlos Williams style, but much less hard-edged; her poems could still be pretty. They had equal doses of two things fashionable at the time—politics and mysticism. . . . It seems only natural now that, as the '70s progressed and she became increasingly a political poet, she would keep only her most dedicated fans. Not that it was entirely a matter of timing: her earlier, more lyrical poems were sometimes better than the new ones. But on the whole, Levertov continued to write well, as one look at **Breathing the Water** shows. The 15th book of her career, it has all her old virtues of musicality, mystery, and directness.

Levertov has access to a part of memory that by its nature is almost always out of reach: details that flicker in the corner of the eye and contain the essential elements of a place or event. She goes a step further in digging up experiences that are themselves just on the edge of awareness. These range from moments of artistic inspiration to childhood memories to spiritual encounters. "Others will speak of her spirit's tendrils," Levertov writes in the elegy **"In Memory: After a Friend's Sudden Death."** "[B]ut I will remember her body's unexpected beauty / seen in the fragrant redwood sauna . . . "

> And I will speak
> not of her work, her words, her
>   search
> for a new pathway, her need
>
> to heedfully walk and sing through
>   dailiness
> noticing stones and flowers,
>
> but of the great encompassing Aah!
>   she would utter,
> entering slowly, completely, into the
>   welcoming whirlpool.

Levertov can wear out her welcome. She goes overboard here with "heedfully," "search," and "dailiness," but even where she keeps the flowerchild under control, the sense of mission remains. There's not a great deal of humor in Levertov and certainly no irreverence, yet she risks writing poems on such difficult-to-pull-off topics as war and poverty, and most of the time she succeeds.

Not surprisingly, Levertov is drawn to holy figures. In her earlier poems she relied on war resisters, but in **Breathing the Water** she's more frankly religious, topping off the book with a series of poems on the 15th century visionary Lady Julian of Norwich. The poet clearly identifies with the lively, independent-minded mystic, whose chief vision reads like the key to Levertov's poetics of miniatures: God places in Julian's hand "the entire world, 'round as a ball, / small as a hazelnut.'" The vision teaches that knowledge and redemption—"the macro-cosmic egg . . . / brown hazelnut of All that Is"—is available to everyone: "As still, waking each day within / our microcosm, we find it, and ourselves." The religious and the social coincide here, since, as Levertov sees it, God's love and mercy make the world's suffering bearable. This is not the poem of a new convert; faith in that love remains something the poet longs for. She doesn't let the tide of feeling overwhelm her sense of the particular. Levertov's gift for detail is matched by the way she can make yearnings and ideas seem almost physical, as if she held them in the palm of her hand. (pp. 58-9)

> *Matthew Flamm, "Holy Muses," in* The Village Voice, *Vol. 32, No. 39, September 29, 1987, pp. 58-9.*

Daniela Gioseffi

Many of the poems in **Breathing the Water,** her eighteenth volume of poetry, continue Denise Levertov's tradition of mingling the personal and the political in a seamless blend that triumphs over non-poetic rhetoric: **"South Africa, 1986,"** or **"Making Peace,"** or **"From the Image Flow—Summer of 1986."** The last, with its epigram on the hope that remained in Pandora's box after she had loosed disaster and affliction on the world, has a Wordsworthian beginning:

> These days—these years—
> when powers and principalities of death
> weigh down the world, deeper, deeper
> than we ever thought it could fall and still
>   keep slowly spinning,
> Hope, caught under the jar's rim, crawls
> like a golden fly
> round and around, a sentinel:
> it can't get out, it can't fly free
> among our heavy hearts—
> but does not die, keeps up its pace,
> pausing only as if to meditate
> a saving strategy . . .

If Levertov is not a poet who sings or chants in the more oral tradition of a Ginsberg, Whitman, or Williams, she is very likely the best poet we have in the tradition of English poetry stemming from British prosody. There's nothing unusual about this, given her early years in the United Kingdom and her first book there in 1946, *The Double Image,* but as a result there is rarely anything startlingly original about her style. Yet she is always highly skillful, and she can be very direct, lucid, and sensual. . . .

It is fitting that the last poem in Levertov's most mature voice invokes Rilke. (There are three poems that do so in the book.) She is, perhaps, the closest poetic equivalent that modern America has produced to a Rilke—a poet of "the stream of perception" who is spiritually and constantly engaged in the search for universal truth along the way. She seems to want to "make sure that no words lie thirsty, bleeding, waiting for rescue," as she says in **"Hunting the Phoenix,"** a cloaked comment on her craft and inner search, the second poem in her new volume.

Levertov's constant "stream of perception" (her own phrase for her work) may be what gives her work the quality that Ursula Le Guin has perceived: "Levertov's writing is like a kind companion in hard times, not trying to sell us anything or scare us or fool us, but going along with us":

> All the long road
> in chains, even if, after all,
> we come to
> death's ordinary door, with time
> smiling its ordinary
> long-ago smile.

Perhaps, also, the serene assurance of knowing that every word she chooses will be read has allowed Levertov to address many of her poems, like intimate letters, to family or friends or figures from history—in a voice that has, like Rilke's, the quality of a monologue of the spirit or communion with others' inner lives, always making the personal touch upon universally shared truths. Like Rilke's, the poet's journey has brought her to view death on the horizon—where it is for all of us, more and more as an opportunity to be deeply touched by every shadowy, fleeting moment, alive in its own unique instant. Unlike Rilke's, though, Levertov's most successful poems seem to be the ones that do not deal with a seemingly Christian reference to God. In the threat of our twentieth-century precarious world, the most satisfying are the ones that realize nature and the Earth itself as the sustainer of our vulnerable human lives. . . .

Breathing the Water might seem to hover between medieval Christian ideas of God and traditional English prosody, but this sort of contemporary spiritual stance is embraced by many of America's women writers involved in the international peace movement and global ideals of feminine feminism. Earth is seen as Goddess of all and nurturer of all that is human. Indeed, the two ideals of God's medieval "agony" and the neo-pagan celebration of "all that is" seem to be reconciled in the long poem just before the end of the new book, **"The Showings; Lady Julian of Norwich, 1342-1416":**

> She lived in dark times, as we do:
> war, and the Black Death, hunger, strife,
> torture, massacre. She knew
> all of this, she felt it
> *sorrowfully, mournfully,*
> *shaken as men shake*
> *a cloth in the wind.*

Poems 1968-72, also issued this year by New Directions, carries forth the record of Levertov's poetic development from *Collected Earlier Poems 1940 to 1960* and *Poems 1960 to 1967.* This new collection gathers together all the poems from *Relearning the Alphabet* (1970), *To Stay Alive* (1971), and *Footprints* (1972), thereby covering Levertov's involvement in the Vietnam war resistance. Testifying to Levertov's growing strength and technical mastery as a poet, the newly collected volume affirms her vision. Here the reader can find grief and nostalgia along with affirmation, remembering those protest years in which so many of us American poets, intellectuals, artists were involved in readings, demonstrations, and activities against the unjust war that Hollywood has now come to rediscover and document with Academy Award-winning films of protest. Here is Levertov's historical resistance and "opposition to the whole system of insane greed of which war is the inevitable expression":

> Heavy, heavy, heavy, hand and heart.
> We are at war,
> bitterly, bitterly at war.
>
> And the buying and selling
> buzzes at our heads, a swarm
> of busy flies, a kind of innocence.

Levertov's *Poems 1968-72* achieves a moving document of those years of protest not easily paralleled in American poetry. She is certainly one of the most highly respected poets of her generation and an essential part of the conscience of American poetry. Though she started her American career with City Lights Books, her style clearly stems from the tradition of an Eliot, Pound, or Lowell, and yet in political sensibility she is closer to a Ferlinghetti or Ginsberg, and infinitely more engaged in the real world than her three American forebears. Most of all, she is Denise Levertov, a poet of intimate vignette and Rilke-like understatement, of emotional power and controlled craft.

> Daniela Gioseffi, "The Stream of Perception,"
> in The American Book Review, *Vol. 9, No. 4,*
> *September-October, 1987, p. 9.*

Diane Wakoski

American poetry, like American culture, has manifested from the beginning an unlikely combination of the material and the spiritual. We are pragmatists, grounded in our physical world, but for some reason we do not accept this as a limitation. We continue to see the spiritual rising out of the material, and our great poets like Whitman talk as if God were in all of us intermingled with the natural world:

> I have said that the soul is not more
> than the body,
> And I have said that the body is not
> more than the soul,
> And nothing, not God, is greater to one
> than one's self is . . .

Levertov's poetry, like most American mysticism, is grounded in Christianity, but like Whitman and other American mystics her discovery of God is the discovery of God in herself, and an attempt to understand how that self is a "natural" part of the world, intermingling with everything pantheistically, ecologically, socially, historically and, for Levertov, always lyrically. Perhaps her search has from the beginning looked like an aesthetic rather than religious quest, though from the beginning she has spoken of God and never seemed to be unwilling to label her own journey as spiritual. But until now her somewhat inconsistent politics, and a stance which certainly embraces no specific religious doctrine or set of religious observances, have confused the issue.

In *Breathing the Water* the linking of body and soul through God is made so clear that even the most obtuse reader can see it. In meditating on the religious mystic Lady Julian of Norwich, Levertov asks that we see the world as a hazelnut placed in the hand in order to understand the relationship between God and humanity:

> God for a moment in our history
> placed in that five-fingered
> human nest
> the macrocosmic egg, sublime paradox,
> brown hazelnut of All that Is—
> made, and belov'd, and preserved.
> As still, waking each day within
> our microcosm, we find it, and
> ourselves.

It hasn't always been so obvious what Levertov was up to, and some of the pleasures of this book come from seeing the focusing of a lifetime career of writing beautiful, lyric poems, interspersed with militant political ones. What becomes apparent in *Breathing the Water* is that a distinct mystical religious vision has informed the poetry from the very beginning, and a struggle to understand God's meaning and intentions for the world.

Levertov's early poetry was a celebration, among other things, of the sexual, Dionysian creative powers of her feminine self and world. In one of my favorites of her lyrical invocations to the powers that be, **"To the Snake,"** from *With Eyes at the Back of Our Heads* (1960), she hangs a snake around her neck and sings to it, telling it that while she reassured her "companions" that the snake was "harmless" in spite of its "cold pulsing throat" which "hissed" at her, she herself "had no certainty" but knew that she needed to hold it there. She releases the snake back to nature, where it "faded into the pattern / of grass and shadows," and concludes the poem "and I returned / smiling and haunted, to a dark morning." In this poem, as in Whitman's lines in *Song of Myself,* "I bequeath myself to the dirt to grow from the grasses I love, / If you want me again look for me under your bootsoles," Levertov longs to identify herself with the natural world, to mingle with it, even though she is not quite sure it will not harm her.

The second section of *Breathing the Water* opens with a poem called **"Zeroing In."** A man and a woman compare the dangers of life to walking in a landscape dotted with bogs. The man tells the story of a dog he had as a boy which had to be put down because it bit a child who touched an injured spot on its head; at the end of the poem the woman says

> "Yes, we learn that.
> It's not terror, it's pain we're talking
> about:
> those places in us, like your dog's bruised
> head,
> that are bruised forever, that time
> never assuages, never."

Life, the snake, in the earlier poem, is only potentially dangerous; in this last book, Levertov shows us how dangerous the natural forces are. Yet no knowledge keeps the speaker from touching the bruised spot, just as no warning keeps the young poet from putting the snake around her neck.

Levertov's single best collection of poems, *Life in the Forest* (1978), included a series of poems about the last year of her mother's life, which was lived in Mexico; that semitropical landscape becomes for Levertov an embodiment of the archetypal Garden. It is in this book that we first begin to see how seriously Levertov has pursued the myth of the Garden from her early sense of herself, like Eve, daring to mingle with it, embracing the snake as a necklace in spite of her friends' warnings. The constant temptations of life never deter her, though she always suspects their danger. In **"Death in Mexico"** her vision of what that danger is emerges. Describing the English-style country garden which her mother has created around her house in Mexico and cultivated carefully over the years, Levertov depicts its rapid crumbling and disintegration after only a few weeks of neglect during her mother's terminal illness. The landscape is returning to its natural jungle state, and in its ruins Levertov sees a primitive reality.

> Gardens vanish. She was an alien here,
> as I am.
> . . .
>   Old gods
> took back their own.

This is what must be feared; that in death, in each personal death, civilization as we know it dies. Perhaps the "Old Gods" are the body, the physical world, always there and always with a primitive power and potentially dangerous capability. Like all mystics, Levertov believes in a God or the knowledge of a God within oneself which is beyond doctrine and organized religion. Sometimes this God takes the face of art or civilization or government or human will, but the marrying of those two elements, the body and the spirit, must be a marrying of the "Old Gods" and the personal God. "Life in the forest" will always be dangerous and primitive, but we cannot resist the beauty of the snake.

One of the loveliest poems in *Breathing the Water* is **"The Well."**

> At sixteen, I believed the moonlight
> could change me if it would.
>   I moved my head
> on the pillow, even moved my bed
> as the moon slowly
> crossed the open lattice.

In this poem, a kind of latter-day "Eve of St. Agnes," Levertov tells us how she religiously (my word; she uses "diligently") "moon-bathed" as others sunbathe. On the dark nights she permitted herself to sleep deeply; it was the bathing in darkness, not the sleepless moonlit nights, which left her feeling refreshed "and if not beautiful / filled with some other power." That "power" by implication is the power of poetry, of creation, and comes neither out of sun nor moon nor any kind of light, but from darkness. . . .

Perhaps one of the reasons no one has noticed that this clergyman's daughter has really been writing religious poetry all these years is that she has always spoken an orthodox Christianity of love while simultaneously offering this vision of the attractive yet terrible dark world of the "Old Gods." Sometimes it is the real world of the "dark morning" Levertov has to return to after the light ecstasy of ex-

periencing the snake, sometimes it is the unfathomable cruelty of war or disease; sometimes it is only sleep, and sometimes it is the stone stairway to the spiritual itself, the Jacob's Ladder. Her ambivalence tests the reader, must constantly puzzle the reader. Is this darkness the unknown? Or God? Or the opposite of God? Is moonbathing a failed spiritual exercise but still necessary? Is the "dark morning" beautiful, or only inevitable?

The vision of a marriage of body and spirit is what allows Levertov to move beyond her politics, her Christian morality and most of all her Romantic fear of the darkness. Levertov offers earth images, Dionysian images, of fertility coming from the buried seed, the physical not the spiritual. (p. 7)

Like Whitman, Levertov implies that "to die is different from what any one supposed, and luckier"; these scenes of darkness, as we fall from the Garden into the possibly dangerous world, are irresistible—like the snake, "glinting arrowy / gold scales," with "the weight of you on my shoulders, / and the whispering silver of your dryness / . . . close at my ears—" which will give her enough pleasure to face "the dark morning." And it is this interaction between the light (the world of breath) and the dark (the refreshment of nothingness, or the water at the bottom of the well) which makes Levertov's mystical vision a religious one. For her, God is the author of paradoxes.

Like Whitman, Levertov's religion is the religion of self, but a cosmic self whose God or approach to God comes through the marrying of body and spirit. It is the human hand that holds God's hazelnut and, as Lady Julian does, understands the immensity of God's love. Like Lady Julian, Levertov refuses to be confounded by war and the darkness of human misery; she tries, as in **"The Well,"** to see it as a source of rest. Her struggle is Lady Julian's struggle, and Job's, to understand God in order to be able to accept contradiction.

In the title poem of *The Jacob's Ladder* (1961), Levertov wrote "The stairway is not / a thing of gleaming strands . . . It is of stone." In the poem, the angels are on the stone steps, brushing their wings against her. In the same collection there is an earlier poem, also called **"The Well."** In that poem "the Muse" wades into dark water, and Levertov finds the word "water" spelled out on her left palm. The purpose of Levertov's long journey as a poet and a spiritual being has been to learn how to "breathe the water," the "water" written earlier on her palm, the water of life, of baptism; how to understand the darkness of the forest she must return to after sensing the beauty of the snake around her neck or bathing in moonlight. It is the fusion of these two that has always been the goal of Levertov's vision: to find a God in this intermingling of flesh and spirit, something, as she says in **"Variation and Reflection on a Poem by Rilke,"** which will "let you flow back into all creation." (p. 8)

Diane Wakoski, "Song of Herself," in The Women's Review of Books, *Vol. V, No. 5, February, 1988, pp. 7-8.*

FURTHER READING

Breslin, James E. B. "Denise Levertov." In his *From Modern to Contemporary: American Poetry, 1945-1965,* pp. 143-55. Chicago: The University of Chicago Press, 1983.

Intensive examination of the evolution of Levertov's poetry.

Christensen, Inger. " 'Hidden Behind Another Nature': Denise Levertov and Organicism." In his *The Shadow of the Dome: Organicism and Romantic Poetry,* pp. 93-116. Bergen, Norway: University of Bergen Press, 1985.

Examines Levertov's work in relation to that of such nineteenth-century writers as Walt Whitman and Samuel Taylor Coleridge.

Jackson, Richard. "A Common Time: The Poetry of Denise Levertov." In his *The Dismantling of Time in Contemporary Poetry,* pp. 187-238. Tuscaloosa: The University of Alabama Press, 1988.

Utilizes theories of Martin Heidegger to study the concept of time in Levertov's poetry.

Levertov, Denise. An interview with Lorrie Smith. *Michigan Quarterly Review* XXIV, No. 4 (Fall 1985): 596-604.

Levertov discusses her recent political and spiritual poetry.

Marten, Harry. "Exploring the Human Community: The Poetry of Denise Levertov and Muriel Rukeyser." *Sagetrieb* 3, No. 3 (Winter 1984): 51-61.

Explores how Rukeyser and Levertov incorporate concepts of community and individuality in their poetry.

————. *Understanding Denise Levertov.* Columbia: University of South Carolina Press, 1988, 219 p.

Marten discusses Levertov's work in terms of her early period, her political poetry, and her spiritual verse. Includes an index and primary and secondary bibliography.

Sakelliou-Schultz, Liana. *Denise Levertov: An Annotated Primary and Secondary Bibliography.* New York: Garland, 1988, 321 p.

Comprehensive analytic bibliography that covers some foreign language sources; includes an index and a chronology of Levertov's life.

David Lynch

1946-

American filmmaker, scriptwriter, cartoonist, and lyricist.

A director who usually writes his own scripts, Lynch is famous for the strange visions expressed in his imaginative, controversial films, which include *Eraserhead* and *Blue Velvet*. His works often focus upon innocent, alienated, or obsessive individuals who reflect either his own personality or those of characters drawn from popular culture and the cinema. By emphasizing protagonists entangled in sinister situations beyond their control, Lynch explores unpleasant and grotesque realities hidden beneath the placid surface of everyday existence. He adopts an intuitive surrealist approach to present viewers with images suggestive of sex, birth, and death—including womblike settings, phallic symbols, and mutilated bodies—while avoiding overt explanation. Although some critics have faulted his nightmarish presentations as sensational, infantile, or meaningless, many concur with David Chute: "Lynch's dreamily evocative visual gifts are a perfectly adequate substitute for intellectualism and analysis. He is such a wizard at infecting us with his creepoid perceptions that he really doesn't need to work through the intermediate steps of figuring out what it all means. As if entranced, he translates his intimations of toxic mortality directly into imagery."

Born in Missoula, Montana, Lynch is the son of a government research scientist who worked in forestry for the United States Department of Agriculture. The settings of his films are often similar to areas in Washington and Idaho, where he was raised before moving to Alexandria, Virginia at the age of fifteen. Determined to become a painter, Lynch attended both the Corcoran School of Art in Washington, D.C. and the Boston Museum School before moving to Philadelphia and enrolling at the Pennsylvania Academy of Fine Arts. In Philadelphia, Lynch witnessed a murder and became both fascinated and repelled by the city's squalor. Lynch commented: "Philadelphia, more than any other filmmaker, influenced me. It's the sickest, most corrupt, decaying, fear-ridden city imaginable. I was very poor and living in bad areas. I felt like I was constantly in danger. But it was so fantastic at the same time." At the Pennsylvania Academy, Lynch completed his first film work, a one-minute animated loop in which six heads repeatedly vomit and catch on fire. During this time Lynch also created *The Grandmother,* a blend of live action and animation in which an abused, bed-wetting boy secretly grows a benign grandmother from a seed in his bed.

In 1970, Lynch moved to Los Angeles to study at the American Film Institute's Center for Advanced Film Studies. There he spent five years creating *Eraserhead,* his first feature-length film. Lynch worked on a small budget largely funded by the American Film Institute and actress Sissy Spacek, and often lived on the set of the film, imagin-

ing himself as part of the world he was projecting. Using grainy black-and-white cinematography, *Eraserhead* draws viewers into a bleak industrial landscape made otherworldly by menacing sounds and images. The film revolves around Henry, a modern Everyman who agrees to wed his girlfriend, Mary, when he discovers she has become pregnant. Their baby, born prematurely, is a squalling, alien creature resembling a skinless animal, its organs bundled together by strips of bandages. Like Lynch himself, whose daughter was born with clubbed feet that required casts to correct, Henry finds the burdens of parenthood unbearable. Whereas Lynch divorced his wife and left his family, however, Henry kills his monstrous offspring and loses himself in the comforting world he imagines behind his radiator. Although a student film, *Eraserhead* achieved cult status at midnight showings across the United States and provoked favorable and negative comparisons to the classic surrealist films *Un chien andalou* and *L'âge d'or* by Luis Buñuel and Salvador Dalí. While some critics faulted the film as sophomoric or obscene, most praised Lynch's ability to create memorable and emotionally effective images.

Lynch's first commercial feature, *The Elephant Man,* also

makes use of black-and-white photography as well as sinister industrial sounds and imagery. The most accessible and the least characteristic of his films, *The Elephant Man* is set largely in Victorian London and is based upon the true life story of John Merrick, a victim of what is today believed to have been neurofibromatosis, a disease of the central nervous system that causes the formation of thick fibrous tissue beneath its victim's skin. Unlike Bernard Pomerance's Broadway play *The Elephant Man,* in which Merrick's deformities are merely suggested through the actor's movements, Lynch's film attempts a more literal rendering based on such nonfiction sources as Sir Frederick Treves's report, *Elephant Man, and Other Reminiscences,* and Ashley Montagu's *The Elephant Man: A Study in Human Dignity.* In Lynch's film, Merrick makes his living as a carnival attraction until he is rescued from his abusive "owner" by Doctor Frederick Treves, a young surgeon who awakens in him a sense of his own dignity.

Because *The Elephant Man* emphasizes the visual aspects of Merrick's disease, some critics charged Lynch with encouraging voyeurism in his audience. However, *The Elephant Man* was nominated for eight Academy Awards, including best director and best adapted screenplay, and garnered wide popular and critical praise for its evocative and compassionate illumination of Merrick's condition. With his next film, *Dune,* Lynch attempted to create a commercial science fiction "blockbuster" that would remain faithful to the complexities of Frank Herbert's 1965 novel on which the film is based. The multimillion–dollar epic proved to be the first commercial and critical failure of Lynch's career. *Dune* was generally faulted as muddled and incomprehensible, and proved unsatisfying both to fans of the original novel and commercial audiences. According to Lynch, the producers of *Dune* cut crucial scenes from his original version, fearing that audiences would not tolerate a film over six hours in length.

Following the failure of *Dune,* Lynch was promised complete creative control over a more modestly budgeted film of his own. The result was *Blue Velvet,* an innovative mystery-thriller that David Chute described as "a nightmarish coming-of-age story, a Hardy Boys thriller with running sores and pustules." Set in Lumberton, a small, fictitious logging community, *Blue Velvet* concerns Jeffrey Beaumont, a young college student who discovers that a sadistic drug dealer, Frank Booth, has kidnapped the son and husband of a local nightclub singer named Dorothy Vallens. Because Dorothy has exhibited suicidal urges, Frank has cut off her husband's ear to remind her of his power and to force her to continue having sex with him, telling her, "Do it for van Gogh." Jeffrey becomes Dorothy's sympathetic lover, but one night he ambivalently indulges her masochistic desire to be hit; following a brutal confrontation with Frank, he is forced to acknowledge his own guilt for victimizing Dorothy. While some critics have faulted the film as sensational and voyeuristic, many acknowledge Lynch's cinematic mastery of mood, style, and image, and *Blue Velvet* earned an award for Best Film from the National Society of Film Critics.

In *Wild at Heart,* Lynch loosely adapts Barry Gifford's novel of the same title to create a stylized black comedy about two lovers in flight from the malevolent spirits of their respective pasts. The film revolves around Lula, a sexually aggressive young woman whose mother orders the contract killing of her boyfriend, Sailor, because he may have witnessed the murder of Lula's father. Sailor, who strives to look, sing, and behave like Elvis Presley, decides to violate his parole and flee to California with Lula. Lynch infuses the travels of Sailor and Lula with allusions to *The Wizard of Oz,* as when Lula's mother appears to her as a wicked witch flying alongside the road. While many critics considered *Wild at Heart* labored, its characters unconvincing, and its symbolism overworked or gratuitously violent, most praised Lynch's craftsmanship and characteristic humor. *Wild at Heart* received the Palm d'or at the Cannes Film Festival.

Lynch's best-known project to date is probably *Twin Peaks,* a television series conceived and cowritten by Lynch and scriptwriter Mark Frost. Named, like such soap operas as *Knots Landing* and *Peyton Place,* for its small-town setting, *Twin Peaks* makes use of multiple characters involved in continuous betrayals, secrets, mysteries, and conspiracies. Early episodes focus upon the efforts of Special Agent Dale Cooper, an eccentric, boyish hero sent to Twin Peaks by the Federal Bureau of Investigation, to aid local law enforcement in locating the murderer of Laura Palmer, a homecoming queen with a secret past. Adultery, drugs, mystic visions and the supernatural all figure in the serial narrative, which also features puns and non sequiturs, odd moments of situation comedy, and eccentric characters such as the Log Lady, a widow who talks to a seemingly prescient log she carries with her. Terrence Rafferty commented: "Everything that happens in *Twin Peaks* is in the normal range of TV serial drama, yet this ordinary stuff is treated with an imaginative intensity that makes it strange and new. It's as if Lynch didn't recognize any difference between the highest movie art and the lowest television craft. The story is banal, but the images grip us with as much power as anything we could see on a big screen."

(See also *Contemporary Authors,* Vol. 124.)

PRINCIPAL WORKS

SCREENPLAYS

Eraserhead   1977
The Elephant Man   [with Christopher DeVore and Eric Bergren]   1980
Dune   [adaptor; from the novel by Frank Herbert]   1984
Blue Velvet   1986
Wild at Heart   [adaptor; from the novel by Barry Gifford]   1990

OTHER

*Industrial Symphony No. 1   [with music by Angelo Badalamenti]   (performance piece)   1990
Twin Peaks   [with Mark Frost]   (television series)   1990-1991

---

*This work is available on VHS videocassette.

Jack Kroll

[In *Eraserhead*], Lynch comes amazingly close to the logic of dreams and nightmares, in which successive layers of reality seem to dissolve, sucking you into a terrifying vortex. The central figure is Henry, a kind of ultimate schlemiel whose towering pompadour is the eeriest coiffure since Elsa Lanchester's electrified marcel in the *Bride of Frankenstein*. Sweetly catatonic Henry lives alone in spartan squalor until he's joined by his equally traumatized girl and their "baby," an inhuman, squalling monster like a horrific parody of the Star-Child in *2001*. The movie clearly deals with an apocalypse, but the apocalypse is not external, not political or technological. It is internal, the ultimate corruption of matter itself throughout the universe.

Eraserhead is strikingly like the writing of the brilliant Argentinian Julio Cortázar, who could have been describing *Eraserhead* when in one of his stories he wrote about cleaving a passage through the glutinous mass that declares itself to be the world." *Eraserhead* is poor Henry's odyssey through deliquescence—a journey Lynch sometimes portrays with grim humor. When the whore across the hall seduces Henry, his ratty bed becomes a kind of sump into whose grisly waters he and the girl slowly sink, until only her hair floats garbage-like on its surface. Henry himself literally loses his head, which is promptly processed into eraser-topped pencils—the organic defeated by the inorganic.

Some of *Eraserhead* is not for the squeamish, especially the baby scenes, which, says a Los Angeles exhibitor, are particularly hard for some parents to stomach. The effects, however, are amazing for a film made on a shoestring, mainly a grant from the American Film Institute. Lynch shot the movie at night in the old stables which are part of the AFI's headquarters in Los Angeles. But, he says, the inspiration was another town, Philadelphia, where he lived for five years while studying painting at the Pennsylvania Academy of the Fine Arts. "Philadelphia is decaying, degenerate, one of the sickest places in the world," says Lynch. "There's a lot of fear in Philadelphia."

Despite this jeremiad, Lynch is an amiable Montana-born 32-year-old who says things like "Aw, shoot." *Eraserhead* is on the midnight screens of New York, Los Angeles, St. Louis and Minneapolis and, next month, San Francisco. "I wasn't thinking of a midnight audience when I made it," he says. "It was a student film. What's happened is unbelievable." Lynch is now earning his keep by playing the bit part of a painter (and doing his paintings) in the forthcoming film about Jack Kerouac, *Heartbeat,* with Nick Nolte and Sissy Spacek, who is Lynch's sister-in-law. Unlike George Romero, Lynch wants to make movies in Hollywood, or anywhere. Unless catatonic Henry is running the movie business, he'll get his chance. (pp. 95, 97)

> Jack Kroll, *"In the Werewolf Circuit," in* Newsweek, *Vol. XCII, No. 11, September 11, 1978, pp. 95, 97.*

Paul Taylor

Arriving home at his squalid apartment [in *Eraserhead*], Henry Spencer is told by the girl across the hall that his girlfriend Mary has phoned to invite him for dinner at her parents' home. There he is confronted with the news that he has fathered a premature, inhuman 'baby'. Mary moves to Henry's place with the increasingly noisy 'baby', but shortly afterwards abandons him to his fantasies about the lady who appears on a lighted stage behind the radiator (which is also in the process of producing some strange organic matter). The 'baby' falls suddenly ill, and Henry is assaulted by strange wormlike creatures. He is seduced by his neighbour. On the stage behind the radiator his head is pushed off by the 'baby' growing inside him. The head falls through space into an urban backstreet, where it is picked up and taken to a workshop, there to be processed into pencil-top erasers. Rebuffed by the girl across the hall, Henry cuts open the bandaged lower half of the 'baby' and stabs at the expanding insides. As 'baby's' head and neck grow and threaten him, Henry is consumed by a planet. Somewhere above and beyond all this, levers are being pulled.

No synopsis could adequately convey the perfect nightmare of David Lynch's extraordinary black-and-white horror: the above is necessarily impressionistic and incomplete; the film itself is an absurdist, surreal treat of repulsive beauty and grisly comedy. Over and above its perverse plot, the film's crisp imagery (often of inexplicable phenomena) and its controlled playing have a unique and eerie suggestiveness. Even though there's material enough in this post-punk dreamscape for an imaginative Freudian to have a field-day, Lynch consistently eschews symbolism and allegory and gives priority to none of the levels of inevitably decomposing 'reality' inhabited by his catatonic hero. He also refuses to indulge in isolated shocks—although the superb effects provide opportunities aplenty—and concentrates on a cumulative, suspenseful grotesquerie. Henry's unique odyssey, finally, is tracked towards an almost intimate apocalypse. Critical shorthand would probably append the work of Bosch and Beckett, and perhaps David Cronenberg and the Kuchars, as tenuous reference points, but *Eraserhead* is a movie to be experienced rather than explained.

> Paul Taylor, *in a review of "Eraserhead," in* Monthly Film Bulletin, *Vol. 46, No. 542, March, 1979, p. 44.*

Robert Asahina

According to the credits, *The Elephant Man* is "based upon the true life story of John Merrick . . . and not upon the Broadway play of the same title or any other fictional account." But truth and drama are at war in this movie, and neither is done justice by the writing or directing.

The eponymous Merrick was a cruelly misshapen cripple who became famous after he was rescued from a freak show in 1886 by a London physician, Frederick Treves (who subsequently went on to be named surgeon-in-ordinary to the Queen and later received a baronetcy from Edward VII). In his 1924 report on the case (reprinted in

The True History of the Elephant Man, by Michael Howell and Peter Ford), Treves gave the following description of his patient:

> The most striking feature about him was the enormous and misshapen head. From the brow there projected a huge bony mass like a loaf, while from the back of the head hung a bag of spongy, fungous-looking skin. . . . The osseous growth on the forehead almost occluded one eye. The circumference of the head was no less than that of the man's waist. From the upper jaw there projected another mass of bone. It protruded from the mouth like a pink stump, turning the upper lip inside out and making the mouth a mere slobbering aperture. . . . The back was horrible, because from it hung, as far down as the middle of the thigh, huge, sack-like masses of flesh covered by the same loathsome cauliflower skin. The right arm was of enormous size and shapeless. . . .

Today it is generally believed that Merrick suffered from neurofibromatosis, a disease of the central nervous system resulting in the formation of the dense fibrous tissue that was partly responsible for his freak-show name. At the time, however, Merrick's condition was tentatively diagnosed as dermatolysis (a loosened condition of the skin) and pachydermatocoele (a tumerous overgrowth of skin). His appellation also owed much to the widely circulated tale (actually his own explanation for his affliction) that Merrick's mother, late in her pregnancy, had been knocked over and terrorized by an elephant from a traveling menagerie.

When Treves eventually discovered that his deformed patient was not an imbecile, as he had at first thought, but an intellectually competent adult who had completed school through the age of 12, the Elephant Man became the star of a new kind of exhibition. London Hospital publicized Merrick's plight in an appeal for charity in the *Times,* and soon high society began trooping to his quarters for a look at, and a talk with, "such a gentle, kindly man, poor thing!" (in the words of Lady Geraldine Somerset, whose journal is quoted by Howell and Ford). Thus until his death in 1890, the Elephant Man found a peaceful refuge as a permanent patient at London Hospital.

This phenomenon of a "normal" man trapped in the body of a beast is a compelling piece of social history and psychology. It is little wonder that numerous accounts of Merrick's life have already appeared, both nonfiction and fiction—most notably, besides the Howell and Ford work, Ashley Montagu's book, *The Elephant Man: A Study in Human Dignity,* and Bernard Pomerance's play, *The Elephant Man,* which opened on Broadway last year. Indeed, the true story is so fascinating that one must wonder why the movie version, despite its claims of authenticity, treats the facts cavalierly.

For example, in the screenplay (by Christopher DeVore, Eric Bergren and David Lynch), Treves discovers Merrick's intelligence shortly after he happens upon him. Once the Elephant Man becomes a celebrity, he is kidnapped by his original exhibitor and again placed on display. In a scene that calls to mind Tod Browning's *Freaks,* the Elephant Man manages to escape while the show is touring the Continent and with considerable difficulty gets back to the hospital. There he briefly resumes his privileged life before committing suicide.

The real sequence of events was significantly different—and even more dramatic. Discovering Merrick in a shop on Whitechapel Road, Treves arranged to have him presented before the Pathological Society of London. As a precaution against any obstacles the grotesque specimen might encounter on the way to the meeting, the doctor gave the Elephant Man his calling card. Following the Pathological Society appearance, Merrick returned to the freak show and its manager, Tom Norman.

Harassed by magistrates who were cracking down on such displays, Norman sent Merrick on a tour of the Continent under the care of an Austrian manager. He abandoned the Elephant Man in Brussels. Penniless and unable to travel without attracting unwelcome attention, Merrick nevertheless succeeded in making his way across the Channel to London. His turning up at Liverpool Street station caused a tumult, but because he still had Treve's card—incredibly, after a year-and-a-half—Merrick was rescued and taken to London Hospital.

It was at this point that the doctor and his strange patient established the relationship that was to confirm the Elephant Man's pathetic humanity and make him a celebrity. He finally died in his sleep when the weight of his skull dislocated his neck. Treves speculated that Merrick, instead of going to sleep sitting up, as he normally did, tried lying on his back in "the pathetic but hopeless desire to be 'like other people.' "

I suspect the screenwriters' rearranging of the facts was inspired by their sense that the Elephant Man's life was essentially a social drama—a kind of metaphor for the ugliness of society at large. In this view Norman, Treves and all the doting upper-class Londoners barely differ from one another; they are drawn to Merrick for their own less than compassionate reasons and see little of the man within the horrible exterior.

The perspective is manifested in David Lynch's direction, . . . [which emphasizes] the horrors of Victorian society in social realist fashion. No chance is missed to linger on ugly scenes of early industrialization (workers toiling, chimneys billowing black smoke, machines creaking and groaning), although they are wholly unrelated to the plot. Nor is any opportunity to equate the doctor with the showman missed. When Treves pays Norman to have Merrick brought to the hospital, the impressario implausibly sneers at the doctor, "We understand each other completely; more than money has changed hands."

Apparently to show the nature of Victorian charity, the script also includes a meeting between the Elephant Man and Madge Kendal, a well-known Victorian actress who was one of his sponsors. This was not mentioned in her published memoirs and probably never took place. Merrick's contact with Kendal seems almost certainly to have been limited to the photographs of her that he requested and she gladly supplied.

Instead of giving us hackneyed sociology, the film could have more legitimately used such long-distance arrangements to focus on the Elephant Man's psychology—particularly his fantasy life. Howell and Ford make clear, as the movie does not, that the poignancy of Merrick's existence was heightened by the limitations his appearance placed on social contact, no matter how frequent or well-motivated. In the movie, there is one brief scene where the Elephant Man is alone in his room, sadly preening in a new suit. But for the most part the filmmakers concentrate on his external relationships, rather than finding some way to dramatize his existential aloneness.

Howell and Ford describe brief walks that Merrick took by himself in the hospital courtyard, under the cover of night, yet not one excursion of this kind is included in the film. Their book notes, too, how reading fiction filled the void in the Elephant Man's experience with the outer world:

> He was apt to speak of novels as if they were factual accounts. . . . He would describe plots as though they were events which happened recently . . . and speak of characters as though they possessed lives of their own, discussing their plights and predicaments with sincere concern.

None of this fascinating "surrogate life" is so much as hinted at in the film.

Unable or unwilling to confront the psychological drama of the Elephant Man's existence, the filmmakers lapse into expressionistic trickery. The movie opens with a fantasy sequence that shows the face of a woman (Merrick's mother, we later learn), then—in a disappointing display of literal-mindedness—a herd of elephants, followed by a shot of the woman writhing on the ground (as if being raped, instead of trampled by the animals), a cloud of smoke, and the sound of a crying baby. The ending is similarly a sort of science-fiction affair: Moments after Merrick expires on screen we actually see stars, then his mother, her face surrounded by a halo, declares gnomically, "Nothing will die." (pp. 18-19)

> *Robert Asahina, "Victorian Bestiary," in The New Leader, Vol. LXIII, No. 17, September 22, 1980, pp. 18-19.*

Vincent Canby

The time [in which *The Elephant Man* is set] is the late 1880's and the place is London, where the beau monde, the rich and fashionable as well as the mannered and the educated who aspire to higher things live in a refinement that's all the more precarious for the assaults of the Industrial Revolution, which is wrecking the social order. . . .

In such a setting it's no surprise that a kind of sad, desperate genteelness was once equated with human dignity. To be kind and polite, in such a landscape, under such circumstances, when the masses were living in such squalor, were reassuring signs of orthodoxy to a threatened London Establishment.

This is one of the vividly unexpected impressions one car-

ries away from *The Elephant Man,* David Lynch's haunting new film that's not to be confused with the current Broadway play of the same title, though both are based on the life of the same unfortunate John Merrick, the so-called Elephant Man, and both, I assume, make use of some of the same source materials. These include Sir Frederick Treves's *Elephant Man, and Other Reminiscences,* and *The Elephant Man: A Study in Dignity* by Ashley Montagu.

When he died in London in 1890 John Merrick was 27 years old. Having been grotesquely deformed at birth from a disease called neurofibromatosis, with a head twice normal size, a twisted spine and a useless right arm, John Merrick made his living exhibiting himself in a freak show until he was saved by Frederick Treves, a London surgeon. The doctor provided a tranquil home for Merrick in the London Hospital, introduced him to society and later wrote his famous book. . . .

[*The Elephant Man* is] a handsome, eerie, disturbing movie.

The Elephant Man uses some of the devices of the horror film, including ominous music, sudden cuts that shock and hints of dark things to come, but it's a very benign horror film, one in which "the creature" is the pursued instead of the pursuer.

Unlike the play, in which the actor playing John Merrick wears no make-up, his unadorned face representing the beauty of the interior man, the audience thus being forced to imagine his hideous appearance, the movie works the other way around. . . . [John Merrick] is a monster with a bulbous forehead, a Quasimodo-like mouth, one almost-obscured eye, a useless arm and crooked torso. . . .

[What] we eventually see underneath this shell is not "the study in dignity" that Ashley Montagu wrote about, but something far more poignant, a study in genteelness that somehow supressed all rage.

That is the quality that illuminates this film and makes it far more fascinating than it would be were it merely a portrait of a dignified freak. Throughout the film one longs for an explosion.

That it never comes is more terrifying, I think, than John Merrick's acceptance of the values of others is inspiring.

> *Vincent Canby, " 'Elephant Man,' Study in Genteelness," in The New York Times, October 3, 1980, p. C8.*

Pauline Kael

The Elephant Man is a very pleasurable surprise. Though I had seen *Eraserhead,* which is the only other feature directed by David Lynch, and had thought him a true original, I wasn't prepared for the strength he would bring out of understatement. It might be expected that the material—the life of John Merrick, the grievously eminent Victorian who is sometimes said to have been the ugliest man who ever lived—would push Lynch into the kind of morbid masochism that was displayed in the various versions of *The Hunchback of Notre Dame* and *The Phantom of the Opera.*

But this young director (he's thirty-four) has extraordinary taste; it's not the kind of taste that enervates artists—it's closer to grace. The movie shows us what the monster feels about himself and what his view of the world is and what he sees when he looks out of the single rectangular slit in his hood (which suggests an elephant's eye). He must see everything framed, as on a screen, and the movie gives us this sense of framed imagery—of action marked off, with curtains drawn over the surrounding material. (The stitching around the slit gives it depth, and at one point, when the hood is hanging on the wall, the camera moves right into the dark opening.) You may find yourself so absorbed that your time sense changes and you begin to examine the images with something of the same wonder that John Merrick shows when he looks at the spire of St. Philip, Stepney, from his window at the London Hospital, where he finds refuge.

The Elephant Man has the power and some of the dream logic of a silent film, yet there are also wrenching, pulsating sounds—the hissing steam and the pounding of the start of the industrial age. It's Dickensian London, with perhaps a glimpse of the processes that gave rise to Cubism. Coming from an art-school background, Lynch has rediscovered what the European avant-garde film artists of the twenties and early thirties, many of whom also came from a painting and design background, were up to, and he has combined this with an experimental approach to sound. In Merrick's fantasy life, his beautiful young mother is trampled by elephants when she is carrying him in her womb, and the sounds of those great beasts as they attack her in his dreams are the hellish sounds of industrial London, whose machines will produce their own monstrous growths. *The Elephant Man* isn't as daringly irrational as *Eraserhead,* which pulls you inside grubby, wormy states of anxiety, but it pulls you into a serene, contemplative amazement. Lynch holds you in scenes with almost no action: Merrick may be alone on the screen preening, or fondling the brushes and buffers in his gentleman's dressing case, or just laying them out in an orderly pattern and waltzing around them, like a swell, and you feel fixated, in a trance.

When Frederick Treves, the doctor who is to become Merrick's friend, first tracks him down in the illegal, hidden sideshow where he's being exhibited as the Elephant Man, Treves goes through what seem to be endless slum passageways and alleys into an abyss—the darkness where the monster huddles. Finally, he sees the pathetic deformed creature, but *we* don't. We see only Treves' reaction, and his tears falling. The grace in Lynch's work comes from care and thought: this is a film about the exhibition and exploitation of a freak, and he must have been determined not to be an exploiter himself. The monster is covered or shadowed from us in the early sequences and we see only parts of him, a little at a time. Lynch builds up our interest in seeing more in a way that seems very natural. When we're ready to see him clearly, we do. By then, we have become so sympathetic that there's no disgust about seeing his full deformity. . . . Even before

Merrick begins to speak to Treves and to recite poetry and to reveal his romantic sensibility, we have become his protectors. He's a large lumplike mass at first, but as we get to know him, and respond to his helplessness, he begins to seem very slight—almost doll-like. There's nothing frightening about him, and he's not repellent either. His misshapen body and the knobby protuberances on his forehead suggest a work of art—an Archipenko or one of Picasso's bulging distortions.

The only horror is in what we experience on his behalf. When a young nurse sees him and screams, it's *his* recoil we respond to. There is a remarkable sequence after Merrick has been kidnapped from the hospital by his London exploiter and taken to be exhibited again, this time on the continent. Too sick to stand and in despair, Merrick doesn't gratify the ticket buyers, and he is beaten so brutally that the other fairground freaks decide to free him. The giant strong man breaks the lock of the cage next to the baboons where Merrick has been put and lifts him out in his arms, and there is a dreamlike procession of the freaks in the woods along a riverbank as they help him to escape. They buy him his passage back to England, and a small group of them take him to the ship. (We're apprehensive then, because he's going to be alone.) He arrives in London by train, and as he makes his way slowly and painfully through the station his cloaked, hooded figure attracts the attention of a puzzled boy, who demands to know why he's wrapped up as he is and pelts him with a peashooter. Other kids follow him and taunt him; with only the eye slit on one side, when he clumsily tries to move faster to get away he inadvertently knocks down a little girl. People begin to chase him, and he rushes down a flight of stairs; on the landing, someone tears off his hood and he runs down more stairs and staggers into a urinal. A mob comes in after him, backing him against a wall; he moans that he is not an animal and collapses. This whole sequence is saved from being a cheap ecstasy of masochism by the fairy-tale design of the shots and the lighting. . . . The smoke that softens everything is like J. M. W. Turner clouds, but carrying poison. . . . [The grays] set a tone of emotional reserve yet make the whites and the sooty blacks, which bleed out of their contour lines, seem very passionate (the way they are in the Londoner Bill Brandt's photographs). The imagery is never naturalistic, and Lynch never pulls out all the stops.

Every time the director does something risky and new or reinterprets something very old, you know you're watching real moviemaking. Though the sound isn't nearly as inventive as it was in *Eraserhead,* whenever it's hyperbolic, like the noise of the big gongs that wake Merrick on his first night at the hospital, it has a disturbing excitement. . . . Lynch is least successful with the conventional melodramatic scenes. When the night porter at the hospital invades Merrick's room with gawkers, and two whores are shoved onto his bed, we want to climb the wall along with Merrick, and not just out of empathy: the staging is crude. And almost all the scenes of the drunken villain, Bytes, the exploiter and kidnapper, seem long, probably because you can read his standard evil piggy expressions a mile away. The scenes of . . . Mrs. Kendal, the actress whose visits to Merrick turn him into a celebrity (which leads to his being taken up by London society), feel obligatory. The first time she's close to Merrick, Mrs. Kendal shows a flicker of disgust that she covers with her actressy poise—that part is good. But after that we need to read her feelings in her eyes, and all we register is her smiley, warm mouth; she's gracious in a great-lady way that doesn't provide any clue to why she becomes involved. (pp. 82-5)

[If Merrick] were not encased in loathsome flesh, we could never believe in such delicate, saintly humility. But the film makes us understand that in a time when ugliness was thought to come from within, Merrick had to become a dandy of the soul in order to feel human. Once he's out of his cloak and into a suit, he has a soft, sidling walk, askew but airy. He's only in his twenties (he died at twenty-seven), and his wish to be good is childlike and a little cracked, but his kindness seems to come from a mystic simplicity. There's no irony in the film when he becomes a society figure—an oddity and a pet to be pampered. We see his sheer delight in being accepted among people with nice manners; his fawning gratitude is from the heart. He isn't concerned with Treves' problems of conscience about whether he, too, is exploiting Merrick's condition. Merrick knows that Treves has brought him from agony to peace. The director doesn't stray from the Victorian framework he constructs; nothing is interpreted (not even the recurrent mother-being-raped-by-elephants dream), and so nothing is sentimentalized in a modern manner.

This is not the usual movie—in which the story supports the images and holds everything together. Lynch's visual scheme is so imaginative that it transcends the by now well-known story, and scene by scene you don't know what to expect. You're seeing something new—subconscious material stirring within the format of a conventional narrative. There is perhaps nothing as eerily, baldly erotic as that moment in *Eraserhead* when two lovers deliquesce into their bed—disappearing in the fluid, with only the woman's hair left floating on top. But there is something indefinably erotic going on here; it's submerged in the film's rhythm and in the director's whole way of seeing. And wherever you look there are inexplicably satisfying images: a little barrel-chested mutt bulldog waddles across a London street with its tail stretched straight out, like a swagger stick; at the medical college, when Treves, assuming a matter-of-fact tone, presents Merrick in all his glorious deformity to the assembled doctors, a man with a big furry beard turns on the light at the start of the presentation and turns it off at the close—a silly detail to remember, but it's part of the texture, like the carriage horse that suggests a phantom, and the illumination on the cobblestones that makes them look like fish scales, and the night scene on the Continent that might be a painting, except that dawn comes up. In Merrick's dream of the trampling elephant feet, the camera swerves and swoops across the bodies of the great beasts in strange panning movements that suggest the way Merrick, who must sleep sitting up with his head on his raised knees (because of its weight), would dream, with his head wobbling and jerking. And in perhaps the most elusive series of effects, when Merrick realizes his lifelong ambition of going to the theatre and sees a Drury Lane performance of the

pantomime *Puss in Boots,* it becomes a fantasy of magical transformations, with ducks and a lion and fairies flying on wires and people who seem to be on horseback, except that the horses' legs are their own, and an ogre behind bars and swans—deliriously snooty cardboard swans. You can't be sure what you're seeing: it's like disconnected memories of the earliest stories you were told. The creatures—animal, human, birds, spirits—are all mixed up together, and the bits of glitter that fall on them have the dreamlike quality of the overturned world in the glass ball that fell from Kane's hand. In this sequence, too, there is a suggestion of the wobbling movement of the heavy head. Late that night, when Merrick, in his fresh nightshirt, smooths his clean white bedsheets—it's like another form of preening—his body seems weightless. He is ready to leave it. (pp. 85-6)

> *Pauline Kael, "The Frog Who Turned into a Prince, The Prince Who Turned into a Frog,"* in her Taking It All In, *Holt, Rinehart and Winston, 1980, pp. 82-6.*

Pauline Kael

When you come out of the theatre after seeing David Lynch's *Blue Velvet,* you certainly know that you've seen something. You wouldn't mistake frames from *Blue Velvet* for frames from any other movie. It's an anomaly—the work of a genius naïf. If you feel that there's very little art between you and the filmmaker's psyche, it may be because there's less than the usual amount of inhibition. Lynch doesn't censor his sexual fantasies, and the film's hypercharged erotic atmosphere makes it something of a trance-out, but his humor keeps breaking through, too. His fantasies may come from his unconscious, but he recognizes them for what they are, and he's tickled by them. The film is consciously purplish and consciously funny, and the two work together in an original, down-home way.

Shot in Wilmington, North Carolina, it's set in an archetypal small, sleepy city, Lumberton, where the radio station's call letters are WOOD, and the announcer says, "At the sound of the falling tree," and then, as the tree falls, "it's 9:30." Not more than three minutes into the film, you recognize that this peaceful, enchanted, white-picket-fence community, where the eighties look like the fifties, is the creepiest sleepy city you've ever seen. The subject of the movie is exactly that: the mystery and madness hidden in the "normal." At the beginning, the wide images (the film is shot in CinemaScope ratio: 2.35 to 1) are meticulously bright and sharp-edged; you feel that you're seeing every detail of the architecture, the layout of homes and apartments, the furnishings and potted plants, the women's dresses. It's so hyperfamiliar it's scary. The vivid red of the roses by the white fence makes them look like hothouse blooms, and the budding yellow tulips are poised, eager to open. Later, the light is low, but all through this movie the colors are insistent, objects may suddenly be enlarged to fill the frame, and a tiny imagined sound may be amplified to a thunderstorm. The style might be described as hallucinatory clinical realism.

When Mr. Beaumont, of Beaumont's hardware store, is watering his lawn and has a seizure of some sort—probably a cerebral hemorrhage—the water keeps shooting out. It drenches his fallen body, and a neighbor's dog jumps on top of him, frisking and trying to drink from the spray. The green grass, enlarged so that the blades are as tall as redwood trees, is teeming with big black insects, and their quarrelsome buzz and hiss displaces all other sounds. When Jeffrey Beaumont, home from college to be near his stricken father and take care of the store, walks back from a visit to the hospital, he dawdles in a vacant lot and spots something unexpected in the grass and weeds: a human ear with an attached hank of hair, and ants crawling all over it. The ear looks like a seashell; in closeup, with the camera moving into the dark canal, it becomes the cosmos, and the sound is what you hear when you put a shell to your ear—the roar of the ocean.

Jeffrey's curiosity about the severed ear—whose head it came from and why it was cut off—leads him to Lumberton's tainted underside, a netherworld of sleazy interconnections. A viewer knows intuitively that this is a coming-of-age picture—that Jeffrey's discovery of this criminal, sadomasochistic network has everything to do with his father's becoming an invalid and his own new status as an adult. It's as if David Lynch were saying, "It's a frightening world out there, and"—tapping his head—"in here."

Wholesome as Jeffrey looks, he's somewhat drawn to violence and kinkiness. But he doesn't quite know that yet, and it's certainly not how he explains himself to Sandy, a fair-haired high-school senior and the daughter of the police detective investigating the matter of the ear. She has become Jeffrey's confederate, and when she questions the nature of his interest in the case he speaks of being involved with "something that was always hidden," of being "in the middle of a mystery." Sandy tantalizes him with what she's overheard the police saying, and he tantalizes her with the strange, "hidden" things he learns about. During their scenes together, an eerie faraway organ is playing melodies that float in the air, and the sound italicizes the two kids' blarney. It's like the organ music in an old soap opera; it turns their confabs into parody, and tells us that they're in a dream world. Sometimes when Jeffrey tells Sandy what he thinks is going on it's as if he had dreamed it and then woke up and found out it had happened. Jeffrey himself is the mystery that Sandy is drawn to (perhaps the tiny gold earring he wears is part of his attraction), and you can't help giggling a little when she turns to him with a worried, earnest face and says, "I don't know if you're a detective or a pervert." She's still a kid; she thinks it's either/or. Jeffrey is soon withholding some of his adventures from her, because they're not just mysteriously erotic—they're downright carnal, and, yes, he's smack in the middle of it all. He has been pulled—with no kicking or screaming—into the inferno of corrupt adult sexuality.

Dorothy Vallens is soft and brunette and faintly, lusciously foreign; she has had a child, and she's enough older than Jeffrey to have the allure of an "experienced woman." A torch singer in a night club outside the city limits, she wears a moth-eaten mop of curls and lives at the Deep River Apartments in musty rooms that look as if they'd sprouted their own furniture. The gloomy walls—mauve gone brown—suggest the chic of an earlier era, when perhaps the building was considered fashionable (and the elevator worked). Sandy has told Jeffrey that the police think Dorothy Vallens is involved in the mutilation case, and have her under surveillance. Jeffrey puts her under closer surveillance. The moviemaker doesn't do any interpreting for you: you simply watch and listen, and what ensues rings so many bells in your head that you may get a little woozy.

Hiding in Dorothy's closet at night, Jeffrey peeks at her through the slatted door while she undresses. She hears him and, grabbing a kitchen knife, orders him out of his hiding place and forces him to strip. When he has nothing on but his shorts, she pulls them down and begins fondling him, but sends him back into the closet when she has a caller—Frank the crime boss, Mr. Macho Sleazeball himself. . . . Frank is an infantile tough-guy sadist who calls her "Mommy," wallops her if she forgets to call him "Daddy," and wallops her harder if she happens to look at him. All this seems to be part of their regular ritual; he demands his bourbon (as if he's sick of telling her), has her dim the lights, and he takes out an inhaler mask (for some unspecified gas) to heighten his sensations during sex. (The gas is probably a booster to whatever drugs he's on.) He also uses a fetish—the sash of Dorothy's blue velvet bathrobe. Jeffrey, in his closet, doesn't make a sound this time; he's transfixed by what he can just barely see. It's like a sick-joke version of the primal scene, and this curious child watches his parents do some very weird things. After Frank leaves, Jeffrey attempts to help the weary, bruised woman, but all she wants is sex. She's photographed in a clinch, with her face upside down and her ruby lips parted in a sly smile that exposes her gleaming front teeth—especially the one that has a teasing chip, as if someone had taken a small bite out of it.

When Jeffrey comes to see her again, he knocks on the door. She greets him eagerly—almost reproachfully—with "I looked for you in my closet tonight." (That line is a giddy classic.) The third night, they're on her bed after a round or two of intercourse. Trying to overcome his reluctance to hit her, she asks, "Are you a bad boy . . . do you want to do bad things?" We know the answer before he does. He's having trouble breathing. (pp. 202-05)

Dorothy is a dream of a freak. Walking around her depressing apartment in her black bra and scanties, with blue eyeshadow and red high heels, she's a woman in distress right out of the pulps; she has the plushy, tempestuous look of heroines who are described as "bewitching." . . . There's nothing of the modern American woman about her. When she's naked, she's not protected, like the stars who are pummelled into shape and lighted to show their muscular perfection. She's defenselessly, tactilely naked, like the nudes the Expressionists painted.

Jeffrey, commuting between Dorothy, the blue lady of the night, and Sandy, the sunshine girl, suggests a character left over from *Our Town.* (He lives in an indefinite mythic present that feels like the past—he's split between the older woman he has sex with but doesn't love and the girl he loves but doesn't have sex with.) (pp. 205-06)

[By contrast], Frank is lewd and dangerous; you feel he does what he does just for the hell of it. (He uses his inhaler to heighten the sensations of murder, too.) . . . [Ben, one of Frank's business associates], is a smiling wonder; you stare at his kissy makeup, the pearly jewel that he wears halfway up his ear, his druggy contentment. Frank refers to Ben as "suave," but that's not the half of it. Miming to Roy Orbison's song "In Dreams," about "the candy-colored clown they call the sandman," he's so magnetic that you momentarily forget everything else that's supposed to be going on.

Actually, it's easy to forget about the plot, because that's where Lynch's naïve approach has its disadvantages: Lumberton's subterranean criminal life needs to be as organic as the scrambling insects, and it isn't. Lynch doesn't show us how the criminals operate or how they're bound to each other. So the story isn't grounded in anything and has to be explained in little driblets of dialogue. But *Blue Velvet* has so much aural-visual humor and poetry that it's sustained despite the wobbly plot and the bland functional dialogue (that's sometimes a deliberate spoof of small-town conventionality and sometimes maybe not). It's sustained despite the fact that Lynch's imagistic talent, which is for the dark and unaccountable, flattens out in the sunlight scenes, as in the ordinary, daily moments between parents and children. One key character is never clarified: We can't tell if Sandy's father is implicated in the corruption, or if we're meant to accept him as a straight arrow out of a fifties F.B.I. picture. Lynch skimps on these commercial-movie basics and fouls up on them, too, but it's as if he were reinventing movies. His work goes back to the avant-garde filmmakers of the twenties and thirties, who were often painters—and he himself trained to be one. He takes off from the experimental traditions that Hollywood has usually ignored.

This is his first film from his own original material since *Eraserhead* (which was first shown in 1977), and in some ways it's linked to that film's stately spookiness. . . . There are also reminders of the musical numbers in *Eraserhead,* which were like a form of dementia. (Lynch used an organ there, too.) With [Dorothy] singing at the club, and vocalists like Bobby Vinton on the soundtrack, and tunes layered in and out of the orchestral score, *Blue Velvet* suggests a musical on themes from our pop unconscious. There are noises in there, of course. . . . The mix of natural sounds with mechanical-industrial noises gives the images an ambience that's hokey and gothic and yet totally unpretentious—maybe because Lynch's subject is normal American fantasy life. Even that fetishized blue velvet robe is tacky, like something you could pick up in the red brick department store on Main Street.

Blue Velvet is a comedy, yet it puts us—or, at least, some of us—in an erotic trance. The movie keeps ribbing the clean-cut Jeffrey, yet we're caught up in his imagination. It must be that Lynch's use of irrational material works the way it's supposed to: at some not fully conscious level we read his images. When Frank catches Jeffrey with "Mommy" and takes him for a ride—first to Ben's hang-

out and then to a deserted spot—the car is packed with Frank's thugs, Dorothy, in her robe, and a large-headed, big-bellied woman in a short, pink skirt who has been necking with one of the guys. When Frank parks and he and his thugs start punching out Jeffrey, the pink-skirted woman climbs up on the roof of the car and, to the sound of that sandman song, dances aimlessly, impassively, like a girl in a topless bar. (She's in her dream world, too.) In a later scene, a man who has been shot several times remains standing, but he's no longer looking at anything; he faces a one-eared dead man sitting up in a chair, with the blue velvet sash in his mouth, and the two are suspended in time, like figures posed together in a wax museum, or plaster figures by George Segal retouched by Francis Bacon. Almost every scene has something outlandishly off in it, something that jogs your memory or your thinking, like the collection of fat women at Ben's joint, who look as if they were objects in a still-life. (pp. 206-08)

It's the slightly disjunctive quality of Lynch's scenes (and the fact that we don't question them, because they don't feel arbitrary to us) that makes the movie so hypnotic—that, and the slow, assured sensuousness of his editing rhythms. This is possibly the only coming-of-age movie in which sex has the danger and the heightened excitement of a horror picture. It's the fantasy (rather than the plot) that's organic, and there's no sticky-sweet lost innocence, because the darkness was always there, inside.

The film's kinkiness isn't alienating—its naïveté keeps it from that. And its vision isn't alienating: this is American darkness—darkness in color, darkness with a happy ending. Lynch might turn out to be the first populist surrealist—a Frank Capra of dream logic. *Blue Velvet* does have a homiletic side. It's about a young man's learning through flabbergasting and violent experience to appreciate a relatively safe and manageable sex life. And when Sandy's father, speaking of the whole nightmarish business of the ear, says to Jeffrey, "It's over now," the film cuts to daylight. But with Lynch as the writer and director the homily has a little zinger. Sandy, who may have watched too many daytime soaps, has dreamed that the morbid darkness will be dispelled when thousands of robins arrive bringing love—a dream that she tells Jeffrey (to the accompaniment of organ music twitting her vision). When a plump robin lands on the kitchen windowsill, it has an insect in its beak. (pp. 208-09)

> *Pauline Kael, "Out There and in Here," in her* Hooked, *E. P. Dutton, 1985, pp. 202-09.*

Terrence Rafferty

[When David Lynch] wants to share his bad dreams with us, he doesn't fool around. *Blue Velvet* is horrifying in ways that genre horror movies never are. If in an ordinary movie, a gunk-spewing alien or a masked slasher appears on the screen, we know how to distance ourselves from our fears—by hiding our eyes, or clutching a companion's arm, or simply giggling at the conventions. None of those responses, though, protect us from the unease that images like these produce: a man having a seizure as he waters the lawn on a sunny day, the green hose gnarling around a branch just before he falls; a bruised, naked woman stumbling out of the suburban darkness to embrace the teenage hero, as his demure girlfriend looks on. . . . This is real nightmare stuff, inexplicable and thus inescapable: we don't know where it's coming from, so we don't know which way to run.

The small logging town of Lumberton, where *Blue Velvet* is set, is a bland American community, as ominous as only places that consider themselves truly safe can be. The streets are so nearly silent that no one notices the persistent, enveloping resonance, the echo, perhaps, of buzzing chainsaws; and because there's no need for much lighting, and the trees are healthy and full, Lumberton by night is voluptuously shadowed, its sidewalks, overhung with branches, like tunnels into a sensuous dark. Every image and every sound in *Blue Velvet* tells us that the ordinary is teeming with unspeakable, innumerable dangers—and some viewers will probably decide, halfway through, that the only safe place is outside the theater altogether, far, far away from the hellish Our Town that David Lynch calls home.

Part, but not all, of what makes *Blue Velvet* so unsettling is that Lynch's nightmare has a sort of irregular, homemade quality, as if it had been cooked up with familiar but not entirely wholesome ingredients—a fresh apple pie with a couple of worms poking through the crust. Lynch tells his story in the form of a boy's detective novel, the kind of tale in which an earnest young fellow happens on a mystery and resolves, on his own, to "get to the bottom of it": in its blunt expository scenes, *Blue Velvet* has the gee-whiz tone of young-adult thrillers, but the bottom of this mystery is *really* the bottom, a long, steep fall away. Lynch's hero, 19-year-old Jeffrey Beaumont, gets involved in his adventure when he finds a severed human ear in a vacant lot; the police, for some reason, figure that this discovery has something to do with a nightclub singer named Dorothy Vallens, and Jeffrey wants to know more. While she sings "Blue Velvet" under a ghastly blue spotlight in a Lumberton dive called The Slow Club, he hides in a closet in her apartment, then spies on her through the louvered door when she comes home. It's a kinky stakeout, disturbingly intimate from the moment she walks in the door: Jeffrey's gaze, and the camera, remain fixed on her as she rips off her wig, strips to black bra and panties, and walks wearily down the long, murky corridor to her bright bathroom.

This hushed sequence has a powerful grip: by this point, Jeffrey's boy-sleuth curiosity has turned into a more intense form of scrutiny, an eroticized alertness to sensual detail. Once Lynch has us watching this way with Jeffrey, really appalling things start to happen, and images seem to enter our minds in a liquid, dreamlike slow motion, one drop of perception at a time, till we're saturated, dazed with experience. What Jeffrey sees from here on is a lurid vision of the adult world, all corruption and cruelty and brutal, scary sex, magnified and made vivid by the shock to his innocence, but a little blurred, too. This stuff is coming at him (and us) out of the blue; and without a context, some link to convention or ordinary experience, nothing can be absolutely clear. When Jeffrey, still lurking in Dor-

othy's closet, watches her being abused, verbally and physically, by a deranged gangster named Frank, the sick little scene is indelible because what Lynch makes us privy to is both too much and not enough. The ugly emotions of the scene come through with overwhelming force, yet we're not quite sure what's at stake in Frank and Dorothy's relationship, and the visual style keeps us off base. From his vantage behind the slats, Jeffrey is right on top of the grotesque couple, but Lynch uses a distorting lens that makes them look farther away and slightly foreshortened—mean and pathetic figures. The lighting and décor are just as disorienting: both Frank and Dorothy have luminously pale flesh, bathed in harsh fluorescence, but neither their clothing nor the apartment's low-to-the-ground, mud-colored 1950s furniture seems to take the light at all. Everything is clear—punishingly direct—yet all the while we're straining to see more.

In passages like these, Lynch achieves a kind of radiant seediness. The drama that's played out before Jeffrey's innocent, greedy eyes, is all the more riveting for being a bit tacky: Lynch has even borrowed, artfully, the look of late fifties nudie movies, with their variable lighting, their peekaboo camera placements, their arsenal of low techniques that keep us gazing avidly, neither sated nor frustrated. *Blue Velvet* is all revealing and concealing, its shutters opening and closing so rapidly we're driven half-mad with excitement. That is to say, it's a real movie, the first one in a long time that turns the viewer's passivity into furious cognitive activity. Every image, even those that seem most shockingly new, teases us with a hint of familiarity, a glimpse of some frayed connection to home. Just as every dream has a thread of reality—corrupted but recognizable bits of remembered life—that keeps us believing in it, *Blue Velvet* maintains a constant, tantalizing hum in the background, a subliminal music like pop melodies dimly recalled. If Lynch's mystery has a key, it's the song "Blue Velvet" itself, or rather the kind of song it is: a trashy romantic ballad that can insinuate itself into the mind and get tangled with deeper, more potent impressions. What we hear in the background of *Blue Velvet,* what we struggle to identify, is Lynch's own warped oldies album of innocence and experience.

Even the roughest, potentially most alienating elements of *Blue Velvet*—the abrupt shifts of tone, the awkward dialogue, the primitive, almost childlike elisions in plot and character development—work for Lynch here, as they didn't in the failed science-fiction spectacle of *Dune,* because they're all his: his dream associations, picked up from the flotsam of 1950s and 1960s pop culture, and carried along on a relentless undertow of obsession, a somnambulist's rhythm. *Eraserhead,* which was also based on an original script by Lynch . . . , had a similar pull, but even that movie, more overtly hallucinatory, was less disturbing than this. It was a midnight movie in more ways than one—so claustrophobic, so unmistakably interior, so dark that it could only have taken place in the small hours of the morning. The more expansive *Blue Velvet,* alternating the 1950s and the 1980s, bland sunlight and rich obscurity, teen-age innocence and ripe adult corruption, is practically a new genre: the demented matinee. (pp. 383-85)

Terrence Rafferty, in a review of "Blue Velvet," in The Nation, *New York, Vol. 243, No. 12, October 18, 1986, pp. 383-85.*

Timothy Carlson

Can moviemaker David Lynch successfully bring the strange and erotically tinged vision of his *Blue Velvet* and *Eraserhead* to prime-time television? Will Lynch's *Twin Peaks,* a kind of Gothic soap opera, hook viewers on his surrealist taste for the warped fantasies that lurk beneath the surface in small-town America?

Listening to those involved in the project, you sense the whole twisted enterprise may just be TV's latest display of doing what it does best: making everything old seem new again. (p. 20)

Twin Peaks takes the dying prime-time soap, révives it with a dose of '90s surrealism and plops it all down in Middle America. In this mythical town (pop. 51,201, located 5 miles from the Canadian border), there's enough sex, family feuding and power grabbing to outdo *Dallas*— but done up in Lynch's inimitable style.

"We're just trying to reimagine the genre of the nighttime soap, the way *Hill Street Blues* did the cop show a decade ago," says Mark Frost, the series' coexecutive producer. "*Dynasty* had a campy quality—outrageously larger than life and glitzy and glamorous. David brings a certain surreal quality."

A quick look at the initial storyline suggests he's right. . . .

[*Twin Peaks* features] FBI agent Dale Cooper, called to Twin Peaks to investigate the murder of the local high school's homecoming queen. As he unravels the mystery of her death, we discover that the girl may have been leading a sordid double life. And it turns out she is hardly the only character in *Twin Peaks* who is not what she seems.

"I've always been interested in secrets. Every human being is a detective, and they are looking for the secret to be revealed."

—David Lynch, 1990

Lynch employs humorous banalities, non sequiturs and other small-town personality quirks to mesmerize the audience—and to make them care about his characters. As in a Fellini film, strange moments abound in *Twin Peaks:* one tall lawman inexplicably cries like a baby at scenes of death; a woman shows up at a public meeting carrying a log, and when Agent Cooper asks who she is, he's told, "We call her the Log Lady."

Sometimes humor emerges from the darkest moments. The camera lingers so long on the murder victim's mother sobbing over her daughter's death that many who have watched the pilot first get nervous, then laugh from tension—when will this woman quit? (p. 21)

All of this weirdness is contained in the two-hour pilot, which was shot for $3.8 million last winter near Seattle. ABC has ordered seven additional one-hour episodes, one of which just might reveal the murderer. But don't absolutely count on it. (p. 22)

David Lynch bristles when he hears that some people think he is "sending up" the soap-opera genre.

"Soap operas to me should not be camp. These are very real characters," he says. The 30-odd townsfolk whose lives will take part in the plot developments all "feel and do what they do with all their heart. Camp is not only not creative, it is putting yourself above something else that has already been done and poking fun at it. To me that is a lower kind of humor."

Many who have seen Lynch's films which are known for their often shocking scenes of violence and perversion, may wonder how a filmmaker with his distinct vision could work within the restrictions of television. Surprisingly, he welcomed the challenge.

"You can't get into certain heavier violence and sexual things that are a part of life but not a part of TV life," he says. "But the added time allows you to pay more attention to more characters, and you can concoct an elaborate tapestry of those lives. That is completely thrilling to me."

So Lynch, who had [Jeffrey Beaumont] discover an attraction for sadomasochistic sex and voyeurism in *Blue Velvet,* has to tiptoe around some more squeamish subjects. And he seems perfectly happy doing a verbal tap dance for ABC's standards-and-practices department.

"We had one line they wouldn't allow—Bobby Briggs says he wasn't going to take any 'crap off that bitch'," says Lynch. "So we rewrote it to have him say he wasn't going to take any 'oink-oink off that pretty pig'."

A strange expression, to be sure, but one Lynch insists is plausible amidst a lot of other picturesque speech in small-town America. Lynch himself was born in Missoula, Mont., and lived in Sandpoint, Idaho, and Spokane, before moving east at age 15. As a result, he has an instinctive grasp of some of the absurd turns of phrase that people use. (pp. 22-3)

"I've always been interested in secrets," says Lynch. "Every human being is a detective, and they are looking for the secret to be revealed."

So will a mass audience get *Twin Peaks,* much less get hooked on its technique? . . .

"The series definitely doesn't insult anyone's intelligence," says Frost. "We have embedded clues for the careful viewer throughout—but it is also rewarding for the casual viewer."

"You just sort of picture this kind of darkness and this wind going through the needles of these Douglas firs, and you start getting a bit of a mood coming along," says Lynch. "And if you hear footsteps, and you see a light in the window, and you start moving toward it, little by little you are sucked in. And this fantastic mood and sense of place comes along, and hopefully you want to go back and feel it each week." (p. 23)

Timothy Carlson, "Welcome to the Weird New World of 'Twin Peaks'," in TV Guide *Magazine, Vol. 38, No. 14, April 7, 1990, pp. 20-3.*

Thomas H. Stahel

[*Twin Peaks*] has been behaving like a real hit. It has not only boffo ratings, that is, but interesting scripts and characters and, above all, an effective style compounded of attention to visual and personal detail (accompanied by a certain offbeat wit), careful pacing and evocative music.

[*Twin Peaks*] is a combined detective story and soap opera that seems, at this early stage, endlessly absorbing. Its creators are David Lynch, best known for his oddly gruesome and now cult movie *Blue Velvet,* and Mark Frost, one of the writers for television's favorite of a few years back, *Hill Street Blues.* As long as these two are creating the scripts, with their peculiar mix of the horrific and the satiric, . . . the programs should hold up. For how long, is another question. How long can the disclosure of Laura Palmer's murderer be delayed? . . .

Agent Cooper, fastidious and brilliant and endowed with a wealth of eccentricities, is the central character, but because this is also a soap, there are a plethora of other odd characters involved in various love duos and trios. Sheriff Truman is seeing Widow Packard. Catherine Martell is sleeping with Audrey's father, Mr. Horne. Before she was murdered, Laura was dating both Bobby and Jimmy, but after her death, her best friend Donna, who had been going with Snake, realizes that she is really in love with Jimmy, too. Jimmy's uncle Ed, married to a harpy with an eyepatch named Nadine, is in love with a diner waitress named Norma. The other waitress, Shelly, is married to Leo but is sleeping with Bobby. Etc.

This is a simultaneous send-up of both the detective story and the soap opera, and that is its underlying wit. Besides, however, there are many goofy details that keep the viewer off-guard and interested: a policeman who cries at the scene of the crime, a phone operator who rejoices in being the feminine helpmate. And the lines. Agent Cooper, into his handheld tape recorder: "Diane, I'm speaking not only as an agent of the F.B.I. but also as a human being: What really happened between Marilyn Monroe and the Kennedys, and who really pulled the trigger on J. F. K.?" Bobby's military father, after slapping a cigarette out of his son's mouth: "To have his path made clear is the aspiration of every human being in our beclouded and tempestuous existence."

Satire is alive on primetime television. We're not dead yet. (p. 433)

Thomas H. Stahel, "Getting Down with Documentaries, Sending Up with Satire," in America, *Vol. 162, No. 16, April 28, 1990, pp. 432-33.*

Stuart Klawans

Like a creature that has developed a single, oversized organ at the expense of the rest of its withered body, Lynch is a misshapen talent, oddly evolved to fit an odd cultural niche. He hasn't the slightest interest in the world around him. His images invariably seem to emerge from a soundstage, even when shot on location. His actors reveal only the gestures and turns of phrase of other actors. You will never feel the shock of recognition in a Lynch film, only shock itself. Nor is there a purpose to the jolt. Though Lynch's abundant stock of absurdities, incongruities and asides sometimes teases the viewer with a hint of profundity, nothing adds up in his pictures. He is as incapable of argument as of documentation. What he *can* do— and he does it supremely well—is draw the viewer into that mood of willful oneirism, using visual effects that are both dazzling and indelible.

Wild at Heart is his latest foray into the land of waking dreams. . . . [The film] is the story of young lovers on the run, from a Carolinas town called Cape Fear to New Orleans to a hellhole known as Big Tuna, Texas. (p. 285)

The proceedings get started with a bang. Immediately after the credits, there's an uncommonly bloody killing, which lands Sailor in jail. On his release—effected with a simple title card, announcing that time has passed—Lula picks him up in a black Thunderbird convertible. Cool cars, sunglasses and plenty of rock music are essential to a filmmaker of Lynch's aspirations. So, too, is dialogue that sounds like *Cliffs Notes* for the movie. Such is Sailor's comment when Lula hands him his beloved snakeskin jacket: "For me, it is a symbol of individuality and my belief in personal freedom." Then it's off for some hot sex, more rock and roll, more hot sex, a few flashbacks of violence. What can the lovers possibly do for a follow-up, except leave the state and break Sailor's parole?

What follows is mannered, arch, empty, labored, expertly made and intermittently thrilling. Though scene flows effortlessly into scene—no one is better than Lynch at transitions—I remember the events in pieces. A man on fire runs through a suburban living room. A young woman, injured in a car wreck, pokes uncomprehendingly at the bloody hole in her scalp. Lula, undergoing an abortion, lies under a doctor's magnifying lamp, her face appearing outsized while her tiny arms thrash helplessly. Many of the shots are enthralling, even when they're without incident—for example, the view of the roadside at night, seen as a horizontal band of shadowy green, rushing past beneath impenetrable blackness. There are also a few sequences, full of incident, that pull you all the way into the dream. The best of them, the great set piece of *Wild at Heart,* is a confrontation in a motel room between Lula and Bobby Peru, Big Tuna's incarnation of evil. It's so intense an encounter that I could all but feel the breath coming through Bobby's rotten teeth.

Then Bobby left. He had shown his power over Lula; and Lynch had demonstrated much the same thing to me. Once more, he had proved he could push my buttons, and once more he'd turned out to have no good reason for pushing them. I felt used. I also felt that this scene, like certain episodes of *Blue Velvet,* exposed the vacuum in Lynch. In its own sick way, *Wild at Heart* is as much a brainless, heartless spectacle as *Indiana Jones and the Temple of Doom.* The difference is that Spielberg engineered his movie-as-rollercoaster for a general audience. Lynch constructs his for an audience that wants to feel wised-up, decadent, better than the Spielbergian middle class.

At this point, Lynch's fans, most of my friends among them, might object that his dreams are so troubled that one's complicit enjoyment of them is itself an act of culpability. By taking to a personal extreme the oneiric and plastic qualities of film, he draws the audience into a more conscious engagement with its desires. It sounds plausible; and if movies are indeed commentaries on a dream rather than mirrors of reality, what more can they honestly offer? So let me suggest a counterexample: Brian DePalma's *Blow Out,* a film so self-enclosed that *The Village Voice*'s J. Hoberman has likened it to a Möbius strip.

Blow Out is, in fact, a circular story with a twist, and it's all surface. Based explicitly on Antonioni's *Blow-Up,* with an added debt to Coppola's *The Conversation,* the picture is at every level a film about film. The protagonist lives within movies. His setting, too, is made up: a mythical city named Philadelphia, central to the history of an imaginary nation called the United States. In this never-never land, the women all have to sell their bodies in one way or another to survive, while the men make a living selling each other pictures of the women. You realize, of course, that this is a fantasy; and DePalma tells you as much in every way he knows how. Still, you leave the theater devastated for these phony characters in their invented country, and for yourself and your own nation as well. For all its artifice, *Blow Out* has weight, purpose, moral power. It's not a balanced film, but it's a great one.

Wild at Heart, on the other hand, is not only lopsided and brilliant but utterly cynical as well. That's a striking conjunction, given the way Lynch's work has been received. His best-known production, *Twin Peaks,* made its mark by providing just what we all want from television—sex, violence and easy laughs—delivering them more amply than the competition and with greater style. So why don't people just say that *Twin Peaks*—and *Wild at Heart* and *Blue Velvet*—are cheap thrills in expensive wrappers? (To take one example out of many: *The New York Times* puffed *Wild at Heart* just before its release by lauding the "unsettling vision" of David Lynch, "the reigning master of locating the bizarre, the surreal and the disturbing in American life.") You'd think, for all the hype, that Lynch's pictures were works of pioneering artistry, suitable to be stuck on a museum wall right next to *Un Chien Andalou.* More likely, though, they're empty artifacts of that cultural niche I mentioned at the beginning of this piece, the milieu of the institutional avant-garde.

Whenever you hear the words *disturbing, transgressive* and *subversive* tossed around, whenever rules are supposedly being broken and authorities challenged, you may assume you're in avant-garde territory. You're among the institutional avant-garde when the transgressors have M.F.A. degrees from good schools and are on a first-name basis with at least three arts administrators. This is the setting in which the avant-garde becomes avant-gardism, one more item in a repertory of styles—an approved, accredited part of the curriculum, to be studied in academies and practiced for the approbation of one's fellow professionals. If Lynch is a pioneer, it's because he has converted this outrage-by-the-numbers avant-gardism into mainstream, commercial success. Think of him as the boy voted Most Likely to Succeed, in a school where the other class notables include Robert Mapplethorpe and Karen Finley.

We might as well forgive the average tourist from Mars for assuming that the names I've just brought together represent America's greatest contemporary artists. Is that entirely a function of notoriety—sought-after and profitable in one case, unwanted in the others, who had their fame thrust upon them by a cabal of sleazoid politicians and Bible-thumpers? Or is there a real resemblance among these classmates? (pp. 285-87)

[If] we can bear for a moment to forget public policy and think about art, we might notice a powerful odor of bad faith arising from the vicinity of the institutional avant-garde. It's the smell of subversion that wants to be risk-free. First comes the self-validating gesture of declaring that all works of art should aspire to the condition of avant-gardism, if they're to be taken seriously; then comes the refusal to play out the consequences. For example: It's shabby to complain that performance artists, those descendants of the Dadaists, will soon have nowhere to perform, given that all the major venues receive government funds. Think of the *real* Dadaists in Berlin, who staged their events not in art galleries or at the local equivalent of Lincoln Center but in churches and bars and cafes, especially the ones where they weren't welcome. Think of the Berlin Dadaist Franz Jung, who in 1923 chose to express himself by hijacking a German freighter in the Baltic and taking it to Petrograd, where he turned the ship over to the Soviet authorities. There's an avant-gardist I can respect.

What I can't respect is work that denies all of the traditional, nontransgressive functions of art while simultaneously turning away from the risks of engagement with the world. Sometimes, on the excuse of favoring strong content over mere style, the artists and their flacks turn against the notion of formal skill. Sometimes, as with David Lynch, formal skill is all the artist provides. In either case, the presumed assault on bourgeois order is safely contained—in an art gallery, at a performing arts center, on the screen. The danger of the image is assumed; the image of danger is all that's demanded.

I came out of *Wild at Heart* feeling sick of images, sick of irony, sick of a copycat avant-garde that's addicted to money and applause. The poor get locked out of their jobs, get tossed out of their homes, get shot by stray bullets at the rate of one a day; and the college-educated play at wanting to be disturbed.

Tourists from Mars, wherever you travel next, try to speak kindly of us. The truth is too great a shame. (p. 287)

Stuart Klawans, in a review of "Wild at

Heart," in The Nation, *New York, Vol. 251, No. 8, September 17, 1990, pp. 284-87.*

Joseph Sobran

Wild at Heart, David Lynch recently conceded, is "not a film for everyone." Maybe he's right. It begins with the hero bashing open the skull of a black who pulls a knife on him. After a brief prison term, he elopes cross-country with the girl he was fighting over; they have frequent and fairly explicit sex along the way. Her mother, who it transpires has tried to seduce him in a public toilet, sends several men to murder him. On the road, the lovers come across a bloody traffic accident. Meanwhile, a rich mobster sits on a toilet talking into his telephone as naked women attend him. During an armed robbery, one man is vividly decapitated; another has a hand shot off, and as he crawls around in his own blood trying to find it a dog trots out the back door holding it in its teeth. At different points in the film, both mother and daughter vomit, and a man is murdered in a sort of voodoo rite. Oh, and the hero gets his nose swollen in a fistfight.

I hope I haven't given the wrong impression: *Wild at Heart* is a comedy.

And believe it or not, it *is* pretty funny. The two lovers, Sailor and Lula, are a pair of losers who are in over their heads. They stick together in dopey devotion as gory misadventures befall them. "This whole world is wild at heart and weird on top," Lula wails. Sailor faces everything with the polite, stoical stupidity of an Elvis Presley, whom he explicitly resembles; in one wonderfully sweet and funny scene, a hard-rock band turns into a backup group for [Sailor's] dead-on Elvis imitation as girls scream and swoon. He proudly wears an outlandish snakeskin jacket, which he says "represents my individuality and my belief in personal freedom," a slightly cracked credo that gets more endearing every time he repeats it. Other eccentric characters keep roaming in and out, most of whom have nothing to do with the plot. Then again Sailor and Lula don't have much to do with the plot either. They more or less outrun it.

But even the jokes have an eerie edge. *Wild at Heart* has Lynch's trademark themes: death, violence, mutilation, deformity, sex, kinkiness, secret traumas—but at the heart of it all, an innocence that escapes being overwhelmed by the monstrosities around it. The innocence is what makes the rest so scary. You never know *what* will happen next in a Lynch film; you feel trapped and fascinated, as in a dream. "Dreamlike" is the word most often used to describe his films. Dreams, disturbing flashbacks, and strange images are his stock in trade. . . .

If there's any sort of philosophy behind his work, it's probably something like what [Lynch] recently told *Rolling Stone* [see reference to David Breskin in Further Reading list]:

> There are too many possibilities for something to go wrong—so you could always worry about that. And there's many things that are hidden and seeming like many, many secrets; and you don't know for sure whether you are being just paranoid or if there really are some secrets. You know little by little, just by studying science, that certain things are hidden—there are things you can't see. And your mind can begin to create many things to worry about. And then once you're exposed to fearful things, and you see that really and truly many, many, many things are wrong—and so many people are participating in strange and horrible things—you begin to worry that the peaceful, happy life could vanish or be threatened.

He's said to have scolded a woman on the set for swearing too much. (p. 38)

Twin Peaks, subject to TV's constraints of decency and decorum, shows that Lynch can give his intuition subtler expression when he doesn't make use of shocking extremes. A girl's body washes up on shore. The town is stunned. Everyone knew her. She turns out to have led a double life. So does everyone else in town.

"Who killed Laura Palmer?" has become a sort of marketing slogan for *Twin Peaks,* but it's hard to imagine a solution. Lynch is about as far from Agatha Christie as you can get. Not only is the tightly woven plot alien to his style; it's not even clear what the ground rules (if any) are in his world.

The real interest of the series lies in the delineation of the populace of Twin Peaks itself. Everyone turns out to have idiosyncrasies. The FBI man who is sent to investigate Laura's death is a little pixilated too; he dictates endlessly into his pocket tape recorder, not omitting such details as what he's snacking on at the moment, and he announces that he plans to crack the case with the use of a Tibetan mystical technique he has learned of. In one sequence he dreams he is several years older, sitting in a red-curtained room with a dwarf and a dead ringer for Laura, both of whom utter nonsequiturs in accents so strange as to require subtitles. Then he bolts up in bed, calls the sheriff, and says he knows who killed Laura—but, having awakened the sheriff in the dead of night, says he won't tell who until they meet in the morning.

It's funny, but in a funny way. There are no mandatory laughs in Lynch's work; even the broadest jokes seem to be private. Good and evil are clearly—even violently—distinguished, but, otherwise, the normal and the abnormal keep close company, even within a single character. Lynch is so interested in loose ends for their own sake that it's almost impossible to conceive of a satisfying resolution for *Twin Peaks.* In the same way, *Blue Velvet's* happy ending, an Ozzie-and-Harriet return to suburban bliss, seemed forced. (p. 40)

Nearly everything that has been said against *Wild at Heart,* and against Lynch generally, strikes me as true enough. There are obvious risks in an eccentric making films about eccentrics. All I can say is that Lynch is something new under the sun. If you can bear to watch him, you can't bear *not* to watch him. For all their violence, his films aren't cruel to the viewer in the manner of *Total Recall* and a hundred slasher movies. They contain indefensible obscenities, but their spirit is monogamous. They move in dangerous territory, but they know right from wrong.

Society doesn't have many secrets left. Individuals do, but each of us knows in principle how strange any of the others may be. In Lynch's films, "normal" is something you act, not something you effortlessly are, and private and secret selves spill out unpredictably. Closely observed, nobody is average. When he keeps this intuition under control, Lynch is funny, scary, and utterly riveting. His awareness of human queerness gives him acres of territory all to himself. His refusal to turn it into a statement means you can't outguess him. Even *he* seems not to know what happens next.

Still, what magic! Life *is* awfully weird, now that you mention it—in America and elsewhere. Someone has noticed! Someone with a camera and an imagination and the wit to spot the specifically American expressions of it, without being anti-American in his attitude toward it all. He'll bear watching. (pp. 40, 52)

> *Joseph Sobran, "Weird America," in* National Review, *New York, Vol. 42, October 1, 1990, pp. 38, 40, 52.*

John Simon

Love, the saying goes, conquers all. But not, I must insist, stupidity, as David Lynch's new film, *Wild at Heart,* amply demonstrates. And I don't mean just the stupidity of its main characters, Lula and Sailor, two near-imbecile juveniles who want nothing from life but continuous sprees and incontinent sex. I mean especially the stupidity of their creator, David Lynch. For that is the overarching characteristic of his oeuvre, from *Eraserhead* through *The Elephant Man, Dune,* and *Blue Velvet,* to the current *Wild at Heart.* I can't speak about *Twin Peaks,* because the one thing I will not stoop to is TV soaps, regardless of how titillatingly unwashed. But I assume that television's self-censorship is powerfully craven enough to sanitize even the most unleashed minds.

Wild at Heart is a cul-de-sac of a road movie in which nothing leads anywhere or makes the barest minimum of sense. Sailor, a shiftless youth with an Elvis complex and prison record, and Lula, a benighted girl with a Marilyn fixation and a demented mother, set out on a wild drive from the Carolinas to California, pursued by the crazily jealous and vengeful mother's bravos (killers, not kudos) and beset by assorted *mauvaises rencontres.* They hit New Orleans, and get as far as Big Tuna, Texas, singing, dancing, fornicating, and exchanging loopy banalities all the way. (Sample: "I'm sorry, Sailor, but the ozone layer is disappearing.") In Tuna, Sailor gets involved in a robbery, is jailed again, but, after serving five years, ten months, and 21 days (the script is maniacally specific about prison terms), rejoins his woman and hitherto unseen son, and, after a brief contretemps, the three of them are off and running again.

This may sound harmless enough, but Lynch throws in every kind of imbecility, perversity, and disgustingness (most of them gratuitous) he can think of, with only the X rating the limit. If he were a less successful filmmaker—this garbage walked, or drove, off with the Golden Palm at Cannes—the movie might indeed have earned an X; as it is, something had to be snipped after Cannes. Why does Lynch win over juries and critics (audiences, alas, are beyond explication and help)? There is a clue in Lula's exclamation in a moment of postcoital pensiveness, "This whole world is wild at heart and weird on top." The typical movie reviewer is weaned on top but child (or infant) at heart.

Characteristic of the film is an incident at the Texas motel. Sailor is away on some fishy Tuna business while Lula, as is her wont, lolls around in bed awaiting their next sexual bout. Only lately she's been feeling queasy (it turns out she's pregnant) and when Sailor, returning, asks why it "smells so terrible," she calmly informs him she's thrown up on the rug. Neither of them makes the slightest move to clean up the mess, not even when, for some time to come, every visitor comments on the stench. (pp. 46-7)

There is no need to review in detail this film that proffers a busted skull with the brain oozing out; a head (another one) blown off with part of it landing near the camera; a set of wired, brown, apocopated teeth on a smiling villain; a car-wreck victim spouting blood in a tight shot; a fellow getting his kicks out of cramming cockroaches into his underwear; Marietta, Lula's mother, smearing her entire face with lipstick till her head becomes a Halloween pumpkin—or, rather, tomato; as well as the odd form of sexual deviation, but kept carefully soft-core. If this stuff were integrated into some sort of schema; if it shed any sort of light, however lurid; if it created at least some plausible atmosphere, very well; but no, Lynch will have no truck with credibility, and uses Barry Gifford's trashy underlying novel only as an excuse for his own aberrations.

Though it may also be sick, Lynch's oeuvre is, above all, stupid. Thus in *The Elephant Man,* Lynch showed us the horribly misshapen hero's face, which the play (on which the film *claimed* not to be based) had the sense to spare us; a disfigurement, by the way, he quite unscientifically turned into a Dumbo head out of some demented version of Disney. Thus *Dune* was a film that could not be followed from one moment to the next. Thus *Blue Velvet,* though likewise utter nonsense, managed, because of its seeming novelty and a semblance of control, to garner almost unanimous raves.

In interviews, Lynch is always mild-mannered, self-effacing, platitudinous, and thoroughly boring. Are his movies, then, the forbidden fantasies of a psychotic Walter Mitty? Or are the interviews the canny dissemblings of a genuine sociopath? There may be a conundrum here, but the movies are too mindless to justify analyzing the mind behind them. "The way your head works is God's private mystery," says one character about another in *Wild at Heart;* it could be any one of them talking about any other. What *is* worth analyzing is the critical mind, which, though largely unimpressed by Lynch's latest, was almost without exception taken in by *Blue Velvet.*

The answer, I reiterate, is infantilism. Film critics—and I cannot in good conscience exempt myself, although I adduce as an extenuating circumstance that I also review most of the other arts—are childish. They spend their time on an art form (and, unlike some highbrows, I insist that it is one) that has lapsed far too early into its second childhood and, at least in America, seems to produce nothing but infantile violence, infantile sex, or infantile humor. To which, latterly, may be added infantile metaphysics: movies about persons who die and come back as ghosts to protect their loved ones or pleasurably scarify the audience, either way indulging folks for whom even this life may be more than they deserve with promises of an afterlife of which they are certifiably unworthy. (p. 47)

The final grossout for me—and the final proof of Lynch's debility—is the running parallel to *The Wizard of Oz.* Lula perceives herself as Dorothy on the Yellow Brick Road, sometimes even wearing the red shoes, and often seeing her mother as, literally, the Wicked Witch pursuing her and Sailor. The dialogue is studded with references to Oz, and the *deus ex machina* comes in the shape of the Good Witch descending in a soap bubble.

If you are still asking why the top prize-winner at Cannes should have been more cinemetic than cinematic, part of the answer may be the European, and more particularly French, attitude toward America. Out of a combination of envy and arrogance, Europeans love to see Americans make pigs and asses of themselves in their movies. It enables the Europeans to cling to a sense of superiority that grows daily less founded. Meanwhile our own audiences enjoy such movies as a spiritual mud bath. Love may be a great leveler, but muck is an even greater one. (p. 48)

John Simon, "Droopy Loves Drippy," in Na-
tional Review, New York, Vol. 42, October 1,
1990, pp. 46-8.

Kathleen Murphy

Back in the days when James Dean was only half a decade dead and Elvis Presley as many years famous, my best friend and I twice played hookey from high school to see Sidney Lumet's *The Fugitive Kind.* On screen in brooding black-and-white, Tennessee Williams' surreal parable—originally *Orpheus Descending*—played like an overheated projection of our small-town dreams and nightmares. Poised to take any road, college-bound in a few months, we imagined in our terrible innocence that it might be possible to beat our way clear of Our Town's soul-killing dumbness and repression. For us, Lady Torrance . . . and Valentine Xavier . . . acted as something like outlaw parents, larger than life in their sexual authority. We understood that this beatnik Adam and Eve could not escape crucifixion by the community's paternalistic thugs: Gardens, artists, blacks, holy sluts and studs—any life that moved and flourished outside the townsfolk's small ken— had to be burned down.

In the ashes of the film's last conflagration, an old black "conjure man" uncovers Brando's signature snakeskin jacket, the advertisement of his wild-child sexuality and the promise of future comebacks. It's Carol Cutrere, a lost soul once jailed as a "lewd vagrant," who falls natural heir to Brando's mantle: "Wild things leave skins behind. . . .

They leave clean skins and teeth and white bones, and these are tokens passed from one to another so that the fugitive kind can follow their kind." When this born-again blonde—a dirty sailor's-cap pulled down over her unkempt hair, her eyes bleared by mascara and too much "jukin' "—slides into her mud-spattered white Jaguar and drives out of town at dawn, she's blessed by more radiance than Lumet's little corner of Hell has yet permitted. Her going is witnessed by a lively bird perched on an overarching branch in the foreground. No bug is being scissored to death in the beak of that robin, if robin it is. For my best friend and me, lewd vagrants that we fancied ourselves to be, *The Fugitive Kind* was a ticket to ride, leaving our Lumberton far behind in the hope that life in a road movie might lead to Heaven.

Thirty years later comes *Wild at Heart,* a film about two cheerfully lewd vagrants for the Nineties, Sailor Ripley and Lula Pace Fortune. And director David Lynch, for whom a road movie is just another birth canal, has deliberately swaddled his hero in that familiar snakeskin jacket. While the deeply romantic narrative of *The Fugitive Kind* labored to deliver a bird from its cage, *Wild at Heart's* storyline takes the form of a snake whose tail ends up in its mouth.

With some few exceptions, this sterile circle breeds only a litter of quotation marks. As voyeurs, we're encouraged to twitch and giggle at bracketed reality: well-known detritus from pop-culture memory; a kind of cinematic vogue-ing that passes for the play of human emotions; and the obligatory directorial grotesqueries that TV's *Twin Peaks* has overdemocratized. Scarcely any character evolution occurs in the space and time between *Wild at Heart's* Cape Fear, the big N.O., and Big Tuna, between Sailor Ripley's first "Stab it and steer!" and the mother-and-child reunion in a traffic jam at film's end. Only the lunatic purity of the performances . . . shines in this postmodernist cul-de-sac.

All of Lynch's work—like Hitchcock's—can be described as emotionally infantile. But when he's in perverse touch with his mommy-Muse, the authenticity of his unweaned (and probably not yet toilet-trained) vision is unimpeachably compelling. Lynch likes to ride his camera into orifices (a burlap hood's eyehole or a severed ear), to plumb the blackness beyond. There, id-deep, he fans out his deck of dirty pictures—flat, bright snapshots a child's shocked eyes might make of an alien landscape charged with inexplicable sex and violence. But the disturbing power of those primary-color Polaroids depends on our fear of the dark. Save for death's roadside attraction and Bobby Peru's Ozian monkey demon, *Wild at Heart* offers only trivial thrills, cheap-jack spooks and mysteries. It's very like a *Saturday Night Live* spoof of Lynchland.

Even when . . . [Lula's mother] Marietta gets Kali-faced, she doesn't make it as the devouring mother of a kid's worst nightmare. Her bloody mask is just a neon smear of lipstick because Ladd plays it like a put-on: there's no night in her. To gauge how far short she falls, one has only to recall the kewpie-doll star of that tacky little theater down in the dark behind the radiator in *Eraserhead*—a pouch-cheeked miniature mommy who whisper-sings . . .

her mesmerizing invitation, "In Heaven everything is fine," while sweetly squashing sperm and inspiring a little man literally to lose his head over her.

In Lynchland, good and bad mommies, witches and fairies, pretty much run the show, keeping the players on a short tether. Such power is mystery, generating a free-floating, primal anxiety that Lynchians breathe in and out like air. . . . In many of Lynch's dreamlike films, there's a strong pull—dreaded and desired—back to the womb. *Eraserhead* begins with what may be a psychotic fantasy of conception: Henry Spencer's floating horizontal head flanked by a sperm-shaped thing that eventually zooms into a heavenly hole, brimming with cosmic light. Later, Henry loses his adult, human head; it's replaced by a mindlessly screaming baby/penis, the twin of his own ever-hungry offspring. Only after he's done away with the baby—his own hot needs—can he get back to Heaven. There he is wrapped in the sticky embrace of his kewpie-doll angel, her halo of frizzy flax far brighter than the hair either of his lubricious mother-in-law or his sexless wife.

In Lynch, anatomy is often indiscriminately sexualized. The nasty parts can change shape or location, even live a life of their own. Mouths are confused with vaginas, noses with phalluses. In the aftermath of the enigmatic rape by *Wild at Heart's* Uncle Pooch, Lula's hymeneal blood

John Nance as Henry in Eraserhead

seems to have migrated north, to her mouth; and Sailor Ripley's nose must be broken to tame him into a family man. Often, Lynch's characters make a desperate bid for self-sufficiency in the form of an obsessive interest in oral gratification, but such appetites only reenact an old attachment. (In *Dune* Lynch achieved a solipsistic extreme by making the Harkonnens an incestuous, all-male hive, every clan member's chest fitted with a "heart plug" that could be readily yanked so that they could drink each other to death at will.)

In the first moments of *The Elephant Man,* the camera touches on a woman's eyes, her mouth, then the full-face portrait of the mother whom John Merrick has deified in his conscious life. But this is uncensored dream, where he hears the sounds of steam pistons lifting and falling while the huge shapes of elephants lumber across the woman's portrait, their squealing and trumpeting an echo of *Eraserhead's* loudly libidinous baby/penis. Mother is now on her back, her head twisting wildly from side to side, in pain or pleasure. Is this sexual orgasm or childbirth, an imagined Oedipal rape or a memory of birth trauma? The truth is as all-inclusive and guilty as that which drives *Blue Velvet's* Dennis Hopper as he sucks on his oxygen mask—a kind of mini-trunk—while staring at the darkness between Isabella Rossellini's legs: "Daddy's coming home." When John Merrick dies, he is transmogrified, like *Eraserhead's* Henry Spencer, into a cloud of dust that returns to that familiar circle of light, euphemized here from heavenly hole to mother's face, then eyes, set among the stars.

Merrick's elephantine disfigurement is the visible stigmata of his failure to be a "good" son to his mother: he has, in dreams, lusted to penetrate her in any way possible. Just before reaching the freakshow corner where Merrick is displayed, Lynch's camera passes a jar in which a foetus floats, labeled "THE FRUIT OF ORIGINAL SIN." What that large-headed worm calls up, along with *Eraserhead's* baby/penis and *Blue Velvet's* oxygen-masked, "I'll fuck anything that moves" enfant terrible, are the down-and-dirty realities that flesh is heir to, and that Lynchians find it difficult to face. "I am not an animal!" Merrick screams as he's cornered in the lavatory, where all the oral and anal evidence of our nonangelic natures emerges. Anti-Darwinian Lynch would like to halt process altogether, shut the steaming flesh-factory down, so that his characters might be forever young and pure, secure in their faith in the Wizard of Oz and Santa Claus.

Thus, John Merrick is more than happy to play Romeo to Mrs. Kendall's sweetly maternal Juliet, and to bury the memory of his monkey-cage sojourn in the magic of her theater full of mythologized beasties and an airborne fairy. Similarly, . . . Sandy, the blond angel in *Blue Velvet,* rescues Jeffrey from any permanent fall into the darkness behind his brain by letting the robins loose against subterranean buglife. (No such cure is offered Lula's cousin Dell . . . in *Wild at Heart* when he enjoys not ants but cockroaches in his pants.)

It's no wonder Lynch's characters are rather short on dramatic will and spontaneity, often freezing into absurd, cartoonlike poses for lack of any whole-hearted sense of self;

their existence is always a function of someone else's more powerful conceptual sway, the mother who made them. In Lumet-Williams' *The Fugitive Kind,* . . . [Valentine Xavier possessed] such powerfully knowing innocence that his snakeskin jacket was an organic part of his being—the earthy balance to the bird-soul that, he explains, touches down only in death. His sexual healing of thwarted mother Magnani and the new life that's born of their union is only partially done in by Death, a rotting, impotent old man—a male version of *Wild at Heart's* Marietta and, like her, responsible for burning a father.

In *Wild at Heart,* lost child Sailor Ripley camouflages himself in the skins of adults: the jacket he compulsively totemizes as "a symbol of my individuality and personal freedom," and the persona of rock god Elvis Presley, a latterday Orpheus who perished in the hell of his own body. Someone called *Wild at Heart* "Elvis and Marilyn on the Road to Oz"; it's apt that the patron saints of Lynch's film should be icons of arrested development, dead of oral gratification. To conflate fictions, Sailor is a Lynchian Peter Pan on the run with Tinker Bell, looking to score eternal, untroubled prepubescence, not from the Wizard of Oz—no male has the power to confer that kind of absolution in Lynchland—but from Glinda, the Good Witch.

Staying on the Yellow Brick Road requires armored innocence on the parts of Sailor and Lula, willed blindness to the facts of life outside fairy tales—those "bad ideas" that are the disease of adulthood. What causes Sailor's psychotic tantrum in the opening moments of *Wild at Heart* is his temptation in the toilet by his mother-in-law, her attempt to make him sink into that subterranean knowledge he keeps at bay with music, sanitized sex, and lots of smokes. When Marietta's minion Bob Ray Lemon, the first of the movie's dark angels, spews dirty talk full in his face, Sailor's flat-toned "Uh oh" signals his censor has kicked in: such bad ideas must be beaten out of mind—literally.

Victorious, he takes time to light up, plugging a pacifier into his mouth before aiming his arm and finger like a gun in primal accusation of the wicked mother above him. It's an archetypal, almost hieratic tableau: mother, daughter, and son/lover paralyzed in a typically Lynchian triangle, the evidence of their complicity momentarily quashed. Here and the two other occasions in *Wild at Heart* when Sailor and Lula teeter dangerously on the verge of epiphany, something like real passion moves in this otherwise bloodless, often silly movie.

In *The Fugitive Kind,* when Marlon Brando sleepily assures Magnani "I can burn a woman down," his flat-out sexual hubris hits home. But *Wild at Heart's* "hotter than Georgia asphalt" sex plays to an audience conditioned to read such bravado as all style and no content. Add to this Lynch's tendency to locate the erotic only in the forbidden, and the heat raised by the couplings of his innocents becomes more a matter of clichéd simile, sex within the parentheses of all-consuming flames, than the real thing. Bathed in the golden or ruddy glow of Lynchian womb-light, Sailor and Lula appear to be locked into commercials for lust rather than sex itself. Like precocious preteens, their climaxes come more in shared smokes and anecdotes than in their bodies' most secret places. Fucking is just the jig they do in bed—can it be as graceless, separate, and lacking in sensuality as their teenybopper crouching and pumping on the dancefloor?

Lula's little-girl mantra—"If we can stay in love for the rest of our lives, the future will be so simple and nice"—depends on a kind of terrible stasis, an idealism that can't survive experience. But booking space on a pop-art Grecian urn turns dicey as Lula and Sailor happen upon Death's roadwork, in a sequence that is Lynch at his hallucinatory best.

Ghostly clothes drift along a night highway. A bloodied figure staggers in and out of the headlights of an overturned car. A girl, scalp awry and dead on her feet, whines that her mother will kill her for losing her purse. Death bares its face, its mouth filling with blood. Self-absorbed to a fault, Lula crosses her fingers and hopes "seeing that girl die doesn't jinx us." Too late: change is in the wind and it carries the stench of morning sickness, and Bobby Peru's bad teeth.

The best thing in *Wild at Heart,* the film's second dark angel is up to the same tricks as the first, but he's less easily exorcised. Every time Bobby Peru skins his lips back from those horrible brown stumps, he rubs our noses in mad monkey-life, the reeking, rutting animal who crouches somewhere in even the most evolved of skulls. Here is mortality at its ugliest, signaled by gross appetite and decay ("My one-eyed jack's a-yearnin' to go a-peepin' in a seafood store"). Lula and Sailor are no match for him; he breaks their fragile faith in themselves and each other. His cold-blooded turn-on of Lula is shot like a dirty movie, graphic and up close in the unadulterated light of day. No amount of clicking her red shoes together can get Lula back to "nice and simple" Kansas. She's been made to acknowledge the unsunny places in her own sexuality, the mindless autonomy of the flesh.

Because Sailor and Lula have been eviscerated of anything like evolving souls, their fates are ultimately settled by a deus ex machina—harpie Marietta having conveniently melted away into a heavenly blond fairy. Lynchland's version of Eden is open for business again, that little Fruit of Knowledge incident forgiven and forgotten. By film's end, Lula seems to have permanently stiffened into Marilyn Monroe's classic posture of infantile ecstasy—knees flexed, chest thrust forward and pelvis back, one arm bent over her head. No amount of let's-pretend can transform this unfallen Eve into a woman once moved by the blood and pain of childbirth. The pitiful itinerary of Sailor's pilgrim's-progress runs from the raw sexual energy of "Love Me" ("Take my faithful heart / tear it all apart / but love me") to the castrated and domesticated "Love Me Tender." From the initial phallic outrage of his stand against the vengeful mother above him (worm's-eye shot), he has been brought low: Glinda approvingly surveys a broken-nosed boy flat on his back, the recipient of "a valuable lesson in life" (god's-eye shot).

In the end, *Wild at Heart* gridlocks the beautiful and terrible dynamics of living in Time. The lessons that might have seasoned Lynch's lovers-on-the-run into something more than eternal thumbsuckers are simply blown away, along with Bobby Peru's awful head (his fate echoing that of the film's first bearer of bad news). **Wild at Heart's** last and only legacy is the equivalent of the familiar Lynchean "keyhole" shot: a little boy looking up, through a car window, at his embracing mother and father . . . the genesis of yet another erotic triangle?

I remember how, in the spring of 1960, *The Fugitive Kind* helped exorcise the Fifties for me, permitting the future to get born. Now, as we slip into yet another new decade, I wonder whether some young small-town dreamer is trying to track the road movie in **Wild at Heart** as it time-trips around in a pastiche of the past, a garish gallery of funhouse mirrors from which there is no exit. I hope not: No matter how hot and bright it seems to burn, David Lynch's paean to arrested development is hollow at heart. (pp. 59-62)

> *Kathleen Murphy, "Dead Heat on a Merry-Go-Round," in* Film Comment, *Vol. 26, No. 6, November-December, 1990, pp. 59-62.*

FURTHER READING

Breskin, David. "The *Rolling Stone* Interview with David Lynch." *Rolling Stone,* No. 586 (6 September 1990): 58-60, 62-3, 98-100.

Interview in which Lynch discusses such topics as his experiences in Philadelphia, recurrent themes in his works, and the artistic process as it relates to psychological aspects of his films.

Bundtzen, Lynda K. " 'Don't Look at Me!': Woman's Body, Woman's Voice in *Blue Velvet.*" *Western Humanities Review* 42, No. 3 (Autumn 1988): 187-203.

Analysis of Lynch's treatment of Dorothy Vallens in *Blue Velvet.* By employing various "stylistic interventions," Bundtzen contends that Lynch forces his audience "to question its own voyeurism and complicity in fetishizing the female body."

Chute, David. "Out to Lynch." *Film Comment* 22, No. 5 (September-October 1986): 32-5.

Article combining critical commentary with an interview in which Lynch addresses such subjects as the auto-biographical origins of *Blue Velvet* and his affinities with filmmaker John Waters and nineteenth-century author Franz Kafka.

French, Sean. "The Heart of the Cavern." *Sight & Sound* 56, No. 2 (Spring 1987): 101-04.

Overview of Lynch's films up to and including *Blue Velvet.*

Griswold, Jeff. "Three Guys in Three Directions: David Lynch Interviewed by Jeff Griswold." *Film Comment* 21, No. 1 (January-February 1985): 55-6.

Interview in which Lynch considers the upcoming release of *Dune* and the commercial and artistic constraints of the film medium.

Holladay, William E., and Watt, Stephen. "Viewing the Elephant Man." *PMLA* 104, No. 5 (October 1989): 868-81.

Evaluates different literary treatments of John Merrick, including Bernard Pomerance's drama *The Elephant Man* and Lynch's film of the same title.

Jameson, Fredric. "Nostalgia for the Present." *South Atlantic Quarterly* 88, No. 2 (Spring 1989): 517-37.

Uses Philip K. Dick's novel *Time out of Joint,* Jonathan Demme's film *Something Wild,* and Lynch's *Blue Velvet* to examine period concepts of small-town life in the 1950s and 1960s.

Jerome, Jim. "David Lynch." *People Weekly* 34, No. 9 (3 September 1990): 79-80, 82, 84.

Incorporates critical commentary with an interview in which Lynch discusses *Twin Peaks* and *Wild at Heart.*

Kuzniar, Alice A. " 'Ears Looking at You: E. T. A. Hoffmann's *The Sandman* and David Lynch's *Blue Velvet.*" *South Atlantic Review* 54, No. 2 (May 1989): 7-21.

Examines "aural and visual discrepancy, castration and the deflected gaze, as well as the structuring device of doubling" in the works of Hoffmann and Lynch.

Pond, Steve. "Naked Lynch." *Rolling Stone,* No. 574 (22 March 1990): 51, 53-4, 120.

Combines comments on *Twin Peaks* by Lynch, co-producer and scriptwriter Mark Frost, and various actors and actresses in the series.

Rose, Lloyd. "Tumoresque: The Films of David Lynch." *The Atlantic* 254, No. 4 (October 1984): 108-09.

Overview of Lynch's films up to and including *The Elephant Man.* Rose calls Lynch "one of the most unalloyed surrealists ever to work in the movies."

Woodward, Richard B. "A Dark Lens on America." *The New York Times Magazine* (14 January 1990): 19-21, 30, 42-3, 52.

Focusing primarily on *Twin Peaks,* Woodward combines critical commentary with statements by Lynch, his friend and fellow director Jack Fisk, and actors and actresses who have worked with him.

Ian McEwan

1948-

(Full name Ian Russell McEwan) English novelist, short story writer, and scriptwriter.

McEwan is widely recognized for the daring originality of his fiction, much of which delineates bizarre sexuality and shocking violence. Frequently centering on deviant anti-heroes, his works explore conflicts between norms and socially unacceptable drives of the unconscious. McEwan predominantly focuses on adolescent characters, depicting them as acutely alienated and prone to cruelty or degenerate behavior. Christopher Ricks observed: "There's a hard sheen to everything [McEwan] does, a combination of fire and ice which chills some people and scorches others, but which, at its best, has the hiss of steel being tempered. With a gaze that is levelled, he looks at cruelty and hardness of heart, and there is to be no flinching."

The son of an army officer, McEwan traveled widely during his childhood, living for several years in northern Africa. In a 1979 interview he acknowledged the influence of travel on his writing: "Travelling rather puts you in the role of author—you're passing constantly through situations without any real responsibility towards them." At the age of eleven, McEwan was sent to boarding school in England for five years, an experience he found stultifying: "[It] was like a long sleep. I was very shy, not noticed by anyone, mediocre in class, usually 20th out of 30." His studies improved, however, and he was admitted to Sussex University; he later enrolled in the newly formed creative writing program at the University of East Anglia, where he studied under writers Malcolm Bradbury and Angus Wilson. Three short stories written for his master's thesis were included in McEwan's initial collection, *First Love, Last Rites,* which won the Somerset Maugham Award and established McEwan as one of England's most promising young writers. However, many critics expressed discomfort with his portrayal of childhood innocence warped by such anomalies as incest and forced transvestism.

McEwan's first novel, *The Cement Garden,* exposes a similarly distorted adolescent world. This work, which examines the deteriorating relationship between four children who are left alone after both parents die, opens with the death of their father. Attempting to cover the family garden with concrete because he is too ill to tend it, the father suffers a heart attack and collapses in the wet cement. The narrator, a homely adolescent named Jack, is unshaken by his father's sudden passing: "I went back outside after the ambulance had left to look at our path. I did not have a thought in my head as I picked up the plank and carefully smoothed away his impression in the soft, fresh concrete." Throughout the novel, Jack's detached voice casts a numbness over horrifying events, which include an incestuous relationship with his older sister and the basement burial of their dead mother. Blake Morrison observed: "This is McEwan's art: flat narration of the absurd or gro-

tesque, the morally extraordinary made ordinary by the indifference or perfunctoriness of the telling." McEwan's second short story collection, *In between the Sheets,* also received praise for its lucid style, which flows from realism to fantasy, horror to comedy. Magic realism permeates the stories, which frequently portray peculiar sexual relationships. For example, "Reflections of a Kept Ape" is narrated by an ape who contemplates his waning affair with his owner, a struggling female novelist. "Dead as They Come" portrays a wealthy, egotistical man who has an "affair" with a mannequin and then destroys her when he believes she has been unfaithful. Emphasizing the collection's theme of destructive sexuality, Terence Winch stated: "Throughout these stories, sex is an invitation not to love, but to violence. It is a weapon used to exert power over others, to possess and objectify them. Love becomes an infantile and destructive force, a source of humiliation."

Many critics consider *The Child in Time* the most complex of McEwan's works, as it presents a political, personal, and metaphysical exploration of childhood. Based on an actual event, *The Child in Time* describes the agony of a father whose daughter is kidnapped from a grocery store. Consumed by guilt and grief, he steadily loses touch with reality, believing he sees his lost daughter everywhere. Many reviewers stressed the novel's theme of lost youth, pointing to a character named Charles Darke, a successful politician who regresses to his childhood and ultimately commits suicide. Roberta Smoodin asserted: "A lost childhood, lost childhood hopes and dreams remain present in the seemingly mature adult, McEwan suggests, not only in memory but in a kind of time that spirals in upon itself, seems to be recapturable in some plausible intermingling of Einstein and Proust, quantum physics and magical realism." Strong political elements also appear in McEwan's depiction of an authoritarian method of childcare prescribed by the state—a government which also requires the unemployed and homeless to wear identification badges.

In McEwan's following work, *The Innocent,* he returns to the macabre; its climactic scene graphically details the dismemberment of a human body. Set in post-World War II Berlin, the novel concerns Leonard Marnham, an awkward young man who is working on a British-American intelligence project. Although he is extremely naive, Leonard's affair with a German woman named Maria soon leads him to explore the darker impulses of his nature, and by the end of the novel he has committed rape and murdered Maria's ex-husband. Reviewers consistently noted McEwan's fascination with the ability of people to commit atrocities while maintaining some degree of innocence. George Stade commented: "In [*The Innocent*], McEwan proves himself to be an acute psychologist of the ordinary mind. He gets our mundane virtues and vices, our craziness and sanities, exactly right, without the distortions of cynicism or sentimentality, so that we see them afresh."

In addition to his short stories and novels, McEwan has written several plays for television. In *Solid Geometry,* adapted from his short story of the same title, a man makes his wife disappear by folding her body into a sequence of positions diagrammed in his grandfather's diary. Only hours before airtime, the production was banned by the British Broadcasting Corporation for "grotesque and bizarre sexual elements." Another television drama, *The Imitation Game,* focuses on a nineteen-year-old woman who questions the menial employment of thousands of women at a World War II decoding operation where only males have access to intelligence information. Comparing his dramas to his fiction, McEwan explained: "For a long time I've wanted to connect up two different sides of my writing: the writing in television plays . . . where my concerns were primarily social and to some extent political, and the writing in prose fiction that tended to be rather dark, rather interior and rather more concerned with the pathology of the mind."

(See also *CLC,* Vol. 13; *Contemporary Authors,* Vols. 61-64, rev. ed.; *Contemporary Authors New Revision Series,* Vol. 14; and *Dictionary of Literary Biography,* Vol. 14.)

PRINCIPAL WORKS

NOVELS

The Cement Garden   1978

The Comfort of Strangers   1981
The Child in Time   1987
The Innocent   1990

SHORT FICTION COLLECTIONS

First Love, Last Rites   1975
In between the Sheets   1978

OTHER

The Imitation Game: Three Plays for Television   1981
Or Shall We Die?   [with Michael Berkeley]   (oratorio) 1983
The Ploughman's Lunch   (screenplay)   1983

Blake Morrison

It is customary to speak of Ian McEwan as a writer who is "out to shock". His two collections of short stories, **First Love, Last Rites** and **In between the Sheets,** have been widely acclaimed, but reservations have been expressed about their author's intentions. Some readers have wondered why so many of the tales should be, in Mr McEwan's own phrase, "histories of perversions", and why the typical McEwan narrator is in some way "abnormal"—a child-molester, a man who lives in a cupboard, an academic who keeps a "beautifully preserved" penis in a jar. Other readers have worried over the seeming implausibility of such stories as **"Dead as They Come"** in which a man buys a shop dummy, and takes it home to be his mistress. What has proved most troubling of all, though, is some of the casual detail in the stories—green snot hanging from the ends of noses, boiling fat poured over someone's lap, a teenage gang preparing to roast a cat.

Ian McEwan is certainly aware that his work sometimes produces feelings of dismay and revulsion. A section from **"To and Fro",** one of the stories from his last collection, looks as if it may have been intended as a sort of apologia: "I claim waking status in my dreams. Nothing exaggerated but fine points of physical disgust and those exaggerated only appropriately". A more substantial answer to his critics is to be found in **The Cement Garden,** Mr McEwan's first novel, and one which, though it may at times shock, could not be accused of doing so gratuitously. There are waking dreams here, and not a little physical disgust (a frog is accidentally trodden on, "a creamy green substance . . . spilling out of its stomach"), but the overall impression of the book is not one of a writer revelling in the fantastic or the grotesque; it is, rather, an impression of care and restraint. **The Cement Garden** should make clearer that the characteristic quality of McEwan's writing is a tension between precise narration and preposterous narrative.

The novel examines the individual developments of, and interaction between, four children left alone following the death first of their father, and then, not long afterwards, of their mother. Worried that, as orphans, they may be separated and taken into care, the children decide to conceal the fact of their mother's death from the outside world. Her corpse is carried down into the cellar, put in a trunk, and covered over with cement. The children struggle to fend for themselves, but it seems only a matter of time before they are found out. As it turns out, they are betrayed by the one intruder into the family, Derek, snooker-playing boyfriend of the elder girl, Julie.

It is a short and devastatingly simple story. Several familiar McEwan elements are present—a teenage male narrator, a strong evocation of adolescent sexuality, an interest in confinement and liberation—but this is a more austere work than his earlier stories. The austerity is discernible not only in the style of the novel (metaphors are so rare that the few allowed into the text—the dead mother "frail and sad in her nightdress lying at our feet like a bird with a broken wing"—come over with real force), but in its tone. McEwan allows himself few jokes: only when Jack is warned about the dangers of masturbation ("Every time . . . you do that, it takes two pints of blood to replace it"), or when the prissy Derek is observed holding the steering wheel of his car "at arm's length and between finger and thumb as if the touch of it disgusted him", is there any clear invitation to laughter.

There is austerity, too, in McEwan's refusal of the more sensational possibilities which the narrative initially seems to offer. Jack's reaction to his mother's death is to feel, as well as loss, "a sense of adventure and freedom," and it seems likely for a time that the novel will develop into a 1970s version of Golding's *Lord of the Flies,* the children running amok in the urban wilderness surrounding their house. But the author imagines quieter and more subtle changes taking place, and concentrates attention on Julie's assumption of authority, on Jack's resentment and lassitude, on Sue's private grief, on the deterioration of the younger boy, Tom. So cool and accurate is this attention that the more disquieting elements in the story—Jack's feeling that he has contributed to his father's death (the death occurs while Jack is masturbating), the girls' habit of dressing Tom up in clothes of the opposite sex, the smell of mother drifting up from the cellar—seem entirely plausible. This is McEwan's art: flat narration of the absurd or grotesque, the morally extraordinary made ordinary by the indifference or perfunctoriness of the telling.

It may be said that the virtues of *The Cement Garden* are those of a short story: there is a compelling central image (the cement cracking to reveal the mother's corpse), but little relish for plot. Whatever its status as a text, however, it should consolidate Ian McEwan's reputation as one of the best young writers in Britain today.

Blake Morrison, "Paying Cellarage," in The Times Literary Supplement, *No. 3991, September 29, 1978, p. 1077.*

William McPherson

Every imaginative writer exhibits a case of arrested development, fixated on some stage in time, some crucial event, around which the rest of his imaginative life loops and circles, straying from the source but always returning to it,

attempting to absorb it, to comprehend it, finally to transcend it (which may not make him so different from you and me). (p. E1)

Take Ian McEwan, a young writer of real talent if I ever read one, whose material is as banal and bizarre as sex and death, whose dreams are circumscribed by his parents' loss, his sister's love. *The Cement Garden* is his first novel and second book. Three years ago he published an extraordinary collection of short stories, *First Love, Last Rites,* unique variations on the same common themes.

The themes may be commonplace but McEwan's handling of them is not. He tells the story through a 14-year-old boy, Jack, who lives, at the beginning, with his barely middle-class parents, two sisters, Julie 16 and Sue 12, and a six-year-old brother in a bleak urban landscape that is, in fact, London, but could as well be Chicago. McEwan has a compelling narrative gift, and *The Cement Garden* is a riveting novel from its opening paragraph:

> I did not kill my father, but I sometimes felt I had helped him on his way. And but for the fact that it coincided with a landmark in my own physical growth, his death seemed insignificant compared to what followed. My sisters and I talked about him the week after he died, and Sue certainly cried when the ambulance men tucked him up in a bright red blanket and carried him away. He was a frail, irascible, obsessive man with yellowish hands and face. I am only including the little story of his death to explain how my sisters and I came to have such a large quantity of cement at our disposal.

How the cement came to be disposed of is the hinge on which the plot turns. It was purchased—15 bags of it—because Jack's ailing father intended to pave over the garden he was no longer well enough to care for, "to surround the house, front and back, with an even plane of concrete." Jack and his father begin the job, but as Jack lingers in the cellar pondering the astonishing new mystery of sex, his father collapses in the wet cement. "The radio was playing in the kitchen. I went back outside after the ambulance had left to look at our path. I did not have a thought in my head as I picked up the plank and carefully smoothed away his impression in the soft, fresh concrete."

So much for father. And so much, eventually, for mother, who fades away in her upstairs bedroom shortly after Jack's 15th birthday, leaving the children to conceal her death in order to prevent the dissolution of their family, which, flawed as it is, is nonetheless all they have.

> "If we tell them," I began again, "they'll come and put us into care, into an orphanage or something. They might try and get Tom adopted." I paused. Sue was horrified.
>
> "They can't do that," she said.
>
> "The house will stand empty," I went on, "people will break in, there'll be nothing left."
>
> "But if we don't tell anyone," said Sue, and gestured vaguely toward the house, "what do we do then?"

What they do then, during their summer of freedom, is to

retain the established structure but change the established roles, parodying the previous familiar model. Jack becomes the sometimes irascible father, Julie the mother who mercilessly babies Tom, the youngest, as if he were a doll, clothing him in wigs and dresses, moving him backwards from bed to crib, protecting him with a fierce, childlike and terrible devotion. Sue giggles with her older sister, and comments on them all in her diary.

To reveal more of the plot which McEwan so skillfully unfolds, planting seeds in the first few pages that he harvests at the end, would be to assume his task and to diminish the reader's pleasure, because in this book you first want to find out what happens next. *The Cement Garden* possesses the suspense and the chilling impact of *Lord of the Flies* but without the philosophy lessons. Its cool, matter-of-fact depiction of child and adosescent sexuality gives it the truth but not the zaniness (nor the psychiatric sessions) of *Portnoy's Complaint.* Its characters are sympathetic, its tone sustained but muted, and its style spare and unadorned, quietly rendering the narrator's sense of the fragility, the impermanence and the mysteriousness of the world.

As one might expect, the flowers that grow from the cracks in a cement garden are ugly—we have to grant a writer his obsessions—but *The Cement Garden* itself is original, memorable, powerful and right. Fortunately too, it is short, because I could not put it down. (pp. E1, E4)

> *William McPherson, "Family Affairs," in* Book World—The Washington Post, *October 29, 1978, pp. E1, E4.*

Ian McEwan [Interview with Christopher Ricks]

Ian McEwan was born in 1948; his father was in the army, so they saw the world—Germany, Tripoli, Singapore—until, at 11, he was sent to a London Educational Authority boarding-school in Suffolk. A dark time, apparently. Things brightened when he went to the University of Sussex, and got brighter still at the University of East Anglia, where he could submit as part of his MA degree three short stories. Then The New American Review *published his story,* **"Homemade."**

There's a hard sheen to everything he does, a combination of fire and ice which chills some people and scorches others, but which, at its best, has the hiss of steel being tempered. With a gaze that is levelled, he looks at cruelty and hardness of heart, and there is to be no flinching. Lately, though—and this is a crucial time for him, as he turns away from his known territory, adolescence, to what is now closer to him and so more difficult to see with perspective—McEwan has turned his sharp eye on tenderness, on the pains of gentleness and of strange love. Near the end of his latest novel, **The Cement Garden,** *the love of Jack and his sister Julie is seen with truth and as truth.*

• • •

[Ricks]: *A lot of people have thought that the world of your stories is a very nasty world. I mean, horrible things are being imagined, and some pretty horrible things are being done. What do you think about the complaint that that's just voguish nastiness?*

[McEwan]: I always find this rather difficult to answer. I suppose if you talk about it in the simplest way possible—and that is if I'm sitting down facing an empty sheet of paper—what is going to compel me into writing fiction is not what is nice and easy and pleasant and somehow affirming, but somehow what is bad and difficult and unsettling. That's the kind of tension I need to start me writing. Beyond that, I suppose, I've always been trying to assert some kind of slender optimism in my stories, and I don't think I can really do that unless I can do it in a world that seems to me to be fundamentally threatening, so what I really worry about is gratuitous optimism, not gratuitous violence.

Your own life has been fairly settled. I was wondering about your childhood, for example. Given the horrifying imaginings about childhood in the stories and in **The Cement Garden,** *what was your childhood like?*

Well, I have a brother and a sister, but they're much older than I am, so in effect I'm an only child. Certainly that stretch of my childhood up to about 11 or 12 was a very secure one, and very happy. I spent a lot of my childhood in North Africa—a very easy, outdoor kind of life. Yes, I think it's true, fundamentally, I was and I think still am a fairly secure person in that sense, and I can let things go when I sit down and enter the rather closed-off special world of trying to make a fiction. I don't feel threatened by my fiction. For example, if I spend a day writing a piece of prose which is ultimately going to be part of a story, and it's going to be something violent or something terrible, at the end of that day what I will feel, if I think I've achieved what I set out to achieve, will be elation and pleasure. It won't have much to do with the content of what I've done.

You write a lot about adolescence, don't you? I know you wouldn't want to be typed as the adolescence man, but you write a lot about that particular hallucinatory clarity of one's physical self, and about masturbation and so on.

I write about adolescence, or I have written about adolescence, because it does provide me with a fairly unique rhetorical standpoint. That is, adolescents are an extraordinary, special case of people; they're close to childhood, and yet they are constantly baffled and irritated by the initiations into what's on the other side—the shadow line, as it were. They are perfect outsiders, in a sense, and fiction—especially short stories, and especially first-person narratives—can thrive on a point of view which is somehow dislocated, removed.

So do you think as you become more a novelist and less a short story writer—am I right in supposing that that's a move you might make, heralded by **The Cement Garden**—*are you likely then to move away from adolescence for something like a technical reason?*

Yes, partly a technical reason. For sure, I think *The Cement Garden* is the last time, certainly in the near future, that I will spend months and months occupying the mind, living inside the mind of a 15-year-old. I was trying to set up a situation where suddenly there were no social controls. Suddenly, children find themselves in the house—there are no teachers, no parents, no figures of authority, they have total freedom—and yet they are completely paralysed. The narrator is at first almost catatonic with freedom—can't move at all. Yes, I would like to broaden out this scope. There's something about why we do have a certain kind of rhetorical freedom by having adolescents as narrators—you do also lock yourself into a fairly small space. That, maybe, is the problem with *The Cement Garden.* There is something of a challenge trying to have the adult world adultly observed, which I think must be faced.

You were abroad a lot, weren't you, as a child? And also, I gather, you used the money from the success of your first story to travel to Afghanistan, and you spent some time in America. What about the freedom of those literally other airs? Do you feel that's affected you a lot?

Yes it has, travel has been very important to me, especially the travel I've done in the last four or five years. I rather like to travel alone, and I suppose that the travel is a way of not doing anything else. I mean, I don't write when I'm travelling, I don't even think about writing. Travelling rather puts you in the role of author—you're passing constantly through situations without any real responsibility towards them. I do find that very exhilarating.

What sort of responsibility do you feel to the places? I think "Psychopolis" is one of your very best stories, and it clearly is about travelling and the particular way in which you're in but not of, without that being irresponsible.

I felt quite free of the responsibility of getting Los Angeles right because I thought it would be better to do it in terms of a series of meetings and then very artificially to bring all the people that your narrator has met into one place to have a conversation and in that way try to represent a city. Somehow I felt so excited about having been in America for the first time, I found myself getting up very early in the morning and itching to write something. I knew that it would have to be about Los Angeles, and I think it was very fortunate that I was only there a couple of days. I'm not a very observant traveller. I don't sort of keep at the back of my mind all kinds of local details, local colour. It made it much easier for me to reconstruct Los Angeles in terms of a city of relations and relationships, rather than as a place that you might describe in the way that Reyner Banham might describe it.

When you write about Los Angeles, one can't help thinking about films, and one of the things that struck me in "Psychopolis" was the way in which the simultaneity of the argument is something which you can do in prose which you couldn't do in a film. That is to say, you know one person is saying this, meanwhile somebody else is competing with him, arguing over it. In a film you wouldn't be able to hear what they were saying.

> 'Wait a minute,' he was saying, 'you can't impose all that Women's Lib stuff on to the societies of thousands of years ago. Christianity expressed itself through available . . . ?'
>
> At roughly the same time Terence said, 'Another objection to Christianity is that it leads to pas-

sive acceptance of social inequalities because the real rewards are in . . . '

And Mary cut in across George in protest. 'Christianity has provided an ideology for sexism now, and capitalism . . . '

'Are you a communist?' George demanded angrily, although I was not sure who he was talking to. Terence was pressing on loudly with his own speech. I heard him mention the crusades, and the inquisition.

'This has nothing to do with Christianity,' George was almost shouting. His face was flushed.

'More evil perpetrated in the name of Christ . . . this has nothing to do with . . . to the persecution of women herbalists as witches . . . Bullshit. It's irrelevant . . . Corruption, graft, propping up tyrants, accumulating wealth at the altars . . . fertility goddess . . . bullshit . . . phallic worship . . . look at Galileo . . . this has nothing to . . . '

I heard little else because now I was shouting my own piece about Christianity.

It's a wonderful conversation, partly because it's such an extraordinarily vital argument.

Yes, I am quite unashamedly proud of those last ten pages of **"Psychopolis."**

One of the things that was in my mind was the question of endings. For example, it's evident to me, and I hope to everybody who reads you, that you've put a tremendous lot of thought into how endings will be—neither smack of firm government, conclusive in a bright, brisk, wrong way, nor, on the other hand, open-minded and vacant and please-make-of-it-what-you-will.

I find endings very difficult. I think they are objectively very difficult. Some endings in my stories I know have just not worked. I feel very uneasy about them. It is walking a kind of tightrope—as you say, you want to avoid a piece of short fiction ending with a great sort of crash like a pianist bringing his elbows down on a piano, and, at the same time, you also want to avoid that feyness of the hanging moment or ending on a hanging participle. You have got to deserve your ending in terms of content, and it has to be worked for. I think, in **"Psychopolis,"** the ending does come off. I spend a lot of time on endings, and I don't write the ending till the end, because I don't usually know the endings till the end. That's another reason why they take up so much time for me—I have to find out what they are.

I take it your first moment of knowing you'd succeeded was when The New American Review *took the story,* **"Homemade."** *Do you think there is some special relation between your writing and American writing? Are you much influenced by American writers?*

I have certainly read all the contemporary major American writers, and there are certainly passages in lots of their books and certain single books that I have liked a great deal. But they do seem quite remote to me in terms of my own work. I suppose writing one does admire is work that you think, well, God, I couldn't have done that—you know, that's something way beyond my own experience or what I could synthesise. Early on, when I first started writing, it was much easier to get going if one moved off with a certain kind of pastiche of what one had read. Both Mailer and Miller provided a taking-off point for **"Homemade,"** a certain kind of voice in Henry Miller, with a cynical, long-winded, rather pompous and yet very funny narrator, which I liked and I hated and wanted to do myself and make it even more pompous.

There's one of your stories, though, that is very different from the others. I'm thinking of **"To and Fro."** *I have to admit it didn't grip me, at first. I now think that was wrong but I still feel that it's a special case. Do you want to say something about that story?*

Yes, I do, because, in a way, it's my favourite. I don't think it got more than one mention in any review of the collection in which it appeared. Normally I've been preoccupied with writing a very accessible, clean kind of prose that anyone could read—I tried to avoid writing anything mandarin or pompously difficult. But **"To and Fro"** is a 55-page story condensed into about eight pages, it seems the only way to solve a particular problem, it's more like a poem. It does require two or three readings. I think I like it most because I know it better than anybody.

Can I ask you about circumstances which I think you might not much like—it has to do with shock in your work. **"To and Fro"** *has a certain experimentalism but is by no means shocking; whereas a lot of your other work, though not shockingly experimental, clearly is, in some way, wishing people to be shocked—shocked by some truth about, at least, their own fantasies and perhaps their own obsession.*

If we're talking about shock, I'm slightly shocked at all this shock, I haven't really met anybody who has told me that they were shocked by my stories. I've met plenty of people who didn't like them; I've yet to meet somebody who said: 'Your stories are so revolting I couldn't read them.' And yet in print what is set out constantly is a reaction of sort of horror and shock, and this is something to do with someone reacting in print. I think, in a public medium like a newspaper, reacting in print to something that's in print, there's a certain kind of artifice about the shock—I mean as artificial as fiction itself. One of my stories has appeared in a lurid pornographic magazine.

It's an anti-pornographic story . . .

Yes, it was, and the story really had some rather pure intentions.

What about contemporary fiction? Do you see yourself occupying a position in this sort of order of monuments, living monuments?

Well, no, I don't—it's very hard to. I don't know if this is a very good time for English fiction. It certainly seems to me that it's a very good time for the theatre, and has been for some years. I know lots of writers and I like them as people, and there are certain of their works, their novels, stories, that I like, but I certainly can't locate myself inside any shared, any sort of community taste, aesthetic ambition or critical position or anything else. I don't really feel part of anything at all.

What about the tradition? I want to pick you up bodily and probably against your will, and put you in a tradition of which the greatest writer is Kipling, and that is short stories of exceptional imagination, of cruelty, humiliation and very traditional moral values. What would you feel about that sort of tradition?

Well I haven't read Kipling—I read "If" when I was 16—so I would say if you wanted to pick me up bodily and do that, that was your prerogative. I'm not sure I would share with you the sense that my fiction has been quite as moral as you would suggest. There are certainly rather frail kinds of statements embodied in them, a rather fragile kind of optimism about life. I hope to avoid any programmatic moral manipulation of the stories, and of the novel, too—I try to keep that sense of the story that is going to be moral in some kind of abeyance, and hope that, through restraint, one will generate a degree of compassion for the right people, even if the right people are in some other sense the wrong people. That is why, in *The Cement Garden,* there is no authorial voice that will tell you that incest is a bad show, don't do it, but neither does it say the other, neither does it recommend that everyone should try, and therefore liberate themselves. I'm not really dealing on that level at all. If I can come back one step: when I'm working, when I'm writing, I do feel extraordinarily free. Even when I'm trying to put together the most unfree situations, I do feel colossal freedom myself. There's nothing more exhilarating than to be writing again—your food tastes better, your step has more spring, the air that fills your lungs seems that much cleaner. (pp. 526-27)

> *Ian McEwan and Christopher Ricks, in an interview in* The Listener, *Vol. 101, No. 2606, April 12, 1979, pp. 526-27.*

Terence Winch

The most dangerous place to be, in Ian McEwan's fictional world, is in between the sheets. At the end of **"Pornography,"** the first story in [the new collection *In between the Sheets*], a cocky young man named O'Byrne finds himself strapped to a bed, awaiting castration at the hands of his two lovers. In **"Psychopolis,"** the last and best story in this book, Terence falls in love with Sylvie and offers to prove his devotion by doing whatever she asks. Sylvie responds by ordering him to urinate in his pants in public.

Terence never winds up in bed with Sylvie. But not so fortunate is the heroine of **"Dead as They Come."** This story is almost an allegorical guide to McEwan's work. It can be read as a comment on male attitudes toward sex, as well as a gruesome example of the materialization of love. In it, a rich man falls in love with a mannequin, his "Helen." At the story's climax (the structural pun would seem to be intended), the man rapes and kills Helen. He enjoys an orgasm as she is dying. He then goes on an orgy of destruction: "I tore, trampled, mangled, kicked, spat and urinated on . . . my precious possessions."

Throughout these stories, sex is an invitation not to love,

but to violence. It is a weapon used to exert power over others, to possess and objectify them. Love becomes an infantile and destructive force, a source of humiliation.

McEwan is a satirist in the tradition of Nathanael West. His stories focus on the extremes and exaggerations of human behavior. McEwan seems to feel that to write of ordinary people would be pointless—such an approach would be boring. No one would listen. This attitude is revealed in another scene from **"Psychopolis"**: an amateur stand-up comedian, at a nightclub for would-be entertainers, tells the sad, depressing story of his very ordinary life. The story is not funny, and the audience is indifferent. The point is that the citizens of the "city of narcissists" are numb to commonplace human suffering. Only extreme, perverted pain attracts attention.

Most mainstream art, McEwan seems to suggest, does little to wake people up, to get through the numbness. In **"Dead as They Come,"** the rich man reflects on his beloved, "I saw once more her genius for *wearing* clothes. I saw beauty in another being as no man had ever seen it, I saw . . . it was art, it was the total consummation of line and form that art alone can realize." Beauty, art, and genius are all here associated with a character who is literally a dummy. Art is something unalive. Beauty is reduced to fashion.

Faced with this kind of situation, McEwan turns to tales of rape, mutilation, and murder. (And, if we include his first two books, incest can be added to the list.) But he is not heavy-handed. His stories are complex and his prose, like Orwell's, is as clear as windowpane. (In fact, one story, **"Two Fragments: March 199–,"** is indebted to Orwell in style and subject matter.) And McEwan's comic edge gives these stories a moral force. They are not meant simply to shock and horrify middle-class readers. Rather, like all good satire, they seek to unmask hypocrisy and cruelty.

In its original meaning, the word "person" meant "mask." People are actors. They play many different roles and wear numerous disguises. Mary, in **"Psychopolis,"** says, "Everyone here has got some kind of act going." This tension between people and the roles they play is a dominant interest in McEwan's fiction.

One of McEwan's favorite techniques is the use of role reversals. In his fictional world, children are often more mature than adults. Many of his child characters are in the "14 going on 40" category. And some of them—e.g., Charmian, a little girl in the title story, who has a bullet-shaped head, a double chin, a "bullish" neck and a faint moustache—are frightening. Men are frequently "the weaker sex," as the unfortunate O'Byrne discovers in **"Pornography."** And an animal, not a human, is the most articulate and sensitive character in any of these stories (read **"Reflections of a Kept Ape"**).

Ian McEwan is a gifted story-teller and possibly the best British writer to appear in a decade or more. His first collection of stories, ***First Love, Last Rites*** (1975), is a brilliant, obsessive book. His only novel to date, ***The Cement Garden*** (1978), is that special kind of book that's difficult to tear oneself away from. If some of these new stories

seem more strained than his earlier work, it is because McEwan is experimenting more with the elements of his fictional world.

That world is a disturbing one, and hard to characterize. McEwan knows about perversion—spiritual as well as sexual. Susan Sontag wrote, "Real art has the capacity to make us nervous." ***In between the Sheets*** is definitely real art. (pp. E1, E3)

Terence Winch, "Writing on The Razor's Edge," in Book World—The Washington Post, *August 5, 1979, pp. E1, E3.*

V. S. Pritchett

Ian McEwan has been recognized as an arresting new talent in the youngest generation of English short story writers. His subject matter is often squalid and sickening; his imagination has a painful preoccupation with the adolescent secrets of sexual aberration and fantasy. But in his accomplishment as a story writer he is an immediate master of styles and structures, his writing transfigures, and he can command variety in subject and feeling. His intellectual resources enable him—and the reader—to open windows in a claustrophobia which otherwise would have left us flinching and no more. Invention, irony, humor, a gift for satirical parody and curiosity give him the artist's initiative. We *do* recognize an underworld—for that is what it is—and it is natural that he has evoked an, albeit distant, connection with Beckett and Kafka. His limitation is that his range of felt experience is confined to his love of his disgusts.

Two stories in his new collection, ***In between the Sheets,*** suggest a new direction. I'll come to those later. The book opens with **"Pornography,"** which begins as a comical account of what goes on between two brothers in a Soho porn shop where customers are nervously trying to get a free furtive glance at the glossy porn. The elder brother is hysterically trying to make a fortune out of his sexual peep show; the younger is crudely dedicated to cunt. He is itching and smells of "clap" and he is having it off with two nurses on alternate days. So far, obsessive observation of Soho grubbiness, cheap lodgings, filthy baths, sulky *macho* manners, nasty smells, bad food, cheap drink. Unhappily, Mr. McEwan surrenders to a well-known fantasy from the world of schoolboy smut. When they discover the young man is deceiving and infecting them, the nurses enact the fantasy of the tart who castrates her man. We leave them at this sadistic feast after one of them has raped the young *macho,* screaming out the war cries of Women's Lib as she jumps him. The melodrama ruins a story whose strength lay in fact, not fantasy. One simply laughs off the schoolboy legend.

In **"Reflections of a Kept Ape"** McEwan is more subtle. It is a droll tale. A pet monkey has been briefly seduced by a young woman who has written a bestseller, and in his eager, lonely, animal way he tells the story of a lust that has faded. . . . From Cervantes to Kafka, now how many writers have tried the puzzled reflections of animals, though not their greedy sexuality; here we notice the change of prose style and especially the notes on the deceits of art. These will recur in McEwan's work.

The ape reflects on the girl's frantic virginal typing of her difficult next book:

> Was art then nothing more than a wish to appear busy? Was it nothing more than a fear of silence, of boredom, which the merely reiterative rattle of the typewriter's keys was enough to allay? In short, having crafted one novel, would it suffice to write it again, type it out with care, page by page? (Gloomily I recycled nits from torso to mouth.) Deep in my heart I knew it would suffice and, knowing that, seemed to know less than I had ever known before.

I must say I object to the new cliché "crafted." But then comes a parody of George Sand-ish self-love when the ape knows she is tired of him: . . .

> My eyes stray to the front door and fix there. To leave, yes, regain my independence and dignity, to set out on the City Ring Road, my possessions clasped to my chest, the infinite stars towering above me and the songs of nightingales ringing in my ears. Sally Klee receding ever farther behind me, she caring nothing for me, no, nor I for her, to lope carefree towards the orange dawn and on into the next day and again into the following night, crossing rivers and penetrating woods, to search for and find a new love, a new post, a new function, a new life.

The ape is an out-of-date Romantic. Ian McEwan is being very clever about the temptations of "literature." That "orange dawn" will reappear in more solemn circumstances: the author is fighting hidden literary tendencies.

"Dead as They Come" is another familiar fable: its merits, as always with Ian McEwan, lie in the half-vulgar elegance in the detail. A rich man falls in love with a beautiful female dummy in a shop window. In a very funny scene he buys her, carries her home; he seduces her, the perfect passive beauty of daydream. Soon he is cuckolded by his chauffeur, who is well drawn. But the point of the story is that it is an attack on the corrupting influence of connoisseur tastes: they turn one into a voyeur. The boss has really been deceived by a juvenile masturbator's tastes for "dead" works of art—for Vermeer, Blake, Richard Dadd, Paul Nash, Rothko. In his jealousy he spits on them, urinates on them, and destroys them. (There is a lot of urination—why not pissing?—in McEwan's stories.) In **"In between the Sheets"** a divorced man, after a chilly scene with his ex-wife, is allowed to take his very young daughter and her child friend back to his house to stay the night. The little child friend is a dwarf-like horror and no sexual innocent. In **"To and Fro"** the style changes again and the story becomes a prose poem. A man and his mistress lie in bed, half asleep after making love. His mind wanders between what went on at the office and night thoughts:

> Sometimes I look at her and wonder who will die first . . . face to face, wintering in the mess of down and patchwork, she places a hand over each of my ears, takes my head between her palms, regards me with thick, black eyes and pursed smile that does not show her teeth . . .

then I think, It's me, I shall die first, and you might live forever.

A little later:

> A voice breaks the stillness, a brilliant red flower dropped on the snow, one of her daughters calls out in a dream. A bear! . . . the sound indistinct from its sense. Silence, and then again, A bear, softer this time, with a falling tone of disappointment . . . now, a silence dramatic for its absence of the succinct voice . . . now imperceptibly . . . now, habitual silence, no expectations, the weight of stillness, the luminous after-image of bears in fading orange.

An exercise for the artist's notebook: an experiment, but probably wasted? You notice that "orange" again.

There are two encouraging breaks with "mean" writing—"mean" in the sense of James Joyce's *Dubliners*—in two long pieces: **"Two Fragments: March 199-"** and **"Psychopolis."** They enlarge his scene. The first is an evocation of a possible London in twenty years time, half-destroyed by war or revolution. The narrative dodges the conventional melodramatic picture of catastrophe. It concentrates on the aftermath of decay. Government offices are still smoldering in a deteriorating wilderness; there is no transport, there is almost no light or heating, food has to be scrounged. People are reduced to living on what fish can be got out of the polluted Thames, and sit around bonfires in the streets or traipse on foot on pointless journeys across the city. Good. The skills of the machine age have gone. Such a fragmented life is simply and exactly suggested and far less sensationally than say, in Orwell's *1984*—though politics are almost missing—and with far greater sense of physical and emotional dissolution. The lovers fall back on memories of things in the happier past: an incurably arty girl thinks that Art Deco may start people learning how to make things again. She is a contemporary bore.

> It was growing colder. We got between the sheets, me with my plans and clean feet, she with her fish. "The point is," I said referring to Marie's age [his child's age], "that you cannot survive now without a plan." I lay with my head on Diane's arm and she drew me towards her breast. "I know someone," she began, and I knew she was introducing a lover, "who wants to start a radio station. He doesn't know how to generate electricity. He doesn't know anyone who could build a transmitter or repair an old one. And even if he did, he knows there are no radios to pick up his signal. He talks vaguely about repairing old ones, of finding a book that will tell him how to do it."

They remember bits of things, like driving a car or taking children to the zoo, forgotten football matches. But cars are now rubbish and the zoo had become a closed ruin years before. The bits are good: catastrophe will be as it was in 1940—bitty. One is struck by McEwan's gift of clarity. It moves easily from fragments of cold reality to fragments of fantasy, from the comic to the threatening. He is moving out of the sexual ennui into one more devastating.

"Psychopolis" takes his traveling mind to Los Angeles,

and here we find him amusing himself with the collision of English and American boastings and opinions as they are thrown out. The finale is excellent. His impressionism is intelligent and he is still a fabulist who keeps clear of journalism. He is always the restless storyteller; every voice or incident moves forward as he follows the interplay of reality and fancy, the inner and the outer, the tender and violent, the banal and the grotesque. The voice (as it must be in the short story) is absolutely distinctive and the means are controlled. (p. 31)

V. S. Pritchett, "Shredded Novels," in The New York Review of Books, *Vol. XXVI, Nos. 21 & 22, January 24, 1980, pp. 31-2.*

Stephen Koch

[For some time, Ian McEwan] has been viewed by certain British critics—A. Alvarez, for example—as a high shining hope for British fiction in our time. . . .

The Cement Garden is a slim, spooky book, involved with the sad perversities of an adolescent boy's first encounters with sex and death. It includes a corpse in the basement. *The Comfort of Strangers* also relies on perversity for its effects, although these have now grown a bit more "adult." It is also in ways a better book. It is better written. The elegance of McEwan's readability and technical skill—invariably much admired—have been brought to a higher luster and intricacy. The prose is richer, more allusive—and McEwan's effects have grown more frightening. McEwan is noted for his jolting moments. True to form, certain pages in *The Comfort of Strangers* sent through this reader a couple of fairly impressive jolts.

Whether the novel thereby fulfills the ambitious claims made on McEwan's behalf is a different matter. I tend to think not. *The Comfort of Strangers* is a kind of highly refined lesson on the virtues and problems of a pure, distilled erotic fantasy as a source of novelistic energy. The book is a sexualized murder story, a kind of sado-masochistic (and much lesser) *Death in Venice*. Vacationing in Venice, a model-pretty, but sexually tepid, youngish British couple, prettily named Colin and Mary, are taken up and courted by an older, "international" couple who call themselves Robert and Caroline. Unknown to the guileless Colin and Mary, Robert and Caroline, ruthless voyeurs, have been stalking the younger pair since their arrival. They have been spying on, and photographing, Colin especially. Their courtship is not social but sexual in intention; moreover, the sexual aim is not mere possession but a ritual murder of Colin, once he has been transformed into a sacrificial male sex-and-death object.

McEwan proceeds through most of this sickly tale with subtlety and promise. He spins an atmosphere of quite real suspense all within an oppressive inexplicable ominousness. Like Mann in the original *Death in Venice,* he exploits effectively the atmospherics of the Emblematic Passerby: Boatmen with strange smiles, couples overhead quarreling in cafes; sexy roughhousing glimpsed on Lido Beach. *Passim,* he touches all kind of subtitles about eros, languor, the workings of desire, much of it in the context

of a kind of feminist-tinted inflection of the sex war, here become a deadly business indeed.

The difficulty is that all this skill is directed toward a climax which, even though it is duly horrific, is sapped by a certain thinness and plain banality at its core. After an impressive wind-up, the sado-masochistic fantasy animating *The Comfort of Strangers* is elaborately revealed as . . . a sado-masochistic fantasy. And not much more. McEwan is anything but a vulgarian, but even he cannot finesse the lurid staginess the fantasy demands: The lascivious Robert and Caroline move in on their prey; the lethal razor glints in their hand; the handsome baffled male's tee-shirt is torn loose; he is murderously fondled, while poor hapless Mary gapes in horror, half-conscious but paralyzed by a secret potion slipped into her herb tea. The fantasized intensity grows first pale, then silly. The lovely hieratic Colin never dies here. It is the novel that dies. Colin merely vanishes in a puff of erotic fancy.

Yet *The Comfort of Strangers* has real interest as a novel. I confess I may not fully understand its strategies, a lapse I would of course rather attribute to McEwan's confusion than my own. In any event, McEwan is an exemplary novelist of our moment—a role in the event both lucky and unlucky. In all his recent fiction, McEwan seems to be reaching toward some new imaginative accommodation to the sexual questions of innocence and selfhood, role and need that have defined, with such special intensity, his generation and mine. I honor him for his effort. At its best, it gives him what interest he has.

Yet I think the issues lose definition here. The sado-masochistic theme is false—too simple, too thin. Moreover, throughout, McEwan alludes to feminist and anti-feminist rhetoric. The unfortunate Mary used to work in a feminist theatrical group, she and Colin, (no feminist, but a Nice Guy), exchange some good boy-girl sparring over the Rhetoric. But elsewhere, the discussion is befogged: Caroline delivers herself hifalutin' intimacies over the joys of submission and pain: the murderous Robert (while displaying hints—and more—of homosexual attraction to Colin) delivers Italianate speeches about the good old days when men were men, and "proud of their sex."

This only clouds issues McEwan has treated better. In a collection of stories, *In between the Sheets* (1978), McEwan published a short story which reads like a trial run of the obsessions that define *The Comfort of Strangers.* The story is called **"Psychopolis."** It is set in Los Angeles, and though it satirizes that city, there is something in the harsh argumentative contested atmosphere of American life that seems to do McEwan good. The story is hard with intellectual acuity and verve; it is a genuinely dazzling achievement, destined surely, for some place in the short story anthologies to come. **"Psychopolis"** is cruel in its vision, but in its 29 pages, it seems to me authentically to grasp the important issues that slip through McEwan's fingers in the novel he has given us here.

Stephen Koch, "Ian McEwan: Visions of Pain and Submission," in Book World—The Washington Post, *June 28, 1981, p. 5.*

Richard P. Brickner

There are novels so generally alert and involving that, if they reveal some dubious point of construction, this possible weakness itself becomes suspenseful. "What is the author doing?" "Why is the author doing it?" "Will the author pull it off?" Questions like these merge with the fundamental "What happens next?" (A reader is a person in a state of hope.)

The Comfort of Strangers, Ian McEwan's second novel, is such a book, well worth reading despite its sometimes arbitrary and implausible nature. It is the price one pays for the book's originality, vividness, wit and power to intrigue. Mr. McEwan's previous novel, *The Cement Garden* (he is also the author of two short story collections), shows a more natural and a more complete dovetailing of subject and story than the new book does. But he is an alluringly gifted writer, whose future work it is a pleasure to anticipate.

The Comfort of Strangers is a nightmare about travel and evil, as it might have been conceived by a Harold Pinter, descended from a Henry James. Colin and Mary, presumably British, are on "holiday" in an Italian city, unnamed but presumably Venice. They are not married, these tourist lovers. Mary has children, whom she guiltily misses, from a marriage now ended. The couple do not relax on their vacation so much as they unravel, together and separately. They get lost all the time, saying, "We should have brought the maps." But the maps themselves are no help. Colin and Mary get lost merely studying the maps. Their personalities are somewhat melted.

So, lost late one night, famished and unable to find an open restaurant, they allow themselves to be taken over by a stranger on the street. Though the stranger's name is Robert, he is evidently Italian. (He says he has lived in England.) Robert "wore a tight-fitting black shirt, of an artificial, semitransparent material, unbuttoned in a neat V almost to his waist. On a chain around his neck hung a gold imitation razor blade. . . . " Myself, I would have insisted on staying lost, but Robert knows just the place, a very good place, and Colin and Mary, only a bit irritated and reluctant, go with him. The place is a bar Robert owns. He brings to the table a bottle of wine, three glasses, "and two well-fingered breadsticks, one of which was broken short." The cook is ill, Robert explains.

A wonderful thing now happens to the reader, if not to the helpless and hungry couple. Robert tells them a psychologically gruesome and somewhat comic story, more or less true, of his childhood as the son of a diplomat stationed in London, a story of the father playing off Robert, the only son, against two of Robert's sisters. The father is a sadist, a family fascist. Robert's intricate, dramatic tale stimulates one's curiosity and makes for unforgettable reading.

Colin and Mary eventually leave the bar, but they still cannot find their way back to their hotel. And they encounter Robert again. (He has, indeed, been following them—and worse.) This time, he brings them to his home and his wife, Caroline, allegedly the daughter of a former Canadian ambassador to England, where Robert had first met her. The

remainder of the novel is an increasingly sinister, macabre, even "ghoulish" account of the reception that Robert gives the tourists. Robert has inherited, in a violent form, his father's cruelty, and Colin and Mary become ruined victims of his pathological punitive personality (Caroline, already his victim, is a pathetic accomplice).

The Comfort of Strangers is Ian McEwan's nasty answer to our comfy adage "travel is broadening." The novel has an epigraph from Pavese: "Traveling is a brutality. It forces you to trust strangers and to lose sight of all that familiar comfort of home and friends. You are constantly off balance. Nothing is yours except the essential things— air, sleep, dreams, the sun, the sky—all things tending toward the eternal or what we imagine of it." I think it is impossible to resist the interest and challenge of the observation; and, even if the observation is untrue or incomplete, it is impossible to deny the interest and challenge of Mr. McEwan's novelistic elaboration.

The book, as it develops, requires the reader to accept a questionably large amount of innocence and acquiescence in Colin and Mary, and what almost seems like a careless overdose of perversity in Robert and Caroline. On the literal level, while not actually unbelievable, *The Comfort of Strangers* is hard to go along with at every moment. As a nightmare, however, it is convincing and clinging. Its details are so imaginative and precise as to be a source of delight.

Richard P. Brickner, "Traveling in Peril," in The New York Times Book Review, *July 5, 1981, p. 7.*

Eliot Fremont-Smith

Alert, lean, lucid prose counts for a lot these days. Ian McEwan's prose is nothing if not efficient; its smooth, classy precision puts us at ease even as we know the effect is calculated to ensnare and scare, to cast uncanny spells. Its very poise poises us for the eerie awfulness that is—*oh, delectably*—impending. . . . Now comes the equally elegant and "compelling" novella, *The Comfort of Strangers* and one must ask what went wrong, why it doesn't work.

The question presupposes the result, which is, alas, mundane. *The Comfort of Strangers* starts with tingles, promises true shivers and the catharsis of shock, and delivers only gore—and not enough of that. It is an unsatisfying suspense-horror, even for an upscale beach read, and therefore quite hateful. This has to do, of course, with resentment—arising from a serious breach of contract between the genre and the reader that no amount of fine writing can paper over. I'll get back to the contract (it's basically about forbidden lust and the promise of transcendence; the breach produces shame, ergo the resentment). But there is also the matter of less being sometimes less. McEwan's very efficiency does him in; admiring the machine, his craftiness (and our art-appreciation of it), one also begins to notice how small and mean it is, not up to the task of shock.

Two lovers come to an unnamed tourist city for a brief and, they hope, renewing vacation. He is Colin, "beautiful" in a slightly androgynous way; she is Mary, whose looks aren't described. They have been lovers for seven years, and the routine, though still accommodating and affectionate, is getting them down. They are English, but their roots are very tenuous: Mary's are a divorced husband and two young kids, Colin's aren't described.

The lovers are vaguely dyspeptic and notably disorganized, incapable of straightening out their hotel room (they leave that to the maid, who sometimes doesn't clean until late afternoon, so they stay out till then) and unable to decipher street maps of the city or even, when hot and thirsty, to locate a drink of water. Hardly aware of their specific surroundings, yet not in great discomfort—Colin's dreams which he recounts to Mary while she does her yoga are "those that psychoanalysts recommend, of flying, . . . of crumbling teeth, of appearing naked before a seated stranger"—they nevertheless sense that something is missing from their lives, or from life, or is anyway not quite right. And on this they have opinions.

Mary claims the key to the malaise lies in the politics of sex, in the continuing patriarchy—"the most powerful single principle of organization shaping institutions and individual lives." Colin argues that "class dominance [is] more fundamental." Mary says, spying a street poster advocating castration for convicted rapists, "It's a way of making people take rape more seriously as a crime." Colin counters, "It's a way of making people take feminists less seriously." McEwan notes that these arguments are less important for their substance than for the glancing abrasiveness they provide—subliminal evidence for Colin and Mary that they still care about each other, at least exist.

So far, so good—meaning so far, so cynical, with deliciously worse to follow. The city is an irritant; it is obviously and unmistakably Venice, so why the no-name pretense? But the victims are in place and perfectly set up for the inevitable. McEwan has also prepared our emotions,—sharpened a passion here, dulled an affect there. We understand and even "relate" to Colin and Mary—they're such ninnies, if anything too sweet and harmless (and there but for the grace of God, etc.)—but not to the degree that could mitigate our rising blood-lust, our erotic eagerness for whatever unspeakable obscenity McEwan has in store for them.

This, incidentally, adheres to a standard clause in the suspense-horror contract. The genre shall, after suitable preparation, expose evil to our excited exploration. But not just any old evil. It is sexual evil that engorges the modern imagination, and offers (vicariously) ultimate thrill. Or evil sexuality—the terms are nearly interchangeable, which is why so many books, and movies too, seem thematically redundant. (Nearly interchangeable does not, however, mean completely interchangeable, and fudging the distinction is a major McEwan error.) It is in a further clause that freedom from guilt is guaranteed, first through the dulling of affect, finally by redemptive shock; it is not the purpose of suspense-horror to make *us* feel bad.

Anyway, one evening Colin and Mary are wandering about, vaguely lost, looking for a place to eat, when a stranger offers assistance. He owns a bar, he says, and will take them there. The stranger's name is Robert; he wears a razor blade on a chain around his neck, but seems both affable and courtly, and soon is telling them all about himself. He's apparently a native of the city but grew up in London, where his father was a diplomat, though at home a sadistic tyrant. Robert was his favorite child and remembers him vividly, and with more than fright.

The evening winds down, Robert excuses himself, and eventually Colin and Mary also leave the bar (which—they scarcely notice—may be gay). But they have trouble finding their hotel, and also get very thirsty. Hours pass. In mid-morning they again meet Robert, who insists that the bedraggled couple come home with him; his wife, Caroline, a Canadian, would also insist. And so they do. They sleep, and then meet Caroline, who is crippled, and only slightly startles Mary by asserting, over brunch, "If you are in love with someone, you would even be prepared to let them kill you, if necessary."

Interruption: I am about to detail, albeit selectively, the inevitable. I wouldn't do this in a recommendation. Take surprise out of the genre, and there isn't much left. Yet there may be some readers who still have hopes for *The Comfort of Strangers*—perhaps have already bought the book—and to them I suggest quitting this review. You will miss some juicy parts, but save energy and stamps; no letters, please.

There are, of course, further encounters. It turns out that Robert and Caroline's attentiveness, which becomes very intense indeed, turns on the lovers. In the privacy of their hotel, Colin and Mary become regular sex machines. It has never been so good. They even joke about it, inventing for each other sex-slave scenarios. In fact, all their senses are heightened; they can even clean up their room (somewhat) and not get lost so much. To some things, however, they are still opaque. For instance, Colin hardly blinks when informed that Robert is going around the city saying they are lovers. And Mary, in the penultimate scene at Robert's house, is only mildly disconcerted to find Robert and Caroline's bedroom adorned with photos of Colin. Caroline explains, even as she slips a mickey into Mary's tea.

It seems that Robert has done his father one better. He is in love with Caroline, but his ardor is indistinguishable from hate. He likes to beat her up. This is why she is crippled. He would like to kill her, and, being true and frank to her (though no feminist), has told her so. This puts Caroline—both of them, really, but especially Caroline—in a bind. She's eager to satisfy her husband (true love demands no less), yet death, aside from being curtains, would destroy a relationship both she and Robert cherish—one based on the *potential* of ultimate sexual violence. So what to do?

Caroline thinks it's just wonderfully lucky that they've bumped into Colin and Mary. Mary can't speak or move because of the debilitating drug (the effect is similar, in a sense, to not being able to read street maps, though more distressing); and so she is unable to warn Colin when he returns to the house with Robert.

The inevitable is over very quickly. As Mary helplessly

watches, Robert and Caroline box Colin in a corner, cut his wrist with a razor, indulge in some extremely brief by-play (Caroline cops a feel, Robert tries a bloody deep-kiss), and then quit the house. (So *that's* why the packed bags were by the door!) Hours pass. By the time Mary recovers enough to get some help, Colin is dead. The police say they've seen this sort of thing before, and surmise that Robert and Caroline want eventually to be caught. There is no suggestion, however, that Robert should be castrated. Mary, understandably all shook up, intends to explain the patriarchy principle, but doesn't; instead after the necessaries, she numbly calls the kids and heads for home. Speculations about Caroline—to what extent an accomplice, to what a victim?—are left to the reader.

Along with a lot of other questions. This is the trouble with *The Comfort of Strangers*—questions that should be suffused in shock spring up. They are expressions of resentment, because the shock has not been sufficient to bury shame, to justify and expiate our willing tumescence for evil. Argue as you like—fantasy is never entirely devoid of moral consequence. But neither is it supposed to be a heavy trip in over-the-counter quality suspense-horror fiction (for that, some people go next door, to pornography). And the trouble with questions, of course, is that they stimulate answers that destroy whatever spell might otherwise linger on. If there's one thing the genre can't survive, it's explanation.

Why is the victim of sexual evil Colin instead of Mary? It makes no sense in terms of Robert's psyche. Colin is patently too weak—remember the hint of androgyny—to be a stand-in for Robert's macho dad. The answer is in McEwan, either because he calculated this kicky twist to be more salable, or for matters that may be both unresolved and libelous to explore. It is not, however, libelous to say that *The Comfort of Strangers* suggests that man's fate is more important (more unsettling) than woman's fate, and that even a hint of androgyny is profoundly subversive to this sophistication, and therefore deserving of the worst fate. But I suspect these things weren't thought through, just plopped.

What clearly was thought through, and worked on, was elegant and restrained prose style (restraint takes over at the end; not enough awful things happen to whoever the victim should have been). But then, why Venice? The answer may be that while an unnamed tourist city is wanted—it fits with Colin and Mary's general and acute astigmatism (a traditional metaphor for innocence)—McEwan is no Ionesco. (He's closer to Robbe-Grillet, if a referent is needed—plus a sizable dash of Pinter.) That is, an *invented* unnamed city of decadence and decay may have been too demanding. And then, too, Venice is where Colin and Mary, being such babes, although "no longer the youngest adults they know," would likely go; they're simply not the type for Florence or Copenhagen or Rhodes. Yet the question nags—Venice, *Thomas Mann's* Venice, but no one is supposed to know, not even the reader? Suspension of disbelief is one thing, suspension of routine synapses, after the age of 21, is another.

Questions and answers—they are not without interest. But they undermine the genre *The Comfort of Strangers* so

classily represents, and are symptomatic of betrayal. Our lust is given in trust, and there's no provision for arbitrating the thing in court—that is precisely what is *not* supposed to happen. In such a setting, the sexuality of evil is indeed transformed into the evil of sexuality. I said this was McEwan's error, and I still think so in terms of our being aware of it. But it may not have been an error. The message may be deliberate: dyspeptic, routine, happenstance sex is bad but survivable, but sharpened, enjoyable, cozy, and *witty* sex invites and is deserving of catastrophe. Maybe yes, maybe no—but I hadn't bargained for a tract.

Eliot Fremont-Smith, "Dearth in Venice," in The Village Voice, *Vol. XXVI, No. 29, July 15, 1981, p. 32.*

Kathy Stephen

At 2:32am London time the telephone rings and an alert, focused voice from a continental hotel room says: "Hello, this is Ian McEwan." . . . He is conscientiously returning a call, at this unearthly hour, to say that due to "complications in Berlin" he would not be able to make our appointment the following day.

Sensing opposition, he talks on smoothly, his voice betraying no sign that it is now 3:34am in Berlin, a time when all but true creatures of the night are asleep. At first he is charming, gracious, apologetic by turns. Then comes a brief outburst of anger, a crucial four-letter word, followed by cold indifference.

At this point he knows he has won. "I think you really *do* want to interview me," he says, as the digital clock flips to 2:37am London time. The meeting will be at a new time of his choosing. After all, he is Ian McEwan, 39, who in his twenties and early thirties was thought to be *the* most promising young writer in Britain: he can behave the way he wants to.

Certainly his fictional characters have behaved controversially. Reviewers murmured at the profane fixations of McEwan's stories but in general applauded the accomplished way he had invented his own version of a world of darkness and peopled it with eerie characters in the grip of erotic obsessions.

Virtually since he started writing at 22, McEwan has staked out his own claim in the terrain of sexual desires, secret cravings and irrational needs of the human psyche. McEwan didn't understand why readers were shocked or why critics "looking for lively copy" (in his words) felt compelled to list thumbnail plots of his stories that sounded like the ABCs of sexual taboos. Nor could he explain *why* he wrote about what he did. He did not feel such explanations were important. "One is at the mercy of one's subject matter," he said later, rather humbly. . . .

In 1983 he was one of the Top Twenty Young British Novelists in a Book Marketing Council promotion. At the time, there seemed a tacit agreement in the group, according to one member, that McEwan, even more than Martin Amis or Salman Rushdie, was the one to watch.

Six years have passed since his last novel, *The Comfort of*

Strangers, appeared, winning a place on the short list for the Booker Prize. Meanwhile, McEwan has proved himself as a screen writer, both for television and the award-winning film, *The Ploughman's Lunch.* But there has been no more sensuously urgent fiction.

Much has happened in his personal life as well in those fictionless years. In 1982 he married his long-time girlfriend, Penny Allen, who has since borne him two sons, the second of which, Gregory, McEwan delivered himself. (p. 36)

The difference between his volatile personality on the phone and the way he is in person among the relaxed confusion of his family is the difference between night and day. For someone so associated with writing about the promptings of the flesh in all its manifestations, he seems to be curiously more of the air than of the earth. He appears to be a gentleman in the literal sense, a hospitable host, and good at dealing with his children. His hair is rather greyer than one might expect of a man whose image has so far been that of the perpetually young talented writer. And he is very thin, pared, like his prose, down to the bone.

McEwan moves among his family—the centre of fresh attention having returned from a week's absence at a literary festival—with enthusiasm and joy. Everyone calls him Ian: the nanny, his children, the impromptu visitors. Lunch is spread out on the lawn near the swimming pool. The underworld of his prose fiction seems very far away.

Finally, in his roomy study overlooking the garden where his children are playing, McEwan talked about his long awaited new novel, *The Child in Time,* which in many ways, he believes, marks the beginning of a new era in his fiction, and yet holds echoes of that instinct for the edge which made his reputation.

"For a long time I've wanted to connect up two different sides of my writing: the writing in television plays and *The Ploughman's Lunch,* where my concerns were primarily social and to some extent political, and the writing in prose fiction that tended to be rather dark, rather interior and rather more concerned with the pathology of the mind."

The Child in Time displays a concern with the theme of responsibility and is written from the perspective of a parent anxious to keep a child safe in a fraught world where criminal intent has devastating, rather than merely interesting, consequences. McEwan is now well-acquainted with the realities of fatherhood—in addition to his own children, he is stepfather to his wife's two daughters, and as he spoke he would get up and look out the window if there was the least sound of crying or shouts from the garden.

His ability to convey desperate feelings is at its height in his description of the event which sends the book's plot in motion: a heart-stopping account of the disappearance of a three-year-old girl during a trip to a South London supermarket with her father.

McEwan based the plot on an incident his parents told him they witnessed in a military grocery store in Germany many years ago when a child disappeared—apparently snatched by a stranger. "The story chilled me so much; it seemed like a loss that was endless. It's a terrible thing to have a child die but you could slowly start to mend. But to know that the child was still around, possibly near you and growing away from you, would be agonising."

The plot surrounding the lost child is only one facet of the new novel. The most complex in structure of all his writing so far, *The Child in Time* is also a novel about politics, social justice, and child-care in Britain—and an attempt at a novel of ideas about the structure of time.

According to McEwan the novel is set "now and not now." Britain of today is recognisable but the unemployed have been given special badges and uniforms and made into official beggars. The government is turning its hand to writing an official childcare manual that will reshape the nation's wayward youth.

"The book's not only about a lost child. It has to do with the loss of childhood in one's self," McEwan said. . . . (pp. 36, 38)

His study is a reminder of the tension between imaginative wildness and intense control found in McEwan's writing. His word processor is to the right of his desk and there is a Freudian-style couch covered with an oriental rug. A bottle of Scotch, one-third empty, is on the coffee table, along with a scattering of books, including *Pride and Prejudice.* Across the room is a Rothko poster and near it, a large black and white school photograph of a huge class of boys.

McEwan was brought up the child of an enlisted soldier who became an army officer and a mother who played the role apparently expected of army wives. He was virtually an only child—a stepbrother and stepsister were over a decade older and away while McEwan grew up in army postings from Libya to Singapore.

Although he describes his home as containing a degree of discipline absolutely standard for the Fifties, it was apparently not home-life, but leaving home for Woolverton Hall School, a council-supported boarding school in Ipswich, that caused McEwan trauma. After school he went to Sussex University, and from there travelled in a van to India with friends, experimenting, he admits, with "psychotropic" drugs. He eventually enrolled in the fledgling creative writing course at East Anglia University—he was the first student—where he met two of his mentors, Malcolm Bradbury and Angus Wilson.

> When I first started writing I was interested a great deal in adolescence—that was the little sea I had just crossed. I would start writing and a voice would be speaking and I realised that this had the innocence of a child and the savagery of an adolescent. And so that just had to be followed.
>
> People who say my stories (have been) all about incest, masturbation, bodily excrescences and so on—the "good copy" list—miss the fact that I'm probably more than anything (he pauses) a moralist, and although that doesn't mean I'm interested in handing out punishments and rewards to characters, I am interested in the way people's

unconscious brings them into conflict with their social structure or the gap between people's presentation of themselves in the outward world and the inner one.

He works slowly: "I'm a labourer rather than someone for whom writing flows. I cut a lot, and I re-write." His short story collections and novels have, so far, been markedly brief. Whether he will complete the transition from prodigy to major writer is a question now staring him squarely in the face.

His wife, Penny, says: "He's got to have something on the go. His work detaches him from the family but in another way, if he's pleased with the way he's working it's better for the family."

Penny McEwan is a former journalist who has become an alternative healer. "I see all physical illnesses as related to mental and emotional aspects of a person. I think Ian may be happier than when we first met. Having children has opened him up a great deal. And possibly that shows itself in the new novel. There is a touch of optimism at the end."

McEwan's Oxford friend, the poet Craig Raine, is also impressed by *The Child in Time* as showing a new phase of fictional concerns:

> Ian McEwan has an extraordinarily meticulous imagination. Better than anyone else of his generation. He can show us not so much how our minds work, but what they really contain. Most of us, reporting on our interior life, resort to headlines and, if we are sophisticated, editorials. McEwan gives us the small print.

McEwan, having been generous with his time, still offers a lift to the station. On the way he talks about his plans: his screenplay of fellow author Timothy Mo's first novel, *Sour Sweet,* is currently being filmed. He is beginning to tinker with another novel. "It will be about outer space, I think. It's about time I got out there." And he is writing another film for an American producer: "They want to call it *The Good Son.* I'd rather call it *Bad Boy.*"

Malcolm Bradbury, novelist and one of the first to see McEwan's work, said:

> Ian was superb at calling up the feelings of the child—something so important for a writer. He wrote with enormous imaginative force. His world was that of adolescence, fantasy and childhood, but it seemed evident there would be a time when he would step on beyond that to write from an adult, worldly point of view.

Ian McEwan's writing has powerfully exhibited the mystery of a psychic puzzle within himself that he wants to explore in fiction rather than understand. He is still clearly in love with the excitement of mischief, but his new novel shows that he knows the child, in time, grows up. (p. 38)

> *Kathy Stephen, "The Bright Young Man Grows Up," in* The Sunday Times, *London, August 16, 1987, pp. 36-8.*

Roberta Smoodin

What greater nightmare can any parent have than that of a stolen child? Such an enormous, capricious loss would unutterably alter any adult life, with the horror and longing, the endless doubts, the fantasies of finding or recognizing the older child, and the desire to discern, in the moment of the ghastly event, what one did wrong, what one might have been able to change, would haunt a parent forever. This is the subject matter of Ian McEwan's new novel, ***The Child in Time,*** and it is powerful, heart-rending stuff. McEwan's dazzling, contrapuntal, subtly mystical gifts as a writer creep out of the subtexts to this single horrible event, and the novel he creates becomes a commentary on marriage, on government, on society, on international relations, parents and children, and even quantum physics and the very nature of time itself.

Like the recent novel *Staring at the Sun* by Julian Barnes, ***The Child in Time*** is set in the very near future, in which the everyday has remained remarkably the same, except for the fact that it is freed, for the writer, from the restraints of our knowledge or preconceptions about our own time. ***The Child in Time*** is also similar to Alice McDermott's *That Night;* both books use a main character's obsession with one past event, an event that shapes each character's life thereafter.

Stephen Lewis, the main character of ***The Child in Time,*** has his toddler daughter stolen from him in a supermarket. The ensuing destruction of his marriage, his professional life (he is a writer of children's books), and his ability to cope with mundane existence makes up the plot of the book. But the book is really about the nature of childhood, positing that many adults have much stronger ties to the children they used to be than one would suspect, particularly adult men. Stephen's boyhood dream of riding in a train's locomotive is fulfilled in the book's magical final chapter. Stephen's friend, Charles, a success in business and politics, hides a frightening connection to the childhood he never had. A lost childhood, lost childhood hopes and dreams remain present in the seemingly mature adult, McEwan suggests, not only in memory but in a kind of time that spirals in upon itself, seems to be recapturable in some plausible intermingling of Einstein and Proust, quantum physics and magical realism.

McEwan uses the literary microcosm, where characters and events recur for thematic reasons, to underscore this magical theory about time. Just as a beggar girl who Stephen gives too much money to turns up later, shockingly, in a train station to teach Stephen yet another lesson about childhood and death. Stephen "turns up" to witness his parents together before they were married, enacting what he will later find out had been the scene that determined his life. Stephen seems to have fallen through some lacuna in the warp and woof weave of time here, and it is eerily beautiful.

The style of this novel is spare, dark, cynical, graceful and cerebral, perfectly suited to the complex themes, but also in surprising and bittersweet contrast to its denouement. The ending wrought from the multilayered, difficult, moving story amazes one with its rightness, but more than this, allows McEwan to transcend the bounds of his style and to leap, with abandon, into new territory. This territory is the possibility of happiness, the continuation of fragile, tenuous life, and even more improbable: love. The gloriousness of this ending, in all its facets—wrapping up Stephen's complicated and mystical realization about his parents, Charles' tragic secret, and Stephen's wife's secret as well, is masterful, even more so because it is so deeply felt, so perfectly crafted.

The nightmare tapestry of the heart-rending loss of a child, which McEwan has woven so beautifully, ends in a splash of golden sunlight. The cautionary nature of all that has come before, about the peril of life and love, has been somewhat redeemed by the continuing, parallel existence of the past. Loss and life exist simultaneously; the past cannot be undone, nor can it be dismissed. Perhaps it is more present and accessible than we ever dreamed, McEwan seems to be hypothesizing in this brilliant novel.

> Roberta Smoodin, *"The Theft of a Child and the Gift of Time," in* Los Angeles Times Book Review, *September 20, 1987, p. 19.*

Michael Neve

Ian McEwan's *The Child in Time* is a novel that meditates on the dead hand of bureaucratic pronouncements on social matters (for example the education of children) and sees the State's use of white paper (and White Papers) as menacing, lifeless ways by which it endorses the nothingness at the centre of the politics of reaction. Famous for his power to denote the sinister things in the world, as well as its political ways, McEwan has not, as has been suggested, "grown up" in *The Child in Time.* Rather, he has deliberately regressed into the childish idea of a pure present, and by so doing is able to indict a bored and cruel society that no longer has the power to look after its children or recover its honest childishness. Despite a certain pretentiousness, not least in the use of a form of hippy physics about wholeness and order, this novel looks to a future which becomes its own midwife, bringing itself into existence by making, not just love, but life.

The novel's protagonist, Stephen Lewis, day-dreams his time away near the centres of power, especially Whitehall, listening to the deliberations of the Official Commission on Childcare, where speakers shuffle through dead wastes of space and time to reach conclusions like "Boys will be boys". Stephen is involved with the Commission through an old friend and contemporary, Charles Darke. A large part of the novel, and of the accusations and distress that it involves itself in, concern Darke, who is close to political power but closer still to mysterious collapse and a refusal to investigate the conditions of that collapse.

Stephen himself is "the father of an invisible child", his daughter Kate, missing not through the fault of others, but his own. In a frightening sequence early on in the novel, Stephen loses Kate, in a supermarket full of ghosts and ghostly commodities. Apparently based on something that McEwan heard from his own parents, this episode and the horror it inspires are to do with what the novel itself addresses: not dead persons, but missing persons.

This losing of Kate puts Stephen into a form of outer space, as when he tells his wife, a musician, of what has happened. He sees her from a high place, down there in South London. This is close to the Empson of the poems, or it may perhaps be seen as a manifestation of the history of drugs and their place in promoting terror. Stephen sees his lost daughter everywhere, in the faces on the street, in schoolrooms, among the now licensed beggars who roam Britain.

The danger facing a book like this is of joining the ranks of narcissistic works that announce the wonder of having children, thereby patronizing all those who have had children without making a fuss, and all those who decided against it because the world is as menacing, full of death and lost identity, as McEwan has always said it is. In fact, McEwan transcends such hymns to domestic life. He has written an English novel that has an almost Continental paranoia about the managerial State, and one moreover, where correct childrearing is the Head of State's deepest, most heartfelt concern. In an England peopled by either champagne-drinkers or broken hustlers, the political task, McEwan seems to suggest, is to protect your own childhood and then that of your child, partly by honouring your parents, partly by not forgiving your collaborationist friends. Stephen watches Charles Darke go strange (in his tree-house in the country) but also listens to Darke's wife Thelma (a brilliant physicist) as she describes field theory and as she refuses to find Charles's collapse (and eventual suicide) instructive. Thelma educates Stephen into the historical time-world that in turn becomes the dream-world where Stephen's broken hopes, his (superbly described) male depression, will lift. To make that journey the novel becomes by turns sentimental (about parents in war) and frightening (as when Stephen is nearly killed in an accident in his car). And much of one's feelings about *The Child in Time*'s success turns on one's view of the resolution that it gives itself, its version of renewal and rebirth. It may be that Stephen delivers his own child, at the end of the novel, in a way too close to the old cultural practice of *couvade,* that "man-childbed" where the man at the point of birth simulates and appropriates the mother, as if giving birth. Or he may be a genuine *accoucheur,* returning to his wife's side without stealing her powers or her memories, as Kate is not forgotten and possibly recreated.

Menaced by dead weather, dumb television, and a sleep-walking, heedless political class, Stephen and his wife have another child (just) in time. Over-convinced of the possibility of personal completion, *The Child in Time* errs on the side of goodness, asking its readers to enter the condensed imprecisions of dreams in order to make a case for a possible future. McEwan was too implausibly horrified at life in some of his early work, and in *The Comfort of Strangers,* downright sadistic. The years that have passed have brought a courageous and socially enraged novel, helping us believe once again "That men may rise on stepping-stones / Of their dead selves to higher things".

> Michael Neve, *"Possible Futures," in* The Times Literary Supplement, *No. 4405, September 4-11, 1987, p. 947.*

Rebecca Goldstein

Before I had reached even its first sentence, Ian McEwan's new novel [*The Child in Time*] managed to startle me. In his acknowledgments, among the three books to which he says he is indebted, is *Wholeness and the Implicate Order,* a highly theoretical and abstract work by the highly theoretical and abstract English physicist David Bohm. The other books are interesting, too: Christina Hardyment's *Dream Babies,* covering three centuries of advice to parents, and Joseph Chilton Pearce's *Magical Child,* a 1977 book promising to reveal the biological plan underlying a child's developing intelligence. As these last two are clearly directed to the child in Mr. McEwan's title, so, I reasoned, must the presence of Mr. Bohm's book signal that the nature of time itself is to be a subject in the novel to follow.

My intention to watch out for time was momentarily forgotten in the powerful grip of the opening pages, in which the central event of the novel unfolds. A 3-year-old girl, on a mundane Saturday morning trip to the local supermarket, is snatched away, literally under her father's nose.

> The checkout girl was already at work, the fingers of one hand flickering over the keypad while the other drew Stephen's items towards her. As he took the salmon from the cart, he glanced down at Kate and winked. She copied him, but clumsily, wrinkling her nose and closing both eyes. He set the fish down and asked the girl for a shopping bag. She reached under a shelf and pulled one out. He took it and turned. Kate was gone.

The narrative that follows takes place largely within the fragmented psyche of the father, Stephen Lewis, a successful writer of children's books, who is transported by his bereavement to the extreme reaches of passivity, alienation and solitude. This is a familiar habitat for characters in Mr. McEwan's fiction, who stalk the bleak and airless site of his imagination with empty eyes and strange desires. But where Mr. McEwan's earlier creations tend to be unlikable misfits—chillingly unwholesome children and adolescents—in this work we are in the company of a sympathetic adult, a parent, devastated by the completeness of his loss.

But the psychic territory is very much the same: a state of distraction so dazed and dispirited that characters are unable to control even their own fantasy life, much less events of the external world. Mr. McEwan is something of a master at representing misery. I particularly admire the lovingly painted details of that disorder that is the natural outward expression of the eviscerated passivity of his characters:

> Mostly he was indifferent to the squalor of his flat, the meaty black flies and their leisurely patrols. When he was out he dreaded returning to the deadly alignments of familiar possessions, the way the empty armchairs squatted, the smeared plates and old newspapers at their feet. It was the stubborn conspiracy of objects— lavatory seat, bedsheets, floor dirt—to remain exactly as they had been left.

And so there is the child of the title, whose loss sets in motion the emotional current of the story. But what of time? I found, on forcing myself to re-read the painfully moving opening section, constant reference to time: "Kate's growing up had become the essence of time itself. . . . Without the fantasy of her continued existence he was lost, time would stop." Thinking how he might have chosen to make love to his wife instead of leaving immediately for the supermarket,

> Stephen was to make efforts to reenter this moment, to burrow his way back through the folds between events, crawl between the covers, and reverse his decision. But time—not necessarily as it is, for who knows that, but as thought has constituted it—monomaniacally forbids second chances. There is no absolute time, his friend Thelma had told him on occasions, no independent entity. Only our weak and independent understanding.

Thelma is a theoretical physicist who wrote her Ph.D. dissertation on the nature of time. I had on first reading hurried past these interesting, if somewhat chill, abstractions, swept along on the swift emotional current of the child's disappearance. However, in the story that follows, as this current slackens, it is abstractions such as these that surface and even take over. It is not just that Stephen's sense of time becomes distorted. Time itself—or, if Thelma would deny the reality of such a thing, at least the time Stephen shares with the other characters in the book— undergoes severe warping. For example, Thelma's husband, Charles Darke, who is wildly ambitious, successful and cynical—in other words, a real grown-up—forsakes his promising political career for a tree house and a reclaimed childhood.

An even more dramatic result of time's activity occurs when Stephen, on the way to visit his now-estranged wife (their old intimacy torn asunder by their shared loss), finds himself suddenly, literally, in the past, witnessing a conversation between his courting parents, during which they consider whether or not to abort him. And this experience is not presented as a figment of his torment. Quite the contrary, he is given outside corroboration that he had been, in some sense, there at that time, that his perceived presence was what determined his mother's decision.

The story, as it proceeds, involves itself more and more with an almost playful meditation on the nature and possibilities of time. And as I stepped back to admire Mr. McEwan's inventive genius, I had to acknowledge that it was a distancing, that his experimentation with the time of the title drew me away from the story flowing from the child of the title. In fact, time's prominence eventually set me to wondering whether the central event, the instantaneous and inexplicable loss of the child, was itself an outcome of the violent action of time, rather than the other way round. Was the child, quite literally, in time? The thought that the central event was constructed of the stuff of science fiction seriously undermined my involvement in Stephen's tragedy, and with those aspects of the book that resonate with psychological reality: the beautifully realized relationships, the tracing of the many-layered love between father and child, husband and wife.

But if the powerful empathetic current set in motion by these elements is occasionally frozen over by something cold and overly calculated, the strongly felt presence of these elements is always enough to get the current moving again, until we are carried to an ending as artfully conceived as it is poignantly realized.

Rebecca Goldstein, "He Turned Around and She Was Gone," in The New York Times Book Review, October 11, 1987, p. 9.

Michael Wood

There is a scene which recurs in several of Hitchcock's films and which could well be in all of them, since it is so central to his favourite fear. An innocent man is discovered in a situation that makes him look hopelessly, undeniably guilty: the corpse in his arms, the knife in his hand. His innocence is both unquestionable (for us) and unbelievable (as far as everyone in the movie is concerned). This man has been framed by appearances, as we all could be; innocence is no defence, innocence doesn't stand a chance.

A complex variant of this scene haunts Ian McEwan's fiction, and creates, among other things, an eerie resonance for the mild-seeming title of his remarkable new novel. For McEwan, the innocent is never entirely innocent, always has a murky relation to the corpse and the knife. But an innocence remains amid the guilt, a bewilderment that no simply guilty person would feel. The children in *The Cement Garden* (1978) have buried their mother in the cellar, and they have committed incest. But they are still children, and they continue to look at each other 'knowingly, knowing nothing.' Innocence is corrupted, complicated by weird cross-currents—'He was innocent,' a character thinks in the new novel, 'but it would take some explaining'—yet only a thorough dose of knowledge (or guilt) could abolish it, and that dose is usually lacking, or in abeyance. Even McEwan's adults are children, sometimes cripplingly so, as in *The Child in Time* (1987), where a politician commits suicide because he cannot bring his residual childhood into line with his frantic public life, where a father cannot mourn his lost daughter without recreating his parents' marriage and his own conception. Knowingness, McEwan keeps telling us, is a flight from knowledge, and knowledge is hard to come by and hard to take.

Hitchcock deals in fear, while McEwan deals in horror, in the Gothic in a rather special sense—in what we might call the Gothic of everyday life. This means that innocence itself has a rather different role to play. In Hitchcock innocence says, 'I didn't do it'; in McEwan it says, 'I may have done it but you have to hear the whole story', or, 'I did it, but only because I was ambushed by some stranger hiding in my personality, some other self I wasn't prepared to meet'.

By Gothic I mean that moment in a fiction when all the emotions go underground, when what seemed like a logical, if extravagant plot turns to nightmare, driven by forces that no one will name. The corpse, for instance, already a practical problem in material reality, takes up its residence in the mind; the monster doubles in size; the aggrieved woman becomes the shrieking harpy, ascends from melodrama into myth—the woman needed appeasing, but the harpy has to be killed. 'The imagination', McEwan memorably says in *The Innocent,* 'was even more brutal than life'. Ancient repressions must be at work here, stoking the imagination with horrors, and the violence which so suddenly surrounds us is surely a distorted reflection of what we are anxious not to know. If we could face what horrifies us, we presumably wouldn't need these Gothic displacements. McEwan's great gift is for getting his characters onto this level of experience by the most casual means: they step into the Gothic the way other people step onto buses, and the sheer ordinariness of their arrival in horror is part of what takes the breath away.

The world of espionage is the perfect place for a writer interested in the difference between knowingness and knowledge, and *The Innocent* is set in Berlin in 1955 and 1956, with a brief epilogue set in 1987. The Voice of America plays "Rock around the Clock," and then "Heartbreak Hotel." This is Berlin before the Wall, torn by memories, littered with ruins, and even more littered with spies, 'between five and ten thousand,' if a report quoted in the novel is to be believed. George Blake, sentenced in 1961 to 42 years in prison for spying, makes a few brief appearances and plays an interesting part in the plot. Intelligence, we learn, is a matter of levels of clearance. One set of persons believes they are building a warehouse. Those whose clearance takes them to the next level know that the warehouse is a radar station. Those at the next level know that the radar station is a cover for a tunnel which will permit the British and the Americans to tap the Russians' telephone cables. And those at the level after that? It's easy to see how espionage runs over into theology, and one American agent here bases a whole theory of human culture on secrecy. 'Secrecy made us possible', he says, meaning that the first human who knew something that others didn't know was the first individual.

Secrecy, of course, can be a cover for ignorance as well as knowledge, the very notion of the secret is a form of bluff. Much intelligence work must be done along these lines. And innocence might then get entangled in secrecy in quite complicated ways—not knowing, for instance, what it thinks it knows, an innocence in spite of itself. I'm not going to describe the plot of this novel—it has too many brilliant surprises, which should not be spoiled—but it won't hurt to look at its chief characters and implications. Our first innocent is a young Englishman called Leonard Marnham, an electrician involved in the wiring of the equipment in the aforementioned tunnel. He meets Maria, an attractive German woman, and McEwan's prose enters a realm of stealthy double-entendre which recalls the hint-filled atmosphere of Henry James—or rather, given the horror of much of what happens later, the atmosphere of a Stephen King who has learned to write like Henry James. 'It had always been certain to start like this. If he was honest with himself, he had to concede that he had always known it really, at some level . . . He thought, correctly as it turned out, that his life was about to change'. The ostensible—and real—subject here is falling in love for the first time, but the carefully unspecific sentences echo already (even if we have read no further) like an elaborate soundtrack of promises. There are other delicately dropped narrative hints ('Many years later,' 'the beginning of the end of Leonard's Berlin days'), which close off some plot possibilities, but still leave us groping, vulnerable to unguessed-at twists of action. Similarly, when Leonard is said to be 'unaccountably happy' or 'uncomplicatedly happy,' we register the feeling—McEwan has made it entirely convincing—but also hear an unspoken threat, as if the old jealous gods were still on the lookout for such happiness. Leonard's innocence ends, in one sense, when he finally understands the emotions which link him to Maria—McEwan's account of the ugly, troubled emotions Leonard *doesn't* understand is a *tour de force* of precision and lucid imagination—but in another sense his innocence, of the political world, of the vast domain of chance, of the way the past can highjack the present, is just beginning.

There are other innocents in the novel—notably the Americans, who remain naive even when they are up to complicated things, and are both dangerous and decent for that reason. Their minds, as Maria says of one of them, are 'too simple and too busy.' Is the 'special relationship' between America and Britain a relationship between innocence and knowingness, or between brands of innocence? Between brands of innocence which are also brands of knowingness, perhaps. Little knowledge either way. And in a disturbing sense the Germans, too, are innocent—this is the subtlest, most glancing implication in the book. Leonard, who was 14 when the war ended, enters a bar on his first night in Berlin and hears a group of men talking. His poor German and his historical superstitions are enough to make him believe the men are unrepentantly discussing genocide, and he is quite wrong: the conversation is innocent. Later, though, when an "innocent" character has been caught up in unimaginable butchery, he thinks, 'I am no different from you, I am not evil', and we half-believe him. Or, rather, we believe he is different from us only because the Gothic has got him, but hasn't (yet) got us. He is not a German, but the terms of his defence apply more closely to the Germans than to anyone else in the novel.

'His dreams were starting without him'; 'The numerous small anxieties associated with preparing a three-course meal animated her face'; 'They knew one another much as they knew themselves, and their intimacy, rather like too many suitcases, was a matter of perpetual concern'; 'It hurts. Hunched by the window with his empty glass, Stephen let his thoughts wither to those two words'. These sentences, taken from three of McEwan's four novels, are a form of signature. His writing is characteristically patient, sympathetic, inventive, intelligent, attentive to detail. The tone is always steady, even (especially) when it deals with repellent material. The books are also funny, in a macabre way, particularly *The Innocent,* where quite ghastly bits of behaviour keep stumbling across the structure of farce, as if farce were in the end the natural form of horror—horror's home.

In the face of all this, it seems absurd (and ungrateful) to complain that things are sometimes *too* well done. The bookshops are full of novels that aren't 'done' at all, and what would 'too well done' mean, anyway? But there is some sort of risk of claustrophobic neatness in McEwan's work, a sense of too many suitcases. It arises, for example, in the way Leonard's experience of love and his work in the tunnel are brought together in a series of images about burrowing, borders and the like—when he is said to miss the tunnel 'almost as much' as he misses Maria. These images in turn tie up with espionage when Leonard, wanting to hold a difficult conversation in the dark, assumes 'that he was safer under cover.' Similarly, in *The Child in Time,* a brilliantly described but gratuitous-seeming motor accident reveals its purpose when a baby is born in much the same way that a man was released from the wreckage of the crash. Accident, birth, damage, danger, life, death—got it? The problem isn't, at least for me, the rather dogged ingenuity at work here, or the implied meanings, which seem rich and interesting enough. It is the sense of what in a less accomplished writer would be under-confidence, an unwillingness to leave well (or more often, wonderfully-rendered ill) alone. There is one occasion on which both McEwan's elegant and stringent style and his tilt into overkill are nicely displayed. Leonard doesn't want to leave Maria, but his injured pride is dragging him away, he is 'drawn to his own defeat': 'Here he was, insisting on leaving. It was the behaviour of a stranger and he could do nothing, he could not steer himself in the direction of his own interests. Self-pity had obliterated his habitual and meticulous good sense, he was in a tunnel whose only end was his own fascinating annihilation'. The image of a man failing to steer himself towards his interests seems witty and exact, as does the opposition between self-pity and good sense—which of us, in the right mood, wouldn't instantly prefer self-pity?—and it is (just) possible that the tunnel has crept in as a casual, unpremeditated metaphor, the product of the writer's busy unconscious, putting in a little overtime. The effect, though, is to dump the whole complicated sign-system of the novel on this small moment: tunnel, spies, underground, secrets, knowledge, innocence, history, all come bouncing into Leonard's private life, when the connection has already been plentifully made. The writer at this point seems keener on Meaning than on meaning, and we are too busy with our admiration (or irritation) to attend to other feelings.

But this is a small distraction, McEwan's own lapse into knowingness. Otherwise, *The Innocent* is a haunting investigation into the varied and troubling possibilities of knowledge. The sheer cleverness of the book is dazzling, and only fully to be appreciated as you turn the last page: but then cleverness is a real virtue here, the best guide possible to the questionable territory between innocence and whatever comes after. (pp. 24, 26)

Michael Wood, "Well Done, Ian McEwan," in London Review of Books, *Vol. 12, No. 9, May 10, 1990, pp. 24, 26.*

James Buchan

Nine pages into *The Innocent,* Ian McEwan's newest novel, the reader will get a jolt. Up to then, it's been smooth going: a routine Cold War setting, English and American intelligence officers with well-defined national characteristics, Berlin street names, stuff in German, evidence of mugged-up history:

> That's Fritz. They all get called Fritz. One of Gehlen's men. You know who I mean?

This particular reader was in clover. I thought: is Ian McEwan, of all people, throwing it in to write a spy thriller? Do I get paid all this money just for reading a sort of high-brow *Funeral in Berlin?* Then, at the top of page nine, comes the jolt. The intelligence officers are having coffee:

> From across the landing, through the open door, came the urinous scent of burnt toast smelled at a distance.

The word urinous is pure McEwan, his weird preoccupations breaking into the flat narrative and knocking the reader sideways. Everything comes back in a rush: *The Comfort of Strangers,* the short stories, the lav, the smelly sex, the blood all over the place. That urinous: it is as if the fairground operator had slipped the ratchet on the roller-coaster. You regret getting on. You want to get off. You don't mind about the money. You wave wildly at the glum young man. But the safety bar is down, and you are already moving, picking up speed, and there is nothing to do but hang on through scenes of unexampled horror and foulness till the fellow hands you out, legs shaking, sick with fatigue, at the end of the book.

With *The Innocent,* Ian McEwan has abandoned the speculative interests of *The Child in Time* (published in 1987) and gone back to his first love, which is carving up his characters. Once again, he chooses a well-frequented literary setting for those acts of fictional outrage. In *The Comfort of Strangers,* published in 1981, it was tourist Venice, with its safe bustle of characters from Thomas Mann or Daphne du Maurier. This time, we get Berlin in 1955-56, a place teeming with literary spies and double agents. For all the ponderous efforts of local and out-of-town critics, McEwan gets away with horrible murder both times.

In *The Innocent,* Leonard Marnham is a young and awkward Post Office engineer newly arrived in Berlin to work on a clandestine project known as Operation Gold. This was a tunnel dug by the CIA and MI6 into the Soviet sector of Berlin in the hope of tapping underground cables carrying secret communications. (The tunnel was evidently betrayed by George Blake, who makes a true cameo appearance in this book: sharply cut, coruscating.)

In a bar and dance hall called the Resi, while drinking with his new associates and carrying a rose behind his ear, Marnham receives a note from another table by pneumatic tube. It is from a girl called Maria Eckdorf, who has survived the liberation of Berlin and a brutal husband, lives in Kreuzberg, and is lonely. They fall in love. The story does not depend for its effect on my not giving away the plot, no sir, but I don't suppose I should anyway. Somebody gets killed, carved up and carried around in a box. The tunnel is betrayed. Thirty-one years later, Marnham returns to Berlin and thinks troubled thoughts about the end of the Cold War.

This simple story shows McEwan's tremendous strengths as a writer. He is good at portraying complex relationships, between an official driver and his passenger, say, or between lovers. McEwan can still describe a man's first love affair with the teenager's queasy and tumultuous pride:

> If Leonard needed proof of his dedication to a passion it was in the matted thickness of his grey socks, and the aroma of butter, vaginal juices and potatoes that rose from his chest when he loosened the top button of his shirt. The excessively heated interiors at the warehouse released from the folds of his clothes the scent of over-used bed-sheets and prompted disabling reveries in the windowless room.

This sort of thing caused a sensation when McEwan's first book of stories, *First Love, Last Rites,* come out in 1975. McEwan has refined it a bit, cutting out the eels and the rats, but it remains as direct as ever.

McEwan is also good at creating small private spaces for his characters: Marnham's government-issue apartment, his cramped room at the tunnel warehouse, the piled-high bed in Maria's freezing flat. What is strange about this novel is that the larger settings are all wrong. Neither Berlin nor the 1950s come across at all. This is an untypical weakness. His Venice in *The Comfort of Strangers* is maddening and claustrophobic and he creates an England of authoritarian Thatcherism and farm monoculture for *The Child in Time.* It is as if McEwan had taken the Berlin setting off the peg.

Again, in *The Comfort of Strangers,* the reader is led in with great care, undermined, demoralised until he starts at the smallest thing: I remember a harmless swim off the Lido which had me turning pages in handfuls. Here there are long passages where nothing much happens at all. (I liked these, for reasons which will become clear.)

In describing the tunnel, which a journeyman thriller-writer could do in his sleep, McEwan writes as if he is translating from Arabic: . . .

> At the base, cut into the wall of the shaft, was a round black hole, the entrance to a tunnel. Various lines and wires fed into it from above. There was a ventilation pipe which was connected to a noisy pump set well back against the basement wall. There were field telephone wires, a thick cluster of electrical cable, and a hose streaked with cement which fed into another smaller machine which stood silent beside the first.

The last-minute smear of McEwanite cement can't disguise a curiously vague and uninteresting piece of description.

I suspect the problem is that McEwan doesn't give a toss about the tunnel, Berlin or the Cold War. The themes of loyalty and betrayal so efficiently worked by John Le Carré and others do not figure in *The Innocent.* What this book is about is packing and unpacking things with a hangover, first 150 Ampex tape-recorders, then a male body.

The tape-recorders are horrible enough. There is no writer alive who can instill so much nastiness into inanimate objects:

> He drew the hunting knife from its sheath and plunged it in. The cardboard yielded easily, like flesh, and he felt and heard something brittle shatter at the knife's tip. He experienced a thrill of panic. He cut away the lid, pulled clear handfuls of wood shavings, and compressed sheets of corrugated paper. When the cheesecloth wrapping round the tape-recorder had been cut away he could see a long diagonal scratch across the area that would be covered by the spools. One of the control knobs had split in two.

But nothing in McEwan's writing, or any literary fiction I know, prepares the reader for what is to come.

The murder and the carve-up and disposal of the body occupies pages 135-215 of this novel. Though I read the book twice, I could not bring myself to read this passage a second time, even to copy it out in quotation. That it is an extraordinary piece of writing goes without saying. I still don't know what to make of it.

There is quite a lot of journalism in this book—McEwan thanks people for research and comments and stuff, always a bad sign in a novel—and the description of the body is as precise as you would expect. But I cannot believe these 80 pages are there for the sake of information, to tell us how to cut up and dispose of a body. McEwan himself is quite snooty about journalistic novels (in *A Child in Time*):

> . . . international best-sellers, the kind of book whose real purpose was to explain the workings of a submarine, an orchestra or a hotel.

Nor is the carve-up designed as a stress to test his characters. They scarcely meet after the deed is done. Fictional time moves on and the novel's loose ends have to be tied up with a long Dear John letter in the last chapter.

I think the dismemberment and disposal of the body is simply a literary task McEwan set himself, and for which the rest of the book is merely a frame (or box). He succeeds brilliantly in his task. These pages carry a feeling of oppression, sadness and guilt that I know only from one or two nightmares. For this intensity, people will no doubt pay good money, but it is all a bit dispiriting. With *The Innocent,* our best young, or youngish, novelist has created a new publishing category: literary slasher fiction. (pp. 36-7)

> *James Buchan, "Getting Away with Murder,"*
> *in* The Spectator, *Vol. 264, No. 8444, May 12,*
> *1990, pp. 36-7.*

Laurie Muchnick

McEwan is part of a now-approaching-middle-aged generation of male British writers who have changed their country's literature from one of genteel domestic excavations to a muscular, wide-ranging examination of the (post) modern condition. The Brit Pack—Martin Amis, Julian Barnes, Salman Rushdie, Kazuo Ishiguro, Bruce

Chatwin, McEwan—has produced some of the most exciting fiction and quasi-fiction of the last 10 years, and has evolved from a bunch of young upstarts to a still provocative yet highly commercial literary establishment. Just how commercial will be proved by McEwan's impending ubiquity on the screen: three of his books are in various stages of production.

Paramount is planning a film version of *The Innocent,* which, while slightly twisted by Hollywood standards, is McEwan's most commercial book by far. Set in mid-1950s Berlin, where the occupying World War II victors have become bitter Cold War bedfellows, the book can be read as a semi-conventional thriller cum bildungsroman. The innocent of the title is Leonard Marnham, a 25-year-old British telephone technician who has never lived without his parents, never had a girlfriend, never met an American—until he's dispatched to work on a British-American intelligence operation in Berlin.

Leonard likes being involved in espionage. He acquires several secrets, which make him feel a lot more grown up. For one thing, he starts spying on the Americans for his fellow Brits. He also begins an affair with an older, divorced German woman, Maria, who initiates him into the mysteries of human relations as well as of sex. "There's a curious myth—which literary fiction promotes—that you lose your innocence when you first have sexual experience," McEwan told me. "In fact, I think it's the beginning of innocence. It's the beginning, not the end, of the process of learning; it's the emotions that are so difficult to learn how to deal with. So it isn't first sex that transforms Leonard, it's having to explain himself to Maria for the first time."

Before long, he has a lot of explaining to do. Leonard can't forget he's in a defeated city, that he represents not only the winners of the Second World War but also the good guys of the Cold War. He's not used to being anything but a humble civil servant, and his newly discovered potency coupled with his hero status gives him delusions of power. Once the novelty of sleeping with Maria wears off, he starts having fantasies of dominating her: "She was the defeated, she was his by right, by conquest, by right of unimaginable violence and heroism and sacrifice. What elation! To be right, to win, to be rewarded." He daydreams about raping her: "He wanted his power recognized and Maria to suffer from it, just a bit, in the most pleasurable way." She would enjoy it, of course. But Leonard miscalculates, because what attracted Maria to him in the first place was his innocence, the way she doesn't have to be physically scared of him. What for Leonard is a fantasy of domination is for Maria a stark memory of war, of fear and humiliation. When Leonard tries to play out his fantasy, Maria panics and sends him away.

McEwan has always excelled at describing the dynamics of relationships. In *The Comfort of Strangers,* he paints the small irritations that affect Colin and Mary on their vacation:

> As individuals they did not easily take offense; but together they managed to offend each other in surprising, unexpected ways . . . and with

each step the city would recede as they locked tighter into each other's presence.

Sex figures prominently in these relationships, and while it can be ecstatic, it's always fraught with danger. In his earlier books, it tends to be all incest and perversion, while the later novels find room for domestic warmth:

> [Stephen] took Julie some tea. . . . She said something which was lost to the pillows. He put his hand under the bedclothes and massaged the small of her back. She rolled over and pulled his face towards her breasts. When they kissed he tasted in her mouth the thick, metallic flavour of deep sleep.

But even this tranquil, loving scene from *The Child in Time* turns into a nightmare: when Stephen goes to the supermarket instead of making love with his wife—so they'll have more time later—his daughter is snatched from the checkout line. "Later, in the sorry months and years, Stephen was to make efforts to reenter this moment, to burrow his way back through the folds between events, crawl between the covers, and reverse his decision." Was Kate kidnapped because her parents didn't have sex? In *The Comfort of Strangers,* Colin and Mary change their vacation routine to make love before dinner one night; they "had never left the hotel so late, and Mary was to attribute much of what followed to this fact." What follows is a chance meeting with a seductive stranger, a compulsive involvement in a sadomasochistic duet, and, eventually, the erotically charged murder of Colin right in front of Mary. In McEwan's world, having sex (or not having sex) can make all the difference.

An act of sex—interrupted, in this case—is as pivotal in *The Innocent* as it was in the earlier books, leading to a grisly fight, murder, and the oft-mentioned dismemberment scene. Leonard manages to patch things up with Maria, and they decide to get married. While in bed, preparing to consummate their engagement, they hear the sound of breathing in the dark. Maria's ex-husband, Otto, a belligerent drunk who appears periodically to demand money and beat Maria up, has broken in and passed out in the closet. If they hadn't decided to make love at that moment, if they had stayed out later and given Otto a chance to sober up . . . perhaps the horror that followed would never have occurred?

McEwan says "the idea that this is a European century of fantastic violence" figures greatly in *The Innocent.* "We had in the first half of the century a scale of human cruelty that's beyond any historical comparison. . . . And it wasn't just people like Hitler and Himmler and Goebbels, those moral monsters; most of the people directly involved in that mayhem were fairly ordinary people who became transformed step by step by events." Leonard isn't a monster, but he becomes enmeshed in the banality of evil. There is a moment after he has killed Otto, hacked him up, and stuffed his body into two suitcases "when Leonard suddenly had the measure of the distance [he] had traveled, . . . and how all along the way each successive step had seemed logical enough, consistent with the one before, and how no one was to blame."

McEwan's viewpoint isn't unremittingly bleak, however.

The Innocent ends on an optimistic note, with Leonard returning to Berlin as the Wall is about to come crashing down. As with many nonorganic endings, like the newspaper account that ends [Tom Wolfe's] *The Bonfire of the Vanities* and the science-fictionish academic conference at the end of [Margaret Atwood's] *The Handmaid's Tale,* the last chapter feels tacked on, not quite necessary. So why is it there? McEwan says the new optimism isn't because he's feeling better about the world—quite the contrary. "Maybe it's because I feel more alarmed about the world that I feel a responsibility to locate what is good. . . . I cling to the idea that people are always better than the systems in which they live." I hope McEwan doesn't get too nice—I'd be afraid to read his next book if the characters never lose their innocence.

> Laurie Muchnick, "You Must Dismember This: Ian McEwan's Shock Treatment," in The Village Voice, Vol. XXXV, No. 35, August 28, 1990, p. 102.

John Banville

Ian McEwan's *The Innocent* was not on the short list for the 1990 Booker Prize—and should have been. This is not to say that I think very highly of the novel; that damn prize, which obsesses us so much on this side of the Atlantic, is no certain measure of literary worth; McEwan's book, in a poor year for novels, should certainly have been among the finalists; but, then, Booker judging panels are notorious for the eccentricity of their decisions.

Ian McEwan is one of the younger generation of English novelists who learned their craft at Malcolm Bradbury's creative-writing course at the University of East Anglia—indeed, McEwan was Bradbury's first student. The creative-writing course is an institution in the United States, but in England the East Anglia school was revolutionary and, to many, a preposterous venture: preposterous because it struck at one of the cherished tenets of English life, which is that professionalism is bad, or in bad taste at least, and that only the gentleman amateur can achieve anything worthwhile. East Anglia, however, was a further stage in the rebellion against the old order begun in the late 1940s by the "red brick" generation of writers (Amis père, John Wain, John Osborne, etc.) which aimed at ousting the Oxford and Cambridge swells and setting in their places the new literary meritocrats. (How far off the whole business seems now, a Spenserian mock-battle played out in fields not yet paved over; never such innocence, as Philip Larkin has it, never such innocence again.)

Much was expected from Ian McEwan. His collection of stories, *First Love, Last Rites,* was one of the most startling debuts since the war. Here was a talent as cold and gleaming as a new alloy, the potential of which no one could be quite sure of yet. A second story collection, *In between the Sheets,* showed that the first was no fluke. However, the novels that followed—*The Cement Garden, The Comfort of Strangers,* even the very powerful *The Child in Time*—somehow did not live up to expectations. There is ice at the heart of these books; however, the cold they exude does not thrill, but numbs, rather.

If Brian Moore set out to write a moral fable in the form of a thriller, Ian McEwan in *The Innocent* seems to have done the opposite, though this is unlikely to have been his intention. The book is set in Berlin in 1955, with the cold war at its coldest. Leonard Marnham, the innocent of the title, a young technician from the British Post Office, arrives in the city as part of the Anglo-American secret intelligence team. . . . (pp. 24-5)

On a pub crawl one night . . . , Leonard meets and falls in love with a young married German woman, Maria. Their affair, literally a source of warmth in one of the worst winters Berlin has known, is described with tender precision. Of course, the idyll, like all literary idylls, cannot last. Maria's sot of a husband turns up, and the affair ends in violence.

Remarkable violence, in fact. The high (or low, depending on the state of your nerves and your digestion) point of the book is a long and clinically detailed description of the murder of Otto and the dismemberment and disposal of his body. It is a chillingly bravura passage, which McEwan has brought off with steely confidence and skill.

Otto appears, not as a *deus ex machina* but a *diabolus ex wardrobe* (this is a nail-biting and undeniably comic chapter-ending), and a fight ensues between him and Leonard:

> He put his fists up, the way he had seen boxers do it. Otto had his hands by his side, like a cowboy ready to draw. His drunk's eyes were red. What he did was simple. He drew back his right foot and kicked the Englishman's shin. Leonard dropped his guard. Otto punched out, straight for his Adam's apple. Leonard managed to turn aside, and the blow caught him on the collarbone. It hurt, it really hurt, beyond reason. It could be broken. It would be his spine next.

Despite Otto's superior fighting skill . . . , Leonard wins the fight, and Otto goes down: "The cobbler's last still protruded from his head, and the whole city was quiet."

At Maria's urging, and out of his fear of being convicted as a murderer and sent to prison, Leonard with Maria's help sets about cutting up Otto's corpse. In writing the description of this dissection, McEwan, it is said, consulted a pathologist—and it shows:

> He took up the saw and untucked Otto's shirt, exposing the back just above the waistband of the trousers. Right on the spine was a big mole. He felt squeamish about cutting through it and positioned the blade half an inch lower. His saw cut now was the whole width of the back, and again the vertebra kept him on track. He was through the bone easily enough, but an inch or so further in he began to feel that he was not cutting through things so much as pushing them to one side. But he kept on. . . .

> There was a glutinous sound that brought him the memory of a jelly dessert eased from its mould. It was moving about in there; something had collapsed and rolled onto something else.

At length he gets through to the last bit of belly:

> The top half swung on its hinge of skin toward the floor, exposing the vivid mess of Otto's digestive tract and pulling the bottom half with it. Both tipped to the floor and disgorged onto the carpet.

I hasten to say that I have spared you the severing of the legs and arms, the removal of the head, and much else. The entire process takes up some seven closely detailed pages.

This passage, and the horridly funny one that follows, in which Leonard staggers off through the streets of Berlin with Otto's remains in a pair of suitcases, left me with a feeling of unease, an unease that was more than mere squeamishness before the prospect of all that blood and hacked bone. Something is out of balance in this book, some moral weight is missing. Here, one must tread warily. Certainly I am not looking for a "message," for profound coments on East-West relations, or on anything else, for that matter (the artist, says Kafka, is the man who has nothing to say). All the same, a work of art is by nature a moral act.

Perhaps my worry is that Ian McEwan has concentrated too much of his artistic energy on the surface of his story, has burnished it to such a high finish that not only the eye but the mind slides over and, ultimately, off the page.

Despite all that, I have to say that *The Innocent* is marvelously entertaining, filled with dark irony, with horror and regret. McEwan catches the period with what feels like uncanny precision; the book fairly reeks of bad food and sour underwear. The characters of Leonard, of . . . Maria, are superbly drawn; even real-life figures, such as the spy George Blake, are convincing, a fictional trick that is always difficult to bring off. Yet for all its artistry and cunning, my feeling at the end of this book was very like that queasy sensation one sometimes experiences after hearing an elegantly recounted but singularly tasteless joke. (p. 25)

John Banville, "In Violent Times," in The New York Review of Books, *Vol. XXXVII, No. 19, December 6, 1990, pp. 22-5.*

FURTHER READING

Batchelor, John Calvin. "Killer Instincts on the Facts on the Family Hour." *Village Voice* XXIII, No. 50 (11 December 1978): 110.
> Compares *The Cement Garden* to works by Julia Markus and Ellen Schwamm.

Davies, Hunter. "Inside the Novelist's Shell." *The Sunday Times, London* (6 February 1983): 14.
> Chronicles formative events in McEwan's life and career.

Johnstone, Richard. "Television Drama and the People's War: David Hare's *Licking Hitler,* Ian McEwan's *The Im-*

itation Game, and Trevor Griffith's *Country.*" *Modern Drama* 28, No. 2 (June 1985): 189-97.

> Discusses *The Imitation Game*'s commentary on World War II.

Ricks, Christopher. "Playing with Terror." *London Review of Books* 4, No. 1 (21 January-3 February 1982): 13-14.

> Explores the style, themes, and plot of *The Comfort of Strangers.*

Sampson, David. "McEwan/Barthes." *Southern Review* 17, No. 1 (March 1984): 68-80.

> Extensive Freudian critical analysis of *The Cement Garden.* Highly academic.

Smith, Amanda. "Ian McEwan." *Publishers Weekly* 232, No. 11 (11 September 1987): 68-9.

> Interview in which McEwan discusses his life and writing, particularly his novel *The Child in Time.*

Tonkin, Boyd. "Trials of a War Baby." *New Statesman & Society* 3, No. 100 (11 May 1990): 18-19.

> Examines the plot and themes of *The Innocent,* emphasizing its depiction of post-World War II Britain.

Yourgrau, Barry. "Snot, Sex, and Something New." *Village Voice* XXIV, No. 35 (27 August 1979): 88.

> Positive review of *In between the Sheets* highlighting several stories.

Flannery O'Connor

1925-1964

(Full name Mary Flannery O'Connor) American short story writer, novelist, and essayist.

The following entry presents criticism on O'Connor's novel *Wise Blood* (1952). For criticism on O'Connor's complete career, see *CLC,* Vols. 1, 2, 3, 6, 10, 13, 15, 21.

O'Connor is considered one of the foremost short story writers in American literature. She was an anomaly among post-World War II authors—a Roman Catholic from the Bible-belt South whose stated purpose was to reveal the mystery of God's grace in everyday life. Aware that not all readers shared her faith, O'Connor chose to depict salvation through shocking, often violent action and characters who are spiritually or physically grotesque. Commenting on this tendency toward bizarre action and caricature, she explained: "To the hard of hearing you shout and for the almost blind you draw large and startling figures." While O'Connor used exaggeration to express her ideas, her prose is considered compressed and brilliantly polished. Moreover, her penchant for employing ironic detachment and mordant humor prompted some critics to classify O'Connor as an existentialist or nihilist. She skillfully infused her fiction with the local color, regional dialect, and rich comic detail of her southern milieu. A complex system of symbolism and allegory adds further resonance to O'Connor's work.

O'Connor began writing *Wise Blood* in 1947-48 while living at the Yaddo writers' colony in upstate New York. She later lived briefly in New York City and Ridgefield, Connecticut, before her independence ended at age twenty-five when she suffered her first attack of disseminated lupus, a hereditary degenerative disease that had taken her father's life in 1950. Following the onset of this illness, O'Connor lived with her mother on a small dairy farm outside Milledgeville, Georgia. While her mother ran the farm, O'Connor maintained a slow, steady writing pace, publishing her first novel, *Wise Blood,* in 1952.

Several critics have connected *Wise Blood* with the tradition of caustic satire and black humor exemplified by Nathanael West's *Miss Lonelyhearts* (1933), a novel O'Connor greatly admired and reportedly read while composing *Wise Blood.* Set in fictional Taulkinham, Tennessee, during the mid-twentieth century, O'Connor's novel focuses on the tragicomic spiritual odyssey of Hazel "Haze" Motes. Described by O'Connor in a note to the second edition of *Wise Blood* as "a Christian *malgre lui*" (a Christian in spite of himself), Haze unsuccessfully attempts to eradicate the influence of Jesus Christ from his life. After losing his faith while in the Army and returning to find his home in Eastrod, Tennessee, inexplicably uninhabited, Haze devotes himself to preaching nihilistic sermons from the hood of his car. These homilies represent Haze's attempt to purge himself of the guilt inflicted by his fiercely religious mother and evangelist grandfather.

As minister of his self-proclaimed "Church of Christ Without Christ," Haze attracts an array of bizarre followers: Hoover Shoats, an obnoxious, materialistic radio evangelist; Asa Hawks, a charlatan preacher who pretends to have blinded himself to prove his faith; Hawks's teenage daughter, Sabbath Lily, who eventually seduces Haze; Enoch Emery, a retarded boy who works as a zoo guard and worships a mummy exhibited in the museum there; and Solace Layfield, a young man who impersonates and is later killed by Haze.

Critics have viewed Haze's tenets as ironic indictments of the modern secularization of religion, and his sermons express unconventional ideas: "Nobody with a good car needs to be justified"; "there was no Fall because there was nothing to fall from and no Redemption because there was no Fall and no Judgment because there wasn't the first two. Nothing matters but that Jesus was a liar"; and "I believe in a new kind of jesus . . . one that can't waste his blood redeeming people with it, because he's all man and ain't got any God in him." Denying the existence of sin, Haze spends his first night in Taulkinham with a prostitute and later sleeps with the fifteen-year-old Sabbath Lily Hawks. However, sin and blasphemy do not pacify Haze.

Through the "wild ragged figure" of Christ, who moves "from tree to tree in the back of his mind," O'Connor suggests that it is impossible to avoid the power of Christ. Asa Hawks warns Haze that he "can't run away from Jesus. Jesus is a fact."

Enoch Emery is often described by critics as Haze's doppelganger. When Haze calls for "a new jesus," Enoch responds by stealing the mummy from the zoo's museum and offering it to Haze and Sabbath Lily, who are living together. Several commentators have analyzed this scene as a mock version of the Nativity. Repulsed by Enoch's gesture, Haze destroys the mummy, an act that signifies his emerging doubts about his anti-Christian beliefs. Significantly, Haze wears his mother's glasses while smashing the false idol. He had also taken her glasses with him into the Army, along with a Bible, in case his vision diminished. Enoch later experiences religious fulfillment when he murders a man wearing a gorilla suit, steals the costume, and then dons it. Enoch's actions have been generally regarded as a parody of Haze's spiritual search and symbolic of a regression into primitivism. According to Miles Orvell, Enoch "helps define, by contrast, the sense in which Hazel is a Christian hero." While Haze is seeking a higher truth, Enoch is merely seeking friends. Also, Enoch's obsession with animals and O'Connor's frequent use of animal imagery underscore her theme that, as William Rodney Allen noted, "the world, without its spiritual dimension, is merely a prison for an odd collection of inmates—a zoo for the human animal."

A prevalent theme in *Wise Blood* is the paradoxical nature of blindness and vision. Blindness is viewed as proof of spiritual insight. Asa Hawks, whom Haze once considered a possible savior because he blinded himself to affirm his belief in Redemption, is later revealed as a confidence man who feigns blindness and piety to cheat people out of money. Haze Motes's name itself suggests blurred vision: Hazel means "one who sees God"; and mote, a speck of dust, is referred to in the New Testament (Matthew vii, 3, 5)—"And why beholdest thou the mote that is in thy brother's eye, but considerest not the beam that is in thine own eye? / . . . Thou hypocrite, first cast out the beam out of thine own eye; and then shalt thou see clearly to cast out the mote out thy brother's eye." Critics have observed that Haze truly "sees" only after he has blinded himself with quicklime as penance and to demonstrate his belief in Christ. At the novel's conclusion, Haze dies from self-mortification and a beating by police, and is returned to his landlady, Mrs. Flood. She looks into his eyes and sees "him moving farther and farther into the darkness until he was the pin point of light." According to some, this passage implies that Haze's faith will be transferred to Mrs. Flood, a greedy, materialistic woman who intended to marry Haze for his Army pension.

Many critics have commented, some unfavorably, on the exaggerated grotesqueness of the characters in *Wise Blood*. Early in the novel, Haze is described as a puppet. Obsessed with Christ and the notion of original sin, Haze has a mechanical rigidity and monomaniacal obsession with beliefs that are absurdly comic. While some commentators found O'Connor's portrayal of Haze cartoonish,

others argued that realism was not her intention in *Wise Blood*. Lewis A. Lawson explained that Haze was conceived "as an exemplum, as a vehicle whose attitudes and actions would personify a spiritual view which [O'Connor] wished to reveal." Lawson added that Haze represents an example "of the deadly effect that Southern fundamentalism could have on the soul, warping and terrorizing it so completely with its perversion of Christian doctrine that the soul in rebellion rejects entirely the idea of orthodox Christianity." However, some critics have found O'Connor's fictional world implausible. The abundance of absurd and outrageous events, characters, and statements in *Wise Blood* compelled Isaac Rosenfeld to remark that O'Connor "writes of an insane world, peopled by monsters and submen." Some commentators have considered Haze a madman unable to redeem others or to be redeemed himself. Consequently, these critics question whether *Wise Blood* can be treated seriously as great literature.

Initial reviewers of *Wise Blood* praised O'Connor's rich imagery, powerful symbolism, and skillful rendering of Southern dialect, but found her characterizations two-dimensional and shockingly monstrous. Later critics generally discussed the book's satirical, theological, and ironic elements, the quest motif, and whether Haze is finally redeemed. While most believe that he is saved, others concur with Ben Satterfield: "Those who claim Haze is redeemed mistake his acts of penance, if that is what they are, for the goal they are employed to achieve; they mistake the means for the end. But atonement is not redemption and should not be confused with it." Satterfield has accused some critics of guilelessly accepting O'Connor's own comments about her work and of being too eager to find redemption in everything she wrote. However, most critics agree with Richard Giannone, who stated: "[In] his own mental way Haze is a martyr in the original sense of the word as giving testimony to the truth, sealed in his own suffering and unwise blood. . . . [Affliction] implements the promise held out in his name *Hazel,* he who sees God." *Wise Blood* remains a provocative novel that continues to inspire diverse critical reaction and myriad analyses.

(See also *Short Story Criticism*, Vol. 1; *Contemporary Authors*, Vols. 1-4, rev. ed.; *Contemporary Authors New Revision Series*, Vol. 3; *Dictionary of Literary Biography*, Vol. 2; *Dictionary of Literary Biography Yearbook: 1980; and Concise Dictionary of American Literary Biography: The New Consciousness, 1941-1968.*)

PRINCIPAL WORKS

SHORT FICTION COLLECTIONS

A Good Man Is Hard to Find   1955
Everything That Rises Must Converge   1965

NOVELS

Wise Blood   1952
The Violent Bear It Away   1960

OTHER

Mystery and Manners: Occasional Prose (nonfiction)
    1969
The Habit of Being: Letters of Flannery O'Connor   1979
Flannery O'Connor: Collected Works (fiction, criticism,
    letters)   1988

William Goyen

Written by a Southerner from Georgia, this first novel
[*Wise Blood*], whose language is Tennessee-Georgia dialect expertly wrought into a clipped, elliptic and blunt
style, introduces its author as a writer of power. There is
in Flannery O'Connor a fierceness of literary gesture, an
angriness of observation, a facility for catching, as an animal eye in a wilderness, cunningly and at one sharp
glance, the shape and detail and animal intention of enemy
and foe. The world of *Wise Blood* is one of clashing in a
wilderness.

When Hazel Motes, from Eastrod, Tenn., is released from
the Army at the age of 22, he comes to a Southern city
near his birthplace. He falls under the spell of Asa Hawks,
a "blind" street preacher who shambles through the city
with his degenerate daughter, Lily Sabbath Hawks, age
15. The encounter with Hawks turns Hazel Motes back
into his childhood traumatic experience with his grandfather who was a preacher traveling about the South in an
old Ford. The story of this novel, darting through rapid,
brute, bare episodes told with power and keenness, develops the disintegration and final destruction of Hazel who
physically and psychologically becomes Hawks and par-
rot-preaches (in vain) to the city crowds from the hood of
his second-hand Essex.

In a series of grim picaresque incidents Hazel struggles to
outfox and outpreach Hawks. He announces a new religion called "The Church Without Christ."

In Taulkinham, U. S. A., the city of Fiendish Evangelists,
one is brought into a world not so much of accursed or victimized human beings as into the company of an ill-
tempered and driven collection of one-dimensional creatures of sheer meanness and orneriness, scheming landladies, cursing waitresses, haunted-house people, prostitutes, fake blind men who take on, as they increase in
number, the nature and small size of downright skuldug-
gery and alum-mouthed contrariness. One is never convinced of any genuine evil in these people, only of a sourness; they seem not to belong to the human race at all, they
are what the geneticist calls a race of "sports."

The stark dramatic power of the scenes is percussive and
stabbing, but Miss O'Connor seems to tell her story
through clenched teeth in a kind of Tomboy, Mean-Moll
glee, and a few times she writes herself into episodes that
have to contrive themselves to deliver her out of them, and
then he is compelled to go on too far beyond or in the direction of sensationalism.

Miss O'Connor's style is tight to choking and as direct and
uncompounded as the order to a firing squad to shoot a
man against a wall. It perfectly communicates this devilish
intent of the inhabitants of Taulkinham to be mean, or
cadge or afflict each other. One cannot take this book
lightly or lightly turn away from it, because it is inflicted
upon one in the same way its people take their lives like
an indefensible blow delivered in the dark. Perhaps this
sense of being physically struck and wounded is only the
beginning of an arousal of one's questioning of the credibility of such a world of horror.

In such a world, all living things have vanished and what
remains exists in a redemptionless clashing of unending
vengeance, alienated from any source of understanding,
the absence of which does not even define a world of darkness, not even that—for there has been no light to take
away.

> *William Goyen, "Unending Vengeance," in*
> The New York Times, *May 18, 1952, p. 4.*

Harvey C. Webster

The cast of unrealistic characters [in *Wise Blood*] is interesting. Haze Motes, the protagonist, has been "converted
to nothing instead of to evil"; he maintains he is clean because he believes in neither Jesus nor sin; he preaches the
Church Without Christ "where the blind don't see and the
lame don't walk and what's dead stays that way," that nobody "with a good car needs to be justified," that "In
yourself right now is all the place you've got" (nihilistic
existentialism?).

Those Haze encounters and opposes include: Asa Hawks,
who lives in shame because he did not fulfill his promise
to put out his eyes for the love of Christ; his ugly daughter,
Lily, who sees salvation in sexual intercourse; Hoover
Shoats, who wants to turn Haze's church into a money-
making proposition; Enoch Emery, whose "wise blood"
makes him a sub-human very much like O'Neill's hairy
ape; equally unreal others whom you can believe in once
you realize that all the characters are symbols, like
Kafka's K or, more exactly, like the salesman in Wilder's
Heaven's My Destination.

The slender and plausible plot shows Haze's progress from
one improbable act to another. After experiencing death
from poverty and death from war and being converted to
the gospel of nothingness, he loves a whore (for nobody
needs Christ who has one), preaches unsuccessfully on the
streets (his blunt presentation of what the people believe
alienates them), buys a forty-dollar automobile, succumbs
to Lily Hawks's nymphomania, refuses the shrunken
mummy of a man Enoch presents to him as the new Jesus,
puts out his eyes and otherwise tortures himself to prove
he's a saint in the church that believes in nothing and has
only himself as preacher and member. Perhaps it's wrong
to say none of this could have happened, yet the nightmare
atmosphere of the whole book makes one feel even the
early, not unusual acts of Haze improbable by the standards of daylight—though they are wonderfully probable
actions in a dream that illuminates what we normally do
and feel, just as the subconscious, when we penetrate it,
makes us more vividly conscious.

Deprived of faith in God and the destination of Heaven, it seems to take characters almost as strong-willed as John Dewey to persist in morality and unbelief. Confronted by contemporary awfulness within and without, remembering what was taught of sin and salvation in youth, many—perhaps the many—long to be converted to either nothing or something. And, in the absense of eloquent or widespread humanist gospels; in the presence of Asa Hawks, who can speak but not act his faith; of Hoover Shoats, who makes religion into money; they founder between a wish for crass sensation uninhibitedly enjoyed and a half-conscious desire for dignity that would be salvation.

It is greatly to Miss O'Connor's credit that her first novel illuminates so universal a modern dilemma. Yet *Wise Blood* is not totally satisfactory as a novel. Often she seems not quite sure how far realistic detail should be used to make her expressionism plausible. (p. 23)

A more serious fault is a faintly precious striving for a multiplicity of symbols. The shrunken man as the modern Jesus is admirable; the human in gorilla clothing and a lot of lesser symbols set the reader to wondering what they mean and confuse him out of following the story, which usually conveys its core of meaning clearly. Still, this is an excellent first novel—both a promise and an achievement. . . . (p. 24)

> *Harvey C. Webster, "Nihilism as a Faith," in* The New Leader, *Vol. XXXV, No. 25, June 23, 1952, pp. 23-4.*

Isaac Rosenfeld

There is an unfortunate tendency among religious writers to take everything as grist for the mill; and this is particularly unfortunate when, as in Miss O'Connor's novel, the extremely important distinction between religious striving and mania is ground away. The theme of *Wise Blood* is Christ the Pursuer, the Ineluctable, with a satire on Protestantism thrown in. Hazel Motes, a Southern preacher, preaches the "church without Christ." To prove his un-faith, Motes sins conscientiously, the way one might prepare for a civil service exam, and in the end, in a supreme act of faith, this unbelieving believer puts out his eyes with lime. It is quite clear what Miss O'Connor means to say by this (though like most paraphrases it sounds unconvincing). Hazel Motes' mutilation is the inevitable consequence of his religious position; there is no escaping Christ. But the author's style, in my opinion, is inconsistent with this statement. Everything she says through image and metaphor has the meaning only of degeneration, and she writes of an insane world, peopled by monsters and submen, Motes the first among them—a world cut off from God, where the escape is complete. In plain words, Motes is plain crazy, and Miss O'Connor has all along presented him this way. Now I don't see how one can maintain that his madness lies in the effort to deny Christ, for he is wholly mad. Nor can one argue that this is what happens to all men, Protestants included, who deny Christ, for it certainly does not. How then can one take his predicament seriously? With pity, yes, sympathy, aversion, fear—all the emotions the insane call out apply

in Mote's case, but he is nothing more than the poor, sick, ugly, raving lunatic that he happens to be. If one takes him to be a valid representative of the religious mind, one might as well say openly that all religious people are crazy.

I may have drawn some faulty observations—*Wise Blood* is not a clear book to read. It has almost no surface, the few figures one can make out in it show in a pallid light reflected mainly, I should say, from Faulkner and Carson McCullers, and most of the transactions are conveyed in a symbolism which does not derive from the underlying meaning of the novel, but rather works the other way, constructing its meaning as it goes along. None of this makes for lucidity, and what I take to be the confusion in its religious ideas is no help. (p. 19)

> *Isaac Rosenfeld, "To Win by Default," in* The New Republic, *Vol. 127, No. 1, July 7, 1952, pp. 19-20.*

R. W. B. Lewis

The interest of Flannery O'Connor's *Wise Blood* arises from a curious tension in the novel between a rather horridly surrealistic set of characters and incidents and a remarkably pure, luminous prose. The book, which has no real plot, consists chiefly of the private twitchings of several almost totally dislocated individuals; while the language circles about them in a sane and steady flow. The characters seem to be grotesque variations on each other, as even their names suggest: Hazel Motes, Hoover Shoats, Asa Hawks—names uttered antiphonally, in dying echoes, by persons just out of range of each others' voices; like the washerwomen in *Finnegans Wake*. These partial, truncated personalities never suspect that they may be members one of another; though most of them are engaged in grotesque variations of the same evangelical enterprise: the mission of the prophet or the preacher or the Christ. Possibilities of expiation and atonement agitate them all, though from what or for what, no one can say; unless it is the dreadful fact of being alive. It is in the prose that there echoes the promise of health and reunion extravagantly denied to the characters by themselves.

In the world of Miss O'Connor's novel—the Kafkian village removed to the American South—there are nothing *but* eccentrics, individuals who pass their time hoping to trick somebody into shaking hands with them. The principal eccentric is one Hazel Motes, and it is his career that we mainly follow: as he preaches the Church without Christ; as he carefully and without expression murders a rival magician; as he promptly and with no more expression performs the penitential act of blinding himself; as he sinks reticently into death. Hazel Motes has affinities with Nathanael West's crucifixion-seeking Miss Lonelyhearts, though Hazel is regarded with an extra portion of quirky humor. But Hazel has affinities too with [Ernest Hemingway's] old man, [Ralph Ellison's] invisible man and the others. For while communication is rarely achieved by any of them, the records of their comic or tragic pilgrimages do communicate among themselves and within the same world. (p. 150)

> *R. W. B. Lewis, "Eccentrics' Pilgrimage," in*

The Hudson Review, *Vol. VI, No. 1, Spring, 1953, pp. 144-50.*

Robert M. Rechnitz

[*In the following excerpt, Rechnitz designates* Wise Blood *as a quest novel and discusses how Hazel Motes's pilgrimage deviates from those of protagonists in traditional quest novels.*]

[*Wise Blood*] is a quest novel. As diligently as Christian, Hazel Motes endeavors to make his pilgrimage "unto the gate of glory." Yet, unlike Christian, Hazel, pathetic creature of the twentieth century, spends the greatest portion of his energy, not in moving toward a specific goal, but in attempting to discover just what the goal should be.

As a child, Hazel listened to his grandfather, "a circuit preacher, a waspish old man who had ridden over three counties with Jesus hidden in his head like a stinger." The grandfather would on occasion point to his grandson and cry to the crowd about him that Jesus would not forget even so insignificant a soul as this boy:

> Did they know that even for that boy there, for that mean sinful unthinking boy standing there with his dirty hands clenching and unclenching at his sides, Jesus would die ten million deaths before He would let him lose his soul? He would chase him over the waters of sin. . . . That boy had been redeemed and Jesus wasn't going to leave him ever. . . . Jesus would have him in the end!

Having heard this time after time, Haze had become convinced that the only way to avoid this terrifying Saviour was to avoid sin. To his own satisfaction, he managed to do this for a while; but the task became more difficult while he was in the army. Often tempted by his friends, Haze maintained his innocence by asserting that he was "from Eastrod, Tennessee, . . . that he was going to be a preacher of the gospel and that he wasn't going to have his soul damned. . . ." (p. 310)

Broadly speaking then, the preliminary action of the novel is composed of Haze's early indoctrination in the religious fundamentalism of his grandfather, and his rejection of this religion. This prefaces the major movement of the novel, his quest for atheistic certainty and his eventual return, after great suffering, to a belief in God, a ruthless, demanding God who will not let Haze lose his soul. Put another way, the novel portrays Haze's painful discovery that being "converted to nothing" is the spiritual equivalent of being converted to evil. When he makes his eventual discovery that this is so, Haze, in a desperate act of expiation, blinds himself. Yet is this so? In his decisive act there is an essential ambiguity. Is his act of mutilation one of expiation or is it one of rare commitment to his atheism? We must attempt to answer this question.

After his period in the army is completed, Haze sets out on his quest for truth. It is this quest which constitutes the major portion of the novel. In Taulkinham Haze buys a dilapidated car, from the hood of which he, like his grandfather, preaches his faith. But it is a faith his grandfather would not have recognized, for it is faith in a new church: the Church of Truth without Jesus Christ Crucified, or as he later comes to call it, the Church Without Christ. . . . With no Christ there can be no damnation. "I'm going to preach there was no Fall because there was nothing to fall from and no Redemption because there was no Fall and no Judgment because there wasn't the first two. Nothing matters but that Jesus was a liar." In such a manner, with syntax flying, Haze attempts to convert others to his belief in Nothing.

His ministry is threatened from three directions. First, the very fundamentalism from which Haze earlier rebelled threatens him in the person of the blind evangelist, Asa Hawks. Hawks, a shouting, fanatical old man reminiscent of Haze's grandfather, scoffs at Haze's disbelief. Convinced, or so Haze thinks him, that the "mark of a preacher" has been left on Haze and that the boy has been drawn to the evangelist as a disciple, Asa commands him to repent and adds, "Listen boy, you can't run away from Jesus. Jesus is a fact." Each time the two men meet, Haze's conviction that there is no Jesus is deeply threatened, for Asa is blind, his eyes covered by dark glasses, his cheeks streaked with scar tissue. And Asa's blindness is self-inflicted, done "to justify his belief that Christ Jesus had redeemed him." The knowledge of such a depth of commitment haunts Hazel; in the face of so violent an action Haze is forced to question his own easy disbelief. Within those burned-out sockets, Hazel thinks, may lie not proof of the existence of God, but rather the hieroglyphics of commitment. Haze is not susceptible to theistic proofs, but he is to evidence of total commitment; for this reason he picks the lock to Asa's room.

> He . . . opened the door. His breath came short and his heart was palpitating. . . . He stood just inside the room until his eyes got accustomed to the darkness and then he moved slowly over to the iron bed. . . . Hawks was lying across it. . . . Haze squatted down by him and struck a match close to his face and he opened his eyes. The two sets of eyes looked at each other as long as the match lasted; Haze's expression seemed to open onto a deeper blankness and reflect something and then close again.

Thinking to uncover the mystery of commitment, Haze gets but a dispiriting glimpse of hypocrisy. Religious orthodoxy as Haze knows it can no longer stay him from his quest. Yet the *idea*, the necessity, of unbounded commitment remains with him, and the vision of sightless eyes returns to Haze when he recognizes the evil he has been guilty of committing.

The second threat to Haze's ministry comes from the false prophets and guileful ministers of his own "sect." Haze has been preaching only a week or so, standing on the hood of his car, addressing the crowds in front of motion picture theatres, having no luck at all in gaining followers, when one evening he notices one member of his audience listening closely:

> The man was plumpish, and he had curly blond hair that was cut with showy sideburns. He wore a black suit with a silver stripe in it and a wide-brimmed white hat pushed onto the back of his

head, and he had on tight-fitting black pointed shoes and no socks. He looked like an ex-preacher turned cowboy, or an ex-cowboy turned mortician. He was not handsome but under his smile, there was an honest look fitted into his face like a set of false teeth.

This is a wonderfully comic portrait, and it exhibits Miss O'Connor's great skill in fusing disparate characteristics into a single, explosive simile. Onnie Jay Holy is a grotesque combination of human and mechanical characteristics, perfect for his sometime-occupation of radio-preacher, a con artist who uses all available mechanical aids in dishing out religion to the gullible and the helpless. And all of this is vigorously implied in the "false teeth" simile.

Onnie Jay immediately draws a tremendous crowd about himself and Haze. In a matter of seconds he is well on his way to show Haze how the preaching business ought to be handled. Two months before, he tells the growing crowd, he was unhappy; but then he met "this Prophet here." Onnie Jay continues to pervert all of Haze's ideas, while Haze loudly protests. Concluding his sermon Onnie starts to take up a collection at which moment Haze finally masters the situation and drives away.

The following night Haze is again interrupted by Holy, who this time has brought his own prophet, an emaciated man dressed exactly like Haze. Looking at him, Haze seems to be looking at himself.

> [Haze] was so struck with how gaunt and thin he looked in the illusion that he stopped preaching. He had never pictured himself that way before. The man he saw was hollow-chested and carried his neck thrust forward and his arms down by his side; . . . Then he began to cough. He had a loud consumptive cough that started somewhere deep in him and finished with a long wheeze. He expectorated a white fluid at the end of it.

Haze has seen himself and is horrified: the man he has seen, his double, is dying.

In the latter portion of the book, Haze, still determined to remain committed to his atheism, strikes down the false prophet, and as the man is dying Haze questions him: " 'You ain't true,' Haze said. 'What do you get up on top of a car and say you don't believe in what you do believe in for?' " Without being aware of it, Haze is talking to himself.

> "You ain't true," Haze said. "You believe in Jesus." . . . "Two things I can't stand," Haze said, "—a man that ain't true and one that mocks what is."

Haze's quest for the truth is jeopardized because, as he discovers, he is his own false prophet. But the realization that this is the case is more fully and painfully brought home to Hazel Motes by the third threat to his quest: his true disciple, Enoch Emery.

The misadventures of this eighteen-year-old simpleton take up about half the novel. Enoch, too, is on a quest; and his pursuit of friends and happiness supplies a comic-grotesque subplot to the principle action. Enoch is first seen listening raptly to a sidewalk salesman. The reason for Enoch's deep interest is made almost immediately clear; to the casual onlooker this salesman may be hawking potato peelers, but as Miss O'Connor describes it, his card table becomes an altar. He is a priest, and Enoch is having what amounts to a minor religious experience.

Throughout the novel Enoch searches for some strange god who will bestow upon him the boon of friendship and importance. Unlike Haze, Enoch has no unconscious yearning for Christ. He knows all about Him, but wants nothing to do with Him. Enoch had been forced to attend the "Rodemill Boy's Bible Academy," but it "won't no relief, Sweet Jesus, it won't no relief." Now he is searching for something new, and when he meets Hazel, he knows he has found it. Enoch knows that Haze is the one man in the city to whom he must show the mystery which he visits everyday and which lies at the heart of the city.

> Everyday he looked at the heart of it; and he was so stunned and awed and overwhelmed that just to think about it made him sweat. There was something, in the center of the park, that he had discovered. It was a mystery, although it was right there in a glass case for everybody to see and there was a typewritten card over it telling all about it. But there was something the card couldn't say and what it couldn't say was inside him, a terrible knowledge like a big nerve growing inside him. He could not show the mystery to just anybody; but he had to show it to somebody. Who he had to show it to was a special person.

But when Enoch takes Haze to the museum to see the mystery, Haze sees only a mummy, the object itself, with no aura of the numinous about it.

Later, however, Enoch hears Haze preaching from atop the hood of his battered automobile, which serves Haze as a traveling pulpit. Haze, in explaining the finer points of his Church Without Christ calls for something to take the place of Jesus. Something that will speak the plain truth. "The Church Without Christ don't have a Jesus but it needs one! It needs a new jesus! It needs one that's all man, without blood to waste, and it needs one that don't look like any other man so you'll look at him. . . . Then you'll know once and for all that you haven't been redeemed. Give me this new jesus, somebody. . . ."

And Enoch begins "shouting without a sound." "Listen here, I got him! I mean I can get him! You know! Him! Him I shown you to. You seen him yourself." Then Enoch, prompted by the persuasive preaching of Hazel, steals the mummy which he brings to Haze.

Enoch has fulfilled his function as the faithful disciple. He labors to promote the teachings of his master, and in so doing he becomes the chief agent of Haze's quitting his ministry. The sight of the "new jesus" shocks Haze into a recognition of the purport of his teachings. The Church Without Christ recommends the worship of nothing, a nothing which is embodied in the torn and broken mummy, the "new jesus." The Church Without Christ leads but to death.

With this recognition Haze commits his last and irrevocable act, he blinds himself. Is this act of mutilation one of expiation or is it one of commitment to his atheism? It is both, we must answer, because it bears a third meaning of deeper significance comprising the others and more. His mutilation is an indictment of intellectual and spiritual passivity. It is a condemnation of the amoral drift which characterizes our age.

Positively, his action is a gesture affirmative of man's stature in the universe. Man, Haze insists, is a force of such colossal proportions that his behavior has cosmic significance. Sufficiently committed man can create God. Indeed, this Haze has done. Out of his commitment Haze has created God in the image of the "new jesus."

Hazel's self-mutilation is but the inevitable outcome of this same commitment, and as such it is profoundly paradoxical: total commitment to his atheism becomes his highest affirmation of God's existence.

Moral commitment of such intensity, maintained unswervingly beyond ordinary human endurance lifts its agent, even as Haze is lifted, to tragic proportions. This, indeed, is perhaps the most impressive feature of the novel: Haze, at first a ridiculous figure, rises steadily in our estimations until his ultimate transformation in the final chapters into a hero of no little nobility.

Commitment, Haze learns, is the ultimate gift and the direst curse of God. A life of animal happiness and freedom is for most men much to be preferred. Haze acknowledges this when to his landlady's insistence that she is as good "not believing in Jesus as a many a one that does," he replies: " 'You're better,' . . . 'If you believed in Jesus, you wouldn't be so good.' " For some men the easy way exists as a possibility, but not for Hazel Motes. He is fated to be pursued by God, a God merciless in His mercy. This is the God that his grandfather preached and of which Hazel, with accurate foresight, we may now say, was so afraid. Try though he would, he could not escape Him; and, in the final pages of the novel, he is possessed by this God, just as his grandfather prophesied he would be, years before. (pp. 310-16)

> *Robert M. Rechnitz, "Passionate Pilgrim: Flannery O'Connor's 'Wise Blood',"* in The *Georgia Review, Vol. XIX, No. 1, Fall, 1965, pp. 310-16.*

Lewis A. Lawson

[*An American educator and critic, Lawson co-edited* The Added Dimension: The Art and Mind of Flannery O'Connor *(1966). In the excerpt below, Lawson attributes* Wise Blood's *success to O'Connor's unconventional characterization of Hazel Motes, which is partially based on the legend of St. Anthony.*]

Offering itself as the most grotesque work in all of Southern fiction, Flannery O'Connor's *Wise Blood* is a novel only in the widest possible sense of the word. It is a prose fiction of considerable length, but beyond that requirement none of the standard elements of the novel is to be found. The development of character, the exploration of character interaction, and the development of plot are unimportant. Such action as occurs is often without motivation, leads nowhere, and is almost always absurd. Any resemblance to the world of objective reality is certainly incidental. Yet, when these things are said, the book still remains one of the most impressive creations of the School of the Grotesque, or School of Southern Gothic. That the book is rewarding despite its unconventionality can be attributed to the author's singular vision and style. Miss O'Connor several times commented upon her vocation: her mission, as she saw it, was to depict the reality of Christianity to an audience for whom nothing transempirical is real. She wrote, "I don't think you should write something as long as a novel around anything that is not of the gravest concern to you and everybody else and for me this is always the conflict between an attraction for the Holy and the disbelief in it that we breathe in with the air of the times." Her style, it follows, is effective only if it serves her intention. She was uninterested in the felicities of the art of conventional fiction, and felt completely free to use absurdity, paradox, and illogicality, if those were the only media which would carry her vision.

The main character of *Wise Blood,* the Tennessean Haze Motes, is an example of the complete artistic freedom which Miss O'Connor allowed herself. Uninterested in creating a rounded character, she concentrated instead upon constructing a caricature whose flatness continually reminds us that he is unreal. To the charge that such a technique weakened her fiction, Miss O'Connor would have replied that any other technique would weaken her vision. She had no interest in Haze Motes as a human being; he was conceived, and his creator would have insisted that he remain, as an exemplum, as a vehicle whose attitudes and actions would personify a spiritual view which she wished to reveal. To make sure that we view Haze properly, she twice describes him as a puppet. . . . (p. 137)

There are suggestions at times that the structure of the gospels is consciously being used: an abstract idea will first be introduced and then made concrete, as in the parables of Christ. Haze Motes was, in his creator's eyes, an exemplification of the deadly effect that Southern fundamentalism could have on the soul, warping and terrorizing it so completely with its perversion of Christian doctrine that the soul in rebellion rejects entirely the idea of orthodox Christianity. Since the creation of a character whose premise lay in normality and logicality would encourage us to identify with him and thus blunt the effectiveness of her attack, Miss O'Connor wisely felt free to make her foil as bizarre, as distasteful, as ridiculous, as she thought necessary. In a day when she saw such actions and attitudes as Haze Motes represents taken for normal behavior, she felt that only by extreme departure from what is expected in both content and style could her characterization achieve its goal. . . .

Miss O'Connor takes very little time sketching the background of Haze Motes. His mother is described: "She wore black all the time and her dresses were longer than other women's . . . She had a cross-shaped face and hair pulled close to her head." His grandfather is mentioned:

" . . . a circuit preacher, who had ridden over three counties with Jesus hidden in his head like a stinger." These two people are representatives of the guilt-obsessed culture which terrified Haze so completely as a child that he had walked in shoes filled with stones. One of his first utterances in the novel, offered casually to a woman on a train, reveals that he is its true heir: "I reckon you think you been redeemed."

In such a culture, where Calvin, though probably unknown to most of its members, is more influential than Christ, guilt overshadows love as the quintessential aspect of Christianity, and Christianity has more an Old Testament flavor than a New. The preacher then assumes a somewhat Mosaic role of wrathful pursuer, hunting man down to confront him with the absolute sinfulness of his condition. And, emphasizing guilt, the fundamentalist preacher seems to find his motive force more often in hatred and vindictiveness than in love and charity. (p. 138)

With such familial and cultural influences, Haze early decides upon two courses of action: he will be a preacher, but he will avoid Jesus Christ, in his mind "a wild ragged figure motioning him to turn around and come off into the dark where he was not sure of his footing, where he might be walking on the water and not know it and then suddenly know it and drown." In his reasoning, if he can successfully deny Christ, then he can also deny man's original sin: "There was no Fall because there was nothing to fall from and no Redemption because there was no Fall and no Judgment because there wasn't the first two." To Miss O'Connor the reality of Christ was the idea underlying all preaching; the idea of what is to be preached is implicit in the idea of preaching. (pp. 138-39)

In Haze Motes, then, Miss O'Connor deliberately constructed an oxymoron as character. In this manner she escaped the danger inherent in using a caricature: that it will become predictable once its mannerisms are known. Since by nature there is an unavoidable tension between the mutually contradictory elements of an oxymoron, Haze Motes has a vitality that will last either until one element overcomes the other or until the tension destroys him.

The paradox at the center of her character's nature is further suggested by his name. Originally, when an early draft of part of the novel was published, Haze's surname was "Weaver." But "Motes" suggests Christ's injunction, in the King James Version of the Sermon on the Mount (Matthew vii, 3-5), against officious intrusion. . . . The name "Haze" also suggests that Miss O'Connor wished her character to be conceived as one of cloudy vision who nevertheless insolently attempts to guide others. (p. 139)

Since Miss O'Connor's main purpose in **Wise Blood** was to warn against defective spiritual vision, it seems almost inescapable that one of the most effective themes of the book is that of sight versus blindness. Its first sentence describes the demobilized Haze, on his way to Taulkinham, sitting at a forward angle on the green plush train seat, suggesting at once his intensity and the possibility that his sight may be impaired. Physical sight becomes associated with spiritual vision soon afterward, when we are told that Haze had used his mother's glasses to read the Bible. He had taken the glasses with him when he was drafted, and he had put them on the first time that he had felt he was being led into temptation, to preach to his tempters. Before he was discharged, "he had all the time he could want to study his soul in and assure himself that it was not there." Thereafter, he puts aside the glasses.

On his second night in Taulkinham, Haze meets a "blind" street preacher, an incident that allowed Miss O'Connor to establish a thematic paradox that continues throughout the novel: those without sight can see and those with sight cannot see, an echo of Christ's words (John ix, 39): " . . . I am come into the world, that they which see not might see; and that they which see might be made blind." The "blind" preacher, Asa Hawks, and his daughter move off down the street, and Haze, in his obsession to taunt the preacher about his beliefs, walks across the street against the light, endangering his life and angering the policeman there. When the policeman sarcastically inquires if Haze knows the purpose of the signal light, Haze replies, "I didn't see it." Here again Haze's obsession with religious delusion, to the exclusion of everything else in the world around him, is suggested by his defective and inattentive sight.

When Haze catches up with the pair, he is told to pass out fundamentalist pamphlets for them, as a crowd pours out of an auditorium. But that command is abhorrent: "I'll take them up there and throw them over into the bushes! . . . You be watching and see can you see." The "blind" man replies, "I can see more than you . . . You got eyes and see not, ears and hear not, but you'll have to see some time," echoing Christ's words (Mark viii, 18): "Having eyes, see ye not? and having ears, hear ye not? . . . " The irony of the "blind" preacher's words operates on both a superficial and a profound level; physically he can in fact see, and spiritually Haze will not see until he has blinded himself. Raging because of the preacher's words, Haze begins himself to preach to the emerging crowd: "Listen here, I'm a preacher myself and I preach the truth . . . Don't I have eyes in my head? Am I a blind man?" Again as Miss O'Connor well knew, in terms of Christ's words to the Pharisees (John ix, 41), who were also denying His reality, Haze is not blind: "If ye were blind ye should have no sin: but now ye say, We see; therefore your sin remaineth."

The ancient forty-dollar rat-colored Essex that Haze buys also contributes to the theme of blindness versus sight. The car comes to represent Haze's attitude of deliberately wishing not to accept the reality of Christ. As he tells Sabbath Lily Hawks, the "blind" preacher's ugly daughter, "Nobody with a good car needs to be justified." Then he voices his need for the car: "I knew when I first saw it that it was the car for me, and since I've had it, I've had a place to be that I can always get away in." And from its hood Haze preaches his perverted vision.

His reliance upon the car for escape is especially clear in a scene after Sabbath seduces him. Always before, Haze had considered himself guiltless of sin, for how could one be sinful if one did not believe in redemption? But Sabbath teaches him how to be sinful: "Yes sir! . . . I like being that way, and I can teach you how to like it." Haze does.

The next morning he is described "lying on his cot," however, "with a washrag over his eyes; the exposed part of his face . . . ashen and set in a grimace, as if he were in some permanent pain." The washrag foreshadows his blinding of himself, when he has come to see. The triumphant Sabbath then enters to show Haze the dried, shrunken corpse, which Enoch Emery had stolen from the museum, in answer to Haze's pleas for someone to give him a new jesus. Just as Sabbath enters, Haze has decided to leave; he begins to pack his duffel bag, accidentally touching the case with his mother's glasses in it, and he stops for a moment to put them on. When Haze sees the mummy through his mother's glasses, his response is so violent and apparently absurd that it can only have symbolic meaning. To see any jesus through his mother's glasses would be to accept the guilt that her religion emphasized and that he had rejected. He flings the new jesus out of doors and the glasses right behind it, refusing to look, for, as he chokes out, "I don't want nothing but the truth! . . . and what you see is the truth and I've seen it! . . . I've seen the only truth there is!" And when Sabbath asks his destination, he shouts, "To some other city, . . . to preach the truth. The Church Without Christ! And I got a car to get there in, . . . "

Before Haze attempts to flee the city, he murders Solace Layfield, whose Puritan name suggests what he represents. One night on the street Haze had preached, "Your conscience is a trick . . . it don't exist though you may think it does, and if you think it does, you had best get it out in the open and hunt it down and kill it, because it's no more than your face in the mirror is or your shadow behind you." At that moment a double-figure, the True Prophet, Solace Layfield, who works for the confidence man Hoover Shoats, is introduced. The resemblance between the two is so striking that a woman asks Haze, "Him and you twins?" And Haze, watching Solace, in *his* glare-blue suit preaching from the hood of *his* rat-colored car, furiously replies: "If you don't hunt it down and kill it, it'll hunt you down and kill you." The night after his seduction, Haze follows Solace home. When the two cars reach the countryside, Haze demolishes the car by forcing it off the road, and Solace, uninjured, comes back to the window of the Essex to ask, "It ain't nothing wrong with that car . . . Howcome you knockt it in the tich?" Haze replies, "You ain't true, . . . What do you get up on top of that car and say you don't believe in what you believe in for? . . . You ain't true, . . . You believe in Jesus." Haze then runs Solace down with his car to kill him. Again apparently meaningless violence has symbolic meaning. Both the True Prophet and the Essex are objectified mental attitudes: Haze's deliberate attempt not to see the truth (the Essex) is still able to overcome his conscience (the double, Solace Layfield), in which remain his childhood guilt and belief in the reality of Christ.

The next morning, beginning his trip to the new city, Haze stops at a filling station, where he tells an attendant who questions the condition of his car that "nobody with a good car needed to worry about anything." His words quickly prove to be untrue, for he runs afoul of the law for the second time; as soon as he reaches the highway, a patrolman, with an apparently meaningless act, orders Haze out of his car, which is then pushed over a cliff. "Was you going anywheres?" he asks Haze, and when Haze answers, "No," the patrolman even repeats the question: " 'You hadn't planned to go anywheres?' Haze shook his head. His face didn't change and he didn't turn it toward the patrolman. It seemed to be concentrated on space." This Saul does not become a Paul; with his hope of denying Christ gone, Haze returns to the city, there to blind himself, as a sign that he can now see his guilt.

With the theme of deliberate self-delusion concluded, the theme of blindness versus vision continues, to end, as it had begun, the novel. People other than Sabbath Lily had noticed Haze's eyes. The woman on the train, Mrs. Wally Bee Hitchcock, had also scrutinized them: "Their settings were so deep that they seemed, to her, almost like passages leading somewhere and she leaned across the space that separated the two seats, trying to see into them." Trying to see into Haze's eyes is repeated when Haze's landlady is fascinated by his self-inflicted blindness and his other punishments of the body. She asks why he walks with rocks in his shoes, and when he answers that he must pay, she persists, "But what have you got to show that you're paying for?" Fully conscious now of the paradoxical truth of Christ's words, " . . . I am come into the world, that they which see not might see; and that they which see might be made blind," Haze answers, "Mind your business, . . . You can't see." From then on, the landlady is obsessed with his scarred eye sockets, and after his murder by the two policemen the novel ends with a description of her final attempt to fathom them: "She sat staring with her eyes shut, into his eyes, and felt as if she had finally got to the beginning of something she couldn't begin, and she saw him moving farther and farther away, farther and farther into the darkness until he was the pin point of light."

As I have indicated, much of the action of the novel is at first apparently extraneous, excessively violent, and meaningless. The plot, such as it is, relates the story of Haze Motes' unsuccessful attempt to fight off a belief in Christ; it is buried, however, in a welter of extraneous action that almost always has an unexpected outcome, sometimes quite hilarious and often gruesome. The novel immediately suggests the quest motif, but when Haze returns home after demobilization, the only thing which happens to him is that a board falls on him during the night. Haze's quest is further mocked, when he steps out on the platform at one stop and misses the train. Finally, the ridiculousness of the quest is confirmed, when Haze, arriving at Taulkinham, has no place to go, until he sees the name of Mrs. Leora Watts on a lavatory wall: "The friendliest bed in town! Brother." And so on, throughout the novel, one unexpectedness follows another: the blind see, the innocent are guilty, and the clean are unclean. (pp. 140-43)

Character relationships are equally meaningless and abortive. Haze meets the "blind" preacher, and apparently the predominant conflict of the book is to be between these two, until the preacher leaves town to take a job on a banana boat. Enoch Emery appears in a fairly large portion of the novel, but he wanders off to steal a gorilla suit, in which he scares people rather than making friends as he had expected. Sabbath Lily Hawks is placed in a juvenile detention ward. Onnie Jay Holy, Haze's first disciple, becomes Hoover Shoats, the confidence man, and then he, too, disappears. Solace Layfield appears only long enough to be murdered.

There is, then, really only one character; the others are personifying figures, used as exempla and then dropped. And in Miss O'Connor's aesthetic, this method was the only one which would not weaken her vision. If any of these figures were rounded and involved in a meaningful conflict with Haze, the emphasis in the book would be upon man's relation to man, whereas in Miss O'Connor's view, the only reason for writing a novel is to explore man's dependence upon Christ.

If the content of *Wise Blood* seems bizarre and ludicrous, the rhetoric only reinforces that appearance. Extremely incongruous images, oxymorons, and synesthesia convince us that here indeed is a strange new world. Objects are like humans and animals, human beings are like animals and insects, and animals are like human beings. But the unconventional rhetoric is not an embellishment pasted upon a basically conventional view of the world. It is indeed a warped world, one which has been likened to a Chagall painting, and the comparison of the novel to the modern painting seems especially apt for Miss O'Connor often appears to share modern painting's preoccupations. Her world frequently is that of a dream (in keeping with her topsy-turvey aesthetic, dreams are perhaps the most lucid and conventional parts of the book), with characters who transpose themselves, with aimless action endlessly performed, with bizarre mixtures of the known and the unfamiliar. (pp. 143-44)

Miss O'Connor believed that it was her Catholicism which prompted her to describe the world as a bizarre and sinister dream: "My own feeling is that writers who see by the light of their Christian faith will have, in these times, the sharpest eyes for the grotesque, for the perverse, and for the unacceptable." She further thought that such a specific vantage point suggested the themes with which she worked: "I will admit to certain preoccupations that I get, I suppose, because I'm a Catholic; preoccupations with belief and with death and grace and the devil." But while belief and grace offered spiritual incentive to her writing, death and the devil offered the human terrors which make fiction remarkable. "I'm born Catholic," she said, "and death has always been brother to my imagination. I can't imagine a story that doesn't properly end in it or in its foreshadowings." Her statement is borne out by the fact that *Wise Blood* begins and ends with a *memento mori:* "The outline of a skull under his skin was plain and insistent" and "The outline of a skull was plain under his skin and the deep burned eye sockets seem to lead into the dark tunnel where he had disappeared."

But, for all that has been said, there may linger a suspicion that content and form are not joined in *Wise Blood.* Nearly everyone who has commented on the novel has noticed the malformed characterizations, the complete absurdity of action and event, and other features which depart from convention. Is it not, then, a farfetched story, which the author has attempted to dignify by grafting on a highly

unconventional rhetoric? I think not. Given the author's many statements of her intentions, we must assume that she would have expected her work to be judged by its communicability, and would not have departed from the conventional structure and treatment of the novel, if she had thought innovations in style or absurdities in content would detract from her vision.

I have suggested elements of symbolism which seem to join content and form and which give qualities of coherency and unity to the work, but I believe that there is yet a motif to be traced which serves as a first ironic and later serious basis for the conception of Haze Motes, a motif which serves as a coagulant for the diverse aspects of the work. If one cannot create the perfect form perhaps the next best thing is to create the perfect deformity. Satirists have always chosen the latter course, and that seems to have been Miss O'Connor's choice. In her view, the only conflict that would sustain for her a work as long as a novel was that of belief versus disbelief. She could have, then, chosen to narrate the story of a modern saint. But such a story would have had the quality of sentimental and intrusive moralism, of preaching, about it which would have alienated the very audience which she wanted to reach. She could have, then, chosen to analyze the rather normal man's attempt to establish a meaningful spiritual relationship in a world where disbelief, especially in the guise of belief, is rampant. But the trouble with this approach would be that the character might be so like his audience that it would not have perceived his problem. That leaves, then, the opposite of the saint: the active disbeliever. Here a demonic figure could have been constructed, but a demonic figure would be without the desire to believe in the first place, and so there would have been no conflict. The ideal figure, it seems, would be a saint who disbelieved, that is, one who was actively searching for religious meaning (as opposed to the majority who passively accept the traditional view, although they secretly regard it as nonsense) but who did not find it in the established beliefs.

What would be better, then, than to posit the form first and then let the character grow to fit it? In this manner the possibility of ironical treatment is available at first, when the character differs completely from the form, when he does the right thing for the wrong reason. Then, as the character is inevitably forced into the form, it receives straight-forward treatment; rather than work by opposites the author can then work by similarities, thus effecting the supreme irony: the only possibility of actively rejecting an idea to which the majority pays lip-service is through the same behavior as that of actively accepting the idea, that is, both disbeliever and believer are "outsiders," in that they seriously think about their spiritual life, whereas most people are so immersed in a materialistic life that they neither accept nor reject religion.

The legend of St. Anthony could be the form. An Egyptian monk of the third century who was evidently a visionary, Anthony gave up his worldly property to go into the desert to live as an ascetic. Here the Devil, often in the guise of animals, continually tempted him. (pp.144-45)

Haze Motes at first seems an unlikely St. Anthony figure. But the wide differences in time and place become unimportant when the essentially similar natures of the two men are seen. Both are possessed with an overpowering sense of the importance of religious belief as the only force which can give order and meaning to their lives. And both use self-abasement to express their realization of the gulf which separates the human from the spiritual. One accepts a saint as a flagellant, but one is at first surprised that Haze Motes, the illiterate Tennesseean, unconsciously knows of the centuries-old method of chastising the flesh to purify the soul.

Once the suggestion is implanted that Haze is to be regarded seriously as a seeker after divine truth, rather than as just another Bible-beating Southerner, the departure from the form is begun. Whereas Anthony had renounced civilization to find God in the desert, it is in the desert that Haze finds his substitute for God; the army "sent him to another desert and forgot him again. He had all the time he could want to study his soul in and assure himself that it was not there." And where Anthony's confrontation with God had left him humble, Haze's false truth goads him into pride; his actions at first betray his contemptuousness of other people, who may believe in the fiction that he has discarded, but soon his words reveal the prideful unbeliever: " 'I'm going to do some things I never have done before,' he said and gave her a sidelong glance and curled his mouth slightly."

Haze also departs from the form when he seeks the city; "God made the country but man made the town" is at least as old as St. Augustine, but for Miss O'Connor, who always conceives of the city as Sodom, such a moral geography is still valid. When Haze reaches the city, his life once again parallels St. Anthony's; according to the legend, St. Anthony was subjected to harassment by all sorts of demons, and the invention of all kinds of demonic forms became the distinguishing characteristic of paintings which used the Temptation as a subject. Haze, too, is bordered on all sides by monsters. With figure of speech, with description, and even with suggestive names—Hawks, Shoats—the author emphasizes that Haze has plunged himself into a chaos filled with every kind of monstrous apparition.

All of the characters have some animalistic aspect to their natures, and all represent some type of worldly threat to Haze's unworldly quest. (pp. 145-46)

Once the tension between the form, St. Anthony, and the departure from it, Haze Motes, has been established, there is little need for its constant emphasis. Rather, the novel is a series of events, or panels of a painting as it were, showing Haze being tormented by the symbolically-different weird beasts. The motif is not reintroduced until near the end of the novel, when Haze has been forced to see that there is no escape from Christ. Structurally, of course, it is at this point when the departure from the form becomes the form. For the description of Haze's final, saint-like actions, the point of view is shifted to the eyes of Haze's horsy, love-sick landlady. After the destruction of his car, of his delusion, Haze returns to blind himself. Thereafter his landlady, mainly because of his large disability check (which is one hundred per cent and suggests that Haze was a mentally exhausted victim of the war),

takes great interest in Haze and observes him closely: "He could have been dead and get all he got out of life but the exercise. He might as well be one of them monks, she thought, he might as well be in a monkery." When she learns that Haze walks in shoes filled with rocks and broken glass and wears strands of barbed wire wrapped around his chest, she is convinced of his insanity. . . . (p. 147)

Flannery O'Connor was . . . perhaps the writer of the modern Southern school most conscious of the chaotic world caused by the declining belief in older religious institutions. Thus her satire was the most desperate, for to her it was most obvious that the old order was crumbling. But she saw that the old order in religion remained a husk; therefore she had to attack those people who play out their lives within the old form without giving allegiance to it and those people who have gone over more obviously to some other allegiance. There was no place in her world for any norms; from her vantage point the entire world did look grotesque, since her audience did not recognize the normative value of faith. (pp. 147,156)

Lewis A. Lawson, "Flannery O'Connor and The Grotesque: 'Wise Blood'," in Renascence, *Vol. XVII, No. 3, Spring, 1965, pp. 137-47, 156.*

Carter W. Martin

[An American educator and critic, Martin is the author of The True Country: Themes in the Fiction of Flannery O'Connor *(1968). In the following excerpt from that book, Martin analyzes the relationship between Hazel Motes and his landlady, Mrs. Flood.]*

[It] is not surprising that some critics have mistakenly taken Mrs. Flood, Hazel Motes's landlady in *Wise Blood,* to be a voracious, avaricious woman steeped in evil [Jonathan Baumbach], "a caricatured portrait of Bible Belt morality" [Melvin J. Friedman]. Mrs. Flood, however, is also in a relatively neutral moral situation; her evil is the practical concern with herself and her needs, typifying her insensitivity to the absolute morality of sacrificing one's self for all other men. Her petty conniving to get more of Haze's government check by raising his rent is counterbalanced by her frequent display of kindness, sympathy, and generosity toward him. Thus the characterization reveals culpability but not irredeemable malice. Mrs. Flood undergoes conversion progressively as she witnesses Hazel Motes's Oedipus-like blinding of himself. When he tells her of his intention, she is completely unable to understand the meaning of it. Her own solution to "feeling that bad" would have been suicide, she thinks, and one sees a parallel to Jocasta in *Oedipus Rex* (which Flannery O'Connor read for the first time during the writing of this novel), who hangs herself rather than live with the terrifying knowledge of her wretchedness. Unlike Jocasta, Mrs. Flood is not aware of her wretchedness and so lives to pursue greater knowledge of herself—and ultimately of God—being carried inexorably on by the nagging suspicion that Haze, though blind, sees something that she does not. As in Sophocles' tragedy, sight imagery is highly significant; Mrs. Flood considers herself to be "clear-sighted": "She didn't like the thought that something was being put over her head. She liked the clear light of day. She liked to see things." Early in this sequence of the novel, "it occurred to her suddenly that when she was dead she would be blind too," but the meaning of her observation is slow in coming to her. She begins to study Haze as if he were a question and imagines that if she were blind she would listen to the radio, eat cake and ice cream, and soak her feet; whereas Haze, inexplicably to her, lives an ascetic life in contempt of the world.

Her movement toward knowledge begins most significantly after Haze explains to her that "If there's no bottom in your eyes, they hold more," and that she cannot understand his acts of mortification because, "You can't see." Although her petulance toward him continues, so does her gradual penetration into the heart of the mystery that he represents:

> She could not make up her mind what would be inside his head and what out. She thought of her own head as a switchbox where she controlled from; but with him, she could only imagine the outside in, the whole black world in his head and his head bigger than the world, his head big enough to include the sky and the planets and whatever was or had been or would be. How would he know if time was going backwards or forwards or if he was going with it? She imagined it was like you were walking in a tunnel and all you could see was a pinpoint of light. She had to imagine the pinpoint of light; she couldn't think of it at all without that. She saw it as some kind of star, like the star on Christmas cards. She saw him going backwards to Bethlehem and she had to laugh.

Even though Mrs. Flood is not aware of it, her description of Haze's condition shows almost mystical religious insight in encompassing the divine timelessness and limitlessness of Haze's vision of God. (pp. 116-19)

She recognizes, though she expresses it in a "voice of High Sarcasm," that Haze, in spite of the name of his church, demonstrates his belief in Jesus through his unusual behavior. Mrs. Flood's own conversion to Hazel's thinking is foreshadowed by her wish to marry him, not to get his pension or to commit him to the state institution, as she had earlier planned, but to "keep him. Watching his face had become a habit with her; she wanted to penetrate the darkness behind it and see for herself what was there."

Although she broaches her marriage proposition to him as a hedge against the emptiness of the world, . . . her ignorance of the place of holiness in matrimony does not diminish her sincerity. Indeed, the imagery suggests the traditional Christian analogy between Christ and the church, Haze in this instance standing as a Christlike bridegroom and Mrs. Flood (her name associating with the descendants of Noah) taking her position as the expectant bride soon to be assimilated into the one flesh of God—the concept that makes marriage a sacrament and extends the bridegroom imagery to approach the significance of the partaking of Christ's body in the Mass. The consummation of the proposed marriage is figuratively accomplished

when two policemen bring Hazel's dead body to Mrs. Flood and place it in her bed. "I see you've come home!" she says, and talks to him as if he were alive. Only through his death does she understand the meaning of his life, as through Christ's death the universal church finds salvation. As she examines Haze's face, her sight turns inward upon the truth for the first time. Although she stares intently at his eyes, only when she closes her own does she realize the meaning of Hazel's action. Mrs. Flood feels helpless to act upon the truth, but she has witnessed it.

Hazel Motes's conversion is quite different in nature from his landlady's; his change is not one from ignorance or innocence such as hers and that of the others like her. Instead, he is one of a large group of O'Connor characters whose epiphanies follow experiences dominated by entrenched pride, willful sin, deliberate rejection of God, or possibly all three. (pp. 119-20)

At the opening of *Wise Blood,* the very name of Hazel Motes's evangelical crusade, the Church Without Christ, certifies his vehement disavowal of God's grace. His background includes exposure to stringent religious practice and subsequent traumatic guilt: his stern mother, the evangelist grandfather with Jesus in his head like a stinger, the obscene sideshow at the carnival, Hazel's attempt to purify himself through mortification. Even as a child his ingrained religion has the marks of fear rather than faith; though trying to emulate his grandfather, he feels that he must avoid sin in order to avoid Jesus. Such religious thinking illustrates the profound spiritual pride that leads man to believe himself capable of achieving his own salvation; it is an outstanding heresy in Christian thought. Haze has such "strong confidence in his power to resist evil" that Jesus is expelled from his dialectic even before he embraces a dedicated belief in blasphemy and nothingness. . . . (pp. 120-21)

Even the vestiges of orthodox faith are lost when Haze is in the army. Having carried with him symbols of that faith, "a black Bible and a pair of silver-rimmed spectacles that had belonged to his mother," he is rigidly defensive of his soul against the threats of the government, foreign places to which he might be sent, and priests taking orders from the Pope. But he is not immune to the skepticism of other soldiers who inform him that he has no soul. Wanting to believe them and suffering the physical and psychological wounds of war, Haze gets rid of his soul by converting his proud heterodox belief "to nothing instead of to evil."

When Haze returns home to Eastrod, Tennessee, aware that all those of his family who have created his character and against whom he has rebelled are dead, the next stage in the almost medieval drama of his soul's fortune occurs. His disappointment upon finding only an empty skeleton of a house remaining suggests that he expected to find the dead resurrected, as he had expected both his father and mother to rise up in their coffins and deny death in the midst of their funerals. . . . It is apparent, then, that Haze's violent rejection of Jesus arises from his literal hope for immediate physical resurrection in this world and his subsequent sense of betrayal when his hope is shattered.

Once he leaves Eastrod, Haze begins an almost systematic program of spiteful blasphemy against what he considers to be the source of his injury. Apropos of nothing, he tells a strange woman on the train that he does not believe in Jesus and would not "even if He existed. Even if He was on this train." In Taulkinham he patronizes Mrs. Leora Watts, the prostitute, to prove through action that he does not believe in sin; and he buys a car, a dilapidated Essex, as a defiant replacement for his soul, contending that "Nobody with a good car needs to be justified." The Essex becomes for him the rock of his gospel from which he disseminates the truth of his Church Without Christ. He preaches the doctrines of nothingness from the car with as much vigor and threatening directness as Haze's grandfather had summoned in Christ's name, and the young prophet's conviction is borne out in his burdenlike profession, sometimes capitalized, "I am clean." Thus Haze's rejection of innate corruption through Adam, mortal sin of any kind, and the total scheme of Christian redemption becomes apparent.

Nevertheless, Haze is subconsciously driven to regain his lost faith. His hope is apparent not only in the fact that he protests too much, but in his fascination with the hypocritical pseudo-blind preacher Asa Hawks. His interest in Hawks's blindness is thematically similar to Mrs. Flood's curiosity about Haze's blindness later in the novel; Haze suspects that the old man is not blind, but he paradoxically entertains the hope that someone has had faith enough to choose inward vision in preference to outward sight. Thus the discovery that Hawks is not blind renews Haze's commitment to evil and impels him to succumb to the corruption of Sabbath Lily Hawks.

For this grotesque saint, submission to Sabbath Lily is a dark night of the soul. Haze emerges from the experience with his eyes burned clean enough to see through the fraudulence around him and with his will strengthened sufficiently to act decisively in carrying out his still-blasphemous, but sternly moral, beliefs. His first act is the destruction of the new jesus—the mummified shrunken man brought by Enoch Emery and coddled like a living child by Sabbath. Haze proves here his earlier contention that the new jesus is a metaphor, not an objective thing; in this acknowledgment one can discern intellectual progress beyond his previous literal-mindedness (although one should be cautious to avoid attributing to Flannery O'Connor any doubts as to the actuality of resurrection—to her it is not a metaphor). Hazel Motes's next significant act is to seek out and destroy Solace Layfield, his rival hired by Hoover Shoats. Layfield, the false prophet of blasphemy, is a kind of anti-antichrist who represents to Haze the lowest form of dishonesty—he claims not to believe in Jesus when he actually does. Haze murders Solace by running him down repeatedly with the Essex, suggesting allegorically an action of his perverse new soul.

After the murder, Haze decides to leave Taulkinham, go to another city, and make a new beginning with the Church Without Christ. Preparing the Essex for the trip, Hazel amazes the mechanic with his doctrines, relating the car's dilapidated condition to his own spiritual condition. Five miles into the country, a patrolman stops him

and genially and methodically pushes the car over an embankment, thus committing Hazel's symbolic soul to a grotesque, red-clay grave, presided over by a hunch-shouldered buzzard.

The change in Haze on this occasion is very subtly conveyed. To the policeman's questions, he replies only that he was not going anywhere anyway; in the thematic context, he is admitting that *nothing* is *nowhere,* that the Church Without Christ is a spiritual cul-de-sac. His epiphany is not marked by a vision or a suddenly violent and revelatory experience; he knows the meaning of the destroyed car, returns to town on foot, buys a bucket and a sack of quicklime. Undramatically he answers Mrs. Flood's question about his intention: " 'Blind myself,' he said and went on in the house." To the casual reader, Hazel Motes's blinding of himself might be interpreted as an act of despair rather than faith; such a reader would probably make the same mistake about Oedipus. But the novel denies such misreading in its detailed account of Haze's humble acts of contrite mortification, in his explicit acceptance of the Christian scheme by altering his previous refrain to "I'm not clean," and in the conversion of Mrs. Flood effected by his example. Finally, in "The Author's Note to the Second Edition," Flannery O'Connor herself explains Haze as "a Christian *malgre lui*":

> That belief in Christ is to some a matter of life and death has been a stumbling block for readers who would prefer to think it a matter of no great consequence. For them Hazel Motes' integrity lies in his trying with such vigor to get rid of the ragged figure who moves from tree to tree in the back of his mind. For the author Hazel's integrity lies in his not being able to.

(pp. 121-25)

Carter W. Martin, in his The True Country: Themes in the Fiction of Flannery O'Connor, *Vanderbilt University Press, 1969, 253 p.*

Joyce Carol Oates

[*Oates is an American fiction writer and critic who is perhaps best known for her novel* them, *which won a National Book Award in 1970. In the following excerpt from her* New Haven, New Earth: The Visionary Experience in Literature *(1974), Oates views Hazel Motes as a soul searching for freedom by rebelling against traditional Christianity and his own fate.*]

O'Connor's two novels [*Wise Blood* and *The Violent Bear It Away*] deal with essentially the same subject: the romance of the "mad shadow of Jesus" and the soul that demands freedom. As Lewis A. Lawson has noted in his excellent study of *Wise Blood,* [see excerpt above], she uses the construction of the parable, introducing an abstract idea that will be made concrete, as in the parables of Christ. Hazel Motes, the Christless preacher of *Wise Blood,* represents by his very being the contradictory elements of modern society—pushed, of course, to comic and morbid extremes. It is not necessary to assume, along with Lawson, that O'Connor feels Mote's fundamentalism to be "perverted." In other of her stories (**"The River,"** for one) the vitality and passion of the fundamentalist is contrasted favorably with the skepticism of the "civilized." Motes embodies the soul in rebellion, not simply against Christ but against his own destiny. He is the grandson of a preacher and the son of a woman, both of whom were consumed with religious feeling. "He had gone to a country school where he had learned to read and write but that it was wiser not to; the Bible was the only book he read." In the sterility of a government institution—the army— Motes is told he has no soul, and is anxious to believe this. "He saw the opportunity here to get rid of it without corruption, to be converted to nothing instead of to evil." The choice Motes wants to make, like modern man, is not between good and evil but between the reality of both good and evil, and nothing: for an absolute nothing would seem to insure man's freedom. Clearly, O'Connor is as fascinated by this theme as is Dostoyevsky, and one cannot resist assuming that the battle fought so bravely and hopelessly by her heroes is in part her own battle.

Motes tries to achieve the sterility of absolute freedom by rejecting his destiny. Yet everywhere he goes, people mistake him for a preacher. Even the fake blind man can recognize him: "I can hear the urge for Jesus in his voice." Enoch Emery, a kind of parody of Motes as a searcher for truth, says: "I knew when I first seen you you didn't have nobody nor nothing but Jesus." Mrs. Watts, the prostitute who is "so well-adjusted that she didn't have to think any more," says when she sees Motes: "That Jesus-seeing hat!" When Motes rages to himself, he is actually praying without knowing it. His blasphemous words are punctuated with "Jesus" and "Jesus Christ Crucified." We do not know what O'Connor thought of Freud's vision of man, but apart from its atheistic implications it is quite compatible with her apparent psychology. She sees man as dualistic: torn between the conventional polarities of God and the devil, but further confused because the choice must be made in human terms, and the divine might share superficial similarities with the diabolical. Indeed, it is difficult for the average reader at times to distinguish between the two in her fiction. Freud's anatomy of the mind, involving a dynamic struggle of the conscious ego or self to maintain its individuality against the raging forces of the primitive unconscious and the highly repressive reservoir of civilization is a classic one. It is the struggle of Oedipus with his fate, the struggle of Hamlet with his, and, on a lesser dramatic level, the struggle of O'Connor's perverse saints with the saintly that is in them. It is not the devil they wish to defeat, but grace in them that prevents them from being "free." In all cases it is a struggle toward knowledge— forbidden knowledge. Freud's rationalism has alienated existential writers—Ionesco, for one—because his absolute commitment to a psychology that wants to explain the inexplicable runs counter to the age-old belief in the sanctity of the unconscious or of divine mystery. D. H. Lawrence, no existentialist, hated Freud for these reasons, and we might assume that O'Connor would have shared this reaction. Freud bears too close a resemblance to her intellectual parodies—Rayber of *The Violent Bear It Away* and Joy-Hulga, the Ph.D. with the wooden leg, in **"Good Country People."** But the constant seesawing between the conscious and the unconscious, the ego-dominated and the repressed, and, above all, the struggle of the ego to maintain itself in a dreamlike world of abstractions made concrete (the usual machinery of the dream) is Freudian drama of a unique type.

What is original, at least for our time, is O'Connor's commitment to the divine origin of the unconscious. Despite her elegance as a stylist, she is a primitive; she insists that only through an initiation by violence does man "see." Paradoxically, it is after his blinding that Motes "sees"; he is also a murderer, but is that relevant? If the novel were realistic, yes, for in realistic or naturalistic fiction everything must be tabulated and accounted for. But if his murder of the fake Motes is seen to be a murder of that side of himself, then the purely symbolic nature of the story is made clear. Motes is an allegorical figure, however exaggerated and ridiculous. He represents contemporary man torn between the religion of his past (the Christianity of the modern West) and the religion of the present (the worship of science—the reliance upon sense-data). There can be no reconciliation of the two. If man cannot make a choice between them, as the completely adjusted have— those lucky people who no longer need to think—man must be destroyed. This is man as hero, however, and not as clown. O'Connor dresses her saints in outlandish costumes, gives both Motes and Tarwater absurd black preacher hats that signal their fates, and plays upon the reader's conventional feelings for these signs of oddness. As metaphysical device, the extreme intellectuality of these back-country preachers is not surprising; if they are taken as representatives of the South, they are unbelievable. O'Connor dares to present conventionally absurd figures as heroes and does not sentimentalize their plights. It is no wonder, then, that she is misunderstood. Her fiction seems to make no compromise with tradition, unless one assumes the larger tradition of Christianity. . . . It is necessary to be a misfit, the religious temperament has always told us. Catholicism presents a clear compromise between unbridled religious emotion and an orderly religious system. Had O'Connor not been born a Catholic, this combination of passion and order would surely have appealed to her, for this "rage for order" is evident in each of her works. (pp. 149-52)

> *Joyce Carol Oates, "The Visionary Art of Flannery O'Connor," in her* New Heaven, New Earth: The Visionary Experience in Literature, *The Vanguard Press, Inc., 1974, pp. 141-76.*

John V. McDermott

[In the excerpt below, McDermott examines O'Connor's use of ironic language in Wise Blood.*]*

In **Wise Blood** a polarization exists between words and the Word and between what man says and what he truly believes. Hazel Motes, the protagonist, says, "I don't believe in anything," but Sabbath Hawks knows him better, "I seen you wouldn't never have no fun or let anybody else because you didn't want nothing but Jesus!" This dilemma of fragmented man is directly related to Flannery O'Connor's theory of man's "conflicting wills" and is specified by her frequent use of verbal and dramatic irony. She uses Enoch Emery as the prototype of the fragmented personality who simultaneously says one thing and does the opposite. . . . As fragmented man, Emery serves as a counterpart to Hazel Motes, who becomes a totally integrated man as the story concludes.

The dichotomy of words to the Word calls for a dramatic reversal, a spiritual fusion on the part of man, if the spiritual malaise, caused by man's commitment to artificial values, is to end. It is Hazel Motes who finally gives reality to his own words when he repudiates his ambiguous self-image. Just before and after he blinds himself, he sees how far he has ventured from the reality of the Word. His painful, personal decision leads to a cohesion between himself and the Word. He achieves integration with Jesus Christ by having his thoughts and feelings coalesce in a significant decision of his will. This perfect coalition of thought and feeling, followed by the decision to act on such, is the sign he has achieved *Wise Blood.*

Enoch Emery is the man of unwise blood. He taunts Hazel Motes, "You act like you think you got wiser blood than anybody else, , , , but you ain't! I'm the one has it. Not you. Me." But as the model of debilitated man, Enoch Emery is wrong. For him wise blood consists only of intuition. He never thinks. In gently satiric terms, Miss O'Connor ridicules his obtuseness: "he was not a foolhardy boy who took chances on the meanings of things."

But Enoch Emery is not the only one without insight. "No one was paying attention to the sky." No one is paying attention to the core of reality. Rather, they see only the surface of being. . . . Like Enoch, many people see only with their eyes. They say, like the blind preacher, Asa Hawkes, "Jesus is a fact." But to this preacher and to the numerous other preachers in the story, this is a simple statement without reality. The words have no true meaning to those who utter them. Hazel Motes denies vehemently any association with being a "preacher," "I'm no goddam preacher." He knows the hypocrisy of their words.

But on his journey to integration with the Word, he becomes what he so vehemently denies. Miss O'Connor writes,

> but no one had followed him. There had been a sort of follower but that had been a mistake. That had been a boy about sixteen years old who had wanted someone to go to a whorehouse with him because he had never been to one before. He knew where the place was but he didn't want to go without a person of experience, and when he heard Haze, he hung around until he stopped preaching and then asked him to go.

Like the others, he does not see "the sky." He has not yet been filled with the Holy Spirit, symbolized by the cloud-bird image in the story. . . . His journey toward unification with the Word is at a standstill, "there was only one truth—that Jesus was a liar."

Ironically it takes the action of a man motivated by hatred to dispel Hazel Motes' illusions. " 'I wasn't speeding,' Haze said. 'No,' the patrolman agreed, 'you wasn't.' 'I was on the right side of the road.' 'Yes you was, that's right,' the cop said. 'What you want with me?' 'I just don't like

your face,' the patrolman said. 'Where's your license?'. . . 'I don't have a license.' 'Well,' the patrolman said,'. . . I don't reckon you need one.'. . . The patrolman got behind the Essex and pushed it over the embankment. . . . The car landed on its top." The patrolman then asks the staring Motes, "Was you going anywheres?" Haze finally realizes the truth and answers simply, "No." His decision then to blind himself to this world in order that he may see the eternal reality of the Word quickly follows. He is now moving in consonance with the bird. He has divested himself completely from the vision of an Enoch Emery. "Enoch's eyesight was very poor." Enoch as the man without vision cared nothing for birds. "Come on, we don't have to look at theseyer birds that come next.' He ran past the cages of birds. . . . 'Oh, Jesus,' Enoch groaned . . . 'Come on!' but Haze didn't move from where he was looking into the cage." He stares into the eye of an owl and protests, 'I AM clean [but] the eye shut softly and the owl turned its face to the wall." The owl like the "sixteen year old boy" recognizes the insubstantiality of his words. Haze's condition at this point in the novel is symbolized by the "shrunken man," the epitome of evil. He is equated with the shrunken man: "he [Haze] made a noise. It might have come from the man inside the case. In a second Enoch knew it had." Haze admits at this point, "if Jesus existed, I wouldn't be clean."

Later, after murdering Solace Layfield, the despicable image of himself, retribution, as I mentioned, moves ironically in when the patrolman destroys his car, the vehicle he had used to escape from himself. He had told his hateful self-image, "Two things I can't stand, . . . a man that ain't true and one that mocks what is. You shouldn't ever have tampered with me if you didn't want what you got." In this act of retribution against his evil self-image, he moves in the direction of the bird. His next decision, to blind himself, so that he may not delude himself again, puzzles his landlady, " 'What possible reason could a sane person have for wanting to not enjoy himself any more?' She certainly couldn't say." But Hazel Motes now knew that "to enjoy" meant satisfaction of the self only. He finally realizes how utterly vapid this expression really is. He is finally able to admit to himself, "I'm not clean." He has turned full circle and has made Enoch Emery a prophet on at least one point, "I knew when I first seen you you (Hazel) didn't have nobody nor nothing but Jesus."

Hazel Motes' journey to Christ has been accomplished by means of long and painful experiences. He did not, as Thomas LeClair suggests [see *CLC,* Vol. 13, p. 420], acquiesce to the admonitions of his mother. He won his victory through a fusion of thought and feeling, deliberate thought and intense feeling which precipitated in him an unwavering decision to act. His "many wills" were no longer in conflict. His will had become one with the will of God. He had finally achieved *Wise Blood* in this integration of his spirit with Christ. "She saw him moving farther and farther away, farther and farther into the darkness until he was the pinpoint of light." Very early in the novel do we see this result foreshadowed. "He wanted it all dark, he didn't want it diluted." His words were now in full consonance with the Word—no longer does he suffer from the malaise, caused by a polarity of matter and spirit that envelopes all the others in **Wise Blood.** In merging his "conflicting wills" and deciding to be one with and in Christ, he has gained **Wise Blood.** He has moved from a negative belief, his inability to run away from Christ, to a positive belief, his decision to blind himself to the things of this world. Man's "integrity" then lies as much in his inability to run away from Christ as in his desire to seek Him out. His "integrity" then is ambivalent in nature. He moves, as it were, on a treadmill, but in the end he must leap from it into Christ's arms, if he is to be saved. His negative "integrity" must become positive. His "conflicting wills" must become one. (pp. 163-66)

> *John V. McDermott, "Dissociation of Words with the Word in 'Wise Blood',"* in *Renascence, Vol. XXX, No. 3, Spring, 1978, pp. 163-66.*

Margaret Peller Feeley

[*In the following excerpt, Feeley interprets* Wise Blood *as a comedy about the quest for salvation through negation.*]

In her preface to **Wise Blood,** Flannery O'Connor calls it a "comic novel about a Christian *malgré lui*," a rather audacious assertion about a book in which the protagonist endures spiritual suffering, commits murder, blinds and mutilates himself and finally dies in a ditch. It does not take the reader long to realize that he is a good way from the comic world of Fielding. Hazel Motes is a comic hero obsessed with God, an intellectual whose reason denies God but whose bones will not forget Him. "The outline of a skull under his skin was plain and insistent," reminding himself and everyone else of mortality and the Christian answer to man's condition. The modern indifference to religion permits a double-edged blade of satire: the author parodies the agnosticism and existentialism that characterize the intellectual trend of the fifties while she also parodies Haze as a Bible Belt hick who is a figure of absurdity, incongruous in his time.

Haze is exactly the type of comic protagonist that Henri Bergson describes in his famous essay, "Laughter": the machinelike individual who is rigid and monomaniacal. Flannery O'Connor brought her experience as a college cartoonist to her descriptions of Hazel as a mechanical toy that works by its own laws, oblivious to the world around it. . . . His physical rigidity underscores his obsession with Jesus that is obvious to everyone but himself. He is constantly being mistaken for a preacher when he insists he's not, and even Enoch Emery who is a near-moron understands Haze better than he does himself: "I knew when I first seen you you didn't have nobody nor nothing but Jesus." The result is comedy of the *idée fixe* or humor which always seems irrelevant or out of sorts with the world around it.

Wise Blood is a novel which draws upon an eclectic group of influences: humors and black comedy, Greek tragedy, and the traditions of the romance and of the grotesque. Gilbert H. Muller, in *Nightmares and Visions,* has pointed out many elements of Nathanael West's *Miss Lonelyhearts,* which Flannery O'Connor read while writing **Wise**

Blood. Her grotesque treatment of death and coffins certainly recalls *As I Lay Dying,* one of her favorite novels. Her reading of the Oedipus cycle at this time probably accounts for the striking visual imagery in **Wise Blood,** and there are, as well, many thematic parallels between the novel and the ancient drama. Like Oedipus, Haze is engaged in a flight from truth that also seems like a quest for it, a flight/quest that may be seen both as a heroic attempt to escape one's fate and as an attempt, rooted in some deep, mysterious, natural faith, to discover the meaning of true obedience to God. O'Connor, who was probably her own best critic, thought of herself as an inheritor of the romance tradition as employed by Hawthorne and spoke of combining in **Wise Blood** the "dark and divisive romance-novel with the comic-grotesque tradition." The formula worked: **Wise Blood's** two-dimensional characters, highly colored plot, symbolic (rather than realistic) plausibility of events are very receptive to the comic exaggeration which is an essential ingredient of the grotesque.

This paper seeks to examine **Wise Blood** as comedy in still another sense, as a Christian *commedia* in which the action begins at the level of low comedy but becomes increasingly other-worldly. The protagonist gradually draws away from human experience altogether until finally he is abstracted into "a pin point of light" by which the corrupt society may be redeemed. The path which Haze walks as a Christian pilgrim is a well-worn one, a comic version, sometimes inversion, of the Negative Way (*via negativa*) or the Way of Rejection. The Way of Rejection is one of the two chief Christian modes of approach to God—the other is the Way of Affirmation—consisting [wrote Charles Williams] "generally speaking, in the renunciation of all images except the final one of God himself, and even—sometimes but not always—of the exclusion of that only Image of all human sense." The Negative Way has had particular appeal for the alienated, for those who are out of sorts with the time they live in, as if the soul must go backwards when the culture that is supposed to nurture it is in trouble. . . . It is my intention . . . to emphasize the universal and archetypal in a novel that has been neglected, I think, because it has been considered a sort of *isolato:* too weird and eccentric to have any real connection with life. Hazel Motes is simply the most recent pilgrim who, to use the paradoxical rhetoric of the Negative Way, arrives at what he is not by going through the way in which he is not. (pp. 104-06)

The subplot concerning Enoch Emery's quest for a "new jesus" serves as a foil to Hazel's quest for truth. Enoch's buffoonery contrasts with Haze's *commedia*. As Haze is a medieval character in a modern world, Enoch seems to be Flannery O'Connor's parody of a primitive man. While Haze is a man of intellect, Enoch is a man of instinct whose "wise blood," an intuitive gene inherited from his father, is much more highly developed than his brain. O'Connor loves to poke fun at him: "His blood was more sensitive than any other part of him; it wrote doom all through him except possibly in his brain, and the result was that his tongue, which edged out every few minutes to test his fever blister, knew more than he did." in fact, his "wise blood" is just as foolish as the rest of Enoch; it is probably meant to evoke and contrast with the blood of

Redemption (man can know nothing without the help of his Redeemer). While Haze is trying to create a world without Redemption, an unsacred world, Enoch lives in a sacred *cosmos* just like a preindustrial person: "The park was the heart of the city. He had come to the city and—with a knowing in his blood—he had established himself at the heart of it. Everyday he looked at the heart of it; every day, and he was so stunned and awed and overwhelmed that just to think about it made him sweat." The omphalos or navel of this world is the "dark secret center of the park," the MVSEVM, which has a name so sacred (like Yahweh) that Enoch cannot even pronounce it. The MVSEVM is the shrine of a mummy which Enoch idolizes. The very fact that he would worship the object of a primitive cult shows that he is something of an anachronism. O'Connor marked this telling passage in Jung: "The archetypal image of the wise man, the savior or redeemer, lies buried and dormant in man's unconscious since the dawn of culture; it is awakened whenever the times are out of joint and a human society is committed to a serious error." This image is awakened in Enoch and he fervently pursues its incarnation in a godless world that heaps abuse on him.

Because Enoch is too inarticulate to express the sacred knowledge, he can only call others to be witness to it. His "wise blood" informs him that Haze will seek him out to share his mystery. When Haze does seek him in pursuit of Asa Hawks, Enoch seizes the opportunity to drag Haze to the MVSEVM. He always precedes his visits with a set, unvarying ritual that may be read as the parody of a religious order (or the parody of Haze's stages on the Negative Way), so that even though Haze is impatient and unaccommodating, each step must be carried out precisely.

First, the ritual orgy: he leers at the women bathers at the park swimming pool. Next the feast: he gulps a milkshake at the Frosty Bottle. Finally, he watches the animals in the zoo, as if his blood were searching out its totem. After Haze rejects Enoch, Enoch breaks into the MVSEVM and steals the mummy for which he has prepared a gilded tabernacle out of a cabinet meant for a slopjar. But the object does not bring him the revelation, the supreme moment he thinks he is entitled to. He expects the "new jesus" to turn him into "an entirely new man, with an even better personality than he had now," and when this transfiguration fails to take place, he takes the mummy to Haze who is now living with Sabbath Lily Hawks. The girl gazes at the mummy and thinks: "She had never known anyone who looked like him before, but there was something in him of everyone she had ever known, as if they had all been rolled into one person and killed and shrunk and dried." The "new jesus" is the incarnation of all people who reject the true God and make a god in their own image: shrunken in stature and spiritually dried up. Haze instantly recognizes the worthlessness of the false idol and throws it out the window.

Enoch, meanwhile, has finally tracked down his totem in Gonga the Gorilla, a man dressed in an ape-suit whose job it is to shake hands with children under movie marquees. The urge to possess the ape-suit now replaces Enoch's obsession with the "new jesus." Discovering where Gonga will stop next on his tour of theaters, he hides in the star's van, murders the man in the ape-suit and jumps out of the van with his treasure at the outskirts of the city. As with Haze, murder means getting rid of the old self, though Enoch is unconscious of what he is doing in trading his clothes for the animal skin: "Burying his clothes was not a symbol to him of burying his former self; he only knew he wouldn't need them any more." Enoch de-evolves, from primitive man back to apehood in which he finally basks: "No gorilla in existence, whether in the jungles of Africa or California, or in New York City in the finest apartment in the world, was happier at that moment than this one, whose god had finally rewarded it." But Enoch is again denied his epiphany. All along, he has been searching for a friend. Spurned by Haze, he now approaches a pair of lovers looking at the city skyline, confident in his new identity, hand outstretched in friendship. But when the couple catch a glimpse of him, they flee screaming. Our last view is of a forlorn gorilla sitting on the rock that the lovers have abandoned and staring across the valley as Haze does at his moment of revelation.

Many critics have voiced complaints about the barrenness and ugliness of the O'Connor landscape in the stories and novels. Martha Stephens has been particulary vehement about the stupidity and meanness of all the characters in **Wise Blood,** major and minor. Certainly they are unattractive. Hazel has a "nose like a shrike's bill" and moves like a robot, Mrs. Leora Watts has green teeth, Enoch resembles "a friendly hound dog with light mange," Asa Hawks is "a tall cadaverous man" with "the expression of a grinning mandrill," Onnie Jay Holy is a drugstore cowboy, and Mrs. Flood is "a tall bony woman, resembling the mop she carried upside-down." They look like things or birds or animals, but a kind of spiritual yearning that possesses all of them—with the exception of Mrs. Watts who is too "well-adjusted" to think—humanizes them and makes them something more than cartoon figures. In O'Connor's favorite story, **"A Good Man Is Hard to Find,"** she writes that "the trees were full of silver-white sunlight and the meanest of them sparkled." In **Wise Blood** the "meanest" characters also have a spark of something, an often barely conscious quickening to the mystery and wonder that are the springs of religion, however they manage to pervert it. Hawks is cynical and crooked, but like Haze, he has faith in spite of himself: "You can't run away from Jesus. Jesus is a fact." Other characters have feelings that go deeper than the language they have to express them. For Enoch, the idea of a Redeemer represents "a terrible knowledge without any words to it," and Sabbath silently cradles the "new jesus" like a grotesque madonna. Onnie Jay Holy's blatant commercial approach to religion—"You know, friend, I certainly would like to see this new jesus. . . . I never heard a idear before that had more in it than that one. All it would need is a little promotion"—would suggest that he is a complete opportunist. Yet even he yearns for something beyond the concrete. When Haze explains to him that the "new jesus" is just a metaphor—"There's no such thing as any new jesus. That ain't but a way to say something"—Onnie Jay is genuinely disappointed: "That's the trouble with you inner-leckshuls,' Onnie Jay muttered, 'You don't never have nothing to show for what you're saying'."

Haze is often the focus of the other characters' spiritual curiosity. The secular world may be shy of religion, but it wants to take a peek. His deepset dark eyes represent a mystery that others wish to penetrate. Mrs. Wally Bee Hitchcock can't avert her eyes from Hazel's: "Their settings were so deep that they seemed, to her, almost like passages leading somewhere and she leaned halfway across the space that separated the two seats, trying to see into them." And Sabbath observes, "I like his eyes. . . . They don't look like they see what he's looking at but they keep on looking." As others pursue Haze, Haze pursues Hawks until he has peered into the eyes of the false blind man.

Hazel's point of view dominates most of *Wise Blood,* but after he blinds himself we see through the eyes of Mrs. Flood, his landlady. Many of the names in *Wise Blood* have an ironic truth: Hazel has motes in his eyes, Hawks is predatory, his daughter is a stained and wilted Sabbath lily, Hoover Shoats alias Holy is an unholy pig, Solace takes solace in Jesus as he is dying, and Mrs. Flood evokes the generation of the Flood which "was corrupt in God's sight" (Genesis 6:11). Mrs. Flood is as avaricious and grudging "as if she had once owned the earth and been dispossessed of it." Dispossession, as we have seen, is a key motif in *Wise Blood,* marking the beginning of Christian pilgrimage. T. S. Eliot cautions, "You must go by the way of dispossession," and Haze echoes, "Nothing outside you can give you any place."

Mrs. Flood has a materialist world view that parallels Haze's at the time he preached that "it was not right to believe anything you couldn't see or hold in your hands or test with your teeth." When she sociably asks Haze what he is going to do with a bucket of lime he is carrying and he answers, "Blind myself," she begins to meditate, but censors herself when the thoughts become too uncomfortable:

> A woman like her, who was so clear-sighted, could never stand to be blind. If she had to be blind she would rather be dead. It occurred to her suddenly that when she was dead she would be blind too. She stared in front of her intensely, facing this for the first time. She recalled the phrase, 'eternal death,' that preachers used, but she cleared it out of her mind immediately with no more change of expression than the cat. She was not religious or morbid, for which every day she thanked her stars.

Mrs. Flood's development, like Haze's, begins after the recognition of her own mortality which she at first avoids facing. Haze, with his ravaged eye sockets, is too brutal a reminder, and she is tempted to tell him to leave her home. But later "she would find herself leaning forward staring into his face as if she expected to see something she hadn't seen before," just as Haze used to stare at Asa Hawks and Mrs. Hitchcock at Haze. Haze disturbs her because "the blind man had the look of seeing something" that she couldn't, "the look of straining toward something" that Sabbath first observed, and she is sure that she is being cheated somehow. She steams open his war injury compensation checks from the government to see how much money he is getting, and although she raises his

rent, she still feels cheated. Tentatively, in spite of herself, she begins to question the limitations of matter and tries to conceptualize eternity and infinity in one of the finest passages in the book:

> She could not make up her mind what would be inside his head and what out. She thought of her own head as a switchbox where she controlled from; but with him, she could only imagine the outside in, the whole black world in his head and his head . . . big enough to include the sky and planets and whatever was or had been or would be. How would he know if time was going backwards or forwards or if he was going with it? She imagined it was like you were walking in a tunnel and all you could see was a pin point of light. She had to imagine the pin point of light; she couldn't think of it at all without that. She saw it as some kind of star, like the star on Christmas cards. She saw him going backwards to Bethlehem and she had to laugh.

The imagery expresses the inversion and paradox that characterize the Negative Way. Her meditation about time recalls the lines from "Burnt Norton" and Haze's sermon. Mrs. Flood imagines the universe filling Haze's head until "time" could be "going backwards." She also imagines Haze "going backwards" and we recall that one of our first glimpses of him "was a thin nervous shadow walking backwards. She laughs at her vision of him "going backwards" to Bethlehem but it is exactly how he comes to Jesus, by first learning what God is not, by rejecting all His images. The "pin point of light" evokes the circle of light, God's glory, which Dante sees in the *Paradiso* once he is beyond the limitations of time and space. Mrs. Flood, however, imagines the pin point of light as a star on a tacky Christmas card, a relic of the complacent life that she is gradually leaving behind, but fights to retain: "I'm as good, Mr. Motes . . . not believing in Jesus as a many a one that does," she tells Haze, who answers sarcastically, recognizing his old self in her: "You're better. . . . If you believed in Jesus you wouldn't be so good."

Self-blinding is consistent with the Negative Way. Charles Williams writes that Jesus' "counsel to pluck out the eye is a counsel of the rejection of images." Denied access to Haze's point of view, we can only guess why he blinded himself. Was it because of his vision at the edge of the embankment? Eliot says in "Burnt Norton": "human kind / Cannot bear very much reality." O'Connor gives us another clue in her introductory statement that choice involves "many wills conflicting in one man." Haze appears to have committed the act as a medieval mystic might have fasted or confined himself for contemplative purposes, to simplify consciousness by withdrawing from all distractions. He spends his time walking around the block alone or silently rocking on the porch. He also seems to have blinded himself as an act of penance (for murder? for denying God? for a multitude of sins?) because this act is followed by other penitential acts which have parallels in his childhood.

Mrs. Flood discovers with horror that he throws away the money left over from his check each month. Next she discovers pebbles in his shoes (as a little boy he walked on rocks to repent), and finally sees him lying in bed with barbed wire—his version of the hair shirt—wrapped around his chest. First she decides to marry him and have him committed to a mental hospital so that she can inherit his money, "but gradually her plan had become to marry him and keep him." Her possessiveness instead drives him away; weak with influenza he goes out into the storm to escape the urgency of her appeal: "Nobody to care if you live or die but me! No other place to be but mine!" "In my beginning is my end," writes Eliot in "East Coker"; Haze is at last offered a home, a "place to be" but homeless he begins and homeless he ends.

After Haze leaves, Mrs. Flood's love becomes less manipulative. She weeps and would hunt him out and follow him on his pilgrimage instead of demanding that he conform to her terms. After two policemen find the dying man in a ditch, club him ("We don't want to have no trouble with him," and return him dead to Mrs. Flood, she gazes at him and then shuts her eyes: "She felt as if she were blocked at the entrance of something. She sat staring with her eyes shut, into his eyes, and felt as if she had finally got to the beginning of something she couldn't begin, and she saw him moving farther and farther into the darkness until he was the pin point of light." The language of paradox, "she had finally got to the beginning of something she couldn't begin," is the language of the Negative Way. Here Mrs. Flood who, until Haze, has comfortably existed all her life without a soul, now takes up the cross to begin her own quest, to experience "the life of the spirit" anew for herself. Haze merges with "the pin point of light" to become Mrs. Flood's star, to guide her through the darkness as she hoped he would, as the image of Beatrice guided Dante.

The conclusion of *Wise Blood* (like the body of the novel) has suffered many critics' tendency to emphasize its brutal, gloomy and eccentric aspects. To me, *Wise Blood* is the most relevant and affirmative of Flannery O'Connor's works. Charles Williams writes that "the tangle of affirmation and rejection which is in each of us has to be drawn into some kind of pattern, and has so been drawn by all men who have ever lived." At the end of *Wise Blood,* the Negative Way merges with the Way of Affirmation. Hazel rejects Mrs. Flood's love—his final "rejection of images"—and dies, but his death, while brutal, is not premature; it is the martyrdom we have been prepared for. He has lived the arc of an entire experience. And in his death he continues to promote growth and change in Mrs. Flood. That so limited and venal a creature can be moved signifies hope for all. In her stories, Flannery O'Connor seems to dangle the possibility of salvation in front of her characters and then, with a bitter twist, snatch life away. . . . *Wise Blood,* O'Connor's first novel, perhaps was written out of youthful idealism about human possibilities for change. It is nice to know that ten years later she found the novel "still alive." (pp. 114-22)

Margaret Peller Feeley, "Flannery O'Connor's 'Wise Blood': The Negative Way," in The Southern Quarterly, Vol. XVII, No. 2, Winter, 1979, pp. 104-22.

Sura Prasad Rath

[*In the following excerpt, Rath discusses comic aspects of* Wise Blood.]

In 1962, when *Wise Blood* "reached the age of ten," Flannery O'Connor countered the early reviewers' opinion of the novel by saying that it was "a comic novel about a Christian *malgre lui,* and as such, very serious, for all comic novels that are any good must be about life and death." With this clarification, critics have since highlighted the general comic effect of the grotesque in O'Connor's writings, and her reputation as an ironist has been secured. The most common critical approach has been to juxtapose her grotesque scenes of Georgia life against O'Connor's devout Catholic background, and examine the humor implicit in the exaggerated counterpoint. On the thematic level, the grotesque is seen as a social or religious aberration, and the comic as a regional element; on the level of character, the comic is regarded as O'Connor's device to present the paradoxical proportions of belief and action represented by her characters. (p. 251)

In this essay, I will discuss *Wise Blood,* her first novel and the seed of all her later work, as an archetypal comic novel, and suggest that its comic effect results from confrontations among characters which form comic polarities within the framework of the story.

In his essay on "The Mythos of Spring: Comedy," Northrop Frye builds upon the three comic character types listed in the *Tractatus Coislinius:* the *eirons,* or self-deprecators; the *alazons,* or impostors; and the *bomolochoi,* or buffoons, clowns, and fools. This list, he points out, is closely related to a passage in the *Ethics* which contrasts the buffoon with a character whom Aristotle calls *agroikos* or the churl. According to Frye, the *eiron* character is the self-deprecating hero or the protagonist who appears to be less than he is or assumes more guilt than he is responsible for. The *alazon* figure, on the other hand, is the impostor who pretends or tries to be something more than he is, the most popular type being the *miles gloriosus*—the braggart soldier, the learned crank, the obsessed philosopher, and the mad scientist. The buffoon is characterized as a parasite (Mosca in Johnson's *Volpone,* for example) or a loquacious host, and the churl as a snobbish or priggish "killjoy who tries to stop the fun." Frye goes on to suggest that "we may reasonably accept the churl as a fourth character type" and thus form two opposed pairs: "The contest of *eiron* and *alazon* forms the basis of comic action, and the buffoon and the churl polarize the comic mood."

In spite of the variety of characterization in *Wise Blood,* the major characters resemble these conventional comic archetypes. We recognize the first two polarities, *eiron* and *alazon,* in the characters of Hazel Motes and Enoch Emery. The comic action emanates from the process by which Haze's mask of naiveté and seriousness dupes Enoch, Asa Hawks, Hoover Shoats, and even Mrs. Flood. The novel begins with Hazel riding the train to Taulkinham where he "will do something" he has never done before, presumably challenge the authority of God and Jesus Christ. O'Connor skillfully acquaints us with his background, something unknown to any of the characters involved in the action. A veteran of World War II, Haze has returned with a serious injury to an empty home to live the rest of his life on a government pension. Yet, ironically, his present appearance—the "stiff black broad-brimmed hat" on his lap and the "glaring blue" suit with its price tag still attached—gives him the air of a country preacher. To resolve this duality between actual inner experience and his external image, he takes on the mask of an introvert outsider and begins his new life at a whorehouse, Leora Watts's, which is on the periphery of the Taulkinham society. In the rest of the novel, he journeys inward toward the center of Taulkinham which forms the comic world of *Wise Blood.* As the self-deprecating protagonist, he ridicules the boastful residents of this world as he confronts them, and the resulting conflicts between the wit and the fools, between self-knowledge and self-deception, structure the comic plot.

Haze initiates the action in the novel by withdrawing himself and his true identity from other characters. On the train, he resists all the overtures of Mrs. Wally Bee Hitchcock to start a conversation. Once he reaches Taulkinham, he turns away into a shrinking world, the world of his inner self, running away from people and objects that project on him a false public image. In the second chapter, he rejects such an image before the cab driver and later before Mrs. Watts. The cab driver remains unconvinced, and Mrs. Watts accepts him with condescension. In Chapter 3, he meets his counterpart, Enoch Emery, who accuses him of being unfriendly and shunning company. In Chapter 9, he tries to protect his mask from Hoover Shoats, and in Chapter 14 from Mrs. Flood. One extreme of this self-deprecation is his initial denial that he is a preacher, a role which he plays for a while on the sidewalks, and the other extreme is his final admission to Mrs. Flood that he is not clean. His admission of sin and acceptance of responsibility for this sin is in direct contrast to the professed or pretended ritual of cleanliness other characters practice in life.

An enigma surrounds Hazel. His mask of disinterestedness is the key to his low profile and his apparent serene wisdom, because the more detachment he cultivates the more he attracts the impostors around him. Enoch, who takes him to be a rich man at first, soon changes his mind:

> "Your jaw just crawls," he observed, watching the side of Haze's face. "You don't never laugh. I wouldn't be surprised if you wasn't a real wealthy man."

Similarly, Asa Hawks, the self-styled redeemer of souls, presumes that Haze is poor in spirit. He says he hears "the urge for Jesus in his [Haze's] voice." Haze's success in the use of this mask of self-deprecation prompts him to expand the mask to cover a wider sphere of his disbelief, and he begins preaching for the Church Without Christ. But he is misunderstood again, for Hoover Shoats, alias Onnie Jay Holy, proposes to manage this religious enterprise by re-naming the Church Without Christ as the Church of Christ Without Christ and by making Haze a false prophet, another Jesus. Later, even the blinded Haze, a modern Georgian Oedipus arousing comic emotions of sympathy

and ridicule, has an erotic appeal to Mrs. Flood, for whom his apparent insanity is charming.

Yet Haze baffles all the characters in the novel. Onnie Jay, the master impostor in Taulkinham, accepts his defeat, though with his characteristic boastfulness: " 'My name is Hoover Shoats,' " he says, " 'I known when I first seen you that you wasn't nothing but a crackpot." This discovery is Onnie Jay's self-identity, for, ironically, he is the symbol of Haze's failure in preaching. When Haze attempts to shed his mask and preach his inner self, he fails miserably. His efforts at getting a disciple or a follower for the Church Without Christ yield nothing but an impostor who tries to outdo the master by re-masking him as a new prophet. Onnie Jay's scheme, to get a preacher for the Church of Christ Without Christ, is a deception, a negation of a negation. Haze recognizes the parasite in Onnie Jay and knows the boundary beyond which such buffoons cannot proceed. He remains silent when Onnie Jay plans to bring his "own Jesus" and "prophets for peanuts" into the market place to compete with the Church Without Christ, and waits to see the other "True Prophet," Solace Layfield.

The only character who sees through Haze's masks is Sabbath Hawks who represents what Alfred Kazin has called "the neutral figure of The Child" in O'Connor's writings. Sabbath, who is not so much a child after all, points to Haze's oblique vision: " 'I like his eyes' " she tells her "blind" father. " 'They don't look like they see what he is looking at but they keep on looking.' " What she sees on his face is his mask of indifferent withdrawal. She later accuses him:

> "I knew when I first seen you you were mean and evil. I seen you wouldn't let nobody have nothing. I seen you were mean enough to slam a baby against a wall. I seen you wouldn't never have no fun or let anybody else because you didn't want nothing but Jesus."

" 'I don't want nothing but the truth,' " he shouts back in reply, " 'and what you see is the truth and I've seen it.' " Haze's penetrating eyes are a contrast to Asa Hawks's which do not perform the function they are capable of. Asa is a comic caricature of Haze: one pretends blindness and claims to see; the other sees and pretends blindness to everything.

Haze's violent rejection and brutal murder of Solace Layfield are foreshadowed in the first encounter the two "prophets" have in front of the Odeon Theater. Solace appears in a "glare-blue suit and white hat," and a fat woman standing next to Haze asks him if the two are twins. Haze's instantaneous response is a slow muttering to himself: " 'If you don't hunt it down and kill it, it will hunt you down and kill you.' " Many perceptive readers have read Solace as Haze's double, yet his role in the story is in sharp contrast with Haze's. He is, to use Frye's term, the "straight" rustic with a wife and six children, who is duped by Hoover Shoats into playing the "True Prophet" for some easy money, unaware of the danger that comes with the territory. Haze's reason for killing him is ideological, not psychological: " 'Two things I can't stand,' " he tells Solace, " '—a man that ain't true and one that mocks what is.' " While Solace highlights the manipulative nature of Hoover Shoats, he entertains the audience, and, like Asa Hawks, provides the comic mood of the novel. In their unwitting vulnerability to being the laughing stock in the public eye, both Solace and Asa are churlish characters who are close to Enoch Emery, the *alazon* figure in **Wise Blood.**

In contrast to Hazel, Enoch claims to be larger than he is. His awareness that he has "wise blood like his daddy" is a mockery of his ignorance and self-deception. O'Connor makes it clear that Enoch is in the tradition of tall talk. . . . Unlike Haze, he searches for the new Jesus with the conviction that it is "not right to believe anything you couldn't see or hold in your hands or test with your teeth." So, with the foppish wisdom of his blood, he decides to steal the shrunken human mummy from the museum and offer it as the new Jesus to Haze. The conflict in character between the two, the fool and the wit, extends to the level of action. Each seeks to become a prophet—the fool by reconstructing a prophecy, the resurrection of the Christ child, with rags and a mummy, and the wit by denying the possibility of redeeming prophets. As expected, Haze rejects Enoch's new Jesus the same way he rejects Solace Layfield—with violent outburst and murderous intent. His destruction of the shrunken Jesus, as predicted, by slamming it against the wall manifests the polarity of belief and disbelief between Enoch and him.

It is ironic that Enoch enters the scene of the novel at a sales pitch for potato peelers on the sidewalk, and when we leave him he remains motionless in a stolen gorilla suit, perched on a rock just off the highway and staring "over the valley at the uneven skyline of the city." He survives his search without being converted. Apparently, there is no conversion for wise bloods like him, but neither is there a conversion for the Taulkinham society which is constructed by or around Enoch and variations of him. The blighted nirvana of his restless spirit in its swift passage into obscure oblivion comes as the closest approximation to the success of the Taulkinham community in its thwarted quest for a workable god. The most visible symbol of this passage is Enoch's regression toward an affected apehood.

The other character who shares some of Enoch's pedantry and runs parallel to him is Asa Hawks. An itinerant preacher and a pretender who has to live with his blasphemous caricature of self-blinding, Asa is an anti-*eiron* figure. In archetypal comic plots, the *eiron* character banishes himself, takes on a disguise, or distances himself from action (Prospero in *The Tempest* or Duke Vincentio in *Measure for Measure,* for example) in order to watch from a vantage point the dramatic action among other characters. Such plots are marked by an initial voluntary withdrawal of the protagonist and a subsequent return to the plot at an opportune or crucial moment when the comic verges on the tragic. Asa's failed attempt to blind himself is a defeat of his will to withdraw from action; even more ironic is the fact that he seeks to use his fake blindness as a means of integrating himself into the plot. So, in place of the witty comic hero who oversees and controls the comic action and laughs at it, we see in him a foolish knave who has lost his vantage point in order to be laughed at. Asa is a victim of his plot.

Yet Asa is a more rounded character than one would expect of a coxcomb. He is less naive than Solace Layfield and more stupid than Hoover Shoats. He is a "heavy father" type who, instead of blocking the advance of other characters toward his daughter, seeks to exploit her as though violation of the girl—and the resulting image of an induced Virgin Mother—would help him expiate his failure and guilt. His accomplishment, as it were, is to be a seeing blind man as opposed to the blind seer Tiresias of classical tragedy. He is parasitic because of his dependence, both physical and financial, on his daughter, Sabbath; so, when he attempts to maneuver her destiny for his own purpose, the trick rebounds on himself. Sabbath runs away from him to Haze. Haunted by a profane suicidal motif, Asa can neither die nor live with honest pride. Like Hoover Shoats and Solace Layfield, he provides choric entertainment. As a country preacher making his living in a city, he shares the fate of the *agroikos,* Solace Layfield, as well as the fate of the buffoon, Hoover Shoats.

Hoover Shoats has a significant role in the novel. He has all the qualities of Hazel in reverse.. . . . Hoover epitomizes everything that Hazel could become and thus is a temptation and a threat to the latter's inner quest. Of all the impostors in **Wise Blood,** Hoover has the most potential to disrupt Hazel's mask by making the mask a reality. Hoover's attempt to make Hazel a fantasy prophet for the Holy Church of Christ Without Christ ironically makes Haze aware of the dangers of preaching on the sidewalks or in front of moviehouses.

Hoover is the archetypal buffoon, the parasite, the business agent who lives off a public performer of our time. His success in gathering and holding a crowd, and even making a living from sidewalk preaching, is a reflection on the nature of Taulkinham society. His character emerges most clearly through the dialogue in the brief scene in Chapter 9 where he offers Haze a package of preaching philosophy and religion. O'Connor presents the classic conflict in this dialogue in obvious terms:

> "Listen here," Haze said, "you get away from here. I've seen all of you I want to. There is no such thing as any new jesus. That ain't anything but a way to say something."
>
> The smile more or less slithered away from Onnie Jay's face. "What you mean by that?" he asked.
>
> "That there is no such thing or person," Haze said. "It wasn't nothing but a way to say a thing." He put his hand on the door handle and began to close it in spite of Onnie Jay's hand. "No such thing exists," he shouted.
>
> "That's the trouble with you innerlecktuls," Onnie Jay muttered, "you don't never have nothing to show for what you are saying."

Hoover's "True Prophet," we realize at this point, is another form of Enoch's shrunken mummy. It is an object to satisfy the empiricist as the words of preaching are there to please the rationalist. They do not have any impact on Haze's nihilism.

The cast of characters in **Wise Blood** thus reveals a chain of tensions between Hazel Motes, the introspective outsider who comes from the war to Taulkinham, on the one hand, and the native citizens who make the comic society of this town, on the other. The action begins with society's members attempting to typecast the stranger and ends with their rejection of Hazel's perspectives. Hazel's death in the hands of the two policemen inside the squad car, symbols of the people and the place of Taulkinham's authorities of justice, suggests a resolution, howsoever crude, of the conflicts arising from this interaction. O'Connor does not give us a conventional sense of "living happily ever after," but the recognition Mrs. Flood has at the end of the novel suggests a comic ending and some understanding:

> She shut her eyes and saw the pin point of light, but so far away that she could not hold it steady in her mind. She felt as if she were blocked at the entrance of something. She sat staring with her eyes shut, into his eyes, and felt as if she had finally got to the beginning of something she couldn't begin, and she saw him moving farther and farther into the darkness until he was the pin point of light.

Since the comic action begins with the arrival of the *eiron* figure (Haze) in town, it is dramatically appropriate that it should conclude with his departure through death. Yet we notice the contrast O'Connor uses in the ways Hazel and Enoch leave the scene: one moves into the darkness and becomes the pin point of light; the other sits, immobile and static, and darkness envelopes him.

The open ending, since it does not include feasting and merry-making, has led readers to suspect the justness of the story's comic resolution. The *alazon* (Enoch), the buffoon (Hoover), and the churls are left to survive, because they continue to constitute the Taulkinham society. Taulkinham does not disintegrate; its values linger on. Yet the ending is not only appropriate to the structure of the comic mood in the novel, it is also necessary to reinforcing the ironic nature of O'Connor's comedy, one that keeps us laughing even after we have finished reading the novel. The elements of Catholicism, Southern regionalism, and the grotesque evolve into a mystical superstructure of comic irony in the novel, and our recognition of the dimensions of each comic type in this process helps us see O'Connor beyond her immediate Georgian background. (pp. 252-58)

Sura Prasad Rath, "Comic Polarities in Flannery O'Connor's 'Wise Blood'," in Studies in Short Fiction, *Vol. 21, No. 3, Summer, 1984, pp. 251-58.*

Richard Giannone

[*In the excerpt below, Giannone compares Hazel Motes's development from "a pharisee into an apostle" to that of St. Paul and St. Francis of Assisi.*]

Flannery O'Connor believes that the only human story worth telling recounts the heart's turning in full seriousness to God. Her conviction is univocal. "It seems to me," O'Connor writes to her friend *A*, "that all good stories are about conversion, about a character's changing." The remark doubles as a guide to O'Connor's own development as a writer. The question of the human person's position before God is *the* question of her work. To consider her total treatment of conversion is to follow the deepening of theological thought behind the growth of her artistry.

The simplicity of O'Connor's statement, however, belies the bold way in which she begins her canonical attention to her rule. **Wise Blood** (1952), her first novel and least admired book, goes out of its way to explore extreme boundaries of conversion. She creates a hero who believes in nothing. By temperament he is as ill-disposed as possible to experience God's inward working of grace. O'Connor names him Hazel Motes. *Hazael* in 1 and 2 Kings is the king of Damascus remembered for brutality against Israel. He persecutes God and his people. Hazel Motes in **Wise Blood** continues the battle of his namesake against God. If to be converted means to come under the power of the Mighty One, then all of Hazel Motes's energy steels him against conversion. Most readers find his behavior so pathological that a slight moderation toward sanity would be welcome. As for turning his eyes to God, that shift would seem out of the question. But *Hazel* in Hebrew means *he who sees God*. And Hazel Motes does see God.

Fighting God and seeing God stand in significant relationship to each other in **Wise Blood,** generating the hero's acute inner conflict. Fear, rebellion, injured pride, all the inducements to oppose God have a tight grip on Hazel Motes. At the same time, a vision of Jesus on the cross, which Hazel cannot dispel, draws him to God. These powers collide when the car Hazel cherishes is demolished. He sees in the wreckage the nothing that he believes in. With this experience of emptiness, he surrenders to the vision. When the satanic hold loosens, the cold discipline which deprives Hazel of his warm humanity reverses its direction and leads him godward. In the end, O'Connor converts the nihilist Hazel Motes into a saint for our unbelieving time.

The word *saint* requires explanation. My usage is scriptural rather than medieval. The saints of the Middle Ages, whose statues adorn houses of prayer, all yield legends and provide incentives. The moral direction they offer, however, invariably comes with the feeling that these holy perfections are inaccessibly far above us. Biblical sanctity is more down-to-earth. Paul gives the essence of such sanctity in Romans 8:19-39. In early Christianity the saint is a person who believes, who loves and obeys, who shares in Jesus' power, and who, with divine help, repeats what Jesus accomplished. The saint struggles to withstand Satan. In doing so, the saint makes actual within the individual's own sphere the kingdom of God.

Hazel Motes numbers among those persons whom God calls most decisively to follow him. O'Connor stresses the wonder of Hazel's call by setting his story against that of St. Paul. The evolution of a pharisee into an apostle serves O'Connor's purposes. Here is an instance of a man with notorious fury making his way to tranquility. Love consumes his former anger. Hazel needs to find precisely that peace, must pass through just that fire. During such a trial, dogma lends no support; faith is all. O'Connor uses Paul's conflict and the felt belief that it bears; she does not hold him up as a specimen of vulgarized holiness or as a man settled in the truth. She takes the apostle as he takes himself. Paul in his irascible letters sees himself as seeking, but not having attained, the full measure of the stature of Christ. His vehement search is what interests O'Connor.

Paul comes up twice in *Wise Blood.* Both references occur on the same occasion. The evangelist Asa Hawks is trying to persuade Hazel Motes that Hawks's blindness marks him as a chosen instrument of God. He identifies himself with the Damascus Christophany. " 'He blinded Paul,' " protests Hawks. It takes Haze a while to discover that Hawks is a fraud, but O'Connor wants the reader to know the facts. We soon learn that at a Saturday night revival meeting ten years earlier Hawks was preaching on Paul's blindness when, overcome by his own zeal, the diviner streaked his face with lime. All for effect, the showman is careful to keep the caustic solution from his eyes. But the stunt backfires. A moment of misdirected fervor costs him a lifelong anguish. His face is maimed, and he must live out a lie to go with the scars. Converted to his own self-deception, "the fake blind man" inflicts more enduring wounds on himself than God does on Paul, who is blind only for three days and lives on in grace.

O'Connor expands the importance of Hawks's sacrifice by setting it on October 4, one of the few instances of her underscoring an event with an exact date. October 4 is the Feast of St. Francis of Assisi. In the background we have a legendary picture of the gentle medieval fantasist preaching to wolves and taming them with blessings. In the foreground a crass con artist preaches to an assembly of cynics who are not even aroused by gore. The effect is pointed. Where Francis gives up great wealth to live by the will of God, Hawks tries to tell God what to do by mimicking Paul for profit. The spirit obeys a different will, however. Francis gains the richness of God's favor, whereas Hawks deepens his poverty and pain. Hawks becomes what he worships. As he tries to make God a commodity he can peddle, he ends up a two-bit street hustler. The October 4 spectacle epitomizes the extreme forms that change can take in *Wise Blood.* On the day honoring the saint who achieved supernatural joy through obedience to suffering, Asa Hawks enacts the negative conversion of self-mutilation.

The disparity between the spiritual ideal and the inept human groping for it depicts more than the twisting of reality we have come to describe as grotesque in O'Connor's art. This travesty conveys the novel's theology. The Paul who inspires Hawks on October 4 also engages the mind of the artist telling the story. In fact, O'Connor's attraction to negations and failures and distortions recalls Paul's analogous practice of explaining the reign of Christ Jesus by showing the wrathful state of life without the gospel. O'Connor works the same way. Her manner derives from her subject in *Wise Blood.* In technique as well as in theme *Wise Blood* draws upon the first Christian *malgré lui,*

Paul, to portray a contemporary Paul *manqué,* Hazel Motes. They converge in Taulkinham through Francis.

Wise Blood spans the last months of Haze's life. He is twenty-two years old. Two days before the novel begins he is discharged from the army after a four-year hitch. Duffel bag on his neck, free at last from the government with its war and other tricks "to lead him into temptation," Haze goes home to Eastrod, Tennessee. Home is but a "skeleton of a house." He spends a night among the bones and hops a train south. While the train pauses at a junction, Haze is left behind chasing his hat. He takes another train and lands in Taulkinham. The city is the end for him. He dies in Taulkinham a short while later. Haze dies as he lived, convinced "that the way to avoid Jesus was to avoid sin." Since he brings his entire biography to these final days, we need only to know this crucial period of his life to grasp the meaning of his longstanding avoidance of Jesus. Time, too, is Pauline in *Wise Blood.* O'Connor's handling of time is more interior than clockwork, akin to Paul's sense of time as decisive moments of the soul's journey.

The fourteen chapters of *Wise Blood* follow a simple movement. Chapter 1 is a preface. It gives the biographical details from Haze's past which launched him on his flight from sin and Jesus. With Chapter 2 he begins to learn about sin. His recognition comes in two stages. Chapters 2 through 7 show Haze's willed immersion in the life of sin. By choosing to sin, he tries to make sin a function of his will rather than an offense against God's will. The second stage runs from Chapters 8 through 13. Here the way opens for Haze to see the untruth of his denial of sin. As he sees through the falseness in others who serve themselves in the name of serving God, the hero comes to see his own complicity. He moves from immersion to conversion. As Chapter 1 prepares for his change, Chapter 14, the last chapter, contemplates the effects of it. Taken together, the fourteen chapters suggest that in his retreat from God Haze nevertheless goes along the fourteen stations of the cross.

Roughly put, Haze's relationship to sin composes a pattern of denial and flight which leads into perception and judgment of his sinfulness that prompt his confession and deliverance. "As sin came into the world through one man and . . . death spread to all men" (Rom. 5:12), so in *Wise Blood* another man makes the reverse passage back through the world to sin, and then through guilt into a new life.

One way to see how Paul and Francis impinge on Haze's backward progress is to consider the telling moments of his life and then to pay special attention to their culmination in Chapter 7 and Chapter 14 into two phases of his spiritual adventure. Haze's desire to escape sin and to avoid Jesus begins as a reaction to his righteous family. At ten he sneaks into a forbidden carnival tent, where he sees his father writhing with delight over a fat woman squirming in a black coffin. The arrant eroticism confounds the boy's trust in his father's moral strictness. Distrust confuses all of Haze's emotions until the guiltless but shamed son takes on the guilt of his shameless father. When he arrives home, his mother, draped in her usual long black dress, incarnates the boy's fear of a vindictive Jesus. Without knowing that her son saw the forbidden woman, she beats him with a stick across his legs. " 'Jesus died to redeem you," she drones. As his mother victimizes Haze to alleviate her own festering prudery, his grandfather uses him to harangue against a world he despises. A circuit preacher, the old man wants each stone soul before him to know that Jesus would "die ten million deaths" to save a soul, even that of the undeserving abomination with clenching dirty fists standing near them. The young Haze is that unclean object.

His family's rectitude cripples Haze. His legs retain the pang of his mother's stick. The pattern of guilt and pain they established persists until he dies. He tries to avoid the image of his personal wickedness instilled by his grandfather by avoiding the Jesus who atones for that evil. After his mother strikes him, he tries to satisfy "the nameless unplaced guilt" through self-mortification. Only ten, Haze fills his sabbath shoes with stones and small rocks to grind away his hurt as he hobbles a mile into the woods. O'Connor gives no hint that Haze learns how to make contact with others, or to share their conflict or suffering. Each step in his life hereafter is haunted by his inherited belief that his personal evil is the one thing that matters. Every encounter is an obstacle to escape. Everyone will come to be his enemy or an instrument in his battle. Like Saul of Tarsus, who had always striven to be "blameless" (Phil. 3:6) in the eyes of others, Haze will persecute those whom he thinks disobey the law.

The army brings out the resemblance to Saul as he becomes Paul. Haze feels bound to a government willing "to have his soul damned." They send him from one desert "to another desert." The desert ordeal extends the spiritual warfare he began in Tennessee against that sin which implicates him in Jesus's death. "Put on the whole armor of God," Paul exhorts the embattled converts in Ephesus, "that you may be able to stand against the wiles of the devil" (Eph. 6:11). Haze may carry the shield of dread to protect himself against the devil, but he does stand up against the principalities and powers of "this present darkness" (Eph. 6:12). He has a scar too, shrapnel he received in his chest. Even after the surgeon removes the pieces of metal, he feels a fragment rusting away, "poisoning" his insides. The residual shred of ammunition is Haze's thorn in the flesh (2 Cor. 12:7). Medicine cannot reach this wasting away, and we can tell from the pressure of Haze's skull against his skin that this ache is no phantom pain. Job complains that his "bones cleave to my skin and to my flesh, and I have escaped by the skin of my teeth" (Job 19:20). The shrapnel is Haze's Joblike affliction, making him old in suffering though young in years. The Tennesseean, like Paul and Job, sustains a blow from a messenger of Satan. No medal or monthly check from the government can compensate for the sting of this adversary. Yet, there is a benefit. Paul explains the way to make amends. He understands his chronic debility as denoting a possible spiritual turning. The thorn could be remedial in that those "delivered to Satan," the author of physical ills, "may learn not to blaspheme" (1 Tim. 1:20). Under the power of Satan's wound, the sufferer may be moved to repentance.

The turning place is Taulkinham. The city covers the gamut of corruptions through which Paul explains the essence and effect of sin. Body, flesh, soul, psyche, heart, and mind, each provides a different perspective on the total rule which sin has over Taulkinham. O'Connor gives us a small-time Corinth, a town synonymous with lowlife. She conducts Haze through the city by following Paul's distinction between "our outer nature" and "our inner nature" (2 Cor. 4:16). Haze begins with the carnal and works his way down into the mental.

The city greets Haze with the graffiti in the men's toilet of the train station, inviting him to Mrs. Leora Watts of 60 Buckley Road, "The friendliest bed in town!" Mrs. Watts is an enormous woman, glistening with grease and draped in a pink nightgown. She sits cutting her toenails in perpetual expectation of old friends paying a call. Flesh (*sarx*) for Paul denotes the domination by earthly desires, not simply those of sex. Mrs. Watts incarnates total submission to the physical. The entire world is a boudoir. Haze comes to her to prove that he does not believe in anything. Mrs. Watt's hospitality subsumes all desire in the usual business of lust. She does what she always does. " 'That's okay, son,' she said. 'Momma don't mind if you ain't a preacher.' " She mothers Haze into the sinful life of Taulkinham.

The best time to catch that life is on Thursday night, when the stores are open late and their wares are displayed. Haze's nighttown excursion reads like a modern documentation of Paul's sketch of depraved heathenism in Romans (1:18-32). As Paul balances his reminder of God's wrath with a reassurance that God has shown his invisible nature in the created universe, O'Connor opens Chapter 3 with a poetic description of the seen things that manifest the divine character of the world.

> The black sky was underpinned with long silver streaks that looked like scaffolding and depth on depth behind it were thousands of stars that all seemed to be moving very slowly as if they were about some vast construction work that involved the whole order of the universe and would take all time to complete.

Here is the first of many revelations of sacred history. Mystery fills Thursday night. Though redemptive activity shines for all to see, "No one was paying attention to the sky." Humanity ignores God. Corruption arises from this negligence.

The cardboard boxes from which a vendor sells potato peelers serves as the "altar" for the shoppers. Asa Hawks appears to work the crowd for a few nickels. Dark glasses, facial scars, white cane, the inevitable tin cup, a girl sidekick with tracts headlined "Jesus Calls You," Hawks is the clichéd pardoner for our time. His spiritual role is assigned by providence, which suffers pardoners in each age for a greater use. While the gogglers watch the potato-peeler man argue with Hawks over business rights to the crowd, Haze stares at the blind man's scars and the girl's tracts. The girl herself is giving Haze a fast eye. Hawks sizes up Haze right away as perfect for his act. Haze's visible and audible severity lends itself to Hawks, just as his hostility served his grandfather's homiletic purpose.

Hawks charges Haze with fornication, blasphemy, and corruption, and challenges Haze to repent. Each accusation contains an accidental truth which Haze must deny in order to preserve the image he has of himself as clean and therefore not in debt to Jesus, that soul-hungry pursuer who is Haze's real summoner. The exchange dissolves into a theological can-you-bottom-this. Though Hawks bears witness only to the money he begs, his message contains a truth despite his fraudulence. He calls all to repent; he confronts Haze with his sinfulness, announces Jesus's love, and foretells that Haze " 'will have to see some time' " though now he has eyes and sees not. The old indictment of his grandfather swells in Haze, who combats Hawks with the annunciation of universal blamelessness: " 'Every one of you people are clean. . . . ' " He has a church to go with the doctrine that precludes the need for church. " 'I'm going to preach a new church—the church of truth without Jesus Christ Crucified.' "

Haze's proclamation enshrines negation. All his personal stumbling blocks—the incarnation, the solidarity of sin, the crucifixion—are surmounted. Guilt is removed. Belief costs nothing. What remains, though, is the pain which drives Haze to assert his cleanness in the first place. His theology is not so much a contradiction as it is a self-punishment. Haze's vehemence measures what Paul calls the "hard and impenitent heart . . .storing up wrath" (Rom. 2:5) for itself. Haze refuses to subject himself to Jesus. He wants to command himself. " 'What do I need with Jesus? I got Leora Watts.' "

Haze's boasting is theologically telling. "Do you not know that he who joins himself to a prostitute becomes one body with her?" warns Paul to the Corinthians (1 Cor. 6:16). The issue for Paul is not sexual, as it never is for O'Connor. The evil consists in replacing the relationship one should have to God with that relationship one sets up with the body. Where the Christian is exalted by cleaving to the Lord, the fornicator is degraded by the soiled flesh of the partner. Leora Watts, in O'Connor's scheme, is culpable not for who she is but for Whom she replaces.

Enoch Emery is Mrs. Watt's male counterpart. As she embodies flesh without the spirit, Enoch is mind without spirit. He emerges from the hard-hearted society which shaped him—on shopping night, naturally. He has spent his entire life looking for a human connection which is never made. " 'This is one more hard place to make friends in,' " he tells Haze. His life story bespeaks a helpless innocence misshapen by sin but without the facility of reason to be responsible for sin. It also indicts society. A welfare woman " 'traded me from my daddy.' " Then he was remanded to the Rodemill Boys' Bible Academy, where they had the papers on him and kept him in line with threats of the penitentiary. His life is a cycle of escape and incarceration, broken only by his giving his latest captor a heart attack. He is a forsaken, runaway bondman fated to search out mockery, which is the only recognition a brutal society can give him. The image of bondage which Paul uses as an analogy for the life of sin is the very condition of bondage for Enoch.

In calling Enoch a "moron" O'Connor aligns herself with Paul, who associates bondage with want of mental whole-ness. Paul characterizes "doing evil deeds" with being "estranged and hostile in mind" (Col. 1:21). Neither Paul nor O'Connor is deriding mental subnormality. On the contrary, they are considering the total state of human sin from the aspect of mental deficiency to point out how much more humanness involves. Human life sold into sin is moronic in that it is life without spirit. O'Connor brings the mind darkened in understanding (Eph. 4:17-18) to life in Taulkinham as the consumers and moviegoers pass by. Caught in their feeblemindedness, they remain defective in grasping the vast airy construction work that gives purpose to the human share in "the whole order of the universe." Moronism is the human mind locked into its own limitations and therefore cut off from an awareness of those silver extensions in the sky that make us wholly human.

Enoch knows " 'a whole heap about Jesus' " and has no faith. As Jesus is used as a weapon by his captors, Enock's knowledge of Jesus is used to escape punishment from daddy or the welfare woman or the Bible Academy. He serves as a warning both to society and Haze. Whereas the meaning of Jesus' life cannot penetrate Enoch's mind, society will not let it affect theirs. Given the ignorance fostered as wisdom in Taulkinham, Enoch is right to feel special. "He had wise blood like his daddy." As a result, he succeeds in keeping the spirit from integrating his nature. That very night, Haze ends his venture in the bed of Mrs. Watts. Here moronism wears the guise of social accomplishment. "It was plain that she was so well-adjusted that she didn't need to think any more." Haze's throat gets dry and "his heart began to grip him like a little ape clutching the bars of its cage." The flesh entraps Haze. He too can fall captive to the life without spirit. Enoch only works at the zoo; Haze's heart might end up living there.

The image of the heart as a terrified, puny ape cleaving to its cage caps a sequence depicting intellectual refusal (to see the stars, to repent, to confess God) and deceit (Hawks) and mental insufficiency (Enoch, the crowd). The context defines *heart,* not as the faculty of sentiment and affect, but as the power of understanding what can be known about the Creator through the surrounding world. Heart for O'Connor is mind plus the emotional response to intelligent recognition. ***Wise Blood*** dramatizes the crimes of the heart and its anguish. Paul extends the meaning of heart (*kardia*) when he writes that the heart of the person *wills* (Gal. 4:9; 1 Cor. 4:21). In this book O'Connor conceives of the human heart that wills not to accept. She refers to such mulishness as the condition of *wise blood.* That dark power is one of the "many wills conflicting in one man" of which O'Connor writes in her 1962 note to the novel's second edition. Enoch and Mrs. Watts exemplify the dire outcome of that will. That there are multiple wills within human choice makes that will free and mysterious. The unfolding of Haze's conflict lies in his discovery that there are ways to respond to Jesus other than that of childhood flight.

Before Haze can know the anguish resulting from his moronic wisdom of self-willed obstinacy, he must get himself a car. His grandfather had a Ford which served as his pulpit. Fifty dollars buys Haze an Essex. The jalopy ordains him as a preacher. His mission to Taulkinham begins as he zigzags the mechanical ark out of the car lot. Enshrined in his idol, Haze can move "thinking nothing." His wise blood fuels undirected movement. But the imagery alerts the reader to his course. Mindless, like Enoch, Haze sinks into the dark carnival coffin that contains the enshrouding gloom of Mrs. Watt's bedroom. O'Connor also wants us to know that Haze is driving the car without a license, on the move like a Paul propelling himself against the law.

Warnings, such as "Jesus Saves" painted on a boulder, pop up all along Haze's route to spell out the danger of serving his instinct. We can take a short cut to the museum case in "the heart of the city" where a shrunken mummy displays for all to see the death-in-life that comes from choosing to believe in nothing. The shriveled corpse pictures what sin does: it is productive of death (2 Cor. 7-10). Death sucks the body dry of spirit. Where death rules, humanity exists in arid captivity. Before Haze preaches his new church, O'Connor shows in the museum the Church Without Christ. It is out of this dust bin that Enoch will disinter the New Jesus to go with the new dispensation.

If the mummy foretells, it also recalls Haze's moral adventure. He too has been shrinking, recoiling from Jesus, whose misery calls Haze from the hanging ragged figure in the trees in Haze's mind. The heart of Haze that gripped him at Leora's—gripped him with the ape's doleful plea for release—will shrink smaller into beastly hardness unless he changes. He will become the stone soul his grandfather said he was. The mummy is the destiny of life outside Christ. Paul refers to "the sinful body" (Rom. 6:6) also as "this body of death" (Rom. 7:24), from which one is to be delivered. Sin corrupts our true humanity, devolves us back into animality. Haze's retreat carries him in this direction.

The ramshackle car gives him a new impetus for his spiritual regression. He can proclaim the truth that " 'there was no Fall because there was nothing to fall from and no Redemption because there was no Fall and no Judgment because there wasn't the first two. Nothing matters but that Jesus was a liar.' " The logic is flawless. With reasoning that only a backwoods Pharisee could appreciate, Haze transforms salvation back into its opposite. The means of freeing humanity becomes a malediction. Jesus' death creates our sin to account for his passion. The stumbling block behind Haze's thinking and feeling here is the cross—the trees from which the ragged figure pursues him. Haze tries to hide the cross by means of condemnation, or reverse justification. If he can invert Jesus' expiatory death, Haze can feel righteous. The doctrine that God forgives sins on the basis of Jesus' death is handed down through Paul, who puts it this way: "Jesus . . .was put to death for our trespasses and raised for our justification" (Rom. 4:25). But Haze has the Essex, and " 'Nobody with a good car needs to be justified.' " Bragging covers his fear and lays bare his bankruptcy, just as the confidence of the Jewish nation in their prerogatives as God's people (Rom. 2:17) reveals their failure. Boasting is natural but, in Paul's economy, fatal. What is at stake is that in which humanity places trust. Haze prides himself in his car and his

rhetorical boldness. These sources cannot sustain him. Like all boasting of the flesh before God (1 Cor. 1:29), Haze's effort to establish trust in things of this world will prove unfounded.

Our awareness of Haze's regression comes in stages. In keeping with her belief "that moral judgment has to be implicit in the act of vision," O'Connor patterns Chapter 7 so that the reader sees both with and beyond Haze's tunnel vision. Haze has visited Hawks and is out on the road testing his cherished car. O'Connor opens the sequence by casting the reader's eye upward. The sky is bright blue "with only one cloud in it, a large blinding white one with curls and a beard." Haze stares straight ahead, taking no notice of the sky. Nor does he see Sabbath Lily Hawks hidden in the back seat. She and her bastardy interest Haze only as a logical contradiction of her father's boasted justification before God. Sabbath tries to seduce him, but Haze is already so seduced by his lust for a new kind of Jesus that he misses the importuning of Sabbath's heart " 'where Jesus is King.' " During their slapstick love-making, the blinding white cloud moves ahead of them, then to the left until it is before them when they stop on a clay road. Sabbath proves no rival of the Essex, with which Haze has his most intimate relationship. He runs to the car. It fails to start.

A nameless man helps the stranded pair with the dead car. This man acts, gives, and he remains taciturn, unboastful, anonymous. The car is beyond his ability to fix it, but he restarts the machine with a push. He speaks only to refuse payment for his help or his gas. Haze offers a grudging " 'I thank you.' " When out of the man's earshot he pays the man's freely given gift with a boast and an insult. His Essex was not built " 'by a bunch of foreigners or niggers or one-arm man.' " The man, whose slate-blue eyes duplicate the sky, has one arm. Head up high, Haze peers onward unaware of the white cloud above, now transfigured into a bird dissolving in the opposite direction on fine extended wings. The tin lizzie jiggles down the road trailing clouds, clouds of glory.

O'Connor shows Haze's vision falling progressively short of things as they are. Not seeing Lily's temptation is amusing. Mocking the one-arm man is truculent and serious. This servant suffers Haze's ingratitude as much as he suffers a physical loss. Haze cannot see what another suffers for him. It is as difficult for Haze to see the suffering servant as it has been since apostolic times for humankind to accept the suffering servant who made the ultimate sacrifice for all. But not for Haze Motes. He never asked anybody for anything. He stands beyond the cross.

From that self-exalted place Haze cannot see the most primitive and plain reflection of divinity, the cloud. The cloud in the light blue sky makes known the luminous quality of the glory of God. It is large and blinding and white, and Haze still cannot see the cloud. His not seeing the kindness of the one-arm man, whose suffering shares in the invisible glory of God, renders Haze blind to the cloud, God's share in the glory of the earth. Paul understands humanity's "beholding the glory of the Lord" (2 Cor. 3:18) as a progression from recognizing the likeness of God in persons to perceiving the divine likeness in the cosmos. We train ourselves to see by degrees. Haze drives on the other way from the cloud into deeper degrees of blindness, from the ludicrous to the blasphemous. No matter. The cloud cleaves to him even as he denies the spirit. The glory of the cloud resides in its patient hovering. When the eye is ready to catch sight of it, the radiance will be there in saving visibility.

In O'Connor's art the joyous aspect is the implicit one. So much of her warmth and intelligence comes through her poetry here that we do well to reflect on how splendor frames the seventh chapter. The image first appears as it does in Exodus 34:30: the large white cloud with curls and a beard recalls Moses, through whose face God's glory first shone forth to Israel. Then the image concludes the chapter as the dove in the gospels. From Old through New Covenant to now the radiance of God remains undiminished for Flannery O'Connor. The shining mirror was too strong for Israel, so Moses had to veil his face. The hardened mind which obscures truth has not softened. The same veil that Moses used to hide the glory of God now lies over the mind of Haze Motes, who knows that the Essex and not Jesus will save him. Splendor has no significance for Haze. It is a disappearing quirk of nature.

For O'Connor splendor in the exact center of *Wise Blood* limns the vast perspective from which the entire story is to be seen. Appearing as it does at the end of Chapter 7, the perfect number, the bird-cloud manifests the total perfection in which creation participates and against which Haze does battle. The cloud disappears in one direction; that is the way of holiness and blamelessness. Haze races in another; he goes the way of denial. Sacred history assimilates all ways. After Haze passes through his own negations, he will have gone all the way around to meet the imperishable cloud that links his life to the glorious coming.

Chapter 7, in sum, concludes the first part of Haze's journey with an admonition and a promise reified in the same image. The bird-cloud gathers together the assorted crows, parrots, game-hens, eagles, owls, shrikes, and hawks that precede it. All the winged beings suggest the ways in which the characters seek to aggrandize or spiritualize themselves. All, except the ethereal bird, are harbingers of debasement. The swarm is an emblem of vanity, predacity, and greed. The delicate sky-bird points the way to genuine transcendence. But the more Haze relies on his willfulness to drive his high rat-colored Essex, the further away he will fly from the freedom he seeks. Here on the road to Taulkinham, presence is a promise. Though God's glory seems withdrawing, they will rendezvous. When they meet again, the bird, a formidable foe of the serpent of self-adoration, will guide Haze to the meaning he seeks.

The second phase of Haze's attempt to prove that there is nothing to believe in shows what life is like along the road he chose at the cloud crossing. Here, in Chapters 8 through 13, the comic grimness of day-to-day existence in Taulkinham erupts into monstrous moral and physical violence. We watch a Tennessee version of the folly of humankind swapping "the glory of the immortal God for images resembling mortal man or birds or animals or reptiles" (Rom. 1:23). This section traces a descent from glory played out through the theological carnival O'Connor enjoys staging.

Enoch Emery leads the spectacle. When he hears Haze call for a new Jesus " 'that's all man, without blood to waste,' " Enoch decides to steal the mummy and hide it until Haze and his shriveling believers are prepared to receive their god. The seed Haze sows in Enoch gestates in the arms of Sabbath, who cradles the dwarf Enoch delivered. The announcer and the bringer of the new eon delivers one more message to Taulkinham before he fulfills his moral mission and disappears. After being insulted by the ape-star Gonga at a film publicity reception, Enoch, to relieve his humiliation, mugs the man wearing the gorilla suit and puts on the Gonga clothes in a nearby pine grove. The last reference to Enoch reduces him to the beast he wants to be. "It sat down on the rock . . .and stared over the valley at the uneven skyline of the city." His silhouette projects his warning.

Gonga against the sky depicts the failure to come face to face with the enemy within. Anguished and torn inside, Enoch fails to locate the true cause of his pain, attaching it to whatever or whomever is at hand—an ape, a moose, an owl, a waitress, Jesus. When he steals the mummy, he darkens his face and hands with brown shoe polish to put the blame for the theft on a colored person. He feels no guilt. For all his efforts, Enoch cannot shake off humiliation, the feeling of being dragged down into bestiality by the constant pain of ridicule and rejection. He has only his moronic wise blood to aid him, and that impulse intensifies his exclusion. Instinct without spirit, action without responsibility, is brute creation. The Enoch of Genesis may have been translated to heaven (Gen. 5:18-24), but the gorilla on the rock is humanity shorn of glory.

Enter Hoover Shoats—or Onnie Jay Holy, as he is called in the redemption racket. Holy is the evangelist in motley who duncifies the spirit to accommodate the public. For three years he ran Soulease, a fifteen-minute radio program of Mood, Melody, and Mentality; so he knows a good show when he sees it. When he hears Haze preach on the nose of the Essex, Holy knows just the right format to promote the act. Holy goes devotional. Haze becomes the Prophet who saved the forlorn Onnie Jay from suicide by bringing out his " 'natural sweetness.' " To be sure that the crowd understands that Haze's Church Without Christ offers salvation without the Crucifixion, Holy amplifies the name to the Holy Church of Christ Without Christ. The inhabitants of Taulkinham take such muddled church names in stride. Holy proposes a do-it-yourself salvation that sanctifies the self-absorbed life without Jesus which the citizenry has been leading all along.

Holy's sweetness ends in pain for himself and death for another. Since blasphemy is the way to the truth for Haze, he indicts Holy as a liar. Persistent, Holy finally invites Haze's retaliation. Haze slams the car door on the pest's thumb. "A howl arose that would have rended almost any heart." But not Haze's. His hardness prompts Holy to hire Solace Layfield, Haze's look-alike, to take advantage of their resemblance. After Layfield's second night out, Haze pursues him. First one rat-colored car ditches another rat-colored car on a lonesome road. Haze's means of salvation, the car, becomes the instrument of death. Then Haze strips Layfield and runs him down and backs over him. Haze identifies himself with the law.

Several judgments arise from this brutal scene. The first falls on Hoover Shoats. Though he did not run Layfield down, he did set him up. His doctrine of inborn sweetness effects a chain of events which ends in a bitter death. His sweet-talk blinds himself to the lies and harm he brings to others. As with Milton's Lucifer, the absentee originator behind all indirect accomplices, Hoover's coaxing is made more venomous by its deceptive, pleasing taste.

The full blame for murder belongs to Haze. He equates killing Layfield with restoring truth. " 'You ain't true,' " he decrees. The verdict displaces the onus of punishment onto the victim. The refrain makes absolute Haze's subjective view, arrogating and becoming the lawful judgment. He is a judicial murderer. The problem is Pauline. More than any other apostle, Paul had to come to terms with the law and its potential contradictions. The law of Judaism sanctioned Paul's persecution of Christians, and yet that same law in its inadequacy prepares for his conversion to the Christ who brings an end to law. The law which was meant to convert Israel to the will of God leads to the opposite condition of confidence in Israel's own merit apart from God. Paul's warning about the deceptions (Rom. 2:1-20) illumines the dark tension in Haze. Haze uses others for the rigid law of his nihilism, and he uses the law to excuse his evil. If we follow Paul, we will reach Haze's outcome. The law "which promised life proved to be death" (Rom. 7:10). The full impact of Paul's thought on O'Connor's novel comes from his plumbing the habit of mind which leads to self-adoring legalism. Over and over, because the prompting is so human, Paul denounces the pursuit of righteousness separate from God and God's mercy. Such self-centered obstinacy creates the state of alienation that **Wise Blood** dramatizes time and time again. It blinds one to glory; it cripples the young; it impedes an understanding of the gospel; and it kills. O'Connor sees the righteousness that the law promotes as the source of Haze's cold-blooded execution of the false prophet. His moral life is coming full circle: at the age of ten, returning from the carnival, he was blameless and felt massive guilt; at twenty-two, after killing Layfield, he is guilty and feels no blame. The more guilty he is, the less guilt he feels.

Haze reacts to bloodguilt by planning to escape to a new city. Since guilt is torment, the sinner wishes to flee that torment. But the Essex does not totter five miles before Haze gets back what he gave out. The boomerang comes about as Paul says it does for the righteous: through the law. "All who have sinned under the law will be judged by the law" (Rom. 2:12). A black patrol car stops the leaky Essex. With a suavity that only ruthlessness borrows, the cop gets Haze to drive the car to the top of the hill, from which he pushes the car down thirty feet. Like the new Jesus, like the false prophet, the Essex is demolished. The cop dusts off his hands as tidily as Haze wiped away the blood stains from his car after killing Layfield. These shattered forms serve a purpose. They are the "earthen vessels" Paul writes of to the Corinthians, which

show in their defectiveness "that the transcendent power belongs to God" (2 Cor. 4:7) and not to the frail molds of our making.

On the road to Damascus, Paul is jolted out of his rigid Pharisaism; on the road out of Taulkinham, the car is ditched from Haze. Haze's knees buckle, as though struck once again by his mother's stick. He sits on the edge of an embankment looking at his broken parts. "His face seemed to reflect the entire distance across the clearing and on beyond, the entire distance that extended from his eyes to the blank sky that went on, depth after depth, into space." By instinct he resumes the penitential walk of his childhood. For three hours he treads back to Taulkinham, pausing to buy quicklime and a tin bucket. When he reaches the boarding house, he mixes the lime with water and blinds himself. The act is pure Hazel Motes—willful and vehement to the end, for the end. We can only speculate on the rabbinical turn of mind which brings him to burn out his eyes. Since he had eyes and did not see the car for the wreck it was, his legalism might run, he ought not see at all. Now the word *blind* would be true to that spiritual darkness. The idea to use lime, of course, comes from Hawks, who tried to use Paul's psychosomatic blindness as proof of Hawks's election. Haze outdoes them both.

A modern reader not schooled by penitential literature will find Haze's self-mortification "ugly" and "morbid," as does Mrs. Flood, his landlady. Suffering is inimical to the modern sense of life. It is to be obliterated or removed from view. Haze wears the blinders of our age at the beginning when he flees from the ragged figure chasing him from the trees. That escape from suffering belongs now to the false wisdom which lies demolished with the Essex in the trench. Counterpuncher that he is, Haze takes up his struggle against that old belief through repentance. The wet quicklime pouring over his eyes is the opposite affection of submission breaking over him. Haze's first act of contrition goes back to the day Hawks plays Paul, October 4, the feast of St. Francis, a scandal of a man if there ever was one.

Certain facts about Francis would interest the author of Haze Motes. Francis was a soldier who suffered from a longstanding and severe disease of the eye. Blurred in physical sight, he was haunted his entire life by a keen inner vision of Jesus suffering his passion on the cross. The sight made Francis flee. Like Paul, Francis experienced a sudden conversion. When he submitted at last to the hand of God, Francis forsook the world to embark upon a life of self-denial. Before he died he was cauterized from ear to eyebrow, painfully blinded, accepting this anguish with the gratitude with which he received all hardships.

O'Connor does not replicate Francis' life in **Wise Blood**. Haze knows nothing about Francis. He is one of those foreigners. Haze himself is a far cry from the gentle Italian lover of birds who preached community while welcoming solitude and who cared for lepers while refusing aid for his own ills. That contrast points up O'Connor's meaning. In his difference from Francis, as in his difference from Paul, Haze lives out the truth of atonement that shaped their lives. All meet on the ground of affliction. Sorrow opens the way into the space on which Haze "concentrated" after losing his car. It is a country without borders of time and place, a milieu unchanged from apostolic and medieval times. Paul charged into it. Francis embraced it. In the last chapter of *Wise Blood* Haze crawls through this eternal locale. The common *centrum* toward which they gather is the indestructible source of life. (pp. 483-98)

O'Connor's treatment of guilt and conversion puts into theological perspective all the anguish and escape that comprise her first novel. Her view is angular, at odds with how we are now trained to see. It culminates in Mrs. Flood's inner vision of the dead Haze "going backwards to Bethlehem." We need Franciscan sight to take in this picture. Francis too looked at spiritual progress obliquely. He was unable to separate the passion of Jesus from his nativity. Francis made the first crib (in Grecchia, 1224), legend has it, to show the faithful the hardship suffered by the infant. O'Connor too fuses suffering with birth. But her Christmas message is not a greeting readers enjoy receiving. *Wise Blood* moves from Calvary to Bethlehem to argue that Haze must accept guilt and pay his debt in order to be awakened to new life. That paradox confounds his will to the point at which he cannot help himself from becoming a Christian. Haze announces his public ministry by calling for a new Jesus who is " 'all man and ain't got any God in him,' " and he dies fulfilling the conditions of the incarnation.

If Haze's heart matched his head, Haze might have been a St. Francis. But in his own mental way Haze is a martyr in the original sense of the word as giving testimony to the truth, sealed in his own suffering and unwise blood. Haze's passion is not a majestic rise to the cross; he crawls and digs his way. After a brief life, which covers a cruel childhood, a truncated ministry, and a fierce, obedient death, Haze finds his birthplace east of the rood. There affliction implements the promise held out in his name *Hazel,* he who sees God. The night of Bethlehem becomes the light of Calvary. In that hour Taulkinham is the new Bethlehem. (pp. 502-03)

> *Richard Giannone, "Paul, Francis, and Hazel Motes: Conversation at Taulkinham," in* THOUGHT, *Vol. LIX, No. 235, December, 1984, pp. 483-503.*

Victoria Duckworth

[In the following excerpt, Duckworth treats the theme of redemption in Wise Blood *and Alice Walker's* The Color Purple.*]*

Alice Walker and Flannery O'Connor appear to have little in common besides a history which both joins and divides them. For example, we can speak of Walker's feminism, but can we speak of O'Connor's feminism? We can examine the orthodoxy of O'Connor's Catholic faith, but can we examine the orthodoxy of Walker's faith? Where, then, is the link between these two women? I believe that the link lies in their choice of themes. Both women present characters caught in a violent—sometimes grotesquely violent—world, characters who are struggling toward their own redemption, many without any conscious knowledge

of what impels them. While personal redemption is a shared and important theme for these writers, each writer treats it differently. For O'Connor, redemption seems to mean "losing oneself," i.e., being humbled, while for Walker, redemption seems to mean finding and asserting oneself. O'Connor's characters must learn to hear the word of God in their hearts by phasing out the static of their own pride. Walker's characters must learn to shout to get both God's and man's attention.

Wise Blood and *The Color Purple* provide excellent examples of the theme of redemption and the diverse paths to redemption that the individual can see, if he will only open his eyes. Seeing, sight, vision are all-important functions in both novels. More than one critic has noted that seeing is the controlling metaphor in *Wise Blood,* and the title *The Color Purple,* with its emphasis on a quality—color—that only the eyes can register, suggests the importance of "vision" in this world.

First, let us look at *Wise Blood* and its protagonist Hazel Motes, whose name focuses on this quality of vision (*Hazel* means "God sees," and motes are specks of dust or other tiny particles that can blur the sight). Hazel Motes is a man whose "vision" has blurred, and *Wise Blood* is the story of his journey to correct his religious astigmatism. Hazel bears as a burden the heritage of his family's Southern fundamentalist faith, a faith whose Jesus is, in Hazel's eyes, "soul hungry." He wants to escape this Jesus, yet ironically throughout the novel carries along, at the bottom of his duffel bag, reminders of his family's faith: a Bible which he never reads, and his mother's glasses, just "in case his vision should ever become dim." Even in his flight from God, Hazel appears unconsciously to pursue Him.

An episode early in the novel sets up Hazel's continuing conflict. When he is drafted, he sees the war "as a trick to lead him into temptation"; after a few weeks in boot camp, he meets his first major temptation, an invitation by some bunkmates to join them in a brothel. He responds to this temptation with a prepared speech on his soul and damnation, during which he puts on his mother's glasses, in effect, adopting her "vision" of the world. Hazel is laughed at by the other men who tell him that he doesn't have a soul. Instead of being disturbed by this revelation, Hazel becomes thoughtful and even pacified because he actually wants to believe them. If man has no soul, he cannot be corrupted. Without corruption, redemption is unnecessary, and if redemption is unnecessary, so, after all, is Jesus, who was born as man to redeem man from sin.

Hazel's subsequent strategy is one of provocation of his God. Hazel "sins" with Leora Watts, challenging God to punish him, and even starts his own religion, the Church without Christ, built upon blasphemy. However, Hazel, like St. Paul, is a Christian *malgré lui.* Unlike Paul, though, Hazel is not struck by God's blinding light in his flight from God, and God does not announce His purpose to Hazel as He did to Paul. Hazel has to effect his own literal blinding in order to restore his "vision."

Asa Hawks, the false preacher in *Wise Blood,* is Hazel's mirror image; he is a man without real belief who professes to believe, while Hazel is a man yearning to believe who professes not to believe. This Asa, unlike the Old Testament king of Judah who opposed idolatry, is not a true believer, but rather "hawks" his religion for his own gain. Initially, Hazel does not "see" Asa for what he is; he sees instead a man who carries with him the secret of a faith so strong that he was willing to blind himself for it.

Hazel's discovery, later in the novel, of Asa's pretense of blindness is important in Hazel's final and total dispossession. As Walker explains in her essay, "[The] moment of revelation, when the individual comes face to face with his own limitations . . . is classic O'Connor and always arrives in times of extreme crisis and loss." When Hazel loses everything—his Church, his car, and his illusion of Asa's belief—he is ready for a new vision, which, ironically, he achieves by blinding himself. While critics have noted the Oedipal parallels here, I have found no critic that notes the Biblical allusion; in the Gospel of St. Mark, Jesus warns:

> "And if your eye should cause you to sin, tear it out; it is better for you to enter into the kingdom of God with one eye, than to have two eyes and be thrown into hell." (Mark 9:46)

Motes' "vision" carried him away from God; once blinded, he turns inward to complete his journey toward God. As Hazel's landlady, Mrs. Flood, notes near the end of *Wise Blood,* " . . .the blind man had the look of seeing something. His face had a peculiar pushing look, as if it were going forward after something it could just distinguish in the distance." Hazel dies at the novel's end, having recognized his need for redemption, if not redemption itself. Like so many of the other protagonists of O'Connor's fictional world, Hazel must be dispossessed and humbled before peace and blessedness are possibilities in his life.

Gilbert H. Muller in *Nightmares and Visions: Flannery O'Connor and the Catholic Grotesque* summarizes O'Connor's vision well when he writes:

> Her dark preoccupations rarely permit a benevolent God, but rather a severe and demanding one. . . . [who] stands poised over the landscape of the grotesque, ready to wreak vengeance on people in their flight from religious responsibilities. . . . [W]hen the author explores the ways which grace works in the world of the absurd, she does not accommodate herself to benign theological vision.
>
> (pp. 51-3)

Victoria Duckworth, "The Redemptive Impulse: 'Wise Blood' and 'The Color Purple'," in The Flannery O'Connor Bulletin, v. 15, 1986, pp. 51-6.

Ben Satterfield

[*In the excerpt below, Satterfield rejects the widespread critical notion that* Wise Blood *is a novel of redemption; rather, he contends, it is an ironic tale of psychological abnormality.*]

From a literary point of view, Flannery O'Connor's *Wise Blood* is an ironic study in pathology rather than, as so many critics claim, a novel of redemption. The main character, Hazel Motes, is exposed early in life to a fundamentalist religion that is a kind of virulent infection he is unable to shake off; his Christ-obsession drives him through the novel and compels him to make an ironic Christ-like sacrifice of his own life (the other characters, minor and grotesque, are more distorted and perverted than "saved" by their religion). Part of the irony, in terms of consistency, is the lack of meaning in Haze's self-inflicted suffering and his guilt-provoked attempt at atonement.

Only readers who have a sacramental view of life and who read fiction with the analogical lenses provided by religious doctrine see Haze as redeemed. Any critical reading based on analytical principles of literary criticism will differ from this generally accepted, and especially Catholic, interpretation that simultaneously insists upon taking the superficial at face value and upon a kind of reading between the lines that amounts to sheer speculation at best or pure eisegesis at worst. There *are* differing ways to read the novel, of course, and one way—a very popular way—is to view the ending as an example of redemption. . . .

Despite the myriad and matter-of-fact assertions of redemption, no one has shown that Haze's sacrifice is in any sense meaningful, as, for example, is the sacrifice of Randall Patrick McMurphy in *One Flew Over the Cuckoo's Nest.* At least McMurphy's "disciples" assert themselves and leave the hospital to resume or assume responsibility for their own lives; in short, McMurphy has an effect on them that is illustrated in the novel. Haze affects no one; people simply think that he is mad (a reasonable deduction), and his death is a meaningless event heeded by no one except his materialistic landlady, who looks into his blind eyes, "trying to see how she had been cheated or what had cheated her, but she couldn't see anything." Of course she could not see anything, neither could Hazel Motes; blindness is one of the themes of this novel.

No evidence can be found in *Wise Blood* to support a conclusion of redemption. The only thing known for certain is that Haze punishes himself; he suffers and dies, and that is all. O'Connor implies that he does so in a plaintive attempt at atonement, but nothing explicit or certain is stated in the novel. Those who claim Haze is redeemed mistake his acts of penance, if that is what they are, for the goal they are employed to achieve; they mistake the means for the end. But atonement is not redemption and should not be confused with it. Still, readers see what they want to see. Mary Gordon, in reviewing O'Connor's letters, avers that "redemptions occur so frequently in her fiction because they are needed so badly." Gordon does not say by whom they are so badly needed because she makes the mistake of *assumption,* the same error that all the other sectarians make; they superimpose a pattern of redemption on O'Connor's work that is not warranted by the fiction itself. Indeed, Gordon's remark, which more accurately phrased might state that "redemptions *are seen* so frequently because they are wanted so badly," sums up the desperate attitude of religious commentators and helps to explain their unqualified perceptions of redemption. But

Wise Blood is infused with so much irony, as is O'Connor's work in general, that it is difficult to believe Haze's sacrifice to be anything but ironic and consistent with the overall tone of the book. In a letter to John Hawkes, O'Connor herself stated: "I am afraid that one of the great disadvantages of being known as a Catholic writer is that no one thinks you lift the pen without trying to show somebody redeemed."

Yet Jonathan Baumbach not only sees Haze as redeemed but also as a redeemer, claiming the thesis of the novel to be that "if one man is willing to sacrifice himself in Jesus' image, redemption is still possible." Baumbach unequivocally states that, at the end of the novel, "Haze immolates himself, re-enacting, in effect, the redemption of Man." This statement is not only untrue but patently absurd. The redemption of man could never be "re-enacted". The idea is ridiculous; all that can be enacted is the sacrifice. Redemption is in God's province, not man's; or as an old French saying has it, *Homme propose, mais Dieu dispose.*

But Baumbach does not interpret the events of the novel as merely suggesting redemption for Haze, he asserts that Motes achieves redemption not only for himself but "in extension, for all of us." Needless to say, this is impressionistic criticism gone amuck, as has much of the commentary on O'Connor's work. (pp. 33-4)

On the contrary, Ihab Hassan, a critic no one would call imperceptive, feels that Haze is damned, not redeemed, that he "gives up his very salvation" despite his self-torture, because he is a "penitent without a god." And Frederick J. Hoffman claims "his death is a parody of the death of Jesus" [see *CLC,* Vol. 15, p. 410].

Such contradictory readings lead to the central question of what there is in the novel that causes readers, intelligent people of keen perception, to interpret it so differently. The answer is irony and ambiguity. The irony one has to assume is deliberate; the ambiguity may be a result of artistic failure or clumsiness, O'Connor's not being in control of the irony, as a master would be. In this regard, the names of the characters are revealing, for they are both ironic and ambiguous. A "mote" is a speck, a tiny particle, and therefore insignificant; the traditional meaning of "Hazel," normally a name for a female, is "one who sees God," but either Hazel Motes is doubly misnamed or his name reflects an unmanaged sense of irony. The appellation "Hazel" is so unusual for a man that it does not seem fitting, and if the name is not right, then the meaning of the name is not apt for the character. "Haze," the abbreviated form of the name, suggests either that the character is not himself clear or that he cannot see clearly, yet he professes absolute clarity throughout the novel. The evidence is against accepting the name at face value because the names of O'Connor's characters in this book, and in all the stories, reveal that most of them are ironic. For example, Asa Hawks: the last name refers to a bird of prey as well as to one who peddles, both appropriate associations, but "Asa" means "healer," something the charlatan Asa Hawks definitely is not. "Solace Layfield," "Holy," "Shoats," are obviously satirical, and the irony of the choice of "Enoch"—which means "devoted, educated" (and, according to one source, "friend of God")—neither

needs nor deserves comment. In this novel, O'Connor seems not to have known when to pull her tongue in from her cheek, and her unsteadiness creates problems.

"*Wise Blood* runs erratically," says Irving Malin, and he is unarguably right. Many commentators note the heavy (and heavy-handed) satire that suffuses the novel, but when they get to the conclusion, they dismiss any thought of parody, quite arbitrarily deciding that the satire ends here. Making such a decision reasonably rather than emotionally is impossible. From a critical perspective, an ironic sacrifice is in keeping with the overall irony of the book; only a religious view demands that the sacrifice be interpreted as redemptive. A valid literary reason to isolate Haze's sacrifice from the ironic elements does not exist. From an artistic standpoint, consistency is a paramount consideration, and if the events leading to the conclusion are satirical, then the conclusion should likewise be satirical; otherwise, the author creates confusion and the novel will be unfocused, as *Wise Blood* is.

Of course, O'Connor attempts to tie together the separate segments of this novel, which started out unauspiciously as two or three discrete short stories. For instance, the book begins and ends with a *memento mori:* on the second page, O'Connor says of Hazel that "the outline of a skull under his skin was plain and insistent"; and on the penultimate page, "the outline of a skull was plain under his skin. . . . " Most of the writing throughout is just as obvious as this, for O'Connor's hand is indeed heavy in this erratic but widely-read novel of a young man trapped in a world without faith.

O'Connor writes about a South that is different in many ways from that of William Faulkner or Erskine Caldwell but nonetheless familiar. Her characters are generally the still-abundant poor whites, but they are more impoverished spiritually than physically, and some of them are as driven as any Faulkner conceived while others are more animal-like than the basest character Caldwell ever imagined. The Southern milieu, while rendered in realistic terms, is composed of various Gothic elements, from a deserted house to a haunted landscape. The Gothic devices are neither extraneous nor melodramatic but serve to underscore the horror of reality, the gross ugliness of living in a godless world. The language is appropriately realistic, naturalistic, earthy; it is concrete and generally free from abstractions; likewise the imagery is always physical and specific, never of the spiritual or intangible.

In addition to profuse nature imagery, there is a superabundance of animal references, associations, and imagery throughout the novel. . . . (pp. 35-6)

Wise Blood is teeming with animal imagery, so much so that its usage is abused, leading as it does to what [Martha Stephens] referred to as the "gross animalism of the whole book." It is Haze's need to transcend the merely animal that creates all the problems, of course, for in O'Connor's works human beings without faith, without sacraments, without the blessing of God's grace, which burns, are nothing but animals, and ugly, disgusting animals at that.

Many of the characters (the peripheral ones are hardly more than creatures) behave as animals; Enoch Emery, for instance, wants little more than to *become* an animal—apparently because of his averse reaction to imposed religiosity—and one of his expressions is " 'I'll be dog.' " Enoch believes that he has wise blood, and his blood wants nothing more for him than to return to a primigenial state, so he is transmogrified into a gorilla, then forgotten. Undoubtedly this evolutionary reversal is O'Connor's way of dismissing people such as Enoch (as she does him in the novel) who want to turn backward rather than reach upward. Haze, however, has a need to transcend the animal, and it is his desire for elevation that is so troublesome. This need is created by a natural fear of death and an unnatural extreme guiltiness over human passion which is instilled by his Bible-belting mother: "Jesus died to redeem you." Religion, since it offers solace in its promise of salvation and everlasting life, provides the means of transcendence, and certainly the obsessed can believe in it. Haze's grandfather, a circuit preacher, believed in it but suffered the fate of all mortals: "When it was time to bury him, they shut the top of his box down and he didn't make a move." The conflict in Haze, as in so many O'Connor characters, is between what is perceived of the natural world and what is taught of the spiritual. There is more than a suggestion in O'Connor's fiction that the two cannot be reconciled.

Haze's frustration becomes an obsession that takes the form of denial, a perfervid denial of Christ who is obviously "in his mind like a stinger." Setting up his own church (a high rat-colored car) to preach against Christ, Haze exhorts strangers to take counsel from their blood, from the animal, the instinctual. His preaching, although presented in parodic terms, is existential, a reaction formation, and totally devoid of anything Haze is able to accept. When Enoch Emery presents him with a "new jesus"—a stolen mummy, which represents man's pathetic attempt at immortality—Haze sees the futility of his behavior and, yielding to the fever in his blood, commences to punish himself for his apostasy. Like a beast whose will is not his own, Haze is driven by his blood, a blood infected and inflamed with religious madness, a madness that culminates in his gory sacrificial death.

O'Connor uses animal imagery to create unfavorable, unappealing impressions and thereby to manipulate the reader's responses. Virtually all of the animal imagery is negative, as it is in most fiction, but here it is especially so because O'Connor's vision of humanity is negative. The author, a devout Catholic, has a decidedly sour view of mankind in general, a view that is not the least bit aided by her religious and cultural parochialism. Here is a pious Christian writer who believes according to the dictates of her faith that man is created in God's image, yet what she portrays are creatures that are hardly more than brute beasts, or men driven mad by the very faith that is supposed to sustain them. Something is amiss, and it appears that O'Connor was never able to reconcile what she saw of real life with what she wanted to believe—not an uncommon problem in literature or religion—and it is this unreconciled conflict that creates confusion in *Wise Blood.*

The book is patchy, uneven, but the last two chapters especially are troublesome, beginning with the scene in which

Haze is deprived of the automobile that is his "church" by a highway patrolman who, in an act of gratuitous malevolence, pushes it off an embankment at the top of a hill. Dorothy Walters, in her study of O'Connor, insists that "when the lawman sends Haze's ancient auto crashing over the cliff, Haze recognizes that God has at last given him a 'sign.' " Her putting the word "sign" in quotation marks would seem to be a concession to credibility; nevertheless, her reasoning is that because of this "sign" from God, Haze "returns to town and blinds himself as a drastic act of atonement for his futile efforts to flee from grace."

The scene referred to is a crucial one and is worth close examination:

> The patrolman got behind the Essex and pushed it over the embankment and the cow stumbled up and galloped across the field and into the woods; the buzzard flapped off to a tree at the edge of the clearing. The car landed on its top, with the three wheels that stayed on, spinning. The motor bounced out and rolled some distance away and various odd pieces scattered this way and that.
>
> "Them that don't have a car, don't need a license," the patrolman said, dusting his hands on his pants.
>
> Haze stood for a few minutes, looking over at the scene. His face seemed to reflect the entire distance across the clearing and on beyond, the entire distance that extended from his eyes to the blank gray sky that went on, depth after depth, into space. His knees bent under him and he sat down on the edge of the embankment with his feet hanging over.

His church has gone into the abyss, and what Haze sees is nothing, or nothingness. Tired of seeing "nothing," he blinds himself, possibly hoping to see more, or at least something of a different order, even something metaphysical; as he says later, "if there's no bottom in your eyes, they hold more." There is no evidence in the text to indicate that "in the patrolman's destruction of his car, Haze detects the unmistakable hand of God," as Walters resolutely avows.

A less assertory view can be found in the astute and well-balanced *The Question of Flannery O'Connor* by Martha Stephens, who cautiously states: "The reader senses that Hazel is at long last overcome with the enormous failure of his attempt to escape Christ into disbelief and that the wrecking of the car is to be seen as an act of grace. . . . " According to Stephens, God has "in a sense" rewarded Haze. The language is justly qualified. But God's hand does not have to be invoked because Haze is ready to give up his apostasy; all his rebellious efforts have been futile and now that his church has been destroyed and he sees the emptiness of his life, he yields to the fever in his blood rather than struggle against it further. He gives up the fight, literally and figuratively. God did not have to do anything, and if God did do something, he would have no way of knowing. To be sure, the book would make more sense and be more meaningful, both in literary and religious terms, if the events occurred without divine intervention.

Even if O'Connor meant the destruction of Haze's car as a sign from God, objective readers can no more believe it than they could believe a person who accosts them at the airport and says the plane's being late is a sign from God or that a stopped watch is a warning. Of course, people who are inclined to see "signs" see them all the time, and since perception is intentional, whatever is "seen" is subject to interpretation. But in this case, if O'Connor is providing signs, she is doing God's work in a grossly manipulative fashion.

Wise Blood is fiction, not Scripture, and fiction is like a deck of cards that can be stacked by the dealer. The reader, if alert, can tell whether the deal is straight or not, and if the patrolman's action is supposed to be a sign from God, then the deal is unmistakably crooked: the deck is stacked. But many critics appear to have some mystic ability to perceive things that are not in the book. Walters flatly states that Haze has "at last seen God" and therefore proceeds directly home to blind himself and commence his expiation. Baumbach agrees that "in blindness he achieves at least spiritual sight," another statement that is pure conjecture, wishful addition of meaning. According to Louis D. Rubin, Jr., Haze blinds himself "to shut out the vision of sin." Obviously, no reader can state positively what, if anything, Haze sees other than what the text specifies, which is "the blank gray sky that went on, depth after depth, into space." But commentators read into that depth of space a range of meaning from God to Nothing. On this literary Gordian knot, Nathan Scott tugs carefully: "Once his car is gone, Haze is, it seems, utterly undone, and having faced the agnosticism and unconcern and mendacity of the world, there is nothing left for him to do but to destroy his capacity to see more."

If the words of the text are to be accepted, Haze sees a lot of empty space and that is all, but he apparently connects that emptiness with his own life. At this point he literally gives up, because when the patrolman asks him if he were going anywhere, he answers "No." . . . Three times the officer asks Haze about his destination, and the response Haze gives indicates that he realizes he was truly going nowhere. His behavior supports this reading, for he gives up his struggle. Either he recognizes the futility of fighting against a power that does not exist, as he had previously proclaimed to do, or he realizes the futility of fighting against God if God does exist. Only Haze's futility is made clear in the text, not the reason for it, and any claim that Haze "sees God," no matter how strongly it is urged, cannot be supported.

Preston Browning asserts that "Haze is brought to acceptance of salvation" and a "radical renunciation of his destiny;" however, he does not believe that Haze sees God because the sky "seems to contain nothing at all, nothing to rebel against, nothing to rest in" [see Further Reading list]. Although Browning states that Haze "accepts redemption," he claims "it is impossible to specify" exactly what Haze moves toward at the end of the novel. In *The World of Flannery O'Connor*, Josephine Hendin argues that Haze is "engulfed in a sense of nothingness, a mental

emptiness broken by ambiguous, irrelevant symbols" and that he punishes himself to feel an animal pain that anchors him to life. But Hendin seems unable to resolve the ending, which is an enigma for many readers. Irving Malin assays the problem:

> We are not prepared for this transformation, unless we take it ironically as another act of grotesque narcissism. Perhaps the conflict we feel arises from the fact that Miss O'Connor herself is torn by the "needs" of the grotesque *and* Christian faith. *She gives up one for the other, unable to hold both at the end of her novel.*

The ending is decidedly ambiguous, notwithstanding the assertions—unsubstantiated, to be sure—that Haze is "undoubtedly redeemed." To Baumbach and Walters, this is "fully evident," but for readers who draw their conclusions from what is in the text, no evidence of redemption exists. Nevertheless, critical interpretation of Haze's behavior at the end of the novel covers the spectrum of possibility—from the belief that Haze receives a divine revelation to the antipodal opinion that Haze sees a "total blankness" that confirms his denials of Christ—or as an early reviewer [John W. Simons] commented, "nobody here is redeemed because there is no one to redeem."

In a footnote, Walters claims that "the meaning of Haze's final course as a return to God through acts of extreme expiation" is clearly established. To support this claim, she cites O'Connor's note to the second edition, which she thinks "should dispel any final doubts as to Haze's intentions." In this note, O'Connor says that Haze is a Christian *malgré lui* and that his integrity does not lie in his vigorous attempt "to get rid of the ragged figure who moves from tree to tree in the back of his mind" but in his *inability* to do so. The note affirms O'Connor's outlook and tells the reader how to interpret the novel, but a statement of Haze's helplessness does not clarify his "intentions."

More importantly, if Haze is a Christian in spite of himself, then his Christianity is in no sense meaningful. In other words, the words of the author, Haze cannot help himself, he is driven by his blood. Apparently, the author believed that Christianity is such a powerful and compelling force that it cannot be resisted; in a letter to John Hawkes dated September 13, 1959, she wrote: "Haze is saved by virtue of his having wise blood; it's too wise for him ultimately to deny Christ. Wise blood has to be these people's means of grace—they have no sacraments." That is didacticism with a vengeance, but if what the author says is accepted as fact, then the novel is about a man who cannot help doing the things he does, and is therefore silly both as literature and religious propaganda.

Allegory, symbolism, or parable are all things easily accepted and expected in art, but not dogmatism. For example, when [Dorothy Tuck McFarland] writes that "O'Connor characteristically uses the sun as a symbol of transcendent power" no reader should find difficulty in accepting that statement, for it seems perfectly reasonable. But when asked to believe that a character is redeemed, or receives grace, or gets a sign from God, many readers will resist not out of obstinacy, wrongheadedness, or any other deprecatory term likely to be applied to them by

O'Connor devotees but because such interpretations, aside from being so arbitrary, defy knowledge and perception and violate an overall sense of reality. If realistic fiction serves as a surrogate for the actual world and if the ideological function of realistic fiction is to clarify the beliefs and behavior of a cultural community, then what is true in it should be equally true about the world, and such is not the case in O'Connor's fiction. (pp. 36-41)

Wise Blood is faulty in the same way as **"A Good Man Is Hard to Find"** and many of the other stories because the reader is not prepared for the transformation that O'Connor says occurs. In order to believe that Hazel Motes experiences redemption or to see the wrecking of his car as an act of grace, and so forth, readers must disbelieve most of the things O'Connor says about him throughout the book. It is difficult to assume that God has "rewarded" Haze for his disbelief. The message of Christianity is just the opposite: believers are rewarded, and unbelievers are doomed.

If critics evaluate *Wise Blood* in terms of purpose and achievement, and assume that O'Connor's artistic goal was to show Haze redeemed after an act of grace, then O'Connor failed in literary terms because the text does not make such an interpretation evident, much less inevitable. Frederick Asals, a sympathetic critic who rightly considers but is not blinded by O'Connor's religiosity, states: "Hard as one may search for the informing sacramental vision in this novel, no such sustained perspective emerges" [see Further Reading list]. The sectarians cannot have things both ways; if, as the advocates of the sacramental view insist, the stories and novels are to be interpreted as containing moments of grace and redemption, then they are decidedly bad art. (pp. 45-6)

One of the requirements of realistic fiction is that any character's behavior has to be believable. For characters to be credible, their actions must be credible, and any change—certainly any significant change—must be within the possibilities of the characters as presented by the author. But without knowledge of O'Connor and her declared purposes, no one could read *Wise Blood* or **"A Good Man Is Hard to Find"** and conclude that Hazel Motes is redeemed or that the smug grandmother receives grace because the texts do not make such readings inevitable or even reasonable. On the contrary, readers must be told how to read the tales, just as Sunday School children must be told how to read Biblical parables. (p. 46)

It is time to reconsider. As art, O'Connor's work should be judged apart from the author's comments about it, evaluated on its own merits, read as fiction that represents and reflects the real world. Most of the fiction of Flannery O'Connor, judged from a purely literary standpoint, is inferior, like that of Lloyd C. Douglas, and unworthy of association with Faulkner, Hemingway, James Joyce, and others of the first water. It is time to recognize that no sound artistic reason exists to continue inflating her reputation, and it is past time to cease stuffing critical (and not so critical) journals with glowing anagogical interpretations that use her fiction as a springboard for a dive into mystical speculation that is not justified by the work itself.

If the things the sectarian critics have written about O'Connor have any validity, then her work is undeniably more concerned with doctrine than art, and most likely the future chroniclers of American literature will place her accordingly: a religious propagandist of minor importance who wrote didactic fiction, or at least thought she did. (p. 48)

> *Ben Satterfield, " 'Wise Blood', Artistic Anemia, and the Hemorrhaging of O'Connor Criticism," in* Studies in American Fiction, *Vol. 17, No. 1, Spring, 1989, pp. 33-50.*

FURTHER READING

Allen, William Rodney. "The Cage of Matter: The World as Zoo in Flannery O'Connor's *Wise Blood.*" *American Literature* 58, No. 2 (May 1986): 256-70.

> Holds that O'Connor's fusion of animal and confinement imagery intensifies the theme of her novel: "that the world, without its spiritual dimension, is merely a prison for an odd collection of inmates—a zoo for the human animal."

Asals, Frederick. "Early Work and *Wise Blood.*" In his *Flannery O'Connor: The Imagination of Extremity*, pp. 9-64. Athens: The University of Georgia Press, 1982.

> Explores the influence of Nathanael West, Edgar Allan Poe, and existentialism on *Wise Blood.*

Browning, Preston M., Jr. "*Wise Blood.*" In his *Flannery O'Connor*, pp. 25-39. Carbondale and Edwardsville: Southern Illinois University Press, 1974.

> Asserts that *Wise Blood* "is organized around a nexus of opposites. . . . The tension generated by these opposites functions to bring the protagonist Hazel Motes ever closer to a revelatory moment when the scales fall from his eyes and he achieves the vision of a mystic or saint."

Byars, John. "Mimicry and Parody in *Wise Blood.*" *College Literature* 11, No. 3 (1984): 276-79.

> Details "how people, objects and animals mimic and parody Hazel's simultaneous flight from, and pursuit of, God."

Cook, Martha E. "Flannery O'Connor's *Wise Blood:* Forms of Entrapment." In *Modern American Fiction: Form and Function*, edited by Thomas Daniel Young, pp. 198-212. Baton Rouge: Louisiana State University Press, 1989.

> Argues that Hazel Motes is ultimately a positive character because he acknowledges his spiritual heritage.

Desmond, John F. "*Wise Blood:* The Rain of History." In his *Risen Sons: Flannery O'Connor's Vision of History*, pp. 51-62. Athens: The University of Georgia Press, 1987.

> Maintains that *Wise Blood* "concerns the problem of how to make the Christian historical vision manifest in the present irreligious world, how to incarnate it."

Gentry, Marshall Bruce. "The Eye and the Body: *Wise Blood.*" In his *Flannery O'Connor's Religion of the Grotesque*, pp. 119-41. Jackson: The University Press of Mississippi, 1986.

Examines the religious significance of eye and body imagery in *Wise Blood.*

Gregory, Donald. "Enoch Emery: Ironic Doubling in *Wise Blood.*" *The Flannery O'Connor Bulletin* 4, (1975): 52-64.

Suggests that Enoch Emery underscores the tragic life of Hazel Motes by serving as a comic foil to him.

HopKins, Mary Frances. "The Rhetoric of Heteroglossia in Flannery O'Connor's *Wise Blood.*" *Quarterly Journal of Speech* 75, No. 2 (May 1989): 198-211.

Using critic Mikhail Bakhtin's theory of heteroglossia, the author explores how the diversity of dialects spoken by characters in the novel conveys O'Connor's themes.

Kunkel, Francis L. "Wrestlers with Christ and Cupid." In his *Passion and the Passion: Sex and Religion in Modern Literature,* pp. 129-56. Philadelphia: The Westminster Press, 1975.

Analyzes the conflict between theological and erotic concerns in *Wise Blood.*

O'Donnell, Patrick. "The World Dactylic: Flannery O'Connor's *Wise Blood.*" In his *Passionate Doubts: Designs of Interpretation in Contemporary American Fiction,* pp. 95-115. Iowa City: University of Iowa Press, 1986.

Investigates "the crucial hermeneutic battle enacted in *Wise Blood*—a battle where the singularity of an authorial intention is placed against the ironies generated by the signs O'Connor employs in fulfilling that intention."

Orvell, Miles. "*Wise Blood.*" In his *Invisible Parade: The Fiction of Flannery O'Connor,* pp. 66-95. Philadelphia: Temple University Press, 1972.

Detailed study of Hazel Motes's spiritual quest and how it affects his relationship with other characters in *Wise Blood.*

Sembène Ousmane

1923-

(Also cited as Ousmane Sembène) Senegalese scriptwriter, novelist, short story writer, and editor.

Ousmane is renowned for films and novels that address social ills in his native Senegal. Based on Marxist-Leninist ideology, most of his works depict underprivileged groups or individuals facing opposition from a corrupt, bureaucratic system. Ousmane denounces the burgeoning, westernized elite he sees in post-colonial Senegal, as well as such traditional Sengalese customs as polygamy and belief in superstition. Robert A. Mortimer observed: "Each [of Ousmane's films] has a dramatic integrity, using well-chosen visual images which move the viewer to a sense of injustice, to an awareness of the need to solve some basic problems. [Ousmane] does not seek to provide set answers to these social problems; never does he lapse into a cinema of slogans or revolutionary demonstrations. He recognizes that the film is a medium for shaping ideas and attitudes as the viewer reflects upon the story he has seen."

Ousmane left school at the age of fourteen, after a fistfight with his school principal, and later served in the French colonial army during World War II where he participated in the Allied invasion of Italy. Ousmane's later experiences as a longshoreman and union organizer in Marseilles, France, led to his first novel, *Le docker noir,* about a black stevedore who writes a book that is stolen by a white woman. While not considered one of Ousmane's strongest novels, *Le docker noir* established a pattern for his subsequent works, which depict Africans who fall victim to a corrupt social or political system. Most of Ousmane's fiction is based on actual events; for example, a newspaper article on the suicide of a black maid in France became the basis of *Le noire de . . . (Black Girl*); Ousmane's film version of the novel won a Cannes Film Festival Special Prize. Another work, *Les bouts de bois de Dieu (God's Bits of Wood)*, recounts the railworker strikes of 1947-1948 on the Dakar-Niger line, in which Ousmane participated. Critics acclaimed *God's Bits of Wood* for successfully portraying both the dominant social and economic concerns of the union as well as the individual sentiments of workers and their families. A reviewer for the *Voice Literary Supplement* commented: "In [Ousmane's] best-known book, *God's Bits of Wood . . .*, modern history, tribal customs, ordinary lives, great scenes of mass battle, and several love stories are thrown together in a marvelous stew that simmers and boils with life."

Realizing that his novels reached only a limited readership in Senegal, where the majority of people are illiterate and speak the indigenous Wolof language, Ousmane turned to filmmaking. He saw film as an effective medium for mass communication, and spent a year studying cinematography in the Soviet Union under noted filmmaker Marc Donskol. For his first short film, *Borom Sarret,* which details one tragic day in the life of a cart driver, Ousmane

won the Tours Film Festival prize in 1963 for best first work, and thereafter began adapting his short stories and novels for the screen.

Ousmane's novel *Xala,* later adapted for film, treats two of his dominant themes: corruption of the African elite and failings of polygamy. After appropriating government funds to finance his third marriage, the protagonist, El Hadji Abdou Kader Beye, is cursed with *xala,* or impotence, by a group of mendicants he has routinely mistreated. Unable to consummate his new marriage, El Hadji loses the respect of his family and colleagues. To remove the *xala,* he ultimately succumbs to the demands of the beggars, who spit on him while his first wife and her children watch. Ten scenes were cut from the film by Senegalese government censors; however, Ousmane countered by distributing fliers to the theatergoers describing the missing segments.

Although his works are often subject to censorship in Senegal, Ousmane has gained a widespread viewership for his films in Africa and abroad, prompting Guy Hennebelle to dub him "the pope of African cinema." Ousmane is involved in all facets of filmmaking: writing, directing, producing, editing, casting, and collaborating on the soundtracks. *Mandabi* (*The Money Order*), which won awards for best foreign film at the Venice Film Festival in 1968 and the Atlanta Film Festival in 1970, was the first film written and directed by an African to be commercially released in Senegal and is considered the first African film to reach an international audience. Like many of Ousmane's works, *The Money Order* was released in both a French and a Wolof version. This film, based on his novella *Le mandat*, recounts the troubles experienced by Ibrahima, a poor, illiterate Senegalese man, who attempts to cash a money order sent from his nephew in France. A bureaucratic banking system and greedy neighbors cheat Ibrahima of his money, leading him to assert that "honesty has become a crime in this day." Ousmane concludes many of his films on a similar note of despair; *Emitai* (*The God of Thunder*), for example, describes a heroic resistance against French rule by the small Diola population of Senegal but closes with a massacre of the villagers by the French.

Most critics contend that the collective movements in Ousmane's works—by communities, unions, and women—offer a sense of hope for positive societal change, yet others compare his works to Jean-Paul Sartre's existential play *No Exit,* in which there is no promise of escaping existing social frameworks. In Ousmane's view, the bleakness of his works only mirrors that of the African world he observes. The artist, he maintains, "can neither invent anything or receive anything. We must see and know our society. We have to be within and without at the same time. Within in order to feel the heartbeat, and without to create the image that society gives to us. And it's from there that we take a position. But our role stops there because the artist alone cannot change society. He can, however, help to orient the society."

(See also *Contemporary Authors,* Vols. 117, 125 and *Black Writers.*)

PRINCIPAL WORKS

NOVELS

Le docker noir   1956
O Pays, mon beau peuple!   1957
Les bouts de bois de Dieu   1960
   [*God's Bits of Wood,*   1962]
L'harmattan, Volume I: Réfêrendum   1964
Xala   1973
   [*Xala,*   1976]
Dernier de l'empire   1981
   [*The Last of the Empire,*   1983]

SHORT FICTION COLLECTIONS

Voltaïque   1962
   [*Tribal Scars and Other Stories,*   1974]
Véhi-Ciosane; ou, Blanche-Genèse, suivi du mandat   1965
   [*The Money-Order; With White Genesis,*   1971]

SCREENPLAYS

Borom Sarret   1964
Niaye   1964; adapted from his short story "Véhi-Ciosane"

La Noire de . . .   1966; adapted from his short story "La Noire de . . . "
   [*Black Girl,* 1969]
Mandabi   1968; adapted from his novella *Le Mandat*
   [*The Money Order,* 1969]
Tauw   1970
Emitai   1971
   [*The God of Thunder,* 1973]
Xala   1974
   [*Xala,* 1975]
Ceddo   1977
   [*Ceddo,*   1978]

The Times Literary Supplement

There is no doubting the reality of [the setting of Sembene Ousmane's *God's Bits of Wood*], as it is an imaginative reconstruction of the effects of the strike on the Dakar-Niger railway in Sénégal in 1947-48. The peoples are carefully delineated, Ouolof, Bambara, Peul, Berber, Toucouleur, *colon,* and the complexities of the linguistic situation are not only never shirked but even made integral. For it is through this very insistence on diversity in the struggle that one is made aware how one of the triumphs of this episode of trade unionism in West Africa was that large numbers of people from different ethnic groups were brought together to achieve aims greater than tribal ambition. And not merely ethnic groups, the novel is at pains to insist, but also generations and sexes. The scene shifts from Dakar to Thiès and Bamako and back and the book concentrates on the effects of the strike on individuals like the self-sufficient, determined strike leader, Bayayoka, his large household in their various roles, the subservient old watchman despised by the strikers, neglected by the women, and eaten by the very rats he tries to make himself hunt and consume. Sembene Ousmane handles terror and tenderness with equal sureness, moving from the bewildered European management, most affronted by the polygamous strikers' demands for family allowances, to the hungry children, and above all to the desperate women, who discover in themselves new power and militancy, old and young, blind beggar woman and whore. Sembene Ousmane has in abundance what both [T. M.] Aluko and [Robert] Serumaga lack: the ability to control a wide social panorama, without once losing sight of, or compassion for, the complexity and suffering of individuals.

> *"Tribal Unions," in* The Times Literary Supplement, *No. 3581, October 16, 1970, p. 1184.*

Robert A. Mortimer

In the fall of 1969, a banner was unfurled across bustling Avenue William Ponty in Dakar to herald an unprecedented event. Emblazoned boldly upon the banner was MANDABI, the Wolofized version of the French "Le Mandat" or "the money order," the title of an award-winning film by the talented Senegalese filmmaker, Ousmane Sembene. The publicity celebrated a cultural and political event of considerable significance: for the first time, the work of a Senegalese director was being shown commercially in Senegal. West African filmmaking was moving beyond the select audience of international film festivals to reach a mass African audience. Therein stands a major landmark in the history of the black man and the film medium.

Film is obviously an attractive medium of expression for artists in countries with high rates of illiteracy. Indeed Sembene, the filmmaker, is the current *persona* of Sembene, the highly regarded novelist; his own personal itinerary from writer to cineast bears testimony to the relevance of the film as a vehicle of education and liberation in contemporary Africa. (p. 26)

Sembene's remarkable career is in itself a living document of the forces of social change in recent African history. Born in 1923 into a poor family in Ziguinchor, the main city of the Casamance region of southern Senegal, Sembene is an essentially self-educated man. He recalls having exercised thirty-five different trades from fisherman to mechanic to soldier on his way to becoming a cineast. Clearly the major experience of this formative period was the decade spent as a longshoreman on the docks of Marseille after World War II. Here he became a union organizer among the black workers, and he has continued to consider himself as a Marxist-Leninist. His profound concern and identification with the common man have been evident throughout his artistic career.

His first novel drew upon his life in Marseille. Published in 1956, *Le docker noir* ("The Black Dockworker") was, according to one critic, "very badly written." Each succeeding work, however, exhibited a polishing of style which soon established Sembene as one of the finest and most original writers in Africa. In 1957, he completed a second novel, *O Pays, mon beau peuple* ("Oh Country, My Beautiful People") which described the efforts of a Casamancais to create a modern, independent business in his own country against the pressures of the colonial merchants and the caste prejudices of the traditional peasant society. Peasants and workers came together in his third work, *Les bouts de bois de Dieu.* This major novel vividly recounts the story of the African laborers' strike on the Dakar-Bamako railway line in 1947-48, incorporating Sembene's concern with progressive social change into a work rich in its portrayal of the physical and social setting of West African semi-urban life.

Foreshadowing his artistic versatility, Sembene shifted effectively to the medium of the short story when he published *Voltaïque* in 1962, a collection acclaimed for the poetic tone and psychological insights in characterization that it revealed. One of these stories later became the subject of a film, as did the two novellas published a few years later as *Véhi-Ciosane* and *Le Mandat.* Although he published yet another novel in 1964 (*L'harmattan,* an interpretation of the political events surrounding the 1958 referendum in which [Leopold] Senghor decided against voting for immediate independence), it seems that by the early 1960's, Sembene, the writer, was already thinking in terms of creations that might be carried to the screen.

Sembene has described his transition into filmmaking as follows: "I became aware of the fact that using the written word, I could reach only a limited number of people, especially in Africa where illiteracy is so deplorably widespread. I recognized that the film on the other hand was capable of reaching large masses of people. That is when I decided to submit applications to several embassies for a scholarship to pay for training in filmmaking. The first country to respond favorably was the Soviet Union. I spent a year at the Gorki Studio in Moscow, where I received a basically practical instruction under the direction of Marc Donskol." This decision to master the film medium, then, was prompted by Sembene's profound commitment to a socially relevant art. His literary subjects were the common people of Senegal struggling to cope with the oppression of colonialism and the disrupting forces of social change brought about by modernization. He was not content that the ideas and lessons contained in his art be limited to the African elite. As a socialist critical of the emerging post-colonial bureaucratic elite on the one hand, and a progressive critical of certain traditional practices on the other, Sembene had a message to convey. He concluded that movies offered a greater opportunity than books to "crystallize a new consciousness among the masses." The step into filmmaking was as much a political act as an artistic choice. The image was to teach a lesson of liberation, but at the same time Sembene was determined not to sacrifice his artistic integrity in taking that step toward a cinema of genuine decolonization.

Each of Sembene's films tells a movingly sad story. His protagonists are humble people exploited in one way or another by the disruption wrought upon their society by colonialism or its neocolonial vestiges. Each film has a dramatic integrity, using well-chosen visual images which move the viewer to a sense of injustice, to an awareness of the need to solve some basic problems. Sembene does not seek to provide set answers to these social problems; never does he lapse into a cinema of slogans or revolutionary demonstrations. He recognizes that the film is a medium for shaping ideas and attitudes as the viewer reflects upon the story he has seen.

Sembene's first production, *Borom Sarret,* runs but nineteen minutes. Slowly paced and filmed in a semi-documentary style, Sembene uses these nineteen minutes to take us through the wearisome day of a *bonhomme charette* or cart-driver, who seeks to make a living from a horse and buggy taxi service. The driver transports a pregnant woman to the hospital, and then a father to the cemetery to bury his dead baby. The poverty of his passengers, his own rumpled old hat, the dusty street of the medina—all add up visually to a day in which no client is able to pay his fare. Finally a well-dressed young man persuades him to cart some of his belongings into a comfortable residential neighborhood in which horse and buggy wagons are prohibited. There a policeman appears, fines the driver, and confiscates his wagon. The victim returns sadly home without a franc, deprived of his means of livelihood. His wife leaves the children with him and goes out saying, "We must eat tonight . . ."

It is a tribute to the director's skill that in this rather short footage, Sembene is able to convey the heavy weight of poverty, the growing demoralization of an unproductive day, the frustration of the struggle to survive in a setting marked by the gap between the rich who make the law and the poor who suffer its inequities. The cart-driver tries his best to support his family only to have his wife thrown back upon her own resources at the end. The mood of the film is one of pathos, not of revolution, but the impact of the story is strong and troubling. For this film, the Tours Film Festival awarded Sembene its prize for the best first work in 1963.

In 1964, he transformed his short novel *Véhi-Ciosane* into a film entitled *Niaye*, a stark vision of the disintegration of traditional rural life under the dual pressure of outmoded authority relationships and colonial interference. As in the novel, the physical focus of the film is the central place of the village, the perfect visual image of rural Senegal, where the men gather beneath a tree to discuss village matters, or to gossip and listen to the *griot*, the traditional story-teller. The *griot* recounts a sordid tale of incest, suicide, murder, and corrupted power. The peaceful appearance of the countryside contrasts sharply with the underlying reality as the viewer learns that the village chief has impregnated his daughter to the despair of his humiliated wife who kills herself when she realizes that no one has the courage to avenge her by rebelling against the chief's authority. Their son later returns home traumatized by his military service in Indochina; the chief's cousin, covetous of his power, persuades the deranged young man to murder his father. The colonial administration legitimizes the conspiracy by naming the guilty cousin as the new chief with the approval of the village elders. At the end we see, however, that the *griot* and the daughter are overwhelmed by this corrupt hypocrisy, and decide to leave the village. The daughter momentarily considers abandoning her infant until she sees vultures circling overhead—a grim image summing up much of the film. She gathers up the baby, and much like the wife of the cart-driver, departs to an uncertain future.

Niaye is a strong dose of social criticism, perhaps too heavily administered to be convincing. The preface to the novel makes it clear that Sembene conceived the work as an attack upon uncritical glorifications of the past, a category within which he includes the doctrine of negritude. The film incorporates this same harsh message. Yet the novel, for all its violence, has a poetic quality—in its contrast between innocent victims and those corrupted by power, and in the dignity expressed by the *griot's* anguish at the disintegration of the ancestral legacy—which Sembene sought to capture on film. He passionately desired that *Niaye* be seen by its primary audience, the peasants of Senegal. As he had no commercial outlet for the work, he undertook the responsibility of distribution himself, touring the country to project and discuss the film personally. Thus he achieved the direct contact with his audience that had drawn him into filmmaking. He recalls with pleasure the long evenings spent discussing the problems raised by *Niaye* in the improvised "open-air theaters" of rural Senegal.

His third movie brought Sembene considerable international recognition as a cineast. *La Noire de . . .* won prizes at film festivals in France and Tunisia as well as at Dakar's special 1966 Festival of the Negro Arts. Adapted from one of the stories in *Voltaïque*, this was Sembene's first direct cinematic treatment of the theme of black-white relations. The story is based in fact, drawn from an incident which Sembene read about in the French press. It portrays the tragic isolation and eventual suicide of an African girl taken to France as a maid. Two images in particular struck many viewers: the *marché aux bonnes* or "maid market" at which the French technical assistance family finds the maid—uncomfortably reminiscent of a slave market as filmed by Sembene—and the recurrent image of an African mask which the maid purchases as a toy for the European child and which comes to symbolize her cultural identity as she grows more despondent over her objectification by the French family.

Sembene himself was most struck by the expressiveness of the face of Thérèse Moissine Diop who plays the girl. In all of his cinema, Sembene has drawn remarkable performances from non-professional actors. As the illiterate and lonely maid rarely speaks to the family (her thoughts being expressed in background monologues), the camera must convey much of the inner turmoil she feels in this racist *huis-clos* [no exit].

La Noire de . . . is a moving portrait of racial exploitation. Sembene believes that the "maid trade", however, is a symbol of a larger issue: the neocolonial attitudes of the new African bureaucratic elite who condone such a relationship in return for European financial aid and technical assistance. In portraying poignantly the human consequences for one person caught up in this neocolonial system, Sembene sought to provoke thought upon the larger situation, and to raise questions about the content of genuine African independence.

Mandabi, the production of which was made possible by the artistic success of *La Noire de . . . ,* takes up this same theme in a quite different story. It is the first work which Sembene produced in color (although he experimented with some color sequences which he eventually cut from *La Noire de . . .*) and he uses color to great advantage in presenting a visual panorama of life in modern Dakar. As anyone who has visited Senegal's capital will readily recall, the city is a palate of splendid colors. Sea, sky, flowers, open markets, and brilliant light provide the setting for the brightly colored fabrics of the women whose long *pagnes* and highly wound kerchiefs bob and wend their way through the busy downtown streets.

Sembene explodes this color in a visual assault upon the viewer as his hero Ibrahima Dieng goes upon his quest to cash a money order. In one of the striking early scenes, the viewer is overwhelmed by a sea of boubous as the men pour out of Dakar's impressive Grand Mosque. The long, flowing, often handsomely embroidered boubou of the traditional Senegalese man becomes a symbol of Ibrahima's traditional dignity; as he sets off upon a difficult errand or is rebuffed by an arrogant clerk, he majestically swishes his boubou into its proper stately fit to reassure himself of his worth and decency.

Mandabi is a political film lightly disguised as a farce. Mamadou Gueye, the Dakar office-worker whom Sembene turned into an international film-star in the lead role, renders an amusing Ibrahima. There are many comic sequences as Ibrahima and his wives Mety and Aram seek to capitalize upon the sudden "fortune" sent by their nephew in France. Yet the comedy and the color gradually fade in significance as the more somber shades of life in Dakar's shantytown emerge. The tribulations of a simple man as he confronts the post-independence bureaucratic establishment (a visual carbon copy of the French administrative system) become painfully serious matters. Ibrahima encounters red tape at the post office, disdain at the city hall, cheating as he seeks the photograph required for his identity card, and finally venality from the young college-educated relative to whom he turns for assistance. At the same time, he becomes fair game for every neighbor who gets wind of the impending "wealth" out of which he is finally cheated. Humiliated by the nascent bourgeoisie of his country, Ibrahima cries out desperately in the film's closing scene that "honesty has become a crime in this day."

The impact of the film is strong. The characters are authentic, and the story is simple and convincing. From the first image of the nephew, a streetsweeper in Paris, dropping the money order into a mail box, to the closing image of Ibrahima's lamentation, one senses the concern with social and economic inequality that pervades Sembene's work. Once again the director does not give us a revolutionary figure, yet the film conveys its message of the need for change. Sembene's critique is implicit in the contrasting images of the shantytown and the well-to-do neighborhoods, or the honest but unemployed man and those who exploit the privileges of a seat behind a desk. The humor and the deft portrayal of ordinary family life allow Sembene to reach a large audience; without turning the movie into a manifesto, the director nevertheless employs his medium to teach a lesson. It is this effective combination plus its technical excellence that make *Mandabi* an artistic success as well as a landmark.

Sembene's most recent work is a short color film, commissioned by American churchmen to illustrate some of the profound dilemmas of modernization in contemporary Africa. Conceived essentially for western audiences, *Tauw* reiterates several themes already familiar from his earlier films. It focuses upon urban youth, faced by the dual problems of unemployment and changing values. The title character is a young man without prospects, engaging in petty thievery (snitching *croissants* from a carrier's tray) while wandering about Dakar in search of work, unable to purchase the ticket which would admit him to the docks for a possible job. He quarrels with his traditionalist father and breaks with his family; one senses as the film ends that Tauw stands on the verge of vagrancy or anomie. While this quasi-documentary short feature reflects issues to which Sembene has earlier drawn attention, he has further ideas for new work. He has already shot some footage in his native Casamance for a film treating the clash of temporal and spiritual authority. Another project calls for a major historical film on the nineteenth-century Malinke resistance leader, Samory Toure. These further themes

suggest Sembene's conception of how the film can continue as a vehicle of growing African self-understanding. (pp. 26, 64-6)

> *Robert A. Mortimer, "Ousmane Sembene and the Cinema of Decolonization," in* African Arts, *Vol. 5, No. 3, Spring, 1972, pp. 26, 64-8, 84.*

John Updike

Xala, by Sembène Ousmane, describes itself, on the dust jacket, as "the basis for a highly acclaimed film of the same title which received accolades at the 1975 New York Film Festival." It is as short as a scenario (one hundred fourteen pages), flows in a succession of scenes without any chapter subdivisions, and contains bits of "business"— "Her tight-fitting dress split, a long, horizontal tear which exposed her behind"—that might be hilarious in a movie but fall rather flat in prose. The stills from the film bound into the book exist on the same continuum as the text, and help us to read it, rather than (as in most illustrated fiction) set up an irrelevant static of alternative visualization. Yet the novel is not thin. Its basic subject, the problems of polygamy in an urban society, resonates eerily in our own society of families extended by divorce and remarriage, of romantic renewals obtained at the price of multiplied obligations. The reality of magic in Mr. Ousmane's interweave of erotic farce and stern social comment suggests, to a Westerner, what magically fragile constructs our personal pretensions are.

A *xala* (pronounced "hala") is a curse that produces impotence; one is laid upon the hero, a Senegalese businessman called El Hadji Abdou Kader Beye, on the night of his wedding to his third wife, the young and voluptuous N'Gone. El Hadji is "fifty-odd" and prosperous enough to keep his two other wives, Adja Awa Astou and Oumi N'Doye, in separate villas in the fashionable part of Dakar, and to provide a minibus for the transportation of his eleven children. Within the minibus, we are told, the children of each mother take a separate bench: "This segregation had not been the work of the parents but a spontaneous decision on the part of the children themselves." There are a number of such fascinating details of how polygamy works in urban Africa. "In the town, since the families are scattered, the children have little contact with their father. Because of his way of life the father must go from house to house, villa to villa, and is only there in the evenings, at bedtime. He is therefore primarily a source of finance . . . " The set time he spends with each wife is called a *moomé;* the first wife is given the title of *awa,* after the Arab word for "first woman on earth." "The first wife implied a conscious choice, she was an elect. The second wife was purely optional." El Hadji's second wife, the sharp-tongued, Frenchified Oumi, has the position of sexual favorite to lose to the third, so she is suspected as the source of the *xala.* When, after many futile trips to marabouts who cannot lift the curse, El Hadji finds one, deep in the bush, who succeeds, it is Oumi who has the benefit of his momentarily revived potency. The plot takes some pains to keep young N'Gone virginal, so that she can, without serious offense to sexual propriety, be discarded, as El Hadji's luxuriant world slips from him. His impotence poisons all his existence. "Day after day, night after night, his torment ate into his professional life. Like a waterlogged silk-cotton tree on the riverbank he sank deeper into the mud." The source of the *xala,* when finally revealed, is perhaps less surprising in the film, where the sound track has repeatedly placed the culprit before us; but the ritual exaction for the curse's removal, and the story's abrupt swerve into social protest, must surprise everyone not immersed in Africa's sense of communal responsibility or familiar with the moral indignation visited there upon elites busy aggrandizing themselves in the approved capitalist manner.

El Hadji's rise, overreaching, and fall are intelligible without magic. He is impotent with his third, much younger wife out of stagefright—the jocular chaffing at the wedding and the postnuptial inspection of the bed linen lend intimacy an intimidating public dimension—and out of fright of his own hubris. His financial status collapses with his sexuality, because he is everywhere overextended. The pre-urban institution of polygamy, wherein the patriarch on the strength of his warrior potential alone ruled his docile compound of subsistence farmerettes, has been intolerably weighted by the Western conceptions of husband, lover, and (of Western goods) provider. El Hadji's metropolitan attempt to combine status and gratification breaks his resources, which, we are reminded in a forceful parenthesis, are pathetically slender:

> (It is perhaps worth pointing out that all these men who had given themselves the pompous title of "businessmen" were nothing more than middlemen, a new kind of salesman. The old trading firms of the colonial period, adapting themselves to the new situation created by African Independence, supplied them with goods on a wholesale or semi-wholesale basis, which they then re-sold.)

El Hadji's vain tour of marabouts for cure is now recast as a vain search for credit; his cars and villas are repossessed. He stands finally before us naked, covered with spittle. Nakedness, Sembène Ousmane seems to say, is man's natural condition. The keen African body-sense supplies a rapture of precision to El Hadji's moment of relief from the *xala:*

> Hadji listened to the clicking of the beads as they fell at regular intervals onto one another. He looked up at the curved roof. Suddenly he felt as if he were on edge. A long-forgotten sensation made him break into bursts of shivering. It was as if sap was rising violently inside his body, running through its fibres and filling it right to his burning head. It went on coming in waves. Then he had the impression that he was being emptied. Slowly he relaxed and a liquid flowed through his veins toward his legs. All his being now became concentrated in the region of his loins.

Not all the writing is this vivid and fluent. The translator seems to have brought to the French some English awkwardnesses: words such as "fulsome" and "exhibitionism" are used in their root, rather than usual, meanings, and

more than one word seems off in a passage like "Her eyes were lifeless, they had a deep inscrutability that seemed like a total absence of reaction. But there was the strength of controlled inertia burning in them." Such eyes have successfully defied description. Not so these: "The lack of sleep showed at the edge of his eyelids and bathed his eyes in a reddish lustre crossed by threads which according to the time of day or the place would take on the colour of stale palm-oil." Generally, the texture of Mr. Wake's translation answers well to Mr. Ousmane's tone—that light, level accent of French Africa's fiction, which voices its perceptions, however withering, with a certain pleasant dispassion, with a thinking man's articulations. (pp. 677-80)

> *John Updike, "The World Called Third," in his* Hugging the Shore: Essays and Criticism, *1983. Reprint by Vintage Books, 1984, pp. 676-722.*

Jonathan A. Peters

A Senegalese fable tells the story of three encounters by Fene-Falsehood and Deug-Truth who were companions on a journey. At the first village they are thrown out by a man whose wife is discourteous to both the strangers and her husband because Deug, when asked, suggests that she is the worst wife he has seen. An honest answer to the chief's enquiry in the second village similarly lands them in trouble: Deug tells him that the children are in charge in the village because they are the ones who share out the meat, reserving the choicest portions for themselves. But in the third, the king is forced to part with half of his wealth because Fene, now their spokesman, dupes him into believing that he can bring back to life not only his dead favourite, but his father and grandfather as well. The present king does not want to have to deal with the problems of three kings in a single kingdom, especially since his father had been a tyrannous king whom his son helped to put away. When they set out on their journey Fene had observed that God loved Deug-Truth more than him. But when he obtains half of the king's wealth as a result of his untruths he concludes that God may be on the side of truth but falsehood was the best way to succeed with men.

Sembène Ousmane, the internationally famous film-maker from the village of Ziguinchor, Senegal, has suffered much the same fate as Deug-Truth in terms of the reception of his fiction and his films. After more than two decades of artistic output he has so far received comparatively little critical attention deserving of his seven books of fiction and at least an equal number of films; for, if numbers do not provide a compelling reason for serious study, the issues he raises as well as the artistic quality of his fiction—to say nothing of his films which earn him first place among African film-makers—are sufficient to deserve more extensive analyses of the kind that some writers with certainly no greater contribution to African letters have received. One reason, perhaps, for his neglect among English-speaking writers and readers stems from the fact that some of his early works have never been translated into English while, among those translated, only his most widely praised novel, *Les bouts de bois de Dieu* was almost immediately available in translation under the title *God's Bits of Wood.*

Another more significant reason may be that what he sees and expounds on repeatedly is the uncomfortable and even repelling 'truth' that black people are still undergoing a form of slavery in this, the latter portion of the twentieth century. . . . The intensely moral tone of many of [Sembène's] works is in keeping not only with the role of a truth-seeker, but also (more importantly) with the function of that truth-telling bard of old—the griot—who, in Sembène's own words, 'was not only the dynamic element in his tribe, clan or village but also the living witness of every occurrence . . . placing before all at village gatherings the facts about each in full detail'. The story of truth and falsehood provides an excellent reference point for examining Sembène's griot role as exemplified in his two novelettes, *Le Mandat* and *Véhi-Ciosane; ou, Blanche-Genèse,* both of which have been made into films.

The major theme in both *The Money-Order* and *White Genesis* turns on the conflict between truth and falsehood in human affairs. The two stories in fact are studies on the value of morality. *White Genesis* is more tragic in its development but its end holds out the hope that truth, in bondage over a long period, will again be resurrected. *The Money-Order,* depicting somewhat humorously the misfortunes that surround its hero, ends on a note of pessimism. It is a structural parallel of the story of truth and falsehood in that its hero, Dieng, decides to give up his truthfulness and honesty in favour of deception and lies. The preference for falsehood evident in the society portrayed in *White Genesis* is constantly undermined by the griot-hero to the point where Sembène is able to suggest a new beginning through the illegitimate child of Khar Diob. In *The Money-Order,* after a series of misfortunes in which Dieng loses more than the value of the money-order sent by his nephew from Paris, he also loses his gullibility declaring: 'I am going to put on the skin of the hyena. . . . Why? Because it is only cheating and lies that are true. Honesty is a crime nowadays.'

White Genesis is a griot's story. Sembène himself remarks in the introduction that it is as old as the world itself. It is a story of incest set in the village of Santhiu-Niaye. Sembène introduces the story by describing the setting of the village close to the Atlantic Ocean in Senegal. The very monotony of this region which defies definition in terms of savannah or delta, steppe, grassland, etc., gives a parallel to the lack-lustre morality which permeates the village, threatening its life as much as the migration of its young men to the city in search of a better life.

The longest section of *White Genesis* gives us an extended view of Ngone War Thiandum, the mother of Khar Madiagua Diob. Before the story opens Khar had become pregnant and at first the responsibility of her pregnancy had been laid on the *navetanekat,* a migrant labourer called Atoumane. In spite of his denials the Diob family had wanted him killed on the strength of the accusation that he has violated their family honour. Since he is poor and perhaps of a low caste marriage with Khar would be undesirable; so the gravity of his offence in getting a girl pregnant whom he could not marry and who would for

ever be tainted by this episode in her life, is quite obvious. Khar's brother, the mad Tanor who served time during the Second World War, destroys the labourer's groundnut crop and a crowd of villagers (which include Khar's uncle Medoune Diob) pursues and hunts the *navetanekat* for several days and nights. The identity of Khar's real violator is only gradually revealed. In fact, Ngone War Thiandum is one of the last people in the village to know. The scene in which she finds out that her husband is the father of the child their daughter, Khar, is expecting is depicted by means of a flashback. Gnagna Guisse, the wife of the shoemaker-griot, Dethye Law, can then no longer deny the truth when Ngone War Thiandum confronts her with it.

The whole story of *White Genesis* is overshadowed by events which have taken place long before the commencement of the story. By presenting these past occurrences through the mind of Ngone who is herself only just finding out the truth, Sembène is able to concentrate the action of the story into the few days when things reach a climax. The climax itself is the scene in which Khar delivers the baby, but already in this first major encounter with Ngone and her family we have the major outlines of the conflict.

In the opening portion of this episode we see Ngone in bed with her husband, Guibril, whom she is now forced by circumstances to despise. There is a delicate balance, however, between this sense of contempt and the genuine warmth of affection that contact with her husband's body conjures up in her through pleasant memories of their past relationship. The closing scene of this episode is the accouchement of Khar and it fittingly ends the long section, promising a resolution of one kind or another to this drama of incest.

The theme of incest in *White Genesis* is connected with themes of honour and nobility as well as morality and justice; it is also related to the theme of truth on which the Senegalese fable I referred to earlier is based. Sembène manages to interweave all these themes together to form a moral world not only as things are or as they used to be but, perhaps more important, as they should be. In accordance with this vision, Sembène makes a statement used first as an epigraph to the story and then recalled in the following reflection by Ngone War Thiandum at the end of our first encounter with her:

> The words of the sage came, luminous, into her mind: 'Sometimes a child is born into the most ordinary low caste family who grows up and glorifies his name, the name of his father, of his mother, of his whole family, of his community, of his tribe. More often, in a so-called high caste family which glorifies in its past, a child comes into the world who, by his actions, sullies his entire heritage, and even robs the individual diambur-diambur [freeborn] of his dignity.' She repeated these words to herself, but still she hesitated to act.

The whole purport of the passage reflects Sembène's belief that honour and nobility are not a typical characteristic of people of high birth, operating in a closed circuit. Rather, honour and dishonour are qualities that mark out individuals whether they are of humble or noble origin. The reference to 'so-called high caste' emphasizes Sembène's point.

Although Ngone is anxious to preserve the good name of her family, this duty and desire are not confined to those of her rank only. Indeed the most outspoken and uncompromising seeker after truth is not a member of a high caste, but one who acknowledges his lowly status. It is Dethye Law the griot-shoemaker who incorporates in his character the old virtues which had made their society great and which are now being trampled upon. The inherent truth behind the words of the sage is dramatized through the story. What Sembène is saying, in essence, is that Guibril Guedj Diob who was born into a family with a noble past, disgraces the reputation of not only his own high lineage but also the ordinary free-born citizen like Dethye Law. At the same time, we can say that someone like Dethye Law, born into an ordinary home, a low-caste griot home, can ennoble his community by his steadfast witness to the truth. It is this simple truth that *White Genesis* is designed to demonstrate.

Sembène Ousmane goes to great pains to document the inbreeding that takes place within a society where truth is seen as the prerogative of a particular class, one in which morality is a stylized process of maintaining dignity even if this means disguising or denying the truth. The crime of Guibril and his daughter Khar, an exception to this rule, is open for all to see. But the machinations of his brother, Medoune Diob, first of all instigating the invocation of the death penalty for Guibril Guedj Diob and his daughter and when this fails inciting the mad Tanor to kill his father are the kind of concern that the griot has. This concern with the truth is displayed throughout the story by Dethye Law as well as by others like Massar. Thus following the deaths of Guibril Diob at the hand of his son and the suicide of Ngone War Thiandum, Dethye Law makes an attempt at leaving which is designed to test the will of the villagers to uphold the truth.

Dethye has always spoken against those who have left the village because their desertion threatens the very survival of Santhiu-Niaye. But when the machinations of Medoune Diob go on unchallenged and even condoned by the present Imam, Dethye begins to be afraid that people like him who speak the truth will be threatened: the unscrupulous will not hesitate to eliminate those who speak against them once the moral will of the people is broken. His announcement that he is going to leave is followed by . . . exchanges which emphasize above all the fact that freedom and truth are not confined to the rich or those of noble ancestry. . . . At the time that the hero, Dethye Law, engages in this dialogue the climax of the story has already been reached. Khar has delivered her baby. Her mother, true to her guelewar upbringing and motto—'Rather die a thousand deaths in a thousand ways each more terrible than the other than endure an insult for a single day'—has already committed suicide. And Guibril Guedj Diob has been killed by his son Tanor, at the instigation of his uncle Medoune Diob. Tanor cannot succeed his father, not only because of his madness but also because of his patricide. Besides, the last we see of him is the scene where he is tied

to a tree; the last we hear of him is Medoune's statement to the toubab-commandant that he has left for the city like many of the young men. Medoune Diob has now inherited everything. He has the chieftaincy, the pomp of receiving dignitaries like the white commandant on a tax-collecting mission—even Guibril Guedj's colourful parasol which Tanor, returning home from the war in Indochina, had brought his father. In the light of these developments—especially the role of Medoune Diob in the liquidation of the incestuous Guibril—Dethye's decision that he can no longer live in Santhiu-Niaye is understandable.

Dethye Law is right on another point. The inhabitants of Santhiu-Niaye are not ready, in spite of their village's increasing desolation, to sacrifice the truth completely—yet. At the mosque where the faithful respond to the griot's intoning of the call to prayer five times a day, almost all the adherents desert the present conniving Imam in favour of Palla, his old rival for the position. The shifting of religious adherents also reflects the political scene, for Medoune Diob becomes ostracized in much the same way as Guibril was isolated when his incest became established. The changed situation also gives added significance to Dethye's comment that in the past the caste system made members of his family servants to the Ndiobene's. Thus, a society will prosper only if it dedicates itself to truth not as 'a gift, nor an inheritance' but as an ideal since 'the blood of truth is always noble, whatever its origin'. If we adopt this view, many of the roles in the story are immediately reversed. Dethye's unflagging efforts to preserve the truth make him a man of noble blood while the blood of the Ndiobene's has become tainted by the attempts to destroy the truth no less than by the sin of incest. This is the core of Sembène's message in the story.

For the cleansing to be complete, however, the new leadership has to banish Khar and her child from the village. Before her death, Ngone War Thiandum had hoped that this grandchild/stepchild would be a boy. But it is a girl that Khar brings into the world amid the injurious gossip that goes on about her. Unlike the gossip-mongers and even Ngone herself, Sembène is careful throughout to avoid making either father or daughter the seducer in their incestuous crime. Since the two of them say very little in *White Genesis,* we are forced to hold them equally guilty. Yet it is this act of banishment that holds out hope in an otherwise bleak ending. In a very short space of time Khar ceases to be a child and becomes a woman. She becomes even more precipitately an orphan caring for a new-born infant whose future, like hers, is unknown. Her attempt to abandon the child which would only handicap her bid to begin life afresh in a new environment, is merely a reflection on her dilemma. The instinctual maternal attachment of this child-mother-orphan to her daughter, Vehi-Ciosane Thiandum, restores the balance to the natural cycle. The child, then, becomes the symbol of hope, the nonracial 'white genesis' after a prolonged rule of dishonesty, corruption and evil.

The moralizing tone of the novelette is inevitable because of the virtual identity of subject and theme, and the signal role of Dethye Law as an exponent of these, a role of griot-moralist that echoes Sembène's own. All the same, a good portion of *White Genesis* concentrates on the lives of villagers outside the Ndiobene-Thiandum household. The favourite meeting spot for the men is under the shade of the beintan tree where the griot-shoemaker works. It is in its shade that intense contests take place between Badieye and Gornaru, two inveterate players of *yothe* (the local version of draughts complete with dry donkey droppings for counters) while the habitués discuss everything under the sun, from the moral dilemma that engulfs the village to bawdy dexterities. . . . Such episodes give body to the otherwise slim story of human calamity. It is essentially an internal conflict, for none of the strangers—the *nave-tanekat* or the white official and his retinue—change the dynamics of the village in any way. All the change comes from within. And the end of the story returns us to the sandy flats as Khar, unselfpityingly braces herself for the trip to a new life in Ndakaru with a child of infamous ancestry but who may well grow up to glorify an entire people.

The locale in *The Money-Order* shifts from a desolate rural setting to Dakar, capital of Senegal, for which Khar Madiagua Diob is headed at the end of *White Genesis.* There is a difference also in the central conflict between the two novelettes. The one in *White Genesis* is, as we have seen, primarily an internal village conflict, the nexus of which is the high caste family of the Ndiobene-Diob which is completely shattered at the end. By contrast, the inhabitants of the same quarters as Ibrahima Dieng, the central character of *The Money-Order,* are virtually indistinguishable in terms of birth and caste on account of their common misery. They help and hurt each other by lending or sharing small portions of the meagre foodstuffs and loans they manage to scrounge out of the over-priced store of Mbarka; by exchanging and spreading news and malicious gossip about the changing society and about each other; and by their jealous outrage against the petit bourgeois whose members include Mbarka and the new western educated elite. The central conflict is, however, a personal one. An external agent in the form of a money-order from Paris forces the jobless Dieng outside his familiar world into the unfamiliar world of the Dakar bureaucracy, leaving him disillusioned in the end.

Perhaps the most emphatic distinction between *White Genesis* and *The Money-Order* is one of tone. The intensely moralistic tone of the former is probably suited to the intention of Sembène to deal with a very serious issue affecting the health and welfare of a whole society. The tone is in fact not confined to the sermonizing hero, Dethye Law, but extends to others as well. Thus, Ngone War Thiandum tells her family griot, Gnagna Guisse (wife of Dethye Law): 'It is a sin to lie. It is unfriendly to lie to me.' And Gnagna Guisse defends to herself the prolonged cover-up of the truth by recalling the wisdom of the appropriate sage: 'Any truth that divides and brings discord among the members of the same family is false. The falsehood that weaves, unites and cements people together is truth.' In the middle of his frustrations over the money-order, Ibrahima Dieng's wife, Mety, spreads the rumour in the neighbourhood that their husband was robbed after he had cashed the money-order. Dieng rebukes her in this way: 'You must always speak the truth. However hard it

is, you must always speak the truth.' But even as he says this, Dieng's faith in the truth is beginning to wear thin. He will soon change his mind about the truth when, ironically, he is robbed of the money not by pickpockets but by a relative of Mety who pretends to be a friendly and honest helper. It is this element of irony which most distinguishes *The Money-Order* from *White Genesis.* In *White Genesis* Sembène is involved with his hero. In *The Money-Order,* he is somewhat detached. (pp. 88-97)

[In] addition to his financial loss, Dieng also suffers from a broken nose at the hand of a practised apprentice of Ambrose, loses his credibility with many of those in his immediate circle and, above all, becomes cynical like the rest following his humiliation and his disillusionment with the truth.

What we have in *The Money-Order* is a crisis of faith. But it is not a crisis that is morbidly presented; rather we have a sequence in which Sembène places a good many characters, including Dieng himself, in ironic situations which point up the exploitative relationships that exist in the society at and between its successive levels. The role of protagonist fits Dieng because he remains one of those who have not yet become corrupted by the malaise and the indigence which permeate the quarter. Even his two wives are much wiser in the ways of the world than their husband whom they acknowledge as master in conformity with custom. In the face of the impatience that even his own wives show for his scruples and the vicious treatment he receives from the parasitic neighbours, the greatest plea for tolerance towards Dieng comes from Sembène himself in this comment about his hero:

> We must try and understand Ibrahima Dieng. Conditioned by years of blind, unconscious submissiveness, he fled from anything likely to cause him trouble, be it physical or moral. The blow of the fist he had received on his nose was an *atte Yallah:* the will of God. The money he had lost, too, it was ordained that it was not he who should spend it. If dishonesty seemed to have the upper hand, this was because the times were like that, not because Yallah wanted it so. These were times that refused to conform to the old tradition. In order to rid himself of his feeling of humiliation, Ibrahima Dieng invoked Yallah's omnipotence: for he was also a refuge, this Yallah. In the depths of his despair, and of the humiliation to which he had been subjected, the strength of his faith sustained him, releasing a subterranean stream of hope, but this stream also revealed vast areas of doubt. He did not, however, doubt the certainty that tomorrow would be better than today. Alas! Ibrahima Dieng did not know who would be the architect of this better tomorrow, this better tomorrow which he did not doubt.

The moral suasion of Dieng, when coupled with his simple approach to situations, stands in bold relief against a background of general cynicism, corruption and dishonesty. It is a major prop onto which much of the irony in the novelette is latched.

Although a good deal of the irony with which *White Genesis* is laced is verbal, this type of irony is often buttressed by irony of situation. We have already seen the ironic twist that the cashing of the money-order takes when Mbaye tells Dieng he has been robbed of his money. Mbaye uses the same story that Mety and Aram had invented to keep the neighbours from wheedling the money out of Dieng once it is cashed. In actual fact, Dieng has himself provided Mbaye with the story, after the dispute with Mbarka. Mbaye (a prototype for El Hadji Abdou Kader Beye, the hero of *Xala,* 1974) does not surprise us in his actions because we have been prepared for this outcome by Sembène's description of him as a member of the 'New Africa' generation, a breed of 'men who combined Cartesian logic with the influence of Islam and the atrophied energy of the Negro.' Since no difficulty is beyond him, it is easy to appreciate the enterprising solution he brings to bear when he disabuses Dieng of the bulk of the money.

Dieng has throughout the story a good deal of difficulty in establishing his identity, because at every turn the bureaucratic functionaries 'want a piece of paper to prove who I am.' This problem of identity is explored on other levels. It is related to his 'fine clothes' which Mbarka tells him are 'just wind'. When he is mauled by Ambrose's apprentice, he returns home via the back alleys so that his neighbours will not see him in his present undignified state. But these very clothes provoke some derisive remarks and help create his identity crisis. Thus the prostitute tells him that he looks like a marabout; the letter-writer charges him with impersonating a marabout when he fails to pay fifty francs for having his letter read; Ambrose's apprentice calls him a 'fake marabout;' and in his reply to his nephew, Abdou, he himself promises to consult a 'real marabout' on Abdou's account. But the incident that tops all is the one in which he recites verses from the Koran as he thanks his Dakar nephew for the great assistance he has given him. Sembène comments thus:

> The distant cousin let him have his way. Out of the corner of his eye, he saw a policeman approaching them, feeling his chest pocket. When he reached them, the policeman looked at the two pairs of hands, at the man's face, then at the marabout (for he thought Dieng was one), and he joined his hands to theirs. Dieng took hold of one of his thumbs. He raised his forehead and his lips moved. Two passers-by stopped and held out their hands. When he had finished murmuring, Dieng sprayed saliva all around. They all replied, 'Amine! Amine!' and rubbed their faces as they broke up.

Sembène's consistent depiction of Dieng and other characters in situations that are both ironical and laughable implies his conscious employment of satire. In a sense, it increases our sense of his detachment from the hero's predicament, in contrast to his apparent attachment to the moral stance of Dethye Law, the protagonist of *White Genesis.* The subtlety which characterizes the gently satiric tone of Sembène shows how painstaking and ingenious a craftsman he is. One will find *The Money-Order* full of structural irony only if one is ready to delve below the surface so as to discover the subterranean echoes and situational parallels that punctuate the narrative. Indeed, so replete is this work with satire and irony, that even the noble (if also humble) profession of griot is not left unscathed.

Unlike Dieng's unintentional performance as a marabout, the unscrupulous Maissa, who is so determined to bilk Dieng of as much money as possible from whatever source without giving away any of his own, suddenly becomes a posturing griot 'extolling the noble lineage of a young man dressed in European clothes: the beauty of the women, the boundless generosity and bravery of the men, the nobility of their conduct, all of it redounding on the young man, pure blood . . . from the purest of blood.' Although the young man is indifferent to traditional praises, he is embarrassed enough to slip Maissa a hundred-franc note in the middle of his intoning that he sings not for money but 'to keep the tradition alive.' And Dieng the 'marabout' who is at the police station trying to obtain an identity card admits that he knows 'nothing about life today', being 'overcome by Gorgui Maissa's lack of dignity in pretending to be a griot.'

Dieng's naïveté is crucial in achieving Sembène's goal of social criticism in *The Money-Order.* Yet, in spite of the exaggerations necessary to satire and such absurdities as the small amount of money which so completely dominated Dieng's world—25,000 francs CFA was the equivalent of approximately forty dollars in 1965—what Cameroonian writer Mbella Sonne Dipoko describes as 'dynamic realism' permeates this 'minor masterpiece'. This realism is even more poignant in the film. Indeed, Sembène has been widely praised and also widely upbraided, in the latter case for touches like the belching of Makhouredia Gueye (as Dieng) and an almost exclusive focus on the depressed areas of Dakar. Ironically, he has also been criticized for a lack of realism in his choice of costumes that are sometimes too colourful or dressy for the people portrayed in this and other films. The much wider audience that Sembène's films have received in both Senegal and elsewhere in Africa, justifies his badge of 'la meilleure école du soir' (the best night school) for the cinema in his country, where illiterates (like the bewildered Ibrahima Dieng) account for virtually eighty-five per cent of the population. His didactic purpose is better realized in the film than in the short novel, because the longer film is largely in Wolof with occasional dialogue in French among the educated Senegalese. An example of his subtle touches shows Mbaye callously carrying on a telephone discussion in French with a prospective buyer for a house while its unwitting and fiercely possessive owner, Dieng, is trustingly sitting down waiting for Mbaye's help.

The use of Wolof in *Le Mandat,* Sembène's first colour film, also serves a political function. Sembène has declared himself in favour of 'un cinéma militant'. The bold use of a national language such as Wolof consequently represents a significant achievement in terms of breaking free from colonial domination, even though dependence on French came through in the process of making the film: the Wolof dialogue had to be written in French phrases that were literal translations of the as yet unwritten language of Wolof. (pp. 97-101)

Taken together, *The Money-Order* and *White Genesis,* the stories on which these two films are based, provide interesting, complementary and artistic case studies on justice, morality and honesty. Sembène is interested in a society where there will be social equality, not one in which women, as wives, will be lorded over by husbands or have to share their spouses with one or more co-wives; nor one in which people will be divided into high and low classes or professions by virtue of their birth. Still far short of this ideal, society is now encumbered by a resigned fatalism which accepts every misfortune as the will of Yallah. It is moreover, a morally and religiously bankrupt society where, according to an elder in **White Genesis:**

> The scriptures are a dead letter. For never in this village, nor in the whole of Senegal, where mosques nevertheless proliferate, not once have the penalties laid down by the holy scriptures been carried out. Go and see the authorities! We respect them and we cherish them; that seems to be all. That leaves us with the adda, the heritage of our fathers.

In **The Money-Order** it is not just that the scriptures are set aside, but that the very day-to-day communications constantly operate in a climate of mutual distrust. Mety, one of Dieng's two wives, observes at one point, 'Tell them the truth? They wouldn't believe it. It's simple: the truth isn't any use any more!' Dieng himself falls prey to the malaise when he implicitly affirms Mety's fabrication of the robbery: 'I have difficulty myself in believing it. Yet . . . well, honesty is a crime nowadays in this country.' The sponging Maissa tells his neighbour that 'people must help one another' and that 'man's remedy is man,' but he deserts Dieng at a time of need. The group solidarity shown by neighbours when they bring gifts to Dieng after the faked robbery is a fragile truce. The postman's assurances to Dieng that in concert they will change society is a wan hope, recalling us to Mety's observation at the outset that hope can kill. For the moment, all the dissimulation and lies help to preserve a society turned against itself, a society in which a small group of 'children'—young bureaucrats and insolent functionaries—is, in distributing the meat of prosperity reserving the choicest bits for itself and distributing the remnants unevenly among the masses. Sembène, as artist-griot, lays bare a society which subscribes to the moral of the fable that men (in spite of Gorgui Maissa) love falsehood rather than truth. (pp. 101-02)

> *Jonathan A. Peters, "Sembène Ousmane as Griot: The Money-Order with White Genesis," in African Literature Today, No. 12, 1982, pp. 88-102.*

Harriet D. Lyons

In this essay I wish to examine the film **Xala**, a work by a contemporary Senegalese novelist and film-maker, Ousmane Sembene, who has explicitly rejected the "atavistic" tendencies of the Négritude movement in favor of Marxist social realism. I hope to demonstrate not only that our understanding of the film can be increased by a knowledge of West African folk traditions but also that Dorson's notion of a "hidden" folk tradition is particularly useful in understanding an avowedly Marxist work. For Dorson believes that some of the themes and motifs of African folklore are not only pan-African but also international in distribution (in a context in which the values of the folklore-

producing masses were always juxtaposed [and sometimes opposed] to those of an elite). Without this juxtaposition, Dorson believes there is no folklore; moreover, the cultural hegemony of the élite assures that all folklore is to some degree covert. Though this position may be extreme, Dorson has described a very important element of much folklore.

I shall argue that in Sembene's work the "covertness" of the folk material takes the form of suppression of detail combined with the retention of essential values. Sembene is thereby able to use folk elements in such a way as to give the work political implications that go well beyond the preservation and/or revival of a local tradition. One can, therefore, examine the folk elements of **Xala** without fear of consigning yet another expression of African creativity to the museum of primitive art. (p. 320)

At the end of Sembene's film **Xala,** the hero (or anti-hero), El Hadji Abdou Kader Beye, is forced to submit to a ritual of humiliation made all the more spectacular by its urban setting and the use of the trappings of upper-middle class life under neo-colonialism. El Hadji suffers from the *xala,* a form of impotence caused by the curse of one who holds a grievance toward the victim. In an attempt to cure his *xala,* El Hadji has already travelled further and further from the comforts of elite, urban Dakar to seek out the services of ever more remote magical and religious practitioners. These have ranged from one who was a comic fraud, advising the middle-aged El Hadji to crawl toward the bed of his adolescent third wife carrying grotesque charms in his teeth, to Sereen Mada, a marabout, or Islamic hermit saint, renowned for his piety. The latter actually cures El Hadji's affliction, but his asceticism does not prevent him from restoring it when El Hadji's cheque bounces.

The denouement of this film and of the novel on which it is based raises a number of interesting questions, which commentators on the whole have been unable to answer and which might perhaps best be approached armed with a knowledge of certain prevalent themes in pre-colonial narratives and rituals of this region of West Africa.

One such question is why Sembene, a Marxist and a critic of some aspects of the Négritude movement's attachment to the irrational, should end a film with a ritual at all. It is apparently not the result of a sudden conversion; indeed, in the novel **Xala,** Sembene's comment on the prayers of El Hadji's pious first wife is an almost verbatim recapping of Marx's dictum on religion: "As others isolate themselves with drugs, she obtained her own daily dose from her religion."

One critic of the novel, Dorothy Blair, sees a disjunction between the bulk of the story and the ending. She suggests that Sembene, in his satirical portraits of El Hadji's circle, promises us comedy and instead "treats us to an emetic" in his sombre portrayal of El Hadji's downfall and the ritual designed to reverse it. In that ritual, El Hadji must submit to being spat upon by beggars, lepers, cripples, and assorted rejects of society. Blair sees the ritual as part of a particularly disquieting ending, in that there appears to be little hope that El Hadji will modify the corrupt ways which had led him (more than twenty years before) to cheat the beggar who leads the band out of his patrimony and, more recently, to sell rice intended for famine relief in order to finance his third marriage. Does the ritual serve any purpose, we may ask, once we rule out the possibilities that it represents either a testament to the author's religious faith or a genuine act of contrition on the part of the character?

In the program "Ousmane Sembene, Cinéaste and Novelist" broadcast by the Canadian Broadcasting Corporation (CBC) on 7 October 1980, the question was raised of a possible contradiction between Sembene's Marxism and his use of religious themes in his work. The question was answered by a reminder that, while Sembene himself is not religious, the lower-class African audience he desires to reach is religious. Themes from religion and folklore are vehicles which Sembene consciously employs to carry his message. Can we say anything, then, about Sembene's choice of ritual themes and the responses which they are likely to evoke in a West African audience? Do these themes provide a link between the social realist film and the surrealist, ritual ending? We may, perhaps, begin with the *xala* itself.

It is obvious that, as a literary conceit, the *xala* stands for the impotence of the Senegalese élite in the period which has followed independence. "What are we?" El Hadji asks the Chamber of Commerce, "Mere agents, less than petty traders. We merely redistribute. Re-distribute the remains the big men deign to leave us."

The artifice by which impotence is made a secular symbol of political and economic conditions is a modern device which will almost certainly call forth in Sembene's audience associations belonging to an older system of ideas, a belief system appropriate to an enchanted universe but in certain crucial ways equivalent in its moral judgements to Sembene's own ideology. These ideas are not specific to the Wolof or to any other Senegalese group. Rather, they may be found in the mythology, folklore, and traditional exegeses of peoples throughout Francophone West Africa and perhaps other regions. In fact, much of my data is drawn from literature on the very similar traditions of the Dogon and the Bambara. The Bambara, according to A. Adu Boahen's Introduction to the English paperback edition of ***God's Bits of Wood,*** have retained more of non-Islamic religion than any of the other groups who commonly figure in Sembene's work; and they have brought some of those preserved items into the life of Sembene's urban milieu.

Throughout the region in question, myth and ritual draw connections between impotence, arrogance, and failure in self-control, particularly control over one's sexual impulses. Mythology and folklore are full of various sorts of tricksters who challenge God, are voracious in their lust for food and women, and are punished with actual or symbolic emasculation. One cycle of legends which draws heavily upon these themes concerns a mythic werewolf who can alternate between hyena and human form. (pp. 321-23)

Hyena-men are murderers, rapists, and thieves of food supplies. Significantly, however, they can be conquered by women or by men who use women's tools or women's wiles. Often, their insatiability is itself used by these feminine figures to lure them to their downfall. In one tale collected from a Bambara girl, a monster accosts a girl on her way home after having her hair done and threatens to eat her. She agrees to return with him to his cave, where he puts his head on her knee and demands that she search for lice (a service traditionally performed by spouses or lovers). She waits till he falls asleep and kills him with her spinning equipment.

In a hyena-man myth collected among the Bozo of Mali, impotence is attributed ironically to desire for all the trappings of powerful masculinity. In this story, a stranger arrives in a village which has been terrorized by a hyena-man who murders young husbands and then rapes and kills their wives. The stranger agrees to kill the hyena-man but only if the local chief will promise to give him his office and his wives if he succeeds. The stranger assumes female form to entrap the hyena-man and is about to kill the monster during the sexual act when the latter tells him that if he does so he must remain a woman until he dies. The two finally agree that the stranger may kill the hyena-man and resume male form if he consents to permanent impotence. He does so and returns to the village, where he emasculates the chief in lieu of extracting the wives and title for which he no longer has any use. This, the widely known tale tells us, is the origin of impotence among men.

In this story about two characters who are in many ways spiritual cousins of El Hadji, the sacrifice of masculine prerogative is the price of power over the hyena-man, who himself knows no checks on his maleness. Ultimately, power over the hyena-man is power over both spiritual and physical decay. Hyena-men are followed by flies because they smell of excrement and are forbidden access to water, a medium which is not merely purifying but sacred in this region on the fringes of the Sahara.

It is interesting to see how many elements parallel to ones found in these tales crop up in the story of El Hadji and his ritual cure. The *xala* itself is impotence suffered as a result of greed and abuse of male sexual privilege. El Hadji has cheated the people of rice to take a third wife; he has cheated the beggar of his heritage to finance his early business ventures.

In other myths of this region, the act of incest is seen as a symbolic encapsulation of greed, arrogance, and unbridled lust. The most important Trickster of the Dogon and Bambara mythologies rapes his mother, the earth, attempts to rape his twin sister, vies for power with the creator God, and attempts to steal the seeds of all the plants meant to be food for men. He is punished by enforced circumcision, which traditional exegesis links to castration, and by permanent sterility, both of himself and of his crops. The theme of incest has been used by Sembene in ***White Genesis*** as a symbol for the total degeneration which has, in the case of some individuals, accompanied social change and the loss of rural values. The offender is a man of noble birth; his incestuous relationship with his daughter strips him of all moral entitlement to his privileged position. In ***White Genesis,*** the community discusses killing the incestuous father, but his family griot (a person of low caste who acts as a combination praise singer and court jester to a noble) argues that, whatever the letter of the Koran may say, every man who marries a woman as young as his daughter—a category which includes a number of pillars of the community—is guilty of incest.

El Hadji, of course, does marry such a girl. El Hadji's marriage, which is of a type Sembene has elsewhere suggested may be essentially incestuous, precipitates his downward slide. It even involves him in the theft of food grains in the form of rice belonging to the National Grain Board.

It is interesting to compare the role of the griot in **White Genesis** and in **Xala,** since Sembene has been widely quoted (for example, on the CBC program mentioned earlier) as saying that the role of the filmmaker in contemporary West Africa is akin to that of the traditional griot. The griots sang the praises of their noble patrons and also attempted to defend them against accusations by others. Conversely, they had the right to speak out and rebuke their superiors for misdeeds. Their accusations could lead to purification from sin, particularly violations of sexual restrictions and abuses of privilege, though they were of a despised caste, forbidden to marry with the free-born. Purification could thus be attained through submitting to verbal abuse from the lowly. As "griot," Sembene the novelist and filmmaker is exposing his society's misdeeds in the hope of effecting purification. The actual griots in the film, unlike the admirable griots in **White Genesis,** have been reduced to mere cyphers and entertainers. Female griots wear money pinned to their dresses while greeting guests at El Hadji's wedding, an event which epitomizes the greed, lust, and addiction to power of El Hadji and his circle.

Speechmaking at ceremonies marking changes of status (for example, at weddings or funerals) was one of the griot's traditional functions. These speeches were often highly satirical. The use of satire links the griot with joking relatives who throughout Africa have assumed the function of purification from sin and who have the privilege of insulting and abusing each other when they meet. Insult, joking, and the licence to tell the truth about another's character thus possess the power to remove sin and the afflictions caused by sin. We have already seen that in this region "sin" is largely equated with sexual lust, greed, and unmerited arrogance. The real griots in the film become greedy flatterers like the rest of society. Sembene, who aspires to the griot's role, constructs a new ritual of purification. This ritual employs a number of symbols very much in keeping with the ways prescribed for combatting pollution by traditional myth and ritual as well as with Sembene's view of social reality. Thus, the ritual does not come as an abrupt departure from the social satire of the rest of the film. It is a restatement of that socially purifying satire in terms of a few widely recognizable visual symbolic images.

This is not to say that Sembene requires belief in a theology. Indeed, Sembene has said that his film is an attack on a "double fetishism," the traditional fetishism of the marabouts and the contemporary fetishism of western commodities. To an audience familiar with their context, certain items in Sembene's ritual are simply symbolic restatements of the message that purification comes from listening to the truths known by those your society despises, abandoning greed, and ceasing to use one's status and one's sex as means for assuming the privileges of the gods. Such traditional scholarly distinctions as that between "magic" and "religion" are irrelevant to Sembene; his quest is for elements of traditional belief and practice which articulate with his own moral vision. As various types of structural and semiotic analyses of film and literature have made clear, a carefully chosen symbolic item like a child's sled and the relationship of that item to other items, present or absent, can suggest, largely unconsciously, a whole chain of associations not actually spelled out on the page or screen, and thus deliver a complex message within the confines of a poem or a film, neither of which allows for much didactic commentary.

Thus, it does not matter whether El Hadji, Sembene, or the audience "believes" in El Hadji's cure; what matters is the associations which will be evoked by the symbols employed in effecting it, particularly upon persons of West African cultural background. Moreover, since some of the items, such as a special mystic virtue adhering to the lowly, are part of the European tradition as well, some of the messages will be decoded by non-African audiences. Indeed, many of these are among the messages which Dorson sees as embedded in folk traditions generally.

What, though, *are* the precise symbols and messages in Sembene's urban proletarian ritual? Here we must look at the specific images employed in the light of our mythic themes.

In the myths and legends we have mentioned, excessive maleness must be curbed if real power over evil is to be achieved. The stranger must accept impotence (or total femininity) to conquer the hyena-man. In the trickster myths, the sequel to the forced circumcision of the trickster, which simply deprives him of male power, is a voluntary castration on the part of a god, which paradoxically restores fertility to the world. To rid himself of his *xala*, El Hadji must, like some of the opponents of hyena-man, accept an appurtenance of femininity—one, moreover, belonging to a female he had hoped to conquer and had given to him in her stead. While the beggars spit on him, he must wear the crown from his third wife's wedding veil. Crowns on weddings veils are, in fact, a European symbol, which in this context may be associated with two different social ironies: the lowering of status, which Africans accept when they seek the tokens of prestige of their oppressors; and the subordination to a master, which women have traditionally accepted when they put on stately garments for their wedding ceremonies. In the traditional African context, the male acceptance of the feminine principle in order to acquire power over pollution was not intended to effect the emancipation of women; indeed, the statement made by males in such roles depends upon an equivalence between femininity and subordination. It takes, however, only a slight twist to add a new secular meaning to this symbolism. If the gods are not to step into the power vacuum left by men who acknowledge their limitations, as was traditionally the case, women may move

Ousmane directing the wedding party scene in Xala.

into that gap. This would certainly be consistent with Sembene's generally intense concern and respect for African women, upon which many critics have remarked.

Not only does El Hadji wear a woman's wedding crown, but the pajama bottoms he clutches around his waist and his massive wristwatch adjacent to his naked chest accord him less dignity than the total nudity allowed him in the novel. They are pathetic trappings of former glory, their incongruousness a product of his harboring of toys of the colonizer and the dependency such harboring has brought about.

During the spitting, the foreground of the set is occupied by rows of empty bottles which once contained the soft drinks and mineral waters which El Hadji, at the height of his arrogance, employed to separate himself from even the waters of his native land. Hyena-men and other evil forces in myth are punished by being banned from the rivers and by the failure of rain to water their crops; the action of **Xala** takes place against a background of devastating drought. It is symbolic of the entire nature of El Hadji's "power" that he has been dependent upon bottled water from Europe even to wash his car; the car washing scene and the ritual scene are linked visually by the presence in both of a plastic pail, prominently placed on the right side of the screen. When El Hadji is finally forced to share his foreign waters with his countrymen, the fluid from the empty bottles is returned to him in the form of their spit.

Those who would assume high status in African societies, that is to say nobles and divine kings, are frequently forced to undergo abuse from those over whom they would elevate themselves. The griots' privilege of abusing their betters to remind them of their duties is one example of this type of social fact; in all cases, the spiritual well-being of the entire community depends on the abuse. A secular equivalent of this sort of practice is very evident in the ritual degradation of El Hadji. He is surrounded by a total cross-section of the lower orders of society, those over whom his kind have assumed superiority: beggars, cripples, his disinherited kinsman, and a peasant who has been robbed of his entire community's pathetic savings by the cowboy-hatted successor to El Hadji's seat in the Chamber of Commerce. There is even a student in jeans and workshirt. Like El Hadji, he has adopted European dress, but it is not the evening dress or business suit of El Hadji's cronies; rather it is the universal uniform which the international student community donned at a certain point in its history to demonstrate solidarity with the oppressed. This student, with his Wolof language newspaper, strikes a somewhat discordant note among the rags of the beggars. (Sembene's treatment of El Hadji's student activist daughter throughout the film has indicated that he appreciates both the good intentions and the limitations of children of the privileged classes who wish to lead revolutions.)

These are the people who strip El Hadji down to size, but in this case there is no noble role to which he may then return, suitably purified. He, too, has become one of the wretched of the earth, but the house and furniture which he has been prudent enough to put in his wife's name will insulate him from the full purifying effect of his wretchedness.

Traditional resolutions of the paradoxes of power depended upon the good will of gods whose existence Sembene does not recognize; a modern resolution to our ritual drama would require political good will which is equally nonexistent. Sembene can only use ritual trappings to define the terms of what Wole Soyinka has called his "aggressive, secular vision." Because he cannot accept the false resolution of mystification, either traditional mystification or that revived by the Négritude movement, Sembene is left still awaiting a real solution to the paradoxes whose symbols he has forced us to observe. Meanwhile, he will attempt to use the cinema to restore a voice to those whose claims were heard in folklore and ritual but whom colonial and post-colonial discourse have silenced. (pp. 323-27)

Harriet D. Lyons, "The Uses of Ritual in Sembene's 'Xala'," in Canadian Review of African Studies, *Vol. 18, No. 2, 1984, pp. 319-28.*

Meredith Tax

Everything is there for a reason in the novels of Ousmane Sembene, the Senegalese writer, filmmaker, and sometime political prisoner. His style, simple realism on the surface, has remarkable symbolic depth. In his best-known book, **God's Bits of Wood,** about the 1947 railway strike on the Dakar-Niger line, modern history, tribal customs, ordinary lives, great scenes of mass battle, and several love stories are thrown together in a marvelous stew that simmers and boils with life. **God's Bits of Wood** has one of the best-drawn revolutionary heroes in fiction, the strike leader Bakayoko. Here is his speech at the great public meeting in Dakar, called by the French governor and trade union leaders to prevent a general strike after the railroad management has refused to negotiate with the union:

It seems that this strike is the work of a little group of black sheep, led by foreigners. If this is so, there must be a lot of black sheep in this country; and you, who know us all, look at me and tell me who are the foreigners. It seems also that we are incapable of creating anything by ourselves, but we must be of some use because, since we stopped working, the trains have stopped running . . .

Monsieur le gouverneur, Monsieur le deputé, the

old lady you see there before you is Grandmother Fatou Wade. She lost her husband in the first war and her older son in the second. They gave her these medals, which have no value to her, and now they have put her younger son in prison because he was on strike. She has nothing left. *Monsieur le gouverneur, Monsieur le deputé,* take back these medals and give her her son and her daily rice in exchange!

Naturally a general strike is declared after a speech like this. One of the main demands of the strikers is pay equal to that of the trainmen in France. They want family allowances as well. The French refuse to consider this: Senegal is Moslem, and many of the trainworkers are polygamous. Why should the French have to pay for more than one wife, much less all those children: "to give in on the question of family allowances was much more than a matter of agreeing to a compromise with striking workers; it would amount to recognition of a racial aberrance, a ratification of the customs of inferior beings. It would be giving in, not to workers but to Negroes," and that they would not do. The family allowance is one of the chief demands of the women because they are starving.

One morning a woman rose and wrapped her cloth firmly around her waist and said, "Today, I will bring back something to eat." And the men began to understand that if the times were bringing forth a new breed of men, they were also bringing forth a new breed of woman.

At the beginning of the novel, these women are still living traditionally, despite the changes wrought by the white men and their machines. Then comes the six-month strike: famine, danger, their water supply cut off by the French. One day old Ramatoulaye kills and butchers an enormous ram belonging to her rich brother, El Hadji Mabigue; the animal has rampaged around the courtyard and eaten the children's few grains of rice. Within hours the police have surrounded her courtyard.

The women were on the verge of panic. They scarcely recognized the woman beside them as the Ramatoulaye they had always known, and they asked themselves where she had found this new strength. She had always been quiet and unassuming and gentle with the children. . . . Where, then, had this violence been born? . . . The answer was as simple as the woman herself. It had been born beside a cold fireplace, in an empty kitchen.

She took a step toward the white officer. "Go away now," she said in French. "This is a house for us, not a house for white men . . . "

On all sides of her the other women began brandishing bottles filled with sand, flatirons, and clubs of all shapes and sizes. In a few minutes the group of policemen was completely encircled.

By participating in the strike, these wives, like the women in *The Salt of the Earth,* come to a place they have not been before. Society can never again be as it was.

Though crowds of angry women have been a force in historical novels since *A Tale of Two Cities,* it is only in our own time that such a crowd could become not just background or local color, but part of that collective hero, the people. If the historical novel finds new life in the United States, you can be sure that women, workers, and third world peoples will be more than extras in these dramas. For that is a central meaning of the history of our times and of the promise we hold for the future. (pp. 8-9)

> *Meredith Tax, in a review of "God's Bits of Wood," in* VLS, *No. 41, December, 1985, pp. 8-9.*

Brenda F. Berrian

If there is one enduring presentation in African literature it is the African mother. From the Soundiata epic to the epistolary novel, *Une si longue lettre* (1979) by the deceased Mariama Bâ, reverence for the African mother is expressed in various forms. In the past, the traditional African mother has been a Queen Mother, a trader, a soldier, an organizer of protest demonstrations, and the nurturer of future generations of children. Cognizant of the role that the mother plays in African societies is Ousmane Sembène, who prefers to set his female characters in their traditional settings as mothers and wives, in order to illustrate specific political and social points of view. Through the women, Sembène notes that in order for them to have new perceptions of themselves and to develop a more defined self-awareness, their men should no longer be the determining factor in their lives. Sembène is convinced that changes in social and political structures and attitudes in Africa are necessary if the African woman is to realize her full potential and importance in the future of her country.

A self-taught man, writer, and filmmaker from Senegal, Sembène is devoted to writing about African people and their aspirations. Most importantly, he is one of the first African writers to move his female characters from a secondary role, in which they compliment their men, to a primary one in which they express their feelings, hurts, joys, and think and react to pressing situations. For instance, in four selected short stories from *Voltaïque. Nouvelles* (1962) [*Tribal Scars*], Sembène introduces his mother who demands custody of her children at a divorce hearing; the mother who defies a tyrannical king in defense of her daughter; the mother who confronts her neglectful husband with his callousness, and finally, the mother who comes to terms with her marriage to a much older man.

In the short story, **"The Bilal's Fourth Wife,"** Sembène slips in modern ideas about marriage and divorce in a traditional village setting where he presents the couple, Suliman and Yacine. Suliman, a man past middle-age, takes great pains to present himself as a pious, devout Moslem and family man before the public whereas, in private, he berates and beats his three wives unmercifully. His appetite for women younger than his daughters has not waned, and he takes advantage of his position as the bilal of the village mosque to make lecherous remarks and to fondle them. Because of his carefully preserved public image as a humble man and a guardian of polygamy, the young victimized women dare not complain expecting that their cries of outrage would not be believed. As the story prog-

resses, Suliman is so consumed with his lust for young women that he fails to keep the mosque clean. Sympathetic male villagers take it upon themselves to find a fourth wife for Suliman in the person of the young, Yacine N'Doye.

Yacine, a 20-year-old former "tomboy," is deemed to be a good candidate for Suliman's fourth wife for she has frightened the young men in the village with her outspokenness. Presumably, an older man like Suliman will be able to tame and mold her into a submissive wife, since it is assumed that she is naive and ignorant of her rights and sexual desires as a woman. Although Yacine would have liked to raise some objections, she follows her father's wishes and marries Suliman. Later, after three years of marriage and a son, the bored Yacine takes Suliman's nephew as her lover, as Suliman's sexual drive is diminishing. Her decision to take a lover is justifiable, for, in her mind, she is in her physical prime and married to a man she does not love. However, this triangle—wife, husband, and lover—becomes the main topic of village gossip when Yacine bears a son for her lover. In an attempt to salvage his tarnished image and manhood, Suliman vents his rage and jealousy upon his three wives and demands a divorce from Yacine. To his surprise, his demand receives a rebuttal from Yacine.

In **"The Bilal's Fourth Wife"** Sembène, with great humor, pokes fun at Senegalese attitudes toward divorce. He attacks the practice of double moral standards, which place women at a disadvantage. Sembène uses the character of Yacine to question and to disagree with the patriarchal Moslem marriage rules drawn up by males centuries ago. In spite of the rumors and intense external pressures, Yacine reveals a tremendous self-confidence. First, she refuses to be coerced by Suliman and her family into a divorce. Second, she is adamant about being treated on equal footing as a woman by the Cadi (special council of male elders called to review her case). Third, she questions why the woman is not free to take a lover when a man in a Moslem society can have four wives with the approval of the Koran and legal laws. These unyielding stances force the male elders to accept, with reluctance, the fact that there are two sides to every marital disagreement, and the woman's position is just as important as the man's.

As for Suliman, he has been made the laughing stock of the village by his inability to control his wife. His ego suffers a beating due to his physical limitations of not satisfying his young wife's sexual needs. What is at stake is Suliman's determination to humiliate Yacine publicly, for she has flaunted her relationship with his nephew with the birth of a child. Double standards, which govern the behavior of men and women in a Moslem polygamous marriage, are addressed again when Suliman asks for custody of his "son" and the return of the dowry.

Suliman does not regard Yacine as a human being who has feelings and rights, but as one of his possessions who is expected to boost his ego. A woman's place, he feels, is to obey her husband and to build her life around him. When his possession (Yacine) no longer brings him pleasure or bends to his needs, he must squash or beat it into submission as he has done with the other three wives. Since Yacine will not conform and retreat into the expected docility, Suliman tries to use psychological pressure and works within the traditional legal system to bring about her downfall. He becomes obsessed with the need to cause Yacine deep pain. Yacine's indiscretion must be exposed to draw attention away from his own inadequacies.

As mentioned before, through Yacine's protests and the divorce hearing, Sembène brings forth the argument that traditional Moslem marriage laws should be reevaluated and rewritten to protect the rights of women too. In support of Sembène's argument, Yacine demands that Suliman should return her virginity knowing full-well that virginity is highly prized and is linked to one's honor and esteem. With this brave announcement, she makes clear that something precious has been taken away from her—her honor and respectability.

Yacine's request to have her virginity returned is a clever tactic and approach in presenting her case in court. She knows that she was more valuable when she was chaste and that her value dropped with her affair with Suliman's nephew, making her second-hand merchandise. Suliman too cannot bear knowing that his wife has been handled by somebody else. His pride and respect have been challenged. He also fears Yacine's power over him—the power of informing the villagers of his sexual weakness.

Since Suliman cannot physically return Yacine's virginity and make her "pure as spring water" again, Yacine hopes that her request will enable the villagers to be more sympathetic toward her. The question then becomes why should women in Moslem marriages hand over the custody of their children to their former husbands. Fortunately, Froh-Toll, the head of the Cadi, is wise enough to debate the custody topic and rules in favor of Yacine with the statement:

> So by what right does Suliman demand custody
> of the child? There can always be doubt as to
> who is the father of a child. But never as to who
> is the mother.

With this pronouncement, Froh-Toll supports women's child rearing rights, which is an admirable step.

In Moslem societies, attitudes toward adultery are one-sided. Traditional customs tend to endorse the fact that married men engaged in extra-marital affairs cannot commit adultery, only women. The Senegalese society is built upon a patriarchal system with a Moslem/Christian/Animist religious foundation. As a consequence, the person who passes judgement on men and women is a man; the society, in which men and women operate, is male dominated. In the eyes of traditional Moslem law, the man's word is accepted as being truthful and binding, but the woman's word does not have the status and legitimacy. So while Suliman is not chastised for engaging in a sexual act with a young woman in the village, the villagers agree that Yacine should be punished for her affair. Yacine's actions upset the value system, which supports the idea that women must be faithful to their husbands. Consequently, her conscious revolt becomes a social act against the antiquated Moslem divorce laws and ingrained value systems.

Sembène's short story, **"The Mother,"** is another example of the application of double moral standards in a Moslem society in Africa. This point is presented through the personnage of the tyrannical king. The king, who has no intentions of cultivating the love and respect of his constituents, alienates himself and evokes the hatred and fear of his subjects to the point that they dream about seeing him burnt alive. Meanwhile, these same subjects are passive and obey the king's orders to murder men over fifty-years old. Thus, the king thinks that he owes no allegiance to anyone. He proceeds to pass a law that he will deflower every virgin before she is married. Over the years, only a few brave mothers succeed in saving their daughters from such a fate. When it is time for the king's daughter to marry, he repeals the law—separate rules for the poor and rich.

For the king, women represent danger, and he wishes to destroy them. By his actions, it appears that he harbours a deep hatred for women and cannot resist raping them. This psychological deviant is confused, insecure, and enjoys exerting his power through violent means. The king obviously likes inflicting pain upon women, because they are said to be the weaker sex.

Since nobody has the courage to defy the king's orders, the people's fears increase. It is only when the king travels that he encounters open resistance to his overtures from a young woman he fancies. In anger he has her locked up. The young woman's mother, a woman of "certain age," fights and pushes past the six feet tall servants to gain an audience with the king. The mother verbally battles and accuses him of outlandish and unfit behavior. Further, she courageously looks the king directly in his eyes and attacks him for not showing any respect for the mothers in the kingdom. She makes the point that without the love and tenderness of his mother he would not have been born. The king responds by slapping her face.

The subjects jump to the mother's defense after the king's display of anger and guilt. The mother's words had hit their target shaming the remaining males in the kingdom for their cowardice and failure to protect their women folk. The king's rule has been divisive and had led to the distrust of one another to the detriment of the society. This exhibition of internal strength and resilience by the mother topples the king's government. One conclusion is that anyone, male or female, who abuses power will not keep it.

Clearly, the king and the mother during their confrontation had struck each other in their most vulnerable spots, he on her face, and she at his ego. Yet a reversal of roles emerges for the so-called weak, defenseless mother becomes the stronger of the two. Without his bodyguards to shield him, the king, like most bullies, is defenseless. His deliberate attempt to limit the freedom of women ultimately results in the loss of his kingdom as a consequence of the words spoken by the African mother.

There is another interesting aspect in the Mother's depiction. One could say that Sembène has succumbed to one of the biased attitudes directed toward women when he describes the mother as ugly. However, it could also be said that Sembène deliberately calls the mother ugly, be-cause of its common use in Senegalese society for strong-willed women. In African literature the good woman, who stays in her place, is always gentle, kind, and beautiful, but the woman, who possesses the courage to debate male pre-rogatives, is frequently labeled or pictured as a physically ugly person. Thus Sembène ends this story by singing praises in honor of mothers who rise up to protect their children.

This particular story argues that one's biological origin and sex do not alleviate one's responsibility to the collec-tive community. Making the female character in **"The Mother"** bigger than life is characteristic of Sembène in both his films and literary works to convince and draw at-tention to the African woman's special place in contempo-rary African society. The men, in the story **"The Mother,"** were paralyzed with fear and failed to challenge the mani-acal orders of the king. They also did nothing to over-throw the king-dictator. It was the woman, the mother, who came to the men's rescue. By magnifying the charac-ter of the mother Sembène scolds the men for their moral impotence and reproaches them for their lack of position action to oppose the king's oppressive policies.

The mother has done what is necessary to save and protect her daughter. She is, as [Anne] Lippert would say, "super human in her love." The mother may be ugly on the out-side, but she is beautiful inside with her concern for her child's misfortune. She possesses spiritual qualities which allow her to look directly into the king's evil heart. This special power permits the mother to weave a hypnotic spell on the male listeners, causes them to grab the king, and renders them half-conscious of the fact that they have aided the mother in her triumph over the king.

Mores of another kind are explored in the short story, **"Her Three Days,"** where one meets Noumbé, the third wife of Mustapha. When the story opens Noumbé is pre-paring for her husband's visit during her allotted three days as dictated by the Koran. Drawing upon his film-making skills Sembène zooms in on Noumbé to show her haggard face, her weakened body after the bearing of five children in rapid succession, her anxieties and fears of being replaced by the fourth wife, and her fight to handle a heart condition. Although Noumbé is still young, she looks older because of her full financial duties of providing for her children.

In a sympathetic voice Sembène attacks the misuse of po-lygamy. If a man marries more than one wife, he is to treat them equally and not differentiate between them. This is a difficult task and even the best of men find that there is always one wife that he prefers among the group. For this reason, the remaining wives do not enjoy their husbands' companionship on an equal basis. In **"Her Three Days"** Mustapha prefers his fourth and youngest wife. It is his fourth wife's turn to be flattered and spoiled by him, and he casts aside his other three wives.

Relying upon a technique that worked successfully in *Les bouts de bois de Dieu* (1960), Sembène delays Mustapha's entrance until the last pages of the short story. In this way, Mustapha is seen through Noumbé's eyes and thoughts.

Hence, Mustapha is known before he actually appears in the text. Leaving Mustapha's entrance until the end of **"Her Three Days"** creates the necessary suspense and en-ables the sensitive reader to feel the internal struggles and pains that Noumbé undergoes during her long wait for Mustapha. With this combination of sympathy for Noum-bé and tension it is not impossible to understand why she lashes out at Mustapha on the eve of his arrival on the third day.

During these three days of waiting Noumbé has cooked Mustapha's favorite dishes, beautified herself, dressed with extreme care, saved the meat, and borrowed money from her next-door neighbor to ensure Mustapha's com-fort. When Mustapha does not show after two days and fails to send a message, Noumbé's physical pain is almost as great as her mental pain. While dosing herself with medicine to prevent a heart attack, Noumbé wonders why she and her three co-wives allow themselves to be Mustapha's playmates and wives of one man. She contem-plates divorce, the hypocrisy of the co-wives in their pre-tense of happiness, and ponders how to escape from such an unsatisfying and demeaning relationship.

Apparently, these thoughts frighten Noumbé somewhat because they are in contradiction with her upbringing. She has been raised to be a submissive wife dependent upon her husband's whims, just as Mustapha's personality and behavior have been formed by years of indoctrination that the male is the dominant person in a male/female relation-ship. As his "right" and with the support of Moslem doc-trines the acquisition of four wives is linked with his viril-ity and manliness. As for Noumbé she has achieved status and esteem with her marriage and the births of her five children. Companionship, mutual respect, and sharing are not part of the bargain.

Mustapha has an exaggerated sense of his ego and mascu-linity. With an air of impatience he comes to see Noumbé at the end of the third day demanding that she serve him and his two male companions. No words of comfort or apologies pass across his lips. In response, Noumbé dis-plays a sarcastic side of her personality in an attempt to preserve some shred of dignity. This small rebellious act brings on a mild heart attack, and Mustapha calmly leaves Noumbé to fend for herself while announcing his horror and disbelief that the Malian government has just passed a resolution condemning polygamy.

The collectivity of female support in the compound is demonstrated when the women rush to Noumbé's aid. It is characteristic of Sembène to show how the women come together and lend each other their strength and advice. On the first day of Noumbé's three days of waiting the women sing to share Noumbé's happiness and unconcealed joy. When Mustapha fails to show up, Aida, the next-door neighbor, kindly helps Noumbé and offers to keep her company. For fear of hurting her feelings the women stay away from Noumbé and avoid meeting her eyes so that she can save "face." However, they all run to her defense when she collapses from the strain of asserting herself be-fore Mustapha. In short, the women come together be-cause they know that their turn to be the displaced wife is coming. Still, Noumbé is resolved to be a mother and resigned to joining ranks with her abandoned co-wives. She once loved Mustapha, but she now rejects him. Her sense of self-worth is linked with common sense and necessity; therefore, she will not leave Mustapha for she is entrenched in Moslem traditions.

Without a doubt, Sembène wants his readers to note that Noumbé is a victim of circumstances. At the same time, he wants his readers to know that African women are also guilty of accepting rules imposed upon them and are responsible for some of the social evils. Noumbé's physical pain ties in with her timid knowledge that she is not pleased with her marriage. She submerges the thought that she is a playmate, since it is uncharacteristic for a devoted wife to question her plight. All of her life Noumbé has been groomed to be a good wife and mother, but not at the expense of her dignity. The waiting and the slow disintegration of hope cause her to mock Mustapha, who throws around his authority. Sembène's silent suggestion is that it is up to African men and women to solve their difficulties and take the initiative to improve their lot.

By lingering over Noumbé's suffering, jealousy, loneliness, and anger Sembène pleads the case against the African male's misuse of polygamy: their failure to treat each wife equally in all ways, including their failure to provide each with adequate financial, temporal and emotional support.

Like Noumbé, Nafi in **"Letters from France"** has been raised in a patriarchal society where man rules over woman, and one class over another. Viewed as a second-class citizen by her society and father, she is tricked into marrying a 73-year old man, who lives in Marseilles, France. The topic of love is not entertained for marriage is based on loneliness, a wish to live in France, and an old man's desire to retain his lost youth. Nafi, the young wife, will serve Demba, her husband, be an instrument for his pleasure, bear his children, greet his friends, and care for him in his old age. By selecting a young wife, like Suliman in **"The Bilal's Fourth Wife,"** Demba hopes that she will be easier to control and thereby gain much from the unbalanced relationship. Unfortunately, the carefully laid plan backfires when Demba succumbs to cancer.

Alone in a damp room with four walls in Marseilles, Nafi has plenty of time to reflect upon her situation and to examine, in a proper perspective, the social and moral values that are imposed upon Senegalese women. What she sees and comes to terms with (as Yacine and Noumbé did) is that she has to bear some of the blame for her marriage. She also must admit that she was initially pleased with the possibility of living in France, and smitten with the picture of a handsome young Senegalese man. The adjustment and the astonishment occur when Nafi arrives in Marseilles to learn that the young man in the photo is actually seventy-three-years old.

In isolation for the first time in her life, cut off from sunshine, gaiety, and human warmth, Nafi rebels through the medium of letters to her girl friend in Senegal. She implores her anonymous girl friend, who is her link with the happy past, to believe in her. Nafi feels that she has touched "rock bottom" with her marriage to Demba. She is furious that she has married an old, unemployed man

without a pension, cannot bear for him to touch her, and even wishes to contract a mysterious disease. As the story develops, Nafi is reduced to begging for a job for her husband with a shipping company, when she learns that she is pregnant. Divorce is contemplated, but she has no independent means and no friends to turn to for aid in Marseilles. Nafi's future brightens, however, when Demba is given a short-term job on a ship, sends money to her, and asks a young dock worker, Arona, to watch over her. Closed in with a crying baby, sad to find that Demba has cancer upon his return, but miserable enough not to play the role of a grieving wife, **"Letters from France"** reaches a melodramatic climax when Nafi tells Demba, on his death bed, that she is returning to Senegal.

Demba's elderly friends are greatly disappointed in Nafi for her failure to conform and exhibit some compassion for Demba. Nafi's explanation is that she is in an incompatible marriage locked in by loneliness. Her dreams to be independent and her own mistress haunt her. Nafi is not ashamed to confess to her girl friend that she had wished for Demba's death in order to be free. Nevertheless, her release does not come until the same elderly friends of Demba meet to decide her fate. Thanks to Arona's intervention she does not have to be hypocritical by mourning Demba for the required 40 days. The decision is that she will be sent back home.

With bitterness and relief, Nafi's past, present, and future have been monitored by male decisions. She is basically shy and innocent in Marseilles and finds it difficult to relate to the French and other Blacks. Nafi, who has some formal education, is a traditional young woman, who is not satisfied with her life. Although she protests loudly to her girl friend in her letters, she lacks the independence to rebel. Without recognizing it, Nafi is tied to her beliefs in the security of the clan and the extended family. There is an awareness that times are changing, but this does not lead her to disobey her father and husband. It is Demba's death that frees her from despair and makes it possible for her to return to Senegal.

Martin T. Bestman notes that: "Sembène paints the image of Africa that is convulsive, a world that questions its norms and values." Indeed, Sembène does not hesitate to take to task such explosive topics as child paternity, adultery, arranged polygamous marriages, tyrannical men, divorce, child custody, and the imposition of double moral standards upon women. He identifies these issues and explores them in his fiction as a committed social critic. Sembène is committed to defending the rights of African women by insisting that they need to reclaim the economic, political, and social positions that they had held in the past. He is not afraid to expose the contradictions that control people's actions, and the collision with their menfolk that occurs when women assert themselves.

Sembène's female characters are not losers. In the four short stories each woman triumphs no matter how small the victory. By presenting such women Sembène opens up opportunities for African women to develop a more positive self-awareness and to draw upon capacities that have laid dormant within themselves. In order for Senegalese women to move forward, they must cast off outdated ideas and modes of behavior and view their plight realistically. In short, they must place themselves on the outside in order to look in. By doing so, they may begin to take steps to eliminate ignorance and mass illiteracy and improve their status in the twentieth-century. All four women—Yacine, the mother, Noumbé, and Nafi—challenge the traditional order, which condemned them to a secondary role. They, as mothers, are believable as characters. They, as mothers and women, through the prism of social and political contexts, will turn their faces to the future with hope for the future generation, their children. (pp. 195-204)

> *Brenda F. Berrian, "Through Her Prism of Social and Political Contexts: Sembène's Female Characters in 'Tribal Scars',"* in Ngambika: Studies of Women in African Literature, *edited by Carole Boyce Davies and Anne Adams Graves, Africa World Press, Inc., 1986, pp. 195-204.*

FURTHER READING

Bayo, Ogunjimi. "Ritual Archetypes—Ousmane's Aesthetic Medium in *Xala*." *Ufahamu: Journal of the African Activist Association,* No. 3 (1985): 128-38.
    Examines Ousmane's use of cultural motifs to express modern social structures.

Harrow, Kenneth. "Art and Ideology in *Les Bouts de bois de Dieu:* Realism's Artifices." *The French Review* 62, No. 3 (February 1989): 483-93.
    Assesses the structure of *Les bouts de bois de Dieu* as a realist technique.

Iyam, David Uru. "The Silent Revolutionaries: Ousmane Sembène's 'Emitai,' 'Xala,' and 'Ceddo'." *The African Studies Review* 29, No. 4 (December 1986): 79-87.
    Examines characters in *Emitai, Xala,* and *Ceddo* whose personalities remain indeterminate for much of the films. In this way, according to Iyam, Ousmane "is able to stem the empathy of the audience while leaving it free to make its decisions according to the general flow of the story."

McGilligan, Patrick and Perry, G. M. "Ousmane Sembene: An Interview." *Film Quarterly* XXVI, No. 3 (Spring 1973): 36-42.
    Interview with Ousmane on the role of the artist and the state of cinematography in Africa.

Ojo, S. Ade. "Revolt, Violence and Duty in Ousmane Sembene's *God's Bits of Wood*." *Nigeria* 53, No. 3 (July-September 1985): 58-68.
    Discusses *God's Bits of Wood* as a Marxist-inspired protest novel.

Ousmane, Sembene and Weaver, Harold. "Interview." *Issue* 11, No. 4 (Winter 1972): 58-64.
    Ousmane answers questions about his film *Emitai*.

Pfaff, Françoise. *The Cinema of Ousmane Sembene, A Pioneer of African Film*. Westport, Conn.: Greenwood Press, 1984, 207p.
    Study of Ousmane's career and influences, including detailed analyses of individual films.

Sevastakis, Michael. "Neither Gangsters Nor Dead Kings." *FLQ: Film Library Quarterly* 6, No. 3 (Summer 1973): 13-23, 40-48.
    Examines Ousmane's films *La Noire de . . . , Borom Sarret, Mandabi, Tauw,* and *Emitai* as products of a "cautious revolutionary" who offers his characters no escape from their plights.

Dawn Powell

1897-1965

American novelist, short story writer, playwright, scriptwriter, and critic.

Powell was praised for her biting satirical wit and trenchant social observations in her work but never attained the popular or critical reputation that many, including such literary figures as Ernest Hemingway and Edmund Wilson, felt she deserved. Her best known books are set in New York City's Greenwich Village from the 1930s to the 1960s, and typically focus on the glamorous yet decadent lifestyles of bohemians, barflies, social climbers, and other types who populate that area. Diana Trilling remarked on Powell's anonymous literary status: "Miss Powell, one of the wittiest women around, suggests the answer to the old question, 'Who really makes the jokes that Dorothy Parker gets the credit for?' " Gore Vidal attributed Powell's lack of popularity to a male-dominated literary elite and to the notion that "she was that unthinkable monster, a witty woman who felt no obligation to make a single, much less a final, down payment on Love or the Family; she saw life with a bright Petronian neutrality, and every host at life's feast was a potential Trimalchio to be sent up."

The daughter of a traveling salesman, Powell was largely raised by relatives in different parts of the Midwest following the death of her mother when she was six years old. Her father later married a woman who one day, according to Powell, "burned up all the stories I was writing, a form of discipline I could not endure. With thirty cents earned by picking berries I ran away, ending up in the home of a kind aunt in Shelby, Ohio." In 1918, Powell escaped the small-town existence she later described as monotonous in her books by traveling to New York City as a member of the Red Cross. Remaining in the city following World War I, Powell published her first novel, *Whither,* after several failed attempts to become a dramatist. This work drew scant critical attention, but Powell gained a growing readership beginning with her next novel, *She Walks in Beauty.* Set in a small midwestern town, *She Walks in Beauty* focuses on two daughters; the elder, Linda, is a narcissist who is ashamed of her impoverished life at her Aunt Jane's boardinghouse, while the younger, Dorrie, embraces her situation. *Dance Night,* a novel set in Lamptown, "the toughest town in Ohio," explores lovelessness through its depiction of Morry, the disatisfied son of a traveling salesman, and Jen, an orphan whom he befriends. The bleakness of the characters' lives is emphasized in the conclusion when Morry's mother kills his father after years of tolerating false accusations of adultery. Mary Ross commented: "[*Dance Night*] is unusually direct and unassuming work, clear and sturdy in its grasp of homely, even hateful things. But in this sturdiness there is a kind of joy in living, in feeling experience whole, that gives illuminating delicacy to its handling of emotion. It

has that fundamental respect for human nature which is the essence of sympathy."

Beginning with *Turn, Magic Wheel,* Powell initiated a series of books set in and around Manhattan and Greenwich Village that some critics have designated her New York cycle. Her emphasis on exposing the foibles of New York society led many reviewers to classify these works as satires. However, Powell insisted that "I don't think satire is what I do. I think it's realism. It's not making fun. It's just telling the truth." She also stated: "[My] novels are based on the fantastic designs made by real human beings earnestly laboring to maladjust themselves to fate. . . . I give them their heads. They furnish their own nooses." *Turn, Magic Wheel* revolves around the Manhattan world of publishers and writers, of the wealthy and the famous, and of those who aspire to wealth and fame. Effie, a charming, middle-aged woman, has organized her life around the seemingly futile belief that her husband, Andrew Callingham, a famous novelist presumably based on Ernest Hemingway, will return to her after fifteen years' absence. Dennis Orphen, an inventive young novelist and recurring character in Powell's narratives whom Gore Vidal called "a male surrogate for Powell herself," believes he has treated her pathetic situation realistically in an unauthorized *roman à clef.* As is typical in Powell's works, however, expectations are defeated, and Callingham returns to Effie. *The Happy Island* centers on Prudence Bly, an intelligent, witty young woman who is prompted by her lover's infidelity to reassess her lifestyle. After becoming involved with an unassuming young playwright from her home town in Ohio, Prudence rejects the pressures of urban life and moves with him to the countryside. She soon tires of rural life, however, and returns to New York City after realizing she has adapted better to urban values.

Powell's next novel, *Angels on Toast,* focuses upon two philandering businessmen who travel to Chicago and become involved in secret love affairs that end in farces of cross-purposes. The machinations of urban society are the subject of *A Time to Be Born,* in which a beautiful and opportunistic young woman becomes the celebrated wife of a powerful publisher by exploiting the abilities and ideas of others. Rose Feld commented on *A Time to Be Born:* "To say it's brilliant, it's witty, it's penetrating, it's mature isn't enough. . . . Because there is something more in this volume than the exercise of a mind that is as daring as it is keen; there is emotional flavor and pungency which make it greater than an intellectual tour de force." In her autobiographical novel *My Home Is Far Away,* Powell relates the story of three children who are passed amongst their relatives following the death of their mother. When their father remarries and the children are subjected to the arbitrary discipline of a neurotic stepmother, the most self-reliant daughter decides to pursue her literary ambitions in Cleveland.

Powell's later novels, in which she subtly portrays the demise of New York café society, are generally regarded as more exact in subject, execution, and style than her earlier works. *The Locusts Have No King,* for example, depicts the frustrations of a typical group of rootless Manhattanites. This work features Frederick Olliver, a shy, indigent young writer living in Greenwich Village who appears in several of Powell's novels. In *The Locusts Have No King,* Frederick is driven by a failed love affair with a sensitive young female playwright to become involved with a self-absorbed, promiscuous woman who serves as an appropriate target for Powell's venomous wit. Her next novel, *The Wicked Pavilion,* is set in and around the Café Julien, a fictional locale similar to New York City's Lafayette Café, where Powell and other bohemian figures of her circle often met for drinks and conversation. As the Café Julien is destroyed at the book's conclusion, Dennis Orphen recognizes the event as heralding the end of an era. Powell's last novel, *The Golden Spur,* is named for an old New York bar where Jonathan Jaimison, a provincial from Ohio, journeys after discovering that he was the illegitimate child of a famous man. Jonathan's search eventually involves three men, each of whom attempts to play the prospect to his own advantage.

(See also *Contemporary Authors,* Vols. 5-8, rev. ed.)

PRINCIPAL WORKS

NOVELS

Whither 1925

She Walks in Beauty 1928
The Bride's House 1929
Dance Night 1930
The Tenth Moon 1932
The Story of a Country Boy 1934
Turn, Magic Wheel 1936
The Happy Island 1938
Angels on Toast 1940; also published as *A Man's Affair* [revised edition], 1956
A Time to Be Born 1942
My Home Is Far Away 1944
The Locusts Have No King 1948
The Wicked Pavilion 1954
A Cage for Lovers 1957
The Golden Spur 1962

OTHER

Big Night (play) 1933
Jig-Saw (play) 1934
Sunday, Monday and Always (short stories) 1952

Edith H. Walton

Although she has lampooned metropolitan manners in her plays, Dawn Powell is best known as a novelist of small-town life. This label, obviously, is too limited. . . . Miss Powell is as wickedly at home in the city as ever she was in the hinterland. ***Turn, Magic Wheel,*** an ironic comedy of Manhattan, carries a cruel flavor of authenticity in every satirical line. Miss Powell's approach differs from John O'Hara's, but about the side of New York which she knows best she is almost equally biting. Amusing and witty as it is, this tale of publishers and writers, of night-club addicts and the padded rich, is not precisely comfortable to read.

Miss Powell's heroine, and the character whom she takes most seriously, is a charming, gracious woman in her early forties who has based her whole existence on a delusive dream. Fifteen years ago Effie's husband deserted her for another woman, and she, in the best tradition of sportsmanship, bade him godspeed. Since then Andrew Callingham, in his self-imposed exile abroad, has become a novelist of extraordinary repute, and Effie, at home, proudly and loyally upholds his legend. . . . [She] cherishes a secret, romantic hope that some day he will return to her.

To Dennis Orphen, a clever young novelist with a ravenous curiosity about other people's lives, Effie's romantic story offers tantalizing material. Though they are intimate friends, seeing each other daily; though he has an angry pity for her, though his attitude is one of half-worshiping affection, Dennis cannot resist the temptation of putting Effie into print. Under the thinnest of disguises he writes a book about the Callinghams, exposing Andy as an egotistical bounder, proving that Effie's life is founded on sterile lies.

While Effie, whom he despises himself for hurting, is attempting to rally her forces, Dennis has his own emotional problems. For several years he has had a mistress, a pretty, vapid little creature named Corinne, who deceives her prosperous husband with the blandest air of innocence. For all her willfulness and essential stupidity, Dennis is tied to Corinne by a close physical bond; he has no illusions about her, yet she is necessary to him. Corinne, then, can rouse his passion and his jealousy, but—by a strange quirk—it is to Effie that his loyalty is given.

Such is the situation which Miss Powell outlines—a situation which remains fairly static until Andy Callingham's return to America galvanizes it into fresh life. One sees Dennis veering between his two magnetic poles of attraction; one watches Effie stanchly concealing her pain; one follows the febrile moods of shallow little Corinne. None of these people have privacy for their emotions. They move against a feverish background of cocktail parties and night clubs. . . .

Under such circumstances even tragedy becomes tarnished, and Miss Powell is right, of course, in ironically emphasizing the fact. To some extent, however, she defeats her purpose by an excess of wit. If there is to be any real sting in her story, one must be able to take her characters at least half seriously, but this—for a good part of the time—one is unable to do. Just at a point where they achieve reality and a certain poignancy, Miss Powell is all too apt to wander off into a scene of malicious burlesque.

After all, however, this does not seem to matter very greatly. The point about **Turn, Magic Wheel** is that it is a barbed and immensely entertaining satire on a certain phase of New York's literary life. Read about the young publisher who discovered the possibilities of proletarian literature; read Miss Powell's analysis of how to write quaint little *prosies* for the "Manhattanite"; read her deliciously comic descriptions of night-club binges and literary teas. Miss Powell's wit, if somewhat overexuberant, has a peculiarly sharp and ruthless edge. She has some deadly things to say about the cormorant aspects of the intelligentsia, and though her actual story—despite its moving moments—is a little synthetic, her book as a whole rings savagely true.

> *Edith H. Walton, "An Ironic Comedy of Lit'ry Manhattanites," in* The New York Times Book Review, *February 23, 1936, p. 7.*

Jerre Mangione

Of the half-dozen novels that Dawn Powell has written, **Turn, Magic Wheel** is the first to reveal her vast talent for writing good burlesque in fiction form. What makes Miss Powell as a lady wit seem more promising than either Tess Slesinger or Dorothy Parker is that, as an experienced novelist, she has developed a sense of structure, shown in her ability to go beyond the *bon mot* and invent characters and situations that are comic in themselves. Thus, although her main target is the dizzy literary world of Manhattan, her comedy emerges from original people and predicaments, rather than from mere caricatures of well known writers in better known quandaries.

Miss Powell's burlesque has a firm basis of truth. Her chief protagonist, Dennis Orphen, the novelist who writes a novel about a famous novelist and his first wife, is a group photograph of any number of young writers who get their private lives snarled up in their search for material. Dennis' physical source of consolation, Corinne, is easily recognizable as the dumb but intuitive sort. She is realistically and hilariously portrayed along with her diversified accessories, such as her conveniently stupid Wall Street husband and her poisonous girl friend, who is favored with whisperings of Corinne's most intimate doings. One of the funniest characters is Johnson, the publisher's partner—the And Company who was exactly like all the other And Companys and was never able to achieve any individuality until he grew a hair-colored moustache and dyed it black with his wife's eyebrow pencil. He is a comic portrait whose authenticity will startle most publishing young men.

At times when the author is dealing with such people as Effie, the faded and self-sacrificing first wife of the famous novelist, and his neglected second wife dying of cancer, it becomes clear that Miss Powell's tongue isn't always in Miss Powell's cheek. Her treatment of Effie's mental anguish in its various stages involves long stretches that are sentimental and out of tune and generally hurdy-gurdy. It is only when Dawn Powell is completely unserious that she becomes a serious novelist. (pp. 80-1)

> *Jerre Mangione, "The Almost Perfect Scream," in* The New Republic, *Vol. LXXX-VII, No. 1121, May 27, 1936, pp. 80-1.*

Edith H. Walton

If we absolutely must have novels about that none too alluring phenomenon known as cafe society, it is as well that Dawn Powell should write them. She has the sardonic wit which is needful for the job; she is quite immune to the glitter in which her giddy worldlings move. Likewise, of course, she has already jabbed her scalpel into the night life of Manhattan—having carved up nicely, in **Turn, Magic Wheel,** an outlying segment of the true cafe crowd. Her victims in that instance were New York's literati. Cruelly as she treated them, their follies and absurdities did at least have spice. One cannot, unfortunately, say the same for **The Happy Island.** The playboys and playgirls who cavort through its pages are such essential dim-wits that they end up as bores. Even Miss Powell cannot succeed in making them overly amusing. They resist satire—as the columns of Lucius Beebe resist attempts at parody.

The world of **The Happy Island** is not, however, quite the world of Mr. Beebe's diligent chronicles. Society, so called, is rather conspicuously absent. What one has left is a strange lunatic medley of real and would-be celebrities, all eager to forget their out-of-town origins. "They were born, so far as each other knew, with a canapé in one hand and a dry martini in the other." There are night-club singers, radio artists, playwrights, musicians. There are dilettantes and professional beauties. There are silly little bourgeois couples, clutching feverishly at the coat tails of these luminaries. Above all—and in great numbers—there are bevies of "Doubtful Men," together with quite a few others whose status is not even questionable. What unites this crew is their pursuit of a brassy notoriety. Always, at any cost, they must be seen in the best places.

As for the plot of *The Happy Island,* it is so extremely negligible that one hardly needs to dwell upon it. Chiefly it revolves around a singer named Prudence Bly, who is the darling of the night clubs and a star in the gossip columns. Famous as well for her deadly, destructive wit, Prudence is seemingly invulnerable. Even a cafe favorite has, however, her setbacks, and Prudence receives a serious one when her lover two-times her. Her prestige, her vanity, are both undermined by the defection of Steve Estabrook, a radio impresario. It is partly as a reaction from this public humiliation that Prudence falls recklessly for one Jefferson Abbott—a dour young playwright from her forgotten home town. . . .

Lest anything that I have said should sound too disparaging, there is, of course, much that is clever, hilarious, biting, in this gaudy satire-farce. Gyrating aimlessly from bar to bar, from night club to night club, from one lush party to another, these characters of Miss Powell's have a certain featureless vitality. As they gossip and backbite, betraying one another's secrets and stealing one another's loves, they hold one half mesmerized by their extremities of caddishness. They are like bright-painted animals in a particularly febrile zoo. Also, despite the vapidity of her creatures, Miss Powell manages often to be funny at their expense. Read her on "the Cosies"—that tight-knit group of aging college gals. Or on little Jean Nelson—an idiotic blonde—who fights it out with Prudence for Steve Estabrook's heart.

When all is said, however, I am afraid that *The Happy Island* is greatly inferior to *Turn, Magic Wheel.* It is neither so trenchant nor so funny. While it would be impertinent to suggest that Miss Powell is less familiar with the cafe crowd than she is with the literati, that is certainly the impression she creates. Her caricatures in this case are overdone, over-farcical, monotonous. With only a few exceptions—notably the tragic Dol Lloyd—there is hardly a character in her book who seems really human. Stinging contempt and a wicked sense of humor have gone into the making of *The Happy Island.* Somehow or other, however, Miss Powell's material has betrayed her. One is left with a covert suspicion that it was hardly worth her time.

> *Edith H. Walton, "Cafe Society," in* The New York Times Book Review, *September 4, 1938, p. 7.*

William Soskin

It may not be long now before Miss Dawn Powell starts writing books about dogs, or old silver, or the rivers of America, or anything not human, for it becomes increasingly apparent in her novels that the smell of men and women is a stench in her nostrils. True, she chooses scarcely human levels of life for her sparkling stories, such as the literary sector of New York which was beautifully done and basted in bitter aloes in her novel, *Turn Magic Wheel.* True also, she contrives to make her revolting peo-

ple and their sophisticated convolutions thoroughly entertaining and spacious vehicles for her cutting wit. Beyond these considerations of good theater and verbal gayety, however, there is the undeniable fact that Dawn Powell's comedy involves a vast disillusion, an almost clinical skepticism regarding people's most fundamental experiences and emotions. *The Happy Island* illustrates that thesis. . . .

[In *The Happy Island,* the people of Manhattan] seem to have only one thing in common—an inability to know on which side their bed is buttered. As a result of this communal trait, they are involved in such a series of promiscuities, adulteries, double-crossings, neo-perversions and Krafft-Ebing exercises as would make the towns of Sodom and Gomorrah seem like mere suburbs of li'l old New York.

It is no sadistic impulse that drives the author to probe beneath the well-massaged hides of these people. Miss Powell simply cannot stand such people in organized social cliques, and she is a sufficiently superb reporter, and enough of a lively mimic and enough of a merciless surgeon to give us all their antics and all their horror in a comic hyperbole. She has, this writer, what the reviewers like to call a good ear. In the flesh I take it Miss Powell's ear is pinkish, delicate and pearly; but as an organ of hearing it is deadly accurate, and all encompassing. Whether she is recording the sibilances of the pseudo-English, suburban Oxford vernacular which the café crowds affect in their drawing rooms, or the mincing accents of the nice boys who pomade their hair, or the torrential gush of spinster Vassar graduates, or the lingo of West Forty-seventh Street near Broadway—she does it with most telling effect.

Her eye, if we may refer to Miss Powell's eyes in the singular, is a fiendish arrangement of lenses and refractions and reflections by which lovely chiffon ladies are reduced to icy, grasping creatures, by which all the pretensions and bluffs and pathetic poses of the sad people who ride the treacherous waves of New York success are pricked sharply and competently. She knows the social pattern in which these creatures wander. She knows that they are for the most part boys and girls from Oklahoma, Ohio, Wisconsin and North Carolina, people who came from farms and mining camps and village poolrooms and are without roots in a hothouse city that permits their orchidaceous blooming for a few months or a few years.

In the center of all the high jinks Miss Powell puts Prudence, a night club singer from a small town, who is intelligent, sensitive and sturdy, but who has been burned by the currents of sexuality and boredom and fashion which permeate her environment. Also there is Jeff Abbott, a good man from the same small town, a playwright and a serious worker. A little like Clifford Odets, but from Silver City instead of The Bronx. Jeff not only has drive and ambition and a supreme contempt for the shallowness of Prudence's crowd. He also has virility and good looks and Prudence goes for him. Eventually she goes back to Silver City for him, and you wonder if Miss Powell is relenting and leading to a happy hometown solution.

Not Dawn Powell. It isn't long before Prudence sits in her

bare farm house and thinks how she'll tell in the future about "the kind of simplicity he loved; a big house with no maids to interfere with his flow of thought, so all the simplicity had to be worked out by the little woman."

It's a beautiful sardonic climax, and I admire Miss Powell for the fine way she takes the only good man, the only virtuous man, the only idealist in the book and reduces him to a priggishness and stuffiness far worse than the frivolous futility of the rest of the characters. You've got to be able to take such wholehearted disillusion with some laughter, otherwise you can't stand it. And Dawn Powell can supply that laughter in large gusts. Her comedy is intelligent, ironic, bitter—and bright.

> William Soskin, "Laughing Amid Café Society," in New York Herald Tribune Books, September 11, 1938, p. 3.

Rose Feld

[*Angels on Toast* is] an intriguing book compounded of wit and hardness and satire. With the exception of Mary Donovan, all the characters are on the make, and if they are not sweet and beautiful they are devastatingly real and human. Miss Powell pulls no punches, plays no favorites. When the little comedy she develops with acid acumen is finished, as far as the book is concerned, there are neither victors nor spoils. They're all ready to start over again with the same problems, the same shabbiness of spirit, the same greed.

First there was Lou Donovan, promotor of hotel chains and services, rich in fees and rake-offs from the various firms to whom he threw his business. He had started as a bellboy, he had acted in vaudeville, he knew everything sordid there was to know about life. Now he was a big-shot in Chicago. . . .

Second, there was Jay Oliver, Lou's friend and confidant in and out of business. Jay was in cotton; hotels needed sheets and towels and such things, so Jay and Lou made a good thing out of the friendship. Jay was married to Flo, who thought nothing was important but money, and, considering Jay, she wasn't very far wrong. The only thing that burned her up was that Mary Donovan snubbed her and Jay and didn't invite them to her home. Jay didn't care much; he liked drinking with Lou in hot spots, preferably without his wife around. Best of all, he liked going to New York with Lou, where he could be with Ebie.

Jay had lots of girls, how could he help it traveling around so much, but Ebie was the one he really loved. She was a commercial artist who had the brains, in spite of looking like a tart, to know she'd never be anything in the world of art galleries and shows. Ebie had stuck to Jay for ten years, unhappy that he wouldn't leave his wife but philosophic about men and love. When Flo surprised Jay on one of his visits to New York, Ebie went out with Lou and was slightly startled and a little ashamed to find him with her when she awoke the next morning. They both knew Jay wouldn't like it; it was unimportant anyway, so nothing was said about it.

Then there was Mr. Rosenbaum, rich entrepreneur, friend and advisor of men who had millions to invest. Mr. Rosenbaum had to stay married to the good and dull woman who had climbed to success with him, but he loved Trina Kameray, the sweet little trick from Russia and points west. When Rosenbaum turned over a big deal to Lou, the promotion of a smart hotel where no Jews would be allowed, he suggested that Lou might find a job on his staff for a friend of his, a brave little woman from Europe. Lou did and before long Mrs. Kameray and Lou were taking little trips together.

These are the main characters and these the complications in this extremely clever and bitter book. The story moves in a crisscrossing of relationships of drinking, sleeping, quarreling. With the exception of Mary [Donovan], who remains a stilted figure, the characters have the lushness and the poverty of their emotions and deeds. Best of all is the dialogue, crisp and sharp and brutal. And excellent is Miss Powell's penetration of character when she gives Lou's philosophy in his relationship with his wife:

> Talking things out was what made people so sore at each other. They were madder at the things they said talking to each other than they were over the original misunderstanding. He and Mary, thank God, could misunderstand each other and never have to speak of it.

It ends up with everybody getting what he didn't want. Which is Miss Powell's own idea of the way things are.

> Rose Feld, in a review of "Angels on Toast," in New York Herald Tribune Books, October 6, 1940, p. 12.

Otis Ferguson

Angels on Toast is the story of one of those promotion fellows who has learned to move in fast and sell some business man an idea he should have had himself for more money than the venture should net, taking a cut every way you could throw a knife; and then move on, still fast. He is paying now as much for a tie as he used to for a suit in the years when he was one jump ahead of the installment collector on it, and change for tips is when you break a hundred-dollar bill. He has got on top, which is about the only thing that the people in this story are interested in. He has a business friend and they both have wives, mistresses, chippies here and there, and trouble. These interrelationships are what keep the story going, when it *is* going.

The story is not always going because Miss Powell is more ambitious than that: you learn much about the people and their operations in the flash-backs of reverie. There is chaff and there are parties; there are a lot of hole-and-corner types for good measure. Miss Powell likes what you might call the parquet type of novel: one scene starting here, then another at right angles to it, then something else laid alongside that. Unless this is done rigorously, of course, the emphasis shifts around too much. Minor characters or situations prove too much fun; old spots revisited too full of detailed memories. She is sufficiently non-rigorous here so that the total and finished pattern is more like a blur. . . .

Dawn Powell is one of the few writers with a first-class wit who has the kind of understanding that combines appreciation with analysis, a curious ear and eye for everything that goes on, with an endless capacity for getting around. The logic of her general background is good, and her characters so natural in it that they continue acting like heels without stirring resentment. Miss Powell has an eye like a hawk but also the quality of forgiveness, which is actually a good deal rarer in novelists than it is in real life.

> *Otis Ferguson, "Far From Main Street," in* The New Republic, *Vol. 103, No. 18, October 28, 1940, p. 599.*

Rose Feld

The difficulty with reviewing Dawn Powell's new novel, *A Time To Be Born,* is that, first of all, you want to quote from it continually. To say it's brilliant, it's witty, it's penetrating, it's mature isn't enough. You want to prove it by giving examples but then, having chosen your quotes, you find they do not add up to all the book holds and means. Because there is something more in this volume than the exercise of a mind that is as daring as it is keen; there is emotional flavor and pungency which make it greater than an intellectual tour de force. Not only does Miss Powell portray a woman of the hour so that you can see the hidden dynamo of ambition which makes her roar her way across the scene of world affairs, but she is equally successful in creating sympathetic little people with modest desires who serve as instruments of her downfall.

A Time To Be Born is the story of Amanda Keeler Evans, beautiful and brilliant novelist, columnist, radio commentator, and chairman of every committee designed to mobilize the nation's activities in a time of stress and indecision. Amanda had this in common with the heart of the people—she came by her success the same way a chorus girl is generally believed to rise to stardom. In other words, Amanda, renowned for her brilliant mind, used her beautiful body to reach the spotlight. Her producer, or creator, as he preferred to think of himself, was Julian Evans, publisher of a powerful syndicate of newspapers. Having, as he erroneously believed, seduced Amanda, he felt he owed it to her and to himself to divorce his comfortable first wife and make the glamorous Amanda his second.

Not only did Amanda thus assure her success as the writer of a best seller whose authorship was not entirely in the clear, but Amanda soared to heights of fame which, for a time at least, convinced the hero-making little publisher that his instincts were as profitable as they were honorable. Through her meteoric rise as a public figure, aided in no small measure by the publicity she received in his own newspapers, the name of Evans gained new glory and prestige.

Amanda was at the zenith of her career as the woman of American destiny when a bit of chaff from her humble past in Lakeville, Ohio, was wafted to New York. When Amanda out of calculated kindness undertook to place Vicky Haven in a job and in an apartment she didn't know that this bit of chaff, to retain the figure of speech, would get into her eye. Certain of her power over Ken Saunders,

the lover she had discarded for the powerful Evans, she used Vicky as a tool. How Vicky and Ken, two insignificant but very real persons whose names meant nothing to anybody but themselves, formed the combination which sent Amanda toppling makes the plot of Dawn Powell's tale.

But it isn't the plot, joyous as it is, which is the essence of this bitingly clever story. It is the stinging characterization of a fraud, the portrait of a woman who ruthlessly picks the brains of others and presents the results as the product of her own genius. . . .

Amanda on the make, Amanda glaringly successful, Amanda cornered by her own emotions, Amanda belatedly trying to catch the train of world affairs—all of these flow together in a series of detailed close-ups that give you the complete woman. As is usual with novels nowadays, Miss Powell states at the beginning that "all of the characters in this book are the invention of the author and have no living counterpart." But this is still a free country, God be praised, and if you think you recognize the beautiful Amanda who sprang full-armored for front-page news from the love-befuddled brain of the publishing Zeus, who is to say you nay?

> *Rose Feld, "Glitter Girl in the Spotlight," in* New York Herald Tribune Books, *September 6, 1942, p. 5.*

Beatrice Sherman

Dawn Powell's new book [*A Time to Be Born*] maintains and probably tops her record for writing very enjoyable books about very disagreeable people. Her wit is sharp, shrewd and biting, and it finds a pretty mark in the stuffed shirts, male and female, of *A Time to Be Born.* Her book is mighty timely, for no one, even on the sidelines of [World War II], can fail to see that a number of people are exploiting its possibilities for profit to themselves as if it were a happy windfall or a special godsend marked "Personal."

Amanda Keeler Evans was a brilliant exponent of this game. Slender, olive-skinned, golden-haired, she used every feminine wile to advance her career. And her grasping, opportunist bent of mind made her quick to seize on other people's capabilities and use them as her own. . . .

She had written a "sword and lace romance" called *Such Is Legend,* for which she had picked the brains of various intelligent but impecunious people. The book was a happy escape from the prospect of being bombed; it was systematically exploited by the great newspaper magnate, Julian Evans; and it proved to be a world-beating best-seller. "Such fabulous profits from this confection piled up for the pretty author that her random thoughts on economics and military strategy became automatically incontrovertible." Ladies' clubs, editors, broadcasting companies in droves begged for Amanda's opinions and pronouncements on every burning issue of the day, from the campaign in Russia to the future of America, at fancy prices.

To top it all, she married the great newspaper publisher, Julian Evans, though he already had a perfectly satisfactory and comfortable middle-aged wife. The great man was so dazzled by his pretty and brilliant new wife that he used all the machinery of his far-flung enterprises to promote her to further glories. . . .

Vicky Haven of Lakeville found herself drawn into Amanda's orbit because Vicky had a broken heart. Ethel Carey, a friend of both Vicky and Amanda, thought it would be a good thing to get Amanda to find Vicky a New York job, so she would forget her heartbreak, and that this would be a good excuse to have a look at Amanda in her new magnificence. It suited Amanda to place Vicky in a smart magazine office, and poor Vicky's one claim to distinction or even notice thereafter was as a friend of the famous career woman. Amanda chose to use her protégée as a blind for renewing an affair with a cast-off lover, and it was not Vicky's fault that she fell in love with the young man herself. Amanda's bad temper over Vicky's independence and her growing detestation of the famous Julian led her to recklessly jeopardize all her carefully built career—but not without an eye on something bigger and better.

Miss Powell has done a fine piece of satiric and witty writing on the Evans pair. She has a stinging drive. One would hate to be speared on the shaft of her wit, but it is a joy to see Amanda and Julian get theirs.

There is no warmth or sentiment or illusion in her writing. Even Vicky, who, as a modest, generous, companionable person rates the reader's liking and sympathy, is drawn with a cool hand. She granted what passes for a happy ending to her love story, but even that has a characteristic stinger in it.

You may lament the lack of anything verging on integrity or nobility in Miss Powell's cast of characters, for she takes delight in shooting the props out from under every sort of illusion; but you can't help but be delighted with the skillful way in which she does it. *A Time to Be Born* should be prescribed as an antidote for overindulgence in inspirational or romantic books.

> *Beatrice Sherman, "Miss Powell's 'A Time to be Born' and Other Fiction," in* The New York Times Book Review, *September 6, 1942, p. 6.*

Diana Trilling

Miss Powell, one of the wittiest women around, suggests the answer to the old question, "Who really makes the jokes that Dorothy Parker gets the credit for?" The central figure of *A Time to Be Born*—you certainly can't call her the heroine—is the fabulous Amanda Keeler Evans, blond and beautiful, the author of a successful novel and the wife of a publishing power; she knows exactly what she wants, which is everything, and she is in a fair way to getting it. The world is her oyster, and the war, on which she is solemnly articulate, is the perfect break for her career. A ruthless debunking and the quintessence of cattiness, Miss Powell's book is at least one instance in which female venom becomes a social force-for-good. She cries out to be quoted, not one sentence at a time, either, like "A gypsy should be required to be wrong, or else she becomes an af-

front to science," or "She was thirty-two, but she looked like a woman of forty so well-preserved she could pass for thirty-two," but whole paragraphs and pages. Her description of the women's-magazine formula for how to cure a broken heart, her picture of women girding themselves for war, her analysis of contemporary literary trends are not only funny; they proclaim the educated, no-nonsense intelligence that lies behind them. It all adds up to a first-rate satiric talent, and one wonders what went wrong for *A Time to Be Born* to fall apart as it does in the middle. Perhaps it is because there is no proper satiric tradition nowadays for Miss Powell to work in; so that she loses heart and dubs in, as a backdrop to her satire, the kind of love story—nice little small-town girl wins away the great big tough newspaperman from the glamorous big-time beauty—that she would be the first to ridicule. At any rate, the wee note of cynicism she introduces into her love idyl doesn't save it. (pp. 243-44)

> *Diana Trilling, in a review of "A Time to Be Born," in* The Nation, *New York, Vol. 155, No. 12, September 19, 1942, pp. 243-44.*

Edmund Wilson

Dawn Powell's new novel, *My Home Is Far Away* sounds like something between fiction and a memoir. It is the story of three little girls, the children of a travelling salesman in Ohio. Their father is a great fellow when out with the boys and brings home wonderful presents, but spends most of his time on the road, seriously neglects his family, and is always having to look for a new job. The mother dies of tuberculosis and the girls spend some miserable years, during which they are passed around from one relation to another and have a period of living more or less on their own in a room in one of those Western hotels that are part of the railroad station. At last, their father marries again, becomes manager of a furniture store, and, using his wife's money, establishes the family in an ample house and plays the rôle of solid citizen. Now the girls have respectability, but find themselves imprisoned and persecuted by a hateful, neurotic stepmother, who makes their lives more wretched than ever. When the town builds a new high school and it is decided to charge tuition, they find that they will not be allowed to finish their education, and the two oldest girls run away. The second daughter, Marcia, is bright—she has always been so good at her lessons that her teacher thought she was cheating, and she has done so much reading and writing that her relatives say she is "loony." She makes friends with a Chautauqua lecturer, scrapes together a little money, and, relying on his help in the city, slips off to Cleveland alone.

That is all there is to the story, but Dawn Powell has made out of it a chronicle of small-town Middle Western life that is touching without sentimentality and amusing with only rare lapses into caricature and farce. One of the best things that Miss Powell does is her sordid or shabby interiors, such as the railroad hotel and the rooming house which the girls' grandmother keeps in Cleveland—and one remembers the small, intimate New York hotel, with its cocktail-drinking old ladies, which figures in her *Angels on Toast.* She gets out of these unpromising backgrounds a humor and a fairy-tale poetry that have something in common with Dickens. The contemporary she most resembles is probably Sinclair Lewis, but she takes human life more calmly, more genially, and less melodramatically. Her quality, however, is all her own: an odd blend of sharp sophistication with something childlike, surprised, and droll—a point of view, in fact, very much like that of the alert, dispossessed little girls in this book.

Miss Powell has so much talent and of a kind that is so uncommon that one is always left rather disgruntled at her not making more of her work than she does. Three of her recent novels—*Angels on Toast* and *A Time to be Born,* as well as this latest one—have all been in some ways excellent, but they sound like advanced drafts of books rather than finished productions. It is not only that they are marred by inaccuracies, inconsistencies, and other kinds of careless writing; Miss Powell, in the space of one page, gets her heroine's great-grandmother mixed up with her great-great-grandmother; she uses "phenomena" as if it were singular, she mistakes the meaning of "perquisites;" and she is addicted to such usages as "imbecilic" and "normalcy." These errors might not be important; Scott Fitzgerald in his best work sometimes misused words even more seriously. But her carelessness extends also to the organic life of the story. Miss Powell has a way of resorting, in the latter parts of her novels, to violent and sudden incidents which she needs for the machinery of the action but has not taken the trouble to make plausible; and in the case of this latest novel, these incidents—the death of the grandfather from walking into a third rail and the killing off of another of the characters by an abortion—are particularly unconvincing, owing to the fact that the rest of the narrative seems to run pretty close to experience. Miss Powell has simply not allowed herself time to smooth these gashes and hummocks out. And the whole book, as I say, gives the impression of being merely an all-but-final draft which represents the stage at which the writer has got all his material down but has not yet done the sculptural rehandling which is to bring out its self-consistent contours and set it in a permanent pose.

If we compare *My Home Is Far Away* with the stories of a childhood in Texas in Katherine Anne Porter's *The Leaning Tower,* we see the difference between fiction that is interesting because of its implications and satisfying because of its art, and fiction which—though Miss Powell is more lively and can fill in her picture more densely—leaves us feeling that we do not quite know and that the author herself does not know what moral she wants to point with her story or what emotion she wants to convey. This is a genuine disappointment, because Miss Powell, like Marcia in her novel, is a born literary temperament, with an independent point of view that does not lend itself to clichés of feeling, and a life of the imagination that makes writing, for her, an end in itself. She will never be a popular purveyor of the daydreams of feminine fiction. She does not hold up the public for laughter, excitement, or sobs. But, as a writer, she has never yet quite grown up. She appeals to the intelligent reader, but she appeals, again, like the perceptive little girl, who entertains you with breathless dashes of talking but whose vivid improvisations betray, by their falterings and their occasional

whoppers, that her imaginative world has not yet been developed to include all of adult experience. (pp. 87-8)

Edmund Wilson, in a review of "My Home is Far Away," in The New Yorker, *Vol. XX, No. 39, November 11, 1944, pp. 87-8.*

Ruth Page

Dawn Powell has extended her claims to versatility in this new novel of Ohio. *My Home Is Far Away* is a considerable accomplishment in an area distinguished for its mediocre products. Stories of American family life of a few decades ago have enjoyed a tremendous vogue both in fiction and on the stage for some time now, but, for one reason or another, have failed to produce more than one or two memorable examples.

All the familiar props are here—the embroidered Sunday dresses, the fringed surrey, Papa's mustache, Mother's old songs—right in the opening scene; and they accumulate throughout—a balloon ascension, an actress, the first phonograph, the hair-do's, the blue silk sashes, Papa's saloon, and so on. The novel invokes an atmosphere identical with that of a dozen recent books which leap to mind. Like these others, it is simple and unpretentious in style, and, in its mixture of humor and pathos, belongs generally to the variety of book known to some as "cockle-warming." There the resemblance stops.

The characteristic of novels which warm the cockles of the heart is their sentimentality; there is nothing sentimental about *My Home Is Far Away* except that it is set in an era which we tend to regard with sentiment. Miss Powell does not. Her view of the world and of human character is sharp and uncompromising. It is, in fact, the combination of surface warmth and generally humorous tone with a more or less acrid reading of character which gives this novel its quality. The three little motherless girls who are bandied about among their affectionate but really uncaring relatives are gay creatures, but their situation is not. The pathos lies in the fact that even very kindly adults, including parents, are blind to the realities of a child's world, and callous to a child's emotional life.

It is no injustice to say that Dawn Powell's novel lies almost exactly between the kind of thing Sally Benson turns out so easily in her St. Louis sketches and the kind produced so perfectly by Katherine Anne Porter in her Miranda stories. She is a more perceptive writer than the first and a less finished one than the second.

Ruth Page, "Surrey Ride, Minus the Sentiment," in The New York Times Book Review, *November 19, 1944, p. 4.*

Florence Haxton Bullock

In *The Locusts Have No King* Dawn Powell impishly assaults you in your ticklish midriff with the absurd performances of her prime young to middle-aging successful and not-quite-so-successful New Yorkers. And while you are engaged in wiping away the tears of irresponsible laughter from your eyes over their foolish antics, you feel a sudden stabbing pain and realize that the merry and merciless Miss Powell has given you a deep thrust in your own unguarded ribs. The follies at which she pokes such ribald and satiric fun are in a manner of speaking your follies too. For the rootlessnes of these typical Manhattanites, and their want of serious purpose in life larger than the single, selfish one of getting on and up in the world, are certainly everywhere the weaknesses of these our times. Miss Powell spreads them out before you in bounteous array.

Among the merry, self-seeking rounders in *The Locusts Have No King* are the bright and busy Tyson Bricker, proponent of streamlined culture in radio and classroom; Murray Cahill, a pleasant fellow whose alcoholic nocturnal habits come in frequent conflict with his daytime jobs; his wife who chooses to live alone and like it; Dodo Brennan, who is not precisely a nymphomaniac, as one of the men in the story points out, but just a girl who thinks she has lollipops enough for all. There are career girls who busily spark the world of merchandise by day and are definitely out for fun at night and on week ends, the while lamenting in their hearts the husbands that once were theirs. . . . Miss Powell presents them all with an almost shocking photographic accuracy, while she indicates through the bright facades of their prides and busy pretentions the lonely emptiness beneath. For all its merry surfaces, *The Locusts Have No King* is a sad book and definitely meant to be that.

Frederick Olliver, the personable young man in the foreground of the novel, is actually a very able fellow. A writer of serious purpose, by nature something of a recluse, Olliver's rather lonely and impoverished life in Greenwich Village, Bohemian style, is at the beginning of the story anchored to his work and his love affair with the young playwright Lyle Gaynor. But Mrs. Gaynor's busy social and professional life, and the exactions of her marriage to an invalid husband-collaborator leave little time for her very genuine love affair with Olliver. Misunderstandings, disappointments, quarrels result, and in the opening chapters of *The Locusts Have No King* young Olliver slips his emotional moorings to Mrs. Gaynor and takes out after Dodo Brennan, the Pooh-on-you girl. Dodo is obsessed with meeting the biggies, with going to the Stork Club, to celebrity parties, to the all night bars on Rubber Leg Square. The months that follow are a rather grim round for Olliver, but he is pathetically grateful to find himself an acceptable escort for the avid Dodo. His chase after the little tramp through bistros, bars and nightclubs is, naturally, expensive, so Olliver puts aside his serious writing to edit a profitable comic called *Haw*. The year-long fling with Dodo, with futility following on frustration, costs the infatuated Olliver much in peace of mind, also. At the end of the novel, Miss Powell, in the deftest fashion in the world, liquidates the situation and gets Olliver back in the groove again. But meanwhile he—and you—have been given a lot to think over.

Florence Haxton Bullock, "Grim Round of Pleasure," in New York Herald Tribune Weekly Book Review, *May 2, 1948, p. 6.*

Diana Trilling

The scarcity of satiric fiction in this country is something this department has often lamented. Aldous Huxley—if he can now be claimed as an American—Helen Howe, Dawn Powell: with three novelists we about exhaust the list of names associated with the form. And of these, Huxley has increasingly subdued his brilliant satiric gifts to his religious message, and Helen Howe indicates a desire to sacrifice hers to social piety. As a matter of fact, even Dawn Powell, with her last book, deserted satire entirely in favor of sentimental childhood reminiscence. Evidently the business of poking serious fun at ourselves is uncongenial to present-day taste: our hard times are to be approached only in a spirit of grim salvationism, or wholly evaded by ducking back to a gentler past.

But though we are prepared to welcome Dawn Powell's return to satiric writing with her new novel, *The Locusts Have No King,* I am afraid the reception cannot be as wholehearted as might be wished. There are many wonderful things in Miss Powell's book, such as her admirers have come to expect in her work—passages of great intelligence and fiercely courageous wit. The novel as a whole, however, quite fails to sustain the excitement promised by its best moments. It would be convenient to place the blame for this disappointment on a general cultural situation which lays too heavy a burden of responsibility upon the writer and gives too little license to gaiety. Certainly this describes our present literary condition. But unfortunately it is my sense that *The Locusts Have No King,* instead of reflecting our generally difficult literary state, reflects only Miss Powell's own problems as a writer.

The clue to the matter lies, I think, in Miss Powell's choice of characters, or—more accurately—in the discrepancy between the power of mind revealed on virtually every page of her novel and the insignificance of the human beings upon whom she directs her excellent intelligence. *The Locusts Have No King* is about a group of contemporary New Yorkers who, most of them, live directly or indirectly by association with the arts—playwrights, publishers, press agents, culture-promoters, painters. A shabbier crowd of hangers-on and bar flies it would be hard to find. Not a single individual among them either positively or negatively, either by the nature of his ambition or the distance of his fall from glory, suggests any human ideal which justifies a writer's bothering with the human race at all. Even Miss Powell's scholarly hero, Frederick Olliver, or her playwright heroine, Mrs. Gaynor, the two people who stand for the best that Miss Powell can say for our species, can scarcely be taken to represent a correction of their fellows which is worth our concern—though Miss Powell offers them as such; for neither of them ever evokes any image of dignity or stature. But this is death to satire. The size of a satire necessarily derives from the size of the object satirized, which in turn derives from the ideal vision of life against which the author sets his picture of a faulty reality. We are always, after all, only as big as the things we laugh at, and if we choose to mock some poor pub crawler or some silly little Southern tart trying to make her way in the big city, who are we to say that life owes us any better possibility for ourselves?

In her last satiric novel, *A Time to Be Born,* Miss Powell at least chose as the chief object of her wit someone equal to it—a very powerful woman, able to destroy her betters. But in the previous book, too, Miss Powell's principle of correction represented no correction at all but merely an act of sentimentality. In the degree that we were invited to pillory the tycooness of *A Time to Be Born* we were also invited to give our affection to a pair of utterly inconsequential young lovers—an unnecessary, indeed an impossible, choice for anyone as intelligent as Miss Powell to force on her readers.

But, as I say, here is the nub of Miss Powell's difficulty—in the curious disparity between what one might call her abstract intelligence and the human material on which, for the most part, she expends it. One wonders why anyone with so much strength and passion of mind, and so much clarity about the debasement of intellectual values in our society, should have so poor a notion of what constitutes the kind of person worth scorning or fearing or respecting. Perhaps, though one hesitates to stress the point, the imbalance springs from the anomalous role which an intelligent woman still plays in our culture—the myriad subtle pressures exerted on her to prove her "womanliness" by disproving her seriousness, to disarm male hostility by asserting a basic frivolity. Certainly no man of Miss Powell's intellectual endowment would fritter away his powers on the small-time creatures to whom Miss Powell devotes herself, or be guilty of the sentimental gestures that so markedly diminish the value of her keen social perceptions. (pp. 611-12)

> *Diana Trilling, in a review of "The Locusts Have No King," in* The Nation, *New York, Vol. 166, No. 22, May 29, 1948, pp. 611-12.*

Frederic Morton

Dawn Powell's parish, as her followers know, is wealth-infested, mink-mad Manhattan. Her arsenal, as [*The Wicked Pavilion*] proves, retains its fire-power—including the most exquisite acid since Dorothy Parker and a fastidious pair of pincers with which to tweak the soul.

For her picaresque morality Miss Powell has assembled her customary cast. This time, it features a middle-aged heiress who subsidizes painters—not to encourage their genius on canvas but their industry as lovers. There's a young couple instantly and easily infatuated with one another, yet uncertain, in our supersonic borough, about how to fall solidly and lastingly in love. There are two attractive young ladies busy with turning their charms into cash. There are three weather-worn but fanatically Bohemian artists, juggling mistresses, debts and the Muse. . . .

The theme of the sermon, also traditional to Miss Powell, is intoned by her alter ego in the novel, a writer named Dennis Orphen:

> If this is the way the world is turning, let us get off the cosmic Ferris wheel. Allow us the boon of standing still until the vertigo passes. Give us a respite to gather together the scraps of what was once us—the old longings for what? for

whom? that gave us the wings and the chart for our tomorrows. There must be some place along the route where the runners may pause and ask themselves why they run, what is the prize and is it the prize they really want? What became of beauty, where went love?

Miss Powell tells us how one of the three painters declares himself dead while the other two profit from "finding" his posthumously enriched canvases. We learn how the first of the two ladies of negotiable loveliness found a perfect paramour in the man who would not share her apartment. We see just how a straggling romance between an heiress and an esthetics drummer graduates into a marriage of precisely dove-tailed greeds.

Miss Powell can sound the tiniest Tom Collins ice cube clink as a knell of doom. She can retranslate the "hello-*darling!*" hug into an overture of malice. The pompous must wilt under the volleys of her wit, since no pretense escapes her. Yet, strangely, disappointingly, it is often shadows we laugh at and not human beings.

Why should that be? For one thing, her brilliances are random, incomplete. Just as she seems on the point of demolishing a charlatan, she packs up her dynamite kit and begins affixing charges elsewhere. Her forte is not the dramatically sustained scene but a sparkling miscellany of needle-prickly essays. But what appears most fundamentally lacking is the sense of outrage which serves as engine to even the most sophisticated satirist. Miss Powell does not possess the pure indignation that moves Evelyn Waugh to his absurdities and forced Orwell into his haunting contortions. Her verbal equipment is probably unsurpassed among writers of her genre—but she views the antics of humanity with too surgical a calm.

> *Frederic Morton, "And Where Went Love?" in* The New York Times Book Review, *Vol. LIX, No. 36, September 5, 1954, p. 5.*

Brendan Gill

If what you hope for in a novel is that, witty and yet serious, it will depict interesting people stumbling into and struggling out of interesting dilemmas and yet will neither break your heart nor leave you in a state of post-soap-operative shock, you are advised to try *The Wicked Pavilion,* the latest novel by Dawn Powell. Miss Powell is witty and serious, and her outlook is neither Kafka-black nor Rinso-white. . . . [Her territory] lies in the Washington Square-Greenwich Village quarter, and its inhabitants are for the most part those congenital unemployables—painters, sculptors, writers, and hangers-on—to be seen walking through the Square or along Eighth Street any night this week, or this year, or this century. . . . Miss Powell's characters are not in business, and if they were, they would not succeed at it. Money, though it passes through their hands, is something other people have. Then how do they survive? An accomplished writer and a seasoned guide to Washington Square, Miss Powell stingingly and sometimes touchingly shows us how some do and some don't.

The wicked pavilion of the title is the Café Julien, the fixed center about which the many separate sections of the novel turn. The café is, to the life, the old front room of the Lafayette, with its tiled floor and marble-topped tables and bleak bentwood chairs, and it is not the least of Miss Powell's virtues that her evocation of that lost landmark is both loving and unsentimental. Having seated herself at a table just inside the door, she strikes, like so many lighted matches, her little sparks ("Hoff Bemans was an old rear avant-gardist with an inky finger in all the arts, who had set himself up as a general handyman for the twenties." "They had nothing in common, but friendship had spread under them like an invisible net waiting for the certain catch"), and by their light fits together the jagged pieces of a plot that is often close to melodrama. Then, being too intelligent to be satisfied with melodrama, she draws back from the jagged pieces, surrenders her table, and, still sharp-eyed and perfectly composed, still taking at any cost the comic view, marches out into the Square.

> The Café Julien was gone and a reign was over. Those who had been bound by it fell apart like straws when the baling cord is cut and remembered each other's name and face as part of a dream that would never come back.
>
> (pp. 155-56, 158)

Brendan Gill, "Rough and Smooth," in The New Yorker, *Vol. XXX, No. 35, October 16, 1954, pp. 155-56, 158.*

Morris Gilbert

Dawn Powell for some decades has been whipping up successive human comedies of the most fastidious disenchantment. With her, the comic spirit is a mordant one; her knowingness is proverbially satanic. She has always had a precocious and highly esteemed gift for outrage. In *The Golden Spur,* she is again at her most outrageous, and again goes swinging on her patented Ohio-New York pendulum—a thoroughly familiar one for her, a native of little Shelby, Ohio, and a habitué of the metropolis. As early as 1940, a reviewer was observing that her eight novels (to that date) "have progressed steadily from Ohio sunshine to Manhattan madness."

Here it is still the case—not to imply any suggestion of repetitiveness. The phenomenon that New York is filled and possessed, year in, year out, with successions of provincials who presently become New York's New Yorkers is like a law of nature. Hence, variations on that basic theme are limitless.

This time, apart from all else, the author has hit upon one of the happiest imaginable and most original of plot contrivances. Three men of mature years are separately caused to suspect that during their long-gone, gay-dog youth in Greenwich Village they had sired a son, out of holy wedlock. With extreme pleasure, for diverse reasons, each of them ardently hopes to prove his dishonest fatherhood, and to turn the circumstance to his own uses.

The source of this unusual agitation is a personable young man, a Silver City, Ohio, Candide, in search of traces of his beloved dead mother—and, indeed, of a true father. Jonathan Jaimison has only recently learned, from his

mother's cryptic diary, the real state of affairs, when Connie Birch had suddenly departed the Village in the late twenties, especially a glamorous (to her) cafe, The Golden Spur, to marry her small-town sweetheart.

The Golden Spur, plus two—make it three—Village girls of astonishingly raucous behavior, a number of artists and writers, good and bad, and the trio of philoprogenitive elders, are vitally affected by young Jonathan's advent. He in turn absorbs the roaring Village of today with sangfroid and finds himself in all innocence initiated into its most intimate and delirious milieu without blinking. An unanticipated denouement brings this tale to a dizzily amusing end.

Miss Powell might have concentrated more on those three old boys and less on other figures, in whose treatment one detects certain *longueurs.* With it all, there are new notes—more than a trace of nostalgia for other Village days, and an occasional distinctly autumnal coloration in the human landscape. But the author's pyrotechnic wickedness is still guaranteed to satisfy.

Morris Gilbert, "In Search of a Father," in The New York Times Book Review, *October 14, 1962, p. 40.*

Edmund Wilson

Why is it that the novels of Miss Dawn Powell are so much less well known than they deserve to be? This is, I believe, partly due to her complete indifference to publicity. . . . No effort has been made to glamorize her, and it would be hopeless to try to glamorize her novels. For in these novels—another reason that they have not been more popular—she does nothing to stimulate feminine daydreams. The woman reader can find no comfort in identifying herself with Miss Powell's heroines. The women who appear in her stories are likely to be as sordid and absurd as the men. There are no love scenes that will rouse you or melt you. It is true that in her more recent books she has been relenting a little. In *The Locusts Have No King,* she did close on a note of enduring affection, though an affection sorely tried and battered—"In a world of destruction," the author concludes, "one must hold fast to whatever fragments of love are left, for sometimes a mosaic can be more beautiful than an unbroken pattern"— and in her last book but one, *A Cage for Lovers,* there are actually a young man and a young woman who, though kept apart by an ogress, are benevolently united at the end.

But love is not Miss Powell's theme. Her real theme is the provincial in New York who has come on from the Middle West and acclimated himself (or herself) to the city and made himself a permanent place there, without ever, however, losing his fascinated sense of an alien and anarchic society. Like Miss Powell, who was born in Ohio, these immigrants find themselves vividly aware of elements of Manhattan life that the native of New York takes for granted, since he has usually no very intimate experience of anything else to contrast with them. To such fresh arrivals, the New Yorkers seem giddy and unreliable, their activities confused and often pointless, yet once the transplantation has taken root, they may enjoy in the very amorality of this life a certain relaxation and freedom, a certain convivial comfort in the assurance that, whatever you do, no one . . . is really going to call you to account. Such a world has great comic possibilities if one has enjoyed it on its own terms and yet observed it from a point of view that does not quite accept these terms as normal, and Miss Powell has exploited its possibilities with a wit, a gift of comic invention, and an individual accent that make her books unlike any others. The mind, the personality behind them, with all its sophistication, is very stout and self-sustaining, strong in Middle Western common sense, capable of toughness and brusqueness; yet a fairyland strain of Welsh fantasy instills into everything she writes a kind of kaleidoscopic liveliness that renders even her hardheadedness elusive.

Miss Powell has explored several New York milieux. In *A Time to Be Born,* she was dealing with a successful uptown world of big journalistic publishing and insatiable careerist women; in *Angels on Toast,* with a somewhat lesser world of delirious advertising men and their equally unstable mates; in *A Cage for Lovers,* with the weight of inherited money in an isolated mansion on the Hudson. But in her new book, *The Golden Spur,* she returns to a favorite field, which has figured in others of her novels: the bohemian downtown world of writers, painters, and professional drinkers, with their feminine consorts and hangers-on, which has its center in Greenwich Village. She has rendered, in these various books, the Village in several of its phases. Of the earlier romantic and radical phase, which was certainly the most creative, she has had little first-hand knowledge, and she has not attempted this, but she has condensed the atmosphere of its later ones in images that do not always keep their contours yet that live as they are blown down the wind; and it is a proof of her quality as a literary artist that she does not depend directly on gossip and never writes a *roman à clef.* The reviewer has been pretty well acquainted with many of the same kind of people who have provided Miss Powell's material, yet he has never found Miss Powell exploiting a personality among them whom he recognized. She has imagined and established for her readers her own Greenwich Village world, which is never journalistic copy and which possesses a memorable reality of which journalistic fiction is incapable. Her chronicle extends from the days of such old-fashioned resorts as the Brevoort and the Lafayette, with their elegant and well-served French restaurants and domino-playing cafés, which encouraged the dignity of love and art and provided a comfortable setting for leisurely conversations . . . her chronicle, perhaps rather her poem, extends from the era of this tranquil quarter, now almost entirely destroyed to make way for huge apartment buildings, to the era of those noisy, abysmal bars, which, though graded from better to worse, have all a certain messy turbidity, in which the hack writer, the talentless artist, the habitual cadger of loans can drift on in a timeless existence of lamplit embothed drinking, with a backdrop of rich-looking bottles standing by like a smartly costumed guard against the mirror that expands the room beyond its crowded narrow limits in space, and in the casual but dependable companionship of the bartender and the other habitués, while the girls who inspire speculation by their constant exchange of partners and their possible availability laugh and brighten after leaving the office or perfunctorily keeping house in the studio, and thus provide a fitful play of romance.

In *The Golden Spur* we see the Village at a point of its decline that is rather squalid: bearded beatniks and abstract painters have seeped in among the Guggenheim fellows, the raffish N.Y.U. professors, and the adult-education students. It is a phase with which Miss Powell is evidently not so intimate and not so sympathetic as she was with the Village of an earlier time but which she nevertheless accepts as still more or less cozy and more or less fun in the good old Village tradition. If one does not have the benefit at one's favorite bar, as one sometimes did with the cafés of the past, of a lobby with a telephone girl who always knew whom everybody was looking for, and who would never be indiscreet, one can still give it as a mailing address or a place where one can be reached by telephone and be granted a certain latitude in the matter of hanging up tabs.

The Golden Spur is such a bar, which dates, however, from an earlier period. Jonathan Jaimison, of Silver City, Ohio, has learned from an aunt at home that he is an illegitimate child, the son of his now deceased mother by someone she had known in New York during a legendary time in her youth when she had had a brief fling in the East. She had supported herself by typing and thus had met distinguished people of whom she was to talk ever after. But she had never told anyone who her lover was, and the boy has come on to find out, with no clues save a few names and the knowledge that the Golden Spur had been a place that his mother had frequented. Gradually he makes connections with her former employers and friends: a clever alcoholic professor who leads rather a miserable life between a wife who has tricked him into marrying her and a mistress who wants to marry him; a successful, somewhat stuffed-shirt lawyer with a wife who has taken him over and set him up in suburban Connecticut; and a demoralized best-selling novelist whose pride receives a serious blow when the wife whom he has ridiculed and neglected runs away on a yacht with a title. None of them has a son, and when the first and the last of the three come to understand that Jonathan is looking for a father, they try to imagine that they may have begotten him in some now forgotten moment: it would give them a new bond and interest, help to bolster up their disappointing lives. . . . I ought not to reveal whose son the boy unexpectedly turns out to be, but Miss Powell, who has sometimes been criticized for the formlessness of her novels and their inconclusive endings, has constructed here a very neat plot, and for once in her career played Santa Claus and made her hero a generous present. She then has him reject, however, the privileges of the social position to which he is now entitled and flee from the opening of an uptown gallery that he has undertaken to subsidize, in company with an erratic and much esteemed painter—you never know in Miss Powell's novels whether the painters are really any good—who has become its principal star but who prefers to the patronage of the affluent a lodging in a rickety warehouse near Houston Street, on the lower West Side. Jonathan escapes to the Golden Spur, to which by this hour, as he knows, "the old crowd must be heading . . . for post-mortems and wakes." In the cab with him and the painter is the lawyer's unappreciated daughter, who has succeeded in persuading her parents to let her live in New York on her own, and who has even managed to go on the stage without their knowing about it; who has, in fact, been leading a double life between suburban correctitude on the one hand and abandoned bohemianism on the other. Jonathan, who has met her in both of her roles, has fallen deeply in love with her, and he doesn't really care at that point that she has also been sleeping with the painter and lying to him about it. . . . (pp. 233-36)

I have said that Dawn Powell must be less at home in the "beat" than in the old Village, yet it is interesting to find that in *The Golden Spur* she has succeeded in modulating without too much strain from the charming Lafayette café to its so much less distinguished successor, and that the beatnik's dread of the "square" comes to seem here the natural extension of the old Greenwich Villager's attitude toward the traditional artists' enemy—"uptown."

I hope that the tone of this article—sociological and somewhat nostalgic—will not obscure the fact that Dawn Powell's novels are among the most amusing being written, and in this respect quite on a level with those of Anthony Powell, Evelyn Waugh, and Muriel Spark. Miss Powell's success in England shows, I think, that she is closer to this high social comedy than to any accepted brand of American humor—and the English do not insist on having the women in their fiction made attractive. Miss Powell's books are more than merely funny; they are full of psychological insights that are at once sympathetic and cynical, and they have episodes that are rather macabre, which seem to represent an all-but-embitterment. The recurring types in these books—with whom the innocent provincial is confronted—are the discouraged alcoholic, the creepy homosexual, the unscrupulous feminine operator, and the tyrannous woman patron, and Miss Powell can make them all look very gruesome. All are present in *The Golden Spur,* but not in their most repellent forms, and here, as elsewhere, one can always be sure that some sudden new comic idea will give a twist to the situation, which has seemed to be irretrievably uncomfortable, and introduce an arbitrary element that will give to the proceedings a touch of ballet. There are few real happy endings in Dawn Powell's novels, but there are no real tragedies, either. These beings shift and cling and twitch in their antic liaisons and ambitions, on their way to some undetermined limbo out of reach of any moral law. But don't those wide-eyed young men and girls from Ohio survive and redeem the rest? Don't be too sure of this. (pp. 236, 238)

> *Edmund Wilson, "Dawn Powell: Greenwich Village in the Fifties," in* The New Yorker, *Vol. XXXVIII, No. 39, November 17, 1962, pp. 233-36, 238.*

Gore Vidal

For decades Dawn Powell was always just on the verge of ceasing to be a cult and becoming a major religion. But despite the work of such dedicated cultists as Edmund Wilson and Matthew Josephson, John dos Passos and Ernest Hemingway, Dawn Powell never became the popular writer that she ought to have been. In those days, with a bit of luck, a good writer eventually attracted voluntary readers, and became popular. Today, of course, "popular" means bad writing that is widely read while good writing is that which is taught to involuntary readers. Powell failed on both counts. She needs no interpretation while in her lifetime she should have been as widely read as, say, Hemingway or the early Fitzgerald or the mid O'Hara or even the late, far too late, Katherine Anne Porter. But Powell was that unthinkable monster, a witty woman who felt no obligation to make a single, much less final, down payment on Love or The Family; she saw life with a bright Petronian neutrality, and every host at life's feast was a potential Trimalchio to be sent up.

In the few interviews that Powell gave, she often mentions, surprisingly for an American, much less a woman of her time and place, *The Satyricon* as her favorite novel. This sort of thing was not acceptable then any more than it is now. Descriptions of warm mature heterosexual love were—and are—woman's writerly task, and the truly serious writers really, heart-breakingly, flunk the course while the pop ones pass with bright honors. Although Powell received very little serious critical attention (to the extent that there has ever been much in our heavily moralizing culture), when she did get reviewed by a really serious person like Diana Trilling [see excerpt above dated 1948], La Trilling warns us that the book at hand is no good because of "the discrepancy between the power of mind revealed on every page of her novel [*The Locusts Have No King*] and the insignificance of the human beings upon which she directs her excellent intelligence." Trilling does acknowledge the formidable intelligence but because Powell does not deal with Morally Complex People (full professors at Columbia in mid journey?), "the novel as a whole . . . fails to sustain the excitement promised by its best moments."

Apparently, a novel to be serious must be about very serious even solemn people rendered in a very solemn even serious manner. Wit? What is that? But then we all know that power of mind and intelligence count for as little in the American novel as they do in American life. (p. 52)

Powell herself occasionally betrays bewilderment at the misreading of her work. She is aware, of course, that the American novel is a middlebrow middle-class affair and that the reader/writer must be as one in pompous self-regard. "There is so great a premium on dullness," she wrote sadly (Robert van Gelder, *Writers and Writing,* 1946), "that it seems stupid to pass it up." She also remarks that

> it is considered jolly and good-humored to point out the oddities of the poor or of the rich. The frailties of millionaires or garbage collectors can be made to seem amusing to persons who are not millionaires or garbage collectors. Their ways of speech, their personal habits, the peculiarities of their thinking are considered fair game. I go outside the rules with my stuff because I can't help believing that the middle class is funny, too.

Well, she was warned by four decades of book chatterers.

My favorite was the considered judgment of one Frederic Morton [see excerpt above]:

> But what appears most fundamentally lacking is the sense of outrage which serves as an engine to even the most sophisticated [*sic*] satirist. Miss Powell does not possess the pure indignation that moves Evelyn Waugh to his absurdities and forced Orwell into his haunting contortions. Her verbal equipment is probably unsurpassed among writers of her genre—but she views the antics of humanity with too surgical a calm.

It should be noted that Mr. Morton was the author of the powerful, purely indignant, and phenomenally compassionate novel, *Asphalt and Desire*. In general, Powell's books usually excited this sort of commentary (Waugh *indignant?* Orwell hauntingly *contorted?*). The fact is that Americans have never been able to deal with wit. Wit gives away the scam. Wit blows the cool of those who are forever expressing a sense of hoked-up outrage. Wit, deployed by a woman with surgical calm, is a brutal assault upon nature—that is, Man. Attis, take arms!

Finally, as the shadows lengthened across the greensward, Edmund Wilson got around to his old friend [see excerpt above]. One reason, he tells us, why Powell has so little appeal to those Americans who read novels is that:

> She does nothing to stimulate feminine daydreams [Sexist times!]. The woman reader can find no comfort in identifying herself with Miss Powell's heroines. The women who appear in her stories are likely to be as sordid and absurd as the men.

This sexual parity was—is—unusual. But now, closer to century's end than 1962, Powell's sordid, absurd ladies seem like so many Mmes. de Stael compared to our latter-day viragos.

Wilson also noted Powell's originality:

> Love is not Miss Powell's theme. Her real theme is the provincial in New York who has come on from the Middle West and acclimated himself (or herself) to the city and made himself a permanent place there, without ever, however, losing his fascinated sense of an alien and anarchic society.

This is very much to the (very badly written) point. Wilson finds her novels "among the most amusing being written, and in this respect quite on a level with those of Anthony Powell, Evelyn Waugh, and Muriel Spark." Wilson's review was of her last book, *The Golden Spur;* three years later she was dead of breast cancer. "Thanks a lot, Bunny," one can hear her mutter as this belated floral wreath came flying through her transom.

Summer, Sunday afternoon. Circa 1950. Dawn Powell's duplex living room at 35 East Ninth Street. The hostess presides over an elliptical aquarium filled with gin: a popular drink of the period known as the martini. In attendance, Coby—just Coby to me for years, her *cavalier servente;* he is neatly turned out in a blue blazer; rosy-faced; sleek silver hair combed straight back. Coby can talk with charm on any subject. The fact that he might be Dawn's lover has never crossed my mind. They are so old. A handsome young poet lies [asleep] on the floor, literally at the feet of E. E. Cummings and his wife Marion, who ignore him. (pp. 52-3)

[In] my memory, the poet is forever asleep on the floor while on a balcony high up in the second story of Dawn's living room, a gray blurred figure appears and stares down at us. "Who," I ask, "is that?"

Dawn gently, lovingly, stirs the martinis; squints her eyes; says, "My husband, I think. It is Joe, isn't it, Coby?" She turns to Coby, who beams and waves at the gray man, who withdraws. "Of course it is," says Coby. "Looking very fit." I realize, at last, that this is a *ménage à trois* in Greenwich Village. My martini runs over. . . .

[One of the few studies of Powell's work is an unpublished] doctoral dissertation by Judith Faye Pett (University of Iowa, 1981). Miss Pett has gathered together a great deal of biographical material for which one is grateful. I am happy to know, at last, that the amiable Coby's proper name was Coburn Gilman, and I am sad to learn that he survived Dawn by only two years. The husband on the balcony was Joseph Gousha, or Goushé, whom she married November 20, 1920. He was musical; she literary, with a talent for the theater. A son was born retarded. Over the years, a fortune was spent on schools and nurses. To earn the fortune, Powell did every sort of writing, from interviews in the press to stories for ladies' magazines to plays that tended not to be produced to a cycle of novels about the Midwest, followed by a cycle of New York novels, where she came into her own, dragging our drab literature screaming behind her. As *doyenne* of the Village, she held court in the grill of the Lafayette Hotel—for elegiasts the Lafayette was off Washington Square, at University Place and Ninth Street. . . .

[In her dissertation], Miss Pett provides bits and pieces from correspondence and diaries, and fragments of book chat. Like most writers Powell wrote of what she knew. Therefore, certain themes recur, while the geography does not vary from that of her actual life. As a child, she and two sisters were shunted about from one Midwestern farm or small town to another by a father who was a salesman on the road (her mother died when she was six). The maternal grandmother made a great impression on her; and predisposed her toward boarding-house life (as a subject not a residence). Indomitable old women, full of rage and good jokes, occur in both novel cycles. At twelve, Powell's father remarried; and Dawn and sisters went to live on the stepmother's farm. "My stepmother, one day, burned up all the stories I was writing, a form of discipline I could not endure. With thirty cents earned by picking berries I ran away, ending up in the home of a kind aunt in Shelby, Ohio." After graduating from the local high school, she worked her way through Lake Erie College for Women in Painesville, Ohio. I once gave a commencement address there and was struck by how red-brick New England Victorian the buildings were. I also found out all that I could about their famous alumna. I collected some good stories to tell her. But by the time I got back to New York she was dead.

Powell set out to be a playwright. One play ended up as a movie while another was done by the Group Theater in 1933, *Big Night.* But it was the First World War not the theater that got Powell out of Ohio and to New York in 1918, as a member of the Red Cross: the war ended before her uniform arrived. Powell wrote publicity. Married. Wrote advertising copy (at the time Goushé or Gousha was an account executive with an advertising agency). Failure in the theater and need for money at home led her to novel writing and the total security of that five-hundred-dollar advance each of us relied on for so many years. Powell's first novel, *Whither,* was published in 1925. In 1928 Powell published *She Walks in Beauty,* which she always maintained, mysteriously, was really her first novel. For one thing, the Ohio heroine of *Whither* is already in New York City, like Powell herself, working as a syndicated writer who must turn out 30,000 words a week in order to live (in Powell's case to pay for her child's treatments). In a sense, this New York novel was premature; with her second book, Powell turns back to her origins in the Great Western Reserve, where New Englanders had re-created New England in Ohio; and the tone is dour Yankee, with a most un-Yankeeish wit.

The Ohio cycle begins with *She Walks in Beauty,* which is dedicated to her husband Joe. The story is set in Powell's youth before the First War. The book was written in 1927. Popular writers of the day: Thornton Wilder had published *The Bridge of San Luis Rey* in the same year as Powell's first but really second novel. Louis Bromfield received the Pulitzer Prize for *Early Autumn* (a favorite Bromfield phrase, "candy pink and poison green," occasionally surfaces in Powell) while Cather's *Death Comes for the Archbishop* was also published in 1927. The year 1925, of course, had been the most remarkable in our literary history. After satirizing life in the Midwest, Sinclair Lewis brought his hero Arrowsmith to New York City, a pattern Powell was to appropriate in her Ohio cycle. Also in that miraculous year alongside, as it were, *Whither:* Theodore Dreiser's *An American Tragedy,* Dos Passos's *Manhattan Transfer,* Fitzgerald's *The Great Gatsby.* It is interesting that Dreiser, Lewis, Hemingway, Fitzgerald, Dos Passos, and the popular Bromfield were all, like Powell, Midwesterners with a dream of some other great good place, preferably Paris but Long Island Sound and social climbing would do.

Powell briskly shows us the town of Birchfield. Dorrie is the dreamy plain bright sister (always two contrasting sisters in these early novels); she stands in for Powell. Linda is the vain chilly one. Aunt Jule keeps a boarding house. The Powell old lady makes her debut:

> She pinned her muslin gown at the throat, dropped her teeth with a cheerful little click in the glass of water on the table, and turned out the gas.

The "cheerful" launches us on the Powell style. The story is negligible: who's going to make it out of the sticks first. In the boarding house there is an old man who reads Greek; his son has already made it to the big city where he is writing a trilogy. (p. 53)

Dorrie observes her fellow townspeople—nicely?

He had been such a shy little boy. But the shyness had settled into surliness, and the dreaminess was sheer stupidity. Phil Lancer was growing up to be a good Birchfield citizen.

Points of view shift wildly in Powell's early books. We are in Linda's mind, as she is about to allow a yokel to marry her. "Later on, Linda thought, after they were married, she could tell him she didn't like to be kissed." The book ends with Dorrie still dreaming that the trilogist will come and take her off to New York.

In 1929 came *The Bride's House.* One suspects that Powell's own wit was the result of being obliged for so long to sing for her supper in so many strange surroundings:

> Lotta's children arrived, . . . three gray, horrid-looking little creatures and their names were Lois and Vera and Custer. . . . "We've come to stay!" they shouted. . . . "We've come to stay on the farm with Uncle Stephen and Aunt Cecily. Aren't you glad?"

No one is, alas. But these children are well-armored egotists.

> "She tells lies," Lois hissed in George's ear. "I'm the pretty one and she's the bright one. She told the conductor we lived in the White House. She's a very bad girl and mother and I can't do a thing with her. . . . Everything she says is a lie, Cousin Sophie, except when it hurts your feelings then it's true."

A child after absolutely no one's heart.

Unfortunately, Powell loses interest in the children; instead we are told the story of Sophie's love for two men. The grandmother character makes a dutiful appearance, and the Powell stock-company go rather mechanically through their paces. Powell wants to say something original about love but cannot get the focus right:

> A woman needed two lovers, she finally decides, one to comfort her for the torment the other caused her.

This is to be a recurring theme throughout Powell's work and, presumably, life: Coby versus Joe? or was it Coby *and* Joe?

Dance Night (1930) is the grittiest, most proletarian of the novels. There are no artists or would-be artists in Lamptown. Instead there is a railroad junction, a factory, the Bon Ton Hat Shop, where the protagonists, a mother and son, live close to Bill Delaney's Saloon and Billiard Parlor. Like the country the town has undergone the glorious 1920s boom; now Depression has begun to hit. Powell charts the fortunes of the mother-milliner, Elsinore Abbott, and her adolescent son, Morry. Elsinore's husband is a traveling salesman; and affects jealousy of his wife, who has made a go of her shop: but given up on her life.

Morry gets caught up in the local real-estate boom. He also gets involved with a waif, Jen, from an orphanage, who has been adopted by the saloonkeeper as a sort of indentured slave. Jen dreams of liberating her younger sister, Lil, from the home where their mother had deposited them. Jen is not much of an optimist:

People last such a little while with me. There's no way to keep them, I guess, that's why I've got to go back for Lil because I know how terrible it is to be left always—never see people again.

It took Powell a long time to work all this out of her system. Happily, farce intrudes. A young swain in a romantic moment

> slid his hand along her arm biceps and pressed a knuckle in her arm-pit. "That's the vein to tap when you embalm people" he said, for he was going to be an undertaker.

The highest work for a Lamptown girl is telephone operator, then waitress, then factory-hand. Powell has a Balzacian precision about these things; and she remembers to put the price-tag on everything. Money is always a character in her novels, as it was in Balzac's. In fact, Powell makes several references to him in her early books as well as to his *Eugénie Grandet.*

Morry grows up and his mother hardly notices him:

> She had moved over for Morry as you would move over for someone on a street car, certain that the intimacy was only for a few minutes, but now it was eighteen years and she thought, why Morry was hers, hers more than anything else in the world was.

This revelation shatters no earth for her or for him; and one can see how distressing such realism must have been—as it still is—for American Worshipers of the Family, Love, too.

Morry gets involved with a builder who indulges him in his dreams to create handsome houses for a public that only wants small look-alike boxes jammed together. Meanwhile, he loves Jen's sister Lil while Jen loves him: a usual state of affairs. The only bit of drama, indeed melodrama, is the return of Morry's father; there is a drunken fight between father and son; then a row between father and Elsinore, whom he accuses, wrongly, of philandering. Finally, "wearing down her barriers" she reaches for a pistol:

> This was one way to shut out words. . . . She raised the gun, closed her eyes and fired.

Although everyone knows that she killed her husband, the town chooses to believe it was suicide, and life goes on. So does Morry, who now realizes that he must go away: "There'd be no place that trains went that he wouldn't go."

In 1932, Powell published **The Tenth Moon.** This is a somewhat Catheresque novel composed with a fuguelike series of short themes (the influence of her ex-music critic husband?). Connie Benjamin is a village Bovary, married to a cobbler, with two daughters; she once dreamed of being a singer. Connie lives now without friends or indeed a life of any kind in a family that has not the art of communication with one another. Connie daydreams through life while her daughters fret ("They went to bed at ten but whispered until twelve, remembering through all their confidences to tell each other nothing for they were sisters"). The husband works in amiable silence. Finally,

Connie decides to have a social life. She invites to supper her daughter's English teacher; she also invites the music teacher, Blaine Decker, an exquisite bachelor, as adrift as Connie in dreams of a career in music that might have been.

Powell now introduces one of her major themes: the failed artist who, with luck, might have been—what? In dreams, these characters are always on stage, in life, they are always in the audience. But Blaine has actually been to Paris with his friend, a glamorous one-shot novelist, Starr Donnell (Glenway Westcott?). Blaine and Connie complement and compliment each other. Connie realizes that she has been "utterly, completely, hideously, unhappy" for fifteen years of marriage. Yet each pretends there are compensations to village life and poverty. (pp. 53-4)

Although the dreamers "talked of music until the careers they once planned were the careers they actually had but given up for the simple joys of living," knowing "success would have destroyed us," Connie goes too far. First, she tries indeed to sing and, for an instant, captures whatever it was she thought that she had: and promptly hemorrhages—tuberculosis. Second, she confides to Blaine that she lost a career, home, virginity to Tony the Daredevil, a circus acrobat, who abandoned her in Atlantic City where the kindly cobbler met and married her. He needed a wife; she could not go home. Blaine is made furious by the truth.

Then daughter Helen runs off with a boy, and the dying Connie pursues her. She finds that Helen has not only managed to get herself a job with a theatrical stock company but she is about to drop the boy; and Connie "knew almost for a certainty that Helen would climb the heights she herself had only glimpsed." Connie goes home to die, and Powell shifts to the dying woman's point of view:

> When Dr. Arnold's face flashed on the mirror she thought, "This must be the way one dies. People collect on a mirror like dust and something rushes through your mind emptying all the drawers and shelves to see if you're leaving anything behind." . . . What a pity, she thought, no one will ever know these are my last thoughts—that Dr. Arnold's mouth was so small.

At the end Connie is spared nothing, including the knowledge that her husband never believed that she came of a good family and studied music and only fell once from grace with an acrobat. Blaine goes off to Paris as a tour guide.

With **The Story of a Country Boy** (1934) she ends the Ohio cycle. This is the most invented of the novels. There is no pretty sister, no plain sister, no would-be artist, no flight from village to city. Instead Powell tells the story of a conventional young man, a country boy, who becomes a great success in business; then he fails and goes home to the country, no wiser than before. Ironically, Powell was doing the exact reverse in her own life, putting down deep lifelong roots in that village called Greenwich, far from her own origins. In a sense, this book is a goodbye to all that.

Again, one gets the boom and bust of the Twenties and

early Thirties. Chris Bennett is the All-American boy who makes good. He is entirely self-confident and sublimely unaware of any limitations. Yet, in due course, he falls, largely because he lacks imagination. There is a good deal of Warren Harding, Ohio's favorite son, in his makeup. He is more striking-appearance than reality. Also, Powell was becoming more and more fascinated by the element of chance in life, as demonstrated by Harding's incredible election (those were simple times) to the presidency. "Chris could not remember ever being unsure of himself except in little details of social life where his defects were a source of pride rather than chagrin." He also wonders "if pure luck had brought him his success." He is right to wonder: it has. When he finally looks down from the heights he falls. No fatal flaw—just vertigo. (p. 55)

[Powell has] developed an essayistic technique to frame her scenes. A chapter will begin with a diversion:

> In the utter stillness before dawn a rat carpentered the rafters, a nest of field mice seduced by unknown applause into coloratura ambitions, squeaked and squealed with amateur intensity. . . . Here, at daybreak, a host of blackbirds were now meeting to decide upon a sun, and also to blackball from membership in the committee a red-winged blackbird.

Unfortunately, her main character is too schematic to interest her or the reader. In any case, except for one final experiment, she has got Ohio out of her system; she has also begun to write more carefully, and the essays make nice point counterpoint to the theatricality of her scene-writing.

The theater is indeed the place for her first New York invention, *Jig-Saw* (1934), a comedy. The gags are generally very good but the plotting is a bit frantic. Claire is a charming lady, whose eighteen-year-old daughter, Julie, comes to stay with her in a Manhattan flat. Claire has a lover; and a best woman friend, to make the sharper jokes. Julie "is a very well brought up young lady—easy to see she has not been exposed to home life." Again it takes two to make a mate: "It takes two women to make your marriage a success." To which Claire's lover, Del, responds, "Have it your way—then Claire and I have made a success of my marriage to Margaret."

A young man, Nathan, enters the story. Both mother and daughter want him. Julie proves to be more ruthless than Claire. Julie moves in on Nathan; and announces their coming marriage to the press. He is appalled; he prefers her mother. But Julie is steel: "I can make something of you, Nate. Something marvelous." When he tries to talk her out of marriage, she declares, "I expect to go through life making sacrifices for you, dear, giving up my career for you." When he points out that she has never had a career, she rises to even greater heights: "I know. That's what makes it all the more of a sacrifice. I've never had a career. I never will have. Because I love you so much." Nate is trapped. Claire wonders if she should now marry Del but he advises against it: "You're the triangular type. . . ." With a bit of the sort of luck that so fascinated Powell by its absence in most lives, she might have had a successful commercial career in the theater. But that luck never came her way in life, as opposed to imagination. Finally, Powell's bad luck on Broadway was to be our literature's gain.

The New York cycle begins (1936) with *Turn, Magic Wheel* (dedicated to Dwight Fiske, a sub-Coward nightclub performer for whom Powell wrote special material). Powell now writes about a writer, always an edgy business. Dennis Orphen is a male surrogate for Powell herself. He is involved with two women, of course. He is also on the scene for good: he reappears in almost all her books, and it is he who writes finis to *The Golden Spur,* some twenty years later, as the Lafayette Hotel is being torn down and he realizes that his world has gone for good. But in 1936 Dennis is eager; on the make; fascinated by others: "his urgent need to know what they were knowing, see, hear, feel what they were sensing, for a brief moment to *be* them." He is consumed by a curiosity about others which time has a pleasant way of entirely sating.

Corinne is the profane love, a married woman; Effie is the sacred love, the abandoned wife of a famous writer called Andrew Callingham, Hemingway's first appearance in Powell's work. Effie is a keeper of the flame; she pretends that Andrew will come back: "Why must she be noble, frail shoulders squared to defeat, gaily confessing that life was difficult but that was the way things were?" Dennis publishes a *roman à clef* whose key unlocks the Callingham/Hemingway story and he worries that Effie may feel herself betrayed because Dennis completely dispels her illusion that the great man will return to her. As Dennis makes his New York rounds, the Brevoort Cafe, Longchamps, Luchows, he encounters the ubiquitous man about town, Okie, who will reappear in the New York novels, a part of their Balzacian detail. Okie edits an entertainment guide magazine; writes a column; knows everyone and brings everyone together. A party is going on at all hours in different parts of the town and Powell's characters are always on the move, and the lines of their extramarital affairs cross and recross. The essays now grow thoughtful and there are inner soliloquies:

> Walter missed Bee now but sometimes he thought it was more fun talking to Corinne about how he loved Bee than really being with Bee, for Bee never seemed to want to be alone with him, she was always asking everyone else to join them. In fact the affair from her point of view was just loads of fun and that was all. She never cried or talked about divorce or any of the normal things, she just had a fine time as if it wasn't serious at all.

(pp. 55-6)

There are amusing incidents rather than a plot of the sort that popular novels required in those days: Effie is hurt by Orphen's portrayal of her marriage in his book; Corinne vacillates between husband and lover; the current Mrs. Callingham goes into the hospital to die of cancer. There are publishers who live in awe of book reviewers with names like Gannett, Hansen, Paterson. One young publisher "was so brilliant that he could tell in advance that in the years 1934-35 and -36 a book would be called exquisitely well-written if it began: 'The boxcar swung out of the yards. Pip rolled over in the straw. He scratched himself where the straw itched him.' " Finally, the book's real protagonist is the city:

> In the quiet of three o'clock the Forties looked dingy, deserted, incredibly nineteenth century with the dim lamps in dreary doorways; in these midnight hours the streets were possessed by their ancient parasites, low tumble-down frame rooming houses with cheap little shops, though by day such remnants of another decade retreated obscurely between flamboyant hotels.

That city is now well and truly gone.

> Fleetingly, Effie thought of a new system of obituaries in which the lives recorded were criticized, mistaken steps pointed out, structure condemned, better paths suggested.

This is the essence of Dawn Powell: the fantastic flight from the mundane that can then lead to a thousand conversational variations; and the best of her prose is like the best conversation where no *escalier* ever muffles wit. As a result, she is at her best with The Party; but then most novels of this epoch were assembled around The Party where the characters proceed to interact and the unsayable gets said. Powell has a continuing hostess who is a variation on Peggy Guggenheim, collecting artists for gallery and bed. There is also a minor hostess, interested only in celebrities and meaningful conversation: she quizzes Dennis. " 'Now let's talk,' she commanded playfully [Powell's adverbs are often anesthetic preparatory for surgery]. 'We've never really had a nice talk, have we, Dennis? Tell me how you came to write? I suppose you had to make money so you just started writing, didn't you?' " Callingham himself comes to The Party. Powell's affection for the real Hemingway did not entirely obscure his defects, particularly as viewed by an ex-wife, Effie, who discovers to her relief, "There was no Andy left, he had been wiped out by Callingham the Success as so many men before him had been wiped out by the thing they represented." Effie frees herself from him and settles back into contented triangularity with Dennis and Corinne. Cake had; ingested, too.

In 1938, with *The Happy Island,* the Powell novel grows more crowded and The Party is bigger and wilder. This time the rustic who arrives in the city is not a young woman but a young man. Powell is often more at home with crude masculine protagonists, suspecting, perhaps, that her kind of tough realism might cause resentment among those who think of women as the fair sex.

A would-be playwright, Jeff Abbott (related to Morry?), arrives on the bus from Silver City; a manager has accepted his play with the ominous telegram, CASTING COMPLETE THIRD ACT NEEDS REWRITING [like that of *Jig-Saw*] COME IMMEDIATELY. Jeff has two friends in the city. One is Prudence Bly, a successful nightclub singer; the other is Dol, a gentleman party-giver and fancier of young men. At the book's end, Dol gives great offense by dying, seated in a chair, at his own party. How like him! guests mutter.

Prudence is the most carefully examined of Powell's women. She is successful; she drinks too much; she is seldom involved with fewer than two men. But it is the relationships between women that make Powell's novels so funny and original. Jean Nelson, a beautiful dummy, is Prudence's best friend; each needs the other to dislike. At the novel's beginning, Jean has acquired Prudence's lover Steve. The two girls meet for a serious drunken chat over lunch. "You aren't jealous of me, are you, Prudence?" "*Jealous?* Jealous? Good God, Jean, you must think this is the Middle Ages!" Prudence then broods to herself:

> Why do I lunch with women anyway? . . . We always end up snivelling over men and life and we always tell something that makes us afraid of each other for weeks to come. . . . Women take too much out of you, they drink too much and too earnestly. They drink the way they used to do china painting, and crewel work and wood burning.

In the restaurant things grow blurred: " 'You're so good to everyone,' sighed Jean. 'You really are.' Nothing could have enraged Prudence more or been more untrue." Finally, Jean goes: "Prudence looked meditatively after Jean as she wove her way earnestly through tables and knees. The girl did look like a goddess but the trouble was she walked like one, too, as if her legs had been too long wound in a flag."

Prudence's forebears include, yet again, the eccentric grandmother. This one is rich, and "Prudence was always glad her grandmother had been neither kind nor affectionate." The escape from Silver City had been easy. The grandmother was indifferent to everyone, including "her surly young Swedish chauffeur." A great traveler, Mrs. Bly

> always wanted to buy one dinner with two plates, as if he were a Pekinese, and, more alarming still, to take one room in the hotels where they stayed. . . . After all, she explained, she always slept with her clothes on so there was nothing indecent in it."

In addition, Mrs. Bly is a sincere liar, who believes that she was on the *Titanic* when it was sunk; and was courted by the czar.

Jeff Abbott and Prudence meet. They have an affair. Jeff is sublimely humorless, which intrigues Prudence. He is also a man of destiny, doomed to greatness in the theater. " 'I never yet found anything to laugh at in this world,' said Jeff. 'You never heard of a great man with a sense of humor, did you? Humor's an anesthetic, that's all, laughing gas while your guts are jerked out.' " Since they are not made for each other, marriage is a real possibility. Prudence is growing unsure of herself:

> She could not find the place where the little girl from Ohio, the ambitious, industrious little village girl, merged into the *Evening Journal* Prudence Bly, *The Town and Country* Bly. There were queer moments between personalities, moments such as the hermit crab must have scuttling from one stolen shell to the next one. . . . Prudence Bly was not so much a person as a conspiracy.

Then, Powell, in a quick scuttle, briefly inhabits her own shell:

> Prudence slew with a neat epithet, crippled with a true word, then, seeing the devastation about her and her enemies growing, grew frightened of revenges, backed desperately, and eventually found the white flag of Sentimentality as her salvation. For every ruinous *mot* she had a tear for motherhood.

The failure of Jeff's powerful play does not disturb him; and Prudence is somewhat awed since worldly success is the only thing that makes the island happy. But

> he belongs to the baffling group of confident writers who need no applause. For them a success is not a surprise but cause for wonder that it is less than international. . . . A failure proves that a man is too good for his times.

When he says he wants to buy a farm in the Midwest and settle down and write, Prudence is astonished. When he does exactly that, she goes with him. Integrity at last. No more glamour. No more happy island. Only fields, a man, a woman. In no time at all, she is climbing the walls; and heading back to New York where she belongs. Since Jean has let go of Steve, he receives her amiably (but then hardly anyone has noticed her departure). The book ends with: "Prudence's looks, [Steve] reflected with some surprise, were quite gone. She really looked as hard as nails, but then so did most women eventually." That excellent worldly novelist Thackeray never made it to so high a ground.

Angels on Toast (1940); war has begun to darken the skyline. But the turning wheel's magic is undiminished for Ebie, a commercial artist, whose mother is in the great line of Powell eccentrics. Ebie lives with another working woman, Honey, who "was a virgin (at least you couldn't prove she wasn't), and was as proud as punch of it. You would have thought that it was something that had been in the family for generations." But Ebie and Honey need each other to talk at, and in a tavern

> where O. Henry used to go . . . they'd sit in the dark smoked-wood booth drinking old-fashioneds and telling each other things they certainly wished later they had never told and bragging about their families, sometimes making them hot-stuff socially back home, the next time making them romantically on the wrong side of the tracks. The family must have been on wheels back in the Middle West, whizzing back and forth across tracks at a mere word from the New York daughters.

Brooding over the novel is the downtown Hotel Ellery. For seventeen dollars a week Ebie's mother, Mrs. Vane, lives in contented genteel squalor.

> BAR and GRILL: it was the tavern entrance to a somewhat medieval looking hotel, whose time-and-soot-blackened facade was frittered with fire-escapes, . . . its dark oak-wainscotting rising high to meet grimy black walls, its ship windows covered with heavy pumpkin chintz. . . . Once in you were in for no mere moment. . . .

> The elderly lady residents of the hotel were without too much obvious haste taking their places in the grill-room, nodding and smiling to the waitresses, carrying their knitting and a slender volume of some English bard, anything to prop against their first Manhattan . . . as they sipped their drinks and dipped into literature. It was sip and dip, sip and dip until cocktail time was proclaimed by the arrival of the little cocktail sausage wagon.

In its remoteness, this world before television could just as easily be that of *St. Ronan's Well.*

It is also satisfying that in these New York novels the city that was plays so pervasive a role. This sort of hotel, meticulously described, evokes lost time in a way that the novel's bumptious contemporary, early talking movies, don't.

> Another curious thing about these small, venerable, respectable hotels, there seemed no appeal here to the average newcomer. BAR and GRILL, for instance, appealed to seemingly genteel widows and spinsters of small incomes. . . . Then there were those tired flashes-in-the-pan, the one-shot celebrities, and, on the other hand, there was a gay younger group whose loyalty to the BAR and GRILL was based on the cheapness of its martinis. Over their simple dollar lunches (four martinis and a sandwich) this livelier set snickered at the older residents.

Ebie wants to take her mother away from all this so that they can live together in Connecticut. Mrs. Vane would rather die. She prefers to lecture the bar on poetry. There is also a plot: two men in business, with wives. One has an affair with Ebie. There is a boom in real estate; then a bust. By now, Powell has mastered her own method. The essay-beginnings to chapters work smartly:

> In the dead of night wives talked to their husbands, in the dark they talked and talked while the clock on the bureau ticked sleep away, and the last street cars clanged off on distant streets to remoter suburbs, where in new houses bursting with mortgages and the latest conveniences, wives talked in the dark, and talked and talked.

The prose is now less easygoing; and there is a conscious tightening of the language although, to the end, Powell thought one thing was different *than* another while always proving not her mettle but metal.

Powell is generally happiest in the BAR and GRILL or at the Lafayette or Brevoort. But in ***A Time to Be Born*** (1942) she takes a sudden social leap, and lands atop the town's social Rockies. Class is the most difficult subject for American writers to deal with as it is the most difficult for the English to avoid. There are many reasons. First, since the Depression, the owners of the Great Republic prefer not to be known to the public at large. Celebrities, of the sort that delight Powell, fill the newspapers while the great personages are seldom, if ever, mentioned; they are also rarely to be seen in those places where public and celebrities go to mingle. "Where," I asked the oldest of my waiter-acquaintances at the Plaza (we've known each other forty years), "have the nobles gone?" He looked sad. "I'm told they have their own islands now. Things," he was vague, "like that."

As I read my way through Powell I noted how few names she actually does drop. There is a single reference to the late Helen Astor, which comes as a mild shock. Otherwise the references are no more arcane than Rockefeller equals money (but then John D. had hired the first press agent). In a sense, Midwesterners were the least class-conscious of Americans during the first half of the twentieth century and those who came from the small towns (Hemingway, Dreiser, Powell herself) ignore those drawing rooms where Henry James was at home amongst pure essences, whose source of wealth is never known but whose knowledge of what others know is all that matters. Powell, agreeably, knows exactly how much money everyone makes (not enough) and what everything costs (too much). As for value, she does her best with love, but suspects the times are permanently inflationary for that over-hyped commodity. Powell never gets to Newport, Rhode Island, in her books but she manages Cape Cod nicely. She inclines to the boozy meritocracy of theater and publishing and the art world both commercial and whatever it is that 57th Street was and is.

But in *A Time to Be Born,* she takes on the highest level of the meritocracy (the almost-nobles) in the form of a powerful publisher and his high-powered wife, based, rather casually, on Mr. and Mrs. Henry Luce. At last Powell will have a fling at those seriously important people Diana Trilling felt that she was not up to writing about. But since one person is pretty much like another, all are as one in art, which alone makes the difference. Humble Ebie is neither more nor less meaningful than famous Amanda. It's what's made of them in art. Powell does have a good deal of fun with Julian and Amanda Evans, and the self-important grandeur of their lives. But Powell has no real interest in power or, more to this particular point, in those whose lives are devoted to power over others. Powell is with the victims. The result is that the marginal characters work rather better than the principals. One never quite believes that Julian owns and operates sixteen newspapers. One does believe Vicki Haven, who comes from the same Ohio town as Amanda, authoress of a *Forever Amber* best seller that has been written for her by the best pen-persons and scholar-squirrels that Julian's money can buy. (pp. 56-8)

Powell sets the *A Time* (Magazine?) *to Be Born* in that time *not* to be born, the rising war in the West:

> This was a time when the true signs of war were the lavish plumage of the women; Fifth Avenue dress shops and the finer restaurants were filled with these vanguards of war. Look at the jewels, the rare pelts, the gaudy birds on elaborate hair-dress and know that war was here; already the women had inherited the earth. The ominous smell of gunpowder was matched by a rising cloud of Schiaparelli's *Shocking*. The women were once more armed, and their happy voices sang of destruction to come. . . . This was a time when the artists, the intellectuals, sat in cafés and in country homes and accused each

other over their brandies or their California vintages of traitorous tendencies. This was a time for them to band together in mutual antagonism, a time to bury the professional hatchet, if possible in each other. . . . On Fifth Avenue and Fifty-fifth Street hundreds waited for a man on a hotel window ledge to jump; hundreds waited with craning necks and thirsty faces as if this single person's final gesture would solve the riddle of the world. Civilization stood on a ledge, and in the tension of waiting it was a relief to have one little man jump.

I know of no one else who has got so well the essence of that first war-year before we all went away to the best years of no one's life.

Again the lines of love and power cross and recross as they do in novels and often, too, in life. Since Julian publishes newspapers and magazines and now propaganda for England, much of it written in his wife's name, there is a Sarrautesque suspicion of language in Powell's reflections. A publisher remarks, "A fact changes into a lie the instant it hits print." But he does not stop there. "It's not print, it's the word," he declared. "The Spoken Word, too. The lie forms as soon as the breath of thought hits air. You hear your own words and say—'That's not what I mean. . . .'" Powell is drawing close to the mystery of literature, life's quirky—quarkish—reflection.

Amanda's power world does not convince quite as much as the Village life of Vicki and Ken and Dennis Orphen. Earlier readers will be happy to know that cute Corinne "had considered leaving her husband for Dennis Orphen for two or three years, and during her delay" the husband had divorced her "with Corinne still confused by this turn of events. . . . She wanted a little more time to consider marrying Dennis." When in doubt, do nothing, is the Powellesque strategy for Ken goes back and forth between Amanda and Vicki. For a time Amanda is all-conquering:

> She knew exactly what she wanted from life, which was, in a word, everything. She had a genuine distaste for sexual intimacy . . . but there were so many things to be gained by trading on sex and she thought so little of the process that she itched to use it as currency once again.

This time with the great writer-hunter Callingham. As it is, ironically, she gets knocked up by Ken and falls out with Julian. But she is never not practical: on the subject of writing, she believed that "the tragedy of the Attic poets, Keats, Shelley, Burns was not that they died young but that they were obliged by poverty to do all their own writing." Amanda's descendants are still very much with us: sweet lassies still saddened at the thought of those too poor to hire someone who will burn with a bright clear flame, as he writes their books for them.

It is plain that Powell was never entirely pleased with the Ohio cycle. She had a tendency to tell the same story over and over again, trying out new angles, new points of view, even—very occasionally—new characters. Finally, in mid-war, she made one last attempt to get Ohio (and herself) right. *My Home Is Far Away* (1944) is lapidary—at least compared to the loose early works. New York has polished her style; the essays glitter convincingly. The rural family is called Willard (*Winesburg, Ohio?*). A Civil War veteran for a grandfather; missing the odd eye, limb. Two sisters again. Lena the pretty one. Marcia the bright one (Powell again holds up the mirror to her past): "The uncanniness of [Marcia's] memory was not an endearing trait; invariably guests drew respectfully away from the little freak and warmed all the more to the pretty unaffected normalcy of little Lena." The book begins when father, mother, daughters leave a contented home. Suddenly, there is a nightmare vision: a man in a balloon floats across a starry sky. Home is now forever faraway.

Too clever by more than half and too much obliged throughout a peripatetic childhood to sing for a supper prepared by tone-deaf strangers, Powell hammered on the comic mask and wore it to the end. But when the dying mother has a horrendous vision of the man in the balloon, the mask blinks—for the last time.

Aunt Lois has a boarding house. The girls work. The old ladies are more than ever devastating. " 'A grandmother doesn't like children any more than a mother does,' she declared. 'Sometimes she's just too old to get out of tending them, that's all, but I'm not.' " Lena goes first. Then Marcia leaves town, as Powell left town, and catches that train which will go everywhere on earth that is not home. On a foggy pane of glass, she writes, with her finger, *Marcia Willard*. Dawn Powell.

After the war, Powell returned to the New York cycle for good. She published a book of short stories, **Sunday, Monday and Always** (1952). There are occasional ill-omened visits back home but no longer does she describe the escape; she has escaped for good. There are some nice comic moments. Edna, a successful actress, comes home to find her rustic family absorbed in radio soap operas. Although she is quite willing to describe her exciting life, the family out-maneuvers her. " 'Well, Edna,' cackled Aunt Meg, hugging her. 'I declare I wouldn't have known you. Well, you can't live that life and not have it show, they tell me.' " The "they tell me" is masterful. Powell's ear for the cadences of real-life talk only improved with time.

The final New York novels, **The Locusts Have No King** (1948), **The Wicked Pavilion** (1954), and **The Golden Spur** (1962), demonstrate Powell's ultimate mastery of subject, art, self. Where the last two are near-perfect in execution, **The Locusts Have No King** ("yet they, all of them, go forth by bands": Proverbs) shares some of the helter-skelterness of the early books. It is as if before Powell enters her almost-benign Prospero phase, she wants to cut loose once more at The Party.

This time the literary scene of the Forties gets it. The protagonist, Frederick Olliver, is a young man of integrity (a five-hundred-dollar-advance man) and literary distinction and not much will. He has been having an affair with Lyle, part of a married team of theater writers: Lyle is all taste and charm. But Frederick Olliver meets Dodo in a bar. Dodo is deeply, unrepentantly vulgar and self-absorbed. She says, "Pooh on you," and talks baby-talk, always a sign for Powell of Lilithian evil. They meet in one of Powell's best bars downtown, off Rubberleg Square, as she

calls it. The habitués all know one another in that context and, often, no other: parallel lives that are contiguous only in the confines of a cozy bar.

Frederick takes Dodo to a publisher's party (our old friend Dennis is there) and Dodo manages to appall. Lyle is hurt. Everyone is slightly fraudulent. A publisher who respects Frederick's integrity offers him the editorship of *Haw,* a low publication which of course Frederick makes a success of. Lyle writes her husband's plays. There is a literary man who talks constantly of Jane Austen, whom he may not have read, and teaches at the League for Cultural Foundations (a.k.a. The New School), where "classes bulged with middle-aged students anxious to get an idea of what it would be like to have an idea." But under the usual bright mendacities of happy island life, certain relationships work themselves out.

The most Powellesque is between two commercial artists, Caroline and Lorna:

> Ever since their marriages had exploded Caroline and Lorna had been in each other's confidence, sharing a bottle of an evening in Lorna's studio or Caroline's penthouse. In fact they had been telling each other everything for so many years over their cups that they'd never heard a word each other had said.

Revelations bombard deaf ears. "Frequently they lost interest in dinner once they had descended below the bottle's label and then a remarkable inspiration would come to open a second bottle and repeat the revelations they had been repeating for years to glazed eyes and deaf ears." Finally, "Both ladies talked in confidence of their frustrations in the quest for love, but the truth was they had gotten all they wanted of the commodity and had no intention of making the least sacrifice of comfort for a few Cupid feathers." Powell was a marvelous sharp antidote for the deep warm sincere love novels of that period. Today she is, at the least, a bright counterpoint to our lost-and-found literary ladies.

Powell deals again with the, always to her, mysterious element of luck in people's careers. When one thinks of her own bad luck, the puzzlement has a certain poignancy. But she can be very funny indeed about the admiration that mediocrity evokes on that happy island where it has never been possible to be too phony. Yet when Frederick, free of his bondage to Dodo, returns to Lyle, the note is elegiac: "In a world of destruction one must hold fast to whatever fragments of love are left, for sometimes a mosaic can be more beautiful than an unbroken pattern." We all tended to write this sort of thing immediately after Hiroshima, *mon assassin.*

The Wicked Pavilion (1954) is the Cafe Julien is the Lafayette Hotel of real life. The title is from *The Creevey Papers,* and refers to the Prince Regent's Brighton Pavilion, where the glamorous and *louche* wait upon a mad royal. Dennis Orphen opens and closes the book in his by now familiarly mysterious way. He takes no real part in the plot. He is simply still there, watching the not-so-magic wheel turn as the happy island grows sad. For him, as for Powell, the café is central to his life. Here he writes; sees friends; observes the vanity fair. Powell has now become masterful in her setting of scenes. The essays—preludes, overtures—are both witty and sadly wise. She also got the number to Eisenhower's America, as she brings together in this penultimate rout all sorts of earlier figures, now grown old: Okie is still a knowing man about town and author of the definitive works on the painter Marius; Andy Callingham is still a world-famous novelist, serene in his uncontagious self-love; and the Peggy Guggenheim figure is back again as Cynthia, an art gallery owner and party-giver. One plot is young love: Rick and Ellenora who met at the Cafe Julien in wartime and never got enough of it or of each other or of the happy island.

A secondary plot gives considerable pleasure even though Powell lifted it from a movie of the day called *Holy Matrimony* (1943) with Monty Woolley and Gracie Fields, from Arnold Bennett's novel *Buried Alive*. The plot that Powell took is an old one: a painter, bored with life or whatever, decides to play dead. The value of his pictures promptly goes so high that he is tempted to keep on painting after "death." Naturally, sooner or later, he will give himself away: Marius paints a building that had not been built before his "death." But only two old painter friends have noticed this, and they keep his secret for the excellent reason that one of them is busy turning out "Marius" pictures, too. Marius continues happily as a sacred presence, enjoying in death the success that he never had in life: "Being dead has spoiled me," he observes. It should be noted that the painting for this novel's cover was done by Powell's old friend, Reginald Marsh.

A new variation on the Powell young woman is Jerry, clean-cut, straightforward, and on the make. But her peculiar wholesomeness does not inspire men to give her presents; yet

> the simple truth was that with her increasingly expensive tastes she really could not afford to work. . . . As for settling for the safety of marriage, that seemed the final defeat, synonymous in Jerry's mind with asking for the last rites.

An aristocratic lady, Elsie, tries unsuccessfully to launch her. Elsie's brother, Wharton, and sister-in-law, Nita, are fine comic emblems of respectable marriage. In fact, Wharton is one of Powell's truly great and original monsters, quite able to hold his own with Pecksniff:

> Wharton had such a terrific reputation for efficiency that many friends swore that the reason his nose changed colors before your very eyes was because of an elaborate Rimbaud color code, indicating varied reactions to his surroundings. . . .

> Ah, what a stroke of genius it had been for him to have found Nita! How happy he had been on his honeymoon and for years afterward basking in the safety of Nita's childish innocence where his intellectual shortcomings, sexual coldness and caprices—indeed his basic ignorance—would not be discovered. . . . He was well aware that many men of his quixotic moods preferred young boys, but he dreaded to expose his inexperience to one of his own sex, and after certain cautious experiments realized that his ane-

mic lusts were canceled by his overpowering fear of gossip. . . . Against the flattering background of Nita's delectable purity, he blossomed forth as the all-round He-man, the Husband who knows everything. . . . He soon taught her that snuggling, hand-holding, and similar affectionate demonstrations were kittenish and vulgar. He had read somewhere, however, that breathing into a woman's ear or scratching her at the nape of the neck drove her into complete ecstasy. . . . In due course Nita bore him four daughters, a sort of door prize for each time he attended.

The Party is given by Cynthia now, and it rather resembles Proust's last roundup: "There are people here who have been dead twenty years," someone observes, including "the bore that walks like a man." There is a sense of closing time; people settle for what they can get. "We get sick of our clinging vines, he thought, but the day comes when we suspect that the vines are all that hold our rotting branches together." Dennis Orphen at the end records in his journal the last moments of The Wicked Pavilion as it falls to the wrecker's ball:

> It must be that the Julien was all that these people really liked about each other for now when they chance across each other in the street they look through each other, unrecognizing, or cross the street quickly with the vague feeling that here was someone identified with unhappy memories—as if the other was responsible for the fall of the Julien.

> (pp. 58-60)

In 1962, Powell published her last and, perhaps, most appealing novel, *The Golden Spur*. Again, the protagonist is male. In this case a young man from Silver City, Ohio (again), called Jonathan Jaimison. He has come to the city to find his father. Apparently twenty-six years earlier his mother, Connie, had had a brief fling with a famous man in the Village; pregnant, she came home and married a Mr. Jaimison. The book opens with a vigorous description of Wanamaker's department store being torn down. Powell is now rather exuberant about the physical destruction of her city (she wrote this last book in her mid-sixties when time was doing the same to her). There is no longer a Dennis Orphen on the scene; presumably, he lies buried beneath whatever glass and cement horror replaced the Lafayette. But there are still a few watering holes from the Twenties, and one of them is The Golden Spur where Connie mingled with the bohemians.

Jonathan stays at the Hotel De Long, which sounds like the Vanderbilt, a star of many of Powell's narratives. Jonathan, armed with Connie's cryptic diary, has a number of names that might be helpful. One is that of Claire van Orphen (related to Dennis?), a moderately successful writer, for whom Connie did some typing. Claire now lives embalmed in past time. She vaguely recalls Connie, who had been recommended to her by the one love of her life, Major Wedburn, whose funeral occurs the day Jonathan arrives at the De Long. Claire gives Jonathan possible leads; meanwhile, his presence has rejuvenated her. She proposes to her twin sister, Bea, that they live together; and gets a firm no. The old nostalgia burned down long ago for the worldly Bea. On the other hand, Claire's career is revived, with the help of a professionally failed writer who gets "eight bucks for fifteen hundred words of new criticism in a little magazine or forty for six hundred words of old criticism in the Sunday book section." He studies all of Claire's ladies' magazine's short stories of yesteryear; he then reverses the moral angle:

> "In the old days the career girl who supported the family was the heroine, and the idle wife was the baddie," Claire said gleefully. "And now it's the other way round. In the soap operas, the career girl is the baddie, the wife is the goodie because she's better for *business.* . . . Well, you were right. CBS has bought the two you fixed, and Hollywood is interested."

Powell herself was writing television plays in the age of Eisenhower and no doubt had made this astonishing discovery on her own.

Jonathan is promptly picked up by two girls at The Golden Spur; he moves in with them. Since he is more domestic than they, he works around the house. He is occasionally put to work in bed until he decides that he doesn't want to keep on being "a diaphragm-tester." Among his possible fathers is Alvine Harshawe alias Andrew Callingham alias Ernest Hemingway. Alvine is lonely: "You lost one set of friends with each marriage, another when it dissolved, gaining smaller and smaller batches each time you traded in a wife." Alvine has no clear memory of Connie; but toys with the idea of having a grown son, as does a famous painter named Hugow. Another candidate is a distinguished lawyer, George Terrence, whose actress daughter, unknown to him, is having an affair with Jonathan. Terrence is very much school of the awful Wharton of *The Wicked Pavilion,* only Terrence has made the mistake of picking up a young actor in the King Cole Bar of the St. Regis Hotel; the actor is now blithely blackmailing him in a series of letters worthy of his contemporary Pal Joey. Terrence welcomes the idea of a son but Jonathan shies away: he does not want his affair with the daughter to be incestuous.

Finally, Cassie, the Peggy Guggenheim character, makes her appearance, and The Party assembles for the last time. There are nice period touches: girls from Bennington are everywhere. . . . Cassie takes a fancy to Jonathan, and hires him to work at her gallery. He has now figured out not only his paternity but his maternity and, best of all, himself. The father was Major Wedburn, who was, of course, exactly like the bore that his mother Connie married. The foster father appears on the scene, and there is recognition of this if not resolution. As for Connie, she had slept with everyone who had asked her because "she wanted to be whatever anybody expected her to be, because she never knew what she was herself." Jonathan concludes, "That's the way I am." At an art gallery, "I have a career of other people's talents."

The quest is over. Identity fixed. The Party over, Jonathan joins Hugow in his cab. "He was very glad that Hugow had turned back downtown, perhaps to the Spur, where they could begin all over." On that blithe note, Powell's life and life-work end; and the wheel stops; the magic's

gone—except for the novels of Dawn Powell, all of them long since out of print, just as her name has been erased from that perpetually foggy pane, "American Literature." (p. 60)

> *Gore Vidal, "Dawn Powell, the American Writer," in* The New York Review of Books, *Vol. XXXIV, No. 17, November 5, 1987, pp. 52-60.*

Michael Dirda

Isaac Babel once remarked that there is no iron that can enter a human heart like a period in just the right place. He might have been describing Dawn Powell's novels: the killer aphorisms and sharp observations rain down like well-placed sniper fire. Turning the pages of these satiric group portraits of New York bohemians and Babbitt-like businessmen is like listening to, say, Gore Vidal at his most serenely malicious. Certainly it is no accident that Vidal has been Powell's champion—he calls her our finest comic novelist—and the efficient cause behind the republication of several of her books.

Dawn Powell (1897-1965) wrote 15 novels, a couple of plays and was sometimes unkindly called the second Dorothy Parker. She spent most of her adult life in Greenwich Village, where much of her fiction takes place. Not quite period pieces, her novels are bittersweet screwball comedies, where the characters all drink like maenads at a bacchanal and the race under the table is always to the wittiest.

Powell's books typically take the reader on a tour of some glamorous, decadent locale, and feature dozens of characters. Sometimes there's a sympathetic central figure, but more often everyone is on the make, on a roll or falling down drunk. She is exceptionally dazzling in her descriptions, often the dullest parts of modern novels. A young gold-digger in a bar "was evidently proud of her extreme slenderness for her gray-striped green wool dress followed every bone and sinew snugly, and from the demure way she thrust out her high-pointed breasts you would have thought they were her own invention, exclusive with her."

This darling, Dodo by name, soon snuggles up to a public relations man who "might be engaged in the world's most degrading occupation but at least he was better at it than anyone else." Later she tricks the novel's hero, a medievalist named Frederick Olliver, into taking her to a soiree held by a rich but stingy publisher. Frederick eventually escapes her clutches to find himself

> peacefully wandering around the Beckley library in the upper reaches of the house, looking at the glass cabinets of rare manuscripts, viewing the sumptuous canyons of books, the portraits of beagle-nosed Beckleys each firmly clasping an exquisitely bound book as if to keep the artist from stealing it.

All these quotes occur in the first 20 pages of *The Locusts Have No King* (1948), and the remaining 250 pages are just as wicked. Powell claimed that *The Satyricon* was her favorite novel and she adopts very much its style in her own work: life as a sideshow; terrific party scenes; easy sexual liaisons; an atmosphere of brittle wit, desperation and venality; an airy, tart prose; plot developments growing out of continual misunderstanding; mini-disquisitions about art, life, fortune. In truth, you don't so much read these satiric romances as look down into them from some quite lofty Olympian heights. Your friend Dawn merely points out the antic goings-on, as you both chuckle and weep and mumble "What fools these mortals be!"

In *Locusts* Lyle Gaynor, who loves Frederick, is married to a creepy bed-ridden playwright. The invalid makes a pitch to go on a trip to the Southwest. "I could ride through the mountains," he explains, "and join up with the Penitentes, maybe, offer myself for crucifixion, really enjoy myself, for once." Hoping for some help with his career, Frederick meanwhile visits a book-chat wheeler-dealer named Tyson Bricker who

> beamed at Frederick with the honest affection one could feel toward a man who will never be a rival, a man one is sure will never be anything but a distinguished failure, a man one can praise freely and honestly without danger of sending him zooming up the ladder ahead of oneself.

As it happens, Frederick unexpectedly becomes a literary hot ticket and after a series of contretemps drifts away from his beloved Lyle; he then finds himself infatuated with Dodo. Powell is especially fine in describing love gone wrong, the birth of jealousy and the gray sorrowfulness that invades the soul. Frederick breaks Lyle's heart and then admires "the new pallor emphasizing the contrast of brown eyes and red-gold hair" while "the aura of secret sadness made her extraordinarily beautiful." Later, in a paragraph worthy of Proust, he gets on a bus to go back to his office, as Lyle crosses the street:

> He caught a glimpse of her from his window and before he was conscious of it the old aching rush of love for her swept over him. He saw how thin she was, how sad her face, and as he watched she made a troubled gesture toward her eyes. He wanted to cry out to her, to beg her to wait, only wait—but for what? Tears came to his eyes as the bus carried him on.

Most of *Locusts* is powered by the various misunderstandings that prevent these two lovers from getting back together, but this simple device—straight out of French farce—allows the novel to embrace most of artsy New York during the late '40s: Spanish poets, magazine editors married to Russian emigres, ad execs, camp followers, night school litterateurs. Eventually Frederick starts to quarrel with Dodo; once while they are getting ready for bed, he shivers before "her slim body in the half unfastened purple jersey as taut as an arrow about to whizz through him." The affair finally over, Frederick finds himself "so exhausted that he could not trust his sense of relief. It was the relief of the tired mother when the baby stops crying at last; the realization of its death comes later." Anyone could write the first part of that last sentence; it takes genius to add the final chilling twist.

Brilliant as *The Locusts Have No King* is, its excellence is typical of Powell. *The Golden Spur*—her last book, published in 1962—is somewhat softer, kinder, in its portrait of New York ways. A young Candide comes to a bar called The Golden Spur looking for his real father among the New Yorkers his long-dead mother once hung out with. Naive, handsome and winning, he soon attracts the attention of a couple of young sophisticates who invite him to move in with them: Lize, with her close-cropped hair and boyish figure, "drew the interest of men of all sexes"; while Darcy seemed to exemplify midwestern practicality. . . .

A classic innocent, Jonathan Jaimison changes the life—for the better—of everyone he meets. The faded lady novelist, the hack writer, the desperate art dealer, the legendary painter, the aspiring actress, the alcoholic professor, the haunted attorney, the world-famous novelist—all of them decide to be a mother or a father or a lover to the young man. It's just like a fairy tale, told by Scott Fitzgerald, with a suitable happy ending for Jonathan in the arms of a young girl in the back of a taxi heading for The Golden Spur.

Besides these forays into bohemia (another is *The Wicked Pavilion*), Powell's range also includes business satire à la John O'Hara or Tom Wolfe. In *Angels on Toast* she eviscerates a pair of two-timing businessmen who ride the night trains back and forth between Chicago and New York, balancing love affairs, wives, mistresses, elaborate schemes and golden daydreams. As usual she sets up a full dramatis personae, shifting among its members to make her satirical thrusts. At one point, the two anti-heroes encounter a pseudo-British, name-dropping sharpy named T.V. Truesdale. Powell captures him forever in a sentence:

> He paid for his beer very carefully from a frayed ancient pigskin wallet, and this too he fondled as he had his briefcase, as if these were all that had been rescued of his priceless treasures when the palace was destroyed.

Everything is wonderful in that sentence, from the balance of phrases to the simile that makes us smile. A writer as good as this merits more than rediscovery: She deserves readers. Lots of them.

> *Michael Dirda, "Satyricon in Manhattan," in* Book World—The Washington Post, *March 18, 1990, p. 10.*

Joseph Coates

Rediscovering a good but neglected writer is both exhilarating and depressing. Here is this terrific novelist, Dawn Powell, a contemporary of Hemingway and Fitzgerald and more prolific than the two put together, who has left a whole shelf of funny, entertaining books that few had ever heard of before fellow novelist Gore Vidal's act of reclamation in the *New York Review of Books* a few years ago [see excerpt above]—part of which is reprinted to introduce *Angels on Toast, The Wicked Pavilion* and *The Golden Spur.* To anyone who reads a lot, finding those books, and Powell's *The Locusts Have No King* is like striking oil while spading the garden.

But it's depressing because here is an outstanding writer

who nearly slipped through the cracks—or canyons—of critical attention into an oblivion as profound as the one that swallowed up, say, Frank Yerby, who for that matter far outsold Powell in her own time (1897-1965). Vidal attributes her failure to achieve more than cult status to the fact that

> she was that unthinkable monster, a witty woman who felt no obligation to make a single, much less a final, down payment on Love or the Family; she saw life with a bright Petronian neutrality, and every host at life's feast was a potential Trimalchio to be sent up.

That Powell's favorite writers were (according to Vidal) the author of *The Satyricon* and Balzac means that she was great on parties, on "sleeping around" (as it used to be called) and on the sweet and sour smells of success, failure and everything in between. It also helps explain why she created characters so prodigally and was so convivially willing to follow them anywhere, usually to another bar. She was the Gibbon of saloon life, unsurpassed even by John McNulty or A. J. Liebling, often to the structural detriment of her novels.

Especially in her early books, the drinking is torrential, but anyone of a certain age who managed to survive that scene will corroborate both the accuracy of her bar-scapes and her perfect pitch for the kind of insane conversations that spiraled up like swamp gas in those dim and smoky places. In *The Locusts Have No King* (1948), perhaps her most bibulous book,

> A red-haired girl named Buffy was weeping loudly that she had been double-crossed by Larry Glay, but one thing she would bet her bottom dollar on was that he would never marry that little tramp, who followed him onto the plane, because he had told her personally that was all off. Anyway, his wife had gotten divorced from him twice before and they always got married again.
>
> "You'd think they'd get tired of the blood tests," she said.

In *Angels on Toast* (1940) there is an elderly antique dealer and slumlord who palms off her dubious finds on her helpless tenants, conducting all business from the bar of the Hotel Ellery in consultation with the bartender, Albert.

> "Here's a message from 4A," she says. "Says the butterfly sofa I brought her from Pittsfield was filled with baby mice. Ridiculous on the face of it."
>
> "Must have been a mother mouse there somewhere," agreed Albert.

Beneficiary of a classically bad Midwestern childhood, Powell during World War I forsook the bleak villages of Ohio for Greenwich Village, which remained her base of operations for the next 45 years or more. Consequently, most of the New York novels reprinted so far center on a young provincial arriving in the Big Apple, improvising a life and finding his or her true self in the process. (The exception is *Angels,* half of which is set in Chicago and contains a vivid portrayal of what must be the old Club Alabam on Rush Street as it was until at least the 1960s.)

There is usually a love story, but often it has no more importance to the book than the "romantic interest" that was routinely folded into a Marx Brothers movie, and the novels usually end with the kind of benedictory reunions of true lovers that we see in Shakespearean comedy. The real payoff in reading Powell is the acuteness of her psychology. Her specialty is showing us the comic implications of the fact that friendships between members of the same sex often consist mostly of standard (and expected) betrayals and how those betrayals differ from the ways in which men and women consistently double-cross each other.

Thus, the young model and girl-around-town Jerry Dulaine in *The Wicked Pavilion* (1952) loses her early friend and sponsor Tessie because the latter's "men friends were taken in by her praise [of Jerry] and went so far as to prefer Jerry to her prettier self." The young women separate, "Tessie to marry a natty-looking promoter named Walton simply to stop him making passes at Jerry, who honestly detested him and had not wanted to offend Tessie by rebuffing him."

In *The Golden Spur* (1962), young Jonathan Jaimison ends up rooming with two art-groupies who have just been jilted in succession by the painter Hugow.

> It was a lesson in female psychology to hear that although Hugow had cruelly deserted each of them they bore him no grudge, for he had more than atoned by treating the other badly too.

And in the same book, the failed writer Earl Turner visits the opulent digs of his immensely successful boyhood pal, Alvine Harshawe, (a good imitation of Hemingway as he was in the '50s) and wishes "that Alvine would get sore at him, dignify him with a little decent jealousy. . . . [T]hey were each other's oldest friends. Not that it meant they liked each other. Some old friends went to their graves without learning to like each other, without even getting to know each other."

A remarkably good-natured satirist, Powell neither denounces nor proselytizes, seems to have no particular agenda in mind and obviously likes most of her people—not least for giving her such great comic targets. She told a British publisher that her

> novels are based on the fantastic designs made by real human beings earnestly laboring to maladjust themselves to fate. . . . I give them their heads. They furnish their own nooses.

Nevertheless, it's probably the sharpness of her eye as much as anything else that precluded her greater popularity. Her great skill was in showing how people con themselves into trouble, and every reader will probably find himself somewhere in her gallery of self-deceits.

The enlightened modern reader will have no trouble laughing at why Chicago hustler Jay North in *Angels* would never marry his mistress: "you can't marry a woman that makes love as well as Ebie. . . . You know that, Lou." But how many can laugh without wincing at the "middle-aged students (in *Locusts*) anxious to get an idea of what it would be like to have an idea"?

Hardier readers, however, will be rewarded by at least two laughs per page of Powell, whom Vidal accurately calls "our best comic novelist," plus a goldmine of period lore, ranging from late '30s to late '50s, and a cumulative statement about the gradual erosion of spirit, individuality, and eccentricity in the American character since the end of World War II. People don't act much like this anymore, nor do they write novels this funny.

> *Joseph Coates, "Forgotten No More," in* Chicago Tribune—Books, *April 22, 1990, p. 3.*

FURTHER READING

Feingold, Michael. "New York Stories: Dawn Powell's Acid Texts." *The Village Voice Literary Supplement,* No. 86 (June 1990): 12-14.
> Favorable retrospective overview of Powell's career.

Josephson, Matthew. "Dawn Powell: A Woman of *Esprit.*" *The Southern Review* IX, No. 1 (Winter 1973): 18-52.
> Detailed biographical and critical overview.

John R. Powers

1945-

(Born John James Powers) American novelist and journalist.

Set during the 1950s and 1960s, Powers's strongly autobiographical novels wryly satirize the trials of growing up Catholic in the strict pre-Vatican II era. His farcical views of the parochial educational system contain sardonic humor and sentimentality, yet his caustic views of Catholicism and its quirks have been considered blasphemous by some. However, most reviewers praise his quick-witted reminiscences and exaggerated characterizations. Pamela Marsh commented: "Somebody—could it have been those nuns?—taught [Powers] how to handle the English language with superb, justified confidence."

Powers's fiction is set in Chicago, where he was born and raised. The predominantly Catholic south side neighborhood where he grew up is featured in his first two novels, *The Last Catholic in America: A Fictionalized Memoir* and its sequel *Do Black Patent Leather Shoes Really Reflect Up?* These works follow the narrator and protagonist, Eddie Ryan, through his elementary and high school years. At St. Bastion's Grammar School, Eddie is contented: he is dimly aware of the unexplained mysticism and superstitions of Catholicism and does not question his faith. Eddie is a thinly disguised portrait of Powers, who has described himself as "a product of sixteen years of Catholic education" and claims to be the only student in his school's history to flunk music appreciation. A mediocre student at best, Eddie must contend with low grades, the traumas of his first confession and first communion, and nuns who openly favor obsequious students. Some of the nuns are given nicknames like "Boom-Boom Bernadine" and "Cyril the Savage," but one, Sister Lee, is so menacing and domineering that none will do her justice. Sister Lee, Eddie says, "was ninety years old when I began first grade and she didn't decide to die until I was nearly twenty."

In *Do Black Patent Leather Shoes Really Reflect Up?,* Powers offers a more potent satire of Catholicism. Older and wiser, Eddie now attends the all-male Bremmer High School, an institution sorely lacking in basic educational facilities. For example, the only sex education the students receive, a film explaining the life cycle of the polar bear, only makes them desperate for real sexual knowledge and experience. The novel's title refers to the popular notion that the reflection in patent leather shoes allows boys to see up girls' dresses. Although several critics found the humor in this work sophomoric, others noted that Powers's protagonist is mature enough to realize the unfair caste system of the high school and to comprehend the potential cruelty of his fellow adolescents. The novel was later adapted for the stage and became both a critical and commercial success. Powers's next work, *The Unoriginal Sinner and the Ice-Cream God,* focuses on collegiate life

and the anxiety-ridden entance into mainstream society. Tim Conroy, the wise-cracking, confused narrator, enrolls in a Chicago commuter college during the turbulent era of the Vietnam War. His many questions about life, death, and religion are fielded by a friend named Caepan, an atheistic garage mechanic who doubles as Tim's personal, earthbound God. More bittersweet and realistic than Powers's previous novels, *The Unoriginal Sinner and the Ice-Cream God* was acclaimed for its poignant use of humor to convey significant issues.

(See also Contemporary Authors, Vols. 69-72, rev. ed.)

PRINCIPAL WORKS

NOVELS

The Last Catholic in America: A Fictionalized Memoir 1973
Do Black Patent Leather Shoes Really Reflect Up? 1975
The Unoriginal Sinner and the Ice-Cream God 1977

Publishers Weekly

[In *The Last Catholic in America: A Fictionalized Memoir,* on] an impulse triggered by a chance conversation with a seatmate, Powers stopped off between planes to visit the section of Chicago's South Side where he grew up; before the 1920s this had been a town called Seven Holy Tombs—which suggests how utterly Catholic a community it had been before Chicago engulfed it. Clearly Powers was stirred by the ghosts of boyhood past in seeing Sarah's Snack bar and the now-dead sights and relics of his mischievous years in "St. Bastion's" parish and school. He tries to recall his experiences through childlike eyes, telling everything he can remember—and, one suspects, exaggerating some episodes—about the "pain" of being a boy and a Catholic at the same time: bullying priests, sadistic nuns, sex learned two ways—from schoolmates like "Felix the Filth Fiend" and from Father Vendel. Powers adds nothing new to the *genre* of Catholic nostalgia; Catholics in fact, may feel his people are caricatures. His altar-boy experiences are amusing, however, and his writing is lively and colorful. (pp. 64-5)

> *A review of "The Last Catholic in America: A Fictionalized Memoir," in* Publishers Weekly, *Vol. 203, No. 4, January 22, 1973, pp. 64-5.*

Paul Kiniery

Mr. Powers refers to . . . [*The Last Catholic in America*] as *A Fictionalized Memoir.* It gives us a day-by-day account of Eddie Ryan at St. Bastion Grammar School in an area on Chicago's South Side in the 1950's. On the first day of school, Eddie found himself with other beginning children in the basement of the school. "All the boys were on one side and all the girls on the other. Everyone was sitting as if they had been painted into their folding chairs. No one talked." Then Father O'Reilly, the pastor, arrived. The author observes: "If it had been a Bing Crosby movie, the priest would have been smiling and he would have said, 'Greetings, Children. It's certainly nice to see all your happy faces today. My name is Father O'Reilly and I would like to welcome you to St. Bastion Grammar School. We have a lovely school here which I'm sure you will enjoy.' " Mr. Powers then adds: "That's not the way it was. Father O'Reilly didn't introduce himself. He didn't have to. Through his years of self-sacrifice, hard work, determination, Hell-preaching, and pure intimidation, parishoners had come to fear Father O'Reilly even more than they feared God." Then Eddie continues: "Although we first graders believed there was a God, we KNEW there was a Father O'Reilly. He didn't smile."

Going upstairs, Eddie found himself, as he reports, in a classroom that had "eighty-five kids in it. The nun, Sister Eleanor, spent half that first day bragging how she had over ninety kids the year before. Since at that time I couldn't count past four, neither number impressed me." fifteen chapters, most of them very funny, are required to tell of Eddie's progress through the eight grades. Mr. Powers has the gift of putting himself in Eddie's place as Eddie faces life's problems. . . .

Like many young people, Eddie may have been unduly critical of some of his teachers, but when Sister Edna died he realized that he had lost a truly helpful friend. Even though you may not have attended a parochial school, you will probably enjoy this book. I didn't, and I did.

> *Paul Kiniery, in a review of "The Last Catholic in America," in* Best Sellers, *Vol. 33, No. 2, April 15, 1973, p. 42.*

Martin Levin

Out of the questionable experience of elementary school, John R. Powers has salvaged a delightful reminiscence [*The Last Catholic in America*]. This puts the author one up on the run of survivors of childhood, who—as a rule—have nothing to show for their misery but undeserved nostalgia.

Mr. Powers's memories of growing up Catholic on the South Side of Chicago in the 1950's are a well-balanced mixture of pleasure and pain. To wit: the pain of getting your head shaved as a dandruff cure—and the ecstasy of being named a traffic-patrol boy on the strength of your new haircut. The pain of corporal punishment from any one of a troop of nuns at St. Bastion's school. The pleasure of reading forbidden paperbacks and the pain of getting caught. The zenith of sensuality at the Swank roller skating rink, where a foxtrot, accompanied by live organ music, could lead to a mixture of seventh heaven and severe injury.

The author's fictional hero, a schoolboy named Eddie Ryan, makes it bravely through the eighth grade, sharing with the reader some of the wisdom picked up along the way. ("First graders are easily recognizable. They are the only ones who have mittens clipped to their coats in October.") You can't go home again, as Eddie Ryan finds out years later. Mr. Powers's book makes it beautifully clear why you shouldn't want to.

> *Martin Levin, in a review of "The Last Catholic in America," in* The New York Times Book Review, *April 22, 1973, p. 28.*

Martin Marty

Powers, a young Chicago writer and media man, looks back on the Second City Catholicism of the 1950s in *The Last Catholic in America: A Fictionalized Memoir.* The genre is becoming quite familiar. Numbers of authors inscribe sheaf upon sheaf of memories of Catholic childhoods and present them as books. . . . Some look back in rage, in the mood of the Kavanaugh Klan. I suppose there are some in the *Twin Circle* circle who picture pre-Vatican II churchdom as "the good old days."

More common is the mood that comes naturally to Powers, one for which the dustjacket people find the word "bittersweet" most appropriate. Powers has talent; his may not be a great book, but it is often funny. We successfully read out several chapters in the family reading circle, and we don't long fool around with someone who cannot hold attention instantly and constantly. Catholics can compare notes as he describes his perceptions of nuns, parochial routines, fears, confessions, old habits.

A ghetto Catholicism this was: it represented a self-contained world. Non-Catholics hardly ever came into the ken of Powers' young anti-hero as he made his way through eight years of parochial school in the "Seven Holy Tombs" area of Chicago, at "St. Bastion's" church. The atmosphere seemed to include both claustrophobia and security. Powers there learns the way of survival, as a gentile *Schlemihl* who gives up thumbsucking for Lent—in the third grade, fumbles his way into the less profound mysteries of sex, and endures tragedies as steadfastly as did earlier progressing pilgrims.

Two families of thought kept returning to me during the reading. One: how irrevocable is that world of twenty years ago! That world he described surrounded me when I first wandered into the city at the beginning of a career a score of years ago. That vestiges of ghetto-Catholicism are strong in Chicago I know; that it has little real future, I also know. The other family: how structurally functionally similar this urban Catholicism was to the rural Protestantism in which I grew up. The same comforting and threatening legalism, the repressive atmosphere which the hardier somehow transcended, the grotesqueries and good times were so similar to his worlds! Will Powers' children and mine ever know a similarly intact world over against which to define themselves? (pp. 82-3)

> *Martin Marty, in a review of "The Last Catholic in America: A Fictionalized Memoir," in* The Critic, *Chicago, Vol. 31, No. 5, May-June, 1973, pp. 82-3.*

Kirkus Reviews

[*Do Black Patent Leather Shoes Really Reflect Up?* is another] pre-Vatican II rag, which follows closely the elbow jab approach of the author's elementary parochial school reminiscences in *The Last Catholic in America* (1973) and this time "Eddie Ryan" undergoes four years of a Catholic boys' high school. Predictably there are accounts of dating and dances when the girls were warned not to wear shiny shoes which might reflect "up"; lectures on sex (a mimeo sheet titled "Concerning Making Out, What You Should Know"); sports events prefaced by Hail Marys; retreats ("School retreats were like Holiday Inns . . . they were always the same."), etc. There are anecdotes concerning classmates (the beasts, the "sex-fiends," the victims and wiseacres), the teachers (those who hit and those who seem several worlds removed), first and interim adolescent loves, and those unique once-in-a-school-lifetime moments—at the victory sock hop, the day's outstanding football player slugged the homecoming queen during the award presentation. Fond, self-indulgent memories, a bit damp in spots, which could be matched by any middle-aged Catholic school grad. (pp. 978-79)

> *A review of "Do Black Patent Leather Shoes Really Reflect Up?" in* Kirkus Reviews, *Vol. XLIII, No. 16, August 15, 1975, pp. 978-79.*

Publishers Weekly

Powers follows his *The Last Catholic in America* with another winner [*Do Black Patent Leather Shoes Really Reflect Up?*]. In this free-wheeling fictionalized memoir, he is as funny as a good stand-up comedian. His outlandish description of his four years at St. Patrick Bremmer High may sometimes leave the reader punch-line drunk, but will not soon be forgotten. He remembers a not-too-bright teacher, who played "straight man to 40 comedians," and Brother Sofeck, whose suggestion to burn oneself with a match when temptation was too great demonstrated "that the tactics of the Mafia and the Catholic Church were so alike." Black patent leather shoes, Catholic girls were warned, enabled boys to see up their dresses. Places with white tablecloths were to be avoided because they reminded boys of bed. The book is a cornucopia of laughs. (pp. 291-92)

> *A review of "Do Black Patent Leather Shoes Really Reflect Up?" in* Publishers Weekly, *Vol. 208, No. 8, August 25, 1975, pp. 291-92.*

Cathy Klein

John Powers has provided us with yet another book of "fictionalized memoirs" on growing up in the Catholic parochial school system. His first chronicle, *The Last Catholic in America,* covered grammar school and with *Do Black Patent Leather Shoes Really Reflect Up?,* he picks up the thread at eighth grade and follows it through senior year in a Catholic boys high school.

The odd query of the title refers to the alleged warning Catholic girls received in class lectures on modesty that "a boy could see up a girl's dress by looking into her black patent leather shoes." A corny locker room joke, but, in fact, Powers' book abounds in corny jokes and neato gags of the sort that one might expect to overhear on the Chicago Transit Authority from some wise-guy freshmen on their way home from algebra class.

As the scene opens, Eddie Ryan, the protagonist of Powers' previous book, has just finished eighth grade and is about to take that big step forward into high school. He is naive and already deeply absorbed in the issues of early adolescence: pimples and curfews and the rigid caste system of athletes, scholars, school spirit "nuts," and those pariahs—the homely kids.

Power paints his characters, with only a very few exceptions, as incredible eccentrics. The world of his teen-agers is a world of droll clowns, freaks and oddballs. Witness Felix the Filth-Fiend Lindor, "proud possessor of the world's dirtiest mind . . . a mind that worked like the floor of a livery stable." Or the ancient, unwashed Latin teacher, Brother Coratelli, who was "nicknamed among the students as 'Sort-a-Smelli.'" Or, Crazy Freddie LeGrand, who when his parked car was hit by a truck, "jumped up and ran out his front door holding his neck and screaming, 'Whiplash!'" One must persist in patient reading to find what might pass for a believable teen-ager in this book. Powers gives us a parade of such over-blown caricatures, such hyperbolic creatures that we are number to the intended satire. In fact, it is never clear throughout the book if he offers these characters with irony intended or if he is just piling up wisecracks. Those characters who by rights should have our sympathy are made laughable by the author for their misfortune.

> Girls like Dolores Crosley make it a point to hang around with a group of fat and ugly girls. That night at St. Bastion's, though, Dolores Crosley was with only one fat and ugly girl. The standard procedure in such a situation was that one guy asked the gorgeous girl to dance while one of his friends asked the same of the fat and ugly girl. If you just asked the gorgeous girl, she would give the excuse that, gee, she'd like to, but right now she was talking to her friend. So one of your friends had to get the fat and ugly girl out of the way. Everyone, including the fat and ugly girl, was aware of this social maneuver. That was, after all, the only reason a fat and ugly girl bothered to be seen at a mixer with one of her gorgeous friends: to catch the crumbs.

Or,

> Fat and ugly kids never took gym; nor, like other students, did they have to give excuses to the coach for not doing so. If a normal person wanted to skip gym, he would have to bring a note from his family doctor stating that he was suffering from a terminal disease and that playing basketball was detrimental to his health. But fat and ugly kids didn't have to bother with notes. They just didn't take gym. The reason, though never officially stated, was apparent. Why get everyone else sick to their stomachs by having fat and ugly kids all over the locker room?

As in Powers' first book, the real theme of this one also, is a sarcastic put-down of Catholic education as he knew it. The parochial school system in Powers' day *was* laden with much silliness and provides a ripe target, in retrospect, for spoof and satire. It is here that Powers succeeds. One chapter entitled simply "Catholic Girls" explores some of the old-fashioned views on sex as taught in his high school days. Powers explains matter-of-factly:

> The Church had such a hatred for sex that it refused to even mention the name. If you thought about doing it, then it was called an 'impure thought.' If you went ahead and did it, it was referred to as an 'impure act,' a 'prurient interest,' or an 'illicit activity.' If you did it with your wife, it was the 'Marriage Act' or 'the privileges of marriage.' If you thought about doing it with your neighbor's wife, then it was called 'coveting thy neighbor's wife.' If you did it with your neighbor's wife, then it was 'adultery.' If you did it alone, it was 'self-abuse.' And if you didn't do it at all, it was called 'holiness.'

The intended spirit of *Do Black Patent Leather Shoes Really Reflect Up?* is ostensibly something like: "It was tough when we had to go through it but now that it's all over let's all have a good horselaugh over the whole experience." But despite the occasional masterful passage, Powers is too bitter and a little too enamored of corny gags to pull it off and give us the colorful touch of Catholic nostalgia that would make enjoyable reading. (pp. 82-4)

Cathy Klein, in a review of "Do Black Patent Leather Shoes Really Reflect Up?" in The Critic, *Chicago, Vol. XXXIV, No. 3, Spring, 1976, pp. 82-4.*

Dennis Vellucci

Powers' "fictionalized memoir" [*Do Black Patent Leather Shoes Really Reflect Up?*] is an example of nostalgia at its worst. A sentimental, cliché-ridden account of the author's experience at a Catholic boys high school, the book thrives on the type of humor that would not be out of place on a second-rate television situation comedy. It is hardly original to say that the Latin teacher was so old, "it was a strong possibility that Latin was his native tongue." The humor could have been copied right off the wall of a stall in any Catholic high school john.

Powers tells us nothing that makes his high school experience unique. His anti-academic bias ("Unless you plan on becoming a priest, there is no reason in the world to learn Latin.") and his clearly pre-Vatican II mentality are disturbing. There are predictable cheap shots at an old-fashioned Catholic morality that has become obsolete. "Timmy Heidi's parents were extremely good Catholics," Powers writes. "They had eleven children. Their religious fervor had been restrained only by the onset of Mrs. Heidi's menopause." When Powers' sophomoric brand of humor subsides, poor taste and cynicism take over. For Powers "Catholicism was always having to say 'I'm sorry.' "

It is sad that Powers' own perspectives on his religion and his education were ever so limited, and sadder still that they remained that way.

Dennis Vellucci, in a review of "Do Black Patent Leather Shoes Really Reflect Up?" in Commonweal, *Vol. CIII, No. 8, April 9, 1976, p. 253.*

Kirkus Reviews

[*The Unoriginal Sinner and the Ice-Cream God* is a further reflection] on Growing Up Catholic Recently from the author of *Do Black Patent Leather Shoes Really Reflect Up?* (1975), this time moving into fiction and on to college—Chicago's Engrim University, a commuter-college in an old hotel that alter-ego-narrator Tim Conroy reaches by filthy subway: "Even the air is dirty, as if each person had taken turns chewing it." Amiable classroom anecdotes are mixed in with amusement-park dating traumas, neighborhood events like Leonard Cohen's grandmother's 85th birthday party, part-time jobs (bun packer, freight-car painter under the "Da Vinci of the freight yard"), and—above all—Caepan. Caepan is Conroy's longtime spiritual mentor, a master garage mechanic with a common-sense approach to everything, including God ("a jerk"); and Conroy uses him as an alternate God, writing questions ("Is sex as immoral as everyone says it is?") and getting answers (" 'Immoral,' an interesting word"). College graduation brings the Patterson Public Relations Co. and intensified what's-life-for pangs, especially since girlfriend Sarah has dropped him, friend Leonard has rebelled against "Thou shalt be a doctor," and Caepan—God—is dead. An attempt to add weight via a surprise epilogue doesn't alter the fact that this is a supremely mild and derivative stew, skillfully prepared, and spiced with one-liners (in a singles bar: "I wouldn't buy a tie under these lighting conditions") by a Catholic Woody Allen who sometimes only manages to be a Catholic Henny Youngman.

> *A review of "The Unoriginal Sinner and the Ice-Cream God," in* Kirkus Reviews, *Vol. XLV, No. 16, August 15, 1977, p. 877.*

Publishers Weekly

The author of **The Last Catholic in America** and **Do Black Patent Leather Shoes Really Reflect Up?** has a rollicking new novel [**The Unoriginal Sinner and the Ice-Cream God**] about the trials and tribulations of growing up male. Tim Conroy is the narrator-hero. We follow his adventures and misadventures from his attack of laughter at Great-Uncle Elmer's funeral when Tim is 13 to his post-college job at the Thomas Patterson Public Relations Company. En route we are treated to a hilarious look at growing up Roman Catholic on Chicago's South Side: education by nuns, unrealized yearning to be a baseball star, extracurricular learning through friends, happenings, accidents. Tim's mentor is a crusty gas station owner, Caepan. Caepan in his own sardonic offhand way proves to be Conroy's greatest friend and teacher: his course is life and he considers imponderables in unusual fashion. Powers has a gift for one-liners and laughter. Though his book has its flaws there are enough good moments to make it worth the price of admission.

> *A review of "The Unoriginal Sinner and the Ice-Cream God," in* Publishers Weekly, *Vol. 212, No. 9, August 29, 1977, p. 353.*

Joe Vinson

[**The Unoriginal Sinner and the Ice-Cream God**] is a story of growing up in contemporary Chicago. It is the witty tale of the coming of age of Tim Conroy, who is not quite comfortable in the world others insist he enter. For example, when Conroy was thirteen, the Funeral Director of his uncle's funeral said, 'Will everyone please come up and take a look at the deceased and then pass out.' "Giggles began gurgling in my throat. I didn't realize it then, but I was a victim of my age. The younger ones didn't get it and the older ones didn't care to." "Mine was a family of practicing Catholics and though I practiced constantly, I never got any better."

He dreams of being a Chicago White Sox baseball player and feels that God had predestined him for baseball— "There was only one thing that God had forgotten— talent." Conroy meets Caepan, the messiah of mechanics. Caepan is no atheist—he just doesn't like God. "God is a jerk" because He does "sloppy work." There follows throughout the book a delightful correspondence between

Conroy and Caepan in which Caepan gives the answers he thinks a God who isn't a jerk would give, such as

> Dear God: What would it be like if Christ came back today?

> Dear Conroy: Joseph would write a book, Mary would do shampoo commercials and Christ would appear on the Johnny Carson Show with a film clip of his latest miracle.

> Dear God: What do people mean when they say that "It's God's Will"?

> Dear Conroy: I don't know. I never felt the need to write one.

> Dear God: Why do there seem to be so many people around who love to suffer?

> Dear Conroy: Years ago, one of my employees started telling people that the only way they were going to enjoy death was if they didn't enjoy life. Amazingly, they believed him. Ever since, the supply of crosses has never been able to keep up with the demand.

Conroy, not knowing what to do, does the usual thing and goes to college. He enters Engrim University, a Chicago commuter college, where he meets an assortment of characters, including Leonard Cohen, a Jew.

> Conroy: I happen to know for a fact that they found your fingerprints on the cross.

> Leonard: So what did you want us to do? Fine him a thousand loaves and fishes and give him six months probation?

He falls in love with Sarah, whom he might never have met had she not held Number 26 in the line at Betterman's Bakery. She finally convinces him that "Life is a lousy spectator sport."

This book is a treasure—full of one-liners, zingers, and chucklers. Although cast in a humorous vein, it runs the gamut of human emotions from ectasy to despair.

> And Heaven? Ah, that'll be a lot of laughs.

So was this book, but like Heaven, it is more, much more.

> *Joe Vinson, in a review of "The Unoriginal Sinner and the Ice-Cream God," in* Best Sellers, *Vol. 37, No. 9, December, 1977, p. 266.*

Evie Wilson and Michael McCue

Powers, whose irreverent, witty memoirs delighted teenagers in two earlier books, continues his tale here [in **The Unoriginal Sinner and the Ice-Cream God**]. Tim Conroy, the narrator, is an average fellow in most respects, except for his biting wit and his friendship with Caepan, a neighborhood gas-station owner. To Caepan, Conroy reveals his self-doubts and his seeming inability to find a niche in life. Young adults will relate to his aspiration to play baseball, despite the fact that he is an inferior athlete; they'll empathize with the ups and downs of his relationship with his girl friend, Sarah; they'll understand his queries to Caepan because the subjects are universal. In Conroy,

Powers has captured the flavor of the successes and doubts of the teenage experience. The laugh-out-loud humor that characterized the earlier books is still very much in evidence. Yet this is also Powers's most serious work, in which he has much to say to young adults on the human condition.

Evie Wilson and Michael McCue, in a review of "The Unoriginal Sinner and the Ice-Cream God," in Wilson Library Bulletin, *Vol. 52, No. 5, January, 1978, p. 415.*

Susan M. Eckert

Novelists J. F. and John R. Powers could be father and son. Both grew up in Illinois and attended Northwestern University. Both are Roman Catholic, and write about present-day church problems. J. F. is about thirty years older than John R. But they aren't related. Their work reveals that they are strangers in fact, philosophy, style, and temperament. (p. 32)

John R. Powers . . . deals with the individual, but his most important characters come from the other side of the confessional window—the youngsters whose views of God are shaded by priests much like those in the elder Powers's books.

In his thirties, he has published two "fictionalized memoirs"—***The Last Catholic in America*** and ***Do Black Patent Leather Shoes Really Reflect Up?***—and a novel, ***The Unoriginal Sinner and the Ice-Cream God.*** Without the aid of national critical attention, he has captured a widespread audience. Apparently, when John R. Powers writes about growing up Catholic in America, he reflects others' feelings as well as his own.

John R. Powers chooses his victims among clergy and laity and pole-axes them: "He was our shepherd and we were his sheep. And if a sheep got out of line, Father O'Reilly cut his head off." "My religion teacher in junior year was Brother Falley . . . Every day when we came to class he'd tell us to . . . study and he'd be with us in a moment. Then he'd pick up a book from his desk and start reading. The 'moment' never arrived. (Later that year) Brother Falley walked through a glass door and nearly cut his head off. At that time, he was reading a book." This destructive satiric vision, along with a lack of symbolic language, is what separates John R. from J. F., who handles satire like a rapier. He carves away at the attitudes and actions of priests without skewering individuals in whom lie the seeds of grace.

Powers's books document the spiritual path along which a Catholic education leads him. ***Last Catholic,*** set in a parochial elementary school, emphasizes the church's legalistic teachings: catechism class and first confession. ***Patent Leather Shoes*** continues in the same vein, detailing the watering of "that seed of solid guilt, buried deep within my cranium, which would shortly grow into a full-size Catholic conscience."

There are plenty of Catholics in Powers's books, as well as Protestants, Jews, religious people, and agnostics, but there is only one Christian—Gordon Feldameano, who goes out of his way to amuse the fat and ugly girls at school dances. "Gordon had a soft spot in his head. He was a Christian." Powers is capable of recognizing a Christian when he sees one; he just doesn't encounter many.

In spite of the hope that glimmers through some of the characters, and in spite of Powers' humorous and irreverent style, his underlying preoccupation with the shortness of life draws each of the books to a wistful, vaguely depressing conclusion.

J. F. Powers's priests are aware, even at their least sanctified moments, of where the truth can be found. There is a strong scriptural underpinning that is missing from the younger Powers. In fact, many of J. F. Powers's stories seem on one level to be written to illustrate particular biblical passages. For example, the two published stories that form the basis for his novel-in-progress depict a priest unwilling or unable to fulfill the requirements for a bishop found in I Timothy 3:1-5.

"A saint is not an abnormal person. He is simply a mature Christian. Anyone who is not a saint is spiritually undersized—the world is full of spiritual midgets," Powers said in 1943. But his priests are more accurately spiritual runts, able to grow to sainthood simply by feeding on the Word they know so well.

The true spiritual midgets are John R. Powers's characters, permanently stunted by the neglect of priests more interested in career, golf game, or joking around with the parishioners than they are in teaching the Word of God. If there is an indictment against Catholicism in any of these works, it lies here. (pp. 32-3)

Susan M. Eckert, "The Sage and the Cynic: Two Views of the Priesthood," in Christianity Today, *Vol. XXIII, No. 16, May 25, 1979, pp. 32-3.*

Philip Roth

1933-

(Full name Philip Milton Roth) American novelist, short story writer, essayist, critic, autobiographer, and memoirist.

The following entry presents criticism on Roth's novel *Portnoy's Complaint* (1969). For discussions of Roth's career, see *CLC,* Vols. 1, 2, 3, 4, 6, 9, 15, 22, 31, 47.

One of contemporary literature's most prominent and controversial writers, Roth focuses on conflict, alienation, and the search for self-identity in his explorations of the modern Jewish-American psyche. While such acclaimed authors as Saul Bellow, Bruce Jay Friedman and Bernard Malamud—with whom Roth is often identified—frequently concentrate on similar themes, Roth is singularly credited with propelling Jewish-American fiction into the realm of popular culture with his outrageous novel *Portnoy's Complaint.* Critics believe the book's widespread appeal is largely due to Roth's insight into human nature, his gift for satire, his authentic use of Jewish-American dialect, and his nefarious sense of humor. Originally appearing as a series of sketches in *Esquire, Partisan Review,* and *New American Review, Portnoy's Complaint* generated immediate controversy and commentary upon publication. The novel takes the form of a profane, guilt-ridden confession spewed by Alexander Portnoy to a silent psychoanalyst, Dr. Spielvogel. Decrying his Jewish upbringing, Portnoy wrestles with his Oedipal complex, his obsession with Gentile women, and his sexual fetishes in an attempt to come to terms with his ambivalent feelings toward Judaism. After the character furiously vents his emotions, however, Roth implies that his problems have merely started, as the novel ends with the doctor's first words: "So. . . . Now vee may perhaps to begin. Yes?"

As in his other works, Roth draws upon his own experiences for the plot, settings, and characterizations of *Portnoy's Complaint.* Like his protagonist, Roth was raised in a predominantly Jewish, lower middle-class neighborhood in Newark, New Jersey, where his father worked as an insurance salesman. The omniscient Dr. Spielvogel, according to Roth, is based on his own psychoanalyst. However, *Portnoy's Complaint* is generally considered a psychological exploration rather than an autobiography. Throughout the novel Roth refers to various Freudian theories, the most easily discernible of which is Portnoy's Oedipal complex. Portnoy also considers himself an expert on psychoanalysis, frequently condescending to his doctor and offering self-diagnoses, and one chapter, titled "Civilization and Its Discontents," satirizes Freud's essay on the conflict between an individual's instinctual urges and society's demand for restraint. Portnoy's rage and confusion, stemming mainly from his mother's domination, manifests itself in self-hatred and resentment toward what he views as Jewish hypocrisy and anxiety. At the time of the novel's publication, rabbis throughout the United States, horri-

fied by Portnoy's attitude, promptly labeled Roth an anti-Semitic Jew and instructed their congregations not to read the work. Despite this rabbinical ban, *Portnoy's Complaint* soon became the best-selling book in the nation and remains Roth's best known work to date. While some initial critics expressed distaste at the novel's sexual frankness and scatological language, most praised Roth's ethnic humor and adroit mimicry of dialogue, as well as his psychological insight. A reviewer from *Time* commented: "[The] success of Roth's monologues rests not on the author's familiarity with [Jewish life], but on the fact that few writers of his generation can match his ability to perceive and record manners and minutiae, or equal him in relating life's inner tumult to its outward appearances of order."

Portnoy is Roth's most flamboyant depiction of an individual searching for an independent identity. The author once noted in an interview that "Portnoy wasn't a character for me, he was an explosion." The protagonist, a thirty-three-year-old bachelor, is used to excelling. A high school honor student who graduated first in his law school class, he works as the Assistant Commissioner for Human Opportunity in New York City at the time of the novel's main action. The appropriateness of Portnoy's job is emphasized frequently by critics, who note that the downtrodden classes for whom he works reflect his negative self-image. His accomplishments mean little to him and his relationships with women are destructive because he is plagued by self-loathing and guilt. Portnoy's most frequent choice for sexual gratification, masturbation, has been construed by some as a desperate attempt at autonomy. Simultaneously pursuing and evading commitment, longing to erase the impotent hysteria and fear that have pervaded his life since childhood, Portnoy seeks analysis because he feels that he is living his life "in the middle of a Jewish joke!" "Please, who crippled us like this?" he asks Dr. Spielvogel. "Who made us morbid and hysterical and weak? . . . [What] do you call this sickness I have? Is this the Jewish suffering I used to hear so much about? . . . I can't stand any more being frightened like this over nothing! Bless me with manhood! Make me brave! Make me strong! Make me *whole!* Enough being a nice Jewish boy, publicly pleasing my parents while privately pulling my putz! Enough!" Roth's use of stream-of-consciousness monologue drew accolades from reviewers, who noted that the style allowed the author more artistic freedom while at the same time effectively expressing his protagonist's erratic personality. Portnoy's earthy language and manic delivery have been likened to that of a stand-up comedian's, and the character's neuroses, sharp wit, and self-destructive tendencies have further elicited comparisons to comic Lenny Bruce, who also candidly scrutinized sex, immorality, and the tortured psyche of the contemporary Jew.

Roth employs social satire throughout *Portnoy's Complaint,* variously ridiculing politics, government, and the habits and values of middle-class Jews and WASPs. Portnoy often idealizes the Gentile community, which was somewhat mysterious to him during his youth, while feeling ambivalent toward Judaism—a problem that arises from his difficulties with his family. While his father is the source of his few warm memories of childhood, Portnoy generally regards the man as spineless and perpetually constipated, forever kowtowing to his Gentile bosses and his overbearing wife. Portnoy's mother, an overprotective, cloistered woman whose life revolves around her son (and *not* around her slightly overweight daughter), is Roth's primary satirical target—a classic portrait of the formulaic Jewish Mother. Several critics found the character demeaning, but many concurred with a reviewer from *Time,* who asserted: "She surpasses the grotesque stereotype simply because Roth plays her absolutely straight, making her totally and comically unconscious of the unconscious." A master of hypocrisy, Mrs. Portnoy regards herself as a seasoned sage of life's traumatic experiences despite her overwhelming fear of the unfamiliar. Portnoy first discusses his mother with Dr. Spielvogel in a segment of the book entitled "The Most Unforgettable Character I've Met," a parody of the hackneyed grammar school essay theme. The use of profanity in *Portnoy's Complaint,* while offensive to some, is considered intrinsic to an understanding of the novel's Oedipal theme: Portnoy constantly swears because it violates everything his mother represents and he wants to rebel against her influence and, indeed, forget this "unforgettable character."

Mrs. Portnoy induces a maelstrom of conflicting emotions in her son and he mimics her illogical nature constantly, using impeccable dialect which many reviewers contend to be the main strength of the novel: "DON'T RUN FIRST THING TO A BLONDIE, PLEASE! BECAUSE SHE'LL TAKE YOU FOR ALL YOU'RE WORTH AND THEN LEAVE YOU BLEEDING IN THE GUTTER! A BRILLIANT INNOCENT BABY BOY LIKE YOU, SHE'LL EAT YOU UP ALIVE!" Furious at his mother's self-proclaimed superiority and inability to defend the religion she so blindly follows, Portnoy rebels against Judaism and its established values. As a youth, he escapes into a vivid Gentile fantasy life where his dream girl is a blonde ice-skater named Thereal McCoy. As an adolescent growing up during World War II, Portnoy is bombarded with guilt concerning the Nazi concentration camps. He longs to assimilate into the dominant WASP culture but cannot rid himself of the remorse and martyrdom he associates with Judaism. In a passage widely regarded as expressing the principal theme of the novel, he implores: "Jew Jew Jew Jew Jew Jew! It is coming out of my ears already, the saga of the suffering Jews! Do me a favor, my people, and stick your suffering heritage up your suffering ass—*I happen also to be a human being!*"

Portnoy's problem has been interpreted by many critics as a metaphor of the human condition in the twentieth century, while others believe *Portnoy's Complaint* to be an archetypal literary treatment of the post-World War II Jewish-American dilemma. In the era following the war, when American Jews were becoming better educated and moving into middle-class Gentile suburbs, many were faced with the predicament of either embracing an ethnic heritage increasingly removed from their American identity or assimilating into Gentile society. Such writers as Bellow, Malamud, and Roth began exploring these conflicts and resulting feelings of alienation and confusion. In Roth's novel, although Portnoy abhors everything associated with his hypocritical upbringing, he is incensed—but cannot explain why—when a non-Jewish girlfriend he plans to marry refuses to convert. Portnoy confesses that by sleeping with Gentile women he is not only conquering *them* but trying to conquer America. His ambivalence toward his Jewish heritage is compounded by feelings of rootlessness. Both desiring and despising non-Jews, Portnoy is an example of the postwar "alienated Jew"; his attempts to assimilate into the dominant culture have alienated him from his own. *Portnoy's Complaint* is not only a vivid portrait of an individual's suffering, but a powerful treatment of a modern cultural conflict, illuminating serious issues through humor, pathos, and irony.

(See also *Contemporary Authors First Revision,* Vol. 2; *Contemporary Authors New Revision Series,* Vols. 1, 22; *Dictionary of Literary Biography,* Vols. 2, 28; *Dictionary of Literary Biography Yearbook: 1982;* and *Concise Dictionary of American Literary Biography, 1968-1988.*)

PRINCIPAL WORKS

NOVELS

Letting Go   1962

Time

Any work by Philip Roth commands attention. Lately, the author of *Goodbye, Columbus, Letting Go* and *When She Was Good,* one of the best of America's younger novelists, has chosen to exhibit his new fiction piecemeal in various magazines. His theme—the psychological problems of a modern Jewish-American—is not exactly new. But to judge from what has appeared so far, Roth's latest work [*Portnoy's Complaint*] looks like the most brilliant piece of radical humor in years.

It takes the form of a series of monologues ranted by a patient at his psychoanalyst. The patient is a 33-year-old bachelor named Alexander Portnoy, high-school honor student from Newark, first in his law-school class, and now assistant human-rights commissioner in New York City. At first glance, the chronicle of Portnoy's pain, rooted as it is in Jewishness and the urban environment, may appear to have only specialized appeal, but Roth gives it a universality that reaches beyond ethnic boundaries. It is a coda of rage and savagely honest self-lashing reminiscent of the performances of the late Lenny Bruce. No detail is varnished, no lust or act nice-Nellied as Portnoy complains, clowns and laments in his desperate efforts to claw his way to sanity. The result is a spontaneous emotional release of enormous authenticity and power.

The first monologue appeared in the April 1967 issue of *Esquire* under the title **"A Jewish Patient Begins His Analysis."** It is a short, tame outline of Portnoy's problems. Things loosened up in a hurry with the 6,000-word installment published last August in *Partisan Review;* called **"Whacking Off,"** it is a frantic confession of boyhood sin. Portnoy recalls how, as an adolescent, he always had to please his parents publicly, while he privately and obsessively masturbated to please himself; this experience sentenced him to a chronic condition of shame, which he begs his analyst to cure. **"The Jewish Blues,"** which re-

veals the Portnoy family guilts and secrets even further, appeared the following month in the first issue of *New American Review.* The fourth and by far largest section (28,000 words) appears in the *Review's* current issue. Titled **"Civilization and Its Discontents,"** after Freud's famous essay on the conflict between the individual's instinctual urges and society's demands for restraint, the latest monologue is the freest, funniest, most touching—and terrifying—of the lot.

Roth sees Portnoy's life as "a masochistic extravaganza," and no one is more aware of this than Portnoy himself. In one of his many hysterical bursts of insight, he cries that he is "torn by desires that are repugnant to my conscience, and a conscience repugnant to my desires." He views himself as the victim in a grim Jewish joke. "Doctor, Doctor," he pleads,

> *please.* I can't live any more in a world given all its meaning and dimension by some vulgar nightclub clown. By some—some *black humorist!* Because that's who the black humorists are—of course!—the Henny Youngmans breaking them up down there in the Fontainebleau, and with what? Stories of murder and mutilation! 'Help, help,' cries the woman running along the sand at Miami Beach, 'my son the doctor is drowning!' Ha ha ha—only it is *my son the patient,* lady.

His family still haunts him. "Good Christ," he cries, "a Jewish man with parents alive is a 15-year-old boy and will remain a 15-year-old boy till *they die!*"

Portnoy wears his Oedipus complex as if it were a festering good-conduct medal that had been stapled to his sternum. But his is a tragedy in which Oedipus is played by Groucho Marx. Mother Portnoy is a vibrant orange-haired vision who has never given up trying to smother her son in the warm pudding of her ample bosom. She surpasses the grotesque stereotype simply because Roth plays her absolutely straight, making her totally and comically unconscious of the unconscious.

Portnoy recalls her with emotions that are swollen with love and loathing. . . . He relates the telephone conversation he had with her after returning from his European vacation: "Well, how's my lover?" she asked, as his father listened on an extension. "And it never occurs to her," says Portnoy, "if I'm her lover, who is he, the *shmegeggy* she lives with?"

This and scores of remembrances are freely juxtaposed with precise details of Portnoy's adult sex life, particularly his exertions with a girl he calls "The Monkey," a beautiful and insatiable ex-hillbilly who is the fulfillment of every sex fantasy that Portnoy ever had. The only trouble is that The Monkey thinks of Portnoy as her way out of the depravity that he is working so hard to sink into. Hence, more guilt, which is the source of the comedy and the source of his sufferings. He tells of the time that he and The Monkey picked up a whore in Rome and took her to bed. "I can best describe the state I subsequently entered as one of unrelieved busy-ness. Boy, was I busy! I mean there was just so much to do."

What elevates the character of Alexander Portnoy far above the usual black-comedy victim is his insistence on knowing why he is in such pain, and his willingness and ability to examine every inflamed nerve ending. Portnoy's upbringing is not exclusively Jewish: it was a characteristic carryover from a time in the '20s and '30s when many immigrants and first-generation Americans saw their sons as Columbuses who would lead the family to security and status in the New World. The burden of these aspirations has left many of those Columbuses with painful kinks.

But the success of Roth's monologues rests not on the author's familiarity with this kind of sociology, but on the fact that few writers of his generation can match his ability to perceive and record manners and minutiae, or equal him in relating life's inner tumult to its outward appearances of order. (pp. 102-04)

> *"The Perils of Portnoy," in* Time, *New York, Vol. 91, No. 20, May 17, 1968, pp. 102-04.*

Therese Pol

The subject of the Jewish family in general and the Jewish mother in particular—with its catastrophic consequences for all those who move within their orbit—can no longer be regarded as a literary endeavor on the American scene. It has become a big industry, nearly as threatening as the military-industrial complex. In this sense Philip Roth, the author of **Portnoy's Complaint,** is merely the latest, if enormously successful, tycoon.

It was Philip Wylie who started the mother-kicking bit with his crusade against momism. With brutal impartiality he condemned *all* American mothers. Reviewers across the land have already praised Roth's new book as the culmination of the Jewish mother motif, apparently forgetting that Bruce Jay Friedman beat him by several miles in *A Mother's Kisses.* Friedman did a final demolition job.

Now comes the culmination of the culmination—Roth's resurrection of this type of woman. The best that can be said of his accomplishment is that Mama Portnoy is a caricature drawn by a master cartoonist, but she's no more than that.

That is not to say that Roth has not added other touches to the overall picture of Jewish family life which, as depicted, must be the most destructive form of living known to mankind. Some of Roth's scenes are outrageously funny. Alex Portnoy has an obsessively Jewish father, who is an insurance salesman in New Jersey, and chronically constipated (not as irrelevant as it sounds). The bathroom becomes for a while the center of the fun, with papa spending many unsuccessful hours on the john and Alex, the kid, masturbating himself into near lunacy. Roth's treatment of constipation is a scream—but how much mileage can you really get out of constipation?

Roth's book is a long monologue addressed to a hypothetical psychoanalyst (does the man listen?), in which Alex dissects his stifling childhood (mother, father, the whole damn Jewish neighborhood, come under the microscope) and his subsequent, and practically preordained, troubles with sex. Because all the girls he yearns for are Gentiles.

Alex drank in the longing for Gentile sex, whatever that is, with his Jewish mother's milk. Alex, the adult, a successful civil servant of sorts, has the worst experiences with his women. He really picks them. The Monkey, an illiterate high-fashion model from West Virginia, blackmails him with suicidal impulses. The Pumpkin, straight from the Corn Belt, is wonderfully American but becomes a bore. The Pilgrim, a Mayflower product, has too much class for her own good, and is incapable of giving Alex oral gratification (of which there is a great deal in this book, in case anyone wants to brush up on it). The novel ends with a five-line scream of *ahhh,* and a slapstick suggestion from the analyst to the effect that perhaps now the treatment might begin in earnest.

The pacing of Roth's book is frantic, which gives it a one-dimensional quality. It is filled with orgies of various kinds, saved from total tedium only by Roth's comic vein. The melancholy truth about orgies is that in the long run they are dull, even funny orgies. The barrage of four-letter words is also getting to be a pain in the ass, to use Roth's idiom, although he has justified it on the highest artistic grounds. In effect, Roth has created the same permanent Jewish joke that his Alex so bitterly complains about in the novel, complete with Jewish self-loathing and guilt far beyond anything Saul Bellow ever had to offer, but certainly nothing brand-new. . . .

Some people profess to see the depths of despair—both Jewish and cosmic—in Roth's book. Maybe so. But Thomas Mann once said that irony can become so dense that it is no longer recognizable as such. So it is with Roth's despair. There is something else wrong with it: it is basically trivial because it is rooted in endless self-examination, leading nowhere in particular, which no amount of stylistic cleverness can disguise. And his occasional gallant attempt to pass from the ridiculous to the sublime without losing his balance simply does not come off.

The main trouble with the Jewish family theme is that it has been overwritten. Unlike the plague in the Middle Ages or the pogroms in Czarist Russia, the Jewish mother goes on and on, spawning more mother-smothered Jewish girls, who in turn will inevitably smother their own brood. It is a vicious circle which can be broken only by a moratorium on the whole subject, guilt included.

Enough already.

> *Therese Pol, "The Jewish Mama Market," in* The Nation, *New York, Vol. 208, No. 10, March 10, 1969, p. 311.*

J. Mitchell Morse

[The] congregation will please rise and sing All Hail the Power of Portnoy's Name. As I write he is for the time being Lord of all, the hottest brand name in the market. By now everybody knows enough about him, and I don't find him worth discussing at length. Philip Roth belongs in the same abject bag as Leo Rosten, Harry Golden, Myron Cohen and Sam Levenson: like Leslie Fiedler's Montana ranch hand who on Saturdays gets all dressed up in a cowboy suit and walks the streets of Butte or Missoula as "the pimp of his particularity," a professional Jew-boy gets his kicks from catering to condescension.

In order to sell a particularity, we must simplify it, idealize it, and make it conform to popular preconceptions. This involves reducing it to a set of easy formulas that don't allow for any personal uniqueness. Though the conventions are different, *Portnoy's Complaint* is as conventional as the fiction in *Woman's Day,* where all adolescent daughters have braces on their teeth and all pre-adolescent sons have freckles. Portnoy is the ideal character toward whom a type of contemporary American novel has been working: The Neurotic Jewish Liberal Intellectual who is *nothing but* The Neurotic Jewish Liberal Intellectual. His mother is The Jewish Mother, Contemporary Comic Variety, whose life is limited to the kitchen and the bathroom. His father is The Jewish Lower-Middle-Class Father, Contemporary Comic Variety—constipation, flat feet and all. Alex Portnoy himself is nothing but a collection of contemporary clichés. He makes all A's in school. He is not athletic. He has all kinds of sexual difficulties because of his mother's smothering love. On his first try with a prostitute he is for aesthetic reasons impotent—just like Holden Caulfield [in *Catcher in the Rye*]. His mistresses are the standard goyische assortment: The Nice Middle-Western Corn-Fed Idealist, The Whorish Underwear Model, and The Liberal Connecticut Aristocrat. These people move in a swirl of contemporary clichés about Jews in general: Jews Have A Strong Family Life. Jewish Family Life Is Hell. Jews Are Either Extraordinarily Intelligent Or Extraordinarily Stupid And Gross. Some Intelligent Jews Are Also Gross. Some Stupid Jews Have An Innate Refinement—If Only They Could Have Gone To College. Jews Are Not Athletic. Jews are Musical. Jews Are Sad. Jews Get Drafted Into The Army And Die In Battle Just Like Everybody Else. Jews Are Not All Communists. Jews Are Not All Rich. There Are Reactionary Jews. Jews Are Not Acquisitive. Jews Are Extraordinarily Generous. Jews Are Extraordinarily Kind. Jews Understand. Jews are Nervous. Jews Are Neurotic. Jews Are Sensual. Jews Are Over-Sexed. Jews Are Over-Sensitive.

Since the defeat of the Nazis, the clichés of anti-Semitism among intellectuals have been largely replaced by these more benign ones. They are not equally harmful, but they are equally stupid, and they make me as a Jew almost as uncomfortable. Moreover, as is well known, group stereotypes tend to have a compulsive force: people tend to do what is expected of them, to play the role assigned to them; and if the role is undignified, the effort of rejecting it also conduces to a self-consciousness that would otherwise be unnecessary. Any attribution whatever of group characteristics, to any group whatever, threatens the individuality of members of the group, and to that extent is a form of hostility to them as individuals, however benign and friendly the attributors may feel. No man should have to keep fighting off clichés about himself. Or ignoring them either. As my son recently told an acquaintance, who was surprised that he wasn't interested in playing the stock market, "You've got your stereotypes confused. Jews steal watermelons and have natural rhythm." Philip Roth has the disease of masochistic conformity. He is a

servile entertainer. *Portnoy's Complaint* is supinely acquiescent in every way: a series of burlesk skits. Many years ago I went to Boston to cover the trial of *Forever Amber,* and my background research took me to the Old Howard Burlesk Theater. There—five minutes from the courthouse—I heard a droopy-pants comedian singing "The Shithouse Blues" and saying aside to the audience between stanzas, "I'm Jewish." In my mind's eye now he seems to have the face of Philip Roth. (pp. 320-21)

> *J. Mitchell Morse, in a review of "Portnoy's Complaint," in* The Hudson Review, *Vol. XXII, No. 2, Summer, 1969, pp. 320-21.*

On his family's reactions to criticism of *Portnoy's Complaint*

"They were stunned. They were hurt. They heard a lot about my inadequacies from their hoity-toity neighbors. They would go to a lecture about me at their temple, expecting a star to be pinned on their boy just like back in grade school. Instead they'd hear from the platform that sleeping in my bedroom all those years, and eating with them at their table, was a self-hating anti-Semitic Jew. My mother had to hold my father down in his seat, he'd get so angry. No, they were all right. They recognized too many folks they knew to think such people as I'd described had never walked around New Jersey."
—*Philip Roth, 1985*

Theodore Solotaroff

[*Solotaroff is an American editor, critic, and author who met Roth at the University of Chicago in 1957. The two became friends and "wary" critics of each others' work. The essay excerpted below takes the form of a personal memoir in which Solotaroff praises Roth's classic tragicomic treatment of the American Jewish experience in* Portnoy's Complaint.]

A few months after *When She Was Good,* [an unsuccessful novel concerning a Protestant female protagonist], Roth published a sketch in *Esquire.* It was a memoir of a Jewish boyhood, this time told to an analyst, and written with some of his former verve and forthrightness. Even so, it ventured little beyond a vein that had been pretty well worked by now: the beleaguered Provider who can't even hold a bat right; the shatteringly attentive mother; the neglected, unhappy sister; the narrator, who is the star of every grade and the messiah of the household. In short, the typical second-generation Jewish family; and after all the writers who had been wrestling with it in the past decade. Roth's latest revelations were hardly news. Nor did a psychoanalytic setting seem necessary to elicit the facts of Jack Portnoy's constipation or Sophie's use of a bread-knife to make little Alex eat. After five years of reading manuscripts at *Commentary,* such stuff was coming out of my ears. Perhaps Roth was only taking a small writer's vacation from the labor that had gone into his last novel or returning to the scene of his early success for a quick score. I hoped so.

But soon after came **"Whacking Off "** in *Partisan Review:* hysterical, raw, full of what Jews call self-hatred: excessive in all respects: and so funny that I had three laughing fits before I had gone five pages. All of a sudden, from out of the blue and the past, the comedian of those Chicago sessions of nostalgia, revenge, and general purgation had landed right in the middle of his own fiction, as Alex Portnoy, the thirteen-year-old fetishist:

> Jumping up from the dinner table, I tragically clutch my belly—diarrhea! I cry. I have been stricken with diarrhea!—and once behind the locked bathroom door, slip over my head a pair of underpants that I have stolen from my sister's dresser and carry rolled in a handkerchief in my pocket.

Discovery is always imminent. This time the sperm lands everywhere ("I am the Raskolnikov of jerking off !"). But a few minutes later, Alex is back at the scene of the crime, doubled over his flying fist, his sister's bra stretched before him, while as his parents stand outside:

> "Alex, I want an answer from you. Did you eat French fries after school? Is that why you're sick like this?"
>
> "Nuhhh, nuhhh."
>
> "Alex, are you in pain? Do you want me to call the doctor? Are you in pain, or aren't you? I want to know exactly where it hurts. *Answer me.*"
>
> "Yuhh, yuhhh—"
>
> "Alex, I don't want you to flush the toilet," says my mother sternly. "I want to see what you've done in there. I don't like the sound of this at all."
>
> "And me," says my father, touched as he always was by my accomplishments—as much awe as envy—"I haven't moved my bowels in a week. . . . "

This was new all right, at least in American fiction—and, like the discovery of fresh material in *Goodbye, Columbus,* right in front of everyone's eyes. Particularly, I suppose, the "Jewish" writers' with all that heavily funded Oedipal energy and curiosity to be worked off in adolescence—and beyond. And having used his comic sense to carry him past the shame that surrounds the subject of masturbation, and to enter it more fully than I can suggest here. Roth appeared to gain great dividends of emotional candor and wit in dealing with the other matters in **"Whacking Off."** The first sketch had kept a distance of wry description between Portnoy and his parents, but here his feelings—rage, tenderness, contempt, despair, and guilt—bring everything up close and fully alive. And aided by the

inadvertent comedy team of Jack and Sophie Portnoy, the familiar counters of Jewish anxiety (eating hamburgers and french fries outside the home leads directly to a colostomy; polio is never more than a sore throat away: study an instrument, you never know; take shorthand in school, look what it did for Billy Rose; don't oppose your father, he may be suffering from a brain tumor) become almost as hilarious as Alex's solo flights of passion. Against the enveloping cloud of their fear and possessiveness, his guilt, and their mutual hysteria, still unremitting twenty years later, Alex has only his sarcasm and, expressive phrase, private parts. He summons the memories of his love as well as of his hate for them, but this only opens up his sense of his vulnerability, and from that, of his maddening typicality:

> Doctor Spielvogel, this is my life, my only life, and I'm living it in the middle of a Jewish joke! I am the son in the Jewish joke—*only it ain't no joke!* Please, who crippled us like this? Who made us so morbid and hysterical and weak? . . . Is this the Jewish suffering I used to hear so much about? Is this what has come down to me from the pogroms and the persecution? . . . Oh my secrets, my shame, my palpitations, my flushes, my sweats! . . . Bless me with manhood! Make me brave! Make me strong! Make me *whole!* Enough being a nice Jewish boy, publicly pleasing my parents while privately pulling my putz! Enough!

But Portnoy had only begun to come clean. Once having fully entered his "Modern Museum of Gripes and Grievances," there was no stopping him. Or Roth. Having discovered that Portnoy's sexual feelings and his "Jewish" feelings were just around the corner from each other and that both were so rich in loot, he pressed on like a man who has found a stream full of gold—and running right into it, another one. Moreover, the psychoanalytic setting had given him now the freedom and energy of language to sluice out the material: the natural internal monologue of comedy and pain in which the id speaks to the ego and vice versa, while the superego goes on with its kibitzing. At the same time, Portnoy could be punched out of the analytic framework like a figure enclosed in cardboard and perform in his true role and vocation, which is that of a great stand-up comic. Further, those nagging concerns with close relationships, with male guilt and female maneuvering, from his two novels could now be grasped by the roots of Portnoy's experience of them and could be presented, not as standard realistic fare, but in a mode that was right up to date. If the background of *Portnoy's Complaint* is a classical Freudian one, the foreground is the contemporary, winging art and humor of improvisation and release, most notably that of Lenny Bruce.

In short, lots of things had come together, and they had turned Roth loose. The rest of *Portnoy* was written in the same way—as a series of "takes"—the next two of which were published in *New American Review,* the periodical which I was now editing. It may be no more than editorial bias speaking here, but I think these are the two richest sections of the book. **"The Jewish Blues"** is a sort of "coming of age in Newark, New Jersey," beginning with the erotic phenomena of the Portnoy household and carrying through the dual issue of Alex's adolescence: maleness and rebellion. On the one hand, there are those early years of attentively following Sophie Portnoy through her guided tour of her activities and attitudes, climaxed by a memory of one afternoon when, the housework all done "with his cute little assistance," Alex, "punchy with delight" watches his shapely mother draw on her stockings, while she croons to him "Who does Mommy love more than anything in the whole wide world?" (a passage that deserves to live forever in the annals of the Oedipal Complex). On the other hand—"Thank God," breathes Portnoy—there are the visits with his father to the local bathhouse, the world of Jewish male animal nature, "a place without *goyim* and women [where] I lose touch instantaneously with that ass-licking little boy who runs home after school with his A's in his hand. . . . " On the one hand, there is the synagogue, another version of the dismal constraints and clutchiness of home; on the other, there is center field, where anything that comes your way is yours and where Alex, in his masterful imitation of Duke Snider, knows exactly how to conduct himself, standing out there "as loose and as easy, as happy as I will ever be. . . . " This is beautiful material: so exact in its details, so right in its feeling. And, finally, there is the story of his cousin Heshie, the muscular track star, who was mad about Alice Dembrowsky, the leggy drum majorette of Weequahic High, and whose disgraceful romance with this daughter of a Polish janitor finally has to be ended by his father, who informs Alice that Heshie has an incurable blood disease that prevents him from marrying and that must be kept secret from him. After his Samson-like rage is spent, Heshie submits to his father, and subsequently goes into the army and is killed in action. But Alex adds his cause to his other manifold grounds of revolt, rises to heights of denunciation in the anti-bar-mitzvah speech he delivers to Spielvogel (". . . instead of wailing for he-who has turned his back on the sage of *his people,* weep for your pathetic selves, why don't you, sucking and sucking on that sour grape of a religion. . . . "), but then is reminded by his sister of "the six million" and ends up in his native state of ambivalence.

Still circling back upon other scenes from his throbbing youth, as though the next burst of anger or grief or hysterical joking will allow him finally to touch bottom, Portnoy forges on into his past and his psyche, turning to his relations with those mysterious creatures known as *shikses* as his life moves along and the present hang-ups emerge. His occupation is that of Assistant Commissioner of Human Opportunity in the Lindsay Administration, but his preoccupations are always with that one thing his mother didn't give him back when he was four years old, and all of his sweet young Wasps, for all of their sociological interests, turn out to be only an extension of the fantasies of curiosity and self-excitement and shame that drove Alex on in the bathroom. Even "the Monkey," the glamorous fashion model and fellow sex maniac, the walking version of his adolescent dream of "Thereal McCoy," provides mostly more grist for the relentless mill of his narcissism and masochism. All of which Portnoy is perfectly aware of: he is the hippest analysand since Freud himself; but it still doesn't help him to give up the maddeningly seductive voice inside his head that goes on calling "Big

Boy," or to end the maddening debate in his head between the contemporary American male ("everything is permitted") and the ancestral Jew ("Look who wants to be an animal!"). And so, laughing and anguishing and analyzing away, he goes down the road to his breakdown, which sets in when he comes to Israel and finds that he is impotent.

I could go on writing about *Portnoy,* but it would be mostly amplification of the points I've made. It's a marvelously entertaining book and one that mines a narrow but central vein more deeply than it has ever been done before. You don't have to be Jewish to be vastly amused and touched and instructed by *Portnoy's Complaint,* though it helps. Also you don't have to know Philip Roth to appreciate the personal triumph that it represents, though that helps too. (pp. 70-2)

Theodore Solotaroff, "The Journey of Philip Roth," in The Atlantic Monthly, *Vol. 223, No. 4, April, 1969, pp. 64-72.*

The Times Literary Supplement

What is *Portnoy's Complaint?* A *cri de coeur* from a Jewish adolescence, a load of specifically Jewish guilt, a casebook of the Jewish blues. It is the most zany, zestful novel Philip Roth has written and, with all its seeming *non sequiturs,* a classic comic statement of the Jewish condition:

> What was it with these Jewish parents—because I am not in this boat alone, oh no, I am on the biggest troop ship afloat . . . Only look in through the portholes and see us there, stacked to the bulkheads in our bunks, moaning and groaning with such pity for ourselves, the sad and watery-eyed sons of Jewish parents, sick to the gills from rolling through these heavy seas of guilt . . .

Oh, cameradoes! This is no longer a *Life with some goyische Father,* but inevitably a *Life with Momma*—a life of every nice bright little Jewish boy, publicly pleasing his parents, while privately pulling his "putz". Locked in self-love and self-hatred, Alexander Portnoy sits enthroned on the lavatory, masturbating; and the bitter joke is that *all* his fantasies—to his shame—come true. Between a kosher kitchen and these dreams of Onan, what bridge? What salvation? . . . While everybody else has been marrying nice Jewish girls, and having children, and buying houses, and (in his father's phrase) *putting down roots,* he has been chasing women, and *shikse* women, to boot!

Thirty-three years old, *nel mezzo del cammin,* Alexander Portnoy is still roaming the streets with his eyes popping. In Newark and the surrounding suburbs there is apparently only one question on everybody's lips: "When is Alexander Portnoy going to stop being selfish and give his parents, who are such wonderful people, grandchildren?" If this were just the old masochistic spiral of sexual degradation, these confessions to a psychoanalyst (Spielvogel, O. "The Puzzled Penis", *Internationale Zeitschrift für Psychoanalyse,* Vol. XXIV p. 909) might verge on pornography. . . . Yet it is the comedy which is triumphant—a peculiarly Jewish comedy on the borderlines of fantasy and despair, exhibitionism and strongly felt ethical impulses, sexual lust and overriding feelings of shame.

It is the same borderline territory where Charlie Chaplin teetered on his tightrope path, or Svevo's Zeno amiably stumbled. Only this, being an American farce, is fiercer, blacker, more outspoken. All are spiritual clowns, wrestling with the swingdoors of a world of matter; all are degraded, only to rise and return as self-appointed saviours. Zeno, too, consulted a psychoanalyst to discover he had an Oedipus Complex. But Portnoy, way ahead of Freud, exclaims:

> Dreams? If only they had been! But I don't need dreams, Doctor, that's why I hardly have them—because I have this life instead. With me it all happens in broad daylight! . . . Doctor, maybe other patients dream—with me, *everything happens.* I have a life *without* latent content. The dream thing *happens!* Doctor: *I couldn't get it up in the State of Israel!* How's *that* for symbolism, *bubi?*

For his tale ends, with blackest irony, in *Eretz Yisroel.* "Im-po-tent in Is-rael, da da daaah"(to the tune of "Lullaby in Birdland"), the Jew of the diaspora must return into exile. Thus the irony travels full circle, recalling the pompous rabbi of Portnoy's bar mitzvah for whom no word in the English language had less than three syllables, "not even the word *God*"; and *Israel* sounded as long as "refrigerator".

But who is this other rabbi, playbird, Spielvogel? "Doctor, my doctor, what do you say, LET'S PUT THE ID BACK IN YID! Liberate this nice Jewish boy's libido, will you please? Raise the prices if you have to—I'll pay anything! Only enough cowering in the face of the deep, dark pleasures!" Portnoy is the victim of a psychological disease and neither his Jewishness nor assimilation (*alias* Alton Christian Peterson, Al Port, Al Parsons), neither Manhattan nor Zionism, can save him. A universal Messiah (Assistant Commissioner of Human Opportunity for the City of New York) tormented by lust, he destroys himself by a torturing stream of self-analysis: "Spring me from this role I play of the smothered son in the Jewish joke!" Unsuited to *any* coherent Jewish role, he bungles his life: reaching for *shikses* he is drowned in *goyim nachus.* Hypochrondriac son of a constipated Life Insurance salesman, he loses his birthright.

Where Bernard Malamud has repeatedly explored fables of the quest for fatherhood achieved, for adult responsibility won through suffering, Philip Roth has triumphantly turned the tables. His is the anguished comedy of Jewish fatherhood evaded and perverted. Alexander Portnoy is the *schlemiel* quester who fails to win his freedom. His suffering is for nothing, his life devoid of meaning, since he has not yet learnt that true freedom lies in the willing acceptance of others. The secret source of his humour, in Mark Twain's words, "is not joy but sorrow. There is no humour in heaven."

> *"Who Needs Dreams?" in* The Times Literary Supplement, *No.3503, April 17, 1969, p. 405.*

Barry Wallenstein

Philip Roth's third novel, **When She Was Good,** seemed an advance over the sprawling **Letting Go.** Its non-Jewish subject matter implied a widening of range. His newest novel, **Portnoy's Complaint,** strikes deeper, pleases on more levels and, if such a consideration still matters, seems truer than all of Roth's previous books.

The book is an extended dramatic monologue of Alexander Portnoy, one of the "fallen psychoneurotic Jewish men," and his many complaints which are terrible, sad, hilarious, bawdy and, I think, universal—and his Complaint. (Traditional poetic usage: a lament over 1) the unresponsiveness of his love (in this case, his mother), 2) the unhappy condition of his life and 3) the sorry state of the world.) The Complaint is usually the unhappy lover's appeal for help from some lady or divinity. This modern utterer of wail and woe rejects the gods, but has discovered an equivalent: "Doctor. . . . Bless me with manhood! Make me brave! Make me whole!" **Portnoy's Complaint** suggests the traditional modes of its genre while, at the same time, transcending the form through a more literal and colloquial expression of modern life's frustrations.

From the beginning the book flirts with one danger, that of becoming a case study. Allusions to Freud abound, as the hero reveals his story to a psychoanalyst. This clinical approach is obvious from Roth's own prefatory note:

> "Portnoy's Complaint (PORTNOIŹ KƎM-PLĀNT)
>
> *n . . . .* A disorder in which strongly felt ethical and altruistic impulses are perpetually warring with extreme sexual longings . . . often of a perverse nature. . . . It is believed that many of the symptoms can be traced to the bonds obtaining in the mother-child relationship."

Yet the psychological study is relieved by Roth's fine sense of mimicry, his ethnic humor:

> of me my mother would say, with characteristic restraint, "This *bonditt?* He doesn't even have to open a book—'A' in everything—Albert Einstein the second!"
>
> And how did my father take all this? He drank—of course, not whiskey like a *goy,* but mineral oil and milk of magnesia; and chewed on Ex-Lax; and ate All-Bran morn—and night—He suffered—did he suffer!—from constipation.

(Often the humor is more epigrammatic: "The perfect couple: she puts the id back in Yid, I put the *oy* back in *goy.*") The patient's compassion for his father's suffering—for suffering peoples everywhere—provides a pathos which goes beyond the literal complaining of the clinical survey.

But after all, the book *is* Portnoy's Complaint and to the substance of that complaint the reader must first and last address himself. Portnoy is the victim of his parents' carelessness (to use that word in a special sense). They treat the young boy to love, affection and material comforts. The ties of love are stronger than blood, but these ties are unaccompanied by respect for the son as a human being with feelings, thoughts and needs which may be *totally separated from those the parents ever had!* Portnoy is left shattered, a cripple, a potential suicide, a sex maniac who, luckily, is able to channel his frustrations by becoming a kind of artist, a tormented leader of a motley society. He holds the position of Assistant Commissioner for the City of New York Commission on Human Opportunities. His exalted post, though, does not save him from being crippled by an overwhelming sense of unworthiness and an overwhelming sense of love for his mother *and* father, a love that will always be strange and maddening.

Portnoy developed a singular defense: "My —— was all I really had that I could call my own." In the chapter, "Whacking Off," Alexander Portnoy begins confession of a sex life laden with guilt. His familial situation necessarily produced guilt, and all his subsequent relationships (onanistic and heterosexual) and fantasies are designed (unconsciously) to produce a similar condition. Often the unconscious and the conscious merge and Portnoy discovers that the only way to deal with guilt is to become more guilty—"to . . . sink into the slime." This marvelous comic chapter is a kind of analysis of guilt. It is an extravaganza, finally a metaphor for Portnoy's many terrors to be developed, by stages, throughout the book: "I grab that battering ram to freedom. . . . " Soon he hears the words "apologize and apologize and apologize"—words heard into his nightmares by another guilty boy, Stephan Dedalus, another who suffered, but was able to fly from the crippling environment in "a house poorly provided."

The reader must face sexual details, most of which would be obscene in any context of Romantic Love. Here, the context naturally calls for Roth's handling. Sex is used in the book as poverty was used in the social protest novels of the 1930's. The details of sex (like those of poverty) are but the manifestations of a condition. By studying the manifestations, *e.g.,* sexual excesses and perversions, the condition itself is cast into light. Unlike poverty in the social protest novel, however, sex is here treated with a gusto and self-mockery that never worry us. We become aware of the grimness of Portnoy's condition *despite* his complaining, not by way of it. When Portnoy complains, "a Jewish man with parents alive is a fifteen-year-old boy and will remain a fifteen-year-old boy till *they die!,*" we learn less of his (and the "Jewish") condition, than we learn of his anger, his frustration, his sense of having been grossly hurt.

After much complaining, venting anger as well as distress against his parents, he moves toward a more general, a more lyrical complaint: "*Oy,* civilization and its discontents!" (Freud again.) Here he is a sacrificial and suffering figure, thirty-three years old (Christ and Joe Christmas). By this time we see that his own personal pains are microcosms of macroscosmic suffering. He is the outcast and the outsider. As a Jew, his identity in America is always dubious. He explains: "What I'm saying, Doctor, is that I don't seem to stick my —— up these girls, as much as I stick it up their backgrounds—as though, through ——, I will discover America."

Identifying with his environment is a problem not tangential but intrinsic to his greater psychological distresses. *Portnoy's Complaint* is a book about personal anguish, but it is also about the social instability of an entire people *and* the universal social implications these specific conditions suggest.

In the final chapter, "In Exile," Portnoy is flying over Tel Aviv airport and suffers, joyfully suffers, memories of his past—not the archetypal memories of his suffering people, but simpler memories of himself with his father. For a short time, all his awareness of damaged ego and broken heart is suspended. He then has a fantasy of himself "settling down" with a Jewish wife who will bear a son who will carry on. . . . This is the only positive fantasy Portnoy has admitted. Pathetically, this is the one fantasy he is unable to put into action. All the others (and they are mainly of sexual performances) are sadly fulfilled in the real world. As he tells Dr. Spielvogel, "the dream thing really happens."

The book thus ends in *stasis.* The monologue has changed nothing. Only the reader may benefit from such revelations. Many, though, suffer such helplessness as Portnoy; their only hope is that from the Doctor and his therapy may come magic. (pp. 129-30)

> Barry Wallenstein, "Remembering Mama with Rue," in The Catholic World, *Vol. 209, No. 1251, June, 1969, pp. 129-30.*

Patricia Meyer Spacks

How can one write seriously about a dirty book, a million-dollar best-seller, a comic dirty Jewish novel; is it necessary to analyze the symbolic significance of each masturbation, each grope, each joust of member and orifice? How does criticism of such a book avoid turning into a joke?

No one seems to have found much in the way of significance, and the nature of this novel makes it oddly embarrassing to look. It has been assumed that the importance of *Portnoy's Complaint* must have something to do with its being a Jewish novel, that it represents either the last gasp or the fine flowering of the form. But it can be argued—I'd like to argue—that the detail of the novel, social and sexual, fills out a metaphor of the human condition in the twentieth century. Portnoy sees his own problems as products of his Jewishness, but readers are not obliged to share his view. Indeed, they are invited to understand that the suffering and the comedy of Alexander Portnoy are the suffering and the comedy of modern man, who seeks and finds explanations for his plight but is unable to resolve it, whose understanding is as limited as his sense of possibility, who is forced to the analyst to make sense of his experience.

The closest affinities of *Portnoy's Complaint* with a traditional novelistic form are with the picaresque novel. *Portnoy* begins in New Jersey, proceeds to Israel, but the journey it relates is not physical, despite excursions as far afield as Iowa and Rome. The novel's looseness of sequence and apparent incoherence of detail recall the picaresque tradition, as do the nature and role of its central character, whose psychic journeyings, circular though they are, are the substance of the narrative. "The basic situation of the picaresque novel," wrote Claudio Guillén, "is the solitude of its principal character in the world." The essential characteristics of its hero, Robert Alter adds, is that he "is a man who does not belong, a man on the move, and a man who takes things into his own hands." Alexander Portnoy is, like the orthodox picaro, a rogue. Unlike some of his predecessors in the genre, he worries—he is, after all, a modern man; and a Jew: modern man intensified—about his roguery. He moves not toward self-knowledge (he starts and concludes with almost the same amount) but toward self-confrontation; he moves toward despair.

Like other picaresque novels, *Portnoy's Complaint* is shaped by successive conflicts between innocence and experience. In this novel, though, the roles keep shifting. The hero (and he *is* a hero, not an anti-hero), unlike Huck Finn or Don Quixote, does not always exemplify natural virtue. Sometimes he seems to embody natural vice. He locks himself in the bathroom to masturbate; his mother concludes that he has diarrhea. How did Melvin Weiner give himself colitis, his mother wants to know; Portnoy replies, *"chazerai"* (indiscriminate eating: in his mother's definition, eating commercial hamburgers). It's the right answer but the wrong tone, the tone of cynicism: the proper note is that of innocent conviction. His mother has simple faiths: lobster is prohibited by Jewish dietary law because it makes you throw up your *kishkas,* Gentile girls want only to trap Jewish boys, hamburgers and French fries spell doom. She is thus the innocent; her son, living through the complexities of adolescence, is by comparison corrupt in his inescapable knowledge. Her faith in his virtue can only intensify his awareness of his own complicated and necessary wickedness. It intensifies, in fact, not only awareness, but the wickedness itself.

But Portnoy is also the perpetual innocent confronted by profound racial experience in which he feels himself an unwilling or incomplete participant. "Do me a favor, my people," he cries, "and stick your suffering heritage up your suffering ass—*I happen also to be a human being!*" It is a theme line of the novel: yet the suffering heritage of the Jews remains an ineluctable fact. The "wisdom" of "his people" is a burden, reinforcing his sense of inadequate experience. At the end of the chapter about his adolescent encounters with Gentile girls, he tells of an abortive episode with Bubbles Girardi, a youthful Italian whore. It ends in disaster for Portnoy, and leaves him still frustrated in his longing to know what women are really like. The boys who remain on the scene have more satisfying experiences with Bubbles, and it is to them that Portnoy finally, rhetorically, appeals: "What is it like! Before I go out of my head, I have to know what it's like!" The cry is strangely moving. It announces another of the novel's themes: the passionate yearning for experience and the knowledge it brings. There is the experience of the Jews, and the experience one is cut off from by being a Jew. Standards shift, and possibilities, and Portnoy struggles to find out what it's like, what he's like, what the world's like, and women. He is an innocent desperate for experience, and experienced sinner yearning for innocence.

The confusions of his position are most apparent in his encounter with the Israeli girl Naomi, with whom he finds himself impotent. She declares herself the representative of natural virtue (i.e., innocence) and Portnoy hopelessly corrupt; he accepts her estimation. But it is equally true that she exemplifies that racial wisdom he can neither comprehend nor accept, and that he by comparison, with his obsessive talk about sex, seems a child. He is both too experienced and too innocent to deal with her. To Portnoy the episode seems a disaster, a self-indictment. *"I couldn't get it up in the State of Israel!"* he tells his doctor, believing that the fact proves his hopeless decadence. But his judgment, once more, is far from ours. Naomi illustrates [psychologist and author] Bruno Bettelheim's thesis that children of the kibbutz have difficulty forming one-to-one relationships and are often incapable of intimacy. Portnoy, too, is lacking in these respects, and perhaps unable to recognize Naomi's manifest inadequacies because he concentrates on his own even more manifest ones. Naomi, whose opinions are impeccable, seems no more than the sum of her opinions. Portnoy's opinions are irrelevant, but we like him better than Naomi because, however limp, he is more fully alive.

Almost at the mathematical center of the novel is the effort at heightened experience which takes place when Portnoy and his female companion, The Monkey, entice an Italian whore—a grown-up one this time—to join them in a small-scale hotel-bedroom orgy. His shame at having involved himself in this sordidness is exceeded only by his shame at being shamed. He tries again the next day: "If I'm going to do it, I thought, I'm going to do it! All the way! Everything! And no vomiting, either!" Experience must, he believes, bring wisdom, or happiness, or sophistication or *something.* But it brings impotence; no end to innocence; it brings the psychoanalyst. Lina, the whore, embodies experience accepted, not considered; The Monkey shows experience considered and resented. Portnoy, caught between the two, can neither fully accept nor fully resent his own experience.

But if we respond to Portnoy as hero—or partial hero, would-be hero—it is not on the basis of considerations so abstract as his relation to innocence and experience, but as an immediate reaction to his overflowing vitality. The nominal subject of *Portnoy's Complaint* is the neurotic inadequacies of its central figure, but the book makes us aware also of his unquenchable energy. That hopeful energy manifests itself most vividly in his odyssey from bed to bed. "Do I really experience this restlessness, this horniness, as an affliction—or as an accomplishment?" Portnoy asks his doctor. "Both? Could be. Or is it only a means of evasion?" It is manifestly all three, but the second definition is most crucial. Erik Erikson, at the end of *Childhood and Society,* suggests that a saving remnant of indignation is necessary to analyst and patient alike in order to make a cure more than "a straw in the changeable wind of history." This is indignation directed outward, a defiance of things as they are, of the inequities and horrors of the human condition, of the need for analysis and of the final impossibility of analysis. Portnoy is splendidly indignant: at being trapped by his history, at his inability to be content, at the impossibility of making people what he wants them to be. His affliction is also his accomplishment, his indignation the enemy of resignation. Unable to accept *shikse* or Jew, he refuses to compromise; his impotence in Israel is evidence of his inability to settle for the surface appearance of exemplary femininity.

One may argue that to embody the hero's unwillingness to compromise, his limitless aspiration, in the responses of a man traversing only the arid wastelands of sexual perversity is a diminishment which makes it impossible to take Portnoy seriously as hero. "He is obscene," Roth commented in an interview, "because he wants to be saved." The possibilities of salvation and of damnation are for Portnoy, mid-twentieth-century man, only sexual. The wanderings of Odysseus and of Don Quixote invite—or at least make possible—allegorical interpretation. The impediments such heroes face emblemize their psychological and social problems and suggest the kind of possibility they believe in. Portnoy is imagined with no such scope as they, but his problems, too, have social as well as psychological significance, although his apparent unawareness of this fact is another of his conspicuous intellectual limitations. He inhabits a world of diminished possibility and demands that it yield meaning; his experience suggests the limitations inherent in such a world.

The prevalence of pornography in our time means more than that pornography has become permissible. It reflects a widespread preoccupation with sexuality as perhaps the only arena for action remaining within individual control. If sex is significant, maybe individuals are important. But pornography, building on the preoccupation with sex, denies the optimism which may be implicit in it. Dealing with people as objects, instruments of gratification for one another, it suggests the debasement of possible human contact, the meaninglessness of terms beyond the physical. It is a genre of despair.

Portnoy's Complaint is not pornography, but it depends on pornographic material with apparent awareness of its dark implications. In Portnoy's society there are no new worlds to conquer, only new women. The Assistant Commissioner for Human Opportunity can talk of the elimination of social problems, but he cannot believe in it. . . . The limitations of his world are exemplified by the limitation of his experience: variety of partners, but monotony of endeavor, defining—like the grander exploits of happier heroes—the precise meaning of his condition. Possibility exists only in adolescent fantasy; realized, when wet dreams come to life, it creates images of sterility and monotony. Traditional religious sanctions against the forms of perverse sexuality rest on the assumption that sex should serve fecundity, that modes of sexuality unrelated to generativity are therefore morally unsound. *Portnoy's Complaint* demonstrates, for all its gusto in recounting perversities, that they are emotionally unsound as well.

But this account of Portnoy's achievement, limitation, and hope has a certain aura of unreality because it is still one degree removed from the novel's fundamental ground of appeal. The reader is in fact most conscious of Portnoy not as hero or would-be hero but as teller of his own story, creator—or re-creator—of his own myth. What he says is more important than what he does; what he says transforms what he does. He wishes to tell the truth; the convention of the analyst establishes this fact. His version of truth makes the mundane, repetitive, perverse facts of his experience into a lyric of comic outrage.

The line between novel and poem becomes harder and harder to draw in the twentieth century. Beckett, Borges, Barth have accustomed us to fiction lacking plot, dependent on linguistic self-awareness and patterning for its crucial effects. *Portnoy's Complaint,* full of people and actions, seems a novel of a very different kind from theirs. Yet it, too, is shaped by style more than by content; its language gives meaning to and at times is identical with its substance.

The point is most obvious in the book's comedy, which, despite its subject matter, is the high comedy of style. It often derives from the same contrast between innocence and experience which shapes the action, a contrast exemplified in incongruities between language and subject. Portnoy relates an episode which exemplifies the perverse experience of his adulthood in language which reminds us of the innocent gusto he retains from childhood. Here he is describing his first encounter with The Monkey:

> Did I eat! It was suddenly as though my life were taking place in the middle of a wet dream. There I was, going down at last on the star of all those pornographic films that I had been producing in my head since I first laid a hand upon my own joint . . . 'Now me you,' she said, '—one good turn deserves another,' and, Doctor, this stranger then proceeded to suck me off with a mouth that might have gone to a special college to learn all the wonderful things it knew. What a find, I thought, she takes it right down to the root! What a mouth I have fallen into! Talk about opportunities!

The comedy depends on tonal manipulation, the close blending of a wonder amounting almost to awe with the deflating self-awareness which recognizes the ludicrousness of the situation. The language enforces the reader's consciousness of the ludicrous with its incongruous conjunctions, its comic restoration of literal force to dead metaphor ("What a mouth I have fallen into!"), its introduction of the term *stranger* into an intimate context, its explicit recognition of the adolescent fantasy level in this adult experience. The last sentence is rich in comic reverberation, for Alexander Portnoy, Assistant Commissioner of Human Opportunity for New York City, talks about opportunities by profession. His account does not only reveal the self-punishing irony familiar from Jewish jokes; it is not only, or even mainly, self-deprecating; it *is* self-aware. The fullness of awareness, and of its linguistic rendition, creates the richness of comedy. (pp 623-29)

The linguistic energy of *Portnoy's Complaint* affirms the vitality which is the novel's most important positive value and enables it to escape the restrictiveness of pornography. Pornography uses dead language to describe lively action; it keeps reality at a distance in order to encourage fantasy. Books like *Lady Chatterley's Lover,* on the other hand, with their "redeeming social importance," relate sexual events to larger human contexts, insist that sex is vital to relationship but that its meaning is more than physical. *Portnoy,* like the pornographic novel, depicts a world dominated by sexual imaginings and events; unlike

Lady Chatterley, it does not describe sexual union as a basis for enduring relationship. It relies heavily and explicitly on fantasy, although it may not encourage further fantasy. Accepting as given a world in which meaningful individual action seems impossible, in which all sexual activity is essentially masturbatory, in which one is ever conscious of incipient despair, it demonstrates through the vigor of its language the continued possibility of transcendence. The true center of Portnoy's heroism is his speech. As Don Quixote rises from his bout with a windmill to fight the next improbable enemy, so Portnoy, bewildered, ashamed, and proud of his condition, continues to talk. Through verbal contact with the analyst he hopes to be saved. Through verbal contact with the reader he reminds us that language, too, remains within the control of individuals, and that there is enduring power in the word. The sexual activity described in the novel is not just disgusting (as it is in summary: people who have only seen accounts of the book are often more shocked than those who have read the novel itself) because it is transformed through language.

That language is in fact a highly literary construct. It is not really a rendition of speech, although it often creates the illusion of the extemporaneous. "I don't think I've spoken of the disproportionate effect The Monkey's handwriting used to have upon my psychic equilibrium," Portnoy says, or is purported to say. It is not a sentence one can readily imagine spoken aloud, despite its informalities; it has the structure and tone of a carefully organized topic sentence. Or, in a rather more "literary" mode: "He wears square steel-rimmed spectacles, and his hair (which now I wear) is a wild bush the color and texture of steel wool; and those teeth, which sit all night long in a glass in the bathroom smiling at the toilet bowl, now smile out at me, his beloved, his flesh and blood, the little boy upon whose head no rain shall ever fall." The calculated rhythms and ironies, the tonal mixture of nostalgia, affection, amusement, even the punctuation—all suggest the formalities of written rather than oral communication. It is true that the freedom of spoken language here combines with the control of the written form. Like Norman Mailer in *Why Are We in Vietnam?* (and, to my ear, far more successfully), Roth exploits the language of obscenity to comment on the social and psychological conditions which produce it. But even when he duplicates the rhythms of the spoken word ("Enough being a nice Jewish boy, publicly pleasing my parents while privately pulling my putz!"), blatant alliteration and structural parallelism remind us that this is a literary version of colloquialism.

The last quotation brings to mind an informal tabulation I undertook of terms Portnoy uses to refer to his penis (or, on one occasion, his father's). I doubt if it is exhaustive, but it is impressive: dong, upright, cock, *shlong,* prick, peter ("LET MY PETER GO! There, that's Portnoy's slogan."), joint, putz, wang, dick. In addition to this collection of locker room terminology, he employs kennings of his own such as "silky monster" and "idiot macrocephalic." The distance between the two kinds of language suggests the book's linguistic range, and a special purpose its language serves. The colloquial nouns Portnoy applies to the sexual organ belong to the idiom of casual sexual refer-

ence; in most contexts they reflect a tendency to take sex lightly, to relegate it to the realm of animality. These are the nouns of sex as opposed to love, of bawdiness, not "significance." In Roth, they take on significance. In their abundance, ease, and energy, they testify Portnoy's vigor, his refusal to be put down; they declare his lack of verbal inhibition as he recounts his lack of inhibition in action; at the same time they suggest his partial contempt for his own sexual acrobatics. Portnoy's more witty and individual terminology makes similar points, offering evidence of his inventiveness while conveying a rather affectionate self-condemnation. When Lawrence allows Mellors to revel in Anglo-Saxon sexual terminology, he uses dirty words as evidence of his hero's moral freedom and the beauty of that freedom. In Roth, obscenities define not only the hero's freedom but his bondage. Roth's purposes, unlike Lawrence's, are not didactic; his language is never self-consciously "beautiful" or "noble"; his faith in the value of sexual liberation seems eroded. But like Lawrence he appears to believe in sexual activity as a metaphor for the human condition. Portnoy can conceive of and indulge in a broad range of sexual practices, but their meaning for him is restricted. The wider conditions of his existence are describable in similar terms: he can do what he likes, but find little meaning in the doing. For Mellors, sexual union generates a sense of meaning which becomes the focus of a full life; no other kind of "doing" is necessary. Significance is imaginable; and it is sexual.

The crucial difference between **Portnoy's Complaint** and Lawrence's novels. . . . is that Roth's novel is, as I have suggested, a linguistic construct more importantly than a record of action. The prospect of the movie to be made from it is embarrassing, as the novel itself is not. The act of telling, the mode of telling, is the novel's main source of interest. We do not wish to see on a movie screen the blonde *shikses* with whom Portnoy dreams of skating; they are as much creatures of fantasy as Portnoy's dreamwhore, Thereal McCoy, and it is as beings of fantasy that we respond to them. (pp. 630-32)

Although [**Portnoy's**] subject is a man unable altogether to grow up, its author is an adult. His is the artistry that structures the novel and judges its central character. The structure of events, neither sequential nor logical, is yet meaningful. When Portnoy turns round in mid-sentence ("My bladder may be distended to watermelon proportions, but interrupted by another presence before the stream has begun [you want to hear everything, okay I'm telling everything] which is that in Rome, Doctor . . . ") his shift helps to define his shame over the Rome episode of sex *à trois* and to suggest the persistence with which the women in his life have made him feel inadequate. The first part of the sentence concerns the inhibition caused by his mother's early tickling of his genitals in an effort to make him urinate like a man; the last part introduces the story of The Monkey and the Roman whore, who tickle him in rather different fashion and make him feel the limitations of his own sexual daring.

The apparent inconsequence of structure on a larger scale serves similar purposes. In the chapter called "The Jewish Blues," Portnoy moves from his undescended—or reascended—testicle to his mother's role as his would-be lover to his association with his father and other large Jewish males in the steam bath. The sequence of association is transparent and revealing: to contemplate isolated Jewish masculinity after a vivid image of the man-destroying female is to see the steam bath in a rather special light. The chapter ends by moving from Portnoy's adolescent rejection of Judaism and his personal objections to the rabbi to his insistence—perfectly opaque to his mother—on equal treatment for Negroes: and one understands in a new sense what it means that Alexander Portnoy is Assistant Commissioner for Human Opportunity. Like a poem, this novel operates by suggestive conjuctions of images. Lacking plot in the ordinary sense, it proceeds by the collocation of Portnoy's discrete visions of reality—the objective correlatives for his sense of emotional maiming. These images are memorable in themselves: Portnoy's mother obsessively washing the utensils the colored girl has used or brandishing a knife over her child or locking him out for his misdeeds; The Monkey, in full evening regalia, watching her rich husband at his perversions; Portnoy himself dreaming of his *shikse* and skating into the shore. They define what Portnoy has seen, and how he sees; thus they tell us who he is. And they shape the novel as poem, reflecting a modern understanding of human life: not an ordered progress of action with definable beginning, middle, and end, climax and dénouement, but a series of moments whose meaning and order depend on their perceiver. Plot is falsification; *Portnoy* attempts poetic truth.

This book is a rendition of a consciousness more than of a series of events; it concerns itself with events only as existent in that consciousness and reported by the voice the consciousness produces. Its novelistic skill manifests itself in making the consciousness reveal more about itself than it knows. The pleasure of the novel is partly the pleasure of understanding: not simply Portnoy, but the events he relates, whose multi-textured meanings (the meanings of the facts and of Portnoy's mode of rendering them) we absorb as though by intuitive response. In the best parts of the book, episodes succeed one another with such speed, are related with such gusto, that there is no time to think about them. One merely responds to emotional and intellectual complexities too subtle and life-like for rational paraphrase.

Conversely, the literary weaknesses of *Portnoy's Complaint* become apparent when Portnoy's self-analysis is most insistent and his piling of detail wanes: in the novel's last chapters, where the author imposes meanings of a more conventional and orderly sort. The conjunctions of imagery in the accounts of Portnoy's adult Gentile girlfriends, and particularly of his trip to Israel, lack the poetic suggestiveness of earlier sequences. They seem calculated and sometimes forced. When Portnoy recalls the Sunday baseball games of his youth, he tells us that he recollected them as he approached Israel by air, and he tells us why: he had always dreamed of growing up to be a conventional Jewish man; the return to the homeland reminds him of this dream. So obvious an association, so carefully located and described, supplies no energy of suggestion, although the loving richness of individual details gives authenticity to the remembered games. Similarly, the sequence of girls—Midwestern Kay Campbell, aristocratic Sarah Maulsby, the two Israelis with whom Portnoy is impotent—suggests little meaning beyond the stated one: Portnoy is either unsatisfied or unsatisfactory. The girls are memorable, and precisely rendered, but their presentation lacks structural significance. Roth supplies expert writing but inadequate perspective; we feel trapped in the wilds of Portnoy's psyche, and it's a dreary environment. Portnoy himself insists on meanings: he asserts, for example, the "ethical impulses" which appear in his doctor's diagnosis of his "complaint" but never become real in the novel. Assertion does not engineer conviction; we cannot believe just because we are told. Portnoy dwells on the symbolic scene of Naomi standing over him, points to the symbolism of her kicking him in the heart—but a symbol pointed to is not a symbol felt. If our judgment of Naomi is more complex than his, it still remains true that the last part of *Portnoy's Complaint* is less real, less compelling, less evocative (and, not coincidentally, less funny) than the rest because it is not true to the technique earlier evolved or to the implications of that technique.

What is most real about Portnoy is his fantasies. He is incapable of intimacy—it is difficult to believe even in the Vermont idyll with The Monkey—because other people are not real to him. Everyone in the book seems his projection. What could be more fantastic than the mother he remembers, fears, loves, and creates? The Monkey is explicitly a fantasy come to life; when her fantasies (of married life in the country) make her real and conflict with Portnoy's, he can no longer stay with her. Even the other Gentile girls and the Israeli ones in Portnoy's rendition take on mythic simplicities and proportions. He makes his world unreal but vivid in telling about it; he helps to create the limitations which trap him by the limitations of his own imagination, emotion, powers of perception. The novel's final sequence exemplifies the technique, the comedy, the horror of the book. Portnoy, who has been talking of his misery, which, he feels, has gone beyond the power of language to express, begins to meditate about the tag on new mattresses that forbids its own removal. He imagines himself tearing it off, the police approaching with drawn guns, himself defiant though doomed; finally, in imagination tormented beyond language, he screams. There is real pain here—the pain of partial awareness, of paranoia, perhaps of persecution. It is hidden behind the comedy of pure fantasy, the mind dwelling on the trivial, forcing logic to absurdity, glorying in its capacity to follow out consequences. It is the same mind that we have encountered throughout the novel: always inventive, elaborating, discovering the comedy which conceals pain itself slightly ridiculous. Have all Portnoy's concerns been at the level of mattress tags—concerns with reality, but with the minute and trivial to the exclusion of real significance? As his mind presents experience, it also forms meanings. If Portnoy defines himself as hero by his storytelling, he also defines himself as neurotic—a conjunction peculiar to our time. Philip Roth, offering not merely a series of jokes but a highly self-conscious narrative, has found the form which sharply reveals this conjunction and its multifarious meanings. (pp. 632-35)

Patricia Meyer Spacks, "About Portnoy," in

The Yale Review, Vol. 58, No. 4, June, 1969, pp. 623-35.

On Fame

"What distinguishes the merely famous from a celebrity or a star has usually to do with money or sex or, as in my case, with both. I was said to have made a million dollars, and I was said to be none other than Portnoy himself. To become a celebrity is to become a brand name. There is Ivory soap, Rice Krispies, and Philip Roth. Ivory is the soap that floats; Rice Krispies the breakfast cereal that goes snap-crackle-pop; Philip Roth the Jew who masturbates with a piece of liver. And makes a million out of it."
—Philip Roth, 1981

Bruno Bettelheim

[Bettelheim is a psychologist and author. In the following excerpt, which purports to be therapy notes found in Portnoy's psychiatric file, he assumes the persona of Dr. O. Spielvogel, Portnoy's psychoanalyst.]

Monday, The first hour: A troublesome—aren't they all?—new patient, 33 years old, raised in Newark. Typical petty bourgeois Jewish Orthodox background. He is highly intelligent, a compulsive talker, extremely narcissistic and exhibitionistic. His intellectual arrogance he hides behind ironic self-deprecation. He cannot stop the diarrhea of talk, since it is his way of denying his essential constipation, his total inability to give of himself or of anything else. His working for the underdog (some kind of public human relations work for the poorest) is not only a denial of his own exploitativeness, but reflects the feeling he has that only the most miserable could possibly accept him.

He gave me no chance to explain what psychoanalysis is all about, claims to be well familiar with it, and proceeds to show that he lacks even the slightest understanding. He seems to think it is a self-serving rattling off of complaints, of accusations leveled at others and himself, instead of serious introspection and the contemplation that it evokes. He is capable of neither, because he feels himself so worthless that he cannot be serious about anything that touches him—neither his own self, nor his parents, nor those he cohabitates with. He wants to do everything himself without any relation to, or contribution by, another person, in a typical masturbatory phallic fixation. He permits no one, including me, to make any contribution to his life. (p. 3)

Despite his long account of all that went wrong in his life beginning with infancy, there is absolutely no realization of his sickness: that he simply cannot relate to other persons. And how can he, since all he sees of the world are his own projections which he is certain are true pictures of reality?

He sees psychoanalysis as one vast catharsis, without the need for any deeper insight or internalization. Everything is just one huge ejaculation. So much so, that I doubt if he can establish even the minimal transference that would enable him to analyze. Probably his selecting me for an analyst typifies his unwillingness to give up his bondage to his Jewish past. (pp. 3-4)

Since he thinks his need is to spill out, uninterruptedly, I shall let him, for a full week. Then we shall see if he can stop the spilling enough for analysis to be possible.

He carries on as if to convince me that all the clichés of a spoiled Jewish boyhood are indeed valid: the overpowering, overindulging, overprotective mother and the ineffectual father. Essentially the hour was one long alibi. I am to understand that if he cannot meet life, cannot relate to another human being, it's not because of how he construes things, but because of his parents and their ritual background, along with two specific traumata. He is a master of the alibi, and like the clever lawyer he is, plays both sides of the road. He blames his misery on both kinds of trauma: the physical (an undescended testicle) and the psychological (his mother's threat of desertion, and with a knife). He must be certain I will see him as the suffering victim, no matter what kind of theories I hold about physical or emotional trauma as causing behavior like his. It is neither one, but only his self-hatred that forces him to defeat all those who love him (his parents, his sexual partners, etc.).

The tirade against his parents, especially his mother, is uninterruptable. A few times I indicated the wish to say something, but he only talked on the more furiously. It was like a satire on the complaints of most of my patients, and on the tenets of psychoanalysis: that of a dominating and castrating father, and of a mother too involved in herself and her own life, to pay much attention to her son. This extremely intelligent young Jew does not recognize that what he is trying to do, by reversing the Oedipal situation, is to make fun of me, as he does of everyone, thus asserting his superiority over me and psychoanalysis itself. His overpowering love for his mother is turned into a negative projection, so that what becomes overpowering is the mother's love for him. Overtly he complains that she could never let him alone, was all intrusive—behind which lies an incredibly deep disappointment that she was not even more exclusively preoccupied with him. While consciously he experienced everything she did as destructive, behind it is an incredible wish for more, more, more; an insatiable orality which is denied and turned into the opposite by his continuous scream of it's being much too much. (p. 4)

Having to listen all day to the endless complaints of my patients about mothers who were never interested in whether they ate or did not eat, whether or not they defecated, whether or not they succeeded in school, it should have been refreshing to listen to an hour of complaints about a mother who did exactly that—but it was not. Because it was so obvious that he, too, felt cheated at not being given enough. No doubt, he is tortured by memories of his past, and by his present inability to be a man, to enjoy normal sex. But nowhere do I see any effort to free himself of this bondage to the past. He certainly makes the most of it. Obviously he expects my magic and that of psychoanalysis to do it for him.

An important clue, later to be followed up: He is fascinated by his father's constipation, which is so stark a contrast with his excessive masturbation and incessant, diarrhea-like talk. It seems like an interesting fixation at the phallic level, where the father's constipation made him so anxious about the ability to produce that to compensate, he produces without interruption—whether by masturbating, talking, or intellectual achievement. If he does not learn to hold in, to store, but continues the indiscriminate discharge, analysis will certainly fail.

If I should give a name to this first hour, I would call it *The most unforgettable character I've met.* Not because the patient thinks this is true of his mother, as he sees her (as it is of everyone and his mother) but because, while he wishes to believe this, his major effort is to impress me with himself as "The most unforgettable character I've ever met." Poor soul. Instead of trying to get from me the help he so desperately needs, he tries to impress me with his uniqueness. Everything he accuses his mother of, he is himself, in the extreme. She exploited him because she loved him so much. He exploits everyone because he loves no one.

Tuesday, The second hour: Despite the same incessant stream of talk, little new material. Speculations arrived by at the end of the last hour seem borne out today. As a child, he masturbated, preferably on the toilet, in line with the father's constipation which emerges ever more as a central experience leading to a negative identification. The father cannot let go. The son cannot hold anything in, or hold onto anyone. The father, out of incessant fear for the future, chose and stuck to his job of life insurance salesman. This is internalized by the son as fear for his masculinity. And for this he finds only one defense: the excessive masturbation that seems to prove his body is working, but at the price of self-disgust. Because what he wants is not a penis that gives pleasure, but an instrument that expels its content, a seeking of self-assurance, which his kind of masturbation cannot give him. Otherwise, it was a repetition of the first hour's contents. In the deliberately vulgar language of the patient, I would title this session *Whacking off.* He uses obscenity to impress others and fools himself into thinking himself liberated, while actually he expresses his loathing for himself.

Wednesday, The third hour: It becomes more and more clear that he has read too much about psychoanalysis, and understood nothing—for example about castration anxiety and the effect of seeing menstrual blood. What he does not see is how desperately he wishes he *had* a castrating father, how deeply disappointed he is because what he encounters instead is only what he experiences as a castrating mother. But even as he complains of how castrating she is, he cannot help admiring her inner strength, which alone seems to sustain the entire family. One gets the feeling that he has to see her as castrating, because he needs

to see her as being strong enough to protect him. It becomes more and more clear that his true sickness is the refusal to recognize his parents' deep love for him, because that would mean the obligation to love them back, and later, other human beings. Instead he clings to his vision of all human relations as exploitative power plays.

A characteristic memory: The athletic cousin, Heshie, gets into a physical fight with his father. Although considerably the stronger, he lets the father pin him down and then defeat him in physical combat. My patient wonders and wonders about it. He cannot understand why his cousin lets this happen. He cannot see what, in his unconscious, he obviously senses: that while the father kept his son from marrying the gentile girl he loved, which led to the fight, the father's motive was deep love for his son. This cousin could realize, consciously or unconsciously, that to be overpowered by the deep love of another for oneself is the greatest victory possible in human relations, even if outwardly it seems like defeat. This my patient, unfortunately, is unable to consciously accept, and I fear never will. If he could, it would mean his problems were over and his analysis done.

That he could never have the closeness there was between Heshie and his father, that he can neither let go of nor enjoy the specific Jewishness of his background, that he denies what he craves—all this gives him the particular *"Jewish Blues"* that formed the leitmotif of this session.

Thursday, The fourth hour: He connects his exhibitionary masturbation on the bus to his having eaten un-Kosher food (lobster) for the first time. In his unconscious he thus recognizes the connection between oral and phallic anxiety, and how much of his sexual acting out is based on oral anxiety, how like the baby who shows off his phallus. From here, his associations move to what an anxious person his mother really is, with her endless stories of how she tries everything once only to find that any venturing out in the world leads to immediate punishment, if not destruction. Even an explicit memory—her first attempt to drive, which led to an accident and to so much anxiety that she never drove again—brings no realization of how anxiety-ridden she is. Because such an insight would destroy his image of her as the all-powerful, castrating woman. He has no realization that what he identifies with in his mother is not her strength, but her abysmal fear of life.

From talking of his resentment at the feeling that he owes his parents something—to get married and provide them with grandchildren, or to be a success in life they can brag about, as their friends and relatives do—he associates to his sexual desire for gentile girls. That is, he can only have sex if it is sex that his parents disapprove of. He is so tied to them that he cannot feel he has a separate existence unless he does something to hurt them. Of course this does not work, and even in the midst of having intercourse he is already dissatisfied, is already longing anxiously for the next girl to have sex with.

Clearly his promiscuity is one big effort to keep from his parents what they so much want, while making certain he is punished for it by getting nothing that is meaningful to him. For all his reading of psychoanalysis, he does not see that his promiscuity, particularly with gentiles, is one big reassurance that he is not having incestuous relations with his mother. By keeping his women ever-changing and meaningless to him, he remains faithful to his mother—not because she won't let him go but because he won't let go of her. Having enslaved himself to her, he projects the relation to see it as if she, or both parents, had enslaved him to them.

Another crucial memory: A fifteen year old boy is pushed too hard by his ambitious mother to perform, and hangs himself. Pinned to his shirt is a message he took for his mother: that she is to take the mah-jongg rules along when she goes out that night. My patient can see in it only the boy's obedience, and not the lethal venom at his mother who dares to enjoy a game with her friends instead of doing nothing all day except cater to her son.

As is typical for patients totally unable to form any human relations, they complain endlessly of the deficiency of human relations in their childhood and try to provide for others what is, in fact, totally absent in their own lives. So this patient, it turns out, is Assistant Commissioner of the New York Committee on Human Opportunity, concerned in his work with improving the lives of others. In his professional life he tries to prevent the poor from being exploited, while all he chases in his personal life is the chance to sexually exploit others.

The worst part of it is that he, who is so lacking in ego and the capacity to give, who is so driven to act out his uncontrolled instinctual tendencies, thinks he is suffering from a deficiency of the id. At one point he makes clear what he wants from me: to put the id back into this particular Yid. That is, he does not really want to analyze himself; does not want to get ego control over superego and id. All he wants of me is to rid him of all the pangs of conscience he still feels about his selfish and asocial behavior. This is how he conceives of the purpose of psychoanalysis. Indeed he offers to pay me an even higher fee if only I could do that for him. (pp. 5-7)

The only enjoyment he seems to get out of sex is cunnilingus. Like his incessant talking and his pleasure in four letter words, so it is with his preference for this perversion. All indicate that he was so intensely satisfied by the oral pleasure his mother provided, that he cannot conceive of its coming from anything else. He is, I am tempted to say, crazy in his efforts to wring oral satisfaction out of sex. In the language of the patient, this session exemplifies his *"cunt craziness."*

Friday, The fifth hour: He begins the session by referring to Freud's paper on the misuse of sex to degrade the partner. Which leads to memories of his sexual relations with some upper-class gentiles. He recognizes that his feelings of Jewish inferiority, his resentment of anti-Semitism, are why he cannot find sexual satisfaction except through seducing his gentile partners into practices which to him are degrading. (pp. 7-8)

Since he has never known true empathy for anyone, he cannot see that these gentile girls had sex with him precisely because he lived up to their stereotyped notions of the dirty, sex-crazy Jew. Forcing them into what they view as perverted sex, proves to them they were right about Jews in the first place. They have selected this highly intelligent, thus seemingly very worthwhile Jew, because being specially admirable he threatened their image of Jews as inferior beings. But if even this very bright, this nice, concerned Jew wants nothing so much as to degrade them in sex, then their initial image of the "dirty" Jew is again confirmed. And my patient does his best to oblige. Still thinking he degrades only them, he degrades himself even more. This mutual exploitation extends also to what the pair use each other for: to defeat their parents. For my patient the worst he can do to his parents is to live with a gentile girl. While to sleep with a Jew is probably the worst these girls can do to their parents. How these neurotics always find each other! How they help each other act out their neurosis so there is no need to face it! His sex experiences certainly seem like an illustration to Freud's: *The most prevalent form of degradation in erotic life.*

Saturday, The sixth hour: Were I to see my patients only five hours a week, like most of my American colleagues, and not also on Saturdays, this patient's story might have developed very differently. Last night, going over my notes up to now, I came close to deciding that his narcissistic self-involvement, his deep oral fixation, his inability to relate, etc., would make analysis impossible and had pretty much decided to tell him so at the end of today's hour. I hoped that the shock might, later on, permit him to seek out another analyst; I planned to suggest a gentile one. With him he might begin to analyze, instead of misusing him as a prop to get rid of his guilt, while continuing to destroy all who have positive feelings for him.

If he had had to wait till Monday, probably nothing would have changed. Maybe that this was a Saturday, *the Sabbath,* had something to do with it. This I shall find out later. Anyway, today was an entirely different hour. Instead of regaling me with his sexual successes—in masturbation, cunnilingus, fellatio—he finally became a bit more human in recounting his sexual defeats, all by Jewish girls. It began with his recalling how he admired Jewish men like his father, their Sunday morning ball game, how he wished to identify with them but could not, because he wanted even more to possess his mother. From his girlfriend, the "Monkey," he had to run because as soon as he had gotten a girl to the point where no further degradation was likely to occur, all attraction was gone. Unable as always to come through when the love of others for him was so obvious he could no longer deny it, his only solution was to run away. Blaming them for trying to put him in bondage—though all he wishes is to see them in bondage to him, and with him having no return obligation—he flees to Israel, the mother country.

There unconsciously (but so close to consciousness that I feel analysis may begin after all) he realizes that if he is no longer a Jew in a gentile world, if he can no longer blame on it (and with it justify) his whole pattern of demanding and receiving without ever giving, if he must manage without these excuses, he is nothing—cannot even manage an erection.

In desperation he tries to seduce a kibbutz girl by reversing the methods he used with his gentile girls. Them he had degraded and their debasement had made them extremely attractive to him, but also useless. Here instead, it is he who submits to debasement, particularly when the girl tells him what should long have been obvious: that his self-degradation is the more despicable because he is a man of such high intelligence. To her telling him how little she thinks of him, he reacts by inviting her to have intercourse with him. Blaming others as always, he tries to pin his impotence on his mother, claiming the kibbutz girl reminds him of her. He believes it to be the Oedipal (but genital) attachment that makes him impotent, while it is really his oral attachment, his wish to remain the suckling infant forever.

The long-suffering Jewish mother who suffers herself to be blamed for everything, is willing to thus serve her son. Never will he have to feel guilty about anything he does because he can always blame it on her. And in a way he can; but not as he thinks. He can blame her for what she has led him to believe: That whatever he wants he must immediately be given. This, the central theme of his life, he screams out at the kibbutz girl: "I HAVE TO HAVE." It is she who finally tells him that this belief of his—that he has to have what he wants, whatever it may cost the other—is not valid.

In a fantasy of being judged for his crimes, he realizes, at least for a moment, that blaming his mother will not get him off, cannot justify his behavior to others. This raises the hope that analysis might just succeed. So, instead of dismissing him, as I had planned, I said, "Now we may perhaps begin." Only the future will tell if I was not much too optimistic.

One more thought: He is very clever at presenting himself, and right after the first session I had the uneasy feeling that he wants to impress me as the most unforgettable patient I ever had. What if all he said so far was carefully prepared and selected? His determination not to permit me to interrupt with questions or interpretations suggests the possibility that he was afraid that any interference might throw him off his only seemingly stream of consciousness-like talk, while it was actually a carefully prepared story, designed to impress me. What if all he presented as the outpourings of his unconscious and preconscious, of his id and superego (the self-criticism, the fantasy about his being judged) would have been conscious ego productions? Was he trying to test me in order to find out whether I am smart enough not to mistake what was essentially a literary production for an effort at analysis?

If so, did I do the right thing not to insist on interrupting him, or on directing his associations, and tell him at the end of the last session that it is time to stop being a man of letters so that, through analyzing himself, he might finally become a man? Again, we shall see.

But even though what has happened so far was not more than an effort to tell a good story, it is significant that it is the "monkey" who emerges as having the greatest dignity. Though born desperately poor, social success means nothing to her. Having been married to one of the richest men of France meant nothing to her. When she felt used by him, she left him without another thought. Though aspiring to culture, she is not at all impressed by its trappings, nor by being invited to the mayor's mansion, because what is important to her is to be with him, not to attend a formal dinner. This she makes clear by having sex with him within view of the mayor's house, not caring what others may think of her or what she does there, while he is deathly afraid of how all this may look to others. He, as always, being involved only in himself, does not recognize that she is not motivated by any hedonist impulsiveness, but by the anxious question: "Are you taking me to the mayor's reception because you love me and want me near you, or because I am ornamental and therefore useful in your social climbing?"

If it was a literary production, what view must he have of himself as a person and as a Jew if social and sexual honesty, that is if true humanity—in his eyes—resides only in the poor "monkey"? Is it just another case then of the self-hating Jew living *in exile*? (pp. 8-10)

Bruno Bettelheim, "Portnoy Psychoanalyzed,"
in Midstream, *Vol. 15, No. 6, June-July, 1969,*
pp. 3-10.

Irving H. Buchen

Portnoy's complex is a complaint because the business of complaining or *kvetching* is an inextricable part of the complex. Complaining is a special way of hurting, and maybe even a special way of enjoying the hurting. In Yiddish and in the context of the novel, it is almost a whine of the bowels; not accidentally a considerable portion of the book centers on the bathroom. *Kvetching* is a form of emotional constipation (or diarrhea) as if a whine is the only acceptable form of anger. It also is made the characteristic response of people who always feel put upon, conspired against, doomed to sacrifice. It thus is a bit of superstition, as if one cannot openly take triumph in achievements or assets lest they be snatched away from you. So the *kvetch* frustrates the evil eye with a special magic: what you have you constantly denigrate as if it did not belong to you; or if it clearly came to you, then it did so, unworthy person that you are, only by accident or chance but never because you earned or deserved it. Portnoy's complaint in part then is: what does one do with a rooster that *kvetches* instead of crowing?

The style of Portnoy's problem—*the kvetching*—expresses a chronological crisis as well. The book is written when Portnoy is 33 (a *kvetching* Christ?); that is, when Portnoy like Dante has reached the mid-point of his life. Why midpoint? Because enough of the past has accumulated to show the end of things. When a life begins to take on the shape of a pattern, it is like an encounter with death. The pattern of the past looms as tyrannical and projective and yet at mid-point there is enough time ahead to change or to experience the despair of continuity. When Dante at mid-point took his life tremblingly into his hands, he descended to the "Inferno" with the aid of Virgil. When Portnoy begins to handle his life, he moves into his hell with the contemporary helpmate, the psychiatrist, a Dr.

Spielvogel; a master of the *spiel,* of the twisting routine, and a bird to boot who takes the measure of the soul.

And what does Portnoy ask of his guide? How is it that the girls I desire I cannot love and the girls I love I cannot desire? How is it that I am told I am the smartest *kopt,* the best prince, the biggest brain and that at the same time that I am an ingrate, a Mr. Big Shot, a worthless brat? What belongs to me alone? Above all—and this is a generational cry—how was I so fitted for success and so unfitted for existence?

The answers—they are more like accusations—are entangled in Portnoy's parents. Portnoy presents his mother in a chapter entitled, "The Most Unforgettable Character I've Met." It is a delightful parody of that favorite school theme assignment and yet it is also an infinitely sad title precisely because he cannot ever forget his mother—she is truly and terribly unforgettable. To be unable to forget is to be unable to forgive. Memory then functions, as it does in the novel, as a perpetual lacerating faculty that binds Portnoy to his mother in such a way that he is incapable of **Letting Go** (the title of Roth's first novel). (pp. 98-9)

What makes Sophie Portnoy so unforgettable? Mostly dreadful things. She threw Alex out of the apartment into the hall when he was bad and thus hit upon one of the principal fears of the child—abandonment. She held a knife over him when he refused to eat and explicitly released another fear of the male child—castration. She regularly holds a tribunal during which she wants to know what terrible crimes she and her husband have committed (to speak of crimes is already to enjoy exoneration) that this bad behavior should be their reward? She asks the young boy to assume the burdens of their lives before he is even able to assume the burden of his own. She constantly whines and reminds young Alex that they have made themselves worthless apart from their children and that whatever worth they do have, they have solely through their children—so that to turn out bad or a bum is to wreck three lives and to bring disgrace on all the Jews. She sings the song of the maimed and the persecuted and the suffering. She wails the wail of 2000 years of pogroms.

And how does Alex respond? He looks around him in America and he does not see much suffering or privation. He sees wealthy and successful Jews moving out to the suburbs. He sees others who are not that well off, but after all this America where a Jew can pull himself up by his *titzis.* And he is too generally ignorant of Jewish history and too far removed geographically and culturally from Europe to share what may be his own parents' guilt that they are here and not in the concentration camps. What is thus set up from the outset is a split. There are the things he owes and there are the things he wants. The things he owes belong to his parents: to be a success and to be a Jew. The only thing that belongs to him and to h im alone is his penis. So what is set in motion is a dichtomy between his wants and his needs, so that he wants no thing and no one for his own sake but for the sake of his parents. And what he needs, he merely needs, for all wants have been apportioned to his parents as the gifts of a dutiful son. Later, this split takes on the classic formulation of Freud

whom Portnoy quotes: "When such men love they have no desire, and where they desire they cannot love."

And what about his father, Jack Portnoy, who ironically sells life insurance? I say ironically because Alex believes his father is more comfortable with death than life, just as later Alex himself seems at odds with his own attempts to advance Human Opportunity. Unlike the relationship with his mother, there is genuine ambivalence in Alex's reaction to his father. Alex longs and hopes for his own liberation as a means of also freeing his father. And yet he hates his father for being emasculated. Alex says, "What he had to offer I didn't want—and what I wanted he did not have to offer." Nevertheless, how much he is his father's son appears in a number of ways. Alex acknowledges, in fact, that "To this day our destinies remain scrambled in my imagination." Then while his father suffers from constipation, Alex claims he has diarrhea. Both are expressions of suppressed anger, and that takes us to the emotional and sexual center of Portnoy's complaint.

The predominant emotion of the novel is one of rage. It is not only the strongest emotion Alex feels, but often his only one. At one point Alex wishes to send his father "howling from the land of the living." Throughout the novel, Alex's two basic desires are to screw and to scream: "what I need most of all, is to howl. A pure howl, without any more words between me and it!" It is the fusion of this screaming screw or screwing scream that propels the entire novel along and that, in transmuted form, releases the foul language and black humor.

Alex lives up to his last name by being a black humorist but it is also his mother's legacy, for Portnoy's burlesque hysteria is a version of his mother's *kvetch.* Portnoy's rage is converted into foul language and often foul sexuality because when Alex wishes to tell the truth about himself the truth, to be the truth, has to be brutal. His sexuality is also brutalizing; his use of four letter words is not spoken with the kind of comfortable maturity D. H. Lawrence hoped for, but in punitive fashion as a way of denigrating and even dirtying sex. (Almost all writers on perversion have a dual fascination with sex and excrement.) The humor is a bit trickier, actually a strategy of sublimation; for its components are rage, and self-contempt released through the safety valve of absurdity. But here, too, there is exhibitionism—the telling of the truth sideways. The many imagined headlines in which the entire world will read the real truth about Portnoy are hilarious devices for turning his screwing into screaming accusations to punish his parents.

What then is the legacy of parents where the mother acts like a father and the father acts like mother? The result according to Roth is the syndrome of the maimed man who has suffered such a deep and perhaps permanent psychic wound that he is unable to love anyone or anything. Psychologically and sexually Portnoy is an arrested adolescent who has never really left the bathroom of masturbation. Significantly, his first encounter is a masturbating one. And when she cannot bring off his climax, he takes over, the old expert, and quickly ejaculates. Who does it as well as oneself, he asks? Nobody, of course, but that is not real sex—what one does to and for oneself. The later fallatio and voyeurism are variations on masturbation. He wants to see what is being done while feeling it as well; he wants to be the sensation giver (or observer) and the sensation receiver. The oral unions are frequently associated with food—with eating and being eaten. Portnoy is never able to accept a woman's difference. Above all, he is never able to accept the fact that sexually and emotionally a woman (not a monkey) grants him what he can never give himself. Women to Alex are sexual holes, sexual mouths; or objects of Jewish revenge, American Pumpkins and Pilgrims. A woman is never presented by Portnoy as having an identity and integrity of her own equal to that of a man. Thus, when Alex fantasies about marriage (in order to reject it) and pictures his long-suffering wife staying home with tears in her eyes while he is monkeying about, there is never any mention that she might be off on her own horsing around. In short, Portnoy the man is really Portnoy the adolescent . . . ; and his sexuality is really masturbating sexuality employed more often than not to degrade, to revenge and to heap contempt on himself and on women.

What imparts a further turn of the screw to Portnoy's problem is the novel factor that what has made him this way is not hidden from him. He screams, quite accurately, that hardly anything about his history is latent—he has a wide-open, explicit Jewish Oedipus Complex. Portnoy's shock may have been duplicated earlier when Freud, putting together the pattern of the Oedipus Complex, found it all out in the open in Sophocles's play. In other words, an important aspect of Portnoy's complaint—and Roth is prophetic on this point—is that it partakes of a historical moment and that if the book is case history it is also generational history.

It is Portnoy's sad and comic fate to be the incarnation of the generation gap itself. The generation that his parents belong to is not responsive to the language and vilification that Roth presents. The new younger generation shows little interest in the book except to point to the hang-ups of the presiding generation and establishment. There is thus always present in the novel the pathos of being caught between two extremes of unresponsiveness. And yet without the ends of that spectrum, there could never be the terrible and stark clarity of Portnoy's generational limbo. The parental generation provided him with the problem, the new generation with the sexual freedom to write about it. The paternal generation bequeathed the fantasies, the new generation with the desire to live them. Portnoy is thus a curious historical freak: an underground man who has surfaced. He is sadly expendable, a vanishing generation at middle age and life: do-gooders with vile thoughts, servicable men with secret contempt, hollow men who are nevertheless versatile. His rage joins him to the *HOWL* of Allen Ginsberg and the Students for a Democratic Society; but his obedience and dutifulness tie him to the generation of his parents. (pp. 100-04)

[Another] historical matter, and for many the most disturbing, has to do with the Jewish content of the book or more accurately with the indictment of Judaism. To be sure, the book is no more a rejection of Judaism than it is a rejection of all religion. Nevertheless, it is clearly an indictment of the Jewish mother and the Jewish family

and my own judgment is that the indictment is both just and unjust.

It is just in that it is an indictment of ghetto psychology, of excessive fear of rocking the boat, of spitting on the *goyim,* of enormous sacrificing for the children, of emasculated men and dominating women, of raising dutiful sons to be both successful and obedient husbands and fathers. Significantly, it is Naomi, the Israeli Pumpkin, who most painfully makes Portnoy and the Jewish reader aware of how anemic is Portnoy's Jewishness. As such, Naomi speaks for a new historical situation in which Israel serves as a real alternative for Jews.

The standard explanation for Portnoy's impotence in Israel is that Naomi is Jewish and hence a threatening Oedipal substitute for his mother. That is only part of the explanation. Equally as important is the fact that Naomi is the only real woman in the novel. She is not some sick chippie or some frowsy "debutramp." She is not some spoiled brat, Short Hills Jewish matron whose Jewishness is a social grace. Naomi is a strong, highly individualistic, passionate and intelligent woman who is not religiously or sexually hung-up. As a result she rejects Portnoy's whining and pretensions, and for the first time in the entire novel, Portnoy receives from her all the accusations that readers have stored up or written in margins throughout the book. Above all, Naomi presents Portnoy with a Jewishness that is vigorous, passionate and robust. To realize the extent to which many American Jews are like Portnoy, all one need do is think back to the beginning of the Six Day War in Israel. Many, many Jews thought Israel was doomed and were ready to recite the memorial service for the dead. Indeed, Israel probably would have been doomed if the Portnoys were in Israel. No, it must be admitted that Roth's indictment of Jewishness is just—it is a timid, spineless Judaism, devoid generally of knowledge and generosity, increasingly hopeless and peripheral. My personal judgment is that the castrating mother has emerged as the religion itself became emasculated.

The indictment, however, is unjust in that by going so far, by raging and lacerating so unmercifully, Roth goes beyond the human, to of all things, the stereotype! Portnoy is furious because of the crimes committed against him. But who can live a lifetime and especially in a family without crimes being committed against one? Has not Kafka redefined original sin as that which you do not do but is done to you? Crimes are committed against us and we commit crimes against others. Sophie Portnoy did terrible things to her son. But what about the terrible things the son does to the Monkey (as grotesque as the mother), to the *shikses,* to the socialite?

And what is also unjust about the indictment is that the faults of Portnoy's parents are only in part Jewish faults. Insofar as Sophie Portnoy is assimilated, she acts out the faults of America as well. Indeed, in this respect, Roth comes closest to echoing the young who are rebelling against all institutionalized images of the adult-parent. The American pursuit of success, the dislocation or dilution of meaningful traditions and values, the loyalty oaths to country and parents, the stress put upon the best schools, professions and tax-dodges—all these and more represent a confluence of Jewish and American faults. In fact, it is precisely because Jewish-American writers have had this personal and intimate way to larger American and even international issues that their works often stake out the kind of comprehensive historical typicality that also pervades Roth's novel.

In the final analysis the book, nevertheless, is a great book, not because of its vile language or acts, not because of its passing off a strain of Judaism as all of Judaism, and certainly not because of its unsympathetic and unfair attack on parents; but rather because it is a passionate, honest and comprehensive portrait of a man and generation in anguish. Moreover, because Roth has presented that dilemma with the fullest range of its despair, not only for all that he has suffered so far, but also for all that he and Judaism may yet suffer in America, the result is not merely the identity crisis of a single precious man, but the tragic awakening to waste of an entire generation in history. And when a writer with honesty and artistry confronts such a crucial issue, shall we begrudge him his achievement merely because he does not say nice things about the Jews or is on the best seller lists? (pp. 104-07)

> *Irving H. Buchen, "Portnoy's 'Complaint' of the Rooster's 'Kvetch',"* in Studies in the Twentieth Century, *No. 6, 1970, pp. 97-107.*

Jesse Bier

If I mention a "symbolic" level in Philip Roth's ***Portnoy's Complaint,*** I hope people will not wince, for I do not mean to abuse the term and subtilize the blatant material of Roth's book out of all recognizability. Still, once we get past the embarrassing, shocking and otherwise extravagant sexual subject matter of ***Portnoy's Complaint,*** there is a plane of general and highly significant meaning underlying the tawdry goings-on. Portnoy's actual experiences and frame of mind are, abstractly speaking, true for Americans at large: our loving is essentially *self*-centered and functional. Portnoy's whole career represents almost anything at all but a love story, and therein, for all of the sexual gymnastics and overflowing onanism, lies Roth's basic, reverberating theme. Too many of his countrymen are also fundamentally barred from love.

Everything confessed and described in the book is an extravagant seriocomic view of basic experience in America, as Roth sees it by now: filled with sexual busy-ness but with a tell-tale lack of human affection and connection. These larger implications in the book allow for all the forlorn lyric cries—and the more than occasional rage, too—that intermittently pierce the novel; they are not simply tonal variations from the outlandish comedy but part and parcel of the work. Even the comedy itself, which is mainly one-liner humor and exaggerated self-centered anecdote, is necessarily precious and self-conscious, quite proper to theme and character this once in Roth's writings. Portnoy is precisely a kind of standup comedian, always and exquisitely center stage, giving his solo performance before a neutral if not alienated audience: before an alienist, in fact. The self-punishing comic monologue, which is always a psychiatric testimony, illustrates at first

a triumphantly wayward but then bitterly unconnected personality. The portrait grows steadily larger than itself because, among other things, it concentrates a national lovelessness in the character. That is one of the reasons that the book, like most recent portrayals of disintegrating Jewish-American families, has impact on the American public at large. It is Portnoy's secret interior relevance finally, not his outer flagrant sexual exploits, that shocks us more fundamentally than any novelistic Kinseyism could.

The lovelessness or the corrupted love that Roth imputes to Portnoy and to the modern Jewish family in the United States used to be attributed solely to *goyim.* The greatest difference between the two groups—at least, in the traditional Jewish view—was never really religious or ethnic, but psychological or temperamental. Jews were an emotional group, in the best sense, motivated and exercised by a Love whose archetypes were, first, family relatedness and, then, social justice or compassion. Historical victims of hatred and prejudice, they consolidated an ethic of love and held themselves distinct from a hard-hearted and merely functional and status-conscious world of gentiles. But what happened, especially in the materialistic, self-serving and class-conscious society of the United States, is that instead of the minority's remaining proof against the rest, it was subverted and overcome. Thus all Jewish-American jokes about "My son, the Doctor . . . "— marvelously transmuted to "My son, the Patient" for Portnoy—have come to represent a basic capitulation to ruling mores of WASP status-consciousness. And in Roth's novel, when Portnoy's Jewish mother locks her little boy out from home, she is also modish in the American way and most un-Jewish, having taken certain pragmatic and cynical American ploys insidiously and thoroughly to herself; she has her old cultural stridency yet, but no longer the old resistant values of parental warm-heartedness and the like. We finally see that, in a sense, there is nothing for a Portnoy to go home *to* anymore. His alternatives now effectively bar him from a genuinely human life: on the one side, a confused and decaying family system and corrupted temperament; and on the other, either an absurdly over-idealized WASP world (the blond *shiksas,* Mayor Lindsay, etc.) or stark abasement ("the Monkey," etc.). Either way, he stands to be un-manned or dehumanized, or both. Sexual castration, alienation, obsessive masturbation, episodes of grimly comic and mechanical love play, and, finally, both a literal and psychological impotence are the intense personal experiences that illustrate a general dilemma and malaise. (pp. 49-50)

[Roth] must be placed with what is by now a veritable tradition of Jewish-American literature since World War II. He and his predecessors and colleagues provide a clear general perspective on the collapse of the Jewish family unit and system of values. All of these writers together have been reporting the fact that minority resistance has been overborne or has sold itself out to cultural assimilation; minority groups have lost their own special acculturing importance in America, which was to fortify the individual against false social values at large in the country quite as much as to indoctrinate the individual with the best of democratic national values. The family—especially the minority family, and especially the warm and strongly self-identified Jewish family—has historically been a bulwark against excesses of patent American myths; it has been a social unit operating best when screening out the absurd and dehumanizing from the vital and sustaining values of American society in general. But in contemporary times the minority family has abandoned its resistant and critical role, and the tragicomedy that has resulted accounts for the central subject matter of Bernard Malamud, Saul Bellow, Bruce Jay Friedman and others as well as Roth. (p. 51)

[Since the 1950s] Jewish writers have written more and more explicitly about the actual and complete breakdown of the putatively strong and independent Jewish family structure, with no solutions whatever to offer.

Portnoy's break from both his family and his Jewish tradition is signaled most readily, though superficially, by his atheism. His abandonment of piety, however, is less important than his phony morality (his social service work in New York City), since in a real way he is profoundly anti-social. His public organizational morality and his essential disconnection represent the basic triumph of the wrong American ethos over the right but decayed Judaic ethic. In addition, the old orthodox sanctions of sexual love based on self-respect—the body as "temple"—are also lost now, the vacuum filled by mere American functionalism. It is not too much to say that the hernia of young Portnoy symbolically expresses the filling up of interior spaces of the spirit and affections with mere wayward sexual machinery.

But the chief loss has been the loss of an altruistic and true parental love, which should normally foster proper self-love and later normal sexuality, with subsequent marriage and new families. Portnoy's father is impotent in his bowels—that is, in essential self-control or personal autonomy—and of course, considering what the unsatisfied Mrs. Portnoy has become, in his own sexual capacity. For her part, Portnoy's mother not only threatens her son with a carving knife and periodically locks him out of the house and generally weighs upon him in the dominating way of "the Jewish mother," but in her own frustrate and Oedipal fashion she abuses her son in provocative sexual undress and semi-temptations, a sign of the decadence of stern Jewish values or of their utter evaporation. The boy's masturbation is psychic compensation for the weakness and corruption of an identity-giving tradition. The onanism is a twofold symbol—of a mechanical functionalism displacing normal sexual love, and of an incurable self-centeredness substituted for the psychological power of attachment. All in all, according to Martin Buber's coordinates, Portnoy is fixated at "I" and cannot normally develop to "Thou." And, consistently, for all of his later urgencies and wild sexual desperations. Portnoy remains encapsulated in self, never freed in true self-regard, but condemned to tragicomic and intense self-consciousness, unfulfilled in his orgies and obsessions, a mechanical and retarded hypocrite instead of a grown man (son, citizen, lover, husband, etc.). Without having been essentially defined and nurtured by parental love, itself welling out of a sanctioned communal background, Portnoy is vulnerable to the most dehumanizing psychological ravages of

prevailing mores in American society. (Roth even asks us to consider his hero as crucified, since he stipulates Portnoy's age as 33 and is all along suggesting the frustration of the powers of love in his character. It is an extra inside joke, of course, to contemplate a Christ-like Jewish protagonist, that is, in such a context as Roth presents).

Portnoy—perhaps Roth himself—is still bourgeois enough to make so much of his irregular practices, which are not really so abnormal in their nature, we all know, but only in the frequency and obsessiveness with which Portnoy pursues them. The fact is that *he* is scandalized somewhat by his life—a fact that makes the book far more middle class, by the way, than truly liberated or shocking or transcendentally pornographic. On a psychological, as well as sociological, level, Portnoy is always and everywhere the object of his own attention, his self-absorption a psychic counterpart to his masturbatory behavior, which he still fundamentally indulges even when he has a sexual partner. In any case, the effect is, remarkably, a series of either vulgar or comic experiences but nothing ever really sensuous. The steady portrayal of outlandish but mere functionalism in sex and of Portnoy's relentless self-consciousness hold the work from any truly sexual episodes, which are requisite for a really inflammatory book, meant to arouse the emotions with genuine excitement. There must be a quantum of sensual passion as a requirement for even lust as well as love. But Portnoy's story never explodes in this fundamentally individual, class-less and liberated way.

Portnoy is locked too deeply in himself, in his own skin. His background condemns him now to such insularity. He is as profoundly cut off, unresponsive, functional and unfeeling, as the ungraced gentiles used to be characterized from within the fold of the older Jewish consciousness. He is even worse off, since some benighted *shikses,* like the Monkey, try to fight back into human love or devotion, while the Portnoys of the modern scene heartlessly run out on them. Portnoy is ultimately more loveless and unremittingly *self*-ish than his allegedly professional West Virginia queen; he is still in the throes of his prostituting and impotent self at the end of the novel, though there is hope for him if he is at the analyst's at all; while his denigrated lover has been humanized enough to threaten suicide for love, at least *needing* love that much now.

In the end, Portnoy's own "complaint" is not a plain Yiddish "kvetch," for it signals lament or lamentation just as much as neurotic whining. The fantasial sex play and masturbatory perversity are an extravagant but apt image for the narcissism to which Portnoy, along with millions of other countrymen of his, is fated. Still, his virtual and representative case history is so filled with a schizoid intensity of love-and-hate, of protective comedy and sharp fury, that there is life yet, excruciating as it is. ***Portnoy's Complaint*** certainly conveys despair as well as slapstick; much of the novel is a "scream" in the two senses of the word. But neurotic hysteria is better than psychotic withdrawal and betokens hope. At all events, we must get past our alternating repugnance and laughter, past the surfaces of downright and cheap action, to the subtler and sometimes poignant human cry that is a basic undertone of the work and a redeeming symbol of Roth's larger intentions.

Just that conjunction, of unlooked for subtlety together with indecently overt and pre-emptive action, is what certifies the American-ness of the book. And the profound complaint, the element of old lingering protest against a whole way of living, the sounds of unlikely eloquence balancing off cynical self-deflations and extravagance, are all marks of its vestigial but implicit Jewish nature, quite as much as the contingent setting. Taken together, these strengths, which come to Roth from his linkage to the contemporary Jewish-American literary school, account for the technical virtues and extra dimension in *Portnoy's Complaint.* In this light the work perhaps signals the fact that its author may be in the very act, now, of transforming himself from prodigal to prophet. (pp. 51-3)

> *Jesse Bier, "In Defense of Roth," in* Études *Anglaises, Vol. XXVI, No. 1, January-March, 1973, pp. 49-53.*

Philip Roth

[*The essay excerpted below originally appeared in the July-August 1974 issue of* The American Poetry Review.]

Portnoy's Complaint took shape out of the wreckage of four abandoned projects on which I had spent considerable effort—wasted, it seemed then—in the years 1962-67. Only now do I see how each was a kind of building block for what was to come, and was abandoned in turn because it emphasized to the exclusion of all else what eventually would become a strong element in *Portnoy's Complaint* but in itself was less than the whole story. Not that I knew then why I was so dissatisfied with the results I got at the time.

The first project, begun a few months after the publication of *Letting Go,* was a dreamy, humorous manuscript of about two hundred pages titled *The Jewboy,* which treated growing up in Newark as a species of folklore. This draft tended to cover with a patina of "charming" inventiveness whatever was genuinely troublesome to me and, as in certain types of dreams and folktales, intimated much more than I knew how to examine or confront in a fiction. Yet there were things that I liked and, when I abandoned the book, hated to lose: the graphic starkness with which the characters were presented and which accorded with my sense of what childhood had felt like; the jokey comedy and dialogues that had the air of vaudeville turns; and a few scenes I was particularly fond of, like the grand finale where the Dickensian orphan-hero (first found in a shoebox by an aged *mohel* and circumcised, hair-raisingly, on the spot) runs away from his loving stepparents at age twelve and on ice skates sets off across a Newark lake after a little blond *shikse* whose name, he thinks, is Thereal McCoy. "Don't!" his taxi-driver father calls after him (taxi driver because fathers I knew of invariably had cried out from behind the wheel at one exasperated moment or another, "That's all I am to this family—a taxi driver!") "Oh, watch it, sonny"—the father calls after him —"you're skating on thin ice!" Whereupon the rebellious

and adventurous son in hot pursuit of the desirable exotic calls back, "Oh, you dope, Daddy, that's only an expression," already, you see, a major in English. "It's only an expression"—even as the ice begins to groan and give beneath his eighty-odd pounds.

The second abandoned project was a play entitled *The Nice Jewish Boy.* Still more about a Jewish family, their son, and his shiksa—in its way a less comforting, more aggressive *Abie's Irish Rose.* A draft of the play was eventually read as a workshop exercise at the American Place Theatre in 1964, with Dustin Hoffman, then an off-Broadway actor, in the title role. The trouble with it was that the realistic dramatic conventions I had adopted rather unthinkingly (and strictly) didn't provide me with the room I needed to get to the character's secret life. My unfamiliarity and timidity with the form, and the collaborative effort itself, inhibited and conventionalized my own sense of things, and so rather than proceeding to a production, I decided after the reading to cut my losses. Again somewhat sadly. The comic *surface* of the play (what father said to mother, what mother said to son, what son said to *shikse*) seemed to me accurate and funny; yet the whole enterprise lacked the inventive flair and emotional exuberance that had given *The Jewboy* whatever quality it had.

So: the struggle that was to be at the source of Alexander Portnoy's difficulties, and motivate his complaint, was in those early years of work still so out of focus that all I could do was recapitulate his problem *technically,* telling first the dreamy and fantastic side of the story, then the story in more conventional terms and by relatively measured means. Not until I found, in the person of a troubled analysand, the voice that could speak in behalf of both the "Jewboy" (with all that word signifies to Jew and Gentile alike about aggression, appetite, and marginality) and the "nice Jewish boy" (and what that epithet implies about repression, respectability, and social acceptance) was I able to complete a fiction that was expressive, instead of symptomatic, of the character's dilemma.

While making abortive forays into what was going to emerge years later as *Portnoy's Complaint,* I was intermittently writing equally shadowy drafts of a novel that was variously titled—as theme and emphasis shifted—*Time Away, In the Middle of America,* and *Saint Lucy,* and that was published in 1967 as *When She Was Good.* This continuous movement back and forth from one partially realized project to another is fairly typical of how my work evolves and the way I deal with literary frustration and uncertainty, and serves me as a means of both checking and indulging "inspiration." The idea, in part, is to keep alive fictions that draw their energy from different sources, so that when circumstances combine to rouse one or another of the sleeping beasts, there is a carcass around for it to feed on.

After the manuscript of *When She Was Good* was completed midway through 1966, I almost immediately began to write a longish monologue, beside which the fetid indiscretions of *Portnoy's Complaint* would appear to be the work of Louisa May Alcott. I did not have any idea where I was going, and playing (in the mud, if you like) more accurately describes my activity than does writing, or "experimenting," that much–used catchall with its flattering implications of courageous pioneering and disinterested self-abandonment.

This monologue was delivered by one of those lecturers who used to go around to schools, churches, and social groups showing slides of natural wonders. My slide show, delivered in the dark and with a pointer, and accompanied by running commentary (including humorous and illustrative anecdotes), consisted of full-color enlargements of the private parts, fore and aft, of the famous. Actors and actresses, of course, but primarily—since the purpose was educational—distinguished authors, statesmen, scientists, etc. It was blasphemous, mean, bizarre, scatological, tasteless, spirited, and, largely out of timidity, I think, remained unfinished . . . except that buried somewhere in the sixty or seventy pages were several thousand words on the subject of adolescent masturbation, a personal interlude by the lecturer, that seemed to me on rereading to be funny and true, and worth saving, if only because it was the only sustained piece of writing on the subject that I could remember reading in a work of fiction.

Not that at the time I could have deliberately set out to write about masturbating and come up with anything so pointedly intimate. Rather, it would seem to have required all that wildness and roughhousing—the *merriment,* which is how I experienced it—for me just to *get* to the subject. Knowing that what I was writing about President Johnson's testicles, Jean Genet's anus, Mickey Mantle's penis, Margaret Mead's breasts, and Elizabeth Taylor's pubic bush was simply unpublishable—a writer's hijinks that might just as well not see the light of day—was precisely what allowed me to relax my guard and go on at some length about the solitary activity that is so difficult to talk about and yet so near at hand. For me writing about the act had, at the outset at least, to be as secret as the act itself.

More or less in tandem with this untitled exercise in voyeurism—which purported to enlarge and examine upon an illuminated screen the sexual parts of *others*—I began to write a strongly autobiographical piece of fiction based upon my own upbringing in New Jersey. For lack of anything more inspired, simply as a kind of genre title, it was called in its first rough draft of several hundred pages *Portrait of the Artist.* By sticking closely to the facts, and narrowing the gap between the actual and the invented, I thought I could somehow come up with a story that would go to the heart of the particular Jewish ethos I'd come out of. But the more I stuck to the actual and the strictly autobiographical, the less resonant and revealing the narrative became. Once again (as I now see it) I was oscillating between the extremes of unmanageable fable or fantasy and familiar surface realism or documentation, and thereby holding at bay what was still trying to become my subject, if only I would let it. I had already described it, unknowingly, in the antipodal titles of the two projects previously abandoned: the argument between the Abel and Cain of my own respectable middle-class background, the Jewboy and the nice Jewish boy.

Somewhere along the way in *Portrait of the Artist,* in order to broaden the scope and relieve the monotony, I invented some relatives to live upstairs from the family, loosely modeled upon my own, who were to have been at the center of the book. These upstairs relatives of "ours" I called the Portnoys. In the beginning the Portnoys were modeled, about as loosely, upon two or three families in whose apartments I used to play and snack and sometimes sleep overnight when I was a boy. In fact, an old boyhood friend of mine, who was interviewed by his local newspaper at the time of my book's publication, was quoted as saying that my family certainly did not seem to *him* to resemble the Portnoys; "but," he added, "I suppose Phil didn't see it that way." That there was a family which in certain aspects Phil did see that way, and, I suspect, which this old boyhood friend of mine sometimes saw that way as well, he did not, for reasons of filial discretion and personal modesty, let on to the reporter.

Though actually the family the Portnoys looked most like to me, as I became increasingly taken by them and began to allow them to take hold in the novel, was a family I had described in passing in an essay published in *American Judaism* some five years earlier. The essay had grown out of a talk I had given at a B'nai B'rith Anti-Defamation League symposium in Chicago in 1961, in which I had attacked what I took to be the unreality and silliness of Jews who were being popularized around that time in books by Harry Golden and Leon Uris. The family was not called the Portnoys then, nor were they as yet the product of my own imagination. Rather, I had come upon them, in various disguises and incarnations, in my reading. Here (abridged somewhat) is what I said at the A.D.L. symposium in 1961:

> . . . There are several Jewish graduate students in a class I teach at the Writing Workshop of the State University of Iowa, and during this last semester three of them wrote stories about a Jewish childhood . . . Curiously, or perhaps not so curiously, in each story the hero is a Jewish boy, somewhere between ten and fifteen, who gets excellent grades in school and is always combed and courteous . . . [This] Jewish boy . . . is watched—he is watched at bedtime, at study time, and especially at mealtime. Who he is watched by is his mother. The father we rarely see, and between him and the boy there seems to be little more than a nodding acquaintance. The old man is either working or sleeping or across the table, silently stowing it away. Still there is a great deal of warmth in these families—especially when compared to the Gentile . . . family [in the story]—and almost all of it is generated by the mother . . . [But] the fire that warms can also burn and asphyxiate: what the hero envies the Gentile boy is his parents' *indifference,* and largely, it would seem, because of the opportunities it affords him for sexual adventure . . . I hasten to point out that in these short stories the girls to whom the Gentile friend leads the young narrator are never Jewish. The Jewish women are mothers and sisters. The sexual yearning is for the Other . . .

Here then was the folktale—transmitted to me by my students as an authentic bit of American-Jewish mythology—that began to enlarge my sense of who these Portnoys might be . . . or become. Now it even made a nice kind of sense that in that first slapdash draft of *Portrait of the Artist* I had imagined them to be "relatives" living "upstairs": here were the fallible, oversized, anthropomorphic gods who had reigned over the households of my neighborhood; here was that legendary Jewish family dwelling on high, whose squabbles over French-fried potatoes, synagogue attendance, and *shikses* were, admittedly, of an Olympian magnitude and splendor, but by whose terrifying kitchen lightning storms were illuminated the values, dreams, fears, and aspirations by which we mortal Jews lived somewhat less vividly down below.

This time, rather than choosing as I had in *The Jewboy* to treat this folklore *as* folklore—emphasizing the fantastic, the charming, the quaint, the magical, the poetic—I determinedly took off in the opposite direction. Under the sway of the autobiographical impulse that had launched *Portrait of the Artist,* I began to ground the mythological in the recognizable, the verifiable, the historical. Though they might *derive* from Mt. Olympus (by way of Mt. Sinai), these Portnoys were going to live in a Newark and at a time and in a way I could vouch for by observation and experience.

(With this sleight-of-hand, if I have to say so myself, I seemed to have succeeded all too well. Among the several hundred letters I received after the book's publication, there was one from a woman in East Orange, New Jersey, who claimed to have known my sister when she and my correspondent's daughter were classmates together at Weequahic High in Newark, where the Portnoy children went to school. She remembered what a sweet, lovely, polite girl my sister was, and was shocked that I should be so thoughtless as to write as I had about her intimate life, especially to make jokes about her unfortunate tendency to gain weight. Since, unlike Alexander Portnoy, I happen never to have had a sister, I assumed it was some other Jewish Athena with a tendency to gain weight to whom my correspondent was alluding.)

However, it was to be a while yet before I began to feel so constrained by the conventions I had imposed upon myself in *Portrait of the Artist* that I abandoned that manuscript in its turn—and thus released the Portnoys from their role as supporting actors in another family's drama. They would not get star billing until sometime later, when out of the odds and ends of *Portrait of the Artist* I liked best, I began to write something I called **"A Jewish Patient Begins His Analysis."** This turned out to be a brief story narrated by the Portnoys' son, Alexander, purportedly his introductory remarks to his psychoanalyst. And who was this Alexander? None other than that Jewish boy who used to turn up time after time in the stories written by those Jewish graduate students back in the Iowa Writers' Workshop: the "watched-over" Jewish son with his sexual dream of The Other. Strictly speaking, the writing of *Portnoy's Complaint* began with discovering Portnoy's voice—more accurately, his mouth—and discovering, along with it, the listening ear: the silent Dr. Spielvogel. The psychoanalytic monologue—a narrative technique whose rhetorical possibilities I'd been availing myself of for years, only not on paper—was to furnish the means by

which I thought I might convincingly draw together the fantastic element of *The Jewboy* and the realistic documentation of *Portrait of the Artist* and *The Nice Jewish Boy*. And a means, too, of legitimizing the obscene preoccupations of the untitled slide show on the subject of sexual parts. Instead of the projection screen (and the gaping), the couch (and the unveiling); instead of gleeful, sadistic voyeurism—brash, shameful, masochistic, euphoric, vengeful, conscience-ridden exhibitionism. Now I could perhaps to begin. (pp. 33-41)

> *Philip Roth, "In Response to Those Who Have Asked Me: 'How Did You Come to Write That Book, Anyway?' " in his* Reading Myself and Others, *Farrar, Straus and Giroux, 1975, pp. 33-41.*

Sheldon Grebstein

In the surge of Jewish-American fiction that began about twenty-five years ago—a body of writing comprising perhaps the most significant and visible movement in American literature since World War II—three novels occupy a special eminence. Bernard Malamud's *The Assistant* remains, after two decades, its most powerful moral statement of the basic Jewish-American theme of redemptive suffering, as well as a superlative example of the ethnic style which fuses Yiddish and English. Saul Bellow's *Herzog* stands as the Jewish movement's leading novel of ideas, as well as perhaps its most accomplished work of art in the richness and variety of craft and materials. Philip Roth's *Portnoy's Complaint* must be recognized as the comic masterpiece of this body of writing, and a remarkably funny, irreverent, daring book by any standards.

Humor is hardly Roth's exclusive domain. From its inception the Jewish movement has been characterized by a strong component of comedy: often dark, as in Malamud's story "The German Refugee," which mixes the death camps, suicide, and hilarious mimicry into a peculiar but compelling synthesis; frequently naughty, as in the long passage in *Herzog* which recounts the hero's after-dinner seduction by the delectable Ramona; sometimes manifestly self-hating and anti-Semitic, as in Bruce Jay Friedman's *Stern*. But until *Portnoy's Complaint* no single literary work had treated the subject of being Jewish in modern America with such brutal candor and comic genius. The major topics of *Portnoy's Complaint*—sexuality, family life, and Jewish self-hatred—frequently inspire comic treatment in the work of Bellow, Malamud, Singer, Friedman, Herbert Gold, and other Jewish-American writers, but nowhere with Roth's concentration, intensity, or profane gusto.

To approach *Portnoy's Complaint* as a "literary work" seems a little artificial and pretentious. The word "performance" appears to be much more appropriate. No voice quite like Portnoy's had ever spoken to us from the pages of an American book. What is immediately evoked for most readers is the "live" performance of stage and nightclub, the attractive-repulsive, brilliant-neurotic, awful-hilarious, aggressive-self-destructive Jewish stand-up comedian, perhaps epitomized in Lenny Bruce, who also exploited sexuality, obscenity, the burden of being Jewish, and the display of his tortured ego for painful laughs. (pp. 152-53)

Even Portnoy's manner of delivery resembles that of the stand-up comic: the *shpritz* (literally "spray" or "outpouring"), which has been defined as "the spontaneous satire that gathers momentum and energy as it goes along, spiraling finally into the exhilarating anarchy of total freedom from inhibition." Of course, this release is never obtained by Portnoy as a psychological condition; rather, it is expressed as the bravado to open up dark and fetid cellars of experience and to utter words forbidden to respectable folk.

The kinship between the routines of popular Jewish comedians and Roth's performance in *Portnoy's Complaint* may be documented further. Theodore Solotaroff, who knew Roth from graduate school days at the University of Chicago, recalls the comic gift Roth often displayed at parties in recounting "Jewish jokes and caustic family anecdotes" with "fantastic mimicry and wit." For Solotaroff, who published two of the episodes of *Portnoy* in *New American Review* before the novel was completed, "the comedian of those Chicago sessions of nostalgia, revenge, and general purgation had landed right in the middle of his own fiction" [see Solotaroff's excerpt]. Solotaroff also remarks on the similarity between the novel's method and that of the stand-up comic: "the contemporary winging art and humor of improvisation and release."

Paradoxically, Roth himself denies the direct influence of popular comedy. . . . Instead, Roth pays homage to "a sit-down comic named Franz Kafka." For Roth, "guilt as a comic idea," an idea derived from Kafka, provided the momentum he needed to release himself from the more conventional concerns of his earlier work. There is an element of self-contradiction in Roth's denial, however, for . . . [in] observations on *Portnoy's Complaint* he refers to his hero's life as "drama, or vaudeville skit," and to the hero himself as "babbling sinner/showman seeking absolution/applause." Who has not conceived the same thought while watching some driven, demonic comic or emcee lash himself into ever more frenetic and vulgar self-revelations as the audience howls, part in laughter, part in shame? (pp. 154-55)

[The] novel's organization can . . . be seen as analogous to a series of improvisations. Just as no patient can prepare and follow a precise script in a visit to the analyst, the novel proceeds by the loose association of what Roth himself called "blocks of consciousness." The very randomness and unpredictability of what is narrated, the sudden shifts in time, locale, and situation, create exactly that ambience of fluidity and surprise which is most congenial to the genre of low comedy. Central to this is an incessant stream of dramatizations or skits, with Portnoy playing all the roles as well as that of commentator.

There are three basic kinds of skits in *Portnoy's Complaint:* elimination (bathroom) skits, eating (kitchen) skits, and sex (bedroom) skits. These physical functions are, of course, fundamental and archetypal sources of comedy, especially slapstick and burlesque. In his unrestrained imagination, Roth often intermixes all three. For example, in the series of masturbation skits which provide the novel's raunchiest and most daring comedy, the adolescent Portnoy barricades himself in the family bathroom—purportedly in the throes of digestive upset, which his intolerably solicitous mother blames on the gorging of bad food (*chazerai*); actually, he is frantically relieving his lusts. For better or worse, this epic masturbation skit, which features the whole family—constipated father and worried mother alternately pounding on the bathroom door, while young Portnoy strives to bring himself off into his sister's bra—is unique in the annals of comic writing. Or Portnoy makes love to various comestibles: e.g., a cored apple, or a piece of liver later served as the family's dinner. The latter are not actual skits but outlines or scenarios, sketched in a few lines of evocative prose.

As boy becomes man, masturbation-food skits develop into oral sexuality. The first encounter with the delectable Monkey begins with this form of sexual gusto, and such intimacies continue to characterize their torrid relationship. In the background of this food-sex association there hover Jewish injunctions against both Gentile girls and non-kosher food. As dramatizations of Portnoy's case history, masturbation, pursuits of the forbidden *shikse,* and the predilection for giving and receiving oral gratification interweave and contrast with the childhood recollections of home and kitchen ruled by mother. As Mark Shechner has pointed out [in his essay "Philip Roth"], "Food is to Jewish comedy and Jewish neurosis what drink is to the Irish." In the comic logic of the novel, the food skits are Jewish—as in Mrs. Portnoy's dramatic rendition of her perilous encounter with lobster—while the sex skits are *goyish.* Father Portnoy suffers the worst fate that can befall a decent Jewish man, constipation. For the son, as he imagines in a characteristically funny and awful juvenile fantasy, the worst fate is the loss of his organ: transformed by venereal disease (contracted beyond the Pale) into a petrified object which disengages itself from Portnoy's body and drops with a clink to the kitchen floor.

These materials, particularly the vivid re-creations of Portnoy's sexual adventures, border on the pornographic. Certainly the affair with Monkey, in its emphasis on the orgiastic, on her easy readiness and lubricity, and on Portnoy's own redoubtable virility, resemble some of the formulaic elements of porn. It is a risk deliberately taken by Roth, this teetering along the edge of the grossly obscene. But if many of his readers were offended—especially those with presuppositions about what was fitting for a Jewish writer and his creations—others were delighted by Roth's skill. If the novel's skits and situations are often crude, the presence of phenomenal wit, inspired wackiness of invention, and dazzling turns of language deflect our attention from the vulgarity. As in the richest comedy, we respond not so much to what is happening in front of us (which may be quite awful), but to its mode of happening.

The language of *Portnoy's Complaint,* as of all comic fiction, is essential to its mode of happening. While the skit and the incongruous juxtaposition of ideas and values are important, language is more important. The live performer has gesture, voice, timing, facial expression, and group dynamics to work with, and often the drumbeats and sound effects provided by a musical back-up; the writer has only the written language and the limited resources of typography. In fact, with these relatively sparse means Roth attempts to transform the visual medium into the aural, to imitate the distinctive voice so crucial to the delivery of the stand-up comic. For example, a series of exclamatory sentences, often interspersed or in combination with a series of interrogatives that are really declarations, convey the rising tone, rhythm, and effect of the build-up to climax, a type of *accelerando* which requires either a scream or a laugh to release. I quote a relatively innocuous and "clean" passage to illustrate this speed-effect and necessary comic discharge:

> I am something called "a weekend guest"? I am something called "a friend from school"? What tongue is she speaking? I am "the *bonditt*," "the *vantz*," I am the insurance man's son. I am [Rabbi] Warshaw's ambassador! "How do you do, Alex?" To which of course I reply, "Thank you." Whatever anybody says to me during my first twenty-four hours in Iowa, I answer, "Thank you." Even to inanimate objects. I walk into a chair, promptly I say to it, "Excuse me, thank you." I drop my napkin on the floor, lean down, flushing, to pick it up, "Thank you," I hear myself saying to the napkin—or is it the floor I'm addressing? Would my mother be proud of her little gent. Polite even to the furniture!

The most intense passages, which aspire to a roaring and painful hilarity, are skits or bursts of mimicry conducted at peak volume, as conveyed by sentence patterns, italics, exclamations, capital letters, and a chorus of impersonated voices dubbed in by that expert ventriloquist, Alexander Portnoy. Portnoy's favorite impressions are, of course, of his parents, especially Mother, as in this brief example: "DON'T RUN FIRST THING TO A BLONDIE, PLEASE! BECAUSE SHE'LL TAKE YOU FOR ALL YOU'RE WORTH AND THEN LEAVE YOU BLEEDING IN THE GUTTER! A BRILLIANT INNOCENT BABY BOY LIKE YOU, SHE'LL EAT YOU UP ALIVE!"

But the zaniest and most feverish of these full-blast episodes are the events and imaginings devolving from the visit to Bubbles Girardi, Portnoy's first adolescent sexual encounter. In a fantasy sequence Portnoy returns home blinded; the scene concludes with a frantic torrent of questions to Ba-ba-lu Mandel, summarizing Alex's boyhood erotic flights. In another fantasized episode the Devil (another ghost from Portnoy's puberty, Rabbi Warshaw) indicts Portnoy for sexual selfishness, chains him to a toilet bowl, and condemns him to masturbate for eternity.

Another sort of mimicry dependent on high-volume, high-speed techniques is the interjection of imagined newspaper headlines that evoke the tabloid approach. The screaming banner, a subhead, and a photo contain most of the story worth telling (i.e., the *New York Daily News* method). Portnoy tends to visualize his fate, particularly his sexual fate, in a series of these catchy headlines:

> ASST HUMAN OPP'Y COMMISH FOUND HEADLESS IN GO-GO GIRL'S APT.

> INSURANCE MAN'S SON LEAPS TO DEATH.

> ASST HUMAN OPP'Y COMMISH FLOGS DUMMY, Also lives in Sin, Reports Old School Chum.

> JEW SMOTHERS DEB WITH COCK, Vassar Grad Georgetown Strangulation Victim; Mocky Lawyer Held.

Or, as a variation of the banner headline, Portnoy will issue a slogan reminiscent of advertising or political campaigning, for example, LET'S PUT THE ID BACK IN YID! (pp. 162-65)

In addition to his adaptation of newspaper and advertising styles for comic purposes, Roth exploits radio and film. Profuse allusions to radio shows and popular movies are augmented by skits, dramatizations, and fantasized scenes. Such bits have long been staples in the patter of stand-up comics.

Portnoy has several favorite radio voices; among his expert impersonations are those of sportscasters such as Red Barber and the patriotic narrators of Norman Corwin's dramas. Portnoy uses these voices early on to establish his adolescent ideals of sports hero or super-citizen and achiever, then later juxtaposes them comically against his lowered adult ethnic and sexual preoccupations. Again, this is just the kind of routine we can easily imagine witnessing in a nightclub, rather than in a book; the impersonated voice helps transmute it from the literary sphere to the live. Here Portnoy stages a bedroom encounter in the manner of a prizefight announcer—suggestive also of the serious business of sexual combat which lurks behind the burlesque:

> In the black pubic hair, ladies and gentlemen, weighing one hundred and seventy pounds, at least half of which is still undigested halvah and hot pastrami, from Newark, N.J., The Shnoz, Alexander Portnoy! And his opponent, in the fair fuzz, with her elegant polished limbs and the gentle maidenly face of a Botticelli, that ever-popular purveyor of the social amenities here in the Garden, one hundred and fourteen pounds of Republican refinement, and the pertest pair of nipples in all New England, from New Canaan, Connecticut, Sarah Abbott Maulsby!

Many of Portnoy's boyhood fantasies of romantic conquest of Gentile girls are cast as film scenes, as asexual and All-American as the actual movies of the 1940's which inspire him. In these fervid imaginings, which combine dreams of assimilation with the first rites of adolescent passage, we have the sardonic paradox of a young American Jew trying to hide his Jewishness because of the propaganda of Hollywood films produced in Jewish-dominated studios. Portnoy's pubescent American Dream of Success thus provokes as much pathos as it does laughter: "O America! America! It may have been gold in the streets to my grandparents, it may have been a chicken in every pot to my father and mother, but to me, a child whose earliest movie memories are of Ann Rutherford and Alice Faye, America is a *shikse* nestling under your arm whispering love love love love love!"

It is interesting, as well as amusing, that although Portnoy savagely berates his parents and his Jewish origins for warping his personality and denying him freedom from guilt, he obviously takes great pleasure in exploiting his meager though vivid vocabulary of Yiddish terms. It is also significant that Roth supplies no glossary, obviously on the assumption that the general audience has become familiar with these terms, largely via Jewish comedians. *Goy, shikse*—repeated dozens of times throughout the novel—everyone knows, of course. Many of the others are almost equally familiar: *kishkas, chazerai, shvartze, shmattas, kvetching, meshuggeneh, shlepped.* Most of the rest are obscene, especially synonyms for the male sexual organ: *putz, shlong, shmuck, shvantz.* For the one Yiddish sentence the novel contains, that familiar folk epigram which is also a simple diagnosis of Portnoy's complaint—*Ven der putz shteht, ligt der sechel in drerd*—Roth supplies an accurate but awkward translation. The same wisdom has sometimes been rendered into apocryphal Latin: *penis erectus non conscientiam habet.*

The Yiddish terms serve a range of stylistic and comic functions. Primarily they are a constant reminder of character, one of Portnoy's basic "languages" or voices. The paucity of his vocabulary, yet the persistence, even obsessiveness, with which he uses some of these terms, form a paradigm of his divided self. He knows his heritage and identity poorly and tries to escape it, but he cannot. Its voice breaks through, not only in vocabulary but also in syntax and sentence rhythms. This voice is Roth's able version of that dialect style developed and perfected by Malamud and Bellow. However, where the older writers use this style for serious or even epic effects, as well as for comedy, Roth largely turns it back to the original functions of American dialect styles: local color, satire, and humor. But Roth's skill prevents the dialect style from culminating in reductive stereotype or mere mockery. It combines with standard English, even rather formal English at one extreme, and pungent street argot at the other. The result is great fluency, constant modulation, considerable variety, and frequent surprise, as we saw above in Monkey's suicide-scene fantasy. I am tempted to offer a formulaic analysis: that Portnoy talks "Jewish" only when he speaks of his parents or his home experiences; otherwise he talks like a lawyer, or, on the subject of sex, like a street tough. But formulas do not apply. In fact, the language is unpredictable. It soars, swoops, swerves, wanders as often as his memories. (pp. 166-68)

Roth does so well with what Yiddish he has in *Portnoy* (about fifty words, the minimum supply for a Jewish comic), it's a shame he doesn't have more. Perhaps the same could be said about Roth's Jewishness. Certainly Roth's hostile critics, and especially those who cried out against what they saw as the anti-Semitism and shameful filth of *Portnoy's Complaint,* would wish him a larger and more satisfying share of his ethnic heritage. Yet, paradoxically, the portion he does claim, and has chosen to work with, yields him a distinctive place in the Jewish movement. In a sense, the major line of development of Roth's career—as well as his reply to all the attacks from the Jewish establishment—can be summarized in this Portnovian declaration: "Jew Jew Jew Jew Jew Jew! It is coming out

of my ears already, the saga of the suffering Jews! Do me a favor, my people, and stick your suffering heritage up your suffering ass,—*I happen also to be a human being!*" There can be no doubt about Roth's own awareness of his role in this movement, and his consciousness of his relationship to Bellow and Malamud. Yet from the beginning of his career, and most notably in *Portnoy,* he has stubbornly followed his own calling. Obviously more remote than Bellow and Malamud from Judaism as a total lifestyle and worldview, Roth is more directly concerned with personality than with fate. Unlike their work, his reflects no glimmers of transcendence, metaphysics, superstition, awe. For Portnoy, as for most of Roth's protagonists, the most intense experiences are through human love. In these respects his work is intrinsically closer to comedy.

But none of these comparisons intend to discredit the novel's Jewish authenticity. Roth's cultural value is precisely his difference from the other writers. His is the "inside view," the exposé of the contemporary quasi-assimilated Jew. Thus *Portnoy* gives us the most comprehensive, graphic, and detailed account of the texture of the Jewish-Oedipal family experience and the results of that experience, mainly guilt. The book also presents the clearest and most vivid statement of how Jewish righteousness, intellectual superiority, and ethical sensitivity—as represented by Portnoy—are engendered by his very guilt. As part of this exposé of Jewish character and personality, Roth gives us the most explicit account to date of how Jews despise Gentiles while slavishly imitating and pursuing them. Still another kind of revelation, one strangely resembling Portnoy's attitude toward Gentiles, is that of Jewish misogyny. What may be perceived as far back as Abraham Cahan, and running through Bellow and Malamud as a latent attitude and motif, is at last made manifest by Roth. In *Portnoy,* as elsewhere in Jewish-American fiction, women are man's chief temptation and source of misery. Roth is the first to say it blatantly, humorously, and at length. Finally, *Portnoy's Complaint* renders explicitly another recurrent suggestion in Jewish-American writing, one only whispered elsewhere: that to be Jewish is to be neurotic.

The compensation for these bitter messages is less uplifting in *Portnoy's Complaint* than in those other remarkable books, *Herzog* and *The Assistant,* but it is far funnier. Because Jews have absorbed so many cultures, it would be difficult to prove the existence of a specifically Jewish humor, irrespective of time and place. Two elements do persist, however, and they are both superbly exemplified in *Portnoy;* marginality (i.e., the Jew's sense of the precariousness and strain of his status in any given society), and the anti-heroic figure of the *schlemiel,* who is an incarnation of Jewish destiny—the archetypal Jew. I would define the *schlemiel* as an aware loser, who complains as he loses but doesn't quit. Alexander Portnoy, who breaks a leg pursuing *shikses,* ejaculates into his own eye as the climax to his first big sex experience, and finds himself at last inert in Israel, is surely a *schlemiel.* But at least he is the funniest of his kind in American literature. True, his *shpritz* can be messy and discomfiting, as any *shpritz* will be if it happens to hit you. But a really good *shpritz* can also be refreshing, even liberating. (pp. 169-71)

Sheldon Grebstein, "The Comic Anatomy of 'Portnoy's Complaint'," in Comic Relief: Humor in Contemporary American Literature, *edited by Sarah Blacher Cohen, University of Illinois Press, 1978, pp. 152-171.*

"I would never have written a book as farcical as *Portnoy's Complaint* if I had any devotion to the cause of sex; causes don't thrive on self-satire. Causes expel you for self-satire. Nor was I a soldier in the cause of obscenity. Portnoy's obscenity is intrinsic to his situation, not to my style. I have no case to make for dirty words, in or out of fiction—only for the right of access to them when they seem to the point."
—Philip Roth, 1981

Helge Normann Nilsen

The Jewish-American fiction written after World War II naturally reflects the changes that occurred in American society and in the lives of the Jews as an ethnic group. Living conditions improved dramatically, and many Jews entered the middle class. The writers, like so many others, were better educated and began to merge into the mainstream of American life. At the same time they retained their commitment to humanistic values and their ancestral awareness of the tragedy of human existence. Thus the stage was set for the exploration of important conflicts between the Jewish sensibility and the agnostic consumer mentality of the larger society. J. D. Salinger's *The Catcher in the Rye* is a striking example of this clash, and there are also traces of it in Bellow's *Dangling Man* and Malamud's *The Assistant.* At the same time Jewish writers did not advocate any return to ethnic orthodoxy, being products of the modern age and regarding themselves as Americans, or humanists first and Jews second. Nevertheless, the basic conflict between their ethnic heritage and the wholly secularized environment emerges in various ways in much of the fiction that was produced. The early immigrants had embraced America, but for the writer of the fifties and sixties the situation had become more complex. No simple response or solution was possible any longer.

There had been uncertainties before the war, but there had also been valid alternatives. Jew or American, radical or moderate, these were some of the possibilities. But in the work of Nathanael West there is a tendency to discard all alternatives and embrace nihilism, and it is his voice that speaks most clearly for those who came after him. Philip Roth and Bellow may not be quite so bleak in their despair, but their work shows a rootlessness and scepticism which can be seen as the hallmark of contemporary Jewish-American prose fiction. For the first time, the effects of assimilation and Americanization are fully felt by writers of Jewish descent, and their Jewish heritage is per-

ceived either as an impediment or a type of sensibility rather than any set of beliefs. *The Assistant* may be said to affirm Jewishness, but only in the vaguest of terms.

Portnoy's Complaint is thought of as a novel that is typical of the sixties, of a generation in rebellion against established values, but it has a curious resemblance to the immigrant school of Jewish-American fiction. Its hero rejects all things Jewish and struggles to become integrated into what he regards as a desirable, secular and liberal way of life. 'His is a late version of the old story of the newcomer struggling to become an American, bent on full assimilation, away from ghetto identity and towards American identity with its much wider horizons of possibility' [Tony Tanner, *City of Words: American Fiction 1950-1970*]. However, the focus is different. The protagonists in immigrant fiction were caught up in a historical process of upward mobility that prevented them from concentrating too much on their individual psyches. In the case of Alexander Portnoy, Jewishness is above all a psychological burden that he labors to rid himself of. The intensity of his struggle is evidence of the power both of the tradition and the larger culture that is opposed to many of its mores and attitudes. Generally speaking there is much to be said for the view that Portnoy's battle against his heritage ends in a draw. It is a modern paradox that the hero cannot quite escape from a tradition that he no longer believes in and thus is doubly victimized.

Roth's novel has a great deal of psychological awareness built into it. The hero is prodigiously intelligent and well versed in his Freud and Marx, but his knowledge is of no help to him. Instead, he employs it as the instrument of an endless self-analysis that becomes an exercise in masochism. (pp. 495-96)

The novel consists of an uninterrupted monologue by the protagonist, with the psychoanalyst Dr. Spielvogel as silent audience. However, the principle of free association is discarded in favor of a coherent presentation by Portnoy of his conviction that his problems have been mainly caused by his background and his parents, especially his mother. Psychoanalysis becomes a vehicle for his attack on Jewish customs and values. The aim of analysis, to obtain emotional insight and experience catharsis, is largely subverted by a Portnoy who is bent on polemic and revenge rather than therapeutic breakthroughs. His portrait of his parents and the Jewish neighborhood is one-sided, to put it mildly, and even if he is right in his criticism, his relentless attacks serve as an escape from himself and his own share in the continued existence of his problems.

One might question Alex's reliability as a narrator who is also a patient undergoing analysis, and it is clear that he is not wholly perceptive with regard to the nature of his condition. Also, he sees others largely in terms of his own needs and reactions. One cannot take everything he says at face value, but at the same time there is a persistent pattern of rejection in his reaction to the Jewish milieu. On the intellectual level, at least, he leaves no doubt as to his complete lack of enthusiasm for all the basic tenets of Judaism and the attitudes that go with them. There is a quality of sincerity in his abandonment of Jewish beliefs which seems to belong to a norm which is stronger, as it were, than the troubled hero himself, or remains unaffected by his problems. It may be here that Roth, as implied author, is perceived most clearly in the novel, whereas Alex, the narrator, generally suffers from a lack of distance between himself and much of his experience. This trait may weaken **Portnoy's Complaint** as a protest novel, but it makes the hero very convincing as a psychological portrait. Another indication of the author's distance from the narrator is Dr. Spielvogel's remark at the end of the book, where he suggests that Alex's treatment is yet to begin.

Alex's parents are close enough to the immigrant experience to cling to certain old world viewpoints, but they are also in a stage of transition, having moved into the suburbs and apparently also withdrawn themselves from Jewish religious activities. Portnoy senior has no higher education and seems to have only vague notions about the culture of his own race, yet he looks upon 'the saga' of the Jewish people with great reverence. But the atmosphere in the household is far from orthodox, and the Portnoys have been more strongly influenced by American values than they seem to be aware of. In fact, the greatest achievement they can think of is material success, and they persecute their son with demands that he fulfill their expectations and establish himself as a respectable citizen with a wife and family. They protest against his atheism, but they are not in any position to teach him Jewish cultural and religious values. The only active remnant of these are certain dietary bans on shellfish and hamburger meat which are ferociously upheld by Mrs. Portnoy. (pp. 496-97)

Given such a background, the striving of Alex toward integration and secularization is a natural one, notwithstanding the horrified reactions of his parents. Seen in the larger context of the historical development from oppression in Europe to freedom in America, the entire Portnoy family have been moulded by the greater forces that have shaped the destiny of Jews in the United States. In Europe there was the misery of poverty, but the land of opportunity also exacts its price. It takes hard work to get ahead, and the family breadwinner has labored, 'in that ferocious and self-annihilating way in which so many Jewish men of his generation served their families'. This is the trap that Alex wants to escape from, but he finds that he carries a burden of remorse and loneliness that may be the price that he will have to pay for his freedom.

Jack Portnoy is proud of his success as an insurance salesman and speaks with great respect of the Anglo-Saxon gentlemen who run the corporation that he works for. But he also feels their prejudice very keenly and is occasionally overcome with fury at these supercilious snobs. Similarly, Alex dreams of non-Jewish girls and wants to obliterate his ethnic background in order to become acceptable to them, although his sister Hannah warns him, arguing that he cannot escape his background. Being a Jew is an historical fact which the surrounding world will never allow to be forgotten. The argument is a time-honored one, but Alex refuses to accept it. He continues to protest and rebel, and it is hard to refute his indictment of the possessive and domineering ways of his mother. They were a source of torment for him when a child and have no doubt

contributed to the formation of his present problems and anxieties.

Alex's main charge against his father is that he is weak and submissive and allows himself to be dominated both by his non-Jewish employers and his overpowering wife. He is a man who gives up any attempt at discovering and asserting his individuality and therefore becomes a negative example to his son. The elder Portnoy wants his son's love and to give him the same, but the latter cannot accept the premises: 'But what he had to offer I did not want—and what I wanted he did not have to offer'. The father has gone too far in his acceptance of the rules laid down by the mother for Alex to be able to communicate with him. He is too much a man of his generation, for whose members conventional success was of overwhelming importance, to be able to allow his son to develop in his own way. Moreover, he has a strong sense of his tradition as a Jew, although he cannot formulate his commitment very well, and thus feels impelled to see his son as one who will fulfill the father's ambitions and be a Jew of the kind that he himself would have wanted to be.

But the son turns against what he regards as the tyranny of the entire older generation of Jewish middle class citizens and singles out two prominent cases of parental oppression among them. His cousin Heshie had decided to marry a girl of Polish descent, but his father compelled him to relinquish her because she did not belong to the tribe. Soon after Heshie was killed in the Great War. This tragedy is eloquent testimony to the dark underside of the Jewish family feeling and sense of togetherness, that is, an intolerance and prejudice that are just as deplorable as anti-Semitism. The story of Ronald Nimkin, the obedient Jewish boy who commits suicide because of his parents' 'selfishness and stupidity', is a pathetic one, though the question of who is responsible for the tragedy is not as clear here as in the case of Heshie. The causes of Ronald's death may be more complicated than Alex is ready to allow for, but then his whole approach to the Jewish milieu is that of the prosecutor rather than the impartial observer. But he no doubt has a valid point when he draws attention to the self-righteousness of the Jews and their imaginary moral superiority.

However, when looking back on his past, Alex is aware that there is another and more positive dimension that was also part of his childhood. There is never any doubt that the Portnoys loved their children, though Alex finds is easier to focus on certain happy moments with his father than recollecting similar ones with his mother. He does remember such episodes with his mother, too, and the pleasure associated with them is more poignant than anything else, but he had also been all too familiar with her threats of withdrawal of motherly love. But the story of how his father had taken Alex swimming one day in summer at the seashore is so full of tenderness that it seems almost incongruous amidst the welter of angry accusations that make up the major portion of the novel. Alex also asserts that he has many more such happy memories of his parents, and in that case the question inevitably arises why he concentrates so intensely on the negative influences of his early life. It seems unsatisfactory to argue that he does this because he is a social critic whose purpose it is to expose the shortcomings of a certain environment. The enormous self-concern of Roth's protagonist is not easy to reconcile with the intentions of the literature of social protest because it diverts the attention from the problems in question to the person who is complaining about them. Even if his personality is considered relevant as evidence of what a narrowminded upbringing can lead to, a certain detachment is required when dealing with the narrator's own condition in order to convey successfully the idea that social criticism is the main concern of the novel.

Alex's relationships with women follow a pattern that is established in his battles with his mother. She uses a technique of alternately smothering him in love and threatening to cast him out of her life altogether, all in the name of giving him a good upbringing. In any case, this is how Alex remembers her behavior. He is extraordinarily sensitive and dependent on women's favors, but at the same time he is afraid of being trapped by them, thus loosing his independence and even identity. His need for love is as strong as his desire for freedom from commitment, and the only 'solution' that seems possible for him as an adult is to lead a life of promiscuity. During his adolescence he indulges in frequent masturbation both as a means of satisfying his sex drive and of asserting his rebellious individuality in the face of the many taboos that the home and the entire environment impose upon him. At the deepest level, his sexual excesses may be regarded as part of his struggle to free himself of his identity as a Jew.

Alex is ambivalent in his feelings towards his parents, but not towards everything they stand for. He cannot forget the moments of love and bliss, but he is unequivocal in his rejection of their use of emotional blackmail and their sentimental and primitive attachment to Jewish customs and beliefs. Above all, Alex abandons the religion of his tribe, indeed, all religions, in favor of an atheism that is combined with a radical political commitment. He is also politically naive, with his belief that 'the rights of man' are realized in the Soviet Union, but he is sincere in his rationalism and atheism, and there is no sign that he ever recants from this position. His own experience supports his views, in that the Jews he has observed have accepted many of the secular standards of the surrounding society and uphold them with a zeal that is second to no other group. Alex is merciless, but also to the point, in his analysis of the function of religion. It is an 'opiate' for the ignorant masses, and the clergy, of any denomination, has an economic interest in maintaining the status quo. It is generally difficult to find any flaws in Alex's arguments against the intolerance, superstition and backwardness of the people of his parents' generation, and he is lucid and consistent in his criticism. His scepticism and rationalism are convincing and based on a keen understanding of human realities and motivations. But his maturity in this field is offset by his inability to utilize his insights in the area of his own emotional problems. Here he seems to be the victim of forces beyond his control, a helpless spectator to a conflict within him that he can analyze but not resolve.

No one can be more eloquent in his diagnosis of his condition than Alex himself. His is the conflict of Western culture, between duty and pleasure, conscience and transgression. But his goal, however difficult, is to rid himself of his own taboos and lead a life according to his own convictions. He wants to follow his own desire and enjoy it, but he has to admit that he is oppressed by 'shame and inhibition and fear'. . . . Every rebellious act is followed by guilt and remorse, no matter how much Alex hates his own inhibitions and knows that they have no rational foundation.

With regard to religion, dietary laws, tribal prejudices and materialistic obsessions, Alex has quite a good case against all of them, but this is not so clear in questions of sexual morality. His promiscuity may be an attempt to establish sexual freedom for himself, and even for others, but the project is utopian. People seem to need emotional security and stability also, even Alex, and besides, his many affairs cannot even provide him with a lasting sense of self-esteem. As far as sex is concerned, he is up against a deep-seated division within himself which is a major cause of his sufferings. He wants to be a swinger, a carefree hedonist, but his sexual and emotional egotism leads to disappointments and disillusion both for himself and his partners.

The women feel exploited by Portnoy, and with reason. He is an attractive man and quite successful in the social sense, but he has very little regard for the women's feelings if they fall in love with him and want to marry. He blames himself for having an overdeveloped superego in sexual matters, but he does not actually experience much remorse in connection with his various colorful sexual experiences, whether with his mistress, the Monkey, or prostitutes and other girls. Alex gives himself too much credit here, perhaps to cover up for an insensitivity and sheer coarseness in him which do not fit the image of himself that he wants to preserve. He experiences a fantasy of ending up in Hell for his sins and of being castigated for his lack of regard for others. He is told here in no uncertain terms that 'suffering mankind' means nothing to him and that the only feelings he has ever experienced have been located in his sexual organs. These charges have an unmistakable ring of truth about them. However, they are not expressed directly by Portnoy to himself, but by the Devil in the shape of Rabbi Warshaw, a character whom Alex regards as a pompous fraud. Thus he manages to take some of the edge off this self-criticism. Moreover, he skilfully draws the attention away from his own flaws by constantly finding fault with his partners, the Monkey in particular. He attacks Naomi, the Israeli girl, for criticizing him, but his own attitude to everyone he meets, including the women once he starts reacting to their personalities, is hypercritical, if not downright misanthropic.

The Monkey is unbalanced and sometimes even hysterical, but this must be seen in relation to her frustrated love for Alex. He is unable to respond to this feeling in her, and his behavior is almost entirely mechanical and sex-oriented. She justly accuses him of lack of feeling and involvement and stands out, in contrast to him, as a person who is alive and human in a broader sense than he is. . . . Alex is right in condemning the idiocies of his Jewish background, but in the process of liberating himself from it he has largely lost the warmth and ability to care for each other that the people of the tribe possessed.

Alex pursues non-Jewish girls as status symbols out of a sense of inferiority that derives partly from his minority origins. When he becomes acquainted with families and institutions different from his own, his reaction is highly ambivalent. He accepts an invitation to visit the family of his girlfriend Kay Campbell in Iowa, and he is impressed by their politeness and cool self-confidence. But his description of them is satirical, if anything, and during the Thanksgiving celebrations he has to admit to a feeling of homesickness. In spite of himself, Alex reacts like a Jew among Gentiles. He plans to marry Kay and . . . suggests that she must then convert to Judaism, but when she refuses he becomes furious, much to his own surprise. But in fact he reacts in a fashion shared by many of his brethren to what he perceives as the haughty dismissal of the *goy,* or non-Jew, of his Jewish heritage. . . . (pp. 497-501)

Clearly, the liberation from Jewishness is a more complex process than Alex has reckoned with. His relationship with Kay also deteriorates when he begins to find her boring and predictable. Her placid demeanour is foreign to him, as he is used to the more tempestuous relations between people that he has witnessed in his own family. The Monkey does provide him with the sort of drama in question, but his own fear of commitment ultimately proves stronger than anything any woman can offer. Moreover, when he leaves a woman behind, he cannot help feeling gratified by the hurt that he inflicts on her. Beginning with his mother, he has developed an attitude of excessive dependence on female attentions and a consequent vulnerability towards women which is bound to stir resentment against them within him. Another complicating factor is that he mixes romance with social climbing in Gatsby-fashion; in his flight from Jewishness he falls in love with the background of the Sarah Maulsbys and Kay Campbells. The Monkey's main attraction in sexual, and she has a lower-class background, but her case parallels the others in that Alex establishes an object relationship to both categories of women. When Sarah refuses to perform fellatio on him, he feels doubly wounded because he thinks her refusal is an expression of anti-Semitism. But when he looks back on their affair, he demonstrates a keen insight into the reasons why he failed to love her: 'Intolerant of her frailties. Jealous of her accomplishments. Resentful of her family'. However, when she finally gives in to his sexual demands, he does not really appreciate that this is her way of expressing her love for him. He registers and portrays vividly female suffering, but he does not take it quite seriously and detaches himself from it. He tries to excuse himself by regarding his behavior as a revenge upon the Wasps for their treatment of his father, but it seems obvious that he does this for motives of his own.

Alex complains to Dr. Spielvogel about the fatal flaws of the Jewish race: 'Please, who crippled us like this? Who made us so morbid and hysterical and weak?' His identification of the problem here verges on a deterministic acceptance of the very stereotypes that he otherwise passionate-

ly rejects. In other words, he comes to surrendering not only to his Jewish weakness as a phase that can be overcome but as an ineradicable historical fact. It is at the point of this recognition that Arthur Levy in Ludwig Lewisohn's *The Island Within* goes the other way and embraces his heritage, whereas Portnoy balances on the sharp edge that divides his sense of hopelessness from his determination to transcend the limits that his background threatens to impose upon him. But he also reveals the influence of his birth in the contradiction between the self-contempt that he expresses and the pride he also feels as a Jew in his culture and its accomplishments, being secretly convinced that he is mentally superior to most non-Jews.

These and other examples suggest that Alex is endowed with a set of attitudes that define him as Jewish though he is wholly sincere in his rejection of the ancestral heritage. (pp. 501-02)

The firmness of Alex's assimilationist stand may be a reason for the vehement reactions against the novel demonstrated by a number of Jewish-American readers of the novel. Irving Howe recognizes the basic thrust of Roth's book when he argues that it is not anti-Semitic or an expression of a 'traditional Jewish self-hatred'. [In Abraham Chapman's *Jewish-American Literature: An Anthology of Fiction, Poetry, Autobiography, and Criticism*] Howe argues that 'What the book speaks for is a yearning to undo the fate of birth', and this may be what Alex wants. But Howe proceeds from analysis of content to direct polemic when he goes on to say that this wish is a mere fantasy that any Jew worth his salt can only 'dally with' for a moment before rejecting it. Such a dogmatic assertion that ethnicity equals fate is hardly in keeping with reality and is as much an admission of defeat as a recognition of the value of Jewish identity. Ruth Wisse aptly argues [in the same anthology] that *Portnoy's Complaint* 'presents the schlemiel condition as unbearable', rejecting a traditional Jewish way of turning pain into laughter and concentrating on revealing the pain to the fullest possible extent. But Wisse still shares the view expressed by Howe that assimilation is impossible and speaks of Alex's 'rather self-loving notion that we could be better if only we tried, the tired but persistentthesis of the little engine that could'. It is no wonder that Alex is tired, given the magnitude of the task, but the novel does not support the idea that the objective is impossible. For all his outpourings about guilt and feeling hampered by his background, Alex's daily life seems to have virtually no 'Jewish' content at all. During his visit to Israel he dutifully sees all the sights and immerses himself in the atmosphere of the homeland of the Jews, but he has no sense of contact or identification with the land and its people. His trip rather seems to be his final and successful test of his own seriousness as an apostate. For him, Israel turns out to be a disappointment in the most vital sense when he discovers that he is impotent with one of its women.

Portnoy's position at the end is quite clear. He intends to leave Jewishness behind, although this does not mean that he wants to replace it with any new ideology or set of beliefs. Rather, he seeks to lead a life based on certain rational insights and values that he regards as having a much broader basis than any kind of tribal grouping. One may disagree with his generally liberal and left-oriented outlook, but there is no reason to deny that an individual, whether Jewish or not, can adhere to such views, even if someone like Portnoy will probably never be able to rid himself of his irrational reactions and sentiments. But he is ready to pay the price of assimilation more in full than the earlier generation who felt so greatly rewarded in the new homeland that the loss of ethnic traditions was softened in its impact. Moreover, at that stage in history those values were more intact, taken for granted and perhaps carried along in an unconscious or unthinking manner even as a wholly new life was taking shape for the Jews in America. (pp. 502-03)

> *Helge Normann Nilsen, "Rebellion against Jewishness: 'Portnoy's Complaint',"* in English Studies, *Netherlands, Vol. 65, No. 6, December, 1984, pp. 495-503.*

Jeffrey Berman

[*The following discussion of* Portnoy's Complaint *is excerpted from Berman's highly academic study* The Talking Cure: Literary Representations of Psychoanalysis. *In his introduction to the work, Berman notes that "Roth writes with a clinical expertise few creative writers can equal and, while his feelings toward psychoanalysis are typically equivocal, the therapeutic setting has given rise to many of his finest and most authentic stories." The chapter on Roth's work excerpted below was originally a paper read to the Western New York Psychoanalytic Society in June, 1984.*]

Portnoy's Complaint is not only Roth's most celebrated psychoanalytic monologue but the novel which brought the analytic couch into the living rooms of millions of American families. Alex's attitude toward [psychoanalysis], the talking cure, may be gleaned from his reading habits, both by what and how he reads. Describing the set of Freud's *Collected Papers* he has bought, he remarks: "since my return from Europe, [I] have been putting myself to sleep each night in the solitary confinement of my womanless bed with a volume of Freud in my hand. Sometimes Freud in hand, sometimes Alex in hand, frequently both." Freud as a soporific? Or as an aphrodisiac? Portnoy reads Freud's writings for the usual reasons—intellectual curiosity, historical awareness, personal self-discovery— yet, he embraces psychoanalytic theory primarily for self-justification. The analyst becomes for Portnoy an erotic plaything, a masturbatory sex object, a handy "how-to" book. As [Doctor] Spielvogel's name suggests in German, he is a "playbird" to be stroked, serenaded, seduced.

Portnoy thus transmutes Freudian ideas into imaginative self-play, the first of many instances in which Roth transforms clinical case studies into the stuff of art. Portnoy's preference for orthodox Freudian psychoanalysis, uncorrupted by revisionist doctrine, reveals the same purist impulse that allows him to quote freely from other great classical writers—Shakespeare, Dostoevsky, Kafka. Portnoy reads Freud's seminal essay, "The Most Prevalent Form of Degradation in Erotic Life," and then confides to us

erotic fantasies and past exploits that would make the Viennese physician blush. In holding up the Freudian mirror to life, Roth's hero is bedazzled by what he sees and by the tantalizing possibilities of life imitating the psychiatric case study. Contemporary analysts speak of fusion with the lost object, but Portnoy's story is an example of a character in search of the author of the *Standard Edition* (or the less epical *Collected Papers*), from which he quotes with Mosaic authority. The promised land for Portnoy is not Israel, toward which he ambivalently moves, but the rich landscape of textbook Oedipal fantasies. Rendered impotent in his mother country, he suffers no loss of verbal potency or bravado when journeying through virgin psychoanalytic territory.

It is obvious from the manic comic tone of the novel that Portnoy hungers not for redemption, as he mistakenly asserts, but for applause and validation. Humor aside, Portnoy does not exist. To question his "illness" seems to be in bad taste, as if to perform an autopsy on a good joke or to translate a pun from another language. . . . Nevertheless, we may wonder whether Portnoy's reading of Freudian theory allows him to chart new imaginative territory or merely to restrict his vision. The question is not how much psychoanalytic theory Portnoy has studied but the uses and misuses of his knowledge. Accordingly, we may analyze one of the most intriguing aspects of the novel, Portnoy's transference relationship to Spielvogel. The inexperienced Libby knows enough about transference in ***Letting Go*** to call it by its proper name. Portnoy, however, seems indifferent to the transactional nature of psychoanalysis. Indeed, he refuses to allow Spielvogel to speak until the last line of the novel. The patient monopolizes the session in a dizzying display of Freudian virtuosity. He allows nothing to interrupt his monologue, neither doubts about psychoanalytic theory nor queries addressed to Spielvogel. All of Portnoy's questions are rhetorical.

Portnoy's transference relationship to Spielvogel suggests the desire to match his Freudian expertise against the analyst's, to compete with him, secure his approval, and ultimately to replace him as an authority. The intense identification with Spielvogel reveals the urge to incorporate him, as if Portnoy were digesting a book. Although he addresses him as "Your Honor" and "Your Holiness," the patient usually regards him as an intellectual equal. "Surely, Doctor, we can figure this thing out, two smart Jewish boys like ourselves." Portnoy never relinquishes his superiority. Identifying himself with Freud's famous case studies, he cites an illustrious artist whose fantasies coincide with his own. "I have read Freud on Leonardo, Doctor, and pardon the hubris, but my fantasies exactly: this big smothering bird beating frantic wings about my face and mouth *so that I cannot even get my breath.*" Later Portnoy challenges Spielvogel (his own "playbird") to another competition, singing the songs of the service academies. "Go ahead, name your branch of service, Spielvogel, I'll sing you your song! Please, allow me—it's my money." ***Portnoy's Complaint*** is itself a raucous anthem to the psychoanalytic process, with the patient paying homage to His Majesty Spielvogel while at the same time making plans for his own succession to the throne.

What does all this mean? To the extent that Portnoy attempts to win his analyst's love and to usurp his magical potency, he recreates Spielvogel into an idealized father figure—a judge, lawgiver, king—the antithesis of his constipated and passive real father, Jack Portnoy. But insofar as Portnoy refuses to surrender verbal control to Spielvogel, thus enforcing silence and passivity upon the analyst, he attempts to manipulate him into his father's submissive position. The transference relationship is consequently an accurate reflection of his life. Portnoy's cocky attitude toward Spielvogel is a disguised attempt to usurp the Oedipal father, to castrate him. Roth's hero never sees the irony. Nor does he comment upon the hidden meaning behind the exhibitionistic impulse to perform or spill forth to the analyst. In his nonstop verbal pyrotechnics, his quest for perfectionism and omnipotent self-control, his unceasing self-mythologizing, and his need to instruct Spielvogel with years of inherited wisdom, Portnoy becomes his own Jewish mother. The irony is crucial. Portnoy criticizes his seductive overprotective mother for overwhelming her docile son; but the son, now a grown man, has internalized his mother's values to the extent that even while rebelling against her, he cannot prevent himself from similarly overwhelming the analyst-father. The mother uses food to overnourish her son; Alex uses a more symbolic form of orality, language, to satiate his analyst. The words never cease. In its unrelenting intensity, Alex's language suggests love and hate, nourishment and suffocation.

And so despite his impressive reading of psychoanalytic theory, Portnoy misses the significance of his ejaculative performance to Spielvogel. "I lose touch instantaneously with that ass-licking little boy who runs home after school with his A's in his hand, the little over-earnest innocent endlessly in search of the key to that unfathomable mystery, his mother's approbation. . . ." Portnoy's colorful language offers the hope of rigorous self-examination and increased narrative perspective; yet, he still does not recognize that, instead of rejecting the mama's-boy values he professes to despise, he has unconsciously transferred these values to Spielvogel, whose approbation he is now demanding. Only now it is an "A" in psychoanalysis he is pursuing in his independent study.

How should Dr. Spielvogel react to Portnoy's artful monologue? In a satirical article entitled "Portnoy Psychoanalyzed," Bruno Bettelheim offers his interpretation of Spielvogel's responses [see Bettelheim's excerpt]. Portnoy's "diarrhea" of talk, observes Bettelheim's analyst, represents a reaction formation to his father's constipation of character. The patient's problem is reflected in his indiscriminate sexual and verbal discharge, a frantic defense against the threat of being unmanned. Accompanying Portnoy's castration fear is the contradictory wish to *have* a castrating father to restore his wounded image of male power. Portnoy's confession is self-indulgent, claims Bettelheim's Spielvogel, because he regards psychoanalysis as a quick and easy catharsis rather than as a difficult process of self-healing through self-discovery. The analyst suggests additionally that although Portnoy believes his psychic impotence arises from an Oedipal attachment, the oral attachments to the mother determine his wish to remain a child forever. Bettelheim's most provocative insight is that Portnoy's complaint of an overprotective mother disguises the disappointment that she was not more exclusively preoccupied with him. "While consciously he experienced everything she did as destructive, behind it is an incredible wish for more, more, more; an insatiable orality which is denied and turned into the opposite by his continuous scream of its being much too much."

Ironically, Bettelheim's Spielvogel is as perceptive in analyzing Portnoy's transference relationship as he is imperceptive in admitting to his own negative countertransference. Unable to concede any sympathy for his "troublesome—aren't they all?—new patient," the analyst is filled with anger, contempt, and intolerance, as if the patient's narcissistic defenses have triggered off his own. He fails to acknowledge anything worthwhile about Portnoy's character. Reading "Portnoy Psychoanalyzed," one is unable to explain the vitality and wit of the Rothian hero, not to mention the novel's linguistic brilliance. Angered by his inability to break through Portnoy's monologue, and worried (rightly, as it turns out) that he will be unable to establish a minimal transference necessary for analysis to succeed, Bettelheim's Spielvogel never admits that countertransference is the key problem.. . . .He is offended by Portnoy's vulgar language, ingratitude toward his parents, inferiority complex, narcissistic rage, and failure in interpersonal relationships. Why, then, is the patient in analysis if he is not to work through these conflicts? In his narrow clinical judgments, threatening tactics, and European condescension, Bettelheim's Spielvogel becomes an unconscious parody of a self-righteous, withholding parent. Indeed, Roth could not have imagined a more unflattering portrait of an analyst. And the absence of authorial distance between the eminent psychoanalyst and his fictional creation makes "Portnoy Psychoanalyzed" more disturbing.

Bettelheim's hostility toward *Portnoy's Complaint* may derive in part from the psychoanalytic community's defensiveness of its image in literature. The angry denunciations of [Peter Shaffer's] *Equus* suggest this, though certainly the play's flaws justify criticism. A more serious problem of "Portnoy Psychoanalyzed" is its unawareness of the satirical art of *Portnoy's Complaint* and Bettelheim's reduction of Roth's novel to a psychiatric case study. Only at the end of the essay does the author consider the possibility that *Portnoy's Complaint* is a literary production, not a clinical confession. He concedes that at best it is "not more than an effort to tell a good story." But he places no value on a good story. He also wishes to tell Portnoy—and his creator—that "it is time to stop being a man of letters so that, through analyzing himself, he might finally become a man." Behind Spielvogel's hostility toward Portnoy lies, of course, Bettelheim's rejection of Roth. Roth's own Spielvogel in *My Life as a Man* demonstrates greater compassion and understanding than the Spielvogel of "Portnoy Psychoanalyzed," which is to say that Roth is a better psychoanalyst than Bettelheim is a literary critic.

Despite its appearance as a psychiatric case study, *Portnoy's Complaint* retains its allegiance to the interior monologue developed by Joyce, Faulkner, and Virginia Woolf. Beginning with *Portnoy's Complaint* and proceeding through *The Breast, My Life as a Man,* and *The Professor of Desire,* Roth has evolved his own narrative form in which the interior monologue is wedded to a contemporary psychoanalytic setting. The analyst, heard or unheard, becomes the recipient of the comic or anguished utterances of a patient searching for psychic relief and moral redemption. The free-association technique, the recurrent phallic-and-castration imagery, the Oedipal triangles, the idealization of the analyst, and the multilayered texture of Portnoy's consciousness help to create the psychoanalytic authenticity. "The style of *Portnoy's Complaint,*" Sheldon Grebstein observes, "is the rhetoric of hysteria, or perhaps the rhetoric of neurosis" [see Grebstein's excerpt].

Roth's prose style also captures perfectly the nuances of psychoanalysis. His language is analytic, restlessly interrogative, self-mocking. The prose is always capable of anticipating the objections of an implied listener who usually turns out to be, of course, an analyst. The language is attuned to the nuances of spiritual imprisonment and moral ambiguity, capable of distorting small humiliations into traumatic injustices, and straining for a release that never quite comes. The voice bespeaks a romantic disillusionment that rarely frees itself from the suspicion that, contrary to what an analyst might say, an unruly personal life is good for a novelist's art. There is a self-lacerating quality about Roth's prose that has remained constant over the years. David Kepesh's observation in *The Professor of Desire* holds true for all of Roth's heroes. "I am an absolutist—a *young* absolutist—and know no way to shed a skin other than by inserting the scalpel and lacerating myself from end to end." Roth's stories dramatize the struggle between the impulse for sensual abandon, on the one hand, and the capacity for pain-filled renunciation, on the other. And the novelist is always willing to incriminate himself in the service of art, preoccupied as he is in novel after novel with illicit and ungovernable passions at war with a rigid conscience.

Does Portnoy discover anything about himself in the course of the novel? The circular form of *Portnoy's Complaint* undercuts the illusion of self—discovery. Roth's comments in *Reading Myself and Others* indicate the contradiction between the realistic and satirical elements of the story. "It is a highly stylized confession that this imaginary Spielvogel gets to hear, and I would guess that it bears about as much resemblance to the drift and tone of what a real psychopathologist hears in his everyday life as a love sonnet does to the iambs and dactyls that lovers whisper into one another's ears in motel rooms and over the phone." The simile reveals Roth's own spirited love affair with psychoanalysis, at least during the creation of *Portnoy's Complaint.* In *My Life as a Man,* he will strive for and achieve stark realism in the treatment of the patient-analyst relationship, but, in *Portnoy's Complaint,* he uses a psychoanalytic setting mainly as the context for his protagonist's lyrical confessions. Never has confession sounded as poetic as this, as free and spontaneous and inventive as these artful outpourings. Portnoy has acquired his psychoanalytic armor before the novel opens, and he seem disinclined to lay down his defenses as the story closes. Consequently, he reaches few if any real insights, nothing comparable to a Joycean epiphany.

Patricia Meyer Spacks has pointed out the affinities of *Portnoy's Complaint* to the picaresque novel [see Meyer Spacks's excerpt], but Roth's story also recalls the dramatic monologue. Robert Langbaum has called the dramatic monologue "the poetry of experience," the doctrine that the "imaginative apprehension gained through immediate experience is primary and certain, whereas the analytic reflection that follows is secondary and problematical." Nearly all of Langbaum's observations in *The Poetry of Experience* apply to *Portnoy's Complaint,* including the tension between our sympathy and moral judgment for a speaker who is outrageous or reprehensible. They apply to the circular rather than linear direction of the narrative. ("The speaker of the dramatic monologue starts out with an established point of view, and is not concerned with its truth but with trying to impress it on the outside world.") Also, they apply to the gratuitous but lyrical nature of the speaker's utterance. "The result is that the dramatic situation, incomplete in itself, serves and ultimately self-expressive or lyrical purpose which gives it its resolution." And so it is with Portnoy's complaint. Interpreted as a Browningesque dramatic monologue, the novel ceases to be a psychiatric case study. The self-indulgent confession gives way to an internally structured monologue, the psychomoral complexity shifts away from Portnoy as a character or object onto the reader's problematic relationship to him, the patient's self-analysis becomes linked to self-deception, and Portnoy's failure to achieve a therapeutic cure is offset by his refusal to have acknowledged any illness.

Nowhere is the reader's troubled relationship to Portnoy better demonstrated than by the enormous controversy the novel has generated. Portnoy shrewdly anticipates the accusations of his critics. "I hear myself indulging in the kind of ritualized bellyaching that is just what gives psychoanalytic patients such a bad name with the general public." Do we praise his candor or criticize his rationalization? Or both? How do we respond to his next set of questions? "Is this truth I'm delivering up, or is it just plain *kvetching?* Or is *kvetching* for people like me a *form* of truth?" The answer depends upon the reader's sympathy for Portnoy, but of course this evades the prior questions of how and why the reader's sympathy for Portnoy is or is not engaged. Irving Howe's influential indictment of *Portnoy's Complaint* in *Commentary* remains the most caustic evaluation. "There usually follows in such first-person narratives a spilling-out of the narrator which it becomes hard to suppose is not also the spilling-out of the author. Such literary narcissism is especially notable among minor satirists, with whom it frequently takes the form of self-exemptive attacks on the shamefulness of humanity." This remains an extreme position, however, and amidst the claims and counterclaims of Roth's critics, a reader is likely to become confused. As Mark Shechner has noted in an admirable essay ["Philip Roth"], one's enthusiasm for Roth's fiction is complicated though not necessarily diminished by the discovery that one's loyalty to *Portnoy's Complaint* as a version of the truth is not widely shared by other readers.

Paradoxically, despite Portnoy's incessant complaints, it is hard to take seriously his demand for therapeutic relief. He may gripe that his parents have psychically crippled him, but they have also been responsible for shaping an imagination that never wavers in its comic inventiveness and vitality. The novel is less a complaint than a celebration. Why should Portnoy be cured of fantasies that are so entertaining? The exuberance of his language works against his claims for deliverance. The voice never assumes the flatness, fatigue, or disconnectedness that is symptomatic of depression. Narcissism notwithstanding, Portnoy realizes that he is not the center of the universe, and Roth's ability to conjure up a rogue's gallery of minor characters testifies to his escape from solipsism. Portnoy's voice never falters in its curiosity and delight in commentary. "The true center of Portnoy's heroism is his speech," Patricia Meyer Spacks has observed [see Meyer Spacks's excerpt]. It is true that Portnoy has not figured out all the psychoanalytic dynamics of his situation. He prefers to discuss Oedipal fixations rather than pre-Oedipal narcissistic injuries. However, if he is consumed by guilt, he seems to be thriving on his imaginative disorders.

The delight in reading **Portnoy's Complaint** lies not in the analysis of a diseased mind but in the appreciation of one of the most fertile imaginations found in contemporary literature. Unlike *The Catcher in the Rye,* which ends with Holden Caulfield's psychotic breakdown, institutionalization, and uncertain return to society, **Portnoy's Complaint** concludes with the protagonist as an outpatient. Spielvogel's punch line, "So. . . . Now vee may perhaps to begin. Yes?", perfectly satirizes Portnoy's bookish self-analysis. Through Spielvogel's one-liner, Roth tells us that Portnoy's psychoanalytic (or pre-psychoanalytic) monologue is both inadequate and incomplete. The analyst has the last word and the last laugh. Yet, Portnoy has discovered one crucial truth that will prepare him for psychoanalysis or any other introspective activity. He has casually dropped upon us (in a parenthesis, no less) the moral of his story: "Nothing is never ironic, there's always a laugh lurking somewhere." **Portnoy's Complaint** appropriately ends with a Joycean "yes." And in the spirit of *Ulysses,* which also climaxes with Molly Bloom's final affirmation as she drifts off to sleep dreaming autoerotic visions of past and present lovers, so does Roth's self-reliant hero, far from being drained or limp from his imaginative foreplay, return to Freud, on the one hand, and himself, on the other, ready to play with his Spielvogelian truths. (pp. 243-51)

Jeffrey Berman, "Philip Roth's Psychoanalysts," in his The Talking Cure: Literary Representations of Psychoanalysis, *New York University Press, 1985, pp. 239-69.*

David H. Hirsh

[The essay excerpted below was originally published in Volume 29 of the Jewish Book Annual.*]*

During the decade of the fifties the state of Jewish letters flourished in America. There were some ironies in all this success, however, which are only now becoming fully apparent. For one thing, the achievement of Jewish writers was partly owing to a general weakening of nineteenth-century "Jewishness" throughout American society, a weakening which numbered among its symptoms a jparadoxical nostalgia for the old ways. This weakening of Jewishness was, and is, primarily apparent in the disappearance of faith, a universal Western phenomenon, and in the disappearance of Yiddish, the language through which Jewish culture had been transmitted for nearly a thousand years. Writing in the language of the dominant culture, and from the vantage point of liberal humanism, Saul Bellow, Bernard Malamud, and Philip Roth entered the mainstream of American culture.

In the sixties, novels by Jews about Jewish subject matter continued to appear, but the three novelists who established their reputations in the previous decade must still be counted as the major figures in this sub-genre, and it is to the work of these three that I shall address myself here. All three have tried in some way to come to terms with that most elusive of concepts so far as Americans are concerned—Jewish Identity. And all three have tried to cope with the problem of Jewish suffering, specifically, with the problem of how Jewish suffering can be related first to American experience (which by and large has not been an experience of unusual suffering) and ultimately to universal human experience. Finally, all three of these writers have interpolated, to a greater or lesser extent, consciously or unconsciously, the rhythms of Yiddish into English. (pp. 47-8)

Throughout the fifties and sixties it was customary in liberal circles to speak about alienation and about the Jew as the archetypal alienated man, because of his inevitable estrangement from the hostile societies in which he found himself forced to live. But while all the talk was going on, the position of the Jew in America was undergoing significant, though apparently undetected, changes. Philip Roth, it seems to me, is the writer who had the deepest and most honest insight (perceivable as early as 1959 in the story **"Eli the Fanatic"**) into these changes. Distasteful though Roth's vision may be, its truth is now being attested to by what is being widely lamented as a lost generation of Jewish youth. The irony that I believe Roth saw, and embodied in his fiction, is that the Jew, who has for millennia been alienated because he has not "fitted into" the dominant culture, is very well assimilated into the general culture; but now he is alienated because he can no longer fit himself into Jewish culture, partly because nobody knows for sure any longer just what that culture is supposed to be, and partly because of the ease with which it is possible to assimilate into and collect the hefty rewards offered by American culture. Roth desentimentalizes Jewish suffering and also Jewish dialect. The language that possesses a charming quaintness when used by Malamud's characters becomes, when used by Roth's characters, an irritant.

[In **Portnoy's Complaint**], Alexander Portnoy is the type of this new alienated Jew, alienated not from gentiles but from other Jews, including his own immediate family. Like Morris Bober [the Jewish grocer in Malamud's *The Assistant*], Portnoy suffers, but he takes no satisfaction in his suffering. Moreover, suffering does not bring him any closer to his Jewish identity. Morris says of the Jews that "they suffer because they are Jews." Portnoy sees Jewish suffering only as a possible cause of sexual difficulties. The "pogroms and the persecution" are meaningless to him, and to pretend otherwise would be hypocrisy and sentimentalism. In fact, he finds himself persecuted not by gentiles but by Jews.

Portnoy is a male Helen Bober (Morris's daughter, who also finds it impossible to experience sexual satisfaction), the humanist ethic drawn to its ultimate conclusion. He is the Jewish liberal intellectual *par excellence,* the glass of fashion and the mold of form, fully equipped with a social consciousness and an Oedipus complex. Malamud's Jews accept suffering because it is, they think, part of being Jewish, but Roth sees that suffering—even (or maybe especially) Jewish suffering—is repulsive when it is not redemptive. And since redemption is impossible in a secular world, what is left in Roth's novel is a massive and ubiquitous repulsion.

There is a passage in Portnoy's recollections that is most revealing in this regard. He has a memory of having seen his mother's menstrual blood " . . . shining darkly up at me from the worn linoleum in front of the kitchen sink." Joined to this memory (this "icon" of his mother, as Portnoy calls it) is another memory of

> an endless dripping of blood down through a drainboard into a dishpan. It is the blood she is draining from the meat so as to make it kosher and fit for consumption. Probably I am confusing things—I sound like a son of the House of Atreus with all this talk of blood—but I see her standing at the sink salting the meat so as to rid it of its blood, when the attack of "woman's troubles" sends her, with a most alarming moan, rushing off to her bedroom

And immediately following this recollection there reappears the ever-present knife, "the bread knife with which my own blood would be threatened when I refuse to eat my dinner."

I trust I am not the only reader who finds this passage repulsive, a repulsiveness in no way diminished by labelling it black humor. But its repulsiveness is not gratuitous, as Roth indicates when he has Portnoy bring up the House of Atreus, a family line plagued with incest, parricide, fratricide, infanticide, cannibalism, etc. But the allusion to the House of Atreus is also somewhat misleading, because the link between the menstrual blood and the tradition of Koshering meat to remove the blood is one that may be found in the Bible itself. Chapter fifteen in the Book of Leviticus gives instructions for dealing with a woman in the "days of her impurity." Two chapters later, the children of Israel are instructed not to eat blood: "For the life of the flesh is in the blood; and I have given it to you upon the altar to make atonement for your souls; for it is the blood that maketh atonement by reason of the life" (Lev. 17:11). In Portnoy's image (the icon of his mother) there is a grotesque paradox: the mother purifying the flesh that is to be eaten is herself struck with the periodic impurity of the flesh womankind is heir to. In Portnoy's mind the two taboo objects have somehow run together—the taboo woman and the taboo flesh. The forbidden woman has become one with the forbidden flesh that she alone can purify.

But there is, after all, a precedent for this grotesquely exaggerated situation, a precedent much more fearful than the situation depicted by Portnoy. I am thinking, of course, of the testing of Abraham. In that moving narrative, Abraham is required to demonstrate his faith by offering as a sacrifice that which is most dear to him. And he does what is required without question or complaint.

In Portnoy's imagination—and perhaps in modern life—a displacement has occurred. It is not the father who proves his faith by offering his only son whom he loves, but the mother, the impure woman, even that mother who purifies the flesh by removing the blood from it, it is that mother who threatens to offer Portnoy up as a sacrifice—to let *his* blood because he refuses to eat.

But what is most striking about the Biblical echoes is their hollowness. Abraham becomes the Knight of Faith, not only for Jews, but for Christians; Portnoy's father becomes an object of contempt and ridicule. In the Biblical narratives, even in the seemingly endless lists of commandments and ordinances of Leviticus, the everyday and the commonplace are elevated to the level of the sublime. We see man firmly planted in the dust that nurtured him, but his vision is directed toward heaven. Even the most sordid human activities have the capacity to glow with the Divine radiance. Ralph Waldo Emerson expressed this condition in these words: "What would be base, or even obscene, to the obscene, becomes illustrious, spoken in a new connection of thought. The piety of the Hebrew prophets purges their grossness. The circumcision is an example of the power of poetry to raise the low and offensive."

To *Portnoy's Complaint,* Emerson's words may be applied in reverse. If we can say of the prophets that their piety purges their grossness, what we would want to say of Portnoy's world is that an absence of piety makes even the purest of things gross. If Biblical man stands rooted in the dust with his eyes straining heavenward, the people of Portnoy's world stand gazing at their genitals. The key lies in Portnoy's language. Emerson's assertion, "The circumcision is an example of the power of poetry to raise the low and offensive," means that even circumcision, a physical act no less involved with blood and sex than menstruation, is beautiful when it is used as a symbol of spirit, or of man's spiritual aspirations.

Roth's characters cannot employ such symbols. Spirit is a dimension that does not enter their lives. They are hopelessly earth-bound and earth-centered, so that even the most spiritual of human concepts, love, has become debased: " . . .The word love has only to be whispered in our house for all eyes immediately to begin to overflow." The Yiddish words that Portnoy uses—*bonditt, goy, kishkas, shkotzim, pishachs, dreck, chazerai*—and the context in which he uses them, reflect an excremental vision. "And once," Portnoy tells his psychiatrist, "I saw her menstrual blood . . .shining darkly up at me. . . . " The image is of someone looking downward in fascination, while from the earth itself emanates a mysterious force that binds him to that which is below. Roth uses American Jewish life as a metaphor for the general emptiness of modern life. There are many who feel that Roth's novel is anti-Jewish and self-hating but I think it is not so much anti-Jewish as a reflection of the spiritual poverty of our secular society. Portnoy's dreams of bliss, the most lyrical passages in the novel, are enclosed within the secular society—dreams of playing "twenty-one innings of softball" before going home "to Sunday dinner"; "to be a center fielder, a center fielder—and nothing more."

Roth draws Jewish liberalism out to its logical conclusion. Rejecting revelation and transcendence, Portnoy turns away from Jewish history and Jewish suffering and institutional Judaism, all of which interfere with his desire to enjoy the pagan pleasures of the flesh: "Renunciation is all, cries the koshered and bloodless piece of steak my family and I sit down to eat at dinner time. Self-control, sobriety, sanctions—this is the key to a human life, saith all those endless dietary laws." (pp. 50-4)

> *David H. Hirsch, "Jewish Identity and Jewish Suffering in Bellow, Malamud and Philip Roth," in* Saul Bellow Journal, *Vol. 8, No. 2, Summer, 1989, pp. 47-58.*

Lawrence E. Mintz

That Philip Roth is essentially a comic writer has not gone unnoticed by his critics. Newspaper writers and some at-large intellectuals allow themselves the distraction of evaluating Roth as a chronicler of the American Jewish experience, or to appropriate the punch line of a well-known Jewish joke, they debate whether "he is good or bad for the Jews." Scholarly analysts quite properly go beyond the discussion of Roth's comedy to an appreciation of his status as an American writer, invoking the traditions of literary realism from Twain to James to Sinclair Lewis to Fitzgerald and beyond, or they place him, with his assistance and encouragement, in the company of Kafka, Flaubert, Mann, Joyce and other modern writers of consequence. But the best discussions of his fiction begin with an acknowledgement of Roth as a humorist, linking him to traditional stylistic devices in American comedy from its earliest manifestations, and framing him in the contexts of the American comic novels of Bellow, Malamud, Updike, Barth, Reed, Coover, and a host of others.

However, identifying Roth as a comic writer is a beginning, not a conclusion, for it is necessary to appreciate the many different ways he uses humor. Humor is a very broad, inclusive term, embracing simple sounds and images which provoke laughter or amusement, and a host of more complex phenomena including satire, fantasy, exploration of the absurd and the grotesque, and a "comic" *weltanschauung* or perspective on life itself. Susan Sontag has recognized the problem of trying to understand as multifaceted a concept as humor: "actually humor is an umbrella term sheltering many different notions, some complementary, some quite contradictory. A term that is used to describe both physical slapstick and verbal wit (such as punning), that embraces romantic comedy as well as burlesque, is obviously a capacious term. As an umbrella term it is not worth trying to define. A definition would have to be either reductive or extremely abstract." Philip Roth's literary applications of humor span the entire range, from playful fun with language and description, to ironic assessment, to scathing ridicule and expression of anger disguised and contexted as humor. As a comic novelist he reaches still further, to complex, sophisticated appreciation of the nature of human life as fundamentally incongruous and to the assertion that the understanding of this comic truth is a prolegomenon to coping, to transcending and achieving self-understanding and a modicum of self-control.

Roth's own comments on his humor, expressed in various places in the collection, **Reading Myself and Others,** reflect this range. He lays claim to a "broadly comic" style of Olsen and Johnson, the Marx Brothers, the Three Stooges, Laurel and Hardy, Abbott and Costello and the like and to Henny Youngman. His critics supply additional names including Buddy Hackett, Lenny Bruce, Alan King, Shelley Berman, Sid Caesar, Charlie Chaplin, and of course Woody Allen, among the many other standup comics and popular artists in whose company Roth might be comfortable. The author also cites one Jake the Snake, a "middle-aged master of invective and insult, and a repository of lascivious neighborhood gossip" in an encomium to the local *shpritz* artist as comic influence. . . . If Roth is not quite the *toomler* of the Borscht Belt circuit, he can certainly do a pretty good imitation (as can Herbie Bratsky, his toilet-mimicking *toomler* in **The Professor of Desire**).

But Roth tells us that he prefers to be placed in the roll of "sitdown comics" including Kafka, Rabelais, Swift, Mann, Flaubert, and Hogarth and Daumier, among other practitioners of that wonderful oxymoron, "serious comedy." He instructs us that "Sheer Playfulness and Deadly Seriousness are my closest friends. . . . I am also on friendly terms with Deadly Playfulness, Playful Playfulness, Serious Playfulness, Serious Seriousness, and Sheer Sheerness," and ultimately, "that perhaps Mr. Roth's view of life is more hidden from certain readers in his wide audience than they imagine, more imbedded in parody, burlesque, slapstick, ridicule, insult, invective, lampoon, wisecrack, in nonsense, in levity, in *play*—in, that is, the methods and devices of Comedy, than their own view of life may enable them to realize."

It is not easy, of course, to separate or to isolate the various qualities of humor in Roth's writing. Roth makes a claim in places for a comedy which "exists for the sake of no higher value than comedy itself . . .", and in the very same quotation he considers this comedy "for the fun of it" as a "destructive, or lawless playfulness." Obviously destructiveness and lawlessness are not meaningless, not "just kidding." The many dimensions of humor, satire, and comedy are not really mutually exclusive or unconnected. The process of humor is largely a matter of style, of the manipulation of sounds and images, but the very act of manipulating perception and expectation inevitably has a tendentious, or purposeful dimension. A survey of Roth's humor will uncover jokes and funny business which should not really be separated form the discussion of satire, or of his approaches to fantasy, the grotesque and the absurd. Just about all of Philip Roth's literary creations incorporate the entire spectrum of the comic, from the ridiculous to at least a quest for, a consideration of the possibility of, the sublime.

As a humorist, Philip Roth uses some very old and very basic devices to get laughs. He is not a consistent dialect comedian, in the sense of American humor's tradition of wise fool columnists and literary comedians such as Artemus Ward or Mr. Dooley or H*y*m*a*nK*a*p*l*a*n. Nor is he a "dutch" vaudeville character. But Roth knows that Yiddish accents, inflections, sentence structures, expressions, and ironic moods are inherently, inevitably funny, at least to twentieth-century American ears. When Neil Klugman's Aunt Gladys sniffs, "Patamkin I don't know," [in *Goodbye, Columbus*], or when Sophie Portnoy runs on and on about the devastating effects of the *chazerai* which she believes is responsible for her son's frequent trips to the toilet, Roth has orchestrated a climate of amusement. As he tells us in *Reading Myself and Others,* he uses this climate of comedy to shape the reader's idea of the characters. We know that Dr. Spielvogel's famous understated response to the diatribe that is *Portnoy's Complaint* is the "punch line," because the author tells us that it is. But would it be as funny if it weren't rendered, "So [*said the doctor*]. Now vee may perhaps to begin. Yes?" (pp. 154-56)

One of the purposes to which Roth directs his humor is of course social satire. As a satirist, Roth's exaggerations and distortions, as well as his anger, his ridicule, his invective, are licensed as intentions to criticize, to correct. Satire can be relatively mild, gentle, an ironic look at something which is strange, silly, not entirely deserving of admiration or respect. Or it can be a full force denunciation of an evil, with but a modicum of humor, of a ridicule which provokes some kind of scornful laughter to distinguish it from pure criticism. Once again Roth's canon exhibits the entire range. His targets include the Northeastern Jewish middle class world of his background, the Midwest and its WASP inhabitants, academia, literary criticism, male-female encounters in sex-poisoned America, the government and related political nightmares, and a few other matters which manage to engage his attention along the way.

It is as the satirist that Roth gets in trouble with some of his readers, particularly when he considers Jews. As Ted Solotaroff notes in ["American Jewish Writers: On Edge Once More"], "most of Philip Roth's stories in *"Goodbye, Columbus*. . .are devoted to an aggressive and astute exposure of the moral ghetto of Jewish ethnocentrism centered by self-righteousness that his young protagonists are trying to escape." That Roth is turned off by bad taste, hypocrisy, stupidity and ignorance, nouveau riche posturing, and other universally acknowledged evils is not admissible or inadequate in defense according to some of his detractors. Alex Portnoy's disgust with his archetypal Seymour Schmuck (alternately named Aaron Putz or Howard Schlong) is directed toward his "six different split-level ranch-type houses made all of flagstone . . ." and his

"eighty-million dollar tour of seven thousand countries, some of them you never even heard of, that they made them up just to honor Seymour," rather than his ethnic identity, though that is not at all in doubt from the description. Roth's protagonists are in revolt against the American middle class as much as against a specifically Judaic environment, or the Jewish religion, per se, and they are just as alienated and just as critical wherever they find themselves. But this fact of universal negativity is often held to be irrelevant to the claim that Roth's wicked portrayal of Jewish characters and Jewish lifestyles in America is reprehensible. Philip Roth may just engender more passionate hostility than any writer in America, at least from some quarters.

Curiously Roth avoids invoking satiric license when he defends himself against the attacks that he is anti-Semitic or that he should self-censor his writing in such a way that he does not associate the negative behavior he wants to expose with primarily or particularly Jewish characters and environments. He seems to prefer to defend himself by pointing out that his descriptions are plausible, even readily recognizable, or by (the often rather easy) demonstration that his critics are shrill, paranoid, excessive, and in other ways ad hominem unworthy of our serious consideration. . . . (pp. 158-59)

Portnoy's Complaint is Roth's most famous satire, indeed his most famous novel, largely because of the satiric caricature of the Jewish mother, in Sophie Portnoy (and, of course, the "good parts" in which Alexander Portnoy's sexual adventures are detailed). Sophie is Roth's primary target. She is ridiculed for her obsession with food, her overprotectiveness, and her excessive praise and love for her son which is constantly contradicted by her bossing him around, by her insistence that she knows what is best for him and that she is ultimately the authority in his life. Mrs. Portnoy's energy, strength, courage, and domestic skills are acknowledged, somewhat wryly if admiringly, but there is no mistaking that Alexander Portnoy attributes his sexual problems as well as his other neurosis essentially to his love-hate relationship with his much larger than life mother.

But the case against Sophie Portnoy is a generic class action suit rather than an individual indictment. So that the reader understands that Sophie is a generic Jewish mother rather than a unique creation, Roth gives us Mrs. Nimkin, a smothering mother whose child-prodigy pianist son, Ronald, hangs himself, but first pins a note to his jacket informing his mother that Mrs. Blumenthal had called to ask her to bring her Mah-Jongg rules to their game that night! Alex rages, "only in America, Rabbi Golden, do these peasants, our mothers, get their hair dyed platinum at the age of sixty, and walk up and down Collins Avenue in Florida in pedalpushers and mink stoles—and with opinions on every subject under the sun." And it isn't just Mommie Dearest. Jack Portnoy is also ridiculed, again with a grudging acknowledgment of his love, his devotion to his family, his loyalty to his job (despite an exploiting WASP employer and a thankless constituency), and his other virtues. He is nonetheless weak, constipated, defeated. He is the "little man" of the comic strips and "golden age" American magazine and movie humor, without much in the way of ironic victory to redeem him.

Portnoy's complaint transcends the personal as well. His diatribe on the Jewish dietary laws flies:

> Oh, and the *milchiks* and *flaishiks* besides, all those *meshuggeneh* rules and regulations on top of their own private craziness! It's a family joke that when I was a tiny child I turned from the window out of which I was watching a snow-storm, and hopefully asked, 'Momma, do we believe in winter?' Do you get what I am *saying?* I was raised by Hottentots and Zulus! I couldn't even contemplate drinking a glass of milk with my salami sandwich without giving serious offense to God Almighty.

His hostility and anger toward his Judaic upbringing recures in many diatribes during the novel. He caricatures Rabbi Warshaw (one of several rabbis Roth satirizes) as '. . .a fat, pompous, impatient fraud, with an absolutely grotesque superiority complex . . .'' who speaks in drawn out, self-important tones: "I-a wan-tt to-a wel-come-a you-ew tooo thee sy-no-gawg-a." Portnoy's *pièce de résistence,* designed to blast himself out of his anger and pain, is his "Jew Jew Jew Jew Jew Jew! It is coming out of my ears already, the saga of the suffering Jews! Do me a favor, my people, and stick your suffering heritage up your suffering ass—*I happen also to be a human being.*"

The several tirades or diatribes in the novel are explained as a part of Portnoy's analysis, as an aspect of his need to express his pain and his anguish over his impotence. These satiric flights are actually examples of the oldest recorded comic traditions; they recall Archilocus, Juvenal, Horace and the *flyting* traditions of early English and Irish poetry. They have been compared, as well, to Lenny Bruce's monologues, especially late in the comedian's career, when his anger was greater than his professionalism, and there are other standup satirists, Dick Gregory, Richard Pryor, Whoopie Goldberg and Brother Theodore, for instance, as well as other writers, e.g. Barth, Barthelme, Reed, Mailer, Tom Wolfe, who also use strong waves of words for comic power and satiric effect. All the same, it is not too difficult to see why readers who do not either share, to some degree, Portnoy's perspective or who are unwilling to allow the satirist the traditional license of violating taboos, stating the unstatable, and in other ways behaving abnormally to make a point are so unwilling to accept Roth's denunciations as comic or even satiric. (pp. 160-62)

From the beginning of Roth's career, he has presented us with quests by protagonists, anti-heroes, who are uncomfortable with what is and uncertain about what might be. . . . [They] are all, in a sense, "trapped in a Jewish joke." They must first come to grips with the contradictions, the frustrations, and the ridiculousness of the world in which they were raised and its effects on their personalities. They must face up to the devils and angels warring within them, the sexual urges and the civilized restraints and the paradox of demand and impotence it engenders. The comic protagonists almost desperately seek and desperately evade commitment (marriage, paternity, perma-

nence of job or place), because they are narcissistic and insatiable. Their wants are enormous, yet again paradoxically, they are intelligent enough to see the flaws in everything (and everyone, including themselves) they encounter. (p. 165)

Portnoy's long-winded confession is so that "vee may perhaps to begin," after all. If Roth has returned to the saga of Nathan Zuckerman so many times, it is because Nathan is still working things out. Roth does not give us "happy endings," but his characters, like Chaplin's tramp and the other classic "little men" of American humor, refuse to fold under the pressures of their lives, or to pretend that the realities they see and feel are anything other than what they are. Humor is at the very core of their existence and their quest. Their creator is truly one of the great masters of American humor. (p. 166)

> *Lawrence E. Mintz, "Devil and Angel: Philip Roth's Humor," in Studies in American Jewish Literature, Vol. 8, No. 2, Fall, 1989, pp. 154-67.*

FURTHER READING

Collier, Peter. "Portnoy's Compliance." *Ramparts* 7, No. 12 (May 1969): 29-31.
  Early article considers Roth's novel representative of the ambivalence which marked the post-World War II Jewish condition in America.

Cooperman, Stanley. "Philip Roth: 'Old Jacob's Eye' with a Squint." *Twentieth Century Literature* 19, No. 3 (July 1973): 203-16.
  Discusses moral choices made by the protagonists of Roth's early novels.

Donaldson, Scott. "Family Crises in the Popular Novel of Nixon's Administration." *Journal of Popular Culture* VI, No. 2 (Fall 1972): 374-82.
  Examines the intertwining of sexual and psychological elements in four novels, including *Portnoy's Complaint.*

Fiedler, Leslie A. "Cross the Border—Close the Gap." *Playboy* (December 1969): 151
  Maintains that *Portnoy's Complaint* marks the passage of the Jewish-American novel into the genre of popular culture.

Finkielkraut, Alain. "The Ghosts of Roth." *Esquire* 96, No. 3 (September 1981): 92-7.
  Insightful interview in which Roth comments on literature, discusses his personal background, and defends himself and his works against charges of sexism and anti-Semitism.

Friedman, Alan Warren. "The Jew's Complaint in Recent American Fiction: Beyond Exodus and Still in the Wilderness." *Southern Review* VIII, No. 1 (January 1972): 41-59.
  Explores self-conscious Jewish protagonists in the works of Saul Bellow, Bernard Malamud, and Roth, asserting that these characters are "cultural schizophrenics" who

attempt to assimilate their heritage into that of modern society.

Girgus, Sam B. "Portnoy's Prayer: Philip Roth and the American Unconscious." In *Reading Philip Roth,* edited by Asher Z. Milbauer and Donald G. Watson, pp. 126-43. London: Macmillan Press, 1988.

    Regards *Portnoy's Complaint* as a breakthrough work due to its treatment of guilt, repression, sexuality, and the human psyche.

Gordon, Lois G. *"Portnoy's Complaint:* Coming of Age in Jersey City." *Literature and Psychology* XIX, Nos. 3 & 4 (1969): 57-60.

    Examines the abundance of Freudian psychology in the novel.

Gross, Barry. "Seduction of the Innocent: *Portnoy's Complaint* and Popular Culture." *Melus* 8, No. 4 (Winter 1981): 81-92.

    Explores the lure of Gentiles for Portnoy and his excursions into their society.

Hyman, Stanley Edgar. "The Book of the Year?" In *The Critic's Credentials: Essays and Reviews by Stanley Edgar Hyman,* edited by Phoebe Pettingell, pp. 112-17. New York: Atheneum, 1978.

    Discusses the numerous initial reviews of *Portnoy's Complaint* and asserts that the novel has more faults than virtues.

Kliman, Bernice W. "Names in *Portnoy's Complaint.*" *Critique: Studies in Modern Fiction* XIV, No. 3 (1973): 16-24.

Interprets the symbolism of characters' names in the novel. See brief excerpt in *CLC,* Vol. 3, p. 438.

Lee, Hermione. "The Art of Fiction LXXXIV: Philip Roth." *The Paris Review* 26, No. 93 (Fall 1984): 215-47.

    Lengthy, introspective interview in which Roth discusses many subjects, including his writing methods and the personal aspects of his works.

Michel, Pierre. *"Portnoy's Complaint* and Philip Roth's Complexities." *Dutch Quarterly Review of Anglo-American Letters* IV, No. 1 (1974): 1-10.

    Elucidates Portnoy's ambivalence toward Jews, his journey toward self-discovery, and Roth's moral commentary throughout the novel. Claims that *Portnoy's Complaint* is striking because of Roth's careful merging of comic and tragic elements.

Schmitz, Neil. "Epilogue: In the Snare of Mother-Wit." In his *Of Huck and Alice: Humorous Writing in American Literature,* pp. 241-59. Minneapolis: University of Minnesota Press, 1983.

    Analyzes Portnoy's relationships with women and his intellectual and physical wants.

Segal, Alan. *"Portnoy's Complaint* and the Sociology of Literature." *British Journal of Sociology* XXII, No. 3 (September 1971): 257-68.

    Sociological study of Roth's novel. Segal maintains that Portnoy's actions and motives are made comprehensible through an understanding of the character's social condition.

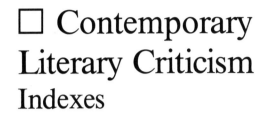

☐ Contemporary
Literary Criticism
Indexes

Literary Criticism Series
    Cumulative Author Index
Cumulative Nationality Index
Title Index, Volume 66

This Index Includes References to Entries in These Gale Series

Contemporary Literary Criticism

Presents excerpts of criticism on the works of novelists, poets, dramatists, short story writers, scriptwriters, and other creative writers who are now living or who have died since 1960.

Twentieth-Century Literary Criticism

Contains critical excerpts by the most significant commentators on poets, novelists, short story writers, dramatists, and philosophers who died between 1900 and 1960.

Nineteenth-Century Literature Criticism

Offers significant passages from criticism on authors who died between 1800 and 1899.

Literature Criticism from 1400 to 1800

Compiles significant passages from the most noteworthy criticism on authors of the fifteenth through eighteenth centuries.

Classical and Medieval Literature Criticism

Offers excerpts of criticism on the works of world authors from classical antiquity through the fourteenth century.

Short Story Criticism

Compiles excerpts of criticism on short fiction by writers of all eras and nationalities.

Poetry Criticism

Presents excerpts of criticism on the works of poets from all eras, movements, and nationalities.

Children's Literature Review

Includes excerpts from reviews, criticism, and commentary on works of authors and illustrators who create books for children.

Contemporary Authors Series

Contemporary Authors provides biographical and bibliographical information on more than 97,000 writers of fiction and nonfiction. *Contemporary Authors New Revision Series* provides completely updated information on active authors covered in *CA. Contemporary Authors Permanent Series* consists of listings for deceased and inactive authors. *Contemporary Authors Autobiography Series* presents specially commissioned autobiographies by leading contemporary writers. *Contemporary Authors Bibliographical Series* contains primary and secondary bibliographies as well as analytical bibliographical essays by authorities on major modern authors.

Dictionary of Literary Biography

Encompasses four related series. *Dictionary of Literary Biography* furnishes illustrated overviews of authors' lives and works. *Dictionary of Literary Biography Documentary Series* illuminates the careers of major figures through a selection of literary documents, including letters, interviews, and photographs. *Dictionary of Literary Biography Yearbook* summarizes the past year's literary activity and includes updated entries on individual authors. *Concise Dictionary of American Literary Biography* comprises six volumes of revised and updated sketches on major American authors that were originally presented in *Dictionary of Literary Biography*.

Something about the Author Series

Encompasses three related series. *Something about the Author* contains well-illustrated biographical sketches on juvenile and young adult authors and illustrators from all eras. *Something about the Author Autobiography Series* presents specially commissioned autobiographies by prominent authors and illustrators of books for children and young adults. *Authors of Artists for Young Adults* provides high school and junior high school students with profiles of their favorite creative artists.

Yesterday's Authors of Books for Children

Contains heavily illustrated entries on children's writers who died before 1961. Complete in two volumes.

Literary Criticism Series
Cumulative Author Index

This index lists all author entries in the Gale Literary Criticism Series and includes cross-references to other Gale sources. References in the index are identified as follows:

AAYA: *Authors & Artists for Young Adults,* Volumes 1-6
CAAS: *Contemporary Authors Autobiography Series,* Volumes 1-13
CA: *Contemporary Authors* (original series), Volumes 1-132
CABS: *Contemporary Authors Bibliographical Series,* Volumes 1-3
CANR: *Contemporary Authors New Revision Series,* Volumes 1-33
CAP: *Contemporary Authors Permanent Series,* Volumes 1-2
CA-R: *Contemporary Authors* (revised editions), Volumes 1-44
CDALB: *Concise Dictionary of American Literary Biography,* Volumes 1-6
CLC: *Contemporary Literary Criticism,* Volumes 1-66
CLR: *Children's Literature Review,* Volumes 1-24
CMLC: *Classical and Medieval Literature Criticism,* Volumes 1-7
DC: *Drama Criticism,* Volume 1
DLB: *Dictionary of Literary Biography,* Volumes 1-104
DLB-DS: *Dictionary of Literary Biography Documentary Series,* Volumes 1-8
DLB-Y: *Dictionary of Literary Biography Yearbook,* Volumes 1980-1988
LC: *Literature Criticism from 1400 to 1800,* Volumes 1-16
NCLC: *Nineteenth-Century Literature Criticism,* Volumes 1-31
PC: *Poetry Criticism,* Volumes 1-2
SAAS: *Something about the Author Autobiography Series,* Volumes 1-12
SATA: *Something about the Author,* Volumes 1-64
SSC: *Short Story Criticism,* Volumes 1-8
TCLC: *Twentieth-Century Literary Criticism,* Volumes 1-41
YABC: *Yesterday's Authors of Books for Children,* Volumes 1-2

Author Index

Author Index

Author Index

Author Index

CLC Cumulative Nationality Index

Nationality Index

Nationality Index

CLC-66 Title Index

Title Index

493